TORTS

ELEVENTH EDITION

STEVEN L. EMANUEL

Founder & Editor-in-Chief, *Emanuel Law Outlines* and
Emanuel Bar Review
Harvard Law School, J.D. 1976
Member (ret.), NY, CT, MD and VA bars

The *Emanuel® Law Outlines* Series

Copyright © 2024 Aspen Publishing. All Rights Reserved.

No part of this publication may be reproduced or transmitted in any form or by any means, electronic or mechanical, including photocopy, recording, or utilized by any information storage or retrieval system, without written permission from the publisher. For information about permissions or to request permissions online, visit us at www.AspenPublishing.com.

To contact Customer Service, e-mail customer.service@aspenpublishing.com, call 1-800-950-5259, or mail correspondence to:

    Aspen Publishing
    Attn: Order Department
    1 Wall Street
    Burlington, MA 01803

Printed in the United States of America.

1 2 3 4 5 6 7 8 9 0

ISBN 978-1-5438-0757-8

This book is intended as a general review of a legal subject. It is not intended as a source for advice for the solution of legal matters or problems. For advice on legal matters, the reader should consult an attorney.

About Aspen Publishing

Aspen Publishing is a leading provider of educational content and digital learning solutions to law schools in the U.S. and around the world. Aspen provides best-in-class solutions for legal education through authoritative textbooks, written by renowned authors, and breakthrough products such as Connected eBooks, Connected Quizzing, and PracticePerfect.

The Aspen Casebook Series (famously known among law faculty and students as the "red and black" casebooks) encompasses hundreds of highly regarded textbooks in more than eighty disciplines, from large enrollment courses, such as Torts and Contracts to emerging electives such as Sustainability and the Law of Policing. Study aids such as the *Examples & Explanations* and the *Emanuel Law Outlines* series, both highly popular collections, help law students master complex subject matter.

Major products, programs, and initiatives include:

- **Connected eBooks** are enhanced digital textbooks and study aids that come with a suite of online content and learning tools designed to maximize student success. Designed in collaboration with hundreds of faculty and students, the Connected eBook is a significant leap forward in the legal education learning tools available to students.

- **Connected Quizzing** is an easy-to-use formative assessment tool that tests law students' understanding and provides timely feedback to improve learning outcomes. Delivered through CasebookConnect.com, the learning platform already used by students to access their Aspen casebooks, Connected Quizzing is simple to implement and integrates seamlessly with law school course curricula.

- **PracticePerfect** is a visually engaging, interactive study aid to explain commonly encountered legal doctrines through easy-to-understand animated videos, illustrative examples, and numerous practice questions. Developed by a team of experts, PracticePerfect is the ideal study companion for today's law students.

- The **Aspen Learning Library** enables law schools to provide their students with access to the most popular study aids on the market across all of their courses. Available through an annual subscription, the online library consists of study aids in e-book, audio, and video formats with full text search, note-taking, and highlighting capabilities.

- Aspen's **Digital Bookshelf** is an institutional-level online education bookshelf, consolidating everything students and professors need to ensure success. This program ensures that every student has access to affordable course materials from day one.

- **Leading Edge** is a community centered on thinking differently about legal education and putting those thoughts into actionable strategies. At the core of the program is the Leading Edge Conference, an annual gathering of legal education thought leaders looking to pool ideas and identify promising directions of exploration.

Abbreviations Used in Text

CASEBOOKS

D,H&B Csbk (7th) — Dobbs, Hayden & Bublick, *Torts and Compensation* (West Academic, 7th Ed, 2013)

Dobbs & Hayden (5th) — Dobbs & Hayden, *Torts and Compensation* (West, 5th Ed, 2005)

E&S (12th Ed) — Epstein & Sharkey, *Cases and Materials on Torts* (Wolters Kluwer, 12th Ed., 2020)

E&S (10th Ed) —Epstein & Sharkey, *Cases and Materials on Torts* (Wolters Kluwer, 10th Ed., 2012)

Franklin — Franklin, Rabin & Green, Tort Law and Alternatives (Foundation Press, 9th Ed., 2011)

H,P&S — Henderson, Pearson and Siliciano, *The Torts Process* (Wolters Kluwer, 8th Ed., 2012)

K,S&S — Keeton, Sargentich & Steiner, *Tort and Accident Law* (West, 3rd Ed., 1998)

P,W&S (14th) — Prosser, Wade & Schwartz, *Cases and Materials on Torts* (Foundation Press, 14th Ed., 2020)

P,W&S (12th) — Prosser, Wade & Schwartz, *Cases and Materials on Torts* (Foundation Press, 12th Ed., 2010)

HORNBOOKS, TREATISES & OTHER REFERENCE MATERIALS

ALI Study — American Law Institute, *Reporters' Study: Enterprise Responsibility For Personal Injury* (ALI, 1991)

D,H&B Trts — Dobbs, Hayden & Bublick, *The Law of Torts* 4-volume treatise (West Practitioner Treatise Series, 2d Ed., West, 2011)

Dobbs — Dan Dobbs, *The Law of Torts* (West Hornbook Series, 2000)

Epstein Tbk — Epstein, *Torts* (Aspen Publishers, 1st Ed. 1999) (Textbook)

H,J&G — Harper, James & Gray, *The Law of Torts* (Little, Brown, 2nd Ed., 1986, with 1994 Cumulative Supplement)

P&K — Keeton, Dobbs, Keeton & Owen, *Prosser & Keeton on Torts* (West, 5th Ed., 1984, with 1988 Supplement)

Rest. 3d — American Law Institute, *Restatement Third of Torts:* Liability for Physical and Emotional Harm (2005); Liability for Economic Harm (Tent. Dr. #2, 2014); Products Liability (1998) and Apportionment (2000)

Rest. 2d — American Law Institute, *Restatement Second of Torts* (1965-1979)

W&S — White & Summers, *Uniform Commercial Code* (West, 4th Ed., 1995)

SUMMARY OF CONTENTS

TABLE OF CONTENTS

Chapter 1

INTRODUCTION

Chapter 2

INTENTIONAL TORTS AGAINST THE PERSON

Chapter 3

INTENTIONAL INTERFERENCE WITH PROPERTY

Chapter 4

DEFENSES TO INTENTIONAL TORTS

Chapter 5

NEGLIGENCE GENERALLY

Chapter 6

ACTUAL AND PROXIMATE CAUSE

Chapter 7

JOINT TORTFEASORS

Chapter 8

DUTY

Chapter 9

OWNERS AND OCCUPIERS OF LAND

Chapter 10

DAMAGES

Chapter 11

DEFENSES IN NEGLIGENCE ACTIONS

Chapter 12

VICARIOUS LIABILITY

Chapter 13

STRICT LIABILITY

Chapter 14

PRODUCTS LIABILITY

Chapter 17

DEFAMATION

Chapter 18

MISCELLANEOUS TORTS

Preface

Thank you for buying this book. I've worked hard on this new edition to make it more tightly focussed on just those topics that are important in today's Torts courses.

In addition to the comprehensive main Outline, the following special features of this book will help you succeed in your Torts course.

- **Casebook Correlation Chart** — This chart, located just after this Preface, correlates each section of the Outline with the pages covering the same topic in three of the leading Torts casebooks.

- **Capsule Summary** — This is a 114-page summary of the key concepts of the law of Torts, specially designed for use in the last week or so before your final exam.

- **Quiz Yourself** — At the end of nearly every chapter we give you short-answer questions so that you can exercise your analytical muscles. There are nearly 100 of these questions. Most are from the *Law in a Flash* Torts title. Also included are 30 multiple-choice questions (with detailed answers) in the style of questions on the Multistate Bar Exam. These questions begin on p. 529.

- **Exam Tips** — These alert you to the issues that repeatedly pop up on real-life Torts exams, and the factual patterns commonly used to test those issues. I created these Tips by looking at literally hundreds of multiple-choice and essay questions asked by law professors and bar examiners.

- **Essay Exam Q&As** —These are actual past Harvard Law School Torts essay questions, together with our suggested model answers.

I intend for you to use this book both throughout the semester and for exam preparation. Here are some suggestions about how to use it:[1]

1. During the semester, use the book in preparing each night for the next day's class. To do this, first read your casebook. Then, use the *Casebook Correlation Chart* to get an idea of what part of the outline to read. Reading the outline will give you a sense of how the particular cases you've just read in your casebook fit into the overall structure of the subject. You may want to use a yellow highlighter to mark key portions of the *Emanuel*.

2. If you make your own outline for the course, use the *Emanuel* to give you a structure and to supply black letter principles. You may want to rely especially on the *Capsule Summary* for this purpose. You are hereby authorized to copy small portions of the *Emanuel* into your own outline, provided that your outline will be used only by you or your study group, and provided that you are the owner of the *Emanuel*.

3. When you first start studying for exams, read the *Capsule Summary* to get an overview. This will

---

1. The suggestions below relate only to this book. I don't talk about taking or reviewing class notes, using hornbooks or other study aids, joining a study group, or anything else. This doesn't mean I don't think these other steps are important — it's just that in this Preface I've chosen to focus on how I think you can use this outline.

probably take you about one day.

4. Either during exam study or earlier in the semester, do some or all of the *Quiz Yourself* short-answer questions. You can find these quickly by looking for *Quiz Yourself* entries in the Table of Contents. When you do these questions: (1) record your short "answer" on the small blank line provided after the question, but also (2) try to compose a "mini essay." Remember that the only way to get good at writing essays is to write essays.

5. Three or four days before the exam, review the *Exam Tips* that appear at the end of each chapter. You may want to combine this step with step **4**, so that you use the Tips to help you spot the issues in the short-answer questions. You'll also probably want to follow up from many of the Tips to the main outline's discussion of the topic.

6. The night before the exam: (1) do some *Quiz Yourself* questions, just to get your thinking and writing juices flowing; and (2) re-scan the *Exam Tips* (spending about 2-3 hours).

My deepest thanks go to my long-time editorial colleagues, Barbara Lasoff and Barbara Roth, who have helped greatly to assure the quality of this edition. Warm thanks also to the excellent publishing team at Aspen Publishing, Nicole Pinard, Joe Terry and Natalie Danner.

By the way, the ***full text of this book***, plus the full text of many other study aids, is available ***online*** as part of a single low-cost monthly subscription at **www.EmanuelAYCE.com.** "AYCE" stands for "All You Can Eat" — we named it that way because you get ***unlimited access*** to the full-text of:

❏ This and the other *9 Emanuel Law Outlines* titles that I write;

❏ All *9 Emanuel CrunchTime* titles that I write;

❏ *Emanuel Law in a Flash* flash-card titles in *13* subjects;

❏ *Casenotes Legal Briefs* for *50* of the leading casebooks; and

❏ Over 1300 *multiple-choice questions and answers.*

Good luck in your Torts course. If you'd like any other Aspen publication, you can find it at your bookstore or at **www.AspenPublishing.com.** If you'd like to contact me, you can email me at **semanuel@westnet.com**.

Steve Emanuel
Larchmont, NY
December 2023

CASEBOOK CORRELATION CHART

(**Note:** general sections of the outline are omitted from this chart. **NC** = not directly covered by this casebook.)

Emanuel's Torts Outline *(by chapter and section heading)*	Epstein & Sharkey Cases and Materials on Torts (12th Ed. 2020)	Prosser, Wade & Schwartz's Cases and Materials on Torts (14th Ed. 2020)	Franklin, Rabin, Green et al Cases and Materials on Tort Law and Alternatives (11th Ed. 2021)
CHAPTER 1 **INTRODUCTION**			
I. Nature of Tort Law	75-86, 96-126	1-2	1-2
II. Categories of Torts	86-141	3-17	2-10, 30-36
III. Sources of Law	NC	NC	NC
CHAPTER 2 **INTENTIONAL TORTS AGAINST THE PERSON**			
I. "Intent" Defined	3-11, 25-29	17-33	902-909
II. Nominal and Punitive Damages	827-828	581	908
III. Scope of Liability	NC	335-337	405-427
IV. Battery	4-15, 59-60	34-42	908-917
V. Assault	4-15, 55-59	43-46	908-912
VI. False Imprisonment	60-65	47-58	917-923
VII. Infliction of Mental Distress	65-73	59-78	924-932
CHAPTER 3 **INTENTIONAL INTERFERENCE WITH PROPERTY**			
I. Trespass to Land	11-15	79-87, 544-551	941-948
II. Trespass to Chattels	554-562	87-94, 610-611	948-957
III. Conversion	563-576	94-106, 609-612	948-957
CHAPTER 4 **DEFENSES TO INTENTIONAL TORTS**			
II. Consent	15-29	108-122	958-961
III. Self-Defense	33-37	122-126	962-965
IV. Defense of Others	37	126	NC
V. Defense of Property	37-43	127-133	965-969
VI. Recapture of Chattels	43	133-137	969
VII. Re-Entry on Land	NC	NC	NC
VIII. Necessity	44-55	138-144	970-975
IX. Arrest and Other Authority of Law	NC	145-146	989-993
X. Discipline	NC	146-148	NC
XI. Justification	81-85	148-150	964
CHAPTER 5 **NEGLIGENCE GENERALLY**			
II. Components of Cause of Action	143-145	153-154	NC
III. Unreasonable Risk	168-170	153-161	46-55
IV. The Reasonable Person	145-166	170-195	55-63, 87
V. Malpractice	200-234, 333-334	206-232	366-377, 735-749
VI. Automobile Guest Statutes	NC	233-234	NC
VIII. Violation of Statute (Negligence *Per Se*)	230-244	237-261	NC
IX. Procedure in Jury Trials	244-258	261-272	9-20, 64-69
X. *Res Ipsa Loquitur* — Creating an Inference of Negligence	261-283	272-289	94-117

CASEBOOK CORRELATION CHART (cont.)

CASEBOOK CORRELATION CHART (cont.)

Emanuel's Torts Outline (by chapter and section heading)	Epstein & Sharkey Cases and Materials on Torts (12th Ed. 2020)	Prosser, Wade & Schwartz's Cases and Materials on Torts (14th Ed. 2020)	Franklin, Rabin, Green et al Cases and Materials on Tort Law and Alternatives (11th Ed. 2021)
CHAPTER 11 **DEFENSES IN NEGLIGENCE ACTIONS**			
I. Contributory Negligence	286-314	660-666	443-449, 452-472
II. Comparative Negligence	334-352	667-679	449-455
III. Assumption of Risk	315-334	679-686	956-957, 648-665
IV. Statute of Limitations	NC	693-702	
V. Immunities	1129-1165	702-781	988-1001
CHAPTER 12 **VICARIOUS LIABILITY**			
II. Employer-Employee Relationship	649-666	752-761	21-35
III. Independent Contractors	657-666	761-769	27-35
IV. Joint Enterprise	656	769-773	667-671, 800
V. Auto Consent Statutes, the "Family Purpose" Doctrine and Bailments	150, 855-856	773-776	800-802
CHAPTER 13 **STRICT LIABILITY**			
II. Animals	576-585	784-792	40
III. Abnormally Dangerous Activities	585-603	792-810	533-544
IV. Limitations on Strict Liability	114, 585-592	810-818	558-559
V. Worker's Compensation	876-902	1340-1349	831-900
CHAPTER 14 **PRODUCTS LIABILITY**			
I. Negligence	667-697	822-823	569-589
II. Warranty	681, 689-693	824-835	575-587
III. Strict Liability	683-689, 691-693	784-818, 835-841	576-617
IV. Design Defects	718-741	846-858	591-618
V. Duty to Warn	741-765	858-887	618-641
VI. Who may be a Defendant	705-713	885-897	626-636, 686
VII. Interests that may be Protected	683-686	906-908	660-673
VIII. Defenses Based on Plaintiff's Conduct	765-773	874-884	646-649
IX. Defenses Based on Federal Regulation, including Preemption	773-791	882-884	508-516
CHAPTER 15 **NUISANCE**			
II. Public Nuisance	637-649	913-921	703-715
III. Private Nuisance	603-637	921-929	687-703
CHAPTER 16 **MISREPRESENTATION**			
II. Intentional Misrepresentation ("Deceit")	1108-1115, 1124-1131	1172-1187, 1228-1232	1251-1256
III. Negligent Misrepresentation	1144-1155	1172-1173, 1179-1192	1264-1265, 1289-1296
IV. Strict Liability	NC	1187-1196	NC

CASEBOOK CORRELATION CHART (cont.)

Emanuel's Torts Outline *(by chapter and section heading)*	Epstein & Sharkey Cases and Materials on Torts (12th Ed. 2020)	Prosser, Wade & Schwartz's Cases and Materials on Torts (14th Ed. 2020)	Franklin, Rabin, Green et al Cases and Materials on Tort Law and Alternatives (11th Ed. 2021)
CHAPTER 17 **DEFAMATION**			
I. **General Principles**	923-925	944-946	1003-1004
II. **Defamatory Communication**	926-940, 951-958	946-967	1004-1023, 1037-1044
III. **Libel vs. Slander**	958-961	968-974	1026-1030
IV. **Publication**	925-939	975-986	1044-1054, 1089-1120
V. **Intent**	936-947, 961-962	998-1011	1052-1140
VI. **Privileges**	985-1039	1044-1055	1035-1052, 1202-1207
VII. **Remedies**	963-974	665-671	1003-1004,1024-1027
CHAPTER 18 **MISCELLANEOUS TORTS**			
I. **Invasion of Privacy**	1033-1083	1071-1124	933-939, 1155-1207
II. **Misuse Of Legal Procedure**	NC	1149-1170	NC
III. **Interference with Advantageous Relations**	1166-1178	1233-1288	1286
IV. **Interference with Family and Political Relations**	NC	1284-1288	940-941

CAPSULE SUMMARY

This Capsule Summary is intended for review at the end of the semester. Reading it is not a substitute for mastering the material in the main outline. Numbers in brackets refer to the pages in the main outline where the topic is discussed.

CHAPTER 1

INTRODUCTION

I. GENERAL INTRODUCTION

A. Definition of tort: There is no single definition of "tort." The most we can say is that: (1) a tort is a *civil wrong* committed by one person against another; and (2) torts can and usually do arise *outside of any agreement* between the parties. [1]

B. Categories: There are three broad categories of torts, and there are individual named torts within each category: [2]

    1. Intentional torts: First, *intentional* torts are ones where the defendant desires to bring about a particular result. The main intentional torts are:

        a. *Battery.*

        b. *Assault.*

        c. *False imprisonment.*

        d. *Infliction of mental distress.*

    2. Negligence: The next category is the generic tort of *"negligence."* Here, the defendant has not intended to bring about a certain result, but has merely behaved *carelessly*. There are no individually-named torts in this category, merely the general concept of "negligence."

    3. Strict liability: Finally, there is the least culpable category, *"strict liability."* Here, the defendant is held liable even though he did not intend to bring about the undesirable result, and even though he behaved with utmost carefulness. There are two main individually-named torts that apply strict liability: [3]

        a. Conducting of *abnormally dangerous activities* (e.g., blasting); and

        b. The *selling* of a *defective product* which causes personal injury or property damage.

C. Significance of categories: There are two main consequences that turn on which of the three above categories a particular tort falls into: [4]

    1. Scope of liability: The three categories differ concerning D's liability for *far-reaching, unexpected, consequences*. The more culpable D's conduct, the more far-reaching his liability for unexpected consequences — so an intentional tortfeasor is liable for a wider range of unexpected consequences than is a negligent tortfeasor. [4]

    2. Damages: The *measure of damages* is generally broader for the more culpable categories. In particular, D is more likely to be required to pay punitive damages when he is an intentional tortfeasor than when he is negligent or strictly liable. [4]

D. Exam approach: First, review the fact pattern to spot each individual tort that has, or may have been, committed. Then, for each tort you have identified:

1. Prima facie case: Say whether a prima facie case for that tort has been made.

2. Defenses: Analyze what *defenses* and justifications, if any, D may be able to raise.

3. Damages: Finally, discuss what *damages* may be applicable, if the tort has been committed and there are no defenses. Pay special attention to: (1) punitive damages; (2) damages for emotional distress; (3) damages for loss of companionship of another person; (4) damages for unlikely and far-reaching consequences; and (5) damages for economic loss where there has been no personal injury or property damage.

CHAPTER 2

INTENTIONAL TORTS AGAINST THE PERSON

I. "INTENT" DEFINED

A. Meaning of intent: There is no general meaning of "intent" when discussing intentional torts. For each individual intentional tort, you have to memorize a different definition of "intent." All that the intentional torts have in common is that D must have intended to bring about some sort of physical or mental effect upon another person. [5-6]

1. No intent to harm: The intentional torts generally are *not* defined in such a way as to require D to have intended to *harm* the plaintiff. [7]

Example: D points a water gun at P, making it seem like a robbery, when in fact it is a practical joke. If D has intended to put P in fear of imminent harmful bodily contact, the "intent" for assault is present, even though D intended no "harm" to P.

2. Substantial certainty: If D *knows with substantial certainty* that a particular effect will occur as a result of her action, she is deemed to have intended that result. [6]

Example: D pulls a chair out from under P as she is sitting down. If D knew with "substantial certainty" that P would hit the ground, D meets the intent requirement for battery, even if he did not desire that she do so. [*Garratt v. Dailey*]

a. High likelihood: But if it is merely "highly likely," not "substantially certain," that the bad consequences will occur, then the act is not an intentional tort. "Recklessness" by D is not enough.

b. Act distinguished from consequences: For "substantial certain" and "intentional," distinguish betwwen D's act, and the *consequences* of that act. The *act* must be intentional or substantially certain, but the *consequences* need not be. [7]

Example: D intends to tap P lightly on the chin to annoy him. If P has a "glass jaw," which is broken by the light blow, D has still "intended" to cause the contact, and the intentional tort of battery has taken place, even though the consequences — broken jaw — were not intended.

C A P S U L E   S U M M A R Y

B. Transferred intent: Under the doctrine of *"transferred intent,"* if D held the necessary intent with respect to person A, he will be held to have committed an intentional tort against **any other person** who happens to be injured. [7]

> **Example:** D shoots at A, and accidentally hits B. D is liable to B for the intentional tort of battery.

II. BATTERY

A. Definition: Battery is the *intentional infliction of a harmful or offensive bodily contact*. [9]

> **Example:** A intentionally punches B in the nose. A has committed battery.

B. Intent: It is not necessary that D desires to physically **harm** P. D has the necessary intent for battery if it is the case **either** that: (1) D intended to cause a harmful or offensive bodily contact; or (2) D intended to cause an *imminent apprehension* on P's part of a harmful or offensive bodily contact. [9]

> **Example 1:** D shoots at P, intending to hit him with the bullet. D has the necessary intent for battery.

> **Example 2:** D shoots at P, intending to miss P, but also intending to make P think that P would be hit. D has the intent needed for battery (i.e., the "intent to commit an assault" suffices as the intent for battery).

C. Harmful or offensive contact: If the contact is "harmful" — i.e., it causes pain or bodily damage — this qualifies. But battery also covers contacts which are merely *"offensive,"* i.e., damaging to a *"reasonable sense of dignity."* [10]

> **Example:** D spits on P. Even if P is not "harmed" in the sense of being caused physical pain or physical injury, a battery has occurred because a person of average sensitivity in P's position would have her dignity offended.

D. P need not be aware: It is *not* necessary that P have *actual awareness* of the contact at the time it occurs. [11] (*Example:* D kisses P while she is asleep. D has committed a battery.)

E. Contact beyond level consented to: Battery can occur where P *consents* to a certain level of bodily contact, but D *goes beyond the consented-to level* of contact. At that point, the consent becomes invalid, and battery results. Look for this "beyond the consented-to level of contact" scenario when the facts involve either a *sporting event* or a *medical/surgical procedure.* [10]

> **Example:** In a pick-up ice hockey game in a park, P and D are skirmishing for the puck near the side wall of the rink. D intentionally delivers a hard body check that throws P into the wall, and the collision between P and the wall badly injures P. D sues P for battery.

> If D intentionally delivered a body check (a body contact) that went beyond the level or type of contact D knew or should have known P was impliedly consenting to, then it would constitute battery.

III. ASSAULT

A. Definition: Assault is the intentional causing of an *apprehension* of *harmful or offensive contact*. [12]

C
A
P
S
U
L
E

S
U
M
M
A
R
Y

Example: D, a bill collector, threatens to punch P in the face if P does not pay a bill immediately. Since D has intended to put P in imminent apprehension of a harmful bodily contact, this is assault, whether D intends to in fact hit P or not.

B. Intent: There are two different intents, either of which will suffice for assault:

   1. Intent to create apprehension: First, D intends to put P in ***imminent apprehension*** of the harmful or offensive contact, even if D does not intend to follow through (e.g., D threatens to shoot P, but does not intend to actually shoot P); [12] or

   2. Intent to make contact: Alternatively, D intends to in fact ***cause*** a harmful or offensive bodily contact.

     Example: D shoots a gun at P, trying to hit P. D hopes P won't see him, but P does. P is frightened. The shot misses. This is assault.

   3. Summary: So D has the requisite intent for assault if D either "intends to commit an assault" or "intends to commit a battery." [12]

C. No hostility: It is not necessary that D bear malice towards P, or intend to ***harm*** P. [13]

     Example: D as a practical joke points a toy pistol at P, hoping that P will falsely think that P is about to be shot. D has one of the two alternative intents required for assault — the intent to put P in imminent apprehension of a harmful or offensive contact — so the fact that D does not desire to "harm" P is irrelevant.

D. "Words alone" rule: Ordinarily, ***words alone*** are not sufficient, by themselves, to give rise to an assault. Normally there must be some overt act — a physical act or gesture by D — before P can claim to have been assaulted. [13]

     Example: During an argument, D says to P "I'm gonna hit you in the face." This is probably not an assault, if D does not make any gesture like forming a fist or stepping towards P.

   1. Special circumstances: However, the ***surrounding circumstances***, or D's past acts, may occasionally make it reasonable for P to interpret D's words alone as creating the required apprehension of imminent contact. [13]

E. Actual contact or apprehension required: Assault requires an ***effect***: P must either actually ***undergo*** a harmful or offensive contact, or be put in ***immediate apprehension*** of such a contact.

   1. Unsuccessful prank or bluff: So where D is pulling a ***prank or making a bluff***, if P believes or knows that no imminent harmful or offensive contact will really occur, and none does occur, there is no assault. [13]

     Example: D, holding a revolver, walks into P's office and says, "I know you've been having sex with my wife, and I'm gonna blow your head off." The particular gun that D is holding is a toy replica that cannot fire anything, and P knows this because W has told him so on a previous occasion. D has not committed assault — even if D intended to put P in fear of an imminent harmful contact (a bullet), the "result" requirement for assault has not been met because P has not in fact been put in apprehension of such contact.

F. Imminence: It must appear to P that the harm being threatened is ***imminent***, and that D has the ***present ability*** to carry out the threat. [15]

     Example: D threatens to shoot P, and leaves the room for the stated purpose of getting his revolver. D has not committed an assault on P.

G. P unaware of danger: P must be *aware* of the threatened contact. [15]

H. Threat to third persons: P must have an apprehension that *she herself* will be subjected to a bodily contact. She may not recover for her apprehension that *someone else* will be so touched. [16]

> **Example:** P sees D raise a pistol at P's husband. D shoots and misses. P cannot recover for assault, because she did not fear a contact with her own body.

I. Conditional threat: Where D threatens the harm only if P does not obey D's demands, the existence of an assault depends on whether D had the *legal right* to compel P to perform the act in question. [16]

> **Example:** P, a burglar, breaks into D's house. D says, "If you don't get out, I'll throw you out." There is no assault on P, since D has the legal right to force P to leave.

IV. FALSE IMPRISONMENT

A. Definition: False imprisonment is defined as the intentional infliction of a *confinement*. [17]

> **Example:** D wants to have sex with P, and locks her in his bedroom for two hours hoping that P will agree. She does not, and D lets her go. This is false imprisonment, because D has intentionally confined P for a substantial time.

B. Intent: P must show that D either *intended* to confine him, or at least that D *knew with substantial certainty* that P would be confined by D's actions. The tort of false imprisonment cannot be committed merely by negligent or reckless acts. [17]

> **Example:** D, a shopkeeper, negligently locks the store while P, a customer, is in the bathroom. This is not false imprisonment, since D did not intend to confine P.

C. "Confinement": The idea of confinement is that P is held *within* certain limits, not that she is prevented from entering certain places. [18]

> **Example:** D refuses to allow P to return to her own home. This is not false imprisonment — P can go anywhere else, so she has not been "confined."

D. Means used: The imprisonment may be carried out by direct physical means, but also by *threats* or by the assertion of *legal authority*. [19-20]

1. **Threats:** Thus if D threatens to use force if P tries to escape, the requisite confinement exists. [19]

2. **Assertion of legal authority:** Also, confinement may be caused by D's assertion that he has *legal authority* to confine P — this is true even if D does not in fact have the legal authority, so long as P reasonably believed that D does, or is in doubt about whether D does. [19]

> **Example:** Storekeeper suspects P of shoplifting, and says, "I hereby make a citizen's arrest of you." Putting aside whether Storekeeper has a privilege to act this way, Storekeeper has "confined" P, if a reasonable person in P's position would think that Storekeeper had the authority to make such an arrest, even if under local law Storekeeper did not have that authority.

E. P must know of confinement: P must either be *aware* of the confinement, or must suffer some actual harm. (*Example:* P is locked in her hotel room by D, but P is asleep for the entire three-hour period, and learns only later that the door was locked. This is probably not false imprisonment.) [21]

V. INTENTIONAL INFLICTION OF EMOTIONAL DISTRESS (IIED)

A. Definition: This tort is the intentional or reckless infliction, by ***extreme and outrageous conduct***, of ***severe emotional or mental distress***, even in the absence of physical harm. [21]

> **Example:** D threatens that if P, a garbage collector, does not pay over part of his garbage collection proceeds to D and his henchmen, D will severely beat P. Since D's conduct is extreme and outrageous, and since he has intended to cause P distress (which he has succeeded in doing), D is liable for infliction of mental distress. [*State Rubbish Collectors Assoc. v. Siliznoff*]

B. Intent: "Intent" for this tort is a bit broader than for others. There are three possible types of culpability by D: (1) D ***desires*** to cause P emotional distress; (2) D knows with ***substantial certainty*** that P will suffer emotional distress; and (3) D ***recklessly*** disregards the high probability that emotional distress will occur. [21-24]

> **Example:** D commits suicide by slitting his throat in P's kitchen. D, or his estate, is liable for intentional infliction of mental distress because although D did not desire to cause distress to P, or even know that distress was substantially certain, he recklessly disregarded the high risk that distress would occur. [*Blakeley v. Shortal's Est.*]

   1. Transferred intent: The doctrine of ***"transferred intent"*** is applied only in a very ***limited*** fashion for emotion distress torts. So if D attempts to cause emotional distress to X (or to commit some other tort on him), and P suffers emotional distress, P usually will not recover. [22]

>   **a. Immediate family present:** The main exception is that the transferred intent doctrine is applied if: (1) D directs his conduct to a member of P's ***immediate family***; (2) P is ***present***; and (3) P's presence is ***known*** to D.
>
> > **Example:** While P is present, and known to D to be present, D beats up P's father. If P suffers severe emotional distress, a court will probably allow her to recover from D, even though D's conduct was directed at the father, not P.

C. "Extreme and outrageous": P must show that D's conduct was ***extreme and outrageous***. D's conduct has to be "beyond all possible bounds of decency." [24-25]

> **Example:** D, as a practical joke, tells P that her husband has been badly injured in an accident, and is lying in the hospital with broken legs. This conduct is sufficiently outrageous to qualify. [*Wilkinson v. Downton*]

   1. Bill collectors: A common fact pattern in which D may be liable for intentional infliction of mental distress is where D is a ***bill collector***. The collector's conduct can and often will be sufficiently extreme and outrageous to trigger IIED (e.g., repeated abusive phone calls at night; or denouncing P to P's boss or neighbors as a "deadbeat"). And it's no defense to an otherwise proper IIED action that P ***really owed the money*** that D was trying to collect. [25]

D. Actual severe distress: P must suffer ***severe*** emotional distress. P must show at least that her distress was severe enough that she ***sought medical aid***. Most cases do not require P to show that the distress resulted in bodily harm. [25-28]

E. Constitutional limits on IIED awards: The *First Amendment of the U.S. Constitution* places some important *limits* on the right of a state to impose liability for IIED. If the conduct by the defendant that causes the distress is the delivery of a *message or communication*, a state's act of awarding damages against the defendant for IIED may well violate the defendant's First Amendment freedom of speech.

    1. P is a public figure; rule from defamation cases: For instance, a plaintiff who is a *public figure* (essentially, a famous or newsworthy person) may succeed with a claim for *IIED* based on a communication only if P shows that the defendant either *knew that his speech was false or recklessly disregarded whether it was true.* [*Hustler Magazine v. Falwell*] [27]

        Example: *Hustler Magazine* satirizes religious leader Jerry Falwell as a drunken hypocrite who has sex with his mother. *Held*, Falwell cannot recover against *Hustler* for IIED unless he shows that *Hustler* made a false statement about him with knowledge of its falsity or with reckless disregard of its falsity. [*Hustler Magazine v. Falwell*]

    2. Statement on a matter of public concern: Another way a tort recovery for IIED can violate the defendant's First Amendment rights is if the alleged distress stems from the communicative impact of the defendant's speech, and the speech involves a matter of *public concern.* [*Snyder v. Phelps*] [27]

        Example: P is the father of a Marine, Matthew Snyder, recently killed in Iraq. The Ds are members of the Westboro Baptist Church, a church that thinks God punishes the U.S. military for tolerating homosexuality. During the course of Matthew's funeral in Maryland, the Ds, from a public place nearby, carry picket signs with messages like "God hates fags," and "Thank God for Dead Soldiers." (The Ds apparently believe that Matthew was killed because of God's desire to punish the military for not rooting out homosexuality.) P brings a suit against the Ds for intentionally causing him emotional distress. The jury awards P $4 million in damages, based on its conclusion that the Ds' conduct was "outrageous."

        Held (by the U.S. Supreme Court on appeal), for the Ds. Since the Ds' speech was on a matter of "public concern," their First Amendment rights allowed Maryland to regulate that speech only in a "content neutral" manner. Since the jury likely reached its verdict without observing the required "content neutrality," enforcing the resulting damage award against the Ds violated their First Amendment rights. [*Snyder v. Phelps, supra*]

CHAPTER 3

INTENTIONAL INTERFERENCE WITH PROPERTY

I. TRESPASS TO LAND

A. Definition: As generally used, *"trespass"* occurs when either: (1) D *intentionally enters P's land*, without permission; (2) D *remains* on P's land without the right to be there, even if she entered rightfully; or (3) D *puts an object on* (or refuses to remove an object from) P's land without permission. [39]

B. Intent: The term "trespass" today refers only to *intentional* interference with P's interest in property. There is no strict liability. [40]

Example: D, a pilot, loses control of the aircraft, and the aircraft lands on P's property. This is not trespass to land.

1. **Negligence:** If D *negligently* enters P's land, this is generally treated as the tort of negligence, not trespass. [40]

2. **Effect of mistake:** If D has the intent to commit a physical contact with P's land, D will have the requisite intent for trespass even if his decision to make the contact is the result of a *mistake*. Thus D's mistake about *legal title* or *consent* won't block liability. [40]

    a. **Reasonableness irrelevant:** This is true even if the mistake is *reasonable* (assuming the mistake wasn't induced by anything P did or said).

        Example: D, an absentee owner, visits his property, which is a farm. He drives a tractor on what he reasonably thinks is his parcel, but unbeknownst to him (and without negligence on his part), he drives over what is really P's land. This is trespass, despite D's reasonable ignorance of the fact that the land he is entering belongs to someone other than D.

C. **Particles and gasses:** If D knowingly causes *objects*, including particles or gases, to enter P's property, most courts consider this trespass. [43]

    Example: D's factory spews pollutants onto P's land. This is a trespass. [*Martin v. Reynolds Metals Co.*]

D. **Air space:** It can be a trespass for a plane to *fly over* P's property. However, today most courts find liability only if: (1) the plane enters into the *immediate reaches* of the airspace (below federally-prescribed minimum flight altitudes); and (2) the flight *substantially interferes* with P's use and enjoyment of his land (e.g., by causing undue noise, vibrations, pollution). [43-44]

II. TRESPASS TO CHATTELS

A. **Definition:** "Trespass to chattels" is defined as any *intentional interference* with a person's *use or possession* of a chattel. [45] D only has to pay damages, not the full value of the property (as in conversion, below).

1. **Loss of possession:** If P *loses possession* of the chattel for any time, recovery is allowed even if the chattel is returned unharmed. [46]

    Example: D takes P's car for a five-minute "joy ride" and returns it unharmed. D has committed trespass to chattels.

2. **Electronic trespass on computer:** If D *interacts with P's computer* without permission, whether this is trespass to chattels depends on the *type of harm* that occurs. [46]

    a. **No harm to computer or data:** Where D's conduct *does not harm P's computer or the data on it,* most courts say trespass to chattels does *not* occur even though D's interaction with P's computer was uninvited and P is bothered.

        Example: D sends lots of emails to P's computer, which P has to take time to delete, but which don't damage the computer or data on it. This is probably not trespass to chattel.

    b. **Harm done:** But if D's conduct *does* harm the computer or data on it, then trespass to chattels does occur.

        Example: D puts "spyware" on P's computer that tracks P's keystrokes and slows down the computer's functioning. This is probably trespass to chattels.

Note: The above discussion assumes that the computer data constitutes *"property"* for trespass-to-chattels purpose. Most courts today agree that computer files *are* property for this purpose. [47]

III. CONVERSION

A. Definition: Conversion is an *intentional* interference with P's possession or ownership of property that is *so substantial* that D should be required to pay the property's *full value*. [48]

> **Example:** D steals P's car, then seriously (though not irreparably) damages it in a collision. D is liable for conversion, and will be required to pay P the full value of the car (though D gets to keep the car).

B. Intent: Conversion is an intentional tort, but all that is required is that D have intended to take possession of the property. Mistake as to ownership will generally not be a defense. [48]

> **Example:** D buys an old painting from an art dealer, and reasonably believes that the art dealer has good title. In fact, the painting was stolen from P years before. D keeps the painting in his house for 10 years. D is liable for conversion, notwithstanding his honest mistake about title.

C. Distinguished from trespass to chattels: Courts consider several factors in determining whether D's interference with P's possessory rights is severe enough to be conversion, or just trespass to chattels. Factors include: (1) duration of D's *dominion* over the property; (2) D's *good or bad faith*; (3) the *harm* done to the property; and (4) the *inconvenience* caused to P. [49]

D. Different ways to commit: There are different ways in which conversion may be committed: [50-52]

    1. Acquiring possession: D takes *possession* of the property from P.

        a. Bona fide purchaser: Most courts hold that a *bona fide purchaser* of *stolen goods* is a converter, even if there is no way he could have known that they were stolen. [50]

    2. Transfer to third person: D can also commit conversion by *transferring* a chattel to one who is not entitled to it. [51]

    3. Withholding good: D may commit conversion by *refusing to return* goods to their owner, if the refusal lasts for a substantial time. [51-52]

    4. Destruction: Conversion may occur if D *destroys* the goods, or fundamentally alters them.

E. Intangibles, including computer files: As with trespass to chattels, if the item is *"intangible"* property, check to make sure that in the state in question, the item counts as property for conversion purposes. Most courts today say that *computer files count.* Therefore if D permanently deprives P of access to files P owns, D will be liable for conversion in most states. [49]

F. Forced sale: If P is successful with her tort suit, a *forced sale* occurs: D is required to pay the *full value* of the goods (not just the amount of the use or damage, as in trespass to chattels), but gets to keep the goods. [52]

CHAPTER 4

DEFENSES TO INTENTIONAL TORTS

I. CONSENT

A. Express consent: If P expressly *consents* to an intentional interference with his person or property, D will not be liable for that interference. [58]

> **Example:** P says to D, "Go ahead, hit me in the stomach — I'll show you how strong I am." If D does so, P's consent prevents P from suing for battery.

B. Implied consent: Existence of consent may also be *implied* from P's conduct, from custom, or from the circumstances. [59-60]

> **1. Objective manifestation:** It is the *objective manifestations* by P that count — if it reasonably seemed to one in D's position that P consented, consent exists regardless of P's subjective state of mind. [59]

C. Lack of capacity: Consent will be invalidated if P is *incapable* of giving that consent, because she is a child, intoxicated, unconscious, etc. [60-61]

> **1. Consent as a matter of law:** But even if P is incapable of truly giving consent, consent will be *implied* "as a matter of law" if these factors exist: (1) P is unable to give consent; (2) immediate action is necessary to save P's life or health; (3) there is no indication that P would not consent if able; and (4) a reasonable person would consent in the circumstances. [60-61]
>
> > **Example:** P is brought unconscious to the emergency room of D, a hospital. D can perform emergency surgery without P's actual consent — consent will be implied as a matter of law. Therefore, P cannot sue for battery.

D. Exceeding scope: Even if P does consent to an invasion of her interests, D will not be privileged if he goes substantially *beyond the scope* of that consent. [61]

> **Example:** P visits D, a doctor, and consents to an operation on her right ear. While P is under anesthetic, D decides that P's left ear needs an operation as well, and does it. P's consent does not block an action for battery for the left-ear operation, since the operation went beyond the scope of P's consent. [*Mohr v. Williams*]

> **1. Emergency:** However, in the surgery case, an *emergency* may justify extending the surgery beyond that consented to. [62]

> **2. Athlete's consent:** Participating in a usually-violent *sport*, like football or hockey, is generally *not* considered to constitute consent to all injuries which may be inflicted by an adversary. Instead, there is an increasing tendency to hold that a player who *intentionally attacks or injures* his opponent may be liable in tort. [63]

> > **a. Scope of implied consent:** So if P impliedly consents to some types of harmful or offensive contact during the sport, fellow-participant D won't be liable for contacts falling within the scope of that implied consent, but *will* be liable for contacts going *beyond* the ones impliedly consented to.

> > **b. Significance of sport's rules and customs:** In determining what contacts the player impliedly consented to, most courts attach great weight to the *rules or customs* of the sport. Decisions recognize at least three major *categories* of contact, and tend to draw dif-

CAPSULE SUMMARY

ferent conclusions about whether the plaintiff "impliedly consented" to the contact based on the category the contact falls into:

[1] **Conduct allowed by rules:** The first category consists of contact that is *expressly allowed* by the rules and customs of the sport. Where the case falls into this category, in virtually all courts the plaintiff will be held to have *impliedly consented* to this type of contact, even if in the particular situation the result is an unexpectedly grave injury. [63]

[2] **Conduct punishable but not "beyond the bounds" of the sport:** The next category consists of conduct that *violates the rules* of the sport, but is considered to be essentially *within the ordinary give-and-take of the sport.* Conduct would likely fall into this category if it is subject to *some minor penalty*, but not to a severe punishment like automatic ejection or a multiple-game suspension. Again, most courts would likely hold that such conduct, while against the rules, is of a type that is sufficiently common (and in most instances insufficiently physically dangerous) that the plaintiff should be *deemed to have impliedly consented to it.* [63]

Example: P and D are playing in an NBA basketball game. D commits a "flagrant foul" on P by grabbing P's arm from behind and throwing him to the ground to prevent him from scoring. (The foul ruling gives P two foul shots, and does not result in D's being ejected or suspended.) P falls, suffering a freak career-ending knee injury when his knee hits the floor. P sues D for battery.

The court would likely hold that judging by the relatively un-severe penalty imposed by the referee, this type of foul is sufficiently ordinary — and sufficiently unlikely to cause severe personal injury — that it should be deemed to be the type of contact to which P implicitly consented by joining the league.

[3] **Reckless or intentionally-harmful conduct beyond the usual bounds:** The final category consists of conduct that not only violates the rules of the sport, but constitutes a *flagrant violation* by means of actions that are *unrelated to the normal method of playing the game*, and that are done *without any competitive purpose*. Scenarios where D *intends to physically harm* his opponent (or *recklessly disregards* the danger of such harm), without any *bona fide* belief that D is advancing his own team's competitive interest, are typical of this category. If the case falls into this category, most courts *allow* a tort suit (typically one for battery) to be brought by the injured player against the opponent who committed the violation, and/or the teams that employed that opponent. [64]

Example: P and Clark are NFL players on opposing teams. (Clark plays for the D team.) At the end of a play that goes well for P's team, while P is kneeling and watching the end of the play, Clark comes up behind P and uses his forearm to hit P on the head and neck. Clark strikes this blow (he later testifies) not because he thinks it might help his team, but out of frustration at the play and the fact that his team, D, is losing. The blow fractures P's neck. Therefore, P sues D for the tortious act committed by their employee (Clark). The trial judge, sitting without a jury, rules that P assumed the risk of Clark's conduct, on the theory that "professional football is a species of warfare[.]" P appeals.

Held (on appeal): for P — case remanded for a retrial. The rules and customs of the NFL prohibit the intentional striking of blows. Where one football player intentionally inflicts a serious injury on another, the injured player won't be deemed to have assumed the risk of such a conduct. [*Hackbart v. Cincinnati Bengals, Inc.*] [65]

Note: However, a few cases have *found for the defendant* as a matter of law even where the defendant *intentionally tried to harm* the plaintiff, or *recklessly disregarded the high risk* that the plaintiff would be harmed. These few cases have reasoned that if players and teams have to worry about being held liable in tort for their aggressive on-field acts, their incentive to compete vigorously but lawfully — a desirable thing — will be chilled. [See *Avila v. Citrus Community College District*, holding that P, a varsity college baseball hitter, assumed the risk that the opposing pitcher would intentionally hit him with a pitch as retaliation for the fact that the pitcher's teammate was previously hit by the pitcher for P's team.] [65]

   c. **A mere negligent violation of rules:** Where D's conduct in violating the sports rule manifests *mere negligence* as to the risk of injury to P (rather than an intention to hurt P or reckless disregard of P's physical safety), *few if any cases allow recovery*. [65]

E. **Consent to criminal acts:** Where D's act against P is a *criminal act*, courts are split. The majority rule is that P's consent is *ineffective* if the act consented to is a crime. [67-68] (*Example:* P and D agree to fight with each other. In most states, each may recover from the other, on the theory that consent to a crime — such as breach of peace — is ineffective.)

II. SELF-DEFENSE

A. **Privilege generally:** A person is entitled to use *reasonable force* to prevent any threatened *harmful or offensive bodily contact*, and any threatened *confinement or imprisonment*. [68]

B. **Apparent necessity:** Self-defense may be used not only where there is a real threat of harm, but also where D *reasonably believes* that there is one. [69]

C. **Only for protection:** The defense of self-defense applies only where D uses the force needed to *protect himself* against harm. [69]

   1. **Retaliation:** Thus D may not use any degree of force in *retaliation* for a tort already committed. [69]

      Example: P hits D with a snowball. Ten minutes later, D hits P with a snowball, in retaliation. D has committed battery on P, because D's act was not done in true self-defense.

   2. **Imminence:** D may not use force to avoid harm which is *not imminent*, unless it reasonably appears that there will not be a later chance to prevent the danger. [70]

      Example: P says to D, "I will beat you up tomorrow." D cannot beat P up today, to prevent tomorrow's attack, unless it appears that there will be no way for D to defend tomorrow.

   3. **Verbal provocation:** D may not use self-defense in response to *verbal provocation*, such as *taunting or insults*. Self-defense is purely a forward-looking idea: D is entitled to prevent imminent future harm, not redress past harm, especially purely verbal harm. [69]

      Example: P calls D a liar and a cheat in front of D's friends. (Assume that D is not a liar and a cheat, and that P's words constitute slander for which D could recover.) P then says to D, "What're you gonna do about, you coward?" D hits P in the face. P can recover for

CAPSULE SUMMARY

battery, and D cannot successfully claim self-defense. That's because provocation does not justify self-defense in tort law; only the prevention of imminent bodily harm can justify it.

D. Degree of force: Only the *degree* of force necessary to prevent the threatened harm may be used. If D uses more force than necessary, he will be liable for damage caused by the excess. [70]

    1. Deadly force: Special rules limit the use of *deadly force*, i.e., force intended or likely to cause death or serious bodily injury. [70-71]

        a. Danger must be serious: D may *not* use deadly force unless he himself is in danger of *death or serious bodily harm*.

        Example: P attacks D with his fists, in a way that does not threaten D with serious bodily harm. Even if there is no other way for D to prevent the attack, D may not use his gun to shoot P, even if the shot is intended only to injure P — D must submit to the attack rather than use deadly force.

E. Retreat: Courts are split on whether and when D has a *"duty to retreat"* (i.e., to run away or withdraw) if the threatened harm could be avoided this way. [71]

    1. Restatement view: The Second Restatement holds that: (1) D may use *non-deadly force* rather than retreating; but (2) D may not use *deadly force* in lieu of retreating, except if attacked in his *dwelling* by one who does not reside in the dwelling. [71]

        Example: If P attacks D on the street with a knife, under the Restatement D may use his fists rather than running away, but may not use a gun rather than running away if running away would avoid the danger. If the attack took place in D's home, where P was not also a resident, then D could use the gun.

III. DEFENSE OF OTHERS

A. General rule: A person may use reasonable force to defend *another person* against attack. The same rules apply as in self-defense: the defender may only use reasonable force, and may not use deadly force to repel a non-deadly attack. [72]

    1. Reasonable mistake: The courts are split on the effect of a *reasonable mistake*. Older courts hold that the intervener "steps into the shoes" of the person aided, and thus bears the risk of a mistake. But Rest.2d gives a "reasonable mistake" defense to the intervener. [72]

IV. DEFENSE OF PROPERTY

A. General rule: A person may generally use reasonable force to *defend her property*, both land and chattels. [73-76]

    1. Warning required first: The owner must first make a *verbal demand* that the intruder stop, unless it reasonably appears that violence or harm will occur immediately, or that the request to stop will be useless. [73]

B. Mistake: The effect of a *reasonable mistake* by D varies:

    1. Mistake as to danger: If D's mistake is about whether force is necessary, D is protected by a reasonable mistake. [73]

        Example: D uses non-deadly force to stop a burglar whom he reasonably believes to be armed. In fact, the burglar is not armed. D can rely on the defense of property.

2. Privilege: But if the owner's mistake is about whether the intruder has a *right* to be there, the owner's use of force will not be privileged. [74]

> **Example:** D reasonably believes that P is a burglar. In fact, P is a friend who has entered D's house to retrieve her purse, without wanting to bother D. Even non-deadly force by D will not be privileged.

C. Deadly force: The owner may use *deadly force* only where: (1) non-deadly force will not suffice; and (2) the owner reasonably believes that without deadly force, *death* or *serious bodily harm* will occur. [74]

> **Example:** D sees P trespassing in P's backyard. D asks P to leave, but P refuses. Even if there is no way to make P leave except by shooting at him, D may not do so, since P's conduct does not threaten D with death or serious bodily harm.

1. Burglary: But a homeowner is generally *allowed* to use deadly force against a *burglar*, provided that she reasonably believes that nothing short of this force will safely keep the burglar out. [74]

D. Mechanical devices: An owner may use a *mechanical device* to protect her property only if she would be privileged to use a similar degree of force if she were present and acting herself. [75-76]

1. Reasonable mistake: An owner's right to use a dangerous mechanical device in a particular case will be measured by whether deadly force could have been used against *that particular intruder*. [75]

> **Example:** D uses a spring gun to protect his house while he is away. If the gun shoots an actual burglar, and state law would have allowed D to shoot the burglar if D was present, then D will not be liable for using the spring gun. But if a neighbor, postal carrier, or someone else not engaged in a crime happened to enter and was shot, D would not have a "reasonable mistake" defense — since D could not have fired the gun at such a person directly, the spring gun may not be used either.

V. RECAPTURE OF CHATTELS

A. Generally: A property owner has the general right to use reasonable force to *regain* possession of *chattels* taken from her by someone else. [76-78]

1. Fresh pursuit: The privilege exists only if the property owner is in *"fresh pursuit"* to recover his property. That is, the owner must act without unreasonable delay. [77]

> **Example:** A learns that B has stolen a stereo and is in possession of it. A may use reasonable force to reclaim the stereo if he acts immediately, but not if he waits, say, a week between learning that D has the property and attempting to regain it.

2. Reasonable force: The force used must be reasonable, and *deadly force* can never be used. [77]

3. Wrongful taking: The privilege exists only if the property was taken *wrongfully* from the owner. If the owner parts willingly with possession of the property, and an event then occurs that gives him the right to repossess, he generally will not be able to use force to regain it. [77]

Example: O rents a TV to A. A refuses to return the set on time. O probably may not use reasonable force to enter A's home to repossess the set, because A's original possession was not wrongful.

B. Merchant: Where a merchant reasonably believes that a person is stealing his property, many courts give the merchant a privilege to *temporarily detain* the person for investigation. [77]

   1. Limited time: The detention must be limited to a short time, generally 10 or 15 minutes or less, just long enough to determine whether the person has really shoplifted or not. Then, the police must be called (the merchant may not purport to arrest the suspect himself). [77]

VI. NECESSITY

A. General rule: Under the defense of *"necessity,"* D has a privilege to harm the property interest of P where this is *necessary* in order to prevent *great harm* to third persons or to the defendant herself. [79-81]

B. Public necessity: If interference with the land or chattels of another is necessary to prevent a disaster *to the community* or to many people, the privilege is that of "public necessity." Here, no compensation has to be paid by the person doing the damage. [79]

   Example: Firefighters demolish D's house, in which a fire has just barely started, because that is the best way to stop the fire from spreading much further. The firefighters, and the town employing them, probably do not have to pay, because they are protected by the privilege of public necessity.

C. Private necessity: If a person prevents injury to himself or his property, or to the person or property of a third person, this is protected by the privilege of *"private* necessity," if there is no less-damaging way of preventing the harm. [80-81]

   Example: A, while sailing, is caught in very rough seas. To save his life, he may moor at a dock owned by B, and will not be liable for trespass.

   1. Actual damage: Where the privilege of private necessity exists, it will be a complete defense to a tort claim where P has suffered no actual substantial harm (as in the above example). But if actual damage occurs, P must *pay for the damage* she has caused. [81]

      Example: On the facts of the above example, if A's boat slammed into B's dock and damaged it, A would have to pay.

   2. Owner may not resist: The main purpose of the doctrine of private necessity is to prevent the person whose property might be injured from defeating the exercise of the privilege. [81]

      Example: P moors his ship at D's dock, to avoid being shipwrecked by heavy seas. D, objecting to what he thinks is a trespass, unmoors the ship, causing the ship to be harmed and P to be injured. P may recover from D, because P's mooring was privileged by private necessity and D, therefore, acted wrongfully. [*Ploof v. Putnam,* 80]

VII. ARREST

A. Common law rules:

C
A
P
S
U
L
E

S
U
M
M
A
R
Y

1. **Arrest with warrant:** Where a police officer executes an arrest with an ***arrest warrant*** that appears to be correctly issued, he will not be liable even if it turns out that there was no probable cause or the procedures used to get the warrant were not proper. [82]

2. **Arrest without warrant:** [82]

   a. **Felony or breach of peace in presence:** A police officer may make a warrantless arrest for a ***felony*** or for a ***breach of the peace***, if the offense is being committed or seems about to be committed ***in his presence***. A citizen may do the same.

   b. **Past felony:** Once a felony has been committed, an officer may still make a warrantless arrest, provided that he reasonably believes that the felony has been committed, and also reasonably believes that he has the right criminal. A citizen may make an arrest only if a felony has ***in fact*** been committed (though the citizen is protected if she makes a reasonable mistake and arrests the wrong person).

   c. **Misdemeanor:** At common law, no warrantless arrest (either by an officer or by a citizen) may be made for a ***past misdemeanor not involving a breach of the peace***.

3. **Reasonable force:** One making an arrest may not use more ***force*** than is ***reasonably necessary***. [82]

   a. **Prevention:** Where the arrest is made to ***prevent a felony*** which threatens human life or safety, even deadly force may be used, if there is no other way to prevent the crime. But where the felony does not involve such danger, deadly force may not be used.

   b. **Apprehension after crime:** If a crime has already been committed, the police may use ***deadly force*** only if the suspect poses a significant threat of ***death or serious physical injury*** to others. (***Example:*** Officer spots Burglar escaping after his crime. Officer knows that Burglar is unarmed and unlikely to be violent. Officer may not shoot at Burglar to arrest him, even if there is no other way to make the arrest.)

VIII. JUSTIFICATION

A. **Generally:** Even if D's conduct does not fit within one of the narrower defenses, she may be entitled to the general defense of ***"justification,"*** a catch-all term used where there are good reasons for exculpating D from what would otherwise be an intentional tort. [83]

CHAPTER 5
NEGLIGENCE GENERALLY

I. COMPONENTS OF TORT OF NEGLIGENCE

A. **Generally:** The tort of "negligence" occurs when D's conduct imposes an ***unreasonable risk*** upon another, which results in injury to that other. The negligent tortfeasor's mental state is irrelevant. [96]

B. **Prima facie case:** The five components of a prima face case for negligence are: [96]

1. **Duty:** A legal ***duty*** requiring D to conduct himself according to a certain standard, so as to avoid unreasonable risk to others;

2. **Failure to conform:** A failure by D to conform his conduct to this standard. (This element can be thought of as *"carelessness."*)

3. **Cause in fact:** A showing that D's failure to act with reasonable care was the *"cause in fact"* of the injury to plaintiff. Generally, "cause in fact" means a *"but for"* cause, i.e., a cause without which the injury wouldn't have occurred.

4. **Proximate cause:** A sufficiently close causal *connection* between D's act of negligence and the harm suffered by P that it's fair to hold D liable, as a matter of policy. This is *"proximate cause."*

5. **Actual damage:** *Actual damage* suffered by P. (Compare this to most intentional torts, such as trespass, where P can recover nominal damages even without actual injury.)

> **Note:** When we say that these five elements make up a *"prima facie case"* for negligence, what we mean is that if as part of P's case in chief, P fails to prove any of these five elements, D will be entitled to a directed verdict by the judge (and the jury won't even get to deliberate).

II. UNREASONABLE RISK

A. **Generally:** P must show that D's conduct imposed an *unreasonable risk of harm* on P (or on a class of persons of whom P is a member). [97]

   1. **Not judged by results:** It is not enough for P to show that D's conduct resulted in a terrible injury. P must show that D's conduct, viewed *as of the time it occurred*, without benefit of hindsight, imposed an unreasonable risk of harm. [97]

B. **Balancing:** In determining whether the risk of harm from D's conduct was so great as to be "unreasonable," courts use a *balancing test*: "Where an act is one which a reasonable [person] would recognize as involving a risk of harm to another, the risk is unreasonable and the act is negligent if the risk is of such magnitude as to *outweigh* what the law regards as the *utility* of the act or of the particular manner in which it is done." [97]

   1. **Small risk of big harm:** Under the balancing test, if a reasonable person would realize that a potential injury, if it came to pass, would be *extremely grave*, there may be liability even though it was relatively *unlikely* that the accident would occur. [98]

      > **Example:** Suppose that D encounters a yellow traffic light while driving his heavy truck into Times Square. He has to decide whether to speed up to make the light, though in any event he intends to keep within the speed limit. D knows that the truck's brakes have been sporadically malfunctioning recently. Assume that D realizes or should realize that if the brakes fail at that moment, numerous people will likely be killed or maimed.
      >
      > Even if D reasonably believes that there is only, say, a 2% chance that the brakes will fail at that moment, the potential harm is so great, and the burden of stopping at the yellow light so small, that his conduct in speeding up is probably negligent despite the unlikeliness of a brake failure. [98]

C. **Warnings:** One of the ways the risks of conduct can be reduced is by giving *warnings* of danger. The fact that D gave a warning of dangers to P in particular, or the public in general, is thus a factor that will make it less likely that D will be found negligent when the danger that was warned of results in an accident. [99]

1. **Failure to warn can itself be negligent:** If D *fails* to give a warning of a danger that he knows about, and the warning could have been easily given, the mere failure to warn can itself *constitute negligence.*

2. **Does not immunize D:** However, it's clear that even if D *does* give a warning, this *does not immunize D* from negligence liability — if D's activity is unreasonably dangerous (evaluated by balancing its benefits against its risks) despite D's warning to P, D will still be liable.

   Example: Dave, while moving out of his second-floor apartment, throws an old television out the window, aiming for a dumpster on the ground below the window. Just before he throws the TV, he yells out "Look out below." Paula, a pedestrian, does not hear the warning because she is talking on her cellphone. Dave can be found negligent despite having given the warning — it is so dangerous to throw a heavy object out of an upstairs window, and so easy to discard the object by safer means, that the giving of the warning did not make the total benefits of Dave's conduct outweigh its dangers.

III. THE REASONABLE PERSON

C
A
P
S
U
L
E

S
U
M
M
A
R
Y

A. **Objective standard:** The reasonableness of D's conduct is viewed under an *objective standard*: Would a *"reasonable person* of ordinary prudence," in D's position, do as D did? D does not escape liability merely because she intended to behave carefully or thought she was behaving carefully. [100]

B. **Physical and mental characteristics:** The question is whether D behaved reasonably "under the circumstances." "The circumstances" generally include the *physical characteristics* of D himself. [100-103]

   1. **Physical disability:** Thus if D has a physical *disability*, the standard for negligence is what a reasonable person with that physical disability would have done. [101]

      Example: P is blind and is struck while crossing the street using a cane. If the issue is whether P was comparatively negligent, the issue will be whether a blind person would have crossed the street in that manner.

   2. **Mental characteristics:** The ordinary reasonable person is *not* deemed to have the particular *mental* characteristics of D. [102] (*Example:* If D is more stupid, or more careless, than an ordinary person, this will not be a defense.)

   3. **Intoxication:** Intoxication is no defense — even if D is drunk, she is held to the standard of conduct of a reasonable *sober* person. [103]

   4. **Children:** A *child* is held to the level of conduct of a reasonable person of that *age* and *experience*, not that of an adult. [103-104]

      a. **Adult activity:** But where a child engages in a potentially *dangerous activity* normally pursued only by *adults*, she will be held to the standard of care that a reasonable adult doing that activity would exercise.

         Example: Suppose D, a 12-year old, operates a motorboat. This is an activity that is potentially dangerous and normally pursued by adults. Therefore, D must match the standard of care of a reasonable adult boater.

C. **Custom:** Courts generally allow evidence as to *custom* for the purpose of showing presence or absence of reasonable care. However, this evidence is generally *not conclusive.* [105]

1. **Evidence by D:** Thus where D shows that everyone else in the industry does things the way D did them, the jury is still free to conclude that the industry custom is unreasonably dangerous and thus negligent. [105]

   > **Example:** D operates a tugboat without a radio. The fact that most tugboats in the industry do not yet have radios does not prevent the jury from holding that D's lack of a radio was negligent. [*The T.J. Hooper*]

2. **Proof by plaintiff:** Conversely, proof offered by P that others in D's industry *followed* a certain precaution that D did *not*, will be suggestive but *not conclusive* evidence that D was negligent. [105]

D. **Emergencies:** If D is confronted with an *emergency*, and is forced to act with little time for reflection, D must merely behave as a reasonable person would if confronted with the same emergency, not as a reasonable person would with plenty of time to think. [106]

   > **Example:** D is a cab driver. A thief jumps in the cab, points a gun at D's head, and tells him to drive fast. D, in a panic, mistakenly puts the car in reverse and injures P. The issue is whether a cab driver confronted with a gun-pointing thief would or might have behaved as D did, not whether a cab driver in ordinary circumstances would have behaved that way.

E. **Anticipating conduct of others:** A reasonable person possesses at least limited ability to *anticipate the conduct of others*. [107-110]

   1. **Negligence:** D may be required to anticipate the possibility of *negligence* on the part of others. [107]

      > **Example:** It may be negligence for D to presume that all drivers near him will behave non-negligently, and that these others will not speed, signal properly, etc.

      a. **Parental supervision:** A *parent* has a duty to exercise reasonable care to *supervise the conduct of his or her minor child*, to prevent the child from intentionally harming others or posing an unreasonable risk of harm to others. [107]

         i. **Direct liability:** This principle does *not* make the parent *"vicariously liable"* for the child's torts. Instead, it constitutes *direct* negligence by the parent not to use reasonable care in controlling the child, where the parent has the ability to control the child, and knows or should have known of the risk being posed by the child's conduct.

            > **Example:** As Mom is aware, Kid, her 10-year-old son, is skateboarding on the sidewalk in front of their house, in a way that poses great danger to pedestrian passersby. Mom knows that she could control Kid to prevent him from skateboarding in this manner, but she unreasonably decides that the risks posed by Kid are small enough to make it not worth Mom's while to intervene. Kid runs into P, a little old lady, who is badly injured.
            >
            > P can recover against Mom, for failing to use reasonable care to prevent Kid from dangerous skateboarding, given that Mom both (1) knew or should have known that she had the ability to control Kid and (2) knew or should have known that Kid's behavior was risky to pedestrians.

   2. **Criminal or intentionally tortious acts:** Normally the reasonable person (and, hence, D) is entitled to presume that third persons will *not* commit *crimes* or intentional torts. [108-110]

a. Special knowledge: But if D has a *special relationship* with either P or a third person, or special knowledge of the situation, then it may be negligence for D not to anticipate a crime or intentional tort.

> **Example:** It may be negligence for D, a psychiatrist, not to warn P that a patient of D's is dangerous to P. [*Tarasoff v. Regents,* 108]

IV. MALPRACTICE

A. Superior ability or knowledge: If D has a *higher degree* of *knowledge*, skill or experience than the "reasonable person," D must *use* that higher level. [110]

> **Example:** D, because she is a local resident, knows that a stretch of highway is exceptionally curvy and thus dangerous. D drives at a rate of speed that one who did not know the terrain well would think was reasonable, and crashes, injuring her passenger, P. Even though D's driving would not have represented carelessness if done by a reasonable person with ordinary knowledge of the road, D was responsible for using her special knowledge and is negligent for not doing so.)

B. Malpractice generally: Professionals, including doctors, lawyers, accountants, engineers, etc., must act with the level of skill and learning *commonly possessed by members of the profession in good standing.* [110-113]

1. Good results not guaranteed: The professional will not normally be held to guarantee that a *successful result* will occur, only that she will use the requisite minimum skill and competence. [110]

2. Specialists: If D holds herself out as a *specialist* in a certain niche in her profession, she will be held to the minimum standard of that specialty. [111]

> **Example:** An M.D. who holds herself out as an ophthalmologist must perform to the level of the minimally competent ophthalmologist, not merely to the minimum level of the internist or general practitioner.

3. Minimally qualified member: It is not enough for P to prove that D performed with less skill than the *average* member of the profession. D must be shown to have lacked the skill level of the *minimally qualified member* in good standing. [111]

a. Novice: One who is just *beginning* the practice of his special profession is held to the same level of competence as a member of the profession generally. [113]

> **Example:** A lawyer who has just passed the bar does not get the benefit of a lower standard — he must perform at the level of minimally competent lawyers generally, not novices.

4. Community standards: Traditionally, doctors and other professionals have been bound by the professional standards prevailing in the *community in which they practice*, not by a national standard. [111]

a. Change in rule: But this rule is on its way out, and many if not most courts would today apply a *national* standard. In "modern" courts, P may therefore use expert testimony from an expert who practices outside of D's community.

5. Informed consent: In the case of a physician, part of the professional duty is to adequately disclose the *risks* of proposed treatment to the patient in advance. The rule requiring adequate disclosure is called the rule of *"informed consent."* The doctor must disclose to the patient all risks inherent in the proposed treatment which are sufficiently *material* that a reasonable patient *would take them into account* in deciding whether to undergo the treatment. Failure to get the patient's adequate consent is deemed a form of malpractice and thus a form of negligence. (In some cases, usually older ones, failure to get informed consent transforms the treatment into battery.) [112]

V. AUTOMOBILE GUEST STATUTES

A. Generally: A minority of states still have "automobile guest statutes" on their books. These generally provide that an owner-driver is not liable for any injuries received by his *non-paying passenger*, unless the driver was grossly negligent or reckless. [113]

VI. VIOLATION OF STATUTE (*NEGLIGENCE PER SE*)

A. "Negligence *per se* " doctrine: Most courts apply the *"negligence per se"* doctrine: when a *safety statute* has a sufficiently close application to the facts of the case at hand, an unexcused *violation* of that statute by D is "negligence *per se*," and thus *conclusively establishes that D was negligent*. [114]

1. **Restatement standard:** The Third Restatement articulates the doctrine this way: "An actor is *negligent* if, *without excuse,* the actor *violates a statute that is designed to protect against the type of accident the actor's conduct causes*, and the accident *victim* is *within the class of persons the statute is designed to protect*." [115]

    > **Example:** D drives at 65 m.p.h. in a 55 m.p.h. zone. While so driving, he strikes and injures P, a pedestrian. Because the 55 m.p.h. limit is a safety measure designed to protect against accidents, and because pedestrians are among those the statute aims to protect, the fact that D has violated the statute without excuse conclusively establishes that D was negligent — D will not be permitted to argue that it was in fact safe to drive at 65 m.p.h.

2. **Ordinances and regulations:** In virtually all states, the negligence *per se* doctrine applies to the violation of a *statute*. Where the violation is of an *ordinance* or *regulation*, courts are split about whether the doctrine should apply, but most courts still apply it. [115]

B. Statute must apply to facts: The negligence *per se* doctrine will apply only where P shows that the statute was intended to guard against the *kind of injury* in question. [115-120]

1. **Protection against particular harm:** This means that the statute must have been intended to protect against the *particular kind of harm* that P seeks to recover for. [115-117]

    > **Example:** A statute requires that when animals are transported, each breed must be kept in a separate pen. D, a ship operator, violates the statute by herding P's sheep together with other animals. Because there are no pens, the sheep are washed overboard during a storm. P cannot use the negligence *per se* doctrine, because the statute was obviously intended to protect only against spread of disease, not washing overboard. [*Gorris v. Scott,* 116]

2. **Class of persons protected:** Also, P must be a member of the *class of persons* whom the statute was *designed to protect*. [116]

Example: A statute requires all factory elevators to be provided with a certain safety device. The legislative history shows that the purpose was only to protect injuries to employees. P, a business visitor, is injured when the elevator falls due to lack of the device. P cannot use the negligence *per se* doctrine, because he was not a member of the class of persons whom the statute was designed to protect.

C. Excuse of violation: The court is always free to find that the statutory violation was *excused*, as long as the statute itself does not show that no excuses are permitted. [117-119]

1. **Typical reasons:** Some typical reasons for finding D's violation to be excused are:

[a] D was reasonably *unaware* of the *"factual circumstances"* that make the statute applicable;

Example: A statute prohibits any contractor from doing excavation within 10 feet of a high-voltage power line. D, a contractor, excavates within 6 feet of such a line. However, D reasonably fails to realize that the line is present because it is obscured by heavy foliage. D knocks down the line, injuring P, a bystander.

Because D neither knew nor should have known of "the factual circumstances" that made the statute applicable to his particular excavation session, the negligence per se doctrine will not apply to his conduct.

[b] D made a reasonable and diligent *attempt* to comply;

[c] The violation was due to the *confusing way* the requirements of the statute were *presented to the public*;

Example: A road sign on Main St. says "No Left Turn." The sign is placed just before two roads turn off of Main St., Maple and Oak. A reasonable driver could be confused about whether the sign means that left turns are prohibited onto Maple, Oak, or both. D, reasonably believing that the sign applies to Maple but not to Oak, turns left onto Oak, and collides with P. D would not be subject to liability under negligence per se, because the confusing nature of the sign would excuse his non-compliance.

[d] Compliance would have involved a *greater risk of harm*.

D. Contributory negligence *per se*: If the jurisdiction recognizes *contributory negligence*, D may get the benefit of contributory negligence *per se* where P violates a statute. [119] (*Example:* Cars driven by P and D collide. If P was violating the speed limit, and the jurisdiction recognizes contributory negligence, D can probably use the negligence *per se* doctrine to establish that P was contributorily negligent.)

E. Compliance not dispositive: The fact that D has *fully complied* with all applicable safety statutes does not by itself establish that he was *not* negligent — the finder of fact is always free to conclude that a reasonable person would take precautions beyond those required by statute. [120]

VII. PROCEDURE IN JURY TRIALS

A. Burden of proof: In a negligence case (as in almost all tort cases) P bears the "burden of proof." This is actually two distinct burdens: [120-121]

1. **Burden of production:** First, P must *come forward* with some evidence that P was negligent, that P suffered an injury, that D's negligence proximately caused the injury, etc. This

burden is known as the ***"burden of production.""*** This burden shifts from P to D, and perhaps back again during the trial. [120-121]

2. **Burden of persuasion:** Second, P bears the ***"burden of persuasion.""*** This means that as the case goes to the jury, P must convince the jury that it is ***more probable than not*** that his injuries are due to D's negligence. [121]

B. Function of judge and jury

1. **Judge decides law:** The judge decides all questions of ***law***. Most importantly, the judge decides whether reasonable people could differ as to what the facts of the case are. If reasonable people could not differ, the judge will direct a verdict. [122-123]

> **Example:** In a car accident case, if the judge decides that D drove so fast that no reasonable person could believe that D acted non-negligently, he will take this issue away from the jury. That is, he'll tell the jury that they *must* find D negligent.

2. **Jury decides facts:** The jury is the finder of the ***facts***. In a negligence case (assuming that the judge does not direct a full or partial verdict), the jury decides: (a) what really happened; and (2) whether D breached his duty to P in a way that proximately caused P's injuries. This means that it is the jury that usually decides whether D's conduct satisfied the "reasonable person" standard. [123]

VIII. *RES IPSA LOQUITUR* — CREATING AN INFERENCE OF NEGLIGENCE

A. Generally: The doctrine of *res ipsa loquitur* ("the thing speaks for itself") allows P to point to the fact of the accident, and to create an ***inference*** that, even without a precise showing of how D behaved, D was ***probably negligent***.

> **Example:** A barrel of flour falls on P's head as he walks below a window on the street. At trial, P shows that the barrel fell out of a window of D's shop, and that barrels do not fall out of windows without some negligence. By use of the *res ipsa loquitur* doctrine, P has presented enough evidence to justify a verdict for him, so unless D comes up with rebuttal evidence that the barrel did not come from his shop or was not dropped by negligence, D will lose. [*Byrne v. Boadle*] [123]

B. Requirements for: Courts generally impose four requirements for the *res ipsa* doctrine: [124]

1. **No direct evidence of D's conduct:** There must be ***no direct evidence*** of ***how D behaved*** in connection with the event. [124]

2. **Seldom occurring without negligence:** P must demonstrate that the harm which occurred ***does not normally occur*** except through the negligence of someone. P only has to prove that ***most of the time***, negligence is the cause of such occurrences. [124]

> **Example:** If an airplane crashes without explanation, P will generally be able to establish that airplanes usually do not crash without some negligence, thus meeting this requirement.

3. **Exclusive control of defendant:** P must demonstrate that the instrumentality that caused the harm was at all times within the ***exclusive control*** of D. [126-128]

Example: P, while walking on the sidewalk next to D hotel, is hit by a falling armchair. Without more proof, P has not satisfied the "exclusive control" requirement, because a guest, rather than the hotel, may have had control of the chair at the moment it was dropped. [*Larson v. St. Francis Hotel*]

    a. **Not always required:** But not all courts require P to show that the instrumentality was under D's exclusive control, and the Third Restatement has dropped this requirement. [126]

    b. **Multiple defendants:** Also, if there are *two or more defendants*, and P can show that at least one of the defendants was in control, some cases allow P to recover. This is especially likely where all of the Ds participate together in an integrated relationship.

        Example: P is injured while on the operating table, and shows that either the surgeon, the attending physician, the hospital, or the anesthesiologist must have been at fault, but is unable to show which one. P gets the benefit of *res ipsa*, and it is up to each individual defendant to exculpate himself. [*Ybarra v. Spangard*]

  4. **Not due to plaintiff:** P must establish that the accident was probably not due to his *own* conduct. [128]

  5. **Evidence more available to D:** Some courts also require that *evidence* of what really happened be *more available to D* than to P. [128]

    Example: This requirement is satisfied on the facts of *Ybarra, supra*, since the Ds obviously knew more than the unconscious patient about who was at fault.

C. Expert testimony: As noted, plaintiff has to to show that the type of accident is one that does not normally happen in the absence of negligence by someone, as well as that more likely than not the negligence was probably that of the defendant(s). If the facts are complex or involve *specialized knowledge* (e.g., *technology*), insight into whether the accident would probably have happened without negligence may be *beyond the expertise of the jury*. In this scenario, most courts today *allow* the plaintiff to *use expert testimony* to establish these preconditions for *res ipsa*.

  1. **Medical malpractice:** Thus expert testimony to show that the requirements for *res ipsa* are satisfied is often allowed in *medical malpractice* cases, for instance. [129]

    Example: The three Ds are all members of a surgical team that operates on P's back. P gets a serious infection at the surgical site, and sues on a *res ipsa* theory. *Held*: P may offer expert testimony by other doctors that this sort of surgical-site infection doesn't generally happen without negligence, and that usually the surgical-team members are the ones in control of what infection-control measures are used. [*Sides v. St. Anthony's Medical Ctr*] [129]

D. Effect of *res ipsa*: Usually, the *effect* of *res ipsa* is to permit an inference that D was negligent, even though there is no direct evidence of negligence. *Res ipsa* thus allows a particular kind of circumstantial evidence. When *res ipsa* is used, P has *met his burden of production*, and is thus entitled to go to the jury. [129-130]

E. Rebuttal evidence:

  1. **General evidence of due care:** If D's rebuttal is merely in the form of evidence showing that he was *in fact careful*, this will almost never be enough to give D a directed verdict — the case will still go to the jury. [130]

2. Rebuttal of *res ipsa* requirements: But if D's evidence directly disproves one of the requirements for the doctrine's application, then D will get a directed verdict (assuming there is no prima facie case apart from *res ipsa*). [130]

> **Example:** If, in a state that requires exclusive control by D, D can show that the instrument that caused the harm was not within his control at all relevant times, the doctrine will not apply, and D may get a directed verdict.

F. Typical contexts: Here are a couple of contexts in which the *res ipsa* issue is especially likely to arise:

1. Airplane accidents: A commercial ***airplane*** accident in which the plane ***crashes into an obstruction*** like a mountain, often furnishes a good illustration of *res ipsa*. [130]

  a. *Res ipsa* applies: Today, airplanes don't usually fly into obstructions without someone's negligence, at least in clear weather. Therefore, the estate of a dead passenger will normally be deemed to have established negligence merely by showing that the plane crashed into an obstruction in good weather.

   i. Rebuttal: But the airline is always free to try to ***rebut*** the evidence, such as by showing that an unforeseeable explosion caused the airplane to veer off course into the obstruction.

2. Car accidents: Plaintiffs often attempt to apply *res ipsa* to ***car accidents***. The analysis varies sharply with whether there are multiple vehicles involved or just one. [131]

  a. Multiple vehicles: *Res ipsa* usually does ***not*** apply to car crashes involving ***multiple vehicles.*** In most multi-vehicle crashes, it generally cannot be said that that type of accident does not happen without someone's negligence. Furthermore, even if someone's negligence were probable, usually the negligence of persons other than the defendant (e.g., the plaintiff, driving in a separate car) cannot be sufficiently eliminated by the evidence.

  b. Single-car accident: On the other hand, if the accident is a ***single-vehicle one*** (e.g., between a driver and a pedestrian), then *res ipsa* will often ***apply***, since such accidents usually involve driver negligence.

  > **Example:** P, a pedestrian walking along the road, is struck from the rear by D's car. P is probably entitled to use *res ipsa* to create an inference of D's negligence, since such accidents usually involve driver negligence.

   i. Rebuttal evidence: But D is always free to come up with evidence ***rebutting*** the *res ipsa* inference of negligence (e.g., that D had an unforeseeable heart attack just before the accident, or, in the above example, that P veered directly in front of D just before the accident).

CHAPTER 6

ACTUAL AND PROXIMATE CAUSE

I. CAUSATION IN FACT

A. Generally: P must show that D's conduct was the ***"cause in fact"*** of P's injury. [141]

B. "But for" test: The vast majority of the time, the way P shows "cause in fact" is to show that D's conduct was a *"but for"* cause of P's injuries — *had D not acted negligently, P's injuries would not have resulted.* [141]

> **Example:** P takes her prescription for a medication to D, her local pharmacy. D mistakenly fills the prescription by giving P pills containing 30 mg of the active ingredient rather than the 20 mg called for by the prescription. After taking the pills, P suffers serious heart arrhythmia, and sues D for this harm. P can recover only if she proves that had D provided the correct, 20 mg, pills, P would not have suffered the arrhythmia. In other words, for P to recover, the trier of fact must be satisfied that the wrong pills were the "but for" cause of P's arrhythmia. [141]

1. Joint tortfeasors: There can be *multiple* "but for" causes of an event. D1 cannot defend on the grounds that D2 was a "but for" cause of P's injuries — as long as D1 was also a "but for" cause, D1 is viewed as the "cause in fact." [142]

C. Concurrent causes: Sometimes D's conduct can meet the "cause in fact" requirement even though it is *not* a "but for" cause. This happens where two events *concur* to cause harm, and either one would have been sufficient to cause substantially the same harm without the other. *Each* of these concurring events is deemed a cause in fact of the injury, since it would have been sufficient to bring the injury about. [142]

> **Example:** Sparks from D's locomotive start a forest fire; the fire merges with some other unknown fire, and the combined fires burn P's property. Either fire alone would have been sufficient to burn P's property. Therefore, D's fire is a cause in fact of P's damage, even though it is not a "but for" cause. [*Kingston v. Chicago & N.W. Ry.*]

D. Proof of actual cause — generally: The plaintiff bears the burden of proving that the defendant's conduct was the cause in fact of his injury, just as he must bear the burden of proving the other parts of his *prima facie* case. However, he must demonstrate this actual causation merely by a *preponderance of the evidence.*

1. Proof of "cause in fact" aspect: Thus the plaintiff does not have to prove with absolute certainty that had it not been for the defendant's conduct, the injury would not have occurred. All he has to do is to show that it is *probable* (*more likely than not*) that the injury would not have occurred without the defendant's act. [143]

E. Actual cause – the "value of a chance" problem: We just saw (in Par. 1 immediately above) that P merely has to show that it's "more likely than not" that D's act was a cause in fact of the injury to P. But now, let's consider the *converse* situation, in which P definitely suffered an injury, but there is a *less than 50/50 chance* that D caused that injury. In this scenario, application of the traditional "more likely than not" requirement for recovery would mean that P would *recover $0.* Do modern courts strictly apply this often-harsh requirement? The answer is generally *"yes,"* except for one special case (medical malpractice), which we discuss in Par. 2 below. [146]

1. The traditional rule: Thus outside of the special medical-malpractice scenario, if the plaintiff proves that there is a substantial but less than 50/50 chance that the defendant negligently caused the (undisputed) injury, the plaintiff is *completely out of luck — she recovers $0.* [147]

2. The medical malpractice scenario: But there is one *exception* to the general rule that where P proves a real but less than 50/50 chance that D caused her harm P recovers nothing. The exception arises in the area of *medical malpractice.* Recall (C-24) that a patient who proves that the treatment she received from her doctor failed to conform to the reasonable standard of care owed by physicians may recover for medical malpractice, a special type of negligence action. Now, suppose that the nature of the malpractice is that the physician failed to provide a ***timely diagnosis or treatment of the patient's disease,*** and that this delay causes the patient to ***die or suffer a worse medical outcome.*** Suppose further that had the treatment or diagnosis been done promptly and without negligence, there is a real, ***but less than 50/50,*** chance that either the bad outcome would have been delayed, or the patient would have been cured.

a.   **Traditional approach denies recovery:**   Notice that if the traditional approach is applied, P would be deemed to have failed to prove by the required "preponderance of the evidence" standard (i.e., more likely than not) that D was the cause in fact of her harm, so she recovers nothing.   And indeed, a ***substantial minority*** of states still apply this traditional approach. [147]

b.   **The "value of a chance" doctrine:**   But a ***majority*** of the states that have considered the problem in the last couple of decades have ***declined to follow the traditional rule*** denying all recovery, and instead allow plaintiff P who shows a less than 50/50 chance that prompt-and-appropriate treatment would have avoided the bad outcome to recover for a ***special type of injury,*** namely an injury characterized as being ***"the loss of the opportunity for a better outcome,*** rather than the death or worse outcome." This approach is commonly called the *"loss of a chance" approach*. Thus in these majority states, P is permitted to recover an amount equal to:

> the ***value the claim would have had*** if the injury was proved more likely than not to have been caused by the malpractice *times*

> the ***percentage chance that a favorable result would have occurred*** had there been no malpractice.

Example: When P begins having some initial symptoms of a stroke, he seeks treatment at D, a physicians' group. D negligently fails to give P timely and adequate stroke-prevention care. P suffers a catastrophic stroke that results in permanent brain damage. Medical evidence demonstrates that in ***one-third*** of the cases where the patient has initial stroke symptoms like P's, proper and prompt treatment enables the patient to suffer no or reduced stroke complications thereafter. P sues D in Oregon state court to recover for value of this "loss of a chance at recovery." D counters that because P cannot prove that it's "more likely than not" that prompt treatment would have prevented the brain damage, P is not entitled to any recovery at all.

Held (by the Oregon Supreme Court), for P. A "limited loss-of-chance" theory of recovery should be recognized in negligence cases involving medical malpractice in Oregon. Under this theory, "a plaintiff who demonstrates that a physician's negligence reduced his chance of a favorable medical outcome from 33% to 0% [can] recover damages based on the unfavorable medical consequences suffered, but only to the possible extent of ***33% of the damages*** resulting from the adverse medical outcome." [*Smith v. Providence Health & Services*] [148]

C
A
P
S
U
L
E

S
U
M
M
A
R
Y

F. Multiple fault: If P can show that each of two (or more) defendants was at fault, but only one could have caused the injury, the ***burden shifts*** to each defendant to show that the other caused the harm. [150]

> **Example:** P, D1 and D2 go hunting together. D1 and D2 simultaneously fire negligently, and P is struck by one of the shots. It is not known who fired the fatal shot. The court will put the burden on each of the Ds to show that it was the other shot which hit P — if neither D can make this showing, both will be liable. [*Summers v. Tice*]

1. The "market share" theory: In ***product liability*** cases, courts often apply the ***"market share"*** theory. If P cannot prove which of three or more persons caused his injury, but can show that all produced a defective product, the court will require each of the Ds to pay that percentage of P's injuries which that D's sales bore to the total market sales of that type of product at the time of injury. The theory is used most often in cases involving prescription drugs. [150]

> **Example:** 200 manufacturers make the drug DES. P shows that her mother took the drug during pregnancy, and that the drug caused P to develop cancer. P cannot show which DES manufacturer produced the drug taken by her mother. *Held*, any manufacturer who cannot show that it could not have produced the particular doses taken by P's mother will be liable for the proportion of any judgment represented by that manufacturer's share of the overall DES market. [*Sindell v. Abbott Laboratories*] [151]

a. Exculpation: Courts are split on whether each defendant should be allowed to ***exculpate*** itself by showing that it ***did not make*** the particular items in question — some more modern cases hold that once a given defendant is shown to have produced drugs for the national market, no exculpation will be allowed. [151]

G. Increased risk, not yet followed by actual damage: Where D's conduct has increased the ***risk*** that P will suffer some later damage, but the damage has ***not yet occurred***, most courts ***deny*** P any recovery for that later damage unless he can show that it is more likely than not to occur eventually. But some courts now allow recovery for such damage, discounted by the likelihood that the damage will occur. [149]

II. PROXIMATE CAUSE GENERALLY

A. General: Even after P has shown that D was the "cause in fact" of P's injuries, P must still show that D was the ***"proximate cause"*** of those injuries. The proximate cause requirement is a ***policy determination*** that a defendant, even one who has behaved negligently, should not automatically be liable for ***all*** the consequences, no matter how ***improbable*** or ***far-reaching***, of his act. Today, the proximate cause requirement usually means that D will not be liable for the consequences that are very ***unforeseeable***. [153]

> **Example:** D, driving carelessly, collides with a car driven by X. Unbeknownst to D, the car contains dynamite, which explodes. Ten blocks away, a nurse who is carrying P, an infant, is startled by the explosion, and drops P. P will not be able to recover against D, because the episode is so far-fetched — it was so unforeseeable that the injury would occur from D's negligence — that courts will hold that D's careless driving was not the "proximate cause" of P's injuries.

1. **Multiple proximate causes:** Just as an occurrence can have many "causes in fact," so it may well have more than one proximate cause. [153] (***Example:*** Each of two drivers drives negligently, and P is injured. Each driver is probably a proximate cause of the accident.)

III. PROXIMATE CAUSE — FORESEEABILITY

A. **The foreseeability rule generally:** As the idea is traditionally stated, D is generally liable only for those consequences of his negligence which were ***reasonably foreseeable*** at the time she acted. [154]

> **Example:** D's ship spills oil into a bay. Some of the oil adheres to P's wharf. The oil is then set afire by some molten metal dropped by P's worker, which ignites a cotton rag floating on the water. P's whole dock then burns. *Held,* D is not liable, because the burning of P's dock was not the foreseeable consequence of D's oil spill, and thus the oil spill was not the proximate cause of the damage. This is true even though the burning may have been the "direct" result of D's negligence. [*Wagon Mound No. 1*] [155]

1. **Third Restatement:** The Third Restatement applies the same basic concept as the above "foreseeability" principle, but formulates it slightly differently: a defendant is "not liable for harm ***different from the harms whose risk made the [defendant's] conduct tortious.***" [158]

> **Example 1:** Consider the above example of the oil spill that catches fire. The Third Restatement would presumably agree with the result in the above example: what made D's oil spill tortious was that it was a nuisance (and perhaps a trespass) that risked junking up the wharf with a foreign substance. The risk of a fire from the spill was *not* one of the risks that made the spill tortious, so D isn't liable for it.

> **Example 2:** D gives a loaded pistol to X, an 8-year-old, to carry across the room and put in a cabinet. While X is carrying the pistol, he drops it. The gun lands on the bare foot of P, X's playmate, and because of its one-pound weight breaks P's toe.

> Under the Third Restatement's "harms that made D's conduct tortious" test, D would not be liable to P, since what made the entrustment of the gun by D to a child negligent was the risk of *shooting* (including a shooting caused by dropping of the gun), not the risk of a foot injury from the weight of the gun if the gun was dropped. [161]

B. **Function of judge and jury:** Is it the ***judge*** or the ***jury*** who decides the issue of proximate cause? The answer is that *both* the judge and the jury participate in deciding this issue, but they participate in different ways.

1. **Judge formulates the legal rule:** It is up to the ***judge*** to ***formulate the appropriate legal rule*** in the form of an instruction to the jury.

a. **Judge's "gatekeeper" function:** Although the judge doesn't make the factual determination of whether D proximately caused P's injuries, the judge exercises an important ***"gatekeeper"*** function. That is, the judge can and should ***prevent the case from ever being decided by the jury,*** if the judge decides that ***no reasonable jury could find that the plaintiff has established each element of her prima facie case*** by the required preponderance of the evidence. [171]

Therefore, if the judge decides that on the proof offered by the plaintiff, ***no reasonable jury could decide that it is more likely than not that the defendant proximately caused the plaintiff's injuries***, the ***judge will decide the case*** in favor of the defendant on a motion for summary judgment or for a directed verdict — the jury will **never get a chance to decide** whether D proximately caused P's injuries.

2. **Factual determination left to the jury:** But in most negligence cases, the judge will **not exercise** her right to **short-circuit the case** by taking the decision on proximate cause away from the jury. That is, usually the judge will decide that a reasonable jury could **go either way** on this issue; in that case, the judge will instruct the jury on the test for determining proximate cause, and **will leave it to the jury to apply that test in deciding the factual issue** of whether the defendant's failure to use due care was so tenuously connected with the harm that proximate cause should be found lacking.

C. **Unforeseeable plaintiff:** The general rule that D is liable only for foreseeable consequences is also usually applied to the **"unforeseeable plaintiff"** problem. That is, if D's conduct is negligent as to X (in the sense that it imposes an unreasonable risk of harm upon X), but not negligent as to P (i.e., does not impose an unreasonable risk of harm upon P), P will not be able to recover if through some fluke he is injured. [156-158]

> **Example:** X, trying to board D's train, is pushed by D's employee. X drops a package, which (unknown to anybody) contains fireworks, which explode when they fall. The shock of the explosion makes some scales at the other end of the platform fall down, hitting P.
>
> *Held*, P may not recover against D. D's employee may have been negligent towards X (by pushing him), but the employee's conduct did not involve any foreseeable risk of harm to P, who was standing far away. Since D's conduct did not involve an unreasonable risk of harm to P, and the damage to her was not foreseeable, the fact that the conduct was unjustifiably risky to X is irrelevant. D's conduct was not the "proximate cause" of the harm to P. [*Palsgraf v. Long Island R.R. Co.,* 156]

D. **Extensive consequences from physical injuries:** A key **exception** to the general rule that D is liable only for foreseeable consequences is: once P suffers any foreseeable impact or injury, even if relatively minor, D is liable for **any additional unforeseen physical consequences**. [159]

1. **Egg-shell skull:** Thus if P, unbeknownst to D, has a very **thin skull** (a skull of "egg-shell thinness"), and D negligently inflicts a minor impact on this skull, D will be liable if, because of the hidden skull defect, P dies. The defendant **"takes his plaintiff as he finds him."** [159]

E. **General class of harm but not same manner:** Another exception to the "foreseeable consequences only" rule is that as long as the harm suffered by P is of the **same general sort** that made D's conduct negligent, it is irrelevant that the harm occurred in an **unusual manner**. [161]

> **Example:** D gives a loaded pistol to X, an eight-year-old, to carry to P. In handing the pistol to P, X drops it, injuring the bare foot of Y, his playmate. The fall sets off the gun, wounding P. D is liable to P, since the same general kind of risk that made D's conduct negligent (the risk of accidental discharge) has materialized to injure P; the fact that the discharge occurred in an unforeseeable manner — by the dropping of the gun — is irrelevant. (But D is not liable to Y, since Y's foot injury was not foreseeable, and the risk of it was not one of the risks that made D's conduct initially negligent.)

F. **Plaintiff part of foreseeable class:** Another exception to the foreseeability rule: the fact that injury to the particular plaintiff was not especially foreseeable is irrelevant, as long as P is a **member of a class** as to which there was a general foreseeability of harm. [161]

Example: D negligently moors its ship, and the ship breaks away. It smashes into a draw bridge, causing it to create a dam, which results in a flood. The Ps, various riparian owners whose property is flooded, sue. *Held*, these owners can recover against D, even though it would have been hard to foresee which particular owners might be flooded. All of the Ps were members of the general class of riverbank property owners, as to which class there was a risk of harm from flooding. [*Petition of Kinsman Transit Co.*]

IV. PROXIMATE CAUSE — INTERVENING CAUSES

A. Definition of "intervening cause": Most proximate cause issues arise where P's injury is precipitated by an *"intervening cause."* An intervening cause is a force which takes effect *after* D's negligence, and which contributes to that negligence in producing P's injury. [162]

    1. Superseding cause: Some, but not all, intervening causes are sufficient to prevent D's negligence from being held to be the proximate cause of the injury. Intervening causes that are sufficient to prevent D from being negligent are called *"superseding"* causes, since they supersede or cancel D's liability. [162]

B. Foreseeability rule: Generally courts use a *foreseeability* rule to determine whether a particular intervening cause is superseding. [162]

    1. Test: If D should have *foreseen* the possibility that the intervening cause (or one like it) might occur, *or* if the *kind of harm* suffered by P was foreseeable (even if the intervening cause was not itself foreseeable), D's conduct will nonetheless be the proximate cause. But if *neither* the intervening cause nor the kind of harm was foreseeable, the intervening cause will be a superseding one, relieving D of liability. [162-163]

C. Foreseeable intervening causes: Often the risk of a particular kind of intervening cause is the *very risk* (or one of the risks) which made D's conduct negligent in the first place. Where this is the case, the intervening cause will almost never relieve D of liability. [162-165]

    Example: D leaves his car keys in the ignition, and the car unlocked, while going into a store to do an errand. X comes along, steals the car, and while driving fast to get out of the neighborhood, runs over P. If the court believes that the risk of theft is one of the things that makes leaving one's keys in the ignition negligent, the court will almost certainly conclude that X's intervening act was not superseding.

    1. Foreseeable negligence: The *negligence of third persons* may similarly be an intervening force that is sufficiently foreseeable that it will not relieve D of liability. [163-165]

    Example: D is a tavern owner, who serves too much liquor to X, knowing that X arrived alone by car. D also does not object when X gets out his car keys and leaves. If X drunkenly runs over P, a court will probably hold that X's conduct in negligently (drunkenly) driving, although intervening, was sufficiently foreseeable that it should not absolve D of liability.

    2. Criminally or intentionally tortious conduct: A third person's *criminal conduct*, or *intentionally tortious acts*, may also be so foreseeable that they will not be superseding. But in general, the court is more likely to find the act superseding if it is criminal or intentionally tortious than where it is merely negligent. [164]

C
A
P
S
U
L
E

S
U
M
M
A
R
Y

D. Responses to defendant's actions: Where the third party's intervention is a ***"normal" response*** to the defendant's act, that response will generally ***not*** be considered superseding. This is true even if the response was not all that foreseeable. [164-168]

1. Escape: For instance, if in response to the danger created by D, P or someone else attempts to ***escape*** that danger, the attempted escape will not be a superseding cause so long as it was not completely irrational or bizarre. [165]

Example: D, driving negligently, sideswipes P's car on the highway. P panics, thrusts the wheel to the right, and slams into a railing. Even though most drivers in P's position might not have reacted in such an extreme or unhelpful manner, P's response is not sufficiently bizarre to constitute a superseding cause.

2. Rescue: Similarly, if D's negligence creates a danger which causes some third person to attempt a ***rescue***, this rescue will normally not be an intervening cause, unless it is performed in a ***grossly careless*** manner. D may be liable to the ***person being rescued*** (even if part or all of his injuries are due to the rescuer's ordinary negligence), or ***to the rescuer***. [166-167]

3. Aggravation of injury by medical treatment: If D negligently injures P, who then undergoes ***medical treatment***, D will be liable for anything that happens to P as the result of negligence in the medical treatment, infection, etc. [167]

Examples: After being initially injured by D in a car accident, P is further injured when the ambulance carrying her gets into a collision, or when, due to the surgeon's negligence, P's condition is worsened rather than improved. D is liable for this worsening.

a. Gross mistreatment: But some results of attempted medical treatment are so ***gross*** and unusual that they are regarded as superseding. [166]

Example: While P is hospitalized due to injuries negligently inflicted by D, a nurse kills P by giving him an injection of morphine which she knows may be fatal, because she wants to spare him from suffering. D is not liable for P's death because the nurse's conduct is so bizarre as to be superseding.

E. Unforeseeable intervention, foreseeable result: If an intervention is neither foreseeable nor normal, but leads to the ***same type of harm*** as that which was threatened by D's negligence, the intervention is usually ***not*** superseding. [168]

Example: D negligently maintains a telephone pole, letting it get infested by termites. X drives into the pole. The pole breaks and falls on P. A properly-maintained telephone pole would not have broken under the blow. Even though the chain of events (termite infestation followed by car crash) was bizarre, X's intervention will not be superseding, because the result that occurred was the same general *type* of harm as that which was threatened by D's negligence — that the pole would somehow fall down. [*Gibson v. Garcia*]

F. Unforeseeable intervention, unforeseeable results: If the intervention was not foreseeable or normal, and it produced results which are *not* of the same general nature as those that made D's conduct negligent, the intervention will probably be ***superseding***. [169-170]

1. Extraordinary act of nature: Thus an ***extraordinary act of nature*** is likely to be superseding. [169]

Example: Assume that it is negligent to one's neighbors to build a large wood pile in one's back yard, because this may attract termites which will then spread. D builds a large wood pile. An unprecedentedly-strong hurricane sweeps through, takes one of the logs, and blows it into P's bedroom, killing him. The hurricane will probably be held to be a superseding intervening cause, because it was so strong as to be virtually unforeseeable, and the type of harm it produced was not of the type that made D's conduct negligent in the first place.

G. Dependent vs. independent intervention: Courts sometimes distinguish between *"dependent"* intervening causes and *"independent"* ones. A dependent intervening cause is one which occurs only in *response* to D's negligence. An independent intervention is one which would have occurred even had D not been negligent (but which combined with D's negligence to produce the harm). Dependent intervening events are probably somewhat more foreseeable on average, and thus somewhat less likely to be superseding, than independent ones. But a dependent cause can be superseding (e.g., a grossly negligent rescue attempt), and an independent intervention can be non-superseding. [170]

H. Third person's failure to discover: A third person's *failure* to *discover and prevent* a danger will almost never be superseding. For instance, if a manufacturer negligently produces a dangerous product, it will never be absolved merely because some person further down the distribution chain (e.g., a retailer) negligently fails to discover the danger, and thus fails to warn P about it. [173]

   1. Third person does discover: But if the third person does *discover* the defect, and then willfully and negligently fails to warn P, D may escape liability if D took all reasonable steps to remedy the danger.

      Example: D manufactures a machine, and sells it to X. D then learns that the machine may crush the hands of users. D offers to X to fix the machine for free. X declines. P, a worker for X, gets his hand crushed. X's failure to warn P or allow the machine to be fixed by D probably supersedes, and relieves D of liability because D tried to do everything it could.

CHAPTER 7
JOINT TORTFEASORS

I. JOINT LIABILITY

A. Joint-and-several liability generally: If more than one person is a proximate cause of P's harm, and the harm is *indivisible*, under the traditional approach *each defendant* is liable for the *entire harm*. The liability is said to be *"joint-and-several."* [183]

   Example: D1 negligently scratches P. P goes to the hospital, where she is negligently treated by D2, a doctor, causing her to lose her arm. P can recover her entire damages from D1, or her entire damages from D2, though she cannot collect twice.

   1. Modern trend cuts back on joint-and-several liability: But there has been a very sharp trend in recent decades to *cut back*, or even completely *eliminate*, *joint-and-several liability*. This has been mainly due to the rise of comparative negligence as a replacement for contributory negligence. (See *infra*, p. C-61.)

    a. Few states keep traditional rule: As of 2000, only 15 jurisdictions maintained pure joint-and-several liability.

    b. Hybrids: About 20 states have replaced joint-and-several liability with one of several *"hybrid"* schemes that combine aspects of joint-and-several liability with aspects of pure several liability. [184]

    ❏ **Hybrid joint-and-several liability with reallocation:** The most common hybrid scheme is this: all defendants are jointly-and-severally liable, but if one defendant turns out to be judgment-proof, the court *reallocates the damages* to all other parties (including the plaintiff) in proportion to their comparative fault. [184]

    Example: P sues D1, D2 and D3 for an indivisible harm. P's damages are $100,000. The jury concludes that P is 10% responsible, D1 40%, D2 25% and D3 25%. D1 turns out to be judgment-proof. The court will reallocate based on D1's insolvency, so that D2 and D3 are each jointly-and-severally liable for 50/60ths of $100,000 (i.e., $83,333). The effect is that P and the remaining Ds will *share the burden* of D1's insolvency in a ratio to their relative fault.

    c. Pure several liability: 16 states now have *pure several liability* — in these states, a defendant, regardless of the nature of the case, is liable only for her share of total responsibility.

B. Indivisible versus divisible harms: Even where the traditional rule of joint-and-several liability is in force, it applies only where P's harm is *"indivisible,"* i.e., not capable of being *apportioned* between or among the defendants. If there is a rational basis for apportionment — that is, for saying that some of the harm is the result of D1's act and the remainder is the result of D2's act — then *each will be responsible only for that directly-attributable harm.* [185]

    1. Rules on apportionment: Here is a summary of the rules on when harms will or won't be capable of being apportioned:

    a. Action in concert: If the two defendants can be said to have acted *in concert*, each will be liable for injuries directly caused by the other. In other words, apportionment does not take place. [161]

    Example: D1 and D2 drag race. D1's car swerves and hits P. D2, even though his car was not part of the collision, is liable for the entire injuries caused by D1's collision, because D1 and D2 acted in concert.

    b. Successive injuries: Courts often are able to apportion harm if the harms occurred in *successive incidents*, separated by substantial periods of time. [186]

    Example: D1, owner of a factory, pollutes P's property from 1970-1990. D1 sells to D2, who pollutes P's property from 1991-2000. The court will apportion the damage — neither defendant will have to pay for damage done by the other.

    i. Consequence of non-apportionability: If P is harmed in successive incidents involving multiple Ds, courts will usually place the *burden of allocating the damages* on the *Ds*, not on P. In other words, if no one proves how much of P's damages from the two successive torts are reasonably allocated to D1 and how much to D2, the court will typically make the Ds jointly and severally liable, so that the tortfeasors, not the innocent plaintiff, bear the "burden of unallocability." [187]

Example: D1 and D2 each separately pollutes a stream, poisoning P's livestock, and damaging P by $100,000. Neither D (nor P) offers proof allocating the damages as between D1 and D2. A court will likely hold D1 and D2 jointly and severally liable, on the theory that the uncertainty about how damages should be allocated between the two should hurt them, not P.

    ii. Overlapping: It may be the case that D1 is jointly and severally liable for the harm caused by both her acts and D2's, but that D2 is liable only for his own. This is especially likely where D2's negligence is in *response* to D1's. [187]

    Example: D1 negligently breaks P's arm. D2 negligently sets the arm, leading to gangrene and then amputation. D1 is liable for all harm, including the amputation. D2 is only liable for the amount by which his negligence worsened the condition — that is, he's liable for the difference between a broken and amputated arm.

  c. Indivisible harms: Some harms are *indivisible* (making each co-defendant jointly and severally liable for the entire harm, in a jurisdiction following the traditional approach to joint liability).

    i. Death or single injury: Thus the plaintiff's *death* or any *single personal injury* (e.g., a broken arm) is *not divisible*. [187]

    ii. Fires: Similarly, if P's property is *burned* or otherwise destroyed, this will be an indivisible result. [187]

    Example: D1 and D2 each negligently contribute to the starting of a fire, which then destroys P's house. There will be no apportionment, so D1 and D2 will each be liable for P's full damages in a state applying traditional joint-and-several liability.

C. One satisfaction only: Even if D1 and D2 are jointly and severally liable, P is only entitled to a *single satisfaction* of her claim. [188]

  Example: P suffers harm of $1 million, for which the court holds D1 and D2 jointly and severally liable. If P recovers the full $1 million from D1, she may not recover anything from D2.

II. CONTRIBUTION

A. Contribution generally: If two Ds are jointly and severally liable, and one D pays more than his *pro rata share*, he may usually obtain partial *reimbursement* from the other D. This is called *"contribution."* [189]

  Example: A court holds that D1 and D2 are jointly and severally liable to P for $1 million. P collects the full $1 million from D1. In most instances, D1 may recover $500,000 contribution from D2, so that they will end up having each paid the same amount.

  1. Amount: As a general rule, each joint-and-severally-liable defendant is required to pay an *equal share*. [190]

    a. Comparative negligence: But in *comparative negligence* states, the duty of contribution is usually *proportional to fault*.

Example: A jury finds that P was not at fault at all, that D1 was at fault 2/3 and D2 at fault 1/3. P's damages are $1 million. P can probably recover the full sum from either D. But if P recovers the full sum from D1, D1 may recover $333,000 from D2.

B. Limits on doctrine: Most states *limit* contribution as follows:

1. **No intentional torts:** Usually an *intentional* tortfeasor may *not* get contribution from his co-tortfeasors (even if they, too, behaved intentionally). [190]

2. **Contribution defendant must have liability:** The contribution defendant (that is, the co-tortfeasor who is being sued for contribution) must *in fact be liable* to the original plaintiff. [190]

> **Example:** Husband drives a car in which Wife is a passenger. The car collides with a car driven by D. The jury finds that Husband and D were both negligent. Wife recovers the full jury verdict from D. If intra-family immunity would prevent Wife from recovering directly from Husband, then D may not recover contribution from Husband either, since Husband has no underlying liability to the original plaintiff.

C. Settlements:

1. **Settlement by contribution plaintiff:** If D *settles*, he may then generally obtain contribution from other potential defendants. (Of course, he has to prove that these other defendants would indeed have been liable to P.) [191]

2. **Settlement by contribution defendant:** Where D1 settles, and D2 — against whom P later gets a judgment — sues D1 for contribution, courts are split among two main approaches [191]:

   a. **Traditional rule:** The traditional rule is that D1, the settling defendant, is *liable* for contribution. This is a bad approach, because it sharply reduces a defendant's incentive to settle — she knows that if she settles early, she may be dragged back into extra liability in the form of contribution to the non-settling co-defendants.

   b. **"Reduction of P's claim" rule:** Today, most courts deal with this problem by taking two steps. First, they *deny contribution* to non-settlers (or later settlers) from the early settler. But second, they *reduce the amount of P's claim* against the non-settlers to reflect the earlier settlement. These courts vary in how they do this [191]:

      i. **Pro tanto reduction:** Some courts reduce P's claim by the *dollar amount* of the settlement (*"pro tanto"* reduction).

      ii. **Proportional reduction:** On the other hand, some reduce it by the *proportion* that the settling defendant's responsibility bears to the overall responsibility of all parties (the *"comparative share"* approach.

III. INDEMNITY

A. Definition: Sometimes the court will not merely order two joint-and-severally-liable defendants to split the cost (contribution), but will instead completely *shift* the responsibility from one D to the other. This is the doctrine of *"indemnity"* — a 100% shifting of liability, as opposed to the sharing involved in contribution. [192]

B. Sample situations: Here are two important contexts in which indemnity is often applied:

1. **Vicarious liability:** If D1 is only *vicariously liable* for D2's conduct, D2 will be required to indemnify D1. [192]

> **Example:** Employee injures P. P recovers against Employer on a theory of *respondeat superior*. Employer will be entitled to indemnity from Employee; that is, Employee will be required to pay to Employer the full amount of any judgment that Employer has paid.

2. **Retailer versus manufacturer:** A *retailer* who is held strictly liable for selling a defective injury-causing product will get indemnity from others further up the distribution chain, including the *manufacturer*. [192]

CHAPTER 8
DUTY

I. DUTY GENERALLY

A. Concept: Generally, a person owes everyone else with whom he comes in contact a general *"duty of care."* Normally, you don't have to worry about this duty — it is the same in all instances, the duty to behave with the care that would be shown by a reasonable person. But there are several situations in which courts hold that the defendant owes plaintiff *less* than this regular duty. The most important of these situations are:

[1] D generally has no duty to take *affirmative action* to help P;

[2] D generally has no duty to avoid causing unintended *mental suffering* to P; and

[3] D has no duty to avoid causing *pure economic loss* to P in the absence of more tangible types of harm such as physical injury. [197]

II. FAILURE TO ACT

A. No general duty to act: A person generally cannot be liable in tort solely on the grounds that she has *failed to act*. [198]

1. **Duty to protect or give aid:** This means that if D sees that P is in danger, and fails to render assistance (even though D could do so easily and safely), D is *not liable for refusing to assist*.

> **Example:** D, passing by, sees P drowning in a pond. D could easily pull P to safety without risk to D, but instead, D walks on by. D is not liable to P.

B. Exceptions: But there are a number of commonly-recognized *exceptions* to the "no duty to act" rule: [199-206]

1. **Special relationship:** A duty to give assistance may arise out of a *"special relationship"* between D and P. [199] Here is a list (from the Third Restatement) of relationships that impose such a duty of care [200]:

[a] the relationship of "a *common carrier* with its *passengers*";

[b] "an *innkeeper* with its *guests*";

[c] "a *business* or other possessor of land that *holds its premises open to the public* with

those who are *lawfully on the premises*";

> **Example:** P gets his finger stuck in an escalator operated by D, a store where P is a customer. If D does not give P assistance, D will be liable.

[d] "an *employer* with its *employees*";

[e] "a *school* with its *students*";

[f] "a *landlord* with its *tenants*"; and

[g] "a *custodian* with *those in its custody*, if the custodian is required by law to take custody or voluntarily takes custody of the other and the custodian has a *superior ability to protect* the other." (*Example*: The duty of a jailer to a prisoner.)

   a. Transient or "ad hoc" relationships: Plaintiffs have sometimes tried to persuade courts to extend the above list of "special relationships" by adding certain *"ad hoc"* relationships, i.e. *transient relationships* that were formed shortly before the episode in question. But courts have generally *rejected* these attempts.

      i. No relationship based on "witnessing an emergency": For example, some plaintiffs have argued that the court ought to recognize a special relationship as existing between a *person who faces a sudden life-threatening injury* and another person who *witnesses that injury at close proximity* and has the *opportunity to summon help.* But this argument has generally been *rejected* by the courts, on the theory that recognizing this type of relationship as imposing a duty to summon assistance would swallow up the "no duty to assist" general rule, and would present *no logical stopping point.*

> **Example:** P and D used to be a couple, but have broken up. P enters D's trailer without permission, shoots himself, and falls to the floor. D finds P, thinks he has merely pretended to shoot himself, and doesn't call 911, though she could do so easily. P dies, and the facts indicate that he could have been saved if D had called 911 as soon as she found him on the floor. P's estate argues that the court should recognize a special relationship as arising whenever a witness discovers an acute injury to another; such a witness should be found to have the limited duty to use due care in summoning assistance.
>
> *Held*, for D; the court will not recognize the "witness to an emergency" relationship urged by the estate. The relationship asserted here does not have either of the elements present in other relationships that have been recognized as creating a duty of assistance: (1) it didn't exist prior to the present occasion; and (2) it did not involve a defendant who had control over either the person in peril or the premises where the peril arose. Imposing a duty to contact emergency assistance on anyone who witnesses another's injury would be a "duty without any practical limit." [*Estate of Cilley v. Lane*] [201]

2. Defendant involved in injury: If the danger or injury to P is *due to D's own conduct*, or to an instrument under D's control, D has the duty of assistance. This is true today even if D acted without fault. [201]

Example: A car driven by D strikes P, a pedestrian. Even though D has driven completely non-negligently, and the accident is due to P's carelessness in crossing the street, D today has a common-law duty to stop and give reasonable assistance to P.

3. **Defendant and victim as co-venturers:** Where the victim and the defendant are engaged in a *common pursuit*, so that they may be said to be *co-venturers*, some courts have imposed on the defendant a duty of warning and assistance. For instance, if two friends went on a jog together, or on a camping trip, their joint pursuit might be enough to give rise to a duty on each to aid the other. [202]

4. **Assumption of duty:** Once D *voluntarily begins* to render assistance to P (even if D was under no legal obligation to do so), D must *proceed with reasonable care*. [202-203]

   a. **Preventing assistance by others:** D is especially likely to be found liable if he begins to render assistance, and this has the effect of *dissuading others* from helping P.

      Example: If D stops by the roadside to help P, an injured pedestrian, and other passers-by decline to help because they think the problem is taken care of, D may not then abandon the attempt to help P.

   b. **Mere promise:** Traditionally, a mere *promise* by D to help P (without actual commencement of assistance) was *not* enough to make D liable for not following through. But many modern courts would make D liable even in this situation, if P has a reliance interest.

      Example: D promises P that while P is away on a two-week trip, D will visit P's apartment every day and feed P's dog. D then forgets to do this, and the dog is seriously injured. Today, many courts (and the Third Restatement) would say that D is liable to P, because once he made the promise to render the assistance, he was required to fulfill the promise with reasonable care. [203]

5. **Duty to control others:** If D has a duty to *control third persons*, D can be negligent for failing to exercise that control. [205]

   a. **Special relationship:** A duty to control a third person may arise either because of a special relationship between D and P, or a special relationship between D and a third person. For instance, some courts now hold that any *business* open to the public must protect its patrons from wrongdoing by third parties.

      Example: D, a storekeeper, fails to take action when X, an obviously deranged man, comes into the store wielding a knife. P, a patron, is stabbed. Most courts would find D liable for failing to take action.

III. MENTAL SUFFERING

A. **Pure mental suffering without physical impact or injury:** Suppose the defendant's negligence is the cause in fact of intense *mental suffering* to the plaintiff, but this suffering has been produced *without any physical impact* upon the plaintiff. Does the absence of any physical impact itself bar plaintiff from recovery? As we'll see, the answer is, "not necessarily." [210]

1. **Several categories:** We'll look at several distinct types of scenarios:

   [1] P suffers a physical impact or direct physical injury, and seeks to *"tack on"* to her claim a recovery for emotional distress (though this is not one of the "pure emotional distress"

scenarios). (See Par. B below.)

[2] P witnesses an accident; she *never fears* for the physical safety of either herself or anyone else during the episode, but suffers emotional distress anyway, for which she seeks to recover. (See Par. C below.)

[3] P witnesses an accident or near-accident, and is *sufficiently close* to the dangerous event herself that she is for a time in *danger of immediate bodily harm*. She escapes the bodily harm, but suffers mental distress from the episode. (See Par. D below.)

[4] P witnesses a *close relative*, X, suffer a serious bodily injury; P never fears for her own physical safety but nonetheless suffers emotional distress (on account of her concern for X's welfare), for which she seeks to recover. (See Par. E below.)

[5] Same as [4], but the person, X, that P witnesses suffer a serious bodily injury is *not P's close relative*. Again, P suffers emotional distress for which she attempts to recover. (See Par. F below.)

[6] P suffers emotional distress without ever being himself at risk, and without directly witnessing serious injury to anyone else, but because of the *special relationship* between P and D (or between D and a third person, X, who suffers injury), for policy reasons the courts allow P to recover for her own emotional distress. (See Par. G below.)

B. Mental distress damages "tacked on" to case involving physical injury: First, let's consider a situation that does not really fall into our "pure mental suffering" category, but that we'll want to compare with the various pure-mental-suffering scenarios we'll be considering. This is the situation in which D causes an *actual physical injury* to P's person (or to P's property), and P suffers not just physical injuries but, in addition, mental distress arising out of the episode. [212]

1. **P may recover:** In this scenario, it's always been clear, in all American courts, that *D is liable* not only for the physical consequences of the impact but also for virtually *all the emotional or mental suffering* that flows naturally from it. This includes fright at the time of the injury, "pain and suffering" stemming from the injury, anxiety about possibility of a repetition, humiliation from disfigurement, etc. The mental distress claim is said to be *"tacked on"* to the claim for physical injury. [212]

2. **"Parasitic" damages:** Such "tacked on" damages from mental suffering are often called *parasitic* — they "attach" to the claim for physical injury, analogously to the way a parasite attaches to the host. The usual reason for allowing parasitic damages is that the existence of a physical injury to P provides sufficient assurance that *the claim of suffering is not being feigned*.

C. Emotional distress, unaccompanied by fear of impact on oneself or others: Next, let's look at the scenario which furnishes probably the *weakest* case for allowing P to recover: P *witnesses* an accident or near-accident caused by D's negligence, but the danger takes place *far enough* from P that she *never fears an imminent impact* with her own body, or even with the body of anyone else nearby. Nonetheless, P later suffers mental distress from the episode. In this situation, virtually *no* American courts will allow P to recover for her emotional distress, even if that distress has physical manifestations. [212]

Example 1: P is walking in New York City's Times Square. Twenty yards ahead of her, she sees a taxi driven by D speed through a red light, lose control, and crash into a storefront, though miraculously neither D nor anyone else is physically injured. At no time does P believe that she or anyone else is likely to be hit by the cab. Nonetheless, P keeps reliving the near-disaster. She develops nightmares, symptoms of PTSD, and an ulcer.

It is unlikely that *any* American court would allow P to recover. As we'll see, there are several exceptions to the general rule against "stand-alone" recovery for negligent infliction of emotional distress. But here, where P never even briefly feared that either she or anyone else was likely to be hit by the cab, none of these exceptions applies. [212]

1. **"Boundless liability" fear:** Courts' universal rejection of a stand-alone distress claim like the one in the above example stems in part from courts' fear that if such claims were allowed, there would be a *flood of litigation*, with no way for courts to distinguish genuine claims from *feigned* ones. For instance, in the above example letting P recover would raise the possibility that hundreds of similarly-situated people walking or riding in Times Square might bring suit, and there would be no line logically dividing those who should recover from those who shouldn't.

D. **P is within the "zone of danger," and suffers distress:** Our next category is where P witnesses an accident or near-accident, and is *sufficiently close* to the dangerous event that she herself is at some point in *danger of immediate bodily harm*. She escapes the bodily harm, but suffers mental distress from the episode. Courts often describe this situation as one in which the plaintiff was *"within the zone of danger."* [213]

1. **Most courts allow:** In this "zone of danger" scenario, most courts today *allow* the plaintiff to recover for her emotional distress, if plaintiff shows that the distress was *severe*. [213]

2. **Third Restatement allows:** The Third Restatement similarly allows the plaintiff to recover in this zone-of-danger situation: "An actor whose negligent conduct causes *serious emotional harm* to another is subject to liability to the other if the conduct: (a) places the other in *danger of immediate bodily harm* and the emotional harm results from the danger[.]"

   Example 2: Same facts as Example 1 above. This time, however, when the taxi driven by D goes out of control, P is standing two feet away. She jumps out of the path of the oncoming cab and barely avoids being hit. If P suffers severe mental distress from constantly re-living the near-accident, most courts (and the Third Restatement) will allow her to recover for that distress, because she was within the "zone of danger." [213]

E. **P is a "bystander," and sees a close relative suffer bodily injury:** Now, let's turn to the first of two categories in which the plaintiff is a *"bystander"* who from a position of safety *watches another person suffer bodily injury* due to the defendant's negligence. In the present category, the injured third person is a *close relative of the plaintiff*, such as the plaintiff's *parent, sibling,* or *child*.

As in the above situation illustrated by Example 2 (where the plaintiff was herself within the "zone of danger"), in the present "bystander watching a close relative be injured" scenario, most courts today *allow the plaintiff to recover* for her own distress. [213]

1. **Rationales:** There are two rationales for allowing recovery here: (a) we don't have to worry much about *fraudulent claims*, since it's highly likely that a person who watches a close relative be injured has indeed suffered great distress; and (b) we don't have to worry about a *flood of claims*, since the number of people suffering a bodily injury from a given tortious event will be limited, and therefore the number of close relatives watching those injuries occur will also be limited.

2. **Third Restatement allows:** Again, the Third Restatement agrees that the plaintiff should be allowed to recover: [214]

> An actor who negligently causes ***sudden serious bodily injury to a third person*** is subject to liability for serious emotional harm caused thereby to a ***person who***:
>
> (a) ***perceives the event contemporaneously***, and
>
> (b) is a ***close family member*** of the person suffering the bodily injury.

> **Example 3:** P is walking with her 6-year-old son, S, in a cross-walk in Times Square. As P watches, horrified, a taxi negligently driven by D jumps a red light and runs over S, killing him instantly. P suffers severe mental distress from watching the accident and re-living it. Most courts (and the Third Restatement) will allow P to recover against D for her own distress. This recovery is entirely separate, conceptually, from S's estate's right to recover for his bodily injury. [214]

3. **Meaning of "close relative":** Courts vary in ***how close the family relationship must be*** between the bystander/plaintiff and the third person who suffers serious bodily harm.

C
A
P
S
U
L
E

S
U
M
M
A
R
Y

   a. **Sibling, parent, child or spouse:** A bystander who is the ***sibling, parent, child,*** or ***spouse*** of the person who suffers the bodily harm is likely to be found to be sufficiently closely-related that the bystander can recover for distress. [214]

   b. **More distant relative:** But if the relationship is even a little more ***distant***, courts are likely to ***deny*** recovery. Thus one who witnesses the death or serious injury of a ***fiancé***, a ***cohabiting*** significant other, a ***son-in-law***, or an ***aunt*** or ***uncle*** (even one who has raised the child who suffers the bodily injury) is likely to be ***denied recovery***.

4. **Perception must be "contemporaneous":** Most courts insist that the bystander must ***perceive*** the accident (the bodily harm to the bystander's close relative) ***"contemporaneously."*** In other words, it's not enough that the bystander learns of the accident very soon ***after*** it occurs. [214] So the following two examples produce opposite legal outcomes:

> **Example 4:** P, sitting on his front porch, watches a car negligently driven by D strike, and badly injure, P's 6-year-old son, S, in the street in front of P's house. Because P has "contemporaneously" perceived the physical injury to S, P will be entitled to recover for P's own mental distress. [214]

> **Example 5:** P is sitting in the kitchen of his house, which looks out only into P's back-yard. The doorbell rings, and P's next-door neighbor, X, tells P, "I just saw your son S be hit by a car on the street; the ambulance just took S to the hospital." P rushes to the hospital, where he sees S lying badly injured in the ER. In most courts — and under the Third Restatement — P will not be allowed to recover for his emotional distress, because P did not "contemporaneously" perceive the event that caused the harm to P's close relative.

   a. **Can "perceive" by another sense:** Ordinarily, the contemporaneous "perception" will be by ***sight*** — P observes the accident with his eyes. But ***other senses***, such as ***hearing***, may also suffice, as long as the "perception" is "contemporaneous." [215]

> **Example 6:** Same facts as Example 4 above, except that P, while sitting on his front porch, does not have his distance glasses on, and therefore cannot see what is happening in the street with any detail. But P knows that his son S is playing in the street. P then hears the squeal of D's brakes, and hears S's screams after he is run over. P has suffi-

ciently "perceived" (through his sense of hearing) the event that caused the serious bodily harm to S that he will be permitted to recover for his mental distress.

b. **Perception that occurs remotely rather than in person:** It's not clear whether the contemporaneous perception has to occur **"in person,"** as opposed to via some **remote, electronic means**. For instance, if P is **video-Skyping** with X and sees X hit by a car driven by D, has P met the "contemporaneous perception" requirement? There is little if any case law on the issue so far.

5. **Bodily harm witnessed must be serious:** The bodily harm that the bystander witnesses must generally be **serious**. So witnessing a close relative's **death**, significant permanent **disfigurement**, or loss **of a body part or function** will almost always be sufficient. But **bruises, cuts, single simple fractures**, and **other injuries that do not require immediate medical treatment** will **rarely be sufficient**. [215]

6. **Bodily injury must be "sudden":** The serious bodily harm suffered by the third person in the plaintiff/bystander's presence must occur in a **"sudden and dramatic manner,"** according to most courts. [215]

> **Example 7:** W works for years at a warehouse owned and operated by D. D negligently stores toxic chemicals there, to which W is unwittingly exposed. Over a period of months, W's health gradually deteriorates, and eventually she is left in a coma. Her husband, H, observes the deterioration with horror, and sues D for distress.
>
> Even though H has been a "bystander" who has directly witnessed the serious bodily harm suffered by his wife, W, a court will probably *not* allow H to recover for distress, because W's bodily harm was not "sudden."

7. **P need not be in "zone of danger" or fear for own safety:** In the bystander scenario, most courts that allow bystander recovery at all do **not** require that the **bystander himself have ever been in the "zone of danger,"** i.e., at risk of direct physical harm. In other words, as long as the bystander "contemporaneously perceives" the injury to a close relative, the bystander's own lack of physical danger does not ruin the claim. [216]

> **Example:** Recall Example 4 on p. C-42, where P sits on his porch and watches as his son S is struck down by D's car. The fact that P was never in any physical danger himself during the episode does not nullify P's distress claim.

F. **P is a "bystander," and sees a non-close-relative suffer bodily injury:** Now, let's consider the other major category in which a bystander might try to recover: the bystander witnesses serious bodily harm to another person, but this time the bystander and the physically-injured person are **not close relatives**. In this scenario, *few if any courts allow* the bystander to recover for mental distress. [213]

1. **Rationale:** This is one of those situations in which courts fear that allowing recovery will produce a **flood of claims**, with no easy way to determine which ones are genuine, and no way to avoid subjecting the defendant to potentially boundless liability.

> **Example 8:** Same basic facts as Example 1 on p. C-40. Now, however, P sees the runaway cab strike and kill X, a stranger to P. As in Example 1, P is far enough away (20 yards) from the cab that she never fears that she herself will or may be hit by the cab. Virtually all U.S. courts would deny P the right to recover for her mental distress, even if that distress unquestionably stemmed from seeing the accident and resulted in physical mani-

festations like ulcers. The same fears of boundless liability and false claims that would result in courts' rejection of P's claim in Example 1 would be cited here. [216]

2. **P not within zone of danger:** The fact that the bystander and the physically-injured person are not close relatives makes the most difference when *the bystander is never within the zone of danger.* That's because, in most courts, if the bystander *is* himself within the zone of danger, that fact will *allow* the bystander to recover for emotional distress from the entire episode — the court will typically not try to distinguish between distress from the bystander's own narrow escape and distress from the injury to the nearby non-relative. [216]

G. **Special relationship or special activity:** Finally, there are a few types of *"special" situations*, scenarios that involve either a *special activity* or a *special relationship among the parties*, such that courts have decided that the general rule against recovery for negligently-inflicted emotional distress should *not apply* even though none of the above exceptions to the general no-liability rule applies. In these special categories, courts have concluded that the *risk* of emotional harm to the plaintiff is *so great*, and the *number* of affected plaintiffs likely to be so *small*, that the court should not worry about either feigned distress or a flood of claimants.

C
A
P
S
U
L
E

S
U
M
M
A
R
Y

1. **Two main categories:** There are two main scenarios that courts have long recognized as being "special categories" where pure emotional harm should be recoverable:

   a. **Mishandling of bodies:** One is the scenario in which a *hospital or funeral home* negligently *mishandles a corpse*, thereby causing emotional distress to a close relative of the deceased. [218]

   Example: Hospital negligently misidentifies a corpse (that of X), causing the corpse to be cremated instead of sent to a funeral home for burial. X's immediate family learns of the error, and suffers great distress because of it. Most courts would allow the family to recover against Hospital.

   b. **Telegrams announcing death or serious illness:** The other is the scenario in which a *telegraph company* negligently and incorrectly announces that *A* is dead or seriously ill, and the telegraph is delivered to *B*, *A*'s intimate family member. [218]

2. **Extension to other situations:** In recent decades, courts have often recognized *other situations* as calling for allowing an emotional distress claim that does not fall within either of the above categories, or within any of the physical-impact categories we discussed earlier. [218]

   a. **Factors required:** Here are a few examples, taken from actual cases in which the court declined to rule as a matter of law that P may not recover for distress:

   [1] D, a *medical clinic* that has run a blood test on P, negligently (and incorrectly) *informs P that she is HIV positive*;

   [2] D, an *obstetrician*, negligently mishandles a *pregnancy* of P, a patient, leading to a *stillbirth* that causes P great emotional harm;

   [3] D, a *fast food chain*, negligently serves P a hamburger with human blood on the bun.

H. **The "at-risk plaintiff":** Claims for negligent infliction of purely emotional distress are sometimes raised by *at-risk plaintiffs."* That is, it is often possible to say that a particular plaintiff, by virtue of his exposure to a certain substance, has suffered an *increased likelihood of a particular disease* (e.g., cancer). May such a plaintiff recover for the purely emotional harm of being *dis-*

tressed by this increased likelihood of illness, assuming that there are no symptoms of the illness itself?

1. **"Cancerphobia":** Liability for emotional distress due to future illness is often referred to by the umbrella (and not-always-accurate) term *"cancerphobia."* For simplicity, we'll use this term here.

2. **Hard for P to win:** Plaintiffs have *rarely succeeded i*n recovering for pure cancerphobia, i.e., cases where the plaintiff cannot show that he has actually suffered bodily harm. Courts put various obstacles in the path of cancerphobia plaintiffs — including obstacles summarized in Pars. 3, 4 and 5 below— and it's the rare plaintiff who can overcome all of these obstacles. [219]

3. **Need actual exposure in toxic cases:** Most of the cases raising the issue of recovery for cancerphobia are *"toxic tort"* cases, i.e., cases in which the plaintiff has been or may have been exposed to some toxic substance, whether it is the AIDS virus, hazardous environmental waste, or some other damaging substance. In this situation, most courts have insisted, at a minimum, that plaintiff show *actual exposure* to the substance, not merely the *possibility* of exposure. [219]

    Example: Suppose that D is a physician who has open lesions on his hands and arms, and who examines many patients, including P, while having those lesions. P later learns that at the time D examined her, D knew that he had AIDS. P has not yet developed AIDS, and there is no evidence that she has had HIV virus particles pass into her body. However, P is very frightened that she will develop AIDS from her exposure to D.

    A court would probably hold that P loses on her "fear of AIDS" theory, because she cannot show that she was "actually exposed" to the HIV virus from D. That is, she will lose unless she can show that more probably than not, some virus particles actually passed from D's body into her own.

4. **Some courts require showing of actual illness:** Some courts have gone even further, and have required that the cancerphobic plaintiff show that more probably than not, he will *actually contract the illness* that he is frightened of. In other words, fear of a less-than-probable illness, no matter how devastating the illness would be if it occurred, will *not suffice*, in these courts. [219]

    Example: In such a court, P in the above example would presumably lose unless she showed not only that she was actually exposed to the HIV virus by D but that she had a greater than 50% chance of contracting AIDS.

5. **Need for danger of "immediate" bodily harm:** Another way that courts often make it hard or impossible to recover for emotional harm from fear of future illness is by insisting that the danger of bodily harm be *"immediate."* [220]

    a. **Third Restatement:** Thus the *Third Restatement* denies recovery for cancerphobia. The Restatement's requirement that the plaintiff can't recover unless she was placed in "immediate" physical danger by the defendant's negligence means that under the Restatement, recovery is *not allowed* in cancerphobia cases. [220]

6. **Accompanying physical harm:** But always keep in mind that if there is *some physical harm* arising from the episode, the emotional distress will *also* be compensable. [220]

C
A
P
S
U
L
E

S
U
M
M
A
R
Y

Example: Many workers exposed to *asbestos* have developed a lung abnormality known as "pleural thickening." This thickening is not by itself life-threatening, nor does it even directly impair the patient's life. But courts tend to consider as a form of "bodily harm." And it has been statistically linked to a much higher than normal incidence of certain cancers.

A plaintiff who has suffered pleural thickening is likely to be permitted to recover substantial sums from manufacturer of asbestos to which plaintiff was exposed. Such an award would compensate plaintiff not just for his current physical harm from the pleural thickening itself, but also for his distress at knowing that he has a high risk of future harm.

IV. UNBORN CHILDREN

A. Modern view: Most courts have now rejected the traditional view that an infant injured in a pre-natal accident could never recover if born alive. Today, recovery for pre-natal injuries varies:

   1. Child born alive: If the child is eventually *born alive*, nearly all courts *allow* recovery. [221]

       Example: D makes a drug that is taken by P's mother while she is carrying P in utero. P is born with serious birth defects resulting from the drug. Nearly all courts would allow P to recover.

   2. Child not born alive: Courts are *split* about whether suit can be brought on behalf of a child who was *not* born alive. Usually, a court will allow recovery only if it finds that a fetus never born alive is a "person" for purposes of the wrongful death statute. [221]

   3. Pre-conception injuries: The above discussion assumes that the injury occurred while the child was *in utero*. Suppose, however, that the injury occurred before the child was even *conceived*, but that some effect from the injury is nonetheless suffered by the later-conceived child. Here, courts are *split* as to whether the child may recover. [221-222]

       Example: P's mother, before getting pregnant with P, takes a drug made by D. The drug damages the mother's reproductive system. When P is conceived, P suffers from some congenital disease or defect (e.g., sterility) as a result. P's mother can clearly recover from D for her own injuries, but courts are split as to whether P can recover against D for these pre-conception events. [*Enright v. Eli Lilly*]

   4. Wrongful life: If a child is born illegitimate, or with an unpreventable congenital disease, the child may argue that it should be entitled to recover for *"wrongful life,"* in the sense that it would have been better off aborted. But almost no courts have allowed the child to make such a wrongful life recovery. Courts do, however, often allow the *parents* to recover for their medical expenses, and perhaps their emotional distress from the child's condition. [222]

V. PURE ECONOMIC LOSS

A. The problem generally: Suppose that D behaves negligently towards X, in a way that causes X personal injury or property damage. Suppose further that D's conduct also injures P, but P's only loss is *economic*, not personal injury or property damage. May P recover in tort from D? As we will see, the traditional general answer is *"no,"* but there are some important exceptions.

   1. Tacking on of economic loss to personal or property damage: Before we begin examining the "three party" situation referred to in the prior paragraph, let's first consider a simpler "two party" situation: D behaves negligently towards P, and causes P both personal injury and economic loss. In this situation, all courts agree (and have always agreed) that P, in addition to recovering for his personal injury, *may "tack on" his intangible economic harm as an additional element of damages*.

> **Example:** P owns a retail store, which he personally operates. P is injured by the negligence of D, a careless driver who hits P while P is walking. P can of course recover damages for his physical harm (e.g., his medical bills plus pain and suffering). Once P shows that he has suffered physical harm, he will be permitted to "tack on," as an additional element of damages, his loss of profits from being unable to operate the store. In other words, P's suffering of physical harm qualifies him to recover for the full range of damages which he has suffered, including intangible economic ones.

a. Property damage: Similarly, if P suffers *property damage* (even if he does not suffer personal injury), this property damage will qualify him to tack on intangible economic loss as well. Thus suppose, on the facts of the above example, that P's car was struck by D's car, and that as a result: (1) P's car was damaged; (2) P himself was not physically injured; and (3) P lost two days of profits at the store because he could not commute to the store. Once P showed that he suffered direct property damage from P's negligence, all courts would allow him to recover his loss-of-business damages, even though those are purely intangible economic losses.

B. Standard rule disallows pure economic losses: Now, let's return to the three-party situation, in which D's negligence causes physical injury or property damage to *X*, but only economic loss to *P*. Nearly all courts agree that *P may not recover anything for his economic losses*, since he has not suffered any personal injury or property damage. This is true even though D is clearly a tortfeasor (vis-à-vis X), and even though D's negligence has quite clearly, and foreseeably, brought about the injuries to P. As the idea is often put, a person may not recover for unintentionally-caused *"pure economic loss."*

1. Restatement 3d follows this rule: The Third Restatement of Torts follows this general no-recovery principle: apart from a few exceptional circumstances:

> a claimant cannot recover for *economic loss* caused by (a) *unintentional personal injury to another party*; or (b) *unintentional injury to property* in which *the claimant has no proprietary interest*.

a. Rationales: There are some strong *policy reasons* behind this general rule barring recovery for pure economic loss. Here are two of the leading rationales:

i. Indeterminate and disproportionate liability: Most importantly, if courts allow recovery for economic loss that is not accompanied by personal injury or property damage to the plaintiff, the likely result is *indeterminate and disproportionate liability*.

ii. Other ways for claimants to protect themselves: Second, courts reason that the victims of economic injury can often *protect themselves effectively by means other than a tort suit*. For instance, they may be able to *buy insurance* against their losses.

2. Contexts in which rule is applied: Here are some of the contexts in which the rule barring recovery for pure economic losses is frequently applied:

C
A
P
S
U
L
E

S
U
M
M
A
R
Y

C
A
P
S
U
L
E

S
U
M
M
A
R
Y

a. Blocking of highways or streets and thus access to P's business: Where the defendant negligently causes a *street, highway or waterway to be closed*, business owners whose property is not directly damaged have often sued, seeking recovery for lost business due to *customers' inability to get to the owner's premises.* Most cases find against the plaintiff, in a straightforward application of the rule denying recovery for negligently-caused pure economic loss. [224]

b. Toxic torts affecting land or water: In another common scenario, the defendant negligently *spills toxic substances or pollutants* onto either a waterway or land, and this "toxic tort" interferes with the economic activities of persons or businesses whose person or property are not directly and physically impacted by the spill. Again, most courts apply the general rule to these non-physically-impacted plaintiffs — unless the plaintiff can show that the defendant negligently created a public nuisance, and that the harm suffered by the plaintiff is *different in kind* from the harms suffered by other businesses in the area, the plaintiff may not recover for its *"pure economic loss."* [225]

Example: D ("SoCalGas") supplies millions of people with natural gas from various storage facilities including Aliso, a subterranean former oil reservoir. Because natural gas is odorless, D has added a nausea-causing chemical so that people will notice if a leak happened. A leak from Aliso occurs, releasing 55 tons of natural gas every hour. Residents of the nearby community, Porter Ranch, suffer from unpleasant odors, headaches, dizziness, respiratory problems, nosebleeds and vomiting. While the leak is still flowing, the county health department orders D to establish a relocation program available to any Porter Ranch resident who lives within a certain radius (initially, 5 miles) of the leak site. Altogether, about 15,000 people are eventually relocated, to locations dozens or hundreds of miles away.

The Ps, various businesses in the Porter Ranch area, seek to bring a class action consisting of all persons or entities conducting business within 5 miles of the Aliso facility. They allege that the leak was caused by D's negligence, and that the resulting relocation has deprived many area businesses of customers, causing the class-member businesses to suffer lost earnings. But *none* of the class member businesses alleges *personal injury or property damage* — every class member seeks recovery for "pure economic loss."

Held (by the California Supreme Court), for D. The court applies the general rule that a defendant has *no tort duty to guard against negligently causing "purely economic losses."* So class member businesses that have not suffered non-economic (e.g., physical or property damage) injuries cannot recover anything, because D *did not owe them any duty* to avoid negligently causing them economic harm. Pure economic losses are "not self-limiting," so allowing recovery for such losses would "threaten liabilities that are *indeterminate and out of proportion* to [a defendant's] culpability." [*Southern California Gas Leak Cases*], Cal. Sup. Ct. 2019). [225]

c. Tort against employee or employer causing economic loss to the other: Similarly, if D *negligently injures P's employee,* X, P may not recover for P's economic losses stemming from X's unavailability. And the converse is also true – if D negligently damages X, a business, then P, an employee of X who is deprived of work because of the damage to X *may not recover lost wages* from D. [227]

Example: Goalie is a star soccer player with a long-term contract to play for Metro, a professional soccer team. Driver negligently injures Goalie in a car accident, causing Goalie to miss Metro's season. Assume that by the terms of the Goalie-Metro contract, Metro has to pay Goalie his salary for the season despite his unavailability. Even if Metro can demonstrate with near certainty that Goalie's unavailability has cost Metro $1 million in ticket sales for the season, Metro cannot recover anything at all from Driver.

That's because, although Driver's negligence has caused physical injury *to Goalie* (for which Goalie himself can of course recover against Driver), Metro has suffered only economic loss, unaccompanied by personal injury or damage to Metro's "property."

d. Interruption to power or supplies: Similarly, if D's negligence causes an interruption of the *flow of goods or services* that are needed for P's business, but there is no contractual relationship between D and P (and no physical damage to P's property), the general rule prevents P from recovering for its losses.

Example: Contractor, doing excavation work on private property two buildings away from P's factory, negligently severs the power lines that serve the factory, putting P's factory out of business for a day. Assume that the power outage does not cause any damage to P's building or equipment. The rule against recovery for pure economic losses prevents P from recovering from Contractor for these losses.

C. Situations that are exceptions or fall outside of the rule: But there are some important situations that are either deemed to fall outside of the scope of the general no-liability-for-pure-economic-loss rule, or to be exceptions to the rule. Two of the more important such situations are (a) where P has a *"proprietary interest"* in property that is physically damaged by D's negligence; and (b) where D has created a *"public nuisance,"* and P has suffered harm from the nuisance that is "different in kind" from that suffered by other nearby persons.

1. P has a proprietary interest: Since the general rule we're discussing bars recovery only for "pure" economic loss, it's not surprising that a plaintiff can recover economic-loss damages if the plaintiff can also show that *"property" in which she has a "proprietary" interest* was damaged by the D's negligence, leading to the economic loss. [228]

a. P owns and possesses the damaged property: If P both *owns and possesses* the tangible property damaged by D's negligence, it's easy to see how P can recover for economic losses that stem directly from the property damage.

Example: BargeCo, the owner/operator of a barge, negligently spills chemicals into a harbor. The spilled chemicals flow into the innards of a new custom-designed drill owned by Contractor, a building contractor who is using the drill to finish a construction project owned by Owner at the edge of the harbor. Repair of the drill costs Contractor $10,000, and the process takes a month. Contractor also loses $40,000 because the month's delay causes Contractor to forfeit a "timely completion" bonus in that amount that Contractor would have otherwise received from Owner. (No replacement drill was reasonably available to Contractor sooner because of the drill's custom design.)

Because Contractor suffered direct damage to its tangible property (the drill), Contractor is entitled to recover from BargeCo not only the repair costs, but the intangible economic loss (the $40,000), since that loss stemmed directly from the same negligent act by BargeCo that caused the property damage.

b. P has possession but not ownership; the "proprietary" test: Where P does *not own* the property that's physically damaged, but has the right to *use or possess* that property, P can recover for economic loss directly resulting from the episode that damages the property if and only if P's arrangement with the owner included at least one (and in some courts both) of the following attributes:

[1] *control* of the property, and

[2] the responsibility for *maintaining and repairing* the property.

Example 1 (right to recover economic loss): P rents one floor of a building from O. D, a contractor working for O on the exterior of the building, negligently causes a wall to cave in, blocking P's employees from work for two weeks. Most courts would say that P, as the tenant of a floor of the building, had enough control of its part of the premises to be deemed to have a "proprietary" interest in those premises. In such a court, P would be permitted to recover its economic losses (lost production) for the period when its employees couldn't come to work. [228]

Example 2 (no right to recover economic loss): P is a railroad that, along with two other railroads, has the right to use a bridge owned and maintained by O. A tugboat owed by D negligently damages the bridge, causing P to have to re-route its shipments for several weeks, at greater cost to P.

A court would probably say that although P had a non-exclusive right to use the bridge, P's lack of complete control (and of the obligation to maintain) the bridge prevented P from having the required proprietary interest in the bridge. If the court so concluded, the court would probably bar P from recovering its economic losses from D, under the general rule preventing recovery of pure economic losses. [229]

2. Public nuisance with special harm: Courts generally recognize an exception to the no-recovery-for-pure-economic-losses rule if the defendant's actions create a *public nuisance,* but only if the type of economic harm suffered by the plaintiff is *qualitatively different* from that suffered by other members of the community.

a. Taken from law of nuisance: This "exception" is really a recognition that the tort of public nuisance has special features that sometimes call for a private right of action for pure economic loss. (See *infra*, p. C-95, for a more detailed discussion of private rights of action for public nuisances.)

b. "Distinct in kind" requirement: The requirement for private suits that the plaintiff's losses be *"distinct in kind* from those suffered by members of the affected community in general" has quite a lot of bite — where the nuisance has some sort of economic impact on a *significant number of businesses*, a plaintiff generally *won't be able to meet* the "distinct in-kind" requirement merely by showing that her losses are of *greater magnitude* than those of most other community members. Rather, the plaintiff typically has to show that something about her situation — usually tied to her particular location — makes her losses of a *"different kind," not just "different magnitude"* — from other nearby businesses' losses. The following two examples illustrate the kinds of situations that will or won't meet this "different in kind" requirement.

Example 1 (not different in kind): A building negligently constructed by D collapses, causing street closings that prevent customers of the Ps (nearby retail stores) from reaching the Ps' premises. The Ps seek to fit within the public-nuisance exception to the no-recovery-for-pure-economic-loss.

The Ps have ***not*** shown the requisite "special injury beyond that suffered by the community at large." (Even if the Ps can show that their ***dollar losses were greater*** than those of nearly every other person or business in the area, it's unlikely that the court would find that the "different in kind" requirement has been satisfied.) [229]

Example 2 (different in kind): Restaurant is located on the bank of a river. Many of Restaurant's customers arrive by boat, and moor their boat at a dock owned and maintained by Restaurant. Logger floats logs down the river, and negligently allows the logs to become stuck on the river bank near Restaurant's dock, so that Restaurant's customers can no longer arrive by boat. (The log blockage is not located at or immediately adjacent to any part of Restaurant's property.) No other person or business is affected by the blockage.

A court would likely find that Restaurant has suffered the requisite "distinct in kind" harm. If the court so concluded (and if the court also concluded that the stock logs constituted a public nuisance), the court would allow Restaurant to recover damages for its lost business from logger. [230]

c. **Commercial fishers as a special case:** Some courts allow ***commercial fishers*** to recover their lost business when the defendant wrongfully pollutes the waterway in which the fishers have been fishing. In such suits, the courts typically conclude that the fishers have met the requirement of showing that their harm is "different in kind" from the losses suffered by the community in general.

D. **Special statutes:** The "rule" barring liability for pure economic losses is a judge-made doctrine, and as such can be overruled by a legislature for all or certain scenarios. And, indeed, there are some important contexts in which state and federal ***statutes overturn*** the common-law no-recovery rule.

1. **Oil spills and the OPA:** For instance, Congress has enacted a special statute that in large part reverses the standard no-recovery-for-pure-economic-losses rule for persons who suffer economic loss as the result of an ***oil spill***. This is the ***Federal Oil Pollution Act of 1990*** (***"OPA"***), 33 U.S.C. § 2702 et seq.

   Example: Suppose Hotel is located near (but not on) a beach that is fouled by an oil spill, and Hotel loses business because customers cancel their visit when they realize they won't be able to use the beaches. Hotel and its employees can probably both recover under OPA. [231]

E. **Other contexts involving pure economic loss:** Here, we've talked about just one aspect of courts' reluctance to award damage to a plaintiff who has suffered only economic loss — the "three party" scenario in which D tortuously causes personal injury or property damage to *A*, but only economic loss to *B*, who nonetheless sues. But there are a number of ***other scenarios*** that similarly raise the issue of whether a plaintiff who has suffered only economic loss may recover, including scenarios in which the defendant has behaved tortiously only to one person (the one who is now bringing suit). These other scenarios — where the court may or may not award liability for pure economic loss — include misrepresentation, products liability, and interference with contract.

CAPSULE SUMMARY

CHAPTER 9
OWNERS AND OCCUPIERS OF LAND

I. OUTSIDE THE PREMISES

A. Effect outside: There are special rules lowering a landowner's standard of care. However, these rules do not apply to conduct by the landowner that has effects *outside* of his property. Therefore, the general *"reasonable care"* standard usually applies to such effects. [238-239]

1. **Natural hazards:** However, if a hazardous condition exists *naturally* on the land, the property owner generally has *no duty* to remove it or guard against it, even if it poses an unreasonable danger to persons outside the property. But in an urban or other thickly-settled area, courts are less likely to apply this traditional rule. [238]

> **Example:** O allows a tree to grow in such a way that it may hit a tall truck passing on the roadway. Traditionally, O may not be held liable to the driver of the truck. But in an urban or suburban context, O might be liable.

2. **Artificial hazards:** Where the hazardous condition is *artificially* created, the owner has a general duty to prevent an unreasonable risk of harm to persons outside the premises. [239]

II. TRESPASSERS

A. General rule: As a general rule, the landowner owes *no duty to a trespasser* to make her land *safe*, to *warn* of dangers on it, to avoid carrying on dangerous activities on it, or to protect the trespasser in any other way. [240]

> **Example:** P trespasses on D railroad's track. His foot gets caught, and he is run over by a train. Even if the reason that P caught his foot was that D negligently maintained the roadbed, P cannot recover because D owed him no duty before discovering his presence. [*Sheehan v. St. Paul Ry. Co.*]

B. Exceptions: There are three main *exceptions* to the general rule that there is no duty of care to trespassers:

1. **Constant trespass on a limited area:** If the owner has reason to know that a *limited portion* of her land is *frequently used* by various trespassers, she must use reasonable care to make the premises safe or at least warn of dangers. This is the *"constant trespass on a limited area"* exception. [241]

> **Example:** If trespassers have worn a path across a railroad, the railroad must use reasonable care, such as whistles, when traversing that crossing.

2. **Discovered trespassers:** Once the owner has *knowledge* that a particular person is trespassing, the owner is then under a duty to exercise reasonable care for the trespasser's safety. [241]

> **Example:** A railroad's engineer must use reasonable care in stopping the train once he sees P trespassing on the tracks.

3. **Children:** The owner owes a duty of reasonable care to a trespassing *child* if: (1) the owner knows that the area is one where children are likely to trespass; (2) the owner has reason to know that the condition poses an unreasonable risk of serious injury or death to trespassing

children; (3) the injured child either does not discover the condition or does not realize the danger, due to his youth; (4) the benefit to the owner of maintaining the condition in its dangerous form is slight weighed against the risk to the children; and (5) the owner fails to use reasonable care to eliminate the danger. [242-244]

> **Example:** O knows that children often swim in a swimming pool on O's land. One part of the pool is unexpectedly deep. It would not cost very much for O to install fencing. P, a child trespasser, walks on the bottom of the pool, panics after suddenly reaching the deep part, and drowns. O is probably liable to P on these facts.

> **Note:** Traditionally, some or all of these elements are summarized by saying that O is liable for maintaining an *"attractive nuisance."*

a. **Natural conditions:** The court is less likely to find liability where the condition is a *natural* one than where it is artificial. [244]

b. **No duty of inspection:** The child trespass rules do not generally impose any *duty of inspection* upon O. [244]

III. LICENSEES

A. **Definition of licensee:** A *licensee* is a person who has the owner's *consent* to be on the property, but who does *not have a business purpose* for being there, or anything else entitling him to be on the land apart from the owner's consent. [244]

B. **Duty to licensees:** The owner does *not* owe a licensee any duty to *inspect for unknown dangers*. On the other hand, if the owner *knows* of a dangerous condition, she must *warn* the licensee of that danger. [245]

> **Example:** Rear steps leading from O's house to her back yard contain a rotten wood plank. If O knows of the rotten condition, she must warn P, a licensee, if P cannot reasonably be expected to spot the danger himself. But O need not inspect the steps to make sure they are safe, even if a reasonably careful owner would do so.

C. **Social guests:** The main class of persons who qualify as licensees are *"social guests."* [244]

> **Example:** Even if P is invited to O's house for dinner, P is a "licensee," not an "invitee."

IV. INVITEES

A. **Duty to invitee:** The owner *does* owe an *invitee* a duty of *reasonable inspection to find hidden dangers*. Also, the owner must use reasonable care to take *affirmative action* to remedy a dangerous condition. [246]

B. **Definition of "invitee":** The class of invitees today includes: (1) persons who are invited by O onto the land to conduct *business* with O; and (2) those who are invited as members of the *public* for purposes for which the land is held *open to the public*. [246-246]

1. **Meaning of "open to the public":** The *"open to the public"* branch of invitees covers those who come onto the property for the purposes for which it is held open, even if these people will not confer any economic benefit on the owner. [247]

Example: P, a door-to-door sales representative, pays an unsolicited sales call on D, a storekeeper. D in fact never buys from such unsolicited callers. However, since P reasonably understood that the premises were held open to salespeople, P is an invitee.

2. **Scope of invitation:** If the visitor's use of the premises goes *beyond* the business purpose or beyond the part of the premises held open to the public, that person will change from an invitee to a licensee. [247]

> **Example:** P visits O's store to buy cigarettes. O then allows P to use a private bathroom in the back of the store not held open to the public. Even though P was an invitee when he first came into the store, he became a licensee when he went into the private bathroom. [*Whelan v. Van Natta*]

C. **Duty of due care:** The owner owes an invitee the duty of *reasonable care*. [247] In particular:

1. **Duty to inspect:** The owner has a duty to *inspect* her premises for hidden dangers. O must use *reasonable care* in doing this inspecting. This is true even as to dangers that existed before O moved onto the premises. [247]

2. **Warning:** The giving of a *warning* will often, but not always, suffice. If O should realize that a warning will not remove the danger, then the condition must actually be remedied. [248]

3. **Control over third persons:** Reasonable care by O may require that she exercise *control over third persons* on her premises. [248]

D. **Firefighters and other public-safety personnel:** Under the common-law *"firefighter's rule,"* *firefighters, police officers* and other *public-safety officials* who come onto private property in the performance of their duties are treated as *mere licensees*, so that the owner does not owe them a duty to inspect the premises or to make the premises reasonably safe. The most common application of the common-law doctrine is that a firefighter who is injured while fighting a blaze cannot recover from the owner of the premises, *even if the owner's negligence caused the fire*. [249]

1. **Status of rule:** A number of states have in recent years expressed dissatisfaction with the firefighters rule. Some have *eliminated* it by statute; others have limited it to the case of firefighters, and have refused to extend it to other rescue workers (e.g., paramedics). Still others limit it to suits against *landowners*, terming it a rule of "premises liability," not a broad rule against suits by rescue workers. [249]

   a. **Most apply:** But most states *continue to apply the rule*, at least in the core case: a firefighter injured fighting a fire may not recover against a negligent fire-setter who owns the premises where the injury occurred.

V. REJECTION OF CATEGORIES

A. **Rejection generally:** A number of courts have *rejected* the categories of trespasser, licensee and invitee. These courts now apply a general single "reasonable person" standard of liability. California [*Rowland v. Christian*] and New York are included in this group. [250]

1. **Half the states give social guests benefit of duty of due care:** Between the rejection of categories, and other changes in legal rules, *social guests* are in a much better position today than at common law. About half the states have either *included social guests in the invitee cate-*

gory or have completely or partially ***abolished the categories***, so that ***all or most non-trespassing social guests are entitled to reasonable care under the circumstances***. [250]

    a. Not followed as to trespassers: But most states have been ***unwilling*** to abolish the categories when it comes to ***trespassers***. Most states continue to apply the common-law rule that an owner owes a trespasser no duty of care, and only the duty to refrain from maliciously injuring the intruder. [250]

VI. LIABILITY OF LESSORS AND LESSEES

A. Lessee: A ***tenant*** is treated ***as if she were the owner*** — all the rules of owner liability above apply to her. [251]

B. Lessors: In general, a ***lessor*** is ***not*** liable in tort once he transfers possession to the lessee. However, there are a number of exceptions to this general rule:

    1. Known to lessor, unknown to lessee: The lessor will be liable to the lessee (and to the lessee's invitees and licensees) for any dangers existing at the start of the lease, which the lessor ***knows or should know about***, and which the lessee has no reason to know about. (This usually does not impose on the lessor a duty to ***inspect*** the premises at the start of the lease.) [251]

    2. Open to public: If the lessor has reason to believe that the lessee will hold the premises ***open to the public***, the lessor has an affirmative duty to ***inspect*** the premises to find and repair dangers before the lease starts. [251]

    3. Common areas: The lessor has a general duty to use reasonable care to make ***common areas*** (e.g., the lobby or stairwells of an apartment building) safe. [252]

    4. Lessor contracts to repair: If the lessor ***contracts***, as part of the lease, to keep the premises in good repair, most courts hold that the landlord's breach of this covenant to repair gives a tort claim to anyone injured. However, P must show that D failed to use reasonable care in performing — it is not enough to show that D breached the contract. [252]

    5. Negligent repairs: The landlord may incur liability even without a contractual repair obligation if she ***begins*** to make repairs, and either performs them unreasonably, or fails to finish them. This is clearly true where the landlord worsens the danger by performing the repair negligently. Courts are split about what happens where the landlord starts the repair, then abandons it, without worsening the danger. [252-253]

    6. General negligence standard: Courts that impose a general negligence standard on occupiers of land often impose a similar general requirement of due care upon lessors. [254]

VII. VENDORS

A. Vendor's liability: Generally, a ***seller*** of land is released from tort liability once he has turned over the property. But there are some ***exceptions***:

    1. Danger to one on the property: First, suppose the accident happens to one ***on the property*** (e.g., a tenant of the new buyer). Here, you only have to worry about an exception (i.e., post-closing liability of seller to persons on the property) if the seller ***knew or should have known*** of the condition and its dangerousness. If that condition is satisfied, then the duration of the

C
A
P
S
U
L
E

S
U
M
M
A
R
Y

seller's post-closing liability varies depending on whether the seller actively *concealed* the danger:

   a. Seller actively conceals: If the seller *actively concealed* the condition, her liability persists after sale until the buyer *actually discovers* the condition and has a reasonable opportunity to correct it (whether the buyer takes the opportunity or not). So here, there's no cut-off if the buyer negligently fails to discover (or fix) the problem. [255]

   b. Seller doesn't conceal: If the seller *didn't actively conceal* the condition, the seller's liability continues only until the buyer "has had *reasonable opportunity to discover*" the condition and correct it. In other words here, the seller's liability is *cut off* as soon as the buyer *should have* discovered and fixed the problem, even if the buyer negligently failed to actually discover it.

  2. Danger to one outside the property: Essentially the same rules apply to a seller's post-closing liability to one *outside the property*, except that the seller has longer liability not only for active concealment but for having *created* the artificial condition. [256] Thus:

   a. Seller conceals or created: If the seller *actively concealed* the condition, *or originally created* the condition, her liability persists after sale until the buyer actually discovers the condition and has a reasonable opportunity to correct it (whether the buyer takes the opportunity or not). So here, there's no cut-off if the buyer negligently fails to discover (or fix) the problem.

   b. Seller doesn't conceal or create: If the seller *neither* actively concealed the condition nor created it, the seller's liability continues only until the buyer "has had *reasonable opportunity to discover*" the condition and correct it. In other words, here the seller's liability is cut off as soon as the buyer should have discovered and fixed the problem, even if the buyer negligently failed to even discover it.

CHAPTER 10
DAMAGES

I. PERSONAL INJURY DAMAGES GENERALLY

  A. Actual injury required: In any action based on negligence, the existence of *actual injury* is required. Unlike intentional tort actions, *nominal* damages may *not* be awarded. [261]

   1. Physical injury required: Furthermore, P must usually show that he suffered some kind of *physical* harm. [262]

     Example: D nearly runs P over. P suffers emotional distress, but no physical manifestation or bodily symptoms from the distress. P may not recover since P had no physical symptoms.

   2. Elements of damages: But once physical harm has been proven, a variety of damages may be recovered by P. [262] These include:

    a. Direct loss: The value of any direct loss of bodily functions. (*Example:* $100,000 for the loss of a leg.)

    b. Economic loss: Out-of-pocket *economic losses* stemming from the injury. (***Examples:*** Medical expenses, lost earnings, household attendant.)

    c. Pain and suffering: *Pain and suffering* damages.

    d. Hedonistic damages: Damages for loss of the ability to *enjoy* one's previous life. (***Example:*** Compensation for loss of the ability to walk, even if loss of that ability has no economic consequences.)

B. Hedonistic damages: As noted, most courts now allow a jury to award ***hedonistic damages***, i.e., damages for the loss of the ability to *enjoy life*. [262]

    1. Consciousness required: Courts are *split* about whether P must be *conscious* of the loss in order to be able to recover damages. Some states (e.g., New York) do not allow hedonistic damages where P is in a coma. [262]

C. Future damages: P brings only ***one action*** for a particular accident, and recovers in that action not only for past damages, but also for likely *future* damages. [263-264]

    1. Present value: When P is recovering future values, courts generally instruct the jury to award P only the *"present value"* of these losses. [263]

    2. Periodic payments: Some states now allow D to force P to accept *periodic payments* in certain situations. These payments generally terminate upon P's death. [264-264]

        Example: In New York medical malpractice cases, where the judgment is for more than $250,000, D may pay the judgment by purchasing an annuity for P, which will terminate on P's death.

D. Tax: Any recovery or settlement for personal injuries is *free* of *federal income tax*. [264]

E. The collateral source rule: At common law, P is entitled to recover her out-of-pocket expenses, even if P was *reimbursed* for these losses by some *third party*. This is known as the *"collateral source rule."* [265-266]

    Example: P has hospital bills of $100,000. A health insurance policy owned by P pays every dime of this. When P sues D, and establishes liability, P may recover the whole $100,000 even though in a sense she has collected twice.

    1. Statutory modifications: Nearly half the states have *modified* the common law collateral source rule in one way or another. [266]

    2. Subrogation: Where the common law rule remains in effect, P may not get a windfall after all. An insurance company that makes payments to P will normally be *subrogated* to P's tort rights. That is, it is the insurance company, not P, who will actually collect any judgment from D up to the amount of the payments made by the insurer. [266]

F. Mitigation: P has a *"duty to mitigate."* That is, P cannot recover for any harm which, by exercise of reasonable care, he could have *avoided*. In particular, P cannot recover for any harm which would have been avoided had P sought *adequate medical care*. [266]

    1. Seat belt defense: In some states, failure to use a *seat belt* may deprive P of recovery under the duty to mitigate — if D can show that P would not have been seriously injured had P worn a seat belt, D may escape liability for the avoidable injuries. [267]

II. PUNITIVE DAMAGES

A. Punitive damages generally: Punitive damages can be awarded to penalize a defendant whose conduct is particularly *outrageous*. [267]

    1. Negligence cases: In cases of negligence (as opposed to intentional torts), punitive damages are usually awarded only where D's conduct was *"reckless"* or *"willful and wanton."* [268]

        a. Product liability suits: Punitive damages are also frequently awarded in *product liability suits*, if P shows that D knew its product was defective, or recklessly disregarded the risk of a defect.

        b. Multiple awards: In a product liability context, a defendant who has made many copies of a defective product may face *multiple suits*, each awarding punitive damages. The possibility of multiple awards by itself generally does not mean that such awards should not be made. But many courts take into account the possibility of multiple awards in fixing the amount of punitive damages in each case.

    2. Constitutional limits: The U.S. Constitution places some — but not severe — limits on the award of punitive damages. [270]

        a. Due process: A defendant might be able to show that a particular punitive damages award violated its Fourteenth Amendment *due process* rights.

            i. Ratio of actual to punitive: One of the most important factors in whether an award of punitive damages violates due process is the *ratio* of the *punitive damages* to the *compensatory damages.* The higher this ratio, the more likely it is that a due process violation will be found. [269]

            Example: D, an insurer, refuses in bad faith to settle a claim by X against P, its policy owner. This refusal temporarily places P in fear of having to pay an excess judgment of $136,000. (D eventually pays the judgment all by itself). A state court awards P punitive damages of $145 million, on top of a $1 million compensatory award. *Held*, this award violated D's due process rights. *"Few awards* [significantly] exceeding a *single-digit ratio* between punitive and compensatory damages ... will satisfy due process." [*State Farm Mut. Auto. Insur. Co. v. Campbell*]

III. RECOVERY BY SPOUSE OR CHILDREN

A. General action by spouse: Most states allow the *spouse* of an injured person to bring an independent action for his or her own injuries. [270-271] (***Examples:*** A spouse of the injured person may recover for loss of companionship or loss of sex.)

B. Recovery by parent: Similarly, nearly all jurisdictions allow a *parent* to recover *medical expenses* incurred due to injury to the child. Also, there may be an action for loss of companionship (e.g., the child is in a coma). [271]

C. Child's recovery: Some — but still not most — courts allow a child to recover for loss of companionship or guidance where the parent is injured. [271]

        Note: The discussion in paragraphs A, B and C above assumes that the victim is only injured, not killed. Where the victim is killed, the "wrongful death" statutes discussed below apply instead.

C
A
P
S
U
L
E

S
U
M
M
A
R
Y

D. Defenses: In such third-party actions, generally any *defense* which could have been asserted in a suit brought by the injured party may be asserted against the plaintiff. [271] (*Example:* In a suit by Husband for loss of companionship and sex due to injuries to Wife, D may assert that Wife was comparatively negligent.)

    1. Defenses against plaintiff: Furthermore, defenses may be asserted against the plaintiff even though these could not have been asserted in a suit brought by the victim. [271]

        Example: Husband drives and collides with D; Wife is injured. If Husband sues for loss of companionship, D can raise Husband's comparative negligence as a defense, even though this would not be a defense in a suit brought by Wife.

IV. WRONGFUL DEATH AND SURVIVOR ACTIONS

A. Wrongful death distinguished from survivor: Most states have two types of statutes which take effect when a personal injury victim dies. The "survival" statute governs whether the victim's own right of recovery continues after his death. The "wrongful death" statute governs the right of the victim's survivors (typically, spouse and children) to recover. [272]

B. Survival statutes: The *survival* statute in most states provides that when an accident victim dies, his estate may sue for those elements of damages that the victim himself could have sued for had he lived. Thus a survival statute typically allows the estate to sue for pain and suffering, lost earnings prior to death, actual medical expenses, etc. In many states, if death is *instantaneous*, there is no survival action at all, since all damages are sustained on account of or after the death. [272]

C. Wrongful death: Most states have *"wrongful death"* statutes, which allow a defined group to recover for the loss they have sustained by virtue of the decedent's death. Typically, the decedent's *spouse* and *children* are covered. If the decedent has no spouse or children, usually the *parents* are covered. [273-274]

    1. Elements of damages: In a wrongful death action, the survivors may recover for: (1) the *economic support* they would have received had the accident and death not occurred; and (2) usually, the companionship (including sexual companionship) and moral guidance that would have been given by the decedent. Some — but not most — states also allow the survivors to recover for *grief.* [273]

        a. Recovery by parent where child is dead: Many courts now allow a parent whose child has died to recover for the loss of companionship of that child. [273]

    2. Defenses: In a wrongful death action, D may assert any defense which he would have been able to use against the decedent if the decedent was still alive and suing in her own name. [274] (*Examples:* The decedent's contributory negligence, assumption of risk, consent, etc. will all bar an action for wrongful death by the survivors.)

CHAPTER 11

DEFENSES IN NEGLIGENCE ACTIONS

C
A
P
S
U
L
E

S
U
M
M
A
R
Y

I. CONTRIBUTORY NEGLIGENCE

A. General rule: At common law, the doctrine of *contributory negligence* applied. The doctrine provided that a plaintiff who was negligent, and whose negligence contributed proximately to his injuries, was *totally barred from recovery*. [277-278]

> **Example:** P, while crossing the street, fails to pay attention. D, travelling at a high rate of speed while drunk, hits and kills P. Had P behaved carefully, he would have been able to get out of the way. Even though D's negligence is much greater than P's, in a traditional contributory negligence regime P will be totally barred from recovery because of his contributory negligence.

B. Standard of care: The plaintiff was held to the *same standard of care* as the defendant (i.e., the care of a *"reasonable person* under like circumstances"). [278]

C. Proximate cause: The contributory negligence defense only applied where P's negligence *contributed proximately* to his injuries. The same test for "proximate causation" was used as where D's liability was being evaluated. [279]

> **Example:** On the facts of the above example, suppose that D was travelling so fast that even had P been careful, D would still have struck P. P will not be barred by contributory negligence, because his negligence was not a "but for" cause, and thus not a proximate cause, of P's injuries.

D. Claims against which defense not usable: Since the contributory negligence defense was based on general negligence principles, it could be used as a bar only to a claim that was itself based on negligence. [280-281]

    1. Intentional torts: Thus the defense could not be used where P's claim is for an *intentional tort*. [280]

    2. Willful and wanton: Similarly, if P's conduct was found to have been *"willful and wanton"* or *"reckless,"* the contributory negligence defense would not be allowed. (But if D's negligence was merely "gross," contributory negligence usually would be allowed.) The idea is that the defense did not apply where D disregarded a *conscious* risk. [280-281]

II. COMPARATIVE NEGLIGENCE

A. Definition: A *"comparative negligence"* system rejects the all-or-nothing approach of contributory negligence. It instead attempts to divide liability between P and D in proportion to their *relative degrees of fault*. P is not barred from recovery by his contributory negligence, but his recovery is reduced by a *proportion* equal to the ratio between his own negligence and the total negligence contributing to the accident. [281]

> **Example:** P suffers damages of $100,000. A jury finds that P was 30% negligent and D was 70% negligent. P will recover, under a comparative negligence system, $70,000 — $100,000 minus 30% of $100,000.

   1. **Commonly adopted:** 46 states have replaced contributory negligence with some form of comparative negligence. So *contributory* negligence has largely been ***abandoned*** in American law.

B. **"Pure" versus "50%" systems:** Only 13 states have adopted "pure" comparative negligence. The rest completely bar P if his negligence is (depending on the state) ***"as great"*** as D's, or ***"greater"*** than D's. [282-283]

C. **Multiple parties:** Where there are ***multiple defendants***, comparative negligence is harder to apply:

   1. **All parties before court:** If all defendants are joined in the same lawsuit, the solution is simple: only the negligence due directly to P is deducted from his recovery. [283]

      Example: Taking all negligence by all parties, P is 20% negligent, D1 is 50% negligent, and D2 is 30% negligent. P will recover 80% of his damages.

   2. **Not all parties before court:** If not all defendants are before the court, hard questions arise concerning ***joint-and-several liability***. The issue is whether the defendant(s) before the court, who is/are found to be only partly responsible for P's loss, must pay for the whole loss aside from that caused by P's own fault. [283-284]

      Example: P's accident is caused by the negligence of D and X. P sues D, but can't find or sue X. The jury finds that P was 20% responsible; D, 30% responsible; and X, 50% responsible. P's damages total $1 million. It is not clear whether P can collect the full $800,000 from D. Under traditional "joint-and-several liability" rules, P would be able to collect this full $800,000.

      a. **Total abolition:** About 1/3 of the states have ***completely abolished*** the doctrine of joint-and-several liability in comparative negligence cases. In these states, all liability is "several." That is, each defendant is ***only required to pay his or her own share*** of the total responsibility. (So in such a state, P in the above example could collect only $240,000 from D, i.e., his 30% share of the overall $1 million in damages.)

      b. **Hybrid:** An additional significant number of states have replaced traditional joint-and-several liability with some sort of ***"hybrid"*** approach, which combines aspects of joint-and-several liability and aspects of several liability. (See *supra*, C-34, for a discussion of these hybrids.)

D. **Last clear chance:** Courts are ***split*** about whether the doctrine of ***last clear chance*** should survive in a comparative negligence jurisdiction. [284]

E. **Extreme misconduct by D:** If D's conduct is not merely negligent, but ***"willful and wanton"*** or ***"reckless,"*** most states nonetheless will reduce P's damages. [284]

   1. **Intentional tort:** But if D's tort is ***intentional***, most comparative negligence statutes will *not* apply. [285]

F. **Seat belt defense:** The ***"seat belt defense"*** is increasingly ***accepted*** in comparative negligence jurisdictions. In this defense, D argues that P's injuries from a car accident could have been reduced or entirely avoided had P worn a seat belt; P's damages should therefore be reduced. [286]

1. **Contributory negligence jurisdictions:** In most ***contributory*** negligence jurisdictions, courts ***refuse*** to allow the seat belt defense at all. That is, P's failure to wear a seat belt does not count against his recovery in most courts. [286]

2. **Comparative negligence jurisdictions:** But in states that have comparative negligence, the seat belt defense is more successful. There are various approaches: (1) D is liable only for those injuries that would have occurred even had P worn a seat belt; (2) D is liable for all injuries, with a reduction made equal to the percentage of P's fault; and (3) D is liable for all injuries, but P's fault reduces his recovery for those injuries that would have been avoided. [287-288]

   a. **Effect of statute:** Thirty-two states have ***mandatory*** seat belt use statutes. But the majority of these either prohibit the seat belt defense completely or make the defense almost valueless by allowing only a small reduction of damages. [288]

G. **Imputed comparative negligence:** Occasionally, the fault of one person (call her *A*) may by ***imputed to another*** (*B*), to as to reduce *B*'s recovery.

   1. **"Both ways" rule:** But under the so-called ***"both ways" rule,*** this imputation will happen ***only*** if *B* would be vicariously liable (see *infra*, p. C-68) for *A*'s torts. As the Third Restatement puts it, "The negligence of another person is ***imputed*** to a plaintiff ***whenever the negligence of the other person would have been imputed had the plaintiff been a defendant[.]"*** [288]

      a. **Employer/employee:** The both ways rule means that if suit is brought by an ***employer*** for damages arising out of an accident involving the employer's ***employee***, any fault by the employee will reduce the plaintiff employer's recovery.

      Example: Company hires Worker to drive a delivery truck for Company's business. (Assume that Company is not negligent in selecting or training Worker for this role). Worker has a collision with a car driven by Dave, which damages Company's truck. Company sues Dave for the damage to the truck.

      If Worker was negligent in driving the truck, this negligence will be imputed to Company under the both ways rule. That's because, if Company were the defendant in a suit by Dave, Company would have been vicariously liable for Worker's negligence under the ***respondeat superior*** doctrine. Therefore, in a comparative-negligence jurisdiction, Company's recovery will be reduced by the percentage of fault attributable to Worker.

      b. **Not attributed from parent to child:** Suppose a ***child is the plaintiff***, the child's parent has contributed to the accident (e.g., by a ***failure to supervise***) and some third party has also been negligent. The both ways rule normally means that any fault attributable to the child's parents ***won't reduce the child's recovery against the third person***. [289]

      Example: Kid is injured in a playground accident, due in part to Guard's failure to supervise rough playing between Kid and Ted, another child. The accident is also due in part to a negligent failure of supervision by Dad, Kid's father, who is also present. Kid has suffered $10,000 in damages, and sues Guard for this sum.

      Kid can collect the entire $10,000 from Guard, without reduction for any percentage of fault due to Dad. That's because: (1) Dad would not be vicariously liable for Kid's negligence if Kid were a defendant in an action brought by Ted (since parents are not vicariously liable for their children's torts); (2) consequently, under the "both ways" rule, Dad's fault won't be attributed to Kid, and can't reduce Kid's recovery against either Guard or Dad; and (3) therefore, Dad and Guard are jointly and severally liable, and Guard can be required to pay the whole amount. (Guard could then seek contribution from Dad.)

c. **Driver-passenger scenario (rule not applied):** But there is one major scenario in which courts and/or legislatures usually ***decline to apply*** the both ways rule. Where the ***owner of a vehicle would be vicariously liable for negligence by the driver,*** but the ***owner/plaintiff is a passenger who is injured***, most modern decisions say that the owner's ability to recover from the negligent third-party will ***not be barred or reduced on account of the driver's negligence.*** [290]

   i. **Restatement approach:** Thus the Third Restatement of Torts, although it generally applies the both ways rule, ***does not apply the rule against the owner-passenger of a vehicle who is injured by a third party*** — the driver's negligence will not be imputed to the plaintiff owner/passenger, even though state law makes the owner liable to third parties for the negligence of a driver who is driving with the owner's permission. See Rest. 3d of Torts (Apport.), § 5, Comment c and Illustration 6.

   Example: P is the owner-passenger in a car driven by her husband (H). H drives the car to a restaurant parking lot. While P remains seated, H stops in a travel lane opposite a parking space occupied by a truck driven by D. While H goes into the restaurant to pick up the couple's take-out order. D backs his truck out of his parking space and strikes P's car, injuring her. P sues D for negligence in Maryland court (Maryland being one of the few states still applying contributory negligence). In Maryland, a driver's negligence is imputed to the owner of the vehicle if the driver has the owner's permission to drive it. Therefore, D defends on the grounds that: (1) H was contributorily negligent for leaving the car in the travel lane, and (2) under the both ways rule, H's negligence must be imputed to P, blocking P from any recovery.

   Held (by the Maryland Supreme Court), for P. In this special owner-passenger scenario, for public policy reasons the state's general both ways rule ***should not be applied***. The traditional rule imputing the driver's negligence to the owner-passenger was a way of ensuring that if a third party is injured by the driver's negligence, that third party could recover against ***the party most likely to be financially responsible:*** the vehicle's owner (covered by compulsory vehicle owner's insurance). But here the roles are switched: it's the ***third-party driver*** (here, D) whose negligence is a but for cause of injuries to the owner-passenger P, and it's X (the driver operating the car with P's permission) who has also been negligent. Application of the both ways rule here would mean that X's contributory or comparative negligence would bar or reduce P's ability to recover from third-party driver D. This result would be at odds with the imputed negligence doctrine's original purpose, which is to supply a solvent party from whom the injured passenger can recover. *Seaborne-Worsely v. Mintiens* (Md. 2018). [290]

III. ASSUMPTION OF RISK

A. Definition: A plaintiff is said to have *assumed the risk* of certain harm if she has *voluntarily consented* to take her chances that harm will occur. Where such an assumption is shown, the plaintiff is, at common law, completely barred from recovery. [292]

B. Express assumption: If P *explicitly* agrees with D, in advance of any harm, that P will not hold D liable for certain harm, P is said to have *"expressly"* assumed the risk of that harm. [292] (*Example:* P wants to go bungee jumping at D's amusement park. P signs a release given to him by D in which P agrees to "assume all risk of injury" that may result from the bungee jumping. If P is injured, he will not be able to sue D, because he has expressly assumed the risk.

1. **Exceptions:** There are three important *exceptions* to the general enforceability of express agreements to assume risk:

   ❏ first, when the party protected by the clause (typically the defendant) either *intentionally causes* the harm, or else brings about the harm by acting in a *reckless or grossly negligent* way;

   ❏ second, when the *bargaining power* of the party protected by the clause is *grossly greater* than that of the other party, typically a status the court finds to exist only when the good or service being offered is *"essential"* (e.g., the services of public carriers or public utilities);

   ❏ finally, where the court concludes that there is some *overriding public interest* which demands that the court refuse to enforce the exculpatory clause.

      Example: Even if P signs a contract with D, her doctor, saying, "I agree not to sue you for malpractice if anything goes wrong with my operation," no court will enforce this promise, because of the overriding public interest in not shielding doctors from their own negligence for medical procedures.

   [*Seigneur v. National Fitness Institute, Inc.*] [292]

C. Implied assumption of risk: Even if P never makes an actual agreement with D whereby P assumes the risk, P may be held to have assumed certain risks *by her conduct*. Here, the assumption of risk is said to be *"implied."* [294]

1. **Two requirements:** For D to establish implied assumption, he must show that P's actions demonstrated that she: (1) *knew of the risk in question*; and (2) *voluntarily consented* to bear that risk herself. [294]

   Example: D owns a baseball team. D posts big signs at the gates warning of the danger of foul balls. P has attended many games, and in each game buys a seat right behind home plate, a place where she and all other fans know many foul balls are hit. If P is hit by a foul ball, she will not be able to recover against D even if D negligently failed to screen the home plate area. This is because P knew of the risk in question, and voluntarily consented to bear that risk.

2. **Knowledge of risk:** The requirement that P be shown to have *known* about the risk is strictly construed. For instance, the risk must be one which was *actually* known to P, not merely one which *"ought to have been"* known to her. [294]

3. **Voluntary assumption:** The requirement that P consented *voluntarily* is also strictly construed. [295]

C
A
P
S
U
L
E

S
U
M
M
A
R
Y

    a. Duress: For instance, there is no assumption of the risk if D's conduct left P with ***no reasonable choice*** but to encounter a known danger.

        Example: P rents a room in a boarding house from D. She has to use a common bathroom at the end of a hallway. After the lease starts, a hole in the floor leading to the bathroom develops, and D negligently fails to fix it. P knows about the hole, but nonetheless steps in it while going to the bathroom. P will not be barred from recovery by an implied assumption of risk, because D's conduct left P with no reasonable alternative but to walk down the hallway to get to the bathroom.

    b. Choice not created by D: Where it is ***not D's fault*** that P has no reasonable choice except to expose herself to the risk, the defense ***will*** apply.

        Example: P is injured and needs immediate medical help. She asks D — who had nothing to do with the injury — to drive her to the hospital, knowing that D's car has bad brakes. P is deemed to assume the risk of injury due to an accident caused by the bad brakes. That's because P's dilemma (does she take the ride in D's car with the bad brakes or not?) is not one that D put P into as the result of any wrongdoing by D. (But there would be *no* assumption if D had caused P's original injuries, because D would then be the cause of P's dilemma.)

4. Distinguished from contributory negligence: Often, P's assumption of risk will also constitute contributory negligence.

        Example: P voluntarily, but unreasonably, decides to take her chances as to a certain risk.

    a. Reasonable assumption of risk: But this is not always true: sometimes conduct that constitutes assumption of risk is *not* contributory negligence.

        Example: P, injured, asks for a ride to the hospital in D's car, which P knows had bad brakes. This is assumption of risk, even though P has behaved perfectly reasonably in view of the lack of alternatives.

    b. Defense to reckless conduct: Distinguishing between assumption of risk and contributory negligence may be important where D's conduct was ***reckless***: contributory negligence is not a defense to reckless conduct, but assumption of the risk generally is.

5. "Primary" versus "secondary" assumption: Distinguish between ***"primary"*** implied assumption of risk and ***"secondary"*** implied assumption. In the "primary" case, D is never under any duty to P at all. [297] (***Example:*** Foul balls at a baseball game.) In the "secondary" case, D would ordinarily have a duty to P, but P's assumption of risk causes the duty to dissipate. (***Example:*** P, injured, asks for a ride to the hospital in D's car, which P knows has bad brakes.)

    a. Effect of comparative negligence statute: Where there is a ***comparative negligence*** statute, most states eliminate the "secondary" assumption doctrine, but not the "primary" assumption doctrine.

        Example 1: In a comparative negligence state, P, knowing of the risk of foul balls, goes to a baseball game and is hit by one. D can still raise assumption of risk as a complete defense, because the assumption here was a primary one — it prevented D from ever having any duty to protect P from foul balls. [297]

C
A
P
S
U
L
E

S
U
M
M
A
R
Y

Example 2: In a comparative negligence state, Landlord negligently allows Tenant's premises to become highly flammable, and a fire results. Tenant reenters the premises to try to rescue his child, and is injured. This is a "secondary" implied assumption of risk situation. Therefore, most courts would merge assumption of risk into comparative negligence. If Tenant behaved reasonably, his recovery will not be reduced at all. If Tenant behaved unreasonably, his recovery will be reduced only by the percentage of fault. [297]

    b. Sports and recreation: Within the context of *sports* and *recreation*, *one participant* sometimes *injures the other*. If the risk of this sort of inter-participant injury is found to be "inherent" in the sport or activity, then even in a comparative negligence jurisdiction the plaintiff will not be allowed to recover against the one who injured him, on the theory that the defendant owes no duty to the plaintiff to avoid that sort of risk. [298]

        i. Ordinary carelessness: Most courts now hold that in such co-participant sports, *ordinary carelessness* is *inherent* in the game (and thus covered by "primary" assumption of risk), so that an injured co-participant may recover only if the injury was *intentional* or so *reckless*ly inflicted as to be *totally outside the range of ordinary activity in the sport.* For a more extensive discussion, see *supra*, p. C-11.

IV. STATUTE OF LIMITATIONS

A. Discovery of injury: If P does not *discover* his injury until long after D's negligent act occurred, the statute of limitations may start to run at the time of the negligent act, or may instead not start to run until P discovered (or ought to have discovered) the injury. [298-300]

    1. Medical malpractice: In *medical malpractice cases*, statutes and case law today frequently apply the "time of discovery" rule. [298]

        Example: D performs an operation on P in 1970, and leaves a foreign object in P's body. P discovers the problem in 2008, and sues immediately. The statute of limitations is six years on tort actions. Many, probably most, states today would allow P to sue, on the theory that the statute only started to run at the earliest time P knew or should have known that the object was left in his body.

    2. Sexual assaults: Some states also apply the "discovery" rule to toll the statute of limitations in *sexual assault* cases. [299]

        Example: P is sexually abused by D, her father, when P is five years old. P represses the whole episode, but rediscovers it under psychoanalysis at the age of 30. A modern court might allow P to sue at age 31, on the theory that the statute of limitations was tolled until P remembered, or should have remembered, the abuse.

V. IMMUNITIES

A. Family immunity: The common law recognizes two *immunities* in the family relationship: between *spouses*, and between *parent and child*. [300-302]

    1. Husband and wife: At common law, inter-spousal immunity prevented suits by one spouse against the other for personal injury. [300]

        Examples: If W is injured while a passenger in a car driven negligently by H, W cannot sue H. If H intentionally strikes W, W cannot sue for battery.

a. Abolition: But over half the states have now completely *abolished* the inter-spousal immunity, even for personal injury suits. Other states have partially abolished it (e.g., not applicable for intentional torts, or not applicable for automobile accident suits).

2. Parent and child: At common law, there is an immunity that bars suit by a *child against his parents* or vice versa. Again, many (though not most) states have abolished this immunity, and others have limited it. [301-302]

B. Charitable immunity: *Charitable organizations*, as well as educational and religious ones, receive immunity at common law. [302-304]

1. Abolished: But more than 30 states have now abolished charitable immunity. Others have cut back on the doctrine (e.g., abolished as to charitable hospitals, or abolished where there is liability insurance). [303]

C. Governmental immunity: At common law, there is *"sovereign immunity,"* preventing anyone from suing the *government*. [303-307]

1. United States: Suits against the *federal government* are generally allowed today, under the Federal Tort Claims Act (FTCA). But the FTCA does not allow certain types of tort suits. [303-305]

a. Discretionary function: Most important, no liability may be based upon the government's exercise of a *discretionary or policy-making function*, even if the discretion is abused.

Example: The U.S. government conducts underground testing of biological weapons. The tests are carried out as carefully as can be done, but the government behaves negligently in making the basic decision that such tests can be done safely. Since this high-level decision is "discretionary," P, injured by escaping gas, probably cannot sue under the FTCA.

2. State governments: State governments have traditionally had similar sovereign immunity. But most have either completely abolished that immunity, or *waived* it selectively. [305]

3. Local government immunity: Local government units (cities, school districts, public hospitals, etc.) have traditionally had sovereign immunity as well. [305-306]

a. "Proprietary" functions: But even at common law, where a local government unit performs a *"proprietary"* function, there is no immunity. Proprietary functions are ones that have not been historically performed by government, and that are often engaged in by private corporations.

Examples: The running of hospitals, utilities, airports, etc., is generally proprietary, since these are revenue-producing activities; they can therefore be the subject of suit for personal injuries. Police departments, fire departments and school systems are not proprietary, and cannot be sued at common law.

b. Abolition: In any event, most states have abolished the general local government immunity, and some that have not done so allow suits where there is liability insurance.

4. Government officials: Courts often grant *public officials* tort immunity, even where their public employer could be sued. [306]

Examples: Legislators and judges generally receive complete immunity, as long as their act is within the broad general scope of their duties.

CHAPTER 12

VICARIOUS LIABILITY

I. EMPLOYER-EMPLOYEE RELATIONSHIP (*RESPONDEAT SUPERIOR*)

A. *Respondeat superior* **doctrine:** If an employee commits a tort during the *"scope of his employment,"* his employer will be *liable* (jointly with the employee). This is the rule of *"respondeat superior."* [315]

   1. Applies to all torts: The doctrine applies to *all* torts, including intentional ones and those in which strict liability exists, provided that the tort occurred during the scope of the employee's employment. [316]

B. **Who is an "employee":** *Respondeat superior* is applied to all cases involving *"employees,"* but *not* to most cases involving *"independent contractors."* You must therefore distinguish between these two. [316-316]

   1. Distinction: The main idea is that an employee is one who works *subject to the close control* of the person who has hired him. An independent contractor, by contrast, although hired to produce a certain result, is not subject to the close control of the person doing the hiring. [316-316]

   a. Physical details: The "control" required to make a person an employee rather than an independent contractor is usually held to be control over the *physical details* of the work, not just the general manner in which the work is turned out.

   Example: A "newspaper boy" is likely to be an independent contractor, not an employee, because the newspaper usually controls only the general terms of employment — such as the time by which the deliveries must take place — not the physical details, such as whether the work should be done by bike or automobile.

C. **Scope of employment:** *Respondeat superior* applies only if the employee was acting *"within the scope of his employment"* when the tort occurred. The tort is within the scope of employment if the tortfeasor was acting with an *intent to further his employer's business purpose*, even if the means he chose were indirect, unwise or even forbidden. [316-319]

   1. Trips from home: Most courts hold that where an accident occurs where the employee is travelling *from her home* to work, she is not acting within the scope of her employment. If the employee is *returning home* after business, courts are divided. [317]

   2. Frolic and detour: Even a *detour* or side-trip for personal purposes by an employee may be found within the scope of employment in many courts, if the deviation was "reasonably foreseeable." [318]

   Example: While D, a salesperson, is taking a two-hour trip to visit a business prospect, she makes a five-minute detour to buy a pack of cigarettes. If an accident occurred during the detour, this would probably be held to be "within the scope of employment," so that D's employer would be liable. But a two-hour detour for personal business while on a one-day trip would probably not be within the scope of employment.)

   3. Forbidden acts: Even if the act done was expressly forbidden by the employer, it will be "within the scope of employment" if done in furtherance of the employment. [318]

Example: D, a storekeeper, expressly orders his clerk never to load a gun while showing it to a customer. The clerk ignores this rule and loads the gun, the gun goes off and the customer is hurt. D will be liable because the loading, though forbidden, was done in furtherance of the employer's business purposes, i.e., sale of guns.

4. **Intentional torts:** The fact that the tort is an *intentional* one does not relieve the employer of liability. [318-319]

> **Example:** X is a bill collector for D. X commits assault, battery and false imprisonment on P in attempting to collect a debt. D will be liable.

   a. **Personal motives:** But if the employee merely acts from *personal motives*, the employer will generally not be liable.

> **Example:** Nurse at D hospital has always hated P because of a prior fight. While P is in the hospital, Nurse kills P. D will not be liable, because Nurse has obviously acted from personal motives, not in an attempt to further D's business.

II. INDEPENDENT CONTRACTORS

A. **No general liability:** As a very general "default" rule, a person who *hires an independent contractor* is *not* generally liable for the torts of that person.However, there are a number of significant *exceptions* to the no-liability general rule. [319]

1. **Distinguished from employee:** An independent contractor is one who, although hired by the employer to perform a certain job, is not under the employer's immediate control, and may do the work more or less in the manner he himself decides upon. See *supra*, C-68.

B. **Exceptions to non-liability:** There are two important exceptions to the rule that an employer is not liable for the torts of his independent contractor.

1. **Employer's own liability:** First, if the employer is *herself* negligent in her own dealings with the independent contractor, this can give rise to employer liability.

   a. **Negligent selection:** For instance, suppose the employer *negligently selects* an inappropriate contractor, given the requirements of the work — for instance the contractor does not have adequate *experience* in doing the type of project *safely*. The employer will be directly liable for her negligence in selection, and for the consequences of that negligence. [320]

> **Example:** Employer selects Contractor to do certain construction renovation work in Employer's store. A reasonable initial investigation by Employer of Contractor's credentials and work experience would have demonstrated that Contractor was not reasonably qualified to do the work safely. Contractor does the work negligently, and the negligent work causes physical injury to P.
>
> Employer is directly liable for negligently tasking Contractor to do the work, and will therefore be responsible for P's damages.

2. **Vicarious liability for non-delegable duties:** Second, there are some duties of care that are deemed so important that the delegator is liable for negligence by an independent contractor the delegator hires, even if the delegator used all due care in selecting that particular contractor. These are called "*non-delegable duties,*" and the delegator/employer is *vicariously liable* for the contractor's negligent performance of those non-delegable duties.

CAPSULE SUMMARY

a. **Most important scenarios:** Here are the most important situations in which the duty will be non-delegable and will thus lead to vicarious liability on the employer's part:

[1] **"Peculiar risk" of harm:** The work is likely to involve a *"peculiar risk"* of physical injury or property damage to others unless special precautions are taken. [320]

Example: D owns a private football stadium and the semi-professional team that plays in it. D hires Contractor to install new high-voltage lighting poles in the parking lot. D is not negligent in picking Contractor for this job, since Contractor has adequate experience and safety credentials. Contractor negligently does the work, leaving a pole in such an uninsulated condition that if someone were to touch it, they would be likely to get a high-voltage shock. P, a patron, touches the pole and is shocked.

Since there is a "peculiar risk" (i.e., a risk of a non-typical type of injury) from high-voltage electrical work that is done without adequate precautions, D will be vicariously liable for Contractor's negligence, in a suit brought by P against D. [321]

[2] **Abnormally dangerous:** The work is *abnormally dangerous* (i.e., ultrahazardous), so that the employer would be strictly liable if he did the work himself (see *infra*, p. C-73) rather than via the independent contractor. [321]

[3] **Land possessor:** The employer is a *possessor or lessor of land,* and owes a duty of care to the *public*. If because of that duty the employer would be liable for negligence in altering or repairing the property himself, the employer will be vicariously liable for comparable negligence committed by the contractor he selects. [321]

Example: O owns a department store. O hires Contractor (properly credentialed) to replace a broken skylight. Contractor does the work negligently. Two months after Contractor turns the repaired area back to O, the skylight falls, injuring P, a patron.

O as the owner of premises open to the public owed a duty of reasonable care to ensure the safety of customers. O will therefore be vicariously liable for the actual negligence of Contractor, since O would have been directly liable for his own negligence if O had done the work himself.

Note about while work is being done: But there's an important clarification to the above rule: it doesn't apply to the contractor's negligence during the period when the contractor is *actively doing the work,* and has *taken over the details of handling of the job* from the owner. [322]

Example: Same facts as above example. Now, however, assume that Contractor has negligently installed the skylight, but is still in physical possession of, and has responsibility, for the skylight area. (O has let Contractor deal with the details of how the work is to be done safely.) P, a customer, wanders in from an area not under Contractor's control, and is injured when the skylight falls on him. Contractor has also not posted any warning signs.

Since Contractor, not O, was in control of the daily work at the time of the accident, O won't be vicariously liable for Contractor's negligence. (Rationale: We want O to delegate the daily care to the person actually doing the work, and we don't want to encourage micromanagement and meddling by O in that work.) [322]

C
A
P
S
U
L
E

S
U
M
M
A
R
Y

[4] **Public place:** The work is done in a *"public place,"* such as a road, sidewalk, park, etc.

Example: LightingCo hires Contractor to repair a street light (on a public street) that LightingCo. owns and is responsible for illuminating. Contractor negligently does the work, and the streetlight fails soon after. P steps in a pothole which he would have seen had the streetlight been working. Since LightingCo. had the responsibility for maintaining the streetlight in a public place, it is vicariously liable for Contractor's negligence in doing the contracted-for maintenance work. [322]

III. JOINT ENTERPRISE

A. **Generally:** A *"joint enterprise,"* where it exists, may subject each of the participants to vicarious liability for the other's negligence. A joint enterprise is like a partnership, except that it is for a short and specific purpose (e.g., a *trip*). [322-323]

   1. **Use in auto cases:** The doctrine is used most often in *auto accident cases*. The negligence of the driver is imputed to the passenger (either to allow the occupant of a second car to recover against the passenger, or to prevent the passenger from recovering against the negligent driver of the other car under the doctrine of imputed contributory negligence). [322]

B. **Requirements for joint enterprise:** There are four requirements for a joint enterprise: (1) an *agreement*, express or implied, between the members; (2) a *common purpose* to be carried out by the members; (3) a *common pecuniary interest* in that purpose; and (4) an equal right to a *voice* in the enterprise, i.e., an equal right of control. [323]

IV. AUTO CONSENT STATUTES, THE "FAMILY PURPOSE" DOCTRINE AND BAILMENT

A. **Consent statutes:** About one quarter of the states have enacted statutes, called *"automobile consent statutes,"* which provide that the owner of an automobile is *vicariously liable* for any negligence committed by one using the car with the owner's *permission*.

B. **Automobile insurance omnibus clause:** The need for automobile consent statutes is eliminated, in many states, by the fact that the standard *automobile liability insurance policy* covers not only the named insured (usually the head of household, who is also generally the owner or co-owner of the automobile), but also any *member* of the named insured's household, and any other person who *uses* the automobile with the consent of the insured. So the user of the car becomes financially responsible himself, making liability on the part of the owner unnecessary (at least up to the policy limits. [324]

C. **Judge-made doctrines:** A number of *judge-made doctrines* accomplish the same objective of making the car owner vicariously liable for the negligence of one she permitted to use the car.

   1. **Joint enterprise:** Often the *joint enterprise* doctrine (*supra*, C-71), can be used to make one member of the enterprise (e.g., the vehicle owner) vicariously liable for the negligence of another member (e.g., the driver).

   2. **Family purpose doctrine:** Another important judge-made doctrine is the *"family purpose doctrine."* The doctrine, in force in about 12 states, provides that a car owner who lets *members of her household* drive her car for their own personal use has done so in order to further

a "family purpose" or family objective, and is therefore vicariously liable. (The doctrine is also sometimes called the *"family car"* doctrine.)

D. Bailments: In the absence of a consent statute (and assuming the family purpose doctrine doesn't apply), the mere existence of a *bailment* does *not* make the bailor vicariously liable for the bailee's negligence. [324]

> **Example:** D lends his shotgun to X. X, while hunting in the woods, negligently fires without noticing P nearby. Even though D is a bailor (he has lent his personal property to X), D does not thereby become vicariously liable for X's negligent use of the bailed property.

1. Negligence by bailor: But the bailor may, of course, be negligent herself in entrusting a potentially dangerous instrument to the bailee where she *should know that the latter may use it unsafely.* In this situation, the claim is directly against the bailor for *"negligent entrustment,"* and there is no vicarious liability. [324]

> **Example:** In the above example, if D knew that X often hunted while drunk, D's act of entrusting the shotgun to X might itself be negligent, in which case D would be directly (not vicariously) liable to P for the injuries caused by X.

CHAPTER 13

STRICT LIABILITY

I. STRICT LIABILITY GENERALLY

A. Generally: Apart from the special situation of defective products, there are three major contexts in which D can have *"strict liability"* — that is, liability regardless of D's intent and regardless of whether D was negligent. We examine those contexts in this chapter. They are:

- ❑ strict liability for keeping *wild or other dangerous animals*;

- ❑ strict liability for carrying out *abnormally dangerous* (or *"ultrahazardous"*) *activities*; and

- ❑ strict liability on the part of an employer for the *employee's on-the-job injuries*, a liability that is enforced by *"workers compensation"* statutes enacted in all states.

II. ANIMALS

A. Trespassing animals: In most states, the owner of livestock or other animals is liable for property damage caused by them if they *trespass* on another's land. This liability is "strict" — even though the owner exercises utmost care to prevent the animals from escaping, he is liable if they do escape and trespass. [330]

B. Non-trespass liability: A person is also strictly liable for non-trespass damage done by any *"dangerous animal"* he keeps. [330]

1. Wild animals: A person who keeps a *"wild"* animal is strictly liable for all damage done by it, as long as the damage results from a *"dangerous propensity"* that is typical of the species in question. (*Example:* D keeps a lion cub, which has never shown any violent tendencies. One day, the cub runs out on the street and attacks P. Even if D used all possible care to prevent the cub from escaping, he is liable for P's injuries, because the cub is a wild animal and

C
A
P
S
U
L
E

S
U
M
M
A
R
Y

the damage resulted from a dangerous propensity typical of lions, that they can attack without warning.) [330]

2. **Domestic animals:** But injuries caused by a *"domestic"* animal such as a cat, dog, cow, pig, etc., do not give rise to strict liability unless the owner **knows** or has **reason to know** of the animal's dangerous characteristics. [330] (***Example:*** Same facts as above example, except that the animal is a dog. If the dog has never attempted to bite anyone before, D is not liable. But if D knew or had reason to know that the dog sometimes attacks people, he would be liable.)

III. ABNORMALLY DANGEROUS ACTIVITIES

A. **General rule:** A person is strictly liable for any damage which occurs while he is conducting an *"abnormally dangerous"* activity. [332-333]

1. **Six factors:** Courts generally consider six factors in determining whether an activity is "abnormally dangerous":

   [1] there is a **high degree of risk** of some harm to others;

   [2] the harm that results is likely to be **serious**;

   [3] the risk **cannot be eliminated** by the exercise of reasonable care;

   [4] the activity is **not common**;

   [5] the activity is not **appropriate** for the place where it is carried on; and

   [6] the danger outweighs the activity's **value** to the **community**. [332]

2. **Requirement of unavoidable danger:** Probably the single most important factor is that the activity be one which **cannot be carried out safely**, even with the exercise of reasonable care. [302]

   Example: D, a construction contractor, carries out blasting operations with dynamite, to excavate a foundation. D uses utmost care. However, a piece of rock is thrown out of the site during an explosion, striking P, a pedestrian on the street. Blasting is an abnormally dangerous activity, in part because it cannot be conducted with guaranteed safety. Therefore, D will be strictly liable for the injury to P.

B. **Examples:** Here are some types of activities that are generally held to be abnormally dangerous:

1. **Nuclear reactor:** Operation of a **nuclear reactor** [333];

2. **Explosives:** The use or storage of **explosives** (see above example) [334];

3. **Crop dusting:** The conducting of **crop dusting** or spraying [335];

4. **Airplane accidents:** There usually is *not* strict liability in suits by passengers for **airplane accidents**. Therefore, in a suit by the estate of a passenger against the airline, the plaintiff must show negligence. (But most courts do impose strict liability for ground damage from airplane accidents.)

5. **Use of firearms:** Similarly, the use of **firearms** is usually found **not** to be abnormally dangerous, because they can be used very safely if good techniques are employed.

[335-336]

IV. LIMITATIONS ON STRICT LIABILITY

A. Scope of risk: There is strict liability only for damage which results from the *kind of risk* that made the activity abnormally dangerous. [337-338]

> **Example:** D operates a truck carrying dynamite, and the truck strikes and kills P. P must show negligence. Transporting dynamite may be ultrahazardous, but P's death has not resulted from the kind of risk that made this activity abnormally dangerous.

1. Abnormally sensitive activity by plaintiff: A related rule is that D will not be liable for his abnormally dangerous activities if the harm would not have occurred except for the fact that P conducts an *"abnormally sensitive"* activity. [337]

> **Example:** D's blasting operations frighten female mink owned by P; the mink kill their young in reaction to their fright. D is not strictly liable, because P was conducting an abnormally sensitive activity. [*Foster v. Preston Mill Co.*]

B. Contributory negligence no defense: Ordinary *contributory negligence* by P will usually *not* bar her from strict liability recovery. [338]

1. Unreasonable assumption of risk: But *assumption of risk* is a defense to strict liability. Thus if P *knowingly and voluntarily* subjects herself to the danger, this will be a defense, whether P acted reasonably or unreasonably in doing so. [339]

> **Example:** P, an independent contractor, agrees to transport dynamite for D. P understands that dynamite can sometimes explode spontaneously. If such an accident occurs, P cannot recover from D in strict liability, because P has assumed the risk; this is true whether P acted reasonably or unreasonably.

V. WORKERS' COMPENSATION

A. Generally: All states have adopted *workers' compensation* (WC) statutes, which compensate the employee for *on-the-job* injuries without regard either to the employer's fault or the employee's. [339-343]

1. No fault: The employer is liable for on-the-job injuries even though these occur *completely without fault* on the part of the employer. Even if the employee is contributorily negligent, the statutory benefits are not reduced at all. [340]

2. Arising out of employment: A typical statute covers injuries arising out of and in the *course of employment*. Thus activities which are purely personal (e.g., injuries suffered while the employee is travelling to or from work) are typically not covered. [340]

3. Exclusive remedy: The WC statute is the employee's *sole remedy* against the employer. The employee gives up his right to sue in tort, and does not recover anything for *pain and suffering*. [341]

a. Intentional wrongs: But if P can show that the employer *intentionally* injured him, the employee may pursue a common-law action.

> **Example:** A few cases have allowed the employee to sue where the employer has wilfully disregarded safety regulations. But most have held that the employer's failure to observe safety regulations or to keep equipment in good repair does not amount to an intentional act, and thus does not permit the employee to escape WC as the sole remedy.

C A P S U L E   S U M M A R Y

b. Third parties: The WC statute does not prevent the worker from suing a ***third party*** who, under common-law principles, would be liable for the worker's injuries.

Example: At P's job, P uses a machine manufactured by D and sold by D to Employer. If P is injured on the job, he cannot bring a common law action against Employer, but can bring a product liability suit at common law against D.

CHAPTER 14

PRODUCTS LIABILITY

I. INTRODUCTION

A. Three theories: "Product liability" refers to the liability of a seller of a tangible item which, because of a defect, causes injury to its purchaser, user, or sometimes bystanders. [349] Usually the injury is a personal injury. The liability can be based upon any of three theories:

1. *Negligence;*

2. *Warranty;*

3. *"Strict tort liability."*

II. NEGLIGENCE

A. Negligence and privity: Ordinary negligence principles apply to a case in which personal injury has been caused by a carelessly manufactured product. [348]

> **Example:** D, a car manufacturer, carelessly fails to inspect brakes on a car that it makes. P buys the car directly from D, and crashes when the brakes don't work. P can recover from D under ordinary negligence principles.

1. **Privity:** Historically, the use of negligence in product liability actions was limited by the requirement of ***privity***, i.e., the requirement that P must show that he contracted ***directly*** with D. But every state has now ***rejected*** the privity requirement where a negligently manufactured product has caused personal injuries. It is now the case that ***one who negligently manufactures a product is liable for any personal injuries proximately caused by his negligence.*** [348-349]

> **Example:** D manufactures a car, and negligently fails to make the brakes work properly. D sells the car to a dealer, X, who resells to P. While P is driving, the car crashes due to the defective brakes. P may sue D on a negligence theory, even though P never contracted directly with D.

a. **Bystander:** Even where P is a ***bystander*** (as opposed to a purchaser or other user of the product), P can recover in negligence if he can show that he was a "foreseeable plaintiff."

> **Example:** A negligently manufactured car driven by Owner fails to stop due to defective brakes, and smashes into P, a pedestrian. P can sue the manufacturer on a negligence theory.

B. Classes of defendants: Several different classes of people are frequently defendants in negligence-based product liability actions:

1. **Manufacturers:** The manufacturer is the person in the distribution chain most likely to have been negligent. He may be negligent because he: (1) carelessly *designed* the product; (2) carelessly *manufactured* it; (3) carelessly performed (or failed to perform) reasonable *inspections* and tests of finished products; (4) failed to package and ship the product in a reasonably safe way; or (5) did not take reasonable care to obtain quality *components* from a reliable source. [349-350]

2. **Retailers:** A *retailer* who sells a defective product may be, but usually is *not*, liable in negligence. The mere fact that D has sold a negligently manufactured or designed product is *not by itself* enough to show that she failed to use due care. The retailer ordinarily has *no duty to inspect* the goods. Thus suit against the retailer is now normally brought on a warranty or strict liability theory, not negligence. [350-351]

3. **Other suppliers:** *Bailors* of tangible property (e.g., rental car companies), *sellers* and *lessors* of real estate, and suppliers of product-related *services* (e.g., hospitals performing blood transfusions) may all be sued on a negligence theory. [351]

III. WARRANTY

A. General: A buyer of goods which are not as they are contracted to be may bring an action for *breach of warranty*. The law of warranty is mainly embodied in the *Uniform Commercial Code* (UCC), in effect in every state except Louisiana. There are two sorts of warranties, *"express"* ones and *"implied"* ones. [351]

B. Express warranties: A seller may *expressly represent* that her goods have certain qualities. If the goods turn out not to have these qualities, the purchaser may sue for this breach of warranty. [352-353]

> **Example:** D, a car dealer, promises that a particular car has "shatterproof glass." While P is driving the car, a pebble hits the windshield, shatters the glass, and damages P's eyes. P can sue D for breach of the express warranty that the glass would be shatterproof. [*Baxter v. Ford Motor Co.*]

1. **UCC:** UCC §2-313 gives a number of ways that an express warranty may arise: (1) a statement of *fact* or promise about the goods; (2) a *description* of the goods (e.g., "shatterproof glass"); and (3) the use of a *sample or model*. [352]

   a. **Privity:** There is usually *no* requirement of *privity* for breach of express warranty.

   > **Example:** D manufactures a car, and prepares a brochure stating that the glass is "shatterproof." D sells the car to Dealer, who resells it to P. P never reads the brochure, and is injured when the glass is not shatterproof. P can recover against D for breach of express warranty, because there is no privity requirement, and D's statement was addressed to the public at large.

2. **Strict liability:** D's liability for breach of an express warranty is *a kind of strict liability* — as long as P can show that the representation was not in fact true, it does not matter that D reasonably believed it to be true, or even that D could not possibly have known that it was untrue. [353]

C. Implied warranty: The existence of a warranty as to the quality of goods can also be *implied* from the fact that the seller has offered the goods for sale. [353-357]

  1. Warranty of merchantability: The UCC imposes several implied warranties *as a matter of law.* Most important is the warranty of *merchantability.* Section 2-314(1) provides that *"a warranty that goods shall be merchantable is implied in a contract for their sale if the seller is a merchant with respect to goods of that kind."* [353-354]

   a. Meaning of "merchantable": To be *merchantable*, the goods must be "fit for the ordinary purposes for which such goods are used."

   Example: A car which, because of manufacturing defects, has a steering wheel that does not work, is not "merchantable," since it is not fit for the ordinary purpose — driving — for which cars are used.

   b. Seller must be a merchant: The UCC implied warranty of merchantability arises only if the seller is a *"merchant with respect to goods of that kind."* Thus the seller must be *in business* and must regularly sell the *kind of goods* in question.

   Examples: A consumer who is reselling her car does not make any implied warranty of merchantability; nor does a business person who is selling a piece of equipment used in that person's business rather than held in inventory.

  2. Fitness for particular purposes: A second UCC implied warranty is that the goods are *"fit for a particular purpose."* Under §2-315, this warranty arises where: (1) the seller knows that the buyer wants the goods for a particular (and not customary) purpose; and (2) the buyer *relies on the seller's judgment* to recommend a suitable product. [354]

   Example: Consumer tells Shoe Dealer that he wants a pair of shoes for mountain climbing. Dealer recommends Brand X as having good traction. If the shoes don't have good traction, and Consumer falls, he can sue Shoe Dealer for breach of the implied warranty of fitness for a particular purpose.

  3. Privity: States have nearly all *rejected* any *privity* requirement for the implied warranties. [354-356]

   a. Vertical privity: Thus *"vertical"* privity is not required. In other words, a manufacturer's warranty extends to *remote purchasers* further down the line.

   Example: Manufacturer sells a widget to Distributor, who sells to Dealer, who sells to Owner. Owner resells to Buyer. Buyer is injured when the widget does not behave merchantably. In all states, Buyer can sue Manufacturer, despite the lack of any contractual relationship between Buyer and Manufacturer.

   b. Horizontal privity: Similarly, *"horizontal"* privity is usually not required. In all states, any member of the *household* of the purchaser can recover if the member uses the product. In most states, *any* user, and even any foreseeable *bystander*, may recover.

D. Warranty defenses: Here are three *defenses* unique to warranty claims:

  1. Disclaimers: A seller may, under the UCC, *disclaim* both implied and express warranties. [357-358]

   a. Merchantability: A seller may make a written disclaimer of the warranty of merchantability, but only if it is *"conspicuous"* (e.g., in capital letters or bold print). Also, the word "merchantability" must be specifically mentioned. (Also, the circumstances may give rise to an implied disclaimer, as where used goods are sold **"as is."**)

2. Limitation of consequential damages: Sellers may try to **limit the remedies** available for breach (e.g., "Our sole remedy is to repair or replace the defective product"). But in the case of goods designed for personal use ("consumer goods"), limitation-of-damages clauses for **personal injury** are automatically **unconscionable** and thus unenforceable. UCC §2-719(3). [357]

E. Where warranty useful: Generally, any plaintiff who could bring a warranty suit will fare better with a strict liability suit. But there are a couple of exceptions:

1. Pure economic harm: If P has suffered only **pure economic harm**, he will usually do better suing on a breach of warranty theory than in strict liability. For instance, loss of profits is more readily recoverable on a warranty theory. [358]

2. Statute of limitations: The **statute of limitations** usually runs sooner on a strict liability claim than on a warranty claim. [358]

IV. STRICT LIABILITY

A. General rule: Nearly all states apply the doctrine of **"strict product liability."** The basic rule is that a **seller** of a product is **liable without fault** for personal injuries (or other physical harm) caused by the product if the product is sold in a **defective condition**. Once a defect is shown to have existed, the seller is liable even though he used all possible care, and even though the plaintiff did not buy the product from or have any contractual relationship with the seller. [359]

Example: Manufacturer makes a car with defective brakes. Manufacturer sells that car to Dealer, who resells it to Owner, who resells it to Consumer. Consumer is injured when the car crashes because the brakes don't work. Consumer can recover from Manufacturer in "strict tort liability," by showing that the brakes were in a defective condition unreasonably dangerous to users at the time the car left the plant. This is true even though Manufacturer used all possible care in designing and building the car, and even though Consumer never contracted with Manufacturer.

1. Non-manufacturer: Strict product liability applies not only to the product's manufacturer, but also to its **retailer**, and any other person in the distributive train (e.g., a wholesaler) who is in the business of selling such products. [359] (**Example:** On the above example, Consumer can recover against Dealer, even though Dealer merely resold the product and behaved completely carefully.)

2. Manufacturing, design and failure-to-warn defects: There are three different types of defects that may exist: (1) a **manufacturing** defect; (2) a **design** defect; and (3) a **warning** defect. It's important to decide which type of defect is or may be at issue, because there are different rules of law governing what constitutes a defect of each type. Here's a brief summary of what each type of defect looks like:

a. Manufacturing: In a **manufacturing** defect, a particular instance of the product is different from — and more dangerous than — all the others, because the product **deviated from the intended design**.

Example: D makes a bicycle which, because of an air bubble that gets into its front fork during manufacture, has an invisible crack that causes the fork to break while P is riding

C A P S U L E S U M M A R Y

it. This is a manufacturing defect — this bike is different from the other bikes of the same model, in an unintended way.

   b. Design: In a ***design*** defect, all of the similar products manufactured by D are ***the same***, and they all bear a feature whose design is itself defective, and unreasonably dangerous.

   Example: D makes a particular model step-ladder that, when more than 150 lbs. is placed on it, is likely to crack because the wood used is a poor grade. This is a design defect — all the ladders of this model have the same poor wood and the same risk of breakage when used for the intended purpose.

   Design defects are discussed beginning on p. C-82.

   c. Warning: In a ***failure-to-warn*** case, the maker has neglected to give a warning of a danger in the product (or in a particular use of the product), and this lack of a warning makes an otherwise-safe product unsafe.

   Example: D, a prescription drug maker, fails to warn users that the drug causes a serious allergic reaction in 2% of the people who take it.

   Failure to warn is discussed beginning on p. C-83.

B. What product meets test: A product gives rise to strict liability only if it is ***"defective."*** [360-361]

   1. Meaning of "defective": In the usual case of a manufacturing (as opposed to design) defect, a product is "defective" if the product ***"departs from its intended design*** even though ***all possible care was exercised*** in the preparation and marketing of the product." (Rest. 3d.) [361].

C. Unavoidably unsafe products: A product will not give rise to strict liability if is ***unavoidably unsafe,*** and its benefits outweigh its dangers.[362]

   1. Prescription drugs: For instance, a ***prescription drug*** is not "defective" merely because it causes some side effects and may in an individual case cause more damage than it cures. This is also true of ***vaccines***. In fact, under the new Third Restatment rule, drugs, vaccines, and medical devices will be non-defective (unavoidably unsafe) as long as there is ***even a single group of patients*** for whom the product's ***benefits outweigh its harms.*** [363]

   a. Consequence: This seems to mean that as long as the drug has a net benefit for one group of patients, the maker doesn't need to make the drug as safe as it could be with reasonable effort! For this reason, many courts have ***rejected*** the Third Restatement drug rule as extreme, and require manufacturers to make reasonable efforts to make the drug as safe as possible. [364]

D. Unknowable dangers: Similarly, if the danger from the product's design was ***"unknowable"*** at the time of manufacture, there will be no liability. See Rest. 3d: a design defect will exist only "when the ***foreseeable*** risks of harm posed by the product could have been reduced or avoided by the adoption of a reasonable alternative design" — so if the risk of harm from the design is unknowable at the time of manufacture, there was no "foreseeable risk" and thus no design-defect liability. [364]

   1. Failure to warn: Similarly, there can be no ***"failure to warn"*** liability (see *infra*, p. C-83) for a danger whose existence was unknowable at the time of manufacture.

C
A
P
S
U
L
E

S
U
M
M
A
R
Y

E. Food products: Where the product is *food*, most courts apply a *"consumer expectations"* test. Under that test, the food product is defective if and only if it contains an ingredient that *a reasonable consumer would not expect it to contain*.

> **Example:** D manufactures a chicken enchilada. P, a consumer, chokes on a chicken bone in the enchilada. Under the prevailing view, the bone constitutes a "defect" if and only if a reasonable consumer in P's position would not have expected to find a bone in a chicken enchilada. (But in a minority of courts, P would lose because the bone was "natural" for that type of food product, even though a reasonable consumer might not expect to find the bone there.)

F. Obvious dangers: The fact that a danger is *"obvious"* may have an impact on whether the product is deemed defective, and thus on whether D is liable. The treatment of obviousness depends on whether the defect is a manufacturing defect, a design defect, or a failure to warn. [365-367]

  1. Manufacturing defect: Where the defect is a *manufacturing* defect, the fact that the danger or defect is obvious probably *won't* block P from recovering (though under comparative fault — generally applicable in products liability cases, see *infra*, p. C-90 — it might reduce P's recovery).

  > **Example:** D makes a can of tuna fish, which contains a sliver of metal in it. P fails to notice the metal and is injured when he swallows it. Even if an ordinary consumer would spot the metal and not eat it, the "obviousness" of the danger won't stop the product from being defective, and P will be able to recover.

  2. Design defect: If what's alleged is a *design* defect, under the modern view the obviousness of the defect is a *factor* bearing upon liability, but it *doesn't automatically* mean that P can't recover. Instead, the question is whether the design's *benefits outweigh its dangers*, considering possible alternative designs — if the answer is "no," P can recover even though the dangers were obvious.

  > **Example:** Suppose that D manufactures cigarettes using a particular type of tobacco and a particular curing process, that produces very high tar and nicotine, and thus high risk of cancer. P gets cancer from smoking D's cigarettes. Even if P was perfectly aware of how dangerous D's cigarettes were, this fact won't (in most courts) bar the court from finding that the cigarettes were "defective" and thus from allowing P to recover in products liability.
  >
  > So, for instance, if P can show that a cigarette made with a different process would taste as good and have less cancer risk, P could win. (But the test will be a cost-benefit analysis: if P shows merely that a safer cigarette could have been made by reducing the elements that give the cigarette the flavor that most smokers expect, D's process won't be found to be "defective" and P will lose, since the safer cigarette won't have the same "benefits" as D's dangerous one.)

  3. Failure-to-warn: If the defect or danger is obvious, this will normally *prevent failure-to-warn liability*. That's because if P is actually aware of the obvious danger the warning won't add anything, and if P isn't aware of the obvious danger he's unlikely to notice or respond to the warning either. [366]

G. Proving the case: P in a strict liability case must prove a number of different elements:

❏ that the item was *made or sold by the defendant*;

❏ that the product was *defective*;

❏ that the defect *caused* the plaintiff's injuries; and

❏ that the defect *existed* when the product *left the defendant's hands.*

We consider each element in turn.

1. **Manufacture or sale by defendant:**   P must show that the item was in fact manufactured, or sold, by the defendant. [367]

2. **Existence of defect:**   P must show that the product was *defective*. [367-368]

    a. **Subsequent remedial measures:**   Most courts *do not* allow defectiveness to be proved by evidence that D subsequently *redesigned* the product to make it safer.

    b. **Toxic torts:**   In the case of a *"mass toxic tort,"* plaintiffs often use *epidemiological* evidence of defectiveness.

        Example: To prove that the pregnancy drug DES causes cancer, P offers expert testimony that daughters of women who took DES in pregnancy have a much higher incidence of cancer than those whose mothers did not. This is admissible evidence of defect and causality.

3. **Causation:**   P must show that the product, and its defective aspects, were the *cause in fact*, and the *proximate cause*, of her injuries. [369-370]

    a. **Epidemiology:**   In *toxic tort* cases, causation will often be the key element in controversy. Plaintiffs in such cases often attempt to prove this element, like existence of a "defect," by *epidemiological* evidence. [370-372]

        i. **"General" vs. "specific" causation:**   Courts often use the terms *"general" and "specific" causation* in toxic tort cases: general causation is a substance's tendency to increase the general incidence of a given disease, and specific causation is the substance's having caused plaintiff's own disease.

        ii. **Specific causation required:**   Courts normally require *proof of specific causation* as part of the plaintiff's prima facie case. However, if plaintiff's only direct proof on the causation issue is proof of general causation, courts will nonetheless permit the jury to *infer* specific causation if the proof of general causation is sufficiently strong, so long as there is also some evidence that the plaintiff was *actually exposed* to the agent.

            Example: P suffers from a rare cancer. In a suit against D, the maker of a drug called DES, P shows that her mother took DES while pregnant with P. P presents expert testimony showing that daughters of women who took DES in pregnancy are 10 times as likely to get that form of cancer as those whose mothers did not. This proof of "general causation" would probably suffice to allow the jury to infer that DES was the specific cause of P's cancer.

        iii. **The "doubling" rule:** Many courts impose the so-called *"doubling rule"*: the jury will be permitted to infer specific causation if and only if P shows that the agent *more than doubles the incidence of the disease* in the population as a whole. These courts reason that without a doubling, it is not "more likely than not" (the relevant preponderance-of-the-evidence standard) that the agent caused P's particular disease. [371]

4. Defect existed in hands of defendant: Finally, P must show that the defect existed *at the time the product left D's hands*. [369]

    a. *Res ipsa:* But an inference similar to *res ipsa loquitur* is permitted — once P shows that the product did not behave in the usual way, and the manufacturer fails to come forward with evidence that anyone else tampered with it, the requirement of defect in the hands of defendant is satisfied.

H. Bystanders and other non-user plaintiffs: *Any person who is injured* due to a dangerously defective product may recover, even if the plaintiff never bought the product. Thus *family members of buyers, bystanders,* even *rescuers,* may all recover if their injuries are proximately caused by the defect in the product. As the idea is sometimes put, *"privity"* is *not required* for strict product liability. [372]

    Example: Consumer buys a car from Dealer. The steering wheel fails due to a manufacturing defect, causing the car to swerve and hit Ped, a pedestrian walking on the sidewalk. Ped can recover from Dealer in strict product liability, because his physical injuries were proximately caused by a defective product sold by Dealer. The fact that neither Ped nor any member of his family ever purchased the product in question doesn't matter.

V. DESIGN DEFECTS

A. Definition of "design defect": A *"design defect"* must be distinguished from a "manufacturing defect." In a design defect case, all the similar products manufactured by D are the same, and they all bear a feature whose design is itself defective, and unreasonably dangerous. [372]

B. Negligence predominates: Most design defect claims have a heavy *negligence* aspect, even though the complaint claims strict liability. As the 3d Restatement puts it, a product has a defective design "when the *foreseeable risks of harm posed* by the product *could have been reduced or avoided by the adoption of a reasonable alternative design* by the seller or other distributor . . . and the omission of the alternative design *renders the product not reasonably safe*." [373]

    1. Practical other design: So P must show that there was a *"reasonable alternative design"* (*RAD*). In deciding whether P's proposed alternative qualifies as an RAD, the court will consider the cost and utility of the alternative, compared with the *cost and utility* of D's design.

        Example: D makes a bullet-proof vest, the Model 101, that covers only the wearer's front and back, not sides. P, a police officer, is shot in the side while wearing D's vest. At trial, P says that a design with side protection was an RAD, and that the no-sides design is therefore "defective." Suppose that the side-protection design would have weighed five pounds more and cost twice as much. A court is likely to conclude that the side-protection design is not an RAD, because its cost-benefit ratio is not clearly superior to the Model 101's, since many wearers would prefer the lighter cheaper design over the greater protection. [374]

C. Types of claims: Two types of common design-defect claims are as follows:

    1. Structural defects: P shows that because of D's choice of materials, the product had a *structural weakness*, which caused it to break or otherwise become dangerous. [377]

C
A
P
S
U
L
E

S
U
M
M
A
R
Y

2. **Lack of safety features:** P shows that a *safety feature* could have been installed on the product with so little expense (compared with both the cost of the product and the magnitude of the danger without the feature) that it is a defective design not to install that feature. [377]

   a. **State of the art:** D will be permitted to rebut this by showing that competitive products similarly lack the safety feature. This is the *"state of the art"* defense. But such a showing will *not* be *dispositive* — the trier of fact is always free to conclude that all products in the marketplace are defective due to lack of an easily-added feature.

D. **Suitability for unintended uses:** D may be liable not only for injuries occurring when the product is used as intended, but also for some types of injury stemming from *unintended uses* of the product. [378-379]

   1. **Unforeseeable misuse:** If the misuse of the product is *not reasonably foreseeable*, D has no duty to design the product so as to protect against this misuse. [378]

   2. **Foreseeable misuse:** But if the misuse is *reasonably foreseeable* by D, D must take at least reasonable design precautions to guard against the danger from that use. (Alternatively, a *warning* to the purchaser against the misuse may sometimes suffice.) [378]

      Example: A car is not "intended" to be used in a collision, and most collisions are in a sense "misuse" of the product. Nonetheless, a car manufacturer must design a reasonably *crushworthy* vehicle if it is feasible to do so, because collisions are reasonably foreseeable.

E. **Military products sold to and approved by government:** If a product is *sold* to the *U.S. government* for *military use*, and the government *approves* the product's specifications, the manufacturer will generally be immune from product liability even if the design is grossly negligent. [*Boyle v. United Technologies Corp.*] [380]

F. **Regulatory compliance defense:** Suppose the manufacturer has *complied with federal or state regulations* governing the design of the product. At common law, this compliance does *not* absolve D of product liability — regulatory compliance is an item of *evidence* that the jury may consider, but it is not dispositive. [380]

   1. **Labeling:** Thus if government requires that a substance be *designed* or *labeled* in a particular way, and the manufacturer follows that requirement, under the common-law approach P may still be able to bring a product liability suit on the theory that the design or labeling was inadequate and constituted a design defect.

      a. **Preemption:** But if the design or labelling requirement was imposed by *Congress*, and the court finds that Congress intended to *preempt* the states from requiring stricter or different designs or warning labels, then D has a defense. For more about preemption, see C-92 *infra*.

VI. DUTY TO WARN

A. **Significance of the duty to warn:** The *"duty to warn"* is essentially an *extra* obligation placed on a manufacturer. [382-383]

   1. **Manufacturing defect:** Thus if a product is *defectively manufactured, no warning can save D from strict liability*. [382]

C
A
P
S
U
L
E

S
U
M
M
A
R
Y

2. **Design defect:**   Similarly, if a product is ***defectively designed***, a warning will generally ***not*** shield D from strict product liability. [382]

3. **Properly manufactured and designed product:**   If a product is ***properly designed*** and ***properly manufactured***, D must nonetheless give a warning if there is a ***non-obvious*** risk of personal injury from using the product. Similarly, in this situation, D may be liable for not giving ***instructions concerning correct use***, if a reasonable consumer might misuse the product in a foreseeable way. [382]

> **Examples:** Prescription drugs, even when properly designed and properly manufactured, must contain warnings about side effects. Similarly, a household utility like a lawn mower, if it poses a non-obvious risk of personal injury such as cutting a foot, must contain instructions concerning correct use.

B. **Risk-utility basis:**   Liability for failure-to-warn is usually based on a negligence-like ***risk-utility analysis.***

1. **Restatement Third approach:**   Thus under the Third Restatement, a product will be deemed defective on account of "inadequate instructions or warnings" "when the ***foreseeable risks of harm*** imposed by the product could have been reduced or avoided by the provision of ***reasonable instructions or warnings*** . . . and the omission of the instructions or warnings renders the product ***not reasonably safe***." This sounds very much like the traditional negligence standard, used here to determine what warnings must be given.

C. **Drug cases:**   The most common category of failure-to-warn cases involves ***prescription drugs***.

1. **Learned intermediary doctrine:** Most courts, and the Third Restatement, recognize a defense that makes the manufacturer's duty to warn in prescription drug cases easier-to-satisfy: the *"learned intermediary"* defense. Where the defense is allowed, the manufacturer's duty is generally limited to warning the ***prescribing physician*** rather than the patient. The physician is viewed as a "learned [i.e., highly trained] intermediary" between the manufacturer and the user; the rationale is that the physician is, in most cases, in the best position to decide whether a drug should be prescribed and when and how its risks should be disclosed. [384]

   a. **Restatement adopts:** The Third Restatement basically ***applies*** the learned intermediary rule as the default rule. The Restatement imposes failure-to-warn liability on a drug or medical device maker only if ***"reasonable instructions or warnings*** regarding foreseeable risks of harm" are ***not provided*** to ***"prescribing and other health-care providers*** who are in a position to reduce the risks of harm in accordance with the instructions or warnings."

      i. **Exception:** But the Third Restatement includes an important ***exception*** to this general acceptance of the learned intermediary defense: The language quoted above indicates that if health-care providers will *not* be a position to pass on warnings, the manufacturer has a duty to give the warnings and instructions ***directly to the patient***. So, for instance, if the product is sold over-the-counter to consumers with a mass-media campaign, then warnings must be made to the consumer (e.g., in packaging inserts and/or on TV ads), not just to physicians who might recommend the item to patients. [384]

   b. **Exceptions:** Most courts that accept the learned intermediary doctrine recognize several ***exceptions*** to it. The most important one is the one mentioned above in connection with the Restatement: if the health-care provider for that drug will typically not be in a position to pass on the manufacturer's warnings (e.g., because the prescriber will generally not be meeting with the patient about that particular drug), then the doctrine does not apply and the manufacturer must see to it that warnings actually reach the end-user. [384]

2. **Adequacy of warning:** When a warning directly to the end-user is required, the manufacturer must provide, in language comprehensible to a lay person, a warning conveying a fair indication of the ***nature, gravity and likelihood*** of the known or knowable risks of the drug.

3. **Failure-to-warn as main basis for liability:** In the usual situation where a prescription drug is of net benefit to some class of patients, ***defective-design*** liability will not exist. (See *supra*, p. C-79.) In these situations, therefore, failure-to-warn is the *only* basis for liability. Thus most product liability suits brought against drug companies are premised upon the failure to warn.

4. **Warnings about generic drugs:** *Generic* drugs pose a special issue concerning warnings, due to the special way that warnings on generic drugs are regulated by the federal government.

   a. **Regulation of warnings:** First, let's look at how the regulation of warning labels by the federal Food and Drug Administration (FDA) *varies* as between labeling on the brand-name drug and that on the generic version.

      i. **Warnings on brand-name drugs:** When a company makes and proposes to market a ***brand-name*** prescription drug, federal law places on the manufacturer the responsibility for drafting the label for the drug; the label must contain all sorts of federally-dictated information, including such matters as usage instructions (e.g., recommended dosages), contraindications to use, and a listing of the most-common and/or most-serious adverse reactions. [385]

      ii. **Warnings on generic drugs:** By contrast, the maker of a ***generic*** drug has far less — essentially zero — responsibility for drafting the warning label for that drug. In brief, the generic maker must place ***"the same" label*** on the drug as the one the FDA has currently approved for the brand-name version. So, for instance, if either the brand-name maker or the generic maker learns of some ***new hazard*** posed by the drug, the generic maker ***may not modify*** the label to warn of the new hazard until the FDA approves the new language (whereas the brand-name maker may, indeed must, ***unilaterally*** change the label, subject to subsequent FDA review). [385]

   b. **Possible right to sue brand-name maker if P took the generic:** What happens when a plaintiff who has taken an arguably-mislabeled *generic* drug seeks recovery not from the maker of the generic, but from the ***maker of the branded version,*** perhaps on a misrepresentation theory? After all, it's the branded manufacturer who has written the label and has the responsibility to update the label based on any newly-discovered hazards. But the American law of product liability has always implicitly restricted product liability suits — even suits based on inadequate warning labels — to ones brought against defendants who either ***manufactured*** the particular instance of the defective product that harmed the plaintiff, or who were ***part of the chain that distributed*** that instance. So letting the patient injured by an improperly-labeled generic drug recover from the creator/maker of the branded version would require abandoning this central requirement of product-liability law. [386]

    i. **Majority rule says that P is out of luck:** Indeed, the substantial majority of courts to have considered the issue have held that the plaintiff who took the generic version is *simply out of luck:* in these states, there is *no* drug-maker from whom the plaintiff can recover. These courts have *rejected* the theory that the plaintiff should be able to recover against the *brand-name manufacturer* based on fraud or negligent misrepresentation in creating and disseminating the incorrect labeling. [387]

    ii. **Minority approach allows recovery against branded manufacturer where P took the generic:** But a few recent cases have reached the *opposite result*, by *allowing* the plaintiff who consumed an arguably mislabeled generic drug to seek recovery on a *fraud or misrepresentation theory against the brand-name manufacturer* who drafted the text of the label used on the generic drug, even though that defendant did not manufacture or distribute the generic drug taken by the plaintiff. [*T.H. v. Novartis Pharmaceuticals Corp.*] (Cal. 2017). [388]

D. Unknown and unknowable dangers: If D can show that it *neither knew* nor, in the exercise of reasonable care *should have known* of a danger at the time of sale, most courts hold that there was *no duty to warn* of the unknown danger. [388]

    Example: If D sells a prescription drug without having any ability to know of a particular side effect, failure to warn of that side effect will not give rise to strict product liability.

E. Danger to small number of people: If the manufacturer knows that the product will be dangerous to a *small number* of people, the need for a warning will usually turn on the *magnitude* of the danger; if the danger is great enough, even a small number of potential bad results will require a warning.

F. Government labelling standards: The scope of D's duty to warn may be affected by the fact that the *government* imposes certain *labeling* requirements. [389-389]

    1. Evidence: If D can show that it has complied with a federal or state labelling requirement, most courts permit this to be shown as *evidence* that the warning was adequate. But in most courts, this evidence is not dispositive — the jury is always free to conclude that a reasonable manufacturer would have given a more specific, or different, warning. [389]

    2. Preemption: But where the labelling requirement is imposed by the *federal government*, and the court finds that Congress intended to *preempt* more-demanding state labelling rules, then compliance with the federal standard *is* a complete defense to P's "failure to warn" claim. [389-389]

G. Post-sale duty to warn: Courts have disagreed about the extent to which a manufacturer has a duty to make a *post-sale* warning about dangers of which the manufacturer was not aware at the time of manufacture.

    1. Duty to warn when manufacturer learns of the risk: The most common approach is to hold that if the manufacturer eventually *learns about the risk*, it has an *obligation to give a post-sale warning,* assuming the risk is great and the user of the product can be identified. In this situation, a duty to warn probably exists even though the defect was *not knowable at the time of manufacture*. [391-393]

    2. Duty to monitor: Some courts have held that the manufacturer has a duty not only to warn about dangers or defects that it learns about, but also an affirmative duty to *"keep abreast of the field"* by *monitoring the performance and safety* of its products after sale. Such an affirmative duty of monitoring and testing is most likely to be found in cases involving ***prescription drugs***. [392]

H. Obvious danger: If the danger is ***obvious*** to most people, this will be a factor reducing D's obligation to warn. But where a warning could easily be given, and a substantial minority of people might not otherwise know of the danger, the court may nonetheless find a duty to warn. [389]

I. Hidden causation issue: In any failure-to-warn scenario, be sure to check that the requirement of a ***causal link*** between the failure to warn and the resulting injury is satisfied. If the provision of a warning ***would not have prevented the accident*** from occurring, then the defendant will ***not*** be liable for failing to warn. [393]

1. **Plaintiff who does not read warnings or ignores them:** For example, in a case in which the injured plaintiff is the one who was the user of the product, and the claim is based upon the defendant manufacturer's failure to place a warning label on the product, evidence that the plaintiff ***never read any warning labels*** would prevent failure-to-warn liability. Similarly, if there is evidence that even had plaintiff read the warning, plaintiff would have ***ignored the warning*** and used the product in the same way so that the accident would have happened anyway, failure to warn will not be the basis for liability.

VII. WHO MAY BE A DEFENDANT

A. Chattels: In any case involving a ***"good"*** or ***"chattel,"*** both strict and warranty liability will apply to ***any seller*** in the ***business*** of selling goods of that kind. [394]

1. **Retailer:** This means that a ***retail dealer*** who sells the good, but has not manufactured it, will have strict liability as well as warranty liability, even if she could have done nothing to discover the defect. But this is true only if the seller is in the ***business of selling goods of that type*** (so that a private individual selling a good, or a business person selling outside of the usual course of his business, will not have liability). [394]

   a. **Indemnity:** If the retailer is held liable in this way, she will be entitled to ***indemnity*** from the manufacturer or wholesaler, as long as the retailer was not herself negligent.

2. **Used goods:** Courts are split as to whether there is strict or warranty liability for the seller of ***used goods***. Probably most courts would hold that there is no such liability. [395]

   Example: Dealer, a used car dealer, sells a used car to X. The brakes are defective, and X is unable to avoid hitting P, a pedestrian. Most courts would not allow P to recover in strict liability against Dealer.

3. **Fulfillment services:** The rise of ***Internet retailing*** has led to an important issue about who is a seller. We'll focus here on ***Amazon***, the overwhelmingly-dominant Internet merchant (but what we say applies to other internet retailers as well). [396]

   a. **Amazon takes title and re-sells:** Often, Amazon.com acts as a true classic retailer: it buys the product from a supplier, thereby ***taking title*** to the product; it then advertises the product as being sold by Amazon and fulfills the order. Here, it's clear that Amazon is the actual seller of the product and will be strictly liable if the product causes personal injury or property damage, just like a brick and mortar store that sells the product. [396]

   b. **Amazon acts as fulfillment agent:** But the substantial majority of product sales that occur on Amazon.com are made under the company's ***Fulfillment by Amazon,"*** or

"FBA," program. Under this program, Amazon *never takes title:* the merchant who holds title to the goods (1) ships them in bulk to Amazon for storage in an Amazon warehouse; and (2) relies on Amazon to *receive the order* on the Amazon.com website, "pick" the goods for the order and *ship* them to the customer. In this FBA scenario, is Amazon is a *"seller"* of the product for purposes of strict product liability?

i. **Cases split:** Cases dealing with this issue are quite *split*. Here's a summary as of 2022: "By and large, U.S. courts have held that Amazon is *not strictly liable* for the goods sold by third parties on Amazon's website. … With that said, the tides may be *turning*, with several recent decisions *holding Amazon liable* for defective products sold by third-party sellers on its website." [400]

One of the recent cases finding that Amazon is a seller in these FBA situations is set out in the following example.

Example where Amazon loses: P goes to Amazon.com (D) and buys a dog collar listed by a seller named "The Furry Gang." (Before the sale, The Furry Gang had sent the collar to Amazon's warehouse for storage.) Amazon ships the order without ever taking title to it and remits the sale price to The Furry Gang after subtracting fees. The collar badly injures P, who brings a strict product liability suit. P's suit is solely against Amazon, in part because P can't locate The Furry Gang for service. Amazon defends on the grounds that since it never took title, it cannot be a "seller."

Held, for P. The court will not be guided by who held title. Instead, the court will consider these public-policy factors: [1] whether D was the *only member of the marketing chain available to the injured plaintiff for redress*; [2] whether the imposition of strict liability on D would serve as an *"incentive to safety"*; [3] whether D is in a *better position than the consumer t*o *prevent the circulation of defective products*; and [4] whether D *can distribute the cost of compensating for injuries* resulting from defects (e.g., by charging more or adjusting the sale terms). Here, all four of these factors cut in favor of treating Amazon as a seller for strict product liability purposes. [*Oberdorf v. Amazon.com Inc.* (3d Cir. 2019)] [398]

B. **Lessor of goods:** Courts frequently impose strict liability upon a *lessor* of defective goods. [400] (*Example:* A *car rental* company may be strictly liable if it rents a defective car and that car injures a pedestrian due to the defect.)

1. **Negligence or warranty liability:** The lessor may also be liable for negligence in failing to discover the defect, or on an implied warranty theory by analogy to the UCC. [400]

C. **Sellers of real estate:** Sellers of *real estate* have also sometimes been subjected to strict and warranty liability when the property turns out to be dangerously defective. But probably only a *professional builder*, not a consumer who resold the house, would be subject to such liability (unless the consumer actively concealed the facts of which he was aware). [400]

D. **Services:** One who sells *services*, rather than goods, generally does *not* fall within standard strict liability nor within the UCC implied warranties. [395-396]

1. **Product incorporated in service:** However, if a product is furnished *in combination with a service*, then most courts (and the Restatements) *will* apply strict liability if the product turns out to be defective. [402]

> **Example:** P goes to D's beauty parlor to get a permanent. D uses a solution made by a cosmetics company, which badly burns P's scalp. A court will probably hold D strictly liable for the defective solution, even though the product is being furnished in combination with services.

2. **Services by professionals:** But where the services are rendered by a *health professional,* she will almost never be liable in either strict tort or warranty, even if she uses a product which is defective. [402]

> **Example:** D is a surgeon, who puts a defective pacemaker into P's heart. D will almost certainly not be held strictly liable for the product defect.

VIII. INTERESTS THAT MAY BE PROTECTED

A. **Property damage:** All the above analysis assumes that P's injury consists of *personal* injury. If P's damages consist only of *property damage*, special rules may apply [403-404]:

1. **Strict liability and negligence:** P may generally recover in *strict liability* and *negligence* even though his damage consists only of property damage rather than personal injury. [403]

   a. **Warranties:** But he might not win on a *warranty* theory. If P is suing a *remote defendant* (one with whom he did not contract), two of the three alternative versions of UCC §2-318 do *not* allow P to recover for property damage unaccompanied by personal injury.

2. **"Property damage" defined:** Since the rules for recovering for property damage are easier for the plaintiff to satisfy than those for recovering "pure economic" damages, the two must be distinguished.

   a. **Property apart from the defective product:** If P's property apart from the defective product is destroyed (e.g., the product causes a fire that burns down P's house), this obviously *counts* as property damage, and is recoverable in strict liability. [403]

   b. **Damage to the product itself:** But where the defect causes the *product itself* to be destroyed or visibly harmed (e.g., an automobile catches on fire due to a defective radiator), this is probably *not* property damage, and thus *not recoverable* in strict liability. Instead, it's intangible economic loss, which as described below usually isn't recoverable in strict liability. [404-404]

   c. **Loss of bargain:** Similarly, if P's damages stem from the fact that the product simply *doesn't work* because of the defect, or is *worth less* with the defect than without it, most courts treat this as unrecoverable intangible economic harm (discussed below).

B. **Intangible economic harm:** Where P's damages are found to be solely *intangible economic* ones (as opposed to personal injury or property damage), P will find it much harder to recover. [404-406]

1. **Direct purchaser:** If P is suing the person who sold the goods to him:

   a. **Warranty:** P can readily recover for breach of *implied or express warranty*. P can recover the difference between what the product would have been worth had it been as warranted, and what it is in fact worth with its defect. He can also generally recover consequential damages, including lost profits.

   b. **Strict liability and negligence:** P probably won't be able to recover for the intangible economic harm in *strict liability* or *negligence* — the court will probably hold that the

UCC warranty claims were intended as the ***sole remedy*** for intangible economic harm by a purchaser against his immediate seller.

2. **Remote purchaser and non-purchaser:** Where P is suing not his own seller, but a ***remote person*** (e.g., the manufacturer), he will probably ***not*** recover anything if his only harm is an intangible economic one. [405-406]

   a. **Warranty:** Most courts would deny an implied ***warranty*** claim, on the grounds that P must sue his own immediate seller for such breaches.

   b. **Strict liability:** Almost all courts would deny recovery to the remote buyer for economic harm on a ***strict liability*** theory.

   c. **Negligence:** Most courts deny P recovery in ***negligence*** for pure intangible economic harm.

   d. **Non-purchaser:** The same is true where P is ***not a purchaser at all*** (e.g., P is a ***bystander***) — P probably can't recover on any theory for his intangible economic loss.

   > **Example:** P owns a restaurant, located next door to an office building that is owned by X Corp. and occupied exclusively by X Corp's employees. D manufactures a faulty boiler, which it sells to X Corp. The boiler explodes, damaging X Corp's building extensively. The building damage causes X Corp. to suspend operations for one month while repairs are made. During that month, P's restaurant loses 50% of its revenues, and all its profits, due to the absence of X Corp. employees as customers.
   >
   > Even though the defective boiler has caused property damage to X Corp. (for which X will be able to recover on a strict liability theory), *P* will not be permitted to recover in strict liability (or, for that matter, in negligence or warranty) because she has suffered only intangible economic harm. [406]

   e. **Combined:** But remember that if P can show that he has received either physical injury or "property damage," he may then be able to ***"tack on"*** his intangible economic harm as an ***additional*** element of damages. This would certainly be the case in a negligence action, and might possibly be true in a strict liability or warranty action.

IX. DEFENSES BASED ON PLAINTIFF'S CONDUCT

A. **General rule of plaintiff's negligence applies:** Early product liability decisions hesitated to make P's contributory or comparative negligence a defense. But under the modern approach, this has changed: usually, ***whatever*** the jurisdiction's standard method of dealing with plaintiff's negligence is (typically comparative negligence of one sort or another), ***that method applies to product-liability actions***. [407]

   > **Example:** In a typical comparative-negligence jurisdiction, P's comparative negligence in using a defective product will reduce, but not eliminate, D's liability in a strict product liability action.

B. **Different types of negligence by P:** There are a number of different ways in which a plaintiff might behave negligently with respect to a product.

   1. **Failure to discover the risk:** First, P might ***"negligently" fail to discover that there is a defect at all.*** Here, the modern approach essentially agrees with that of the earlier approach: if P's only fault is to fail to discover the defect, this is probably ***not really "negligence" at all***,

C
A
P
S
U
L
E

S
U
M
M
A
R
Y

since a person is normally entitled to assume that a product is not defective. Therefore, in the ordinary case P's failure to discover the defect will not cause any reduction in her recovery. [407]

2. **Knowing assumption of risk:** Second, P might be fully aware of a product's defectiveness (whether of a manufacturing or design nature), yet voluntarily and unreasonably decide to **"assume the risk"** of that defect. In this situation, the modern trend is to **treat assumption-of-risk as a form of comparative negligence**: to the extent that P's decision to use the product in the face of the known risk was **unreasonable**, it will cause plaintiff's recovery to be reduced proportionately (and will **not** serve as an **absolute bar** to recovery). [408]

   Example: P is driving a new car manufactured by D. A warning light suddenly flashes, saying "Overheated engine. Stop immediately." P knows that an overheated engine can often lead to an explosion, with consequent physical danger. P then looks under the hood, and sees that a water hose has ruptured, causing the engine to receive too little water. (Assume that this rupture constitutes a manufacturing defect for which D will be liable under standard strict-liability doctrine.) Nonetheless, P continues to drive for 100 more miles in 90 degree temperatures, even though he is merely taking a pleasure drive. The engine explodes, injuring P.

   Under the Third Restatement and modern approach, P's conduct — though it consists of a voluntary encountering of a known risk — will be treated the same as any other type of plaintiff's negligence. In a pure comparative negligence jurisdiction, therefore, P's recovery will be reduced by an amount representing P's portion of the combined "responsibility" of P and D, but P will still be allowed to make some recovery.

3. **Ignoring of safety precaution:** Suppose P **consciously fails to use an available safety device**, and is then injured by a product defect that would not have led to injury had the safety device been used. In some situations, the safety device is one provided by the manufacturer of the defective product; in other cases, it is provided by a third party. The analysis is pretty much the same in both types of situations — in most courts the plaintiff's failure to use an available safety device is generally fault that **reduces** (but does **not eliminate**) plaintiff's recovery. [409]

   Example: P, a consumer, purchases a Slicer-Dicer made by D. The Slicer-Dicer is designed to slice, dice, chop, and puree a variety of household products. The Slicer Dicer comes with a hand guard, which when installed prevents the user's hand from getting near the cutting blades. The hand guard is purposely designed to be removable for easy cleaning; the device and its instruction manual both contain a bold-faced warning that the device should not be operated without the hand guard. P removes the hand guard because he finds it easier to use the machine without it; he realizes that there is a greater danger of cutting his hand, but decides to risk it. P's hand slips, and is severely cut by the blades. P sues D on the theory that D's permitting the guard to be removed for separate cleaning constituted a design defect.

   In a modern comparative-negligence jurisdiction the court will probably hold that P's use of the product without the guard should reduce, but not eliminate, his recovery.

4. **Use for unintended purpose:** If P totally **misuses** the product, D will not be relieved from liability unless the misuse was so **unforeseeable** or **unreasonable** that either: (1) the misuse

couldn't reasonably be warned against or designed against, or (2) the misuse is found to be *"superseding."* [410-412]

> **Example:** D makes a chair with bars across the back. The chair is designed for seating, not climbing. P takes the chair and uses the bars across the back as a step-ladder; he then falls and hurts himself badly. A court would probably hold that the misuse here is so unforeseeable and unreasonable that the risks the design presents (the risk of unsafe climbing) need not be designed against or warned against. [410]

X. DEFENSES BASED ON FEDERAL REGULATION, MAINLY THE DEFENSE OF PREEMPTION

C
A
P
S
U
L
E

S
U
M
M
A
R
Y

A. Preemption: Federal regulation of product safety can have an important impact on consumers' state product-liability rights. In particular, under the doctrine of *"preemption,"* federal regulatory action may *limit the states' freedom to apply their usual rules of tort liability* to cases involving the regulated product. [412]

1. **The Supremacy Clause:** The concept of preemption is based on the *Supremacy Clause* of the U.S. Constitution. That clause says, in essence, that federal law *takes priority over conflicting state law*.

2. **Preemption, generally:** Here is a brief summary of how preemption works in the context of product-liability law:

   a. **Express preemption:** First — and usually easiest to apply — is *"express"* preemption. This occurs when Congress explicitly says that it intends to take away the states' ability to regulate in a particular way. When it is clear that Congress has meant to do this, the Supremacy Clause nullifies any attempt by a state to do what Congress has said the state may not do. [413]

      i. **Express preemption in medical-device cases:** Express preemption is likely to be found, for instance, where the Food and Drug Administration *pre-approves* a newly-developed *medical device* such as a pacemaker or heart valve. Once this happens, a user of the device will generally not be permitted to recover under state tort law for the device's defectiveness. That's because the court will likely conclude that the federal approval expressly preempts a state from awarding tort damages premised on the device's defectiveness. [*Riegel v. Medtronic Inc.*] [413]

   b. **Implied preemption:** Most real-life controversies involving preemption in tort law, however, involve *"implied"* rather than express preemption. That is, Congress (or a federal agency acting under direction from Congress) does not explicitly tell the states that they may not take a particular tort-related action. Instead, Congress or the federal agency enacts a statute or regulation, and a litigant (usually the manufacturer of the product) argues that the federal enactment should be interpreted as displacing a particular state tort-law rule. There are two different ways in which implied preemption can occur in a tort-law context, a *direct conflict* and a federal decision to *occupy* an *entire field*.

      i. **Direct conflict:** Sometimes analysis of the federal law and the state law shows that the two are in *direct conflict*. When this happens, as you'd expect, the state law must yield. The direct conflict can be of two sorts:

(1) It is *impossible* for the maker of a product to *comply simultaneously* with the federal regulation and the state regulation; or

(2) the *objectives* behind the federal regulation and the state regulation are *inconsistent*. [413]

Example of (1) (compliance with both is impossible): Suppose that Congress says that every package of cigarettes must contain a label stating, "the Surgeon General has determined that smoking may be hazardous to your health." Suppose then that North Carolina, a tobacco-growing state, passes a statute saying "No health warnings are required in this state on any package of cigarettes." Obviously there is a direct contradiction between the federal and state regulatory schemes — a given cigarette package cannot comply with both. Therefore, the state regulation is invalid.

Example of (2) (conflicting objectives): Suppose that Congress says, "it is the desire of Congress that auto manufacturers be encouraged to install airbags in every automobile produced after the date of this act." To further that objective, Congress gives auto manufacturers a $200 tax credit for every car that is made with an airbag. Texas then passes a statute saying, "in any tort litigation in which the occupant of a vehicle alleges that he or she has been injured by the inappropriate inflation of an airbag, the burden of proving the non-defectiveness of the airbag shall be placed upon the manufacturer." A court might well hold that in view of the strong federal interest in encouraging airbag installation, the Texas statute has a sharply conflicting objective — making airbag installation more burdensome to manufacturers — and that the Texas statute should therefore be deemed impliedly preempted by the federal legislation.

ii. **Occupation of entire field:** The second form of implied preemption occurs where the federal government is found to have *intended to occupy an entire field of regulation*. If such an intent is found, then even a state law that does *not directly conflict* with the federal law will be preempted. [414]

(1) Need for uniformity: When a court is deciding whether Congress intended to occupy the entire field, the court will give special weight to indications that Congress perceived a need for a *uniform national rule*, rather than varying state rules. So, for instance, in the medical-device-labelling field, the need for manufacturers to have a *single nationwide system of labels* (not state-by-state variations) would be an important factor pointing a court towards the conclusion that Congress intended to occupy the entire field.

c. **Implied preemption of state common-law tort remedies:** Sometimes a manufacturer succeeds with the argument that federal regulation preempts the states from allowing a plaintiff to recover for a *common-law tort*. Here, the defendant manufacturer is typically making the argument that merely *allowing a plaintiff to recover in tort* would itself constitute an *implicit* sort of "regulation" that is inconsistent with the federal regulatory scheme. So these are cases of "implied" (rather than "express") preemption of state law by federal law. [414]

i. **Needs direct conflict or impeding of federal enforcement:** It is *not easy* for a manufacturer to defeat a common-law tort claim by use of an implied preemption defense.

As a good rule of thumb, the manufacturer (D) will win with such a defense *only* if it can show that *either:*

[1] the conduct that P argues D was required to take under state common-law rules *conflicts* with the federal regulation; or

[2] allowing the tort recovery sought by P *would impede enforcement* of the federal regulatory scheme.

Manufacturers will often have a tough time making either of these showings.

ii. **Implied preemption in prescription-drug cases:** Cases involving *prescription drugs* will often be found to involve only *"implied"* preemption. Although Congress has given the FDA authority to regulate prescription drugs just as it allowed the agency to regulate medical devices like the one in *Riegel* (*supra*, p. C-92), Congress has *not expressly dealt with preemption* in the prescription-drug context. Therefore, prescription-drug cases are harder for the defendant manufacturer to win on a preemption theory than are medical-device cases, because an implied-preemption defense tends to be harder to establish than an express-preemption one. [*Wyeth v. Levine*] [416]

B. **Compliance with government standards:** Don't confuse the defense of federal preemption of state law with a separate defense, the so-called *"regulatory compliance"* defense. The latter defense asserts that because a product complies with a particular government regulation scheme, that compliance automatically means that the product is not defective. Most jurisdictions do *not* accept this defense — the plaintiff is free to show that even though the product meets the relevant federal regulatory requirements, the product is nonetheless defective. (However, nearly all states at least allow the fact that the product meets federal regulatory requirements to be admitted as non-dispositive *evidence* of non-defectiveness.) The regulatory compliance defense is discussed *supra*, p. C-83.

CHAPTER 15
NUISANCE

I. NUISANCE GENERALLY

A. **Type of injury:** The term "nuisance" refers not to a type of tort, but to a *type of injury* which P has sustained. In the case of "public nuisance," the injury is the loss of any right that P has by virtue of being a "member of the public." In the case of "private nuisance," P's injury is interference with his *use or enjoyment of his land.* [429]

1. **Three mental states:** A suit for nuisance may be supported by any of the three defendant mental states: (1) intentional interference with P's rights; (2) negligence; or (3) abnormally dangerous activity or other conduct giving rise to strict liability. [429]

II. PUBLIC NUISANCE

A. Definition: A *"public nuisance"* is an interference with a *"right common to the general public."* [429-431]

    1. Examples: We talk more below about what is a right "common to the general public." Generally, activities that interfere with *public waterways, air purity,* or *public roads and facilities,* are the most likely to be found to satisfy this standard.

    2. Factors: Courts look at a number of factors in deciding whether something is a public nuisance, including the *type of neighborhood,* the frequency/duration, the degree of damage, and the social value of the activity. [430]

        a. Substantial harm required: A public nuisance will not be found to exist unless the harm to the public is *substantial.*

    3. Need not be a crime: It is no longer the case that for conduct to be actionable as a public nuisance, it must also be a *crime* (though the fact the conduct *is* a crime will make it more likely to be held to be a public nuisance). [430]

B. "Right common to general public": The key element of a claim of public nuisance is that the right that is being unreasonably interfered with must be a "right that is *common to the general public.*" [430]

    1. Has impact: This requirement of a right common to the general public has considerable *impact,* in that it prevents many widespread harms from being eligible to be considered public nuisances. As the Second Restatement puts it, to be a right common to all members of the general public the right must be "*collective in nature* and *not* like the *individual* right that everyone has not to be assaulted or defamed or defrauded or negligently injured." [430]

        a. What qualifies: As the idea is sometimes put, the term "public right" is limited to those *"indivisible resources shared by the public at large,* such as *air, water, or public rights of way.*" [430]

            i. Interference with just some people: Even if the interference *is* with a shared resource like air or water, the interference won't qualify if by its nature it affects *only a few isolated landowners, not the public at large.* Thus the Restatement says, "the pollution of a stream that merely deprives 50 or 100 lower riparian owners of the use of the water for purposes connected with their land does not for that reason alone become a public nuisance. If, however, the pollution prevents the use of a public bathing beach or kills the fish in a navigable stream and so deprives *all members of the community* of the right to fish, it becomes a public nuisance." [430]

            ii. Interference that takes place within individual private properties: The "common right" requirement means that typically, a claim that a product has had a particular effect on a piece of *privately-owned real estate not accessible to the public* at large will *fail* the common-right test.

            Examples: Thus claims that manufacturers have infiltrated *guns* into neighborhoods, or that manufacturers of *paints* have failed to remove lead from them and thus injured children living in buildings painted with these paints, have tended to fail the "common right" standard. [430]

C. Requirement of particular damage: Courts sometime say that a private citizen may recover for his own damages stemming from a public nuisance, but only if he has sustained damage that is different in *kind*, not just degree, from that suffered by the public generally. However, it's not clear how much impact this so-called requirement has anymore; many newer decisions seem to ignore it.

> **Example:** P is a tenant of a small novelty store on the boardwalk opposite a famous beach; the boardwalk contains hundreds of merchants. D, an oil exploration company, negligently causes an offshore oil spill that fouls the beach for the entire summer, causing P's profits to drop 50% or $20,000, and doing approximately the same to hundreds of the other merchants. It's likely that P can recover from D in public nuisance for his lost profits, notwithstanding that hundreds of other merchants have suffered the same sort of harm to their collective right to an unfouled beach. [431]

D. Within "control" of defendant at time of harm: For public nuisance, courts require that the defendant have had *control over the instrumentality* at the *time of damage* — it's *not* enough that defendant had control at some *earlier* point (e.g., at the time of a sale of a product).

> **Example:** In a case by a state against makers of lead-paint that poisoned children in aprtment buildings, the Ds (the paint manufacturers) would likely escape liability if the state can't show that when the child plaintiffs were ingesting the lead, the Ds still had the right to abate the nuisance by removing the paint. The fact that the Ds had been in control of the contents of the paint at the time of the much earlier sales to the building owners would be irrelevant — the "control at the time of the harm" requirement is what counts, and is what's not satisfied here. [431]

III. PRIVATE NUISANCE

A. Nature of private nuisance: A *private nuisance* is an *unreasonable interference* with P's *use and enjoyment* of his *land*. [431]

1. **Must have interest in land:** P can sue based on a private nuisance only if he has an *interest in land* that has been affected. [432]

   > **Example:** A fisherman whose boat is injured by an oil spill that occurs when he is out at sea cannot sue for private nuisance, because no interest in land held by him is affected.

   a. **Tenants and family members:** But a fee simple is not necessary — a *tenant*, or members of the *family* of the owner or tenant, may sue.

2. **Elements:** P must demonstrate *two* elements in order to recover: (1) that his *use and enjoyment of his land* was interfered with in a *substantial way*; and (2) that D's conduct was either *negligent, abnormally dangerous*, or *intentional*. [432]

B. Interference with use: The interference with P's use and enjoyment must be *substantial*. If P's damage is merely a small *inconvenience* (e.g., somewhat extra noise, mildly unpleasant smells), there will be no recovery. [432]

C. Defendant's conduct: There is *no general rule of "strict liability" in nuisance*. P must show that D's conduct fell within one of the three classes for tortious defendant conduct: *negligence, intent*, or *abnormal dangerousness*. [433-433]

[left margin vertical text: CAPSULE SUMMARY]

Example: D, a utility, suddenly spews polluted smoke onto the land of P, a nearby owner. Unless P can show that D was careless in allowing the pollutants, intended to pollute, or was carrying out an abnormally dangerous activity, P cannot recover for private nuisance.

1. **Intentional:** In nuisance cases, D's conduct will be deemed "intentional" even though D did not *desire* to interfere with P's use and enjoyment of her land, as long as D *knew with substantial certainty* that such interference would occur. [433]

   Example: In the above example, if P put D on notice that pollution was occurring, and D continued with the conduct, the continuing conduct would be deemed intentional, and D could be liable for nuisance.

2. **Unreasonableness:** D's interference with P's interest must be *"unreasonable."* [433]

   a. **Test for unreasonableness:** The interference will be deemed unreasonable if *either*: (1) the harm to P outweighs the utility of D's conduct; *or* (2) the harm caused to P is greater than P should be required to bear without compensation.

   Example: On the above pollution example, even though operation of a utility is socially beneficial, and even if the social benefits outweigh the damage to P from the pollutants, D probably will have to pay for the polluting because it is not fair that P should have to bear the burden of this pollution without compensation.

3. **Nature of neighborhood:** One important factor in determining whether D's conduct is "unreasonable" is the kind of *neighborhood* in which D and P are located — the more commercial or industrial the neighborhood, the less likely given conduct is to be a nuisance. [434]

D. **Remedies:** P may be entitled to one or both of the following *remedies* for private nuisance:

1. **Damages:** If the harm has already occurred, P can recover *compensatory damages*. [435]

2. **Injunction:** If P can show that damages would not be a sufficient remedy, she may be entitled to an *injunction* against continuation of the nuisance. (But to get the injunction, P probably has to show that the harm to her and to all others similarly situated *outweighs* the utility of D's conduct.) [436]

E. **Defenses:** P's conduct may give rise to the defenses of contributory negligence and/or assumption of risk. [436]

1. **Contributory negligence:** Where the claim is based on D's *negligent* maintenance of the nuisance, contributory negligence will normally be a defense. [436]

2. **Assumption of risk:** The defense of *assumption of risk* is generally applicable to nuisance cases. [436]

   a. **"Coming to the nuisance":** Most commonly, the defense arises where D claims that P *"came to the nuisance,"* i.e., P purchases property with *advance knowledge* that the nuisance exists. Today, "coming to the nuisance" is not an absolute defense, but merely *one factor to be considered* in determining whether P should win. [437]

   Example: P, a developer, buys a parcel next to D's cattle feed lot, and sells off some of the parcels as homesites. D will be enjoined from operating the feed lot — the manure from which creates flies and odor — even though P came to the nuisance, because the rights of innocent parties, including the homeowners, are at stake. [*Spur Industries, Inc. v. Dell E. Webb Development Co.*]

CHAPTER 16

MISREPRESENTATION

I. INTENTIONAL MISREPRESENTATION ("DECEIT")

A. Definition: The common law action of *"deceit"* or "fraud" corresponds to what we today call *"intentional misrepresentation."* [442]

    1. Elements: To recover for intentional misrepresentation, P must establish the following elements [442]:

        a. A *misrepresentation* by D;

        b. *Scienter* (i.e., a culpable state of mind — either knowledge of the statement's falsity or reckless indifference to the truth);

        c. An *intent to induce the plaintiff's reliance* on the misrepresentation;

        d. *Justifiable reliance* by P; and

        e. *Damage* to P, stemming from the reliance.

B. Misrepresentation: D must make a *misrepresentation* to P. Normally, this will be in *words*. [442-445]

    1. Actions: But D's *actions* may also constitute a misrepresentation. [442] (*Example:* A used car dealer turns back the odometer on a car.)

    2. Concealment: If D intentionally *conceals* a fact from P, he will be treated the same way as if he had affirmatively misstated that fact. [442-442]

    3. Non-disclosure: If D simply *fails to disclose* a material fact (as opposed to taking positive steps to conceal it), it is harder for P to establish the requisite misrepresentation [443-444]:

        a. Common law: At common law, failure to disclose was almost never a misrepresentation.

        b. Modern view: In modern courts, the general rule remains that failure to disclose by itself does *not* constitute misrepresentation. [443]

            i. Exceptions: But modern cases recognize some *exceptions*, including:

                [1] matters that must be disclosed because of a *fiduciary relationship* between the two parties (e.g., lawyer/client);

                [2] matters that must be disclosed in order to prevent a *partial* statement of the facts from being *misleading*;

                [3] *newly acquired* information, which, if not disclosed, would make a previous statement misleading; and

                [4] facts *basic to the transaction*, if the party with knowledge knows of the other's reliance and knows that the other would reasonably expect a disclosure of those facts.

                Example: A homeowner who fails to disclose to the buyer the presence of *termites* will today often be found to have made a misrepresentation — this is a fact

CAPSULE SUMMARY

basic to the transaction that, as the seller should know, a buyer would normally expect to be told about. This represents a change from the common-law rule.

C. Scienter: P must show that D had that culpable state of mind called ***"scienter."*** D acts with scienter if he either: (1) knew or believed that he was not telling the truth; (2) did not have the confidence in the accuracy of his statement that he stated or implied that he did; or (3) knew that he did not have the grounds for a statement that he stated or implied that he did. [444-445]

   1. **Negligence not enough:** Scienter does not exist where D was merely ***negligent*** in making the misrepresentation. (In this instance, a claim for negligent misrepresentation, discussed below, must be brought.)

D. Third-party recovery: Where the fraudulent misrepresentation was not made to P, but to some third person, the rules have changed [445-446]:

   1. **Common law rule:** At common law, D was liable only to those persons whom he ***intended*** to influence by his misrepresentation, and not to others, even though their reliance may have been foreseeable. [445]

      Example: The Ds, directors of a company, prepare an intentionally false prospectus, intending to influence people who buy stock at the initial public offering. P later buys "used" stock from an existing stockholder, and relies on the misrepresentation. At common law, P may not recover against D, because D did not intend to influence P, even though P's reliance was quite foreseeable. [*Peek v. Gurney*])

   2. **Modern rule:** But modern cases make it easier for P to recover. Even if D did not intend to influence P, P can recover if she can show that: (1) she is a member of a class which D had ***reason to expect*** would be induced to rely; and (2) the transaction is of the ***same sort*** that D had reason to expect would occur in reliance. [446-447]

      Example: D falsely claims to have good title in an auto, and sells the car to X, who D knows is wholesaler. X resells to P, repeating the misrepresentation. Under modern law, P could recover against D, because P is a member of a class — ultimate buyers — whom D had reason to expect might rely on the misrepresentation, and the transaction is of the same sort — sale of the car — as D had reason to expect would occur in reliance. [*Varwig v. Anderson-Behel Porsche/Audi*]

E. Justifiable reliance: P must also show that he in fact ***relied*** on the misrepresentation, and that his reliance was ***justifiable***. [446-448]

   1. **Investigation by P:** If, after receiving D's misrepresentation, P makes his ***own investigation***, and ***relies totally*** or almost totally upon this investigation, P will be held not to have met the reliance requirement. (But if the misrepresentation is a ***substantial factor*** in inducing the reliance, P can recover even though his own investigation was also a substantial factor.) [446]

   2. **Justifiability:** P must show that his reliance was ***justifiable***. [447]

      a. **No general duty to investigate:** P has no ***duty to investigate*** on his own, even where an investigation could be easily done, and would disclose the falsity of D's statements. (But P may not overlook the ***"obvious"*** — if he does, his reliance is unjustifiable.)

   3. **Materiality:** P must show that the fact that he relied on was ***material*** to the underlying transaction. [447]

F. Opinion: It is hard for P to recover for a statement that is fairly characterizable as an *"opinion."* [448-450]

1. **Adverse party:** It is especially hard for P to recover where D was an *"adverse party"* to P at the time of the misstatements. But even here, P may be justified in relying on D's expression of opinion in one of these special situations:

   a. **Special knowledge:**   D "purports to have *special knowledge* of the matter" that the plaintiff does not have and D then actively *conceals material information.* [448]

   Example: The Ps, experienced restaurant operators, negotiate with D, a company that owns a vacant building that the Ps propose to lease for use as a restaurant. During the negotiations, D's representative, Powell, tells the Ps, "The building is in perfect condition. ... There [has] been nothing wrong with the place at all." After the Ps sign the lease and begin remodeling the property, they learn from multiple sources that there was previously a hamburger restaurant there, whose operations were harmed by the building's "very very bad odor." The Ps sue D to recover damages for fraud. D defends on several grounds, one of which is that Powell's statements were statements of opinion.

   Held, for the Ps: Powell's statements about the building's suitability for the Ps' planned restaurant give rise to a fraud claim. This is true even if, as D argues, Powell's statements are properly considered "pure expressions of opinion." Powell and D had a *one-sided knowledge of past facts.* Where a lessor has *"superior personal knowledge,"* a prospective tenant is entitled to rely on the fact that the lessor *"will not actively conceal material information."* [*Italian Cowboy Partners, Ltd. v. Prudential Ins. Co. of Am.*] [449]

   b. **Fiduciary relationship:** The defendant "stands in a *fiduciary* or other similar relation of trust and confidence" to the plaintiff. [449]

   c. **Confidence:** The defendant "has successfully endeavored to secure the *confidence*" of the plaintiff. [449]

   d. **Other:** There is some other "special reason" to expect that the plaintiff will rely on the defendant's opinion. [449]

      i. **Defendant knows of plaintiff's gullibility:** For instance, if the defendant knows that the plaintiff is particularly *gullible* or unintelligent, and therefore has reason to believe that the plaintiff will be misled by a false statement of opinion, this would be a "special reason" to expect the plaintiff to rely. [449]

   e. **"Puffing" still not actionable:** But *"puffing"* or *"trade talk"* is *not* actionable. (***Example:*** Car Dealer says to Consumer, "This is the best two-door car for the money." In fact, Car Dealer believes that the car is a terrible value. Consumer cannot recover for intentional misrepresentation, because Car Dealer's statement is obviously "puffing.") [449]

2. **Opinion of apparently disinterested person:** If the opinion is expressed not by one of the parties to a business deal, but by someone whom the plaintiff reasonably perceives as being *"disinterested,"* it is *easier* for P to recover. [449]

3. **Opinion implying fact:** The above rules apply only to statements of "pure" opinion. Where an opinion either *expresses* or *implies facts*, P can recover for misstatement of the underlying facts. [449]

   a. **Lack of knowledge of inconsistent facts:** Thus an opinion often contains the implied statement that its maker knows of no facts *incompatible* with that opinion. If P can show that D really knew facts incompatible with his opinion, P can recover. (***Example:*** Seller tells Buyer, "In my opinion, this house is structurally sound." Seller really knows that the foundation is badly cracked. Buyer can probably recover.)

G. Statements about law: Today, statements involving ***legal principles*** are generally treated the same as any other statement. Thus if D's representation of law includes an implied statement about ***factual*** matters, P may rely upon the factual part of the statement. [450]

> **Example:** T is about to become a tenant in a New York City building owned by L. As L knows, T proposes to operate in the building a business that converts restaurant garbage into fertilizer. The lease contains a representation by L that for zoning purposes, the proposed use will be allowed. P signs the lease, moves in, and starts to convert garbage. However, it turns out that the building's zoning prevents T from doing garbage conversion unless T makes expensive modifications. T sues L for fraud. L defends on the grounds that only a misrepresentation of law rather than of fact is involved, and that misrepresentations about whether the law allows a particular use are always statements of pure opinion, for which state law does not allow recovery in fraud.
>
> *Held*, for T. The false statement about the building's zoning status was not a pure expression of opinion about the law, but rather a mixed statement of fact and law: when L said that it knew the premises were in an unrestricted district, T properly understood this to mean that L knew, as a fact, that the zoning code allowed the proposed use. Therefore, the false statement was a statement of fact about the building's zoning, not an "opinion of law." [*National Conversion Corp. v. Cedar Bldg. Corp.*] [451]

H. Prediction and intention

1. Prediction: If the defendant ***predicts*** that something will happen, this will generally be treated as an opinion, which means that in most instances it cannot be relied on. [451]

2. Intention: But where D makes a statement as to her own ***intentions***, this is generally treated as a factual representation that can be relied on. [451]

I. Damages: If the misrepresentation was made directly by D to P, most courts give P the ***"benefit of the bargain"*** measure of damages. [452-453]

II. NEGLIGENT MISREPRESENTATION

A. General: At common law, there was no action for "negligent misrepresentation." Unless P suffered personal injury or direct property damage (thus enabling her to bring a conventional negligence action), P was out of luck. But today, most courts ***do*** allow recovery for negligent misrepresentation, even where only ***intangible economic harm*** is suffered. [454]

1. Same requirements: Most requirements for a negligent misrepresentation action are the same as for an intentional misrepresentation action. [454]

B. Business relationship: Courts are quickest to allow recovery for negligent misrepresentation where D's statements are made in the course of his ***business or profession***, and D had a ***pecuniary interest*** in the transaction. (Thus if D is P's friend, and makes a representation that is not in the course of D's business, P cannot recover.) [454]

C. Liability to third persons: The maker of a negligent misrepresentation is liable to a much ***narrower class*** of third persons than is the maker of a fraudulent misstatement. [455]

C
A
P
S
U
L
E

S
U
M
M
A
R
Y

1. **Persons intended to be reached:** According to the Restatement, D is liable for negligent misrepresentation to a *"limited group of persons"* whom D either: (1) *intends to reach* with the information; or (2) knows the *recipient intends to reach*. [455]

   Example: D runs a stock ticker service, which negligently reports that X Corp has declared higher earnings, when in fact its earnings are lower. P, an investor, learns of the "higher" earnings from a subscriber to D's service, and buys the stock, losing money. P probably cannot recover from D, since they were not in contractual privity, and since P was not a member of a "limited group of persons" whom D intended to reach or whom D knew that its subscriber intended to reach.

   a. **Persons covered:** Even though the class of third persons covered is narrow, it is still important. Examples where liability might attach include: (1) a surveyor knows or should know that his survey will be given to a prospective purchaser, and a purchaser relies on the survey in buying the property; (2) a lawyer drafts a will negligently cutting out a particular intended heir, and the heir sues the lawyer; (3) an accountant negligently certifies the books of X Corp, knowing that X Corp plans to seek a loan from Bank; Bank makes the loan, X Corp goes bankrupt, and Bank sues the accountant.

III. STRICT LIABILITY

A. **Not generally allowed:** Generally, a person has no liability for an *"innocent"* misrepresentation. In other words, as a general rule there is no strict liability for misrepresentations. But there are some exceptions, discussed below. [457]

B. **Sale, rental or exchange:** If two parties are involved in a *sale*, *rental* or *exchange* transaction, and one makes a material misrepresentation to the other in order to close the deal, he will be liable even if the misrepresentation is innocent. [457]

   1. **Warranty:** Usually, the buyer can get as much relief from a claim of *breach* of express warranty as from the tort claim of strict liability for misrepresentation. But P may avoid certain contract defenses by relying on the tort theory rather than the warranty theory (e.g., the parol evidence rule). [457]

   2. **Service transactions:** A few courts have applied strict liability where D sells P a *service*, and makes a misrepresentation. [457]

      Example: An agent for Insurance Co. tells P that the policy he is buying will cover him for liability from drunk driving, and through no fault of the agent, the policy does not in fact cover P for this. Some courts might allow P to recover from the agent.

   3. **Privity:** The sale, rental or exchange must have been *directly* between P and D. [457]

C. **Sale of chattel:** A seller of goods who makes any misrepresentation on the label, or in public advertising, will be strictly liable for any *physical injury* which results, even if the injured person did not buy the product directly from D. [457]

CHAPTER 17

DEFAMATION

I. GENERAL PRINCIPLES

A. **Meaning of "defamation":** The tort called *"defamation"* is actually two sub-torts, "libel" and "slander." These both protect a person's interest in his *reputation*. A state's freedom to define these torts as it wishes is sharply curtailed by the First Amendment. [465]

B. **Prima facie case:** To establish a prima facie case for either libel or slander, P must prove [465]:

1. **Defamatory statement:** A *false* and *defamatory* statement concerning him;

2. **Publication:** A *communicating* of that statement to a person other than the plaintiff (a *"publication"*);

3. **Fault:** *Fault* on the part of D, amounting to at least *negligence*, and in some instances a greater degree of fault;

4. **Special harm:** Either *"special harm"* of a pecuniary nature, or the actionability of the statement despite the non-existence of such special harm.

II. DEFAMATORY COMMUNICATION

A. **Injury to reputation:** To be defamatory, a statement must have a tendency to *harm the reputation* of the plaintiff. [466]

1. **Reputation not actually injured:** For the statement to be defamatory, it need not have *actually* harmed P's reputation. It must simply be the case that, *if the statement had been believed*, it would have injured P's reputation. [466] (But in most cases of slander, and in cases of libel where the defamatory meaning is not apparent from the face of the statement, P has to prove "special damage," i.e., that his reputation was in fact damaged and caused him pecuniary harm — this is not part of the definition of "defamatory," however.)

B. **Meaning attached:** Many statements can be *interpreted in more than one way*. Where this is the case, the statement is defamatory if *any one* of the interpretations which a reasonable person might make would tend to injure P's reputation, and P shows that at least one of the recipients did *in fact* make that interpretation. [466]

C. **Reference to plaintiff:** P must show that the statement was reasonably interpreted by at least one recipient as *referring to P*. [467-467]

1. **Intent irrelevant:** But P does not necessarily have to show that D *intended* to refer to him, rather than to someone else. As a common-law matter (putting aside constitutional decisions), even if D behaved non-negligently and intended to refer to someone else entirely, P can still sue. [467]

2. **Groups:** If D's statement concerns a *group*, and P is a member of that group, P can recover only if the group is a *relatively small one*. [467]

    Example: The statement, "All lawyers are shysters," would not be defamatory as to any particular lawyer, assuming there was no evidence indicating that the statement was intended to refer to P in particular.

3. **Reference need not be by name:** If a non-explicit reference to P is reasonably understood as in fact referring to P, it does not matter that P is referred to by a *different name* or characterization. This is true even if the publication is labelled a "novel." [467]

D. **Truth:** A statement is *not defamatory* if it is *true*. At common law, it is always the *defendant* who has had the burden of proving truth. [468-468]

1. **Matters of public interest:** Today, as the result of constitutional decisions, the *plaintiff* must bear the burden of proving falsity, if: (1) D is a media organization; and (2) the statement involves a matter of *"public interest"* (whether P is a public figure or a private figure). [468]

2. **Private figure, no public interest or non-media defendant:** It is probably the case that the states may still require the *defendant* to bear the burden of proving truth if: (1) the defendant is not a media organization; *or* (2) the plaintiff is a private figure and the statement is not of public interest. [468-469]

3. **Substantial truth:** For truth to be a barrier to recovery, it is not necessary that the statement be *literally* true in all respects. Instead, the statement must merely be *"substantially"* true. [468]

E. **Opinion** [469-471]

1. **Pure opinion:** A statement of *pure opinion* can never be defamatory. [469] (*Example:* "I think Smith is a disgusting person," without any factual basis for this statement either expressed or implied.)

2. **Implied facts:** But if a statement of opinion *implies undisclosed facts*, and a statement of those facts would be defamatory, then the statement will be itself treated as defamatory. [469]

> **Example:** "I think P must be an alcoholic" is probably actionable, because it implies that the speaker knows precise facts about P's alcohol consumption that would justify an opinion of alcoholism.

III. LIBEL vs. SLANDER

A. **Significance of distinction:** Distinguish between "libel" and "slander." It makes a difference only with respect to the requirement of *special harm*: to establish slander, P must show that he suffered pecuniary harm (unless the statement falls into one of four special categories). To prove libel, by contrast, P does not have to show such special harm (except, in some courts, if the defamatory nature of the statement is not evident on its face). [471]

B. **Libel:** Libel consists mainly of all *written or printed matter*. [471-472]

1. **Embodied in physical form:** Most states hold that it also includes any communication embodied in *"physical form."* [471] (*Examples:* A phonograph record, or a computer tape, would be libel in most courts.)

2. **Radio and TV:** Where a program is *broadcast* on radio or TV:

   a. **Written script:** If it originated with a *written script*, all courts treat it as libel.

   b. **No script:** If the program is "ad libbed" rather than coming from a written script, courts are split as to whether it is libel or slander.

C. Slander: All other statements are *slander*. An ordinary *oral statement*, for instance, is slander. [472]

D. Special harm: P may generally establish slander only if he can show that he has sustained some *"special harm."* This harm generally must be of a *pecuniary nature*. [472-473]

> **Example:** P shows only that his friends believed D's defamatory statements, and the friends now socially reject P. If the statement is slander, and does not fall within one of the four "slander per se" categories, P cannot recover.

1. "Slander per se": There are four kinds of utterances which, even though they are slander rather than libel, require *no showing* of special harm [472]:

    a. Crime: Statements imputing morally culpable *criminal behavior* to P.

    b. Loathsome disease: Statements alleging that P currently suffers from a *venereal* or other loathsome and communicable disease.

    c. Business, profession, trade or office: An allegation that adversely reflects on P's fitness to conduct her *business*, trade, profession or office. (*Example:* "P cheats his customers.")

    d. Sexual misconduct: Statement imputing serious *sexual misconduct* to P.

2. Libel: In the case of *libel*, at common law courts do not require proof of actual harm, and can award *"presumed"* damages even without a showing of harm. However, recent Supreme Court decisions cut back on the states' ability to do this [473-474]:

    a. Matters of public concern: If the statement involves a matter of *public concern* or a *public figure*, and recovery is allowed without proof of "actual malice," presumed damages may not constitutionally be awarded.

    b. Matter of private concern: But if the defamatory statement does *not* involve a matter of "public concern" or a public figure, presumed damages *may* be allowed, even without a showing of "actual malice."

> **Example:** D, a credit reporting agency, sends a subscriber a written report falsely stating that P, an ordinary private corporation, is insolvent. Since the statement is not of "public interest," P may recover $50,000 presumed damages without showing any financial loss, and without showing that D knew of the falsity or recklessly disregarded the truth. [*Dun & Bradstreet v. Greenmoss Builders*]

    c. Actual malice: If P does show "actual malice" (that D either knew of the falsity or recklessly disregarded the truth), presumed damages may probably be constitutionally awarded, even if P is a public figure and the matter is one of public interest.

IV. PUBLICATION

A. Requirement of publication generally: P must show that the defamation was *"published."* "Publication" means merely *"seen or heard by someone other than the plaintiff."* [474]

1. Must be intentional or negligent: D's publication must have been either *intentional* or *negligent*. Thus there is no "strict liability" as to the publication requirement. [474]

> **Example:** D makes a defamatory statement to P himself, while in P's office. D does not realize (and isn't negligent in not realizing) that X is standing outside the office listening

through a keyhole. X hears the statement. D has no liability for defamation, because he did not intentionally or negligently publish the statement (i.e., communicate it to one other than the plaintiff).

B. Repeater's liability: One who *repeats* a defamatory statement made by another is held to have published it, and is liable as if he were the first person to make the statement. [475] This is true even if he indicates the source, and indicates that he himself does not believe the statement.

> **Example:** D says, "X told me that P is a thief who steals from his customers, though I doubt it." Technically, D has published the defamatory statement, and can be liable.

V. INTENT

A. Common-law strict liability: At common law, libel and slander were essentially *strict liability* torts. P had to show that the *publication* occurred due to D's intent or negligence, but did not have to show intent or negligence as to any of the other aspects. For instance, it was irrelevant that D had every reason to believe that the statement was *true*. [476]

B. Constitutional decisions: But Supreme Court decisions on the First Amendment have eliminated courts' right to impose strict liability for defamation. The precise mental state which D must be shown to have met depends on whether P is a public figure [476-479]:

1. **Public figure:** If P is a *"public figure,"* he can recover only if he shows that D made the statement with either: (1) *knowledge that it was false*; or (2) *"reckless disregard"* of whether it was true or false. [*New York Times v. Sullivan*] (These two alternate states of mind are collectively called *"actual malice,"* which is a term of art.) [477-478]

   a. **Meaning of "reckless disregard":** For P to show that D "recklessly disregarded" the truth, is *not* enough to show that a "reasonably prudent person" would not have published, or would have done further investigation. Instead, P must show that D *in fact entertained serious doubts* about the truth of the statement. [477]

2. **Private figures:** But if P is *neither* a public official nor a public figure, he is *not constitutionally required* to prove that D knew his statement was false or recklessly disregarded whether it was true or false. [*Gertz v. Robert Welch, Inc.*] [477]

   a. **No strict liability:** However, the First Amendment prohibits a state from applying *strict liability*, even in the "private figure" situation, at least if the suit is against a *media defendant.* In other words, even in suits brought by private figure plaintiffs, if D is a media defendant P must prove that D was at least *negligent* in not ascertaining the statement's falsity.

      i. **Suits by one private person against another:** In suits by a private-figure plaintiff against a *private individual* or other *non-media* defendant, the Supreme Court has never said whether strict liability is constitutionally allowable. However, virtually all states — as a matter of *common law*, not federal constitutional law — refuse to allow private-figure plaintiffs to recover against even non-media defendants unless the plaintiff *shows at least negligence.* In other words, as a common-law matter, all defamation suits require *at least a showing that the defendant negligently failed to make reasonable efforts to ascertain the statement's truth or falsity.* (States are always free to require more than negligence regarding truth, such as recklessness or intent.) [478]

C
A
P
S
U
L
E

S
U
M
M
A
R
Y

Example: D fires P. P seeks a new job from X. X asks D for a reference. D writes back, "We fired P because P sexually harassed a co-worker." If D's belief that P harassed a co-worker was reasonable, under state common-law principles P cannot recover from D for libel, even if P can prove that the accusation was completely false.

VI. PRIVILEGES

A. **Absolute privileges:** An *"absolute"* privilege applies even if D was motivated solely by malice or other bad motives. The following classes of absolute privilege are usually recognized:

   1. **Judicial proceedings:** Judges, lawyers, parties and witnesses are all absolutely privileged in what they say during the course of *judicial proceedings*, regardless of the motives for their statements. [479] (*Example:* D, in a pleading in a civil lawsuit between him and P, calls P a crook. P cannot recover from D for defamation, even if P shows that D knew D's statement was a lie.)

   2. **Legislative proceedings:** *Legislators* acting in furtherance of their legislative functions are absolutely privileged. [479]

   3. **Government officials:** Many *government officials* have absolute immunity for statements issued in the course of their jobs. Thus all federal officials, and all high state officials, have this privilege. [480]

   4. **Husband and wife:** Any communication between a *husband and wife* is absolutely privileged. [480]

   5. **Consent:** Any publication that occurs with the *consent* of the plaintiff is absolutely privileged. [480]

B. **Qualified privilege:** Other privileges are merely *"qualified"* or "conditional" ones. A qualified privilege will be lost if D is acting primarily from *malice*, or from some other purpose not protected by the privilege. [480-484]

   1. **Protection of publisher's interests:** D is conditionally privileged to *protect his own interests*, if these are sufficiently important, and the defamation is directly enough related to those interests. [480-481]

      Example: If D reasonably believes that his property has been stolen by P, he may tell the police of his suspicions. If D's belief is reasonable, he is protected against a slander action by P, even if his suspicions are wrong.

   2. **Interest of others:** Similarly, D may be qualifiedly privileged to act for the protection of the *recipient* of his statement, or some other third person. The issue is whether D's statement is "within the generally accepted standards of *decent conduct*." [481]

      a. **Old boss to new boss:** Thus an ex-employer generally has the right to give information about his *ex-employee* to a new, prospective, employer if asked by the latter.

   3. **Public interest:** D may be conditionally privileged to act in the *public interest*. [481] (*Example:* A private citizen's reasonable but mistaken accusation made to the police that P committed a crime would be covered.)

   4. **Report of public proceedings:** There is a conditional privilege to report on *public proceedings*, such as court cases, legislative hearings, etc. [481-482]

Example: D, a newspaper, accurately reports that in a lawsuit, X has called P a crook and a liar. Even if X's statement is completely untrue and was made with malice, D has a qualified privilege to make the report of the public proceeding, and therefore may not be sued for libel.

    5. **Neutral reportage:** A few cases have recognized a *"neutral reportage"* privilege. Under this privilege, one who *correctly* and *neutrally* reports charges made by one person against another will be protected if the charges are a matter of *public interest,* even if the charges are false. [482-484]

        Example: D, a newspaper, runs a story saying, "Citizen said at a press conference that he saw Mayor Brown take a bribe from a developer." If Citizen really made these charges, D would be protected under the "neutral reportage" privilege even if D had serious doubts about the truth of the charges. This is so even though D's doubts would cause D's conduct to constitute "actual malice" under *New York Times v. Sullivan.*

C. **Abuse of qualified privilege:** Even where a qualified privilege exists, it may be *abused* (and therefore forfeited) in a number of ways. [484-485]

C
A
P
S
U
L
E

S
U
M
M
A
R
Y

    1. **Actual malice:** Most importantly, the privilege will be lost if D *knew that his statement was false*, or acted in *reckless disregard* of whether it was true. [484]

        Example: D, P's ex-employer, is asked for information by X, P's new prospective employer, concerning P's work. D's clerk negligently misreads the file, and asserts that P was fired for dishonesty, when in fact P quit voluntarily. If the clerk is shown to have behaved recklessly, D's qualified privilege — to protect the interest of a third person by commenting on an employee's fitness — will be deemed abused and thus forfeited. But if the clerk was only negligent, the privilege will probably not be lost.

    2. **Excessive publication:** The privilege is abused if the statement is made to persons to whom publication is *not reasonably necessary* to protect the interest in question, or if more damaging information is stated than is reasonably needed. [485]

D. **Statutory privileges:** Many states, and the federal government, have enacted a number of *statutory privileges.*

    1. **Internet Service Providers:** One of the most important of these is the federal immunity given to *Internet Service Providers* (ISPs) under the Communications Decency Act of 1996. Part of the CDA, 47 U.S.C. § 230(c)(1), says that *"no provider or user* of an interactive *computer service* shall be treated as the *publisher or speaker of any information* provided by *another information content provider."* This provision amounts to a grant of *immunity* from state defamation liability for "publishing false or defamatory material so long as the *information was provided by another party."* [*Carafano v. Metrosplash.com, Inc.*] [485]

        Example: D, a corporation, owns the matchmaker.com Internet dating service. Some unknown person posts a dating profile of P (a well-known actress) on the matchmaker.com site, without P's consent. The posting is done in the form of answers to a questionnaire that D requires posters to fill out; many of the questions are in multiple-choice format. The posting includes P's picture, her home address, her e-mail address and various sexually-oriented statements. People who send e-mail to the e-mail address are then given P's home phone number. As a result, P receives numerous phone calls, voice mail messages and e-mails, some of which are sexually explicit or threatening. She sues D in state court for defamation and invasion of privacy. D defends on the grounds that the CDA gives it immunity against all such claims by P. P responds that the CDA immunity does not apply where D supplies part of the defamatory content, and that that is what happened here, since most of the content was formulated in response to matchmaker.com's detailed questionnaire.

Held, for D. The immunity given by the CDA was intended by Congress to be *"quite robust."* It is true that the immunity does not apply where the defendant functioned as an "information content *provider*" for the portion of the statement or publication at issue. But here, the fact that some of the content was formulated in response to D's questionnaire does not mean that D was the provider of the content in question. And the fact that D's site structured and standardized the poster's answers (e.g., by supplying multiple-choice answers for dozens of questions) did not turn D into a supplier of the content in the profile. [*Carafano v. Metrosplash.com, Inc., supra*] [485]

VII. REMEDIES

A. **Damages:** A successful defamation plaintiff may recover various sorts of damages:

1. **Compensatory damages:** First, of course, P may recover *compensatory* damages. These can include [486]:

   a. **Pecuniary:** Items of *pecuniary loss* (e.g., P's lost earnings from being fired from her job, due to D's statement to P's boss that D was dishonest in the last job).

   b. **Humiliation, lost friendship:** Compensation for *humiliation*, lost friendship, illness, etc. (even though these items would not count as "special harm" for purposes of slander).

2. **Punitive damages:** Also, under some circumstances *punitive* damages may be awarded [486-487]:

   a. **Public figure or matter of public interest:** If P is a *public figure*, or the case involves a matter of *public interest*, punitive damages may be awarded only on a showing that D knew his statements were false or recklessly disregarded the truth. (That is, the "actual malice" requirement of *New York Times v. Sullivan* extends, as far as punitive damages go, not only to public figures but also to private figures suing on matters of public interest.) [*Gertz v. Robert Welch*]

   b. **Private figure/private matter:** But if P is a *private* figure and D's statement relates to a private matter, then punitive damages may be awarded even if P shows only that D was *negligent*. (*Example:* D, a credit reporting agency, falsely reports to a few subscribers that P, a corporation, is insolvent. Because P is a private figure and the report did not involve any matter of public concern, punitive damages can be awarded, as a constitutional matter. [*Dun & Bradstreet v. Greenmoss Builders,* 486])

3. **Nominal damages:** Even a plaintiff who has suffered no direct loss may recover *nominal* damages, to "clear his name." Certainly if P shows knowledge of falsehood or reckless disregard of the truth on the part of D, P may recover nominal damages. It is not clear whether or when a plaintiff who shows less than this may recover nominal damages. [487]

B. **Retraction:** Most states have enacted *"retraction"* statutes. Some of these statutes hold that if D publishes a retraction within a certain period, this bars P from recovery. Other statutes merely *require* news organizations to grant a right of response to P, without providing that this eliminates P's defamation action. [487]

CHAPTER 18

MISCELLANEOUS TORTS: INVASION OF PRIVACY; MISUSE OF LEGAL PROCEDURES; INTERFERENCE WITH ADVANTAGEOUS RELATIONS; FAMILIAL AND POLITICAL RELATIONS

I. INVASION OF PRIVACY

A. Four torts: The so-called *"invasion of privacy"* cause of action is essentially four distinct mini-torts. They all involve P's "right to be let alone." The four are:

[1] *misappropriation* of P's name or picture;

[2] *intrusion* on P's solitude;

[3] undue publicity given to P's *private life*; and

[4] the placing of P in a *false light*. [496]

B. Misappropriation of identity: P can sue if her *name or picture* has been *misappropriated* by D for his own financial benefit. [496]

> **Example:** D, a cereal maker, runs an ad containing a photo of P eating D's cereal. P does in fact eat D's cereal, but has never agreed to endorse it. P can recover for appropriation of his picture.

C. Intrusion: P may sue if his *solitude* is *intruded upon*, and this intrusion would be "highly offensive to a reasonable person." [497]

> **Example:** P and D are roommates at college; they share a suite, but each has his own small bedroom. D hides a web-cam in P's room, and uses it to stream video on the Internet of P having sex with X. P (as well as X) will have a claim against D for the intrusion-on-solitude branch of invasion of privacy: the use of hidden electronic equipment to monitor P's private space is an intrusion that would be "highly offensive to a reasonable person." [497]

1. Must be private place: This "intrusion upon solitude" branch is triggered only where a *private place* is invaded. Thus if D takes P's picture in a public place, this will normally not be enough. [497]

D. Publicity of private life: P may recover if D has *publicized* the details of P's *private life*. The effect must be "highly offensive to a reasonable person." [497-498] (*Example:* D, a sensationalist newspaper, prints the details of the extramarital sex life of P, who is wealthy but not a public figure. P can recover against D for publicity of private life.)

1. Not of legitimate public concern: As a constitutional matter, it is probably a requirement for the "publicity of private life" action that the material *not be of legitimate public concern*. [498]

C A P S U L E S U M M A R Y

     Example: If P is on trial for murder, it is not an invasion of his privacy for newspapers to give reports on even minor private details of his past life, such as his sexual history.

E. False light: P can sue if he is placed before the public eye in a *false light*, and this false light would be highly offensive to a reasonable person. [499]

     Example: P is war hero. D makes a movie about P's life, including fictitious materials such as a non-existent romance. D is liable for invasion of privacy, of the "false light" variety.

    1. Actual malice: But at least where P is a public figure, he can recover for "false light" only if he can show that D knew the portrayal was false, or acted in reckless disregard of whether it was. In other words, *New York Times v. Sullivan* applies to false light actions by public figures. [*Time, Inc. v. Hill*] Probably private figures do not have to meet this "actual malice" standard.

II. MISUSE OF LEGAL PROCEDURE

A. Three torts: Three related tort actions protect P's interest in not being subjected to *unwarranted judicial proceedings:* (1) *malicious prosecution;* (2) *wrongful institution of civil proceedings;* and (3) *abuse of process.* [499]

B. Malicious prosecution: To recover for *malicious prosecution*, P must prove the following: (1) that D instituted *criminal proceedings* against him; (2) that these proceedings terminated *in favor of P* (the accused); (3) that D had *no probable cause* to start the proceedings; and (4) that D was motivated primarily by some purpose other than bringing an offender to justice. [499-501]

    1. Initiating proceeding: P must show that D took an *active part* in instigating and encouraging the prosecution. [500] (***Example:*** If D merely states what she believes to be the facts to the prosecutor, and lets the prosecutor decide whether to prosecute, this is probably not "institution" of proceedings. But if D attempts to persuade the prosecutor to prosecute, this will be sufficient.)

    2. Favorable outcome: The criminal proceedings must *terminate in favor of the accused* (P). An acquittal will of course be enough; so will a prosecutor's decision not to prosecute (but a plea bargain to a lesser offense will not suffice). [500]

    3. Absence of probable cause: P must show that D *lacked probable cause* to institute the criminal proceedings. [500]

       a. Reasonable mistake: If D made a *reasonable mistake*, she does not lack probable cause.

       b. Effect of outcome: The fact that P was *acquitted* does not itself establish lack of probable cause. D still has the right to show, in the tort case, by a preponderance of evidence, that P was guilty and that D therefore had probable cause.

    4. Improper purpose: P must show that D acted out of *malice*, or for some other purpose than bringing an offender to justice. [501]

C. Wrongful civil proceedings: In most states, a tort action exists for wrongful institution of *civil* proceedings. The requirements are virtually identical to the "malicious prosecution" action, except that the original proceedings are civil rather than criminal. [501-502]

    1. Elements: Thus P must prove that: (1) D initiated civil proceedings against P; (2) D did not have probable cause to believe that his claim was justified; (3) the proceedings were started for an improper purpose (e.g., a "nuisance" suit or "strike suit," brought solely for the purpose of extorting a settlement); and (4) the civil proceedings were terminated in favor of the person against whom they were brought. [501]

D. Abuse of process: The tort of *"abuse of process"* occurs where a person involved in criminal or civil proceedings uses various *litigation devices* for improper purposes. [502] (*Example:* Even if a civil suit is properly brought by P, if P then uses his power of *subpoena* to harass D or make him settle, rather than for the proper purpose of obtaining his testimony, this is an abuse of process.)

III. INTERFERENCE WITH ADVANTAGEOUS RELATIONS

A. Three business torts: Three related torts protect business interests: (1) injurious falsehood; (2) interference with contract; and (3) interference with prospective advantage. [502]

B. Injurious falsehood: The action for *"injurious falsehood"* protects P against certain false statements made against his business, product, or property. Most important is so-called *"trade libel."* This occurs where a person makes false statements disparaging P's *goods or business*. [502]

1. **Elements:** P must prove the following elements for trade libel [502]:

    a. **False disparagement:** D made a *false statement disparaging* P's goods, business, etc. (*Example:* D falsely states that P is out of business);

    b. **Publication:** P must show that the statement was "published," as the word is used in defamation cases;

    c. **Scienter:** P must show *scienter* on D's part. That is, P must show that D knew her statement was false, acted in reckless disregard of whether it was false, or (in some courts) acted out of ill-will or spite for P.

    d. **Special damages:** P must prove *"special damages,"* i.e., that P suffered *"pecuniary"* harm.

2. **Defenses:** D can raise a number of *defenses*, including [503]:

    a. **Truth:** that the statement was *true*; and

    b. **Fair competition:** that D was *pursuing competition by fair means*. In particular, D is privileged to make *general comparisons* between her product and P's, stating or implying that her product is the better one. In other words, "puffing" is protected. But if D makes *specific* false allegations against P's product, D will not be protected.

C. Interference with existing contract: The tort of *"interference with contract"* protects P's interest in having others perform *existing contracts* which they have with him. The claim is against one who *induces* another to breach a contract with P. [504-506]

> **Example:** P, a theater owner, has contracted to have actor X perform in P's theater on a certain date. D, a competing theater owner, induces X to perform for him on that date instead. P can recover against D for interference with contract.

1. **Privileges:** D can defend on the grounds that his interference was *privileged*. [505]

    a. **Business competition:** D's desire to *obtain business* for herself, however, is *not* by itself enough to make her privileged to induce a breach of contract. (But in most courts, if

C A P S U L E S U M M A R Y

P's contract was *terminable at will*, D is privileged to induce a termination of it for the purpose of obtaining the business for herself.)

D. Interference with prospective advantage: If due to D's interference, P loses the benefits of *prospective, potential* contracts (as opposed to existing contracts), P can sue for *"interference with prospective advantage."* [506-508]

1. **Same rules:** Essentially the same rules apply here as for "interference with contract." The big difference is that D has a much greater scope of *privilege* to interfere. [506]

    a. **Competition:** Most importantly, D's desire to *obtain the business for herself* will be enough to give her a privilege, which is usually not the case where there is an existing contract.

    Example: P and D are competitors. D learns that P has been pursuing a certain prospect for nine months, and is about to sign a long-term supply contract with that customer. D can jump in, and offer a money-losing low price, even if this is for the sole purpose of weakening P.

IV. INTERFERENCE WITH FAMILY AND POLITICAL RELATIONS

A. Family: A family member's interest in having the *continued affections* of the other member of his family is sometimes protected. [508-510]

1. **Husband and wife:** In some states, a jilted *spouse* may bring either of two tort claims against an outsider who has interfered with the marital relation:

    a. **Alienation of affections:** Some states allow P to sue for *"alienation of affections"* against anyone who has caused P's spouse to lose his or her affection for P. (This is usually, but not always, a romantic rival — for instance, the action can be brought against a friend or relative who has convinced the spouse to leave P.) But D has a *privilege* to interfere to advance what D reasonably believes to be the alienated spouse's welfare. [508]

    b. **Criminal conversation:** A person who has *sexual intercourse* with one spouse may be liable to the other for *"criminal conversation."* [509]

2. **Parent's claim:** A *parent* will *not* usually have a tort claim against one who alienates his *child's affections*. But there are a couple of exceptions, where suit is allowed:

    a. **Minor leaves home:** The parent has a claim against the person who has caused his minor child to *leave home*, or not to return home. [509] (*Example:* A parent might sue the members of a cult, if the cult induces the minor child to leave home.)

    b. **Sex:** The parent has a tort claim against anyone who has *sexual intercourse* with the parent's minor *daughter* (but not son).

B. Interference with political and civil rights: There may be a common-law tort action for interfering with P's *political rights* (e.g., his right to vote), his *civil rights* (e.g., his right to make a public protest), or his *public duties* (e.g., his duty to serve on a jury). [510]

1. **§1983 suits for state violation of federal rights:** The most important statute allowing recovery for civil rights violations is the famous federal *"section 1983,"* 42 U.S.C. §1983. Section 1983 allows a person to bring a tort action against any person who, *"under color of" state law*, deprives the plaintiff of "any rights, privileges, or immunities" secured by the *federal Constitution or a federal statute*. So the basic effect of §1983 is to permit a tort suit by

anyone who is injured when a *state or local official* violates the plaintiff's federal rights, typically her *constitutionally-guaranteed civil rights*. Dobbs, §44, p. 82.

a.   Constitutional provisions: Most §1983 actions allege that state or local officials have violated one of these three federal constitutional provisions:

> [1] the 14th Amendment's guarantee of *substantive and procedural due process* of law, and its guarantee of *equal protection* of the laws;
>
> [2] the 4th Amendment's prohibition of *unreasonable searches and seizures*; and
>
> [3] the 8th Amendment's ban on *cruel and unusual punishment*. *Id.*

> **Example (Fourth Amendment):** Suppose that Officer, an officer in the City police force, arrests P without probable cause, and then brutally beats P in an unsuccessful attempt to extract a confession. P can recover tort damages from both Officer and City under §1983. Officer has acted "under color of" state law — that is, he has used his official position as justification for his acts. And Officer's conduct amounts to an "unreasonable seizure" under the 4th Amendment. City is vicariously liable under the doctrine of *respondeat superior* (*supra*, p. 68).

b.   Limitations: Supreme Court decisions over the last few decades have placed two important *limits* on the extent to which suits brought under §1983 can supplement state tort law recoveries.

> **i.   Must show actual damage:** First, compensatory damages may not be awarded based on the abstract *value* or *importance* of the constitutional rights that were violated.
>
> **ii.   Negligence:** Second, where the deprivation of a constitutionally-guaranteed right results from a public official's *negligence* rather than intent, §1983 *may not be used at all*.
>
> > **Example:** P, a prisoner, is attacked by X, a fellow prisoner. Prior to the attack, a prison guard working for D (the state) negligently fails to heed P's warning that X plans to attack him. *Held*, for D: §1983 protects only against intentional, rather than negligent, deprivations of Due Process. So P has only his state-law tort remedies (which, apparently, don't exist here because of sovereign immunity). [*Davidson v. Cannon*]

c.   Implied right of action from constitutional provision: Section 1983 allows only actions against state and local government officials, not federal ones. However, when a federal official violates a citizen's constitutional rights, the citizen is often permitted to bring a federal tort-like suit against the official. This occurs because the court finds an *"implied private right of action"* for violation of the constitutional provision. [511]

> **i.   4th Amendment violation:** For example, suppose that a federal law-enforcement official violates P's 4th Amendment right to be free from unreasonable searches and seizures. The Supreme Court has held that P has an implied right to bring a federal civil-damages suit against the official for this violation. [*Bivens v. Six Unknown Named Agents of FBI* (civil suit for money damages allowed against FBI agents for search and arrest made without probable cause).]

C
A
P
S
U
L
E

S
U
M
M
A
R
Y

CHAPTER 1

INTRODUCTION

I. NATURE OF TORT LAW

A. No satisfactory definition: There is no really useful definition of a "tort" which will allow all tortious conduct to be distinguished from all non-tortious conduct. In fact, courts are constantly changing their view of what constitutes tortious conduct (usually by way of *expansion* of liability). The best that can be done is to identify a few of the main features and purposes of tort law:

1. Not contractual: Tort law, unlike contract law, is not based on the idea of *"consent."* Whereas a contract is an expression of the parties' consent to be bound, every member of society will be liable in tort if he behaves in certain ways, whether he has consented to such liability or not. Thus an automobile driver who drives carelessly will be liable in tort to one he hits, regardless of consent.

2. Compensation: The overall purpose of tort law is to *compensate* plaintiffs for *unreasonable harm* which they have sustained.

a. Societal standard: The unreasonableness of the harm is generally measured from a broad *"social utility"* standpoint. For instance, in determining whether the defendant's conduct is "negligent," the social utility of that conduct (e.g., running a railroad) plays an extremely important role.

b. Economic efficiency: When the law takes into account the "social utility" of the defendant's conduct, courts are to some extent trying to achieve *economic efficiency*. That is, they try to impose on the defendant an *incentive* to make sure that the *costs* associated with her activities do not outweigh the *benefits* from those activities. Normally, a defendant will not engage in conduct whose costs outweigh its benefits anyway; tort law addresses those cases where the defendant gets the benefits, but the costs are imposed on *third parties*.

Example: Assume that D is a driver who is running ten minutes late for an important — and potentially lucrative — business meeting. If D does not face civil liability for driving at 70 m.p.h., and feels that he is completely protected by his airbag, he is likely to speed — all of the benefits from speeding will accrue to him (he gets to the meeting on time, and gets to make the business deal), and the big potential costs from the activity are likely to be imposed on others (e.g., the pedestrian he may run over). Even if the expected financial benefit to D from speeding in this case is fairly small (say, $1,000), and the expected "cost" to others from the speeding is higher (e.g., $200,000 estimated cost of injury to a pedestrian if one is hit, times, let's say, a 1% chance of such an accident occurring, for an expected value of $2,000), D will still have an incentive to speed. Making D responsible for the cost to others from his activity thus induces D to behave "efficiently" (here, by refraining from conduct that has an expected "benefit" of $1,000 versus expected "cost" of $2,000).

3. **Shifting of burden:** Apart from tort law's interest in promoting economic efficiency, this branch of law also has an interest in imposing the cost of accidents on those who can *afford* them. That is, where financial hardship must fall on someone, the courts generally attempt to place it on the party who can best bear it (usually because he is, or could easily have been, covered by *insurance*).

   a. **Not dispositive:** The parties' relative ability to bear the burden is not dispositive; a worker who dashes out into the street and is hit by a U.S. Mail Truck will usually not be able to recover very much from the U.S. (because of his "comparative negligence"), even though he is obviously far less able to bear financial burdens of his injury than would the U.S. government. But ability to bear the burden is certainly one important factor in courts' decisions; this is seen most clearly in cases of "products liability," in which manufacturers and other sellers of defective products are required to bear the cost of injuries caused by these products, regardless of negligence, on the theory that such costs should be treated as simply part of the "cost of doing business." See *infra*, p. 347.

4. **Conflict:** Observe that the goal of "economic efficiency" and the goal of "shifting costs to those who can afford them" will often be *at odds* with each other. Consider the above hypothetical of the worker who dashes carelessly into the street and is hit by a U.S. mail truck. If we want to encourage "economic efficiency" — that is, if we want to give all parties the economic incentive to avoid activities whose economic costs outweigh their economic benefits — we would make sure that the worker cannot recover, because he is the one who had the best opportunity to change the outcome, by not dashing carelessly into the street. If, on the other hand, we want to make sure that costs are imposed on those who can best bear them, we will allow the dasher to recover from the U.S., which obviously has the deeper pocket.

II. CATEGORIES OF TORTS

A. **Three types of defendant conduct:** Most Torts courses and casebooks organize the bulk of tort law into three categories, relating to the nature of the *defendant's conduct*. This is also the approach followed here. Thus we consider, in order: (1) *intentional* torts; (2) the tort of *"negligence"* (i.e., roughly speaking, "carelessness"); and (3) torts in which the defendant's conduct is neither intentional nor careless, but he is made *"strictly liable"* because of the nature of his activity (e.g., abnormally dangerous activity, manufacture of defective products, etc.).

B. **Historical overview:** The relations among these three categories have undergone vast historical development.

1. **Early strict liability:** Under early (15th century) common law, courts often imposed *strict liability*. Thus in *Hulle v. Orynge (The Case of Thorns)*, King's Bench, 1466, the text says, "[i]f a man does a thing he is bound to do it in such a manner that by his deed no injury or damage is inflicted upon others." For instance, as that case stated, if A lifted his stick to defend himself against an attack by B, and the stick accidentally hit C, standing behind A, A would be liable, notwithstanding his carefulness, and the fact that he was engaged in lawful self-defense.

    a. Trespass vs. trespass on the case: A distinction developed between the action of ***"trespass"*** (which was for a ***direct invasion*** of the plaintiff's person or property) and ***"trespass on the case"*** (which was for an indirect invasion of these interests). A classic example was that of a log which falls on the road; if the log hit the plaintiff while she was walking, this was trespass. But if she stumbled on the log after it had landed, this was merely trespass on the case.

    b. Significance of distinction: One important consequence of the distinction between the two causes of action is that for trespass, strict liability existed (as in *Hulle, supra*). For trespass on the case, however, it was normally necessary to show some fault on the defendant's part.

2. Negligence for trespass: But the rule of strict liability for "trespass" began to break down, with respect to certain kinds of trespasses. Thus in *Weaver v. Ward*, 80 Eng. Rep. 284 (K.B. 1616), P and D were soldiers engaged in military exercises. As they were skirmishing, D's musket went off, wounding P. The court held for P, but noted that if D had been able to show that the accident was "utterly without his fault," as would be the case if P had run in front of the gun at the moment of firing, D would not be liable. The burden of proving pure accident was upon D, however, and he did not make such a showing.

3. Shift of burden of proof to plaintiff: Still later, courts began to hold not only that the defendant in a "trespass" case was not liable if he was completely without fault, but also that the ***burden of proving fault*** should be on the ***plaintiff***.

    Example: Two dogs, owned by P and D, are fighting. D, attempting to separate them, raises his stick over his shoulder, hitting P in the eye.

    Held, " . . . if the injury was unavoidable, and the conduct of the defendant was free from blame, he will not be liable. . . . Want of due care became part of the plaintiff's case, and the burden of proof was on the plaintiff to establish it." *Brown v. Kendall*, 60 Mass. 292 (Mass. 1850).

    a. Meaning of "negligent": The courts came to adopt a more-or-less "moral" standard of negligence, by which the defendant would be held to have failed to use due care only if his conduct was somewhat ***blameworthy***. See, e.g., Rest. 2d, §283C, Comment c ("[A]n automobile driver who suddenly and quite unexpectedly suffers a heart attack does not become negligent when he loses control of his car and drives it in a manner which would otherwise be unreasonable; but one who knows that he is subject to such attacks may be negligent in driving at all.")

4. Return of strict liability: But in recent decades, courts have made a sweeping return to the principle of strict liability, at least in many areas. Chief among these are where the defendant engages in an ***abnormally dangerous activity*** (*infra,* p. 332), and where he makes or sells a ***defective product*** that causes physical injury (*infra*, p. 358).

C. Combined torts: Our analysis of liability founded on the three major types of defendant conduct (intent, negligence and strict liability) appears on pp. 5 through 428 *infra*. After that, a number of torts are treated which may be based upon more than one of these three types of defendant conduct. For instance, the torts of nuisance and misrepresentation may be founded on either intent, negligence or strict liability; the same is true for a manufacturer's or retailer's sale of a defective product.

1. **Significance of distinction:** The distinction among these three major types of defendant conduct is most significant, apart from the basic question of liability, with respect to two issues:

    a. **Scope of liability:** First, if the defendant's conduct produces *far-reaching, unexpected, consequences*, will he be liable for these consequences? In general, *the more culpable his conduct, the more far-reaching his liability* for unexpected consequences. Liability for intentional torts, for instance, extends significantly further than that for the tort of negligence; see *infra*, p. 8.

    b. **Damages:** Secondly, what *measure of damages* must the defendant pay once he is found liable? For all torts, he must pay "compensatory damages," i.e., damages whose purpose is to repay the plaintiff for the harm she has suffered. (Obviously, this objective is virtually never realized in cases of personal injury; can $100,000 really repay the plaintiff for loss of an arm?

        i. **Punitive and nominal damages:** But in intentional tort cases, the plaintiff may also sometimes obtain *"punitive damages"* and *"nominal damages,"* both of which are discussed *infra*, p. 8. Punitive and nominal damages are almost never recoverable where negligence or strict liability is the basis for recovery.

D. **Analyzing tort problems:** The student should analyze a tort problem by considering three major questions about each possible tort:

    1. **Basic requirements:** Are the basic requirements (the "*prima facie* case") for the tort satisfied?

    2. **Are defenses available?** Are there any *defenses* or justifications which the defendant can raise that would prevent him from being liable (e.g., self-defense as a defense to a claim of assault, or contributory negligence as a defense to a claim of negligence)?

    3. **What damages?** If the *prima facie* case has been established, and there are no defenses, what elements of *damages* may the plaintiff recover (e.g., medical expenses, lost income, pain and suffering, punitive damages, etc.)?

III. SOURCES OF LAW

A. **Restatement as source of law:** In addition to cases and treatises, the principal sources for the black-letter rules stated in this outline are very influential *Restatements of Torts*, drafted by the American Law Institute.

    1. **Second Restatement:** The *Second* Restatement of Torts was published in the 1960s and 70s.

    2. **Third Restatement:** As of this writing (late 2024), most major torts topics have been covered by a *Third* Restatement, including Liability for Physical & Emotional Harm, Products Liability, Apportionment of Liability and Liability for Economic Harm. We discuss these parts of the Third Restatement where appropriate.

CHAPTER 2

INTENTIONAL TORTS AGAINST THE PERSON

ChapterScope

This chapter is concerned with four "intentional" torts that are committed against "the person" (as opposed to being committed against property): (1) *battery*; (2) *assault*; (3) *false imprisonment*; and (4) *infliction of emtional distress*. (In later chapters, we will consider non-intentional torts related to some of the torts discussed in this chapter. For instance, we will consider the tort of *negligent* infliction of mental distress *infra*, p. 218.) Here are the key concepts in this chapter:

- **Intentional:** Each of the torts covered here is committed only if the defendant acted *"intentionally."* However, the precise meaning of "intent" is different for each of the torts.

- **Transferred intent:** Under the doctrine of *"transferred intent,"* if D held the necessary intent with respect to person A, he will be held to have committed an intentional tort against *any other person* who happens to be injured.

- **Battery:** *Battery* is the *intentional infliction of a harmful or offensive bodily contact*.

- **Assault:** *Assault* is the intentional causing of an *apprehension* of *harmful or offensive bodily contact*.

  ❑ **Imminence:** It must appear to P that the harm being threatened is *imminent*, and that D has a present ability to carry out the threat.

- **False imprisonment:** *False imprisonment* is defined as the intentional infliction of a *confinement*.

- **Infliction of mental distress:** Intentional infliction of mental distress is defined as the *intentional or reckless* infliction, by *extreme and outrageous conduct*, of *severe emotional or mental distress*, even in the absence of physical harm.

I. "INTENT" DEFINED

A. **Intent generally:** What exactly must a tortfeasor intend to do in order for him to commit an "intentional" tort against another person? For instance, suppose that "battery" is defined as the intentional infliction of a harmful or offensive contact (the definition given *infra*, p. 9). Suppose further that we are interested in determining whether a slap given by A to B's face is a battery. Does A have the necessary intent if he merely intended to move his hands through the air as a gesture to make a point, and did not intend either to touch B or to frighten her? What if he did intend to touch her, but did not intend to harm her?

   1. **Summary of rule:** It is difficult to formulate a definition of intent which would apply to the battery example given above, and to all the other torts discussed in this chapter. Therefore, the precise kind of intent required for each of these torts will be discussed when the

other aspects of that tort are treated. However, a general principle applicable to all these torts can be stated:

a. **General principle:** The intent must be at least to bring about some sort of ***physical or mental effect upon another person***, but does not need to include a desire to "harm" that person. Thus the gesture described above would not be a battery, since the person making it did not intend to touch or frighten the person he hit; this is true even though he did intend to move his hand through the air. But the slap that was not intended to "harm" the victim is nonetheless a battery, since there was an intent to ***make the bodily contact***.

2. **Intent to commit different tort:** Suppose a person intends to commit one tort, but in fact commits another. For instance, suppose A intends to frighten B by shooting at him and missing, but she accidentally hits him. She will be held to have had the intent necessary for a battery, even though the only tort she intended to commit was the tort of assault (the intentional infliction of an "apprehension of a bodily contact"). See Rest. 2d §18(1).

a. **Broadly applicable:** The rule that a person who intends to commit one intentional tort and in fact commits another is liable for the tort actually committed, applies ***no matter which kinds of torts are involved.***

Example: If *A* accidentally hits *B* while trying to subject him to false imprisonment, *A* is liable for battery.

B. **"Substantial certainty":** An occurrence is obviously "intentional" if the actor desires to bring it about. But tort law also calls it intentional if the actor didn't desire it, but ***knew with substantial certainty*** that it would occur as a result of his action. See Rest. 2d, §8A.

Example: Brian Dailey, five years old, pulls a chair out from under P as she is sitting down. The evidence at trial shows that he did not desire that she hit the ground, but that he may have known with substantial certainty that she was trying to sit, and would hit the ground.

Held, the case must be remanded the trial court, to determine whether Brian indeed knew with substantial certainty that P would fall. If so, he meets the intent requirement for battery.

On remand, the trial court found that Brian knew with substantial certainty that P was trying to sit when he pulled the chair away, and that there was therefore the intentional tort of battery (defined *infra*, p. 9). *Garratt v. Dailey*, 279 P.2d 1091 (Wash. 1955).

1. **Less than substantial certainty:** But if it is not "substantially certain" that the invasion of the plaintiff's interest in his person will occur, but merely highly likely, the act is not an intentional tort. This is true even though it may be "reckless," and may give rise to liability for negligence.

Example: Suppose Brian Dailey, in the above example, thought it was very probable, but not "substantially certain," that P would hit the ground when he pulled out the chair. His act ("act" defined here as his causing P to hit the ground, since that is the respect in which P's interest in her person was invaded) is not "intentional," and cannot give rise to battery. It might, however, give rise to a cause of action for negligence, if Brian in acting had failed to meet a reasonable standard of care for one of his age.

a. **Act distinguished from consequences:** But while the "act" must be intentional or substantially certain, as distinguished from highly probable, this is not true for the *consequences* of the act. Thus if D intends to tap P lightly on the chin, to annoy him, and unbeknownst to D, P has a "glass jaw," D will be liable for any unforeseeable injury suffered by P as a result of the tap. In other words, the causing of the tap, the contact, must be intentional or substantially certain, but the consequences (the injury), do not have to be intended or substantially certain, or even foreseeable. See the further discussion of this matter, *infra*, p. 8.

C. **No intent to harm necessary:** A person can have the intent necessary for an intentional tort even though he does not desire to *"harm"* the victim, and does not have a hostile intent.

> **Example:** D, a schoolboy, kicks his classmate P. The jury finds that although D intended to kick P, he did not intend to harm him. Nonetheless, P suffers severe injuries. *Held*, whether D intended to harm is irrelevant, as long as D intended to kick P. *Vosburg v. Putney*, 50 N.W. 403 (Wis. 1891), *infra*, p. 8.

1. **Ignorance of the law no excuse:** Similarly, it is irrelevant that the defendant did not know that the action would constitute a tort or a crime. Thus in the law of intentional torts, "ignorance of the law is no excuse."

2. **Insane persons are liable for their torts:** *Insane people* do not automatically escape liability for committing intentional torts.

> **Example:** P, a registered nurse, is charged with the care of D, an insane person. During a fit of rage, D strikes P on the head with the leg of a piece of furniture. P sues for assault and battery.
>
> *Held*, for P. If an insane person is capable of forming an intent to do a harmful act, he may be held liable for the intentional tort just as a normal person would be. The fact that insanity may have been the cause of the intent is irrelevant. Here, the jury could reasonably find that D was capable of intending to strike P. *McGuire v. Almy*, 8 N.E.2d 760 (Mass. 1937).

> **Note:** As indicated by the *McGuire* court, an insane person may be *incapable* of forming the necessary intent. This is particularly likely to be the case with respect to a tort requiring an unusual degree of intelligence or rationality, such as *deceit*. In that event, the insane person would not be liable.

D. **Transferred intent:** In all kinds of intentional torts, the doctrine of *"transferred intent"* may apply. This doctrine holds that as long as the defendant held the necessary intent with respect to one person, he will be held to have committed an intentional tort against *any other person who happens to be injured*. See P&K, pp. 37-39.

> **Example:** D sees Smith and X on D's shed. D throws a stick at Smith or X, and accidentally hits P. *Held*, assuming that D used an unreasonable degree of force, he is liable to P, even though it was not P he was trying to hit. *Talmadge v. Smith*, 59 N.W. 656 (Mich. 1894).

1. **Different kind of tort intended:** We saw above that if a defendant intended to commit an assault, and in fact struck the plaintiff, he will be deemed to have had the intent necessary for battery. This rule applies in the "transferred intent" situation as well. Thus if A intends to frighten B by shooting near her, and the bullet accidentally hits C, A has committed a battery upon C.

II. NOMINAL AND PUNITIVE DAMAGES

A. **Significance of intent:** Often the judge or jury will have to decide whether a defendant's conduct constituted an intentional tort, or merely negligence. Assuming that it is either one or the other, how they decide will have several possible consequences. But the most important is probably the *measure of damages*.

1. **Nominal damages:** If the tort is held to have been an intentional one, the judge or jury may award *nominal damages*, (i.e., a token sum), even if the plaintiff cannot show that he suffered any actual pecuniary harm. But if the tort is merely that of negligence, nominal damages are not awardable, and the plaintiff may recover only the damages that he shows he actually suffered.

   Example: D attempts to shoot P. She misses, but P sees her aiming, and is frightened. This is the intentional tort of assault, and P will be entitled to recover nominal damages (perhaps $1.00) even if he cannot show that he suffered more than a momentary fright of little consequence. But if D had been hunting, and had almost shot P out of negligence, P could not recover nominal damages. He would recover only the actual damages he sustained (though these might include a sum in compensation for fright suffered during and after the episode, so-called "mental suffering" damages).

2. **Punitive damages:** An intentional tort victim may also recover *punitive* damages, if the defendant's conduct was outrageous or malicious. Rest. 2d, §908. Such damages may be very substantial (perhaps even in the hundreds of thousands of dollars), and may be awarded even where little or no compensatory damages are awarded. Thus in the above example of an attempted shooting, P would have a good chance of being awarded substantial punitive damages together with nominal damages and slight or no compensatory damages.

   a. **Negligence:** In ordinary negligence cases, on the other hand, punitive damages are not awardable. Rest. 2d, §908, Comment b.

   b. **Non-outrageous conduct:** Nor are punitive damages awardable in *every* intentional tort case. It is only where the conduct is outrageous or malicious that they will be allowed. For instance, in a situation like *Vosburg v. Putney, supra,* p. 7, where the defendant intended the kick but meant no harm, the court would almost certainly hold as a matter of law that the jury could not award punitive damages.

III. SCOPE OF LIABILITY

A. **Distinction:** Another important consequence of the distinction between intentional torts and negligence has to do with liability for unexpected results. Whereas the negligence defendant will generally be held liable only for those consequences which were at least somewhat fore-seeable, the intentional tortfeasor will be liable for virtually every result stemming directly or even somewhat indirectly from his conduct, however unlikely it might have seemed at the time of his act that this result would follow. Rest. 2d, §435B.

> **Example:** D intentionally hits P on the head intending merely to annoy him. P is slightly injured, and is taken to the hospital. There, by a gross and completely unfore-seeable error, a nurse gives him poison instead of medicine, and P dies. D will be lia-ble for P's death, not just the minor injury. But if D had merely negligently given P the same minor injury, he would not be liable for the unanticipated death. Rest. 2d, §435B, Illustr. 1.

IV. BATTERY

A. Battery generally: Battery is the ***intentional infliction*** of a ***harmful or offensive bodily contact***. See Rest. 2d, §§13, 18.

> **Example:** *A* intentionally punches *B* in the nose. *A* has committed a battery.

B. Intent: Battery cases often turn on subtle questions of ***intent***.

1. Meaning of "intent": Saying that battery is an "intentional" tort does not mean that D must have desired to physically ***harm*** P. D has the necessary intent for battery if it is the case ***either*** that:

[1] D intended to ***cause a harmful or offensive bodily contact; or***

[2] D intended to cause an ***imminent apprehension*** on P's part of a harmful or offensive bodily contact (even if D did not intend to cause the contact itself).

> **Example of [1]:** D shoots at P, intending to hit him with the bullet. D has the neces-sary intent for battery.

> **Example of [2]:** D shoots at P, while facing him, intending to miss P, but also intend-ing to make P think that P would be hit. D has the intent needed for battery. That is, the "intent to commit an assault" (see *infra*, p. 12) suffices as the intent for battery.

2. Intent to create apprehension of contact: Alternative [2] above means that an ***"intent to commit an assault"*** will suffice as the intent for battery. That is, if D intends merely to put ***P in fear of an imminent harmful or offensive contact***, that's a sufficient intent for battery, and it doesn't matter that D does not intend that such a contact actually occur.

a. Prank gone bad: So, for instance, be on the lookout for a ***"prank gone bad,"*** where D tries to trick P into thinking that P will undergo an imminent harmful or offensive contact, but D doesn't intend the contact to actually occur. If something goes wrong and a harmful contact occurs, that's battery of the "intent to commit assault" (i.e., intent to create an imminent apprehension of harmful or offensive contact) variety. See generally, Rest. 2d, §13 and Comment c thereto.

> **Example:** D and P are golfing together. As a prank, D swings his club towards P's head, desiring to make P think (falsely) that the club will strike P. D holds up his swing

at the last instant, but due to a hidden defect in the club the clubhead flies off and strikes P in the fact, injuring him. This is battery, because: (1) D intended to create in P an apprehension of an imminent harmful or offensive contact; and (2) an actual harmful or offensive contact ensued.

C. Harmful or offensive contact: Battery of course includes the infliction of contacts that are truly "harmful," in the sense of causing pain or bodily damage. But it also includes contacts which are merely ***"offensive,"*** i.e., damaging to a ***"reasonable sense of dignity."***

> **Example:** P consults D, an ear doctor, about her right ear. She consents to an operation on that ear, but does nothing about her left ear. During the operation, D discovers that the left ear (but not the right ear) needs surgery, and performs it.
>
> *Held*, the surgery on the left ear was an unauthorized, offensive contact, and constituted battery even though it was not in fact harmful to P's health. *Mohr v. Williams*, 104 N.W. 12 (Minn. 1905).

1. **Reasonableness standard for "offensive" contact:** In determining whether a particular contact is "offensive," the standard is not whether the particular plaintiff was offended, but whether "an ***ordinary person not unduly sensitive*** as to his dignity" would have been offended. P&K, p. 42.

   a. **Ordinary and reasonable contacts:** Thus if A gently pushes past B in a crowded subway, or taps him on the shoulder to ask directions, no battery will be found even if it turns out that B is unduly sensitive and was in fact offended by the touching. But if A uses violence to push past B, this will be battery.

   b. **Where defendant has knowledge of plaintiff's sensitivity:** But suppose that the defendant happens to have known that the plaintiff was an unusually sensitive person (e.g., a Howard Hughes-type who is afraid that being touched by a stranger will infect him). Can the defendant be held liable for a touching which would not be offensive to a normal person? It is not at all clear how such a case would come out — Rest. 2d, Caveat to §19, expressly declines to take a position on this issue.

2. **Contact beyond level consented to:** Battery can occur where the plaintiff ***consents*** to a certain level of bodily contact (see *infra*, p. 61), but the defendant ***goes beyond the consented-to level*** of contact. At that point, the consent becomes invalid, and battery results. Look for this "beyond the consented-to level of contact" scenario when the facts involve either a ***sporting event*** or a ***medical/surgical procedure.***

   > **Example 1:** In a pick-up ice hockey game in a park, P and D are skirmishing for the puck near the side wall of the rink. D intentionally delivers a hard body check that throws P into the wall, and the collision between P and the wall badly injures P. D sues P for battery.
   >
   > If the level of contact between P and D was within the level to which players in this pickup game would be found to have impliedly consented (based on past practices, actual words, etc.), then consent would be a complete defense to P's claim. But if D intentionally delivered a body check (a body contact) that went beyond the level or type of contact D knew or should have known P was consenting to, then it would constitute battery.

Example 2: D, a surgeon, agrees to perform liposuction on P's thighs. While P is under anesthesia, D decides that D could benefit from liposuction on P's arms. Assuming that P is not found to have impliedly consented in advance to the procedure on the arms, that procedure was battery, because it went beyond the scope of the bodily contact to which P consented.

D. Extends to personal effects: A battery may be committed not only by a contact with the plaintiff's body but also by a contact with her *clothing*, an object she is *holding*, or anything else that is s*o closely identified with her body* that contact with it is as offensive as contact with the body would be. See Rest. 2d, §18, Comment c; see also P&K, pp. 39-40.

Example: P, who is black, is attending a luncheon at the Brass Ring Club, located in D hotel. As P is standing in line waiting for his food, one of D's employees snatches the plate from P's hand, and shouts that because P is black, he cannot be served in the club. P is not actually touched, nor is he frightened. He is, however, highly embarrassed.

Held, P has suffered a battery. "The intentional snatching of an object from one's hand is as clearly an offensive invasion of his person as would be an actual contact with the body." Furthermore, P can recover compensatory damages for his mental suffering, even though there was no physical injury. *Fisher v. Carrousel Motor Hotel, Inc.*, 424 S.W.2d 627 (Tex. 1967).

1. Indirect contact: It is not necessary that the defendant touch the plaintiff with his own body. It is sufficient if he causes the contact *indirectly* (e.g., by ordering his dog to attack the plaintiff.) See Rest. 2d, §18, Comment c.

Example: As a prank, D mails P a box of home-made cookies containing peanuts, to which D knows P is highly allergic. P eats a cookie (not thinking it contains peanuts), and suffers severe hives, necessitating a hospital stay. D has committed battery, since he knew with substantial certainty that a harmful contact between the object and P's body would occur. The fact that the contact was indirect (from an object mailed by D instead of from D's body or an object held by D) is irrelevant.

E. Plaintiff's awareness of contact: It is not necessary that the plaintiff have *actual awareness* of the contact at the time it occurs.

Example: D kisses P while she is asleep, but does not awaken or harm her. D has committed battery. Rest. 2d, §18, Illustr. 2.

F. Unforeseen consequences: Once it is established that the defendant intended to commit a harmful or offensive touching (or intends any other tort, such as assault) and such a contact occurs, the defendant is liable for *any consequences which ensue*, even though he did not intend them, and in fact could not reasonably have foreseen them. (This is, as noted above, true for intentional torts generally.)

Example: D is playing golf. P, his caddy, is not paying intention, and D becomes annoyed. Intending to frighten P but not to hurt him, D swings at him with a golf club but stops eight inches from P's head. Because of the negligence of the manufacturer of the golf club, the head of the club flies off and hits P in the eye. D could not have discovered the defect in the club without removing the head. Nonetheless, he is liable to

P for the injury to the eye, since he intended to commit an act which would have been an assault (i.e., the causing of an imminent apprehension by P of a harmful bodily contact). See Rest. 2d, §16, Illustr. 2.

G. **Damages:** If the plaintiff can establish that the intentional harmful or offensive contact occurred, she may, as noted, recover **nominal damages** even if she suffered no physical injury. This might be the case, for instance, where the contact is "offensive" but not "harmful."

1. **Mental disturbance:** Also, she may recover compensation for any pain, suffering, embarrassment, or other **mental effect**, even in the absence of physical harm.

   Example: The plaintiff in *Fisher v. Carrousel Motor Hotel, Inc., supra*, p. 11, was allowed to recover $400 in compensatory damages for his "humiliation and indignity" even though he suffered no physical injury. (He also recovered $500 in punitive damages, a subject discussed immediately below.)

2. **Punitive damages:** If the defendant's conduct was particularly outrageous, the court may, as noted, award **punitive damages**. The subject of punitive damages is discussed more generally *supra*, p. 8.

V. ASSAULT

A. **Definition:** Assault is the intentional causing of an **apprehension** of **harmful or offensive contact**. See Rest. 2d, §21.

1. **Explanation:** In other words, the defendant has committed the tort of assault if he has intentionally caused the plaintiff to think that she will be subjected to a harmful or offensive contact. The interest being protected is plaintiff's interest in freedom from **apprehension** of the contact; thus the tort can exist even if the contact itself never occurs.

   Example: P runs a tavern with her husband. One night when the tavern is closed, D demands wine. P leans out the window to tell him to go away, and D swings at her with a hatchet. He misses, but P is frightened by the attempt.
   Held, D has committed the tort of assault, even though P was not touched. *I. De S. and Wife v. W. De S.* (Eng. 1348).

B. **Intent:** To have the requisite intent, the defendant must either have intended to cause the apprehension of contact, or have intended to cause the contact itself. See Rest. 2d, §21(1)(a) and (b).

1. **Intended apprehension:** Thus if the defendant merely intends to frighten the plaintiff, and does not intend an actual contact, he has the necessary intent.

2. **Attempted battery:** Furthermore, if the defendant intends to commit a battery, and does not intend to put the plaintiff in apprehension of a contact, he also has the necessary intent for assault.

   Example: D sneaks up behind P, intending to shoot her through the back of the head. P happens to turn around just as D is raising the gun. P thinks that D is about to shoot her, but D in fact lowers the gun because he has been discovered. D had the necessary intent for an assault, even though he never intended to put P in apprehension of the bodily contact (and in fact desired that P never know what hit her).

3. **No hostility required:** As in the case of battery, it is not necessary that the defendant bear *malice* or *hostility* to the plaintiff, or intend to harm her. See Rest. 2d §34.

   a. **Pranks:** This means that a *"prank"* can often constitute assault. That is, suppose D tries to induce in P an apprehension of an imminent harmful or offensive contact, without intending to cause an actual contact; then, something goes wrong, and an unintended harmful or offensive contact ensues. We saw that this is battery (see *supra*, p. 9), but it's *also assault*, if P was placed in apprehension of an actual harmful-or-offensive contact, however briefly. So the correct analysis in this kind of fact pattern will typically be that *both* assault and battery have been committed. See Rest. 2d, §34, Illustr. 1.

   Example: D, intending as a prank to cause P to think P is about to be hit in the head (but not intending to make contact), swings a golf club toward P's head. P momentarily thinks that he'll be hit. Then, due to a manufacturing defect, the head of the club flies off, hitting P in the head. Not only is this battery (see *supra*, p. 9), it's also assault, because P momentarily was in apprehension that he'd be hit, and D intended to cause this apprehension. (Indeed, this would be assault even if the head never flew off — once D succeeded in his intent to make P believe he was about to be hit, the tort of assault was complete.)

4. **Transferred intent:** Again, as in the case of battery, the doctrine of *"transferred intent"* applies. Thus if D throws a stone at X, and P, who is standing nearby, is put in fear of being hit, D is liable to P for assault even though he never intended either to hit or frighten P. See Rest. 2d, §33.

C. **"Words alone" rule:** Many cases state the general principle that "words alone are not sufficient to constitute an assault." These cases hold that words must be accompanied by some *overt act*, no matter how slight, that adds to the threatening character of the words.

1. **Qualification:** Some commentators, however, as well as the Second Restatement, suggest that there may be cases where the surrounding circumstances are such that words by themselves, without any overt act, are sufficient to constitute an assault. See Rest. 2d, §31.

   Example: D, a notorious gangster, who is known to have killed others, telephones P and tells him that he will shoot him on sight. Coming around the corner, P encounters D standing on the sidewalk. Without moving, D says to P, "your time has come." D has committed an assault upon P, according to the Restatement. Rest. 2d, §31, Illustr. 4.

2. **Words may negate assault:** Although words by themselves will almost never constitute an assault, their impact must be taken into account, along with any overt act, in determining whether there has been one. Just as threatening words may convert an overt act into an assault where it would otherwise not be one (e.g., D reaches into his pocket, and says to P, "I've got a gun in my pocket and I'm going to fill you full of lead"), words may also *negate an intent* to commit assault.

Example: It is assize time and the travelling judges are in town. P gets into an argument with D, puts his hand on his sword, and says "if it were not assize-time, I would not take such language from you." D then attacks P, injuring him.

Held, P has made no assault, because these words make it clear that despite his gesture of reaching for his sword, he had no intent to commit a present battery or assault. Therefore, D cannot claim self-defense, and is liable for P's injuries. See *Tuberville v. Savage*, 86 Eng. Rep. 684 (Eng. 1669).

D. Actual contact or apprehension required: Apart from the defendant's intent, the tort of assault requires an *effect*: P must either actually **undergo** a harmful or offensive contact, or be put in *immediate apprehension* of such a contact.

1. **Unsuccessful prank or bluff:** So where D is pulling a *prank or making a bluff*, if P believes or knows that no imminent harmful or offensive contact will really occur, and none does occur, there is no assault.

   Example: P has been having sex with D's wife, W, and P knows that D knows this. D, holding a revolver, walks into P's office and says, "I know you've been having sex with my wife, and I'm gonna blow your head off." The particular gun that D is holding is a toy replica that cannot fire anything, and P knows this because W has told him so on a previous occasion. D has not committed assault — even if D intended to put P in fear of an imminent harmful contact (a bullet fired at him), the "result" requirement for assault has not been met because P has not in fact been put in apprehension of such contact.

2. **Feared contact with ground or independent object suffices:** The harmful or offensive contact of which P is placed in apprehension does not have to be with D or an instrumentality under D's control — it can be with the *ground* or some other *free-standing object*.

   Example: While P is driving along a narrow two-lane road which has a stone wall to P's right, D drives up behind P from the same direction. D wants to frighten P into thinking that D will force P's car into the stone wall. D therefore comes up even with the left side of P's car, and veers right-ward until there is just one inch between the right side of his car and the left side of P's. P believes, for an instant, that P will be forced into contact with the wall. Then D veers away, laughs, and drives off. P's car never touches either the wall or D's car. This is assault — D intended to make P believe that P's car (which is part of his person for this purpose) would touch the wall, and D succeeded in that goal, so the tort was complete at the moment P had the "I'm about to hit the wall" belief.

E. Imminence of threatened contact: For assault, it must appear to the plaintiff that the harm being threatened is *imminent*.

1. **Future threats:** Threats of future harm cannot constitute assaults, although they may constitute the tort of intentional infliction of emotional distress (discussed *infra*, p. 21). The dividing line between a threat of imminent harm and one of future harm is hard to define, but the courts and commentators have taken a relatively strict view requiring a

short period between the making of the threat and the time when, according to the threat, the harm will take place. See Rest. 2d §29, Comment c.

> **Example:** A threatens to shoot B, and leaves the room for the stated purpose of getting his revolver. A has not committed an assault on B. Rest. 2d. §29, Illustr. 4.

2. **Present ability to commit harm:** The defendant must have what appears to the plaintiff to be the ***present ability*** to commit the threatened contact. Just as there is no assault if the defendant's words indicate that the threatened harm will not take place imminently, so there will be no assault if it is apparent to the plaintiff that the defendant does not have the ability to commit the threatened harm immediately. See Rest. 2d §29, Comment b.

F. **Plaintiff unaware of danger:** Since the tort of assault protects what is essentially the plaintiff's interest in freedom from a mental condition (apprehension of imminent contact), the plaintiff must be ***aware*** of the threatened contact.

> **Example:** D, standing behind P, raises his gun to shoot P. X, a bystander, sees what is about to happen and disarms D before he can shoot. P then turns around, and realizes for the first time the danger that he has been subjected to. Because P was not aware of the threatened harm at the time the threat existed, he cannot recover for assault, no matter how shaken up he becomes after the fact. See Rest. 2d, §22, Illustr. 2.

G. **Apprehension is not same as fear:** The plaintiff must have "apprehension" of imminent harmful or offensive contact. But "apprehension," as the term is used in the definition of assault, does ***not necessarily mean "fear."*** It is sufficient that the plaintiff believes that if she does not take action, a harmful or offensive contact will occur in the near future. The plaintiff's right to recover is not negated by the fact that she is confident of her own ability to take action to avoid the contact.

> **Example:** "A, a scrawny individual who is intoxicated, attempts to strike with his fist B, who is the heavyweight champion pugilist of the world. B is not at all afraid of A, is confident that he can avoid any such blow and in fact succeeds in doing so." A has nonetheless committed an assault on B. Rest. 2d, §24, Illustr. 1.

1. **Where threat by itself incapable of performance:** But if it appears to the plaintiff that even without action on her or a third person's part, the defendant will be unable to make good his threat of harm, there is no assault.

> **Example:** D points a pistol at P, threatening to shoot. P happens to know that D is holding not a loaded weapon, but a water pistol with no water in it. Because P knows that D will not be able to make good his threat in the imminent future, there is no assault, regardless of how hard D is trying to frighten P.

> **Note:** Suppose, in the above example, that P knew that D was holding a water pistol, but that she also knew that the water pistol was loaded. Would the threat of being sprinkled with water be sufficient to give rise to an action for assault? Remember that P's mental state must be apprehension of an imminent "harmful or offensive" contact; it is quite possible that having water sprayed in one's face would be an offensive contact, although obviously not a harmful one. If so, P would have an action for assault.

H. Unreasonable apprehension: Just as most courts have held that a battery does not exist where it is only because of the plaintiff's unusual sensitivity that a particular contact is offensive, so the courts have generally held that a plaintiff who is unusually timid may not recover for assault where a normal person would not have an apprehension of contact. See P&K, p. 44.

1. Restatement view: The Second Restatement, however, takes the position that as long as the defendant *intends* to put the plaintiff in apprehension of an immediate bodily contact, and succeeds in so doing, there is an assault "although [the] act would not have put a person of ordinary courage in such apprehension." Rest. 2d, §27.

I. Threat to third persons not actionable: The plaintiff must have an apprehension that *he himself* will be subjected to a bodily contact; he may not recover for his apprehension that someone else will be so touched.

> **Example:** P sees D raise a pistol at P's wife. P realizes the danger his wife is in, and manages to disarm D before he fires. P cannot recover for assault, because although he was apprehensive of an imminent bodily contact, it was a contact upon his wife, not upon P himself. See Rest. 2d, §26.

> **Note:** It is anomalous that P in the above example cannot recover for assault, despite the very real fear for the safety of his wife that he feels; yet P, the heavyweight boxer in the example on p. 15, who is confident of his ability to avoid the blow, may recover, despite his absence of fear. This discrepancy is due to historical reasons. P in the above example could, however, probably recover for intentional infliction of mental distress, a modern tort discussed *infra*, p. 21.

J. Ability to carry out threat: We have seen that the plaintiff must believe that the defendant has the ability to carry out his threat of contact unless the plaintiff or some third force intervenes. But it is not necessary that the defendant *in fact* have the ability to carry out the threat.

> **Example:** D points an unloaded pistol at P. If P does not know that the pistol is unloaded, and she is put in apprehension of being shot, she may recover for assault. See Rest. 2d, §33.

K. Conditional threats: Suppose the defendant threatens the plaintiff with immediate bodily harm unless the plaintiff will pay him money, turn over a secret formula, or something of the like. Does the fact that the threat is *conditional* mean that the defendant has not committed an assault?

1. Question of legal right: The Second Restatement and most courts hold that there is nonetheless an assault unless the defendant had the *legal right* to compel the plaintiff to perform the act in question. Since the robber has no legal right to force his victim to turn over his money, and the industrial spy has no right to compel disclosure of the secret formula, they may not use the existence of these demands as an escape hatch from an assault suit.

a. Privilege: But if the defendant is privileged to enforce the condition, there is no assault unless he uses or threatens *unreasonable force in presenting the choice between contact and compliance*.

Example: P, a burglar, breaks into D's house. D surprises him, and says "If you don't get out, I will throw you out." There is no assault, since D has the legal right to throw P out (see discussion of defense of property, *infra*, p. 73). If P were a household employee whom D was firing, and D pointed a pistol at P and said "Get out right now or I'll shoot you through the head," there would be an assault. This is so because although D would be entitled to put P out of the house, he is threatening the use of unreasonable and unlawful force. See Rest. 2d, §30, Illustrs. 1 and 2.

L. Assault is not attempted battery: From the above discussion, it should be clear that an assault is not the same thing as an "attempted battery," despite the tendency of some courts to think that it is. Thus an assault is committed where the defendant intends to frighten the plaintiff by pointing a pistol at her, but does not intend to shoot her; this is clearly not an attempted battery.

M. Abandoned attempt: The tort of assault is complete as soon as the plaintiff suffers the requisite apprehension. It is not negated by the fact that the defendant subsequently has second thoughts, and *abandons* her plan.

Example: D points her pistol at P, intending to shoot P. P sees the danger, and is apprehensive that he will in fact be shot. D changes her mind, lowers the pistol, and says to P, "I was going to shoot you, but I've changed my mind." The tort of assault was complete as soon as P had an apprehension that he would be shot, because D had the requisite intent. (Remember that an intent to commit a battery, like an intent to cause an apprehension of a battery, is sufficient — see *supra*, p. 12). The fact that D changed her mind, and never committed the battery, does not negate the assault.

N. Damages: The rules for damages in the case of assault are the same as in the case of battery.

  1. Nominal damages: Thus nominal damages can be awarded where the plaintiff shows no out-of-pocket loss.

  2. Mental suffering: Similarly, the plaintiff can be awarded compensatory damages based upon his mental suffering. In fact, since the tort of assault is based upon a mental harm, mental suffering forms the principal or sole foundation for damages in most cases. If, however, the plaintiff suffers physical injury or ailment as a result of the assault (e.g., he is frightened, and tries to run away, and is hit by an oncoming car), he may recover for this as well.

  3. Punitive damages: And, if the defendant's conduct is sufficiently outrageous or malicious, punitive damages may be awarded.

VI. FALSE IMPRISONMENT

A. Definition: The tort of "false imprisonment" is defined as the intentional infliction of a *confinement*. It is unclear whether the plaintiff must be aware of the confinement; this issue is discussed below.

B. Intent: Since false imprisonment is an intentional tort, the plaintiff must show that the defendant intended to confine him. As with assault and battery, he can meet this burden by showing that the defendant knew with *"substantial certainty"* that the confinement would result.

C. Transferred intent: Similarly, as with assault and battery, the doctrine of *"transferred intent"* applies.

> **Example:** P is shopping in the D store. D's store detective, an unduly zealous person, erroneously and unreasonably believes that X, who is also shopping in the store, has attempted to shoplift. She orders all exits to the store to be closed. This has the effect of confining P, who the detective does not even know to be in the store. Since the detective had the requisite intent for false imprisonment vis-à-vis X, D will be liable to P as well as to X for false imprisonment, by the doctrine of transferred intent.
>
> **Note:** The reasons for which D is liable to X for false imprisonment, despite the detective's honest though unreasonable belief that X has been shoplifting, are discussed *infra*, p. 77, in the treatment of the defense of recapture of chattels. If D were not liable to X because the detective's belief, although erroneous, was reasonable, it is not clear whether D would be liable to P. Probably, however, the detective would be held not to have had the requisite intent vis-à-vis X, and the doctrine of "transferred intent" would have no application, thereby absolving D with respect to P's suit as well.

D. Nature of confinement: The plaintiff must be confined within *definite physical boundaries*. Blocking of the plaintiff's path is not enough: it is not enough that the path the plaintiff wishes to travel is obstructed by the defendant, or that the plaintiff is prevented from entering a particular place.

1. Confinement: In other words, the essence of the idea of "confinement" is that the plaintiff is held *within* certain limits, not prevented from entering certain places. The distinction is a matter of degree, but most cases will be clear one way or the other. See P&K, p. 47; see also Rest. 2d, §36(3).

> **Example:** A portion of a public road has been reserved for paying spectators of a boat race. P wants to enter the restricted area, but is prevented from doing so by D's police officer.
>
> *Held*, P has been confined in the sense that he was not permitted to go in the spectating area. However, since he was free to travel along the other direction of the road, he has *not* been subjected to false imprisonment. *Bird v. Jones*, 115 Eng. Rep. 668 (Q.B. 1845).
>
> **Note:** The result in the above example is the same regardless of whether D's blocking off of the highway was lawful. See Rest. 2d, §36, Illustr. 11.

E. Means of escape: It is irrelevant that there is some means of escape from the area of confinement, provided that the plaintiff does not know of this means. Rest. 2d, §36(2).

1. Means must be "reasonable":   Even if the plaintiff does know the means of escape, he will not lose his action for false imprisonment unless the means is "reasonable." The Second Restatement (§36, Comment a) takes the view that the means of escape is reasonable only if the plaintiff's use of it would not be physically dangerous to the plaintiff, harmful to his clothing, "offensive" to his "reasonable sense of decency or personal dignity," or dangerous to some third person.

F. Means by which confinement enforced: If the plaintiff is physically confined, as where he is put in a room with all doors locked, the confinement obviously meets the requirements for false imprisonment. But there are other, less explicitly physical, kinds of duress to confine a person, which may also give rise to the tort.

    1. Use of threats: Thus if the defendant threatens to use force if the plaintiff tries to escape (and appears to have the ability to do so), the requisite confinement exists. Rest. 2d, §40, Comment a. This is so whether the threats are explicit, or merely implied by the defendant's conduct (e.g., D displays a gun in a menacing manner).

        a. Plaintiff's desire to clear himself: However, if the plaintiff's confinement is due solely to his own desire to clear himself of suspicion, there is no false imprisonment. Thus, in the usual case where a suspected shoplifter submits to a search or remains for questioning at the store, the existence of false imprisonment will turn on whether the plaintiff submitted to the search or questioning solely to clear himself, or, rather, submitted at least in part because of the threat of implied force.

            i. Possible privilege: But even if the detention of a suspected shoplifter is not voluntary, the detention may be *privileged* if it is brief and the store's suspicion is reasonable. See *infra*, p. 77.

        b. Purely verbal commands: If the plaintiff voluntarily submits to commands that are *strictly verbal*, unaccompanied by force or threats, there is no false imprisonment.

    2. Threat to harm others: Just as a threat to use force against the plaintiff if he tries to escape may give rise to false imprisonment, so may a threat to harm a third person if the plaintiff tries to escape. Thus if the defendant threatens to harm the plaintiff's spouse if the plaintiff does not remain in a particular room, there is false imprisonment. See Rest. 2d, §40A.

    3. Threat to property: Threats to the plaintiff's *property* may also constitute the necessary duress. For instance, if a storekeeper believes that a customer has been shoplifting, and seizes his shopping bag to dissuade him from leaving, there will probably be false imprisonment.

        a. Threats of future harm: But the duress, whatever its nature, must involve *imminent* harm. Threats of *future* harm (e.g., "if you don't stay here in my store and clear yourself of shoplifting, I'll call the police and have them arrest you at your house"), as in the case of assault and battery, are not sufficient. See P&K, p. 50.

    4. Assertion of legal authority: Just as the confinement may be caused by threats of force, so it may be caused by the defendant's assertion that she has *legal authority* to confine the plaintiff. This is so even if defendant does not in fact have legal authority, as long as the plaintiff reasonably believes that she has, or is in doubt about whether she has, such authority. See Rest. 2d, §41.

        Example: D is a private detective who works for Storekeeper. She sees P leaving the store, and chases him down the street. When she catches up to him, she says "I'm a plainclothes police officer, and I hereby arrest you." P believes D's statement, and follows D back to the store for interrogation. D is liable for false imprisonment, even though she used no force.

a. **Validity of asserted authority:** For purposes of determining whether there has been a prima facie case of false imprisonment, it is ***irrelevant whether the asserted legal authority is in fact valid or invalid***. Thus in above example, it is irrelevant whether D was only a store detective who under local criminal law had no authority to make the arrest in question, or was in fact a police officer. As long as the plaintiff ***believes*** that the defendant has legal authority, or is in reasonable doubt about whether the defendant has such authority, there is false imprisonment if the plaintiff submits.

   i. **Defense of valid arrest:** Of course, if a party asserting legal authority in fact has the ***right*** to make an arrest, this will serve as a defense to a false imprisonment claim. (The general rules governing when arrests may be validly made by police officers and private citizens are discussed *infra*, p. 82.)

b. **Actual submission necessary:** The mere assertion of legal authority will be sufficient if the plaintiff in fact submits to the confinement (as P in the above example did by going back to the store). But if the plaintiff refuses to submit, and leaves, the defendant's assertion of legal authority will not be enough to give rise to an action for false imprisonment. Thus in the above example, if P merely walked away from D, D's statement "I arrest you" would not in itself be a false imprisonment. However, if D used force to detain P, that use of force would of itself be false imprisonment.

c. **Instigation in arrest:** If a private citizen participates in an arrest which turns out to have been unlawful (under the rules discussed *infra*, p. 82), she may be liable for false imprisonment even though she was not the one who ultimately made the arrest itself. Thus if the owner of a store tells a private detective to detain a suspect, and the detective purports to "arrest" the suspect in circumstances where she does not have the right to do so, the storekeeper may, like the detective, be liable for false imprisonment.

   i. **Mere filing of complaint:** But a private person who merely files a complaint with the police will not be liable. To incur liability, he must take a more active role than the mere furnishing of information (e.g., urging the police to make the arrest). However, one who furnishes information to the police may, if the information is false, be liable for ***malicious prosecution*** (discussed *infra*, p. 499).

   ii. **Distinction:** Even if the defendant does take an active part in the arrest (as by urging the police to make it), he will not be liable for false imprisonment as long as the requisite legal formalities are met. That is, if the police themselves act lawfully (e.g., they obtain a warrant, or they make the arrest in a situation in which no warrant is required, such as where they have probable cause), the private citizen will not be liable for false imprisonment (though he may be liable for malicious prosecution). But if he actively helps the police, and the police do not follow proper procedures (e.g., they act on information which they know to be false), he will be liable for false imprisonment.

   iii. **Summary:** There are thus two requirements for "instigator" liability for false imprisonment: (1) an unlawful arrest must have occurred (judged against the rules given on p. 82) and (2) the defendant must have actively aided the arrest (i.e., persuaded the authorities to make the arrest, rather than merely giving them information and letting them decide what to do about it). See Rest. 2d, §45A.

G. Duty to aid in escape or release: It may happen that the plaintiff *consents* to an initial confinement (thus negating the tort — see *infra*, p. 58). If so, there will nonetheless be a false imprisonment if the defendant is under a duty to release the plaintiff, or to help him escape, and does not do so. See Rest. 2d, §45.

> **Example:** D induces P to sail with him from Syria to America, promising to let P off the boat as soon as it arrives in the U.S. The boat arrives at a U.S. port, but D refuses to give P a row boat so that she can leave the yacht.
>
> *Held*, P committed false imprisonment, since he had implicitly agreed to furnish P with whatever was necessary (here, a row boat) to enable her to leave the yacht. *Whittaker v. Sandford*, 85 A. 399 (Me. 1912).

H. Necessity that plaintiff know of confinement: We have seen that in the case of assault, the plaintiff must be *aware* of the tort at the time it is committed, but that in the case of battery, he *need not be aware*. In false imprisonment cases, most courts have held that the tort is like assault, and that the plaintiff must be *aware of his confinement* while he is suffering it.

    1. Second Restatement view: The Second Restatement, in §42, holds that *either* the plaintiff must be aware of the confinement, or he must suffer some actual harm. Thus the Restatement states that if a six-day-old child is locked in a bank vault for two days, and suffers from hunger and thirst, he has been falsely imprisoned despite his lack of awareness of the confinement. See Rest. 2d, §42, Illustr. 3.

I. Damages: As in the case of the other intentional torts we have examined, the plaintiff may recover *nominal damages* for false imprisonment, even if he has suffered no actual physical or mental harm. He may also recover for mental suffering, humiliation, loss of time, inconvenience, etc., and where actual malice is shown, he may recover punitive damages. See P&K, p. 48-49.

VII. INTENTIONAL INFLICTION OF EMOTIONAL DISTRESS ("IIED")

A. Definition: Nearly all modern courts recognize the tort of intentional infliction of emotional distress (which we'll sometimes call "IIED" for short). This tort may be defined as the intentional or reckless infliction, by *extreme and outrageous conduct*, of severe emotional or mental distress, even in the absence of physical harm.

B. Intent: In the intentional torts we have examined so far (battery, assault and false imprisonment), we have seen that the requisite intent may exist not only where the defendant *desires* to cause a certain result, but also where she knows with "substantial certainty" that the result will occur. In the case of infliction of mental distress, however, the necessary mental state is *even broader* — there are *three* possible mental states on D's part, any of which will qualify:

[a] D *desires* to cause P emotional distress;

[b] D knows with *substantial certainty* that P will suffer emotional distress; and

[c] D *recklessly disregards the high probability* that emotional distress will occur.

See Rest. 2d, §46(1).

1. **Meaning of "reckless":** For the defendant's conduct to be *"reckless"* (the third mental state listed above), however, it must be in the face of risk that is significantly higher than the risk of harm that would make her conduct "negligent." (Negligent conduct is discussed generally *infra*, p. 95.) In other words, for recklessness it is not enough that the defendant acted despite a risk of causing emotional harm that a person of average prudence would recognize was *unreasonable*.

   a. **Third Restatement's definition:** Thus the Third Restatement says that a person "recklessly" causes harm if (1) the person *"knows of the risk* of harm created by his conduct, or *knows facts that make that risk obvious* to anyone in the actor's situation"; and (2) the precaution that would eliminate or reduce that risk involves *burdens that are so slight* relative to the magnitude of the risk as to render *highly blameworthy* the actor's failure to adopt the precaution." Rest. 3d (Liab. for Phys. & Emot. Harm) §2.

   b. **Typical case:** Here is an example of a case holding that *reckless disregard* of the high chance of causing emotional distress is the equivalent of causing the distress.

      Example: D's wife has left him, and he is a guest in the home of a friend of his, P. While P is away from the house, D decides to commit suicide by slitting his throat in P's kitchen. P returns to find his corpse lying there, in a pool of blood and suffers from nervous shock, and becomes ill. She sues D's estate for intentional infliction of mental distress.

      Held, the jury could find that D "willfully" caused P emotional distress, since he acted in disregard of the high probability that she would suffer the distress. Therefore, the tort may be treated as if it were intentional. *Blakeley v. Shortal's Estate*, 20 N.W.2d 28 (Iowa 1945).

      i. **Application of Third Restatement to *Blakeley*:** Let's see whether the Third Restatement's definition of recklessness, just quoted above, would apply to D's conduct in *Blakeley*. First, whether or not P would be able to show that D actually knew of the risk that P might suffer emotional distress at finding D's body in her kitchen, D surely knew of the fact that P (or some resident of the house) would discover the body, so D "[knew] facts that [made] the risk obvious to anyone in the actor's situation" (satisfying the first prong one of the Restatement definition). Second, presumably it would not have been very burdensome on D to wait until he was somewhere else (e.g., in his own home, or a hotel room) to commit suicide, so that a stranger rather than a friend would find the body. So the second prong of the Restatement definition seems to be satisfied as well. Thus D seems to have acted "recklessly" under the Third Restatement.

2. **"Transferred intent":** The doctrine of "transferred intent" is *not* generally applicable in cases of IIED. That is, if the defendant attempts to cause emotional distress to X, or to commit some other tort upon him, and P suffers emotional distress (e.g., because he witnesses the defendant's attempt and becomes frightened), P will not usually be able to recover.

   a. **Rationale:** The most frequent reason given for this refusal by courts to make the doctrine of transferred intent generally applicable to IIED cases is that it would open too wide the gate for litigation. Prosser, for instance (PW&S, p. 62) suggests that if transferred intent were allowed, three million people watching an assassination of a President on television would be able to sue the assassin.

b. **Exception:** However, the cases have generally recognized at least one exception to the rule that transferred intent is not applicable: if the defendant directs her conduct at a member of the ***immediate family*** of the plaintiff, and the plaintiff is present. Most of these cases impose the further requirement that the plaintiff's presence be ***known*** to the defendant, so that the mental distress could have been reasonably anticipated by the defendant.

Example: P watches her father being beaten up by D, and as a result of seeing this beating, suffers severe emotional distress.

Held, since P does not allege that D knew of her presence (nor that D intended to cause her emotional distress), P's claim does not state a cause of action. *Taylor v. Vallelunga*, 339 P.2d 910 (Cal. App. 1959).

c. **Restatement has more liberal view:** The Second Restatement, however, extends the category of persons who can recover for conduct which they witnessed being directed at others.

    i. **Bodily harm:** Under the Restatement view, any person who is present at a beating, attack, threat, etc. made to another may recover if he suffers "bodily harm" from watching the episode, even if the witness is not a member of the victim's immediate family. (Once the witness shows bodily harm, he may also recover for purely emotional harm.)

    ii. **Relative:** If the witness is a member of the victim's immediate family, he may recover for his purely emotional distress even if he suffers no bodily harm. See Rest. 2d, §46(2).

    Example: P, while walking down the street, is stopped by a stranger, X, who asks him for a match. While P is pulling out his cigarette lighter, X is suddenly shot down by D. As a result, P suffers emotional distress, and becomes physically ill. According to the Second Restatement, P may recover from D on a theory of intentional infliction of emotional distress. See Rest. 2d, §46, Comment l.

3. **Emotional distress where other tort attempted:** We saw (*supra*, p. 6) that if the defendant has attempted to commit an assault or false imprisonment, and in fact commits a harmful or offensive touching, a battery has occurred, even though the touching itself may not have been intentional. A similar rule does ***not***, in general, apply to infliction of emotional distress. That is, if the defendant attempts to commit some other tort, and the only effect on the plaintiff is emotional distress, the tort of IIED has not occurred. Rest. 2d, §47.

Example: D tries to shoot P in the back of the head; she hopes that P will not suspect anything until the bullet actually enters. However, as D is aiming, X knocks the gun away. P, when he learns of what D was trying to do, becomes exceptionally distraught, even though the danger is, for the moment, over. This is not an assault, since P did not learn of the danger until after it had passed — see *supra*, p. 15. Nor is it a battery, of course, since no contact in fact occurred. And, even though emotional distress to P resulted, the tort of intentional infliction of emotional distress has not occurred, because D did not have the requisite intent (i.e., the intent to cause the distress, as opposed to intent to cause bodily harm).

    a. Assault distinguished: But keep in mind that if the defendant attempts to commit battery, false imprisonment, or some other intentional tort, and the plaintiff suffers emotional distress in the form of an "apprehension of imminent harmful or offensive contact," the tort of assault has occurred, and the plaintiff can recover for his mental suffering. Similarly, if the plaintiff has mental distress as the result of a battery, he can recover damages for this distress, even though the separate tort of infliction of mental distress has not occurred.

C. Extreme and outrageous conduct: For the plaintiff to recover, he must show, among other things, that the defendant's conduct was *extreme and outrageous*. It is not enough for him to show that the defendant insulted him, or hurt his feelings. Even the defendant's use of profanity to him will not be enough, unless the relationship of the parties is such that the use of the dirty words is particularly outrageous (see the discussion below of aggravating circumstances).

    1. Restatement test: As the Second Restatement has put the idea, the conduct must be "[s]o outrageous in character, and so extreme in degree, as to go *beyond all possible bounds of decency*, and to be regarded as atrocious, and utterly intolerable in a civilized community. Generally, the case is one in which the recitation of the facts to an average member of the community would arouse his resentment against the actor, and lead him to exclaim, 'Outrageous!'" Rest. 2d, §46, Comment d.

    2. Typical cases: The following are two of the best-known cases in which the defendant's conduct was held to be outrageous, and liability for intentional infliction of emotional distress was found.

        Example 1: D, as a practical joke, tells P that her husband has been badly injured in an accident, and is lying in the hospital with both legs broken. D suggests that P go to the hospital to fetch her husband with two pillows. P suffers nervous shock with consequent serious physical illness, and is at one point in danger of going insane.

        Held, P may recover from D for her emotional suffering and physical harm. *Wilkinson v. Downton*, 2 Q.B. 57 (Eng. 1897).

        Example 2: D is a rubbish collector. The president of P, an association of rubbish collectors, summons D to a meeting of the association, and tells him that he, D, is infringing on territory held by one of P's members. The president tells D that if he does not join P, and pay over a portion of the proceeds of his collections, the members of P will beat him up, burn his truck, and put him out of business. D, intimidated, agrees, and signs some notes for payment of these proceeds. D defaults on the notes, P sues on them, and D counterclaims for intentional infliction of emotional distress.

        Held, D may recover on his counterclaim against P for emotional distress, even though he suffered no physical harm. (Also, P may not recover on the notes.) *State Rubbish Collectors Association v. Siliznoff*, 240 P.2d 282 (Cal. 1952).

3. **Bill collectors:**   A common fact pattern in which the defendant is alleged to be liable for intentional infliction of mental distress is where the defendant is a *bill collector*. The collector's conduct can and often will be sufficiently extreme and outrageous to trigger IIED. And it's no defense to an otherwise proper IIED action that the plaintiff *really owed the money* that D was trying to collect.

> **Example:** D operates a collection agency. He is trying to collect a $1,000 bill for goods sold to P by Store. D goes to P's house and when Sis, P's sister, answers the door, D tells Sis he is there to collect a bill owed by P. Sis tells D that P has been unemployed for six months, and that P will pay the bill as soon as she can. D, in a loud voice, then demands to see P and says to Sis that if D does not receive payment immediately, he will file a criminal complaint charging P with fraud on creditors. P then comes to the door, and D in a loud voice that can be heard by neighbors across the street, repeats his demand for immediate payment and his threat to have P prosecuted.
>
> If P suffers severe emotional distress from D's conduct, she can recover for IIED against him, because D's conduct is extreme and outrageous. And that's true even if P *really does owe* the $1,000 to Store.

4. **Individual circumstances of case:**   In determining whether the defendant's conduct is sufficiently outrageous, the court will take into account the particular characteristics of the plaintiff, and the relationship between him and the defendant.

   a. **Plaintiff's situation:**   Thus if the plaintiff is very young, or retarded, or senile, the defendant's conduct might be held to be outrageous even though it would not be so if the plaintiff were a normal adult. Similarly, if the defendant is or holds herself out to be a police officer in her dealings with the plaintiff, her threats to have the plaintiff arrested might be deemed outrageous, where they would not be if defendant was and appeared to be a private citizen.

   b. **Defendant's knowledge of plaintiff's sensitivity:**   Where the defendant's conduct is outrageous only because of the plaintiff's particular characteristics, it is usually held that the defendant must have been *aware* of these characteristics. See Rest. 2d §46, Comment f.

D. **Actual severe distress:**   Once the plaintiff has shown that the defendant's conduct was extreme and outrageous, he must then show that he, the plaintiff, in fact suffered *severe* emotional distress. See Rest. 2d §46, Comment j.

1. **Medical effects:**   At a minimum, the plaintiff must always show that his mental distress was sufficiently severe that he *sought medical aid.*

2. **Physical harm:**   Some cases even hold that recovery may be allowed only where there is some *physical harm* in addition to emotional distress. See P&K, p. 64. But most modern courts appear not to require physical harm. Thus in *Siliznoff, supra,* the court explicitly held that the recipient of threats of violence could recover even though he suffered no physical harm.

   a. **Restatement view:**   The Second Restatement does not require that the emotional distress be accompanied by any kind of bodily harm. However, it notes that courts may tend to look for bodily harm as a guaranty that the emotional distress is real; but if the outrageousness of the act is clear enough, liability will be found without bodily harm. Rest. 2d, §46, Comment k.

3. **Reasonable standard:** In addition to the requirement that the plaintiff suffer severe mental distress, the defendant's conduct must be such that a ***reasonable person*** would suffer such distress. Thus if the plaintiff turns out to be an unusually sensitive person, who suffers severe distress where a normal person would not, there will be no recovery.

   a. **Exception:** However, this "reasonable person" standard does not apply where the defendant has ***notice*** that the plaintiff is unusually sensitive. In most respects, therefore, this "reasonable person" rule is merely a restatement of the principle, described above, that the defendant's conduct must be "outrageous," taking into account the peculiarities of the plaintiff that are known to the defendant.

      Example: P is a superstitious woman, who believes that there is a pot of gold buried in her backyard. D, as a practical joke, plants a pot, containing things other than gold, in P's backyard. P digs up the pot, and D escorts her in triumph to the town hall, where she opens the pot and is humiliated.

      Held, P may recover against D. *Nickerson v. Hodges*, 84 So. 37 (La. 1920).

   b. **Insulting language:** ***Insulting words***, even if they are profane, will almost never be enough by themselves to give rise to an action for intentional infliction of emotional distress.

      i. **Two rationales:** Some cases refusing relief rely upon the theory that insults by themselves are never sufficiently "outrageous"; other cases reach the same result by holding that insults do not cause "severe emotional distress" in a person of ordinary sensitivity.

      ii. **Special notice:** But again, remember that if the defendant has special notice that the plaintiff is a person of unusual sensitivity, insults by themselves might be enough to establish liability.

E. **Directed at third person:** If D intentionally or recklessly directs extreme and outrageous conduct at ***someone other than P*** (call this third person X), D will nonetheless be liable for IIED to P, if either of two scenarios occurs. (The scenarios differ as to whether D and X were close relatives). In both cases, P will have to be ***physically present*** (and known to D to be present) when the conduct occurs.

1. **P and X are close relatives:** First, suppose P (the person who suffers the severe emotional distress) and X (the one at whom D's outrageous conduct is directed) are members of the ***same immediate family.*** P can recover for severe emotional distress, ***even if it does not result in bodily harm,*** as long as P was ***present***, and known by D to be present.

2. **P and X are not close relatives:** Now, consider the situation in which P (the person suffering the emotional distress) and X (the one at whom the conduct is directed) are ***not members of the same immediate family.*** Here, P can recover only if P satisfies ***two*** conditions:

   ❏ P was ***present*** at the time; *and*

   ❏ The emotional distress suffered by P ***led to bodily harm.***

Example 1 (close relatives): In front of P, D pulls a gun and threatens to shoot X to death. P, who is X's wife, suffers great emotional distress from watching the episode. P can recover from D for IIED, even if P never suffered bodily harm from the distress.

Example 2 (not close relatives): Same facts as Example 1, but now P and X are friends, not relatives. If P suffers great emotional distress without any bodily harm, she (probably) cannot recover from D for IIED. But if P's emotional distress leads to bodily harm (e.g., a miscarriage), she can recover.

F. **Constitutional limits on IIED awards:**   The *First Amendment of the U.S. Constitution* places some important *limits* on the right of a state to impose liability for IIED. Most importantly, if the conduct by the defendant that causes the distress is the delivery of a *message or communication*, a state's act of awarding damages against the defendant for IIED may well violate the defendant's First Amendment freedom of speech.

1. **P is a public figure; rule from defamation cases:** One scenario in which such a First Amendment violation can easily result from an IIED action arises where the plaintiff is a *"public figure."* We'll see when we come to the law of *defamation* (see *infra*, p. 465) that a public figure (essentially, a famous or newsworthy person) can recover only by showing that the defendant either *knew* that his speech about P was false or *recklessly disregarded* whether it was true or false; see *New York Times v. Sullivan* (*infra*, p. 477), the famous Supreme Court case that established this constitutional rule.

    a. **Same rule for IIED:**   The Supreme Court has extended the *Sullivan* principle to hold that, similarly, a plaintiff who is a public figure may succeed with a claim for *IIED* based on a communication only if P makes this same showing that the defendant either *knew that his speech was false or recklessly disregarded whether it was true.* *Hustler Magazine v. Falwell*, 485 U.S. 45 (1998).

        Example: *Hustler Magazine* satirizes religious leader Jerry Falwell as a drunken hypocrite who has sex with his mother. *Held,* Falwell cannot recover against *Hustler* for IIED unless he shows that *Hustler* made a false statement about him with knowledge of its falsity or with reckless disregard of its falsity. *Hustler Magazine v. Falwell, supra.*

2. **Statement on a matter of public concern:**   Another way a tort recovery for IIED can violate the defendant's First Amendment rights is if the alleged distress stems from the communicative impact of the defendant's speech, and the speech involves a matter of *public concern.* The main case on point is *Snyder v. Phelps*, 131 S.Ct. 1207 (2011), whose facts are set forth in the following Example.

    Example: P is the father of a Marine, Matthew Synder, recently killed in Iraq. The Ds are members of the Westboro Baptist Church, a church that thinks God punishes the U.S. military for tolerating homosexuality. During the course of Matthew's funeral in Maryland, the Ds carry picket signs nearby with messages like "God Hates the USA/Thank God for 9/11," "God hates fags," and "Thank God for Dead Soldiers." (The Ds apparently believe that Matthew was killed because of God's desire to punish the military for not rooting out homosexuality; they seem to have believed, though incorrectly, that Matthew was gay.) The picketing takes place entirely on a small plot of public land, 1,000 feet from the church where the funeral is being held. None of the Ds ever enter the church, or interfere with the funeral. P learns of the protest after it's over, when he sees footage of it on the local TV news. P brings a federal-court diversity action against the Ds for IIED, based on Maryland substantive tort law. The jury finds in his favor, based on its conclusion that the Ds' conduct was "outrageous," and was intended to cause P emotional distress. P is awarded a civil judgment for $4 million in combined compensatory and punitive damages. The Ds appeal on First Amendment grounds.

Held (by the U.S. Supreme Court), for the Ds. Allowing P to recover any damages at all would be a violation of the Ds' First Amendment right to speak freely on a matter of "public concern." That's because speech on matters of public concern "occupies the highest rung of the hierarchy of First Amendment values [making it] entitled to special protection." Speech involves a matter of public concern when it either (1) "can be fairly considered as relating to *any matter of political, social, or other concerns to the community,*" or (2) "is a *subject of legitimate news interest.*" The fact that the statement is *"inappropriate or controversial"* is *irrelevant* to the question of whether it involves a matter of public concern.

The messages on the picket signs here were clearly designed to speak on a broad public issue, and indeed, to reach as broad a public audience as possible. Since the speech was of public interest, Maryland could regulate it only in a "content neutral" manner. The substantive tort law of Maryland gave the jury the right to allow recovery for "outrageousness," a concept that is so subjective that the jury was *"unlikely to be neutral* with respect to the content of the speech." Since the jury likely reached its verdict without observing the required "content neutrality," enforcing the resulting damage award against the Ds violated their First Amendment rights. *Snyder v. Phelps, supra.*

G. Public utility and common carrier liability: *Common carriers* and *public utilities* are held to a *stricter standard* of conduct than the rest of the population, with respect to IIED. Whereas insults, no matter how gross, will almost never be held actionable when made by an ordinary person, a utility or carrier will be liable when its employee, during the course of his work, uses highly insulting language to a customer. Rest. 2d, §48.

1. **Hotels:** This rule applies not only to transportation companies, and to the water and power companies that are usually thought of as "public utilities," but also to *hotels*. See Rest. 2d, §48, Comment a. (But it has not generally been applied to ordinary businesses which hold their doors open to the public.)

2. **Rationale:** Originally, the rationale for this rule was the theory that the person who purchased a ticket or paid for services had a *contractual* right to respect. But later cases hold that a carrier or utility is liable for insults made to a *prospective* customer (e.g., one who is seeking to buy a ticket). Thus the liability does not really seem to be based on contract, but instead on a general duty on the part of utilities, common carriers, etc., to treat the public at large with courtesy. See Rest. 2d, §48, Comment a.

Quiz Yourself on

INTENTIONAL TORTS AGAINST THE PERSON *(Entire Chapter)*

1. Juliet is gazing at the stars from her balcony, exclaiming dreamily, "Romeo, Romeo, where art thou, Romeo?" A voice from below responds, "Here I am, you moron, give me a hand up." Juliet looks down and sees Romeo climbing up to the balcony. Before she has a chance to help, Romeo loses his footing, and falls, breaking his arm. Juliet races downstairs and tries to set the arm, even though Romeo tells her that she should wait for a doctor. Juliet makes the break much worse by moving the arm the wrong way. Has Juliet committed a battery even though she was only trying to help? _____

2. Calvin takes his mean-tempered pet tiger, Hobbes, out for a walk to terrorize the neighborhood. He sees little Susie Derkins playing across the street, and yells to her, as he walks toward her, "Hey, you stupid girl! Why don't you come over and say hello to Hobbes!" Calvin's intent is to frighten Susie, but nothing more. Susie stands, frozen with fear. Hobbes snarls at Susie, straining at his leash. The leash breaks, and Hobbes runs over and attacks Susie. Is Calvin liable to Susie for battery? _____

3. Speed Racer takes his squeeze, Trixie, on a wild spin through town in his hot racing car, the Mach 5. Paying more attention to Trixie than the road, Speed carelessly runs a stop sign and narrowly avoids hitting Chim-Chim, a pedestrian who is crossing the street at a crosswalk. Chim-Chim is terrified. Has Speed Racer committed an assault? _____

4. Zorro leaves his valuable cape with the cloakroom attendant at a restaurant. When he returns, the attendant wrongfully refuses to hand over the cape, and threatens to burn it. Zorro stays for two hours before he gets the cape back. Can he successfully claim false imprisonment? _____

5. Pocahontas runs Indian Trader, a novelty shop. It's closing time, and she takes a quick look around the store to see if there are any patrons left. She doesn't see any. In fact, however, John Smith is crouching down behind a counter, looking at the bottom shelf of a display of plastic tomahawks. Pocahontas leaves and locks up the shop, unwittingly locking Smith in the store. False imprisonment? _____

6. To play a joke on his friend Ethel Rosenberg, Max disguises himself as an FBI agent, comes to Ethel's door, and tells her that her husband Julius has just been arrested for spying and is about to be executed. In fact, Max knows that Julius has been out fishing all day, and that Ethel has been scared sick worrying about him. She screams and faints, and is extremely anguished for months afterwards. When she recovers, she sues Max for intentional infliction of emotional distress. Max defends on the grounds that Ethel's distress has not led to any physical illness or injury (a factually correct statement). Will Max's defense succeed? _____

7. Cleopatra and her boyfriend, Marc Antony, have a fight at his house. He storms out. Despondent, Cleopatra goes to his bathroom, gets in the tub, and slashes her wrists. Antony comes back, and finds her in a pool of blood. Shocked and horrified, he rushes her to the hospital. Cleopatra survives. Antony sues her for intentional infliction of emotional distress. She defends on grounds that she didn't intend to distress him. Who wins? _____

8. Jerry Joker, a notorious practitioner of pranks, wants to play one on his friend, Frank Friendly. Jerry takes a real gun and loads it with blanks. He puts a stocking cap over his head so that he cannot be identified. At eleven o'clock at night, he rings Frank's doorbell. When Frank answers, Jerry puts the gun two inches from Frank's temple, says "Greetings from the Godfather," and presses the trigger. Jerry intends that Frank merely be startled by the loud noise. Frank is not startled. However, a small piece of the casing

from the blank breaks loose, and causes a small scratch on Frank's face, which heals quickly. What tort(s), if any, has Jerry committed? _____

9. Timid owes money to Mobster, a loan shark. When the money is overdue, Mobster sends his henchman, Hulk, a large and scary-looking man, to try to collect the debt from Timid. Hulk goes to Timid's house, and while standing in the foyer, says to Timid, "If you don't have the money back by next Thursday, with the 2% per week vigorish, next Friday I'm gonna shoot out both your kneecaps. Think about what it'll be like for a young man like yourself to spend the next thirty, forty years on crutches." Tina, Timid's wife, watches this conversation, and Hulk knows she is watching. Both Timid and Tina become extremely terrified, and go into hiding, where Hulk has been unable to find them. What tort(s) have been committed by Hulk, and against whom? _____

―――――――――――――

Answers

1. Yes. The distinction here is between intent and <u>motive</u>. Intent is the desire to cause a certain immediate result; motive is <u>why</u> the tortfeasor chose to behave a certain way. A battery is the intentional infliction of a harmful or offensive bodily contact. The required intent is the intent to make a contact (or to create an apprehension of a contact). It is not necessary that the defendant desire to <u>harm</u> the plaintiff, as long as he intends the contact and the contact is in fact harmful or offensive. The harmful touching here was mis-setting the arm; Juliet voluntarily set the arm as she did, so she satisfies the intent element of battery. Her *motive* was to help, but that by itself won't relieve her of liability.

NOTE: Motive isn't an element of any intentional tort, but it *can* be relevant. It can aggravate, mitigate, or excuse a tort. For instance, acting with <u>malice</u> can justify "punitive" damages. Acting in self-defense can excuse a tort. But there are other motives that don't have an impact on liability for intentional torts. For instance, say Romeo kissed Juliet without her consent. The fact that his motive was to *compliment* her wouldn't mitigate his liability to her. Similarly, if Juliet pushed Romeo as a joke, the fact that she intended only a joke doesn't change the nature of the act; it's still a battery.

2. Yes. The "intent" requirement for battery is satisfied if D either (a) intended to cause a harmful or offensive contact; *or* (b) intended to cause in another person an <u>apprehension</u> of a harmful or offensive contact. Where D's conduct falls within (b), D will be liable for battery if the conduct causes (directly or indirectly) a harmful or offensive contact. Here, even though the attack itself was unintended, the harmful contact was the result of Calvin's intentional act (taking the mean tiger out and putting it near Susie to frighten her). Since Calvin "set the force [the tiger] in motion," he'll be liable for battery.

3. No. Assault is an "intentional" tort, and the intent required is that D either desired to cause a harmful-or-offensive contact, or desired to place P or another in apprehension of such a contact. Here, Speed Racer may have intended to drive (and even intended to drive extremely fast), but he didn't intend either to hit anyone or frighten anyone, so there's no assault.

RELATED ISSUE: Say that as Speed Racer approaches the stop sign, he sees Chim-Chim, and speeds up with the idea of scaring the bejesus out of Chim-Chim. Since Speed *intends* to scare Chim-Chim, there *would* be an assault.

RELATED ISSUE: Say that as Speed Racer approaches the stop sign, he sees Chim-Chim and, hoping to scare Chim-Chim, aims his car at him, intending to swerve away at the last moment. The car skids and hits Chim-Chim. Speed would be liable for <u>battery</u> (as well as assault) even though he didn't intend to hit Chim Chim, because he intended to *scare* him and he did in fact *touch* him, and that's enough for a battery.

4. **Yes.** A false imprisonment claim requires intentional confinement to a bounded area. The restraint needn't be physical; it can be accomplished by duress. Wrongfully keeping the plaintiff's valuable property is regarded as one type of duress that qualifies.

5. **No.** False imprisonment is the intentional confinement of someone to a bounded area. Here, Pocahontas didn't intend to confine Smith; she did so accidentally. Without intent, she can't be liable for false imprisonment. At best, she'd be liable for <u>negligence</u>.

   RELATED ISSUE: Say instead that Pocahontas is really paranoid about the threat of shoplifting, and falsely and unreasonably believes that Smith stuck one of the plastic tomahawks in his satchel without paying for it. She locks the doors to the shop (intending to confine Smith), and doesn't realize that another customer, John Rolfe, is in the store. If she's liable to Smith for false imprisonment, she'd be liable to Rolfe, as well — even though she didn't <u>intend</u> to confine him. That's because of "transferred intent." When someone intends to commit a tort against one person, but injury to another results, the actor's intent is said to be "transferred" from the intended victim to the actual one for purposes of establishing an intentional tort. Here, Pocahontas confined Rolfe as well as her intended victim, Smith, so her intent towards Smith will be "transferred" to Rolfe. (Note, by the way, that Pocahontas <u>didn't</u> have a right to detain Smith to investigate for shoplifting, because her belief that he stole something was <u>unreasonable</u>. Detention for shoplifting investigations is only permissible if the merchant's suspicion is <u>reasonable</u>. See *infra*, p. 77.)

6. **No.** So long as the defendant's conduct has produced serious emotional distress, the fact that that distress is not manifested by physical symptoms (e.g., sleeplessness, nausea, or ulcers) is not fatal to the claim. (Obviously, the presence of physical symptoms makes the distress easier to prove, but physical harm is not actually required.)

   On the other hand, the distress must be <u>severe</u>; mere unhappiness, humiliation, or a couple of sleepless nights won't suffice. In general, the more objectively outrageous the conduct, the less proof of great distress is required. Max's conduct here is so completely outrageous that Ethel probably won't need very detailed proof of her distress.

7. **Marc Antony, probably.** Even where conduct is not intentional, but only reckless — that is, the defendant proceeds with a conscious disregard of a high probability that emotional distress will result — most courts hold that a claim for IIED will lie. See, e.g., *Blakeley v. Shortal's Estate.*

   NOTE: A minority of courts hold that recklessness is not sufficient, and require intent (that is, <u>intending</u> emotional distress or <u>knowing</u> that it will result from the outrageous conduct).

8. **Battery.** Battery is the intentional infliction of a harmful or offensive bodily contact. Here, the contact by the piece of bullet casing against Frank's cheek was certainly a "harmful contact," even though it was not a very serious one. The nub of the question relates to *intent*. The intent to cause the harmful or offensive contact will of course qualify. But alternatively, the intent to commit an *assault* will meet the intent requirement for battery, if a harmful or offensive contact actually results. Jerry intended to commit an assault, since he intended to put Frank in apprehension of an immediate bodily contact (clearly he intended that when Frank heard the blank go off, Frank would believe that a bullet was simultaneously hitting him). This intent to commit assault will also supply the intent required for battery.

9. **Intentional infliction of emotional distress, against both Timid and Tina.** Hulk's conduct was "extreme and outrageous," and he intentionally caused severe emotional distress to Timid (indeed, that was the purpose of his visit). Since Hulk knew that Tina was present, he is also liable for Tina's distress,

since she is a member of Timid's immediate family. At least under the Restatement view, Hulk is liable even if Timid and Tina did not suffer bodily harm, so long as they suffered severe mental distress. See Rest. 2d, §46(1) and §46(2)(a). (Interestingly, Hulk's conduct does *not* constitute assault. The reason is that Hulk did not put Timid or Tina in apprehension of an ***imminent*** harmful or offensive contact — the threatened contact was not to take place until next week.)

Exam Tips on
INTENTIONAL TORTS AGAINST THE PERSON

For three of the torts covered in this chapter — battery, assault and false imprisonment — you shouldn't have much trouble spotting the tort on an essay exam. The fourth tort — intentional infliction of emotional distress — can be easier to miss. Since these are all "intentional" torts, it's not surprising that the most commonly-tested issues relate to intent. Here are the main things to look for:

☞ Look for a ***battery*** issue whenever you have what seems to be a ***"harmful or offensive contact."***

☞ If you spot a battery problem, introduce your discussion with the following definition: "Battery is the intentional infliction of a harmful or offensive bodily contact."

☞ ***"Intent"*** is probably the most frequently tested sub-issue in battery.

    ☞ One type of intent is "desire to ***cause contact***." That's a pretty obvious and spottable type of intent. (*Example:* D swings at P and hits him.)

    ☞ Another type of intent is "desire to ***frighten***." Remember that even if D didn't intend contact to occur (and just wanted to make P think it would) this "intent to cause assault" is enough for battery, if contact ensues. (*Example:* D swings at P, intending to just miss P's nose, but miscalculates and makes contact.)

    ☞ Finally, there's the ***"substantially certain"*** variety of intent — if D knows that a harmful or offensive contact is "substantially certain" to occur, the fact that D doesn't "desire" that contact is irrelevant. (*Example:* D is repossessing P's car, while P is on the running board — if D knows that P is substantially certain to fall off, that's enough for battery even though D doesn't desire that P fall.)]

      ☞ Remember that for "substantially certain," the test is ***"subjective"*** — the issue is what D really thought, not what he "should" have thought, so even if an ordinary person would have realized that a harmful or offensive contact with P was nearly certain, D is protected if he didn't realize this.

      ☞ Also, "substantially certain" doesn't mean *"very* likely" — it means "almost certain."

    ☞ ***"Transferred intent"*** is often tested — if D tries to make contact with (or frighten)

X, and contact ensues with P, that's enough for battery.

☞ Contact of a *"different sort"* than intended can suffice. (*Example:* D tries to ram his car into P's car, but P swerves into a fire hydrant — since P has come into contact with the fire hydrant, it doesn't matter that this contact is different from the "ramming" contact intended by D; D is still liable for battery.)

☞ The nature of *"contact"* is often tested:

☞ The contact can be either *"harmful"* or *"offensive."* An "offensive" contact means that as long as P's dignity is harmed, *no injury* is necessary. (*Example:* D pushes P while speaking nastily to him — even if there is no physical harm at all to P, there has been an "offensive" contact.)

☞ The contact can be by *indirect* means, i.e., not necessarily D's person touching P's person. (*Examples:* D throws an object at P, or hits P with his car, or lets loose an animal to attack P.) The use of *"mechanical devices"* to protect property is often tested, and will typically involve battery unless the property owner had a privilege. (*Example:* If D puts a security system in his car that administers an electric shock to anybody who tries to touch the car, that's a battery.)

☞ Whenever a person seems to *exceed a privilege*, look for a possible battery. (*Example 1:* D tries to defend himself against an attack from P, but uses excessive force — D is liable for battery. *Example 2:* D uses non-deadly force against one who he thinks is an intruder on D's property, but who is really the mail carrier. Again, that's battery.)

☞ In a *medical malpractice* or *sports* context, consider the possibility that there may be battery.

Example 1: D is a doctor who fails to get the patient's informed consent before performing a certain procedure; he may be found to have battered the patient.

Example 2: P and D play a contact sport (so P impliedly consents to contacts that are within the usual practices or rules of the sport). D hits or tackles P on purpose, and outside of the rules; D probably has committed battery, by going beyond the scope of what P impliedly consented to.

☛ Look for an *assault* issue whenever you have a person who is put in *"apprehension of an imminent harmful or offensive contact"* by another person.

☞ If you have an assault issue, work the following definition into the beginning of your discussion of the issue: "Assault is the intentional causing of an apprehension of harmful or offensive contact."

☞ Anytime you have identified a *battery*, also consider whether there was *first* an assault — there usually was. As long as P *saw was about to happen* there's an assault just before the battery. (*Example:* If D swings at P's jaw, there's an assault just before the impact, as long as P saw D's swing.)

☞ *Intent* issues are sometimes tested in assault:

☞ Remember that there are two distinct intents, either of which can suffice: (1) D intends to commit a battery, but fails; or (2) D intends to put P in apprehension, but not to really cause the contact (so that the intent is "attempt to frighten").

☞ ***"Transferred intent"*** operates in assault cases. Thus if D tries to frighten X (or to make a contact with X), and P thinks that he himself will be hit, then D has assaulted P even if D never intended any effect on P or even saw P.

☞ Remember the ***"words alone"*** rule — words alone can't constitute an assault. But typically, the facts will show at least some small ***overt act***, which will be enough. (*Example:* While saying words, D raises his fist, or steps menacingly towards P — that's enough of an overt act to prevent the "words alone" rule from applying, so that there is an assault.)

☞ The contact must (in P's mind) be ***"imminent."*** (*Example:* P's fear of being beaten tomorrow isn't enough.)

☞ The sub-issues relating to whether P has suffered the requisite ***"apprehension"*** are often tested in assault fact-patterns:

☞ Remember that P must be ***aware*** of the danger before it happens, and it's not enough that contact eventually does happen. Be on the lookout for fact patterns that tell you that something is happening ***behind P's back***, or happening just before P comes on the scene — these are typically a tip-off that P may not have seen the contact coming in advance, thus negating assault. (*Example:* D aims at P from behind, shoots and misses; P then realizes that he was almost hit — there's no assault.)

☞ Especially often tested: P's apprehension must be that there will be a contact with ***herself***, not a contact with a loved one. (*Example:* D shoots at X, while X's mother, P, looks on. If P feared only that the bullet would hit X, not that it would hit P herself, P has not been assaulted.)

☞ P must be apprehensive of a "harmful or offensive contact," but ***not*** necessarily apprehensive of a "battery." That is, if P thinks the contact is some ***natural event*** or some ***unintentional human event***, that can still be enough to satisfy the "apprehension" requirement. (*Example:* P sees a "tarantula" that he thinks is real, and that he thinks will bite him. It's really a fake put there by D to scare P. Even though P doesn't think a human was involved, and thus doesn't think that this is an attempt at "battery," it's still an assault because P has been put in apprehension of a harmful or offensive contact.)

☞ As with battery, consider the possibility of assault whenever someone exceeds the scope of a ***privilege***. (*Example:* D, a homeowner, shoots at P, who D knows is an unarmed burglar. D misses. Since D wasn't permitted to use deadly force here, he had no defense of self-defense or defense of land, so he has committed garden-variety assault.)

☛ Look for the tort of ***"false imprisonment" (FI)*** anytime you see one person ***intentionally confine*** another person ***within boundaries***.

☞ If you spot an FI issue, lead with the following definition: "False imprisonment occurs when the defendant intentionally confines the plaintiff. The plaintiff is 'confined' when his will to leave a place with fixed boundaries is overcome in a way that would overcome the will of an ordinary person in the plaintiff's position."

☞ Here are a couple of particular contexts that should clue you to the possibility of FI:

❑ P is detained in a *store* on suspicion of shoplifting;

❑ P is detained on a *bus* or *train* on suspicion of not having paid the fare;

❑ P is *arrested* (or otherwise detained by a law enforcement official), and placed in a patrol car, or handcuffed to a post or other fixed support.

☞ Remember that the essence of the tort is that P is kept *"in."* Keeping P *"out"* is not enough, even if the place P is being kept out of is a place where he has the right to be, and even if it's P's own *home*. (*Example:* Landlord keeps P out of P's apartment, by changing the lock. Even if Landlord's conduct is wrongful, there is no FI because P is not being kept "in.")

☞ The confinement must be *"enforced,"* i.e., it must be *against P's will*. (*Example:* If P is told to "stay here," but a reasonable person in P's position would believe that nothing bad would happen to P if P left, there's no enforced confinement and thus no FI.) However, remember that "enforcement" may happen even *without force*.

　☞ Thus *threats* of physical harm or prosecution may be enough to constitute "enforcement" of the confinement. Similarly, assertions of *legal authority* to detain P, together with a command that P remain, will usually be enough. (*Example:* "I'm a police officer; get in the patrol car and stay there," would be enough.) The test is always whether an ordinary person in the plaintiff's position would feel that he couldn't leave, or would suffer some harm if he tried to leave.

　☞ When a store detective says, "Wait here," to a suspected shoplifter, that's probably "enforcement," even though P realizes that the detective has no official status. On these facts, P can reasonably anticipate that the detective will use force to confine him, or will call the police.

　☞ If P is given a *"choice"* between staying or leaving, but there is some sacrifice to P's interests that will occur if P leaves, that's still FI if a reasonable person in P's position wouldn't leave. (*Example:* If P is stopped on suspicion of shoplifting, and forced to leave his wallet as "security" that he'll answer charges, that's probably a sufficiently unpleasant choice that if P stays, he has suffered FI. However, it's not FI if P takes the deal and leaves, even if it was wrongful for D to put P to this choice.)

☞ P is generally required to be *aware* of the confinement while it is going on. (*Example:* P is locked in a room while he is asleep; the room is unlocked before P wakes up. This is not FI.) One exception recognized by modern courts and the Restatement: if P suffers *harm* during the confinement, that's FI even if P was not aware of the confinement while it was occurring. (*Example:* P suffers an allergic reaction while locked in his hotel room asleep.)

　☞ Except for this modern exception to the requirement of awareness, FI will occur even if *no damage* to P occurs. (*Example:* If D is wrongfully and unreasonably suspected of shoplifting and detained in the store for one half hour, that's FI even if P does not suffer mental distress or any physical injury.)

☞ If your FI fact pattern involves detention of P as a suspected shoplifter, remember to check out the *"shopkeeper's privilege"* (discussed *infra*) — most courts let a merchant who reasonably suspects P of shoplifting to detain P for the time reasonably needed to conduct an investigation, and there is no FI even if it turns out that P is innocent.

☞ Remember that this tort requires **intent** to **confine**. Mere intent to do an act that has the unexpected effect of confining P is not enough, unless D knew with substantial certainty that confinement would result. (*Example:* While P is on an elevator, D stops the elevator to make repairs; if D did not realize that P was on the elevator, there's no FI because there was no intent to confine.)

☛ Look for the tort of **intentional infliction of emotional distress** (IIED) whenever one person does something to another that seems really **"outrageous,"** and the latter suffers great **anguish**.

   ☞ If you spot an IIED issue, introduce your discussion with the following definition: "The tort of intentional infliction of emotional distress occurs whenever the defendant intentionally or recklessly causes, by outrageous conduct, severe emotional or mental distress in another person."

   ☞ Here are some contexts where you should be on the lookout for an IIED issue:

   ❑ The facts mention that P is **"humiliated"** or "suffers great distress" (especially where the facts tell you that P seeks medical attention for the distress);

   ❑ The facts involve a business dispute where one party spies on another, follows the other, or otherwise **"harasses"** the other;

   ❑ D is a **debt collector** who wrongfully harasses P, or wrongfully repossesses P's goods (or does so rightfully but in an outrageous manner);

   ❑ D commits a major **crime** against P's person or against the person of P's close relative (e.g., D kidnaps P's child); or

   ❑ D plays a really nasty practical joke on P (but in this scenario, you should probably conclude that there is insufficient "outrageousness").

   ☞ P's **mental state** is often tested:

      ☞ Three types of mental state will suffice: (1) D **intended** to bring about the distress; (2) D knew with **substantial certainty** that the distress would result, even if D didn't desire it; or (3) D **recklessly disregarded** the possibility that distress would result. Note that "recklessly disregarded" applies for IIMD even though it does not for the other intentional torts (assault, battery and false imprisonment).

      ☞ Intent to do a particular **physical act** is not sufficient — the intent must relate to P's distress. (*Example:* Suppose D intends to repossess P's trailer home, and does so, but it turns out that P wasn't really in default. The mere fact that D intended the act of repossession is not enough to meet the "intent" requirement — unless D intended to cause P anguish, knew P's anguish was substantially certain to occur, or recklessly disregarded the possibility that P would be anguished, the requisite mental state is not present.)

   ☞ **"Outrageousness"** is the most frequently tested issue for IIED:

☞ *Mere insults* are generally *not* sufficiently outrageous.

☞ P's special *sensitivity* is normally irrelevant — outrageousness is measured by whether D's conduct would cause great distress to a person of ordinary sensitivity. (But if D *knew* of P's special sensitivity, then outrageousness is judged by reference to whether a person of P's sensitivity would have been seriously anguished.)

☞ Publication of a *true story* about P probably is not sufficiently outrageous (unless the publication would also constitute invasion of privacy, and perhaps not even then).

☞ Requirements for the type of *harm* suffered by P are also sometimes tested:

☞ At a minimum, P must seek *medical attention* for the distress. Thus if P is merely "outraged," or somewhat "embarrassed," that's not sufficient (even if the act itself is "outrageous").

☞ Some courts hold that the distress must be severe enough to cause *physical manifestations* (e.g., sleeplessness) in P. Therefore, if there are no physical manifestations, note that this poses an issue (but also say that most modern courts, and the Restatement, do not require physical harm if P has suffered anguish, has sought medical attention, and the act was "outrageous).

☞ Be on the lookout for a situation in which the way D commits the IIED is by a *communication* as to a *"matter of public concern."* Here, you should write that the *First Amendment* prevents the state from allowing P to recover unless the jury's determination that the conduct was "outrageous" was made in a strictly "content-neutral" way (something that is almost impossible for a jury to do).

> *Example:* D pickets P's son funeral, with signs saying "God killed P because he was gay, and God punishes gays." When the jury in P's IIED action considers whether D's conduct was "outrageous," the jury must make this decision without considering the "message" communicated by D, since the message is on a topic of "public concern." Since it will be almost impossible for a jury to find outrageousness without considering the message's content, any verdict in P's favor will almost certainly violate D's First Amendment rights. [Cite to *Snyder v. Phelps*, on similar facts.]

CHAPTER 3

INTENTIONAL INTERFERENCE WITH PROPERTY

ChapterScope

In this chapter, we consider various kinds of intentional interferences with plaintiff's goods and land. We are concerned primarily with three torts: (1) *trespass to land*; (2) *trespass to chattels* (i.e., goods); and (3) *conversion* (the taking of goods). Here are the main concepts in this chapter:

- **Trespass to land:** *Trespass to land* occurs when the defendant *enters the plaintiff's land*, or causes another person or an object to enter the plaintiff's land.

  - ❏ **Intentional trespass:** As a matter of semantics, the phrase "trespass to land" usually covers only *intentional* entry on another's land. (Negligent entry is also a tort, but it is usually classified as an aspect of the general tort of negligence, and is not covered in this chapter.)

- **Trespass to chattels:** The tort of *"trespass to chattels"* occurs when the defendant *intentionally interferes* with the plaintiff's *use or possession* of a *"chattel"* (i.e., a piece of personal property, such as a car or a diamond ring).

  - ❏ **Loss of possession:** The tort occurs when D interferes with the owner's *"possession"* of the good, even if it is a brief interference (e.g., an unauthorized "borrowing" of the item, such as taking a neighbor's lawnmower for 10 minutes, or taking his car for a two-block joy ride).

- **Conversion:** The tort of *conversion* occurs when D so *substantially interferes* with P's possession or ownership of property that it is fair to require D to pay the property's *full value*.

  - ❏ **Dividing line:** So the dividing line between trespass to chattels and conversion is the line between a not-so-serious interference with possession (trespass to chattels) and a serious interference with possession, or complete destruction, of the item (conversion).

I. TRESPASS TO LAND

A. Definition: A trespass to land can occur when the defendant enters the plaintiff's land, or causes another person or an object to enter the plaintiff's land.

  1. Wrongfully remaining: Alternatively, it can occur if the defendant remains on the plaintiff's land without the right to be there, even if she initially entered rightfully.

  2. Failure to remove: Finally, trespass can occur if the defendant fails to remove an object from the plaintiff's land which she is under a duty to remove.

B. Intentional trespass: In this chapter, we are concerned only about *intentional* forms of trespass; the requisite intent is discussed shortly below.

  1. History of trespass: Under English common law, prior to the 19th century, liability for trespass to land was *strict*. That is, the plaintiff did not have to show that the defendant's entry was either intentional or negligent. For instance, if the defendant cut a tree on her own property, without negligence, and the tree accidentally fell onto the plaintiff's property, the defendant was liable.

    a. Rationale: This strict liability for trespass to land was an historical anomaly, probably arising from the fact that the action was usually used to adjudicate title disputes. See P&K, pp. 67-68.

    b. Involuntary acts not included: But even the strict liability theory for trespass required that the defendant's act be *voluntary*. Thus if the defendant was forcibly carried onto the plaintiff's land by third persons, she did not commit trespass, although it would have been a trespass if she had walked onto the land thinking it was her own. See *Smith v. Stone*, 82 Eng. Rep. 533 (K.B. 1647), *infra*, p. 42.

2. Intent: Today, virtually all American jurisdictions have *rejected strict liability* for trespass except where the defendant has been carrying out some "abnormally dangerous activity." Thus the Second Restatement, §166, provides that where entry on land is neither intentional nor negligent, the defendant is liable only if the entry occurred pursuant to his carrying out of an "abnormally dangerous activity."

    Example: D is walking along a sidewalk bordering P's land. Accidentally, and non-negligently, he slips, and falls against and breaks a plate glass window in a store that P has built on the land. D is not liable for trespass (although he probably would have been in 16th century England). See Rest. 2d, §166, Illustr. 1.

    a. Requisite intent: In this chapter, we examine only the tort of intentional trespass; negligent trespass follows the rules described in the material on negligence generally (*infra*, p. 95); strict liability from abnormally dangerous activity is treated *infra*, p. 334.

C. Kind of intent required: As with the other intentional torts, the defendant can have the requisite intent even though he does not intend any *harm* to the plaintiff's property interest.

    Example: D, a nine-year-old boy, is a member of the P Swim Club. While swimming in the pool one day, D raises a metal cover over a drain. Thinking that there is no suction at the time, he inserts a tennis ball into the drain pipe, then replaces the cover. When he returns to get the ball, it is gone. The ball enters a critical part of the pipe and causes the pool not to drain properly, which in turn forces P to close and to make repairs. P sues D for trespass.

    Held, D had the requisite intent if he intended to place the ball in the pipe, regardless of whether he intended to cause any harm, or even knew that harm might occur. The question is whether D "possessed the capability to perform the physical act intentionally without regard to knowledge of possible injurious consequences. . . . " *Cleveland Park Club v. Perry*, 165 A.2d 485 (D.C. App. 1960).

1. Effect of mistake: If the defendant has the intent to commit a physical contact with the plaintiff's land, he will have the requisite intent for trespass even if his decision to make the contact is the result of a *mistake*. Thus D's mistake about *legal title* or *consent* won't block liability.

a. **Reasonableness irrelevant:** This principle that "mistake is no defense to trespass" is true even if the mistake is *reasonable* (assuming the mistake wasn't induced by anything P did or said).

Example: D, an absentee owner, visits his property, which is a farm. He drives a tractor on what he thinks is his parcel, but unbeknownst to him (and without negligence on his part), he drives over what is really P's land. This is trespass, despite D's reasonable ignorance of the fact that the land he is entering belongs to someone other than D.

i. **Induced by P's conduct:** However, if the defendant's mistaken belief is induced by the plaintiff's conduct, this may amount to an implied consent by the plaintiff. See the discussion of consent, *infra*, p. 58. See Rest. 2d, §§163, 164.

D. **Damages:** At common law, the plaintiff who could show that a trespass had occurred was entitled to receive *nominal damages* where no actual harm occurred, whether the trespass was intentional, negligent or accidental.

Example: D enters P's land with a surveyor and chain carriers. They survey the land, and D claims it as his own, but does not mark any trees, cut any bushes, or cause any other physical harm to the property.

Held, P may recover against D for the trespass, even though there was no actual harm. He is entitled to nominal damages. "From every . . . entry against the will of the possessor, the law infers some damage; if nothing more, the treading down the grass or herbage, or as here, the shrubbery." *Dougherty v. Stepp*, 18 N.C. 371 (1835).

1. **Modern view:** Today, only intentional trespass, the variety of trespass being discussed in this chapter, entitles the plaintiff to nominal damages where no harm has occurred. See Rest. 2d, §163. Thus the *Dougherty* case, *supra*, would probably turn out the same way today, since the trespass there was intentional despite D's mistake (he intended to enter the land). But if D had been on his own land, and had negligently or accidently fallen onto P's land, P would today not recover nominal damages, and could recover only for harm she could actually prove.

E. **Scope of recovery:** Once trespass is established, the defendant is liable for virtually *all consequences* of the trespass, no matter how and unpredictable. (This rule apparently still applies to cases of negligent and accidental trespass, as well as intentional trespass.)

1. **Far-reaching results:** Thus in the *Cleveland Park* case, *supra*, even if D reasonably believed that the ball would not be sucked into the pipe, and even if he had no reason to foresee that extensive repairs would be necessary, he is still fully liable for these repairs.

2. **Personal injury and mental distress:** If *personal injury* to the possessor of the property occurs as a result of the trespass, or even injury to the possessor's family, the trespasser will be liable in full for this injury, regardless of how unpredictable it was. Some courts have even awarded the possessor and her family damages for mental distress suffered as a result of the trespass where there was no physical harm. See P&K, pp. 76-77.

F. **Only possessor has claim:** Only the *possessor* of the property has the right to bring an action in trespass. Thus if the owner of an apartment building has rented it to X, and D trespasses in the building, only X, not the owner, can bring a trespass action. (The owner may sue on a modified trespass action for the injury to her right of reversion, but she will have to show actual permanent harm affecting her interest, and cannot recover nominal damages as in a normal trespass action.) See P&K, pp. 77-78.

1. **Possessor who is not owner:** The corollary of this rule is that one who is in possession of property that she does **not own** may nonetheless sue in trespass. Thus a tenant may sue, although she can recover damages only for her interest up to the end of her lease term.

2. **Vacant land:** If the land is unoccupied, the owner may sue in trespass, under the legal fiction that she is in "constructive possession" of the property.

3. **Wrongful possessor:** Even if the plaintiff's possession is **wrongful** because someone else owns the property, he can sue any third person who enters it.

    a. **Suit by rightful owner:** And once the wrongful possessor has held the property for an appreciable period of time, and has a "colorable" (i.e., not completely absurd) claim of ownership, the rightful owner cannot sue **him** in trespass. Instead, the owner must bring the common law action of ejectment, or its statutory equivalent. P&K, p. 78.

G. **Indirect invasions:** If the defendant causes a **tangible object** to enter the plaintiff's land, there is a trespass even though the defendant himself has not made the entry. See p. 432, *infra*.

> **Example:** D intentionally throws a pail of water against P's house, but D himself never steps on P's land. D has nonetheless committed trespass. See Rest. 2d, §158, Illustr. 3.

1. **Entry substantially certain:** It is also a trespass if the defendant does not intend to cause the entry of the object, but knows that it is substantially certain to occur. "Thus one who so piles sand close to his boundary that by force of gravity alone it slides down onto his neighbor's land . . . becomes a trespasser on the other's land." Rest. 2d, §158, Comment i.

2. **Causing entry to third person:** The defendant also trespasses if he causes a **person** to enter the land. Thus in *Smith v. Stone, supra*, p. 40, the court noted that the people who had carried the defendant onto the plaintiff's land themselves committed trespass.

3. **Blasting damage:** Under English common law, trespass existed only if the defendant **directly** caused the entry on the plaintiff's property. Thus if the defendant set off a blast that caused concussion or vibrations on the plaintiff's property, and these caused damages, the plaintiff could not sue in trespass.

    a. **Action on the case:** Instead, the victim of such an indirect entry had to bring an action known as **"trespass on the case."** The essence of this action was that the defendant had indirectly invaded the plaintiff's interest in her property. See *supra*, p. 3. There were some important differences between an action in pure trespass, and an action in trespass on the case. For one thing, in an action "on the case," the plaintiff had to show either intention, negligence, or abnormally dangerous activity, and could not take advantage of strict trespass liability. Also, she had to prove that there was actual harm, and could not recover nominal damages.

b. **Modern view:** Most modern courts reject the distinction between direct and indirect injury. They therefore hold that if the defendant sets off a blast that causes concussion or vibrations, the plaintiff may recover in trespass.

4. **Particles and gasses:** By the same token, most courts now hold that a defendant who has caused *particles*, however fine, or *gasses*, to enter the plaintiff's property, has committed trespass. The court's decision to apply a trespass rather than non-trespassory theory often has important consequences on the applicable *statute of limitations*, as shown by the following example.

> **Example:** D runs an aluminum reducing plant, which causes certain gasses and particles to travel through the air and to settle on P's farm, making it unfit for raising livestock. P sues in trespass for the damage to his land and to his cattle. D contends that at most, a nuisance, not a trespass, occurred.
>
> *Held*, D has committed trespass. "[W]e may define trespass as any intrusion which invades the possessor's protected interest in exclusive possession, whether that intrusion is by visible or invisible pieces of matter or by energy which can be measured only by the mathematical language of the physicist." Therefore, the local six-year statute of limitations for trespass, not the two-year statute applicable to nuisance, applies, and plaintiff can recover for all damages suffered during the six years prior to commencement of the suit. *Martin v. Reynolds Metals Co.*, 342 P.2d 790 (Or. 1959).

H. **Air space:** At common law, it was said that *"cujus est solum ejus est usque ad coelum"* — the one who owns the soil owns all the way to heaven. In other words, the property owner owned the *air space* above the land, and she could recover in trespass against someone who put telephone wires over it, fired shots across it, or otherwise entered it.

> **Example:** D hunts ducks by standing on X's land and shooting over P's land. No bullets land on P's land.
>
> *Held*, for P. D, by firing over P's land, interfered with the "quiet, undisturbed, peaceful enjoyment of the plaintiff," and committed a trespass to the land. *Herrin v. Sutherland*, 241 P. 328 (Mont. 1925).

1. **Air travel:** This theory was obviously impractical once the age of general aviation began. Private owners clearly could not be given the right to block the passage of airplanes, no matter how high above their land. Yet most courts felt that the property owner did have a right not to have planes fly overhead at extremely low altitudes, say 50 feet. In trying to set rules for just how far up the property owner's right to exclusive use of his air space goes, the courts have adopted several different solutions. The confused state of the law can be summarized as follows:

a. **Federal law pre-empts:** The U.S. Supreme Court has held that federal statutes and C.A.B. regulations make the air space above the C.A.B.-prescribed minimum flight altitudes a federal and public domain. Therefore, it seems that federal law has pre-empted this area, and that the state courts may *not award trespass damages* for any flight occurring above these minimum altitudes. See P&K, p. 81, fn. 38.

b. **Nuisance theory:** Even for flights occurring below federally prescribed minimum altitudes, more and more courts are rejecting traditional trespass ideas. Instead, they are permitting the landowner to recover only when she can show *actual* harm from the flights. To do this, the landowner will usually attempt to show that her *use* of the property has been curtailed (e.g., by the noise, vibrations, pollution, etc.) The basis for recovery in these cases is thus either implicitly or explicitly a *nuisance* theory, rather than a traditional trespass theory based on strict liability. See the discussion of nuisance *infra*, p. 429.

  c. Restatement view: The Second Restatement adopts what might be called an "implicit nuisance" approach to plane flights. §159(2) allows the plaintiff to recover in trespass for aircraft overflight only if the plane "enters into the *immediate reaches* of the airspace next to the land," *and* the flight "interferes substantially with the [plaintiff's] *use and enjoyment* of his land."

I. Refusal to leave as trespass: Even if the defendant had permission to enter the plaintiff's land, it will be a trespass if he refuses to *leave* when the permission is terminated. Similarly, if the defendant is authorized to put an object on the plaintiff's land, but then refuses or neglects to remove it when he is supposed to, there will be a trespass. See Rest. 2d, §160.

  Example: P gives the D Board of Road Commissioners permission to put a snow fence on P's property parallel to a road running past P's farm. D agrees that at the end of the winter, the fence will be removed. At the end of the winter, D removes the fence, but leaves behind an anchor post. P's husband, driving a mowing machine, hits the post, is thrown to the ground, and dies.

  Held, D committed a trespass by not removing the anchor post, and is liable to P for the damages she sustained by loss of her husband. *Rogers v. Board of Road Commissioners*, 30 N.W.2d 358 (Mich. 1948).

  Note: Observe that in the above example, the defendant was found to have trespassed even in the absence of a showing that its failure to remove the post had been either intentional or negligent. Apparently this rule of "strict liability" for failure to remove objects is limited to cases where there is actual harm. See PW&S, p. 73, n. 5.

J. Continuing trespass: Where a trespass is caused by the entry of an object on the land, it is often the case that the trespass is a *continuing* one. That is, as long as the object is present on the land, the landowner's harm continues. When this occurs, and the property owner wants to sue, must she sue at one time for all past damages and all *future ones* that she might sustain if the trespass continues? Or may she bring an action for only those damages she has suffered thus far, and then bring a series of later actions for harm after the first suit?

  1. Conflicting law: The law on this question is confused and often conflicting.

    a. New trespass to remove: Where the trespass is such that the defendant would have to commit a new trespass on the plaintiff's land to remove it, the courts usually hold that a single action for all past and future damages must be brought, on the ground that the defendant may not commit a second trespass to eliminate the first one, and that therefore the trespass should be viewed as permanent. This will be true, for instance, if the defendant built a house on the plaintiff's land.

b. Other cases: But if the trespass is indirect (e.g., sewage from the defendant's plant flows onto the plaintiff's land), courts have required a single suit only where the condition seems fairly permanent and unlikely to be abated. See P&K, p. 84.

II. TRESPASS TO CHATTELS

A. Torts against personal property generally: The owner of a chattel (i.e., personal property, as opposed to real estate) may have several possible tort actions against one who interferes with his use or possession of that chattel.

1. **Negligence:** If the interference is negligent, not intentional, the plaintiff's claim would be an ordinary negligence action, and will follow the rules for such actions discussed *infra*, p. 95.

2. **Intentional:** If the interference is intentional, the action will be for either ***trespass to chattels*** or ***conversion***, depending on the severity of the interference. If the interference is so great that it is fair to require the defendant to pay the full value of the chattel (regardless of whether it could be returned in some form to the plaintiff), the action will be for conversion; if the interference is less substantial, the action will be for trespass to chattels.

B. Definition: Any ***intentional interference*** with a person's ***use or possession of the chattel*** is a trespass to chattel. Thus if the defendant takes the chattel out of the plaintiff's possession (e.g., D takes P's car for a joy ride), or harms the chattel (e.g., D intentionally puts a dent in P's car), a trespass to chattel has occurred.

C. Intent: Trespass to chattel is, today, an exclusively intentional tort. (Negligent interference with personal property is treated according to the general rules of negligence.) However, as in the case of trespass to land, it is unnecessary that the defendant had intended to cause harm to the plaintiff's interest in his property. She must merely intend to do an act which turns out to constitute an interference.

> **Example:** D picks up P's book in the library, thinking it is her own. She underlines a few pages, then discovers the error, and returns the book. Although D's mistake was completely innocent, she nonetheless intended the physical act of picking up the book and marking it, and she is liable for trespass to chattels.

D. Must be actual damages: Most courts hold that a trespass to chattels occurs only where the plaintiff can prove some ***actual harm***. In other words, in contrast to the rule for trespass to land, the plaintiff is not entitled to nominal damages where he merely shows that the defendant has touched his property.

> **Example:** P, a four-year-old girl, climbs on the back of Toby, a dog owned by D. P pulls the dog's ears, and the dog snaps at her nose. P sues for damages for the bite. D contends that under local law, P may not recover if P was a trespasser, and that P was in fact committing a trespass to chattels at the time she was bitten.
>
> *Held*, P can recover. She did not commit trespass to chattels, because there was no showing by D that the dog was harmed in any way. *Glidden v. Szybiak*, 63 A.2d 233 (N.H. 1949).

1. **Second Restatement's explanation:** The Second Restatement, §218, Comment e, explains the requirement of actual harm in the case of trespass to chattels as follows: "The interest of a possessor of a chattel in its inviolability, unlike the similar interest of a possessor of land, is not given legal protection by an action for nominal damages for harmless intermedlings with the chattel. . . . Sufficient legal protection of the possessor's interest in the mere inviolability of his chattel is afforded by his privilege to use reasonable force to protect his possession against even harmless interference."

    a. **Criticism:** However, if it is true that the right to use reasonable force to protect against harmless interference is sufficient in the case of trespass to chattels, it is hard to see why this right is not also sufficient to protect against harmless trespasses to land. The requirement of actual harm in one case but not the other is probably due more to the differences in the historical development of the two torts than to any policy reasons.

2. **Loss of possession:** If the trespass to chattels is such that the plaintiff *loses possession* of the chattel for any time, no matter how brief, this loss of possession will be deemed to be an "actual harm," and recovery will be allowed. Some value will then be placed on the temporary loss of possession, and the result will be almost the same as if nominal damages had been allowed. See P&K, p. 87. See also Rest. 2d, §218, Comment i.

3. **Contact not causing dispossession:** On the other hand, where D merely *makes contact* with the chattel, *without taking the chattel out of P's possession,* D is liable only where some *harm* to the chattel, or some interference with P's *use and enjoyment* of the chattel, occurs.

    Example: D, a child, climbs on P's large dog, and pulls its ears. No harm to the dog results. D has not committed a trespass to chattels, because D neither took the dog out of P's possession, nor harmed the dog or P's "use and enjoyment" of the dog. Rest. 2d, §218, Comm. e and Illustr. 2.

4. **Mistake as to ownership:** As with trespass, the required intent *does not encompass details about ownership*. So if D intends to take possession of an object, and does take possession of it, the fact that D *mistakenly believes the object is his own* is *no defense.* That's true even if the mistake is a *reasonable* one.

    Example: D enters a restaurant for lunch and hangs her coat on the coat rack. When she is leaving, she removes from the rack a coat which looks like hers, but which actually belongs to P. (At the time she took it, D believed it to be her own coat.) When D has driven two miles from the restaurant, she realizes that the coat is not hers. D turns around and drives back to the restaurant, where she hands it to P, who has been angrily trying to figure out where her coat has gone.

    D committed trespass to chattels as soon as she took possession of P's coat. The fact that D honestly and/or reasonably thought the coat was her own does not negate the tort, or constitute an affirmative defense.

5. **Electronic trespass on computer:** Suppose D *interacts with P's computer* without permission; when does D's conduct rise to the level of trespass to chattels? The answer generally depends on the *type of harm* that occurs.

a. **No harm to computer or data:** Where D's conduct *does not harm P's computer or the data on it,* courts have generally held that trespass to chattels does *not* occur even though D's interaction with P's computer was uninvited. And the fact that P's *employees* may have been bothered by the intrusion does not change this result, according to most courts: there must be some harm, or at least serious possibility of harm, *to the data or the computer itself* (the "chattel"), for trespass to chattel to occur.

Example: D, a former employee of P (Intel Corp.) sends, on six occasions, e-mails to thousands of P's employees complaining of P's employment practices. On one occasion, the e-mail goes to 35,000 employees. No harm occurs to P's computer systems, but P's employees allegedly suffer a loss of productivity by having to read and delete D's messages. D does not breach any computer security imposed by P, and offers to remove from his future e-mails any recipient who so requests. P sues for an injunction against further e-mails, contending that they constitute trespass to P's chattels.

Held, for D. Trespass to chattels can occur only where there is harm to the personal property in question, or to the possessor's interest in personal property. Here, P is not claiming any injury to its personal property (i.e., to the computers or the data on them), so the tort cannot occur. As to the claim by some computer industry groups as amici that the rules of trespass to real property should be applied to computers (so that any unauthorized intrusion, however harmless, is a trespass), such a rule requiring advance permission would substantially reduce the freedom of electronic communication, and would diminish the social value of networks. *Intel Corporation v. Hamidi*, 71 P.3d 296 (Cal. 2003).

b. **Harm to computer or data:** On the other hand, if the defendant's intrusion *causes harm* to the plaintiff's computer system or data — or even poses a real *risk* of such harm — then that *will* satisfy the requirements for a trespass-to-chattels claim.

Example: P alleges that the Ds tricked P into downloading "spyware" and "adware" software onto P's computer. P claims that this software (1) causes advertising "pop-ups" to appear, and (2) tracks P's computing activities, thereby slowing down P's system and possibly harming P's files. *Held,* the Ds are not entitled to have P's claim of trespass to chattels dismissed, because P has alleged facts which, if proven, would satisfy the harm-to-personal-property requirement for that tort. *Sotelo v. DirectRevenue, LLC*, 384 F.Supp.2d 1219 (N.D. Ill. 2005).

c. **Must be "property":** Keep in mind that a recovery for trespass to chattels based on D's misuse of P's computer files requires that P's interest in these files constitutes *"property"* under the law of trespass to chattels (and the law of conversion, *infra*, p. 48). Courts are split about whether various types of intangibles, including computer data, count as property for these purposes. The issue is discussed further *infra*, p. 49.

E. **Return of chattel:** If the trespasser is still in possession of the chattel at the time suit is brought, she has the right to tender the goods to the plaintiff, in mitigation of the latter's damages. In other words, title is treated as never having left the plaintiff. This is in distinction to the tort of conversion, discussed below, as a result of which title is deemed transferred from plaintiff to defendant, and the defendant is required to pay the full value of the property.

F. Protects possessory interest: Any person in *possession* of the chattel may sue for trespass to chattels, even if he is not the rightful owner. In other words, the defendant is not permitted to use the defense of *"jus tertii,"* i.e., that the plaintiff has no right to sue because some third person really owns the property. The reason for this is that "The maintenance of decent order requires that peaceable possession be protected against wrongdoers with no rights at all." P&K, p. 87. See also Rest. 2d, §219.

1. **Colorable claim:** However, the plaintiff in possession must have at least a "colorable" claim to the property, i.e., a claim that is not completely absurd. Thus Prosser suggests that a thief would not be allowed to recover. P&K, p. 87, fn. 24.

2. **Non-possessor:** A person who *owns* goods but who is *not in possession* of them at the time of the trespass may also sue. This is true whether he is entitled to the goods immediately upon request (e.g., a bailor), or only to possession at some future time (e.g, a lessor). However, in the latter case the owner may sue only for the damages done to his future possessory interest.

> **Example:** Ace Car Leasing leases a car for a two-year period to Lessee. D takes the car for a one-day joy ride, and then returns it unharmed. Lessee could sue for the damage to his possessory interest, even though he is not the owner of the car. Ace, however, could sue only for the damage to its future possessory interest, which in this case would probably be nothing.

III. CONVERSION

A. Introduction: The tort of conversion occurs when the defendant *so substantially interferes* with the plaintiff's possession or ownership of property that it is fair to *require the defendant to pay the property's full value.* See Rest. 2d §222A.

1. **Dividing line:** The dividing line between interferences which are so serious as to constitute conversion and those which are merely enough to constitute trespass to chattels (for which only actual damages must be paid, and as to which there is no "forced sale" to the defendant) is thus a matter of degree. Most of our discussion of conversion will consist of describing where the courts have drawn this dividing line.

B. Intent: As with trespass to land and trespass to chattels, conversion is exclusively an intentional tort, but the requisite intent need not include a desire to harm the plaintiff's possessory interest. An innocent mistake by the defendant as to the ownership of goods, for instance, will not negate the existence of the required intent. (However, innocent intentions may be a factor in determining whether the interference with the plaintiff's rights is so severe as to constitute conversion; this factor is discussed below.) See Rest. 2d, §244.

> **Example:** D, an auctioneer, receives a valuable painting from X, which he reasonably believes X owns. D sells the painting on behalf of X, but it turns out to have been owned by P. D is liable to P for conversion, notwithstanding his honest and reasonable mistake. See Rest. 2d, §244, Illustr. 4.

1. **Negligence:**   But if the defendant's exercise of dominion or control of the plaintiff's property is merely negligent, not intentional, there will be no conversion. Instead, the plaintiff must sue for the tort of negligence.

    Example: P deposits bonds in D Bank as collateral for a loan from the latter. D Bank negligently misplaces the bonds, and is unable to return them to P when the loan is paid off. D has not committed conversion either by losing the bonds or by failing to return them since it did not intentionally do either. See Rest. 2d, §244, Illustr. 1.

C. **What can be converted:** The tort of conversion, like the tort of trespass to chattels, originated as a way to protect *tangible property* only. In recent decades, courts have struggled with whether to allow recovery for trespass or conversion where the "thing" that the defendant has interfered with is an *intangible.*

1. **Document closely associated with right:** Where the "property" in question is a *document* that *embodies* or is highly important to some underlying *ownership right* of the plaintiff, courts will generally hold that the document *can* be the subject of conversion or trespass to chattels.

    Examples: So, for example if D steals from P a stock certificate, a savings account bank book, or a physical insurance policy, each of these documents is likely to be found to be sufficiently tangible — and sufficiently linked to a property right — that P will be deemed to have met the requirement that what was taken be "property." See P&K, p. 91

    a. **Computer files:** The biggest issues arise in the case of *computer files*. Suppose D steals or interferes with files on P's computer. Does the intangible nature of the files prevent them from being the sort of property that can be converted or trespassed upon? In general, the trend has been sharply in favor of answering *no* — the files, although intangible, are usually found to be the sort of property that *can* be converted or trespassed upon.

D. **Character of defendant's act:**   The courts consider several factors in determining whether the defendant's interference with the plaintiff's property is sufficiently great so as to justify requiring the defendant to pay the entire value of it. The Second Restatement lists these factors, among others:

1. **Dominion:**   The extent and duration of the defendant's exercise of *"dominion"* or *"control"*;

2. **Good faith:**   The defendant's *good faith*;

3. **Harm:**   The *harm* done to the property; and

4. **Inconvenience:**   The *inconvenience* and *expense* caused to the plaintiff. See Rest. 2d, §222A.

    a. **Blending of factors:**   In many cases, some of these factors will indicate that conversion should be found, but others will indicate the contrary. The issue is inevitably a relatively imprecise one, but the following examples, taken from the Second Restatement, will indicate how the factors might be reconciled.

Example 1: D, leaving a restaurant, mistakenly picks up P's hat from the coat rack, thinking it is his own. When he gets to the sidewalk, D puts on the hat, realizes that it is not his own, and returns it to the rack. This is not a conversion, because no harm is done, the interference with P's right of control is limited, and D acted in good faith. Rest. 2d, §222A, Illustr. 1.

Example 2: Same facts as above, except that D keeps the hat for three months before discovering his mistake and returning the hat. This is a conversion, due to substantial interference with P's use of his property; this is so despite D's complete good faith. *Ibid*, Illustr. 2.

Example 3: Same as above, except that as D gets to the sidewalk, the hat is blown off his head, and disappears through an open manhole. This is conversion, since P's property interest is completely destroyed, even though D acted in good faith, would otherwise have discovered and returned the hat immediately, and was not negligent in permitting it to be blown away. *Ibid*, Illustr. 3.

Example 4: Same as above, except that D takes P's hat knowingly, intending to steal it. As he leaves the restaurant, he sees a police officer, and immediately returns the hat. This is a conversion, notwithstanding the short interference, because of D's bad faith. *Ibid*, Illustr. 4.

E. **Kinds of interference:** The following are a number of ways in which a conversion may be committed:

1. **Acquiring possession:** The defendant may take ***possession*** of the property from the plaintiff. A claim for conversion thus lies against a ***thief***, or a sheriff who wrongfully levies upon property, or a con artist who obtains goods by ***fraud*** (e.g., by paying with a worthless check.)

   a. **Bona fide purchaser:** Most courts hold that a ***bona fide purchaser of stolen goods*** is a converter, ***even if there is no way he could have known that they were stolen***. However, the courts of New York and a few other states hold that such a good faith purchaser is not liable for conversion if he is willing to give back the goods to the rightful owner upon demand.

   b. **Transfer of goods procured by fraud:** We have seen that one who obtains goods from the plaintiff by fraud is a converter. What is the status of a *bona fide* purchaser of these goods from the defrauder? Because the owner's right to get back the goods is based upon the equitable doctrine of rescission, and because a *bona fide* purchase always cuts off all equitable rights, the purchaser is ***not a converter*** in this situation. P&K, *ibid.*

   c. **Bailment of converted goods:** One who takes goods as a ***bailee***, for purposes of storing or transporting them, is not a converter if the goods turn out to have been stolen or lost. However, since this rule exists only to make it possible to run a parking garage, warehouse, or transportation service, it applies only where the bailee does ***not have knowledge***, at the time she accepts the goods, that someone else is entitled to them. P&K, p. 95.

2. **Removal of goods:** One who *removes goods* from one place to another may be liable for conversion, if the removal constitutes a sufficiently serious interference with the plaintiff's right to possession and control. However, this is a question of degree.

3. **Withholding goods:** The defendant may also commit conversion by *refusing to return goods* to their owner. As with the other kinds of conversion, the existence of conversion will depend on the severity of the interference with the plaintiff's right to the goods. See generally Rest. 2d, §§222A, 237-241.

   a. **Parking garage:** Thus a parking garage which intentionally refuses to give the plaintiff back her car for half an hour would not be liable for conversion, but one which refused to surrender the car for a month would be. See Rest. 2d, §222A, Illustrs. 14-15. Similarly, if the garage delayed only a half hour, but the car was destroyed by fire during that period, there would be conversion, due to the substantial interference with plaintiff's rights. Ibid, Illustr. 16.

      i. **Good faith:** Once again, the defendant's good faith or bad faith may play an important role in determining whether the interference is so substantial as to give rise to conversion. Remember, however, that bad faith is not a prerequisite to liability, and that a parking garage which refuses to deliver the plaintiff's car for a month because it honestly and reasonably believes that the car belongs to someone else would nonetheless be liable. But in close cases, good or bad faith can make the difference.

   b. **Dominion:** If the defendant refuses to return the plaintiff's goods, it is irrelevant that the defendant is not using them for his own purposes, or that no permanent damage to them occurs, provided that the interference with the plaintiff's rights is otherwise sufficiently grave. The essence of the conversion claim is that the defendant has exercised *dominion* over the goods.

      Example: D borrows P's lawn mower, then leaves it locked in D's toolshed without ever using it, and refuses to return it. P has the police help him retrieve the mower 6 months later. Even though D hasn't used (or damaged) the mower, he's liable for conversion. So he'll have to pay P the full value of the mower measured as of the time of his first refusal to return it. (But D will then get to keep the mower.)

      Note: This example illustrates the essence of a conversion action, i.e., that it is a *forced sale* to the defendant.

   c. **Demand:** There is generally no liability for conversion until the plaintiff has *demanded return* of the chattel and has been refused. The defendant is deemed to have "refused" to return the goods not only where he explicitly states that he will not surrender them but also where he equivocates, or falsely promises to return them, or stalls for a substantial time.

      i. **Intentional refusal:** It is only an *intentional* refusal to return the goods that gives rise to an action for conversion. If the defendant is unable to return the goods because he has lost them, the plaintiff's only remedy will be an action for negligence. See Rest. 2d, §237, Comment f.

ii. **Qualified refusal:** Once the plaintiff demands return of his goods, the defendant is entitled to take a reasonable time necessary to *check the validity* of the plaintiff's claim, provided that he gives the reasons for not yielding immediate possession. P&K, pp. 99-100.

4. **Destruction or alteration of the goods:** Perhaps the clearest cases of conversion occur when the defendant *destroys* the goods, or *alters* them in some *fundamental way*.

   Example: P stores his fur coat with D. Without P's knowledge or consent, D alters the coat by reducing its size, so that P can no longer wear it. This is a conversion. But if D had merely repaired a hole in the coat, there would not be a conversion. See Rest. 2d, §222A, Illustrs. 19 and 20.

   a. **Partial alteration:** If only part of a chattel is destroyed or altered, there may not be a conversion of the whole, depending on how hard the partial alteration is to repair. Thus Prosser suggests that if the defendant removes a tire from the plaintiff's automobile, there will not be a conversion of anything except the tire itself if a replacement tire is easily available, but there will be a conversion of the entire car if the episode occurs in the middle of the desert. See P&K, p. 101.

5. **Use of the chattel:** Conversion may occur by virtue of the defendant's *use* of the plaintiff's goods. Again the existence of conversion will be a question of degree, depending on the extent of the use and the harm it causes to the goods.

   Example: P lends her car to D, a dealer, in order for D to sell it. On one occasion D drives the car, on his own business, for 10 miles. This is not a conversion. But if D drove the car 2,000 miles, there would be a conversion. Rest. 2d, §222A, Illustrs. 21 and 22. Similarly, if D intended to drive the car only 10 miles, but it was seriously damaged in a collision during this trip, there would be a conversion, regardless of whether D drove negligently. Rest. 2d, §222A, Illustr. 26.

6. **Assertion of ownership:** A conversion will *not* be found from the mere fact that defendant *asserts ownership* of the goods, where he does not interfere with the plaintiff's possession or other rights. For instance, if the defendant advertises the sale of the plaintiff's car, there is no conversion. But if the defendant actually conducted the sale, and permitted his buyer to gain possession of the car for even a short time, there would be. See P&K, p. 102.

Quiz Yourself on
INTENTIONAL INTERFERENCE WITH PROPERTY *(Entire Chapter)*

10. Miles Standish likes to take long walks every day along what he believes is the edge of his property, Turkey Ridge. The course he travels is actually on land belonging to Chief Big Foot. Has Standish committed a trespass to land? _____

11. Jack T. Ripper jumps into H. G. Wells' time machine, mistakenly believing it's his. He takes it on a whirl through time, realizes his mistake, and returns it. Has Ripper committed a trespass to chattels? _____

12. Icarus asks Orville Wright if he can borrow Wright's wax wings. Wright hands them over, Icarus straps

them on, and soars into the wild blue yonder. Unfortunately, Icarus flies too close to the sun, the wings melt, and Icarus isn't too well off, either. Icarus returns the wings to Wright as one solid mass of wax. Wright claims that Icarus has committed a conversion. Icarus claims that since he rightfully borrowed the wings, he can't be liable for conversion. Who's right? _____

13. Owner leaves his watch with Jeweler for repairs. Jeweler does the repairs, then ships the watch, properly-addressed to Owner, via American Parcel Service (APS). APS mistakenly delivers the package to Neighbor, who lives next door to Owner. APS learns of its mistake one day after making it, immediately retrieves the watch from Neighbor, and delivers it to Owner. What torts, if any, has APS committed against Owner? _____

Answers

10. Yes. Trespass to land requires intentional physical invasion of another's land. It is defendant's simple intent to enter land that in fact belongs to the plaintiff— not defendant's intent to do so <u>wrongfully</u> — that is the basis of liability. To put it another way, a mistake of fact — even a reasonable one — about who owns the land is no defense to a trespass-to-land claim. Thus even if Standish had hired the best surveyor in the county and the surveyor had (mistakenly) told Standish that Standish owned the land in question, Standish would still lose. PK §13 at 73.

RELATED ISSUE: Remember that Big Foot doesn't have to prove damages as part of his prima facie case — damages don't have to be proven in order to prevail on a trespass to land claim (and Big Foot can recover nominal damages if he can't prove actual damages).

11. Yes. Trespass to chattels consists of intentionally interfering with personal property in someone else's possession. The issue here is whether mistake of fact is a defense to trespass to chattels. In fact, it's not. It's intent to do the act which creates the interference that's required — not to do so *wrongfully*.

NOTE: H. G. Wells won't have to prove actual damages here, because the type of trespass involved was "dispossession" as opposed to "intermeddling." Loss of possession itself, regardless of the length of time involved, is sufficient to satisfy the damage requirement of a trespass to chattels claim. Had Ripper merely interfered with the time machine — for instance, by putting a bumper sticker on it — Wells <u>would</u> have to prove actual damages as part of his trespass claim.

12. Wright's right. Conversion is an intentional interference with the plaintiff's personal property that is so substantial that it's fair to require the defendant to pay the property's full value. Severe damage, destruction, or misuse all qualify as a misappropriation serious enough to constitute conversion. It doesn't matter that the initial entrustment of possession to D was with P's consent; so long as the interference with P's possessory rights went beyond what was consented-to (here, Wright didn't consent to a melt-down), there can be a conversion.

SIMILAR SITUATION: Say Fairy Godmother turns Farmer Brown's coach into a pumpkin. She will be liable for conversion, since *substantial change* to the chattel is sufficient to justify the claim.

13. Probably trespass to chattels, but not conversion. Conversion exists only where the owner's rights are so seriously interfered with that it is fair to make the defendant pay the chattel's full value. Here, the one-day interference with Owner's right to use or possess the watch is not sufficiently great. See Rest. 2d, §222A, Illustr. 9 & 10. On the other hand, the deprivation of use is probably great enough that the tort of trespass to chattels has been committed; if so, APS would have to pay Owner the value of one day's use of the watch (compared with having to pay the entire value of the watch, if it had been destroyed while at

Neighbor's.)

Exam Tips *on*
INTENTIONAL INTERFERENCE WITH PROPERTY

In a complex fact pattern, the presence of any of the three torts covered in this chapter (trespass to land, trespass to chattels and conversion) is usually pretty easy to spot. By and large, your problem is to determine whether the tort has in fact been committed. Here are particular things to look for:

☛ Look for *"trespass to land"* whenever one person intentionally comes onto another person's land.

    ☞ If you spot a trespass issue, lead with the following definition: "Trespass to land is the intentional unauthorized entry onto the land of another."

    ☞ Trespass is an *intentional* tort. The intent is the intent to *enter land*, not the intent to harm the defendant or the land in any way.

       ☞ If D knows with *"substantial certainty"* that he is entering (or causing an object to enter) land, the intent requirement is met. (*Example:* Suppose D operates a factory that discharges particles of ash onto P's land, and that D knows that this is happening. D meets the intent requirement for trespass, even though D doesn't "desire" that the particles touch P's land.)

       ☞ The most frequently tested sub-issue in trespass relates to *mistake*. As long as D knows he's entering land, the intent requirement is satisfied, and D's mistaken belief (even his *reasonably* mistaken belief) that his entry is *authorized* is *irrelevant*. (*Example 1:* D thinks he's coming onto land owned by X, who has in fact invited D, but D is really by mistake coming onto land owned by P. That's trespass. *Example 2:* D thinks he has a legal right to enter P's land to repossess P's car, but P is really paid up so D has no right to be there. Again, that's trespass.)

       ☞ Remember that the term "trespass" refers only to *intentional* interference. There is no strict liability. (*Example:* D, a pilot, loses control of the aircraft, and the craft crash lands on P's property. This is not trespass. But if the pilot has a mechanical problem and intentionally selects a particular parcel to emergency land on, that probably is trespass, though the pilot may have the defense of necessity.)

    ☞ Trespass occurs not only where D himself comes onto the land, but also where D causes an *object* to come onto the land. (*Example:* D puts a car onto P's land, or sends pollutant particles onto P's land.)

    ☞ Remember that a landowner is deemed to have exclusive possessory rights to at least some of the *air space* above the land. Whenever you spot one person *flying over* another's land, consider the possibility of trespass.

☞ If D is flying high enough that he is within FAA-defined "navigable air space," the states cannot deem him to be trespassing.

☞ But if D is flying lower than the limits of navigable air space, some states make this automatically trespass. Most states make it trespass *only* if P's use and enjoyment of the land is interfered with (the "implicit nuisance" approach).

☞ Even if there is *no actual harm* to P's land, the tort still takes place as soon as D comes on the property (and P can get *nominal* damages).

☞ Even if D's initial entry is *"authorized"* by P (e.g., P invites D on as a business visitor) the entry will *turn into trespass* if D *remains* after being asked to leave.

☛ Look for *"trespass to chattels"* (T/C) whenever one person intentionally interferes with another's possession of a "thing."

☞ If you spot a T/C issue, lead with the following definition: "Trespass to chattels is the intentional interference with another's possessory interest in a chattel, resulting in damage to that interest."

☞ Most T/C issues relate to *intent*.

☞ The relevant intent is the intent to take possession or otherwise affect the chattel. D's belief about his *right* to do the act, or about who holds *title*, is *not* part of the requisite intent.

☞ Most often tested is the effect of *mistake*. In general, mistake is *never* a defense to T/C. Thus the following types of mistake (even if *reasonable*) will all be no defense.

❑ D believes that the chattel already belongs to D. (*Example:* D takes P's umbrella in a restaurant, thinking it's his own — this is T/C.)

❑ D believes that X has title to the object, and buys the object from X when it really belongs to P. (*Example:* X steals a radio from P and sells it to D, who does not know the radio is stolen. D is liable to P for T/C.)

❑ D is a creditor who wrongly thinks that he has the right to *repossess* P's chattel.

☞ Also, the distinction between intent and *accident* is often tested. If D doesn't intend to even make contact with P's possession, and this contact happens by accident, there's no T/C. But you should still discuss T/C (even though the tort hasn't been committed) in this scenario. (*Example:* D, while driving either carefully or carelessly, hits and damages P's car without intending any contact. That's not T/C.)

☞ The *degree of interference* is sometimes tested. T/C takes place as long as there's some *"damage."* So there are no *nominal damages* as in trespass to land. (*Example:* D picks up P's umbrella, realizes the mistake, and immediately puts the umbrella down. That's not T/C.) But "damage" is deemed to take place even if the only damage is a temporary one to P's right of *"possession,"* and the item is returned unharmed. (*Example:* D picks up P's umbrella, walks around the block with it, and returns it after noticing the mistake.

That's T/C.)

☞ Always distinguish between T/C and *conversion*. Conversion only occurs when the injury to P's interests is so severe that it is appropriate to make D pay for the whole value of the item as opposed to damages for just the interference. (See the discussion of conversion, below, where we cover the factors that go into this distinction.)

☛ Look for *"conversion"* at the same time you look for T/C. Remember that conversion is more "serious" than T/C.

☞ When you spot a conversion issue, use the following definition as your lead-in: "Conversion occurs when the defendant so substantially interferes with the plaintiff's possession or ownership of goods that it is fair to require the defendant to pay the property's full value."

☞ Conversion is an "intentional" tort — the definition of "intent" is the same as for T/C (so D's mistake about the right to possess, or about who has title, doesn't negate his intent).

☞ The main issue in conversion is to *distinguish* it from T/C. Remember the factors that courts consider:

  ☞ The extent and duration of D's *"dominion"* (the greater/longer, the more likely it's conversion). (*Example:* If D keeps the item for three months, that's probably conversion.)

  ☞ D's *good* or *bad faith*. (*Example:* D buys property thinking his seller has good title — this suggests T/C rather than conversion, because D has behaved in good faith.)

  ☞ The degree of *harm* to the property. (*Examples:* If the item is given back to P in an unchanged condition except for the passage of time, this suggests T/C rather than conversion. But if D takes P's car for a 10-minute joy ride, and returns it to P with the front end smashed, this suggests conversion.)

  ☞ The *inconvenience* and *expense* caused to P.

☞ For both conversion and trespass, if the *"property"* in question is an *intangible*, point out that the item must be "property" of the sort required for these torts under state law. But remember that today, in most courts *electronic files* are deemed to be "property" that can be trespassed on or converted.

☞ Remember why the distinction between conversion and T/C makes a difference: in T/C, D just pays for the damage, but in conversion there's a *"forced sale"* — D "buys" the item for the value it had at the time of the conversion (and gets to keep the item).

  ☞ If it's conversion, the value of the item is the *sole* measure of damages — the fact that D may have gotten benefits from the item while using it, or that D physically damaged the item, is *not* added. Since D is "buying" the item, he gets the right to past benefits, or to commit physical damage, at "no additional charge."

  ☞ P can always *"elect"* to sue for T/C (and get the item back plus damages for the harm) even where the facts would support conversion.

Chapter 4

DEFENSES TO INTENTIONAL TORTS

ChapterScope

This chapter discusses various *defenses* that D may raise to P's claim that an intentional tort has been committed. Here are the main defenses considered in this chapter:

- **Consent:** Under the defense of *"consent,"* if P has consented to an intentional interference with his person or property, D will not be liable for that interference. This consent may be either express, or may be *implied* from P's conduct or from the surrounding circumstances.

- **Self-defense:** A person is entitled to use *reasonable force* to prevent any threatened *harmful or offensive bodily contact*, and any threatened confinement or imprisonment. This is the defense of "self-defense."

  - ❑ **Degree of force:** Only that *degree* of force *necessary to prevent the threatened harm* may be used. (Special rules limit the use of *deadly force*, i.e., force intended or likely to cause death or serious bodily injury.)

- **Defense of others:** A person may use reasonable force to defend *another person* from attack. The same general rules apply as in self-defense.

- **Defense of property:** A person may generally use reasonable force to *defend her property*, both land and chattels.

- **Recapture of chattels:** A property owner generally has the right to use reasonable force to *regain* possession of *chattels* taken from her by someone else.

  - ❑ **Merchant:** Where a *merchant* reasonably believes that a person is stealing his property, most states give the merchant a privilege to *temporarily detain* the person for investigation.

- **Necessity:** Under the defense of *"necessity,"* D has a privilege to harm the property interests of P where this is *necessary* in order to prevent *great harm* to third persons or to D herself.

- **Arrest:** The police or a private citizen are entitled to make an *arrest* depending on the circumstances. This arrest may be with or without a warrant. Only that degree of force that is reasonably necessary may be used.

- **Justification:** Even if D's conduct does not fit within one of the above narrow defenses, she may be entitled to the general defense of *"justification,"* a catch-all term.

I. INTRODUCTION

A. **Defenses generally:** This chapter discusses the various defenses that a defendant may raise to the plaintiff's claim that an intentional tort has been committed. These defenses may be broadly grouped into two categories: **(1)** the defense that the plaintiff **consented** to the invasion of his interest; and **(2)** defenses that are imposed as a matter of law.

1. **Privileges:**   The latter group, those imposed as a matter of law, are usually called ***privileges***. The defendant's conduct is said to be privileged where, even though she has damaged the plaintiff by committing actions which would otherwise constitute a tort, she has acted to "further an interest of such social importance that it is entitled to protection. . . . " P&K, p. 109.

2. **Distinguish from *prima facie* case:**   It is up to the defendant to affirmatively plead, and ***bear the burden of proving***, the existence of a privilege. That is, the non-existence of privilege is not an element of the plaintiff's *prima facie* case. Thus whereas the elements of the various torts examined in the previous two chapters are matters which must be affirmatively pleaded and proven by the plaintiff, the plaintiff does not bear the burden of showing that the defendant's conduct was not privileged.

3. **Consent:**   The non-existence of **consent**, on the other hand, **is** part of the plaintiff's *prima facie* case, at least with respect to torts against the person (assault, battery, false imprisonment and infliction of mental distress) and the tort of conversion. Therefore, it is not strictly speaking a "privilege," since that term is generally reserved for exculpatory defenses which the defendant bears the burden of raising and proving. However, consent to trespass to land is usually considered to be a true privilege, and not a part of the plaintiff's *prima facie* case. P&K, p. 112. fn. 2.

B. **Mistake:**   The defendant's conduct will never be privileged solely by virtue of the fact that it arose from a ***mistake***. Thus we have seen that one who intentionally enters land, in the honest and even reasonable belief that it is her own, is nonetheless liable for the intentional tort of trespass; similarly, the doctor who believes he is operating on *A*, and who is in fact performing unauthorized surgery on *B*, is liable for battery.

> **Example 1:** While hunting for wolves, the Ds see P's dog, which resembles a wolf, and kill it. *Held*, the Ds are liable for the damages caused by their mistake, even though they may have been acting in good faith. *Ranson v. Kitner*, 31 Ill. App. 241 (Ill. 1888).

> **Example 2:** D mines coal from under P's land, having mistaken the location of the boundary line. D is liable to P for trespass, even though the mistake is a reasonable one. Rest. 2d, §164, Illustr. 2.

1. **Important factor in privileges:**   However, the existence of a mistake will sometimes be an important ***factor*** in determining whether the defendant's conduct falls under one of the specific privileges discussed in this chapter. For instance, the defendant in a battery case may be able to establish that he is protected by the privilege of self-defense, if he can show that he honestly and reasonably, although mistakenly, believed that the plaintiff intended to cause him bodily harm. The effect of mistake will be examined in the context of each of the privileges discussed below.

II. CONSENT

A. **General rule on consent:**   Generally, if the plaintiff has consented to an intentional interference with his person or property, the defendant will not be liable for that interference. In fact, as was stated above (*supra*, p. 58), most courts take the position that as to all intentional torts except trespass to land, lack of consent is part of the plaintiff's *prima facie* case, and he must plead and prove it.

B. No operation in negligence cases: The doctrine of consent is generally of importance only in intentional tort cases. The policy behind the doctrine, that of letting the parties agree on the relationship between them to a relatively great extent, is in negligence and strict liability cases embodied by the doctrine of **assumption of risk** (discussed *infra* at p. 292 and p. 339).

C. Implied consent: The plaintiff's consent to an invasion of his interests may sometimes be express or explicit, as where he says "I'll be your sparring partner" (thus negating the existence of assault and battery). But the existence of consent may also be *implied* from the plaintiff's conduct, from custom, or from the circumstances.

1. **Objective manifestation:** If it reasonably seemed to the defendant that the plaintiff consented, consent will be held to exist *regardless of the plaintiff's subjective state of mind*. That is, it is the *objective manifestations* by the plaintiff that are taken into account — a not surprising rule, since defendants are not mind readers.

   a. **Manifestations:** These objective manifestations may be not only words spoken by the plaintiff, but any other conduct or even lack of conduct, by him. The test is *whether a reasonable person in the position of the defendant would believe that the plaintiff had consented to the invasion of his interests.*

   Example: As passengers are about to leave a ship owned by the D Ship Co. after a transatlantic voyage, they are told that they may not enter the U.S. unless they have a certificate to show that they have been vaccinated. They are also told that X, a doctor employed by D, will vaccinate anyone who wishes to have this done. P stands in line with the other passengers, and tells X that she has already been vaccinated before. He says that there is no mark and that she should be vaccinated again. She says nothing, and holds up her arm, whereupon he vaccinates her. P sues D for battery, and D claims that P consented.

   Held, for D. It reasonably appeared to X that P consented to the vaccination. Therefore, P is deemed to have consented, regardless of the actual state of her mind. "If the plaintiff's behavior was such as to indicate consent on her part, [the doctor] was justified in his act, whatever her unexpressed feelings may have been. In determining whether she consented, he could be guided only by her overt acts and the manifestations of her feelings." *O'Brien v. Cunard S.S. Co,* 28 N.E. 266 (Mass. 1891).

2. **Real but unmanifested consent:** On the other hand, if the plaintiff *subjectively consents*, and there is some way to prove this, the consent will be effective even though it was never manifested to the defendant. P&K, p. 113.

   Example: "A repeatedly states to members of his own family that he would be glad to have B make use of his tennis court. A makes no such statement to B, does nothing else to manifest his consent, and none of the members of A's family communicate the information to B. B enters A's tennis court and plays on it." A has consented to B's entry and there is no trespass. Rest. 2d, §167, Illustr. 3.

3. **Custom:** If the defendant can show that it was *customary* for one in the plaintiff's position to consent to a certain act by the defendant, there will be consent even if the plaintiff made no objective manifestation of consent in this particular case. See Rest. 2d, §892, Comment d.

    Example: D fishes in a small pond that is almost completely enclosed by P's farm. P sues D for trespass, and D claims that P implicitly consented.

    Held for D. In the jurisdiction in question, it has always been customary to permit the public to fish in small ponds. Therefore, in the absence of any notification by P to the contrary, D reasonably understood the fishing to be consented to, and consent will be found. *Marsh v. Colby*, 39 Mich. 626 (1878).

4. **Inaction:** Similarly, there may be circumstances where the plaintiff's *inaction* by itself indicates consent. Once again, the issue is whether a reasonable person in the position of the defendant would have inferred the consent from the inaction.

    Example: D, a boy, and P, a girl, sit on a park bench together in the moonlight. D says that he is going to kiss P; P says and does nothing, and D kisses her. P will be deemed to have consented by her silence and inaction. P&K, p. 113; Rest. 2d, §50, Illustr. 2.

D. **Lack of capacity to consent:** There are circumstances in which the plaintiff is clearly *incapable* of giving consent. This is so where P is a child, intoxicated, unconscious, etc. In such a case, any objective manifestation of consent by the plaintiff will be ineffective, at least where the defendant knows or should know that the plaintiff is not competent to give a meaningful consent. Nutshell, p. 160.

1. **Exception:** However, the patient's consent will be implied "as a matter of law" if *all* of the following factors exist:

    a. **Incapacitated:** The patient is unable to give consent, either because he is unconscious or for some other reason;

    b. **Emergency:** In order to save his *life* or safeguard his health, *immediate* action is necessary;

    c. **Lack of consent not indicated:** There is no indication that he would not consent if able to; and

    d. **Reasonable person:** A reasonable person would consent in the circumstances.

    Example: P is run over by a train, and is carried unconscious to a hospital where D is the resident doctor. It reasonably appears to D that P will die if his foot is not immediately amputated. D performs the amputation before P regains consciousness, and without procuring the consent of a relative. P will be deemed to have consented to the surgery, because of its vital and emergency nature. Rest. 2d, §62, Illustr. 3.

2. **Consent by relative:** Even if the factors listed above are not all present, a doctor may, if the patient is unconscious or otherwise incapable of consenting, procure the consent of a *close relative* instead. P&K, p. 115. Conversely, even if all these factors are met, the physician may still be under a duty to seek the consent of a close relative if one is at hand.

a. **Minor:**   If the patient is a *young child*, he will usually be held not to be capable of giving consent, and either his parents must consent, or an emergency must exist. But if the patient is a minor who is approaching the age of majority, he will be able to consent on his own, and this consent may be effective regardless of whether the parents also consent. Thus a 17-year-old girl presumably has the ability to consent to a legal abortion, despite the opposition of her parents; if so, she will not be able to sustain a battery action.

b. **Court order:**   If medical care is necessary to save a child's life, and the parents *refuse to consent* (e.g., because they are Jehovah's Witnesses), the doctor or hospital will normally be able to obtain a *court order* overruling the parents. But if such an order is not obtained, the doctor may be held liable (unless there was not enough time to obtain one.)

   i. **Aiding child's comfort:**   If the operation is not necessary to save the child's life, but is a matter of aiding his comfort, the courts are split on whether to overrule the parents. See P,W&S, p. 96, note 12.

c. **Substituted consent when no emergency exists:**   As stated, a parent or guardian generally has the power to consent on behalf of a youthful minor, incompetent, etc., whether or not an immediate emergency exists. But does the parent or guardian have the right to consent to surgery that is not for the patient's benefit, but is instead for the *benefit of some third person?* This question has arisen recently in the case of *kidney transplants*, and has received conflicting answers.

E. **Exceeding scope of consent:**   If the plaintiff does give actual consent to an invasion of his interests, the defendant will not be privileged if she goes substantially *beyond the scope* of that consent. That is, the plaintiff generally consents to the defendant's performing acts of a certain nature, and no others. If the defendant invades the plaintiff's interests in a way that is substantially different from that consented to, she will be liable.

> **Example:** P, while having a few drinks at the local bar, challenges D to "step outside and put up your dukes." They go outside, and D attacks P with a knife, not with his fists. D has gone beyond the scope of P's consent, and will be liable for battery, and perhaps assault, as if consent had not been given. See P&K, p. 118.

1. **Consent to act, not consequences:**   "The consent is to the plaintiff's conduct, rather than to its consequences." P&K, p. 118. Thus in the above example, D's conduct went beyond the scope of what was consented to, since it consisted of the use of a knife rather than a fist. But if D had used his fists, and due to P's weak heart, P had dropped dead, D would not have exceeded the scope of the consent, even though the damage clearly exceeded the scope of what P anticipated.

2. **Surgery:**   The scope-of-consent issue frequently arises in cases involving surgery. As in other contexts, the rule is that the plaintiff patient's consent, if it is to one particular kind of surgery for one particular purpose, *will not constitute consent to another, substantially different, surgical procedure.*

> **Example:** P visits D, an ear specialist. D tells P that she has a diseased right ear, and needs an operation. She consents to such an operation. After D administers the anes-

thetic, D decides that P's right ear is not seriously enough diseased to need surgery, but that her left ear is; he therefore operates on it, without obtaining P's specific permission for this operation. P sues for battery, and D raises the defense that she consented.

Held, P did not consent. No emergency threatened P's life or health. Therefore, there was a technical battery, despite the fact that the operation benefitted P. (However, a new trial should be held as to damages, since the jury's finding of $14,322.50 was excessive.) *Mohr v. Williams*, 104 N.W. 12 (Minn. 1905).

Note: As the appellate court in *Mohr* noted, P's recovery would be dependent upon the extent and the nature of her injury. Although the original trial court awarded P damages in the amount of $14,322, the court in the second trial awarded her only $39, probably because little actual physical harm occurred.

a. **Desirability irrelevant:** As the *Mohr* case shows, it is irrelevant that the additional or different surgery was medically desirable. The physician (and the hospital employing her) are nonetheless liable for battery. The fact that the doctor conformed to standard medical practice by the additional surgery will not be taken into account. Furthermore, even if the patient sustained no actual injury, the court may award nominal and punitive damages. P&K, p. 118-19.

b. **Emergency:** However, an *emergency* may justify extending the surgery beyond that consented to, just as it can justify surgery without consent in the first instance (*supra*, p. 60). The test is a balancing one, weighing the risks of waiting to bring the patient back to consciousness to obtain his consent, against the risks from the additional surgery.

Example: "A consents to a particular operation and for that purpose places himself in the hands of B, a surgeon, and submits to anesthesia. Upon opening A's body, B discovers conditions which make it necessary to extend the operation or to perform a different operation from that consented to. The conditions apparently require the new or extended operation to save A's life or to accomplish the cure desired by him, and its postponement would involve pain and distress to A out of proportion to the risk of the new operation. A reasonable person would consent to the operation if he knew of the conditions discovered by B. B performs the operation." A will be deemed to have implicitly consented to the operation, and B will not be liable. Rest. 2d, §62, Illustr. 4.

Note: Observe that by the standards of the above example, the defendant in *Mohr v. Williams, supra,* might have been able to establish the existence of implied consent. He could have argued that the purpose of the plaintiff's operation was to remove the latter's ear problems in general, and that postponing this until the plaintiff could be revived and her consent obtained would involve trauma and pain out of proportion to the risk of the operation. But the fact that the operation involved a completely different ear (as opposed to an adjoining organ), coupled with the fact that the defendant had had ample opportunity to examine both ears, would probably cause a court to reach the same result as the *Mohr* court did.

c. **Hospital consent forms:** The issue of consent to the scope of an operation is often academic today, since most surgery is performed in hospitals pursuant to extremely general *consent forms*.

d. Broad consent: Even when no general hospital consent form is signed, courts may interpret the plaintiff's consent to an operation as being quite broad, particularly where complete diagnosis is impossible until anesthesia has been applied and the incision made.

    i. Construed as general: Thus one court held that in such cases, unless there is proof to the contrary, the patient's consent "will be construed as general in nature and the surgeon may extend the operation to remedy any abnormal or diseased condition in the area of the original incision whenever he, in the exercise of his sound professional judgment, determines that correct surgical procedure dictates and requires such an extension. . . . " *Kennedy v. Parrott*, 90 S.E.2d 754 (N.C. 1956).

3. Athlete's consent: Participating in a usually-violent *sport*, like football or hockey, is generally *not* considered to constitute consent to all injuries which may be inflicted by an adversary. Instead, there is an increasing tendency to hold that a player who *intentionally attacks or injures* his opponent may be liable in tort (or even subjected to criminal prosecution.) See Rest. 2d, §50, Comment b and Illustrs. 4-6.

    a. Scope of implied consent: So if P impliedly consents to some types of harmful or offensive contact during the sport, fellow-participant D won't be liable for contacts falling within the scope of that implied consent, but *will* be liable for contacts going *beyond* the ones impliedly consented to.

    b. Significance of sport's rules and customs: How, then, should the court decide *which* types of contacts fall within the scope of the plaintiff's "implied consent"? Most courts seem to attach great weight to the *rules or customs* of the sport. Decisions recognize at least three major categories of contact, and tend to make different conclusions about whether the plaintiff "impliedly consented" to the contact based on which category the court thinks the contact falls into:

    [1] Conduct allowed by rules: The easiest category to analyze consists of contact that is *expressly allowed* by the rules and customs of the sport. Where the case falls into this category, in virtually all courts the plaintiff will be held to have *impliedly consented* to this type of contact, even if in the particular situation the result is an unexpectedly grave injury.

    Example: Assume that the rules of professional soccer permit a certain type of "tackle" by a defender, where the defender intentionally slides into the legs of the player with the ball. Assume that in a professional game, while P is dribbling the ball down court, D, a defender, makes a legal tackle that has the unexpected (and unintended) consequence of severing P's ACL ligament, ending his career. Virtually all courts would say that since the tackle by D did not violate any rule or custom of soccer, P impliedly consented to that tackle, and may not recover for battery (or, for that matter, for negligence).

    [2] Conduct punishable but not "beyond the bounds" of the sport: The next category consists of conduct that *violates the rules* of the sport, but is considered to be essentially *within the ordinary give-and-take of the sport.* Conduct would likely fall into this category if it is subject to *some minor penalty*, but not to a severe punishment like automatic ejection or a multiple-game suspension. Again, most courts would likely hold that the conduct, while against the rules, is of a type that is sufficiently common (and in most instances insufficiently physically dangerous) that the plaintiff should be ***deemed to have impliedly consented*** to it.

Example: P and D are playing in NBA basketball game. While P has the ball and has a clear path to a layup, D lunges at P from behind, grabs P's arm, and throws P to the ground. Assume that the referee believes that D's sole motive was to intentionally foul P (and send him to the free-throw line), not to engage in what D thought was an acceptable defensive move. The referee calls a "Flagrant Foul – Penalty 1" (defined in NBA rules as a foul involving excessive contact, but not so culpable as to justify immediate ejection if it is the player's first such foul of the game). As often happens in the case of this type of foul, P falls; but on this occasion, he suffers a freak career-ending knee injury when his knee hits the floor. P sues D for battery.

The court would likely hold that judging by the relatively un-severe penalty imposed by the referee, this type of foul is sufficiently ordinary — and sufficiently unlikely to cause severe personal injury — that it should be deemed to be the type of contact to which P implicitly consented by joining the league.

[3] Reckless or intentionally-harmful conduct beyond the usual bounds: The final category consists of conduct that not only violates the rules of the sport, but constitutes a flagrant violation by means of actions that are ***unrelated to the normal method of playing the game***, and that are ***done without any competitive purpose***. Scenarios where D ***intends to physically harm*** his opponent (or ***recklessly disregards*** the danger of such harm), without any *bona fide* belief that D is advancing his own team's competitive interest, are typical of this category. If the case falls into this category, most courts allow a tort suit (typically one for battery) to be brought by the injured player against the opponent who committed the violation, and/or the teams that employed that opponent.

Example: P plays for the Denver Broncos NFL team, and "Booby" Clark plays for D (the Cincinnati Bengals team). The Broncos intercept a Bengals pass, and P blocks Clark from pursuing the player who had made the interception and was running downfield. While P is kneeling and looking at the run-back, Clark comes up behind him and uses his forearm to hit P on the head and neck. Clark strikes this blow (he later testifies) not because he thinks it might help his team, but out of frustration at the interception and the fact that the Bengals are losing. The blow fractures P's neck. Therefore, P sues D[1] for the tortious act committed by their employee (Clark). The trial judge, sitting without a jury, rules that P assumed the risk of Clark's conduct, on the theory that "professional football is a species of warfare and … so much physical force is tolerated that … injuries [are] not actionable in court." P appeals.

---

1. Because the short one-year statute of limitations for assault and battery had already passed, P did not sue on an assault or battery charge; instead, he based his claim on Clark's reckless disregard of the risk that his action would seriously injure P, a separate negligence-like tort that was not time-barred.

Held (on appeal): for P — case remanded for a retrial. The rules of the NFL prohibit the intentional striking of blows, and the general customs of the sport also prohibit such conduct. These principles "are intended to establish reasonable boundaries so that one football player cannot intentionally inflict a serious injury on another." The trial judge was incorrect to assume that because football involves violence, "all reason has been abandoned"; it cannot be the case that "the only possible remedy for the person who has been the victim of an unlawful blow is retaliation." *Hackbart v. Cincinnati Bengals, Inc.*, 601 F.2d 516 (10th Cir. 1979).

(1) A few cases rule against P: However, a few cases have *found for the defendant* as a matter of law even where the defendant *intentionally tried to harm* the plaintiff, or *recklessly disregarded the high risk* that the plaintiff would be harmed. These few cases have reasoned that if players and teams have to worry about being held liable in tort for their aggressive on-field acts, their incentive to compete vigorously but lawfully — a desirable thing — will be chilled.

Example: P plays varsity baseball for Rio Hondo Community College team. During a preseason game against D (the Citrus Community College Owls), the pitcher for the Owls hits P on the head, cracking his helmet and injuring him. P alleges that the pitch was an intentional "beanball" thrown in retaliation for the fact that a previous Owls batter was hit by the Rio Hondo pitcher. P sues D on various theories, including D's failure to supervise the pitcher. The trial judge holds that P assumed the risk of a pitch like the one that hit him. P appeals.

Held (on appeal), for D. Being intentionally hit by a pitched ball is an "inherent risk of the sport, so accepted by custom that a pitch intentionally thrown at a batter has its own terminology: 'brushback,' 'beanball,' 'chin music.' " It's true that intentionally throwing at a batter is forbidden by the rules of baseball. But despite this prohibition, allowing tort suits for such conduct "might well alter fundamentally the nature of the sport by deterring participants from vigorously engaging in activity that falls close to, but on the permissible side, of a prescribed rule." It's also true that in California, an athlete does not assume the risk of a co-participant's intentional or reckless conduct "totally outside the range of the ordinary activity involved in the sport." But even if the Owls pitcher here intentionally threw at P, his conduct "did not fall outside the range of ordinary activity involved in the sport." Therefore, P will be deemed to have accepted the risk of such an intentional brushback pitch, thereby relieving D of any duty to prevent such a pitch. *Avila v. Citrus Community College District*, 131 P.3d 383 (Cal. 2006).

Note: But don't assume that most courts would agree with the California Supreme Court's holding in *Avila*. See D,H&B Csbk (7th), saying that "*Avila* is one of a *very small number of cases* that suggest even a reckless or intentional harm would be in the range of ordinary activity."

c. A mere negligent violation of rules: All of the above cases and examples of sporting rule violations involved violations in which D either *intended* to injure P or *recklessly disregarded* a high risk that P would be injured. In this situation, as we've seen, the plaintiff has some chance of recovery if the court believes that the defendant's violation was outside of the ordinary range of activities involved in the sport. But where D's conduct in violating the sports rule manifests *mere negligence* as to the risk of injury to P (rather than an intention to hurt P or reckless disregard of P's physical safety), *few if any cases allow recovery*. See D,H&B Csbk (7th Ed.), p. 326: "A growing number of courts say that 'personal injury cases arising out of an athletic event must be predicated on [at least] reckless disregard of safety.' "

Example: P, a famous jockey, is riding in a race in which D is also a jockey. D rides his horse in such a way that P's horse is cut off and jostled, and P is thrown to the ground. P becomes a paraplegic. D's conduct constitutes "foul riding," a violation of thoroughbred racing rules. P sues D for negligence.

Held, for D. The fact that D violated a rule of the sport does not prevent P from having assumed the risk of D's conduct. Here, the claim is merely that D negligently violated the rules, not that he intentionally or recklessly did so. Since foul riding is not "unrelated to the normal method of playing the game," and was not an intentional rules violation, P has assumed the risk. *Turcotte v. Fell,* 502 N.E.2d 964 (N.Y. 1986).

F. **Consent due to mistake:** Suppose the plaintiff's consent would not have been given except for the fact that he is *mistaken* about some material aspect of the transaction. As a general rule, such a mistake is *not* by itself enough to make the consent ineffective.

Example: P and D are on their first date. D, in order to induce P to go to bed with him, tells her that he doesn't have herpes. P is very concerned about the risk of catching herpes, but in reliance on D's statement, consents to sex. Unbeknownst to either P or D, D in fact has herpes, which he transmits to P. Notwithstanding the mistake, P's consent is effective, even though she would never have given it had she known the full facts. Therefore, P cannot sue for battery (although she might be able to sue for negligent misrepresentation, if she could show that D should have known that he had herpes).

1. **Mistake known or induced by defendant:** But if the defendant knew of the plaintiff's mistake, or induced that mistake (as by lying to the plaintiff), then the mistake would vitiate the consent. Thus, in the above example, if D knew that he had herpes, and was lying to P when he said he didn't, P's consent would be ineffective, and she could sue for battery.

Example: P, a woman in labor, summons D1, a doctor, to her house to help her in child birth. To help carry certain essential items, D1 brings with him D2, who is young, unmarried, and not a doctor; these facts are known to D1 but not to P. P permits D2 to be present during the birth, and to hold her hand.

Held, P's consent to D2's presence and contact is ineffective, because it was a mistake induced by D1's and D2's deceit. Therefore, P may recover against both. *De May v. Roberts*, 9 N.W. 146 (Mich. 1881).

a. **Collateral matter:** Even where the defendant induces the plaintiff's mistaken consent, that consent will be ineffective only if the mistake related to some *essential* aspect of the transaction. That is, the mistake must relate to an aspect of the invasion that makes it harmful or offensive, not to some "collateral" matter that induces the consent. See P&K, p. 120.

Example: P consents to have intercourse with D, because D offers her what appears to be a $20.00 bill. The bill turns out to be counterfeit. P's consent is nonetheless effective, because P's mistake related to a collateral aspect of the transaction. See Rest. 2d, §57, Illustr. 1. But if D induced P to have intercourse with him by taking her through a marriage ceremony which he knew was fake and P didn't, her consent would be ineffective, since the married state of the parties would be held to go to the essence of whether the intercourse was offensive. See Rest. 2d, §55, Illustr. 2.

2. **Medical cases:** Questions of mistaken consent often arise in medical cases, where the plaintiff alleges that the defendant did not adequately *inform him* of the *risks* of the proposed treatment.

   a. **Active misrepresentation:** If the physician has affirmatively misstated the existence or probability of risks, most courts hold that this is enough to render the plaintiff's consent to the treatment ineffective, and thus to permit a battery claim. Similarly, the consent will be ineffective if the doctor fails to disclose consequences that she *knows* will definitely follow the treatment. P&K, p. 120.

   b. **Non-disclosure:** But if all the doctor has done is to fail to mention the risk of consequences that may or may not follow the treatment, most courts hold that the doctor's conduct is merely *negligent*, and that only a collateral matter is involved. Therefore, these courts do not allow a battery claim and instead treat the action as one for negligence.

      i. **Consequence:** Hence, the doctor may show that her failure to disclose was *acceptable medical practice* in the community in which she practiced, regardless of whether full disclosure would have altered the patient's decision. The issue of "informed consent" is thus discussed more fully in the treatment of negligence, *infra,* p. 112. (Some cases even hold that the doctor's duty to disclose is not measured by standard medical practice, but rather, by what is reasonable under the circumstances.)

G. **Consent to criminal acts:** If the defendant's act against the plaintiff is a *criminal act,* the courts are split as to whether the plaintiff's consent to that act is effective.

   1. **Majority rule:** Most courts, particularly in older decisions, hold that the plaintiff's consent is *ineffective* if the act consented to is a crime. For instance, where plaintiff and defendant fight each other, these courts hold that each may recover from the other.

      a. **Minority view:** But approximately eight states, and the Second Restatement, take the view that the plaintiff's consent to the defendant's criminal act is *always effective* even where a breach of the peace is involved. This position is expressed by the maxim, *in pari delicto potior est conditio defendentis* ("In equal guilt the position of the defendant is the stronger").

   2. **Certain class protected:** Where the legislature's purpose in making the defendant's conduct a crime is to *protect a class of persons against their own poor judgment,* however, and the plaintiff is a member of the protected class, his consent will generally be ineffec-

tive, even in those jurisdiction that do ***not*** follow the ***majority rule*** (i.e., jurisdictions that do ***not*** agree that the existence of a crime involving a breach of the peace is by itself enough to render the plaintiff's consent ineffective).

> **Example:** D, a boxing promoter, puts on a boxing exhibition between P and X, without a license to do so, and without following the State Athletic Commission's rule on ring padding, fouls, etc. P, who is 18 years old, is injured during the fight, and sues D.
>
> *Held,* P's consent was not effective to bar his suit against D. The state statute making unlicensed boxing matches a crime is concerned primarily with protecting the contestants. Therefore, P is a member of the protected class, and his consent to the fight does not relieve D of liability, "regardless of what the rule may be as between the combatants." *Hudson v. Craft,* 204 P.2d 1 (Cal. 1949).

a. Statutory rape: Where the defendant commits the crime of ***"statutory rape"*** (i.e., intercourse with a person below a certain age, regardless of that person's actual consent), the same rule applies — the victim may sue for battery, and his or her consent is ruled ineffective because he/she is a member of the class for whose protection the statutory rape statute exists.

III. SELF-DEFENSE

A. Privilege generally: Just as the criminal law recognizes the privilege of self-defense, so does tort law. In fact, the rules concerning when the privilege of self-defense exists are virtually the same in the two contexts. See P&K, p. 124, fn. 3.

B. Two issues: In determining whether the privilege exists, there are two questions:

1. Does privilege exist? Was the defendant privileged to use *some kind* of force to defend herself?; and

2. What degree of force? If so, was she privileged to use the *degree* of force that she did?

C. What may be defended against: A person is entitled to use reasonable force to prevent any threatened ***harmful or offensive bodily contact***, and any threatened ***confinement or imprisonment***.

1. Negligent or intentional: This is true whether the threat is ***intentionally imposed*** (i.e. a danger which if it occurs would be an assault, battery, or false imprisonment), or merely ***negligent***.

> **Example:** P, walking along a crowded street, is swinging a cane. D, walking behind him, wants to pass, but realizes that she is in danger of being hit by the cane if she does. There is no room to step in the street, and P refuses to stop swinging. D may use reasonable force to take the cane out of P's hand, in order to protect herself against being hit, even though P's conduct is negligent, and is not the product of an intent to hit her. See Rest. 2d, §64, Illustr. 2.

2. Burden of proof: The defendant bears the burden of proving that the privilege of self-defense existed. P&K, p. 124.

D. Apparent necessity: Self-defense may be used not only where there is a real threat of harm, but also where the defendant *reasonably believes* that there is one.

> **Example:** "A, a notorious desperado, has threatened to shoot B on sight. B sees A approaching him with his hand in his hip pocket. A does not see B and is putting his hand in his pocket to draw out a handkerchief. B mistakenly but reasonably believes that A is about to shoot him." B may use reasonable force to block what he thinks is an attempt to shoot him (e.g., knocking A down and perhaps, if necessary, shooting A). Rest. 2d, §63, Illustr. 7.

1. Contrast: A reasonable but mistaken belief thus has a *very different effect* in cases of self-defense than it does in situations involving most of the *prima facie* torts discussed previously. Recall, for instance, that a person's reasonable but mistaken belief that the land he is entering is his own will not prevent him from being a trespasser, and a practical joker's reasonable mistaken belief that the butt of his joke will not find it a harmful or offensive contact will not shield him from liability for battery. This difference in the significance given to reasonable mistakes has been attributed to the importance courts attach to "self-preservation as the first law of nature." P, W&S, p. 102.

2. Reasonableness: But the defendant's belief that a threat exists must, as noted, be reasonable. Thus in the above example, if B were abnormally timid or paranoid, and a reasonable person in his position would not have believed that A was about to shoot him, B's use of force would not be privileged, no matter how real B's fear was.

E. Protection only: The defendant may use only the force reasonably required to *protect herself* against harm.

1. Retaliation: Therefore, she may not use any degree of force in *retaliation* for a tort already committed on her, or as a punishment.

> **Example:** P, a small boy, throws a snowball at D, hitting her in the eye and causing her severe pain. D may not use force to inflict a beating on P either as a punishment or as a warning against similar misconduct in the future. Rest. 2d, §63, Illustr. 4.

2. Disarmed or helpless adversary: Similarly, once the defendant's adversary is disarmed or helpless after committing an attack, the defendant may not use force against him.

3. Verbal provocation: D may not use self-defense in response to *verbal provocation*, such as *taunting or insults*. In part that's because in tort law, self-defense is purely a forward-looking idea: D is entitled to prevent imminent future harm, not redress past harm, let alone redress purely verbal harm.

> **Example:** P calls D a liar and a cheat in front of D's friends. (Assume that D is not a liar and a cheat, and that P's words constitute slander for which D could recover.) P then says to D, "What're you gonna do about, you coward?" D hits P in the face. P can recover for battery, and D cannot successfully claim self-defense. That's because provocation does not justify self-defense in tort law; only the prevention of imminent bodily harm can justify it.

a. Words alone: So just as *words* of insult by themselves will usually not constitute an assault (see *supra*, p. 13), so they will not by themselves justify the use of any degree of force. But when insults or threats are spoken in combination with any kind of **hostile act** (e.g., the raising of a fist), they may contribute to the defendant's overall belief that she is in imminent danger of physical harm, in which case the defendant *will* have the right to use force in self-defense. P&K, p. 125.

4. **Harm must be imminent:** The defendant may not use force to avoid harm which is *not imminent*, but future, unless it reasonably appears to her that there will not be a later chance to prevent the danger.

    Example: "A draws his sword from his scabbard and says, 'If it were not an assize time, I would run you through, but God help you when the court rises.' B immediately grapples with A and takes his sword from him, wounding him, but not severely." B was not privileged to use force against A, because the harm was a future one, and it should have appeared to B that he would have a later opportunity to defend himself. But if the confrontation had taken place in a tavern, and A had drawn his sword and said, "When you step out of this tavern tonight, I will run you through," B would have been justified in disarming A, since his ability to protect himself stepping out into the dark is limited. See Rest. 2d, §63, Illustrs. 10 and 11.

F. **Degree of force:** Just as no force may be used unless necessary to protect against an imminent harm, so only the *degree* of force necessary to prevent that harm may be used. If the defendant uses more force than was necessary, she will be liable for damage caused by the excess.

1. **Both sides with claims:** As a result of the rule against the use of more force than necessary, it may happen that each party to a fight has a claim against the other. Thus if A attacks B with his fists, injuring him slightly, and B defends himself by seriously wounding A with a knife, B will have a claim against A for his injuries and A will have a claim against B for the knife wounds (which would not have occurred had B limited his response to a reasonable degree of force, such as the use of his own fists).

2. **Minor assaults:** Even if a threatened harmful or offensive contact or imprisonment does not seem likely to lead to more than **minor injury**, the person threatened may use such force as is necessary to avoid it.

    Example: P and D get into an argument. According to D's later testimony, P calls D a liar and makes an attempt to hit him with his fist. D then hits P and injures him.

    Held, D was entitled to use a reasonable degree of force (his fists) so as to prevent P's attack, even though D did not believe that he was in danger of serious bodily harm. Therefore, the trial court's jury instructions limiting the right of self-defense to cases where the defendant believes himself in danger of great harm was incorrect. *Boston v. Muncy*, 233 P.2d 300 (Okla. 1951).

G. **Deadly force:** As we have seen, the general rule is that the defendant may use whatever degree of force is necessary to defend herself against imminent harmful or offensive contact. But there is an exception to this rule: the defendant may **not** use **deadly force** (i.e., force intended or likely to cause death or serious bodily injury) unless she herself is in danger of death or serious bodily harm. Rest. 2d, §§65 and 66. (And, of course, even where the defendant is threatened by such serious bodily harm or death, she may not use deadly force if a lesser degree of force would suffice to dispel the danger.)

> **Example:** P swings his fists twice at D's face, but since P is weak, the blows don't do any real damage. D, instead of retreating (as he could safely do) or swinging his own fists (which he could also safely do), gashes P with a large knife, killing him. P's estate brings a wrongful death claim against D.
>
> D cannot claim self-defense. He was not, nor reasonably seemed to be, in danger of great bodily injury or death. Therefore, he had no right to use deadly force to repel the attack.

1. **May have to submit:** The "deadly force" rule means that even if the defendant *cannot protect himself* against a non-deadly attack without the use of deadly force, he *still* may not use deadly force. Thus even if D in the above example had been a poor street-fighter who couldn't have repelled P's non-deadly attack with D's own fists, and couldn't have retreated, D would still have had to submit to the beating by P rather than use the deadly knife.

2. **"Deadly force" defined:** What constitutes "deadly force" will depend not only upon the weapon, but upon the way it is used. Thus the hand of a black-belt karate expert, if capable of breaking an adversary's neck and used with that intent, will be deadly force; conversely, the use of the butt of a gun merely to stun an opponent would not be. See Rest. 2d, §63, Comment d.

   a. **Rape:** The threat of *rape* or *sodomy* is deemed sufficiently serious that the victim may use deadly force if there is no other way to prevent the attack. Rest. 2d, §65(1)(b).

H. **Retreat:** The general rule, as we have seen, is that force (whether deadly or otherwise) may be used only if necessary to prevent the threatened harm. What if the threatened harm could be avoided merely by running away? The defendant's *"duty to retreat"* has been the subject of much debate, and the courts are split.

1. **One view:** Some courts hold that the defendant may **stand her ground and use deadly force against an attack, even if she could retreat with complete safety**. This view gives priority to the "dignity and sense of honor of the individual." P&K, p. 127.

2. **Other view:** Other courts, "giving priority to the importance of human life" (P&K, p. 127), hold that one who is attacked must retreat if she can do so safely. Even these courts, however, do not require one who is attacked in her *own home* to retreat "from room to room." P&K, p. 128.

3. **Analogy to criminal statute:** Most courts, regardless of precedent, will probably apply in a tort suit the same rule that the legislature has decreed for *criminal* cases. *Id.* The trend in the criminal area is towards requiring retreat where this can be done safely.

4. **Restatement view:** The Second Restatement requires the person who is attacked to retreat (if she can do so safely) in some situations, but not in others:

   a. **Use of non-deadly force:** The person being attacked may **always refuse to retreat**, if she is willing to use **only non-deadly force** to repel the attack. Rest. 2d, §63(2).

b. **Deadly force:** Where the person attacked wants to use deadly force to defend herself, she may not do so if she is attacked somewhere other than her dwelling, and she could retreat to safety. So there's a general duty to retreate before use of deadly force, according to the Restatement. But if the person is attacked *within her dwelling,* she does **not** have to retreat (except that she must retreat if she is being attacked by someone who also lives in the same dwelling, e.g. a spouse). Rest. 2d, §65(2).

5. **Ordinary rules apply in dwelling:** But keep in mind that although the duty to retreat may not exist where a person is attacked in his own dwelling, the other rules regarding self-defense still apply. Thus the homeowner who is robbed at gunpoint may not shoot the robber if there is another, less deadly, way of disposing of the threat.

  a. **Prevention of crime:** But if it does appear to the homeowner that there is no way to prevent a burglary or robbery except by, say, shooting the perpetrator, he may do so **even if he himself is not directly attacked.** This is so because deadly force may be used to **prevent most felonies,** including those involving the breaking and entry of a residence. See Rest. 2d, §143(2).

I. **Injury to third person:** Suppose that in a situation where the defendant is entitled to use reasonable force in his self-defense, he does so, and injures an **innocent bystander.** In this situation, the use of force in self-defense will generally be privileged, assuming that the defendant did not act negligently.

  Example: D is attacked by X and Y. He defends himself by shooting at them, and hits P.

  Held, assuming that D was entitled to use deadly force to defend himself against X and Y, he is not liable to P even if P was merely an innocent bystander. *Morris v. Platt,* 32 Conn. 75 (1864).

IV. DEFENSE OF OTHERS

  A. **General rule:** The common law recognized a person's right to use reasonable force to defend a member of his own family against attack. Today, even if a bystander sees a **complete stranger** being attacked, all courts would allow the bystander to use reasonable force to intervene; P&K, p. 130; Rest. 2d, §76.

  1. **Degree of force:** The intervenor is subject to the same rules of reasonable force as the person being attacked would be. Thus the intervenor may not use deadly force to repel what appears to him to be a non-deadly attack. Similarly, he may not use a greater degree of force than appears necessary to repel the attack.

  2. **Reasonable mistake:** What about *mistake*? Although courts are split, the modern view is that if a person makes a **reasonable mistake about the need for force (including the degree of danger to the third person),** the defense-of-others defense is **not forfeited.** See Rest. 2d §72.

    a. **Unreasonable mistake:** But *all* courts agree that D's belief in the need to use force in defense of another (and D's selection of the level of force to use) **must at least be reasonable.** So if D makes a **negligent mistake** about whether the third person (call her X) is in physical danger, or about whether D's proposed physical contact will help avoid the danger, D will not be able to use the defense-of-others defense.

Example: D, a good samaritan, sees P, a little old lady, who is slowly crossing the street. D believes that P is about to be struck by an SUV, so he pushes P out of the way, causing her to fall and break her hip. If D was negligent in believing that P was actually in danger, D will be liable to P for battery. But if D was reasonable in his belief that P would likely be hit by the SUV if she was not pushed out of the way, and reasonable in the amount of force he used, he will be able to use defense-of-others as a defense to a battery action by P. And that's true even if D was mistaken about the existence of the danger (e.g., because the driver of the SUV saw P and wouldn't have hit her).

V. DEFENSE OF PROPERTY

A. **General rule:** There is a privilege to defend property (both land and chattels) on essentially the same basis as the right to defend oneself.

1. **Reasonable force:** The property owner may use only as much force as appears necessary to protect the property.

2. **Verbal demand required first:** The owner must first make a *verbal demand* that the intruder stop, before using force, unless it reasonably appears that violence or other harm will occur immediately, or that the request to stop will be useless. See Rest. 2d, §77(c).

   a. **Allow time for intruder to obey:** Furthermore, if the owner does make a request to leave, the owner must give the intruder *sufficient time to obey the request,* unless it's clear that the request will not be heeded.

   Example: While O is walking around his rural property, he comes upon Neighbor, who is trespassing. O says, "Get off my property!" Neighbor pauses for two seconds without saying anything, at which point O hits him in the leg with a stick that O is carrying. This is battery, and the defense-of-property defense does not apply, because O was required to give Neighbor a reasonable time to obey the request to leave, unless it reasonably appeared to O (which it didn't) that Neighbor would not obey.

B. **Mistake:** A *reasonable mistake* of fact by the property owner will have different consequences, depending on whether the mistake relates to the existence of the danger, or, instead, to the intruder's own lack of privilege.

1. **Mistake as to danger:** If the property owner mistakenly but reasonably believes that force is necessary to protect her property, her use of force will be privileged, provided that there is a real non-privileged intrusion.

   Example: D is sitting at home one night, when she sees P crawling through an open window in D's house. D mistakenly but reasonably believes that P is armed and might commit violence; accordingly, she rushes at P without warning, throws him out of the window, and slams the window. In fact, P was unarmed, and has never committed the slightest violence during his long career as a cat burglar. D's use of force without warning is privileged, even though in reality no violence was threatened (thereby making this the kind of situation in which a warning before the use of force would ordinarily be necessary); this is so because D's mistake was as to the necessity for using force.

2. Mistake as to intruder's privilege: But if the property owner reasonably believes that the intruder has no right to be there, and it turns out that the intruder's presence was in fact privileged for some reason (see, e.g., the discussion of necessity, *infra*, p. 79), the property owner's use of force will *not* be privileged. P&K, pp. 131-32; Rest. 2d, §77(a).

Example: P's boat goes adrift, and runs aground on D's beach. A storm arises, threatening to carry the boat out to sea. P enters D's land to save his boat (as he is privileged to do under the doctrine of necessity — see *infra*, p. 80). D reasonably but mistakenly believes that P is attempting to steal D's own boat. He therefore blocks P's way and knocks him down. D will be liable for his injuries to P, and for the loss of P's boat, despite the reasonableness of his mistake. This is so because D was mistaken not about the necessity of using force, but about the absence of P's own privilege to enter D's property. See Rest. 2d, §77, Illustr. 1.

C. Deadly force: As stated, the property owner can never use more force than reasonably appears necessary to protect the property. But even beyond this, the owner does *not* have a general right to use *deadly force* even where the intrusion can only be prevented this way.

1. Serious bodily harm: Instead, the property owner may use deadly force against the intruder only if she believes that the latter will, unless he is kept out, cause *death or serious bodily harm*.

a. Certain felonies: However, the property owner may be privileged to use deadly force to *prevent certain felonies*, namely those involving death, serious bodily harm, or the *breaking and entering of a dwelling place*. This is really a separate privilege to prevent certain crimes, and is only indirectly related to the privilege to defend one's property. See Rest. 2d, §143(2).

b. Burglary: This privilege to prevent breaking and entering crimes in dwellings means that a *homeowner may use deadly force against a burglar*, provided that she reasonably believes that nothing short of this force will safely keep the burglar out. Most courts would probably also hold that she has the right to use such force against a burglar who has already entered, again assuming that there is no other apparent safe way of expelling him.

i. Limited to dwelling place: However, this privilege to prevent burglaries and other breaking and entering felonies (e.g., a breaking and entering occurring during the daytime, and therefore not a burglary under many state statutes) applies only in the case of *dwelling places*.

ii. Not applicable to trespassers: And this privilege also does not permit the homeowner to use deadly force (e.g. a shotgun) against one who is merely a *trespasser* on lands belonging to the family homestead. The casual trespasser, in fact, must normally be warned before even *non-deadly force* is used against him.

2. Where expulsion would injure intruder: If the situation is one where the property owner may not use deadly force against the intruder, she may furthermore not *eject* the intruder if this is likely to cause him serious injury. See Rest. 2d, §77, Comment e. See also, *Ploof v. Putnam, infra*, p. 80, where D was held liable to P for unmooring P's boat during a storm and thereby injuring P.

D. Mechanical devices: Property owners frequently make use of various ***mechanical devices*** to protect their property. These include barbed wire, glass shards on top of walls, vicious watch-dogs, and spring guns (guns rigged mechanically to go off when the premises are entered). The general rule regarding such devices is that the owner is privileged to use them ***only if he would be privileged to use a similar degree of force if he were present and acting himself***. Thus to the extent that the devices are likely to cause serious bodily harm, and are therefore to be considered deadly force, they may be used only to protect against serious injury to the inhabitants, or, possibly, to protect against breaking and entering felonies in a dwelling.

1. **Trespasser:** Thus if an electrified fence causes serious injury to a trespasser who has no intent to enter the house, the owner will be liable since he would not have been privileged to use such deadly force personally against the trespasser.

2. **Reasonable mistake:** And regardless of whether the property owner's intent was to pro-tect his home against dangerous felonies (e.g. armed robbery), his right to use the mechan-ical device in a particular case will be measured by considering whether deadly force could have been used against *that particular intruder*. Thus an electrified fence intended to guard only against burglary but which nonetheless severely injures a casual trespasser (not to mention a person with a privilege to enter, e.g. the postman) will give rise to liabil-ity.

3. **Spring gun case:** The most important case involving mechanical devices is one concern-ing a spring gun, described in the following example.

   Example: D owns an unoccupied boarded-up farmhouse. Because the house has been broken into many times and robbed of various household items, D conceals a shotgun in the bedroom, and connects it to the bedroom doorway in such a way that a person entering that room will discharge the gun. P, with a friend, breaks into the house, in order to steal some bottles and fruit jars which they think are antiques. When P enters the bedroom, the gun goes off, and part of his leg is blown away by the blast. P sues for his injuries, wins in a jury trial, and D appeals.

   Held, on appeal, D is liable. A property owner may not use deadly force to defend his property against a trespasser, unless the latter is committing a felony of violence, or is endangering human life by his act. And what a property owner may not do directly, he may not do indirectly by a spring gun or other mechanical device. *Katko v. Briney*, 183 N.W.2d 657 (Iowa 1971).

   A dissent argued that D should be liable only if P showed that D ***intended*** to shoot anyone who entered the bedroom. The dissent contended that P had not met that bur-den, and that, in fact, D had testified that he was only trying to "frighten" intruders, not to shoot them.

   Note: The court in *Katko* approved a jury instruction to the effect that the crime of breaking and entering is not a felony of violence, and therefore does not give rise to the owner's right to use deadly force (unless the inhabitants' safety is threatened for some other reason). This position is contrary to that of the Second Restatement, which explicitly gives a right to use deadly force to prevent the breaking and entering of a *dwelling*. Rest. 2d, §143(2). Note, however, that the Restatement test would have led to the same result here, since the unoccupied farmhouse was not a dwelling.

Note: As stated, the dissent claimed that liability would lie only where it was shown that the property owner intended to injure intruders, not just to frighten them. However, "deadly force" is generally defined to include not only force intended to cause serious bodily injury, but also that which is *likely* to cause such injury, regardless of the user's intent. See Rest. 2d, §79. Therefore, the *Katko* majority seems to have been correct to require D to show that the situation entitled him to use deadly force, a burden which he failed to meet. Also, the jury was free to believe that D knew with "substantial certainty" that injury would result, whether or not he literally intended it. See *Garratt v. Dailey, supra*, p. 6.

4. **Warning:** In the case of non-deadly mechanical devices, (e.g. barbed wire), most courts have held that the owner must post some kind of *warning* of the existence of the device, unless its use in the area is so common that it is reasonable to assume an intruder is aware that it may be present. See Rest. 2d, §84, Comment f. See also P&K, pp. 134-35.

   a. **Deadly devices:** But if a mechanical device constitutes deadly force (i.e. it is intended or likely to cause death or serious injury), and the use of the device meets the other requirements for use of deadly force, listed above, then normally no warning of the existence of the device will be required. See Rest. 2d, §85, Comment c. Thus in *Katko, supra*, the fact that no warning of the spring gun present was posted, seems to have had no effect on the outcome of that case.

      i. **Warning not bar to liability:** But, conversely, if such a deadly device is used against an intruder against whom the owner himself could not use deadly force, the fact that a warning has been posted will not save the owner from liability.

VI. RECAPTURE OF CHATTELS

A. **General right:** Just as a property owner may in some circumstances have the right to use force to defend her possession of land or chattels (discussed *supra*), so she may sometimes have the right to use force to *regain* possession of chattels or land taken from her by someone else. Re-entry on land is discussed *infra*, p. 78. Here, we deal only with recapture of chattels.

B. **Similar to defense of possession:** The right to forcibly recapture chattels is more limited than the right to defend existing possession. This is so because in one case, the owner is merely seeking to maintain the status quo, whereas in the other she is herself the aggressor, disturbing the peace. Therefore, there are several respects in which the right of recapture is circumscribed:

   1. **Reasonable mistake:** If the owner reasonably but *mistakenly* believes that some third person has possession of the former's goods, or if she reasonably but mistakenly believes that force is necessary to retake the goods, it is she, not the third person, who must bear the consequence of her mistake, and *no privilege will exist.* This is somewhat different from

the case of defense of property, where the property owner is not liable for a reasonable but mistaken belief that force is necessary.

   a. **Shoplifting:** However, in the case of a suspected shoplifter, a merchant may be protected against a reasonable but mistaken suspicion under certain circumstances described *infra*, p. 77.

2. **Fresh pursuit:** The privilege exists only if the property owner is in *"fresh pursuit"* to recover her property. P&K, p. 138. If the owner waits a substantial length of time before making his attempt to get the property back (in some circumstances, probably as little as an hour), she can no longer use reasonable force to retake it, and instead must resort to the courts.

3. **Reasonable force:** The force used must be reasonable in the circumstances, and *deadly force* can never be used.

   a. **Resistance:** But if the wrongdoer resists the owner's attempt to get the property back, this resistance may itself give rise to the right to use deadly force in self-defense. This was the case in the *Hodgeden* case, discussed *infra*.

4. **Wrongful taking:** The privilege exists only if the property was taken *wrongfully* from the owner. If the owner parts willingly with possession, and then an event occurs which gives her the right to repossession of the goods, she will generally not be able to use force to regain it.

   > **Example:** Storekeeper sells a TV to Consumer on a chattel mortgage, with the contract providing that Storekeeper may repossess the television if Consumer does not make the monthly payments. Consumer misses several payments, and Storekeeper attempts to break into Consumer's house to repossess the set. He has no right to do so, since the breaking-in constitutes the use of force, and since Storekeeper willingly parted with possession. (He could repossess if this could be done without "breach of the peace," but that is not the case here. See §9-503 of the UCC.)

C. **Detention by merchant:** A merchant who thinks that a customer is shoplifting is put to a difficult choice. If she attempts to stop the customer and search or question him, she may be liable for false imprisonment or false arrest, if it turns out that no crime was committed or attempted. But the alternative, of course, is to let the customer walk away, possibly with the goods. A number of courts have aided the storekeeper in this position by granting her or her employees a privilege to *temporarily detain* for investigation a person who is *reasonably suspected* of stealing property. See P&K, pp. 141-42. See also Rest. 2d, §120A.

1. **Limited privilege:** The privilege is a limited one. First, the detention must be limited to a short time, generally 10 or 15 minutes or less, the time necessary to make a quick investigation.

2. **No coercion:** Also, the storekeeper or detective may not use the detention to attempt to coerce *payment*.

3. **No arrest:** Nor may the merchant or detective purport to *arrest* the suspect — if this occurs, the privilege terminates, and there is liability for false imprisonment and false arrest if a crime was not in fact committed.

4. **No confession:** And the storekeeper may not attempt to obtain a *confession* once it is determined the crime was committed.

5. **Off premises:** Some cases have held that the privilege of detention exists only where the suspect is stopped and detained *on the store's premises*. Thus the Rest. 2d, §120A, in a Caveat, states that no opinion is expressed as to whether the privilege extends to one who has left the premises but is immediately nearby.

   a. **New view:** However, some cases have extended this privilege to cover the area immediately around the store. See, e.g., *Bonkowski v. Arlan's Department Store*, 162 N.W.2d 347 Mich. 1968) (privilege held applicable where store detective stops P who is outside store and walking toward next-door parking lot). A court would probably be more likely to find the privilege applicable if the stop occurred on the store's own property (e.g., a store-owned parking lot) than if it happened elsewhere (e.g., in the street, or in a parking lot not owned by the store).

D. **Entry on land:** Just as an owner attempting to recover her goods may sometimes use reasonable force against the person of the wrongdoer, so she may use reasonable force to *enter the wrongdoer's land* to recover the missing goods.

   1. **Reasonable time and manner:** The entry must be made at a *reasonable time* and in a *reasonable manner*.

   2. **Use of force:** The owner of the goods may use reasonable force to enter, but only if the circumstances are such that she would be allowed to use force against the landowner's person (see *supra*, p. 76).

   3. **Where landowner not at fault:** But if the chattels are on another person's property through *no fault of the latter* (e.g. carried on by storm) the owner has only a limited privilege to enter to recover them — she may enter the land, but she is liable for any actual substantial harm which she causes. This privilege is similar to that of necessity, discussed below.

      a. **Chattel owner's fault:** However, if the goods are on the other person's land because of their *owner's* own fault (e.g. she negligently lets her boat drift onto a neighbor's beach) she may not enter, even if she is willing to pay for actual damage. She must instead bring a court action (usually called "replevin") to get back the property. See Rest. 2d, §200, Comment c.

VII. RE-ENTRY ON LAND

A. **Privilege generally:** A property owner who has been deprived of his possession of his *land* may sometimes recover it by force, just as one deprived of possession of his chattels may, as we have just seen.

B. **Majority rule:** The issue of recovery of real property usually arises in the case of a *tenant who overstays the lease*, and is forcibly thrown out by the landlord. Most American courts hold that a landlord has *no right* to use force (whether it results in bodily harm or not) to eject a tenant. P&K, p. 144. In states following this rule, the tenant may therefore recover for assault and battery, trespass to chattels, etc.

1. **Rationale:**   The majority rule relies in part on the fact that there are almost always summary procedures permitting the landlord to use legal process to obtain a speedy recovery of his property, thus minimizing the need for him to take matters into his own hands.

2. **Mere entry:**   But states following this majority rule usually do allow the landlord to enter the property if he can do so ***without force***. And if the lease itself says that the landlord may use force to re-enter, courts which would otherwise follow the majority rule may nonetheless uphold forcible entry, provided that no more than reasonable force is used.

VIII. NECESSITY

A. **Directed towards innocent person:**   The privileges we have examined so far are generally triggered by wrongdoing on the part of the plaintiff. For instance, it is the plaintiff's attack upon the defendant that triggers the latter's right of self-defense, the plaintiff's wrongful taking of the defendant's chattel that gives the latter the right to recapture it, etc. This being the case, it is not unreasonable to cause the plaintiff to lose his tort action, since he may be fairly said to have brought his injury upon himself. But there are situations in which the defendant is privileged, because of unusual exigencies, to harm the plaintiff, even though the plaintiff himself is completely blameless. This privilege is usually described as that of ***"necessity."***

B. **General scope:**   There are two categories of emergencies which may justify the defendant in harming the plaintiff's property: cases of so called ***"public necessity"*** and those of ***"private necessity"***.

1. **Single rule:**   A single rule applies to both of these categories: the defendant is privileged to harm the property interest of the plaintiff where it is necessary to do so in order to prevent great harm to third persons or to the defendant herself. If the class of persons being protected is the ***public as a whole***, or a substantial number of persons, the privilege is said to be that of "public necessity." If the defendant is only protecting ***her own interests***, or those of a few private citizens, the privilege is that of "private necessity."

2. **Distinction:**   The principal distinction between these two kinds of necessity is that in the "public" case, the defendant does ***not have to pay*** for the damage, whereas in the private case, she does.

C. **Public necessity:**   The privilege of public necessity exists wherever interference with the land or chattels of another is necessary, or reasonably appears necessary, to prevent a ***disaster*** to the community, or to a substantial number of people.

> **Example:** A fire is raging in the houses within the immediate vicinity of P's house, and P is removing goods from it. Although the fire has already passed over P's house, D, the Fire Warden of San Francisco, determines that there is a danger that the fire will spread elsewhere, and in order to prevent this, orders P's house blown up. P sues for the damage to his property.
>
> *Held*, for D. His conduct was privileged, in order to prevent the spread of the fire. "At such times [of emergency], the individual rights of property give way to the higher laws of impending necessity." *Surocco v. Geary*, 3 Cal. 69 (1853).

1. **Act by private persons:** In the above examples, the privileged act was committed by public officials. But even a private individual, if she is acting on behalf of the community, may claim the privilege of public necessity.

   > **Example:** D, a private citizen, breaks into P's house to put out a fire inside it that D reasonably thinks may spread to numerous nearby buildings. D will have the privilege of public necessity.

2. **Apparent necessity:** The privilege will exist as long as the necessity was reasonably apparent, whether or not it in fact existed. (This is true for the privilege of private necessity, as well.) P&K, p. 148.

3. **Compensation:** The person who injures the plaintiff's property, and successfully claims the privilege of public necessity, will never herself be required to reimburse the plaintiff for the damage suffered. And generally, the community as a whole (e.g. the state or town which benefitted) has ***not***, as a matter of common law, usually been required to ***compensate*** the victim.

   a. **Statutes:** However, several states have enacted ***statutes*** providing for compensation to the victim in a case of public necessity. Such statutes are analogous to eminent domain statutes applicable where property has been taken to build highways, public projects, etc. See Rest. 2d, §196, Comment h.

4. **Personal injury:** The privilege of public necessity is usually used to justify injury to the plaintiff's land or chattels. However, in a sufficiently compelling case, it could also justify the infliction of injury to the ***person***. See P&K, p. 148. But remember that as in the case of property damage, the privilege only applies where there is no other less-damaging way of combatting the danger.

D. **Private necessity:** The doctrine of ***private necessity*** is similar to that of public necessity. Any person is privileged to prevent injury to himself or his property, or to the person or property of a third person, by injuring private property, if there is no less-damaging way of preventing the harm.

   > **Example:** P and his family are sailing on a sloop, when a sudden storm arises. P moors at D's dock for safety. D unmoors the boat, causing it to be driven onto the shore, destroying it and injuring P and his family. P sues in trespass and also for negligence.
   >
   > *Held*, P had the privilege of private necessity to moor himself to D's property. Therefore, D had no right to interfere with P's exercise of this privilege, and D is thus liable for the damages his unmooring of the boat inflicted upon P. *Ploof v. Putnam*, 71 A. 188 (Vt. 1908), *supra*, p. 74.

1. **Limited danger:** Whereas public necessity apparently only applies where the danger to the community is severe, private necessity can apply even in less drastically dangerous situations. However, in determining whether the privilege exists in a particular case, the harm to the plaintiff's property interest must be weighed against the severity and likelihood of the danger that the defendant seeks to avoid. See Rest. 2d, §263, Comment d.

2. **Technical tort nullified:** Where the privilege of private necessity exists, it will be a *complete defense* to a tort claim where the plaintiff has suffered no actual substantial harm. Thus a claim for "technical" trespass, alleging merely that the defendant intentionally entered the plaintiff's land, and not showing any actual damages, will be defeated by the privilege of private necessity. (This is what happened in the *Ploof* case, where there was no showing that D's dock would have been harmed by the mooring.)

    a. **Actual damage:** But if the defendant causes *actual damage* to the plaintiff, private necessity provides only a *limited privilege* — the defendant has the right to interfere with the plaintiff's property rights, but she must *pay for the damage* she causes the plaintiff. That's what makes private necessity a more limited privilege than public necessity. See P&K, p. 147; see also Rest. 2d, §263(2).

    Example: D's boat is discharging cargo at P's dock when a storm arises. Because of the severity of the storm, D is unable to move his boat and has his employees moor it tightly to the dock. During the storm, the boat repeatedly knocks against the dock, damaging the latter. P sues D for the damage to the dock.

    Held, D had a right to use the dock to protect its property. However, it also had an obligation to compensate P for the damage caused to P, since D's act was an intentional one and the source of the danger was not an object belonging to P. "Theologians hold that a starving man may, without moral guilt, take what is necessary to sustain life; but it could hardly be said that the obligation would not be upon such person to pay the value of the property so taken when he became able to do so. And so . . . necessity, in times of war or peace, may require the taking of private property . . . ; but under our system of jurisprudence compensation must be made." *Vincent v. Lake Erie Transportation Co.*, 124 N.W. 221 (Minn. 1910).

    b. **Owner may not resist:** If the holder of the privilege of private necessity must pay for any actual damage she causes, one might wonder what the use of the privilege is in such cases. But there is one very significant use — where the privilege exists, the person whose property is being harmed has *no right to use reasonable force* to defeat the exercise of the privilege, and is liable for any damages he causes by using such force. See Rest. 2d, §263, Comment b. Thus in the *Vincent* case, if P had unmoored D's ship (as the dock owner in *Ploof* did), and the ship had been damaged as a result, D presumably would have had a counterclaim for this damage. And D probably would also have been justified in using reasonable force in turn to prevent P from such an unmooring.

IX. ARREST AND OTHER AUTHORITY OF LAW

A. **Generally:** Acts done under *authority of law* are, in general, privileged. For instance, a police officer who executes a valid arrest warrant, and uses proper procedure in doing so, of course has a defense against a false imprisonment suit by the person he arrests. (This is so even if it later turns out that the arrested person committed no crime.)

1. **Difficulties:** However, if the police officer or other official fails to use proper procedures, or enforces a purported legal order which was itself issued without jurisdiction, or

there is some other flaw in the proceedings, it can be very hard to determine whether the privilege of legal authority exists. We examine here in detail only the privilege of *arrest*, since it this privilege that is usually at issue in intentional tort cases.

B. Common law rules: There are a variety of common law rules which govern the privilege of arrest. These have been changed substantially by statute in most jurisdictions, but they nonetheless furnish a general overview of the privilege.

1. **Arrest with warrant:** Where a police officer executes an arrest *with an arrest warrant*, he will be privileged if the court has jurisdiction to issue the warrant, the warrant is "fair on its face" (i.e. is formally complete and consistent), and the officer uses proper procedures in making the arrest. Many modern cases hold that the arrest will be privileged even if the court did not have jurisdiction to issue the warrant (e.g., because it was issued without probable cause). P&K, p. 149.

    a. **Mistaken identity:** Even if the warrant is completely correct, the officer will be liable if he reasonably but mistakenly arrests X when the warrant means Y. P&K, p. 150. Furthermore, the officer is liable if he uses more force than is reasonably necessary to make the arrest (discussed below).

2. **Arrest without warrant:** The rules governing arrest without warrant are complex, and only a few of the general principles are set forth here:

    a. **Felony or breach of the peace in presence:** An *officer* may make a warrantless arrest for a felony or breach of the peace which is being committed or seems about to be committed *in his presence*. A *citizen* may do the same.

    b. **Past felony:** Once a felony has been committed, an *officer* may still make a warrantless arrest, provided that he *reasonably believes* that the felony has been committed, and also *reasonably believes* that he has the right criminal. The arrest is privileged so long as he can show both of these reasonable beliefs, even if it turns out either that there was no crime or that he has arrested the wrong person.

        i. **Citizen:** A *citizen*, on the other hand, has a narrower privilege in the case of a past felony. A citizen's arrest is valid only if a felony has *in fact been committed*. However, the citizen, like the officer, will not lose the privilege by arresting the wrong person, provided that she reasonably believed him to be the right one. P&K, p. 154.

    c. **Past breach of peace:** If there has been a past breach of peace (i.e., a non-felony involving a threat of violence or disorder, such as a threat to make a criminal assault), neither an officer nor a citizen may make a warrantless arrest, unless the breach of peace was committed in his presence, and he is in "fresh pursuit." P&K, p. 154.

    d. **Misdemeanor:** The common law rule with respect to *misdemeanors* not involving the breach of the peace was that neither officer nor citizen could arrest without a warrant. However, some states have allowed an officer to arrest for such a misdemeanor if it is committed in his presence.

3. **Reasonable force:** One making an arrest may not use more force than is reasonably necessary. What is "reasonable" force in various specific circumstances has been the subject of much dispute in the courts.

a. **Prevention:** Where the arrest is made to ***prevent a felony*** which threatens human life or safety, courts have universally held that even deadly force may be used, if there appears to be no other way to prevent the crime. Where the crime does not involve such danger, however, most courts have held that deadly force may ***not*** be used, since it would be out of proportion to the severity of the offense. P&K, p. 155.

b. **Apprehension of suspect after crime:** If a crime has ***already been committed***, the right of the police to use deadly force to effect an arrest is now a ***constitutional*** issue, as the result of a 1985 Supreme Court decision. Deadly force may not be used "unless it is necessary to prevent the escape and the officer has probable cause to believe that the suspect poses a ***significant threat of death or serious physical injury*** to the officer or others." *Tennessee v. Garner*, 471 U.S. 1 (1985). So an officer who uses deadly force to prevent escape of a non-dangerous felon may be liable to the felon for his injuries from the deadly force.

C. **Privilege to use force in resisting arrest:** Just as there may be a privilege to use force in making an arrest, so there may in a few situations be a privilege to use force in ***resisting*** an ***unlawful*** arrest. However, one may never use deadly force to resist arrest, even if unlawful. And in general, the privilege to resist unlawful arrest by force has been very much curtailed in recent years. P&K, pp. 156-57.

X. DISCIPLINE

A. **Generally:** A person who by virtue of her job or status is charged with maintaining ***discipline*** may sometimes be privileged to use force and restraint to ensure that discipline. This is most frequently the case for ***parents, teachers*** and ***military officials***.

1. **Reasonable degree of force:** Predictably, however, the rule is that the person doing the disciplining may not use more force than is reasonably necessary to maintain the discipline. To determine whether the degree of force is reasonable, the severity of the misconduct, the age, strength, sex, etc. of the person being disciplined, the motive of the discipliner, are all to be taken into account.

XI. JUSTIFICATION

A. **Justification as a "catch-all" defense:** Even if the defendant's conduct does not fit within one of the conventional defenses discussed above, he may be entitled to the general defense of ***"justification,"*** a "catch-all" used where there are good reasons for exculpating the defendant for what would otherwise be an intentional tort.

> **Example:** On the last day of the school year, P, 14 years old, is a passenger on a school bus owned by D1, and driven by D2. The 65 to 70 students aboard are in a boisterous and exuberant mood, and a number of them break windows and lights, and cause other damage to the bus. D2, after failing to restore order, bypasses several scheduled stops and takes the children to a police station. P, who did not take part in any of the destruction, sues for false imprisonment.

Held, the Ds should have been allowed to introduce evidence of *justification*. D2, the driver, had a duty to "take reasonable measures for the safety and protection of . . . the passengers and the property," and his conduct may have constituted such reasonable measures. *Sindle v. New York City Transit Authority*, 307 N.E.2d 245 (N.Y. 1973).

Quiz Yourself on

DEFENSES TO INTENTIONAL TORTS *(Entire Chapter)*

14. Anne Boleyn enters the hospital to have her sinuses drained. While she is anesthetized, her doctor, Ryno Plasty, removes her eleventh finger (which doesn't function anyway), as well. Has Plasty committed a tort? _____

15. In an NHL playoff hockey game, Wayne Greatsky gets around the player defending him, Mario Lemeow, and scores. Lemeow, enraged at being scored upon, skates up behind Greatsky and hacks at him with his stick. Greatsky falls, strikes his head on the ice, and suffers a career-ending injury. Greatsky sues Lemeouw for battery. Lemeow raises the affirmative defense of implied consent. Will this defense succeed?

16. Axel Cutioner tells Mary, Queen of Scots, that he is a magician, and offers her a solid gold ring if she lets him saw her in half. She consents, not realizing the gold ring is cheap plastic, and, in fact, still has Cracker Jack candy stuck to it. When she discovers the fraud, she sues him for battery. Does her consent constitute a valid defense? _____

17. Ron is a "responsible" rapist — he never rapes anyone without wearing a condom, and he does not carry a weapon. One night, he attempts to rape Lorena, telling her that he'll be gentle and won't hurt her as long as she doesn't resist. He in fact uses no overt force as he puts on a condom and prepares to assault her. Lorena decides (reasonably under the circumstances) that the least deadly way to prevent intercourse is to use a knife she has hidden in her purse; she does so, and castrates Ron. Ron sues Lorena for battery. She defends on grounds of self-defense. Who wins? _____

18. Fletcher Christian, deck hand on the ship HMS Bounty, plays a practical joke on Captain Bligh. Bligh whips Christian, in violation of Navy regulations. Humiliated, Christian sets Bligh afloat on a raft. When Bligh gets back to civilization and sues Christian, Christian claims he acted in self-defense. Is his defense valid? _____

19. Aaron Burr is sitting in an aisle seat in the bleachers at a baseball game, minding his own business. Alexander Hamilton walks up to Burr, his arms laden with beer, nachos, and bratwurst. Hamilton sneers, "Get out of my way, you stupid butthead." People in nearby seats titter. Burr gets up and decks Hamilton, sending him sprawling backwards. Hamilton sues Burr for battery. Burr defends on self-defense grounds. What result? _____

20. Dorothy is out for a drive with her dog, Toto. A howling storm kicks up, and the visibility decreases to almost nothing. Dorothy is terrified, and says, "Toto, I don't think we're in Kansas anymore." She pulls off the road, into the driveway of the Wicked Witch of the West. She grabs Toto and runs into the garage. Wicked Witch sees Dorothy coming and reasonably believes she's trying to steal Witch's magic brooms, which she keeps in the garage. Witch runs out and beats her up. When Dorothy sues Wicked Witch for battery, will Wicked Witch have a valid "defense of property" privilege? _____

21. Portentia Lardo, circus fat lady, visits the U-Pik-M Meat Market. She browses for a while in the Beef Department. As she leaves, not having purchased anything, a store detective runs up behind her yelling, in front of other shoppers, "Stop! Thief! She has a side of beef under her coat!" She is, indeed, so large that she looks like she's hiding something. Portentia stops, mortified, and the detective catches up to her, saying, "Come with me." She follows him to the store office, where he asks her to take off her coat. She does so. When it's obvious she's only fat and not a thief, he says, "I'm sorry. You can go." Does Portentia have a valid claim against the store? _____

22. The Minnow, a tiny ship, sets sail from a tropical port for a three-hour tour. Shortly thereafter a fearsome storm kicks up, the tiny ship is tossed, and the crew seeks refuge at a private dock belonging to Snively. If Snively sues for trespass, will he win? _____

23. Shakespeare, a playwright, is walking down the street. As he passes a doorway, he sees a woman, Lady Macbeth, standing there. She has a glazed look in her eyes, she's holding a cleaver dripping with blood, and her hands are covered with blood as well. Shakespeare slips surreptitiously into a phone booth, calls the police, and emerges, brandishing a gun. He tells Lady Macbeth that if she moves an inch he'll blow her head off. In fact, Lady Macbeth works at the Titus Andronicus Butcher Shop, and she didn't have a chance to wash her hands before she left work. However, when she tries to tell Shakespeare this, he thinks it's a pile of baloney, and doesn't let her go until the police arrive. She sues Shakespeare for false imprisonment. Can he defend on grounds of legal authority? _____

24. Surgeon believes that Patient is suffering from a non-cancerous growth in his esophagus. Patient agrees to have Surgeon perform surgery for the limited purpose of removing the polyp. After Patient is under a general anesthetic, Surgeon opens him up, and discovers that the polyp is in fact a malignancy that has spread to the stomach. Surgeon realizes that if the malignancy is not removed, Patient's life will be in danger. It would subject Patient to material (though not extreme) extra risk to sew him up, bring him out of anesthesia, get his consent to the extended operation, and then do the operation. Instead, Surgeon simply removes the cancerous growth from the stomach. Unbeknownst to Surgeon, Patient has always told friends and relatives, "If I ever get cancer, I don't want them to cut it out of me — I just want to be left alone to die." Patient recovers, and sues Surgeon for battery. Does Patient win? _____

25. Drug Lord is in the business of selling crack. He has heard rumors in the neighborhood that a man nicknamed Scarecrow is a hit man for a rival drug gang, and that Scarecrow has been given a contract on Drug Lord's life. As Drug Lord is finishing a sale of crack one day, he sees Scarecrow come up to him and draw and aim his pistol at Drug Lord. As Scarecrow is about to say something, Drug Lord shoots him in the hand to disable him. Scarecrow turns out to be an undercover police officer, who wanted to arrest Drug Lord (an arrest which would have been legal in the circumstances). Has Drug Lord committed battery against Scarecrow? _____

26. Pilot is flying her two-engine private jet from New York to Boston. Suddenly, one engine stops working, and Pilot is unable to restart it. Pilot knows that there is a good, but not 100%, chance that she will be able to continue on just the other engine until Boston. However, she decides that it would be more prudent to make an emergency landing sooner. There are no commercial airfields around, so she lands in a meadow owned by Farmer. There is no measurable economic harm done to the meadow. Farmer sues Pilot for trespass. May Farmer recover anything? _____

_____

Answers

14. **Yes, he's committed a battery.** The focus here is on the role <u>consent</u> plays in battery. Consent is a valid defense to almost every tort, but only <u>within the scope</u> of the conduct the victim consented to, or conduct closely related to that consent. Here, Anne gave her consent to having her sinuses drained. Removing her

extra finger would be well outside the scope of her consent, *and since no emergency situation existed to justify it,* Plasty will be liable for battery. (For the rule in an emergency, see Question 23.)

15. **Probably not.** Where people participate in an organized sport, each will be held to have impliedly consented to those harmful or offensive bodily contacts that are an ***ordinary part of the give-and-take of the game,*** even if the contact violates the rules of the game. But a player will generally *not* be held to have impliedly consented to actions by fellow competitors that are "unrelated to the normal method of playing the game," and that are done without any competitive purpose. Here, if Lemeow had, say, tripped Greatsky in an attempt to stop him from scoring, the court would probably hold that Greatsky impliedly consented to that conduct, even though it constituted a foul, because the contact was part of the ordinary give-and-take of professional hockey, and was done for competitive purposes. But when Lemeow struck Greatsky out of frustration, and not until the play was over, a court would likely hold that Lemeow's action was "unrelated to the normal method of playing the game," was not done with a competitive purpose, and was therefore not covered by the consent that Greatsky will be found to have impliedly given by entering the league. Cf. *Hackbart v. Cincinnati Bengals, Inc.* (where one football player strikes another out of anger after the play was over, this was not a contact to which the person struck impliedly consented).

16. **Yes.** The rule on fraud as it relates to consent is that it only invalidates consent if it relates to an *essential* matter, not a collateral one (i.e., an unimportant one). The fraud here relates to a collateral matter, not an essential one; as such, the consent is valid.

    RELATED ISSUE: Had Axel not, in fact, been a magician, the fraud would have related to an essential matter and the consent would have been invalid, and Axel would be liable for battery.

17. **Lorena.** One may not use deadly force (i.e., force <u>intended</u> or <u>likely</u> to <u>cause death or serious bodily injury</u>) unless one is in danger of death or serious bodily harm. Lorena's use of the knife here certainly qualifies as deadly force (even though she was only trying to injure, not kill, Ron). However, courts hold that the threat of rape alone — even if there is no overt threat of additional bodily injury — constitutes a threat of serious bodily injury. Rest. 2d §65(1)(b). Since Lorena did not use more force than the situation seemed to require, she qualifies for the privilege of self-defense.

18. **No.** The privilege of self-defense only allows one to use reasonable force to prevent threatened harmful/offensive contact or confinement. When Christian set Bligh adrift there was no longer a threat of danger; it was <u>retaliation</u>, which is *not* a valid ground for self-defense.

19. **Hamilton wins.** Self-defense gives one the privilege to use reasonable force to prevent threatened harmful or offensive contact or confinement. The focus here is on whether <u>insults alone</u> can justify the use of force in self-defense, and the rule is that they can't. But don't interpret this too broadly! Insults (or other types of words) *can* help create a threat of imminent physical harm, especially when they're accompanied by threatening physical gestures. Say, for instance, that Hamilton hadn't had his hands full, but rather had waved a fist at Burr in a menacing way as he spoke to him. In *that* case, self-defense would probably be justified, because there's a threat of physical harm, and not just verbal provocation. Cf. Rest. 2d of Torts §69.

20. **No.** The focus here is on the how the defendant's *mistake* impacts his assertion of the "defense of property" privilege. The answer depends on what it is the defendant's mistaken about. Mistake *negates* the privilege if the mistake consists of a false (even if reasonable) belief that the intruder is not privileged to enter the land. That's the case here; Dorothy entered Witch's land out of necessity, and that's a privilege. Witch was mistaken about Dorothy's privilege to enter, and that mistake negates Witch's defense of prop-

erty privilege. That means she'll be liable to Dorothy.

RELATED ISSUE: But a reasonable mistake as to *whether force is necessary* will leave the privilege *intact*. For instance, let's say Dorothy really was trying to steal the brooms, but she didn't have any weapons and force wouldn't have been necessary to subdue her. If Witch mistakenly believed force was necessary and it wasn't, and that mistake was reasonable, she'll be able to rely on "defense of property" as a defense.

21. **Yes, because the detention wasn't reasonable; she was needlessly humiliated.** Although stores have a right to temporarily detain those reasonably suspected of shoplifting, the privilege is limited. It cannot be lengthy (the few minutes here seem reasonable); it cannot exceed the scope of a brief investigation (e.g., the storekeeper cannot use the detention to attempt to coerce payment for the items); and it cannot involve public humiliation. Here Portentia was publicly humiliated by the detective, and so she may have an intentional infliction of emotional distress claim. She may also have a slander claim (since other shoppers heard the false accusation).

RELATED ISSUE: A common claim in instances like this is for false imprisonment. However, since Portentia was not held anywhere for an appreciable length of time, such a claim wouldn't exist here. But Portentia could sue for slander.

22. **No.** The crew has a private necessity defense, because it seemed necessary to invade Snively's dock to avoid death or serious harm, and the invasion they committed was substantially less serious than the injury they faced. NOTE: Private necessity is analogous to self-defense, but there the *plaintiff* is the source of the threat.

NOTE: The privilege of necessity means the landowner cannot take even what would otherwise be *lawful* action against the entrant. So if Snively turned the boat out to sea, and it was destroyed, Snively would be liable for conversion.

NOTE: The privilege only lasts until the danger has passed. Any excess = trespass.

RELATED ISSUE: Any loss caused to the landowner must be compensated; the private necessity privilege is *limited*.

23. **No, because Lady Macbeth didn't commit the crime.** When it comes to felonies, a private citizen has a privilege of legal authority only if a felony was in fact committed (with no room for a reasonable mistake), and he's got reasonable grounds to believe the person in question committed it. The problem here is that no felony was in fact committed. As a result, Shakespeare won't have a defense based on legal authority even though his mistake may have been "reasonable."

RELATED ISSUE: Say that Shakespeare had been a police officer, and not a private citizen. Then he would have a defense based on legal authority. That's because the privilege of legal authority for a police officer encompasses a reasonable mistake as to whether a felony was actually committed.

RELATED ISSUE: Say that a murder *had* actually taken place nearby, and the perpetrator had escaped. But let's say that Lady Macbeth is innocent; she really did get bloody at her butcher shop job. Whether or not Shakespeare was a police officer, he would have a good "legal authority" defense. That's because where a felony has in fact been committed, a private citizen won't lose the "legal authority" privilege by arresting the person he reasonably (but wrongly) believes committed the crime.

24. **No.** A patient will be deemed as a matter of law to have consented if all the following conditions are met: (1) the patient was unable to give consent (as where he was under anesthesia); (2) the action was neces-

sary to save his life or safeguard his health; (3) the defendant did not know that the patient would refuse to consent if conscious; and (4) a reasonable person would have consented in the circumstances. Here, these conditions were all satisfied, so Patient is deemed to have consented. The fact that in reality Patient was idiosyncratic — and would not have consented if given the choice — is irrelevant, since Surgeon had no way of knowing this. (But if Surgeon *knew* of this strong desire on the part of Patient not to have cancerous growths removed, and Surgeon went ahead anyway, this would be battery.)

25. **No.** In the circumstances, Drug Lord reasonably believed that Scarecrow was about to kill or seriously wound him. Therefore, Drug Lord had a privilege to use self-defense if it seemed under the circumstances that he could not obtain his safety in any other way (e.g., by retreating). On the facts as known to Drug Lord, retreat would not have reasonably seemed to be a successful strategy. The fact that Scarecrow was actually a police officer who did not intend serious bodily harm is irrelevant — what matters is the reasonableness and genuineness of Drug Lord's belief that he was in imminent peril. Therefore, Drug Lord has a privilege of self-defense. See Rest. 2d, §65.

26. **No.** Under the doctrine of ***"private necessity,"*** a person has a privilege to enter another's property if this is necessary to protect herself (or another) from serious harm. This privilege constitutes a complete defense to Farmer's trespass action. See Rest. 2d, §197, Illustr. 3.

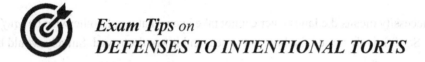

Exam Tips on
DEFENSES TO INTENTIONAL TORTS

Once you spot what appears to be an intentional tort, always check for defenses. The main ones to check for are: (1) *consent*; (2) *self-defense*; (3) defense of *others*; (4) defense of *property*; (5) recapture of *chattels*; (6) *re-entry* on land; (7) *necessity*; (8) *arrest.* Here's what to look for as to each:

☛ Whenever your fact pattern involves an intentional tort, be alert to the possibility that P *consented* (since consent is a defense to all intentional torts).

  ☞ Here are some typical contexts where there is or may be consent:

    ❏ P and D engage in a contact sport, and D then makes a harmful contact with P. As long as the contact was within the rules of the sport, P will be found to have impliedly consented to it. (And even if D *did* violate a rule of the sport, if the contact was part of the *"ordinary give-and-take"* of the sport, and was done for competitive purposes, P will still probably be found to have impliedly consented to the conduct.)

    ❏ P is injured by a mechanical security device (e.g., a spring gun or an electric-shock guard device) — if there's a *warning* sign, which P actually saw, he may be deemed to have consented.

    ❏ P is a suspected shoplifter, who is told to "wait here" by the storekeeper's detective — the circumstances may indicate that P waited voluntarily, in which case there was no true confinement.

❏ P's claim is for conversion, but D reasonably believed that P was letting D have the goods. (*Example:* P has moved out of an apartment shared with D, and D reasonably thinks that P has abandoned his property, so D sells it.)

☞ Remember that the existence of consent is determined by ***"objective,"*** not "subjective," analysis. That is, the question is always what a reasonable person in ***D's position*** would have ***thought*** that P meant, not what P really meant. Thus consent can be "implied" from P's conduct or from the surrounding circumstances. (*Example:* P and D have each consented to the other's practical jokes on past occasions, including frightening "assaults." This may mean that P can't sue for assault when D frightens him with a fake tarantula.)

☞ But in any consent situation, and especially where the consent is "implied" rather than express, be sure that the ***scope*** of consent hasn't been ***exceeded***. (*Example:* Even if P and D have sparred before, giving rise to implied consent for a "fight" on the present occasion, this is not consent to D's use of brass knuckles that he has never used before.)

☞ ***Fraud*** and ***mistake*** are very frequently tested in the consent context.

☞ D's ***fraud*** will vitiate P's consent, if the fraud goes to the ***essence*** (usually, the nature of the contact), but ***not*** if the fraud merely goes to some ***"collateral"*** aspect. (*Example:* If D tells P an electric cattle prod to be used in an experiment won't hurt P when D knows that it will, this fraud goes to the essence of the contact, and thus vitiates P's consent; P can sue for battery. But D's knowingly false statement to P that P will be paid for undergoing the experiment is "collateral," and therefore doesn't vitiate P's consent; therefore, P can't sue for battery.)

☞ P's ***"mistaken consent,"*** i.e., his mistake about the nature of the event that will take place, usually does ***not*** vitiate consent (as long as D wasn't aware of P's mistake). This is true even if P would never have consented had he known the true facts. (*Example:* P consents to have surgery performed on him under anesthetic by D. P is not aware that D has been sued several times for malpractice. D does not realize that P would never consent if he knew these facts. P's consent is valid.)

☞ ***D's mistake*** about whether P has in fact consented depends on the reasonableness of D's belief — D is protected for his reasonable belief (since the test is always the "objective" standard of what one in D's position should reasonably think), but is not protected from his unreasonable mistakes. (*Example:* While in P's store, D reads a sign that says, "Take one" — if an ordinary person would realize that the sign refers to brochures, not the merchandise underneath the sign, D will be liable for conversion for taking the merchandise even though D honestly believed that P was consenting.)

☛ If your facts suggest that X is threatened with a battery or false imprisonment, and X ***responds*** with ***force***, consider whether X can assert ***"self-defense"*** as a defense against liability for battery or assault.

☞ Look out for the possibility of self-defense whenever *two* parties fight. Even if it is not clear who started it, you should consider each fighter's chances of claiming self-defense.

☞ Do your best to identify the *first* to commit battery or assault. Being the first has two consequences: (1) the other can now use self-defense; and (2) the initial aggressor **cannot** respond to the other's self-defense with self-defense of his own. (*Example: A* insults *B*; *B* swings at *A* and misses; *A* hits *B*; *B* hits *A*. Analysis: *A*'s insults aren't enough to trigger *B*'s right to swing; *B*'s swing was therefore tortious; *A* probably then had the right of self-defense; *B* probably didn't have the right of self-defense in return, because his act was in response to *A*'s valid right of self-defense.)

    ☞ But remember that even the "initial aggressor" can use self-defense in response to an inappropriate **escalation** of the level of force. (*Example:* A swings at B without cause; B pulls out a gun; now, A can probably use his own gun in self-defense, because B has gone beyond the scope of reasonable self-defense by answering non-deadly force with deadly force.)

    ☞ **Verbal provocations** (e.g., **insults**) won't by themselves justify self-defense. (See the next-prior example, in which *A* insults *B*, and *B* is not thereby justified in swinging at *A*).

☞ D can use self-defense even if based on a *mistake*, if D's belief in the need for self-defense was **reasonable**. (*Example:* P puts his finger in his pocket and points it at D; if D's belief that P has a gun is reasonable, D can use self-defense even though he is wrong.)

☞ After you determine that D had the right to use self-defense, always examine the **level of force**. This is probably the most commonly-tested area of self-defense. Here's a recap of the general rules:

    ☞ D can't use non-deadly force that's more than is reasonably needed in the circumstances;

    ☞ D can't use deadly force to oppose non-deadly force;

    ☞ Even against deadly force, some jurisdictions say D must **retreat** instead of using deadly force if he knows he can do so safely (but some of these jurisdictions make an exception where the encounter takes place in D's dwelling, in that they allow D to "stand his ground").

    ☞ Many questions require you to determine whether the force used is **deadly** or not. The test is: was the force likely to cause **death** or **serious bodily injury**? This can vary with the circumstances. (*Example:* A's fists could be deadly force if A was very skilled or strong, or if his adversary was unskilled, weak or temporarily incapacitated.)

☛ It's easy to spot a *"defense of others"* (D/O) issue — one person will be coming to the aid of the other, to repel some sort of attack.

    ☞ Almost all of the issues discussed above in self-defense can be present in D/O, and the substantive rules are the same. Especially likely: an issue about level of force.

☞ One special D/O issue: Can you come to the defense of a ***complete stranger***? Most courts now say ***"yes."*** If so, the rules are the same as for defending your relatives or yourself.

☞ Biggest issue specific to D/O: D comes on the scene ***after the fight has already started***, and doesn't realize that X (who D helps out) was really the initial ***aggressor***. Older cases say D ***"steps into the shoes"*** of X, which means that since X as the aggressor wouldn't have had the right to use self-defense, D can't either (even where D's mistake is "***reasonable***"). But modern courts, and the Restatement, usually let D off the hook for a reasonable mistake here.

☛ Whenever X is attempting to ***evict*** someone from his property, consider whether the defense of ***"defense of realty"*** applies. Whenever X is attempting to keep possession of his personal property, think about the defense of ***"defense of chattels."*** The same rules apply (and the same test issues pop up) as to both. Here, we use the phrase "defense of property" (D/P) to cover both.

☞ Remember that D normally cannot use ***deadly force*** to protect his realty or his chattels. (However, some states allow deadly force to be used to prevent the breaking and entering of a dwelling if there is no other way to stop the entry.)

☞ Frequently-tested: D uses a ***trap*** or other ***mechanical device*** to injure or frighten intruders. Sub-issues:

☞ Remember that the case is analyzed as if D had been ***present*** and was using the force in person. So if D couldn't use that particular level of force in person against ***that particular intruder***, he can't do it by mechanical device either. (*Example:* D puts a spring gun in his unoccupied farm house. When P, seeking to steal whatever's inside, breaks in, the gun shoots him. If under state law D would not have been privileged to use deadly force in person to protect a non-dwelling (which this is, because it's unoccupied), D's use of the spring gun is not allowed either. Cite to *Katko v. Briney* for this type of fact pattern.)

☞ Most courts say that D must post a ***warning*** unless the danger is obvious (e.g., barbed wire).

☞ Often, the fact pattern will involve ***unexpectedly severe*** injury to P (the intruder). General rule: if D ***reasonably believed*** that the injuries would be non-existent or not severe, D gets the defense. (*Example:* D rigs a device to give a mild shock to anyone who touches his car; P gets shocked, then has an unexpected heart attack. D wins, since the "take the victim as you find him" rule doesn't apply in determining whether D stayed within the D/P privilege in the first place.)

☞ Other special D/P issue: D is "defending" his land against P's "intrusion," but in reality P is ***privileged*** to be on the land. In this scenario, D has no privilege to evict P, and is liable for battery if he tries.

☞ Usually this scenario occurs when P goes onto D's property to ***reclaim a chattel*** that he reasonably believes D has taken from him. (See "reclaiming of chattel" privilege discussed below.) This scenario can also occur when P is on D's land under the privilege of *necessity* (e.g., the crash-landing of P's plane or boat).

☛ The privilege to *recapture chattels* (or "recapture property" or "reclaim property") can pop up in several different contexts.

☞ The two most likely scenarios in which you should be on the lookout for this privilege are:

☞ D's property is wrongfully taken from him in some sort of street crime (e.g., a mugging), and D either tries to get it back immediately from the criminal's person, or later goes onto the land of the criminal (or the land of some third person who's now in possession of the item) to get it back.

☞ D is a merchant who detains a suspected shoplifter.

☞ *Mistake* is sometimes tested — if D is mistaken about whether P wrongfully took the property (or about whether P is in possession of the item), D loses the privilege even if his mistake was "reasonable." (But this isn't true for the merchant's privilege to detain a suspected shoplifter — see below.)

☞ Remember that D must act *"promptly"* to recapture the item. Essentially, this means that D must be acting in *"fresh pursuit,"* so even a wait of an hour is probably fatal to the privilege.

☞ Most-often tested: the *merchant's* privilege to *detain a shoplifting suspect* while investigating. (You can refer to this as the *"shopkeeper's privilege."*) This is analytically distinct, but related, to the privilege to recapture chattels. Most common sub-issues in the merchant case:

❏ Did D (the merchant) have *reasonable grounds* for suspecting P? (It's not required that P actually have committed the shoplifting, so here a "reasonable mistake" by D is protected — but D's suspicion must at least be "reasonable.")

❏ Did D take *too long* to complete the investigation? (10 minutes or so is usually the maximum allowed.)

❏ Did D stop P outside the *store's property* (e.g., as P got into his car located on the street)? Courts are split about whether the privilege extends beyond the store's own property line.

❏ Was the detention done in a *reasonable manner?* If P was roughed up, handcuffed, or coerced to confess, the privilege is lost.

☛ Be alert for the defense of *"necessity"* whenever D intentionally does something to *protect himself* or others in an *emergency*, and this affects the rights (usually the land rights) of P, an innocent person.

☞ When you write your answer, always say whether the applicable doctrine is *"public"* necessity or *"private"* necessity. "Public" necessity applies only where there's a serious danger to many people; "private" applies where the danger is to D and/or a few others. (The distinction is mainly important on the issue of whether D must pay for the damage caused, as discussed below.)

☞ The two most common contexts for "necessity":

❑ D, who can be either a public official or private citizen, tries to stop the spread of a *fire* by destroying P's house, moving things out of P's building, putting barriers on P's property, etc. Prevention of fire is generally "public" necessity.

❑ D is a *pilot* who makes an "intentional" but emergency landing on P's property. This is usually "private" necessity, at least where the plane is a small private one.

☞ Most common issue: Must D *pay for the harm*? If the necessity is "private," the answer is "yes." (Therefore, private necessity is usually useless unless the landowner physically resists the privilege, or is seeking nominal damages for trespass.) But if the privilege is "public," the answer is "no."

☞ In the private necessity situation, often the question is whether D is liable for *nominal damages* where no actual harm has occurred. Answer: D is not liable. (*Example:* D crash lands on P's open field, but does no significant damage. D pays nothing.)

☞ Most common scenario: *A* comes onto *B*'s land under the privilege/defense of necessity, but *B* resists, injuring *A*. Here, *A* can recover against *B*. (*Example:* A is a pilot who makes an emergency landing on *B*'s property, and is injured. B evicts A, aggravating A's injuries. B is liable to A for the aggravation of the injuries, in addition to being unable to recover nominal trespass damages from A. But B could recover for actual damage to his property that occurred before B resisted, assuming that A's necessity was "private.")

☞ The privileges of *"arrest"* and *"prevention of crime"* will often be found together.

☞ A common scenario for prevention-of-crime: D intervenes to *break up a fight*. Typically, D injures one of the fighters, who turns out to have been a "non-aggressor" who then sues D for battery. Here, D has the privilege, so long as D's belief and level of force were reasonable.

☞ Common scenario for arrest: D is a private individual who makes or tries to make a *"citizen's arrest"* for a felony he sees committed, or believes has just been committed. Generally, D has the privilege to make this citizen's arrest as long as the force he uses is reasonable, even if D makes a reasonable mistake about who did it. (But D loses the privilege if there was no felony committed at all.)

☞ Use of *"deadly force"* is often tested.

☞ Most common sub-issue: May either a police officer or citizen use deadly force to stop a *fleeing suspect*? Answer: neither may use deadly force unless the suspect poses a threat of *death* or *serious physical injury* to others. (*Example:* Neither a homeowner nor the police may shoot a fleeing burglar in the back, unless there is evidence of the burglar's serious dangerousness. Such "serious dangerousness" might be evidenced by the fact that the burglar is armed.)

CHAPTER 5

NEGLIGENCE GENERALLY

ChapterScope

Tort law recognizes a broadly-defined "omnibus" tort called "negligence." The essence of this tort is that the defendant has imposed an "unreasonable" risk of harm on the plaintiff, and the plaintiff has been injured as a result. Here are the most important concepts covered in this chapter:

■ **Negligence generally:** The tort of "negligence" occurs when D's conduct imposes an ***unreasonable risk*** upon another, resulting in an injury to that other. D's mental state is irrelevant.

❏ **Balancing:** In determining whether the risk of harm from D's conduct was so great as to be "unreasonable," courts use a ***balancing test***: if the risk of harm to another from D's conduct is greater than the "utility" of that conduct, the risk is deemed "unreasonable."

■ **The reasonable person:** The reasonableness of D's conduct is viewed under an objective standard: Would a "***reasonable person*** of ordinary prudence," in D's position, do as D did?

■ **"Negligence *per se*" doctrine:** Most courts apply the "***negligence per se***" doctrine: when a ***safety statute*** has a sufficiently close application to the facts of the case at hand, an unexcused violation of that statute by D is "negligence *per se*", and thus conclusively establishes that D was negligent. (But the negligence *per se* doctrine will apply only where P shows that the statute was intended to guard against ***the very kind*** of injury in question.)

■ ***Res ipsa loquitur***: The doctrine of ***res ipsa loquitur*** ("the thing speaks for itself") allows P to point to the fact of the accident, and to create an inference that, even without a precise showing of how D behaved, D was probably negligent.

❏ **Requirements:** P must meet four main requirements to use the doctrine: (1) There must be ***no direct evidence*** as to D's precise conduct; (2) P must show that the harm is of a type that ***does not normally occur*** except through the negligence of someone; (3) P must show that the instrumentality which caused the harm was at all times within D's ***exclusive control***; and (4) P must show that the injury was not due to P's ***own*** negligence.

I. INTRODUCTION

A. Distinguished from intentional torts: In the previous chapters, we have examined a number of distinct, narrowly defined "intentional" torts. We now turn to a much more broadly defined tort, that of "negligence". While a cause of action for negligence has a number of components, which will be listed and discussed below, the tort differs from intentional torts in one particular way: whereas the intentional tortfeasor generally desires to create a certain objectionable result (e.g. a harmful contact with the defendant's person), or at least knows with substantial certainty that such a result will occur, the negligent tortfeasor has no such desire, and may have in fact desperately wished to avoid the harmful result which occurred. To phrase it another way, the intentional tortfeasor's mental state is of the utmost importance, but the negligent tortfeasor's mental state is irrelevant — the essence of his tort is that his **conduct** (without regard to his mind) imposed an **unreasonable risk** upon others.

II. COMPONENTS OF CAUSE OF ACTION

A. **"Negligence" has two meanings:** "Negligence," used in its everyday nonlegal sense, refers to carelessness. And, as we shall see, a failure to appreciate the risks of one's own conduct is one of the components of the tort of negligence. But in addition, there are a number of other elements that together with carelessness make up a **prima facie case** for the tort of negligence. The five components of a *prima facie* case for negligence are as follows:

- ❏ *Duty*;
- ❏ *Failure to conform* to duty;
- ❏ *Causation in fact*;
- ❏ *Proximate cause*;
- ❏ *Actual damage*.

We consider each of these in turn below.

1. **Duty:** Plaintiff must show that defendant owed plaintiff a *legal duty* to conduct himself according to certain standards, so as to avoid unreasonable risks to others;

2. **Failure to conform:** Plaintiff must show a *failure by the defendant* to *conform his conduct to this standard*. This is the aspect of the cause of action that can by itself be thought of as "carelessness" or "lack of reasonable care."

    a. **Significance of duty:** Most negligence cases focus on this aspect, since generally the scope of the defendant's duty is the same: to act with the care that a "reasonable person" would exercise. However, there are kinds of cases in which the defendant owes the plaintiff no duty at all, or only a very limited duty; thus a landowner generally owes a trespasser of whom he is not aware no duty of care at all. In such a circumstance, even if the plaintiff trespasser shows that the defendant was "negligent" in the sense of being careless, she will not establish a cause of action for negligence, since it will be held that the defendant was not under any duty *not* to be careless.

3. **Cause in fact:** Plaintiff must show that defendant's failure to act with reasonable care was the *"cause in fact"* of the injury to plaintiff. Generally, "cause in fact" means a *"but for"* cause, i.e., a cause without which the injury wouldn't have occurred.

4. **Proximate cause:** The plaintiff must also show that there is a sufficiently close connection, or *causal link,* between the defendant's act of negligence and the harm suffered by the plaintiff, to justify holding the defendant liable as a matter of policy. This aspect of the cause of action is generally called *"proximate cause"* or *"legal cause."*

5. **Actual damage:** Finally, the plaintiff must also show that she suffered *actual* damage. Thus the tort of negligence is different from most of the intentional torts discussed previously (which allow a plaintiff who suffered no actual injury to generally recover purely *nominal damages*).

III. UNREASONABLE RISK

A. **Imposition of risk:** To demonstrate that the defendant's conduct failed to meet the duty of care imposed on him (i.e. to show the second of the components listed above), the plaintiff must show that the defendant's conduct imposed an ***unreasonable risk of harm*** on the plaintiff (or on a class of persons of whom the plaintiff is a member). Rest. 2d, §282.

1. **Not judged by results:** To make this showing, the plaintiff cannot simply show that the defendant's conduct resulted in a terrible injury to her. Rather, she must show that the defendant's conduct, viewed ***as of the time it occurred***, without the benefit of hindsight, imposed an unreasonable risk of harm. P&K, p. 170.

   Example: D, a water company, installs water mains in the street, leading to fire hydrants. Twenty-five years after D does so, a hydrant in front of P's house springs a leak caused by the expansion of freezing water, during a winter of unprecedented severity. As a result, P's house is flooded.

   Held, D's conduct was *not* negligent because the risk of such a heavy frost was so remote as not to be the kind of risk an ordinary prudent person would guard against in doing the work. *Blyth v. Birmingham Waterworks Co.*, 156 Eng. Rep. 1047 (1856).

   a. **Inherently dangerous objects:** This "no hindsight" principle is also illustrated by cases in which ***potentially dangerous objects*** are left lying around. Some objects (e.g. a shotgun) are so dangerous that it is negligence to leave them lying around without special handling (e.g., unloading the shotgun.) But other objects pose less of a danger, and it will not be negligence to leave them around ***even if it turns out that, unexpectedly, they cause harm***. The risk is to be evaluated as it reasonably appeared before the accident.

   Example: D1 leaves a golf club lying in the backyard of his house. D2, D1's 11-year-old son, swings the club in order to hit a stone, and in doing so strikes P in the jaw and chin. P sues both D1 and D2 on a negligence theory.

   Held, for D1. A golf club is not so "obviously and intrinsically dangerous" that by leaving it on the ground D1 committed negligence. But D2 was negligent in the way he swung the club. *Lubitz v. Wells*, 113 A.2d 147 (Conn. 1955).

   Note: In some situations, however, it may be negligence not to anticipate the negligence of others. (See *infra* p. 107.) Thus if D1 knew that his son had a history of injuring people, the leaving of the club might have been combined with D1's lack of supervision of D2 to result in D1's liability.

B. **Balancing test:** As the above examples indicate, in determining whether the risk of harm from the defendant's conduct was so great as to be "unreasonable," the test is whether a "reasonable person" would have recognized the risk, and have striven to avoid it. (The attributes of such a "reasonable person" will be examined further below.) However, because it is often exceptionally difficult to tell what a reasonable person would have done in a particular situation, the courts have developed a "balancing test" as a rough guide as to whether the defendant's conduct is so risky as to involve an unreasonable threat of harm to others. The most famous formulation is that stated by Judge Learned Hand: Liability exists if:

$B < L \times P$

where B equals the burden which the defendant would have had to bear to avoid the risk, L equals the gravity of the potential injury, and P equals the probability that harm will occur from the defendant's conduct.

> **Example:** This test was formulated by Judge Hand in a case involving the following facts: P's barge, docked at a pier, broke away from its moorings due to D's negligence in shifting the lines that moored it. D, however, argued that P was also negligent in not having an employee on board the barge, and that, according to the rules of admiralty, the damage should be divided between D and P according to their respective degrees of negligence.
>
> *Held* (on appeal), it is burdensome, to a degree, to have an employee on board at all times. However, there was wartime activity going on in the harbor, and ships coming in and out all the time. Therefore, the risk that the mooring lines would come undone, and the danger to the barge and to other ships if they did, was sufficiently great that P should have borne the burden of supplying a watchman (unless he had some excuse for his absence) during working hours. *U.S. v. Carroll Towing Co.*, 159 F.2d 169 (2d Cir. 1947).

1. **Threat of serious injury:** As the Learned Hand formula implies, the more serious the potential injury, the less probable its occurrence need be before the defendant will be held to be negligent for not guarding against it. Thus if a reasonable person would realize that a potential injury, if it came to pass, would be *extremely grave*, there may be liability even though it was relatively *unlikely* that the accident would occur. See Rest. 2d, §291.

   > **Example:** Suppose that D encounters a yellow traffic light while driving his heavy truck into Times Square. He has to decide whether to speed up to make the light, though in any event he intends to keep within the speed limit. D knows that the truck's brakes have been sporadically malfunctioning recently. Assume that D realizes (or should realize) that if the brakes fail at that moment, numerous people will likely be killed or maimed.
   >
   > Even if D realizes that there is only, say, a 2% chance that the brakes will fail at that moment, the potential harm is so great, and the burden of stopping at the yellow light so small, that his conduct in speeding up is probably negligent despite the unlikeliness of a brake failure.

C. **Calculation of burden:** "*B*" in the above equation, the burden which the defendant would incur in order to avoid the risk, is itself a function of not only the cost to him, but also the broader *social utility* of the conduct which he would have to forego. Hence the courts attempt, in effect, to answer the question: "Would society be better off if all defendants in the position of D were permitted to act as D did, or were instead required to change their conduct so as to avoid the kind of risk which resulted in injury to P?" Only if the answer to this question is that defendants in D's position should be required to change their conduct will the cause of action for negligence lie (assuming that the other requirements are met).

   > **Example:** D Railroad maintains a railway turntable (a rotating platform with a track for turning a locomotive) near a publicly traveled path. P, a child, discovers that the

turntable is unlocked, climbs on it, and while playing on it with a group of children gets his foot caught between the rails and severed at the ankle joint.

Held, it was negligent of D not to keep the turntable locked and guarded. The business of railroading is facilitated by the use of turntables, so the public good demands that their use not be entirely outlawed, since their utility is out of proportion to the occasional injuries which result. But the burden of keeping the turntable locked is so small that the danger of not doing so outweighs this burden. *Chicago, B. & Q. Railway Co. v. Krayenbuhl*, 91 N.W. 880 (Neb. 1902).

D. Restatement standard: The Second Restatement, §291, sets forth the balancing test this way: "Where an act is one which a reasonable [person] would recognize as involving a risk of harm to another, the risk is unreasonable and the act is negligent if the ***risk is of such magnitude*** as to ***outweigh*** what the law regards as the ***utility of the act*** or of the ***particular manner in which it is done.***" In more down-to-earth terms, the question is whether "the game is worth the candle." Rest. 2d, §291, Comment a.

E. Warnings: One of the ways the risks of conduct can be reduced — usually without reducing the social benefits of the conduct very much — is by giving ***warnings*** of danger. The fact that D gave a warning of dangers to P in particular, or to the public in general, is thus a factor that will tend to make it at least somewhat less likely that D will be found negligent if the danger that was warned of results in an accident.

1. **Failure to warn can itself be negligent:** If D *fails* to give a warning of a danger that he knows about, and the warning could have been easily given, the mere failure to warn can itself ***constitute negligence.*** As the Third Restatement expresses the concept, "A defendant whose conduct creates a risk of physical harm can fail to exercise reasonable care by ***failing to warn*** of the danger if: (1) the defendant knows or has reason to know: (a) of that risk; and (b) that those encountering the risk will be unaware of it; and (2) a warning ***might be effective in reducing the risk*** of physical harm." Rest. 3d (Liab. for Phys. & Emot. Harm) §18(a).

2. **Does not immunize D:** However, it's clear that even if D *does* give a warning, ***this does not immunize D from negligence liability*** — if D's activity is unreasonably dangerous (evaluated by balancing its benefits against its risks) despite D's warning to P, D will still be liable. As the Third Restatement puts it, "Even if the defendant adequately warns of the risk that the defendant's conduct creates, the defendant can fail to exercise reasonable care by ***failing to adopt further precautions*** to protect against the danger if it is foreseeable that despite the warning some risk of physical harm will remain." Rest. 3d (Liab. for Phys. Harm) §18(b).

   Example: Dave, while moving out of his second-floor apartment, throws an old television out the window, aiming for a dumpster on the ground below the window. Just before he throws the TV, he yells out "Look out below." Paula, a pedestrian, does not hear the warning because she is talking on her cellphone. Dave can be found negligent despite having given the warning — it is so dangerous to throw a heavy object out of an upstairs window, and so easy to discard the object by safer means, that the giving of the warning did not make the total benefits of Dave's conduct outweigh its dangers. Cf. Rest. 3d (Liab. for Phys. Harm) §18, Illustr. 1, from which this example is drawn.

F. Activity level vs. care level: One of the peculiarities of our negligence system is that it usually focuses on the actor's level of *care* in *carrying out* the activity, but not on the social utility of the actor's decision to *engage in that activity at all*. Consequently, a defendant who engages in a fairly safe activity but does so negligently is likely to be liable for damages, whereas one who engages in a risky-and-not-socially-beneficial activity but does so carefully, will not — this is true even though the net burden on others is greater in the latter situation.

> **Example:** Consider two drivers, *A* and *B*. *A* is a doctor on his way to perform an important operation at a hospital, and there is no other way for him to get there in time. If *A*'s attention wanders, and he strikes P (a pedestrian), *A* is liable — we weigh the "cost" to *A* of paying attention while he drives, and because this cost is small relative to the cost of the injuries to P multiplied by the likelihood of those injuries, we hold *A* liable. Now, consider *B*: *B* is a bored teenager who is not driving anywhere in particular, and is driving merely because it is a moderately pleasurable way to fill the time. *B* drives "carefully," in the sense that he pays close attention. Nonetheless, he strikes P, because his eyes are momentarily blinded by the sun. We would not find *B* negligent, even though there was virtually no social utility from *B*'s decision to drive in the first place — all we focus on is whether *B* drove carefully once *B* decided to drive at all. Yet it may well be that the total social utility of *B*'s conduct — its benefits less its costs — was less than for *A*'s. Consequently, people in *B*'s position will drive "too much," because they are not required to "pay" for the accidents that their excess driving causes. See Epstein, p. 199; see also 9 J. Leg. Stud. 1 (1980).

1. Compare with strict liability: Observe that something quite different happens when the liability scheme is *strict liability* rather than negligence. Under strict liability, an actor who engages in, say, an "ultrahazardous" activity is responsible for *all* injuries that he proximately causes, even if these occur without negligence. Under a strict liability regime, D *does* have an incentive to weigh the social utility from engaging in the activity at all, not just an incentive to behave carefully once having decided to do the activity. In terms of the above example, if we impose strict liability on motorists, *B* would have an incentive not to take the meaningless-but-enjoyable ride. See Epstein, p. 199-200. See the further treatment of strict liability beginning *infra*, p. 329.

IV. THE REASONABLE PERSON

A. Objective standard: The balancing test described above, for weighing burden against risk, is a very abstract one, and neither a jury nor a potential defendant can be expected to use it to evaluate conduct in most instances. Therefore, the negligence issue is usually put to the jury as: "Would a *'reasonable person' of ordinary prudence*, in the position of the defendant, have conducted himself as the defendant did?" This is essentially an objective standard. That is, it does not ask whether the defendant intended to behave carefully or thought he was behaving carefully. However, this hypothetical "reasonable person" does, as we shall see below, bear some of the characteristics of the actual defendant, at least to the extent of some of his physical attributes.

B. Physical and mental characteristics: As we have said, the test for negligence is whether the defendant behaved as a reasonable person would "under the circumstances" that confronted the defendant. "The circumstances" obviously include the external facts of the case, such as the traffic conditions, speed limits, etc., which confront a motorist. But an important question is to what extent "the circumstances" should be deemed to cover the *physical or mental characteristics of the defendant.*

1. **Physical disability:** Most courts have extended "the circumstances" to include the *physical characteristics of the defendant himself.* That is, they have held that the test is whether a reasonable person with the physical attributes of the defendant would have behaved as the defendant did. Thus if the defendant has a *physical disability*, the standard for negligence is what a reasonable person with that physical disability would have done. See Rest. 2d, §283C; Rest. 3d (Liab. for Phys. & Emot. Harm) §11(a).

   a. **Sudden disability:** A key factor will often be whether the disability has struck for the first time immediately preceding the accident. A defendant who reasonably believes himself to be in good health, and who suddenly suffers, for the first time ever, a *heart attack* or *epileptic seizure* while driving, would almost certainly not be held to have negligently caused the ensuing accident. But one who knows that he is subject to such attacks or seizures might well be negligent in driving at all. See Rest.2d, §283C, Comment c.

   b. **Blindness:** Many disability cases have involved *blindness*. Typically, it is the plaintiff who is blind, who has been injured, and *against whom* the defense of *comparative negligence* is asserted. (This defense, discussed *infra*, p. 281, involves roughly the same definition of negligence as on the defendant side, except that this definition is applied to the plaintiff's conduct.) Other times, it is the defendant who is blind. Both for the blind-plaintiff and blind-defendant situation, the usual rule is that the blind person must conduct himself in a way that *a reasonable person would act if he or she were blind.* See Rest. 2d, §283C, Illustr. 1 and 2.

      i. **What is required:** This general requirement of reasonableness means that sometimes, the blind person will have to take *greater precautions* than a reasonable sighted person, sometimes not.

         (1) **Illustrations:** For instance, a blind plaintiff who attempts to cross a street without asking for assistance or carrying a cane might well be found negligent, and thus subject to comparative fault, even though a sighted person who crossed without assistance would not be. Conversely, it would not be negligence for a blind person to step into a depression on the sidewalk, whereas a sighted person who saw the depression would be negligent if he tried to walk through it rather than around it. See Rest. 2d, §283C, Illustr. 1 and 2.

   c. **Strict liability rejected:** Observe that if the definition of negligence did not take into account the actor's physical disabilities, something akin to *strict liability* (see *infra*, p. 329) would be imposed for accidents stemming from such disabilities. For instance, if a driver were held liable for conduct which would otherwise be negligent (e.g., going through a stoplight or off the road), and no account were taken of the fact that he had just suffered an unforeseen heart attack or epileptic seizure, this would not be a true negligence standard at all, but rather, something like the absolute liability for defective products imposed upon manufacturers and sellers (see *infra*, p. 347). But courts do not in fact impose such a strict-liability standard for negligence.

2. **Mental attributes:** The ordinary reasonable person is generally *not*, however, deemed to have the particular *mental* characteristics of the defendant. For instance, the defendant is not absolved of negligence because he is more stupid, hot-tempered, careless or of poorer judgment than the ordinary reasonable person. P&K, pp. 176-77.

> **Example:** D builds a hay rick (a device for drying hay) near the edge of his property. P is afraid that the stack will ignite, burning his nearby cottages. He repeatedly warns D, but D says he will "chance it." The hay spontaneously catches fire, and the resulting conflagration destroys P's cottages.
>
> *Held*, D is not entitled to a jury instruction that he is not negligent if he acted in good faith and according to his best judgment, and that he should not be penalized for not being of the highest intelligence. Such a standard would be "as variable as the length of the foot of each individual," and would be impossible to administer. Instead, an objective standard, the prudence of an ordinary person, must be applied. *Vaughan v. Menlove*, 132 Eng. Rep. 490 (1837).

3. **Imbecility or insanity:** Courts are split about whether a mental state so low that it must be considered *imbecilic* or *insane,* and which prevents the actor from even understanding that danger exists, should be held to render negligence impossible. "Probably the prevailing orthodoxy is that *neither insanity nor mental deficiency relieves the actor from liability*, and that his conduct must *conform to the general standard of care* of a reasonable person under similar external circumstances." Dobbs & Hayden (5th), p. 128.

   a. **Restatement agrees:** The Third Restatement agrees with this "prevailing orthodoxy," and holds that mental deficiency, no matter how severe, may not relieve a person of negligence. See Rest. 3d (Liab. for Phys. & Emot. Harm) §11(c): "An *actor's mental or emotional disability is not considered* in determining whether conduct is negligent, unless the actor is a child."

   > **Example:** D, who suffers from Alzheimer's disease, attacks P, his caretaker at a nursing home. D defends on the ground that he should not be held to the usual standard of due care because of his extreme mental disability.
   >
   > *Held* (on this point) for P. Several policy reasons support holding the mentally disabled to an ordinary standard of care. For example, such a policy "provides incentive to those responsible for people with disabilities and interested in their estates to prevent harm and 'restrain' those who are potentially dangerous." Also, the policy "forces persons with disabilities to pay for the damage they do if they 'are to live in the world'." National policy changes since the 1970s favoring the deinstitutionalization of the disabled — such as the Individuals with Disabilities Education Act and the Americans with Disabilities Act — reflect "a determination that people with disabilities should be treated in the same way as non-disabled persons."
   >
   > (However, a person who agrees to care for a patient known to be combative because of Alzheimer's has *assumed the risk* of injuries from that care. Therefore, P may not recover despite the general rule that the mentally disabled will be held to the usual adult standard of care. *Creasy v. Rusk*, 730 N.E.2d 659 (Ind. 2000).)

i. Child's mental deficiency: However, most courts and the Restatements hold that a *child's* mental deficiency *may* be taken into account. Rest. 2d, §283A; Rest. 3d §11(c).

ii. Same rule for contributory negligence: Whatever the jurisdiction's rule as to whether the mentally disabled are to be held to the usual standard of care, that rule generally also applies to disabled *plaintiffs* against whom **contributory negligence** is asserted. See, e.g., Rest. 3d (Liab. for Phys. & Emot. Harm), Comment e to §11 (stating that that section's "rule ... that an actor's mental disabilities shall be disregarded applies in the context of the actor's contributory negligence as well as the context of the actor's negligence.")

4. Intoxication: A defendant who is intoxicated at the time of an accident is *not* permitted to claim that his intoxication stripped him of his ability to comprehend and avoid the danger; he is held to the standard of conduct of a **reasonable sober person**. P&K, p. 178. See also, Rest.2d, §283C, Comment d.

5. Children: Another exception to the general objective "reasonable person" standard is that *children* are not held to the level of care which would be exercised by a reasonable adult. A child must merely conform to the conduct of a "reasonably careful person of the same **age, intelligence**, and **experience**." Rest. 3d (Liab. for Phys. & Emot. Harm) §10(a).

a. Subjective: Note that this is a somewhat subjective standard, in that if a child is less intelligent that most children of his age, he is held simply to the degree of care which a similarly unintelligent contemporary would exercise. This should be distinguished from the standard for adults, which makes no allowance for the fact that the individual is less intelligent than the average person.

b. Fixed chronological test discarded: Many older cases applied an irrebuttable presumption that a child under the age of seven could not be negligent, a rebuttable presumption that one between seven and fourteen was not negligent, and a rebuttable one that a child between fourteen and twenty-one was capable of negligence. However, the arbitrary divisions stem more from the Bible than from any sound judicial reasoning, and they are no longer used by most modern courts.

c. Definition of "child": At least under the Third Restatement, the special "person of the same age, intelligence and experience" rule applies to *all minors,* not merely to young children. On the other hand, the Restatement's "minor" rule means that in a state where 18-year-olds are deemed to have reached the age of majority, an 18 year-old will *not* get the benefit of the special rule. See Rest. 3d (Liab. for Phys. & Emot. Harm) §10, Comment a.

i. Very young child: At the other end of the spectrum, *very young children* are still deemed to be *incapable of negligence* under the modern/Restatement approach. As noted, the traditional "rule of sevens" (making children under seven incapable of negligence) rarely applies today. But even under modern cases, children under the age of *five* are usually deemed incapable of negligence. See, e.g., Rest. 3d (Liab. for Phys. & Emot. Harm) §10(b) ("A child less than five years of age is incapable of negligence.").

d. **Adult activity:** Another exception to the special rules for children is that where a child engages in a *potentially dangerous activity that is normally pursued only by adults*, he will be held to the standard of care that a reasonable adult doing that activity would exercise. See Rest. 3d (Liab. for Phys. & Emot. Harm) §10(c). This principle has been applied to *driving a car, operating a motorboat,* and even to *playing golf.* See P&K, pp. 181-82.

    i. **Dangerous but not adult:** Suppose the activity is potentially dangerous, but *not* one that is usually engaged in by adults rather than children. The courts are split as to the standard of care which should be applied in this situation. The Third Restatement would apply the child rather than adult standard of care, since the adult standard will be applied to children only if the activity is *"characteristically undertaken by adults."* Rest. 3d (Liab. for Phys. & Emot. Harm) §10(c). For a case following the Restatement approach, see *Purtle v. Shelton*, 474 S.W.2d 123 (Ark. 1972) (deer-hunting will not trigger adult standard, since activity is often pursued by minors).

C. **Knowledge:** Assuming that the general "reasonable person" standard is the one which applies to a case at hand, there a number of basic issues about how a reasonable person generally behaves. One of these troublesome areas has to do with *knowledge* that a reasonable person would possess.

1. **Ordinary experience:** There are obviously many things which every adult has learned; these include such things as that objects will fall when dropped, that flammable materials can catch fire, that other human beings are likely to react in certain ways such as by attempting to rescue a person in danger, etc. These items of knowledge that virtually every adult in the community possesses will be imputed to the "reasonable adult" and thus to the defendant. This is true whether the defendant herself actually knows the fact in question or not. P&K, pp. 182-84. See also, Rest. 2d, §290.

2. **Stranger to community:** Furthermore, facts generally known to all adults in a particular community will be imputed to a *stranger* who enters the community without having had the experience of knowledge in question. Thus a city dweller who visits a farm, and who has never learned that a bull can be dangerous, will nonetheless be held to the standard of behavior that would be exercised by one who did have such knowledge, since that knowledge is common to dwellers in rural areas. P&K, p. 184

3. **Duty to investigate:** Even where a certain fact is not known to members of the community at large, or to the defendant herself, she may be under a duty to end her ignorance. A driver who senses that something is wrong with his steering wheel, for instance, would have a duty to find out what the problem is before an accident is caused. P&K, p. 185.

    Example: As D's car is passing P's car, D has a blowout, causing a collision. There is evidence at trial that D's tires were badly worn.

    Held, D was under a duty to know of the condition of the tires (whether he in fact knew or not), and was also under a duty to know that worn tires are dangerous. *Delair v. McAdoo*, 188 A. 181 (Penn. 1936). See also, Rest. 2d, §290, Illustr. 2.

4. **Memory:** Just as the reasonable person knows certain facts, she also has a certain level of memory. Thus, a motorist who has passed a particular intersection many times will be charged with remembering that it is dangerous in a certain way, whereas one who never or seldom had passed that intersection before would not have the same burden. See Rest. 2d, §289, Illustr. 4.

5. **Distractions:** Similarly, the reasonable person pays attention to what she is doing, and is not *distracted*, unless there is a *legitimate reason* for such distraction. Thus, a driver who turns to look at his passenger and slams into another car would be held to have failed to behave like a reasonably prudent person. See Rest. 2d, §289, Comment k.

6. **Some frailties remain:** The "reasonable person" is not, however, completely without imperfections. Her care for her own safety and that of others is merely reasonable, not *flawless*. For instance, the reasonable person may occasionally become slightly distracted, or may panic slightly in the face of a serious emergency.

D. **Custom:** In litigating the defendant's negligence, one thing that either side may point to is *custom*, that is, the way a certain activity is habitually carried out in a trade or a community. The plaintiff may try to show that the defendant did not follow the safety-motivated custom that others in the same business follow, or the defendant may try to show that he exercised due care by using the same procedures as everyone else in the trade.

1. **Not conclusive:** The vast majority of courts allow evidence as to custom for the purpose of showing the presence or absence of reasonable care, but do not treat this evidence as *conclusive*. Thus, the fact that everyone else in the defendant's industry does a certain thing the same way the defendant did it does not mean that that way was not unduly dangerous, if there are other factors so indicating.

   Example: Two tugboats owned by D are towing cargo owned by P. Most tugboats have not yet installed radio receiving sets, although some have; D's two tugs do not yet have these sets. They are therefore unable to receive messages that a strong storm is overtaking them, and are sunk.

   Held, the fact that most tugs have not installed sets does not conclusively establish that D was non-negligent in not having installed them. For custom is not dispositive on the issue of negligence — "a whole calling may have unduly lagged in the adoption of new and available devices. . . . Courts must in the end say what is required; there are precautions so imperative that even their universal disregard will not excuse their omission." Here some tug owners had already installed the sets, so D's case is even weaker, and was liable. *The T.J. Hooper*, 60 F.2d 737 (2d Cir. 1932), *infra*, pp. 111, 377.

   Caveat: Even though custom is not conclusive on the issue of negligence, it is nonetheless evidence on this question, and if there is no evidence in rebuttal, the fact that the defendant did or did not follow custom may be sufficient for him to prevail.

2. **Advances in technology:** The technological *"state of the art"* at a particular moment is, similarly, relevant to what constitutes negligence. For instance, the defendant's failure to take action to prevent a certain known risk might be either negligent or non-negligent, depending upon whether technology exists that could reduce that risk. Consequently, con-

duct that would be non-negligent in earlier times may have become negligent today due to technological advances.

> **Example:** In the 1920s, little technology was available to keep cars from running off roadways. Therefore, it might not have been negligent for a municipality that built a road to fail to install guardrails strong enough to keep a car from leaving the roadway or crossing over into the other lane. But today, guardrail technology has probably advanced sufficiently that installation of a 1920s'-style guardrail (or none at all) would be negligent.

E. Emergency: As we have seen, the general rule is that the defendant must follow the standard of care that a reasonable person would exercise "considering all of the circumstances." One of the circumstances of a particular case may be that the defendant was confronted with an *emergency*, and was forced to act with little time for reflection. If this is so, the defendant will not be held to the same standard of care as one who has ample time for thinking about what to do; instead he must merely behave as would a reasonable person confronted with the same emergency. See Rest. 2d, §296.

> **Example:** Cab Driver, who drives a cab for the D cab company, is suddenly accosted one day by a thug, who jumps into the cab, puts a gun to the cab driver's back, and tells him to step on it. Meanwhile, a number of pedestrians start shouting, "Stop, thief!" The thug tells Cab Driver that the latter will "suffer the loss of his brains" if he does not obey the thug's orders. Cab Driver then jams on the brakes, puts on the emergency brake, and, leaving the motor running, jumps out. The cab keeps on rolling, and injures P.
>
> *Held*, Cab Driver did not behave negligently, and D is therefore *not* liable (as it would be under the doctrine of *respondeat superior, infra*, p. 315, if Cab Driver had been negligent). "If under normal circumstances an act is done which might be considered negligent, it does not follow as a corollary that a similar act is negligent if performed by a person acting under an emergency, not of his own making, in which he suddenly is faced with a patent danger with a moment left to adopt a means of extrication." *Cordas v. Peerless Transportation Co.*, 27 N.Y.S.2d 198 (N.Y. 1941).

1. **Emergency caused by defendant:** But if the emergency was *caused by the defendant's negligence,* the fact that the emergency leads the defendant into an accident will not absolve him of liability. In such a situation, it is the initial negligence leading to the emergency, *not* the subsequent response to the emergency, that makes the defendant negligent.

2. **Negligence still possible:** Even if the emergency is not of the defendant's own making, he must still live up to the standard of care of a reasonable person confronted with such an emergency. That is, if he behaves unreasonably, even conceding the fact that he had little time for reflection, he will nonetheless be negligent. Thus a person driving on an undivided highway who sees an accident ahead of him, and who swerves left into oncoming traffic instead of right onto a shoulder, might well be held liable notwithstanding the fact that he had little time for reflection.

3. **Activity requiring special training:** There are certain activities which by their nature require an unusual capacity to react well in an emergency. In a case involving such an activity, the defendant will therefore be held to this higher standard of preparedness. A bus

driver, for instance, should by her training be better prepared than the average driver to anticipate various traffic emergencies, and she will be held to this higher standard. See Rest. 2d, §296, Comment c. In fact, even the average motorist will probably be held to bear the burden of being capable of anticipating certain kinds of common emergencies (e.g., a child rushing out into the street after a ball), and will be charged with reacting more quickly in such a situation than if that kind of emergency arose less frequently. See P&K, p. 197.

F. **Anticipating conduct of others:** Just as the reasonable person must possess certain knowledge, so she must possess a certain ability to ***anticipate the conduct of others***. Following are a few kinds of responses by third persons that a defendant may be charged with the burden of anticipating.

   1. **Negligence of others:** The defendant may be required to anticipate the possibility of ***negligence*** on the part of others. Generally, this will be so only if the likelihood of injury is great, or the magnitude of the injury is very substantial. P&K, p. 197. See Rest. 2d, §290, Comment m.

      Example: An automobile driver is normally entitled to assume that other drivers will drive non-negligently. But if she has reason to know that the car ahead of her is being driven by a drunk driver, or if the road conditions are such that a short stop by the driver ahead is very likely to cause the defendant to run over a pedestrian, the defendant will be required to guard extra carefully against these consequences.

      a. **Children:** Furthermore, the defendant is charged with anticipating careless or dangerous conduct on the part of ***children***, since they are commonly known to be incapable of exercising the degree of care of the average adult. Thus one who drives down a street crowded with children playing is not entitled to assume that the children will stay out of the car's path and must take extra precautions to guard against their carelessness. P&K, p. 200.

      b. **Parental supervision:** A ***parent*** has a duty to exercise reasonable care to ***supervise the conduct of his or her minor child***, to prevent the child from intentionally harming others or posing an unreasonable risk of harm to others. Rest. 2d, §316.

         i. **Direct liability:** This principle does ***not*** make the parent ***"vicariously liable"*** (see *infra*, p. 315 for the meaning of vicarious liability) for the child's torts. Instead, it constitutes ***direct*** negligence by the parent not to use reasonable care in controlling the child, where the parent has the ability to control the child, and knows or should have known of the risk being posed by the child's conduct.

            Example: As Mom is aware, Kid, her 10-year-old son, is skateboarding on the sidewalk in front of their house, in a way that poses great danger to pedestrian passersby. Mom knows that she could control Kid to prevent him from skateboarding in this manner, but she unreasonably decides that the risks posed by Kid are small enough to make it not worth Mom's while to intervene. Kid runs into P, a little old lady, who is badly injured.

            P can recover against Mom, for failing to use reasonable care to prevent Kid from dangerous skateboarding, given that Mom both knew or should have known that she had the ability to control Kid and knew or should have known that Kid's behavior was risky to pedestrians.

2. **Criminal and intentionally tortious acts:** The reasonable person, and hence the defendant, is normally entitled to assume that third persons will not commit *crimes* or *intentional torts*, unless she has some reason to believe the contrary as to a particular third person.

   a. **Special relationship:** However, the defendant may have a *special relationship* with either the plaintiff or a third person, such that the defendant will bear the burden of anticipating and preventing intentionally tortious or criminal acts by that third person.

      i. **Psychotherapist-patient relationship:** For instance, in the famous case set forth in the following Example, the California Supreme Court held that the *psychotherapist-patient* relationship is one of those special relationships. So at least in California, the psychotherapist bears a burden to use reasonable care (e.g., has a duty to *warn*) on behalf of a *non-patient* who the psychotherapist learns is at risk of intentional harm at the hands of the patient.

         Example: Poddar is under the care of the Ds, university psychotherapists. He tells them that he intends to kill Tatiana, the Ps' daughter. One of the Ds asks the campus police to detain Poddar, but after he seems rational, they release him. Neither of the Ds warns Tatiana or the Ps. Two months later, Poddar in fact kills Tatiana.

         Held, the psychotherapist-patient relationship between the Ds and Poddar was sufficiently "special" that it created a duty for the Ds to protect third persons such as Tatiana (with whom they had no relationship at all) from reasonably foreseeable harm by Poddar. The Ds therefore had the duty to take reasonable steps to protect her, including probably the giving of a warning to her or the Ps. The university police, on the other hand, had no special relationship to Poddar (even though they detained him) or to Tatiana; they therefore bore no duty to protect Tatiana against harm from Poddar, and the Ps' complaint as against them must be dismissed. *Tarasoff v. Regents of the University of California*, 551 P.2d 334 (Cal. 1976), *infra*, p. 205.

   b. **Premises liability:** One important context in which the special relationship between plaintiff and defendant may impose a duty on the defendant to protect the plaintiff against third-party crimes is *"premises liability."* That is, the owner of *real estate* that is *held open to the public* normally has some sort of duty to *make reasonable protections against crimes* committed by third persons against those legitimately on the property. Thus a *shopping-mall operator*, a *hotel*, or a *school* may be liable for failing to impose reasonable security measures to protect against crimes against shoppers, hotel guests or students.

      i. **Different standards:** Courts are not in agreement on precisely what *standard* to use in evaluating whether the risk of third-party crime was sufficiently foreseeable that the property owner owed a duty to those on the premises to prevent that crime. The two major tests for foreseeability seem to be the *"totality of the circumstances"* test and the *"balancing"* test.

(1) "Totality of circumstances" test: The *"totality of the circumstances"* test, as its name implies, takes a whole variety of factors into account in determining whether the crime that ensued was sufficiently foreseeable that the property owner should have protected against it. When the totality test is used, a very important factor is the number, nature, and location of *prior similar incidents.* When courts use this test, they often focus on the level of crime in the *surrounding area,* and are willing to impose liability even if there has not been much crime on the particular premises, as long as the owner knew that there was significant crime *nearby.*

(2) "Balancing" test: The totality test is often criticized as placing *too great a burden on business owners.* Therefore, a number of courts (including those of California, Tennessee and Louisiana) have adopted the *"balancing"* test. This test "seeks to address the interests of both business proprietors and their customers by *balancing* the *foreseeability of harm* against the *burden of imposing a duty* to protect against the criminal acts of third persons." *Posecai v. Wal-Mart Stores, Inc.,* 752 So.2d 762 (La. 1999). Under the balancing test, a court will often hold that the defendant may not be required to use effective measures to deal with even a foreseeable risk, because of the *high cost of the measures.* D&H, p. 466. For instance, a court using this test would typically hold that a store operator had no duty to post security guards where there had been some crime in the surrounding neighborhood but not much on the actual store premises.

Example: D (Wal-Mart) operates a Sam's Club store in the town of Kenner. After shopping at the store, P goes to the parking lot, where she is robbed of $19,000 of jewelry. P sues D, asserting that D was negligent in not posting security guards in the parking lot during business hours. Evidence shows that the store was adjacent to, but not in, a high-crime area: in the prior six years, there were only three robberies on the store premises, but 83 "predatory offenses" at other businesses on the same block.

Held, for D. The court adopts the balancing test. Under this test, "a very high degree of foreseeability is required to give rise to a duty to post security guards, but a lower degree of foreseeability may support a duty to implement lesser security measures such as using surveillance cameras [or] installing improved lighting or fencing[.]" By this standard, the foreseeability of a robbery in D's parking lot was not sufficiently great to place on D a duty to provide security patrols in the lot. *Posecai v. Wal-Mart Stores, Inc., supra.*

G. Misrepresentation: Just as a defendant's acts may be negligent, so her *speech or other communication* may be. Where the resulting injury is an abstract economic one (e.g., investors' losses due to a financial statement negligently prepared by accountants), special rules apply, generally tending to limit the defendant's liability; these are discussed in a separate section on misrepresentation, *infra,* p. 442.

1. Physical injury: Where, however, a negligent statement leads to physical injury, or to tangible property damage, the case is treated under the same general rules as any other kind of negligence.

Example: D, a truck driver, gives a hand signal to P, driving behind him, to indicate that the way is clear for P to pass D. In fact, D has carelessly failed to notice that there is an oncoming car, which P smashes into. D will be held liable for negligence. P&K, p. 206, fn. 34. See also Rest. 2d, §311, Illustr. 6.

2. **Persons who may sue:** The person to whom the false information is given may, as we have seen, sue. Furthermore, *third persons* who the defendant knew or should have known might rely on the information may also sue. Thus a driver who gestures to one pedestrian to cross, and who should anticipate that other pedestrians nearby will also cross, will be liable to them if she runs them over. See Rest. 2d, §311(1)(b).

3. **Right to rely:** However, the circumstances must be such that the plaintiff is *reasonably justified* in relying on the defendant's information. For instance, "There may be no reasonable justification for taking the word of a casual bystander, who does not purport to have any special information or any interest in the matter, as to the safety of a bridge or scaffold. . . ." Rest. 2d, §311, Comment c.

V. MALPRACTICE

A. **Superior ability or knowledge:** We have seen that the usual standard of care and knowledge is an objective one, based on the level of a hypothetical reasonable person. But what if the defendant in fact has a higher degree of knowledge, skill or experience than this reasonable person — is she charged with using that higher level, so that she will be held for using, say, only the skill of an ordinary reasonable person? The short answer is "yes" — the defendant is charged with making reasonable use of whatever specialized type of knowledge or skill she possesses.

B. **Malpractice generally:** The issue of superior skill or knowledge arises most frequently in suits against professional persons, commonly known as *malpractice* suits. The general rule is that professionals, including doctors, lawyers, accountants, engineers, etc., must act with the level of skill and learning *commonly possessed by members of the profession in good standing*. See Rest. 2d, §299A; P&K, p. 187. There are, however, a number of more specific rules which, in practice, govern the disposition of malpractice suits.

1. **Good results not guaranteed:** The professional will *not* normally be held to guarantee that a *successful result* will occur. She is liable for malpractice only if she acted without the requisite minimum skill and competence, not merely because the operation, lawsuit, etc. was not successful.

Example: The Ds, lawyers, handle a suit for P against an out-of-state insurance company. They make service on the company by serving the State Insurance Commissioner. The trial judge holds that the service is valid. At that point, the Ds elect to stand by this method of service, and not to serve the defendant again by alternate means. The defendant appeals, and it is held that the service was invalid. Under local procedural rules, P is thenceforth barred from bringing a new suit against defendant, since the statute of limitations has run. P then sues the Ds for malpractice.

Held, it was widely assumed by lawyers throughout the state that service on the Insurance Commissioner would suffice; therefore, the Ds were not negligent in failing to use an alternate form of service, even though this later turned out to have been a strategic error. A lawyer is *not* liable for a *"mere error of judgment*, or for a "mistake in a point of law which has not been settled by the court of last resort . . . and on which reasonable doubt may be entertained by well-informed lawyers." *Hodges v. Carter*, 80 S.E.2d 144 (N.C. 1954).

2. **Specialists held to a higher standard:** Where the defendant holds herself out as a specialist in a certain portion of her profession, she will be held to the minimum standards of that specialty (which will obviously be higher than those of the profession at large). This will be true, for instance, for an ophthalmologist or a tax lawyer.

3. **Need for expert testimony:** It is almost always held that the defendant professional's negligence may be shown only through *expert testimony*. That is, in a medical malpractice case, the plaintiff must produce another doctor to testify, another accountant to establish the defendant accountant's negligence, etc. The expert testimony must normally establish both the standard course of conduct in the profession, and that the defendant departed from it.

   a. **Difficult burden:** This is generally an extremely difficult burden for the plaintiff to carry, in view of professionals' notorious unwillingness to testify against each other. It is made even more difficult by the general rule that it is not enough for the expert to say that he would have handled the matter differently from the defendant; he must testify that the defendant's conduct departed from all courses of conduct accepted by some portion of the profession.

   b. **Standard applied:** The correct standard has always been the level of skill of the ***minimally qualified member in good standing***, not the average member. " . . . [T]hose who have less than median or average skill may still be competent and qualified. Half of the physicians of America do not automatically become negligent in practicing medicine at all, merely because their skill is less than the professional average. On the other hand, the standard is not that of the charlatan, the quack, the unqualified or the incompetent individual who has succeeded in entering the profession or trade. It is that common to those who are recognized in the profession or trade itself as those qualified, and competent to engage in it." Rest. 2d, §299A, Comment e.

   c. **Exception where negligence obvious to lay person:** If the defendant's negligence is so blatant that the court determines as a matter of law that a ***lay person could identify it*** as such, expert testimony will not be needed. This would be the case, for instance, if a doctor amputates the wrong leg, injures the patient's shoulder during an appendectomy (*Ybarra v. Spangard, infra*, p. 127), etc.

      i. **Lay person understands obligation:** There may also be no need for expert testimony on negligence where the nature of the professional's obligation is such that a lay person can understand it, and determine whether it has been met, even though its absence is not blatant.

4. **"Standards of the community":** Until the last few decades, doctors and other professionals were almost always held to be bound by the professional standards prevailing in the ***community in which they practiced*** (or similar communities), not by a national professional standard. A reason usually cited for this rule was that education and facilities

varied tremendously from place to place, and allowance should be made for the "country practitioner's" inability to keep up with his city counterpart.

   a. Changing rule: As professional education has become more uniform nationally, however, more and more courts have abolished the "local standards" rule; as a result, the plaintiff may now frequently fulfill his burden of producing expert testimony by calling on an expert from outside the community (who may be more willing to testify). Abolition of the local standards rule has been particularly common where the defendant is a *specialist*. See Rest. 2d, §299A, Comment g.

5. Objective standard for professional: The standard of care for one who engages in a business, occupation or profession is *objective*, not subjective. Thus the defendant's **own training and experience are irrelevant** in determining whether she behaved with due care (at least where she does not hold herself out as a specialist); the issue is whether the defendant matched the standard of care commonly found among other members of the same profession.

6. Informed consent: In the case of a physician, one of the professional standards which must be met is that the *risks of a proposed treatment* must be adequately disclosed to the patient before he consents to that treatment. Older cases held that the physician's failure to make such disclosure vitiated the consent, and paved the way for a battery action (see *supra*, p. 67). More recently, however, courts have generally held that lack of full disclosure constitutes professional negligence, and that the matter must be handled under the general malpractice rules. The doctrine that adequate disclosure of risks must be made is known generally as the rule of "*informed consent*".

   a. Professional standard: Most courts hold that what should be disclosed to the patient is itself a question of professional standards, as to which expert testimony is necessary. The general principle is that the doctor must disclose to the patient all risks inherent in the proposed treatment which are sufficiently *material* that a reasonable patient *would take them into account* in deciding whether to undergo the treatment, provided that the patient's *well-being* would not be unduly disturbed by such disclosure. Also, disclosure of other possible courses of treatment must generally be made.

      i. Causality: Because of the requirement of proximate cause (*infra*, p. 152), the plaintiff must show that he would probably have *declined the treatment* had full disclosure been made. (If the patient would have undergone the treatment even had full disclosure of the risks been made, the lack of informed consent could not have been a proximate cause of the injury.) Some courts have held that what counts is what decision the patient himself would have made (whether a reasonable decision or not), not what some hypothetical "reasonable patient" would have done had full disclosure been made. See, e.g., *Scott v. Bradford*, 606 P.2d 554 (Okla. 1979). Other cases have applied a "reasonable patient" standard to this issue. But observe that even under the *Scott* standard, the jury does not necessarily have to take P's word that he would not have undergone the treatment; the jury may always choose to conclude that P's testimony is not credible.

   b. Exceptions: Of course, if there is an *emergency* and the patient is incapable of giving consent, disclosure will not be necessary; similarly, if the patient is exceptionally high-strung, and the doctor has reason to believe that he will overreact to any risk, and will elect a course of nontreatment which is, in reality, much more dangerous, disclosure may not be necessary.

7. **Novice:** One who is just *beginning* the practice of her profession (e.g., a hospital intern, a lawyer who has just passed the bar, etc.) is nonetheless ordinarily held to the same level of competence as a member of the profession generally, despite her inexperience. This is a special case of the general rule that a beginner at anything (e.g., a beginning automobile driver) may not have the benefit of a lower standard of care. "The law does not require the general public to assume the risk of the neophyte's lack of competence." Nutshell, p. 53.

   a. **Assumption of risk:** However, in the facts of a particular case, the plaintiff may be found to have been aware of the defendant's inexperience, and to have consciously accepted the risk of it. Thus a lawyer who carefully tells her client that she has recently been admitted to practice and knows little about civil procedure may be entitled to some lessening of the standard of performance owed by her in pursuing the plaintiff's lawsuit. But it is hard to believe that this principle would apply to a hospital intern, even if the patient-plaintiff knew full well of the frequent incompetence of such interns.

VI. AUTOMOBILE GUEST STATUTES

A. **Gross negligence and recklessness:** Thus far, we have discussed what might be termed "ordinary negligence". There are a few situations, however, in which the standard for liability is not ordinary negligence but some degree of culpability beyond that; this is sometimes called *"gross negligence"*, or *"willful and wanton disregard"*, or *"recklessness"*, etc. While distinctions have been frequently attempted among these various formulations (see P&K, pp. 211-12), the main thing to keep in mind is that all of these terms refer to a more serious departure from standards of ordinary care than would be required to constitute ordinary negligence. Generally, this departure is more serious because the risk of harm is substantially greater than the risk whose disregard constitutes ordinary negligence. See Rest. 2d, §500.

B. **Automobile guest statutes:** The major context in which a standard of gross negligence or recklessness is applied is that in which a *nonpaying passenger in an automobile* is injured, and sues the *driver-owner* of the car. So-called *"automobile guest statutes,"* at one time in force in approximately half the states, provide that the owner-driver is not liable for injuries received by his nonpaying passenger (whether a family member or not) *unless the driver has been "grossly" or "willfully negligent" or "reckless."*

   1. **Rationale:** Two principle rationales have been advanced for such statutes.

      a. **Ingratitude:** First, at the time most of these statutes were enacted in the 1930s, automobile liability insurance was not widespread, and a driver who was successfully sued by his "guest" was likely to bear the considerable expense himself; most legislatures felt that it was unfair to encourage "ingratitude" by guests.

      b. **Collusion:** Secondly, to the extent that there was insurance, there was (and presumably still is today) a risk that the guest and the driver (who are most probably either friends or relatives) will behave *collusively* in the lawsuit. That is, the defendant-owner, since he will not be paying the bill, may try to help out the plaintiff by conceding that he was in fact negligent.

2. **Constitutional attack:** In the last several decades, a number of the statutes have been repealed, and at least eleven state statutes have been found violative of either or both the *federal or state constitutions*. P&K, p. 216-17 and fn. 86. The most important decision in this area is *Brown v. Merlo*, 506 P.2d 212 (Cal. 1973), holding that the California guest statute violates the Equal Protection clause of the United States Constitution because it is "over-inclusive" — in order to guard against a few collusive suits, it denies recovery to a much larger class of non-colluding plaintiffs.

3. **Present status:** Today, only nine states have guest statutes still in force, and two of these (Texas and Illinois) are of restricted application. See P&K, p. 217, fn. 87.

4. **Intoxication as gross negligence:** It is sometimes held where the host driver drives while *intoxicated*, his conduct constitutes gross negligence, making the guest statute inapplicable.

VII. VIOLATION OF STATUTE (NEGLIGENCE PER SE)

A. **Significance of statutory violation:** In the cases we have examined thus far, the decision as to what a reasonable person would do in the circumstances was left to the judge and jury. Sometimes, however, the *legislature* passes a statute which appears to define reasonable conduct in a certain kind of situation. This is most often true of legislation establishing *safety standards* for industry, transportation, etc. A substantial body of case law has arisen discussing the extent to which the court is required to treat a violation of such legislation as *"negligence per se."*

1. **"Negligence per se doctrine":** Most courts follow the general rule that when a safety statute has a sufficiently close application to the facts of the case at hand, an unexcused violation of that statute is *"negligence per se,"* and the defendant will not be permitted to show that the legislature set an unduly high standard of care.

> **Example 1:** P drives a buggy after dark without lights, in violation of a New York criminal statute requiring lights. The buggy collides with D's automobile, and P is killed. The trial judge instructs the jury that it may consider the lack of lights as some evidence of negligence, but not as conclusive on the question of negligence.
>
> *Held*, in an appellate decision by Judge Cardozo, "We think the unexcused omission of the statutory signals is more than some evidence of negligence. *It is negligence itself.*" Since there was evidence at trial that the absence of lights was causally related to the accident, P's violation was necessarily contributory negligence, and he may not recover. *Martin v. Herzog*, 126 N.E. 814 (N.Y. 1920), *infra*, p. 119.
>
> **Example 2:** D owns a drugstore. His clerk sells a bottle of poison to P without labeling the bottle "poison," as required by statute. P, not knowing that the bottle contains poison, drinks the contents, and dies.
>
> *Held*, D is negligent because he violated the standard of care imposed upon him by statute. P's action is not "statutory"; it is simply based on conduct by D which,

because of the statutory duty of labelling, is deemed by the court to constitute "negligence *per se.*" *Osborne v. McMasters*, 41 N.W. 543 (Minn. 1889).

    a. **Third Restatement:**   The Third Restatement gives a good summary of how the negligence per se doctrine operates:

"An actor is negligent if, ***without excuse***, the actor ***violates a statute that is designed to protect against the type of accident the actor's conduct causes***, and if the accident *victim* is ***within the class of persons the statute is designed to protect.***"

Rest. 3d (Liab. for Phys. & Emot. Harm) §14.

    b. **Three requirements:**   As the above-quoted Third Restatement rule illustrates, there are three main requirements for application of the negligence per se doctrine:

[1] D *violated a statute*;

[2] the statute was ***designed to protect against the same type of accident*** that D's conduct caused; and

[3] the accident *victim* (presumably P) falls within the ***class of persons the statute was designed to protect.***

We'll consider each of these requirements in more detail below.

B. Penal statutes: Some statutes contain an explicit provision that their violation will give rise to civil liability. If this is the case, of course, the court has no choice but to give the statute its intended effect, presuming that it is validly enacted and constitutional. The statutes we are talking about principally here, however, are ones which are solely ***penal*** in nature; that is, they provide that a violation is a crime or a misdemeanor, but they do not say anything about whether civil liability ensures.

    1. **Deference:**   The majority rule that in such situations, the court will apply the statutory standard as a matter of law, is therefore usually explained not by reference to the doctrine of separation of powers, but by the fact that the court is adopting the legislature's determination of what is necessary for safety "voluntarily, out of deference and respect for the legislature." P&K, p. 222.

    2. **Ordinances and administrative regulations:** The negligence per se doctrine ordinarily applies to violations of ***local ordinances*** and ***administrative regulations*** just as to ordinary statutes. Dobbs, p. 316. However, some courts treat such violations as being merely non-dispositive "evidence" of negligence.

C. Statute must apply to facts: Even in states following the majority rule that statutory violations can sometimes be "negligence per se," the courts have set up a series of requirements to ensure that, before the violation will be negligence per se, the statute was intended to guard against the ***kind of injury*** in question.

    1. **Protection against particular harm:**   The first requirement the statute must meet before there is a violation per se is that the statute was intended to protect against the ***particular kind of harm*** that the plaintiff seeks to recover for. See Rest. 2d, §286(b).

        Example: A statute requires that vessels carrying animals across the ocean shall keep them in separate pens. The statute is obviously intended to protect only against the spreading of contagious diseases from animal to animal. P sends his sheep on D's ships, and D violates the statute by herding P's sheep together with other animals. Because there are no pens, the sheep are washed overboard during a storm.

Held, the statutory violation cannot be relied on because "the damage is of such a nature as was not contemplated at all by the statute, and as to which it was not intended to confer any benefit on the plaintiffs." There might have been a recovery, however, had P's sheep been lost through disease because of overcrowding. *Gorris v. Scott*, L.R. 9 Ex. 125 (Eng. 1874). See also Rest. 2d, §286, Illustr. 4.

a. **Keys left in car:** The significance of how the "type of risk" question is resolved is illustrated by cases where *keys* have been left in a parked car, in violation of a statute requiring that keys not be so left, and a theft, and an ensuing accident, have resulted. Where the court has construed the purpose of the statute as being to guard against reckless driving by thieves, negligence per se has been found; where it has been found to be for some other purpose, there has been no such automatic liability. P&K, pp. 224-25.

2. **Class of persons protected:** The second requirement for the application of negligence per se is that the plaintiff must be a member of the *class of persons* whom the statute was designed to protect. See Rest. 3d (Liab. for Phys. & Emot. Harm) §14.

   Example: A statute requires that all factory elevators be provided with a certain safety device. The legislative history, title and details of the statute make it clear that the statute's sole purpose was to protect employees of the factory, not visitors. P1, an employee in D's factory, and P2, a business visitor to the factory, are both injured when the elevator falls, because of a lack of the safety device. The statute will establish that D's failure to have the safety device was negligence as to P1, but not as to P2, because P2 was not a member of the class of persons whom the statute was designed to protect. Rest. 2d, §286, Illustr. 1.

   a. **General interests of state:** A sub-species of this rule is the principle that where the statute is intended to protect only the interests of the *state* or of the *public at large*, and not to protect particular individuals against harm, its violation will not be negligence per se.

      i. **Blue Law:** Thus, a *"Blue Law"*, prohibiting stores from being open on Sunday, would not conclusively establish the negligence of a store owner who opened on Sunday, exercising all reasonable care, but whose customer slipped on the store floor. The law would be held to protect the interest of the public at large in having a day of rest, not to protect individuals who would otherwise shop on Sundays. (Such a statute would also be held not to meet the other requirement, that of protecting against the kind of harm in question, since it is clear that the statute is not designed to protect against Sunday falls in stores.) P&K, pp. 222-23.

   b. **Two classes of persons protected:** But a statute may be held to have been intended to protect both the public at large as well as a particular class of individuals. If so, its violation may be negligence per se if the plaintiff belongs to the particular class.

D. Causal link: Even where the statute is applicable to the facts of the case, the "negligence per se" does not make the defendant liable unless the plaintiff shows that there is a *causal link* between the act constituting a violation and the resulting injury. See P&K, pp. 229-30.

    1. Warnings and safety devices: This principle requiring proof of causation is often important in cases involving *warnings or safety devices* — if D violates a statute requiring a particular type of warning or safety device, but the accident would have happened even if the warning or device had been furnished as required, then the negligence per see doesn't matter.

        Example: A statute requires the manufacturer of a prescription drug to insert into the drug package a warning of adverse side effects. D fails to insert an appropriate warning of a particular side effect, cardiac arrhythmia, in a drug it manufactures. P buys the drug and contracts fatal arrhythmia. P's estate sues D for negligence, arguing that the omission of the warning was negligence per se.

        If D can show that neither P nor anyone in his household ever read warnings that accompany prescription drugs, D should win. That's because D has shown that the statutory violation had no causal connection to the harm (since the harm would have occurred even if the never-to-be-read warning had been placed in the package).

E. Excuse of violation: Once the plaintiff has shown that the statute was designed to guard against the kind of harm that she sustained and that it was addressed to a class of person that included the plaintiff (and assuming that plaintiff carries the more general burden of showing that the act that was violative of the statute was the actual *cause* of the harm), a prima facie case of the defendant's negligence per se has been established. However, in some circumstances, the defendant may then have the right to show that his violation of the statute was *excusable.* If he can do this, the violation will be stripped of its "negligence per se" nature, and will be, at most, evidence of negligence which the jury will weigh, and may disregard.

    1. Absolute duties: There are some statutes which, the court may hold, by their nature and history leave no room for excuses. That is, they impose upon the defendant an *absolute duty* to comply with the statute, and a good faith attempt to do so is not sufficient.

        a. Typical cases: For instance, statutes prohibiting the use of *child labor* have generally been held to fall in this category. Thus an employer who hires a child in violation of the statute will be held liable if an injury occurs of the sort that the act was intended to protect against, and the employer will not be heard to say that he believed in good faith that the child was above the minimum age.

    2. Rebuttable presumption or excuse: Most statutes, on the other hand, are not interpreted to impose an absolute duty of compliance. Courts have chosen two similar (but not exactly identical) ways of preventing statutes from being given this absolute effect. Sometimes, the statute is viewed as merely establishing a *rebuttable presumption* of negligence; the defendant can then introduce evidence of due care in order to rebut the presumption. Other courts treat the statute as establishing negligence per se, but allow certain *excuses* for non-compliance; if one of the available excuses is demonstrated, the violation has no bearing on the issue of negligence. The Third Restatement follows the "excuse" approach. Thus Rest. 3d (Liab. for Phys. & Emot. Harm) §15, lists a number of factors that will excuse a violation:

a. **Disability:** The violation is reasonable because of the defendant's "*childhood, physical disability*, or *physical incapacitation*." §15(a).

   Example: A local ordinance makes it an offense to drive through a stop sign without stopping. After a collision between cars driven by P and D, in which D dies, P sues D's estate for damages. P produces uncontested evidence that D drove through a stop sign, and that that action proximately caused the collision, while P drove properly. D's estate produces undisputed evidence that (1) D had no previously known heart condition; (2) D was driving properly until moments before the accident; (3) D suffered a fatal heart attack a few second before arriving at the stop sign; and (4) that heart attack prevented D from pressing the brake when the car got to the stop sign.

   P will not recover. The only evidence of negligence in the case is D's violation of the stop sign ordinance. But this violation will be excused due to D's incapacity, making negligence per se inapplicable. Therefore, there is no evidence of D's negligence, entitling D's estate to a directed verdict.

b. **Ignorance of need:** The defendant neither knew nor should have known of "the *factual circumstances* that render[ed] the statute applicable." §15(c).

   Example: A statute prohibits any contractor from doing excavation within 10 feet of a high-voltage power line. D, a contractor, excavates within 6 feet of such a line. However, D does not realize that the line is present because it is obscured by heavy foliage (and a reasonable person in D's position would not have realized that the line was or might be present). D knocks down the line, injuring P, a bystander.

   Because D neither knew nor should have known of "the factual circumstances that render[ed] the statute applicable" to his particular excavation session, the negligence per se doctrine will not apply to his conduct. Cf. Rest. 3d (Liab. for Phys. & Emot. Harm) §15, Comment d (giving a hypothetical with essentially these facts).

c. **Reasonable attempt to comply:** Similarly, the violation may be excused because the defendant "exercise[d] *reasonable care in attempting to comply* with the statute," but was unsuccessful. §15(b).

d. **Confusion to public:** The violation may be excused if it was "due to the *confusing way* in which the requirements of the statute are *presented to the public*." §15(d).

   Example: A road sign on Main St. says "No Left Turn." The sign is placed just before two roads turn off of Main St., Maple and Oak. A reasonable driver could be confused about whether the sign means that left turns are prohibited onto Maple, Oak, or both. D, reasonably believing that the sign applies to Maple but not to Oak, turns left onto Oak, and collides with P. D would not be subject to liability under negligence per se, because the confusing nature of the sign would excuse his non-compliance. Cf. Rest. 3d (Liab. for Phys. & Emot. Harm) §15, Comment e ("If a sign or signal is such as to confuse the reasonable motorist, negligence per se is not appropriate.")

e. **Greater risk of harm:** A violation by a person may be excused if compliance would have "involve[d] a *greater risk of physical harm* to the actor or to others than non-compliance." §15(e).

Example: A statute provides that pedestrians walking along the highway shall walk towards oncoming traffic. Ps are walking along a highway one night, when traffic conditions are such that traffic on the left side (where Ps are required by statute to walk) is much heavier than on the right side. They therefore walk on the right side, and are hit by D. D argues that they were contributorily negligent as a matter of law, because of their statutory violation.

Held, Ps's violation will be excused where it would have been more dangerous to comply. *Tedla v. Ellman*, 19 N.E.2d 987 (N.Y. 1939), *infra*, p. 280. See also Rest. 2d, §288A, Illustr. 6.

Note: The court in *Tedla* distinguished between statutes which "define the standard of care and the safeguards required to meet a recognized danger" (as to which the court said no excuse is allowable) and statutes such as the one before it, which "fixes no definite standard of care which would under all circumstances tend to protect life, limb or property, but merely codifies or supplements a common law rule, which has a always been subject to limitations and exceptions." In this latter event, the court held, the statute "should not be construed as intended to wipe out the limitations and exceptions which judicial decisions have attached to the common law duty. . . . " However, Prosser and Keeton suggest that this "implied exception theory" is really a rationalization, and that the true reason the court allowed the exception was simply because "the courts reserve the final authority to determine whether the civil standard of reasonable conduct will always require obedience to the criminal law." P&K, p. 228.

3. **Foolish or obsolete legislation:** There are many statutes on the books which have never been enforced, or which have not been enforced for so long that they may be treated as *obsolete.* In such a situation, the court will often in effect treat the violation as excused, although in reality the court is really simply declining to accept the legislative standard as binding on the civil liability question.

F. **Effect of the plaintiff's contributory negligence:** Even where the defendant's negligence per se is established, he may be able to assert the defenses of *contributory negligence* or *assumption of risk.* However, if the statute is of a sort that is held to impose an absolute duty on the defendant, and therefore to allow no excuses (see *supra*, p. 117) these defenses may not be available. Thus an employer who violates the child labor laws will not be allowed to raise the defense of contributory negligence, since this would defeat the entire purpose of the statute. This limitation upon the defenses of contributory negligence and assumption of risk is further discussed *infra* at pp. 281 and 296, respectively.

G. **Contributory negligence per se:** The defendant may, in an appropriate case, demonstrate that the plaintiff's violation of a statute constitutes *contributory (or comparative) negligence per se.* Generally speaking, the rules are the same for asserting contributory negligence per se as for defendant's negligence per se. See, for instance, *Martin v. Herzog, supra*, p. 114.

1. **Hurdles:** But keep in mind that the hurdles which must be surmounted before negligence per se is established are still imposed; thus if the statute is construed as one which was not intended for the protection of a person in the position of the plaintiff, the violation will not conclusively establish contributory negligence.

2. Speed limits: Generally, however, such statutes as *speed limits* and other traffic regulations are held to be for the purpose of protecting plaintiff drivers who violate them, as well as innocent third persons. See P&K, p. 232.

H. Violation as evidence: Even if the plaintiff (or the defendant, in a case involving contributory negligence) is unable to meet all the requirements of the negligence per se doctrine, the statutory violation may still be taken as *evidence of negligence*.

> **Example:** A statute providing that hogs must be confined by fences of a particular strength is construed to be solely for the purpose of preventing misbreeding. D violates the statute by using less than the required strength of fence to enclose his hogs. One breaks the fence, runs into the highway, collides with P's car, and the resulting accident injures P. Even though the violation is not negligence per se (since the statute was not intended to guard against the kind of harm which occurred) the jury may consider the degree of strength required by the statute as evidence as to how strong a fence is needed to keep hogs from breaking loose. See Rest. 2d, §288B, Illustr. 2.

I. Compliance with statute not dispositive: The converse of the "negligence per se" doctrine does not hold true. That is, the fact that the defendant has *fully complied* with all applicable state safety regulations does *not by itself establish* that he was not negligent. The finder of fact is always free to conclude that a reasonable person would take precautions beyond those required by statute. See, e.g., Rest. 3d (Liab. for Phys. & Emot. Harm) §16(a): "An actor's compliance with a pertinent statute, while evidence of non-negligence, *does not preclude a finding* that the actor is negligent ... for failing to adopt precautions *in addition* to those mandated by the statute."

1. Greater hazard: This rule is especially applicable where the situation at hand was *more hazardous* than the usual situation the statute was designed to govern. See Rest. 2d, §288C.

a. Usual case: But if the situation confronting the defendant was substantially the same as that which the statute was designed to control, the finder of fact may consider the defendant's full compliance with all statutes as significant evidence that nothing more was required of a reasonable person. See P&K, p. 233.

VIII. PROCEDURE IN JURY TRIALS

A. Aspects of procedure: Since most tort cases are tried before juries, it is important to understand at least a few basic aspects of jury trial procedure. Considered here are two principal topics: (1) the *burden of proof*, and (2) the allocation of functions between *judge and jury*. See generally Rest. 2d, Chapter 12, Topic 9.

B. Burden of proof: In a negligence case, as in virtually all tort cases, the plaintiff is said to bear the *"burden of proof."* In reality, the plaintiff actually bears two distinct burdens:

1. Burden of production: First, she must come forward with some evidence that the defendant was negligent, that she, the plaintiff, suffered an injury, that the defendant's negligence was the proximate cause of this injury, etc. This burden is generally known as the *"burden of production."* The burden of production may be defined as the obligation upon a party to come forward with evidence in order to avoid a directed verdict (i.e., an instruction from the judge to the jury telling them that they must decide in favor of the party not bearing the burden of production). This burden can and does shift from the plaintiff to the defendant and possibly back again, depending on the strengths of the proof offered by each side. The following diagram, adapted from Field, Kaplan & Clermont, *Cases and Materials on Civil Procedure*, 7th Ed., p. 672, is illustrative:

Judge	Jury	Judge
Zone 1	Zone 2	Zone 3

a. **Directed verdict for defendant:** The case starts off in Zone 1 — if the plaintiff does not produce any evidence in support of her *prima facie* case, the judge will order a directed verdict for the defendant. That is, she will tell the jury that as a matter of law, it must find for the defendant.

b. **Jury case:** If the plaintiff comes forward with enough evidence in support of her *prima facie* case that a reasonable person could (but would not necessarily have to) decide in the plaintiff's favor, the case is in Zone 2, and will go to the jury. Once the case is in Zone 2, neither party bears the burden of production, since neither party must come forward with additional evidence in order to avoid a directed verdict.

c. **Directed verdict for plaintiff:** It may be, however, that the plaintiff's case is so strong that, unless the defendant comes forward with rebutting evidence, the court will have to order a directed verdict in the plaintiff's favor (i.e., the court will decide that no reasonable person could find in favor of the defendant). If so, the case is in Zone 3, and plaintiff has in effect shifted the burden of production to the defendant.

d. **Effect of defendant's case:** When the defendant puts on his case, he can similarly move the burden of proof from Zone 3 to Zone 2 or 1 (leading to submission of the case to the jury, or a directed verdict in favor of the defendant, respectively). Or, if he starts his portion of the case with the matter in Zone 2, he may produce so little evidence that the case stays in that Zone (and is given to the jury), or enough to get it to Zone 1, directed verdict for himself.

2. **Practical significance:** The judge does not monitor the shifting burden of production throughout the trial. It is really only at two points that evaluation of the burden is significant: first, at the end of the plaintiff's case, the defendant usually moves for a directed verdict; that is, he asks the court to declare that the plaintiff has failed to move the case out of Zone 1, and that the jury should be instructed that it must decide in his, the defendant's, favor. Secondly, at the end of the defendant's case, each side is likely to move for a directed verdict, the plaintiff alleging that the case is in Zone 3, and the defendant that it is in Zone 1.

3. **Burden of persuasion:** The second respect in which the plaintiff begins by bearing the burden of proof is that she bears what is sometimes called the ***"burden of persuasion"***. This means that if the case goes to the jury (i.e., if the case ends up in Zone 2), the plaintiff

must convince the jury that it is *more probable than not* that her injuries are due to the defendant's negligence. To put it another way, the fact that the plaintiff bears the burden of persuasion means that if the jury believes that there is exactly a fifty percent chance that the defendant caused the injuries, the plaintiff loses. The concept is usually expressed by saying that the plaintiff must demonstrate her case *"by the preponderance of the evidence"*.

    a. Not usually shifted: The burden of persuasion, in a negligence case (and, in fact, in almost every kind of case) rests on the plaintiff from the beginning, and almost never shifts.

C. Circumstantial evidence: Sometimes, the plaintiff may be lucky enough to prove her case by direct evidence. For instance, she may be able to produce an eye witness who will testify that the defendant behaved in a particular way, and that the plaintiff was injured in a particular way as a result. But very often, the plaintiff will make her case by *circumstantial* evidence. Circumstantial evidence has been defined as "evidence of one fact . . . from which the existence of the fact to be determined may reasonably be inferred. It involves, in addition to the assertions of witnesses as to what they have observed, a process of reasoning, or inference, by which a conclusion is drawn." P&K, p. 242.

> **Example:** P, departing from a train run by D Railroad, slips on a banana peel left on the railroad platform. No one testifies as to how long the banana lay there prior to the accident (which would bear on whether D's employees were negligent in not yet having picked it up). However, witnesses testify that the banana was, after the accident, "flattened down, and black in color," "dry, gritty, as if there were dirt upon it," etc.
>
> *Held*, the jury could have justifiably inferred, from the appearance and condition of the banana peel, that it had been on the platform for such a long period of time that D's employees would have seen and removed it if they had been reasonably careful. This circumstantial evidence was enough to rebut the possibility that the peel might have been dropped moments prior to the accident by another passenger. Therefore, it was error to direct a verdict for the defendant. *Anjou v. Boston Elevated Railway Co.,* 94 N.E. 386 (Mass. 1911).

D. Function of judge and jury: Both the judge and jury play a significant role in the adjudication of a negligence case. An extended discussion of the allocation of roles between the two is not possible here; however, a few general observations may be made:

1. Judge decides law: The *judge*, of course, decides all *questions of law*. In a negligence case, this means that the judge will decide, typically, the following issues:

    a. State of facts: She will decide, after all the evidence is in, whether that evidence admits of more than one conclusion. If she decides that *reasonable people could not differ* as to what the facts of the case are, she will instruct the jury as to the findings of fact they must make (thus virtually taking the case out of their hands).

    Example: Suppose plaintiff begins a medical malpractice case, and attempts to show that the defendant left a sponge in his body. If the judge decides that reasonable people could differ as to whether the sponge was really left in the plaintiff's body, or as to whether it was really left there by the defendant, the judge will allow the jury to decide this fact question (assuming that the plaintiff has demonstrated the other aspects of his case sufficiently so as to be entitled to go the jury). But if the judge concludes that all reasonable people would agree that the sponge was left in the body, she will instruct the jury that it must so find; similarly, if there could be no doubt that the sponge was not left in the body, she will so instruct the jury. See Rest. 2d, §328D, Illustr. 9.

b. **Existence of duty:**   The judge will also determine what the defendant's *duty* to the plaintiff was. This is done as a matter of law. Thus in a suit by a plaintiff trespasser against a defendant landowner, the court will probably instruct the jury that, provided the defendant did not know of the plaintiff's presence, he owed him no duty of care at all. And in an accident case, the judge will instruct the jury that the defendant owed the plaintiff the duty of care that a reasonable person would exercise in the circumstances.

c. **Directed verdict:**   By deciding aspects of both of these matters, the judge may remove the case from the jury by *directing a verdict.* Thus in an accident case, if the judge concludes that reasonable persons would all agree that the defendant had behaved reasonably, and also decides as a matter of law that the defendant owed only the duty of behaving as a reasonable person would under the circumstances, she will direct the jury to find for the defendant.

2. **Jury's role:**   The jury, it is commonly said, is the finder of the facts. However, since as we have seen the judge may sometimes decide the facts as a matter of law, what this really means is that the jury will be permitted to find the facts only where these facts are in such dispute that reasonable persons could differ on them. If the case is sufficiently unclear that it is permitted to go to the jury, the jury will decide two principle factual issues:

a. **What happened:**   First, what really happened; and

b. **Particular standard of care:**   Secondly, whether the facts as found indicate that the defendant breached his duty of care to the plaintiff, in a way that proximately caused the plaintiff's injuries. See generally, P&K, pp. 235-38.

IX. *RES IPSA LOQUITUR* — CREATING AN INFERENCE OF NEGLIGENCE

A. **Aid in proving the case:**   A plaintiff's tort lawyer often has a difficult task in proving his case. Frequently, it is made particularly hard by the fact that the plaintiff does not have any knowledge of or access to the facts about the defendant's conduct. This section is about a doctrine which, when it applies, makes the plaintiff's task significantly easier. The doctrine of *res ipsa loquitur* (which in English means *"The thing speaks for itself"*) allows the plaintiff to point to the fact of the accident, and to *create an inference* that, even without a precise showing of how the defendant behaved, the defendant was *probably negligent.* See generally Rest. 2d, §328D.

> **Example:** P is walking in the street past D's shop, when a barrel of flour falls on him from a window above the shop. In P's suit against D, his evidence demonstrates only these facts, and shows nothing about any actual acts by D or his employees.

Held, P has presented enough evidence to justify a verdict for him. "A barrel could not roll out of a warehouse without some negligence, and to say that a plaintiff who is injured by it must call witnesses from the warehouse to prove negligence seems ... preposterous. . . . It [is] apparent that the barrel was in the custody of the defendant who occupied the premises, and who is responsible for the acts of his servants who had the control of it; . . . the fact of its falling is *prima facie* evidence of negligence, and the plaintiff who was injured by it is not bound to shew that it could not fall without negligence, but if there are any facts inconsistent with negligence, it is for the defendant to prove them." *Byrne v. Boadle*, 159 Eng. Rep. 299 (Eng. 1863).

Note: It was in this case that one of the judges, Chancellor Pollock, observed that this was a situation "of which it may be said *res ipsa loquitur.*"

B. **Requirements for doctrine:** Virtually all American courts recognize that there are situations in which the doctrine of *res ipsa loquitur* should be applied, thus permitting the plaintiff to create an inference of the defendant's negligence without any direct evidence showing that negligence. The courts generally agree on at least *four requirements* before the doctrine may be applied (see also Rest. 2d, §328D):

1. **No direct evidence of D's conduct:** First, there must be *no direct evidence of how D behaved* in connection with the event.

2. **Seldom occurs without negligence:** Second, the plaintiff must demonstrate that the event is of a kind which *ordinarily does not occur except through the negligence* (or other fault) of *someone*. See Rest. 2d, §328D(1)(a).

3. **In defendant's control:** Third, plaintiff must show that the instrument which caused her injury was, at the relevant time, in the *exclusive control* of the defendant.

4. **Rule out plaintiff's contribution:** Fourth, plaintiff must show that her injury was not due to her *own* action. P&K, p. 244.

5. **Accessibility of information:** Some courts have purported to hold that in addition to establishing these four things, the plaintiff must also show that a true explanation of the events is more readily *accessible* to the defendant than to herself. However, few courts have really relied on this requirement, as is discussed further below.

C. **No direct evidence of D's conduct:** As a threshold matter, most courts insist that there must be *no direct evidence of how D behaved* in connection with the event. *Res ipsa* is only used as an indirect means of inferring that D was probably negligent, so there's no need to use the doctrine if we know the details of D's conduct.

D. **Inference of someone's negligence:** The plaintiff must, as stated, demonstrate that the harm which befell her does not normally occur except through the negligence of someone. This is true of, for instance, falling elevators, escaping gas or water from utility mains, the explosion of boilers, etc. (See Rest. 2d, §328D, Comment c.) The plaintiff is not required to prove that such events *never* occur except through someone's negligence; all she has to do is to show that *most of the time*, negligence is the cause of such occurrences.

Example: P is driving behind a truck driven by D. As the truck goes over some railroad tracks, a heavy spare tire comes out of its cradle underneath the truck and falls to the ground. The truck's rear wheels then cross over the spare, throwing the spare into the air. The spare crashes through P's windshield, injuring him badly. P sues D on a *res ipsa* theory. At trial, D testifies that the tire was secured to the truck's underside by a chain, which he says he inspected before the trip. (The chain cannot be located for the trial.) The judge instructs the jury that it may apply *res ipsa*. The jury finds for P. D appeals on the grounds that this is not the type of accident that would not have occurred without negligence.

Held, for P. "We conclude that the spare tire escaping from the cradle underneath the truck . . . is the type of accident which, on the basis of common experience and as a matter of general knowledge, would not occur but for the failure to exercise reasonable care by the person who had control of the spare tire." *McDougald v. Perry*, 716 So. 2d 783 (Fla. 1998).

1. **Certainty not required:** The plaintiff is *not* required to demonstrate that there were *no other possible causes* of the accident. She must merely prove that *most* of the time, this type of accident is caused by negligence.

   Example: Suppose P's decedent dies in a plane crash over water. P is not required to demonstrate that there was no mechanical failure, or to negate every other possible cause. All P has to do is show that in *most* airplane crashes over water, negligence is a but-for cause. (P will often attempt to do this by expert testimony — in this case, perhaps by testimony from an expert on the causes of plane crashes.)

   a. **Negating non-negligence causes:** The plaintiff may satisfy the "most of the time" requirement in part by *excluding certain causes*: if P can show that certain non-negligence-based causes suggested by the defendant could not possibly have been the cause of the particular accident, these will be taken out of the "more likely than not" computation.

   b. **Proof that one cause is especially likely:** Conversely, if the plaintiff can come up with evidence that a certain cause is *especially likely* to have produced the present harm, this may be enough to *raise* the overall chance of negligence beyond the required 50% threshold. Thus in the following pair of examples given by the Third Restatement, notice how the second one satisfies the plaintiff's burden on the "most of the time" issue:

   > Assume, for example, that the evidence identifies *five causes, of essentially equal likelihood*, for a particular type of accident: *causes A and B* are associated with the negligence of the defendant, while the remaining three causes are not. Given this evidence, res ipsa loquitur should be *denied*, since the probability of defendant negligence is *less than 50 percent*. Assume now, however, that some evidence is available about the defendant's conduct in the particular case that *raises the possibility of cause A* to roughly *40 percent*, while leaving undisturbed the relative likelihood of the remaining causes. Given this evidence, the likelihood of defendant negligence is now *55 percent* (40 percent plus 15 percent), and res ipsa loquitur *can be properly applied.*

   Rest. 3d (Liab. for Phys. & Emot. Harm) §17, Comment d.

2. **Aviation:** It is now generally accepted that where an *airplane crashes* without explanation, the jury may infer that negligence was more than likely the cause. In the early days of aviation, however, where the elements were often sufficient to cause a crash without anyone's negligence, and where there was no body of accident history to justify any conclusion about the general causes of accidents, most courts refused to allow this inference, and the doctrine of *res ipsa loquitur* was therefore not applied. See P&K, pp. 246-47.

3. **Basis of conclusions:** Normally, the fact that a particular kind of accident does not usually occur without negligence is within the *general experience of the jury,* and does not have to be explicitly proved by the plaintiff. However, there are other cases (e.g., *medical malpractice* cases) where the court may conclude that juries don't have enough pertinent experience to decide the issue on their own; thus the court may require plaintiff to provide — as a prerequisite for getting the case to the jury — *expert testimony* to the effect that accidents such as the one that occurred normally do not happen without negligence.

E. **Showing that negligence was defendant's:** The plaintiff must also show, again by a preponderance of evidence, that the negligence was *probably that of the defendant.* In the older cases, this requirement is usually expressed by stating that the plaintiff must demonstrate that the instrumentality which caused the harm was at all times within the *exclusive control* of the defendant.

> **Example:** During the great V-J celebration, P is walking on the sidewalk next to D Hotel, when she is hit by a falling armchair. P proves no other facts at trial.
>
> *Held,* "A hotel does not have exclusive control, either actual or potential, of its furniture. The guests have, at least, partial control." Therefore, P has failed to establish the requirement for *res ipsa. Larson v. St. Francis Hotel,* 188 P.2d 513 (Cal. 1948).

1. **Modern view:** Most modern cases, however, do not express this requirement solely in terms of "exclusive control" by the defendant. Instead, they simply require the plaintiff to show that, more likely than not, the negligence was the defendant's, not someone else's.

   a. **Third Restatement abandons requirement:** The Third Restatement explicitly *abandons* the requirement that the plaintiff show that the instrumentality that brought about the accident was under D's exclusive control. See Rest. 3d (Liab. for Phys. & Emot. Harm) §17, and Comment b thereto. The commentary points out that the concept of the person in exclusive control theoretically functions as a proxy for the likely negligent party, but that "frequently exclusive control functions poorly as such a proxy." *Id.*

   Example: The Restatement gives this example: Consumer buys a new car. The day after the purchase, the brakes fail, and Consumer strikes Pedestrian. Consumer has had exclusive control the car prior to the accident, but there is no reason to believe that Consumer was the negligent one. Rather, there is every reason to believe that the responsible party is the manufacturer. So Pedestrian ought not to have a *res ipsa* claim against Consumer (and ought to have a *res-ipsa*-like claim against the manufacturer) even though the car was under Consumer's exclusive control immediately prior to the accident. *Id.,* Comment b.

2. **Plaintiff's particular evidence:**   To demonstrate that the negligence is more probably that of the defendant, the plaintiff is required to produce evidence **negating other possibilities**. "[H]owever, the evidence need not be conclusive, and only enough is required to permit a finding as to the greater probability." P&K, p. 249. Thus a plaintiff injured by a soda bottle which explodes after she has bought it from a retailer must produce evidence showing that there were no intervening causes, i.e., that the retailer handled the bottle carefully, and that she herself handled it carefully, at all times. *Id.*

3. **Multiple defendants:**   Sometimes the plaintiff sues **two or more defendants** at once, alleging that some or all of them have been negligent. If the plaintiff can demonstrate the probability that the injury was caused by the negligence of at least one of the defendants, but cannot show which of them, may the doctrine of *res ipsa* be applied against all? This has been one of the major questions in the recent history of the doctrine.

   a. **Ybarra case:**   The most famous case holding that the answer to this question can sometimes be "Yes" is **Ybarra v. Spangard**, set forth in the following example.

   Example: P goes into the hospital for an appendectomy. After the operation, his shoulder hurts, and turns out to have sustained a serious injury during the operation. P sues the surgeon, the attending physician, the owner of the hospital, and the anesthesiologist. He demonstrates that at least one of them (or a nurse under the control of one of them) must have been negligent, but is unable to offer any evidence as to which.

   Held, res ipsa may be applied. It would be unreasonable to require the plaintiff to identify the negligent defendant, insofar as he was unconscious throughout the operation. Furthermore, the defendants bore interrelated responsibilities; each of them had a duty to see that no harm befell P. Therefore, each of the defendants who had any control over or responsibility for P must bear the burden of rebutting the inference of negligence by making an explanation of what really happened. (This should be done at a new trial.) *Ybarra v. Spangard*, 154 P.2d 687 (Cal. 1944), *supra*, p. 111, *infra*, p. 150.

   Note: At the retrial, all of the defendants except the hospital owner testified that nothing had occurred during the operation which would explain P's injury. The trial court, without a jury, found against all of the defendants.

   b. **Special relationship:**   The result in *Ybarra* seems to be at least partially due to the fact that the defendants all bore an integrated relationship as professional colleagues, and that all had a responsibility for the patient's safety. Where the multiple defendants are **strangers** to each other, and have only an ordinary duty of care to the plaintiff, *res ipsa* has generally **not** been allowed merely upon a showing that at least one of them must have been negligent.

   Example: P, a pedestrian, is injured by a collision between cars driven by D1 and D2. P shows at trial that automobile accidents do not normally occur without the negligence of someone, but he is unable to show that the accident was more likely due to the negligence of one than the other. P will be unable to obtain application of the doctrine of *res ipsa*, because he has not shown that a particular defendant was, more likely than not, negligent. See P&K, p. 251.

F. Not due to plaintiff: The final requirement for the application of *res ipsa* is that the plaintiff establish that the accident is probably not due to her own conduct.

> **Example:** P is an engineer operating a locomotive of D Railroad. Part of his job is to keep the right amount of water (and therefore the right level of steam) in the boiler. The boiler explodes and kills P. If there is no evidence showing that P was not himself responsible for the explosion (by putting in too much water), *res ipsa* will not apply. But if there is testimony that P acted properly, the doctrine may apply. Rest. 2d, §328D, Illustr. 11.

1. **Contributory negligence:** *Contributory negligence* on the part of the plaintiff will sometimes, but *not always*, constitute a failure to meet this requirement. Thus, in the above example, if it were shown that P was contributorily negligent in his duty to keep the right water level, the doctrine would not be applied. But if the plaintiff's contributory negligence does not lessen the probability that the defendant was also negligent, the requirement may be met.

   > **Example:** P, walking near a construction site, is hit by a falling beam. P proves that beams do not usually fall from construction sites without negligence, and shows that D's employees were at all times in control of all beams. The fact that P may have been contributorily negligent in walking too close to the construction site is irrelevant as far as application of *res ipsa* goes; the doctrine will still apply. (Of course, contributory negligence may bar P from a recovery anyway, but it would not if the jurisdiction is one which applies comparative, as opposed to contributory, negligence — see *infra*, p. 281).

G. Evidence more available to defendant: A number of courts have stated that *res ipsa* will only apply where evidence of what really happened is more available to the defendant than to the plaintiff. This was, for instance, one of the underlying rationales involved in the *Ybarra* case. However, although it is true that application of *res ipsa* helps to "smoke out" the defendant (i.e., forces him to explain or pay), it does not seem to be a real requirement that evidence be more available to defendant than to plaintiff. For instance, in the airplane-crash hypo referred to on p. 126, the reasons for the airplane's crash are no more available to the D airline than to P, yet most courts (and the Restatement) would apply *res ipsa*. See P&K, p. 255.

H. Expert witnesses on negligence issues: Recall that the plaintiff is required to make several showings (*supra*, p. 124) regarding negligence in order to establish a *prima facie* case for getting the benefit of the *res ipsa* doctrine. Thus the plaintiff must show that the accident is one that does not normally happen in the absence of negligence by someone, and must also show that more likely than not the negligence was probably that of the defendant(s). In cases where the facts are complex or involve *specialized knowledge* (e.g., *technology*,) insight into whether the accident would probably have happened without negligence may be *beyond the expertise of the jury*.

1. **Expert testimony usually allowed:** In this scenario, most courts today *allow* the plaintiff to *use expert testimony* to establish that the type of accident in question typically does not occur without negligence, and/or that the defendants were in control of all the most probable causes.

a. **Medical malpractice:** The question arises most often in the case of ***medical malpractice;*** something goes horribly wrong either in surgery or as the result of the patient taking a drug that the defendant manufactures or prescribes. Generally, courts today ***permit*** the plaintiff to show by ***expert medical testimony*** that the requirements for *res ipsa* are satisfied.

Example: P arranges with D1 (an individual doctor), D2 (a medical corporation that employs D1 and other orthopedists) and D3 (a hospital) to have them perform a spinal fusion on P. Shortly after the operation, P is diagnosed with an E. coli infection at the surgical site. She sues all three D's, alleging that they negligently failed to guard against E. coli. She argues that she's entitled to the benefits of *res ipsa*, on the theory that E. coli infections do not normally happen without a negligent failure of infection-prevention, and that the members of the medical team are the ones in control of whether infection-prevention is done adequately. P seeks to offer expert testimony by other doctors that in their opinion these conditions were satisfied here. D says that expert testimony should not be allowed on these points.

Held, for P. The vast majority of courts (and the Second Restatement) endorse the use of expert testimony in medical malpractice cases seeking to invoke *res ipsa*. Using expert testimony helps bridge the gap between "the jury's common knowledge and the complex subject matter that is 'common' only to experts in a designated field." So P may present expert medical opinion that E. coli infections do not normally occur in the absence of negligence, and that the defendants here collectively had a right to control the factors that likely caused the infection. However, the Ds will of course have the right to combat these assertions, including the right to use medical testimony of their own to do so. *Sides v. St. Anthony's Medical Center*, 258 S.W.3d 811 (Mo. 2008).

I. **Effect of *res ipsa*:** The usual effect of the application of *res ipsa* is, as we have seen, to permit an inference that the defendant was negligent, even though there has been no direct, eyewitness evidence that he was. In this respect, *res ipsa* is merely a doctrine that sanctifies the use of a particular kind of ***circumstantial evidence.*** The consequence of the doctrine's application is that the plaintiff has ***met her burden of production***.

Example: P is a guest in a tractor-trailer driven by D. D loses control of the truck, it overturns, and crushes P to death. P sues, and at trial D is unable to explain what caused the accident. Nonetheless, the jury finds for D, and P appeals.

Held, the case was a proper one for *res ipsa loquitur*, since the vehicle was under D's control, and vehicles usually don't suddenly run off the road without negligence. But application of the doctrine merely means that the jury *could* find negligence, not that it was *required* to. Therefore, its verdict in D's favor will not be overturned. *Sullivan v. Crabtree*, 258 S.W.2d 782 (Tenn. 1953).

1. **Diagram:** Putting the problem in terms of the diagram, *supra*, p. 121, P in *Sullivan*, by earning the right to have *res ipsa* apply, moved the case at least into Zone 2 (where it would be sent to the jury). According to the *Sullivan* court, he did not move it to Zone 3, where a directed verdict in his favor would have been required. Occasionally, however, the plaintiff may meet the requirements for the doctrine's application so convincingly that the

court will rule, as a matter of law, that the defendant must have been negligent (i.e., the case will end up in Zone 3).

J. Third Restatement's stripped-down approach: The Third Restatement has a *simplified standard* for *res ipsa*: the Restatement's complete formulation of the doctrine is that "The fact-finder may *infer* that the defendant has been negligent when the accident causing the plaintiff's physical harm is a *type of accident that ordinarily happens as a result of the negligence of a class of actors of which the defendant is the relevant member.*" Rest. 3d (Liab. for Phys. & Emot. Harm) §17.

   1. Requirements eliminated: So the new Restatement eliminates several of the requirements often imposed by courts, including (1) the requirement that there be no direct evidence of how D behaved, (2) the requirement that P show that the injury-causing instrument was in D's exclusive control (see *supra*, p. 126 for more about this), and (3) the requirement that P make an affirmative showing that the injury was not due to her own action. However, the comments to §17 suggest that this new, simpler, phrasing was not intended to alter how the doctrine is applied in most cases.

K. Defendant's rebuttal evidence: Suppose that the plaintiff, in her own case, establishes the elements of *res ipsa* sufficiently that she would, in the absence of any evidence from the defendant, be entitled to go to the jury. (This is the usual effect of application of the doctrine). Now, however, the defendant steps forward with **rebuttal evidence** of his own. What is the effect?

   1. General evidence of due care: If the defendant merely offers evidence to show that he was *in fact careful,* this will almost never be enough to put the case back in Zone 1 (diagram, *supra*, p. 121), entitling the defendant to a directed verdict. The defendant's evidence will therefore usually simply be enough to prevent a directed verdict against him (unless it is so weak that it does not overcome the plaintiff's particularly convincing satisfaction of the three requirements for *res ipsa*), and it will be up to the jury to decide whether the defendant's evidence is enough to negate the inference of negligence stemming from application of *res ipsa*.

   2. Rebuttal of *res ipsa* requirements: But the defendant's evidence may, rather than merely tending to establish the defendant's due care, directly **disprove one of the requirements** for application of *res ipsa*. Thus if the defendant conclusively shows that the accident is not of a sort which normally occurs only as the result of negligence, or shows that all reasonable people must agree that the cause was something other than the defendant's negligence, he will be entitled to a directed verdict. In such a situation, the defendant has really shown that the case is not a *res ipsa* case at all, and the doctrine is out of the case. See Rest. 2d, §328D, Comment o.

L. Typical contexts: Here are a couple of contexts in which the *res ipsa* issue is especially likely to arise:

   1. Airplane accidents: A commercial *airplane* accident in which the plane *crashes into an obstruction* like a mountain, often furnishes a good illustration of *res ipsa*.

      a. *Res ipsa* applies: Today, airplanes don't usually fly into obstructions without someone's negligence, at least in clear weather. And typically, the influence of factors other than the airline won't be pointed to by the evidence. Therefore, the estate of a dead passenger will normally be deemed to have established negligence merely by showing that the plane crashed into an obstruction in good weather.

    i.   **Rebuttal:** But the airline is always free to try to ***rebut*** the evidence, such as by showing that an unforeseeable explosion caused the airplane to veer off course into the obstruction. See the discussion of rebuttal evidence *infra*, p. 131.

2.   **Car accidents:**   Plaintiffs often attempt to apply *res ipsa* to ***car accidents***. The analysis varies sharply with whether there are multiple vehicles involved or just one.

    a.   **Multiple vehicles:** *Res ipsa* usually does ***not*** apply to car crashes involving ***multiple vehicles.*** In most multi-vehicle crashes, it generally cannot be said that that type of accident does not happen without someone's negligence. Furthermore, even if someone's negligence were probable, usually the negligence of persons other than the defendant (e.g., the plaintiff) cannot be sufficiently eliminated by the evidence.

    b.   **Single-car accident:** On the other hand, if the accident is a ***single-vehicle one*** (e.g., between a driver and a pedestrian, or between a driver and some fixed obstruction), then *res ipsa* will often ***apply***, since such accidents usually involve driver negligence. In such a single-vehicle fact pattern, if the defendant (typically the driver) cannot come up with affirmative evidence of his non-negligence, or of some other cause, the plaintiff will not only win, but may be entitled to a directed verdict.

    Example: P, a pedestrian, is struck in broad daylight by a car driven by D, while P is crossing at a crosswalk with the green light in her favor. These are the only facts proven by either side in P's suit against D.

    P will be entitled to a directed verdict. That's because *res ipsa* applies; pedestrians don't normally get hit by motorists while walking in a crosswalk with the light in their favor on a clear day, unless the driver has been negligent. Since *res ipsa* means that P has met her burden of producing some evidence of D's negligence, and since there is no countervailing evidence of D's non-negligence or some other cause, no reasonable jury could find for D. That's enough to entitle P to a directed verdict from the judge. (Even if P might have also been negligent for not spotting D's approaching car, in a comparative negligence jurisdiction P's negligence would not negate D's liability, and would merely reduce P's damages.)

    i.   **Rebuttal evidence:**   But D is always free to come up with evidence ***rebutting*** the *res ipsa* inference of negligence, and in single-vehicle accident cases D will often succeed in doing so. For instance, D may be able to show that he had an unforeseeable ***heart attack*** just before the accident, which is a non-negligent explanation that, if believed, would remove the *res ipsa* inference.

Quiz Yourself on
NEGLIGENCE GENERALLY *(Entire Chapter)*

27. Arthur Fonzarelli is a bored teenager. He rides all over Mayberry on his Harley Davidson just to kill time. Arthur is very concerned about damage to his spotless Harley, so he is always watchful when he rides.

One day, however, he runs over Aunt Bea when he is momentarily blinded by the sun. Aunt Bea sues Arthur for negligence on the grounds that there is no social utility in riding around merely to kill time. Will she win? _____

28. Batman's son, Batboy, is thirteen. One night, while Batman is playing poker with the Commissioner, Batboy sneaks into the Batcave, stuffs a chaw of chewing tobacco in his cheek, jumps into the Batmobile, and takes off like a bat out of hell. Robin is walking his bike across the street at a crosswalk, and Batboy negligently hits him, ruining the bike and injuring Robin. When Robin sues Batboy for negligence, what standard of care will Batboy be held to? _____

29. The Hotten Swettee Nightshirt Company manufactures childrens' nightclothes. The cloth it uses is highly flammable. One youngster, Emma Layshen, wearing a Hotten Swettee nightie, naps a bit too close to her night light and is engulfed in flames. When Hotten Swettee is sued in negligence, Hotten Swettee defends by pointing out (correctly) that the industry custom is to use this same kind of cloth for childrens' nightclothes. Can Emma win? _____

30. The Han-dee Shop-R Grocery Store is open 24 hours a day, seven days a week, in violation of a Sunday closing law. Pierre Lucky is shopping at Han-dee one Sunday, and is injured when he slips on a ketchup slick in Aisle 3, which had been there for hours. Pierre sues Han-dee for negligence on the basis of opening for business in derogation of the Sunday closing law. Will he win? _____

31. The State of Anxiety has a criminal statute requiring that people lock their space saucers when they park them in public places. George Jetson carelessly leaves his keys in the ignition and his space saucer unlocked, when he takes his dog Astro to the park one day. Kibbles Enbitts steals the saucer, and goes for a "joy-fly" in it. Enbitts knocks over Mr. Spacely, who's walking along a sidewalk. Spacely sues Jetson for negligence based on Jetson's violation of the statute. Assuming Spacely can prove the statute was designed to protect pedestrians from being hit by stolen saucers, will Jetson be liable, in most jurisdictions? _____

32. Redd Wightenbleu, soldier, survives six tours of duty in Europe during World War II, and is awarded the Purple Heart for bravery. After the war, he returns, victorious, to the states. During the V-E Day celebrations, he is on a sidewalk in front of the Booby von Trapp Hotel, when an armchair falls on his head from an upper story window. He sues the hotel for negligence. Will *res ipsa* loquitur be applicable? _____

33. In the trucking industry, it is customary to use only a side-view mirror, not a rear-view mirror, on tractor-trailers, since a rear-view mirror is impractical. In recent years, a video camera device has become available, which can be mounted at the rear of the trailer and which transmits the view from the rear of the truck to a monitor next to the driver. Because of the substantial cost ($3,000) of the device, only about 10% of large trucks have been outfitted with the new device. Trucker, an individual who owns his own large rig, has not installed the new camera device and therefore has no ability to see the view from the rear of his truck. One day Trucker sideswipes Driver, who is driving a small car near the rear of Trucker's truck. Even a very careful driver in Trucker's position could not have avoided the accident without the rear camera device. However, if Trucker's truck had had the camera device, a reasonable driver would almost certainly have seen the danger and avoided the accident. Driver sues Trucker for negligence.

  (a) May the availability and growing usage of the camera device be admitted as part of Driver's case, on the question of whether Trucker was negligent? _____

  (b) Assume for this part only that the answer to (a) is "yes." May Trucker introduce evidence that the widely-followed custom in the industry is not to install the cameras, because of their high cost?

_____

   (c) May a jury properly find that Trucker was negligent? _____

34. The federal Food and Drug Act provides that any poisonous substance must be marked with the word "poison" and with a skull and cross-bones at least one-half inch high. Cleaner Co., a manufacturer of various household cleaners, sells DeClog, a very powerful chemical for unclogging drains. Cleaner sells DeClog in a clear plastic bottle which exposes the substance's attractive cherry-red color, similar to the color of Hawaiian Punch. On the bottle, Cleaner includes the required "poison" and skull and cross-bones markings, but takes no other child-proofing precautions. Child, who is two years old, finds a bottle of DeClog underneath the kitchen sink, drinks it, and is horribly wounded. Child sues Cleaner, and Cleaner defends on the grounds that it complied with all applicable warning statutes (a correct assertion). Does Cleaner's statutory compliance bar Child's negligence suit? _____

35. Passenger is aboard an airplane operated by Airline. The airplane disappears over the Mediterranean Sea in clear weather, and no trace is ever found. Passenger's estate sues Airline. The estate does not come forward with any evidence of Airline's negligence. Airline produces testimony that some otherwise unexplained plane crashes turned out to have been caused by plastic bomb devices that even very close security inspection could not have detected. However, Airline does not produce any evidence directly suggesting that this is what happened here. There is no other evidence as to the cause of the accident. Should the judge:

   (a) Direct a verdict for Passenger;

   (b) Direct a verdict for Airline; or

   (c) Send the case to the jury?

_____

Answers

27. No. One of the peculiarities of our negligence system is that it usually focuses on the actor's level of care in *carrying out* an activity, rather than on the social utility of the actor's *decision* to engage in the activity at all. Thus, a defendant who carelessly engages in a socially-useful (and low-risk) activity is likely to be liable for damages; whereas one who carefully engages in a risky activity that is not socially beneficial is not likely to be liable. Even though there was virtually no social utility in Arthur's ride, he rode "carefully," in the sense that he was *attentive*. Therefore, he will not be liable for negligence.

28. The obligation to operate the Batmobile in the way a reasonable <u>adult</u> of ordinary intelligence would have operated it, even though Batboy is only thirteen. Although the duty owed by a child is *generally* measured as that of an ordinary child of like age, intelligence, education and experience, when children undertake adult activities, like driving cars, they are held to an adult standard of care.

29. Yes. Although custom is admissible as evidence of a minimum standard of due care, it is <u>not conclusive</u> because, as here, an entire industry is capable of negligence. The industry standard here is likely motivated by cost considerations and clearly not by safety concerns; as such, the custom cannot control as a minimum standard of care.

30. No, because Han-dee's violating the Sunday closing law was not the cause of Pierre's injuries. In order for a violation of a criminal statute to provide the basis of a civil negligence claim, the breach of the statute must have caused the injury in question. Here, it didn't. Thus, it is irrelevant in determining Han-dee's liability for his injuries.

RELATED ISSUE: If Pierre sued Han-dee for its negligence in not cleaning up the ketchup earlier, he would probably succeed, since the "hours" it had been there suggest that the store was on notice that there was a danger to customers, and Han-dee carelessly ignored it.

31. **Yes, because most jurisdictions view violation of a safety standard embodied in a criminal statute as being conclusive proof of negligence ("negligence per se"),** as long as the statute was formulated for the purpose of preventing the kind of harm in question, and the plaintiff is a member of the class the legislature intended to protect. Since the facts tell you to assume that the statute's purpose is to prevent pedestrian accidents involving stolen saucers, and since Spacely is indeed a pedestrian injured in such an accident, the above requirements are satisfied, and Jetson will be automatically deemed to have been negligent.

There are certain situations in which D's non-compliance with the statute will ordinarily be <u>excused</u> (and negligence per se not applied), but none applies to Jetson here:

1. The violation was reasonable in light of D's childhood, physical disability, or physical incapacitation.

2. D reasonably <u>attempted to comply</u>. (E.g., the doorlock suddenly broke and Jetson couldn't get it to work right away).

3. D neither knew nor should have known of <u>the factual circumstances that rendered the statute applicable.</u> (E.g., after Jetson left the car locked, his friend unlocked it without Jetson's knowing about it).

4. The statute's requirements were <u>presented in a confusing way to the public.</u> (E.g., the statute said that it applied only to "cars," and a reasonable person wouldn't know whether a space saucer was a car.)

5. Compliance with the statute would have been <u>more dangerous</u> than violation.

Rest. 3d (Liab. for Phys. & Emot. Harm) §15.

32. **No.** *Res ipsa loquitur* requires an event that would not normally have occurred in the absence of negligence; the instrumentality must have been in the exclusive control of the defendant; and the plaintiff must not have voluntarily contributed to his injury. The element missing here is the exclusivity of control. Since guests have at least some control over the furniture in hotel rooms, *res ipsa loquitur* doesn't apply here.

NOTE: The hotel *could* be liable in negligence for failing to take reasonable steps to adequately protect passersby; it's just that *res ipsa loquitur* isn't the means by which the negligence claim would be proven.

RELATED ISSUE: The hotel could not be strictly liable for Redd's injuries, even if the actual tortfeasor couldn't be identified.

33. **(a) Yes.** The question is always what a reasonable person in Trucker's position would have done. Evidence that a new safety device was available would certainly be admissible as evidence on whether Trucker was behaving reasonably in choosing not to install the device.

(b) Yes. Conversely, the "custom" in an industry is always admissible as tending to show that a person who followed that custom was acting reasonably.

(c) Yes. Neither the availability of a new safety device not used by the defendant, nor the fact that the defendant was following industry customs, will be dispositive on the issue of negligence. On these facts, a reasonable jury could go either way — by finding that it was not reasonable for Trucker to decline to use an available safety device, or by finding that the lack of widespread adoption of the device meant that a reasonable trucker could decline to use it.

34. **No, probably.** A state or federal safety statute will generally be construed to establish merely a minimum standard. If in the particular circumstances a reasonable person would adopt additional precautions, then failure to so adopt can be negligence. (Occasionally, a federal enactment will be found to have been intended to "pre-empt" state law as to what constitutes reasonable safety or warnings — as is the case with cigarette labeling — but a general statute saying that all poisons must be marked as such would probably not be held to have been intended as pre-emptive.) Since a jury could properly find that a reasonably careful manufacturer of an exceptionally dangerous poison would adopt additional safeguards (e.g., a child-proof cap), Child's case will be permitted to go to the jury.

35. **(c).** The situation is an appropriate one for application of *res ipsa loquitur*: a plane does not normally crash in clear weather except through the negligence of someone, the airplane was in the exclusive control of Airline at the time it crashed, and Passenger himself was almost certainly not at fault. However, in most courts, even if *res ipsa* applies, it does not ***require*** an inference of negligence. Rather, the doctrine merely ***permits*** an inference of negligence; that is, the doctrine allows the plaintiff to be deemed to have met his burden of production, thus entitling him to get to the jury. Therefore, the judge should send the case to the jury and let the jury decide whether it is more probable than not that the crash was caused by Airline's negligence. See Rest. 2d, §328D, Illustr. 3.

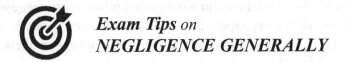

Exam Tips on
NEGLIGENCE GENERALLY

In any fact pattern, you must of course be on the lookout for the distinct tort of "negligence." But the tips in this chapter relate mainly to one sub-issue within the tort of negligence, namely, how to determine whether D "was negligent," i.e., failed to behave with reasonable care.

☞ On any set of facts, check whether each participant may have behaved "negligently," i.e., carelessly. Once you find this, check for **all** of the elements of the tort of negligence:

❏ a *duty* of reasonable care to the plaintiff, i.e., that there was ***foreseeable danger*** if care was not used (covered in the next chapter);

❏ failure by D to *exercise* that *reasonable care*;

❏ *harm* (usually required to be physical harm or at least danger of physical harm) to P; and

❏ *causation*, i.e., that the failure of care actually and proximately caused the harm.

(This chapter only deals with second of the above requirements, that D failed to exercise reasonable care.)

☞ Your main job is to spot situations where D *may* have behaved negligently, and to articulate both sides of this issue. There's rarely a "right" or "clear" answer to the question,

"Was D negligent?" — that's why the existence of due care is almost always a question left for the jury.

☞ Be especially careful to check for negligence when the facts involve a **vehicle accident** — there are few car or truck accidents on exams where there *isn't* a negligence issue.

    ☞ Don't presume that D's conduct is definitely negligence, even though it seems to be. (*Example:* Even if the facts tell you that D took his eyes briefly off the road while driving, consider the possibility that there was a good cause for this, or at least that this was within the range of things that a reasonable driver might do on, say, a long trip.)

☞ One type of negligence often tested is the **failure to warn** another person about a danger. Here the negligence is a form of "omission," so you can miss the issue if you're not looking carefully for it. (*Example:* D has car trouble, and parks his car at the side of the road without placing warning flares around it.)

☞ The issue of **"custom"** comes up often. The fact that a particular precaution is or isn't "customary" in the industry is **evidence** of what would be reasonable care, but it's **not dispositive** either way. (That is, failure to follow a custom that is usually observed for safety reasons, such as the giving of a particular type of warning, doesn't necessarily mean that D's conduct is negligent; conversely, the giving of, say, a customary warning doesn't necessarily mean that D's conduct wasn't negligent.)

☞ Sometimes, the negligence is **"antecedent,"** not carelessness right before the accident. That is, D's negligence lies in having put himself in a dangerous position by **engaging in the activity in the first place**, not in carrying out the activity carelessly. (*Example:* D takes a prescription drug, then drives and gets into an accident while having an allergic reaction; even if D was as "careful" as his condition let him be at the precise moment of the accident, he may have been negligent in getting in the car at all after taking a new drug with a tendency to cause allergic reactions.)

☞ The standard of care for **children** is often tested. This happens both where the child is the defendant and where the child is a plaintiff who might be barred by contributory negligence (or have his recovery reduced by comparative negligence). Remember that in most instances, the test is, "What is the level of care of a **reasonable child** of the **age and experience** of this child?"

    ☞ But remember that a child engaging in an **adult activity** (e.g., water skiing) is evaluated by an adult standard.

    ☞ Related issue: It can be negligence for an adult to **entrust a task** to a child when a child wouldn't normally have the skills. (*Example:* It may be negligence to leave a 12-year-old to watch a one-year-old.)

    ☞ Also, remember that a parent has a duty to exercise reasonable care to **supervise the conduct of her minor child**, to prevent the child from intentionally harming others or posing an unreasonable risk of harm to them. (If the parent doesn't fulfill this duty, she's "directly liable" for her own negligence, not "vicariously liable" — a parent isn't vicariously liable for the torts of her minor child, even ones committed in the parent's presence.)

☞ One of the most-tested negligence issues: D negligently fails to **anticipate the negligence** (or other wrongdoing) of **another person**. *Examples:*

   ☞ D is a car rental agency that fails to verify that X has a license; X then has an accident, hurting P. D is probably negligent.

   ☞ D somehow helps X drive while drunk. Thus D may be a bartender or social host who serves X after X is already drunk, or a passerby who helps X start X's car when X is obviously drunk. D is probably negligent.

   ☞ D imposes some sort of hazard which isn't dangerous to others who are paying attention, but is dangerous to a person who isn't paying attention. (*Example:* D parks his car at the shoulder of a highway, posing a danger only to one such as X who is speeding.) Here, D is probably negligent in not anticipating the negligence of others.

☞ **"Negligence per se"** is one of the very most often-tested issues in all of torts. This is because it's easy for professors to construct fact patterns testing the doctrine, it's easy for students to miss the issue completely (e.g., the statute is buried in a complex fact pattern), and once the student spots the issue, there are still many sub-issues.

   ☞ Whenever you spot a statute in your fact pattern, and the professor gives you the precise language (or even a pretty precise summary) of the statute, that's a tip-off that you should be looking for a negligence per se issue. (In fact, if the statute relates to some safety issue, negligence per se is practically the *only* issue to which the statute is likely to be relevant.)

   ☞ Here's a good statement of the negligence per se doctrine, to begin your answer with: "D is negligent if, **without excuse**, D **violates a statute that is designed to protect against the type of accident D's conduct causes**, and the accident **victim** is **within the class of persons the statute is designed to protect.**" Rest. 3d, §14.

   ☞ The single most commonly-tested sub-issue: Was the **type of harm** that occurred the type of harm the statute was **designed to prevent**? Usually, the answer is **"no,"** but you will often have to speculate about what types of harm the legislature might have had in mind.

   ☞ This issue is especially likely to occur where the statute is essentially **bureaucratic**, such as a **licensing** requirement. *Examples of the "type of harm" problem:*

      ❏ A statute says, "No pilot may take on a passenger for pay unless the pilot has a commercial pilot's license." An accident then happens in flight while P is flying as D's paying passenger, and D has only a regular pilot's license. (Probably you should conclude that the licensing requirement was not enacted for the purpose of avoiding in-flight accidents, in which case the violation would not establish negligence.)

      ❏ A statute says, "No one may leave a parked car with the keys in the ignition." D violates that statute; the car is stolen, and the thief crashes into P. You have to examine why the legislature passed this statute — was it to prevent accidents from thief-driven cars (in which case the per se doctrine applies), or was it to prevent some other harm (e.g., a child's driving the car), in which case the doctrine does not apply.

☞ A related issue: the violation must *"cause"* the accident. (This issue really belongs in the next chapter on causation, but we'll consider it here.) The violation of a regulatory statute — especially a licensing statute — usually is not deemed to be the "proximate cause" of the accident, so the violation gets disregarded.

> *Example:* A statute says, "No one may drive a truck without a $500,000 minimum truck liability insurance policy." An accident occurs to D, an uninsured truck driver. Since the accident would still have happened even with insurance, the causal link between statute violation and accident will probably be found missing. (The same rule usually applies where the violation is not having a required license to engage in the activity.)

☞ Also tested: Was P a *member of the class* that the legislature intended to protect by means of the statute? Don't be too narrow in interpreting the "protected class." In any event, you'll usually not be able to say for sure, and you just want to spot this issue and argue the pros and cons.

> *Example:* The statute says, "No one may leave a vehicle parked and unattended on a part of a street marked 'school zone.'" P is an adult who crashes into D's unattended car parked in such a zone. You can't know what the legislature intended. Therefore, say that if the legislature intended only to protect school children, P will not get the benefit of the negligence per se doctrine. But discuss the possibility that although the statute is tied into a school zone, it may have been intended to protect *any member* of the public (e.g., a child's parent, a visitor to the school, etc.) who is using the street in front of the school, in which case the doctrine would apply.

☞ If the provision is an *ordinance* or an *administrative regulation* instead of a statute, you should note that not all courts apply the negligence per se doctrine here. (But also note that those courts that don't accept the doctrine would probably accept the violation as at least strong evidence of negligence.)

☞ Fact patterns often raise the issue of *"excuse"* of the violation. D is likely to be "excused" from his non-compliance if either: (1) he couldn't avoid the violation even though he was "careful"; or (2) he chose to violate the statute as the lesser of two evils. (*Example:* A statute says, "All drivers must keep their brakes in working order at all times." D's brakes fail suddenly, and he crashes into the car ahead of him. If D shows that he had no advance notice that his brakes were failing, he'll probably be deemed to be excused, and the negligence per se doctrine won't apply.)

☛ Sometimes D's *compliance* with a statute poses the converse issue: Does the fact that D complied with a fairly precise statutory safety rule automatically mean that D *wasn't* negligent? Usually, the answer is "no" — compliance is at most non-dispositive evidence of D's non-negligence.

☛ Look for a *"res ipsa loquitur"* (RIL) issue whenever there's no direct evidence as to whether D was negligent.

☞ Requirements for the RIL doctrine in most courts: (1) there must be ***no direct evidence*** as to D's precise conduct; (2) the event must be one that ***normally doesn't occur without negligence by somebody***; and (3) D must be the ***most likely person*** whose negligence would have caused the event (sometimes clumsily expressed by saying that the event must have been "within D's exclusive control").

  ☞ Most of the time, the existence of a RIL issue is easy to spot. The tougher part is determining whether all conditions for the doctrine are satisfied.

☞ Some contexts where RIL frequently arises on exams (and can be successfully asserted by the plaintiff):

  ❏ The product is grossly defective, and suit is brought in negligence rather than in strict product liability. (*Examples:* Food with a foreign object in it; exploding containers.) In this "product" situation, RIL is most useful where there is no direct evidence that the manufacturer screwed up, i.e., no information about what happened during the manufacture of that particular item.

  ❏ An airplane crashes into the ground, and there are no clues as to what caused the accident.

  ❏ A driver hits a pedestrian from the rear, while the pedestrian is walking along the side of the road; the pedestrian dies or doesn't know how the accident happened. (But RIL usually ***doesn't*** apply to ***multiple-vehicle*** accidents, since you can't say that such accidents usually don't occur without the negligence of the particular driver who's the defendant.)

  ❏ P gets surgery, and something unexpected results (e.g., a surgical tool is left inside P's body, or the wrong part of P's anatomy is removed).

☞ The requirement that D be the person most likely to have been negligent is often tested. It's up to you to spot this issue and discuss it, because the facts won't usually tip you off. (*Example:* P undergoes surgery by D, and a later x-ray shows a surgical tool left in his body. It's up to you to say, "But P will have to show that D was probably the only one who operated on P, or at least that he's more likely than anyone else to have left the tool in P's body.")

  ☞ Because of the "D is the most likely negligent person" requirement, RIL is not usually successfully used against the manufacturer of an airplane or other machine that has to be operated by a third person — since the manufacturer is not in control of the machine at the time of the accident, the doctrine doesn't fit unless negligence can be directly traced to the time of manufacture. (RIL works better against the operator than against the manufacturer, in this operated-machine situation.)

☞ The requirement that the accident be of a sort that ***usually doesn't occur without negligence*** is also sometimes tested. Again, the issue is usually hidden — it's up to you to notice that you've been given no information about whether an accident of this type "usually doesn't occur without negligence." (*Example:* P is killed when a plane piloted by D crashes into a mountain. It's up to you to notice and discuss that you don't know whether this accident is of a type that usually doesn't happen without negligence. You might, for instance, speculate that such accidents may often be due to an undetectablyfaulty altimeter or some reason other than negligence.)

☞ But remember that P doesn't have to show that this type of accident *never* occurs without negligence, only that it *usually* involves negligence. (That's what allows use of the doctrine in airplane-crash-into-ground suits against airlines.)

☞ Also, keep in mind that in technical cases (e.g., *medical malpractice*), P is generally allowed to use *expert witnesses* to show that the accident is one that usually doesn't happen without negligence, and/or that the defendants were the ones in control of whether this type of event occurred.

☞ The doctrine is only used as *indirect evidence* of negligence. Therefore, it's not used when there is *direct evidence* of what caused the episode, or of exactly how D behaved during the event.

☞ Thus if the facts tell you that D "used all possible care" or some such, then RIL is not used.

☞ Similarly, if the facts tell you that the cause of the particular accident was something other than D's negligence, the fact that the accident falls into a "class" in which RIL usually is used is irrelevant. (*Example:* If an airplane crashes, but the facts suggest that a defective altimeter was probably the cause, RIL will not be used in a suit against the pilot.)

☞ If the facts describe D's conduct in detail, and the sole issue is, "Was that conduct reasonably careful?" don't use RIL — it's only used when we don't know the specifics of what D did.

☞ Since the purpose of the doctrine is to produce circumstantial evidence of negligence, it's not used in cases based on a non-negligence theory, such as those based on strict product liability.

Example: The suit involves a product with a foreign object in it. If the suit is brought in strict product liability, we don't use RIL because we only need to know, "Was there a 'dangerous defect?'" not "Did the manufacturer use due care?"

Note: On the other hand, we'll see in the Products Liability chapter that in strict liability cases, courts often give P the benefit of a "res-ipsa-like" inference on the issue of whether the product was defective. Thus here, in the product-with-a-foreign-object-in-it suit, P would get the benefit of an inference that a product with a foreign object in it is usually "defective."

☞ You may want to point out that, in most states, the function of the RIL doctrine where applicable is to treat P as having produced *enough evidence of negligence to get to the jury.* That is, if the RIL is not rebutted, D won't succeed with a motion for a directed verdict alleging that P hasn't proved that D was negligent. (But remember that D is generally allowed to come up with *rebuttal* evidence that he was in fact careful, or that the accident was in fact caused by someone or something else.)

CHAPTER 6

ACTUAL AND PROXIMATE CAUSE

ChapterScope

Once the plaintiff has shown that the defendant behaved negligently, he must then show that this behavior "caused" the injury complained of. Actually, P must make two quite distinct showings of causation:

▪ **Cause in fact:** P must first show that D's conduct was the *"cause in fact"* of the injury. This usually means that P must show that *"but for"* D's negligent act, the injury would not have occurred.

▪ **Proximate cause:** P must also show that the injury is sufficiently *closely related* to D's conduct that liability should attach. This requirement is commonly called the requirement of *"proximate cause"* or "legal cause."

❑ **Foreseeability:** The requirement of "proximate cause" usually means that the injury must have been at least a reasonably *foreseeable* (and not bizarre or extraordinary) result of the defendant's negligence.

I. CAUSATION IN FACT

A. General significance: When the plaintiff alleges that the defendant "caused" his injuries, it is pretty clear what he means — that the injuries were the actual, *factual,* result of the defendant's actions. In most cases, the question of "causation in fact" is a purely factual one, with few legal or policy issues attached to it.

   1. "But for" test: In the vast majority of situations, the defendant's conduct is the (or a) cause of the plaintiff's injuries if it can be said that "Had the defendant not so conducted herself, the plaintiff's injuries would not have resulted." This formulation is sometimes known as the *"sine qua non"* or *"but for"* test.

      a. Third Restatement's formulation: The Third Restatement implements the idea of a "but for" cause. After saying that liability will exist only where the defendant's tortious conduct was a "factual cause" of the plaintiff's injury, the Restatement goes on to express the idea that *a "but for" cause is always a factual cause*: "Conduct is a factual cause of harm when the harm would not have occurred absent the conduct." Rest. 3d (Liab. for Phys. & Emot. Harm) §26.

      Example: P takes her prescription for a medication to D, her local pharmacy. D mistakenly fills the prescription by giving P pills containing 30 mg of the active ingredient rather than the 20 mg called for by the prescription. After taking the pills, P suffers serious heart arrhythmia, and sues D for this harm. P can recover only if she proves that had D provided the correct, 20 mg, pills, P would not have suffered the arrhythmia. In other words, for P to recover, the trier of fact must be satisfied that the wrong pills were the "but for" cause of P's arrhythmia. *Id.*, Illustr. 2.

2. **Broad test:** Observe that the "but for" test casts an extremely broad net. Every injury occurring to a plaintiff has thousands of causes, by this standard, since if any of a thousand things happened differently, there would have been no accident. For instance, in a night-time automobile accident, the fact that one of the drivers worked late at the office that night would be a cause, since had he not, he would not have been at that location in time to be hit by the other car. See P&K, p. 264, fn. 6.

   a. **Multiple negligence:** It follows that a defendant may not claim that she is not an actual cause of the plaintiff's injury merely because *some other person's negligence* also contributed to that harm. This matter is more fully discussed in the material on joint tortfeasors, *infra*, p. 183; the general principle is that each of several joint tortfeasors will be held liable for the entire harm.

      Example: P is a passenger in a car driven by D1. On a stormy night, the car crashes into an unlit truck which has been parked in the middle of the road by D2. There is evidence that D1 was negligent in not seeing the truck, and that D2 was negligent in leaving it parked where and how he did.

      Held, D2 should not be dismissed from the case merely because the accident would not have happened without D1's negligence. "Where separate acts of negligence combine to produce directly a single injury each tortfeasor is responsible for the entire result, even though his act alone might not have caused it." *Hill v. Edmonds*, 270 N.Y.S.2d 1020 (N.Y. App. 1966).

B. **Concurrent causes:** Inclusive as the "but for" test is, it nonetheless rules out one kind of cause which the courts have generally held does constitute a true cause in fact. This is the situation where two events *concur* to cause harm, and *either one would have been sufficient* to cause substantially the same harm without the other. To provide for this case, it is generally stated that *each* of these concurring events is a cause of the injury, insofar as it would have been sufficient to bring that injury about. See Rest. 2d, §432(2).

   Example: Sparks from one of D's locomotives start a forest fire. The fire merges with another fire of unknown origin, and the combined fires burn P's property. The evidence indicates that the fire started by D's locomotives would by itself have been sufficient to burn P's property.

   Held, D is liable for the entire damage to P's property, even though the property would have burned anyway had D not started the fire that it did. Because the fire started by D played a substantial role in the destruction of P's property, it would not be equitable to allow D to escape liability, since the entire loss would then be placed on the innocent P. *Kingston v. Chicago & N.W. Ry.*, 211 N.W. 913 (Wis. 1927), *infra*, p. 187.

1. **"Substantial factor" standard:** Where each of the two events would have been sufficient by itself to bring about the harm, the test for each event is often said to be whether it was a *"substantial factor"* in bringing about the harm. If so, that harm is a cause in fact. Thus in the above example, the spark from D's locomotive was undoubtedly a "substantial factor"

in starting the fire, so it's a cause in fact of the damage to P's property, and we disregard the fact that the spark wasn't a "but for" cause of the damage.

   a.   Third Restatement uses "sufficient causal set" formulation: The new Third Restatement does not use the phrase "substantial factor." But even so, it still applies the traditional rule under which if there are two concurrent causes, each sufficient to produce the injury, each is deemed to be a factual cause. The Restatement does this by saying that "If *multiple acts* exist, *each of which alone* would have been a factual cause ... of the physical harm at the same time, *each act is regarded as a factual cause* of the harm." Rest. 3d (Liab. for Phys. & Emot. Harm) §27.

2.   Caveat: The rule of double liability for concurrent causes, stated above, applies only where *each* of the concurrent causes would be sufficient, by itself, to bring about substantially the same harm as occurred. If the defendant's conduct would not have been sufficient, by itself, to do so, but the other concurrent event *would* have been sufficient, the defendant will not be liable.

3.   Distinguished from apportionable harms: Also, the rule applies only where the concurrent causes produce a single, *indivisible*, harm. If the damage caused by one concurrent cause may be separated, analytically, from that caused by the other, the person causing the former will be liable only for that harm. See the discussion of apportioning harm among joint tortfeasors, *infra*, pp. 185-188.

C.   Proof of actual cause generally: The plaintiff bears the burden of proving that the defendant's conduct was the cause in fact of his injury, just as he must bear the burden of proving the other parts of his *prima facie* case. However, he must demonstrate this actual causation merely by a *preponderance of the evidence.*

1.   Proof of "cause in fact" aspect: Thus the plaintiff does not have to prove with absolute certainty that had it not been for the defendant's conduct, the injury would not have occurred. All he has to do is to show that it is *probable* (*more likely than not*) that the injury would not have occurred without the defendant's act.

   Example: P, a 40-year-old man, has lived his entire life in a house whose insulation was manufactured and installed by D Corp. in 1970. P develops mesothelioma, a rare lung condition. In 2023, P brings a "strict product liability" suit (*infra*, 358) against D. In such an action, P does not have to show that D was negligent but merely that the insulation D manufactured and installed in D's house was "defectively dangerous," and that this installation was the "actual cause" of P's disease. At trial, P offers unrebutted evidence that he has at no time been exposed to asbestos outside of his house, and that there is no asbestos in the house except for the insulation produced by D. He also produces unrebutted medical evidence that 55% of cases of mesothelioma are caused by asbestos. D moves for a directed verdict, on the grounds that there is a 45% chance that P's disease was due to some source other than the asbestos installed by D in P's house; therefore, D contends, P has not "proved" that D's product was the actual (or "but for") cause of P's disease.

   The court will *deny* D's motion. It's true that as part of P's *prima facie* case (*supra*, p. 96), P must "prove" the element of causation in fact, which in this case means proof that D's defectively dangerous asbestos was the but for cause of P's disease. However, in a tort action P merely has to prove all the elements of his *prima facie* case by a ***"preponderance of the evidence."*** Therefore, with respect to the element of causation in fact, P merely needs to show that it is ***more likely than not*** that he would not have gotten mesothelioma except for D's installation of dangerously defective asbestos in P's house. Since P's medical evidence establishes that more than half of all mesothelioma cases are caused by asbestos (and P has also shown that the only asbestos to which he has ever been exposed came from D's plant), the court will allow the case to go to the jury because the jury could properly find that it is more likely than not that D's asbestos was the but for cause of P's disease.

    a. Inference by jury: In fact, most courts do not actually require P to "prove," in any exact sense, even that it is more likely than not that D's conduct act caused the particular damage at issue. Instead, the jury is permitted to make ***common-sense inferences*** that D's conduct caused the damage, as long as such an inference is not unreasonable. Thus in the above example, unless the court would conclude that ***no reasonable jury*** could believe that it was more probable than not that D's dangerously defective insulation was a "but for" cause of P's mesothelioma, P would be permitted to get to the jury.

        i. Dosages in medical malpractice cases: An illustration of this principle arises in ***medical malpractice*** cases where the claim is that the defendant administered an ***unsafely-large dose*** of an otherwise-safe drug. The plaintiff must theoretically prove that the "extra" dose made the difference (i.e., that the recommended dose would not have produced the damage). But the court will be quick to let the jury decide that because dosages are set at particular levels for good scientific reasons, a dose significantly in excess of the recommended level is likely to have caused the damage.

           Example: A doctor working for D (the U.S.) negligently prescribes twice the maximum recommended daily dose of the drug Danocrine for P. P takes the too-high dosage every day for the next month. During that month, she develops various symptoms of illness, and is soon thereafter diagnosed with a rare and fatal disease, primary pulmonary hypertension ("PPH"). After P eventually dies from PPH, her estate sues D. At trial, P's expert medical witness provides good evidence that P's exposure to the Danocrine caused her PPH. But the expert's evidence is much less convincing as to whether the overdose, as opposed to a properly-sized dose, caused the disease.

           Held, for P. "[W]hen a negative side effect is demonstrated to be the result of a drug, and the drug was wrongly prescribed in an unapproved and excessive dosage (i.e. a strong causal link has been shown), the plaintiff who is injured has generally shown enough to permit the finder of fact to conclude that the excessive dosage was a substantial factor in producing the harm." Therefore, P's estate has adequately proved that the excessive dosage was the cause in fact of her death. *Zuchowicz v. U.S.*, 140 F.3d 381 (2d Cir. 1998).

2. D found liable for more than the damage it caused: The rule that the plaintiff must merely prove that the defendant "more probably than not" caused the plaintiff's injury will often lead to the defendant's being found liable, ***across multiple cases,*** for damages

beyond those it caused. That result comes from the fact that over multiple suits, the defendant will be required to pay ***full damages in each,*** even though all the jury has decided in each case is that there was a greater than 50/50 likelihood that the defendant caused the harm.

> **Example:** Consider the mesothelioma example on p. 143. Suppose that D is required to defend 100 similar claims (brought by 100 separate plaintiffs) in front of the same judge sitting without a jury. And assume that in each of these, D is proven to have had had a 55% chance of being the cause of that particular plaintiff's disease. D will be required to pay for the ***full amount of the harm in each*** of those 100 cases, even though we know that D is not likely to be responsible for more than about 55 of the cases.

> This result is simply a consequence of the traditional rule, just discussed, that a defendant who is found to have caused a plaintiff's injury "more probably than not" must pay for the ***entire*** injury, not just for value of the injury times the percentage chance that D caused that injury. D is thus ***"over deterred"*** — forced to pay more than the aggregate value of the injuries it caused. See E&S (12th Ed), p. 404.

3. **Expert testimony:** Sometimes ***expert testimony*** may be necessary to prove actual causation by the defendant. This is frequently true in ***medical malpractice*** cases, where the jury has no knowledge of its own which would permit it to conclude that the defendant's treatment caused the plaintiff's injury.

> **Example:** P, a guest in D's hotel, cuts his forehead on a piece of glass which falls from a broken transom. The injury does not heal, and two years later, a physician tells P that a skin cancer has developed at the point of injury. Two medical experts testify at the trial; one states that there is a remote possibility that a skin cancer could develop from such a wound, and the second declares there is "no causal connection" between P's injury and the cancer.

> *Held*, for D on the issue of liability for the cancer. A mere possibility that the cancer to P was the result of the injury does not provide the requisite causal connection. The jury should not have been permitted to find D liable for the cancer, since the causes of cancer are outside the experience of laymen, and the only relevant medical evidence, that of the two experts, indicated that it was highly unlikely that the injury caused the cancer. *Kramer Service, Inc. v. Wilkins*, 186 So. 625 (Miss. 1939).

4. **Scientific evidence:** Similarly, ***scientific evidence*** often plays a big role in proving causation, especially in ***product liability*** cases. Thus plaintiffs will frequently attempt to prove by ***epidemiological*** evidence that a product manufactured by the defendant is more likely than not to have been the "but for" cause of the plaintiff's injuries. This leads to the question, *How "reputable" or "well established" must scientific theories of causation be before the jury is permitted to hear them?*

   a. **Differing possible approaches:** Courts follow different approaches to this question.

      i. **"Generally accepted" standard:** Some states hold that only ***"generally accepted"*** scientific theories may be presented to the jury. This is the so called *Frye* standard, from *Frye v. U.S.*, 293 F. 1013 (D.C.App. 1923). Under this theory, a scientific theory or piece of evidence that was accepted by only a minority of specialists would not be admissible at all.

ii. **"Relevance" standard:** At the other end of the spectrum, some states allow virtually any scientific theory or evidence to be placed before the jury, so long as it is relevant, and so long as the expert presenting it has reasonable scientific credentials; even a theory or approach rejected by the vast majority of scientists working in a particular area could be presented, if done so by an expert who was one of the few who believed the theory. Under this approach, it is up to the jury how much or little weight to give the evidence.

iii. **Middle approach for federal cases:** The Supreme Court has adopted a *middle* approach for scientific evidence presented in *federal* cases. Under this middle approach, the evidence does not need to be "generally accepted." But it does need to be *"scientific knowledge,"* which means that it must have been *"derived by the scientific method."* Usually, this will mean that the proposition has been, or is at least capable of being, *"tested."* The fact that the theory or technique has or has not been subjected to *peer review* and *publication* is one factor in determining whether it is "scientific knowledge," but this is not a *dispositive* factor. So even a distinctly minority theory or approach that has not yet been published could be admitted under this new federal standard (at least if advanced by scientists with reasonable credentials), but a theory or approach that had been published and rejected by the vast majority of working scientists might well be excluded. *Daubert v. Merrell Dow Pharmaceuticals, Inc.*, 113 S.Ct. 2786 (1993), also discussed *infra*, p. 371.

Example: P sues D, a drug company, after P's children are born with serious birth defects. P claims the birth defects were caused by Bendectin, an anti-nausea drug manufactured and marketed by D for pregnant mothers. To demonstrate causation, P proposes to rely on eight experts, who will testify that a re-analysis of previously published epidemiological studies, plus their own unpublished experiments, suggests that Bendectin can cause birth defects. D, correctly claiming that none of the many published studies on Bendectin ever concluded that the drug could cause birth defects, moves to have the case thrown out on summary judgment.

Held, for P. For federal cases, the test for admissibility of scientific evidence is not whether the testimony is "generally accepted," but merely whether the testimony is "scientific knowledge." The degree to which the testimony or theory has been accepted in the scientific community is relevant, but is not dispositive — new theories that have not yet been generally accepted may nonetheless be "scientific knowledge," in the sense that they have been tested according to the procedures of science. Similarly, the fact that a theory has not yet been published or peer-reviewed is relevant but not dispositive. "Ordinarily, the key question to be answered in determining whether a theory or technique is scientific knowledge . . . will be **whether it can be (and has been) tested**." *Daubert v. Merrell Dow Pharmaceuticals, Inc., supra.*

D. Actual cause – the "value of a chance" problem: On p. 143 *supra*, we discussed the general rule that if D "more likely than not" was the cause in fact of P's injury, D will have to pay for the entire injury, not just a number representing the total value of the injury times a fraction representing the percentage chance that D caused it. Now, let's consider the **converse** situation, in which P definitely suffered an injury but there is a **less than 50/50 chance** that D caused that injury. In this scenario, application of the traditional "more likely than not" requirement for recovery would mean that P would **recover $0.** Do modern courts strictly apply this often-harsh requirement?

The answer is generally **"yes,"** except for one special case (medical malpractice), which we discuss in Par. 2 below.

1. **The traditional rule:** Thus outside of the special medical-malpractice scenario, if the plaintiff proves that there is a substantial but less than 50/50 chance that the defendant negligently caused the (undisputed) injury, the plaintiff is **completely out of luck — she recovers $0.**

> **Example:** Same basic facts as the Example on p. 143 *supra*. Now, however, assume that in the course of suit, the judge concludes that there is about a 45% chance that D was the cause-in-fact of the undisputed case of mesothelioma suffered by that plaintiff. Virtually all courts agree that the 100 Ps **each recover nothing** — even though (statistically speaking) D caused 45 cases of mesothelioma to the group of Ps, D gets away scot free. In the opposite of the Example on p. 143, D here has been **"under-deterred."** Apart from the arguable unfairness to the Ps, this rule means that D is **not incentivized to spend anything** to avoid causing further injuries of this type in the future.

2. **The medical malpractice scenario:** But there is one **exception** to the general rule that where P proves a real but less than 50/50 chance that D caused her harm P recovers nothing. The exception arises in the area of **medical malpractice**. Recall that a patient who proves that the treatment she received from her doctor failed to conform to the reasonable standard of care owed by physicians may recover for medical malpractice, a special type of negligence action. Now, suppose that the nature of the malpractice is that the physician failed to provide a **timely diagnosis or treatment of the patient's disease,** and that this delay causes the patient to **die or suffer a worse medical outcome.** Suppose further that had the treatment or diagnosis been done promptly and without negligence, there is a real, **but less than 50/50,** chance that either the bad outcome would have been delayed, or the patient would have been cured or able to live longer.

   a. **Traditional approach denies recovery:** Notice that if the traditional approach is applied, P would be deemed to have failed to prove by the required "preponderance of the evidence" standard (i.e., more likely than not) that D was the cause in fact of her harm, so she recovers nothing. And indeed, a **substantial minority** of states still apply this traditional approach to the medical-malpractice scenario, depriving patient P of any recovery even if the evidence proves that there was, say, a 40% chance that had the malpractice not occurred, P would have had a more favorable outcome. D, H&B Torts, § 196.

   b. **The "value of a chance" doctrine:** But a **majority** of the states that have considered the problem in the last couple of decades have **declined to follow the traditional rule** denying all recovery, and instead allow plaintiff P who shows a less-than 50/50 chance that prompt-and-appropriate treatment would have avoided the bad outcome to recover for a ***special type of injury,*** namely an injury characterized as being ***"the loss of the opportunity for a better outcome,*** rather than … the death or worse outcome." P,W&S (14th), p. 308. This approach is commonly called the ***"loss of a chance" approach***. *Id.* at 309. Thus in these majority states, P is permitted to recover an amount equal to:

> the ***value the claim would have had*** if the injury was proved more likely than not to have been caused by the malpractice *times*
>
> the ***percentage chance that a favorable result would have occurred*** had there been no malpractice.

See Rest. 3d (Liab. For Phys & Emot. Harm), § 26, Comment n, p. 356.

Example: When P begins having some initial symptoms of a stroke, he seeks treatment at D, a physicians' group. D negligently fails to give P timely and adequate stroke-prevention care.[1] P suffers a catastrophic stroke that results in permanent brain damage. Medical evidence demonstrates that in one-third of the cases where the patient has initial stroke symptoms like P's, proper and prompt treatment enables the patient to suffer no or reduced stroke complications thereafter. P sues D in Oregon state court to recover for value of this "loss of a chance at recovery." That is, he seeks an award equal to:

> the "dollar value" of the difference between P's brain post-stroke and a stroke-free brain, *times*
>
> the one-third chance that timely and non-negligent treatment would have saved P from that injury.

D counters that because P cannot prove that it's "more likely than not" that prompt treatment would have prevented the brain damage, P is not entitled to any recovery at all.

Held, for P. "[A] limited loss-of-chance theory of recovery should be recognized in common-law negligence cases involving medical malpractice in Oregon." Under this theory, "a plaintiff who demonstrates that a physician's negligence reduced his chance of a favorable medical outcome from 33% to 0% [can] recover damages based on the unfavorable medical consequences suffered, but only to the possible extent of 33% of the damages resulting from the adverse medical outcome." (The court does not address the issue of whether the plaintiff in a loss-of-chance suit has to prove that he lost a *"substantial* chance" of a better medical outcome, because the 33% chance claimed to have been lost here is certainly "substantial.") *Smith v. Providence Health & Services,* 393 P.3d 1106 (Ore. Sup. Ct. 2017).

i.   **What injury must be proved:** Those cases, like *Smith,* that recognize the loss-of-chance theory relieve P of the burden of showing that more likely than not, D's negligent treatment was the cause-in-fact (as well as proximate cause) of the bad medical outcome. But the theory ***does not eliminate*** the requirement that P ***prove***

---

1. These facts are as alleged in the complaint — for purposes of D's motion to dismiss, the appellate court's opinion treated these allegations as true.

causation by a preponderance of the evidence. Instead, the theory changes the *nature of the injury* whose dollar value P must prove (by a preponderance) that D's negligence caused. The relevant dollar value is not the full value of *"the bad medical outcome,"* but rather, the *value of the less-than-50/50 chance* that without medical malpractice, the bad medical outcome would have been avoided.

So imagine that Mr. Smith had gone to trial following the court's decision, and had proved only a 40% likelihood that proper medical treatment would have given him a 33% chance of avoiding the brain damage. In that scenario, P would not have proved his "injury" — loss of the chance — by the requisite "more than 50/50 probability"; therefore he would recover *$0, not 13.2%* (i.e., not 40% x 33% of the difference between the value of no brain damage versus the actual brain damage).

   ii. **Incentives:** Some courts adopting the loss-of-chance theory have argued that rejecting the theory and applying the traditional more-than-50/50-likelihood requirement will *disincentivize physicians.* See, e.g., *Holton v. Memorial Hosp.*, 679 N.E.2d 1202 (Ill. 1997): "Disallowing tort recovery in medical malpractice actions on the theory that a patient was already too ill to [likely] survive or recover may operate as a *disincentive* on the part of healthcare providers to *administer quality medical care to critically ill or injured patients.*"

E. **Increased risk that's not yet followed by actual damage:** Now, consider the flip side of the problem discussed in Par. (D) above: Assume — in a non-medical-malpractice case[2] — that the defendant's conduct increased the risk that some later damage would occur, but the actual damage has *not yet occurred.* May the plaintiff recover something on a *"probabilistic"* basis?

   Example: For instance, suppose insulation manufactured by D has increased P's risk of incurring fatal pancreatic cancer from 1% to 15%. P does not yet have pancreatic cancer (though, perhaps, P has some pre-cancerous condition). May P recover now an amount equal to 14% of what he could recover for an actual fatal case of pancreatic cancer? As we'll see immediately below, the typical answer is slowly changing.

   1. **Traditional view:** The traditional approach is to answer *"no"* to this question — unless P can show that it is *more probable than not* that he will incur the harm in the future, P cannot recover anything now, and must wait until he actually incurs the harm, if that ever happens. H,P&S, p. 694. Courts adhering to this traditional view worry that the tort system will be swamped with tens of thousands of claims, especially in toxic-tort situations.

   2. **"Emerging view" allows recovery:** But a few modern decisions (representing what we'll call the "emerging view") have *allowed* recovery where P shows a real, but less than 50% chance, that he will incur the harm in the future.

      i. **Smoothing effect:** Observe that the "emerging view" has a "smoothing" effect compared with the traditional rule. Under the traditional rule, if P has a less than 50% chance of incurring the harm, P gets nothing; if P has a greater than 50% chance, P collects *full* damages (not discounted for the chance that the harm will

---

2. The same issue arises in malpractice suits. The issue in malpractice suits is described in the bullet point and Example just prior to our discussion here.

never occur). Under the emerging view, as it is usually expressed, there should be a discount for the chance that the harm will not occur, whether P's chance of incurring the harm is less than 50% or greater than 50%. So at least in theory, neither side gets a windfall under the emerging view. (On the other hand, a lot more suits probably get brought than under the traditional view, especially in mass-exposure toxic tort scenarios such as a chemical explosion or widespread exposure to a substance like asbestos.)

3. **Surveillance:** Even courts following the traditional view generally allow the plaintiff to recover for the costs of *medical surveillance*. That is, the defendant is required to pay the ongoing costs for *checking* the plaintiff's condition periodically, to determine whether the plaintiff has incurred the condition.

4. **Fears:** Plaintiffs also frequently attempt to recover for *emotional distress* damages, i.e., damages for the *fear* that they will incur the harm in the future. As you might expect, courts following the traditional view that the plaintiff may not recover for a less-than-50% chance of incurring the harm in the future also generally do not permit the plaintiff to recover for his fear of incurring the harm. See the discussion of this topic (sometimes called "cancerphobia") *infra*, p. 219.

F. **"Double fault and alternative liability":** Generally, as noted, the plaintiff must bear the burden of proving actual causation. In one situation, however, the court may thrust this burden on the *defendant* (or defendants). This situation has been termed by Prosser and Keeton that of "clearly established *double fault and alternative liability*." P&K, pp. 270-71. That is, the burden shifts where the plaintiff can show that each of two persons was negligent, but that only one could have caused the injury. In this situation, it is, according to most courts, up to each defendant to show that the other caused the harm. See Rest. 2d, §433B(3).

> **Example:** P, D1, and D2 go hunting together. D1 and D2, at the same time, negligently fire at a quail, and P is struck by one of the shots. It is not known from which gun the bullet was fired.
>
> *Held*, the burden is on each of the defendants to show that it was the other's shot which hit P. The defendants "brought about a situation where the negligence of one of them injured the plaintiff, hence it should rest with them each to absolve himself if he can." Otherwise, P might be left remediless. (The court then analogized to the case of *Ybarra v. Spangard, supra*, p. 111, 127.) *Summers v. Tice*, 199 P.2d 1 (Cal. 1948).

1. **Failure to show negligence:** In *Summers*, it was established that both defendants had behaved negligently. A few courts have apparently extended this rule of shifting the burden of proof onto the defendants to cases where it is *not* so clear that all defendants were negligent. For instance, if the plaintiff is injured by one of two cars involved in a collision, and cannot prove which, a court might impose the burden of proof as to causation on the defendants, even if it was not clear that both had been negligent. However, Prosser and Keeton recommend against such a shift in this situation. See P&K, P. 271.

2. **The "market share" theory:** The "double fault and alternative liability" theory has occasionally been extended to situations involving *three* or more parties. Thus if the plaintiff cannot prove which of three or more persons caused her injury, but can show that all were negligent (or produced a defective product), the court may cast upon each defendant

the burden of proving that he did not cause the injury. This is especially likely to occur in cases of *products liability*, where the plaintiff was injured by her long-ago usage of a product which she can identify only by *type*, not brand name. If a given member of the class of defendants is unable to prove that he did *not* cause the injury, the court may well require him to pay that percentage of the plaintiff's injuries which the defendant's sales of the product bore to the total market sales of that type of product. This is known as the *"market share"* theory of liability.

> **Example:** At least 200 manufacturers use an identical formula to produce DES, a synthetic estrogen. P alleges that her mother took the drug during pregnancy, and that it has caused P to develop cancer. P is unable to show which manufacturer of DES produced the drug that P's mother took. However, she sues five drug companies, who she asserts manufactured 90 percent of the DES ever marketed.
>
> *Held*, P need not identify the single manufacturer of the drug that her mother used, since this would be impossible to do. It is true that it cannot be said with certainty that one of the five D's produced the dosages taken by P's mother. However, the unavailability of proof is not at all P's fault, and is partially attributable to the fact that the D's produced a drug whose bad effects were not visible for many years. Furthermore, "[f]rom a broader policy standpoint, defendants are better able to bear the cost of injury resulting from the manufacture of a defective product," since they can discover and guard against defects, and warn of harmful effects. Thus the rule here will give the D's an incentive to make their products safe.
>
> Each defendant is free to show (but has the burden of proving) that it could not have produced the particular dosages consumed by P's mother. Any defendant who cannot make such a showing will be liable for the proportion of any judgment represented by that defendant's share of the overall DES market. *Sindell v. Abbott Laboratories*, 607 P.2d 924 (Cal. 1980).

a. **No right to exculpate oneself:** In *Sindell*, the court said that if a particular defendant could show that it could not *possibly* have manufactured the drug that P's mother used (e.g., because it didn't start making the drug until later, or never sold in the state where P's mother purchased the drug), D would escape liability. But some later decisions that have applied the market share theory have *not* agreed that the defendant should be allowed to exculpate itself by showing that it did not make the particular items in question.

   i. **Illustration:** For instance, *Hymowitz v. Eli Lilly & Company*, 539 N.E.2d 1069 (N.Y. 1989), was, like *Sindell*, a DES case. The New York Court of Appeals held that the particular defendant could escape liability by showing that it never sold DES for pregnancy use to *anyone*. But, the court held, a defendant should not be permitted to escape liability merely by showing that it could not have possibly produced the DES that injured *the particular plaintiff*: "Because liability here is based on the *over-all risk produced*, and not causation in a single case, there should be *no exculpation* of a defendant who, although a member of the market producing DES for pregnancy use, appears not to have caused a particular plaintiff's injury."

b. National market share: Courts faced with a market share situation have also struggled with the issue of *what market* should control for purposes of divvying-up damages among defendants according to their market shares. For instance, should the relevant market be the national market for the product, or the market in the state where the plaintiff's injury took place? The emerging consensus seems to be that a *national* market concept should be used, since this is easiest to administer.

    i. Consequence: But a quirky consequence of the national-market approach is that a plaintiff injured in New York and suing in New York might be able to recover from D 20% of her damages based on D's 20% share of the national market, even though D never sold a single dosage in New York.

c. No joint-and-several liability: Suppose that some manufacturers who had market share have since *gone out of business*, or are *not before the court* in the present action. Ordinarily, co-tortfeasors are subject to *"joint-and-several"* liability. That is, the plaintiff may recover her *entire* damages from any one defendant, rather than just that defendant's proportionate share of the harm caused. (See *infra*, p. 187.) But courts adopting the "market share" theory are, more and more, *rejecting* the standard joint-and-several liability approach, in favor of allowing a plaintiff to collect from any defendant only that defendant's *proportionate* share of the harm caused.

3. Alternate "enterprise liability" theory: A few courts, instead of applying the market share theory, have imposed liability via what is sometimes called the theory of *"enterprise liability."* As the theory goes, the multiple defendants have engaged in some sort of industry-wide *cooperation* (e.g., delegating to an industry trade association the authority to promulgate labelling or product-safety standards.) By this cooperation, the defendants may be said to have "jointly controlled the risk," so that it is not unreasonable to hold each member of the industry liable.

a. Joint-and-several liability more likely: A court following the "enterprise liability" approach will probably be more apt to impose joint-and-several liability than when using the market share theory, since by hypothesis, the defendants have acted in concert, and tort law has always traditionally awarded joint-and-several liability against co-defendants who acted together. (See *infra*, p. 187.)

II. PROXIMATE CAUSE GENERALLY

A. Scope of problem: Suppose that the plaintiff has established that the defendant was "negligent", in the sense that the defendant acted with an unreasonable disregard of the risks her conduct would impose on others. Suppose further that the plaintiff has succeeded in establishing that the defendant's negligence was the "cause in fact" of the plaintiff's injuries. There remains one more major hurdle for the plaintiff — he must show that the defendant *"proximately"* caused the injuries.

1. Misnomer: This requirement of "proximate cause" is really a misnomer. The word "proximate", when it was first used in this context, meant merely "close in time or space"; yet, as will be seen, this kind of proximity is only one of many factors that go into determining whether the defendant's act was the proximate cause of the plaintiff's injury. Nor does the word "cause" add much — since the plaintiff always has to make a separate showing that the defendant's act was the "cause in fact" of his injury, the limitation on liability imposed by the proximate cause requirement is really not causal at all.

2. **True nature of requirement:** Instead, the proximate cause requirement is a ***policy determination***, arising out of a judicial sense that a defendant, even one who has behaved negligently, should not automatically be liable for ***all*** of the consequences, no matter how ***improbable or far-reaching,*** of her act.

> **Example:** Suppose D, driving carelessly, collides with a car driven by X. Unbeknownst to D, the car contains dynamite, which explodes. Ten blocks away, a nurse who is carrying P, an infant, is startled by the explosion, and drops him. (See *Palsgraf v. Long Island R.R.* [Andrews dissenting] discussed extensively *infra*, p. 156.)
>
> In this situation, all courts would undoubtedly hold that P could not recover against D. This is not because D has not been negligent (since she did impose an unreasonable risk of harm upon X); nor is it because her careless driving was not the cause in fact of P's injury (since without that carelessness, the collision and the explosion would not have occurred). The reason that D will not be liable is simply that the injury is so ***far-fetched*** that courts administering a system based on fault feel it unfair to hold D liable. This feeling is expressed by stating that D's careless driving was not the "proximate cause" of P's injuries.

   a. **"Legal cause" better name:** Many writers feel that the term *"legal cause"* is a more descriptive label than "proximate cause". The Second Restatement uses the former term; see Rest. 2d, §434(2).

3. **Relation to "cause in fact":** The term "proximate cause" is sometimes used to include the concept of "cause in fact"; that is, in holding that the defendant's conduct was not the cause in fact of the plaintiff's negligence, the court may label this a failure of proximate cause. In this outline, however, the term "proximate cause" is not used to include the idea of actual causation, and encompasses only the restrictions on the defendant's liability for consequences that are deemed unduly far-fetched.

B. **Multiple proximate causes:** Just as an occurrence can have many "causes in fact" (*supra*, p. 141-143), so it will also often have more than one proximate cause. For instance, if each of two drivers drives negligently and an accident results, it is quite likely that each will be held to be a proximate cause of the accident.

1. **Joint tortfeasors:** In fact, the whole idea of joint-and-several liability of joint tortfeasors (*infra*, p. 183) is premised on the fact that a tort can have more than one proximate cause, and more than one person legally responsible for it. In general, each possible tortfeasor's actions must be examined, by use of the tests described below, to ascertain whether his acts were so closely related to the resulting damage that he is a proximate cause of it.

III. PROXIMATE CAUSE — THE FORESEEABILITY PROBLEM

A. **Need for dividing line:** Since everyone agrees that the defendant's liability must stop short of the most far-reaching and bizarre consequences, the difficulty is to define exactly where this dividing line should be. It is quite likely that the task of formulating mechanical rules which will apply to all cases is an impossible one, and that the matter must be determined case by case, according to what seems instinctively fair.

1. **Conflicting views:** However, among courts which have tried to resolve the problem, two conflicting views have emerged. One, which might be termed the *"direct causation"* view, would impose liability for any harm that may be said to have directly resulted from the defendant's negligence, no matter how unforeseeable or unlikely it may have been at the time the defendant acted. The other, which could be called the *"foreseeability"* or *"scope of the risk"* view, would limit the defendant's liability to those results that are of the same general sort that made the defendant's conduct negligent in the first place; i.e., results of a generally foreseeable nature, both as to kind of injury and as to person injured.

2. **"Foreseeability" leading contender:** The "foreseeability" view appears to be "on its way to ultimate victory as the criterion of what is 'proximate,' if it has not already achieved it." P&K, p. 297-300. However, there are certain kinds of cases in which this view does not explain the result which is usually reached by the courts. Therefore, an examination of both views, and the leading cases advocating each, is worthwhile.

B. **The "direct causation" view:** The *"direct causation"* view holds that the defendant is liable for all consequences of her negligent act, provided that these consequences are not due in part to what might be called "superseding intervening causes" (discussed *infra*, p. 162). The most significant aspect of this view, contrasted with the "foreseeability" view, is that the former would hold the defendant liable for all consequences, *no matter how far-fetched or unforeseeable,* so long as they flowed "directly" from her act, and not from independent new causes.

1. **Formulation:** One has summarized this "direct causation" view as follows: " [N]egligence is tested by foresight but proximate cause is determined by *hindsight*." *Dellwo v. Pearson*, 107 N.Y. 859 (Minn. 1961). The "direct causation" view is thus sometimes called the "hindsight" theory of proximate cause.

2. **The *Polemis case:*** The most famous case espousing the "direct causation" view is *In Re Polemis*, 3 K.B. 560 (Eng. 1921).

   a. **Facts:** In *Polemis*, the plaintiffs chartered their ship to the defendants. While the defendants were unloading it at the end of the voyage, they negligently dropped a plank into the hold; the plank somehow struck a spark, and this spark ignited petroleum the ship was carrying. The resulting fire destroyed the ship.

   b. **Holding:** It was clear to the court both that the defendants had acted negligently in dropping the plank, and that no one could reasonably have foreseen that dropping the plank would strike a spark, let alone burn up the ship. Nonetheless, because the fire was the "direct" result of the negligent act, the defendants were held liable. "If the act would or might . . . cause damage, the fact that the damage it in fact causes is not the exact kind of damage one would expect is immaterial, so long as the damage is in fact directly traceable to the negligent act, and not due to the operation of independent causes having no connection with the negligent act. . . . "

   c. **Overruled:** The *Polemis* case was, forty years later, overruled in a case known as *Wagon Mound No. 1*, discussed *infra*, p. 155. However, it nonetheless represents a powerful viewpoint, as evidenced by the fact that shortly after *Wagon Mound No. 1*, a case known as *Wagon Mound No. 2*, discussed *infra*, p. 160, very nearly reinstated it.

3. **Rationale:** The "direct causation" rule is often attacked on the grounds that it may result in limitless liability.

> **Example:** D, a railroad, operates one of its engines in a negligent manner. The engine sets fire to D's woodshed, which in turn causes P's house, located nearby, to be consumed by the fire.
>
> *Held*, for D. While the destruction of the woodshed is the "ordinary and natural result" of the negligent operation of the engine, to place liability on D for the destruction of P's house is too remote. "To sustain such a claim . . . would subject D to a liability against which no prudence could guard, and to meet which no private fortune would be adequate." *Ryan v. New York Central R. R. Co.*, 35 N.Y. 210 (1866).

     a. **Who should bear the loss:** However, proponents of the "direct causation" view observe that where the issue arises, the injury has already occurred, and "the simple question is, whether a loss, that must be borne somewhere, is to be visited on the head of the innocent or guilty." *Fent v. Toledo, P. & W. R. Co.*, 59 Ill. 349 (1871).

     b. **Further support:** Further support for this rule stems from the fact that in most cases of far-reaching harm from a single negligent act, the defendant is a large corporation, government, utility, etc., which by *adjusting its prices, obtaining insurance,* or by some other means, is better able to bear the burden of compensation than the plaintiff, who normally had no reason, or ability, to guard against the economic consequences of such a loss. P&K, p. 287.

     c. **Additional consideration:** Furthermore, the imposition of extended liability does not really impose a higher burden of *conduct* upon the defendant. By hypothesis, he has been negligent in some respect toward some person; therefore, we are only asking him to bear the consequences of his negligence, not to conform to a standard of conduct higher than that which would be observed by the "reasonable person." *Id.*

C. **The foreseeability view:** The opposite view is one which seeks to apply the same factors to limit the scope of liability as are used to determine whether the conduct is negligent in the first place. That is, this view would make the defendant liable, as a general rule, only for those consequences of his negligence which were *reasonably foreseeable* at the time he acted.

1. *Wagon Mound case:* This view is clearly articulated in a case usually called *Wagon Mound No. 1*, A. C. 388 (Austral. 1961), *supra*, p. 154, *infra*, p. 160.

     a. **Facts:** In *Wagon Mound*, the defendants' ship spilled oil into a bay. Some of the oil adhered to the plaintiffs' wharf, slightly interfering with the wharf's use. (The interference was so slight that no damage claim was made for it.) Then, however, the oil was set afire by some molten metal dropped by plaintiffs' workers, which ignited a cotton rag floating on the water. Because of this, the whole dock burned.

     b. **Unforeseeable result:** The trial court found that it was not reasonably foreseeable to the defendants that the oil could be set afire on the water. The burning of the wharf was therefore also an unforeseeable result of the spillage.

c. Holding: The appeals court held that, in these circumstances, the defendants were *not liable*. The court rejected the "direct causation" rule, whereby any consequences, no matter how far-reaching, were laid at the defendant's door, simply because they were the "direct" result of his negligence: " . . . It does not seem consonant with current ideas of justice or morality that for an act of negligence, however slight or venial, which results in some trivial unforeseeable damage the actor should be liable for all consequences, however unforeseeable and however grave, so long as they can be said to be 'direct'."

d. Application of foreseeability rule: The court pointed out that it was both simpler, as well as less burdensome to defendants, to apply the same rule to the question of the scope of liability as is applied to determining whether the conduct is negligent to begin with, i.e., whether the result was foreseeable.

2. Unforeseeable plaintiff: *Wagon Mound* involved a plaintiff as to whom the defendant's conduct was clearly negligent in a trivial respect (minor interference with the use of the dock), and the question was whether the defendant should also be charged with more serious, but far-fetched, injury suffered by this same plaintiff. A slightly different kind of situation, but one involving much the same issue, might be termed the *"unforeseeable plaintiff"* problem. Suppose the defendant's conduct is negligent as to X (in the sense of imposing an unreasonable risk of harm upon him), but not negligent as to P (i.e., not imposing an unreasonable risk of harm upon P). If P is nonetheless injured through some fluke of circumstances, may she in effect "tack on" to the negligence against X, and establish the defendant's liability for her injuries?

a. *Palsgraf:* This question was posed, and answered in the *negative,* by the most famous American tort case of all time, *Palsgraf v. Long Island R. R. Co.*, 162 N.E. 99 (N.Y. 1928), also discussed *infra*, p. 197.

  i. Facts of *Palsgraf:* In *Palsgraf*, a man running to board the defendant's train seemed about to fall; one of the defendant's employees, attempting to push him onto the train from behind, dislodged a package from the passenger's arms. The package, unbeknownst to anyone (except perhaps the passenger) contained fireworks, which exploded when they fell. The shock of the explosion made some scales at the other end of the platform fall down, hitting the plaintiff.

  ii. Issue: It was clear from the facts of the case that, although the defendant's employee may have been negligent toward the package-carrying passenger (by pushing him), his conduct did not involve any foreseeable risk of harm to the *plaintiff,* who was standing far away. The issue was whether, given the fact that the defendant had been negligent toward someone, this negligence was enough to give rise to liability to the plaintiff, injured by fluke.

  iii. Holding: The court, in a decision by Judge Cardozo, held that the defendant was *not liable*. "The conduct of the defendant's guard, if a wrong in its relation to the holder of the package, was not a wrong in its relation to the plaintiff, standing far away. Relatively to her it was not negligence at all. Nothing in this situation gave notice that the fallen package had in it the potency of peril to persons thus removed. . . . The plaintiff sues in her own right for a wrong personal to her, and not as the vicarious beneficiary of a breach of duty to another." Furthermore, generally speaking, " . . . [A] wrong is defined in terms of the natural or probable, at least when unintentional."

    iv. "Negligence in the air": Since the defendant's conduct did not involve an unreasonable risk of harm to the plaintiff, and the damage to her was not foreseeable, the fact that the conduct was unjustifiably risky to someone else is irrelevant. *"Proof of negligence in the air, so to speak, will not do."*

    v. "Duty" formulation: The majority opinion phrased its rule in terms of "duty", more than "foreseeability". The question, the court said, was whether the defendants had a duty of care to the plaintiff which was violated by their acts. But this formulation simply poses the same question as to the scope of liability; if the rule is that a defendant will be liable only to a plaintiff as to whom his conduct imposed a foreseeable risk, it will also be the case that the defendant violated no duty to a plaintiff as to whom there was no foreseeable risk. Phrasing the question in terms of duty does, however, have the advantage of not making the question sound like one of factual causation when it is really one of policy. See P&K, p. 281.

  b. Dissent: A famous dissent by Judge Andrews put forth the opposing view (roughly similar to the "direct causation" view discussed above), in what many believe is a more convincing opinion than Cardozo's majority one. The defendant, like every member of society, bears a burden of due care, a burden to "protect *society* from unnecessary danger, not to protect A, B or C alone." When an act imposing an unreasonable risk of harm to "the world at large" occurs, "Not only is he wronged to whom harm might reasonably be expected to result, but he also who is in fact injured, even if he be outside what would generally be thought the danger zone."

    i. Limitation of convenience: The Andrews dissent recognized a need to cut a defendant's liability short of all possible consequences which might stem from his negligent conduct. However, Andrews' limit was not determined by the foreseeability of these consequences, but by a more nebulous test: "What we . . . mean by the word 'proximate' is that, because of convenience, of public policy, of a rough sense of justice, the law arbitrarily declines to trace a series of events beyond a certain point. This is not logic. It is practical politics."

    ii. Factors: Andrews did, however, list some of the factors which he thought courts should consider in determining whether the consequences are so remote that liability should not attach. These included whether there was a "natural and continuous sequence" between cause and effect, whether there was a "direct connection" between them, without "too many intervening causes", whether the result was "too remote from the cause, and here we must consider remoteness in time and space", etc. In any event, Andrews argued, the court in *Palsgraf* should not rule on the record before it that the defendant's negligence was not the proximate cause of the plaintiff's injuries.

  c. Relevance to *Wagon Mound* problem: Observe that the "unforeseeable plaintiff" problem, posed by *Palsgraf*, is extremely similar to the issue posed by *Wagon Mound* (in which a single defendant is subjected to an unreasonable risk of trivial injury, which in fact occurs, as well a risk of more serious damage, which damage is so unlikely as to be "unforeseeable", but which nonetheless occurs).

> **i.** *Wagon Mound* **view:** The *Wagon Mound* court itself thought that these two issues must be resolved by the **same test.** Suppose, the *Wagon Mound* court said, there were two plaintiffs, each of whom had suffered the same unforeseeable injury as the result of a single act by the defendant. It would be unjust to allow one to recover and not the other, merely on the grounds that the former had coincidentally suffered some trivial, but foreseeable, damage from the defendant's action. Thus in the view of the *Wagon Mound* court, and probably in the view of both sides in *Palsgraf,* the same test, whether "foreseeability" or "direct causation" is chosen, should be applied to both the plaintiff unforeseeably damaged by an act which constituted negligence towards someone else, as well as a plaintiff who suffers both foreseeable and unforeseeable injury from a single act by the defendant.

D. Cardozo rule generally followed: Cardozo's "reasonably foreseeable" standard has generally been *followed by American courts*, although only a few cases have involved precisely the *Palsgraf* "unforeseeable plaintiff" problem. P&K, p. 286.

> **1. "Highly extraordinary" test:** Many courts express the Cardozo foreseeability approach by saying that the defendant will not have liability for injuries that are *"highly extraordinary."* Under this formulation, an injury that was a somewhat-unlikely but not completely-unforeseeable consequence of the defendant's negligence can still be a proximate result; but an injury that, viewed after the fact, seems to be an *extraordinarily unlucky or unlikely consequence* will *not* be proximate result. The case set forth in the following example is a good illustration of "highly extraordinary" formulation.
>
> > **Example:** D owns a house, and allegedly makes faulty repairs on a second-floor toilet. P, who is lawfully outside D's house watering D's flowers, receives a severe electric shock when he touches the outside water faucet. P sues D for negligence. It turns out (according to P's complaint) that due to the faulty repairs, the second-floor toilet had overflowed, and the flooding water reacted with the home's electrical system, causing current to flow to the outside faucet. D moves for summary judgment on the grounds that even if events happened the way P asserts, D's negligent repairs were not the proximate cause of P's electric-shock injuries.
> >
> > *Held,* for D. As a matter of law, the injuries sustained by P were such a "highly extraordinary" consequence of the defective second-floor toilet that D could not be required to guard against such injuries. P's assertion that the requirement of proximate cause is automatically satisfied as long as D's negligence can be connected in an "unbroken causal chain" to P's injuries is not correct — if D couldn't reasonably foresee injuries like that befalling P, D's negligence is not the proximate cause of those injuries regardless of whether there was a "unbroken chain." *Hebert v. Enos*, 806 N.E.2d 452 (Mass. App. 2004).
>
> **2. Third Restatement follows Cardozo view:** The various Restatements essentially follow the Cardozo foreseeability view, though with tweaks. Thus the Third Restatement agrees that there should not be liability for very unexpected harms: "An actor's liability is

limited to those physical harms that ***result from the risks that made the actor's conduct tortious.*** " Rest. 3d (Liab. for Phys. & Emot. Harm) §29. We'll call this the ***"scope of risk"*** standard.

Illustration 9 to §29 essentially restates the facts of *Palsgraf*: Bob, an employee of Railroad, jostles passenger Betsy so that she drops a package. Unbeknownst to Bob or Railroad, the package contains explosives, which explode on impact, knocking over a platform scale 30 ft. away. The scale falls on waiting passenger Heather. The illustration agrees with the result in *Palsgraf*: Railroad (and for that matter Bob) is not liable, because the harm to Heather did not result from the types of risks that made Bob's jostling of Betsy negligent — what made Bob's jostling negligent was the risk to the package or perhaps to Betsy's person from direct contact, not the risk of "concussive forces due to an explosion." *Id.*

    a. **No separate rule for "unforeseeable plaintiffs":** The Third Restatement does ***not*** share Cardozo's the view that there should be a ***separate rule*** barring the liability for injury to ***"unforeseeable plaintiffs."*** Comment n to §29 says that the Restatement has no such special unforeseeable-plaintiff rule. Instead, the lack of liability in situations like the *Palsgraf* rewrite in Illustration 9 above derives from the Restatement's *general* rule barring liability for harmful results that are ***outside of the type of harms the risk of which made the conduct negligent.*** (Thus if the explosion had harmed Betsy, the package's owner, presumably the Third Restatement would have still concluded that Bob and the Railroad were not negligent, because what made the jostling negligent was not the risk of an explosion.)

  3. **Exceptions to the foreseeable-consequences approach:** Although courts (and the Restatements) have generally accepted the view of Cardozo in *Palsgraf* that only foreseeable consequences may be recovered for,[3] there are a number of recurring situations in which most courts do *not* follow the *Palsgraf* no-liability view. Here are some of these special situations:

    a. **Extensive results from physical injuries:** Once the plaintiff suffers any foreseeable impact or injury, even if relatively minor, it is universally agreed, even by courts following the foreseeability rule, that the defendant is liable for ***any additional unforeseen physical consequences*** (provided these do not stem from "intervening causes" so unlikely that they should supersede liability — see *infra*, p. 168-169).

      i. **Plaintiff with egg-shell skull:** This principle is most frequently illustrated by the hypothetical case of a plaintiff who, unbeknownst to the defendant, has a ***skull of egg-shell thinness.*** If the defendant negligently inflicts a minor impact on this skull, but because of this hidden defect, the plaintiff dies, the defendant will be liable for his death. See P&K, p. 292. The rule is sometimes expressed by saying that the defendant ***"takes his plaintiff as he finds him."***

---

   3. Of course, as noted above, Cardozo formulated his rule in *Palsgraf* as being a rule of "duty" rather than a rule of "foreseeability." But there is little practical difference between these two approaches. So the generally-stated American rule that there is no liability for "unforeseeable consequences" is usually thought to be the substantial equivalent of the Cardozo / *Palsgraf* "no duty to protect against unforeseeable dangers" rule.

Example: D, a taxicab driver, negligently strikes P, an alcoholic, with his cab. The accident hastens the development of delirium tremens, a condition which only occurs in alcoholics, and P dies from it.

Held, for P. Even though the delirium tremens probably would have resulted in P's death at a later time had D not injured P, D is nonetheless liable, since he negligently aggravated P's condition. *McCahill v. New York Transp. Co,* 94 N.E. 616 (N.Y. 1911).

(1) Rationale: Since the initial physical injury in these "thin skull" cases was foreseeable, the holding that the defendant is liable for the far-reaching physical consequences might be explained as simply a refusal by the courts to divide an essentially indivisible physical harm into foreseeable and unforeseeable components. But these decisions may really be more a function of courts' tendency to carry liability further in cases of personal injury than in cases involving property damage or other, even more abstract, economic loss.

(2) Intentional torts: This tendency is analogous to the tendency referred to previously (*supra,* p. 8) of courts to impose broader liability for unlikely consequences in the case of intentional torts than in the case of negligent ones. This all points up the fact that tort law is largely an instrument of what courts perceive as justice and social planning, and not so much a series of strict legalistic rules of physical causation and compensation.

b. Rescuers: The "foreseeability" rule also seems frequently not to be strictly applied where the plaintiff is a *rescuer* of one who is endangered by the defendant's conduct, and the rescuer is herself injured. These cases are discussed *infra,* p. 165, in the treatment of intervening causes; here, we'll just say that the intervention of the rescuer is often not truly foreseeable, but this has not stopped the courts from imposing liability.

c. Foreseeable but highly unlikely: The foreseeability rule has also been weakened by cases holding that as long as the actual harm to the plaintiff was *remotely foreseeable,* there is liability even though these consequences were highly unlikely.

Example: The same facts as *Wagon Mound No. 1, supra,* p. 155, *infra,* p. 165. This time, however, the suit is brought by the owner of two ships which were docked at the wharf which burned; the defendant is the same as in *Wagon Mound No. 1.* Here, however, there is a finding of fact that it should have been foreseeable to the defendant that discharge of oil posed *some small risk of fire.*

Held, it does not follow from *Wagon Mound No. 1* that merely because the risk was small, the defendant was justified in ignoring it. The defendant should have weighed the risk against the difficulty of eliminating that risk, and avoiding the spillage would have been so unburdensome that it should have been done. Therefore, the defendant is liable. *Wagon Mound No. 2,* 1 A.C. 617 (Austral. 1966) *infra,* p. 165.

Note: Observe that the court here has taken the Learned Hand "balance the risk against the burden" analysis for determining negligence (*supra,* p. 97), and applied it for determining scope of liability. But it is hard to know how far the court meant to go — does liability only extend as to those consequences which by themselves were sufficiently likely and severe, in view of the small burden of avoiding them, that the defendant should have acted differently? Or does it apply to *any* consequence that is remotely foreseeable, even if the risk of that consequence was, by itself, not sufficient to justify the defendant's taking measures to avoid it (and the act was negligent only because of the risks of other consequences that did not materialize)? If the court meant the latter, then Prosser and Keeton seem to be correct in saying that the effect of this case is to "let the *Polemis* case in again by the back door, since cases will obviously be quite infrequent in which there is not some recognizable slight risk. . . . " P&K, p. 296.

d. **General class of harm but not same manner:** The courts have also cut back on the apparent rationale of *Palsgraf* by holding that as long as the harm suffered by the plaintiff was of the ***same general sort*** that made the defendant's conduct negligent, it is irrelevant that this harm occurred in an ***unusual manner.***

Example: D gives a loaded pistol to X, an 8-year-old, to carry to P. In handing the pistol to P, X drops it, injuring the bare foot of Y, his playmate. The fall sets off the gun, wounding P. D is liable to P, since the same general kind of risk that made D's conduct negligent (the risk of accidental discharge) has materialized to injure P; the fact that the discharge occurred by means of an unforeseeable dropping of the gun is irrelevant. D is not liable to Y, however, since his foot injury was not foreseeable, and the risk of it was not one of the risks that made D's conduct initially negligent. See Rest. 2d, §281, Illustr. 3.[4]

e. **Plaintiff part of foreseeable class:** Similarly, it has been held that the fact that injury to the particular plaintiff was not especially foreseeable is irrelevant, so long as the plaintiff is a ***member of a class*** as to which there was a general foreseeability of harm. Both this rule, and the rule just mentioned (that the harm must merely be of the same general class as that the risk of which made the defendant's conduct negligent), are illustrated by the following well-known case.

Example: D1, a shipping company, negligently moors its ship at a dock run by D2. Ice and debris force the ship adrift, and it collides with another ship, which is properly moored. Both ships smash into a drawbridge run by D3, the City of Buffalo, which might have been able to raise the bridge except for the fact that its employees were not on duty at the time. The bridge is toppled, and a dam is created by the collapsed bridge, the two ships, and floating ice. A flood results, and suit is brought by the various owners of flooded riparian property.

Held, all three defendants are liable to the property owners. First, the fact that it would have been impossible to identify in advance precisely which property owners would be harmed is irrelevant; a loose ship surely poses a danger to river-bank property owners in general, and the failure to raise a drawbridge similarly threatens at least

---

4. See also Rest. 3d (Liab. for Phys. & Emot. Harm) §29, Illustr. 3, posing a comparable hypo, and concluding that D is not liable for Y's foot injury because what made the entrustment of the gun to a child negligent was the risk of shooting, not the risk of a foot injury. Illustration 3 does not address the issue of whether a bystander injured when the dropped gun goes off (P in the example in the text) would recover. But under the Third Restatement's "scope of risks" rule, the answer would still be yes — at a general level, D's act was negligent because of the risk of shooting, which is what injured the bystander.

some owners, if only those whose property might be harmed by having the bridge tower fall on them. Since all of the plaintiffs were members of this general class of river-bank property owners, they are within the scope of risk, and are not barred from recovery by *Palsgraf*. Furthermore, the defendants may not succeed with their argument that there is no liability because the precise manner of the accident (i.e., flood damage from the backing up of ice due to the draw bridge's blocking the stream) was not foreseeable. There was a general, foreseeable risk that a loose ship would injure adjoining property, and that a drawbridge's failure to be raised would similarly damage adjoining owners. " . . . Where, as here, the damages resulted from the same physical forces whose existence required the exercise of greater care than was displayed and were of the same general sort that was expectable, unforeseeability of the exact developments and of the extent of the loss will not limit liability." *Petition of Kinsman Transit Co. ("Kinsman No. 1")*, 338 F.2d 708 (2d. Cir. 1964).

IV. PROXIMATE CAUSE — INTERVENING CAUSES

A. **Nature of intervening cause:** Questions of proximate cause arise particularly frequently in cases where the plaintiff's injury is precipitated by what is generally called an *"intervening cause"*. An intervening cause is a force which takes effect *after* the defendant's negligence, and which contributes to that negligence in producing the plaintiff's injury. Rest. 2d, §441(1).

    1. **Superseding cause:** Some, but not all, intervening causes are sufficient to prevent the defendant's negligence from being held to be the proximate cause of the injury. Intervening causes of this kind are usually called *"superseding causes"*, since they supersede, or *cancel,* the defendant's liability. See Rest. 2d, §440.

B. **Foreseeability rule:** In general, the issue of whether a particular intervening cause is a superseding one (i.e., one which prevents the defendant's act from being the proximate cause of the plaintiff's injury) is determined by the application of a test much like the Cardozo "foreseeability" test, described above.

    1. **Test:** If the defendant should have foreseen the possibility that the intervening cause (or one like it) might occur, *or* if the **kind of harm** suffered by the plaintiff was foreseeable (even if the intervening cause was not itself foreseeable) the defendant's conduct will nonetheless be the proximate cause.

        a. **No liability:** But if *neither* the intervening cause nor the harm was foreseeable (or "normal", a somewhat watered-down version of foreseeable), the intervening cause will be a superseding one, relieving the defendant of liability. P&K, p. 302.

C. **Foreseeable intervening causes:** There are situations in which the risk of a particular kind of intervening cause is the *very risk* (or one of the risks) which makes the defendant's conduct negligent in the first place. (Recall that the issue of proximate cause never arises until it is established that the defendant's conduct was negligent, in at least some way toward some person.) When this is the case, the intervening cause will virtually never relieve the defendant of liability. See Rest. 2d, 442A.

    1. **Illustration of scope of risk:** When courts hold that an intervening cause is not superseding because the risk of that intervention was one of the things that made the defen-

dant's conduct negligent, they are really collapsing the concept of proximate cause into that of negligence. This is illustrated by the following Example.

> **Example:** P is riding as a passenger in a car driven by X. A fuel truck driven by an employee of D Oil Co., coming in the opposite direction, skids and blocks the road; X swerves to avoid it, and ends up off the highway. Because the accident occurs near the top of a hill, P gets out of the car to warn drivers coming up the hill from the other direction. While doing so, he is hit by an oncoming car.
>
> *Held*, D's negligence is the proximate cause of P's injury. D's basic act of negligence towards P was in endangering him during the initial near-collision. But one of the extra risks of D's conduct was that P would do exactly what he did, namely, try to warn other motorists. (The court noted that if P had gotten back in the car, and had an accident five miles down the road, D's negligence would not have been the proximate cause because, despite the fact that P would not have been at the fatal intersection had it not been for D's conduct, that conduct would not have increased the risk of the five-miles-down-the-road collision.) P's injury was therefore "not remote, either in time or place", from D's negligence, and D is liable. *Marshall v. Nugent*, 222 F.2d 604 (1st Cir. 1955).

2. **Acts of nature generally:** If the intervening event is an act of nature that is truly "extraordinary," and not foreseeable, it will often be held to be a superseding cause. But one exception to this principle is that if the extraordinary, unforeseeable, act of nature (or *"act of God,"* as such catastrophes are often called, particularly in insurance policies) merely produces the *same result* as was threatened in other ways by the defendant's negligence, the defendant may still be liable. The general rule that the defendant is liable in cases of "unforeseen intervening causes but foreseeable result" is discussed *infra*, p. 168.

3. **Risk of harm must be increased:** For the defendant to remain liable under this "foreseeable intervening cause" rule, it is not enough that the intervening cause was foreseeable. It must also be the case that the *risk of harm* due to this force was *increased* by the defendant's conduct.

> **Example:** P, on a long drive throughout which there is a lot of thunder and lightning, stops because D has carelessly smashed into a tree, blocking P's path. While P is waiting, his car is struck by lightning. D will be held not to be the proximate cause of P's injury. It is true that the lightning is somewhat foreseeable. It is also true that D is a "but for" cause of P's injury, in the sense that had D not blocked P's route, D would have been somewhere else. But P was just as likely to be hit by lightning a few miles further down the road, where he would have been had there been no accident. Thus D's conduct has not increased the risk of damage to P through the foreseeable intervening cause. See P&K, p. 305-06. See also *Marshall v. Nugent*, supra.

4. **Foreseeable negligence:** The *negligence of third persons* may also be an intervening force that is sufficiently foreseeable that it will not relieve the defendant of liability. As was noted previously (*supra*, p. 107), the negligence of others is, in some situations, sufficiently foreseeable that it is negligence on the part of the defendant not to anticipate it and guard against it. In such a situation, it is not surprising that when the third person's negli-

gence does occur, the defendant will be held to be a proximate cause of damage that was immediately precipitated by the third person's conduct.

Example: P is standing in a telephone booth located in a parking lot 15 feet from a major street. D1, while drunk, is driving on that street; she loses control of her car and crashes into the booth, severely injuring P. P would probably have been able to get out of the booth before the crash except that the booth's doors did not open properly. P sues not only D1 but also D2 (the phone company, which built and owned the phone booth). P claims that D2 is liable on both negligence and strict liability theories. D2 defends on the grounds that it was D1's negligence, not any negligence or design defect by D2, that was the proximate cause of the accident.

Held, P has stated a valid cause of action against D2. A jury could find that there was a reasonably foreseeable risk that a hard-to-open telephone booth located near a major thoroughfare might cause a person inside to be trapped and injured in a collision. Nor was D1's gross negligence superseding — "If the likelihood that a third person may act in a particular manner is the hazard or one of the hazards which makes the actor negligent, such an act whether innocent, negligent, intentionally tortious, or criminal does not prevent the actor from being liable for harm caused thereby." Since a jury could find that the risk that the booth would be hit by a negligent driver was one of the very things that made D2's conduct dangerous, P should be allowed to present his case to the jury. *Bigbee v. Pacific Telephone & Telegraph Co.*, 665 P.2d 947 (Cal. 1983).

a. **Liquor sales:** The doctrine that the foreseeable negligence of others will not be superseding also furnishes a rationale for holding *tavern owners* liable for accidents caused by patrons who have been served too much liquor. Many states accomplish this result by statutes known as *Dram Shop Acts*, which make commercial sellers of liquor statutorily and automatically liable for such accidents if they have served a person who they should have realized was already intoxicated. But this result is also sometimes reached by the court acting without a Dram Shop statute.

   i. **Social furnishing of liquor:** But where the defendant is not a commercial tavern or liquor store owner, but one who serves liquor *socially* or as part of *business entertainment*, most states have *not* been willing to impose common law liability.

5. **Criminal or intentionally tortious conduct:** A third person's *criminal conduct* may, similarly, be sufficiently foreseeable that, even though it is clearly an intervening act, it will not be a superseding one. This is also true of *intentionally tortious acts* by third persons, the risk of which the defendant could have foreseen. In practice, however, the plaintiff may find it quite difficult to establish that the risk of criminal or intentionally tortious intervention was so great that it should have been guarded against.

Example: D Railroad negligently derails a tank car full of gasoline, and the gasoline spills into the street. X then throws down a lighted match, which ignites the gasoline, leading to an explosion that injures P. Evidence at trial is conflicting as to whether X was merely negligent in throwing down the match, or rather did it on purpose.

Held, on appeal, if X acted merely negligently (e.g., by lighting his cigar with the match), D is liable, since the risk of such a casual act by someone was one of the risks which made D's derailment negligent. But if X set the fire intentionally, such an intervention was so unlikely that D could not reasonably have been expected to guard against it. Case remanded for a new trial to determine whether X was negligent or criminal. *Watson v. Kentucky & Indiana Bridge & R.R. Co.*, 128 S.W. 146 (Ky. 1910), *infra*, p. 168.

    a. Shifting responsibility: Courts may also avoid holding the defendant liable for intervening criminal or intentionally tortious acts by holding that responsibility for the plaintiff's harm has **shifted** to the intervenor. See the discussion of shifting responsibility, *infra*, p. 172. Thus the court in *Watson*, instead of holding that the intentional-match-throwing was unforeseeable, could have reached the same result by holding that foreseeable or not, this criminal act was so clearly the direct responsibility of X that D should be relieved of liability. See P&K, pp. 317-18.

D. Weakening of "foreseeable": We saw that in courts following the general "foreseeability" approach to proximate cause, the requirement that the type of harm suffered by the plaintiff have been foreseeable has often been watered-down; this was true, for instance, of the decision in *Wagon Mound No. 2, supra*, p. 160, where even a very slight chance that the harm would occur was held to render it foreseeable. A similar weakening of the concept of foreseeability has occurred in cases involving intervening causes; that is, certain intervening causes have been held to be "foreseeable", and thus not superseding, even where the odds that these causes would intervene were very long indeed.

    1. "Normal" intervention: This watering-down of foreseeability has sometimes been expressed by saying that the intervening cause will not be superseding so long as it is a **"normal"** consequence of the defendant's conduct, whether foreseeable or not. See Rest. 2d, §443. This has been particularly true in cases where the intervening cause is a **response** to the danger or harm caused by the defendant. This includes cases of attempted **escape from harm, rescue, aggravation** of the harm by responses such as attempted **medical treatment,** and actions taken under emotional disturbance (including **suicide**). We consider each of these scenarios separately below.

    2. Attempted escape from danger: Thus if, in response to the danger created by the defendant's conduct, the plaintiff or someone else attempts to **escape** that danger, thus causing injury to the plaintiff, the attempted escape will not be a superseding cause so long as it was not completely irrational or bizarre.

        Example: D, driving on the highway, negligently attempts to pass a car driven by P, even though there is a truck approaching from the other direction. To avoid the threatened collision, P turns the car to the right edge of the highway, and hits a railing. X, a passenger in P's car, foolishly goes into an entirely unreasonable panic, opens the door of the car, and throws out his child, injuring her. P's act will not be a superseding cause relieving D of liability for damage to P's car; this is so because P's act was a "normal" (i.e., not extraordinary) response to the danger. (This is the case even if P's act was contributorily negligent, although this might be a defense that could be asserted by D). X's act is so bizarre and abnormal, however, that it will be a superseding cause, relieving D of liability for the injury to X's child. See Rest. 2d, §445, Illustr. 2 (slightly different facts).

3. **Rescue:**   Similarly, if the defendant's negligence creates a danger which causes some third person to attempt a *rescue*, this rescue will normally not be an superseding cause, unless it is performed in a *grossly careless manner.* Assuming that the rescue is not of this latter class, the defendant may be liable either to the *person being rescued* (even if part or all of his injuries are due to the rescuer's ordinary negligence), or to the *rescuer* (if she is injured in her rescue attempt).

   a. **Foreseeability:**   Some cases have held the rescuer not to be a superseding cause on the theory that the rescue was "foreseeable." The most notable such case is *Wagner v. International Railway*, a decision of Judge Cardozo set forth in the following Example.

   > **Example:** P and his cousin Herbert take an electric railway run by D. As the train is crossing a bridge, it lurches violently, and Herbert is thrown out. P leaves the train and walks along the bridge, trying to find Herbert's body; in the dark, he falls off the bridge and is hurt.
   >
   > *Held*, D owed a duty to P as well as to Herbert. "***Danger invites rescue. The cry of distress is the summons to relief.*** . . . The risk of rescue, if only it be not wanton, is born of the occasion. . . . The wrongdoer may not have foreseen the coming of a deliverer. He is as accountable as if he had." (However, a new trial must be had to decide whether P was contributorily negligent.) *Wagner v. International Ry.*, 133 N.E. 437 (N.Y. 1921).

   b. **Gross negligence:**   As noted, if the rescuer's act is *grossly negligent* or otherwise *bizarre*, it will generally be regarded as a superseding cause.

   c. **Firefighters' rule:** If the rescuer is a *firefighter, police officer,* or other public employee *paid to assume particular risks,* most states apply the so-called *"firefighters' rule,"* also known as the *"professional risk takers rule."* Under this rule, a professional risk taker may *not recover* for injuries caused by another's negligence, where "the negligently created risk was the very reason for [the plaintiff's] presence on the scene." Dobbs, §286. Despite the term "firefighters' rule," the rule extends to *police officers* as well, when they are called to premises to perform law-enforcement duties.

   > **Example:** D negligently invites guests to his house, whom he has reason to know often get into fights. Two guests get into a fight, and D calls the police. P, a police officer, responds, and suffers a broken jaw while breaking the fight.
   >
   > Under the common-law firefighters' rule, still in force in most jurisdictions, P will not be able to recover against D. That's because the rule says that a professional risk-taker such as a police officer may not recover in negligence against one who created the peril, if that peril was the very reason for the risk-taker's presence on the scene, and the peril is one of the special risks inherent in the plaintiff's job. The facts here meet these requirements for application of the rule.

      i. **Beyond premises liability:** Originally, the firefighters' rule applied only to premises liability. But those courts that apply it today generally extend it to cover professional rescue efforts that take place ***outside of D's (or anyone's) premises***. And they extend it to non-rescue situations, such as ***chasing suspects***.

Example: D is speeding. P, a police officer, chases him at high speed, and is injured in a collision. If the jurisdiction follows the modern version of the fire-fighters' rule, P will not be permitted to recover against D for creating the peril, because police officers are deemed to have voluntarily accepted the risk of injury from high-speed chases. Dobbs, §285, p. 770.

ii. **Normal risks:** Even among courts that apply the firefighters' rule, the doctrine is generally limited to ***risks*** that are ***inherent in, and special to,*** that particular occupation. Dobbs, §286.

Example: While driving on the job, P, a police officer, is injured in a collision in ordinary traffic with a car driven negligently by D. Even if the jurisdiction applies the firefighters' rule, P can recover against D, because the rule doesn't apply to the collision here. That's because the risk of a collision in ordinary traffic is not one of the special risks inherent in police work.

4. **Aggravation of injury:** If the defendant negligently injures the plaintiff, and as a result of that injury the plaintiff receives a further injury or an ***aggravation*** of the existing one, the defendant is liable for all of this.

   a. **Medical treatment:** Thus if the defendant injures the plaintiff, who then undergoes ***medical treatment,*** the defendant will be liable for anything that happens to the plaintiff as a result of negligence in the medical treatment, infection, or other by-products. *See, infra*, p. 187.

      i. **Bizarre result:** Some results of attempted medical treatment are, however, so ***gross and bizarre*** that they are regarded as superseding. The Second Restatement illustrates this by the example of a nurse who is unable to bear the plaintiff's suffering, and kills him by an injection of morphine which she knows may be fatal. (Rest. 2d, §457, Illustr. 4.)

      ii. **Most malpractice not superseding:** But most of the things that can go wrong in medical treatment are not superseding causes. For instance, if the plaintiff is injured when the ***ambulance carrying him gets into a collision,*** the person causing the initial need for the ambulance will be liable (P&K, p. 310, fn. 86); similarly, if the plaintiff is hospitalized, and then receives an unnecessary operation due to a ***clerical mix-up*** of his records with those of another patient, the defendant who caused him to be hospitalized in the first place will be liable. (Rest. 2d, §457, Illustr. 3.)

      iii. **Lowered vitality:** Similarly, if the defendant causes the plaintiff to become sick or otherwise weakened, and this weakened state leads the plaintiff to ***catch another disease*** which she might not otherwise have caught, the defendant's liability will extend to the results of this subsequent disease. Rest. 2d. §458.

   b. **Subsequent accidents:** And if the defendant injures the plaintiff, and this injury makes the plaintiff particularly susceptible to ***another accident***, which occurs, again there will be full liability.

Example: D negligently runs over P, breaking his leg. Two months later, as P is learning to walk on crutches, he slips, and breaks his arm. D is liable for injuries to the arm as well as the leg. See Rest. 2d, §460, Illustr. 1. (But if P tried to walk on the crutches down a ladder into his basement, and fell, D would not be liable for this fall; the fall would be such an abnormal consequence of the original broken leg that it would be viewed as superseding. *Ibid*, Illustr. 2.)

5. **Suicide:** What if the plaintiff becomes so despondent or pained by the injuries he has received from the defendant's negligence that he *kills himself*? If the plaintiff was *sane* at the time he committed suicide, the courts unanimously hold that the suicide was a superseding cause, and the defendant has no liability for it.

   a. **Insanity:** But if the injury drives the plaintiff *insane,* and the suicide is the product of this insanity, recovery is usually allowed. The requisite insanity has generally been found only where the suicide is shown to be the product of an *"irresistible impulse"* on the part of the plaintiff. This phrase, however, has acquired a broader meaning in recent years.

E. **Unforeseeable intervention but foreseeable result:** The "intervening cause" cases examined above were ones in which the intervention was foreseeable, or at least "normal". What if the intervention is neither foreseeable or normal, but it leads to the *same type of harm* as that which was threatened by the defendant's negligence? The general tendency in such situations is to hold that the intervention is *not a superseding cause.* See P&K, p. 316; see also Rest. 2d, §442B.

   1. **Rationale:** The rationale for this result is that since the defendant has imposed upon the plaintiff an unreasonable risk of the same type of harm as that which occurred, it is unjust to allow him to escape responsibility merely because the harm was in fact produced by an unforeseeable intervention. As Prosser and Keeton put it, this result is compelled by "an instinctive feeling of justice." P&K, *ibid.*

      Example: D Transit Co. runs a trolley system, as part of which it maintains wooden poles. It allows one of these poles to become infested by termites. P is standing near that pole when X, negligently driving his car, collides with the pole, knocking it over onto P.

      Held, if the evidence shows that a properly maintained pole would not have broken under the impact of X's car (so that D's negligence is a cause in fact of the injury), X's negligence will not be a superseding cause, even though it was unforeseeable. Since the general risk imposed by D's negligence is that the pole would, due to its own weight or outside forces, fall on a bystander, and since the same general type of harm occurred (falling pole injures bystander), the fact that the actual precipitating cause was unforeseeable is irrelevant. *Gibson v. Garcia*, 216 P.2d 119 (D.C. App. Cal.1950).

   2. **Criminality or intentional tort:** But if the unforeseeable intervening act is a *crime or intentional tort,* it *will* usually be a superseding cause, even if the injury that results to the plaintiff is the same as that threatened by the defendant's negligence.

      Example: This was the case in *Watson v. Kentucky & Indiana Bridge & R.R. Co., supra*, p. 164 in which the court held that if the explosion of gasoline spilled by the defendant was due to arson on the part of a third person, that arson would a superseding cause.

    a. Rationale: As noted, *supra*, p. 164, the rationale for holding that an intervening intentionally tortious or criminal act is a superseding cause is often that responsibility has *"shifted"* to the third-party criminal or tortfeasor. See the discussion of shifting responsibility *infra*, p. 172. See Rest. 2d, §442B, Comment c.

F. Unforeseeable intervention with unforeseeable results: The last major class of intervening causes consists of those interventions which are not foreseeable (or even "normal"), and which produce results that are not of the same nature as those potential results that made the defendant's conduct negligent. Generally, the courts have treated such intervening causes as superseding. As with the other classes of intervening causes, this result has been reached on basically instinctive feelings of justice; in this case, that it is not fair to hold the defendant liable for a harm that was not within the original risk of her negligent conduct, where that harm was produced through an unforeseeable intervention. See P&K, p. 312.

    1. Extraordinary acts of nature: Thus an extraordinary act of nature ("Act of God") which brings about damage to the plaintiff different from the damage threatened by the defendant's negligence, will relieve the defendant of liability. See Rest. 2d, §451

        Example: In a state where it is a tort to build a "spite wall" (i.e., a wall separating one's land from that of one's neighbor), D builds such a wall. The wall is strong enough to withstand any foreseeable winds, but an extraordinary cyclone blows the wall down, damaging the house of P, D's neighbor. The cyclone will be held to be a superseding cause relieving D of liability, since it was not foreseeable or even "normal", and the risk of damage to the land of his neighbor was not one of the risks that made D's original conduct tortious. See Rest. 2d, §451, Comment a.

    2. Other extraordinary acts: Similarly, intentionally tortious or criminal acts by third persons, gross negligence by third persons, and other highly unusual intervening causes, have been held to be superseding, where they produce a result different from that the threat of which made the defendant's conduct negligent. See P&K, pp. 312-13. Several of the more frequently recurring fact situations in which this rule is applied are as follows.

        a. Key-in-ignition cases: Suppose the defendant leaves his car unlocked, with the *key in the ignition,* and a thief steals it, later running down the plaintiff. Is the thief's act a superseding one? In most circumstances, the courts have answered *"yes,"* whether or not there is a local car-locking ordinance. See P&K, pp. 313-14.

            i. Rationale: The rationale for this result can be expressed as follows: First, the risk of the intervening act (if one defines it as not merely the theft of the car, but the subsequent negligent driving of it) is not one of the risks which makes the defendant's conduct negligent. (His conduct is negligent, if at all, because of the danger to the owner's own car.) Secondly, the kind of result (personal injury or property damage to third persons) is not the kind of result that is threatened by the defendant's negligence.

            ii. Unusual circumstances: But in a particular case, circumstances may be such that the owner should foresee that leaving the keys in the car will materially increase the risk of harm to others. For instance, suppose the owner leaves the car in an area known to have a high crime rate; the owner may well be held to have been on notice of the increased danger of theft and ensuing negligence, in which case the owner would be liable for the later injuries to the plaintiff.

iii. **Negligence per se:** Recall that the car-locking problem arose in the discussion of negligence *per se, supra*, p. 116. There, it was noted that statutes requiring car-locking are sometimes held to be for the protection of third persons, and violations are held to be negligent *per se* towards a bystander who is injured. Where negligence *per se* is found on this basis, the court will normally also conclude that the theft and the thief's negligence are not superseding causes, since their conduct was somewhat foreseeable and was part of the risk that the statute was designed to prevent.

b. **Delays by carriers:** Suppose a *common carrier* negligently *delays the transport of goods,* leading them to be destroyed by a flood, fire, etc. The delay is clearly the cause in fact of the damage, since had there been no delay, the goods would not have been in the place that was flooded or burned. But unless the plaintiff can show that an *increase in the risk* of such a catastrophe was foreseeable as the result of the delay (e.g., the carrier fails to move the goods out of an area where floods have been threatened into a safer one), most courts (and the Second Restatement, §451) would probably hold that the act of nature was a superseding cause.

i. **Minority view:** Other courts might impose liability on the carrier, but this is more properly viewed as the imposition of strict liability (i.e., liability without regard to fault) than as the application of traditional rules of proximate cause and negligence. See P&K, p. 315.

G. **Dependent vs. independent causes:** In deciding whether to treat an intervening cause as superseding, courts have often distinguished between *"dependent"* intervening causes and *"independent"* ones. A dependent intervening cause is one which operates in *response* to the defendant's negligence. An independent intervention is one which would have existed even had the defendant not been negligent (but which, in any case in which the defendant's negligence is a cause in fact of the plaintiff's harm, combined with that negligence to produce the harm.)

Example: Suppose D negligently fails to maintain his tires in a safe condition. If he has a blow-out, and this blow-out makes his car swerve in such a way that P, in an oncoming car, tries to avoid him by going off the road and runs into a fence, P's act of avoidance is a dependent intervening cause. But if P had gently bumped into D prior to the blow-out, and this bump had precipitated the blow-out, P's act would be an independent one, since it would have occurred regardless of the condition of D's tires (although the resulting blow-out might not have occurred).

1. **Significance of distinction:** An intervening cause's status as dependent or independent is *not per se dispositive* as to whether that intervention is superseding. It may well be that dependent causes are generally more foreseeable than independent ones, and are thus more likely to be superseding. But an independent intervening force can certainly fail to supersede (e.g., X's collision with the termite-infested pole in *Gibson v. Garcia, supra*, p.

168, which would have occurred even if the pole had been in good condition), and a dependent cause can be superseding (e.g., a grossly negligent rescue attempt, which would not have occurred but for the danger to the rescued person created by the defendant).

   a. Distinction not important: The student should therefore not place too much attention on the "independent" and "dependent" labels, and should instead ask the question, "Did the defendant's conduct increase the risk either that an intervening cause like the one that occurred would occur and bring damage, or that damage like that which occurred would occur?" If the answer is yes, the intervening cause will generally not be superseding.

H. Function of judge and jury: Is it the *judge* or the *jury* who decides the issue of proximate cause? The answer is that *both* the judge and the jury participate in deciding this issue, but they participate in different ways.

   1. Judge formulates the legal rule: As you would expect, it is up to the *judge* to *formulate the appropriate legal rule* in the form of an instruction to the jury.

> **Example:** Assume that the jurisdiction has adopted the Third Restatement's "scope of risk" formulation (*supra*, p. 159). In that event, assuming the case went to the jury, the judge would instruct the jury in words something like the following: "You may find that the defendant is liable for the physical injuries suffered by the plaintiff only if you conclude that those injuries were the result of the type of risk that made the defendant's conduct unreasonably dangerous to other persons."

   2. Judge's "gatekeeper" function: Keep in mind, however, that although the judge doesn't make the factual determination of whether D proximately caused P's injuries (as we'll see below, that's the jury's job), trial judges can and often do exercise an important *"gatekeeper"* function. That is, the judge can and should *prevent the case from ever being decided by the jury,* if the judge decides that *no reasonable jury could find that the plaintiff has established each element of her prima facie case* by the required preponderance of the evidence. (See *supra*, p. 96, for more about the *prima facie* case.)

   Now, one of the elements of the plaintiff's *prima facie* case is, of course, what we're calling "proximate cause." Therefore, if the judge decides that on the proof offered by the plaintiff, *no reasonable jury could decide that it is more likely than not that the defendant proximately caused the plaintiff's injuries*, the judge will decide the case in favor of the defendant on a motion for summary judgment or for a directed verdict — the jury will *never get a chance to decide* whether D proximately caused P's injuries. And that's true even if the judge believes that the plaintiff has satisfied other elements of her *prima facie* case (e.g., the judge believes that a reasonable jury could properly conclude that the defendant failed to exercise due care as to a duty he owed the plaintiff).

   3. Factual determination left to the jury: But in most negligence cases — at least ones in which the judge believes that the jury could properly find that the defendant failed to use due care, and that the defendant's lack of due care was the cause in fact of the plaintiff's injuries — the judge will *not exercise* her right to *short-circuit the case* by taking the decision on proximate cause away from the jury. That is, in most but not all instances, the judge will decide that a reasonable jury could go either way on this issue; in that case, the judge will instruct the jury on the test for determining proximate cause, and *will leave it to*

the jury to apply that test in deciding the factual issue of whether the defendant's failure to use due care was so tenuously connected with the harm that proximate cause should be found lacking

> **Example:** The Ds, a couple, disassemble a trampoline and place its components in their backyard, 38 feet from an adjacent road. Because they intend to dispose of these parts soon, they do not secure them in place. A few weeks later, a severe thunderstorm blows the top of the trampoline from the yard onto the road. Later, P, driving on the road, swerves to avoid the trampoline top that is obstructing the road, causing him to roll his car into a ditch and injuring him. Prior to the trial of P's negligence suit against the Ds, the Ds move for summary judgment. The trial judge grants the motion, in part on the theory that even if the Ds behaved negligently in not securing the trampoline parts, that negligence was not the proximate cause of the injuries to P because the danger that the unsecured trampoline parts would be displaced by a force of nature from the Ds' backyard to the road was not reasonably foreseeable to them.
>
> *Held* (on appeal), for P: summary judgment reversed, and case remanded for trial. First, the court now adopts the Third Restatement's scope-of-risk formula for handling what has traditionally been called the "proximate cause" inquiry: "An actor's liability is limited to those physical harms that result from the risks that made the actor's conduct tortious." Turning to the issue of whether the trial judge correctly decided that no reasonable jury could find that the harm here resulted from the risks that made the Ds' conduct negligent, the answer is "no." "[T]he question of whether a serious injury to a motorist was within the range of harms risked by disassembling the trampoline and leaving it untethered for a few weeks on the yard less than forty feet from the road is not so clear in this case as to justify the district court's [grant of] ... summary judgment[.]" That's because "[a] reasonable fact finder could determine [that the Ds] should have known high winds occasionally occur in Iowa in September and a strong gust of wind could displace the unsecured trampoline parts the short distance from the yard to the roadway and endanger motorists." *Thompson v. Kaczinski*, 774 N.W.2d 829 (Iowa 2009).

V. SHIFTING RESPONSIBILITY

A. Nature of problem: We have encountered several situations where the defendant acts negligently, and this negligence or other wrongdoing of third persons, in combination produces the plaintiff's injury. As has been noted, there are some situations in which the defendant will be allowed to say, in effect, that responsibility for the dangerous condition created in part by her has ***passed to that third person,*** absolving the defendant of responsibility. That is, the responsibility is said to have ***"shifted"***.

B. No general rule: Prosser and Keeton (P&K, p. 205) and the Restatement (Rest. 2d, §452, Comment f) both agree that it is difficult or impossible to state a general principle about when the responsibility will have shifted. But a few general observations and typical fact situations may be stated.

    1. Contract or other agreement on responsibility: There may be an ***agreement*** between the defendant and the third person expressly or implicitly shifting responsibility to the latter. Such an agreement will not be dispositive, if there are strong policy considerations in favor of not relieving the defendant of liability. Nonetheless, such an agreement will be a factor making it more likely that the court will find responsibility to have shifted in the manner that the agreement refers to. Rest. 2d, §452, Comment e.

2. **Cases where there is no agreement:** Where there is no agreement between the defendant and the third person regarding apportionment of responsibility, the court must make an even more abstract weighing of factors. Among these are the degree to which the defendant should have *foreseen* that the third person might be negligent, the *severity* of the harm which would result if such negligence by the third person occurred, and the *lapse of time.* See Rest. 2d, §452, Comment f.

3. **Third person's failure to discover defect:** One rule that is well-established is that if a manufacturer negligently produces a dangerous product, he will *never* be absolved of responsibility merely because some person further down the distributive chain (e.g., a distributor or a consumer who resells the product) negligently *fails to discover the danger,* and thus fails to warn the plaintiff (the ultimate user) about it. See P,W&S (9th), p. 351, Note 1. See also *infra*, p. 350.

   Example: In 2008, Manu manufactures a power saw that it sells to Factory. The saw contains a hidden design defect that makes the saw blade likely to snap off, potentially injuring the user. In 2010, Manu discovers the problem as the result of consumer complaints. Manu then promptly writes a letter to Factory (addressed to Factory's president) describing the problem and offering to fix it for free. The president negligently throws the letter away, instead of reading it or telling anyone on the shop floor about the danger. In 2013, User, a Factory employee, uses the saw and is injured when the blade breaks.

   A third person's failure to discover a danger will virtually never, by itself, constitute a superseding cause relieving the original tortfeasor of liability. Therefore, the negligence of Factory's president in discarding the letter will not prevent Manu's defective design from being a proximate cause of User's injury, so that negligence won't block User from recovering against Manu in strict product liability.

   a. **Third person does discover:** Even if the third person *does* discover a danger caused by the defendant, the third person's *failure to warn* the plaintiff about that danger usually *won't be superseding.*

   Example: Same facts as above example. Now, however, Factory's president reads the recall letter, then due to press of other business fails to mention it to User or to get the saw fixed. It's unlikely that this third-party failure to warn will be deemed superseding. So Manu's defective design will still likely be considered a proximate cause of User's injuries. (A different result — an interruption of the causal chain — might occur if Manu then called up Factory, or otherwise did everything reasonably in its power to fix the saw, and Factory's president simply refused to allow the saw to be fixed or replaced by Manu for free.)

Quiz Yourself on

ACTUAL AND PROXIMATE CAUSE *(Entire Chapter)*

36. In January 2022 Paula, a 42-year-old woman, asks Doc, a gastroenterologist, to perform a colonoscopy to check for colon cancer. Doc performs the procedure but fails to notice a polyp that, if biopsied, would show Stage 2 colon cancer. A gastroenterologist who performed a colonoscopy with the minimal competency required of G.I. specialists would have spotted the polyp, biopsied it, and recognized that it was cancerous and needed to be removed. In November 2022, a different physician diagnoses Paula with stage IV colon cancer (an invariably fatal condition), and she dies of that disease in January 2023. Had the polyp been removed and standard chemotherapy administered to Paula soon after January 2022, medical statistics show that Paula would have had a 40% chance of being cured and a 60% chance of dying within one year. Her estate is now suing Doc for medical malpractice. Doc defends by arguing (with factual correctness) that even had he correctly spotted Paula's cancerous polyp during the original examination and ensured that she got state-of-the-art treatment for it, more likely than not Paula would have died within a year anyway. Assume that under standard principles for computing damages, if the estate were able to show a more than 50% chance that prompt treatment would have cured her, the appropriate recovery would be $2 million. You represent the estate.

    (a) Identify the legal theory that gives your client the best chance of recovering at least something in the action. _____

    (b) Is the legal theory you identified in Part (a) likely to succeed? _____

    (c) If that legal theory is accepted by the court, what is the appropriate amount of damages that the estate should be awarded? _____

37. King's Man catapults a styrofoam ball at Humpty Dumpty's forehead, intending only to embarrass him. In fact, Humpty falls and cracks his skull, where a normal person would have been unhurt. Will King's Man be liable for Humpty's injuries? _____

38. Things are kind of anxious in Europe, and Gavrilo Princip takes to carrying a gun. He's watching a parade one day, when a man next to him, Dr. Pangloss, carelessly drops a peanut into Princip's gun. When Princip tries to shake the peanut out, the gun goes off, killing Archduke Ferdinand and starting World War I. Rupert, who is badly injured in WWI, sues Pangloss for negligently causing Rupert's injuries. Can Rupert win? _____

39. Vronsky is raking the leaves in his front yard, and he carelessly blocks the sidewalk with a huge pile of leaf-filled bags. As a result, Anna Karenina must walk out into the heavily-travelled street to get around the pile, and she is run over by a driver who negligently fails to stop in time. Will Vronsky be liable for Anna's injuries? _____

40. Sprooss Goose Plane Repairs negligently fixes Amelia Earheart's plane, such that the next time she flies, she crashes and breaks her leg. The leg is set in a cast. Shortly thereafter, she goes rowing on a local lake. The rowboat tips over, and she drowns, the cast pulling her down and making her unable to swim to safety. Will Sprooss be liable for her death? _____

41. Abel, while driving his car, hit the brakes as a child ran into the road. Baker, who was tailgating Abel, slammed into Abel. Carr, who was tailgating Baker, slammed into Baker, causing an additional impact on Abel's car. Abel suffered serious whiplash. Abel sued Baker and Carr for his injuries. No party produces

evidence as to which crash (Baker into Abel, or Carr into Baker and thence into Abel) caused Abel's whiplash. What is the most likely result:

(a) Both Baker and Carr are liable; or

(b) Neither Baker nor Carr is liable?

---

42. With Driver at the wheel, Driver and Passenger motor into town one day. Passenger has fallen asleep during the trip. Driver parks the car in front of a fire hydrant next to a bank, in violation of a municipal statute and also in violation of what motorists all over America know to be prudent practice. Driver goes into the bank to make a quick deposit, while Passenger remains asleep. Trucker, who is driving his truck down the street, suddenly swerves to avoid hitting a dog. Trucker's truck smashes into Driver's car, seriously injuring Passenger. Had Driver parked the car anywhere but in front of the hydrant, Trucker's truck would not have hit Driver's car. Passenger sues Driver for negligence. Will Passenger recover?

---

43. Dan is driving his car with Patti as passenger. Dan negligently runs a red light, and his car is struck by an oncoming car driven by Xavier. Patti is seriously though not fatally injured. An ambulance is called, which rushes Patti to the hospital. The ambulance driver drives at an excessive rate of speed (even considering the need to get Patti to the hospital quickly), and crashes. Patti is killed. Her estate sues Dan. Assuming the estate may recover for the serious but not fatal injuries sustained by Patti during the initial collision, may it also recover for Patti's death? _____

Answers

36. **(a) The "value of a chance" theory**. Under this theory, if accepted by the court, the state is entitled to recover for a special type of injury, namely, the injury of being deprived of the opportunity (or "chance") of obtaining a better outcome (a cure) than the early death that occurred.

(b) Yes, probably. Most courts that have considered the matter in the last few decades apply the value of a chance theory. Therefore, the estate can recover even though it is "less likely than not" that Doc's negligence was the actual and proximate cause of Paula's death. In other words, the usual rule that a plaintiff cannot recover unless she can show that the defendant more likely than not caused her injury is modified in the medical-malpractice situation to view the injury not as being "deprived of a cure," but rather, "deprived of the [less than 50/50] chance of a cure."

(c) $800,000. In value-of-a-chance cases, the court takes the value that the claim would have had if P proved that the injury was more likely than not caused by D's malpractice, and multiplies that number by the percentage chance that a favorable result (e.g., a cure) would have occurred had there been no malpractice. Thus the formula is:

$2 Million [value of claim if there was a more-than-50% chance that Paula would have been saved by competent and timely treatment] *times 40%* [the likelihood that such treatment would have cured her].

See Rest. 3d (Liab. for Phys. & Emot. Harm, § 26, Comment n.

37. **Yes.** The rule is that the defendant is responsible for all personal injury to the plaintiff flowing from his wrongful conduct, even if the injury is surprisingly severe. Here, King's Man committed a battery; he intentionally acted to cause harmful or offensive contact with Humpty, so he is responsible for all per-

sonal injuries flowing from his conduct. This is known as the "eggshell skull" theory — particularly apropos when applied to Humpty Dumpty!

NOTE: Note that it doesn't matter that King's Man only wanted to <u>embarrass</u> Humpty; his <u>motive</u> won't relieve him of liability. His action could still constitute a battery if he intended the act that brought about harmful or offensive contact, or even if he only intended to create the *apprehension* of such contact.

NOTE: The "eggshell skull" theory applies to all intentional torts, as well as negligence. It is sometimes summed up by the phrase "The defendant takes his plaintiff as he finds him."

38. **No.** Negligence requires duty, breach, causation, and damages. There is no negligence here because Pangloss didn't have a duty to Rupert, anymore than he had such a duty to all the other millions who were harmed in some way by the War. An individual owes a duty only to prevent the <u>foreseeable risk</u> of injury to one in plaintiff's position. In this case, injury to millions of war-injured people is not a foreseeable result of dropping a peanut in a gun — which is really saying that, as a matter of policy, Pangloss will not be held liable for such widespread damages on the basis of his act. (This result is often expressed in terms of <u>proximate cause</u> rather than duty: one is liable only for those consequences that one's carelessness proximately caused.)

NOTE: The <u>level of fault</u> bears on the scope of duty. Thus, intentional wrongdoers are commonly held liable for consequences beyond the foreseeable risk created; and, in turn, negligent tortfeasors are responsible for a broader scope of potential damage than those subject to strict liability.

39. **Yes, because one is responsible for those intervening causes that are considered "foreseeable."** The negligence of drivers on heavily-travelled streets, as here, would be considered foreseeable. What this tells you is that others' negligence *can* be considered foreseeable.

40. **No, probably.** Negligent defendants are liable for damages from foreseeable intervening causes. Where plaintiff's initial injury leaves him susceptible to subsequent diseases or injury, defendant will be liable for these. However, Amelia's death here was not the result of her weakened condition. Drowning is so abnormal a consequence of a broken leg that it will probably be considered a "superseding" cause, relieving Sprooss of liability for Amelia's death.

41. **(a) Both liable.** When the conduct of two or more defendants is tortious, and plaintiff proves that the harm to him has been caused by only one of them, but he cannot prove which one, the burden is on each of the defendants to prove that he did not cause the harm. Here, the fact that Baker and Carr were each tailgating the car in front of him, establishes that they were each negligent. Abel has certainly proved that the damage resulted from the negligence of either Baker or Carr. Therefore, the burden was placed on Baker and Carr each to show that his negligence was not the cause in fact of Abel's injury — since neither carried this burden, each is liable for the full amount of Abel's injuries (though of course he may not have a double recovery, so that if he recovers the full amount of his injuries from Baker, he may not recover from Carr, and vice versa). See Rest. 2d, §433B, Illustr. 11.

42. **No.** First, let's analyze the case from the perspective of the negligence per se doctrine. Even though Driver was negligent per se in parking in front of the hydrant, he will only be liable for those consequences which were of a ***type*** the ***risk of which*** the ordinance was enacted to guard against. What makes parking in front of a hydrant prohibited is that fire engines may not be able to get water to put out fires; parking in front of a hydrant does not increase the risk that some other driver will collide with one's own car (since such collisions are equally likely to occur whether there is a hydrant on the sidewalk or not). Because the presence of the hydrant did not increase the risk of such a collision, a court would hold that

Driver's negligence per se was not the proximate cause (or "legal cause") of Passenger's injuries.

A similar analysis applies to whether Driver's conduct was "ordinary" negligence (i.e., negligence independent of the negligence per se doctrine.) Again, Driver's parking in front of the hydrant was negligent only in that it increased the risk that fire trucks couldn't get access to the hydrant to fight a fire. Again, therefore, Driver's negligence has not increased this risk, and therefore is not the proximate cause of Passenger's injuries.

43. Yes. A defendant who behaves negligently will be liable for additional damage caused by foreseeable rescue efforts, even if these rescue efforts were themselves conducted with negligence. It is foreseeable that ambulance drivers will sometimes travel too fast and get in accidents, so Dan's negligence was the proximate or "legal" cause of Patti's death. (But the result would be different if the ambulance driver behaved in a totally bizarre, unforeseeable, and dangerous manner. For instance, if the driver knew that Patti had sustained only mild non-life-threatening injuries that could wait half an hour for medical attention, and the driver travelled at 80 m.p.h. in a 25 m.p.h. zone in order to shorten the trip from 10 minutes to 3 minutes, Dan would not have been liable for Patti's death in the resulting ambulance crash.)

Exam Tips on
ACTUAL AND PROXIMATE CAUSE

D can't be liable for negligence (or any other tort) unless he in some sense "caused" the harm to P. When you deal with causation on an exam, you must always deal with two distinct issues: (1) was D the *"cause in fact"* or "factual cause" of the harm to P?; and (2) was D the *"legal cause"* or *"proximate cause"* of the harm to P?

☞ Even if there's no true "issue" on either of these types of causation, you should *discuss each* at least briefly in your essay answer, since they're part of P's prima facie case. (*Sample answer where both types of causation are clear:* "Since D hit P while driving carelessly, D is clearly the 'cause in fact' of P's broken leg, because that leg wouldn't have been broken had D not driven his car into P. Also, D is clearly the proximate or legal cause of the injuries, since it was quite foreseeable that D's careless driving in this situation might cause injury to a pedestrian like P, and there were no intervening factors.")

☞ Here's what to look for concerning *"cause in fact"*:

   ☞ In virtually every situation except one, use the *"but for"* standard — D's negligent act is the "cause in fact" of the harm to P *if the harm would not have happened "but for" D's negligent act*. (*Example:* "D's speeding was the "but for" cause of P's broken leg, because but for D's speeding, D could have stopped or swerved in time, or P could have jumped out of the way. . . . ")

      ☞ Usually, the fact pattern on an exam is such that the "but for" test is satisfied. But you must look out for the occasional fact pattern where the accident or injury *"would have happened anyway"* even without D's negligence, so the "but for" is not satisfied. (*Example:* D1 negligently maintains a telephone pole so it rots. D2 negligently drives his car into the pole, knocking the pole down so it hits P. You should say on your answer something like, "If D2 hit the pole so hard that it would have fallen even had it not been rotten, then the court will treat D1's negligence as not being the "but for" cause, or cause in fact, of the impact to P.")

☞ The one time you shouldn't use the "but for" test is where the facts disclose two *"concurrent causes," each of which would have been enough by itself* to cause the harm. Here, you should use the *"substantial factor"* test — if one of the causes was a "substantial factor" in bringing the harm about, it's deemed a cause-in-fact even though the other cause could have sufficed alone. (So both causes are likely to be found "causes in fact" on this scenario.) (*Example:* D1 and D2 are each bar-owners. Each serves X enough alcohol to get X legally drunk. X hits P with his car. The facts suggest that even a just-barely-legally-drunk driver probably would have hit P. D1 and D2 are each a "substantial factor" in P's injury, and thus each is a cause-in-fact, even though neither is truly a "but for" cause since the accident would have happened based solely on the drinks served by one.)

☞ Don't forget the *standard of proof* for causation (as well as for the other elements of negligence): P has to prove actual causation by a *"preponderance of the evidence"* (i.e, that it's *"more likely than not"* that P's injury was caused in fact by D's negligence).

  ☞ But in a *medical-malpractice* scenario, be on the lookout for a *"value of a chance"* problem. Even if correct medical diagnosis treatment would have increased P's chance of a good outcome but to less than 50%, P can still recover. What he recovers is the value of a good outcome (versus the bad outcome P actually suffered), but multipled by a fraction representing the percentage-chance that the good outcome would have occurred with adequate and timely treatment.

  Example: Doc fails to catch P's early-stage cancer (which adequate diagnosis would have caught). P dies one year later as a result. Assume that if Doc had caught the cancer at the early stage and treated P right away, P would have had a 30% chance of being cured instead of dying in a year. P can recover an amount equal to:

    (the value of a complete cure) *times*
    (30%, the chance that prompt treatment would have cured him).

☞ You'll often have two *serial* causes. If so, distinguish between two situations:

  ☞ In one situation, both causes are necessary (and neither is sufficient alone) to cause a *single injury*. In that instance, *both* are "causes in fact." (*Example:* D1 drives negligently onto the sidewalk, forcing P, a pedestrian, to jump into the street. D2 comes along driving too fast, and hits P because he can't stop in time. D1's and D2's careless acts are each "but for" causes, and thus "causes in fact," because, as to each, we can say that the impact wouldn't have happened "but for" that careless act.)

  ☞ In the other situation, you have two causes, but you have *two sets of injuries* (an earlier set and a later set). Here, the earlier tortfeasor will be liable for *both* sets of injuries, but the later tortfeasor will typically be liable only for the *later set* of injuries. (*Example:* D1 hits P with his car, breaking P's leg. D2, an ambulance driver, taking

P to the hospital, crashes, breaking P's arm. D1 is the cause in fact of both the leg and the arm injuries, but D2 is the cause in fact of *only the arm injury*.)

☞ You'll often have to **speculate** in your answer about whether D is a cause in fact, based on "what would have happened" if D had behaved differently. Your speculation is especially likely where D's negligence consisted of **failing to act**. Keep in mind that the "but for" element merely has to be established as "more likely than not." (*Example:* D abandons his stalled car in the road, without staying to warn other traffic. P, another driver, hits D's car and injures himself. You don't really know what would have happened if D had stayed around, so you'll have to speculate something like this: "If D had stayed around to warn oncoming traffic, he probably (but not certainly) would have been able to successfully warn P of the danger, thereby avoiding the accident. Consequently, D's failure to stay and warn should probably be treated as the "but for" cause of P's injuries.")

☞ For *"proximate cause,"* here's what to look for:

☞ Proximate cause generally boils down to whether the harm was *"foreseeable."* If it was reasonably foreseeable that D's behavior might (not would, just might) cause an injury somewhat like the one that happened to P, then you should probably conclude that D's behavior was the proximate cause of P's injury.

☞ A good definition of proximate cause to use on an exam is: "Conduct will be deemed to be a proximate cause of harm if the harm was a foreseeable result of the conduct, and if the harm was not brought about by an extraordinary or unforeseeable sequence of events."

☞ D's act (even though negligent) won't be a proximate cause unless it somehow increased the foreseeable risk of an accident *of a type like the one that happened*. You may want to quote the Third Restatement's test: a defendant is "not liable for harm *different from the harms whose risk made the [defendant's] conduct tortious.*"

Example: D builds a building using what he knows to be weak steel. Five years later, an earthquake occurs. The building falls on a gasoline truck, causing gas to leak into the roadway. The gas travels two blocks, to where X is standing. X throws a match, and the ensuing explosion hurts P. P probably loses: The harm whose risk made the use of weak steel negligent might include a building collapse. But it probably doesn't include a building's collapse, during an earthquake, onto a gasoline truck, followed by gasoline spillage that causes an explosion two blocks away. So the injury to P was a "harm different from the harms whose risk made the weak-steel-use negligent," preventing that injury from being the proximate result of D's negligent use of steel.

☞ One common exam fact pattern illustrating this "scope of risks" principle: D's negligence causes someone (D, P or a third person) to be in a particular place at a *different time* — or at a *different place* altogether — than if D hadn't acted. Assuming that being in the place at that different time or being in that different place wasn't inherently and foreseeably more risky, then D's initial act is *not* the proximate cause of the harm that ensues. (*Example:* D is a pilot who misreads his fuel gauge before taking off, and has less gas than he thinks. D is therefore forced to make a landing at an airport that isn't his final destination. While the plane is on the runway, parked properly, P's plane collides with it. D's negligence is not the proximate cause of the crash, because although it put the plane where it wouldn't have otherwise been, this didn't materially increase the risk of a crash — falling out of the sky, not being parked on a particular runway, was the kind of risk that made D's misreading negligent in the first place.)

☞ This "scope of risk" analysis is also used in negligence *per se* cases — if the type of accident that occurred wasn't the type of accident the statute was designed to prevent, then D's violation of the statute isn't the proximate cause of the accident. (*Example:* A motorist who violates a statute requiring a certain amount of insurance has an accident while driving cautiously — the insurance violation is not the proximate cause of the accident.)

☞ In any proximate-cause scenario, be alert to the allocation of **decision-making** as between **the judge and the jury**. Remember, the judge instructs the jury on what legal test to apply in deciding whether D's tortious conduct proximately caused the harm to P (and the jury then applies that test). However, if the judge believes that **no reasonable jury could find** that D's conduct was the proximate cause of the harm, the judge can **take the case away** from the jury (by issuing a directed verdict or summary judgment for D).

    ☞ But say that usually, the judge will conclude that the jury could decide the proximate-cause issue **either way**, in which case the judge will let the jury make the decision.

☞ Unforeseen **medical complications** suffered by P are often tested. Here, as long as D was the proximate cause of **some** harm to P, the fact that the harm was much worse than anticipated is irrelevant. This is the **"eggshell skull"** problem. Quote the classic rule here: "D takes P as he finds him." (*Example:* P has one eye. D's negligence causes P to lose that eye. D is responsible for total blindness.)

☞ Most proximate cause issues involve **intervening events**, either by nature or by people. Whenever you see an initial careless act by one person, followed by another act or event by nature or someone else, that's probably a tip-off to ask whether the first person's act was the proximate cause of the eventual injury.

    ☞ In this "intervening event" situation, the basic issue is still **foreseeability** — if the intervening act/event was reasonably foreseeable, it doesn't block the first event from being a proximate cause. If the intervening act/event was unforeseeable, it's probably **"superseding,"** i.e., it prevents the first act from being the proximate cause.

    ☞ Courts sometimes distinguish between **"dependent"** and **"independent"** intervening acts. (On this view, a dependent act occurs in response to D's act, such as a rescue of a victim injured by D, whereas an independent act would have happened anyway but without the bad consequences.) However, the distinction is not that significant — you may want to classify the particular event, but then you should probably ignore the distinction.

    ☞ Many fact patterns involve D's failure to foresee the **negligence or intentional**

wrongdoing of third persons. Often, the facts will be such that this third-party wrongdoing is foreseeable, and thus not superseding. *Examples:*

❏ D leaves the key in the ignition of his car. The risk that X will steal the car and injure a pedestrian is probably foreseeable (and is probably part of the same general risk that makes leaving a key in the ignition negligence in the first place), so D will be the proximate cause of the injury to the pedestrian.

❏ D leaves explosives around. X, a terrorist, steals them. (This is foreseeable, if one who deals in explosives should know that these are attractive to terrorists or other criminals.)

❏ D leaves his car in an intersection where no parking is allowed. Careful drivers would be able to avoid it, but the car is hit by a careless speeding driver, X. D will still be a proximate cause of the damage. (As a general rule, the negligence of other drivers on the road is probably ***always*** foreseeable, so a third party's negligence in driving is almost never superseding.)

☞ ***Rescuers*** are often part of the fact pattern. General rule: the rescue is a foreseeable response to an accident or injury. Therefore, the initial tortfeasor will still be on the hook when either the injured person is hurt worse, or the rescuer is hurt. This is true even if the rescuer behaves negligently. Quote Cardozo: "Danger invites rescue." (*Example:* D hurts P. P is then injured worse when the ambulance is speeding to the hospital and gets into an accident. D is responsible for the worsened injuries to P.)

☞ But if it's the rescuer that gets hurt, check to see whether she's a firefighter, police officer, or other person "paid to assume" that type of risk. Most states apply the ***"firefighters' rule,"*** under which such ***professional-risk-takers can't recover*** against the person who negligently caused the need for the rescue.

☞ Remember that ***medical malpractice*** is usually deemed foreseeable and thus not superseding. (*Example:* D1 hurts P slightly. D2, a doctor, hurts P worse while treating him. D1 is the proximate cause of the whole set of injuries.) But "gross" medical negligence (e.g., the doctor operates on the wrong leg) is probably superseding.

☞ Sometimes ***"responsibility shifting"*** is tested. If X is ***aware*** of the risk caused by D, but ***consciously disregards*** that risk, then X's going forward generally supersedes, and shifts the risk away from D to X. This principle applies in strict products liability, not just negligence cases. (*Example:* D manufactures a car. Two years later, D discovers that a part was defective, and notifies X (the owner) that D is recalling the car and will fix it for free. X gets the message, but declines to take up the offer. Three years later, X sells the car to P, who is later injured in a crash caused by the defect. X's conscious disregard of the risk will probably be deemed to shift the responsibility away from D to X, so P can't recover from D. (But this probably isn't true where X doesn't get the recall message; here, D's initial fault is still the proximate cause of P's injury.))

CHAPTER 7

JOINT TORTFEASORS

ChapterScope

This chapter deals with situations in which more than one defendant is liable for some or all of the harm suffered by the plaintiff. The key concepts in this chapter are:

- **Joint liability:** If more than one person is a proximate cause of the plaintiff's harm, and the harm is *"indivisible," each defendant* is liable for the *entire harm*. The liability in this situation is said to be *"joint-and-several."*

- **Contribution:** A defendant who has paid to the plaintiff more than his pro rata share of damages will usually be able to recover *partial reimbursement* from the other defendants. Such partial reimbursement is referred to as *"contribution."*

- **Indemnity:** Sometimes, courts will *shift* the entire financial responsibility for the tort from one defendant to the other (even though both are jointly and severally liable). This is done by the doctrine of *indemnity*.

I. JOINT LIABILITY

A. **Joint liability for concurrent wrongdoing:** The chapter on proximate cause was replete with cases in which more than one person behaved negligently, or otherwise wrongfully. When this is the situation, may the plaintiff recover against all of them, and if so, in what amounts relative to her overall injury?

1. **Joint liability for indivisible result (traditional rule):** First, it is necessary to determine whether each of the defendants was a proximate cause of the plaintiff's harm. (Recall that, as stated *supra*, p. 142, the plaintiff's harm may have more than one proximate cause, i.e., two or more events which substantially contributed to it, and which are so closely related to it as to give rise to liability.) If more than one person is a proximate cause of the plaintiff's harm, and the harm is *indivisible,* then under the *traditional common-law rule, each defendant* is liable for the *entire harm*. The liability is said to be *"joint-and-several."*

   a. **Consequence:** Therefore, under this rule the plaintiff may sue and collect from *either* of them or *both* of them. (But of course she is only entitled to recover a sum equal to her overall damages — i.e., she cannot collect twice.)

   Example: D1 and D2, each driving her own car, approach each other at an intersection. Each has a stop sign, and each runs that stop sign. The two cars collide. The resulting force pushes D2's car onto the sidewalk, where it hits P, a pedestrian. P suffers $100,000 in damages. In a jurisdiction following the traditional rule of joint-and-several liability, P will be entitled to a judgment against both D1 and D2 for $100,000. Then, P can recover the full judgment from D1, the full judgment from D2, or part from D1 and part from D2, all at P's sole option. (However, P may not recover a total of more than $100,000.) This is true even if the trier fact concludes that D1 was much more at fault than D2.

    i. Risk of one defendant's insolvency: The biggest effect of the traditional joint-and-several-liability rule is that if one defendant is or becomes ***insolvent***, the risk of that insolvency is ***put on the remaining defendant(s)***, not on the plaintiff. Thus in the above example, if D1 has no assets or insurance, P will still recover her full damages, because she can get them all from D2.

  b. Similar liability for both joint and concurrent tortfeasors: The traditional rule making each defendant liable for the entire indivisible harm applies whether the defendants are ***concurrent*** tortfeasors (those whose ***independent*** acts concurred to proximately cause the injury) or ***joint*** tortfeasors (those who have acted in concert).

2. Indivisible harm: But this traditional rule of joint-and-several liability applies only where the plaintiff's harm is not capable of ***apportionment*** between or among the defendants. If there is a rational basis for saying that some of the harm is the result of one defendant's act, and the remainder the result of the act of the other defendant, then each will be responsible only for that harm attributable to him. See Rest. 3d (Apport.) §26.

3. Modern trend cuts back on joint-and-several liability: There has been a very sharp trend in recent decades to ***cut back***, or even completely ***eliminate, joint-and-several liability.*** This trend has been caused mainly by the near-universal substitution of ***comparative*** negligence for ***contributory*** negligence.[1] (See *infra*, p. 282.) After all, if a plaintiff's recovery is to be diminished precisely in proportion to the ratio between his own culpable conduct and the total culpability of all parties, it seems reasonable to say that each defendant, too, ought to be liable only for her portion of the total culpability.

  a. Few states keep traditional rule: As of 2000, only 15 jurisdictions (Alabama, Arkansas, Delaware, Maine, Maryland, Massachusetts, Minnesota, North Carolina, Pennsylvania, Rhode Island, South Carolina, South Dakota, Virginia, and West Virginia, plus D.C.) maintained pure joint-and-several liability. And five of these 15 are the five states that have retained traditional contributory rather than comparative negligence. So less than one-quarter of comparative-negligence jurisdictions have retained joint-and-several liability. See Rest. 3d (Apport.) §17, Reporters' Note and tables.

  b. Hybrids: Many states have replaced joint-and-several liability with one of several *"hybrid"* schemes that combine aspects of joint-and-several liability with aspects of pure several liability. Here are the three most common types of hybrid schemes:

    ❏ **Hybrid joint-and-several liability with reallocation:** Under this approach, all defendants are jointly-and-severally liable, but if one defendant turns out to be judgment-proof, the court ***reallocates the damages*** to all other parties (including the plaintiff) in proportion to their comparative fault.

---

1. Whereas contributory negligence is an absolute bar no matter how minor plaintiff's fault is, comparative negligence is an apportionment system where, say, a plaintiff whose negligence accounts for 10% of the total fault by both parties has his recovery reduced by 10%.

> **Example:** P sues D1, D2 and D3 for an indivisible harm. P's damages are $100,000. The jury concludes that P is 10% responsible, D1 40%, D2 25% and D3 25%. D1 turns out to be judgment-proof. The court will reallocate based on D1's insolvency, so that D2 and D3 are each jointly-and-severally liable for 50/60ths of $100,000 (i.e., $83,333). The effect is that P and the remaining Ds will *share the burden* of D1's insolvency in a ratio to their relative fault. Cf. Rest. 3d (Apport.) §C21, Illustr. 1.

❏ **Hybrid liability based on threshold percentage:** Under this approach, a tortfeasor who bears more than a certain *"threshold"* percentage of the total responsibility remains jointly-and-severally liable, but tortfeasors whose responsibility is less than that threshold are merely severally liable.

> **Example:** Suppose that the jurisdiction has set a 25% threshold. P sues D1, D2 and D3 for an indivisible harm. P's damages are $100,000. The jury concludes that P is 10% responsible, D1 20%, D2 30% and D3 40%. D3 turns out to be insolvent. D1, because he is below the 25% threshold, is merely severally liable, and must therefore pay only $20,000 (20% of $100,000). Since D2 is above the threshold, he is jointly and severally liable for all the Ds' share (i.e., $90,000). This means that if P collects the $20,000 from D1, D2 can be required to pay $70,000 (i.e., his own share plus the full share of the insolvent D3.) Cf. Rest. 3d (Apport.) §D18, and Illustr. 1.

❏ **Hybrid liability based on type of damages:** Under this approach, liability remains joint-and-several for *"economic"* damages but several for *"non-economic"* damages.

> **Example:** P sues D1 and D2 for injuries arising out of a car accident. P's damages are $100,000, consisting of $40,000 in lost wages and $60,000 for pain and suffering. The jury concludes that P is blameless, D1 is 30% at fault and D2 70%. D2 turns out to be insolvent. In a state applying the economic/non-economic distinction, D1 will be required to pay the full $40,000 for P's lost wages (since these are economic damages for which D1 and D2 are jointly and severally liable), but only $18,000 (30% x $60,000) for P's pain and suffering (since these are non-economic damages, for which D1 and D2 are merely severally liable).

c. **Pure several liability:** 16 states now have *pure several liability* — in these states, a defendant, regardless of the nature of the case, is liable only for her share of total responsibility. See Rest. 3d (Apport.) §17, Table.

B. **No joint-and-several liability for divisible harms:** The traditional rule of joint-and-several liability, even when it applies, does *not apply* to so-called *"divisible"* harms. When two defendants each harm the plaintiff, but the harms can be readily *apportioned* into those caused by one defendant and those caused by the other, the harms are said to be divisible. In that event, each defendant is responsible *only for the harms that he himself caused.*

> **Example:** D1 and D2 each hates P. Acting independently but at virtually the same moment, D1 shoots P in the arm and D2 shoots him in the leg. The leg injuries are sufficiently distinguishable from the arm injuries that the two harms will be deemed to be

divisible. Suppose that the jury concludes that P's damages from the arm shooting should be valued at $10,000 and the leg shooting at $20,000. Because the harms are divisible, joint-and-several liability will not apply even in a jurisdiction that still ordinarily follows the traditional rule of joint-and-several liability. Consequently, P can collect only $10,000 from D1 and $20,000 from D2. If D2 turns out to be insolvent, P, not D1, will bear the burden of this insolvency, by being limited to a total recovery of $10,000.

1. **Action in concert:** But if the two defendants can be said to have acted *in concert*, each will be liable for injuries directly caused by the other, even if the harms caused by each are divisible. See Rest. 3d (Apport.) §15 ("When persons are liable because they acted in concert, all persons are jointly and severally liable. . . .")

   Example: D1 and D2 drag-race against each other on a public highway at twice the speed limit. The Ps are traveling in their car towards the speeding racers. D1, unable to steer his car back into the proper lane, collides with the Ps. D2 is not involved in the accident.

   Held, both Ds are fully liable, even though only one actually struck the Ps. " . . . All parties engaged in a motor vehicle race on the highway are wrongdoers acting in concert and . . . each participant is liable for harm to a third person arising from the tortious conduct of the other, because he has induced and encouraged the tort." *Bierczynski v. Rogers*, 239 A.2d 218 (Del. 1968).

   a. **Burden of proof:** In those situations where the harm is theoretically apportionable, but in practice difficult to do so, usually because of difficulties of proof, courts have sometimes *shifted the burden of proof* onto the defendants to demonstrate a reasonable allocation of harms. See, e.g., Rest. 3d (Apport.) §26, Comment h (stating that the best solution to the problem of proving the appropriate apportionment "is to place the burden of proof on the party seeking to avoid responsibility for the entire injury. . . .")

   Example: The Ps, a group of 37 residents, contend that the Ds, three corporations who own industrial plants, have polluted the air around the Ps' homes. The Ds contend that the Ps may not recover anything, because they cannot allocate responsibility among the various defendants.

   Held, for the Ps. Where, as here, dividing the harm is theoretically possible, but very difficult, the burden of proof as to who is responsible for what is shifted to the Ds. If none of the Ds can produce satisfactory proof as to who is responsible, all will be jointly and severally liable. *Michie v. Great Lakes Steel Div., Nat'l Steel Corp.*, 495 F.2d 213 (6th Cir. 1974).

2. **Successive incidents:** One situation in which courts are often able to apportion harm is where the harms have occurred in *successive incidents*, separated by substantial periods of time. See Rest. 2d, §433A, Comment c.

   Example: D1 operates a factory, and pollutes a stream from 1990 to 2000. The plant is sold to D2, which operates it and pollutes the same stream from 2001 through 2005. In a suit by the owner of land abutting the stream, the court will apportion the damage caused by D1 and that caused by D2 (probably by assessing a certain amount of damage per year of pollution, in which case D1 will pay twice what D2 pays). If the plaintiff is unable to collect the judgment against, say, D1, D2 will *not* be required to pay D1's portion. See Rest. 2d, §433A, Comment c.

a. **Consequence of non-apportionability:** In any scenario in which P is harmed in successive incidents involving multiple Ds, courts will usually place the ***burden of allocating the damages*** on the ***Ds***, not on P. In other words, if no one proves how much of P's damages from the two successive torts are reasonably allocated to D1 and how much to D2, the court will typically make the Ds jointly and severally liable, so that the tortfeasors, not the innocent plaintiff, bear the "burden of unallocability."

Example 1: P suffers upper-back injuries in a collision with D1. Six months later, P suffers lower-back injuries in a collision with D2. At P's trial of claims against D1 and D2 jointly, P is unable to produce evidence allocating her extreme and ongoing back pain between the upper-back injuries and the lower-back ones. Neither D1 nor D2 produces allocation-of-harm evidence.

A court will likely hold that D1 and D2 are jointly and severally liable, because if damages cannot be allocated, the tortfeasor defendants, not the innocent plaintiff, should bear the financial consequence of that impossibility.

Example 2: D1 and D2 both pollute a stream, poisoning P's livestock, and damaging P by $100,000. Neither D (nor P) offers proof allocating the damages as between D1 and D2. A court will likely hold D1 and D2 jointly and severally liable, on the theory that the uncertainty about how damages should be allocated between the two should hurt them, not P.

3. **Overlapping liability:** Even if the harm *is* apportionable among the various defendants, it may still be the case that more than one defendant is liable for all or a portion of the harm. For instance, if the defendant negligently breaks the plaintiff's leg, and a physician negligently treats the leg so that it becomes infected and has to be amputated, the original defendant will be liable for the full harm, including amputation (since he will be held to have been a proximate cause of the entire injury — see *supra*, p. 167); the physician, however, will only be liable for the worsening of the condition due to her negligence (i.e., the damage represented by having a broken leg become an amputated leg.)

4. **Indivisible harms:** Some types of harms, however, are not sensibly divisible into portions caused by each of the defendants. As to these indivisible harms, joint-and-several liability will apply to the extent that it remains in force in the particular jurisdiction.

a. **Death or single injury:** If the plaintiff ***dies***, for instance, as a result of concerted or independent acts by two defendants, each will be liable for the death, because death is not apportionable. This will similarly be the case for any other kind of ***single personal injury***.

b. **Fires:** Similarly, if the plaintiff's property is ***burned*** or otherwise destroyed, this will generally be an indivisible result. Thus in *Kingston v. Chicago & N.W. Ry., supra*, p. 142, in which a fire started by the defendant merged with a fire of unknown origin, and both destroyed the plaintiff's property, the defendant was held liable for the entire result. Recall that in cases involving such "concurrent causes" (*supra*, p. 142), the defendant will generally be liable if his conduct was a "but for" cause (and a proximate cause) of the damage, or a "substantial factor" in producing the result. If the harm is indivisible, then once the defendant is liable at all, he is liable for the whole harm.

   c. **Apportionment between guilty and innocent causes:** But if apportionment is feasible, it may be made between a guilty and an innocent cause, just as between two guilty ones. Thus in *Kingston, supra*, if it had been possible to show that half the plaintiff's property was burned by the unknown fire, and half by the fire caused by the defendant, the defendant would have had to pay only for the value of the half he burned.

II. SATISFACTION

   A. **Only one recovery:** As we have seen, a plaintiff may bring an action against any or all of the potential defendants in order to secure a judgment. However, she is entitled to only one *satisfaction* of her claim. Thus if D1 and D2 are jointly and severally liable for a $1,000,000 judgment in favor of P, and P recovers the full $1,000,000 from D1, she can't collect anything from D2. (D1 is probably entitled to "contribution" from D2; see *infra*, p. 189.)

   1. **Incomplete recovery:** If the recovery from one of the joint tortfeasors does not fully satisfy the claim, the amount received by the injured party is credited to the other defendants who may be liable.

III. RELEASE

   A. **Significance of release:** A plaintiff who has possible causes of action against two or more defendants may *settle* with one while pursuing a lawsuit against the remainder. Until recently, the precise manner in which she settled his claim against the one had grave consequences for her ability to pursue the others.

   1. **Release:** At common law, if the plaintiff gave a *"release"* to one defendant (i.e., a document absolving the latter of all liability), this was held to *release the other defendants as well.* This rule was the product of the common law fiction that a plaintiff had only one, indivisible, cause of action against all the joint tortfeasors, and it could not be extinguished as to one yet alive as to the others.

      a. **Covenant not to sue:** But if the settlement was embodied by a *"covenant not to sue"* (i.e., a contract in which the plaintiff promised not to sue, and would be liable in damages if she did) other defendants were not absolved of liability. Thus careful lawyers used the covenant not to sue rather than the release whenever there was any possibility of continuing the action against some other defendant.

   2. **Majority view:** Only two states, Washington and Virginia, still apply the common law rule that a release of one defendant relieves all others, even if the release explicitly provides otherwise. (On the other hand, most states hold that P's later recovery against the non-settling Ds must be *reduced* to account for the settlement/release. For more about this, see pp. 191-192 *infra*.)

a. **Where release is silent:** Also, most states, either by statute or case law, still completely relieve the non-settling defendants if the release is *silent* on the question of continuing liability of other defendants. See, e.g., *Cox v. Pearl Investment Co.*, 450 P.2d 60 (Colo. 1969).

IV. CONTRIBUTION

A. **Contribution generally:** Suppose that the case is one in which several defendants are theoretically jointly and severally liable (because each was a proximate cause of the plaintiff's indivisible harm). As we have seen, this means that the plaintiff may obtain a judgement against any one of the defendants, and collect the full amount from him. If this happens, does that defendant get stuck with the entire loss? Or may he instead turn to the other defendants and obtain at least a share from them?

1. **Sometimes available:** The answer is that the defendant who has paid more than his *pro rata* share may often obtain partial reimbursement from the other defendants; when he does so, he is said to have received *contribution*.

B. **Historically limited:** It has always been virtually universally held, both in England and America, that a *willful or intentional* tortfeasor has no right to contribution from his fellow wrongdoers. For a variety of historical reasons, this rule was extended during the latter part of the nineteenth century, to prevent contribution on behalf of *any* tortfeasor, even if he was merely "ordinarily" negligent.

1. **Changed by statute:** However, in recent years, more than half the states have enacted statutes permitting contribution among tortfeasors in various situations. These statutes are frequently patterned on the Uniform Contribution Among Tortfeasors Act. Another 9 states or so have judicially accepted contribution in at least some circumstances. See P&K, p. 337, fn. 12.

   Example: The Ps, guests in a car owned and operated by D, are injured when D's car collides with a taxicab, owned by X, and operated by Y, X's employee. The Ps sue X but not D. The jury finds that the accident was caused by the negligence of both D and Y, and awards damages against X on a theory of vicarious liability (see *infra*, p. 315). X, who has brought D into the suit as a third-party defendant, is given the right to collect from D half of the damages, if he pays the Ps the full amount of the judgment.

   Held, on appeal, the grant of the right of contribution to X from D was proper. It is irrelevant that there was no judgment obtained by the Ps against D. The common-law rule disallowing contribution between non-intentional tortfeasors is hereby overruled. Otherwise, the plaintiff and one defendant could gang up on another defendant, and force him to pay for the plaintiff's entire damages. *Knell v. Feltman*, 174 F.2d 662 (D.D.C. 1949).

   a. **Restatement allows:** The Third Restatement follows this majority view of allowing contribution among tortfeasors. See Rest. 3d (Apport.) §22(a): "When two or more persons are or may be liable for the same harm and one of them discharges the liability of another by settlement or discharge of judgment, the person discharging the liability is entitled to recover contribution from the other, unless the other previously had a valid settlement and release from the plaintiff."

2. **Amount of contribution:** To the extent that contribution has been allowed in the absence of statute, many courts have required each defendant to pay an *equal share*. See P&K, p. 340.

    a. **Comparative negligence:** But states adopting *comparative negligence* (see *infra*, p. 281), as the vast majority have now done, have often taken the similar step of making the duty of contribution proportional to fault.

        i. **Restatement agrees:** The Third Restatement agrees that the principles of comparative fault should govern the amounts of contribution that may be recovered by one tortfeasor against another. See Rest. 3d (Apport.) §22(b): "A person entitled to recover contribution [under §22(a), quoted above] may *recover no more* than the *amount paid to the plaintiff in excess of the person's comparative share* of responsibility."

            Example: P sues D1 and D2. The jury finds that P's damages total $100,000, and that P is 10% responsible, D1 is 30% responsible and D2 60%. Assume that the jurisdiction maintains joint-and-several liability in this situation. Assume that P recovers the full $90,000 (i.e., the 90% representing the defendants' collective share) from D1, as he is entitled to do under joint-and-several liability. Now, under the Restatement approach, D1 is permitted to recover only $60,000 in contribution from D2 — that is, D1's contribution recovery is limited to an amount that would put D1 in the position he would have been in had each party borne his own share of the responsibility (since in that event, D1 would have paid $30,000, or 30% of the damage total). See Rest. 3d (Apport.) §23, Illustr 5.

C. **Present limitations:** Use of the contribution doctrine is still limited, however, in certain important respects, even in those states which allow it.

    1. **No intentional torts:** Thus in many courts it is still the rule that an *intentional* tortfeasor may not have contribution from his co-tortfeasors. See P&K, p. 339.

    2. **Contribution defendant must have liability:** The contribution defendant (i.e., the co-tortfeasor who is being sued for contribution) must in fact be *liable to the original plaintiff*. If the contribution defendant has a defense that would bar his liability to the plaintiff, the other defendant may not have contribution against him even if the two acted in concert. And the contribution *plaintiff bears the burden of proving* in the contribution suit that the contribution defendant would have this liability to the original plaintiff.

        a. **Restatement agrees:** The Third Restatement agrees with this requirement that the contribution defendant must be liable to the original plaintiff. See Rest. 3d (Apport.) §23, Comment j, stating that normally, "A person seeking contribution must prove that the person against whom contribution is sought would have been liable to the plaintiff in an amount and share equal to or greater than the amount of contribution."

    3. **Other barriers to suit:** Most courts also bar a contribution suit against the employer of a plaintiff employee where a *Workers' Compensation* statute prevented the plaintiff from suing the employer in tort. (See *infra*, p. 339.) Similarly, where the plaintiff was an injured automobile passenger, who recovers against the driver of the other car involved in a collision, it is usually held that that driver cannot recover against the driver of the passenger's

car, where the passenger would have been barred from suit by an ***automobile guest statute.*** However, the major purpose of such guest statutes is to prevent collusion between passenger and driver, and this objective would not be weakened by permitting a contribution suit by the other driver. See P,W&S, p. 196.

D. Settlements: The most controversial issues in the law of contribution have involved ***settlements.*** There are two distinct issues: First, may a defendant who has settled with the plaintiff recover contribution from other potential defendants? Second, may a defendant who has settled be sued later by other defendants against whom a judgment is recovered?

1. **Settlement by contribution plaintiff:** Where there is no statutory provision on point, it is almost always held that a defendant who settles may turn around and ***obtain contribution*** from other potential defendants. However, he bears the burden of proving not only that he and these other defendants were actually liable, but also that the ***settlement amount was reasonable.*** See Rest. 3d (Apport.) §23, Comment h.

   a. **Restrictive statutes:** Several state statutes, however, allow only those defendants against whom a judgment has been rendered to obtain contribution from potential co-defendants.

2. **Settlement by contribution defendant:** The most controversial question of all is whether a defendant who has settled can later on be sued for contribution by another defendant against whom a judgment has been obtained by the plaintiff.

   a. **Traditional rule:** The traditional, majority, rule has been that the settling defendant ***can*** be later held liable for contribution. This is not a very good rule, however, since it greatly discourages any defendant from settling — he cannot settle and close the file, since he knows he may have contribution liability later on; therefore he has no incentive to settle.

   b. **No contribution, but plaintiff's claim is reduced:** The modern trend is to prevent this problem by imposing two rules:

      (1) the non-settling defendants who are found liable are ***not permitted to get contribution*** against the previously-settling defendant; but

      (2) the ***plaintiff's recovery*** against the non-settling defendants is ***reduced*** to account for the prior settlement.

      See Rest. 3d (Apport.) §23, Comment i (no contribution against prior settlers) and §16 (plaintiff's recovery against non-settlers reduced by proportion of responsibility assigned to settler). See also §8(b) of something called the Uniform Apportionment of Tort Responsibility Act, a uniform act promulgated in 2002 by the Commissioners on Uniform State Laws — §8(b) implements these same two rules.

      i. **How to reduce P's share:** Even within courts following this modern "reduce P's recovery against the non-settling Ds" approach, there is a further sub-issue: should the plaintiff's recovery against the non-settling defendants be reduced by (i) the ***dollar amount*** of the settlement (the ***"pro tanto"*** approach); or (ii) the ***proportion*** that the settling defendant's responsibility bears to the overall responsibility of all parties (the ***"comparative share"*** approach)? The Third Restatement follows the latter (comparative share) approach, as can be seen from the following example.

192 Ch. 7 — JOINT TORTFEASORS

Example: While P is a passenger in D1's car, that car collides with D2's car, and P is injured. P suffers $100,000 in damages. P sues D1 and D2, then settles with D1 for $20,000 before trial. At trial, the jury concludes that P was 20% responsible (because he distracted D1), D1 45% responsible, and D2 35%. Assume that the jurisdiction otherwise enforces joint-and-several liability in this situation. Under the Restatement's "comparative share" approach, D2 will be entitled to a $45,000 credit (D1's 45% share of comparative responsibility times $100,000 damages) on account of the settlement by D1. Therefore, P will only be able to recover $35,000 from D2. See Rest. 3d (Apport.) §16, Illustr. 1. See also Unif. Apport. Tort Resp. Act, §8(b). Compare this result with the result under the "pro tanto" approach, where D2 would get just a $20,000 credit (the dollar amount of the settlement), allowing P to collect $60,000 from him.

V. INDEMNITY

A. Concept of indemnity generally: Contribution is, as we have seen, a sharing of payment for joint liability. There are situations, however, in which, either out of a general sense of fairness, or because of a great difference in the degree of culpability of the two defendants, the court will *shift* the financial responsibility for the tort from one defendant to the other. This is done by the doctrine of *indemnity*; when the one tortfeasor pays some or all of the plaintiff's damages, he is indemnified by the other tortfeasor for *everything* that he paid. Thus indemnity is a 100% shifting of liability, whereas contribution is a sharing.

   1. Restatement's explanation: The Second Restatement, §886B(1), expresses the rationale for indemnity by saying that there shall be a shifting when one tortfeasor has paid the claim (discharging both), and the other would be *"unjustly enriched"* if he were not required to fully reimburse the first.

B. No general rule: It is impossible to state a general rule about when indemnity will be permitted. However, some of the more common situations in which it will be allowed are as follows:

   1. Vicarious liability: If one defendant is only *vicariously liable* for the other's conduct, the former will be indemnified. For instance, an employer is generally liable for the torts of his employee (*infra*, p. 315), and an employer who had to pay for such a tort could recover the full amount of the payment from the employee. See Rest. 3d (Apport.) §22(a)(2)(i).

   2. Retailer versus manufacturer: A *retailer* who is held *strictly liable* for selling a d*efective injury-causing* product will get indemnity from others further up the distribution chain, including the *manufacturer*.

   Example: A dangerously defective product causes injury to P. P sues (in strict product liability) the wholesaler who sold it to the retailer who sold it to P. If the wholesaler has to pay P, the wholesaler can get full indemnity from the manufacturer.

   a. Higher up the chain: In fact, more generally, anyone in the distribution chain who is held strictly liable can probably get indemnity from *anyone higher up in the chain*, especially where the higher-up person is more at fault. See Rest. 3d (Apport.) §22(a)(2)(ii).

Example 1: Manu, a manufacturer of a product whose defective design made it dangerous, is required to pay a strict product liability judgment to P, who was injured by the product. Manu licensed the design for the product from Des, an industrial designer. Manu made the product exactly according to Des' full set of specifications. Manu did not know, or have reason to know, of the product's defective design or dangerousness. Des will be required to fully indemnify Manu for the judgment.

Example 2: EngineCo sells an engine to Pilot for her private plane, and installs it. Due to a defect in the engine, the plane crashes into Paul's building. Paul recovers against Pilot's estate under strict liability for ground damage from airplanes (see *infra*, p. 335). Pilot's estate is entitled to full indemnity from EngineCo for the judgment it had to pay, even if EngineCo acted without fault in selling and installing the engine.

3. **Negligent vs. intentional tortfeasor:** If one tortfeasor is merely ***negligent***, and the other commits an ***intentional*** tort, the intentional tortfeasor will be required to indemnify the negligent one. This can happen, for instance, if D1's negligence consists of not preventing D2 from committing an intentional tort where D1 had an obligation to use reasonable care to prevent such a tort.

   Example: D1 negligently entrusts his car to his friend D2, knowing that D2 is unstable and often violent. D2 takes the car and purposely runs over P, D2's former girlfriend. P's estate recovers in negligence from D1 for entrusting the car to D2. D1 will be entitled to full indemnity from D2 for the judgment, since D2 was an intentional tortfeasor and D1 was merely negligent.

   a. **Dangerous condition on land:** The general principle that one is entitled to indemnity for failing to discover another's misconduct also means that a ***contractor*** who negligently constructs or repairs a building will usually be required to indemnify an ***owner*** who negligently or innocently fails to discover the defect, if the latter is liable to a tenant, guest, etc. who injures herself.

4. **Contract:** A ***contract*** between two tortfeasors may provide that one will indemnify the other. This is a frequent provision, for instance, in building contracts between a general contractor and sub-contractor.

Quiz Yourself on
JOINT TORTFEASORS *(Entire Chapter)*

44. Caesar and Antony are fighting over possession of an asp which slithered into a street from the woods. As they wrestle over it, Cleopatra walks by, and they accidentally bump into her with the snake. It bites her and she is seriously injured. She sues Caesar (but not Antony) in negligence, and recovers a $100,000 judgment from him. Is Caesar likely to be entitled to contribution from Antony? _____

45. Pompeii Canned Goods, Inc., ships cans of Vesuvius Stew to the Volcano Grocery Store. The cans are not properly sealed, and are starting to bulge due to bacteria growth. Volcano doesn't notice and puts them on the shelves anyway. Most of the city comes down with salmonella poisoning as a result of eating the

tainted stew. One purchaser who becomes violently ill, Frequentus Regurgitus, sues Volcano on a strict product liability theory, and recovers a $100,000 judgment. Is Volcano likely to be able to recover the entire $100,000 from Pompeii? _____

46. Aggressive, while riding her bicycle on the sidewalk (instead of on the street where she should be), and riding too fast, nearly hits Bystander. To avoid being hit, Bystander throws himself into the street. Bystander is not seriously injured by the impact with the street. However, before he can get up, Careless, who is driving his car too fast and not paying attention, runs over Bystander, causing Bystander's leg to be amputated. Bystander chooses to sue only Aggressive for his injuries. Under the common-law approach, may Bystander recover the full value of his lost leg from Aggressive? _____

Answers

44. **Yes.** Where joint tortfeasors act in concert and their negligence causes harm, and the plaintiff only sues one of the tortfeasors, that tortfeasor can seek contribution (partial reimbursement) from the other joint tortfeasor(s). If the jurisdiction follows comparative negligence, the court will probably apportion the liability between the two in proportion to their fault. In a non-comparative-negligence jurisdiction (and in some comparative-negligence states), the court will split the liability evenly regardless of which tortfeasor was most at fault. Without the doctrine of contribution (which applies in most but not all states), Caesar could not recover anything from Antony, since this is a case of "joint liability": Caesar and Antony acted in concert, and the damages are indivisible.

NOTE: Since Cleopatra recovered the entire judgment from Caesar, her claim has been "satisfied," and she can't proceed against Antony. Also, note that Cleopatra could have sued Caesar and Antony in the same lawsuit, recovered a judgment against them, and then proceeded to collect from either one or partially from both — her choice — until her claim was satisfied. Finally, note that the rule of "contribution" is not applicable to intentional torts.

RELATED ISSUE: Say Antony and Caesar each had an asp, and each negligently let his asp bite Cleo, injuring her with two separate wounds. The damages would be divisible, and thus joint liability would not apply.

45. **Yes.** Keeping in mind that rules on indemnity vary from state to state, a situation like this is one where indemnity would likely be applied. If the defendant is liable only because he failed to discover another's misconduct, he will normally be entitled to indemnity. A manufacturer who produces defective goods will generally be required to indemnify a retailer who resells the goods and incurs strict liability (as long as the retailer did not *know* of the defect). Volcano can recover the entire $100,000 from Pompeii.

NOTE: Where strict liability is involved, all subsequent suppliers can seek indemnity from those before them in the supply chain, so that the manufacturer — or whoever is responsible for the defect — is ultimately responsible as long as the item was in a defective condition unreasonably dangerous to the user or consumer when it left his control. (Strict liability is liability without fault; that is, liability without regard to how careful the defendant was.")

46. **Yes.** Both Aggressive and Careless were proximate and "but for" causes of the injury to Bystander. Therefore, under the common-law approach they are jointly and severally liable for the damage to Bystander. (The joint-and-several rule applies only where the harm is not capable of apportionment, and a single injury or death is never apportioned.) Because of the joint-and-several liability, Bystander may get a judgment (and collect it) against either Aggressive alone, Careless alone, or both. (However, Bystander may only collect a single time.) See Rest. 2d, §879, and Illustr. 2 thereto. If Bystander collects the full judg-

ment against Aggressive, Aggressive will be entitled to contribution from Careless.

Note, however, that the result would be different in many states today: many states have statutorily abolished joint-and-several liability in many or all contexts, and in such a state Aggressive might be liable for only her pro rata share of the damage (e.g., in a comparative-negligence jurisdiction, her percentage of fault).

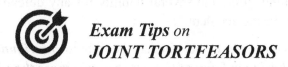

Exam Tips on
JOINT TORTFEASORS

Whenever you have multiple tortfeasors, consider whether they will be *"jointly and severally liable."*

☞ General rule: If more than one person is an actual and proximate cause of P's harm, and the harm is indivisible, each D is liable for the ***entire harm***.

☞ Often-tested issue: "Was the harm to P ***indivisible***?" If not, there is no joint-and-several liability. (*Example:* D1 and D2 shoot at P. D1 hits P in the leg, D2 hits him in the eye. If we can apportion the harm, including pain and suffering — which we can do here — then there's no joint-and-several liability; each D pays only for the harm he himself caused.)

☞ If the harm is theoretically divisible, but P has no allocation evidence (i.e., P can't show which of two or more Ds was responsible for which harm), the court may put the ***burden of proof on the Ds*** to show this. (*Example:* P shows that D1 and D2, acting separately, poisoned his stream by pollution at different times. If P can't come up with evidence of which harms were due to which D's acts, the court may say that it's up to the Ds to produce such proof, and if they can't they're jointly and severally liable.)

☞ If joint-and-several liability applies, then P can collect the ***entire amount*** from whichever single defendant he wishes. Alternatively, he may collect some from each. (P is of course limited to one total recovery.)

☞ Two common contexts for joint-and-several liability:

   ☞ ***Employer/employee*** — each is jointly and severally liable (the employer on a "vicarious liability" theory).

   ☞ Where a ***dangerous product*** injures the consumer, both the ***manufacturer*** and the ***retailer*** will be jointly and severally liable if P recovers in strict product liability.

☞ Very often tested: The interaction between traditional joint-and-several liability and ***comparative*** negligence.

   ☞ If there is no statute dealing specifically with this interaction, then joint-and-several liability ***persists*** as to that portion of the total fault that is not the plaintiff's. (*Example:* P has total, indivisible, injuries of $100,000. The jury finds that P was 30% at fault, D1 was 50% at fault and D2 20%. The jurisdiction has a comparative negligence statute, but no statute addressing joint-and-several liability. P can only collect $70,000, which he can collect all from D1, all from D2 or in a mix.)

☞ Some states now have special statutes limiting joint-and-several liability in connection with comparative negligence. If your facts are silent about whether such a statute is in force, you might want to give the traditional analysis as in the prior paragraph, and then speculate. (*Example:* "But the state may have a statute, as a number of states now do, abolishing joint-and-several liability for any defendant found to be less than 50% at fault for the accident.")

☛ Whenever you have multiple tortfeasors, consider whether one has the right to *contribution* from the other(s). Contribution is a *cost-sharing* in favor of one who has paid *more than his proportionate share* of the total liability.

☞ Under classic common-law contribution, the court makes each defendant pay an *equal* net amount. (*Example:* D1 and D2 are found jointly and severally liable for P's $100,000 in injuries. P collects $70,000 from D1 and $30,000 from D2. Under the common-law approach, D1 can get contribution of $20,000 from D2, since this is the amount needed to equalize their shares.)

☞ No contribution right is given to an *intentional* tortfeasor (even against another intentional tortfeasor).

☞ Most commonly-tested issue: the interaction between contribution and *comparative negligence*. Here, most comparative negligence states have statutes requiring contribution *in proportion to fault*. (*Example:* P has a $100,000 loss. The jury says that P was 25% responsible, D1 25% and D2 50%. Assume that P recovers the whole $75,000 from D1 (which he can, provided the state doesn't have a statute changing the traditional joint-and-several liability rule in comparative negligence cases). In most states, D1 can get contribution of $50,000 from D2, since that's the amount that would adjust the shares of D1 and D2 in proportion to the jury's finding of fault.)

☛ Whenever you have multiple tortfeasors, consider whether one has the right to be *indemnified* by the other(s). Indemnity refers to a *complete reimbursement*, not a cost-sharing. It is usually given where one tortfeasor is clearly less culpable than the other.

☞ Most commonly, the right of indemnity exists where one D is only *vicariously* liable, and the other is directly liable. *Examples:*

❑ Employer can get indemnification from Employee (assuming that employer had no direct fault, and his only liability was vicarious).

❑ Retailer can get indemnity from Manufacturer in a strict product liability case. (In fact, anyone in a distribution chain held strictly liable can recover against *anyone higher up* in the chain — so Retailer can get indemnity from Wholesaler, and Wholesaler can in turn get indemnity from Manufacturer.)

❑ Where Owner is liable for accident by Driver from having allowed Driver to drive Owner's vehicle (this is the result of Owner consent statute), Owner will get indemnity from Driver.

CHAPTER 8

DUTY

ChapterScope

This chapter covers several quite distinct scenarios where courts may hold that P cannot recover because D did not owe P any "duty." The main concepts in this chapter are:

- **Failure to act:** The law does not impose any general *"duty to act."* Therefore, as a general rule, D cannot be liable for merely failing to give P assistance. (But there are many exceptions.)

- **Effect of a contract:** Where the source of D's duty to P lies in a **contract**, courts usually do not allow P to sue in tort for D's failure to perform, and instead require that the suit be brought on a breach-of-contract theory.

- **Mental suffering:** Plaintiffs are sometimes allowed to recover for *mental suffering* caused by the defendant's conduct, even where the plaintiff has not suffered physical injuries. Most controversial is whether P should be allowed to recover for mental anguish at seeing a loved one be injured.

- **Unborn children:** D may be liable for injuries inflicted on a *fetus*.

- **Pure economic loss:** Courts are split as to whether P may recover for *"pure economic loss,"* unaccompanied by physical injury or property damage. The modern view is to allow P to recover for such economic loss (e.g., loss of business profits) if P was a member of an "identifiable class" that D knew or should or have known would be likely to suffer economic loss from D's conduct.

I. "DUTY" GENERALLY

- **A. Introduction:** In the list of elements of a negligence cause of action given on p. 96, *supra*, one requirement was that the defendant owe the plaintiff a *"duty of care"*. In most tort cases, this duty is simply the duty of behaving towards the plaintiff with the degree of care that a reasonable person would exercise in like circumstances. In such cases, the courts devote relatively little attention to this general requirement of duty, since it is so uniform; instead, they spend most of their energies looking at whether the defendant's conduct met this duty.

  1. **Special cases:** There are several classes of cases, however, where the courts have held that the defendant owes the plaintiff something less than or more than the exercise of the degree of care a reasonable person would use. Sometimes, courts have held that the defendant owes the plaintiff no duty at all. For instance, we saw in *Palsgraf, supra*, p. 158, that, under the theory of that case, the defendant owed no duty at all to a plaintiff who was outside the scope of the risk imposed by the defendant's negligence. And we have alluded several times to the rules governing common carriers, who are held to a higher standard of care (the obligation to use extreme care) towards their passengers.

2. **Scope of this chapter:**   This chapter considers several kinds of cases in which, because of either the nature of the plaintiff (e.g. an unborn child), the type of harm suffered (e.g., pure mental suffering, with no physical effects) or the plaintiff's relation to an occurrence (e.g. mere bystander), the defendant is held to have violated no duty to the plaintiff.

    a. **Conclusory term:**   As will be quickly seen in these cases, courts use the concept of "duty" in a highly conclusory manner. That is, because they wish to avoid allowing recovery, they state that the defendant owed no duty to the plaintiff to avoid the harm in question. The concept of duty is thus similar to that of proximate cause, and many of the cases discussed in this chapter could have been treated in the previous one.

        i. **Illustration:** For instance, in a case raising the question whether the plaintiff may recover for emotional suffering not accompanied by physical symptoms (to which the answer is almost always "no"), the case may be decided on the basis of whether the defendant owes the plaintiff a duty to avoid this kind of harm (the approach followed here) or, by contrast, on the basis of whether emotional harm unaccompanied by physical harm can ever be so foreseeable and closely related to the defendant's conduct that the latter should be held to be the proximate cause of the former.

    b. **Other examples:**   Other situations in which the usual standard of duty is modified are considered in other chapters. The most important of these involves *owners and occupiers of land*, treated in a separate chapter beginning *infra*, p. 237. *Vicarious liability* of employers, car owners, etc. may also be seen as a modification of the general duty of care; such liability is discussed *infra*, p. 315.

II. FAILURE TO ACT

A. **No general duty to act:**   Can a person be liable in tort solely on the grounds that she has *failed to act?* The general answer to this question given by the common law, an answer which continues today, is *"no."*

1. **Misfeasance v. nonfeasance:**   Thus the law distinguishes sharply between *misfeasance* (i.e., an affirmative act which harms or endangers the plaintiff) and *nonfeasance* (a mere passive failure to take action). All the cases we have seen thus far involved defendant's conduct of the former category. Many of the cases refusing liability for nonfeasance which we will examine here are generally considered absolutely scandalous by commentators, and are a unique product of Anglo-American law with almost no counterpart in other Western countries.

2. **Duty to protect or give aid:**   Most nonfeasance cases arise when the defendant sees that the plaintiff is in danger, and *fails to render assistance,* even though she could do so easily and safely. As stated, the rule is that unless there is some *special relationship* between the defendant and the plaintiff, the former is *not liable for her refusal to assist.* See Rest. 2d, §314.

    Example: P is rowing his boat on a lake. P falls off, and while struggling, yells for help. D, a passer-by on the shore, sees this, and could easily throw P a life-preserver from the shore. But D does nothing, because she's late for a tennis game. If P drowns and his estate sues D, D will win — since there was no special relationship between D and P, D had no obligation to assist P no matter how vital and easy-to-give this assistance would have been.

B. Exceptions: Courts have, however, carved out an increasing number of *exceptions* to this general rule.

1. **Special relationship:** One category of exceptions involves situations where a plaintiff and a defendant have some *special relationship* to each other.

   a. **Common carriers and innkeepers:** Thus it has always been the case that certain callings imposed a duty to furnish assistance to patrons. This has been true of *common carriers* with respect to their passengers and *innkeepers* with respect to their guests.

      Example: The Ps are passengers on board a bus operated by D, a public common carrier, when a violent argument erupts among a group of other passengers. The bus driver is notified of the situation but continues to drive the bus and fails to take any measures to protect his passengers. The Ps are injured in the violence, and sue D for negligence.

      Held, because of the special relationship between a common carrier and its passengers, D had a duty to use utmost care and diligence to protect the Ps from the assaults. Bus passengers have no control over who enters the bus, and are dependent on the driver to summon help or provide a means of escape if trouble arises. Depending on the situation, this duty of care might be satisfied by a warning to the rowdy passengers, stopping the bus until the trouble subsides, installing a radio to allow contact with the police, or other measures — the point is that the bus company and driver have a duty to do more than merely stand by while passengers are subject to danger. Nor does the fact that D is a public rather than private carrier make any difference — although governments in general, and police departments in particular, are not liable for failing to protect the public against assaults, a common carrier owes such a duty of protection to passengers who have "accepted the carrier's offer of transportation and have put their safety, and even their lives, in the carrier's hands. . . . " *Lopez v. Southern California Rapid Transit District*, 710 P.2d 907 (Cal. 1985).

   b. **Business relationships:** In recent years, most courts have extended this rule imposing a duty of care to *business generally*: anyone who maintains business premises must use reasonable care to furnish warning and assistance to a business visitor, regardless of the source of the danger or harm. See Rest.2d, §314A.

      Example: P, 6 years old, is shopping with his mother in the D Department Store. Through no negligence of D, P's fingers get caught in the escalator and severed. D unreasonably delays calling for an ambulance, thereby aggravating P's injuries.

      P will be entitled to damages for the aggravation of his injuries. Since D operated business premises, D and its employees had an affirmative duty to make reasonable efforts to assist anyone who came into peril on the premises.

   c. **Employer:** Similarly, it has been established for a long time that an *employer* must give warning and assistance to an employee who is endangered or injured during the course of his employment.

d. Third Restatement has seven categories: The new Third Restatement list seven types of "special relationships" that impose a duty of care " with regard to risks that arise within the scope of the relationship." The list includes these relationships:

[1] "a common carrier with its passengers";

[2] "an *innkeeper* with its *guests*";

[3] "a *business* or other possessor of land that *holds its premises open to the public* with those who are *lawfully on the premises*";

[4] "an *employer* with its *employees* who are: (a) in imminent danger; or (b) injured and thereby helpless";

[5] "a *school* with its *students*";

[6] "a *landlord* with its *tenants*"; and

[7] "a *custodian* with *those in its custody*, if a) the custodian is required by law to take custody or voluntarily takes custody of the other; and b) the custodian has a *superior ability to protect* the other." (*Example*: The duty of a jailer to a prisoner.)

See Rest. 3d (Liab. for Phys. & Emot. Harm) §41.

e. Transient or "ad hoc" relationships: Plaintiffs have sometimes tried to persuade courts to extend the list of "special relationships" that will trigger a duty to render assistance. Some of these suggestions concern *"ad hoc"* relationships, i.e. *transient relationships* that were formed shortly before the episode in question. By and large, courts have *resisted* these suggestions — only the types of relationships typically recognized as having legal significance in other contexts, and arising well before the present occasion, are usually found to trigger a duty of due care. (Notice that all of the seven relationships (listed above) recognized by the third restatement fall into this category.)

i. No relationship based on "witnessing an emergency": For example, some plaintiffs have argued that the court ought to recognize a special relationship as existing between a *person who faces a sudden life-threatening injury* and another person who *witnesses that injury at close proximity* and has the *opportunity to summon help.* But this argument has generally been *rejected* by the courts, on the theory that recognizing this type of relationship as imposing a duty to summon assistance would swallow up the "no duty to assist" general rule, and would present *no logical stopping point.*

Example: Jennifer Lane and Joshua Cilley have previously been in a romantic relationship, but have since broken up. Cilley visits Lane's trailer, and Lane asks him to leave. Cilley grabs a rifle, and while Lane is not looking, shoots himself, and falls to the floor. Lane does not see any blood, and does not investigate;

instead, she visits a friend in a nearby trailer, whom she tells that Cilley has "pretended" to shoot himself in her trailer. The friend goes to the trailer, investigates, sees that Cilley is turning white, and calls 911. Cilley is taken to the hospital, where he dies of a single gunshot wound to his abdomen; the ER doctor concludes that Cilley could have been resuscitated if he had arrived at the hospital five or 10 minutes earlier. Cilley's estate sues Lane for negligently failing to call 911. The estate argues that the court should recognize a new form of "special relationship," that between a person suffering an acute injury and one who witnesses that injury – according to the estate, the witness should be held to have the narrow duty to "contact emergency assistance."

Held, for Lane. The "relationship" identified by the estate — the witnessing of an injury — is "unlike any other relationship recognized as sufficient to create a duty of care." The relationships that have been recognized as triggering such a duty all involve either (1) a close pre-existing relationship between the parties, or (2) some measure of control by the person with the duty over either the endangered person (e.g., employer-employee or parent-child) or the location (e.g., a landowner and an invitee who is endangered while on the premises). The relationship asserted here — based solely on "presence at the opportune moment" — does not have either this pre-existing nature or this element of control. Furthermore, the duty urged by the estate would have no obvious limiting point: "each person would be obligated to contact emergency assistance anytime she witnessed another's injury, which would indeed be a duty without any practical limit." *Estate of Cilley v. Lane*, 985 A.2d 481 (Me. 2009).

Note: Observe that the court in *Cilley* missed a relatively easy "peg" on which to hang on Lane a duty to summon assistance. It's true that Cilley was not Lane's "social guest" at the time of the shooting, since she had asked him to leave, making him a trespasser, not an invitee.[1] But many courts impose on the possessor of land a duty to use due care towards a *discovered trespasser*. See, e.g., Rest. 3d (Liab. For Phys. & Emot. Harm), §52(b)(1), placing a possessor of land under a duty to exercise reasonable care where a trespasser "reasonably appears to be imperiled and helpless." Since when Cilley was lying there injured he was on Lane's property, this exception, if recognized in Maine, would seem to have been applicable (at least assuming that Lane recognized or should have recognized Cilley's peril and helplessness). Cf. D,H&B (7th Ed.), p. 501.

2. **Defendant involved in injury:** A second major category of exceptions is that the defendant will have a duty of warning and assistance if the danger or injury is *due to her own conduct,* or to an instrument under her control. See Rest. 2d §314, Comment d.

   a. **Negligence vs. innocent acts:** Originally, this rule applied *only* where the original danger or injury was the result of the defendant's ***negligence or other fault.***

---

1. If Cilley *had* been an invitee, the case would likely have turned out differently, since many courts treat the landowner/invitee relationship as being one of the special relationships creating a duty on the landowner to render reasonable assistance.

i. Modern view: But the modern, and certainly more sensible, view is that if the defendant endangers or harms the plaintiff, *even if she does so completely innocently,* she must render assistance or warning when she discovers the problem. See Rest. 3d (Liab. for Phys. & Emot. Harm) §39 ("When an actor's prior conduct, even though *not tortious*, creates a *continuing risk of physical harm* of a type characteristic of the conduct, the actor has a duty to exercise reasonable care to prevent or minimize the harm.")

Example: The Third Restatement gives this example: D non-negligently runs into P, who is hiking at the side of the road. P, who does not have a cell phone, asks D to use D's own cell phone to call for help. D refuses and drives away. Because D has brought about the situation (even though non-negligently), he has a duty to make the call, and is liable for any worsening of P's condition if he doesn't. See Rest. 3d (Liab. for Phys. & Emot. Harm) §39, Illustr. 5.

ii. Hit and run: A number of *"hit and run"* driving statutes in various states require a driver to render assistance to one whom he has hit (even if non-negligently); these have sometimes been held to result in negligence *per se*, and civil liability, where the driver does not comply with the statute. See P&K, p. 377.

3. Defendant and victim as co-venturers: Where the victim and the defendant are engaged in a *common pursuit*, so that they may be said to be *co-venturers*, some courts have imposed on the defendant a duty of warning and assistance. For instance, if two friends went on a jog together, or on a camping trip, their joint pursuit might be enough to give rise to a duty on each to aid the other.

Example: D and his friend, V, try to engage two women in conversation. They follow the women, and the women complain to friends about D's and V's behavior. In response, six young men chase D and V. D escapes; V does not and is beaten severely. Later, D returns to V, puts some ice on V's head, and drives V around for two hours. He then parks V's car (with V in it, unconscious) at V's grandparents' house. The next morning, V's grandparents find him in the car and take him to the hospital, where he dies several days later. P (V's father) sues D for wrongful death.

Held, for P. D and V were "companions on a social venture." When two people engage in a "common undertaking," they have a special relationship, and each is understood to promise assistance to the other where this can be done without danger. Therefore, since D knew of V's need for help, he had an obligation to give that help. (Alternatively, once D began to give V assistance, under the "assumption of duty" exception he had the obligation to follow through. This exception is discussed further immediately below.) *Farwell v. Keaton*, 240 N.W.2d 217 (Mich. 1976).

4. Assumption of duty ("undertaking"): An additional limitation on the lack of duty to render assistance is that once the defendant *voluntarily begins* to render such assistance (even if she was under no legal obligation to do so) she must *proceed with reasonable care*. This means that the defendant must make reasonable efforts to *keep the plaintiff safe* while he is in the defendant's care, and that she may not *discontinue* her aid if so doing would leave the plaintiff in a *worse position* than he was in when the defendant began the assistance. See Rest. 3d (Liab. for Phys. & Emot. Harm) §42.

Example 1: P becomes sick in the D department store. D's employees attempt to give aid to P, by putting her in the store infirmary. However, they leave her there for six hours, without medical care, and she dies.

Held, it may be that D owed P no duty of assistance in the first place. But once having undertaken to give such assistance, D had a duty to use due care in doing so. *Zelenko v. Gimbel Bros.*, 287 N.Y.S. 134 (N.Y. Sup. Ct. 1935).

Example 2: D promises P that while P is away on a two-week trip, D will visit P's apartment every day and feed P's dog. D then forgets to do this, and the dog is seriously injured. D is liable to P, because once he made the promise to render the assistance, he was required to fulfill the promise with reasonable care. Cf. Rest. 3d (Liab. for Phys. Harm) §42, Illustr. 3.

a. **Preventing assistance by others:** In finding that one who has undertaken to give aid must carry through with reasonable care, the courts have often relied on the fact that a voluntary giving of such assistance *prevents others* (who might do a better job) from giving aid.

Example: P calls a 911 emergency number operated by the police department of D (the county in which P lives). She reports that a burglar is trying to break into her house, and gives her address as "319 Victoria" in the suburb of Kenmore. D's employee writes the address as "219 Victoria" instead of "319 Victoria." Because of this error, the police are delayed in arriving at P's premises. By the time they arrive, P is dead of seven knife wounds; there is evidence that had they gone immediately to the correct address, P might have survived.

Held, D is liable to P for her pain and suffering before death. D voluntarily set up the emergency call system, and induced P to rely upon it. Had P not been told by the 911 operator that help was on its way, she would almost certainly have directly dialed her local suburban police, or asked one of her neighbors for help. Therefore, D's negligence increased the risk to P, making D liable for its negligence in carrying out the duty it assumed. *DeLong v. Erie County*, 455 N.Y.S.2d 887 (N.Y. Sup. Ct. 1982).

   i. **Other factors:** The prevention of aid by others is only one way in which a defendant who voluntarily undertakes to give assistance may become liable. Even where there is no possibility of assistance by third persons, if the defendant behaves carelessly, and the plaintiff's condition is *worsened* as a result, there will be liability. See, e.g., Rest. 3d (Liab. for Phys. & Emot. Harm) §42(a), providing that if D undertakes to help P, then even without reliance on P's part, D must use reasonable care if D's "failure to exercise such care *increases the risk of harm beyond that which existed without the undertaking*."

b. **Pre-employment physical exam:** The "assumption of duty" rationale has been used to impose liability on an employer who gives a job applicant or worker a *physical exam* — while the employer usually does not owe a duty to a prospective employee to see whether he is physically fit for the job, once the employer assumes the duty to examine the applicant, he is liable if the examination is performed negligently (e.g., it misses a disease).

5. What constitutes undertaking: Because of this exception (which arises out of the old common law distinction between misfeasance and nonfeasance), it becomes important to note when the defendant has actually undertaken to give assistance. In general, very little in the way of affirmative action has been necessary to trigger this action.

   a. Past custom: A *past custom* of giving warning or assistance has been held to constitute an undertaking, at least where the plaintiff is aware of the custom. Thus in *Erie Co. v. Stewart,* 40 F.2d 855 (6th Cir. 1930), the defendant railroad maintained a watchman at a crossing, who customarily warned motorists when there was a train approaching. The plaintiff, who was aware of this custom, saw no sign from the watchman, crossed, and was crushed by the oncoming train; the watchman had been otherwise occupied. The defendant was held liable on the grounds that the plaintiff relied on the absence of a warning.

   b. Promise to assist: Until recently, it was almost always held that a mere *promise* to give assistance, unaccompanied by any overt act, was *insufficient*. Thus in the famous case of *Thorne v. Deas,* 4 Johns. 84 (N.Y. 1809), P and D were co-owners of a ship which was about to go on a long voyage. D promised on two occasions to procure insurance on the ship, and P therefore refrained from doing so. The ship was lost at sea; it turned out that D had never obtained the insurance, and D was held not liable — P had no action in contract, because of lack of consideration, and no action in tort, because of the lack of an undertaking (i.e., this was nonfeasance, not misfeasance). See P,W&S (9th) p. 413.

      i. Reliance on promise alone: But modern law, both contract and tort law, has begun to show a willingness to allow recovery based *solely upon a promise to provide assistance*, even if no overt act of performance ever occurs. In contract law, this has been done under the doctrine of "promissory estoppel"; see Restatement Second of Contracts, §90. In tort law, many courts have simply dispensed with the requirement of an overt act by the defendant, where the plaintiff has relied, to his detriment, on the defendant's unperformed promise of assistance.

   Example: P, shopping in D's store, is bitten by D's cat. P asks D to lock the cat up for fourteen days, so that he can be tested for rabies. D promises to do so, but carelessly lets the cat out whereupon it disappears for a month. D is therefore advised by her doctor to undergo a painful and dangerous series of rabies shots. After she completes the treatment, and suffers side effects from it, the cat comes back in perfect health.

   Held, D, by his promise to confine the cat, undertook to do so, and therefore had a duty to use at least reasonable care in seeing that this was done. P obviously relied on D's promise, since otherwise, she could have had local health authorities lock up the cat and test it. *Marsalis v. La Salle,* 90 S.2d 120 (La. 1957).

      ii. Restatement's view: The Third Restatement of Torts agrees that a promise to help will give rise to a duty to furnish that help if plaintiff relies on the problem, even if defendant never carries out an overt act in furtherance of the promise. See Rest. 3d (Liab. for Phys. & Emot. Harm), §42, Comment e: "[A] promise without any action in furtherance of it is [nonetheless] an undertaking subject to the rule [imposing a duty of due care once D makes an undertaking] stated in this section."

So the Third Restatement would agree with the result in *Marsalis*, even though D there merely made promises without any overt act.

6. **Duty to control others:** Nonfeasance may also be tortious where the defendant has undertaken to control *third persons* who then injure the plaintiff. Such a duty may arise either because of a special relationship between the *defendant and plaintiff,* or a special relationship between the *defendant and the third person.*

  a. **Defendant-plaintiff relationship:** Such special defendant-plaintiff relationships include *common carrier-passenger* (with a duty on the carrier to use reasonable care to protect its passengers from attacks or robberies by strangers as in *Lopez, supra,* p. 199); *innkeeper-guest* (e.g., the Connie Francis case, where the Howard Johnson hotel chain was held liable for inadequate room security leading to a rape of the singer); *hospital-patient, school-pupil,* and *parent-child.* See P&K, p. 383.

    i. **Business open to public:** In fact, many courts now hold that *any business open to the public* must protect its patrons from wrongdoing by third parties who are on the premises. (See the discussion of liability to business invitees, *infra,* p. 246).

      Example: D, a storekeeper, fails to take action when X, an obviously deranged man, comes into the store wielding a knife. (Assume that D, because of his martial arts background, could have restrained X with minimal risk to D.) X stabs P, a patron. Most courts would say that D is liable for failing to take reasonable measures to restrain X to prevent the harm to P.

  b. **Defendant-third party relationship:** Alternatively, the relationship between the defendant and the *third party* may be such that the defendant has a duty to control that party and prevent him from harming the plaintiff. This can be so even if the defendant and the plaintiff have no relationship at all.

    i. **Medical professional:** For instance, where D is a *medical* or social-work *professional* who learns that her *patient X poses a specific danger to P*, many courts recognize a duty on D's part to warn P.

Example: The Ds, psychotherapists, have a doctor-patient relationship with Poddar, who tells them of his intent to kill Tatiana, the Ps' daughter. Neither D warns Tatiana or the Ps. Poddar in fact kills Tatiana.

  Held, because of this special relationship between the Ds and Poddar, the Ds had a duty to warn the Ps of Poddar's intentions (intentions which Poddar later carried out) if a reasonable person would have done so. (The Ds did not, however, have a duty to the Ps to confine Poddar, because of a state statute granting doctors immunity with respect to this kind of decision.) *Tarasoff v. Regents of University of California,* 529 P.2d 553 (Cal. 1974) (also discussed *supra,* p. 108).

    (1) **Danger only to patient:** On the other hand, if the medical professional only has reason to believe that the patient is dangerous to *herself* (e.g., is suicidal), then the professional has no duty to warn others (e.g., the patient's family) of that danger. And that's true even if the patient commits suicide and a close family member suffers great emotional distress as a consequence.

    ii. **Other applications:** Similarly, the *owner of a car* owes pedestrians and other drivers the duty of using reasonable care to see that one who drives the car in her presence does not do so negligently. See Rest. 2d, §318. Likewise, a ***surgeon*** in charge of an operation is responsible for preventing negligence on the part of her assistants.

        iii. Only reasonable care required: But the defendant is required only to use ***reasonable care*** to prevent the misconduct of others in this kind of a situation. Thus if she does not know of the danger, she will not be liable (in the absence of some other principle, such as employer liability, *infra*, p. 315, where the liability is essentially without regard to the employer's fault.)

7. Good Samaritan protection for physicians: Because of the nonfeasance/misfeasance distinction, a ***physician*** who refuses to give emergency aid will never have any liability, whereas one who gives aid leaves herself open to a malpractice charge (made all the more likely because of the usual lack of equipment, nurses, etc. in the typical on-the-street emergency). For this reason, more than forty states have passed so called ***"Good Samaritan"*** statutes, which generally relieve a physician who gives assistance at the scene of an emergency from all liability, or from all liability except for gross negligence. See, e.g., §2144 California Business and Professions Code; P&K, p. 378.

        a. "Scene of accident" limitation: Good Samaritan statutes are usually limited to care rendered at the ***"scene of an accident,"*** and do not apply where the emergency care is given at a ***hospital or doctor's office***, even if the emergency occurs there. Often, the statute contains this limitation explicitly; sometimes, a statute that is silent on this issue is interpreted to exclude such in-hospital help.

III. EFFECT OF A CONTRACT

  A. Relation between tort and contract: The borderline between tort law and contract law is not always clear-cut. For instance, P buys a car from D, a dealer. If the car is defective, and injures both P and a bystander, X, are the suits brought by P and X to be in tort or contract? It is not unreasonable for the actions to be in tort, since D may have violated its duty to the world at large not to sell defective products that may foreseeably cause personal injury. On the other hand, especially with respect to the suit by P, the fact that there is a contract between P and D should certainly have some relevance.

    1. Practical significance of distinction: The choice between contract law and tort law is not academic. For instance, the Statute of Limitations may have run on a tort action, but not yet on a contract action (which is usually given a longer period). Conversely, the damages available to one suing in tort are likely to be much broader than for one suing on a contract. (In the latter case, they are limited by the rule of *Hadley v. Baxendale*; see Emanuel on *Contracts*.)

  B. Traditional distinction between misfeasance and nonfeasance: The common law has traditionally been much more willing to find that, where a contract exists, there has been a tort if the defendant was guilty of ***"misfeasance"*** rather than merely ***"nonfeasance."*** (The significance of this distinction is also discussed *supra*, p. 198, in connection with a general failure to act by the defendant). Accordingly, our discussion of the effect of a contract focuses on this distinction, first in the case of a suit brought by one party to the contract against the other, and then in the case of a suit brought by a third person, not party to the contract.

C. Party to the contract; nonfeasance: If suit is brought by a party to the contract, and her claim is that the defendant has simply *failed to perform a promise*, the plaintiff's suit is unlikely to be found to be a tort claim. For instance, suppose that D contracts to sell P a car, and fails to deliver; because of this failure, P has to walk to her destination, and is run over while she does so. P's suit, since it alleges complete nonperformance by D, will be held to be in contract, not tort.

    1. Exception for utilities: The only major exception to this rule is that if the defendant is a *common carrier*, or other public utility, it may be held to have acted tortiously if it fails to honor a contract with a member of the public. Thus if A bought a ticket to ride on the B bus line, and the driver refused to let her board, this might be a tortious act.

    2. Misrepresentation: Also, if the plaintiff can show that the defendant, when he made the promise, had *no intent to perform it*, she may be able to maintain the tort action of misrepresentation, or deceit (*infra*, p. 442).

D. Party to the contract; misfeasance: Once the defendant *starts to perform* his promise, if he fails to complete it, the plaintiff has a much better chance of being able to sue in tort. Consider the common case of a physician, for instance, who is engaged to perform a particular operation. If he performs the operation, but does so negligently, he will be liable in tort (see *supra*, p. 110), notwithstanding that his negligence arose out of a contractual relation between him and the plaintiff.

    1. Election: Thus the plaintiff may have the ability to sue either in contract or tort. In the case of a physician's malpractice, for instance, the plaintiff might, instead of suing for the tort action of malpractice, want to sue for breach of contract (although this would seldom be of practical advantage to her.) In many situations, this choice is left completely to the plaintiff, and she simply *"elects"* which remedy she wishes to pursue, and may even be able to pursue both at once.

        a. Gravamen: But some courts look for the *"gravamen"*, or gist, underlying the plaintiff's claim, and make their own decision about which one of the two theories of recovery, tort or contract, is involved. In a court favoring this approach, for instance, a lawyer's negligent preparation of a will is likely to be considered a breach of contract, whereas a physician's negligent performance of an operation is likely to be considered the tort of negligence. See P&K, p. 666.

    2. Insurer's failure to settle: One increasingly important setting in which a party may be liable in tort for failure to complete a contractual obligation arises where an *insurance company* has the opportunity to *settle* a claim against its insured, but in bad faith refuses to do so, leading to a recovery against the insured for more than the policy limit.

        Example: X falls down the stairs at P's house and sues P. P has insurance coverage of $10,000, and encourages D, her insurance company, to settle. X offers to settle for $10,000 but D only offers $3,000, because D feels that X will not be able to prove that her claimed psychosis was a result of the fall (even though D knows that X has a psychiatrist who will so testify). At trial the jury awards X and her husband $101,000, of which D pays $10,000. P sues D for the $91,000 balance, plus damages for P's mental suffering.

Held, for P. Every liability insurance contract includes a "duty to accept reasonable settlements, a duty included within the implied covenant of good faith and fair dealing." Here, the evidence showed that D knew there was a risk of a recovery substantially beyond the policy limits, and that D considered its own, not P's, interests when it refused to settle for the policy limits. Therefore, D breached its obligations, and is liable for the $91,000 (plus $25,000 for P's mental suffering). *Crisci v. Security Insurance Co.*, 426 P.2d 173 (1967).

3. **Breach of duty of "good faith and fair dealing":** Nearly all courts hold that each party to a contract has a general duty of "*good faith* and *fair dealing*." Some plaintiffs have tried to sue in tort for a violation of this duty. In general, courts have **refused** to recognize tort liability for breach of this general implied covenant of good faith and fairness. (Cases involving an insurance company's obligation to pay or settle claims fairly, as discussed above, represent the one exception to this general rule rejecting tort liability for breach of contractual good faith/fair dealing.)

a. **Employment relationship:** For instance, few if any courts have granted a tort recovery to an *employee* who alleges that he has been discharged in violation of the employment agreement. This is true whether the discharge is alleged to be in violation of the express terms of the contract, or in violation of the implied covenant of good faith and fair dealing.

i. **At-will contracts:** Plaintiffs have often asserted a breach of the duty of good faith and fair dealing when they are fired from *at-will positions,* i.e., positions in which there is no term, and either party can terminate the relationship at any time. For these plaintiffs, a tort remedy is especially important, because typically there would be no contract damages at all even if there were found to be a breach of the duty of good faith (since the employer "could have" terminated the employee at any time). But for such "at will" plaintiffs, as for other types of plaintiffs alleging wrongful discharge in the employment context, court have almost always said, "Your remedy, if any, is at contract, not in tort."

ii. **Whistle blowers and those who refuse to commit wrongdoing:** But there are a couple of *special situations* within the employment context where courts may nonetheless allow a tort recovery. When allowed, the recovery is often said to be for the tort of *"wrongful discharge."* For instance, many states protect *whistle blowers* (those who object to wrongdoing by the employer or by other employees), or those who refuse to engage in *illegality* when asked to do so by their boss. An employee discharged under these circumstances might be found to have a claim in tort, not just contract, because of the strong public interest in deterring illegality.

E. **Non-party to contract; traditional rule as to nonfeasance:** Where the plaintiff is one who is not a party to the original contract, and the defendant is guilty only of *nonfeasance*, traditionally the plaintiff has generally found it hard to recover in either tort or contract. She will not be able to recover in contract unless she is able to show that she is a third party beneficiary (see Emanuel on *Contracts*). As for tort liability, insofar as the courts have traditionally seldom allowed even a party to the contract to sue in tort where there has been nonfeasance, they have been even more reluctant to allow a non-party to sue in tort.

> Example: D, a water company, contracts with the city of Rensselaer to supply water to the city, for use in public buildings, fire hydrants, etc. The contract also indicates that service will be furnished to private parties who pay fixed rates. One day a fire starts, and spreads until it has destroyed a warehouse belonging to P. P sues on the theory that D failed to supply adequate water pressure, which would have enabled the fire department to stop the fire before it burned his warehouse. The suit is brought in tort.

> *Held*, P has no tort cause of action against D. D's action in this case amounted merely to nonfeasance, not affirmative misfeasance. If P were granted a right of action, then "liability would be unduly and indeed indefinitely extended by this enlargement of the zone of duty. . . . Every one making a promise having the quality of a contract will be under a duty to the promisee by virtue of that promise, but under another duty, apart from contract, to an indefinite number of potential beneficiaries when performance has begun." *H.R. Moch Co. v. Rensselaer Water Co.*, 159 N.E. 896 (N.Y. 1928).

> Note: Cases such as *H.R. Moch* have been almost universally criticized by commentators, but they still represent the majority position, that a water company is not liable to private citizens. Observe that D in fact began to perform the contract (it supplied water to most of the city), so it was guilty of misfeasance, not merely nonfeasance. Furthermore, by making the contract with the city, it induced the city and its citizens to forego other opportunities for obtaining an adequate supply of water, and they therefore relied to their detriment (a factor considered in the duty cases discussed *supra*, p. 202).

1. **Non-party to the contract; traditional rule as to misfeasance:** Where the third-party sues on a theory of ***misfeasance,*** rather than nonfeasance, her chance of recovery in tort have traditionally been somewhat better. Nonetheless, courts have historically been reluctant to allow recovery, on the misguided notion that tort recovery is barred because there is no "privity of contract."

F. **Non-party to the contract; modern rule as to nonfeasance and misfeasance:** But within the last fifty or sixty years, courts have largely ***scrapped*** the requirement that a tort plaintiff whose claim arises out of a contract to which the defendant was a party must have been in privity with the defendant.

1. **Sellers of chattels:** This has been most clearly the case with respect to sellers of ***chattels*** that cause physical harm to a person who was not in privity of contract with the seller. Most of the chapter on products liability (*infra* p. 347) is devoted to a discussion of how third parties may recover in tort against one who has supplied defective goods.

2. **Services:** Modern courts also now frequently scrap the privity requirement with respect to persons who supply ***services***. Thus a person, D, who provides services under a contract with *A* may be liable for physical, emotional and even ***economic loss*** suffered by *B* (who is not a party to the contract), if the D-to-*A* contract contemplates that a ***limited group of persons will be benefited*** by D's performance, and *B* is part of that limited group.

a. **Third Restatement:** The Third Restatement's provisions on economic loss agree with this approach of giving protection to members of a *"limited group"* who are intended to be benefited by commercial services performed by the defendant:

> (1) One who, in the *course of his business, profession or employment*, or in any other transaction in which he has a *pecuniary interest, performs a service for the benefit of others*, is subject to liability for pecuniary loss caused to them by their *reliance* upon the service, if he fails to exercise reasonable care in performing it.
>
> (2) The liability stated in Subsection (1) is limited to loss suffered
>
> > (a) by the *person* or one of a *limited group of persons* for whose *benefit the actor performs the service*; and
> >
> > (b) through *reliance* upon it in a *transaction that the actor intends to influence*.

Rest. 3d Torts (Liab. for Econ. Harm, Tent. Dr. 2), §6.

Example: Buyer, a potential buyer of a house owned by Seller, asks Realtor to have the furnace inspected. All parties realize that Realtor is under contract to Seller, not Buyer. But Realtor promises to have the furnace inspected. Realtor negligently selects Amateur to do the inspection, and Amateur fails to discover a defect, and tells the parties that the furnace is in good working condition. Buyer closes, and discovers that the furnace wasn't and isn't working.

Buyer will be able to recover from Realtor for Realtor's negligent selection of Amateur to do the inspection. Even though Realtor's only contractual obligation was to Seller, Realtor conducted the service (procurement of an inspection) in the course of Realtor's business or profession. And Buyer was "the person or one of a limited group of persons for whose benefit" Realtor was performing the service. Therefore, Realtor had a duty to use reasonable care in selecting the person who did the inspection. *Id.*, §6, Illustr. 3.

b. **Will-drafting by lawyers:** *Lawyers'* services in *drafting wills* frequently fall within this principle allowing recovery by non-contracting parties who are part of a "limited class that relies" on the service. Thus the *intended beneficiary under a will* is likely to be allowed to recover her economic loss from the lawyer who prepared the will, if the beneficiary doesn't receive the bequest because of the lawyer's negligent drafting. Despite the fact that there is no privity between lawyer and beneficiary, courts reason that it is extremely foreseeable (even probable) that negligence in the will-drafting process will cause injury to the intended beneficiaries, and that these beneficiaries form a limited class. Therefore, modern courts say, there is no reason to fear boundless liability to large numbers of claimants, a typical reason for traditionally requiring privity of contract between the plaintiff and the defendant who provided the contracted-for services.

IV. MENTAL SUFFERING

A. **Pure mental suffering without physical impact or injury:** Suppose the defendant's negligence is the cause in fact of intense *mental suffering* to the plaintiff. But suppose further that this suffering has been produced ***without any physical impact*** upon the plaintiff. Does the absence of any physical impact itself bar plaintiff from recovery? As we'll see, the answer is, "not necessarily."

1. **Illustration:** Here are two examples of situations in which mental suffering without physical impact might occur:

   Example 1: P is a pedestrian on the sidewalk. D, a driver who is negligently speeding, loses control and the car goes onto the sidewalk near P, missing P before slamming into a storefront. As D's car is hurtling towards her, P believes she is going to be hit and killed, though the car misses her by an inch. P develops Post-Traumatic Stress Disorder (PTSD) as a result. Can P recover from D for her mental suffering?

   Example 2: Same facts as Example 1, except that this time P is walking with her toddler son, S. D's car misses P, but strikes S while P watches, horrified. S barely survives, and P develops PTSD, suffering constant nightmares in which she relives her fear that S is about to be killed. Putting aside S's action against D, can P recover from D for her own mental suffering?

   As we'll see below, in most courts today, there are at least some circumstances in which P *may* recover for her mental distress negligently caused by D, even though P never suffered a physical impact. For instance, in most courts, P would likely be able to recover under both of the above examples. But the topic of recovery for mental suffering in the absence of physical impact is a very complicated one, in that: (1) in a given jurisdiction, slightly differing no-impact scenarios often lead to very different litigation outcomes; and (2) states vary tremendously in how they handle this whole category of cases.

2. **Several categories:** We'll look at several distinct types of scenarios:

   [1] P suffers a physical impact or direct physical injury, and seeks to ***"tack on"*** to her claim a recovery for emotional distress (though this is not one of the "pure emotional distress" scenarios). (See Par. B below.)

   [2] P witnesses an accident; she ***never fears*** for the physical safety of either herself or anyone else during the episode, but suffers emotional distress anyway, for which she seeks to recover. (See Par. C below.)

   [3] P witnesses an accident or near-accident, and is ***sufficiently close*** to the dangerous event herself that she is for a time in ***danger of immediate bodily harm***. She escapes the bodily harm, but suffers mental distress from the episode. (See Par. D below.)

   [4] P witnesses a ***close relative***, X, suffer a serious bodily injury; P never fears for her own physical safety but nonetheless suffers emotional distress (on account of her concern for X's welfare), for which she seeks to recover. (See Par. E below.)

   [5] Same as [4], but the person, X, that P witnesses suffer a serious bodily injury is ***not P's close relative***. Again, P suffers emotional distress for which she attempts to recover. (See Par. F below.)

   [6] P suffers emotional distress without ever being himself at risk, and without directly witnessing serious injury to anyone else, but because of the ***special relationship*** between P and D (or between D and a third person, X, who suffers injury), for policy

reasons the courts allow P to recover for his own emotional distress. (See Par. G below.)

B. Mental distress damages "tacked on" to case involving physical impact or injury: First, let's consider a situation that does not really fall into our "pure mental suffering" category, but that we'll want to compare with the various pure-mental-suffering scenarios we'll be considering. I'm referring to the situation in which D causes an *actual physical impact* to P's person, and P suffers not just physical injuries but, in addition, mental distress arising out of the episode.

   1. **P may recover:**   In this scenario, it's always been clear, in all American courts, that *D is liable* not only for the physical consequences of the impact but also for virtually *all the emotional or mental suffering* that flows naturally from it. This includes fright at the time of the injury, "pain and suffering" stemming from the injury, anxiety about possibility of a repetition, humiliation from disfigurement, etc. See P&K, pp. 362-63. The mental distress claim is said to be *"tacked on"* to the claim for physical injury.

   2. **"Parasitic" damages:**   Such "tacked on" damages from mental suffering are often called *parasitic* — they "attach" to the claim for physical injury, analogously to the way a parasite attaches to the host. The usual reason for allowing parasitic damages is that the existence of a physical injury to P provides sufficient assurance that *the claim of suffering is not being feigned*.

C. Emotional distress, but no fear of impact on oneself or on others: Next, let's look at the scenario which furnishes probably the *weakest* case for allowing P to recover: P *witnesses* an accident or near-accident caused by D's negligence, but the danger takes place *far enough* from P that she *never fears an imminent impact* with her own body, or even with the body of anyone else nearby. Nonetheless, P later suffers mental distress from the episode. In this situation, virtually *no* American courts will allow P to recover for her emotional distress, even if that distress has physical manifestations.

Example 1: P is walking in New York City's Times Square. Twenty yards ahead of her, she sees a taxi driven by D speed through a red light, lose control, and crash into a storefront, though miraculously neither D nor anyone else is physically injured. At no time does P believe that she or anyone else is likely to be hit by the cab. Nonetheless, P keeps reliving the near-disaster. She develops nightmares, symptoms of PTSD, and an ulcer. In her suit against D for having negligently inflicted emotional distress on her, P is able to establish that more likely than not, all of these symptoms arose from her having watched this terrifying accident.

   It is unlikely that *any* American court would allow P to recover. As we'll see, there are several exceptions to the general rule against "stand-alone" recovery for negligent infliction of emotional distress (i.e., recovery for pure emotional distress, in the absence of any claim by P for physical injury or property damage). But here, where P never even briefly feared that either she or anyone else was likely to be hit by the cab, none of these exceptions applies.

   1. **"Boundless liability" fear:**   In part, courts' universal rejection of a stand-alone distress claim like the one in Example 1 stems from courts' fear that if such claims were allowed, there would be a *flood of litigation*, with no way for courts to distinguish genuine claims from *feigned* ones. Allowing someone like P in our example to recover would raise the possibility that hundreds of similarly-situated people walking or riding in Times Square

might bring suit (not to mention thousands of claims from, say, people who later saw the accident on the local TV news and alleged they were similarly traumatized).

   a. Fear for safety of unknown person: As we'll see below, p. 216, the same principle of non-liability applies — for the same reason — if the plaintiff never fears for her own safety but sees someone else be injured or nearly injured, where that third person is not a close relative of the plaintiff.

D. P is within the "zone of danger," and suffers distress: Our next category is the situation in which P witnesses an accident or near-accident, and is *sufficiently close* to the dangerous event that she herself is at some point in danger of immediate bodily harm. She escapes the bodily harm, but suffers mental distress from the episode. Courts often describe this situation as one in which the plaintiff was *"within the zone of danger."*

1. Most courts allow: In this "zone of danger" scenario, most courts today *allow* the plaintiff to recover for her emotional distress, if shows that the distress is *severe*.

2. Third Restatement allows: The Third Restatement, similarly, allows the plaintiff to recover in this zone-of-danger situation. See Rest. 3d (Liab. Phys. and Emot. Harm), §47: "An actor whose negligent conduct causes *serious emotional harm* to another is subject to liability to the other if the conduct: (a) places the other in *danger of immediate bodily harm* and the emotional harm results from the danger[.]"

> Example 2: Same facts as Example 1 above. This time, however, when the taxi driven by D goes out of control, P is standing 2 feet away. She jumps out of the path of the oncoming cab and barely avoids being hit. If P suffers severe mental distress from constantly re-living the near-accident, most courts (and the Third Restatement) will allow her to recover for that distress, because she was within the "zone of danger."

3. Distress at harm to third person: As long as the plaintiff is herself within the zone of danger, the court is likely to allow the plaintiff to recover for all of her emotional harm stemming from the episode, even if that harm is a combination of distress at her own near-injury and her distress at an actual severe injury to someone else present.

   a. Illustration: So, for instance, in Example 2 above, suppose that P not only fears that she herself is about to be hit, but watches X, who is standing a few feet away from P, be killed. P will probably be able to recover for the *entirety* of her severe emotional distress -- the court will not try to subdivide the distress into separate fear-for-P-herself and fear-for-X components. This means that even though X is a *stranger* to P, P's X-related distress will be part of the "package" of damages for which P can recover.

E. P is a "bystander," and sees a close relative suffer bodily injury: Now, let's turn to the first of two categories in which the plaintiff is a *"bystander"* who from a position of safety *watches another person suffer bodily injury* due to the defendant's negligence. In the present category, the injured third person is a *close relative of the plaintiff*, such as the plaintiff's *parent, sibling* or *child*.

As in the above situation illustrated by Example 2 (where the plaintiff was herself within the "zone of danger"), in the present "bystander watching a close relative be injured" scenario, most courts today *allow the plaintiff to recover* for her own distress.

1. **Rationales:** There are two rationales for allowing recovery here: (a) we don't have to worry much about *fraudulent claims*, since it's highly likely that a person who watches a close relative be injured has indeed suffered great distress; and (b) we don't have to worry about a *flood of claims*, since the number of people suffering a bodily injury from a given tortious event will be limited, and therefore the number of close relatives watching those injuries occur will also be limited.

2. **Third Restatement allows:**   Again, the Third Restatement agrees that the plaintiff should be allowed to recover in this "bystander seeing a close relative be severely injured" scenario. See Rest. 3d (Liab. Phys. & Emot. Harm), §48:

   > An actor who negligently causes *sudden serious bodily injury to a third person* is subject to liability for serious emotional harm caused thereby to a *person who*:
   >
   > (a) *perceives the event contemporaneously*, and
   >
   > (b) is a *close family member* of the person suffering the bodily injury.

   Example 3: P is walking with her 6-year-old son, S, in a cross-walk in Times Square. As P watches, horrified, a taxi negligently driven by D jumps a red light and runs over S, killing him instantly. P suffers severe mental distress from watching the accident and re-living it. Most courts (and the Third Restatement) will allow P to recover against D for her own distress. This recovery is entirely separate, conceptually, from S's estate's right to recover for his bodily injury.

3. **Meaning of "close relative":**   Courts vary in *how close the family relationship must be* between the bystander/plaintiff and the third person who suffers serious bodily harm.

   a. **Sibling, parent, child, or spouse:**   A bystander who is the *sibling, parent, child,* or *spouse* of the person who suffers the bodily harm is likely to be found to be sufficiently closely-related that the bystander can recover for distress.

   b. **More distant relative:**   But if the relationship is even a little more *distant*, courts are likely to *deny* recovery. Thus one who witnesses the death or serious injury of a *fiancé*, a *cohabiting* significant other, a *son-in-law*, or an *aunt* or *uncle* (even one who has raised the child who suffers the bodily injury) is likely to be *denied recovery*. D,H&B Trts, Vol. 2, s. 391, pp. 579-580.

4. **Perception must be "contemporaneous":** Most courts insist that the bystander must *perceive* the accident (the bodily harm to the bystander's close relative) *"contemporaneously."* In other words, it's not enough that the bystander learns of the accident very soon after it occurs. Consider the following two examples, which produce opposite legal outcomes:

   Example 4: P, sitting on his front porch, watches a car negligently driven by D strike, and badly injure, P's 6-year-old son, S, in the street in front of P's house. Because P has "contemporaneously" perceived the physical injury to S, P will be entitled to recover for P's own mental distress. Cf. Rest. 3d (Liab. Phys. & Emot. Harm), §48. Illustr. 1 (on essentially these facts).

   Example 5: P is sitting in the kitchen of his house, which looks out only into P's backyard. The doorbell rings, and P's next-door neighbor, X, tells P, "I just saw your son S be hit by a car on the street in front of your house; the ambulance just took S to the hospital." P rushes to the hospital, where he sees S lying badly injured in the ER. In most courts — and under the Third Restatement — P will not be allowed to recover for his emotional distress, because P did not "contemporaneously" perceive the event that caused the harm to P's close relative. Cf. Rest. 3d (Liab. Phys. & Emot. Harm), §48, Illustr. 2 (on essentially these facts).

   a. **Can "perceive" by another sense:** Ordinarily, the contemporaneous "perception" will be by *sight* — P observes the accident with his eyes. But *other senses*, such as *hearing*, may also suffice, as long as the "perception" is "contemporaneous."

   Example 6: Same facts as Example 4 above, except that P, while sitting on his front porch, does not have his distance glasses on, and therefore cannot see what is happening in the street with any detail. But P knows that his son S is playing in the street. P then hears the squeal of D's brakes, and hears S's screams after he is run over. P has sufficiently "perceived" (through his sense of hearing) the event that caused the seriously bodily harm to S that he will be permitted to recover for his mental distress. Cf. Rest. 3d (Liab. Phys. & Emot. Harm), §48, Illustr. 4 (on essentially these facts).

   b. **Perception that occurs remotely rather than in person:** It's not clear whether the contemporaneous perception has to occur *"in person,"* as opposed to via some *remote, electronic means*. For instance, if P is *video-Skyping* with X and sees X hit by a car driven by D, has P met the "contemporaneous perception" requirement? There is little if any case law on the issue so far. The Third Restatement doesn't take a position; it leaves this issue for "future development." Rest. 3d (Liab. Phys. & Emot. Harm), §48, Comment e.

5. **Bodily harm witnessed must be serious:** The bodily harm that the bystander witnesses must generally be *serious*. So witnessing a close relative's "death, significant permanent *disfigurement*, or l*oss of a body part or function* will almost always be sufficient." *Id.*, Comment l. But "*bruises*, cuts, *single simple fractures*, and *other injuries that do not require immediate medical treatment* will *rarely be sufficient*." *Id.*

   Example 6: Same facts as Example 4 above, except that what P observes is that D's car knocks S to the ground, causing P to suffer to bloody knees but no other harm. No matter how emotionally traumatized P is from witnessing the scene, the absence of serious bodily harm to S would prevent most courts, and the Third Restatement, from allowing P to recover from D for his distress.

6. **Bodily injury must be "sudden":** The serious bodily harm suffered by the third person in the plaintiff/bystander's presence must occur in a *"sudden and dramatic manner,"* at least according to the Third Restatement. Rest. 3d (Liab. Phys. & Emot. Harm), §48, Comment m. "*Slow deterioration*, even to a seriously disabling condition or death, is *insufficient* to support liability[.]" *Id.* Most courts would likely agree with the Restatement's "sudden and dramatic" requirement.

   Example 7: W works for years at a warehouse owned and operated by D. D negligently stores toxic chemicals there, to which W is unwittingly exposed. Over a period of months, W's health gradually deteriorates, and eventually she is left in a coma. Her husband, H, observes the deterioration with horror. When he finally realizes that W has been irreversibly poisoned, he suffers great emotional distress, and sues D for that distress.

Even though H has been a "bystander" who has directly witnessed the serious bodily harm suffered by his wife, W, a court will probably not allow H to recover for distress, because W's bodily harm was not "sudden." Cf. *Vosburg v. Cenex-Land O'Lakes Agronomy Co.*, 513 N.W.2d 870 (Neb. 1994) (similar facts; court denies recovery to the children of the slowly-poisoned worker because the worker suffered her injuries gradually, and the children therefore could not have become aware of their mother's injuries in the required "sudden and shocking" manner).

7. **P need not be in "zone of danger" or fear for own safety:** In the bystander scenario, most courts that allow bystander recovery at all do ***not*** require that the ***bystander himself have ever been in the "zone of danger,"*** i.e., at risk of direct physical harm. In other words, as long as the bystander "contemporaneously perceives" the injury to a close relative, the bystander's own lack of physical danger does not ruin the claim. See Rest. 3d (Liab. Phys. & Emot. Harm), §48, Comment j (bystander who perceives the injury to a close relative can recover "even though the [defendant's] negligent conduct does not cause direct physical impact to the [bystander] or cause [the bystander] to have fear or apprehension for his or her own safety.")

   Example: Recall Example 4 on p. 214, where P sits on his porch and watches as his son S is struck down by D's car. The fact that P was never in any physical danger himself during the episode does not negate P's distress claim.

F. **P is a "bystander," and sees a non-close-relative suffer bodily injury:** Now, let's consider the other major category in which a bystander might try to recover: the bystander witnesses serious bodily harm to another person, but this time the bystander and the physically-injured person are ***not close relatives***. In this scenario, ***few if any courts allow*** the bystander to recover for mental distress — this is one of those situations in which courts fear that allowing recovery will produce a flood of claims, with no easy way to determine which ones are genuine, and no way to avoid subjecting the defendant to potentially boundless liability.

   Example 8: Same basic facts as Example 1 on p. 212. Now, however, P sees the runaway cab strike and kill X, a stranger to P. As in Example 1, P is far enough away (20 yards) from the cab that she never fears that she herself will or may be hit by the cab. Virtually all U.S. courts would deny P the right to recover for her mental distress, even if that distress unquestionably stemmed from seeing the accident and resulted in physical manifestations like ulcers. The same fears of boundless liability and false claims that would result in courts' rejection of P's claim in Example 1 would be cited here.

1. **P not within zone of danger:** The fact that the bystander and the physically-injured person are not close relatives makes the most difference when ***the bystander is never within the zone of danger.*** That's because, in most courts, if the bystander *is* himself within the zone of danger, that fact will ***allow*** the bystander to recover for emotional distress from the entire episode — the court will typically not try to distinguish between distress from the bystander's own narrow escape and distress from the injury to the nearby non-relative.[2]

2. **P is an innocent "participant" in the injury:**   Suppose that the plaintiff bystander is not just a passive observer of the injury to the unrelated third person, but is instead in some sense an innocent *participant* in the injury to the third person caused by the defendant's negligence. Does the fact of the plaintiff's participation — which may well increase the plaintiff's distress — change the rule that a bystander who is not within the zone of danger cannot recover for injuries he witnesses to a third person who is not a close relative? Most courts answer *"no"* to this question — lack of a close family relationship between the physically injured person and the bystander is fatal to the bystander's claim, no matter how integrally a part of the episode the bystander is, and no matter how much the bystander's participation may have served to increase his distress.

Example: P drives a motorboat on a lake, while pulling two tow-ropes behind the boat. The tow-ropes are attached to two tubes, ridden by two of P's daughter's friends, Samantha and Aimee. As P is traveling eastwards towards the shore, he sees a jet ski ridden towards him from the south. At the moment P first sees the jet ski, it is 75 yards away. The jet ski is ridden by a 14-year-old boy, Panek (D1), who has been entrusted with it by its owner, Lewis (D2). P never believes that the jet ski will hit him or the boat (he expects the ski to turn away before that happens), but fears that when the rider turns, he may then hit one of the two tubes P is pulling. Indeed, Panek turns the jet ski and drives it into Samantha's tube, plunging her face-down into the water. At the moment of impact, the tube is about 60 feet from the rear of P's boat. P floats Samantha back to shore, but she is dead. P brings his own suit against D1 and D2, seeking damages for the Post-Traumatic Stress Disorder that he suffers from witnessing the accident and unsuccessfully attempting to rescue Samantha.

Held, summary judgment for the Ds. In Nebraska, if P does not suffer any impact or physical injury, P may recover for negligent infliction of emotional distress only if he shows either (1) that he was a bystander who had an "intimate familial relationship" with a seriously injured victim of the defendant's negligence; or (2) that P was a "direct victim of the defendant's negligence" in that P was in the "zone of danger" of that negligence. Showing (2) does not apply, because the jet ski was never closer than 60 feet from P, and by P's own testimony he always believed that the ski would turn before it could hit his boat; thus P was never himself in the "zone of danger." (If he *had* been, he would be able to recover for his pure emotional distress.) And as to showing (1), the physically-injured victim (Samantha) and P did not have an "intimate familial relationship." Therefore, no matter how foreseeable it may have been that one in P's position would suffer emotional distress from this type of accident, P cannot recover. *Catron v. Lewis*, 712 N.W.2d 245 (Neb. 2006).

G. **Special relationship or special activity:**   Finally, there are a few types of *"special" situations*, scenarios that involve either a *special activity* or a *special relationship among the parties*, such that courts have decided that the general rule against recovery for negligently-

---

2. For instance, go back to Example 3 on p. 214, where the runaway cab comes within two feet of striking P, who jumps out of the way. Now, assume that at the same moment the cab just misses P, it strikes and kills X, P's friend, who is nearby. Since P was in the zone of danger, she will likely be able to recover for the full extent of her mental distress — the court will probably not try to apportion damages to distinguish between P's distress at her own near-injury and her distress at seeing her friend killed.

inflicted emotional distress should ***not apply*** even though none of the above exceptions to the general no-liability rule applies. In these special categories, courts have concluded that the ***risk*** of emotional harm to the plaintiff is ***so great***, and the ***number*** of affected plaintiffs likely to be so ***small***, that the court should not worry about either feigned distress or a flood of claimants.

1. **Two main categories:** There are two main scenarios that courts have long recognized as being "special categories" where pure emotional harm should be recoverable:

    a. **Mishandling of bodies:** One is the scenario in which a ***hospital or funeral home*** negligently ***mishandles a corpse***, thereby causing emotional distress to a close relative of the deceased.

       Example: Hospital negligently misidentifies a corpse (that of X), causing the corpse to be cremated instead of sent to a funeral home for burial. X's immediate family learns of the error, and suffers great distress because of it. Most courts would allow the family to recover against Hospital. See Rest. 3d (Liab. Phys. & Emot. Harm), §47, Comment f and Illustr. 3.

    b. **Telegrams announcing death or serious illness:** The other is the scenario in which a ***telegraph company*** negligently and incorrectly announces that *A* is dead or seriously ill, and the telegram is delivered to *B*, *A*'s intimate family member. *Id.*, Comment f. Most courts permit *B* to recover for emotional distress.

2. **Extension to other situations:** In recent decades, courts have often recognized ***other situations*** that call for allowing an emotional distress claim that does not fall within either of the above categories, or within any of the physical-impact categories we discussed earlier.

    a. **Factors required:** Typically, for a situation to be classified as a special one that calls for recovery, one or both of the following must be present: (a) P and D have a special ***fiduciary or expert*** relationship (with D being the fiduciary or the expert), making it especially likely that if D behaves negligently, P will suffer great emotional distress; or (b) D helps P engage in an ***"activity"*** in which, if D behaves negligently, great emotional distress to P is likely. Here are a few examples, taken from actual cases in which the court declined to rule as a matter of law that P may not recover for distress:

        [1] D, a ***medical clinic*** that has run a blood test on P, negligently (and incorrectly) ***informs P that she is HIV positive***;

        [2] D, an ***obstetrician***, negligently mishandles a ***pregnancy*** of P, a patient, leading to a ***stillbirth*** that causes P great emotional harm;

        [3] D, a ***fast food chain***, negligently serves P a hamburger with human blood on the bun.

       All of these examples are from cases cited in Rest. 3d (Liab. Phys. & Emot. Harm), §47, Reporter's Note to Comment f.

H. **The "at-risk plaintiff":** In recent decades, the issue of liability for negligent infliction of purely emotional distress has been raised by a new type of plaintiff, sometimes referred to as the ***"at-risk plaintiff."*** With the increased use of epidemiological and statistical techniques, it is often possible to say that a particular plaintiff, by virtue of his exposure to a certain substance, has suffered an ***increased likelihood of a particular disease*** (e.g., cancer). May such a plaintiff recover for the purely emotional harm of being ***distressed*** by this increased likelihood of illness, assuming that there are no symptoms of the illness itself?

1. **"Cancerphobia":** Cases and commentators often refer to liability for emotional distress due to future illness under the umbrella (and not-always-accurate) term *"cancerphobia."* The term is not always accurate, of course, because a person's fear of illness from exposure to a dangerous substance can encompass illnesses other than cancer. But for simplicity, we'll use the term "cancerphobia" in our discussion.

2. **Hard for P to win:** Plaintiffs have ***rarely succeeded i***n recovering for pure cancerphobia, i.e., cases where the plaintiff cannot show that he has actually suffered bodily harm. Courts put various obstacles in the path of cancerphobia plaintiffs — including obstacles summarized in Pars. 3, 4 and 5 below— and it's the rare plaintiff who can overcome all of these obstacles.

3. **Need actual exposure in toxic cases:** Most of the cases raising the issue of recovery for cancerphobia are *"toxic tort"* cases, i.e., cases in which the plaintiff has been or may have been exposed to some toxic substance, whether it is the AIDS virus, hazardous environmental waste, or some other damaging substance. In this situation, most courts have insisted, at a minimum, that plaintiff show ***actual exposure*** to the substance, not merely the ***possibility*** of exposure.

    Example: Suppose that D is a physician who has open lesions on his hands and arms, and who examines many patients, including P, while having those lesions. P later learns that at the time D examined her, D knew that he had AIDS. P has not yet developed AIDS, and there is no evidence that she has had HIV virus particles pass into her body. However, P is very frightened that she will develop AIDS from her exposure to D.

    A court would probably hold that P loses on her "fear of AIDS" theory, because she cannot show that she was "actually exposed" to the HIV virus from D. That is, she will lose unless she can show that more probably than not, some virus particles actually passed from D's body into her own. See Dobbs, pp. 845-846.

4. **Some courts require showing of actual illness:** Some courts have gone even further, and have required that the cancerphobic plaintiff show that more probably than not, he will ***actually contract the illness*** that he is frightened of. In other words, fear of a less-than-probable illness, no matter how devastating the illness would be if it occurred, will not suffice, in these courts. (In such a court, P in the above example would presumably lose unless she showed not only that she was actually exposed to the HIV virus by D but that she had a greater than 50% chance of contracting AIDS.)

    Example: D (Firestone Tire Co.) sends hazardous waste to a landfill, including two chemicals that are known human carcinogens. The Ps, who live near the landfill, sue D on the theory that although they have no present symptoms of disease, they have suffered emotional distress from the possibility that they may get cancer in the future from their exposure to this hazardous waste.

Held, for D. Unless the Ps can prove that it is ***more likely than not*** that they will get cancer, they cannot recover. "The tremendous societal cost of . . . allowing emotional distress compensation to a potentially unrestricted plaintiff class demonstrates the necessity of imposing some limit on the class. Proliferation of fear of cancer claims in California in the absence of meaningful restrictions might compromise the availability and affordability of liability insurance for toxic liability risks." *Potter v. Firestone Tire and Rubber Co.*, 863 P.2d 795 (Cal. Sup. Ct. 1993).

5. **Need for danger of "immediate" bodily harm:** Another way that courts often make it hard or impossible to recover for emotional harm from fear of future illness is by insisting that the danger of bodily harm be ***"immediate."***

    a. **Third Restatement:** That's how the ***Third Restatement*** denies recovery for cancerphobia. As we've seen (*supra*, p. 219), §47 of the Restatement allows P to recover for emotional harm based on negligently-caused physical danger to the plaintiff if and only if the negligent conduct places the plaintiff "in danger of ***immediate bodily harm*** and the emotional harm results from the danger." Comment k to this section explains that the section's requirement that the person be placed in "immediate" danger means that the section ***does not apply to cancerphobia cases.*** And the Comment indicates that this rule is broadly followed by American courts: "[C]ourts deny recovery in cancerphobia cases, at least during the indeterminate latency period before the person actually suffers bodily injury."

6. **Accompanying physical harm:** But always keep in mind that if there is ***some physical harm*** arising from the episode, the emotional distress will *also* be compensable.

    Example: Many workers exposed to *asbestos* have developed a lung abnormality known as "pleural thickening." This thickening is not by itself life-threatening, nor does it even directly impair the patient's life. But courts tend to consider as a form of "bodily harm." And it has been statistically linked to a much higher than normal incidence of certain cancers.

    A plaintiff who has suffered pleural thickening is likely to be permitted to recover substantial sums from manufacturer of asbestos to which plaintiff was exposed. Such an award would compensate plaintiff not just for his current physical harm from the pleural thickening itself, but also for his distress at knowing that he has a high risk of future harm.

I. **Intentional torts:** Where the defendant's conduct in imposing emotional distress on plaintiff is ***intentional*** or ***"willful,"*** courts have been ***much more willing*** to allow recovery for pure distress than in the above cases where the defendant was merely negligent. (See the discussion of the tort of Intentional Infliction of Emotional Distress, *supra*, p. 21.) For instance, Rest. 2d, §46(1) allows recovery for pure distress where the defendant's conduct is intentional and "extreme and outrageous."

    Example: D commits suicide in P's kitchen. P suffers great shock when she encounters the body, and ongoing distress. P sues D's estate for her distress. At the close of P's case, the trial judge directs a verdict for the estate, in part on the theory that recovery for distress in the absence of physical injury is improper.

Held (on appeal), for P. The estate can properly be held liable for P's shock and distress if D acted "willfully." D's act was "willful" if he either intended to inflict injury (in this case, shock) on P, or recklessly disregarded the risk that injury would occur. On these facts, a reasonable jury could properly find that D acted willfully, so the directed verdict in the estate's favor was improper. *Blakeley v. Shortal's Estate*, 20 N.W.2d 28 (Iowa 1945).

    a. **Rationale:** Courts' more-generous-to-the-plaintiff approach in cases of intentional or willful conduct is probably due to the general tendency of courts to impose a broader scope of liability (see *supra*, p. 8) in cases of intentional torts than in torts of negligence.

V. UNBORN CHILDREN

A. **Scope of problem:** Can one ever owe a duty of care to a child who is, at that time, ***unborn***? Until 1946, all courts agreed that the answer was "no". This meant that, for instance, if the defendant injured a mother in a car accident, and the fetus she was carrying was later born with injuries directly sustained in the accident, the infant could not recover. (The mother, however, could recover for mental distress at having an injured child, medical payments required for treatment of the child's injuries, etc.)

B. **Modern view:** Starting in 1946, one court after another overruled the bar on liability for pre-natal injuries. This now appears to have been universally done, and Prosser and Keeton call this overruling "a rather spectacular reversal of the no-duty rule." P&K, p. 368.

    1. **Viability:** A few cases have implied in dicta that for there to be recovery, the child must, at the time of injury, have been ***"viable"*** (i.e., capable of surviving if placed in an incubator). But all courts directly confronted with the issue seem to have permitted recovery even where the fetus was only a few weeks old at the time of injury. The soundness of this is indicated by the Thalidomide disaster, which proved that external forces can cause drastic injury to an embryo that is far from being viable.

        a. **Restatement cautions:** But the Second Restatement, §869, Comment d, notes that the causal link between the defendant's act and injury to a just-recently-conceived embryo can be extremely speculative and unreliable, and suggests that courts require "convincing evidence" of causation in this circumstance.

    2. **Requirement that child be born alive:** Suppose the fetus, after being injured, is ***stillborn***. May an action for its wrongful death (see *infra*, p. 272-273) be brought? The question usually turns on what the state legislature meant by the use of the word "person" when it provided a statutory right to a wrongful death action on behalf of persons. Most courts have allowed recovery in this situation. But a fair number have not; see, e.g., *Endresz v. Friedberg*, 248 N.E.2d 901 (N.Y. 1969).

        a. **Restatement view:** The Second Restatement, §869(2), would not allow recovery "unless the applicable wrongful death statute so provides."

    3. **Pre-conception injuries:** The above discussion assumes that the injury occurred while the child was *in utero*. Suppose, however, that the injury occurred before the child was even ***conceived***, but that some effect from the injury is nonetheless suffered by the later-conceived child. This scenario can arise where D manufactures a drug or other product that has the effect of injuring P's mother's (or grandmother's) *reproductive system* in some way. Here, courts are *split* as to whether the child may recover.

> Example: Patricia Enright's mother takes the drug DES, manufactured by D, while she is pregnant in 1960. The mother gives birth to Patricia in 1960. Patricia, when she reaches adulthood, has several miscarriages, and then gives birth prematurely to a daughter Karen. Karen has cerebral palsy and other developmental disorders. Patricia and Karen both sue D. The issue here is whether Karen can recover from D for injuries caused to her by the drug ingested by her grandmother.
>
> *Held*, for D. The court declines to change the traditional view that a child has no cause of action for pre-conception torts committed against the mother. "Public policy favors the availability of prescription drugs even though most carry some risks. . . . [W]e are aware of the dangers of overdeterence — the possibility that research will be discouraged or beneficial drugs withheld from the market. These dangers are magnified in this context, where we are asked to recognize a legal duty toward generations not yet conceived." *Enright v. Eli Lilly & Co.*, 570 N.E.2d 198 (N.Y. 1991).
>
> Note: But not all courts have agreed with the no-liability approach of *Enright*. See, e.g., *Renslow v. Mennonite Hospital*, 367 N.E.2d 1250 (Ill. 1977), allowing a child to recover where the defendant negligently transfused blood to the mother nine years before the plaintiff's birth.

4. **"Wrongful life":** One issue concerns what might be called *"wrongful life"* actions. Suppose a child is born illegitimate, or born unwanted because of a faulty contraceptive, or born with a congenital disease which could not have been prevented, but which, had it been diagnosed *in utero*, could have led to an abortion. In this circumstance, may the child argue that it would have been *better off not being born at all,* and is or therefore entitled to damages for life?

   a. **Illegitimacy:** In the case of children born illegitimate, the courts have universally refused to allow an action against the parents, on the grounds that it is better to have been born illegitimate than not to have been born at all.

   b. **Faulty contraception:** If the child is born, healthy but unwanted, due to the defendant's furnishing of a defective contraceptive or performance of a faulty sterilization, courts have sometimes allowed recovery. Apparently no court has allowed the child to recover for "wrongful life." Most courts have, however, allowed the parents to recover. Most courts have limited recovery to the pain, suffering and medical expenses of an unwanted pregnancy, and have denied recovery for the costs of raising a normal child. A minority have allowed even normal child-rearing costs (though these are usually offset by the financial and emotional "benefits" of raising a child). See P&K, p. 372.

   c. **Congenital defect:** The most troubling cases are those in which the child suffers from a severe *congenital defect or disease* which, had it been diagnosed during pregnancy, might have led the mother to abort. Here, the impaired child seems to have a much stronger claim that he would be better off never having been born. Apparently, no court has yet explicitly allowed a "wrongful life" recovery in this situation. However, some (but by no means all) courts have allowed *the parents* to recover for the medical expenses and emotional distress arising from the child's condition.

VI. PURE ECONOMIC LOSS

A. The problem generally: Suppose that D behaves negligently towards X, in a way that causes X personal injury or property damage. Suppose further that D's conduct also injures P, but P's only loss is *economic*, not personal injury or property damage. May P recover in tort from D? As we will see, the traditional general answer is *"no,"* but there are some important exceptions.

    1. Tacking on of economic loss to personal or property damage: Before we begin examining the "three party" situation referred to in the prior paragraph, let's first consider a simpler "two party" situation: D behaves negligently towards P, and causes P both personal injury and economic loss. In this situation, all courts agree (and have always agreed) that P, in addition to recovering for his personal injury, *may "tack on" his intangible economic harm as an additional element of damages*.

        Example: P owns a retail store, which he personally operates. P is injured by the negligence of D, a careless driver who hits P while P is walking. P can of course recover damages for his physical harm (e.g., his medical bills plus pain and suffering). Once P shows that he has suffered physical harm, he will be permitted to "tack on," as an additional element of damages, his loss of profits from being unable to operate the store. In other words, P's suffering of physical harm qualifies him to recover for the full range of damages which he has suffered, including intangible economic ones.

        a. Property damage: Similarly, if P suffers *property damage* (even if he does not suffer personal injury), this property damage will qualify him to tack on intangible economic loss as well. Thus suppose, on the facts of the above example, that P's car was struck by D's car, and that as a result: (1) P's car was damaged; (2) P himself was not physically injured; and (3) P lost two days of profits at the store because he could not commute to the store. Once P showed that he suffered direct property damage from P's negligence, all courts would allow him to recover his loss-of-business damages, even though those are purely intangible economic losses.

B. Standard rule disallows pure economic losses: Now, let's return to the three-party situation, in which D's negligence causes physical injury or property damage to *X*, but only economic loss to *P*. Nearly all courts agree that *P may not recover anything for his economic losses*, since he has not suffered any personal injury or property damage. This is true even though D is clearly a tortfeasor (vis-à-vis X), and even though D's negligence has quite clearly, and foreseeably, brought about the injuries to P. As the idea is often put, a person may not recover for unintentionally-caused *"pure economic loss."*

    1. Restatement 3d follows this rule: The Third Restatement of Torts (Liab. for Econ. Harm), §7, follows this general no-recovery principle: except for a few exceptional circumstances:

        a claimant cannot recover for *economic loss* caused by (a) *unintentional personal injury to another party*; or (b) *unintentional injury to property* in which *the claimant has no proprietary interest.*

2. **Rationales:** There are some strong *policy reasons* behind this general rule barring recovery for pure economic loss. Here are two of the leading rationales:

    a. **Indeterminate and disproportionate liability:** Most importantly, if courts allow recovery for economic loss that is not accompanied by personal injury or property damage to the plaintiff, what is likely to result is *"indeterminate and disproportionate liability"* (Rest. 3d (Liab. For Economic Harm) §1, Comment c(1)). Whereas "physical forces that cause injury ordinarily spend themselves in predictable ways [so that] their lifespan and power to harm are *limited*," economic harm is *not limited* in this way. *Id.*

        Example: Suppose the defendant negligently causes a collision that sinks a ship. This act of negligence will "cause a well-defined loss to the ship's owner; but it may also foreseeably cause economic losses to *wholesalers* who had expected to buy the ship's cargo, then to *retailers* who had expected to buy from the wholesalers, and then to *suppliers*, employees, and customers of the retailers, and so on." Rest. 3d (Liab. For Economic Harm) §7, Comment b. If the courts were to allow claims for all of these types of losses, this would "greatly increase the number, complexity, and expense of potential lawsuits arising from many accidents," and would "result in liabilities that are *indeterminate* and *out of proportion to the culpability* of the defendant." *Id.* And it's doubtful (or so courts say) that there would be commensurate benefits to society from imposing such broad liability.

    b. **Other ways for claimants to protect themselves:** Second, courts reason that the victims of economic injury "often can *protect themselves effectively by means other than a tort suit.*" *Id.* For instance, they may be able to *buy insurance* against their losses, or bring a successful contract suit against someone who in turn has a conventional tort claim against the negligent person who caused the loss. *Id.*

C. **Contexts in which rule is applied:** Here are some of the contexts in which the rule barring recovery for pure economic losses is frequently applied:

    1. **Blocking of highways or streets and thus access to P's business:** Where the defendant negligently causes a s*treet, highway or waterway to be closed*, business owners whose property is not directly damaged have often sued, seeking recovery for *lost business* due to customers' inability to get to the owner's premises. Most cases find *against the plaintiff*, in a straightforward application of the rule denying recovery for negligently-caused pure economic loss.

        Example: Due to the negligent construction by D, a builder, of a building on Madison Avenue in the central business district of Manhattan, a wall of the building collapses, covering the street with bricks and mortar. City officials close 15 heavily-trafficked blocks of Madison Avenue for two weeks. The named Ps are retail businesses, none of which suffered physical damage from the collapse or closure; the Ps lost business because shoppers couldn't get to these stores during the closure. The named Ps (acting for themselves, and all other businesses similarly affected by the closure) bring a class action against D in tort for their economic losses.

Held, for D. The New York courts "have never held ... that a landowner owes a duty to protect an entire urban neighborhood against purely economic losses." If a particular plaintiff business owner were able to show that (a) D created a "public nuisance" and (b) the particular plaintiff "suffered special injury beyond that suffered by the community at large," the plaintiff would be entitled to a private recovery for public nuisance. But none of the plaintiffs here have suffered the requisite "special injury beyond that of the community." "[E]very person who maintained a business, profession or residence in the heavily populated areas of ... Madison Avenue was exposed to similar economic loss during the closure period[]." Therefore, the plaintiffs may not recover for their economic losses, either under nuisance or any other theory. *532 Madison Avenue Gourmet Foods, Inc. v. Finlandia Center, Inc.*, 750 N.E.2d 1097 (N.Y. 2001). See also Rest. 3d (Liab. For Econ. Harm) §7, Illustr. 4, based on *532 Madison*.

2. **Toxic torts affecting land or water:** In another common scenario, the defendant negligently *spills toxic substances or pollutants* onto either a waterway or land, and this *"toxic tort"* interferes with the economic activities of persons or businesses whose person or property are not directly and physically impacted by the spill. Again, most courts apply the general rule to these non-physically-impacted plaintiffs — unless the plaintiff can show that the defendant negligently created a public nuisance, and that the harm suffered by the plaintiff was *different in kind* from the harms suffered by other businesses in the area, the plaintiff *may not recover for its "pure economic loss."* A good example of courts' refusal to allow recovery for pure economic loss caused by a toxic spill is *Southern California Gas Leak Cases*, 441 P.3d 881 (Cal. Sup. Ct. 2019).

   a. **Facts:** *Southern California Gas Leak* involved a massive leak of natural gas into the air and water in the Porter Ranch neighborhood of Los Angeles. The defendant was Southern California Gas Co. ("SoCalGas" or "D"), which supplies millions of people with natural gas from various storage facilities. Its largest storage facility, Aliso, was a subterranean former oil reservoir that the company had used for gas storage for 40 years. Because natural gas is odorless, D added a nausea-causing chemical so that people would notice if a leak happened. Such a leak from Aliso occurred in October, 2015, releasing 55 tons of natural gas every hour. Porter Ranch residents reported unpleasant odors, headaches, dizziness, respiratory problems, nosebleeds and vomiting.

      i. **Relocation:** In November 2015, while the leak was still flowing, the county health department ordered D to establish a relocation program available to any Porter Ranch resident who lived within a five-mile radius of the leak site. Then a month later, while the flow was slowing but still significant, the county board of education relocated students from two public schools; also, D expanded its relocation program to people living outside the initial five-mile boundary. Altogether, about 15,000 people were relocated to locations dozens or hundreds of miles away.

      ii. **The plaintiffs:** Various businesses in the Porter Ranch area sought to bring a class action consisting of all persons or entities conducting business within five miles of the Aliso facility. The Ps alleged that the leak was caused by D's negligence, and that the resulting relocation devastated the local economy. By depriving area businesses of customers, the Ps claimed, the disaster caused the class-member businesses to suffer lost earnings. Named class members whose earnings were harmed included restaurants, gas stations, pharmacies, beauty salons, doctors' offices, a martial arts center, a daycare center, etc. Residential property values were also damaged, reducing the earnings of class-member companies like home mortgage lenders and home improvement businesses.

  (1) No property losses: But *none* of the class member businesses alleged *personal injury or property damage* — every class member sought recovery for "pure economic loss."

b. **Recovery denied:** The California Supreme Court applied the general rule that a defendant has *no tort duty "to guard against negligently causing ... 'purely economic loss[es]'."* [3] So class-member businesses that had not suffered non-economic injuries could not recover anything, because D *did not owe them any duty* to avoid negligently causing them economic harm.

c. **Rationale:** The court relied on the same rationales for denying liability for purely economic losses as does the Third Restatement of Torts (*supra*, p. 223). The court mentioned these rationales, among others:

  [1] **Not self-limiting:** Most of all, "purely economic losses *'proliferate more easily* than losses of other kinds' and are *'not self-limiting'* in the same way."

  [2] **Indeterminate liabilities:** Because of [1], allowing recovery for such losses would "threaten 'liabilities that are *indeterminate and out of proportion* to [a defendant's] culpability.'"

  [3] **Pressure to avoid activity:** That type of indeterminate liability would in turn cause "'exaggerated pressure to *avoid an activity altogether.'*"

d. **The "five-mile limit":** Recall that initially, the only residents who were relocated were those *within a five-mile radius* of the leak. The plaintiffs relied on that fact to limit their proposed class to *businesses operating within* that five-mile radius. But the court said that it was "far from clear why the five-mile limit means anything." The court pointed out that a few weeks after the leak was detected, the evacuation zone was *extended* beyond the five-mile mark. Therefore, the opinion said, "Why businesses operating outside the original boundary but inside the new one should not get to recover their equally real and foreseeable financial losses we do not know." And using the "boundary of an evacuation zone" as a "liability line" would *"lack predictability."* Without a *"workable way to limit geographically"* those who should be allowed to recover pure economic losses, "the dangers of *indeterminate liability, overdeterrence, and endless litigation* are at their *apex*."

  i. **"Dangerous incentives":** Furthermore, the court said, using the evacuation zone as a liability line would *"inject a dangerous incentive into disaster response*

---

3. The court said it was using the term "purely economic loss" as a shorthand for "pecuniary or commercial loss that does not arise from actionable physical, emotional or reputational injury to persons or physical injury to property."

efforts." For instance, there is a risk that defendants would put "overt *pressure on public officials to roll back* or *eliminate a proposed evacuation."*

e. **Unfair line-drawing:** The court conceded that its black-letter rule denying all liability for pure economic losses *"may appear arbitrary in some sense,"* since "[t]he courthouse doors are *open* for people who experience *slight physical injury* — yet closed to others who suffer *devastating purely economic losses."* But "drawing arbitrary lines is *unavoidable* if we are to limit liability and establish meaningful rules[.]" The line based on presence of property damage or physical injury is an "admittedly imperfect legal regime," but it is *"the least-worst rule out there."*

i. **Insurance:** The court noted one "partial solution" to the arbitrariness of its bright-line rule: at least some types of businesses could buy *private insurance* to cover this sort of pure economic loss. For instance, *"business interruption* insurance policies" might cover at least losses when a business is *forced to close down* during a man-made disaster.

3. **Tort against employee or employer causing economic loss:** Here is another common scenario in which the general principle denying liability for negligent infliction of pure economic losses applies: suppose that D *negligently injures P's employee*, X. Under the general rule, P may not recover for P's economic losses stemming from X's unavailability. And the converse is also true — if D tortiously damages X, a business, then P, an employee of X who is deprived of work because of the damage to X, *may not recover lost wages* from D.

Example: Goalie is a star soccer player with a long-term contract to play for Metro, a professional soccer team. Driver negligently injures Goalie in a car accident, causing Goalie to miss Metro's season. Assume that by the terms of the Goalie-Metro contract, Metro has to pay Goalie his salary for the season despite his unavailability. Even if Metro can demonstrate with near certainty that Goalie's unavailability has cost Metro $1 million in ticket sales for the season, Metro cannot recover anything at all from Driver.

That's because, although Driver's negligence has caused physical injury *to Goalie* (for which Goalie himself can of course recover against Driver), Metro has suffered only economic loss, unaccompanied by personal injury or damage to Metro's "property." (An employee is not considered "property" of the employer for this purpose.) Thus the general rule barring recovery for unintentionally-caused pure economic loss applies. Cf. Rest. 3d (Liab. For Econ. Harm) §7, Illustr. 1 (nearly identical facts).

4. **Interruption to power or supplies:** Similarly, if D's negligence causes an interruption of the *flow of goods or services* that are needed for P's business, but there is no contractual relationship between D and P (and no physical damage to P's property), the general rule prevents P from recovering for its losses.

Example: Contractor, doing excavation work on private property two buildings away from P's factory, negligently severs the power lines that serve the factory, putting P's factory out of business for a day. Assume that the power outage does not cause any damage to P's building or equipment. The rule against recovery for pure economic

losses prevents P from recovering from Contractor for these losses. D,H&B Trts. §
647, v. 3, p. 586.

D. Situations that are exceptions or fall outside of the rule: But there are some important situations that are deemed either to fall outside of the scope of the general no-liability-for-pure-economic-loss rule, or to be exceptions to the rule. Two of the more important such situations are (a) where P has a *"proprietary interest"* in property that is physically damaged by D's negligence; and (b) where D has created a *"public nuisance,"* and P has suffered harm from the nuisance that is "different in kind" from that suffered by other nearby persons. We consider each of these two scenarios in turn.

1. **P has a proprietary interest:** Since the general rule we're discussing bars recovery only for "pure" economic loss, it's not surprising that a plaintiff can recover economic-loss damages if the plaintiff can also show that *"property" in which she has a "proprietary" interest* was damaged by the D's negligence, leading to the economic loss.

    a. **P owns and possesses the damaged property:** If P both *owns and possesses* the tangible property damaged by D's negligence, it's easy to see how P can recover for economic losses that stem directly from the property damage.

        Example: BargeCo, the owner/operator of a barge, negligently spills chemicals into a harbor. The spilled chemicals flow into the innards of a new custom-designed drill owned by Contractor, a building contractor who is using the drill to finish a construction project owned by Owner at the edge of the harbor. Repair of the drill costs Contractor $10,000, and the process takes a month. Contractor also loses $40,000 because the month's delay causes Contractor to forfeit a "timely completion" bonus in that amount that Contractor would have otherwise received from Owner. (No replacement drill was reasonably available to Contractor sooner because of the drill's custom design.)

        Because Contractor suffered direct damage to its tangible property (the drill), Contractor is entitled to recover from BargeCo not only the repair costs, but the intangible economic loss (the $40,000), since that loss stemmed directly from the same negligent act by BargeCo that caused the property damage.

    b. **P has possession but not ownership; the "proprietary" test:** Where P does *not own* the property that's physically damaged, but has the right to *use or possess* that property, the analysis is more complicated. In this situation, P can recover for economic loss directly resulting from the episode that damages the property if and only if P's arrangement with the owner included at least one (and in some courts both) of the following attributes: (1) *control* of the property, and (2) the responsibility for *maintaining and repairing* the property. Rest. 3d (Liab. For Economic Harm) §7, Comment c.

        Example 1 (right to recover economic loss): P rents one floor of a building from O. D, a contractor working for O on the exterior of the building, negligently causes a wall to cave in, blocking P's employees from work for two weeks. Most courts would say that P, as the tenant of a floor of the building, had enough control of its part of the premises to be deemed to have a "proprietary" interest in those premises. In such a court, P would be permitted to recover its economic losses (lost production) for the period when its employees couldn't come to work.

Example 2 (no right to recover economic loss): P is a railroad that, along with two other railroads, has the right to use a bridge owned and maintained by O. A tugboat owed by D negligently damages the bridge, causing P to have to re-route its shipments for several weeks, at greater cost to P.

A court would probably say that although P had a non-exclusive right to use the bridge, P's lack of complete control (and of the obligation to maintain) the bridge prevented P from having the required proprietary interest in the bridge. If the court so concluded, the court would probably bar P from recovering its economic losses from D, under the general rule preventing recovery of pure economic losses. Cf. Rest. 3d (Liab. For Economic Harm) §7, Illustr. 6.

2. **Public nuisance with special harm:** Courts generally recognize an exception to the no-recovery-for-pure-economic-losses rule if the defendant's actions create a *public nuisance,* but only if the type of economic harm suffered by the plaintiff is *qualitatively different* from that suffered by other members of the community. See Rest. 3d (Liab. for Econ. Harm) §8, entitled "Public Nuisance Resulting in Economic Loss": D will be liable if its "wrongful conduct harms or obstructs a public resource or public property," but only if P's losses are *"distinct in kind* from those suffered by *members of the affected community in general."*

   a. **Taken from law of nuisance:** This "exception" is really a recognition that the tort of public nuisance has special features that sometimes call for a private right of action for pure economic loss. (See *infra*, p. 431, for a more detailed discussion of private rights of action for public nuisances.) Normally, the preferred remedy for a public nuisance is an action by the government to have the nuisance abated. But courts often allow private plaintiffs to bring suit for both an injunction and damages, on the theory that such a suit is a valid substitute for a government abatement suit, especially in those cases where there is no single government body standing by ready to bring its own suit.

   b. **"Distinct in kind" requirement:** The requirement for private suits that the plaintiff's losses be *"distinct in kind* from those suffered by members of the affected community in general" has quite a lot of bite — where the nuisance has some sort of economic impact on a *significant number of businesses*, a plaintiff generally *won't be able to meet* the "distinct in-kind" requirement merely by showing that her losses are of *greater magnitude* than those of most other community members. Rather, the plaintiff typically has to show that something about her situation -- usually tied to her particular location — makes her losses of a *"different kind," not just "different magnitude"* — from other nearby businesses' losses. The following two examples illustrate the kinds of situations that will or won't meet this "different in kind" requirement.

   Example 1 (not different in kind): Recall the *532 Madison Avenue Gourmet* case, *supra*, p. 225, where the collapse of a building negligently constructed by D caused street closings that prevented customers of the Ps (nearby retail stores) from reaching the Ps' premises. The Ps sought to fit within the public-nuisance exception to the no-recovery-for-pure-economic-loss.

But the court found that the Ps had *not* shown the requisite "special injury beyond that suffered by the community at large" – *"[E]very person who maintained a business, profession or residence* in the heavily populated areas of ... Madison Avenue was exposed to *similar economic loss* during the closure period[]." (Even if the Ps had shown that their *dollar losses were greater* than those of nearly every other person or business in the area, it's unlikely that the court would have found that the "different in kind" requirement was satisfied.)

Example 2 (different in kind): Restaurant is located on the bank of a river. Many of Restaurant's customers arrive by boat, and moor their boat at a dock owned and maintained by Restaurant. Logger floats logs down the river, and negligently allows the logs to become stuck on the river bank near Restaurant's dock, so that restaurants customers can no longer arrive by boat. (The log blockage is not located at or immediately adjacent to any part of Restaurant's property.) No other person or business is affected by the blockage.

A court would likely find that Restaurant has suffered the requisite "distinct in kind" harm. If the court so concluded (and if the court also concluded that the stock logs constituted a public nuisance), the court would allow Restaurant to recover damages for its lost business from logger. Cf. Rest. 3d (Liab. For Economic Harm) § 8, Illustr. 4 (same facts, but assuming, without deciding, that Restaurant's losses are "special," and concluding that on that assumption Restaurant may recover for its pure economic losses).

    c. **Commercial fishers as a special case:** Some courts allow *commercial fishers* to recover their lost business when the defendant wrongfully pollutes the waterway in which the fishers have been fishing. The Third Restatement says that these cases "are usually, and correctly, understood as *suits to remedy a public nuisance."* Rest. 3d (Liab. for Econ. Harm) §7, Comment e(b). In such suits, the courts typically conclude that the fishers have met the requirement of showing that their harm is "different in kind" from the losses suffered by the community in general. *Id.*

E. Some courts reject basic rule: A few courts seem to have simply *rejected the basic rule* barring recovery for economic damages where the plaintiff has not suffered personal injury or property damage. See, e.g., *People Express Airlines, Inc. v. Consolidated Rail Corp.*, 495 A.2d 107 (N.J. 1985), the leading such decision.

    1. **Rare:** But rejection of the general principle barring recovery for pure economic loss is *relatively rare*, and seems not to be becoming more common. (Note that *People Express*, the leading case rejecting the general rule, is now over 30 years old.) See, e.g., Rest. 3d (Liab. for Econ. Harm) §7, Reporter's Note to Comment a, saying that as to §7's general rule barring recovery for pure economic loss, "contrary positions have been taken *only occasionally* in the case law," and citing *People Express* as one of only two such cases.

F. Special statutes: The "rule" barring liability for pure economic losses is, of course, just a *common-law* principle – in other words, it is a judge-made doctrine, and as such can be overruled by a legislature for all or certain scenarios. And, indeed, there are some important contexts in which state and federal statutes overturn the common-law no-recovery rule.

1. **Oil spills and the OPA:** For instance, Congress has enacted a special statute that in large part reverses the standard no-recovery-for-pure-economic-losses rule for persons who suffer economic loss as the result of an *oil spill*. In the *Federal Oil Pollution Act of 1990* (*"OPA"*), 33 U.S.C. §2702 et seq., Congress gave many persons who suffer economic loss from a spill of oil into navigable waters and onto shorelines the right to recover lost profits caused by the spill, even if the plaintiff did not herself own property that was damaged by the spill.

   Example: Suppose Hotel is located near (but not on) a beach that is fouled by an oil spill, and Hotel loses business because customers cancel their visit when they realize they won't be able to use the beaches. Hotel and its employees can probably both recover under OPA. See 30 Miss. C. L. Rev. 335, 374 (2011), saying that OPA probably gives a loss-profits claim to "the hotel owner who loses profits because neighboring beaches and waters that his customers tend to use are polluted, and the employee of that hotel who loses wages because of the hotel's loss of business."

   a. **2010 Gulf of Mexico oil spill:** Thus following the 2010 Deepwater Horizon oil-drilling spill in the Gulf of Mexico, thousands of claimants who suffered only economic harm from the spill filed various sorts of claims against BP, the well operator. As of April 2015, BP had paid out $10 billion in claims to people and businesses in five states who lost income, profit or property because of the spill, much of it on claims that did not involve physical damage to the claimant's property. www.ibtimes.com, April 16, 2015. It seems likely that BP's willingness to make such large payments for pure-economic-loss was due to OPA's overriding of the standard no-recovery-for-pure-economic-losses regime.

G. **Other contexts involving pure economic loss:** Here, we've talked about just one aspect of courts' reluctance to award damage to a plaintiff who has suffered only economic loss — the "three party" scenario in which D tortuously causes personal injury or property damage to *A*, but only economic loss to *B*, who nonetheless sues. But there are a number of *other scenarios* that similarly raise the issue of whether a plaintiff who has suffered only economic loss may recover including scenarios in which the defendant has behaved tortiously only to one person (the one who is now bringing suit). These other scenarios — where the court may or may not award liability for pure economic loss — include negligent performance of a contract for services (*supra*, p. 209), misrepresentation (*infra*, p. 442), products liability (*infra*, p. 358), and interference with contract (*infra*, p. 504). As you will see, judges' fears of unbounded liability surface in these other economic-loss scenarios, too, but those fears are often countered by a judicial instinct to allow recovery where there is only a small class of affected victims.

Quiz Yourself on

DUTY *(Entire Chapter)*

47. Benedict Arnold, diplomat, is out riding, and sees his friend, George Washington, slumped beside a tree. Washington has caught a chill, and Arnold helps him up and takes him back to the Arnold home. There, Arnold applies leeches to Washington, which Arnold believes will suck out Washington's "bad blood"

and cure him. Arnold's not a doctor, but he remembers hearing that applying leeches sucks out a sick person's "bad blood." In fact, however (and as most people know), antibiotics are the only proper way to treat a chill, and leeches are dangerous. Arnold's treatment worsens Washington's condition. When Washington sues him, Arnold defends on the grounds that he was under no duty to act at all, so he can't be liable. Who's correct? _____

48. Patricia is walking with her five-year-old son, Colin, across the street. Doug, driving dangerously fast, is unable to come to a full stop, and lightly hits Patricia. Patricia is knocked to the ground, and suffers minor bruises. She suffers many sleepless nights mentally replaying the accident, and is afraid to cross any of the busy streets in her neighborhood anymore. She sues Doug not only for the bruises but for her emotional distress arising out of the accident. May she recover for this distress? _____

49. Paula and Pam, who are friends, are out on a walk with Paula's 12-year-old daughter Sheila. While Sheila is walking 10 yards ahead of the two women, she starts to cross the street at a cross-walk. Dan, speeding, goes through a red light and strikes Sheila, knocking her down and paralyzing her from the waist down. Paula and Pam watch the whole event, horrified. Neither ever feels personally in danger of being hit, but both suffer symptoms of Post-Traumatic Stress Disorder for years afterward, with constant nightmares in which they relive seeing Sheila be terribly injured. Paula and Pam each sue Dan for their emotional distress. Under the majority approach to the relevant issues:

    (a) Can Paula recover? _____

    (b) Can Pam recover? _____

50. DrillCo is an oil company that drills for oil off the shore of Hilton Head, South Carolina. Due to DrillCo's negligence in performing the drilling, a large blow-out occurs, and oil is spread onto the shore. Some direct beachfront owners have oil wash up onto their property with harmful direct results to the land. Peg owns and runs a hotel that is two blocks from the waterfront; no part of the hotel is directly touched by the spill, and no guest or member is physically injured. Because the beach is rendered unsightly for a one-year clean-up period, occupancy at Peg's hotel (like that of most local hotel keepers) diminishes by 60%, leaving her with a loss of $100,000 in profits compared with the profits in a normal year. Assume that the facts constitute an actionable public nuisance. Under prevailing modern law, may Peg recover $100,000 in damages from DrillCo? (Assume there are no statutes on point.) _____

_____

Answers

47. Washington. Initially, Arnold was under no duty to act — when he first saw Washington, he could have left him as he found him, without incurring liability. But once he took an affirmative act in an effort to help (in torts lingo, once he "undertook" to help), he then had the obligation to do so in a reasonable, non-negligent way. Consequently, he is liable for using a treatment method that an ordinary citizen of reasonable care would have known was unsafe.

48. Yes. If the defendant's negligence has caused a physical impact with the plaintiff's person, the defendant is liable not only for the physical consequences of that impact but also all the emotional or mental suffering which flows naturally from it. Thus Patricia, like any physically injured negligence plaintiff, may recover for "mental suffering" — these mental damages are said to be "parasitic" ones, i.e., ones which attach to the physical injury.

49. (a) Yes. Most modern courts allow a bystander to recover for pure emotional distress, if the bystander watches a close relative be severely injured. See, e.g., Rest. 3d (Liab. Phys. & Emot. Harm), §48, which says that a defendant who "causes **sudden serious bodily injury to a third person**" will be liable for "serious emotional harm" caused to a plaintiff who "**perceives the event contemporaneously**" and who is a "**close family member**" of the third person who suffers the bodily injury. Since the person that Paula watched suffer the "sudden serious bodily injure" was her daughter, Paula meets the "close family member" requirement, and can recover for her pure emotional distress. And that's true even though Paula was never herself within the "zone of danger," i.e., never close enough to the speeding car that she feared that she herself would be hit.

(b) No. If Pam had herself been at some point within the "zone of danger" from the speeding car, most courts would allow her to recover her emotional distress, both distress at the danger to Pam herself and distress at the actual injury to Sheila. But since Pam was never physically in danger, a different rule applies. Under the rule described in sub-paragraph (a) above, Pam would be able to recover for distress at seeing Sheila be injured only if Pam was a "close family member" of Sheila. Since Pam is not a close family member of Sheila, neither the above rule nor any other rule would furnish an exception to the general rule that one may not recover for emotional distress at witnessing, from a safe position, a severe injury to another.

50. No. As a general rule, tortfeasors are not liable to plaintiffs for negligently-caused **pure economic loss**, i.e., loss that does not occur in conjunction with any property damage or physical injury to that plaintiff. See, e.g., Rest. 3d of Torts (Liab. for Econ. Loss), §7, stating the general rule that "a claimant cannot recover for economic loss caused by (a) unintentional personal injury to another party; or (b) unintentional injury to property in which the claimant has no proprietary interest." This rule applies here, because the facts tell us that DrillCo has negligently caused oil damage to the property of certain beach-front owners, but that there has been no direct property damage to any property in which Peg has a "proprietary interest." (There's no indication that she has any financial interest in any of the beach-front property that was physically affected by the spill.) Therefore, the Restatement — and most courts — would not allow Peg to recover for her pure economic loss, despite the fact that DrillCo's negligence was the factual and proximate cause of that loss. There are some exceptions to this general principle of "no recovery for pure economic loss," but none of those exceptions applies here.

Note, by the way, that the question tells you to assume that there are **no statutes** on point. This is an important assumption, because in fact, there *is* a federal statute on point: the federal Oil Pollution Act, 33 U.S.C. §2702 et seq, gives many people and businesses who suffer economic losses from a negligently-caused oil spill into a navigable waterway the right to recover those losses, even if the claimant did not own property that was physically damaged by the spill. So under the OPA, Peg *would* be able to recover her lost profits.

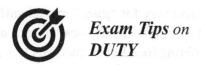 *Exam Tips on*
DUTY

Be on the lookout for three special types of situations: (1) D **fails to act**; (2) P claims "**mental suffering**" without physical impact; and (3) D suffers solely "**intangible economic harm**."

☞ Look for situations where D **fails to act**.

☞ The core rule, of course, is that a person generally has **no duty to assist another**, even where he could do so easily. Occasionally, this general rule is tested — you can spot it because the facts will typically involve a complete stranger who happens to pass by to observe P's peril. (*Example:* D jogs by, sees P drowning, doesn't pull P out or call for help. D is not liable.)

☞ Much more often, however, the **exceptions** to the general rule of "no duty to render assistance" are what are tested. The most important exceptions are:

  ☞ Any **owner of business premises** has a duty to help one who is on the premises, regardless of the source of the danger. (*Example:* If P is choking in D's store, D must attempt to help P even if the choking has nothing to do with D's conduct.)

    ☞ A sub-rule: **Common carriers** have a special duty to help passengers, including protecting them from third-party wrongdoers.

    ☞ Similarly, most courts now recognize a special **university-student** relationship (so that the university must give assistance to a student it knows or should know is in danger, whether the danger is from drug use or from, say, a poorly-lit parking lot).

  ☞ D has a duty to help if **D's conduct created the danger** (even if D did not behave negligently). (*Example:* D's car hits P when P darts into the street. Even if D drove completely carefully, D has a duty to get medical assistance for P.)

  ☞ D has a duty to render assistance if he **"undertakes"** to furnish assistance. "Undertaking" clearly includes the situation where D starts to render assistance, and then doesn't follow through. (*Example:* D drives P partway to the hospital, then puts P off at the side of the road.)

    ☞ Testable issue: Does D's mere **promise** to render assistance bind D? Most courts today find that a promise alone can be an undertaking, if it induces detrimental reliance by P or others (e.g., others declined to help P thinking D is already giving help).

    ☞ But there's only liability on an "undertaking" theory when D leaves P **worse off** than had there been no undertaking ("detrimental reliance"). (*Example:* D passes by, sees P lying injured, and says, "I'll get help." If no one else comes along, until X comes along and gets help, probably D is not liable because he didn't worsen P's status.)

☛ Look for situations where P may have a claim for **"mental suffering."**

  ☞ First, remember that the courts usually don't allow recovery for **"pure"** mental suffering, without any **physical manifestations**. Thus if P suffers no physical impact **and** doesn't get physical symptoms from her asserted suffering (headaches, nausea, etc.), the court is likely to hold that the mental suffering did not merit compensation.

  ☞ Also, remember that if P has **direct physical injuries**, the mental suffering can in all courts be **"tacked on"** as an additional element of recovery. (*Example:* P gets a broken leg from a car accident; P can also recover for suffering the pain from the break.)

☞ Mental suffering thus is an important issue just in those cases where there is **no direct physical injury**. There are two major fact patterns that pop up on exams:

    ☞ First, P is **herself in physical danger**, and is frightened solely for her own safety. Here, all courts allow P to recover. (*Example:* P is about to be run over and jumps out of the way. P can recover for her mental distress, both at the moment and reliving the near-accident.)

    ☞ Second (and more commonly tested), P **witnesses an accident** to another person, and P's mental suffering is mainly her fear **for the other's** safety. Here, your analysis should go through several stages:

        ❏ If P was within the **"zone of impact"** or **"zone of danger,"** virtually all courts will allow P to recover for mental suffering, both for her fear for her own safety and her fear for the safety of any **relative** who may have been hit or almost hit. So if the facts tell you that P was walking alongside of her husband X (or "standing next to" X), and X is run over or otherwise hurt, then P can recover for mental suffering.

        ❏ If P was **not** within the zone of impact/danger, but was "present" and **viewed** an accident to another, **some** (but probably not yet most) courts have abolished the "zone of impact" requirement, and **allow** P to recover for fear for the safety of the injured person. However, these courts almost all require that the injured person be a **close relative**, and also require that P suffer **serious** emotional distress. So on these facts, say that P can recover "if the jurisdiction has abolished the zone-of-impact requirement." (Usually, the facts won't make it clear whether the jurisdiction has abolished the requirement.)

        Note: In courts that have abolished the "zone of impact" requirement, P can recover not only where she is, say, outside and within a few feet of the accident site, but also where she is **inside** and sees the accident through a **window**.

        ❏ If P **does not see** the accident at all, but merely hears about it later (even just a few moments later), no court seems to let P recover for mental distress, even if the injured person (call him "X") is P's close relative. So be on the lookout for a fact pattern reading, "A few moments after the accident, P, X's mother, came on the scene . . . ," or "A neighbor rushed to tell P about the accident to X . . . " — there is **no recovery** for P's distress in these scenarios. If X is badly hurt or killed, P can recover for loss of consortium — but in this chapter, we're talking about situations where X is either not badly hurt, or not hurt at all, and P has merely suffered fear, not permanent loss.

☛ Look out for situations where D suffers pure **"intangible economic harm"** (e.g., **lost business profits**), as distinguished from physical harm or property damage.

    ☞ First, look for the situation where D suffers intangible economic harm **in addition to** physical injury or direct property damage. Here, all courts agree that P may "tack on" his economic loss to the other elements of harm. (*Example:* P gets a broken leg, and can't operate his store for six months. P can collect the profits he would have made operating the store.)

☞ More difficult (and more likely to be tested) is the situation where P suffers *only* intangible economic harm, with no personal injury or property damage.

　☞ First, check that *someone* has suffered personal injury or direct property damage. If there is no such person, then in all courts it's clear that P can't recover for the economic losses.

　☞ Assuming that the person or tangible property of someone other than P was directly injured, then you have an issue about whether P can recover for his pure economic loss from the same episode.

　　❑ Under the ***majority view***, D can't recover at all, because courts fear open-ended liability. (*Example:* P operates a brokerage business. D negligently drives into an electric transformer on the street, knocking out the power to P's business and all others within a 300 yard radius. P can't operate the business for a day, and loses money. Under the majority view, P can't recover, because he has suffered no personal injury or property damage, and his damages are purely economic.)

　　❑ In a few courts, there is no longer any per se rule against recovery of pure economic losses. However, even these courts require that P be part of a relatively small ***"identifiable class"*** that could be foreseen to suffer losses from an act like D's. (*Example:* Under the above brokerage example, P might be able to recover in a few courts, because any business in the relatively small area served by the transformer could be identified in advance as being one that would be economically damaged by D's conduct.)

　☞ Contexts where the issue of intangible economic harm is likely to arise:

　　❑ D launches some ***"public health hazard"*** (e.g., some disease, or some toxic chemical into the air, or some pollutant into the water). (*Example:* The Gulf Oil Spill scenario, where D negligently causes the spill and claims are brought by P, a hotel operator who suffers no direct physical injury or property damage, but loses profits because customers stay away. Under the majority view, absent a statute P cannot recover for this pure economic loss.)

　　❑ D cuts off some ***vital public service*** (e.g., a bridge or highway, electric or water service, etc.).

　　❑ D negligently injures X, a human, and P, X's ***employer***, loses the benefits of X's services for a time, and thus loses profits. (P can't recover from D for P's pure economic losses, even though *X* can recover his lost wages as well as for pain and suffering, medical bills, etc.)

　☞ The "intangible economic loss" problem arises both where the claim is based on negligence, and also where it's based on ***strict product liability*** or ***abnormally dangerous activity***. (But it does not arise where the tort is intentional, since here the liability is wide-sweeping, and probably all courts will give recovery for pure intangible economic loss.)

Chapter 9

OWNERS AND OCCUPIERS
OF LAND

ChapterScope

This chapter summarizes the various common-law rules dealing with the obligations of owners of land, and the more modern rules that have sometimes replaced the common-law ones.

- **Duty to those outside the premises:** A landowner has a general duty to prevent an unreasonable risk of harm to persons *off* the land from *artificial conditions* on the land. (Traditionally, the owner has no duty to remove a *natural* condition that poses risk to those off the land.)

- **Trespassers:** As a general rule, the landowner owes *no duty to a trespasser* to make her land *safe*, to *warn* of dangers on it, or to protect the trespasser in any other way. But there are important exceptions to this rule.

  - ❏ **Children:** Most significantly, the owner owes a duty of reasonable care to a trespassing *child* if certain conditions are met.

- **Licensees:** The common-law recognizes a limited set of duties that a landowner owes to a *"licensee."*

  - ❏ **Definition:** A licensee is a person who has the owner's *consent* to be on the property, but who does *not have a business purpose* for being there. The main class of persons who qualify as licensees are *"social guests."*

  - ❏ **Duty:** The landowner does *not* owe a licensee any duty to *inspect for unknown dangers*, or to *fix* any known danger. However, the owner does have the duty to *warn* the licensee of any danger that the owner *knows* of.

- **Invitees:** At common law, the owner owes a greater set of duties to an *"invitee."*

  - ❏ **Definition:** An invitee, under the modern view, includes: (1) persons who are invited by the owner onto the land to conduct *business* with the owner; and (2) those who are invited as members of the *public* for purposes for which the land is held *open to the public*.

  - ❏ **Duty:** The landowner owes an invitee a duty of *reasonable inspection to find hidden dangers*. Also, the owner must take reasonable efforts to *fix* a dangerous condition.

- **Rejection of categories:** Some (but not yet most) courts have *rejected* the categories of trespasser, licensee and invitee, in favor of a single "reasonable person" standard of landowner liability.

- **Lessors and lessees:**

  - ❏ **Lessee:** A *tenant* is treated *as if she were the owner*, for liability purposes.

  - ❏ **Lessors:** In general, a *lessor* (landlord) is *not* liable in tort once he transfers possession to the lessee. However, there are some important exceptions.

I.   HISTORICAL INTRODUCTION

A.   **Landowner tort law historically:** The common law, up through the nineteenth century, was strongly influenced by the primarily agrarian and rural nature of both the English and American economies. These societies, being sparsely settled as they were, were able to nurture the view that an individual's land was his to do with as he pleased. Consequently, a number of detailed, specialized rules arose concerning the duties of owners and occupiers of land towards other persons, both on and off the premises. These rules were not merely clarifications of what constituted "due care," but were on the contrary rules sharply reducing the duties of landowners and occupiers, holding them to a standard of care markedly lower than that which, to our modern eyes, would be shown by the typical "reasonable person."

    1.   **About this chapter:** This chapter summarizes these various common law rules, and also shows the process whereby modern courts have liberalized and, in some cases, abandoned, these principles in favor of a more general duty of due care.

II.   OUTSIDE THE PREMISES

A.   **Natural v. artificial conditions:**   Whatever socio-economic reasons there have been for imposing a low standard of care upon landowners vis-à-vis persons upon their land, these reasons are less compelling when the landowner's conduct has effects *outside* of his property. Landowners have therefore generally been held liable for conditions upon their land which pose an unreasonable risk to persons outside of it. See Rest. 2d, §§364, 365. There are, however, some exceptions to, as well as special clarifications of, this rule. The most important of these is the distinction between naturally existing hazards and artificially created ones.

    1.   **Natural hazards:**   Where a hazardous condition exists *naturally* upon the land, it has almost always been held that the property owner has *no duty* to remove it or guard against it, even if it poses an unreasonable danger of harm to persons outside the property. See Rest. 2d, §363(1).

        Example: A boulder sits at the edge of D's property, adjacent to (and higher than) P's property. (The boulder has naturally come to that position, without human intervention.) Even though it's obvious to D for some time that the boulder might fall onto P's property, he does nothing. In a strong windstorm, the boulder falls onto P's house, damaging it. Under the traditional rule, D is not liable to P, because the hazardous condition existed naturally on the land, and D therefore had no duty to remove it or guard against it.

        a.   **Trees:**   One frequent setting in which the "natural hazard" issue arises involves *trees*. Traditionally, courts have distinguished between thickly-settled and rural areas. In thickly-settled urban and suburban areas, owners have generally been required to prevent trees on their property from posing an unreasonable risk of harm to persons on the public roads. This means not only that owners must remove rotten trees where they know of the danger, but also that they probably have an affirmative duty to *inspect* to discover such defects. See Rest. 2d, §363(2). In less-densely-populated rural areas, by contrast, owners have generally been held not to have any duty to remove rotten trees or to inspect for defects.

b. **Rural/urban distinction rejected:** But some modern decisions have rejected the rural/urban distinction in fallen-tree cases. In one case, for instance, this distinction was abandoned in favor of a general requirement that the landowner exercise *"reasonable care to prevent an unreasonable risk of harm." Taylor v. Olsen*, 578 P.2d 779 (Or. 1978).

2. **Artificial hazards:** Where the hazardous condition is *artificially* created, however, the owner has a *general duty to prevent an unreasonable risk of harm* to persons outside the premises. This includes not only man-made structures, but also living things which have been artificially placed on the land (e.g. shrubs) as well as changes in the physical conditions of the land (e.g. excavations). Rest. 2d, §363, Comment b.

   a. **Danger to persons on highway:** Most of the cases falling under this rule have involved danger to persons on an *adjoining public road* (usually called a "highway," even if only a seldom-travelled public street).

   b. **Foreseeable deviations:** This duty is owed not only to those who use the public road, but also those who, while using it, predictably *deviate slightly* from it onto the owner's land. Thus a property owner will be liable where she places an unreasonably dangerous excavation next to a public side walk, and the plaintiff unwittingly falls into it. Similarly the defendant will be liable if he places a building next to the sidewalk, with a side door in it which is not locked and which opens into a steep drop to the basement, injuring a person who leans against the door. The issue is whether the plaintiff's deviation is "reasonably foreseeable"; it is usually held that deviations by children are more foreseeable than those by adults.

   c. **Telephone poles and other above-the-ground objects:** But where a property owner maintains a necessary *above-the-ground object*, such as a *telephone pole* or *mailbox*, courts are reluctant to impose liability when a person using the adjoining road collides with the object.

B. **Conduct of others:** The landowner's duty of reasonable care may require her to *control the conduct of others,* whose behavior on her property may cause injury to those off it.

   1. **Employees:** This is of course true with respect to the owner's *employees* under the doctrine of *respondeat superior* (discussed *infra* p. 315).

   2. **Contractors:** Similarly, the landowner may be responsible for the negligence of an *independent contractor*, if the contractor's work is inherently dangerous to those off the premises (see *infra*, p. 319).

   3. **General rule:** But even more generally, the owner is responsible for preventing the activities of anyone on her property if she knows or should know there is danger to outsiders. Thus the owner of a hotel was liable to a passer-by who while on the adjoining sidewalk was hit by an object thrown by a drunken Junior Chamber of Commerce conventioneer staying at the hotel; *Connolly v. Nicollet Hotel*, 95 N.W.2d 657 (Minn. 1958). Similarly, the owner of a baseball park was liable for injury to a pedestrian arising from one of a continual series of foul balls hit by the players; the court asserted that the public has "a right to the free and unmolested use of the public highways," and that the owner was required to take reasonable precautions (e.g., a higher fence) to guard against

such injuries. *Salevan v. Wilmington Park, Inc.*, 72 A.2d 239 (Del. 1950). See Rest. 2d §318.

III. INJURIES ON THE PREMISES GENERALLY

A. **Detailed rules:**   It is where injuries occur *on* the owner's premises that the detailed and restrictive rules on liability referred to at the beginning of this chapter take effect.

    1. **Possessor v. owner:**   These common law rules were designed to encourage the full exploitation of land. Therefore, the beneficiary of the rule is the ***possessor*** of the land, not the abstract legal owner. The most important consequence of this fact is that when a ***tenant*** takes possession of property, even if only for a very short period, he is the one who gets the benefit of these specialized rules. The lessor, once he gives up possession, loses the benefit of these rules, although there are other rules (discussed *infra*, p. 251) which also curtail the degree of care which he is required to show.

    2. **Family and employees of possessor:**   The benefits available to the possessor are also shared, according to most courts, by members of the possessor's ***household*** as well as persons working on the land for his benefit either as ***employees*** or ***independent contractors.*** See Rest. 2d, §384.

    3. **The term "owner" used for convenience:**   In this outline the terms "landowner" or "property owner" are used, for convenience, to designate the person who, as possessor of the land, has the benefit of these special rules.

B. **Three categories:**   The common law evolved a rigid series of categories of plaintiffs, as to each of which the landowner owed a sharply differing duty of care. The three principal classes were ***"trespasser", "licensee"*** and ***"invitee".*** The "trespasser" was one who had no right at all to be on the land; the "licensee" was one who came on the land with the owner's consent, but as a social guest (not a business visitor), and the "invitee" was one who came with a business purpose. The owner's duty of care with respect to the "trespasser" was the least, and that with regard to the "invitee" the greatest.

    1. **Present significance:**   As is discussed *infra*, p. 250, the significance of these three rigid categories, and the duties relative to each, have been rejected or modified by at least some modern courts, but most courts continue to apply them. Therefore, the highly formalistic rules for determining which category a particular plaintiff falls into must be carefully studied.

IV. TRESPASSERS

A. **General rule as to trespassers:**   The general rule is that the landowner owes ***no duty to a trespasser*** to make her land safe, to warn of dangers on it, to avoid carrying on dangerous activities on it, or to protect the trespasser in any other way. The theory behind this view is that a property owner should be entitled to use her land as she wishes, without worrying about the safety of those who have no right to be on it. See Rest. 2d, §333.

Example: P trespasses along D Railroad's track. His foot gets caught in the track bed, and he is run over by one of D's trains, which fails to stop in time P alleges both that the roadbed was negligently maintained, and that D's employees were negligent in not stopping in time.

Held, since P was a trespasser, D owed him no duty of maintaining the roadbed, train brakes or other equipment in a safe condition, or of running the train at low enough speeds to be safe. D may have owed P a duty of reasonable care once his presence was discovered (one of the exceptions discussed below), but as to this duty, the evidence is that D's employees met this standard. *Sheehan v. St. Paul & Duluth Ry. Co.*, 76 F. 201 (7th Cir. 1896).

1. **Invitee who goes beyond scope of invitation:** Keep in mind that a person who starts out being an invitee (one who is on the premises for a business purpose; see *infra*, p. 246) or a licensee (one who has the owner's consent but not a business purpose; see *infra*, p. 244) can become a trespasser by *failing to stay within the scope of the area* in which the premises owner has invited him.

   a. **"Employees only" or "Keep out":** Thus a customer or patron who goes into an area of business premises marked "private" or "employees only" or "keep out" will be a trespasser once she does so, and the owner will no longer owe the customer any duty of reasonable care if the owner is not aware of the customer's presence or peril.

   Example: P is a customer of D, a department store. P sees a door marked, "Men's Room," which bears a sign "Employees only. Customers, please use bathroom on main floor." P enters anyway (unbeknownst to D's employees), and slips on a wet floor. A court will probably hold that although P started by being an invitee, P became a trespasser when he entered the bathroom. In that event, D will be found to have not owed P any duty of care to keep the floor non-slippery.

B. **Exceptions:** There are a number of exceptions to this general absence of a duty of care to trespassers. The more important of these are as follows.

   1. **Constant trespass on limited area:** If the owner has reason to know that a *limited portion* of her land is *frequently used* by various trespassers, as a crossing or path, she must use reasonable care to make the premises safe, or at least, to warn them of dangers which they would probably not otherwise discover. Rest. 2d, §§ 333, 334.

      a. **Railroad crossing:** This principle has been most frequently applied in cases of persons injured while using a well-travelled path across or along a *railroad*; it is held that the trains must be operated with reasonable care (e.g., with warning whistles) to protect the trespassers. See, e.g., Rest. 2d, §334, Illustrations 1-3.

   2. **Discovered trespassers:** The most important exception to the general rule of non-liability to trespassers is that once the owner has *knowledge* that a particular person is trespassing on her property, she is then under a duty to exercise reasonable care for the latter's safety. Rest. 2d, §§ 335, 336.

      a. **Natural conditions:** This exception clearly applies where the danger to the discovered trespasser arises from the owner's physical activities (e.g., running a train), or from "artificial conditions" on the land (e.g., an excavation). Where the condition is a purely ***natural*** one, however, (e.g., a hidden bog), it is not clear whether the exception will apply; see Rest. 2d, §337, Comment b stating that the exception should, in theory, apply.

b. What constitutes discovery: the duty of reasonable care is triggered not only when the owner ***actually*** learns of the trespasser's presence, but also, when she is confronted by evidence which ***should*** reasonably lead her to the conclusion that a trespasser is present and in danger.

c. "Wanton and willful" requirement: Some courts have held that the defendant is liable only if, following the discovery of the trespasser, she disregards the latter's safety ***"wantonly and willfully"***. But this standard has either been rejected by most courts in favor of a simple due care standard, or interpreted in such a way that lack of due care following discovery of a trespasser is automatically deemed "wanton." See P&K, p. 397.

d. Sufficiency of warning: The defendant will often be able to satisfy her burden of due care merely by ***warning*** the trespasser; this will be so where the owner reasonably believes that the trespasser will respond to such a warning.

   i. Warning ignored: But once it becomes apparent that the warning will not be respected (e.g., where the trespasser makes no move to leave the train tracks following the engineer's blowing of the whistle), the duty then becomes to use other means to avoid harm.

3. Trespassing children: More liberal (to the plaintiff) rules have arisen where the trespasser is a ***child***. This is due to several factors: a child is usually less able to appreciate the dangers posed by strange conditions than an adult; children trespass more frequently than adults and therefore danger to them is more foreseeable; and courts are naturally sympathetic to injured children.

a. "Attractive nuisance":   Originally, a child plaintiff got the benefit of a more lenient rule only where his case fell within the so-called "***attractive nuisance***" doctrine. This doctrine imposed liability upon a landowner who maintained an injurious condition on her land which, because it made an enticing plaything, induced children onto the land.

b. Modern view: But most modern courts reject the requirement that the child have been attracted by the particular condition which ends up injuring him. However, there are a number of special conditions which must be met before there will be liability to a trespassing child (assuming this is not one of the situations in which there would also be liability to a trespassing adult, such as the "continued trespass upon a limited area" exception, discussed above). These requirements are set forth in an influential Restatement provision, Rest. 2d, §339:

   i. Likelihood of trespass: First, the owner must have reason to know that the condition in question is in a place on her land where ***children are likely to trespass;***

   ii. Danger: The owner must also have reason to know of the condition, and have reason to know that it poses an ***unreasonable risk*** of serious injury or death to trespassing children;

iii. Children ignorant of risk: The injured child must, because of his youth, either not have discovered the condition or not *realized the danger* posed by it;

iv. Utility: The *benefit* to the owner of maintaining the condition in its dangerous form must be *slight* weighed against the risk to the children, and;

v. Lack of reasonable care: The owner must fail to use *reasonable care* to eliminate the danger or protect the children.

> **Example of Restatement doctrine:** P1, who is five years old, enters the backyard of D, P1's next-door neighbor. D's yard has a previously-drained swimming pool that now contains 6 feet of accumulated rainwater; D has removed the fence that previously enclosed the pool. The rainwater in the pool has become pond-like, with tadpoles and frogs in it. P1 drowns, and P2 (P1's mother) also drowns while trying to save him. D defends on the grounds that since P1 was a trespasser, D owed him only a duty to refrain from wanton and willful misconduct, not a duty of reasonable care.
>
> *Held*, for the Ps: Ohio hereby adopts the attractive nuisance doctrine of Rest. 2d §339. This doctrine "effectively harmonizes the competing societal interests of protecting children and preserving property rights." Therefore, P1 can recover for negligence even though he was a trespasser, if he can show that: (1) D knew or had reason to know that children were likely to trespass into his yard, (2) D knew the pool/pond posed an unreasonable risk to such children, (3) P1 because of his youth did not realize the risk, (4) the utility to D of maintaining the pond-like pool (or the burden to him of eliminating the condition) was slight compared to the risk; and (5) D failed to use a reasonable care to eliminate the danger. (If P1 makes this showing, P2 can also recover, because she was reasonably attempting to rescue P1 from the negligently-caused danger.) *Bennett v. Stanley*, 748 N.E.2d 41 (Ohio 2001).

c. Other issues: Several issues have frequently arisen in connection with the "trespassing children" doctrine.

i. Age of children: How *young* must the child be to gain the benefit of the rule? Originally, many courts imposed a firm rule that the child had to be under twelve. But the modern view seems to be that the child must simply be so young that he is unable to appreciate the risk of the particular condition. This means that where the risk is a familiar one, such as that of drowning in a body of water, a relatively young child may be expected to understand the risk. A power cable, on the other hand, may pose such a sophisticated danger that even a child of sixteen will not be expected to be on his guard, and may recover. See P&K, p. 410.

(1) Subjective and objective aspects: The question apparently has both a subjective and objective aspect. That is, requirement (ii) above in the above list of Restatement requirements is met if the owner has reason to believe that the condition is dangerous to children of the age who are likely to trespass (even if the child who is injured is of a different age category). That's an objective standard. But as to requirement (iii), the actual injured child must not have appreciated the danger, and will be barred from recovery if, say, he had particular knowledge, unusual for one so young, of the danger. That's a subjective standard. (So for instance, a nine-year-old who is the son of a railroad engineer, and has been warned many times of the dangers of railroad turntables, but nevertheless injures himself, doesn't meet requirement (iii). See Rest. 2d, §339, Illustr. 8.)

   ii. **Natural conditions:** The rule recited in the Restatement applies only to "artificial conditions" on the land. As to "activities" carried on upon the land (e.g., the running of a railroad), trespassing children receive no greater protection than adults (and must fall within one of the above exceptions to recover). Where the danger comes from a "condition," but from one which is ***"natural"*** rather than "artificial", the rule is unclear. The Restatement, in §339, has a caveat on this issue, stating that most of the existing cases denying liability for natural conditions are ones where the child ought to have been familiar with the risk (e.g., a body of water), and also, generally, where the condition would have been unreasonably expensive to protect against.

   d. **General negligence standard:** The various requirements of Rest. 2d, §339, really amount to imposition of what is ***almost the usual "reasonable person" standard*** of negligence. Thus in most courts, "child trespasser law [is] viewed as essentially ordinary negligence law," with a few exceptions. P&K, p. 401. This means that the owner does not have to make her premises "child-proof", but must merely take "reasonable measures" to prevent harm; a warning, for instance, may often suffice.

   e. **Child invitees and licensees:** What if the child is not a "trespasser", but a "licensee" or "invitee"? It is universally agreed that such a child should have at least the benefit of the above "child trespasser" rules. Furthermore, she may gain even greater protection by virtue of the rules governing invitees and licensees discussed below; these, however, do not generally make special allowances for children.

   f. **No duty of inspection:** The child trespasser rules do not generally impose any ***duty of inspection*** upon the landowner. She is not required to inspect in order to determine whether children are likely to trespass, nor is she required to inspect to see if there are any dangerous conditions of which she otherwise would not have any reason to know. See Rest. 2d, §339, Comment g.

V. LICENSEES

A. **Significance of being a "licensee":** The next step up from the lowly "trespasser" is the so-called ***"licensee"***. A licensee is a person who has the owner's ***consent*** to be on the property, but who does ***not have a business purpose*** for being there, or anything else entitling him to be on the land apart from the owner's consent. See Rest. 2d, §330. As is outlined below, the licensee is the beneficiary of a somewhat higher standard of care than is the trespasser, but a lower standard than would be owed to a business visitor or other "invitee."

B. **Social guests:** The main class of persons who qualify as licensees are ***"social guests."*** Such a guest, even though he is "invited" by the owner, is not an "invitee", since that term applies only to business guests and other persons identified *infra*, p. 246.

1. **Incidental services:** A social guest will not become an "invitee" even by gratuitously doing *incidental services* (e.g., washing dishes). Nor, generally, has the fact that the guest and host have been involved in cultural or fraternal activities been sufficient to make the guest an invitee; only those activities which devolve to the host's *economic benefit* have generally been sufficient for this purpose.

2. **Rationale:** The principle difference between the duty owed to a licensee and that owed to an invitee is that as to the licensee, there is *no duty to inspect for unknown dangers* (see *infra*). Accordingly, the rationale for holding that a social guest is only a licensee is that such guests commonly understand that the owner will not take any special precautions for their safety. That is, the guest understands that he takes the premises on the same footing as the owner herself. This theory may not be in accord with how hosts and guests usually act, but the conclusion drawn from it, that social guests are not "invitees," is well-established. See Rest. 2d, §330, Comment h(3).

3. **Duties to licensee:** Since, as just noted, courts presume that the licensee takes the premises on the same footing as the owner, the owner is required to use reasonable care to place him in the same position of relative safety as herself. This means in particular that where the owner *knows* of a *dangerous condition*, which she should reasonably anticipate that the licensee may not discover, she must *warn* him of that danger. (But a warning of the danger is all that is required; the owner is not required to remedy what she knows to be a defective condition.)

   a. **Natural conditions:** This general duty to warn includes dangers arising from *natural conditions*, (even though such conditions are exempted where owner liability to persons outside the premises or to child trespassers is concerned). See P&K, p. 417.

   b. **No duty to inspect:** But very significantly, the owner is *not required to take affirmative action* to make the premises safe. This means that she has *no duty to inspect the premises* to find any hidden dangers. Nor is she liable if the premises are unsafe because of faulty construction. See Rest. 2d, §342, Comment d.

C. **Dangerous activities:** Most courts now distinguish between passive conditions on the land (discussed above), as to which the owner has no duty of inspection, and *activities* carried out by her on the land, as to which an affirmative obligation of due care to licensees is required. Thus if the owner runs trains on her property, she has an affirmative obligation to do so with reasonable care for the safety of any licensee; reasonable care in a particular situation may require that the owner actively keep an eye out for licensees, even if she does not know of their presence. (Her duty is thus higher than it is to trespassers, as to whom there is no obligation until they are actually discovered.)

D. **Automobile guests:** A *guest passenger* in an automobile is sometimes held to be bound by the same rules as a licensee upon land. As was noted previously, *supra*, p. 113, the status of an automobile guest is regulated by statute in some states, but where there is no statute, courts have frequently held that the guest (assuming that he is a social, rather than business, guest) is owed no duty of inspection. See P&K, p. 489

1. **Consequence:** This means that if the owner/driver carelessly fails to inspect the car's brakes, and the guest is injured, there will be no liability, on the theory that the defective condition was like a passive condition upon land.

VI. INVITEES

A. Significance of distinction from licensees: As noted, the major difference between "invitees" and "licensees" is that only to the former does the owner owe a duty of reasonable inspection to find hidden dangers, and of affirmative action to remedy such conditions. What she must do to satisfy this burden is discussed below.

B. Who is invitee: The modern view, shared by most courts as well as Rest. 2d, §332, is that the class of "invitees" consists not only of persons who are invited by the owner onto the land to conduct (directly or indirectly) *business* with him, but also those who are invited as *members of the public* for purposes for which the land is held *open to the public*. The former are called by the Second Restatement (*ibid*) "business visitors" and the latter "public invitees".

   1. Old view: A number of courts formerly held that there *had* to be some business purpose in the plaintiff's visit before he could be an invitee. However, this led courts following this view to stretch to unreasonable lengths to find some kind of indirect business purpose.

   2. The modern view: The majority position today includes within the class of invitees *members of the public who come onto land held open to them* and who do so for the *purpose for which the land is held open*. This majority view relies on the fact that such persons *reasonably expect that the premises have been made safe for them*.

      a. Scope of "business visit: " Where the plaintiff tries to come under the "business visitor" branch of invitee status, it is not required that he have engaged in business at the time of his injury, or even on the visit in question, as long as he has a *general business relationship* with the defendant.

      Example: D runs a cigar stand in a building. P, who has been D's customer for many years, loiters in front of the stand one day for fifteen minutes, without making a purchase, and then goes to use a toilet in the building. On the way, he falls into an open trapdoor in a dark hallway. D, argues that P was not an invitee, since he made no purchase on the day in question, and since the toilet was not open to the public (but was intended just for D's employees).

      Held, P had been allowed to use the toilet many times in the past, and there was no indication that it was not a public toilet. Furthermore, P is not blocked from obtaining invitee status merely because he made no purchase on the day in question; anyone who enters a store with the present or future intention of being a customer is an invitee, since the owner implicitly invites him for a potential business purpose. *Campbell v. Weathers*, 111 P.2d 72 (Kan. 1941).

      b. Salespeople and job-seekers: Even in the case of business visitors, the test is whether these visitors reasonably believe that the premises have been held open to them for the *particular purpose* on which they enter. Thus a job- applicant at a department store is an invitee, even if the store rejects his application, as long as the applicant reasonably believes that there is a possibility of employment. The same is true of a salesperson who calls on business premises, in a situation where she reasonably believes that such door-to-door salespeople are sometimes received. But a salesperson paying an unsolicited call to a *private home* is not an invitee at the outset; this is because she cannot reasonably anticipate that the premises have been especially made safe for her. (But if she is invited in, she then becomes an invitee.) See Rest. 2d, §332, Comment b.

3. **Scope of invitation:** Since the theory behind expanded liability to invitees is that the premises have been made safe for such persons and held out to them, it follows that a visitor who is an invitee as to one part of the premises may become a licensee or even a trespasser if he goes to other parts of the premises *beyond his invitation*.

   a. **Implied invitation:** However, the test is always what *reasonably appears* to the visitor; if it reasonably seems to him that the premises are open to the public, he will not cease to be an invitee merely because, unknown to him, the owner intends that portion to be off limits to anyone except employees. Thus in *Campbell, supra*, the plaintiff continued to be an invitee when he went to the toilet, since he had never been informed in the past that it was not for public use.

   b. **Private portion used with owner's consent:** Suppose the invitee receives the owner's explicit authorization to go into a portion of the premises not usually open to the public. If the visitor does so purely for his *own benefit*, he will generally not be an invitee when he does.

      Example: P buys some cigarettes in D's grocery store. P then asks for an empty box for his son, and is told that he can find some in the back room. The back room is unlit, and he falls down a stair well.

      Held, P was only a licensee once he went into the back room. In doing so, he was not furthering the business for which he was originally implicitly invited onto the premises (i.e., to make a purchase). *Whelan v. Van Natta*, 382 S.W.2d 205 (Ky. 1964).

   c. **Time period:** Similarly, a guest will cease to be an invitee if he remains on the premises for a longer *period of time* than reasonably necessary for the business purpose for which he has been invited.

C. **Duty of due care:** The owner must exercise reasonable care for the safety of her invitees. Her duty is in theory no different from that of, say, a driver towards pedestrians. But in the case of land, specific rules define what constitutes reasonable care.

1. **Duty to inspect:** Most importantly, the owner may not impose unreasonable risks of harm upon his invitee, even from dangers as to which the owner is *unaware*. This means that the owner has a *duty to inspect* her premises for hidden dangers. This does not mean that she must, as an absolute matter, find all hidden dangers; it merely means that she must use *reasonable care* in making her inspection. Rest. 2d, §343.

   a. **Construction defects:** The owner may be liable even for dangers stemming from an original *faulty construction or design,* if it poses unreasonable danger to her invitee. And this may be true even if the condition existed *before the owner ever came into ownership* or possession of the property. P&K, p. 426.

2. **Effect of warning:** Will a landowner's *warning* of a peril negate the owner's liability to an invitee if that peril comes to pass? The general answer is *"no"* — a duty to warn about a danger, and a duty to take affirmative steps to prevent the danger from causing harm, can, and often will, *co-exist* as independent forms of the duty to use reasonable care to protect invitees.

a. **Torts by third persons:** This principle is sometimes tested by scenarios in which a third person commits a tort against P while on D's premises. Recall (*supra*, p. 108) that one of the ways a premises owner can fail to render due care to protect an invitee is by failing to provide reasonable security against the torts of third persons that the owner should anticipate. Generally, this duty to protect is ***not negated*** by the fact that the owner has warned its invitees against the kind of third-party tort in question.

    Example: D runs a convenience store that is open 24 hours per day, in an area of town where there are frequent muggings. D posts a sign in the lot, "Warning, there are often thieves in the parking lot; walk here at your own risk." P, a customer, is mugged in the lot at night. The fact that D gave this warning doesn't negate D's obligation to supply a higher level of security (e.g., better lights or a guard) if it would have been reasonable for an owner or operator in D's position to supply that greater security.

3. **Duty varies with use:** What constitutes "reasonable care" on the part of an owner will vary with the use of the premises. Thus the owner of private home, who invites a travelling salesperson in for a consultation, owes a lesser duty of inspection than the owner of a major department store, who must anticipate the thousands of customers whose safety may be at stake. See Rest. 2d, §343, Comment e.

    a. **Sufficiency of warning:** The owner's duty of exercising "reasonable care" will often be satisfied by the mere giving of a ***warning*** of a dangerous condition. This would certainly be true, for instance, of the homeowner/travelling salesperson situation, where a warning "Be careful of the baby's toys" would suffice and it would be unnecessary to clean up the mess instead.

    b. **Sometimes insufficient:** But there are situations in which the owner should know that a warning will ***not suffice to remove the danger;*** if so, she must take other affirmative action to protect the invitee. This may be the case where the owner should realize that the warning (e.g., a posted sign) will not be noticed, or that even if noted, the invitee will still be subject to unreasonable danger.

        i. **Distraction:** One common situation in which a warning is not sufficient is where a storekeeper should know that there is a good chance that a customer will be ***distracted*** from the danger by goods placed on display. See, e.g., Rest. 2d, §343A, Illustration 2.

    c. **Knowledge by invitee:** The same rules apply if the invitee ***knows*** of the danger through his own observation, even in the absence of a warning from the defendant. That is, the defendant normally has no further duty in this situation, but she will have a duty to obviate the danger if even a visitor aware of the danger would be subjected to unreasonable risks. For instance, a train passenger confronted with an icy platform might have no choice except to confront the danger or forego the use of the train; if so, the railroad might be liable for the icy conditions despite the passenger's knowledge of the danger, if the platform could not be crossed with reasonable safety. See Rest. 2d, §343A, Illustrations 6 and 8.

    d. **Control over third persons:** Reasonable care by the owner may require that she exercise ***control over third persons*** on her premises. A storekeeper may, for instance, be required to take reasonable ***security measures*** to ***prevent attacks or thefts*** against her customers. See P&K, p. 428. Similarly, a merchant may be required to at least warn his customers where independent contractors are doing work on the premises which the merchant should know may pose danger to nearby persons.

D. Firefighters and other public-safety personnel: What is the status of *firefighters, police officers* and other *public-safety officials* who come onto private property in the performance of their duties? Under the common-law *"firefighter's rule,"* such workers are treated as *mere licensees*, so that the owner does not owe them a duty to inspect the premises or to make the premises reasonably safe. The most common application of the common-law doctrine is that a firefighter who is injured while fighting a blaze cannot recover from the owner of the premises, *even if the owner's negligence caused the fire*.

1. **Rationale:** Courts recite several justifications for the firefighter's rule. One is that the firefighter or other public servant is *aware of the risks* inherent in his chosen profession, and should therefore be deemed to have *assumed the risk*. Another rationale is that the injured worker will generally be compensated through workers' compensation, and allowing tort recovery would allow *double recovery*. See *Minnich v. Med-Waste, Inc.*, 564 S.E.2d 98 (S.C. 2002) (reciting these rationales, but then concluding that South Carolina ought not to follow the firefighter's rule).

2. **Status of rule:** A number of states have in recent years expressed dissatisfaction with the firefighters rule. Some have *eliminated* it by statute (e.g., Florida and New Jersey) or by judicial decision. Dobbs & Hayden (5th), p. 368. Others have limited it to the case of firefighters, and have refused to extend it to other rescue workers (e.g., paramedics). *Id.* Still others limit it to suits against *landowners*, terming it a rule of "premises liability," not a broad rule against suits by rescue workers. *Id.*

   a. **Most apply:** But most states *continue to apply the rule*, at least in the core case: a firefighter injured fighting a fire may not recover against a negligent fire-setter who owns the premises where the injury occurred. Dobbs & Hayden (5th), p. 366.

   b. **Exceptions:** Even in states following the common-law firefighter's rule, courts recognize several situations in which the rule *does not bar recovery* by the public servant against the wrongdoing landowner:

      ❏ The rule does not prevent recovery against a wrongdoer who acts *intentionally* or *"willfully"* rather than negligently. So, for instance, a firefighter who is injured fighting a blaze may recover against a person who set the fire *intentionally*.

      ❏ The rule does not prevent recovery against a defendant who commits his act of negligence *after learning of the officer's presence.* (*Example*: D, the homeowner, sees P, a uniformed police officer, at P's door. P is there to investigate a missing neighbor. D negligently allows D's dog to run free and bite P while P is on the property. The firefighter's rule would not bar P from recovering from D, because D's act of negligence occurred after D was aware of P's presence.)

      ❏ The rule does not prevent recovery for *risks that are not part of the reason for the officer's presence*. (*Example*: Same facts as above example, involving D's dog. A second reason for denying D the protection of the firefighter's rule is that danger from a dog was not part of the reason for P's presence.)

See Dobbs & Hayden (5th), p. 367.

3. **Non-emergency public employees:** *Non-emergency* public employees, such as *safety inspectors, trash collectors, postal carriers,* etc., are usually deemed to be *invitees*. The theory behind this treatment is that since the visits of such persons are *foreseeable* (at least in general, if not in the sense of anticipation of a particular visit on a particular day), the owner can reasonably be expected to keep his premises safe for them. P&K, p. 428-29.

VII. REJECTION OF CATEGORIES

A. **Rejection of categories:** A number of courts in the last few decades have *rejected* the rigid categories of trespasser, licensee, and invitee, in favor of a general single *"reasonable person"* standard of liability.

> **Example:** P is a social guest in D's apartment. P asks to use the bathroom, and while doing so severs part of his hand on a broken faucet. It turns out that D was aware of the defective faucet, but failed to warn P.
>
> *Held,* by the California Supreme Court, the plaintiff's status as trespasser, licensee or invitee will *not be dispositive* as to the duty of care owed to him. Instead, the test will be "whether in the management of his property [the owner] has acted as a reasonable person in view of the probability of injury to others, and, although the plaintiff's status as a trespasser, licensee, or invitee may in light of the facts giving rise to such status have some bearing on the question of liability, the status is not determinative." *Rowland v. Christian,* 443 P.2d 561 (Cal. 1968), *infra,* p. 254.
>
> **Note:** In the vast majority of jurisdictions, as noted previously, the owner has a duty to warn a licensee of known defects which the licensee may not discover. But California had never, up to the time of *Rowland,* accepted this rule. Therefore, the plaintiff in *Rowland* could not have won if the court had not rejected the invitee/licensee distinction.

1. **Half the states give social guests benefit of duty of due care:** *Rowland* has turned out to be very influential, at least as to *social guests.* "By 2004, about half the states had either *included social guests in the invitee category* or had completely or partially *abolished the categories*, with the result that *all or most non-trespassing entrants upon land are entitled to reasonable care under the circumstances.*" Dobbs & Hayden (5th), p. 371.

   a. **Not followed as to trespassers:** But most states have been *unwilling* to follow *Rowland*'s "reasonable care / abolish the categories" rule when it comes to *trespassers*. Thus the Iowa Supreme Court, in recently reaffirming the common-law rule as to undiscovered trespassers (no duty except to refrain from maliciously injuring them), noted that "Only one court in the last 27 years has abandoned the common-law trespasser rule, [so that] the so-called 'trend' to adopt a universal standard of care for premises liability has clearly lost momentum." *Alexander v. Medical Assoc. Clinic,* 646 N.W.2d 74 (Iowa 2002).

VIII. LIABILITY OF LESSORS AND LESSEES

A. Lessee: A lessee of real estate (usually called a "tenant") becomes the possessor of the property. As such, he is treated as if he were the owner, and all the rules of owner liability discussed previously in this chapter apply to him.

1. **Liability:** This can produce liability where the non-lawyer might not expect it. For instance, an apartment tenant who inherits a dangerous condition from the landlord which the tenant has not discovered (e.g., a faulty ceiling), but which defect could have been discovered by reasonable care, may be liable to an invitee (e.g. a door-to-door salesperson invited in to demonstrate his goods) if the ceiling falls. For this reason, such tenants should have liability coverage in their "homeowner's" insurance policy. (The landlord may also be liable in such a situation, as will be discussed below.)

2. **Common areas:** But the tenant is only liable for those areas as to which he is in actual possession. Thus *common areas*, such as stairways, elevators, corridors, outside grounds, etc., are usually deemed to remain within the control of the landlord, at least where the building is a multiple dwelling, office building, or other structure with multiple tenants. The tenants therefore can have no liability for defects in these areas (except perhaps for a non-possession-related liability for failing to warn of the defect to a person to whom they had a duty of due care, such as a social guest. In this situation, the liability would be based upon general principles).

B. Lessor's liability: Since the lessee is treated as the owner for most purposes, courts generally relieve the lessor of most liability once she transfers possession to the lessee. This is true both as to dangerous conditions existing prior to the lease, and conditions arising thereafter. There are, however, a number of important exceptions to this general rule of non-liability.

1. **Danger unknown to lessee which should be known to lessor:** The lessor will be liable to the lessee (and to the lessee's invitees and licensees) for any dangers existing at the start of the lease, which the lessor *knows or should know about*, and which the lessee has no reason to know about. Rest. 2d, §358.

    a. **No duty of inspection:** This rule is *not* usually interpreted as requiring the lessor to make an *inspection* of the premises. It generally means merely that if she either knows of a hidden danger, or knows of other facts which should reasonably lead her to learn of the danger (e.g. she knows of similar defects in other apartment units in the same building), she must warn the tenant. Rest. 2d, §358, Comment b.

2. **Rented property to be held open to public:** If the lessor has reason to believe that the lessee will *hold the premises open to the public,* and she also has reason to believe that this may occur before a condition which the lessor knows is dangerous has been repaired, the lessor will be liable. The reason for this rule is that where the safety of the public at large is at stake, the lessor has a higher duty than where only casual visitors are expected; the lessor should not be allowed to freely transfer this responsibility onto the lessee.

    a. **Duty of inspection:** Here, it is usually held that the lessor has an affirmative duty to inspect the premises to find and repair dangers. P&K, p. 437.

    b. **Defect must exist prior to lease:** This rule applies only where the dangerous condition exists at the time the lessee takes possession. Thus if the premises are turned over in good condition, and due to the lessee's negligence the structure deteriorates to a dangerous point, the lessor has no liability even if she is aware of the condition. Rest. 2d, §359.

c. Lessee's promise to repair: The lessor is only liable under this rule if she has reason to believe that the lessee will admit the public prior to repair of the dangerous condition. But the lessor does not automatically escape liability merely because the lease contains a promise by the lessee to make the repairs.

i. Express promise: But if the lease contains an express promise by the lessee that he will *not admit the public* until he has made the repairs, this will generally be enough to relieve the lessor of liability. Rest. 2d, §359, Comment i.

3. Common areas kept under control of lessor: As noted previously, the *common areas* of a structure, such as its corridors, stairwells, etc., frequently remain within the landlord's control, particularly where the building has several tenants. As to such a common area, the lessor has a general duty to use reasonable care to make the area safe. If she does not do so, she will be liable not only to an injured tenant, but also to a member of the tenant's household, a social guest, a business invitee, or anyone else who uses the common area with the tenant's or landlord's permission. Rest. 2d, §360.

a. Natural conditions: A majority, but not a large one, of courts hold that the landlord's duty applies even where the condition is a *"natural"* one, such as snow or ice on the front steps of the building. P&K, p. 441.

4. Lessor contracts to repair: If the lessor *contracts,* as part of the lease, to keep the premises in good repair, courts are not in agreement about whether breach of this duty will give rise to a tort action. The tenant himself, of course, can sue in contract for such a breach, but damages in such an action have sometimes been restricted to the reduction in the rental value of the premises due to the breach, with damages for personal injury not allowed. P&K, p. 443.

a. Restrictive rule: Until fairly recently, most courts have *not* permitted an action in tort either by the tenant or anyone else; this means that a member of the tenant's family, a licensee, or anyone else not a party to the original lease would have no recovery against the landlord based on the failure to repair.

b. Majority view: A majority of courts, however, has held that the landlord's breach of her covenant to repair does give a tort claim to anyone injured. But such courts have required the plaintiff to show not only that the landlord failed to perform her contract, but that she failed to use *reasonable care* in performing it. See Rest. 2d, §357(c). Thus the landlord is generally only required to correct the condition within a reasonable time after being notified of it. P&K, p. 443.

5. Repairs negligently undertaken: Even if the landlord has no contractual duty to make repairs, she may incur liability if she gratuitously *begins* to make repairs, and either performs them unreasonably, or fails to finish them. Where the landlord, by doing this, has made the danger actually *worse,* or has lulled the tenant into a false sense of security, most courts agree that the tenant, or anyone else injured while on the premises with the tenant's consent, may recover. P&K, p. 445; Rest. 2d, §362. To avoid liability, however, the landlord does not necessarily have to finish the repairs, or correct them, but merely exercise reasonable care for the safety of persons on the property; a warning may be enough. P&K, *ibid.*

   a. Condition not worsened: But if the danger is not worsened by the landlord's negligent or abandoned repairs, the courts are divided. In some instances, no liability of the lessor has been found, whereas other courts have held that "the mere failure of the lessor to exercise reasonable care under the circumstances is enough for liability." P&K, p. 445.

   b. Knowledge of lessee: Most courts have also held that the landlord is liable only where the lessee does not know that the repairs were negligent or abandoned. See Rest. 2d, §362, Comment d. That is, in the majority view the action is essentially one for "deceit" on the part of the landlord. This means that even a third person (e.g., a social guest) may lose his right to sue the landlord, where the tenant has failed to pass on his knowledge of the landlord's negligence.

      Example: P is a social guest in a house rented by X from D. Water continually drips from the roof of the house onto the front steps, and D begins to fix this problem by repairing the roof. However, he does not finish the repair by installing guttering, and X is aware that the repairs have not been finished. He fails to warn P about the whole problem, and P slips on ice caused by the freezing of the run-off.

      Held, D "could reasonably assume that [X] would inform his guest about the icy condition on the front steps" and D is therefore not liable. *Borders v. Roseberry*, 532 P.2d 1366 (Kan. 1975).

   c. Repairs done by independent contractor: Suppose the lessor hires an ***independent contractor*** to perform repairs. Is she liable for the contractor's negligence? There is dispute about the extent to which the landlord ***delegate*** her responsibility for safe repair. Therefore, if the landlord would be liable for negligent repair work done personally by her, in some situations she will be equally liable for the contractor's negligence. See *infra*, p. 321.

      i. Limitation of liability: But the trend is to limit the owner's liability to situations where the control of the premises is ***not completely entrusted*** to the contractor. Most courts would thus deny liability if, say, the repairs were done after the owner had turned over the daily details of the work to the appropriately-selected and appropriated-instructed contractor. The Third Restatement follows this approach. See Rest. 3d (Liab. for Phys. & Emot. Harm), §62, Comment e and Illustr. 2 thereto, discussed *infra*, p. 322. See also P&K, pp. 445-46.

6. Duty of protection: Does the lessor have the duty to attempt to make the premises safe for her tenants, by the taking of *security precautions?* Most courts have held historically "no." But this attitude seems to have changed over the last several decades, as is evidenced by the following example.

      Example: P is a tenant in a combination office-apartment building owned by D. At the time she became a tenant, the building had a doorman, but D thereafter ceased to furnish one. P is assaulted and robbed in the hallway of the building one night, and sues

D. There is evidence that there had been an increasing number of assaults and thefts in the building.

Held, D had a duty to use reasonable care to protect its tenants from "foreseeable criminal acts committed by third parties." D was in a much better position to take such steps than its tenants; furthermore, it had notice of the dangers. And P was led to "expect that she could rely upon" protection, since there was a doorman when she moved into the building. D is not necessarily required to maintain a doorman, if other procedures (e.g., a tenant-controlled intercom/latch system) could provide the same relative degree of security as that which P relied on. (The court analogized to the duty of innkeepers, discussed *supra*, p. 199, to protect their guests against similar attacks.) *Kline v. 1500 Massachusetts Ave. Apartment Corp.*, 439 F.2d 477 (D.D.C. 1970).

7. **Persons outside the premises:**   It was noted previously, *supra*, p. 238, that owners' liability for harm to persons *outside* of the premises is somewhat broader than that involving harm to persons on the premises. This is similarly true as to lessor's liability to such off-the-premises plaintiffs.

   a. **Danger at time of lease:**   The lessor is liable for unreasonably dangerous conditions that exist on the premises at the time she turns them over to the lessee (e.g., holes in the sidewalk). P&K, p. 437.

   b. **Conditions arising after lease:**   Where the dangerous condition does not arise until after the start of the lease term, the lessor is usually not liable unless she has contracted with the lessee to keep the premises in repair, and has unreasonably breached the contract. See Rest. 2d, §§377, 378.

   c. **Activities carried on by tenant:**   If the tenant carries on *activities* that are unreasonably dangerous to persons off the leased premises (e.g., blasting operations in a quarry), the lessor is liable only if she had reason to believe, *at the time of the lease,* that the activity would occur, and reason to believe that it would be dangerous to such persons. Rest. 2d, §379A.

8. **General negligence standard for lessors:**   Just as some courts have now imposed a *general negligence standard* on occupiers of land (see *Rowland, supra*, p. 250), so a few courts have imposed a similar general requirement of due care upon lessors.

   Example: P, who is assisting D's tenant, is hurt when he leans against a dry-rotted balcony railing which collapses.

   Held, D owed ordinary care to his tenant and to others on the premises with permission. Since modern social conditions no longer support special tort immunity for occupiers of land, there is no logical basis for a general rule of non-liability for landlords either. "It would be anomalous indeed to require a landlord to keep his premises in good repair as an implied condition of the lease [see Emanuel on *Property*], yet immunize him from liability for injuries resulting from his failure to do so." *Pagelsdorf v. Safeco Ins. Co. of America*, 284 N.W.2d 55 (Wis. 1979).

9. **Strict liability for latent defects:**   One court has even imposed *strict liability* on a lessor, where a latent defect in the property resulted in personal injury. In *Becker v. I.R.M. Corp.*, 698 P.2d 116 (Cal. 1985), the California Supreme Court held that P could recover for injuries he incurred when he broke a shower door in an apartment leased to him by D, even

though the average person in D's position inspecting the glass would not have seen that it was of a dangerous "untempered" variety, and even though the glass was already part of the premises when D acquired them.

   a.   Rationale: The California court summarized its holding this way: "A landlord engaged in the business of leasing dwellings is strictly liable in tort for injuries resulting from a latent defect in the premises when the defect existed at the time the premises were let to the tenant." The court relied on the fact that the landlord is in a better position to inspect for latent defects, and on the general rationale — derived from product liability cases, see *infra*, p. 359 — that one who markets a product must bear the cost of injuries resulting therefrom.

IX.   VENDORS AND VENDEES

A.   Vendor's liability: Generally, a *seller* of land is released from tort liability to persons on the property once he has turned over the property to the buyer. But there are exceptions. All these exceptions involve *artificial conditions* that exist on the day of the sale, as to which the seller *knew or should have known* of the danger. The exceptions can apply to a person injured either on the property or outside it. We consider the on-the-property and outside-the-property scenarios separately.

   1.   Danger to one on the property: First, let's assume that the accident happens to one *on the property* (e.g., a tenant of the new buyer). You only have to worry about an exception (i.e., post-closing liability of seller to persons on the property) if the seller *knew or should have known* of the condition and its dangerousness. If that condition is satisfied, then the duration of the seller's post-closing liability varies depending on whether the seller actively *concealed* the danger.

   a.   Seller actively conceals: If the seller *actively concealed* the condition, her liability persists after sale until the buyer *actually discovers* the condition and has a reasonable opportunity to correct it (whether the buyer takes the opportunity or not). So here, there's no cut-off if the buyer negligently fails to discover (or fix) the problem.

   Example: *S* sells a house to *B* on April 1. Prior to the sale date, *S* is aware of a rotten step in the back, and puts wood-colored putty over the rot rather than fix it. Assume that *B* should have immediately, after closing, inspected the step and would have discovered the rot had she done such an inspection. However, *B* never inspects or fixes the step. On Nov. 1, *B* rents to *T*. *T* falls through the step. *S* will be liable, because: (1) he actively concealed the condition; and therefore (2) his liability for negligence to persons on the land persisted until *B* actually learned of the danger (not merely "should have learned"), which had not happened by the time of the accident.

   b.   Seller doesn't conceal: If the seller *didn't actively conceal* the condition, the seller's liability continues only until the buyer "has had *reasonable opportunity to discover*" the condition and correct it. In other words here, the seller's liability is *cut off* as soon as the buyer *should have* discovered and fixed the problem, even if the buyer negligently failed to actually discover it.

Example: Same basic facts as above example. Now, however, assume that *S* knew of the danger but didn't putty it over or actively try to prevent *B* from learning of it (e.g., *S* didn't give *B* false assurances of the step's safe condition). For any accident after the date on which *B* should have learned (but didn't) of the condition prior to *T*'s accident, *S* won't be liable to *T*.

As to both concealment and non-concealment, see Rest. 2d, §353.

2. **Danger to one outside the property:**   Essentially the same rules apply to a seller's post-closing liability to one *outside the property*, except that the seller has longer liability not only for active concealment but for having *created* the artificial condition. Rest. 2d, §373. Thus:

    a. **Seller conceals or created:**   If the seller *actively concealed* the condition, *or originally created* the condition, her liability persists after sale until the buyer actually discovers the condition and has a reasonable opportunity to correct it (whether the buyer takes the opportunity or not). So here, there's no cut-off if the buyer negligently fails to discover (or fix) the problem.

        Example: In 2013, *S* puts a new roof on his house. *S* should have known that several slates were dangerous lose, and risked falling on passersby on the public sidewalk running next to and near the house. *S* sells the property to *B* on Feb. 1, 2014. *S* makes no mention to *B* of the roof's condition, and doesn't attempt to conceal the existence of the loose slates. *B* never inspects or discovers the loose slates, though it is negligence for *B* not to inspect and thus discover the problem. On Sept. 1, 2014, a slate falls off and injures *P*, a passerby on the sidewalk.

        S is liable to *P*, because: (1) *S* created the hazardous condition; and (2) *S* therefore had liability until *B* actually discovered the condition and had an opportunity to fix it (even though it was negligent of *B* not to have discovered it prior to *P*'s accident). *B* would also be liable to *P* in this situation, for having failed to use reasonable care to discover and fix dangers to persons outside the property.

    b. **Seller doesn't conceal or create:** If the seller *neither* actively concealed the condition nor created it, the seller's liability continues only until the buyer "has had *reasonable opportunity to discover*" the condition and correct it. In other words, here the seller's liability is cut off as soon as the buyer should have discovered and fixed the problem, even if the buyer negligently failed to even discover it.

B. **Builder-vendors:**   Where the vendor of a house is the company that *built it*, some courts are now applying general principles of negligence, and holding the vendor liable for *all* injuries by analogy to cases involving negligence in manufactured goods. And others are imposing *strict liability* in this situation, again by analogy to those cases holding a manufacturer of defective goods liable without regard to negligence. The subject of builder-vendor liability is discussed further *infra*, p. 401.

Quiz Yourself on

OWNERS AND OCCUPIERS OF LAND *(Entire Chapter)*

51. Herman Hermit owns property secluded deep in the woods. Tris Passer, a trespasser, enters Hermit's property and stumbles into a snake pit, which Herman has dug as a home for his pet snakes. It is full of thorny plants and disgusting, writhing snakes. When Tris finally escapes, terrified, she sues Herman for negligence. At common law, will she succeed? _____

52. A housing inspector arrives at the home of Snow White and the Seven Dwarfs. He's heard that more than four unrelated people live there, which is a violation of the local housing code. He asks to examine the basement, which is accessible via an unlit stairway. Snow White and the Dwarfs have been out picking apples, and unbeknownst to them a few of the apples are strewn about the stairway. The inspector trips on one of the apples, falls, and breaks his leg. Are Snow White and the Dwarfs liable for the inspector's injuries? _____

53. The Heerr Chick-Chick Fried Chicken Store is on premises rented from the Stately Real Estate Company. Heerr stages a publicity stunt whereby it hires a helicopter to drop chickens over the parking lot, foolishly anticipating that the chickens will drop harmlessly to the ground. The chickens fall, Splat! on the parking lot. One chicken lands on Renee Katzendogs, injuring her. Will Heerr be liable to Renee? _____

54. Farmer owns a relatively small (20-acre) farm. If Farmer had inspected his property even casually after buying it, he would have known that there was an abandoned mine shaft in one corner of it, leading hundreds of feet down with no easy way back to the surface. But because Farmer is a "weekend farmer" who bought the property for its appreciation potential, Farmer has never conducted such an inspection, and thus does not know of the shaft's existence. Had such an inspection been made and the mine shaft discovered, it would have cost very little to fence in the shaft. Farmer in fact knows that children from neighboring farms frequently trespass on his property to play in his barn. Paulette, who is six, comes onto Farmer's property to play in the barn, happens to walk into the mine shaft after dark, and is killed. Her estate sues Farmer. Can the estate recover? _____

55. As the result of snow and rain a day earlier, a platform owned by Railway Co. is covered with ice. Railway has previously posted a prominent sign saying, "Mind your step — platform is icy," but has not removed the ice (which could have been done at reasonable cost). Harried, who is running late for his commuter train, slips on the ice and cracks his skull. He sues Railway for damages. Can Harried recover? _____

Answers

51. No. Negligence requires duty, breach, causation, and damages. The key here is duty, and to what extent Herman as a landowner owed Tris a duty. Tris was a trespasser, of which there are two types: discovered and undiscovered. The facts suggest (though they don't conclusively establish) that Tris was an "undiscovered trespasser." If so, under the common-law rule Herman owed Tris *no duty at all*. An undiscovered trespasser represents the very lowest category — in terms of the owner's duty to him — of individuals who enter land. (The rule which imposes a duty on landowners for natural conditions which the owner has *altered* applies only to people *outside* the land, so it doesn't apply here.)

RELATED ISSUE: A *"discovered"* trespasser is owed the duty of reasonable care for the trespasser's safety, which is generally satisfied by a warning (e.g., a sign) of dangers that are known to the landowner and that are unlikely to be discovered by the trespasser.

NOTE: Had the hazard been natural (instead of man-made), no liability would attach even if Tris had been discovered. The most common exception to the "no liability for natural conditions" rule is the case of urban landowners, who must inspect and maintain trees on their property to ensure the trees will not fall on others' property or on a public highway.

52. **Yes, probably — it depends on whether the inspector was an invitee.** If the inspector was a "licensee" (one who enters the land with owner's consent but without a business purpose), the only duty owed to him was to warn him of known dangerous conditions. So if he's considered a licensee, Snow White & Co. aren't liable for his injuries because they didn't know about the apples. If, however, he was an "invitee" (one who enters by express or implied invitation to conduct business with the owner, or enters for purposes for which the land is held open to the public), he could reasonably expect that the owner had made the premises safe for him. So if he was an invitee, Snow White's duty was to inspect for dangerous conditions *and* warn or make safe (a warning being sufficient under most circumstances). Thus if the inspector is considered an invitee, Snow White & Co. will be liable for his injuries. Most courts treat those who visit during normal hours and under normal circumstances, like this, as *invitees*, making it likely that Snow White & Co. will be liable.

NOTE: If the condition is so obvious that the invitee/licensee should have been aware of it, there is no liability on the landowner (since a warning is superfluous).

53. **Yes.** Lessees of property are liable to the same extent as landowners. Thus, since Renee is an invitee, Heerr must warn her of known dangers ("Warning: Falling Chickens") and inspect the premises to make them safe for her. Dropping a chicken on her head would constitute a breach of Heerr's duty.

54. **No.** Even where all of the conditions are satisfied for imposing on the landowner a duty to use reasonable care to protect trespassing children, the landowner has no affirmative duty to *inspect* his land to discover whether hazardous conditions exist; he merely has the duty to protect against such conditions if he knows or should know that they exist, and knows or should know of the danger to trespassing children. See Rest. 2d, §339, Comment h.

55. **Yes.** Harried was an invitee, since he was on the premises for business purposes. Therefore, Railway had the obligation to make the premises reasonably safe for him. While a warning may in many situations be enough to make the premises safe, here this was not the case — it was quite foreseeable that a patron might be running late, and would either not see or disregard the sign, especially where no safe alternative way was made available by Railway. See Rest. 2d, §343A, Illustr. 8.

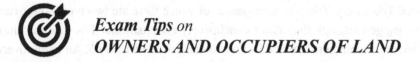

Exam Tips *on*
OWNERS AND OCCUPIERS OF LAND

Nearly every torts exam contains at least one question involving the obligation of *owners of land*.

☞ Remember that a landowner has a duty to prevent an unreasonable risk of harm to persons *off the land* from *artificial conditions* on the land. (*Example:* D burns trash on his land, causing smoke that distracts a driver on the adjacent road; D is probably liable.) Older cases hold that there is no duty to prevent an unreasonable risk from *natural* conditions on the land (e.g., a tree), but modern cases, especially ones from urban states, may disagree.

☛ Many exam questions involve the owner's duty to *trespassers*.

  ☞ The general rule is that the owner owes *no duty* to a trespasser to make the land safe, or even to warn the trespasser of known dangers. But there are some exceptions.

  ☞ If O has *knowledge* of the trespasser's presence, most courts require O to use reasonable care for the trespasser's safety. Usually a *warning* of a specific danger will suffice (but the posting of a general "no trespassers" sign will not).

  ☞ Most commonly tested is the duty to trespassing *children*. Here, O will be liable if five requirements are met: (1) O knows or should know that children are *likely to trespass* on that particular part of his land; (2) O knows or should know that a condition on that part of the land poses an *unreasonable risk* of serious injury to trespassing children; (3) the child has not *discovered* the condition or *does not realize the danger* because of his youth; (4) the utility in maintaining the condition is *outweighed* by the danger to children; and (5) O fails to use *reasonable care* to eliminate the danger or to protect the children. (The list probably applies only to *"artificial"* conditions on the land, not to "natural" conditions; it's not clear whether it applies to "activities" carried out by O on the land.)

  ☞ Examples where O may be liable to trespassing children:

    ❑ O maintains a gravel heap which he knows children sled ride down, with the risk that they'll go onto the adjacent roadway and get run over;

    ❑ O maintains a high-tension wire at the top of a pole. The pole has spikes for climbing, and O knows that children from the nearby school often trespass and climb the pole.

☛ Many questions require you to distinguish between *"licensees"* and *"invitees."*

  ☞ A *"licensee"* is typically a *"social guest."* An *"invitee"* is one who is either invited by O to conduct *business* on the premises, or is a member of the *public* coming onto the land for the purposes for which the land is held open to the public.

  ☞ The key difference between licensee and invitee is that O has *no* affirmative duty to *make the premises safe* for the licensee, including no duty to *inspect* for hidden dangers.

    ☞ Commonly-tested: If P is a police officer, fire fighter or other public *emergency worker*, under the common-law "firefighter's rule" P is probably a licensee, and can't recover for dangers that O should have known about but didn't. (*Example:* O doesn't know there's a loose step on the way to his basement, and P, a fire fighter going to the basement to check out a blaze, falls. O is not liable even if it was negligent of him not to have discovered and fixed the step.)

    ☞ Key point: Even to a licensee, O has an obligation to *warn* of hidden dangers *known* to O. (*Example:* On above example, if O knows the stair is loose, he's got an obligation to warn P, the fire fighter, assuming there's time.)

☞ By contrast, O *does* have an affirmative duty to an *invitee* to *inspect the premises* for hidden dangers, and to *make the premises reasonably safe*.

    ☞ This obligation often includes a duty to protect against wrongdoing — including crimes — by third parties. (*Example:* If O runs a hotel, O probably has a duty to supply reasonable security in the hotel and its parking lot, and O is liable to a business visitor who is attacked by a third person if reasonable security would have prevented the attack.)

    ☞ Keep in mind that even to an invitee, O is *not an insurer*, merely a person having an obligation to behave "reasonably." For instance, if there have been few or no assaults on O's premises previously, O probably isn't liable for failing to have a security officer when an attack finally occurs.

    ☞ Common issue relating to invitee: When O hold his business open to the public, is a P who comes there just to *browse* (without making or intending to make a purchase) an "invitee"? Answer: probably "yes," because O could hope to get economic benefit from P either on that or some later occasion.

    ☞ Similar issue: Is a *worker* or other *independent contractor* engaged by O to work on the premises (e.g., painter or plumber) an "invitee"? Answer: again, probably "yes," because he gives an economic benefit to O.

☞ In any discussion where you mention the trespasser/licensee/invitee distinction, you should allude to the possibility that the jurisdiction has (as many jurisdictions now have) *abolished* this distinction. Say something like: "If the jurisdiction has abolished the distinctions between trespasser, licensee and invitee, it probably imposes a single standard of 'reasonableness under all the circumstances.' In that event, we must consider the foreseeability of P's presence on the premises and the foreseeability of danger to him. O probably would [or would not] be found liable because. . . ."

☛ Questions sometime involve the liability of a *lessor*. The general rule is that the lessor is off the hook once possession is transferred to the lessee.

☞ But there are numerous exceptions, including these three big ones: (1) the lessor is liable to the lessee and to the lessee's invitees/licensees for failure to *warn* about any hidden dangers which the lessor *knows of* at the beginning of the lease (but the lessor has no duty to inspect to find hidden dangers); (2) the lessor remains responsible for *common areas* (e.g., an apartment lobby, stairway, elevator, etc.); and (3) some courts now impose a general duty of reasonable care on landlords as to all who come onto the premises (including the licensees/invitees of tenants).

Chapter 10

DAMAGES

ChapterScope

Every personal injury lawyer knows that having "good damages" in a case is as important as having "good liability." This chapter examines the various components of damages that may be recovered in a persona injury action. The key concepts are:

- **Actual injury required:** In a negligence action, P must generally show that he suffered some sort of *physical* harm (so that he cannot recover damages if he suffered only mental harm with no physical symptoms, and cannot recover nominal damages). But once physical harm has been proven, a variety of damages may be recovered, including the value of any loss of bodily functions, out-of-pocket economic losses, pain and suffering, "hedonistic" damages, and more.

- **The collateral source rule:** Under the *"collateral source rule,"* P is entitled to recover her out-of-pocket expenses, even if she was *reimbursed* for these losses by some third party (e.g., an insurance company).

- **Mitigation:** P has a *"duty to mitigate."* That is, P cannot recover for any harm which, by the exercise of reasonable care, he could have *avoided* (e.g., any harm caused by P's failure to seek prompt medical assistance). Some courts also deny P recovery where he fails to take *advance safety precautions* that worsen his injuries (e.g., he doesn't wear a seat belt).

- **Punitive damages:** *Punitive* damages can be awarded to penalize a defendant whose conduct is peculiarly *outrageous*. In a negligence case, D's conduct must generally be "reckless" or "willful and wanton."

- **Recovery by spouse or children:** Most states allow the *spouse*, *parent* or *child* of an injured person to recover for the losses that they have suffered. (For instance, a spouse of the injured person may recover for loss of companionship or loss of sex; this is called "loss of consortium.")

- **Wrongful death and survivor actions:** Most states provide that when an accident victim dies, his estate may sue for those elements of damage that the victim himself could have sued for (a *"survival"* action); such actions typically include the decedent's pain and suffering before death. Most states also have *"wrongful death"* statutes, which allow a defined group (typically the decedent's spouse and children, or if she has none, her parents) to recover for the losses they have sustained by virtue of the decedent's death.

I. PERSONAL INJURY DAMAGES GENERALLY

A. **Actual injury required:** In any action based on negligence, the existence of *actual injury* is a requirement. Unlike intentional tort actions (e.g. trespass), therefore, *nominal damages* may not be awarded. See Rest. 2d, §907, Comment a.

1. **Physical injury required:**   Furthermore, in the usual negligence case, the plaintiff must show that he suffered some kind of *physical* harm. We have already seen (*supra*, p. 218), for instance, that the plaintiff may not recover where he has sustained only mental harm, with no physical symptoms.

2. **Elements of damages:**   But once physical harm has been proven, a variety of damages may be recovered by the injured plaintiff. In addition to compensation for the physical harm itself (e.g., $100,000 for the loss of a leg), the important general categories of damages are as follows:

   a. **Economic loss:**   The plaintiff can recover his direct out-of-pocket losses stemming from the injury. These include *medical expenses, lost earnings,* and the cost of any labor required to do things that plaintiff can no longer do himself (e.g. a housekeeper).

   b. **Physical pain:**   The plaintiff may also recover for actual *physical pain* suffered from the injuries. (As discussed below, this aspect of damages, like the others, may include both suffering sustained up to the time of the trial as well as an estimate of the suffering which will occur during the future.)

   c. **Mental distress:**   Finally, the plaintiff may recover for various mental consequences of the injury, including:

      i.   *fright and shock* at the time of the injury;

      ii. *humiliation* due to disfigurement, disability, etc.; see "hedonistic damages," *infra*;

      iii. unhappiness and depression at being *unable to lead one's previous life* (e.g. inability to enjoy sex, work, play sports, etc.); see "hedonistic damages," *infra*;

      iv. *anxiety* about the future (e.g. anxiety about the plaintiff's unborn child).

3. **Maximum possible verdict:**   One situation in which allocation of the injuries to the various categories becomes significant is when the court attempts to decide whether the jury's verdict is so unreasonable that it must be set aside as a matter of law (either for being too high or too low). Most of the time, the issue is whether the verdict is too high, and the judge decides this question by evaluating the *"maximum possible reasonable award"*, on an item-by-item basis.

B. **Hedonistic damages:**   Most courts now allow a jury to award *hedonistic damages*, i.e., damages for the loss of the ability to *enjoy life*. This is a type of damage that is, conceptually at least, distinct from pain-and-suffering.

> **Example:** Suppose that P, injured in an accident, loses the ability to run, and thus the ability to play tennis. P earns her living as an office worker, so the injury does not in any way diminish her earning capacity. Furthermore, the injury does not involve any pain. Nonetheless, if P can show that she played tennis frequently, loved the game, and is distraught at never being able to play again, most courts will allow her to recover damages for loss of the ability to enjoy this aspect of life.

1. **Consciousness required:**   Probably the major question concerning hedonistic damages is whether the plaintiff must be *conscious* of the loss in order to be able to recover these damages. In other words, may a plaintiff who as the result of the defendant's fault is ren-

dered permanently *comatose* recover damages for the loss of the ability to enjoy life? Courts are *split* on this issue.

  a. *McDougald* case: The most important decision to date is that of the New York Court of Appeals in *McDougald v. Garber*, 536 N.E.2d 372 (N.Y. 1989), where the court held that *"cognitive awareness is a prerequisite* to recovery for loss of enjoyment of life." The court recognized that its holding would lead to "the paradoxical situation that the greater the degree of brain injury inflicted by a negligent defendant, the smaller the award the plaintiff can recover in general damages." But the court felt that its no-recovery-without-consciousness rule was required in order to further the interest of tort law in compensating victims rather than punishing offenders.

C. Recovery for future damages: The rules of civil procedure require that a plaintiff bring only *one action* for a particular accident, and that he recover in that accident for not only his past damages, but for ones he can be expected to *sustain in the future.* Rest. 2d, §10.

  1. **Absolute certainty not required:** Obviously future losses cannot be exactly calculated. All the plaintiff has to do, however, is to show the *approximate* amount of damages, which, *more likely than not,* he will sustain in the future. Such future damages can include future pain and suffering, future mental distress, future lost earnings, future medical expenses, etc.

  2. **Expert testimony:** To prove his future damages, the plaintiff will usually use various kinds of expert testimony. First, he will try to show that the physical injuries will probably be permanent, or at least long-lasting; expert medical testimony would be relevant on this point. Then, he will try to show facts about what his future prospects would have been had there been no injury. He may use *actuarial tables* to show, for instance, that he has a life expectancy of, say, thirty-five years (assuming that his life expectancy is not shortened by the injuries), and that he must therefore be compensated for thirty-five years of anticipated pain and suffering.

    a. **Lost income:** Also, if the plaintiff is no longer able to work, he may produce an expert in economics to testify about what his income from working would likely have been.

    b. **Shortened life expectancy:** In many states, the plaintiff may also show that his *life expectancy* has been shortened. This will entitle him to recover for the anticipated "value" of these lost years, as well as for the lost income that could have been earned during them.

  3. **Present value:** Future damages are, by definition, compensation for losses which the plaintiff will not suffer until some time in the future. The plaintiff is therefore getting, in a sense, a windfall by collecting now for future losses. To offset this windfall, courts generally instruct the jury to award the plaintiff only the *"present value"* of these losses, at least where lost future earnings and future medical expenses are concerned (though not in the case of damages for physical impairment, pain and suffering, or mental distress). The effect of this discounting is that the defendant receives "interest" on his advance payment. See Rest. 2d, §913A.

Example: Suppose that the jury concludes that P has a life expectancy of twenty-five years, and that he will have anticipated medical expenses during the rest of his life of about $10,000 per year. The jury will be instructed not to award the annual amount times the number of years (i.e. $250,000), but rather, the present value of a $10,000 payment in each of the next twenty-five years. The defendant would be permitted to introduce statistical tables showing that, assuming an interest rate of, say, 6%, the present value of a stream of twenty-five annual payments is only $127,833, not $250,000.

4. **Effect of inflation:** When the jury calculates the plaintiff's anticipated lost earnings or anticipated medical expenses, many courts don't allow the jury to consider the effect that *inflation* would have on these sums. Where this is the case, some courts have similarly refused to require that the award be discounted to present value, on the assumption that inflation and discounting cancel each other out.

5. **Periodic payments:** One way in which states are increasingly dealing with the problem of inflation is by use of *periodic payments* of judgments. That is, the plaintiff's recovery is paid in *installments* over many years, rather than in a lump sum immediately following the judgment. The payments can be indexed to account for inflation. In this way, the plaintiff can be assured of having a constant level of purchasing power over the rest of her life, in a way that will more closely approximate replacement of earnings than would a lump-sum payment.

   a. **Required:** The parties have always been free to agree on such treatment, and the phrase "structured settlement" is frequently used to describe such consensual periodic-payment arrangements. But as part of the "tort reform" movement, some states now allow one party to *force* the other to accept periodic payments, in certain situations. This has happened most commonly in *medical malpractice* cases.

   b. **Terminates on death:** One possible advantage to the defendant of periodic payments is that they can be, and usually are, arranged to *terminate upon the death* of the plaintiff.

6. **Per-diem calculation:** How is the jury to go about fixing a value for pain and suffering, particularly pain and suffering which is prospective in nature? In an effort to give the jury guidance (and to increase the resulting figure), plaintiffs' lawyers often attempt to use what is called the *per-diem* argument. That is, the lawyer suggests to the jury that a particular amount for each day, hour or minute of suffering (e.g. $2.00 per hour) would be fair. The lawyer then multiplies out this figure by the number of days or hours of anticipated suffering (usually the plaintiff's life expectancy) and emerges with a very precise, and large, figure. (For instance, $2.00 per hour, based on a twenty-four hour day, amounts to $525,600 if the plaintiff has a thirty year life-expectancy!)

   a. **Majority rule allows *per-diem* argument:** Most courts *allow* the *per-diem* argument, "assuming that defendant's counsel can point out any flaws in the argument and that the jury will not be misled." P,W&S, p. 536, n. 17. But a substantial minority refuse to allow per diem calculations.

D. **Effect of taxation:** A special section of the Internal Revenue Code, §104, makes any recovery or settlement for personal injuries *tax-free*. This is true even if the damages represent lost past or future earnings (which, of course, would have been taxed). This exemption has given rise to two related questions, on which the courts have been in dispute.

1. **Calculation based on net, not gross, earnings:**   First, should the jury be instructed to base its award for lost past and future earnings on what the net, *after-tax,* amount of these earnings would have been?

    a. **Ordinary taxpayer's future earnings:**   Most courts hold that lost *future* earnings should be calculated on a ***gross, not after-tax, basis.*** These courts point to the uncertain future course of federal taxation, and to other factors in the personal injury litigation system (e.g., the fact that plaintiffs must pay their lawyers out of the award) as reasons for not worrying about this relatively minor windfall.

        i. **Past earnings:**   But where the plaintiff seeks *past* lost earnings, the amount of tax which would have been paid on these earnings can be calculated with some precision. Therefore, many courts require the jury to award only the *after-tax* lost earnings.

        ii. **Restatement view:**   The Second Restatement, in §914A, provides that future earnings of ordinary taxpayers should not be calculated on an after-tax basis, but has a caveat expressing no opinion as to whether past earnings, and future earnings of high-bracket taxpayers, should be so calculated.

2. **Telling the jury about non-taxation of the award:**   The second question is whether the ***jury should be told*** that any award would not be taxable. Proponents of telling the jury are afraid that otherwise, the jury will assume that the award would be taxable, and will award a larger sum so that the plaintiff will come out with a "fair amount" after subtraction of the imaginary tax.

    a. **General rule:**   Courts are split on what, if anything, should be said to the jury. But it seems fair to say that most appellate courts at least permit the trial judge to tell the jury that the award would not be taxable. Some appellate courts even hold that it is reversible error *not* to tell the jury about this.

E. **Reimbursement by third persons:**   As we have seen, the plaintiff is entitled to recover her out-of-pocket expenses, including expenditures for medical care, lost wages, etc. This is so even though the plaintiff is *reimbursed* for these loses by some *third party* (e.g. health insurance). The general common-law rule is that as long as payment for any aspect of harm is not made by the defendant or someone acting on his behalf (e.g. the defendant's insurance company), the plaintiff's recovery from the defendant is *not diminished* by the amount of these payments. See Rest. 2d, §920A.

    1. **Collateral source rule:**   This principle is commonly called the *"collateral source rule."* It applies in the following common situations, among others:

        a. **Employment benefits:**   If the plaintiff misses work, she can recover the wages she would have earned, even if these are reimbursed through *sick pay* furnished by the employer (either voluntarily or under a contract or collective bargaining agreement), statutory disability benefits (e.g. workers' compensation), etc.

        b. **Insurance:**   Any losses covered by the plaintiff's insurance may nonetheless be recovered.

   c. **Social security and welfare payments:**   Payments by the government under social welfare programs (e.g. social security disability benefits, welfare payments, etc.) also do not count against the plaintiff's recovery.

   d. **Free services:**   And even more surprisingly, if the plaintiff receives *free services* (e.g., free medical services from a friend, or free home-care services by her own family), the plaintiff may recover the *reasonable value* of these services.

2. **Rationale:**   There are three major rationales for the collateral source rule.

   a. **Payment by plaintiff:**   First, many of the kinds of benefits listed above are ones for which the plaintiff has indirectly paid. For instance, if she receives payments under a disability or life insurance policy, she has paid the premiums on these policies previously; similarly, if she receives free care from her family, she has contributed to the support of her family. It would be unfair to strip her of the benefits of her investment.

   b. **Aiding wrongdoer:**   Second, courts feel that it is unfair to allow benefits received by the plaintiff (whether she indirectly paid for them or not) to go to the benefit of the tortfeasor, who is obviously the more culpable of the two.

   c. **Subrogation:**   Finally, in many cases the person making the payments is *subrogated* to the rights of the plaintiff,[1] or has a right of reimbursement against her out of any judgment; in this situation, there is no double recovery at all.

3. **Attack on rule:**   The collateral source rule has been subject to a great deal of attack since the 1980s. In fact, nearly half the states have *modified* the common-law collateral source rule in one way or another, generally as part of the 1980s "tort reform" movement. (See ALI Study, v. II, p. 167.) Critics of the collateral source rule argue that it leads to duplicate recovery for some plaintiffs. Furthermore, in cases where subrogation is allowed (see prior paragraph), the collateral source rule simply gives a windfall to the insurer or other person making prior payment to the plaintiff, at the expense of the defendant's insurance company. For these reasons, the ALI Study, v. II, p. 179, recommends the rejection of the collateral source rule. (But the ALI would give the plaintiff a credit for the last two years worth of premiums paid on medical insurance, and would prevent most subrogation claims.)

F. **Mitigation:**   A tort plaintiff, like a contract plaintiff, may not recover any damages which he could reasonably have avoided. This idea is sometimes expressed by saying that the plaintiff has a *"duty to mitigate."* In particular, this means that the plaintiff cannot recover for any harm which would probably have been avoided had he sought *adequate medical care*.

1. **Only reasonable care required:**   But the plaintiff is only required to use reasonable effort and care, and courts are very lenient in construing this. Furthermore, the burden of

---

1. Under the doctrine of subrogation, one who makes payments to or on behalf of another — such as an insurer making payments to or for an insured — succeeds to the insured's rights against the wrongdoer who brought about the need for payment. So in a suit that appears to be by the victim V against the tortfeasor D, the real party in interest on the plaintiff's side may well be V's insurance company, which advanced to V medical expenses, lost wages, etc., and which has now in return been subrogated to (i.e., has succeeded to) V's right to recover for these items, at least up to the amount of the payments made by the insurer to V.

proof is on the defendant to show that the plaintiff's harm could reasonably have been avoided.

2. **Seat belt defense:** Most states apply the "duty to mitigate" rule only to conduct by the plaintiff after the accident. But a few apply it also to some *safety precautions* which the plaintiff should have taken before the accident. In these states, for instance, it may be held that where the plaintiff has failed to wear a *safety belt* or *motorcycle helmet*, injuries which he suffers that would not have been sustained had he taken such precautions are avoidable damages, for which there can be no recovery. See Nutshell, p. 311. (In other jurisdictions, the failure to use a seat-belt can be contributory or comparative negligence — see *infra*, p. 286.)

   a. **Seat belt law:** At least 32 states have *laws* that *require* drivers and/or passengers to wear a *seat belt*. Failure to wear a seat belt in violation of such a law is somewhat more likely to be considered a failure to mitigate damage than where there is no such law. See *infra*, p. 288.

3. **Effect of comparative negligence:** The mitigation-of-damages doctrine is much less important today than formerly, because most states that have adopted comparative negligence no longer apply the mitigation rule, and instead merely treat P's failure to mitigate as a form of fault that reduces but does not eliminate her recovery. See *infra*, p. 285.

G. **Caps on pain-and-suffering awards:** In the 1980s, a number of groups (especially doctors and insurance companies) warned of a "tort law crisis," and lobbied extensively for reform. These groups were strikingly successful in persuading legislatures to put a *cap* on *pain-and-suffering* awards. By 1990, over half the states had enacted some sort of cap on pain-and-suffering damages. See Dobbs, pp. 773-777. Many of these statutes protect only a certain type of defendant (e.g., doctors), but others apply across the board.

1. **Medical malpractice:** The most common type of statute protects *doctors and hospitals* against large pain-and-suffering awards in *medical malpractice* cases. For instance, Cal. Civ. Code §3333.2 sets a $250,000 limit on pain-and-suffering damages for any malpractice action against a "health care provider," including doctors and hospitals.

2. **General:** Other statutes have set a cap on pain-and-suffering awards regardless of who the defendant is. See, e.g., Md. Ann. Code, Ct. & Jd. Proc. §11-108, setting a $350,000 limit on awards for "non-economic damages" in personal injury cases, regardless of the identity of the defendant.

3. **No federal right:** Few if any decisions have found pain-and-suffering caps to be a violation of the *federal* Constitution.

II. PUNITIVE DAMAGES

A. **Punitive damages:** Punitive damages (as noted *supra*, p. 10) are sometimes awarded to penalize the defendant, and deter similar wrongdoers, where the defendant's conduct is particularly outrageous.

1. **Negligence cases:** In cases of negligence, as opposed to intentional torts, punitive damages are usually awarded only where the defendant's conduct was *"reckless"* or *"willful and wanton."*

    a. **Product liability suits:** Punitive damages are now more and more commonly awarded in *product liability suits*. One who sells a defective product may be held "strictly liable," even without negligence. (See *infra*, p. 359.) If all that the plaintiff shows is that the product was defective, and he does not demonstrate negligence, punitive damages are highly unlikely. But if the defendant is the manufacturer, and the plaintiff shows that the defendant *knew* of the defect, and made the product anyway, an award of punitive damages will often be made and sustained. See, e.g., *Fischer v. Johns-Manville Corp.*, 512 A.2d 466 (N.J. 1986).

    b. **Effect of possible multiple suits:** Observe that in the product liability context, if every jury which awarded compensatory damages were also to award significant punitive damages, the defendant might well be bankrupted. This might in turn mean that *later plaintiffs* would be unable even to recover compensatory damages. For instance, early large punitive damages awards have probably contributed to the insolvency of several asbestos manufacturers, including most spectacularly Johns-Manville Corp. Plaintiffs exposed to asbestos produced by Manville and other manufacturers appear, on average, to have gotten smaller awards the later their cases were tried.

        i. **No outright ban:** Even in product liability cases where allowing multiple punitive damages would, as described above, risk of bankrupting the defendant before all later plaintiffs are compensated, courts have rarely if ever used this as a ground for flatly refusing to allow punitive damages. However, some courts have held that the possibility of repeated awards, and the defendant's financial condition, may be taken into account in fixing the amount of punitive damages in the earlier cases, so that individual awards are lowered to preserve funds for later claimants.

2. **Punitive damages against corporation:** A corporation, like any employer, is generally liable for the torts of its employees acting within the scope of their employment (see *infra*, p. 315). Where an employee commits a tort of a nature which would permit punitive damages to be awarded against her, may such damages be awarded against the *employer?* Again, the courts are split. Many follow a "middle" ground, expressed by Rest. 2d, §909. That section allows punitive damages against an employer only where the employer had some personal culpability (either by authorizing the act, recklessly hiring the worker despite his unfitness, or approving the act after the fact) or where the worker was employed in a *managerial capacity*.

3. **Constitutional limits:** As punitive damages awards have risen in frequency and amount in recent years, defendants have begun attacking the *constitutionality* of such awards. Present law can be summarized by saying that the Constitution does place some limits on how and in what amount punitive damages may be awarded, but that only in extreme cases will the award be overturned on federal constitutional grounds.

    a. **"Grossly excessive" standard:** An award will violate the *due process clause* of the federal constitution's Fourteenth Amendment if it is *"grossly excessive."* *BMW of North America v. Gore*, 517 U.S. 559 (1996).

b. **Ratio of actual to punitive:** One of the most important factors in whether an award of punitive damages violates due process is the ***ratio*** of the ***punitive damages*** to the ***compensatory damages.*** The Court has said that "*few awards* [significantly] exceeding a *single-digit ratio* between punitive and compensatory damages ... will satisfy due process." **State Farm Mut. Automobile Insur. Co. v. Campbell**, 123 S.Ct. 1513 (2003).

   i. *Campbell* **case:** For instance, in *Campbell, supra,* the Court found that a punitive damages award of $145 million (*145 times* the $1 million compensatory award) violated the defendant's due process rights.

      (1) **Facts:** In *Campbell,* D (an insurance company) refused to settle a case in Utah against the Ps (the policy holders) for the policy limits, even though there was (the Supreme Court later concluded) a "near-certain probability that by taking the case to trial, a judgment in excess of the policy limits would be awarded." The Ps suffered emotional distress from facing a judgment of $136,000 in excess of the policy limit (though D ultimately paid this whole sum before the Ps-vs.-D suit, thus sparing the Ps from actual financial loss). The trial court in the Ps-vs.-D suit allowed in evidence of 20 years worth of assorted alleged wrongdoing by D in states other than Utah, most of which had nothing to do with the refusal-to-pay-valid-claims practice at issue in the case itself.

      (2) **Ratio too high:** As noted, in striking the award the Court relied heavily on the fact that there was a 145-to-1 ratio between punitive and compensatory damages, far higher than the single-digit ratios that the Court said would usually be the appropriate limit.

      (3) **Irrelevant wrongdoing:** But the Court also objected to the trial court's consideration of evidence of other wrongdoing that *"had nothing to do with"* the type of refusal-to-settle wrongdoing at issue in the case itself. One of the key factors in the due process analysis is the ***reprehensibility*** of the defendant's conduct, and, the Court said, only conduct that is "*similar* to that which harmed [the plaintiffs]" may be considered in determining reprehensibility.

   ii. *Exxon Shipping* **case:** In *Campbell, supra,* the Supreme Court was deciding whether a punitive damages award was so high that under the circumstances it violated the defendant's federal *constitutional* rights. But occasionally, the Supreme Court sits as a ***common law*** court, whose function is to decide what the proper measure of punitive damages ought to be as a matter of ***public policy.*** In one such recent case, ***Exxon Shipping Co. v. Baker***, 128 S.Ct. 2605 (2008), the Court decided that punitive damages ought not to be ***greater than the amount of compensatory damages*** properly awarded in the case. In other words, for the type of case for which the Court was setting a non-constitutional standard — federal maritime cases involving oil spills — the Court set a ***maximum ratio of 1 to 1*** between compensatory damages and punitive damages.

4. **Legislative reform:** Defendants and insurance companies have been more successful in combatting punitive damages in the legislatures than in the courts. Since the late 1980s, at

least 15 states have attempted to put statutory controls on punitive damages. These statutes follow several approaches, including:

❑ *Limits on the amount* that may be awarded. (For instance, in Texas, four times the actual damages or $200,000, whichever is greater, unless the tort is intentional; Tex. Civ. Prac. & Rem. Code §§41.001-009);

❑ Payment of some of the award *to the state* instead of to the plaintiff, to reduce the incentives to seek such awards (e.g., 75% of a punitive damages award in product liability suits, adjusted for litigation expenses, is paid to the state; Ga. Off. Code Ann. §§51-12-5.1(e)(2)); and

❑ Tightening of the *standard of proof* beyond the usual "preponderance of the evidence" standard (e.g., requiring proof "beyond a reasonable doubt," as Colorado Rev. Stat. Ann. §13-25-127(2) does, or proof by "clear and convincing evidence.") .

a. Constitutional attacks: These legislative efforts to curtail punitive damages have often been attacked by plaintiffs on the grounds that the curtailment violates some *constitutional* provision, typically a provision of the *state* constitution. These constitutional attacks have sometimes succeeded, as occurred in Illinois, Ohio, Oregon and Kentucky. See PWS (10th), p. 1226.

i. Right of state to keep award as a "taking": One feature of state reform statutes that plaintiffs have often attacked on constitutional grounds is the requirement (the second one listed above) that *some portion of the award go to the state* instead of to the plaintiff. These attacks, usually made on the basis of a state or federal constitutional ban on *"takings"* without due process, have generally *failed*. See, e.g., *Cheatham v. Pohle*, 789 N.E.2d 467 (Ind. 2003).

III. RECOVERY BY SPOUSE OR CHILDREN OF INJURED PARTY

A. Historical action for husband: The old English common law viewed the husband-wife relationship as a master-servant one. Accordingly, if anyone injured the wife, the husband had a claim for "loss of services" (or *"loss of consortium"*). These lost services might include companionship, sex, housework, earnings outside the home, etc.

1. No remedy for wife: But the wife, being essentially a chattel, had no right to "services" from her husband. Therefore, if he was injured, she could not recover anything at common law; all recovery had to be in his name.

2. Modern view: Today, nearly all states treat the sexes equally with respect to recovery by a spouse. This has occurred through a variety of means, including evolution of the common law and Equal Protection attacks on statutes giving only husbands the right to recover for injuries to a spouse. (A few courts have fostered sexual equality by not allowing *either* sex to recover for injuries to a spouse.) See P&K, pp. 931-33.

a. Double recovery: Where the physically injured party and his or her spouse are both allowed to sue, there is obviously a danger of double recovery. For instance, where it is the woman who is injured, she might recover her medical expenses in one action, and her husband might recover these same expenses in his own action, on the theory that he was really the one paying for them. For this reason, the civil procedure rules of a number of states require that the two actions be brought together, so that double recovery can be guarded against; even where no rules require this, as a practical matter both actions are almost always brought jointly. See Nutshell, p. 316. See also P&K, p. 933.

b. **Unmarried co-habitants:** Starting in the late 1990's, some courts have allowed *unmarried co-habitants* to bring loss-of-consortium claims. Dobbs & Hayden (5th), p. 584, n. 6. Similarly, some states allow *domestic partners* or persons joined by a *civil union* to bring such claims. So far, however, few if any courts have allowed *gay or lesbian partners* to bring loss of consortium claims (though Vermont's statute allowing same-sex couples to enter civil unions expressly changes this result, and Massachusetts' 2003 judicial decision allowing gay marriage may also do so).

3. **Parent's recovery where the child is injured:** Similarly, nearly all jurisdictions allow a *parent* to recover *medical expenses* incurred due to an injury to the child. Also, since the common law rule that a parent is entitled to the *services and earnings* of his minor child has never been repudiated, a parent can recover for loss of these items.

   a. **Loss of companionship:** An increasing number of courts now allow a parent to recover, in addition to the above items, damages for loss of the child's *companionship* or *affection*. Normally, such damages will exist only if the child dies (but they might also be appropriate if the child suffers brain damage). See *infra*, p. 273.

4. **Child's action where parent injured:** Where it is the *parent* who has been injured no courts, prior to 1980, allowed the child to recover for loss of companionship or guidance.

   a. **Rationale:** Courts denying recovery for loss of a parent's companionship have stressed the difficulty of measuring loss, and the problem of duplicative claims.

      i. *Borer* **case:** For instance, recovery for loss of a parent's companionship was denied by the court in *Borer v. American Airlines*, 563 P.2d 858 (Cal. 1977). There, Patricia Borer was the mother of *nine* children who all brought suit for damages for loss of society and companionship after Ms. Borer was injured. The court emphasized the difficulty of placing a value on this type of injury, and "the inadequacy of monetary compensation to alleviate [the] tragedy. . . . "

   b. **Modern developments:** However, since 1980 a few courts have allowed children to recover for the loss of society and companionship stemming from the parent's injury. For example, Massachusetts now allows such damages if the child is both: (1) a *minor* and (2) *dependent* on the parent for nurture and development. *Ferriter v. Daniel O'Connell's Sons, Inc.*, 413 N.E.2d 690 (Mass. 1980).

5. **Defenses:** In such third-party actions, it is usually held that any defense which could have been asserted in a suit by the injured party may be asserted against the plaintiff. For instance, in a suit by a husband for loss of companionship and intercourse due to injuries to his wife, the defendant may assert that the wife was contributorily negligent. See P&K, p. 937.

   a. **Defenses against plaintiff:** Furthermore, there are defenses that can be asserted against the plaintiff himself. For instance, if Husband and Wife are driving together, and Wife is injured in a collision, the defendant to Husband's suit for loss of services can win by showing that Husband drove negligently. See P&K, p. 937.

IV. WRONGFUL DEATH AND SURVIVOR ACTIONS

A. **Consequences of injured party's death:** At common law, when a person who was physically injured by the defendant's negligence died from these injuries, his death had two important consequences with respect to legal recovery. First, the decedent's own tort action was extinguished. Second, third persons injured by his death (e.g., his spouse and children), lost their right to recover, due to an early illogical holding that "in a civil court the death of a human being could not be complained of as an injury". *Baker v. Bolton*, 170 Eng. Rep. 1033 (Eng. 1808).

   1. **Modern statutes:** By not allowing any recovery for death, the result was that "it was cheaper for the defendant to kill the plaintiff than to injure him. . . . " P&K, p. 945. This was remedied in England by the passage of Lord Campbell's Act in 1846; similar statutes were enacted in the U.S. To prevent the injured party's own action from being lost due to his death, all states have enacted what are called "Survival" statutes under which damages are awarded to the deceased's estate. And to give a cause of action to the spouse and children of the decedent, "Wrongful Death" statutes have been passed.

   2. **Common-law modification:** Occasionally, also, courts have supplemented the statutory process by granting common-law relief. For instance, in *Moragne v. States Marine Lines, Inc.*, 398 U.S. 375 (1970), the Supreme Court held that the heirs of a seaman killed on board ship could recover for his wrongful death, notwithstanding the lack of a statute, and despite prior case law holding that he could not. The Court noted that in recent years, every state had enacted a wrongful death statute, and that whatever public policy reasons were originally perceived to make such recovery undesirable no longer existed.

B. **Survival statutes:** Every state has passed a ***survival statute*** to modify the common law rule in at least some respects. In about half of them, the decedent's claim for ***personal injuries*** survives, whether or not the injury was caused by the defendant. P&K, p. 942. (The other statutes sometimes allow continuation only of those actions for injuries which did not lead to death, or for damage to personal or real property, or based upon similar distinctions.)

   1. **No claim for death itself:** In many states, survival actions are accompanied by a separate wrongful death action. Where this is so, there is obviously a danger of double recovery. For this reason, where there are two statutes the survival action generally is restricted to recovery for ***pain and suffering*** by the decedent prior to his death, lost earnings prior to death, actual medical expenses, etc. (i.e., only losses occurring prior to the death). This means that if death is ***instantaneous,*** generally there is no survival action at all in such states, since all damages are sustained on account of or after the death. See Rest. 2d, §926, Comment a.

   2. **Survival of action against dead defendant:** Most survival statutes, regardless of what torts they apply to, hold that just as the plaintiff's action may be maintained after his death, so an action may be maintained after the ***defendant*** has died, or even instituted after his death. Rest. 2d, §926.

C. Wrongful death statutes: As noted, most states have special *wrongful death statutes* which allow a defined group of persons (usually the decedent's spouse and children, and sometimes parents if the decedent has no spouse or children) to recover for the loss they sustained by virtue of the decedent's death. Normally, the decedent's executor or administrator brings the action, but the proceeds go directly to the beneficiaries, with each one generally receiving what the court finds as being his own pecuniary loss from the decedent's death.

1. **Who are proper parties:**   Since the wrongful death action is usually considered to be exclusively a statutory one, courts have been *strict* in construing all aspects of the statute, including the *class of allowable beneficiaries*. Thus it has been held, for instance, that a *step-child* is not an "heir" of the decedent and is thus not permitted to recover anything, even though the child may have suffered tangible losses of economic support and moral guidance from the death.

    a. **Cohabitants, including same-sex couples:**   Where the wrongful death statute gives a right of recovery to the "surviving spouse," generally the decedent's unmarried *"cohabitant"* (live-in lover) will *not* have any rights under the statute. Dobbs & Hayden (5th), p. 618, n. 5. However, if the state permits *civil unions*, the surviving member of such a union may have the right to bring a wrongful death action. Vermont, for instance, not only provides that same-sex couples may enter into civil unions, but also expressly provides that a survivor of such a union has the right to bring a wrongful death action (as well as an action for loss of consortium). See 15 Vt. Stat. §§ 1204(a) and 1204(e)(2).

2. **Elements of damages:**   Elements of damages in a wrongful death action are generally similar to those allowed in actions by a spouse or parent for injuries not leading to death (*supra*, p. 270). Thus, the beneficiaries may recover for the *economic support* they would have received had the accident, and death, not occurred, or for the pecuniary value of *household services* which the decedent performed.

    a. **Recovery for grief:**   It is usually held that recovery under these wrongful death statutes can be had only for items having a "pecuniary value." In recent years, the list of items having pecuniary value has been extended so that it usually includes the *companionship, sexual intercourse*, and *moral guidance* of the decedent. P&K, pp. 951-53. A number of states also allow *grief* or other mental suffering of the survivors as an element of damages, though most do not. See P&K, p. 952.

    b. **Recovery by parent where child is dead:**   Where a *child* has been fatally injured, it is hard to establish true pecuniary loss on the part of the parents, since the cost of raising and educating a child is generally more than any earnings he could be expected to bring home. However, many, if not most courts, are now willing to allow a substantial award for loss of the "companionship" of the child. Although the rule in a few jurisdictions, most notably New York, is to explicitly refuse to allow such non-pecuniary damages, denial of such damages has been the target of severe criticism, and it is likely that fewer and fewer courts will persist in disallowing them. Some courts, in fact, have awarded such damages to the parent of an *adult* child, and even to a parent who had *abandoned* the now-dead child.

        i. **Post-majority support:** Other courts have held, along similar lines, that since damages may be recovered based on what the beneficiary reasonably *expected* to receive from the decedent, not what the decedent was legally bound to provide, support which the decedent child would have given to her parents in their *old age* (after her own emancipation) may be considered.

3. **Defenses that could have been asserted against decedent:** There is a lot of dispute about what *defenses* a defendant may assert in a wrongful death action. It is generally agreed that the defendant may assert any defense which he would have been able to use against the *decedent,* if the decedent was still alive and suing in her own name. Thus the decedent's *contributory negligence* (assuming that defense is applicable in the jurisdiction in question), *assumption of risk, consent*, etc., will all bar an action for wrongful death by the survivors. See P&K, pp. 954-55.

    a. **Statute of limitations:** If the decedent originally had a cause of action, but did not sue while alive until the statute of limitations on this action had run, most courts hold that the wrongful death action is *not necessarily barred*. These courts take the view that the wrongful death action begins to run only from the date of death (and that the applicable statute of limitations on wrongful death actions is the only thing that matters). P&K, p. 957.

    b. **Settlement by or judgment for or against decedent:** Suppose the injured person brings her own action, and settles it, wins it, or loses it before dying. Will any of these things bar the beneficiaries from bringing a wrongful death action? Most courts have held that each of these things will bar the action, on the theory that settlement or judgment dissolves the decedent's claim, and any wrongful death action must "derive" from a live claim on the part of the decedent.

4. **Defenses against beneficiaries:** A second cluster of issues relates to defenses that may be asserted against the *beneficiaries*.

    a. **Effect on individual claims:** Most wrongful death statutes are for the benefit of a defined class of beneficiaries (rather than for the estate itself). Where such a statute is involved, it is usually held that a defense that would be valid against a particular beneficiary (e.g., that beneficiary's contributory negligence, assumption of risk, etc.) bars recovery of the pecuniary loss that that person has suffered. If there is only one beneficiary, against whom there is a defense, this obviously forecloses the action. If there are several beneficiaries, and only some are subject to such a defense, the majority rule now seems to be that their damages may not be recovered as part of the overall wrongful death award, but that the other beneficiaries may recover for their own pecuniary losses. See P&K, pp. 958-59.

D. **Variety of statutes:** Most of the above discussion of survival and wrongful death statutes has focused upon the usual statutory scheme, in which there is both a survival action and a wrongful death action (with actual losses incurred prior to death allocated to the survival action, and all other losses allocated to the wrongful death one). But there are many other statutory schemes in the various states.

    1. **No survival action allowed:** For instance, some states do not allow a survival action at all where the defendant is the cause of the death; instead, the wrongful death action includes recovery for any lost earnings due to shortening of the decedent's life expectancy (without regard to whether these earnings would have been passed on to the decedent's heirs). See Rest. 2d, §925, Comment b(3).

2. **Examine particular statute:** Thus it is extremely important to examine the particular statutory set-up in the state in question.

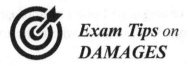

Exam Tips on DAMAGES

Damages issues can and usually will appear as part of virtually every torts essay exam. Here are some things to look for, especially where the question mainly involves a negligence action:

☛ Be on the lookout for applications of the *"collateral source"* rule.

  ☞ Remember that under this rule, D doesn't get a *discount* to reflect the fact that P may have been *reimbursed* for her out-of-pocket expenses associated with the accident from some third party (e.g., a health insurer who pays P's medical bills).

  ☞ For a collateral source issue to be present, the fact pattern will have to tell you that P has received insurance or some other reimbursement payment (e.g., public disability payments, or sick pay from P's employer).

  ☞ Often, a collateral source issue will be *joined* with a comparative negligence and/or joint-and-several liability issue. Don't be distracted — unless the facts tell you otherwise, assume that the common law collateral source rule is in effect, and therefore don't take into account any reimbursements in figuring out who can recover what from whom.

    Example: P's total damages are $100,000. He is reimbursed by a health insurance company for $20,000, representing his hospital bills. The jury says that P is 25% responsible, D1 25% and D2 50%. In a comparative negligence jurisdiction, with no other relevant statutes, how much can P collect from each defendant? Answer: up to a total combined limit of $75,000 from each of D1 and D2. This answer is the same as it would be if P had not gotten any reimbursement.

  ☞ You might want to allude to the possibility that the state has abolished or cut back on the collateral source rule, as some states have done. (*Example:* "Assuming that the state has not abolished the common law collateral source rule, P's recovery will not be reduced. . . .")

☛ Be on the watch for places to apply the plaintiff's *"duty to mitigate"* her damages.

  ☞ In the garden-variety situation, P fails to seek *prompt medical attention*, and his problem (caused initially by D) worsens. Under the duty-to-mitigate rule, P can't recover for any damages that would not have been suffered if P had sought prompt medical aid.

  ☞ More likely to be tested: P fails to take some *advance safety precaution*. Here, some (but not most) courts hold that P has violated the duty to mitigate, and is completely blocked from recovery for those injuries that would have been prevented by the precaution. (Note that this defense is a total one, whereas if P's failure to use the device is treated as comparative negligence P's recovery will be only partly reduced.) (*Examples:* P doesn't wear a seat belt; P doesn't wear a hard-hat while walking in a construction site; P doesn't wear a mask or gloves while working in a hospital.)

☛ Occasionally, you will want to note that *"punitive"* damages are or may be appropriate.

    ☞ If the suit is for an *intentional* tort (including defamation or invasion of privacy, as well as the intentional torts against the person), punitive damages will often be appropriate. This is especially true where D's conduct is "outrageous," such as where the tort is intentional infliction of mental distress.

    ☞ In *negligence* cases, note the possibility of punitive damage only where you conclude that D was *"reckless"* or *"willfull"* in his conduct. Usually, this means that D disregarded what he knew to be a substantial risk of injury to P or others, rather than merely being "inattentive."

    ☞ If the fact pattern tells you that punitive damages awarded by a jury are many times greater than the compensatory damages awarded, you should mention the possibility that the large punitive award violates D's federal *due process* rights because it is *"grossly excessive."*

☛ You should also have a catalog of various *types* of damages in mind, ready to select from as appropriate in the fact pattern. Here is a partial list:

    ❏ Value of a *lost body function* (e.g., loss of an arm).

    ❏ *Pain and suffering*.

    ❏ *Lost earnings*.

    ❏ *Mental distress*.

    ❏ *Hedonistic damages.* (These apply where P loses the ability to engage in a pursuit she enjoyed; courts are split about whether this is allowable where P is in a coma.)

    ❏ Loss of *consortium*. (These apply where the spouse, parent or child of a person who has a physical injury loses some aspect of companionship — thus where H is injured and his wife, W, can't have sexual relations with him, W gets a recovery for the loss of consortium.)

    ❏ *Survival* action. (Even though P is dead, his estate is allowed to recover for his pain and suffering, his medical expenses before death, etc.)

    ❏ *Wrongful death* action. (Survivors, such as a spouse, children or — if there is no spouse and child, parents — get recovery for their grief, their loss of money that the decedent would have earned and given to them as support, etc.)

CHAPTER 11

DEFENSES IN NEGLIGENCE ACTIONS

ChapterScope

This chapter examines various defenses that can be asserted by a defendant in a negligence action. The most important concepts are:

- **Contributory negligence:** At common law, the doctrine of *contributory negligence* applies. The doctrine provides that a plaintiff who is negligent, and whose negligence is a proximate cause of his injuries, is *totally barred* from recovery.

  ❏ **Last Clear Chance:** The doctrine of *"Last Clear Chance"* acts as a limit on the contributory negligence defense. If, just before the accident, D had an *opportunity to prevent the harm*, the existence of this opportunity (the last clear chance) *wipes out* the effect of P's contributory negligence.

- **Comparative negligence:** Most states have replaced contributory negligence with *"comparative negligence."* The comparative negligence system rejects the all-or-nothing approach of contributory negligence, and instead divides the liability between P and D in proportion to their *relative degrees of fault*. P's recovery is reduced by a *proportion* equal to the ratio between his own negligence and the total negligence contributing to the accident.

- **Assumption of risk:** P is said to have *"assumed the risk"* of certain harm if she has *voluntarily consented* to take her chances that the harm will occur. Where such an assumption is shown, the plaintiff is, at common law, completely barred from recovery.

  ❏ **Express and implied:** P can assume the risk either "expressly" or "implicitly." The latter occurs when P indicates *by her conduct* (rather than by her express words) that she knows of the risk in question, and agrees to bear that risk herself.

  ❏ **Effect of comparative negligence statute:** The existence of a *comparative negligence* statute eliminates certain types of assumption of risk, but maintains the "core" variety as a defense. Thus if P's voluntary agreement to bear a certain risk prevents D from ever having any duty to P at all, the existence of a comparative negligence statute does not change this.

- **Immunities:** The common law recognizes certain *immunities* from negligence actions, including: (1) various *intra-family* immunities (e.g., between spouses, and between parent and child); (2) immunity of *charities*; and (3) *sovereign* immunity, i.e., immunity possessed by governmental entities. Each of these immunities has been abolished today in most states.

I. CONTRIBUTORY NEGLIGENCE

A. **Nature of contributory negligence defense:** The contributory negligence defense is much loved by defendants, particularly insurance companies, who fondly refer to it as "contrib".

The essence of the defense is that a plaintiff who is negligent (in the sense of not taking reasonable care to protect his own safety), and whose negligence contributes proximately to his injuries, is ***totally barred from recovery***. The defense is thus a complete one — it shifts the loss totally from the defendant to the plaintiff, even if the plaintiff's departure from reasonable care was much less marked than that of the defendant. Rest. 2d, §467.

1. **Diminishing importance:** Contributory negligence is of much ***less importance*** today than previously. As we'll see (*infra*, p. 282), more than 90% of the states have replaced it with comparative negligence, an apportionment-of-fault device that is much less damaging to plaintiffs.

B. **Historical emergence:** The defense is of judge-made origin. It first appeared in *Butterfield v. Forrester*, 103 Eng. Rep. 926 (K.B. 1809). In *Butterfield*, the defendant had blocked part of a road with a pole; the plaintiff, riding his horse rapidly at twilight, ran into the pole. The court held that plaintiff was barred from recovery, since had he been riding at a reasonable speed and looking out with reasonable care, he would have seen the obstruction and avoided it.

1. **Practical explanation:** The best explanation for the development of the contributory negligence doctrine is probably that at the time the defense evolved, courts were afraid that juries left with a free hand would give unduly large awards, and would impair the growth of industry. An additional factor is that in a comparative negligence system (the major alternative to contributory negligence, by which the plaintiff's recovery is reduced by the relative extent of his own negligence compared with that of the defendant — see *infra*, p. 281), it is necessary to apportion damages between two sources, a process whose complexity scared nineteenth century courts.

C. **Burden of pleading and proof:** In all states still applying contributory negligence, the defendant must ***specifically plead*** contributory negligence as a defense. Furthermore, she must bear the ***burden of proof*** on it; thus if there is no evidence at all (or evenly weighted evidence on both sides) as to the existence of contributory negligence, the defense does not apply. P&K, p. 451.

D. **Standard of care:** The plaintiff is held to essentially the ***same standard of care*** as the defendant, i.e., the care of a "reasonable person under like circumstances." Rest. 2d, §464. See also Rest. 3d (Apport.) §3: "Plaintiff's negligence is defined by the applicable standard for a defendant's negligence."

1. **Possible difference:** Of course, it is possible that the care a reasonable person will exercise to protect his *own* safety might in some circumstances be *less* than that person would reasonably use to protect the safety of others. But such situations should be rare — generally, if conduct would be negligent were the party to do it as a defendant, it is likely to be negligent if done when the party is a plaintiff.

2. **Child plaintiffs:** Where the plaintiff is a *child,* the standard of care to which he is held is that of a reasonable child with similar age, intelligence and experience. This is, in essence, the same "subjective" standard as is applied where the child is a defendant. (See *supra*, p. 103).

3. **Issue left to jury:** In any event, the issue of what constitutes reasonable care on the part of the plaintiff is left to the jury in all but a very few cases.

E. Proximate cause: The contributory negligence defense only applies where the plaintiff's negligence *contributes proximately* to his injuries. In general, the rules for determining actual and proximate causation are the same as those discussed previously in the context of defendants' conduct. (See *supra*, p. 141.)

F. Avoidable consequences: The defense of contributory negligence must be distinguished from that of *avoidable consequences as mitigation,* discussed *supra*, p. 266. The latter is generally held to apply only to conduct by the plaintiff *after the accident* which unreasonably fails to mitigate his damages. Contributory negligence, on the other hand, applies to the plaintiff's conduct *prior to the accident.* Hence, although both the doctrines of contributory negligence and avoidable consequences rest on the policy of requiring the plaintiff to exercise proper care to protect himself, the rule of avoidable consequences is usually held to come into play only after a legal wrong has occurred but while some damages can still be averted.

1. **Apportionment:** Observe that where the avoidable damages doctrine is applied the result is usually an *apportionment* of damages, part to the plaintiff (those that could have been avoided) and the remainder to the defendant. Contributory negligence, on the other hand, is almost by definition a refusal to apportion damages between two causes or two parties.

2. **Exceptions where apportionment allowed:** But there are nonetheless a few situations in which the damage caused by the plaintiff's negligence and that caused by the defendant's are so distinguishable from each other that apportionment *will* be allowed. This might be the case, for instance, if both the plaintiff and the defendant polluted the same stream. See P&K, p. 459.

   a. **Seat belt defense:** Perhaps the most interesting context in which the apportionment issue has arisen is that of the "*seat belt defense.*" In this defense, the defendant argues that the plaintiff's injuries from a car accident could have been reduced or entirely avoided had the plaintiff worn a seat belt. An increasing number of states — though probably not yet a majority — reduce the plaintiff's damages in some way to reflect the fact that the plaintiff's injuries would have been less if he had worn a seat belt. This topic is discussed more extensively *infra*, p. 286.

   b. **Excessive speed:** A similar apportionment issue is presented by accidents in which the plaintiff's car is traveling at an *excessive speed*. If the speed has not increased the risk of the accident, but does increase the damage which results to the plaintiff from it, what is the consequence? Again, as with seat belts, some courts have tried to apportion the damage, and others have not. See P&K, p. 459.

G. Conscious exposure to danger: One way in which the plaintiff may fail to use due care for his own safety is if he *consciously* puts himself in a position of unreasonable danger (as opposed to merely unwittingly and "casually" doing so). For instance, one who agrees to be a passenger in a car driven by a person he knows to be *drunk* may be contributorily negligent. Such conscious exposure to risk also usually gives rise to the defense of "assumption of risk," discussed *infra*, p. 292.

1. **Giving up of right by plaintiff:** Suppose the plaintiff has a *legal right* to act in a certain way, but the defendant's negligence renders that act dangerous. In this situation, the plaintiff's insistence on exercising his right is contributorily negligent only if he acts unreason-

ably; in making this determination, the social value of what he is trying to do will be weighed against the burden of not doing it, and the probability of harm, as in a case involving the defendant's own negligence. (See the Learned Hand test, *supra*, p. 97.)

    a. Highway travel: Thus even though the plaintiff has a legal right to make use of a highway, it may be contributory negligence for him to insist on using it in a situation where the defendant's negligence has blocked the highway and made its use unreasonably dangerous. Whether the danger is "unreasonable" will depend on, among other things, the existence of alternate routes, the importance of plaintiff's trip, etc. See Rest. 2d, §473, Comment b.

H. Claims against which defense not usable: The contributory negligence defense, based as it is upon general negligence principles, may be used as a bar only to a claim that is itself based on negligence.

    1. Intentional torts: Thus, the defense may not be used where the plaintiff's claim is for an *intentional tort*. P&K, p. 462.

    2. Willful and wanton tort: Similarly, if the defendant's conduct is found to have been "willful and wanton" or "reckless", the contributory negligence defense will not be allowed. Prosser and Keeton (P&K) suggest (p. 462) that this is in reality a rule of comparative negligence, with the court "refusing to set up the lesser fault against the greater."

        a. Gross negligence: But if the defendant's negligence is merely "gross" (i.e., differing in degree from that of the plaintiff, but not in kind), contributory negligence will be allowed. Obviously it may sometimes be hard to distinguish between negligence that is merely "gross", and that which is "willful". But the idea is that the latter applies to conduct by the defendant which disregards a *conscious* risk.

            i. Plaintiff's similar conduct: In any event, even if the defendant's conduct is "willful" or "reckless", contributory negligence will be allowed if the defendant shows that the plaintiff's conduct was also "willful", etc.

    3. Strict liability: For a discussion of the use of contributory negligence as a defense to *strict products liability* actions, see *infra*, pp. 406-412.

    4. Negligence per se: Contributory negligence can generally be asserted as a defense even to the defendant's *"negligence per se"*, i.e., his negligence based on a statutory violation. (See *supra*, pp. 114, 119.) Rest. 2d, §483.

        a. Exceptions where responsibility placed on defendant: But there are some statutes which are enacted solely for the purpose of protecting a class of which the plaintiff is a member, and which show an intent to place all responsibility for violations upon the defendant. Where the plaintiff shows a violation of such a statute, contributory negligence may *not* be asserted as a defense.

        Examples: One kind of "special protection" statutes are child labor laws; an employer who hires a child under the legal age may not assert contributory negligence if child is injured. A statute prohibiting the sale of guns to minors might also fall in this category, as do many statutes whose purpose is to protect employees against occupational hazards. See P&K, p. 461.

I. **Last clear chance:** The most significant limitation on the contributory negligence defense is a rule called the "*last clear chance*" doctrine. While the doctrine may or may not apply in a variety of specific situations, the general impact of the rule is as follows: If, just before the accident, the defendant has an *opportunity to prevent the harm,* and the plaintiff does not have such an opportunity, the existence of this opportunity (i.e, this last "clear chance") *wipes out* the effect of the plaintiff's contributory negligence, leaving the defendant liable if she does not take advantage of that last opportunity.

    1. **Rationale:** The doctrine is usually supported by the argument that the defendant's failure to exercise her last opportunity to avoid the harm acts as a *superseding cause,* preventing the plaintiff's negligence from being the proximate cause of the accident.

        a. **Dislike of defense:** But a more realistic explanation of the doctrine is that courts recognize the harshness and frequent unfairness of the contributory negligence defense, and have taken this route, among others, to lessen its use. Rest. 2d, §479, Comment a.

    2. **Plaintiff helpless, defendant discovers danger:** The clearest case for applying last clear chance is where the plaintiff is *helpless* to avoid his predicament, and the defendant *discovers* that predicament but negligently fails to use her opportunity to avoid the danger. In this situation, *all contributory-negligence courts* (even those purporting to reject the last clear chance doctrine) hold that the plaintiff is not barred from recovery. Rest. 2d, §479.

        Example: P negligently attempts to jay-walk across a busy street. He falls, and is unable to move. D, seeing P lying on the street, attempts to hit the brakes, but instead negligently hits the accelerator and runs P over. P's contributory negligence in jay-walking will not bar his recovery, because he was a "helpless plaintiff", and D discovered his predicament, but negligently failed to avoid it.

II. COMPARATIVE NEGLIGENCE

  A. **Rejection of "all or nothing" approach:** Contributory negligence is, of course, an "all or nothing" system — either the plaintiff is not contributorily negligent, in which case he recovers his full damages, or he is, in which case he gets nothing. In recent years, courts and legislatures have come increasingly to feel that such a system is less fair than one which makes an attempt to apportion damages between the plaintiff and the defendant according to their relative degree of fault.

    1. **Jury behavior:** Furthermore, as every tort lawyer knows, juries frequently reject the all or nothing approach, and in effect apportion damages, no matter how clearly the trial judge's instructions attempt to prevent them from doing so. Thus a plaintiff with $200,000 in damages, who the jury believes to have been somewhat contributorily negligent, will frequently be awarded, say, $100,000.

  B. **Comparative negligence defined:** A so-called *"comparative negligence"* system rejects the all-or-nothing approach, and instead attempts to divide liability between plaintiff and defendant, in proportion to their *relative degrees of fault.* As the idea is often expressed in statutes, the plaintiff is not barred from recovery by his contributory negligence, but his recovery is reduced by a proportion equal to the ratio between his own negligence and the total negligence contributing to the accident (i.e., if there is just one plaintiff and one defendant, their combined negligence).

> **Example:** P suffers damages of $100,000. A jury finds that P was 30% negligent and that D was 70% negligent. P will recover, under a comparative negligence system, $70,000 (i.e., $100,000 minus 30% x $100,000).

C. **Historical emergence:** Comparative negligence, in certain kinds of cases, has been around for a long time. English courts have applied it in *admiralty* (i.e., maritime) cases since 1700, and the U.S. Federal Courts, in the exercise of their exclusive admiralty jurisdiction, have followed it. Several Federal statutes have also applied comparative negligence; the most important of these is the Federal Employer's Liability Act (F.E.L.A.), which as early as 1908 applied comparative negligence to any suit for injuries brought by an employee of an interstate railroad against the railroad.

1. **State statutes:** A few states tried comparative negligence early in this century. Mississippi, for instance, did so by statute in 1910, first as to all personal injuries, and then even in suits for property damage. Wisconsin is also an old-time comparative negligence state, having applied the doctrine to all negligence actions since 1913. See P&K, p. 471.

2. **Explosion during 1970's:** But it was not until the 1970's that a virtual explosion of comparative negligence in the state courts began. The number of states with general (i.e., applicable to all or most negligence claims) comparative fault systems went from six in 1963 to *46* by the mid-1990's. "As of the early 21st century, only Alabama, North Carolina, Maryland [and] Virginia [as well as] the District of Columbia [had] failed to adopt comparative fault rules. In those jurisdictions, the plaintiff's contributory fault remains a complete bar." Dobbs & Hayden (5th), p. 276.

   Of the 46 states that have adopted comparative negligence, most have done so by statute, but some have done so by judicial decision.

   a. **California:** The most important of the judicial decisions instituting comparative negligence as a matter of common law was that of the California Supreme Court in *Li v. Yellow Cab Co. of California*, 532 P.2d 1226 (Cal. 1975), infra, p. 284.

      i. **"Pure" applied:** The court in *Li* decided that a *"pure,"* rather than a "50%," comparative negligence system should be applied. In a "pure" system, the plaintiff is allowed to recover (but at a reduced level) even if his fault is greater than the defendant's. In a "50%" system, by contrast, the plaintiff is allowed partial recovery only if his negligence is (depending on the exact wording of the statute or decision) either less than, or no greater than, the defendant's. If he is as negligent or more negligent than the defendant, under such a system he recovers nothing. (As is noted below, most states have adopted this kind of system.) The *Li* court asserted that a 50% system "simply shifts the lottery aspect of the contributory negligence rule to a different ground."

D. **"Pure" vs. "50%" systems:** Only *13* states employ a "pure" form of comparative negligence. These are: Alaska, Arizona, California, Florida, Kentucky, Louisiana, Mississippi, Missouri, Michigan, New Mexico, New York, Rhode Island and Washington. See *McIntyre v. Balentine, supra.*

1. **Various modified systems:** The remaining comparative negligence states have applied one of two basic cut-offs beyond which ***the plaintiff may not recover at all***. Most states bar the plaintiff's claim as soon as his negligence is ***"as great"*** as the defendant's. The remainder bar him when his negligence is ***"greater"*** than the defendant's. Obviously these two systems differ only as to their treatment of the "50-50" case, but given the tendency of juries to regard the negligence of both sides as about the same, this 50-50 case is of considerable importance as a practical matter.

E. **Multiple parties:** Where there are only two parties, a plaintiff and a defendant, the various comparative negligence systems are easy to administer. But what if there is more than one defendant?

1. **All parties before court:** If both (or all) defendants are joined in the same lawsuit, and the system is a "pure" one, the solution is simple. If the total negligence of all parties is determined to be, say, 20% due to P, 50% to D1, and 30% to D2, P recovers 80% of his damages.

   a. **Not pure:** But what if all the defendants are before the court, and the jurisdiction is one in which the plaintiff may recover only if his negligence is less than, or not greater than, that of the defendants? If the plaintiff's negligence is less than that of all the defendants combined, but greater than that of some particular defendant, can the plaintiff recover? Most state statutes leave this question unanswered. It would, however, seem highly unfair to deny a plaintiff all recovery where he is 26% negligent, and three defendants constitute the remaining 74% negligence.

2. **Not all parties before the court:** If not all defendants are before the court in a single action, the problems become even greater. The biggest question relates to ***joint-and-several liability***. May the defendant(s) before the court who is found to be only partly responsible for plaintiff's loss, be required to pay for the whole loss aside from that caused by plaintiff's own fault? Under traditional "joint-and-several liability" principles (see *supra*, p.183), the answer would be "yes."

   Example: P, a pedestrian who is jaywalking, is injured when a car driven by D and a car driven by X collide. P is able to locate D, and sues him in a "pure" comparative negligence jurisdiction. X, a hit-and-run driver, is never found. In the P-D action, the jury finds that P was 20% responsible, D 30% responsible and X 50% responsible. P's damages total $1 million. It is clear that P can collect at most $800,000 total. The question is, may P collect the full $800,000 from D, or only $300,000? Under traditional "joint-and-several liability" rules applicable to joint tortfeasors, P would be allowed to collect the full $800,000 from D. But this would be, at least on the surface, quite unfair to D, who is responsible for only 30% of the total fault.

   a. **Tort reform statutes:** In the 1980s, the "tort reform" movement led to modification of traditional joint-and-several liability principles (at least in situations where comparative fault applies) in most states.

      i. **Total abolition:** About 16 states have ***completely abolished*** the doctrine of joint-and-several liability in comparative negligence cases. In these states, all liability is "several." That is, each defendant is only required to pay his or her own share of the total responsibility.

ii. Hybrid: Most states that have replaced traditional joint-and-several liability, however, have enacted some sort of *"hybrid"* approach, which blends aspects of joint-and-several liability and aspects of several liability. These hybrids — which include the reallocation, threshold and damage-type variants — are discussed in detail *supra*, p. 184.

F. How percentage is determined: In most of the comparative negligence systems, the percentage of fault assigned to the plaintiff seems to be based on the *relative degree to which his conduct deviated from the standard of care*, *not* the relative *contribution* his negligence made. Thus if the plaintiff is only slightly negligent, and the defendant grossly so, the plaintiff will have a relatively small percentage assigned to him, even though, in a causal sense, each person's negligence was clearly a *sine qua non* of the accident. Thus the Third Restatement takes into account "the nature of the person's risk-creating conduct, including any *awareness* or *indifference* with respect to the risks created by the conduct and any *intent* with respect to the harm created by the conduct[.]" Rest. 3d (Apport.) §8(a).

1. Contrary view: But some cases have held that the relative directness of the causal link between negligence and damage may also be considered in assigning the plaintiff his percentage. And even the Third Restatement, after the passage quoted above emphasizing the degree of fault, says that the court may also take into account "the *strength of the causal connection* between the person's risk-creating conduct and the harm." Rest. 3d (Apport.) §8(b).

G. Last clear chance: Does the doctrine of *last clear chance* survive in a comparative negligence jurisdiction, allowing the entire loss to be thrust upon the defendant? Courts are split.

1. *Li* solution: In California, the doctrine does not survive. The court in *Li, supra* p. 282, held that "when true comparative negligence is adopted, the need for last clear chance as a palliative of the hardships of the 'all-or-nothing' rule disappears and its retention results only in a windfall to the plaintiff in direct contravention of the principle of liability in proportion to fault."

2. Opposing view: But other jurisdictions have *continued to apply* the doctrine, sometimes on the theory that where the defendant has had a "last clear chance" to avoid the accident, the plaintiff's conduct is not the proximate cause of the accident. P&K, p. 477.

3. Restatement: The Third Restatement *rejects* the last-clear-chance rule in comparative-negligence cases. See Rest. 3d (Apport.) §3, Comment b.

H. Willful and wanton misconduct by defendant: We saw (*supra* p. 280) that in many jurisdictions, where the defendant's conduct is "willful and wanton" or "reckless", contributory negligence does not apply. In a comparative negligence jurisdiction, does this kind of willful or reckless conduct by the defendant prevent the plaintiff's damages from being reduced in proportion to his own fault?

1. Usual approach: Generally, the statutes have been interpreted to mean that the plaintiff's damages may nonetheless be reduced in this situation (although since the plaintiff's wrongdoing is being compared with the defendant's severe wrongdoing, the percentage of fault assigned to the former will generally be quite low). See Nutshell, p. 111.

2. **Intentional torts:** If the defendant's tort is *intentional*, some jurisdictions do not apply their comparative negligence statute *at all*, under theory that a plaintiff's "mere negligence" should not reduce the significance of the defendant's volitional conduct. But the Third Restatement essentially rejects this view: comparative negligence doctrines *apply even where the defendant's tort is an intentional one.* See Rest. 3d (Apport.) §1, Comment c. Indeed, the Restatement speaks in terms of comparing the plaintiff's negligence to all parties' "responsibility" (not negligence), in part to reinforce the concept that comparative-fault applies in intentional-tort cases. See Rest. 3d (Apport.), §7.

I. **Assumption of risk:** What about the doctrine of *assumption of risk*, discussed beginning on p. 292; does it survive? There is no clear single answer; the subject is discussed on p. 294 (express assumption) and 296 (implied assumption).

J. **Mitigation of damages:** Recall that the doctrine of *mitigation of damages* (*supra*, p. 266) says that P cannot recover for any harm which she could reasonably have avoided. The classic example is the plaintiff who is injured due to D's negligence and who then worsens her injury by *failing to get medical attention* or to follow the doctor's advice. Does the mitigation of damages doctrine survive in a comparative- negligence jurisdiction?

1. **Most courts abolish doctrine:** Most comparative negligence states seem to have *abolished* the mitigation-of-damages doctrine, either by statute or decision. As long as D's negligence and P's failure to take reasonable precautions have combined to produce an *indivisible harm*, most comparative-negligence jurisdictions would probably apply a comparative-fault allocation rather than permitting D to escape liability completely by means of the mitigation-of-damages doctrine.

   a. **Third Restatement agrees:** This is the approach of the Third Restatement, which says in commentary that the general rule of comparative negligence "applies to a plaintiff's unreasonable conduct that aggravates the plaintiff's injuries. No rule about mitigation of damages or avoidable consequences categorically forgives a plaintiff of this type of conduct or categorically excludes recovery." Rest. 3d (Apport.) §3, Comment b.

      Example: D negligently causes P's leg to be broken. P then negligently fails to take antibiotics as prescribed by P's doctor. The leg gets infected, and P is forced to miss two weeks of work, resulting in lost wages of $1,000. The leg would not have gotten infected had P taken the antibiotics (and P would not have missed any work).

      Under the traditional mitigation-of-damages rule, P would not be entitled to recover any of the lost wages, because she would have avoided this harm entirely had she behaved non-negligently. But under the majority (and Restatement Third) approach to comparative negligence, B will be permitted to recover for the lost wages, though her recovery will be reduced by her percentage of fault. See Rest. 3d (Apport.) §3, Illustr. 4, so concluding on essentially these facts.

K. **P's negligence creates the need for D's services:** Now consider what might be thought of as the flip-side of the mitigation-of-damages problem: *P's negligence causes him to need services*, which D then negligently renders. Can D successfully argue that P's recovery should be reduced by P's comparative fault in bringing about the occasion for D's negligence? Most courts have answered *"no."*

1. **Need for medical attention:** The most common illustration of the problem is where P's negligence causes him to *need medical attention* from D, a doctor or hospital — most courts have said that P's "antecedent negligence" *does not reduce his recovery* in this scenario.

    Example: P gets drunk, and then crashes his car. He receives a minor concussion and several facial fractures, and is taken to the D hospital. There, he is put on a respirator to assist his breathing. While P is on the respirator, a nurse for D negligently lets the oxygen run out from the respirator, and P suffers permanent brain jury. D argues that P's recovery should be reduced on a comparative fault basis, because it was P's negligence (driving while drunk) that brought about the occasion for P to need the medical services that resulted in his brain damage.

    Held, for P. "[M]ost jurisdictions have held that a patient's negligence that provides only the occasion for medical treatment may not be compared to that of the negligent physician. ... We ... agree that 'patients who may have negligently injured themselves are nevertheless entitled to subsequent non-negligent medical treatment and to an undiminished recovery if such subsequent non-negligent treatment is not afforded.'" *Mercer v. Vanderbilt Univ.*, 134 S.W.3d 121 (Tenn. 2004).

2. **Third Restatement agrees:** The Third Restatement agrees with the result in cases like *Mercer, supra.* See Rest. 3d (Apport.) §7, Comment m: "[I]n a case involving negligent rendition of a service, including medical services, a factfinder does not consider any plaintiff's conduct that created the condition the service was employed to remedy."

L. **Violation of safety statute by defendant:** Where the defendant violates a safety statute, giving rise to *negligence per se,* we saw that contributory negligence will normally apply. But we also saw that if the statute is construed to protect members of the plaintiff's class against their own negligence, and to place all responsibility on the defendant, contributory negligence will not apply. In this latter situation, in a comparative negligence jurisdiction, may the defendant obtain apportionment?

1. **General view:** Most courts have held that this distinction between the various kinds of statutes is no longer necessary, in the absence of contributory negligence, and that therefore the defendant may obtain apportionment; see Comment to §1 of the Uniform Act.

M. **Seat belt defense:** The *"seat belt defense"* is increasingly *accepted* in comparative-negligence jurisdictions. In this defense, the defendant argues that the plaintiff's injuries from a car accident could have been reduced or entirely avoided had the plaintiff worn a seat belt; the plaintiff's damages should therefore be reduced, the defendant argues.

1. **Contributory negligence jurisdictions:** Before we examine how the seat belt defense has fared in comparative negligence jurisdictions, let us first briefly discuss how the defense has fared in traditional *contributory* negligence jurisdictions. There are three plausible alternatives:

    a. **Complete bar:** In theory, a court could hold that failure to wear a seat belt amounts to garden-variety contributory negligence, thereby entirely barring the plaintiff from recovering. However, virtually no cases have taken this approach. Since the accident would have occurred anyway, and the plaintiff would have sustained *some* damages even if he had been completely careful (by wearing a seat belt), it seems very unfair to give the defendant a complete windfall, so courts don't do it.

    b. **Apportionment:** Some courts have ***apportioned*** plaintiff's damages. These courts hold that failure to wear the belt does not bar recovery entirely, but that damages must be apportioned between those which would have occurred anyway and those which could have been avoided. The plaintiff is then permitted to recover only for damages which would have occurred anyway. A number of states, but probably only a minority of those that have considered the issue, have followed this approach. See, e.g., *Spier v. Barker*, 323 N.E.2d 164 (N.Y. 1974).

    c. **No apportionment:** In most contributory-negligence jurisdictions, courts have refused to allow the seat belt defense at all. That is, plaintiff's failure to wear a seat belt has not been counted against his recovery in any way.

2. **Comparative negligence jurisdictions:** In the more than 40 states that have now adopted comparative negligence, the seat belt defense has been more successful. In general, courts seem to feel that making a partial reduction of the plaintiff's damages for his "fault" in not wearing a seat belt comports with the overall scheme of reducing a plaintiff's damages by a percentage equal to his fault. In the comparative-negligence area, there are at least four ways of handling the seat belt defense:

    a. **Defense rejected:** Some states continue to reject the seat belt defense, just as they did in contributory-negligence times. However, fewer comparative-negligence jurisdictions seem to reject the defense than did so under contributory negligence.

    b. **Causal apportionment:** Some states hold that D can be liable for all of the injuries that would have occurred even had the plaintiff worn a seat belt, but ***not at all*** for injuries that would have been avoided. This is the "causal apportionment" approach.

    Example: D, while speeding, collides with a car driven by P. P is not wearing his seat belt. P suffers a fractured leg, which leads to $20,000 of total damages. P also suffers a brain injury when his head slams into the steering wheel; this results in $80,000 worth of damages. Evidence shows that if P had worn a seat belt, he still would have suffered the fractured leg, but would not have suffered the brain injury. The jury also finds that P was 30% at fault and D 70% at fault.

    Under the "causal apportionment" approach, P may recover the full $20,000 for the fractured leg (since P's "fault" did not worsen this injury in any way), but may not recover any of the brain injury damages. Thus P would recover $20,000.

    c. **Comparative fault without causal apportionment:** Alternatively, D can be held liable for all injuries, with a reduction equal to the percentage of P's fault. Under this approach, no attempt is made to distinguish between damages that would have been suffered anyway and those that would have been avoided had the belt been worn.

    Example: Under this "comparative fault without causal apportionment" approach, on the facts of the above example, P would recover $70,000 ($100,000 total damages, less 30% for P's comparative negligence). No attempt is made to distinguish between the fractured leg which would have happened anyway, and the brain injury which would have been avoided by wearing a belt.

d. Comparative fault after causal apportionment: Finally, D can be held liable for both injuries, but P's fault reduces his recovery for those injuries that would have been avoided.

Example: On the facts of our above example, P would recover the full $20,000 for the fractured leg, since his fault did not increase that injury at all. However, P would recover only $56,000 for the brain injury ($80,000 times 70%), since P's 30% negligence played a part in bringing that brain injury about.

i. View of Third Restatement: This approach — D is liable for both injuries, but P's fault reduces his recovery for the injury that would have been avoided by seat-belt use — seems to be the approach of the Third Restatement. See Rest. 3d (Apport.) §3, Illustr. 3, saying that P's failure to wear a seat belt is "relevant in determining whether [P] was negligent and, if so, in assigning percentages of responsibility for the portion of the plaintiff's injuries caused by the failure to wear the seat belt."

e. Effect of statute: Many states have *statutes* requiring drivers and passengers to wear seat belts, *supra*, p. 267. But these statutes generally don't help defendants who want to use the seat belt defense — just the contrary. Of the 32 mandatory-seat-belt use statutes in effect as of 1989, 16 explicitly prohibited the seat belt defense completely, and four made the defense almost valueless by setting a small limit on the reduction of damages permitted. See generally 102 Harv. L. Rev. 925, 929, n. 37.

N. Strict liability: For the effects of comparative negligence upon *strict liability*, see *infra*, pp. 406-412.

O. Imputed comparative negligence: Occasionally, the fault of one person (call her *A*) may by *imputed to another* (*B*), so as to reduce *B*'s recovery. This is the doctrine of *"imputed comparative negligence."* (In a contributory negligence situation, it's the doctrine of *"imputed contributory negligence."*)

1. "Both ways" rule: But under the so-called *"both ways" rule,* this imputation will happen *only* if *B* would be *vicariously liable* (see *infra*, p. 315) for *A*'s torts. As the Third Restatement puts it, "The negligence of another person is *imputed* to a plaintiff *whenever the negligence of the other person would have been imputed had the plaintiff been a defendant[.]*" Rest. 3d (Apport.), §5. The both ways rule has both a *"positive"* and a *"negative"* application. We'll explore the positive application in Par. 2 immediately below, and the negative application in Par. 3 on p. 289. Then, in Par. 4 on p. 290, we'll discuss an important context — involving *drivers and passengers* — in which most modern courts *no longer apply* the both ways rule.

2. "Positive" application: The *"positive"* application of the both ways rule means that a non-negligent party (call him *A*) who is vicariously liable for *B*'s behavior will be *unable to recover anything against C* for *C*'s tortious conduct, if *B* was contributorily negligent in a situation in which contributory negligence is a *complete bar* to recovery. Similarly, in a *comparative* negligence situation, *A*'s recovery against *C* will be reduced by *B*'s portion of fault.

a. **Employer/employee:** An important scenario in which this positive application of the both ways rule would likely apply is in suits brought by an *employer* for damages arising out of an accident involving the employer's *employee* and a *third party*. In such a scenario, assuming *contributory* negligence still applies, if the employer sues the third-party for negligence, but the employee was also negligent, the employer's recovery will be barred because the *employee's contributory negligence will be imputed to the employer*. Similarly, in a *comparative* negligence scenario, the employer's recovery against the third-party will be *diminished* by the employee's percentage of fault, because the employee's negligence will be *imputed to the employer*.

Example: Company hires Worker to drive a delivery truck for Company's business. (Assume that Company is not negligent in selecting or training Worker for this role.) Worker has a collision with a car driven by Dave, which damages Company's truck. Company sues Dave for the damage to the truck. If Worker was negligent in driving the truck, this negligence will be imputed to Company under the "both ways" rule.

That's because, if Company were the defendant in a suit by Dave, Company would have been vicariously liable for Worker's negligence under the *respondeat superior* doctrine. (See Rest. 3d (Apport.), §5, Illustr. 1, reaching this conclusion on exactly these facts.) Therefore, in a comparative-negligence jurisdiction, Company's recovery will be reduced by the percentage of fault attributable to Worker. And in a contributory negligence jurisdiction, Company will be completely barred from recovery against Dave on account of Worker's contributory negligence.

3. **"Negative" application:** Here's how the *"negative"* application of the both ways rule would work: Assume that, as in Par. 2 above, there is a non-negligent party (again called *A*) who has a relationship with *B*, but now the relationship is such that *A* is *not* vicariously liable for *B*'s behavior. Again, assume that *A*'s property or person is injured in part by the negligence of third party *C*, but that *B*'s negligence is also a significant factor in causing the injury. The negative aspect of the both ways rule means that because *A* is not vicariously liable for *B*'s behavior, then in a suit by *A* against *C*, *A*'s recovery will *not* be barred (in a contributory negligence state) or reduced (in a comparative negligence state) on account of *B*'s negligent behavior.

a. **Not attributed from parent to child:** The negative application of the both ways rule will often apply to a situation involving a *child plaintiff*. Assume that the child is injured, the child's parent has contributed to the accident (e.g., by failing to supervise the child) and some third party has also been negligent in a way that was a significant factor in the injury. The negative application of the both ways rule means that any fault attributable to the child's parents *won't be imputed to the child,* and therefore *won't reduce the child's recovery against the third person*.

Example 1: Kid, riding in a car driven by his father Dad, is injured when the car collides with a car driven negligently by Drive. Kid suffers $10,000 of injuries. Kid was not properly seat-belted. If he had been, he would have had only $5,000 of injuries. Assume that Dad's failure to fasten the seat belt violated a statute designed to prevent or minimize just this sort of injury. Assume also that Dad would not be immune from suit by Kid in the jurisdiction. Kid sues Drive.

Kid can recover all $10,000 of damage from Drive. The recovery won't be reduced by Dad's negligence *per se* in failing to fasten Kid's seat belt. That's because: (1) Dad's fault won't be attributed to Kid (since Kid wouldn't be liable for Dad's torts, so under the both ways rule Dad's fault won't be imputed to Kid); and (2) therefore Dad and Drive are each tortfeasors, and are jointly-and-severally liable. If Drive has to pay for more than his percentage of fault (computed by taking as the numerator Drive's fault and the denominator Drive's plus Dad's fault), Drive will be able to get contribution from Dad.

Example 2: Kid is injured in a playground accident, due in part to Guard's failure to supervise rough playing between Kid and Ted, another child. The accident is also due in part to a negligent failure of supervision by Dad, Kid's father, who is also present. Kid has suffered $10,000 in damages, and sues Guard for this sum.

Kid can collect the entire $10,000 from Guard, without reduction for any percentage of fault due to Dad. That's because: (1) Dad would not be vicariously liable for Kid's negligence if Kid were a defendant in an action brought by Ted (since parents are not vicariously liable for their children's torts; see *supra*, p. 107); (2) consequently, under the "both ways" rule, Dad's fault won't be attributed to Kid, and can't reduce Kid's recovery against either Guard or Dad; and (3) therefore, Dad and Guard are jointly and severally liable, and Guard can be required to pay the whole amount. (Guard could then seek contribution from Dad.)

4. **Driver-passenger scenario (rule not applied):**   There are a few scenarios in which most modern cases *do not apply the both ways rule,* either because of a statute that modifies the common law, or because a court decides to modify the jurisdiction's common (i.e., judge-made) law on account of public policy considerations. The most important of these scenarios in which courts and/or legislatures usually *decline to apply* the both ways rule is where the *owner of a vehicle would be vicariously liable for negligence by the driver,* but the *owner/plaintiff is a passenger who is injured*; most modern decisions say that the owner's ability to recover from the negligent third-party will *not be barred or reduced on account of the driver's negligence.*

   a. **Restatement approach:**   Thus the Third Restatement of Torts, although it generally applies the both ways rule, *does not apply the rule against the owner-passenger of a vehicle who is injured by a third party* — the driver's negligence will not be imputed to the plaintiff owner/passenger, even though state law makes the owner liable to third parties for the negligence of a driver who is driving with the owner's permission. See Rest. 3d of Torts (Apportionment), § 5, Comment c and Illustration 6.

   b. ***Seaborne-Worsely* case:**   A good recent illustration of the modern/Restatement approach of not applying the both ways rule to the plaintiff-owner/operator scenario is ***Seaborne-Worsely v. Mintiens***, 183 A.3d 141 (Md. 2018).

      i. **Facts:**   The case involved an accident in a restaurant parking lot. P was the owner-passenger in a car driven by her husband (H). H had driven the car to the restaurant; while P remained seated, H stopped in a travel lane opposite D's parking space while H went into the restaurant to pick up the couple's take-out order. D

(Mintiens) then backed his truck out of a parking space and struck P's car parked in the travel lane, injuring P.

ii. **The defense:** P sued D, and D defended on the grounds that (1) H was contributorily negligent for leaving the car in the travel lane, and (2) H's negligence should be imputed to P. (Maryland is one of the few states still applying contributory negligence, so if H's negligence were imputed to P, P's suit against D would be completely barred.) Under Maryland law — as in most states — a driver's negligence is imputed to the owner of the vehicle if the driver has the owner's permission to drive it.

iii. **Ruling:** The court (the highest in Maryland) decided that in this special owner-passenger scenario, for public policy reasons the state's general both ways rule ***should not be applied***. Here's how the court explained its decision:

[1] **Rationale for imputation:** In Maryland, as in other states, the traditional rule imputing the imputing the driver's negligence to the owner-passenger is a way of ensuring that if a third party was injured by the driver's negligence, that third-party could recover against ***the party most likely to be financially responsible:*** the vehicle's owner. The justification for this traditional rule is that where the owner is a passenger, and the driver negligently injures a third person, the *"**fiction** that the owner is able to **control the actions of the driver"** justifies allowing the third person to recover against the (presumably solvent) driver. But the rule is also applied to cases where the owner-passenger could not in fact have controlled the driver's actions.

[2] **Problem with both ways rule:** But now assume that (1) the jurisdiction applies the traditional approach of imputing driver X's negligence to owner-passenger O, but (2) this time it's the ***third-party driver*** (call her "D") whose negligence is a but for cause of O's injuries, which stem from an accident in which X is also negligent. If the jurisdiction were to apply the both ways rule, X's contributory or comparative negligence would bar or reduce O's ability to recover from D. Thus applying the both ways rule here would, as the *Seaborne-Worsley* court put it, "lead to results ***at odds with [the imputed negligence doctrine's] original purpose"*** (of supplying a solvent party, the owner-passenger, from whom the injured third party could recover).

[3] **Rationale for not applying both ways rule:** The court in *Seaborne-Worsley* therefore decided, as a matter of public policy, that the both ways rule ***should not apply*** to this ***owner-passenger-as-plaintiff scenario.*** Therefore, P was able to recover from D notwithstanding H's contributory negligence.

iv. **Where exception doesn't apply:** But the court in *Seaborne-Worsley* was careful to point out that its decision did ***not*** mean that an owner-passenger could *never* be contributorily negligent. The only thing that the decision did was simply to "dispens[e] with the ***presumption*** that an injured owner-passenger ***is contributorily negligent because the driver is negligent."*** There would be other ways in which an owner-passenger's ***own*** actions or omissions would be a proximate cause of an accident. For instance, owner-passenger O might have ***"wrest[ed] control of the*** *steering wheel* from the driver"; in that case, O's ability to recover from the third party who was also negligent would be blocked because O herself was contributorily negligent — there would no need to impute any contributory negligence by the driver to O.

III. ASSUMPTION OF RISK

A. Nature of the doctrine: A plaintiff is said to have *assumed the risk* of certain harm if she has voluntarily consented to take her chances that that harm will occur. Where such an assumption of risk is shown, the plaintiff is, under traditional common law principles, completely barred from recovery.

  1. Cutting back of doctrine: However, as will be discussed *infra*, p. 296, most courts which have adopted comparative negligence now hold that assumption of risk is no longer an absolute defense, but merely a consideration to be taken into account in making an apportionment of harm. Furthermore, some states now refuse to accept assumption of risk as a separate doctrine distinct from contributory negligence, and have in effect abolished it.

B. Classes of assumption of risk: There are several very distinct kinds of situations in which the plaintiff is said to have "assumed the risk" of harm. For purposes of our discussion here, these will be divided into two basic categories, *"express"* and *"implied"* assumption.

C. Express assumption: If P *explicitly* agrees with D, in advance of any harm, that P will not hold D liable for certain harm, P is said to have *"expressly"* assumed the risk of that harm. An express assumption of risk (also called a *"contractual limitation of liability"*) is generally *enforceable*, in which case it will completely bar P from recovery.

> Example: P wants to go bungee jumping at D's amusement park. P signs a release given to him by D in which P agrees to "assume all risk of injury" that may result from the bungee jumping. Assuming that none of the exceptions to express-assumption-of-risk (see below) applies, if P is injured he will not be able to sue D, because he has expressly assumed the risk.

  1. Exceptions: There are three important *exceptions* to the general enforceability of express agreements to assume risk:

❑ first, when the party protected by the clause (typically the defendant) either *intentionally causes* the harm, or else brings about the harm by acting in a *reckless or grossly negligent* way;

❑ second, when the *bargaining power* of the party protected by the clause is *grossly greater* than that of the other party, typically a status the court finds to exist only when the good or service being offered is *"essential"* (e.g., the services of public carriers or public utilities);

❑ finally, where the court concludes that there is some *overriding public interest* which demands that the court refuse to enforce the exculpatory clause. (Typically, this category overlaps with the above "unequal bargaining power because the good or service is essential" category.)

Cf. Seigneur v. National Fitness Institute, Inc., 752 A.2d 631 (Ct. Spec. App. Md. 2000).

a. **Private companies:** Where a good or service is offered by a relatively **unregulated private company,** and there are a **number of competitors** offering the plaintiff substantially the same good or service, the court will typically find that an exculpatory clause in the contract should be **enforced** to bar claims for negligence. That's because in this situation, generally none of the three exceptions discussed above will be found applicable.

> **Example:** P signs a contract with D (the operator of a chain of fitness clubs), in which P agrees that D "shall not be liable to me for any ... injuries ... to my person or property[.]" P is injured while working out, and sues. *Held,* for D: None of the above exceptions to the enforceability of express assumptions of risk applies, so P is deemed to have assumed the risk of injury. *Seigneur v. National Fitness Institute, Inc., supra.*

2. **Reduction of liability:** Even in the case of a utility or other regulated public service industry (i.e., in contrast to the "unregulated private company" scenario just discussed), if the defendant makes an honest attempt to **fix a reasonable value** for damages in advance (i.e., liquidated damages), and allows the plaintiff to pay a **graduated fee** based on the value fixed, this arrangement will be upheld. P&K, pp. 482-83.

   a. **Parking lots, baggage storage:** Where the defendant is a parking lot or garage, baggage storage concession, or other private business which because of its location is the only one available to the plaintiff, there is a tendency to apply the same rules. That is, a blanket waiver of liability is against public policy, but graduated fees based upon declared value in advance will be upheld. P&K, p. 483.

3. **Fine print:** The defendant must also show that the terms of the liability limitation were brought home to the plaintiff. This means that the plaintiff must have been actually **aware** of the limitation, or at least that a reasonable person in the plaintiff's position would have been. Thus if a limitation of liability is buried in fine print on the back of a railroad ticket, and the plaintiff reasonably fails to become aware of this clause, it will not be binding on her. P&K, pp. 483-84.

4. **Intentionally or willfully negligent misconduct:** Normally, a waiver of liability for the defendant's "negligence" will be construed so as not to include liability for **"willful and wanton"** or **"gross"** negligence, and certainly not for intentionally tortiously conduct. These may sometimes also be included in the waiver, but only if this is spelled out clearly, and is shown to have been understood by the plaintiff. Rest. 2d, §496B, Comment d.

5. **Health care:** In some contexts, courts simply refuse to allow the plaintiff to assume the risk even if her action is quite voluntary, she is well-informed about what she is doing, she is paying less because of this willingness, etc. The prime example is **medical care:** few courts would uphold even a carefully negotiated contract between doctor and patient in which patient agrees, "In consideration for your charging me a lower fee, and with full awareness of the consequences, I agree to waive any claim I might have against you for malpractice concerning the treatment you are about to give me." See Epstein, pp. 325-28;

see also *Obstetrics & Gynecologists v. Pepper*, 693 P.2d 1259 (Nev. 1985) (patient's agreement with clinic that patient will arbitrate any injury claims not enforceable).

6. **Effect of comparative negligence:** What effect should a state's decision to adopt *comparative negligence* have on this principle that express assumptions of risk will be enforced? Virtually all courts, and the new Restatement, agree that the answer is *"none."* See Rest. 3d (Apport.) §2, Comment b: "[A] valid contractual limitation on liability, within its terms, creates an absolute bar to a plaintiff's recovery from the other party to the contract. A valid contractual limitation on liability does not provide an occasion for the factfinder to assign a percentage of responsibility to any party or other person."

> **Example:** Before attending D's skydiving school, P reads and signs a waiver that states, "I understand that skydiving is highly dangerous, and agree not to seek to recover damages from D even in the event that D behaves negligently." On the plane, P receives a visibly torn parachute from D, but negligently fails to heed D's instructions, "Check your chute for any tears, and ask for a new one if you find any." The chute fails, P freefalls and dies, and his estate sues D. Under the Third Restatement (and in virtually all courts), the fact that the jurisdiction has enacted comparative negligence would *not* lead the court to allow the jury to allocate fault between P and D so that P might receive a partial recovery. Instead, the court will enforce the liability-waiver as written under the doctrine of express assumption of risk, and P as a matter of law will be completely precluded from recovering.

D. **Implied assumption of risk:** Even if the plaintiff never makes an actual agreement with the defendant whereby risk is assumed by the former, she may be held to have assumed certain risks *by her conduct*. In this situation, the assumption of risk is said to be *implied*.

1. **Requirements for implied assumption:** For the defendant to establish such implied assumption of risk, he must show that the plaintiff's actions demonstrate that she *knew of the risk in question* and *voluntarily consented to bear that risk herself*. This consent may be shown by the fact that the plaintiff has chosen to enter a certain place, to remain in a certain place, to work with certain machinery, etc.

> **Example:** D is dangerously setting off fireworks near a public street. P watches at close range, even though she is aware of the danger of doing so, and is injured by a stray rocket. P has assumed the risk of being injured, and cannot recover. See Rest. 2d, §496C, Illustr. 1.

   a. **Distinguished from contributory negligence:** The plaintiff's conduct in assuming risk may also, in many cases, constitute contributory negligence. The connection between these two defenses is discussed *infra*, p. 296.

2. **Knowledge of risk:** For implied assumption of risk to apply, the plaintiff must, as noted, have had *knowledge of the risk*. This requirement is usually quite *strictly construed*.

   a. **Subjective standard:** For instance, the risk must be one which was *actually* known to the plaintiff, not merely one which "ought to have" been known to her.

      i. **Particular risk:** Furthermore, P must have actually known of the *particular type of risk that eventuated*, not some other vaguely-similar risk. So, for instance, in the case of an argument by D that P voluntarily assumed the risk of an absent safety precaution, D must show that P actually knew that the precaution was missing, as well as knew of the specific risk that eventuated.

Example: P, a young woman, agrees to go for a pleasure drive with D, a 21-year-old man. D asks P whether she wants him to drive fast on a "roller coaster" road. She says yes. P does not realize that D is a very inexperienced driver, even as compared with other 21-year-old drivers. D drives at 89 mph, and loses control as the car goes over a bump, resulting in a crash into a side guardrail that a more experience driver would probably not have had even at high speed. The crash causes P to become a quadriplegic.

P's recovery will probably not be reduced at all by virtue of her consent. That is, P will not be found to have impliedly assumed the risk of such a crash. By her consent, P may have implicitly assumed certain risks, such as the risk of hitting her head against the roof of the car during a bump. But she did not know of, or consent to, the specific risk of D's being an inexperienced driver who might lose control under circumstances in which another driver would not. Cf. Rest. 2d, §496C, Illustr. 7.

  b. **Risk of unknown dangers:** Generally, as stated, the plaintiff must have understood the particular risk in question. But there are a few situations in which, by her conduct, she indicates her consent to *unknown risks*. Thus *automobile guests* have often been held to assume the risks of unknown defects in their host's car; see P&K, p. 489. (But many of these holdings have been or will be overruled by more general holdings that, particularly in comparative negligence jurisdictions, there is no separate defense of assumption of risk.)

3. **Voluntary assumption:** The requirement that the plaintiff have consented to the risk *voluntarily* is also strictly construed in implied-assumption scenarios.

  a. **Duress:** For instance, there is no assumption of risk if the defendant's conduct has left the plaintiff with *no reasonable choice* but to encounter a known danger.

  Example: P is D's tenant in a building with an outhouse. One day when she is using the privy, she falls through a hole or door in the floor, and has to be taken out with a ladder.

  Held, P did not assume the risk of the defect in the floor. She "had no choice, when impelled by calls of nature, but to use the facilities placed at her disposal by the landlord. . . . She was not required to leave the premises and go elsewhere." *Rush v. Commercial Realty Co.*, 145 A. 476 (N.J. 1929).

    i. **Existence of reasonable alternative:** But if, despite the defendant's conduct, the plaintiff is left with a *reasonable alternative* to submitting herself to the danger in question, and she voluntarily declines to follow this alternative, she may have assumed the risk. For instance, in the above example, if there had been another outhouse on the property, which, although slightly less convenient (e.g., further away), was feasible to use and safe, the plaintiff might have been held to have assumed the risk when she used the dangerous one (assuming that she knew of the danger).

ii. **Determining reasonableness of alternative:**   Whether the alternative is a reasonable one or not depends on such factors as the dangerousness of the course finally followed by the plaintiff, the degree of inconvenience in using the alternative, the importance of the interest being pursued by the plaintiff, etc. See Rest. 2d, §496E, Comment d. Thus a person whose house is burning down might be held to have assumed the risk if he dashes in to save his hat, but not if he dashes in to save his son; in either case, he has the alternative of not doing anything, but this is a reasonable alternative only in the former case. The weighing of factors in determining "reasonableness" is much the same as is done when the contributory negligence of the plaintiff is at issue.

iii. **Choice not created by defendant:**   Where it is not the ***defendant's fault*** that the plaintiff has really no choice except to expose herself to risk, this is not enough to vitiate the voluntary nature of the plaintiff's act, and the defense will apply.

Example: P is injured in an accident, bleeding badly, and needs immediate medical help. He has no other means of transportation, so he asks D to drive him to the hospital, knowing that D's car has bad brakes. P assumes the risk of injury due to an accident caused by the bad brakes. This is so because P's dilemma (risk of bleeding to death or risk of bad brakes) is not the result of D's wrongdoing. Rest. 2d, §496E, Illustr. 1.

b. **Public accommodation:** Where the accident takes place in a place of ***public accommodation*** (e.g., a ***store***), the court is unlikely to conclude that P impliedly assumed the risk of a negligently-caused accident — there are a limited number of stores or other places of accommodation, so even if P was aware of the risk, this choice is unlikely to have been truly voluntary.

Example: Store, a convenience store, has a parking lot where muggings have often occurred. Store places a sign on the lot saying, "Use this lot at your own risk. Muggings often occur in this lot." P reads the sign, but parks anyway, and is assaulted by X on the way to the inside of Store. P sues Store for negligence. If Store could easily have provided better security, it's very unlikely that P's recovery will be reduced by virtue of implied assumption of risk — P's consent to the risk of being assaulted wasn't truly voluntary, since P had limited places in which to shop.

4. **Statutory violation by defendant:**   Where the defendant's negligence consists of the violation of a statute *("negligence per se")*, most courts have allowed assumption of risk as a defense in those same situations where contributory negligence would be a defense. That is, it is allowed in all cases except those in which the statute is found to have been intended principally for the benefit of a class unable to protect itself (of which the plaintiff is a member), and the purpose of the statute would be defeated by allowing the defense. Rest. 2d, §496F.

5. **Effect of comparative negligence:**   In a state that has enacted comparative negligence, what should be the effect of that enactment on implied assumption of risk? Most courts, and the Third Restatement, say that implied assumption of risk is ***merged into*** — and thus ***replaced by*** — comparative negligence.

Example: P goes to a baseball game at a stadium owned by D (the team). He sits in a portion of the stands where there is no screen preventing foul balls from going into the seats, as there is in other parts of the stadium. P is hit by a foul ball, and sues D for negligence in not installing a screen. D asserts that P impliedly assumed the risk of getting hit by a foul ball. The jurisdiction applies comparative negligence.

A court would very likely hold that the doctrine of implied assumption of risk has been *merged* into comparative negligence, so that the significance of P's fault, if any, in choosing to sit in an unscreened seat will reduce his recovery, *not eliminate it.* See Rest. 3d (Apport.) §3, Illustr. 6, so indicating on these facts.

a. **D may be reasonable in relying:** However, keep in mind that D may so clearly and reasonably believe that P understands the risks (and that P is voluntarily choosing to expose herself to those risks) that this belief *prevents D from being negligent at all.* In that case, *neither assumption of risk nor comparative negligence matters.* As the Third Restatement puts it, "Whether the defendant reasonably believes that the plaintiff is aware of a risk and voluntarily undertakes it may be relevant to whether the defendant acted reasonably. The defendant might reasonably have relied on the plaintiff to avoid the known risk[.]" Rest. 3d (Apport.) §3, Comment c.

Example: On the facts of the above foul ball example, suppose that (a) D has made available many good seats that *are* screened from foul balls; (b) D has placed large signs in the unscreened portions of the stands urging patrons to watch out for foul balls; and (c) P turns down a perfectly good screened seat because he doesn't like having the mesh of the screen interfere with his view of the field. On these facts, a court would probably hold that D was *simply not negligent at all*, because it reasonably believed that a patron who sat in the unscreened seats was knowingly and voluntarily agreeing to assume the risk of being hit by a foul ball. Cf. Rest. 3d (Apport.) §3, Illustr. 6 ("If [D] could reasonably assume that [P] and other fans are aware that balls are occasionally hit into the stands, this fact is also relevant to whether [D] acted reasonably in relying on [P] to watch out for balls instead of constructing a screen or providing warnings.")

Note on "primary vs. "secondary" assumption of risk: In this type of situation — where D simply *never has any duty to P* to avoid the risk because D reasonably believes that P understands that risk and is voluntarily submitting to it — courts sometimes say that the case involves *"primary* assumption of risk," and that primary assumption of risk is a *complete barrier to recovery* even in a comparative negligence jurisdiction.

By contrast, if D *owes* a duty of care to P but P knowingly encounters a risk posed by D's breach of that duty, courts sometimes call this *"secondary* assumption of risk." These courts then say that secondary assumption of risk is *subsumed into ordinary comparative negligence principles.*

b. **P is reasonable in encountering the risk:** You should also keep in mind, conversely, that sometimes P's decision to *place herself in particular danger* is *reasonable*. In that event, P's conduct will simply not be negligent at all, and her recovery will *not be reduced* even in a comparative negligence jurisdiction.

Example: Landlord negligently allows Tenant's premises to become highly flammable, and a fire occurs. Tenant returns to the premises to find them ablaze, with his infant trapped inside. Tenant rushes in to retrieve the child, and is injured. (We shall assume that the state is one which imposes upon landlords a duty of ordinary care for the safety of tenants and others on the premises with permission; see *supra*, p. 254). Under traditional assumption of risk doctrine, Tenant would be barred from recovery, because he assumed the risk, even though he did so reasonably. But in most states that have enacted comparative negligence, Tenant's conduct would be viewed solely from the perspective of comparative fault, not assumption of risk. Since his conduct was reasonable, it is not negligence, and his recovery would not be reduced at all.

However, now assume that Tenant dashes in not to save his child, but to save his favorite hat. Tenant's conduct will be reviewed to see whether his conduct was negligent. Tenant's conduct is clearly negligent, since a reasonably prudent person would not risk serious injury in order to save a relatively unimportant object. Therefore, in most comparative-negligence states Tenant's recovery will be *reduced* (but, in a "pure" comparative negligence state, not completely eliminated) by the proportion of his culpability. See *Blackburn v. Dorta*, 348 So.2d 287 (Fla. 1977) (reciting this hypothetical situation, and reaching this conclusion).

   c.   **Danger from other participants:** Within the context of *sports* and recreation, special problems are posed when *one participant injures the other*. If the risk of this sort of inter-participant injury is found to be "inherent" in the sport or activity, then even in a comparative negligence jurisdiction the plaintiff will not be allowed to recover against the one who injured him, on the theory that the defendant owes no duty to the plaintiff to avoid that sort of risk.

Most courts now hold that in such co-participant sports, *ordinary carelessness* is *inherent* in the game (and thus covered by "primary" assumption of risk), so that an injured co-participant may recover only if the injury was *intentional* or so *reckless*ly inflicted as to be *totally outside the range of ordinary activity in the sport*. For a more extensive discussion, see *supra*, p. 63.

E.   **Burden of proof:**   Normally, the *burden of proof*, and the burden of *pleading*, as to assumption of risk are upon the *defendant*, as they are in the case of contributory negligence. Rest. 2d, §496, Comment g.

IV. STATUTE OF LIMITATIONS

A.   **Discovery of injury:** A frequent defense in tort actions, as in most other legal actions, is the *statute of limitations.* A general discussion of this defense is beyond the scope of this outline. However, there is one aspect of it that has troubled courts for a long time, and as to which the rules are rapidly changing: When the plaintiff does not *discover* his injury until long after the defendant's negligent act occurred, does the statute of limitations start to run at the time of the act, or at the time of the discovery?

   1.   **Medical malpractice:**   The question arises most frequently in *medical malpractice* cases. Suppose, for instance, a surgeon leaves a surgical sponge in his patient. If the rele-

vant statute of limitations is four years, and the patient does not discover the sponge until five years after the operation, is he barred by the statute?

a. **Former view:** Until the early 1970s or so, it was almost always held that the statute started to run as soon as the negligent act was committed, and if the plaintiff did not discover his injury until after the statute had run, that was his hard luck.

b. **Recent view:** But many courts have recently refused to continue this injustice. Several approaches to the problem have been used:

i. **Termination of treatment:** Some courts have held that the statute begins to run when the doctor-patient relationship terminates, even if the plaintiff has not discovered his injury. This gives him at least some extra time.

ii. **Only for objects left in body:** Other courts have applied a time-of-discovery rule, but only where the claim involves an object left in the patient's body, not where the case involves a mistaken diagnosis, or surgery that is negligently performed without leaving an object. P,W&S, p. 617, n. 8.

iii. **All surgical cases:** Many states now apply the time-of-discovery rule to all surgical cases, whether involving foreign objects or not. See, e.g., *Teeters v. Currey*, 518 S.W.2d 512 (Tenn. 1974), holding that the statute begins to run "when the patient discovered, or in the exercise of reasonable care and diligence for his own health and welfare, should have discovered, the resulting injury."

iv. **Discovery of legal claim:** Some courts have even held that the statute of limitations does not begin to run until the plaintiff has (or should have) discovered not only the injury but the fact that it may have been *caused by the defendant's negligence*. (Thus if P develops a disease, but does not immediately discover that it was probably due to improper treatment by his doctor, the claim does not start to run until the latter discovery, in these courts.) See P&K 1988 Pocket Part, p. 25.

v. **Statutory solutions:** A number of states have dealt with the limitations problem by statute. New York, for instance, has shortened the statute for medical malpractice from three years to two and one-half years, but provides that the statute does not begin to run until the date of last treatment (if the treatment is for the same illness as that which gave rise to the malpractice); also, where the claim involves a foreign object left in the body, the patient has *one year* to sue starting with the time the injury was or should have been discovered. As to all other malpractice, the statute runs from the time of injury. C.P.L.R. §214-a.

2. **Other professionals:** A similar issue arises frequently in the case of malpractice by other professionals, particularly lawyers, architects and engineers. The time-of-discovery rule has sometimes been applied in such cases. P,W&S, pp. 617-17, nn. 9, 10.

3. **Sexual assaults:** An especially controversial use of the "discovery" rule for tolling the statute of limitations has recently arisen in a quite different context: that of *sexual assaults*. Suppose that a father sexually abuses his daughter when she is five. Suppose that the relevant statute of limitations for a civil battery action is three years, and that under general limitations principles the time to sue is tolled until the plaintiff reaches 18. The plaintiff would be entitled to sue between the ages of 18 and 21, and would thereafter be

barred. But suppose that the plaintiff has *repressed* her memory of abuse until she undergoes, say, psychotherapy at the age of 30, at which time the memories rush to the surface and she relives the episode. Should some variant of the discovery rule be employed so that the plaintiff may sue, 25 years after the original event and nine years after the limitations period would otherwise have expired? An increasing number of courts have given at least a partial *"yes"* answer.

   a. **Repression plus corroboration:** A court is most likely to apply the discovery rule where both of the following conditions are satisfied: (1) the abuse occurred during the plaintiff's minority and the episode was completely repressed until it was discovered sometime within the statutory period (e.g., less than three years before suit, in a state that has a three year limitation period on battery actions); and (2) there is some independent *corroboration* that the assault actually occurred. See D&H, pp. 286-290.

V. IMMUNITIES

   A. **Definition of immunity:** An immunity is a defense to tort liability that is given to an entire *class* of persons based on their relationship with the prospective plaintiff, the nature of their occupation, their status as a governmental or charitable entity, etc. The common law created a number of virtually complete immunities, but all of these are beginning to break down at least to some extent, either by statutory reform or judicial overruling.

   B. **Intra-family immunity:** The common law recognized two immunities from suit growing out of the family relationship: that between *spouses*, and that between *parent and child.*

   1. **Husband and wife:** At common law, the husband and wife were considered as one person (and, as was often noted, that person was the husband). Therefore, it was considered illogical to allow the husband to bring a tort suit against his wife, or vice versa. Married Women's Acts, passed in the late nineteenth century, giving women property rights and legal identity, were held to allow at least suits between husband and wife regarding *property interests*.

      a. **Personal injury suits:** But the inter-spousal immunity continued with respect to suits for personal injury. This meant that a wife who was injured while a passenger in a car driven negligently by her husband could not sue him; nor could a battered wife recover for her abuse.

      b. **Most states now allow:** But over half the states have now completely *abolished* the inter-spousal immunity, even for personal injury suits. See P, W&S, p. 622, n.1. See also Rest. 2d, §895G.

      c. **Partial abolition:** In those states that have not completely abolished the immunity, a number of *limitations* on it are commonly applied.

         i. **Termination of marriage:** If the marriage has been *terminated* before the suit, the immunity will usually not apply. This is true not only where there has been a divorce, but also where one spouse has died. For instance, the estate of a deceased spouse might sue the surviving spouse in a wrongful death action. See Rest. 2d, §895G, Comment d.

ii. **Tort before marriage:**   Similarly, if the tort occurred *before* the parties were married, some courts do not apply the immunity. Rest. 2d, *ibid.*

iii. **Intentional personal injury:**   If the personal injury derives from an intentional tort (e.g., assault or battery), some courts do not allow the immunity.

iv. **Automobile suits:**   A number of states have abolished the immunity, as to *automobile accident* suits.

d. **Vicarious liability:**   Almost all states that have not abolished the immunity nonetheless permit a husband or wife to sue one who is *vicariously liable* for the other spouse's torts, even if the spouse himself could not be sued. Thus if a husband and wife work for the same employer, and the husband negligently injures the wife in a car crash while they are on a joint business trip, the wife could sue the employer under the doctrine of *respondeat superior* (see *infra*, p. 315), even though the inter-spousal immunity might bar her from suing her husband directly. See Nutshell, p. 353-55.

2. **Parent and child:**   In the United States (but not in England), a common law immunity also developed to bar suit by a *child against his parents* or vice versa. Except for the "oneness" of husband and wife, the same justifications for inter-spousal immunity were usually given to support the parent-child immunity.

a. **Partial abolition:** States have been much slower to abolish parent-child immunity than to abolish spousal immunity. But about a dozen states have completely abolished the immunity (in addition to another seven that never had it). P,W&S (12th), p. 656, n. 1 and 2.

b. **Abolition by some states:**   Beyond the 19 or so states that don't presently recognize parent-child immunity at all, another substantial group have *partially* abolished the immunity, by making it inapplicable to *automobile accident suits*. Cf. P,W&S (12th), p. 657, n. 3(E). In the auto-accident context, those favoring abolition stress that nearly everyone has liability insurance, so that in economic terms such suits usually are not really between members of the family, but between the family and the insurance company.

c. **Exceptions:**   As in the case of inter-spousal immunity, a number of states that have not completely abolished the doctrine have developed *exceptions* to it. Common exceptions include the following:

i. **Emancipation:**   If the child has been legally *emancipated* (i.e., of legal age or where other circumstances indicate that the parent has renounced his right to the child's earnings);

ii. *In loco parentis:*   Where the defendant is a *step-parent or guardian*;

iii. **Relationship terminated by death:**   Where the parent-child relationship has been terminated by the *death* of one or the other prior to the suit;

iv. **Wrongful death of other spouse:**   Where the plaintiff-child is suing his parent for the wrongful death of the other parent;

v. **Intentional or willful:**   Where the tort is *intentional*, or in some cases "willful";

vi. **Property rights or pecuniary loss:**   Where the action is for something other than personal injury (i.e., property loss, pecuniary loss);

vii. **Business activity:**   Where the injury occurred during the course of *business activity* by the defendant;

See generally, P,W&S, p. 630; Rest. 2d, §895H, Comments d-i.

d. **Duty of supervision:**   A big problem with completely abolishing the parent-child immunity is that courts will then have to decide whether to allow children to sue their parents for *negligent supervision* that results in injury to the child. If the jurisdiction decides to allow such suits, there is a risk that courts will find themselves *interfering with traditional parental decision-making*.

   i. **No suit allowed:**   Therefore, the vast majority of courts, even ones that have partially or completely abrogated the parent-child immunity, do *not* allow a child to sue her parent for negligent failure to supervise. See, e.g., *Zellmer v. Zellmer,* 188 P.3d 497 (Wash. 2008) ("The overwhelming majority of jurisdictions hold parents are not liable for negligent supervision of their child[.]")

      (1) **Three theories:** Often the no-liability-for-negligent-supervision rule is carried out by keeping the parent-child immunity in place for negligent-supervision suits. But there are two *alternative* ways that courts often implement a rule against a child's recovery for negligent supervision:

         ❑ First, some jurisdictions give the parent a special *privilege* to exercise judgment about how closely to supervise her child. See, e.g., Rest. 2d §895g, taking this approach.

         ❑ Second, the court can hold that a parent has *no affirmative duty* to supervise her child. Such an approach brings the child's failure-to-supervise suit within the general rule, discussed *supra,* p. 198, that a person will ordinarily not be liable for a failure to act.

      These three methods — based on immunity, privilege and no-duty — all produce the same practical result: a child who is injured cannot recover against the parent (or the parent's insurance company) by arguing, "You negligently failed to supervise me, and if you had properly supervised me, I wouldn't have been injured."

3. **Siblings:**   There is no immunity between *siblings.* See Rest. 2d, §895I. Nor is there any other family relationship (e.g. *grandparent*-grandchild) as to which there is immunity.

C. **Charitable immunity:**   *Charitable organizations*, as well as educational and religious ones, received immunity at common law.

   1. **Rationale:**   Two principal reasons have been given for this:

      a. **Trust fund:**   First, the charity holds the donations it receives in trust, and the donor has not given these funds with the intention that they be used to pay tort claims.

b. Implied waiver: Second, the beneficiary of charity (e.g. one who uses a charitable hospital) has "impliedly waived" his right to sue in tort, by virtue of having accepted this benevolence.

2. **Overruling:** By now, more than thirty states have abolished charitable immunity. See Rest. 2d, §895F.

3. **Limitations:** Those states which have not abolished the immunity completely have carved out a number of limitations upon it:

    a. Abolished as to the hospitals: Some have abolished it as to charitable hospitals, but have kept it concerning religious or educational institutions.

    b. Beneficiaries: Others have maintained the immunity where the plaintiff is a beneficiary of the charity (e.g. a patient at the charitable hospital), but not where she is an employee, stranger, or other non-beneficiary. The theory behind this is presumably that the "implied waiver" doctrine applies only to beneficiaries.

    c. Liability insurance: Still other courts deny liability where a judgment would have to be satisfied out of trust funds, but not where there is liability insurance. This result is reached by recognizing the validity of the trust fund argument, but cutting it back to those cases where it applies directly to the facts. See generally, Rest. 2d, §895F.

D. Governmental immunity: At English common law, "sovereign immunity", i.e., immunity of the king, developed. The doctrine, which was connected to the divine right of kings, was sometimes expressed by saying that "the king can do no wrong."

1. **United States:** Early American courts applied the English rule to hold that the *United States* could not be sued without its consent. The first major and meaningful consent by the United States to tort claims was embodied in the 1946 Federal Tort Claims Act (FTCA). Because this Act continues today to be dispositive of almost all possible tort claims against the government, its provisions are worth looking at in some detail.

    a. General provision: The FTCA provides generally that money damages may be recovered against the United States " . . . for injury or loss of property or personal injury or death caused by the negligent or wrongful act or omission of any employee of the Government while acting within the scope of his office or employment", if the claim is such that the U.S. could be sued if it were a private person. This means that in any situation in which the doctrine of *respondeat superior* (see *infra,* p. 315) would apply if the tortfeasor were a private employee, the U.S. may be sued by use of that same doctrine. 28 U.S.C.A. §1346(b).

    b. Exceptions: However, several exceptions substantially limit the scope of federal tort liability. The most important of these are as follows:

    c. Intentional torts: The U.S. is *not* liable for "any claim arising out of assault, battery, false imprisonment, false arrest, malicious prosecution, abuse of process, libel, slander, misrepresentation, deceit, or interference with contract rights." However, this clause was recently amended to provide that assault, battery, false imprisonment, false arrest, abuse of process, or malicious prosecution, where committed by *"investigative or law enforcement officers"* of the federal government, may be sued upon. Thus a police brutality claim might be brought against the government for a battery committed by an F.B.I. agent, for instance.

d. Execution of statute or regulation: Another exception to the U.S.'s liability is where a government official, using due care, carries out a *statute or regulation* which later turns out to be invalid. 28 U.S.C.A. §2680(a).

e. Discretionary function: But the most important exclusion, which sometimes seems to swallow the whole Act, is that no liability may be "based upon the exercise or performance or the failure to exercise or perform a *discretionary function* or duty on the part of a Federal agency or an employee of the Government, *whether or not the discretion involved be abused*." 28 U.S.C.A. §2680(a). This section was designed to insure that the Government was not prevented from exercising its leadership and planning functions by the institution of tort suits attacking the manner in which this was done.

i. Discretionary v. operational functions: "Discretionary" functions are generally contrasted with "operational" ones. What occurs at the planning stage is usually discretionary, whereas the *carrying out* of the plans is usually held to be operational, and thus not within the exclusion for discretionary functions. Nonetheless, the distinction can be very hard to draw in a particular case.

ii. *Berkovitz:* In a Supreme Court case, *Berkovitz v. U.S.*, 486 U.S. 531 (1988), the Court spoke about this distinction between discretionary and operational functions. The case illustrates that much of the work done by federal health or safety agencies will be deemed to be "operational." Only those governmental actions and decisions that are *"based on considerations of public policy"* will be deemed *"discretionary."* More specifically, a federal agency's decision to set up a certain kind of testing or inspection program may be "discretionary," but once such a program is enacted, the agency's failure to *follow that program* will be deemed "operational," not discretionary, and the government can be liable for that failure.

Example: P takes a dose of oral polio vaccine, and contracts severe polio. P's parents sue the U.S., asserting that the U.S. wrongfully approved the release of the particular privately-manufactured lot that injured P. They assert that the FDA had made a policy decision to test each batch of vaccine, but that the batch here was released without having been tested.

Held, for P. The "discretionary function" exemption applies only to activities involving the "permissible exercise of policy judgment." The FDA's decision about what sort of testing program to use would be protected as a "discretionary" function. But once the FDA decided to test each batch, the subsequent decision of an official to release a particular batch without testing did not involve discretion, and can give rise to liability. *Berkovitz, supra.*

2. State governments: *State governments* have traditionally had a similar sovereign immunity. This immunity too, however, has been largely removed.

a. Generally waived at least in part: Nearly all states have now *waived* their comonlaw sovereign immunity, both for the state itself and for state *agencies* (e.g., hospitals, prisons, etc.). Dobbs, § 268, p. 716. States have typically replaced the common-law immunity with special tort-claims *statutes* that give *partial* immunities.

   i.   **Still immunity for discretionary decisions:** Many states have statutes that are similar to the Federal Tort Claims Act (*supra*, p. 303), in that the state waives immunity for its negligence in carrying out its day-to-day functions, but maintains immunity for *discretionary* decisions, i.e., decisions that are about *public policy.* Dobbs, § 268, p. 717.

   ii. **Caps on liability:** States have also often placed *dollar caps* on their tort liability as part of their tort-claim statutes. Thus Florida caps its liability at $100,000 per claimant (see Fl. Stat. Ann. § 768.28(5)) and Pennsylvania has a $250,000 per person cap (Pa. Consol. Stat. § 8528). See Dobbs, § 268, p. 718.

   iii. **Notice of claim:** States also usually impose special *procedural requirements* on people who sue a state entity in tort. For instance, states usually require the plaintiff to give a *written notice of claim* before filing suit, and the time limits for giving such a notice are often shorter than the general-purpose statute of limitation.

   b.   **Courts, legislatures and policy-makers:** Where the immunity has been judicially or statutorily abolished, there will nonetheless almost never be liability for acts of the *courts* of the state, or its *legislature*. Nor will there be liability for administrative actions which involve a "basic *policy decision*". See Rest. 2d, §895B(3).

3. **Local government immunity:** Units of *local government* have generally had at least partial immunity. Thus a city, school district, local public hospital, etc., when it conducts activities of a governmental nature, has been immune. But where such local units (often called "municipal corporations") perform functions that could just as well be performed by private corporations, there has traditionally *not* been immunity. The distinction is between *"governmental"* and *"proprietary"* functions.

   Example: Operation of a hospital is likely to be considered a "proprietary" function. Therefore, a city that operates a hospital typically won't have sovereign immunity from suits alleging that the hospital behaved negligently.

   a.   **Governmental functions:** Police and fire departments, school systems, health inspectors, and the like, are usually held to be involved in governmental functions. Thus even if a police officer beats up the plaintiff without any excuse, suit cannot be brought against the department or city (assuming that there has been no abolition of local government immunity, as discussed below).

   b.   **Revenue-producing activities:** But activities which produce *revenue* for the government, such as gas or water utilities, airports, garages, etc. are generally held to be proprietary. See P&K, pp. 1053-54.

   c.   **General abolition:** Partly because of the difficulty of distinguishing between "governmental" and "proprietary functions," many courts have abolished the general local government immunity, and at least fifteen others allow suit where liability insurance has been purchased. But legislative and judicial functions continue to be immune, as are administrative policy decisions. Rest. 2d, §895C(2).

d. **Extent of duty:** Assuming a municipality no longer has immunity, what duties does it owe its citizens? In general, the answer has been that the duties are *narrower* than they would be if the defendant were a private corporation. This is due partly because of courts' desire not to second-guess the discretionary and policy decisions made by administrative officials.

Example: P, a young woman, is repeatedly threatened by a suitor, X (a lawyer!), that if she will not marry him, he will fix it so "no one else will want you". P repeatedly asks the police of D (New York City) for protection, which they refuse. X then hires a thug to throw lye in P's face, partially blinding her.

Held, D has no duty to provide police protection to any particular member of the public. If such duty were recognized, and enforced by the courts, this would "inevitably determine how the limited police resources of the community should be allocated and without predictable limits."

A dissent argued that the police's denial of protection to P was not a "conscious choice of policy" but simply "garden variety negligence", which should be actionable. "No one is contending that the police must be at the scene of every potential crime or must provide a personal bodyguard to every person who walks into a police station and claims to have been threatened. They need only act as a reasonable man would under the circumstances," said the dissent. *Riss v. City of New York*, 240 N.E.2d 860 (N.Y. 1968).

   i. **Broadening liability:** But even this "de facto" immunity, stemming from courts' desire not to second-guess administrative officials, seems to be *disappearing* year by year. For instance, a New York court held a county liable for negligence in operating its 911 emergency number service, in *DeLong v. Erie County*, 455 N.Y.S.2d 887 (N.Y.Sup.Ct. 1982), discussed more extensively *supra*, p. 203.

4. **Government officials:** In addition to the immunity sometimes conferred upon governments, *public officials* in their private capacity may also have tort immunity. Such immunity is of common-law origin, and may also exist even where sovereign immunity has been abolished as to the tort in question.

   a. **Rationale for immunity:** The principal rationale for granting at least partial immunity to public officials is that, otherwise, the fear of "vexatious suits" (most of them without merit) will prevent officials from making the necessary decisions and carrying out the duties of government. See Rest. 2d, §895D, Comment b.

   b. **Legislators and judges:** *Legislators* and *judges* receive *complete immunity*, as long as their act is within the broad general scope of their duties. This is so even if such an official is clearly motivated by malice, greed, corruption, etc. The only exception to the rule is that there is no immunity where the act is "wholly beyond the jurisdiction" of the official. But this is true of few acts.

   c. **Administrative officials:** High administrative officials, in many states, receive a similar complete immunity for torts committed within the general scope of their duties. In the other states, however, even such high officials have only a limited immunity, which will not protect them if it is shown that they acted in *bad faith*. P, W&S, p. 656.

d. **Lower officials:** Low-ranking officials, on the other hand, generally receive no immunity at all where the act in question is "operational", as opposed to "discretionary". If the act is discretionary, they usually receive the same treatment as higher officials, whatever that treatment is in the jurisdiction in question. The distinction between operational and discretionary acts is generally done on the same basis as it is with respect to local government immunity (see *supra*, p. 305).

e. **Statutory treatment:** Several Federal statutes directly affect public officials' immunity in certain kinds of actions.

i. **Civil Rights:** The Civil Rights Act of 1871 (42 U.S.C.A. §1983), provides that any person who, "under color of any statute, ordinance, regulation . . . of any state" violates the Federal civil rights of any person, "shall be liable to the party injured in an action at law. . . . " This statute applies to state and local officials, and a similar judge-made rule probably applies to Federal officials. See Rest. 2d, §895D, Comment i.

ii. **Federal Tort Claims Act:** Conversely, the Federal Tort Claims Act provides that in the case of any injury arising out of a Federal employee's operation of a ***motor vehicle***, the ***only*** liability is against the government, and the employee is immune, 28 U.S.C.A. §2679(b).

5. **Government contractors:** Government contractors (independent contractors who perform services for or provide supplies to the government) are not directly protected by the immunity of government officials. In certain situations, however, they are entitled to defenses which in effect draw on the immunity granted to governments. For example, if a military contractor supplies defectively-designed goods to the government, which injure a soldier, the contractor will probably be able to avoid liability if he can show that the design was approved by the government and the product was manufactured according to that design. See *Boyle v. United Technologies Corp.*, discussed *infra*, p. 380.

Quiz Yourself on

DEFENSES IN NEGLIGENCE ACTIONS *(Entire Chapter)*

56. The Hit & Run Railroad Company has tracks running adjacent to Old MacDonald's Farm. It negligently fails to erect fences on either side of the tracks; as a result, Old MacDonald is worried that if he lets his cows graze in the fields surrounding the tracks, they'll wander onto the tracks. But he lets them graze there anyway (he has nowhere else for them to graze), and one of them wanders onto the tracks and is struck by an oncoming train. Old Mac sues Hit & Run; Hit & Run asserts assumption of the risk as a defense. Who wins? _____

57. Al Bundy drives his car to the Mr. Walletwrench Service Station to get the oil changed. He drives the car into the garage, fumbles around in the back seat to get a newspaper, and opens the door to get out. He does not realize that the car has been hoisted ten feet into the air to facilitate the oil change; he steps into mid-air, falls to the ground, and is injured. He sues the station for negligence in hoisting the car with him in it. Mr. Walletwrench defends on contributory negligence grounds. (The jurisdiction applies this doctrine.) Who wins? _____

58. Diamond Jim Potluck visits the N-Palatable Diner. As he walks to the counter, he studies the menu board on the wall, looking for the meatloaf of the day. He does not notice that the cellar door, which opens out of the floor, is open. He falls in, injuring himself. Assuming the Diner was more negligent in leaving the cellar door open than Diamond Jim was in failing to notice it, in a contributory negligence jurisdiction will the Diner be liable for Jim's injuries? _____

59. Paul Revere and William Dawes are each on a casual midnight horseback ride. They run into each other; each is thrown from his respective horse and each is injured. Each sues the other for negligence. Revere suffers $20,000 in damages and is found to be 25% at fault for the accident. Dawes, who was riding faster, is found to be 75% at fault and suffers $30,000 in damages. Who owes what to whom, under a comparative negligence statute holding that a plaintiff who is more negligent than the defendant cannot recover?

_____

60. Perry, an avid hiker, negligently wears very thin-soled shoes, which are inadequate protection for the sharp stones on the mountain trail that he plans to navigate. About halfway up the trail, Perry badly gashes his foot, and passes out in the middle of the trail from lack of blood. Donna, riding a trail bike, arrives at the same point in the trail, sees Perry, negligently believes that she (Donna) has enough room on the trail to get by Perry without hitting him, and because of her miscalculation runs over Perry's foot, crushing it. Perry sues Donna for the crushed foot. Donna raises the defense that Perry's contributory negligence was the proximate cause of Perry's injury, since if Perry had worn proper shoes, he would never have gashed his foot, would therefore not have been lying in the middle of the trail unconscious, and could not have been run over by Donna. The jurisdiction follows the common-law approach to contributory negligence.

(a) What doctrine should Perry assert to rebut Donna's defense? _____

(b) May Perry recover? _____

61. Jay Walker, a pedestrian who is in a hurry, crosses a busy street from between two parked cars in the middle of the street, rather than at a crosswalk. Although this is an act of negligence, it is widely (and properly) perceived as only slightly negligent on this particular street, since crosswalks are few and far between and drivers generally know to be on the lookout for pedestrians doing this. Hard Driver, a hard-driving executive, is driving down the street at 70 m.p.h. in a 40 m.p.h. zone. She never even sees Jay, just slams into him. Jay never even knows that he is in danger, because Hard's car simply comes on too suddenly. Jay is killed in the collision. His estate sues Hard. There are no applicable statutes, and all relevant common-law doctrines are in force. May Jay's estate recover? _____

62. The courts of New York have held that, as a common law matter, any operator of a baseball stadium must furnish each patron with a screened seat so that that patron will not be hit by batted balls. Fan, who is knowledgeable about baseball and the risks associated with it, attends a New York Yokels baseball game at Yokels Stadium. A particular seat sold to Fan by the Yokels is an unscreened seat, and Fan is aware of this fact. The ticket says nothing about the risk of foul balls. Fan sits in the seat, and is hit in the face by a foul ball. The jurisdiction still applies common-law contributory negligence. May Fan recover in a negligence suit against the Yokels? _____

Answers

56. Old MacDonald. Assumption of the risk requires that plaintiff voluntarily and knowingly undertake a risk. In this instance, Old Mac did know the danger, and subjected his cows to it; however, the element missing is the voluntariness. Old Mac has a right to a moo-moo here and a moo-moo there, here a moo, there a moo, everywhere a moo-moo on his own farm, and Hit & Run can't deny him this right.

57. Mr. Walletwrench. Contributory negligence bars recovery where plaintiff doesn't behave reasonably to protect himself from injury, and he is injured as a result. Here, reasonable behavior would include "looking before you leap," so to speak. Since Bundy didn't do so, and this was a substantial factor in his injury, Mr. Walletwrench won't be liable.

58. No. Under contributory negligence, any negligence on plaintiff's part bars recovery, regardless of how insignificant it is compared to defendant's negligence.

59. Dawes owes Revere $15,000. Revere is only entitled to the portion of his damages caused by Dawes. Since he was 25% responsible, he is entitled to 75% of his damages: .75 x 20,000 = $15,000. Dawes gets no offset by virtue of his own claim: under this "modified" comparative negligence statute (P can't recover anything if he's more negligent than D), Dawes-as-plaintiff is more negligent than Revere-as-defendant, and so collects nothing on his claim. Therefore, Dawes must write Revere a check for $15,000.

COMPARE: Suppose the state had had a "pure" comparative negligence statute (i.e., one in which P can recover from D even if his fault is much greater than D's). In that event, Dawes would be entitled to 25% of $30,000 (or $7,500), which would be subtracted from Revere's $15,000, leaving Revere a net recovery of $7,500.

60. (a) Last clear chance. By the doctrine of *"last clear chance,"* if the plaintiff is helpless to avoid his peril, and the defendant discovers that peril and negligently fails to avoid it, the defendant's subsequent negligence (her squandering of her last clear chance to avoid the accident) wipes out the effect of the plaintiff's contributory negligence.

(b) Yes. Perry was helpless to avoid the peril (since he was unconscious), and Donna knew of the peril and negligently failed to avoid it. So the last clear chance doctrine applies, and wipes out the effect of Perry's negligence.

61. No. This is a classic situation in which Jay's contributory negligence would completely bar him from recovery, even though his degree of fault is much less than that of Hard. Also, last clear chance does not apply, because virtually no courts apply the doctrine in this "inattentive plaintiff, inattentive defendant" situation.

62. No. The defendants would be successful in asserting that Fan *assumed the risk*, and was thus barred from recovery. A plaintiff will be barred by the doctrine of implied assumption of risk if he understands a risk of harm to himself, and nonetheless voluntarily chooses to accept that risk, assuming that no strong public policy forbids application of the doctrine. Here, Fan understood the risk of foul balls, and voluntarily chose to expose himself to that danger (rather than either requesting a different seat, or simply declining to attend the game). Also, probably no strong public policy prevents the application of the implied assumption of risk doctrine to foul ball dangers. Therefore, Fan would be barred from recovery. See Rest. 2d, §496C, Illustr. 4.

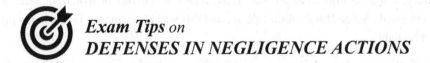

Exam Tips on
DEFENSES IN NEGLIGENCE ACTIONS

Whenever you identify a negligence issue, be sure to look for two very common defenses: (1) contributory/comparative negligence; and (2) assumption of risk.

☛ Always be on the lookout for application of the doctrine of *contributory negligence* (CN).

    ☞ Remember the core principle of common law CN: it's an *absolute defense*, and wipes out P's claim even if D's negligence is much greater than P's.

    ☞ Unless the fact pattern tells you that comparative negligence is used, assume that you must identify and discuss situations where CN would apply. Therefore, examine the behavior of everyone you've identified as a potential plaintiff, and ask, "Did he/she behave with reasonable care?"

        ☞ Usually, CN will consist of P's failing to notice, or disregarding, danger to *himself* (not P's imposition of an unreasonable risk to others). There are two types: (1) P should have noticed the danger, and didn't; and (2) P noticed the danger, and unreasonably decided to encounter it anyway.

            ☞ Type (2) above will also constitute "assumption of risk." (The same conduct can be both CN and assumption of risk, and you should say it's both.) Where P notices the danger and disregards it, remember that this isn't *necessarily* CN — perhaps P's need was so great that P was *reasonable* in subjecting himself to the risk. (*Example:* P needs to get to the hospital, and takes a ride from a somewhat drunk driver — P's conduct may have been dangerous but reasonable, in which case it's not CN.)

            ☞ Look out for situations where P *couldn't have known* of the danger — it's not CN to fail to protect oneself against unknown danger, and the fact that P "could have protected herself if she had known of the danger" is irrelevant.

            ☞ Sometimes the facts will tell you that a certain danger is "in plain view." That's a tip-off for the probable existence of CN.

    ☞ If the facts don't tell you whether the jurisdiction has CN or comparative negligence, discuss *each*. (*Example:* "If the jurisdiction has common law contributory negligence, then P will get no recovery because. . . . If the jurisdiction has comparative negligence, then P's claim will be reduced by the proportion of his fault. . . .")

    ☞ Many fact patterns involve *children*. Remember that the standard is, "What's the reasonable level of care for a child of that age and experience?" Even a child under 10 can be contributorily negligent if he's less careful than an "ordinary" child of that age.

    ☞ Don't forget that CN is only a defense if P's negligence was a *cause* (both cause in fact and proximate cause) of P's injuries. (*Example:* P doesn't wear his seat belt, and crashes due to D's negligence. If P would have died anyway even with a seat belt on, the failure to wear the belt wasn't a cause in fact of P's injuries, and CN will not apply.)

☞ Frequently-tested: Can CN be a defense where D's liability is based upon a ***statutory*** violation (negligence per se)? Answer: yes — negligence per se is just a special form of negligence by D, so P's CN will be a defense just as in any other negligence case.

☞ In any case where you think CN may apply, consider whether the doctrine of *"**Last Clear Chance**"* (LCC) may undo the effect of CN.

  ☞ Remember that under LCC, if P has negligently put himself in a position of risk, and D then sees (or should see) P's peril in time to avoid the problem, D is said to have had a "Last Clear Chance" to avoid the peril, and that LCC wipes out P's CN.

☛ Always be on the lookout for opportunities to discuss ***comparative*** negligence.

☞ Since about 90% of the states have replaced contributory negligence with comparative, you should talk about comparative whenever the facts indicate that P may have been negligent. Assuming the facts don't say whether the jurisdiction has contributory or comparative, you should talk about **both** scenarios, one after the other.

☞ Don't forget that comparative negligence can only apply where the main claim is based on ***negligence***. Thus there is no comparative neg. where P's claim is based on fraud (intentional misrepresentation), strict product liability, breach of warranty, etc.

☞ If the facts don't say what type of comparative statute the jurisdiction has, you should probably mention that the statute could be either *"pure"* or *"modified,"* and say how this would affect the outcome. Remember that this distinction only makes a difference where P's negligence is ***at least half*** the total negligence. Thus if P is found 60% responsible for the accident and D 40%, in a "pure" jurisdiction P collects 40% of her total damages, whereas in a "modified" or "50%" jurisdiction, P gets nothing.

  ☞ If the fact pattern gives you the actual statutory language, you should be able to tell whether the statute is a pure or modified one. You should recognize a "pure" statute by the fact that it doesn't say anything about P's negligence being "as great as" or "greater than" D's. A modified or 50% statute will have to deal specifically with this "as great as" or "greater than" case.

☞ Wherever P has failed to use some ***available safety device*** (e.g., seat belt or helmet), raise the issue of what effect the existence of a comparative negligence statute might have. Courts vary so much on this issue that it's hard to say what the effect might be — the most likely effect is that P's failure to use the device will be just one type of "fault," and that failure will be thrown into the hopper with everything else in computing P's "percentage of fault," which will then be applied to all the injuries.

☞ If you're covering the comparative scenario, you need to look out for possible applications of ***Last Clear Chance***. You should say that courts are split about whether the doctrine applies in a comparative negligence situation. Probably a majority would say that the doctrine no longer applies, so that P's recovery is reduced by her fault even if D had a Last Clear Chance to avoid the accident.

☞ You also need to worry about the interaction between comparative negligence and ***multiple defendants***. There are two main things to worry about:

☞ First, once P's recovery has been reduced by his amount of fault, does P still have the right to recover all the "reduced" award from any ***single*** defendant? That is, does joint-and-several liability persist under comparative negligence?

❏ If all Ds are before the court and are solvent, the answer is clearly "yes."

❏ But if one or more Ds were absent or judgment-proof, courts are split on the effect of comparative negligence.

> *Example:* Assume P 25% at fault, D1 25% and D2 50%; total damages equal $100,000. Assume D2 is judgment-proof. Some courts would allow P to collect the full $75,000 from D1 — so common law joint-and-several liability persists, and D1 suffers the full brunt of D2's unavailability. Other courts say that P and D1 split the burden of D2's unavailability *pro rata*, so that P would collect $50,000 from D1 (i.e., P and D1 would each "suffer" a $25,000 loss from D2's unavailability). Still other courts make the allocation depend on whether P's losses are economic or non-economic, or on some other factor.

> Probably you should just indicate that not all courts honor joint-and-several liability under comparative negligence, if one or more defendants are absent or judgment-proof.

☞ The second issue is each D's right of ***contribution*** against other Ds under comparative neg. Here, it depends on whether the state has passed a special statute. If no special statute has been passed, then the existence of comparative doesn't change each D's common-law right to "equal" contribution from the fellow tortfeasors. But many comparative negligence states have passed statutes applying comparative fault to contribution. (*Example:* Assume $100,000 in total injuries, no fault by P, D1 is found to be 40% at fault and D2 60% at fault. Assume P collects the entire $100,000 from D1. If the state has by statute applied comparative fault to contribution, D1 will be allowed to collect $60,000 contribution, not $50,000, from D2.)

☛ Be prepared to discuss briefly the doctrine of ***"imputed comparative (or contributory) negligence."*** Remember that under the ***"both ways rule,"*** if and only if *B* would would be liable for *A*'s torts, then if *B*'s property or person is injured by *C*, *A*'s contributory or comparative negligence will be imputed to *B*, nullifying or reducing *B*'s ability to recover from *C*.

☛ *Example: B* employs *A* as a truck driver. *C* negligently collides with the truck, while it's driven by *A* on business, but *A* is also negligent. *B* sues *C* for damage to the truck. In a comparative negligence jurisdiction, since *B* is liable for *A*'s negligence under *respondeat superior*, *A*'s negligence will be imputed to *B*. Therefore, *B*'s recovery against *C* will be reduced by *A*'s comparative negligence.

☞ But there are two important scenarios where the both ways rule ***won't be applied*** so as to impute a person's comparative/contributory negligence to a plaintiff even though the plaintiff would be vicariously liable for that person's negligence.

> *Scenario 1:* Parent fails to supervise Child; Child gets hurt due to the negligence of D (but the accident wouldn't have happened if Parent had supervised reasonably). Under the older view: Parent's contributory or comparative negligence is "imputed" to Child, barring (or in a comparative negligence state reducing) Child's recovery. But the pre-

vailing view today is that there's *no* imputed comparative negligence here — so Child can recover in full from D, and it's up to D to get contribution from Parent.

Scenario 2: P is an owner/passenger in a car driven (with P's permission) by Drive. Truck negligently drives his truck into the car, but Drive is also comparatively negligent. The both ways rule won't be applied to P's suit against Truck; therefore, P can recover fully for her injuries from Truck even if under local law Drive's negligence would have been imputed to P on the theory that P could have prevented Drive's negligence.

☛ *"Assumption of risk" (AOR)* is one of those important issues that's quite possible to miss on an exam, because it can be easily hidden in the fact pattern. For this reason, it's often tested.

☞ First, keep the basic definition of AOR in mind: "P may be barred from recovery when an injury results from a danger of which P was *aware* and that P *voluntarily* encountered." (*Example:* D offers P a ride home. P knows that D is slightly drunk. P has other ways to get home, but this way is a little easier. If D crashes because of being drunk, then at common law P is barred from recovery by AOR.)

☞ So look for situations where P knows about a danger in advance, and nonetheless decides to go forward.

☞ Distinguish between *"express"* and *"implied"* AOR. In express, P and D make an explicit agreement that P is taking the risk (e.g., P signs a *waiver* form). In "implied," P's conduct, not his words or documents he signs, establish that he voluntarily and knowingly took the risk.

☞ For *"express,"* the general rule is that P is *bound* by his agreement to assume. (But there are exceptions, such as where D's *bargaining power* is grossly greater than P's, or where D *intentionally or recklessly* caused the danger).

☞ For "implied," P is bound as long as the circumstances demonstrate that he *knowingly and voluntarily* assumed the risk.

☞ Most frequently tested issue (mainly in "implied" cases): Was the risk truly *known* to P?

☞ The test is "subjective" — did P *actually* know of the risk. It's irrelevant that P *should* have known. (*Example:* P is driving on a road. D, who is stopped on the road to fix a flat, has put flares 100 feet before his car. If P sees the flares and understands that they are meant to slow down motorists, then if P drives at regular speed he's bound by AOR because he "knows" of the risk of D's vehicle. But if through inattention or otherwise P doesn't see the flares, he doesn't "know" of the risk, even though a reasonably careful driver would know — AOR does not apply.)

☞ Also, P's knowledge of the risk must be fairly *specific.* (*Example:* D offers P a ride, and P agrees. P is aware that D is an "average" driver who might get in an accident. P has not assumed the general risk of an accident, because his knowledge is not specific enough.)

☞ Questions sometimes test the effect of *comparative negligence* on AOR.

☞ In general, comparative negligence has no effect on the *"express"* case (the rules summarized above still apply).

☞ But in most courts comparative negligence causes *implied* AOR to *disappear* as an independent defense, and to instead be merged into comparative fault analysis. (That is, if P is unreasonable in taking the risk, his unreasonableness is taken into account in fixing his percentage of fault, and AOR has no independent significance.)

☞ Don't forget that there still has to be a *causal link* between P's AOR and the harm to P. (*Example:* If P agrees to drive with D knowing D has bad brakes, and an accident happens because D makes a turn and fails to see another car, AOR doesn't apply — the risk assumed by P, failure to be able to stop, wasn't the cause in fact of the accident.)

☞ If the suit is in *strict products liability*, most courts say that AOR *applies*. Most common scenario: P knows the product lacks a particular *safeguard* that D could have put onto it (e.g., roll bars). Majority rule here: P is stuck with AOR.

☛ Questions concerning *immunity* from tort don't arise very often.

☞ The most you will probably have to do is to spot the occasions when common-law immunity might have applied: (1) *intra-family* immunity (one spouse sues the other, and child sues parent); (2) *charitable* immunity; and (3) immunity of *governmental bodies* ("*sovereign* immunity").

☞ If you spot a situation in which one of these three immunities might have applied at common law, you should probably say something like: "At common law, the suit would have been blocked by [intra-family] [charitable] [sovereign] immunity, but nearly all states today have abolished this immunity." (If your fact pattern involves the *federal* government as defendant, and the claim relates to the government's failure to handle some discretionary or policy-making activity reasonably, you may wish to say that the Federal Tort Claims Act would block the suit because of the *"discretionary function"* exception contained in that statute.)

described as the doctrine of *"respondeat superior"* (which means, literally, "Let the person higher up answer").

1. **Rationale:** Many explanations are given for this doctrine. But the most convincing is that accidents which arise directly or indirectly out of an enterprise ought to be paid for by the entrepreneur in question, as a cost of doing business. As the idea is sometimes put, the employer often has a *"deep pocket,"* whereas the employee is frequently judgment-proof. Furthermore, the employer is in a better position to obtain insurance against work-related accidents than is the employee.

2. **Applies to all torts:** The doctrine applies to *all* torts, including *intentional* ones and also those situations in which *strict liability* exists. But the tort must have occurred during the scope of the employee's employment, a requirement discussed below. Particularly in the case of intentional torts, the employer is often able to avoid liability by showing that the employee was acting completely for his own purposes, not his employer's.

B. **Who is an "employee":** Vicarious liability applies more frequently to torts committed by employees than to those committed by independent contractors (see *infra*, p. 319). Therefore, it is important to be able to tell whether a particular tortfeasor was an employee or independent contractor.

1. **Distinction:** While no single factor is dispositive in all cases, the main idea is that an employee is one who works *subject to the detailed control* of the person who has hired him. An independent contractor, on the other hand, although he is hired to produce a certain result, is not subject to the detailed control of the one who has hired him while he performs his work. He is, in a sense, his own boss.

   a. **Prosser's test:** As Prosser puts the idea, a person is an employee (or a "servant" as older cases call him) "when, in the eyes of the community, he would be regarded as a part of the employer's own working staff. . . . " P&K, p. 501.

   b. **Control over physical details:** The "control" required to make a person an employee rather than an independent contractor is usually held to be control over the *physical details* of the work. It is not enough that the employer exercises control over the general manner in which the work is carried out. See, e.g., *Murrell v. Goertz*, 597 P.2d 1223 (Okla. Ct. App. 1979) (where newspaper publisher sets general rules for a newspaper carrier like route boundaries and time for performance, but leaves details about how to do the deliveries to the carrier, carrier is an independent contractor of the publisher, not an employee).

   c. **Contractual label not dispositive:** The fact that a tortfeasor and his employer have a *contractual agreement*, and that that agreement calls the tortfeasor an "independent contractor" of the employer, will not change their relationship, so the employer can nonetheless be held liable under the *respondeat superior* doctrine. In other words, it is the real working relationship that counts (e.g., the extent to which the employer controls the physical details of the tortfeasor's work), not the *label* applied to the relationship in the employment contract.

C. **Scope of employment:** The most difficult question in the entire area of *respondeat superior* is whether, in a particular case, the employee was acting *"within the scope of his employ-*

ment" when the tort occurred. In general, the tort is within the scope of employment if the tortfeasor was acting with an ***intent to further his employer's business purpose,*** even if the means he chose were indirect, unwise, and perhaps even forbidden. And he will be within the scope of his employment even if his intent to serve his employer is coupled with a separate personal purpose.

> **Example:** Fruit, an insurance salesperson, attends a convention in Alaska run by his employer, the D Insurance Co. He is encouraged to "mix freely" with out-of-state insurance experts who are also at the convention, in order to learn about "sales techniques." One night, after the day's convention activities are over, he goes to a bar in order to look for some out-of-state colleagues, sees that they are not there, and heads back to his hotel. En route, he negligently collides with P.

> *Held*, Fruit was acting within the scope of his employment at the time of the accident. In going to the bar, he was motivated at least in part by a desire to socialize with these experts, whom he had been encouraged to get to know. *Fruit v. Schreiner*, 502 P.2d 133 (Alaska 1972).

1. **Trips from home:**   Most courts hold that where an accident occurs where the employee is travelling *from her home* to work, she is not acting in the scope of her employment; this conclusion is often based on the theory that the employer has no "control" over the employee at that time.

   a. **Returning home:**   Where the employee is *returning home* after her business activities, courts are divided, although most would probably deny liability on the employer's part here as well.

2. **Side trip:**   It frequently happens that, while on a business trip, the employee makes a short *"side trip"* for her own purposes.

   a. **Frolic/detour distinction:**   Traditionally, courts have distinguished between a *"frolic"* and a *"detour."* In courts making this distinction, a "frolic" is "the pursuit of the employee's personal business as a ***substantial deviation*** from or an abandonment of the employment," whereas a "detour" is "a deviation that is ***sufficiently related to the employment*** to fall within its scope." *O'Shea v. Welch*, 350 F.3d 1101 (10th Cir. 2003). Under this analysis, accidents occurring during a *"frolic"* do ***not*** trigger *respondeat superior*, but ones occurring during a *"detour" do* trigger it.

   b. **Modern emphasis on "slight deviation" test:**   Many modern courts have replaced the ambiguous term "detour" with the more descriptive term *"slight deviation"* — if the employee was making only a slight deviation from the tasks required by the employment when the accident occurred, the employer *will* be liable.

      i. **What determines whether deviation is "slight":**   What determines whether a deviation is "slight"? Courts rely on several factors, including (1) the employee's ***intent or purpose*** in making the deviation; (2) the ***"nature, time, and place"*** of the deviation; (3) the ***time consumed*** by the deviation; (4) the ***type of work*** for which the employee was hired; (5) whether the act was ***incidental*** to the work, as reasonably expected by the employer; and (6) how much ***freedom*** was allowed the employee in performing his job responsibilities. *O'Shea v. Welch, supra.*

As you would expect, the use of these factors means that the ***longer*** the deviation took, the ***farther*** from the path dictated by the job the employee was when the accident occurred, the ***further*** the deviation was in ***nature*** from the kind of thing that the employer would reasonably have expected the employee to do, or the ***smaller the freedom*** the employee had on-the-job, the more likely it is that the deviation will be found to be ***substantial*** rather than "slight," and thus not appropriate for vicarious liability.

c. **Foreseeability standard:** Many modern courts have boiled the scope-of-employment problem down to a vague ***"foreseeability"*** standard — the employee is deemed to have been acting within the scope of business if and only if the deviation was "***reasonably foreseeable***." Cf. P&K, pp. 504-05. This standard usually produces pretty much the same result as the six-factor test described above. For instance, the shorter the deviation was in terms of physical distance, the more "foreseeable" it will be deemed to have been, and thus the more likely to trigger *respondeat superior*.

   i. **Smoking and other personal objectives:** A similar "foreseeability" test is often applied to other acts done by employees which are not specifically in furtherance of their employer's business interest. Thus an employee who ***smokes on the job***, or who is on her way to the ***toilet***, would probably be held by most modern courts to be engaged in an activity so foreseeable that it was done within the scope of employment. P&K, pp. 503-04.

3. **Acts prohibited by employer:** Since the whole idea behind *respondeat superior* is that the employer is liable completely ***irrespective of his own negligence***, it follows that employer liability will exist even if the acts done were expressly ***forbidden*** by the employer, as long as it is found that they were done in furtherance of the employment. For instance, even if a storekeeper expressly orders his clerk never to load a gun while showing it to a customer, there will be liability if the clerk does so, since he is furthering the general business purpose of selling the gun. P&K, pp. 502-03.

   a. **Relevant to scope of employment:** But the fact that a particular activity is forbidden by the employer may be *evidence* that that is not what the employee was hired to do at all, and thus was not for a business purpose.

4. **Intentional torts:** *Respondeat superior* may, as noted, apply to intentional torts. Generally, "[T]he master is held liable for any intentional tort committed by the servant where its purpose, however misguided, is wholly or in part to further the master's business." P&K, p. 505.

   a. **Debt collection:** Thus the employer will be liable if his employee attempts to ***collect a debt*** owed to the employer by assault, battery or false imprisonment.

   b. **Personal motives:** But if the employee acts purely from ***personal motives*** (e.g., a violent dislike of a customer), the employer will not be liable. P&K, p. 506.

      i. **Special duty owed by employer:** But even in this "personal motive" situation, the employer may still be liable if he owes an independent duty of protection to the victim. We saw, for instance (*supra*, p. 205), that a common carrier owes its passengers a duty of reasonable care to protect them against torts by third persons.

Therefore, if a railroad conductor attacked a passenger, even though solely for his own motives, the railroad would still be liable, on the grounds that it breached its direct duty of care. P&K, pp. 506-07.

    c. Lost temper: If the employee gets into an ***argument*** during a business transaction, and then loses his temper and commits an intentional tort, most courts hold that the employer is not liable. But a growing minority hold that such a tort really arises out of the employment, and that the employer is therefore liable. P&K, p. 507.

5. Employer's own liability: Keep in mind that in addition to the vicarious liability being discussed here, the employer is also liable for his own direct negligence. It may for instance, be negligence on the part of the employer to hire an employee who the employer should realize is unfit and poses a risk to others. See P, W&S, p. 664, n. 6.

D. Torts by non-employees (e.g., guests and customers): Don't be fooled into thinking that a tort by a ***customer*** of the defendant triggers vicarious liability on the defendant's part. Vicarious liability occurs only when there is an employment relationship (or, occasionally, an independent contractor relationship; see *infra*, p. 319) between the defendant and the tortfeasor. So a defendant can't be vicariously liable for the torts of a customer, or of some ***non-employee*** on the defendant's premises. (The defendant may be liable for not having adequate security, or for having negligently allowed the tortfeasor to come on the premises, but that's direct liability, not vicarious liability.)

Example: While P is shopping at a department store owned by StoreCo, P is assaulted by X, a person who purports to be a customer. StoreCo won't be vicariously liable for X's tort; only if StoreCo is found to have been directly negligent (e.g., by not having adequate security) will StoreCo be liable to P.

III. INDEPENDENT CONTRACTORS

A. No general liability: As a very general "default" rule, a person who ***hires an independent contractor*** is ***not*** generally liable for the torts of that person. P&K, p. 509. However, there are a number of significant ***exceptions*** to the no-liability general rule, and our discussion of liability for torts of one's independent contractors is essentially the discussion of these important exceptions.

1. Distinguished from employee: An independent contractor is one who, although hired by the employer to perform a certain job, is not under the employer's immediate control, and may do the work more or less in the manner he himself decides upon. See the discussion of the distinction between independent contractors and employees *supra*, pp. 316-316.

B. Exceptions to non-liability: Two of the more important exceptions to the rule that an employer is not liable for the torts of his independent contractor involve cases where (1) the employer has ***direct liability*** for her *own* negligence in her handling of the relationship with the contractor; and (2) the employer has ***vicarious liability*** for the contractor's own negligence in doing the work. We discuss each of these areas in turn, even though only the latter (vicarious) liability is a form of the "strict liability" that we are generally covering in this chapter.

By the way, the area of an employer's liability (both direct and vicarious) for torts associated with an independent contractor has been extensively recodified in 2011 in the *Third Restatement* of Torts (Liab. for Phys. & Emot. Harm), references to which are included below.

1. **Employer's own liability:** First, if the employer is *herself* negligent in her own dealings with the independent contractor, this can give rise to employer liability. Rest. 3d (Liab. for Phys. & Emot. Harm) §55 and 56.

    a. **Two common ways:** Here are the two most common the ways in which the employer might be directly negligent in dealing with the contractor:

        [1] **Negligent selection:** The employer *negligently selects* an inappropriate contractor, given the requirements of the work — for instance the contractor does not have adequate *experience* in doing the type of project *safely*.

        Example: Employer selects Contractor to do certain construction renovation work in Employer's store. A reasonable initial investigation by Employer of Contractor's credentials and work experience would have demonstrated that Contractor was not reasonably qualified to do the work safely. Contractor does the work negligently, and the negligent work causes physical injury to P.

        Employer is directly liable for negligently tasking Contractor to do the work, and will therefore be responsible for P's damages.

        [2] **Negligent instruction:** The employer *negligently instructs* (or negligently fails to instruct) the contractor about *how to do the work*.

        Example: Employer non-negligently selects Contractor to do construction work in Employer's retail store. The work consists of replacing a skylight. Employer knows that the replacement work has to be done in a special non-obvious way because of difficulties with how the nearby section of roof handles hard rains. Contractor does the work non-negligently (based on Contractor's limited understanding of the requirements as poorly specified by Employer), but because of the lack of instructions, the skylight weakens and falls, injuring P.

        Employer will be directly liable for P's injuries, because Employer negligently failed to instruct Contractor adequately, and the negligently-given instructions were an actual cause of the injuries.

    Rest. 3d (Liab. for Phys. & Emot. Harm) §55, including Illustr. 1 and 2; §56, Comment b.

2. **Vicarious liability for non-delegable duties:** Second, there are some duties of care that are deemed so important that the delegator is liable for negligence by an independent contractor the delegator hires, even if the delegator used all due care in selecting that particular contractor. These are called "*non-delegable duties*," and the delegator/employer is *vicariously liable* for the contractor's negligent performance of those non-delegable duties.

    a. **Most important scenarios:** Here are the most important situations in which the duty will be non-delegable and will thus lead to vicarious liability on the employer's part:

        [1] **"Peculiar risk" of harm:** The work is likely to involve a "*peculiar risk*" of phys-

ical injury or property damage to others unless special precautions are taken. Rest. 3d (Liab. for Phys. & Emot. Harm), §59.

Example: D owns a private football stadium and the semi-professional team that plays in it. D hires Contractor to install new high-voltage lighting poles in the parking lot. D is not negligent in picking Contractor for this job, since Contractor has adequate experience and safety credentials. Contractor negligently does the work, leaving a pole in such an uninsulated condition that if someone were to touch it, he would be likely to get a high-voltage shock. P, a patron, touches the pole and is shocked.

Since there is a "peculiar risk" (i.e., a risk of a non-typical type of injury) from high-voltage electrical work that is done without adequate precautions, D will be vicariously liable for Contractor's negligence, in a suit brought by P against D. Cf. Rest. 3d (Liab. for Phys. & Emot. Harm), §59, Illustr. 2.

Note: "Peculiar risk" as used here is not the same as "abnormally dangerous activity" (another vicarious-liability category, discussed next below). Abnormally-dangerous liability applies only where the activity couldn't be done with perfect safety no matter how careful the actor was. There will often be "peculiar risk" from an activity even though it *could* be done with utter safety if the right precautions had been followed, which they weren't.

Thus in the above example, installing insulated high-voltage electrical lighting poles is not abnormally dangerous (it can be done perfectly safely), but such installation poses a particular risk of electrocution if the installation is not done properly. So it triggers "peculiar risk" vicarious liability for the person who engages the contractor.

[2] **Abnormally dangerous:** The work is *abnormally dangerous* (i.e., ultrahazardous), so that the employer would be strictly liable if he did the work himself (see *infra*, p. 332) rather than via the independent contractor. Rest. 3d (Liab. for Phys. & Emot. Harm), §58.

Example: O owns land that needs to have trees cleared from it. O hires Contractor to use dynamite to blast away the tree stumps. Contractor uses dynamite, in a non-negligent manner, to blast the stumps. The shock waves damage the plaster of Neighbor's adjacent home. O is vicariously liable in Neighbor's suit against O and Contractor, since blasting is an ultra hazardous activity under the usual "cannot be done with absolute safety no matter how carefully the actor behaves" rules for such activities, *infra*, p. 332.

[3] **Land possessor:** The employer is a *possessor or lessor of land*, and owes a duty of care to the *public*. If because of that duty the employer would be liable for negligence in altering or repairing the property himself, the employer will be vicariously liable for comparable negligence committed by the contractor he selects. Rest. 3d (Liab. for Phys. & Emot. Harm), §62.

Example: O owns a department store. O hires Contractor (properly credentialed) to replace a broken skylight. Contractor does the work negligently. Two months after Contractor turns the repaired area back to O, the skylight falls, injuring P, a patron.

O as the owner of premises open to the public owed a duty of reasonable care to ensure the safety of customers. O will therefore be vicariously liable for the actual negligence of Contractor, since O would have been directly liable for his own negligence if O had done the work himself. Cf. Rest. 3d (Liab. for Phys. & Emot. Harm), §62, including Comment e and Illustr. 3 thereto.

Note about while work is being done: But there's an important clarification to the above rule: it doesn't apply to the contractor's negligence during the period when the contractor is *actively doing the work,* and has *taken over the details of handling of the job* from the owner.

Example: Same facts as above example. Now, however, assume that Contractor has negligently installed the skylight, but is still in physical possession of, and has responsibility, for the skylight area. (O has let Contractor deal with the details of how the work is to be done safely.) P, a customer, wanders in from an area not under Contractor's control, and is injured when the skylight falls on him. Contractor has also not posted any warning signs.

Since Contractor, not O, was in control of the daily work at the time of the accident, O won't be vicariously liable for Contractor's negligence. (Rationale: We want O to delegate the daily care to the person actually doing the work, and we don't want to encourage micromanagement and meddling by O in that work.) Cf. Rest. 3d (Liab. for Phys. & Emot. Harm), §62, Comment e and Illustr. 2 thereto.

[4] **Public place:** The work is done in a *"public place,"* such as a road, sidewalk, park, etc. Rest. 3d (Liab. for Phys. & Emot. Harm), §64, Comment g and Illustr. 3 thereto.

Example: LightingCo hires Contractor to repair a street light (on a public street) that LightingCo. owns and is responsible for illuminating. Contractor negligently does the work, and the streetlight fails soon after. P steps in a pothole which he would have seen had the streetlight been working. Since LightingCo. had the responsibility for maintaining the streetlight in a public place, it is vicariously liable for Contractor's negligence in doing the contracted-for maintenance work. *Id.,* Illustr. 3.

IV. JOINT ENTERPRISE

A. **Nature of joint enterprise relationship:** Another relationship which may give rise to vicarious liability is that frequently called *"joint enterprise"*. A joint enterprise is like a partnership, except that it is generally for a very short and specific purpose (e.g., a *trip*). Once the various requirements for the existence of a joint enterprise are met, the negligence of one "joint enterpriser" (or "joint venturer" as he is sometimes called) is imputed to the other.

1. **Use in auto cases:** The doctrine almost always arises in *automobile accident cases,* in which the negligence of the driver is imputed to the passenger (either to allow the occupant of a second car to recover against the passenger, or, under the doctrine of imputed comparative negligence, discussed *supra,* p. 288 to reduce the passenger's recovery

against the negligent driver of the other car.)

B. Requirements for joint enterprise: There are usually held to be four requirements for a joint enterprise: (1) an *agreement*, express or implied, between the members; (2) a *common purpose* to be carried out by the members; (3) a *common pecuniary interest* in that purpose; and (4) an equal right to a *voice* in the enterprise, i.e., an equal *right of control*. Rest. 2d, §491, Comment c. Most litigation has revolved around the third and fourth requirements.

   1. **Pecuniary interest:**   In courts requiring a common pecuniary interest, the result is that a mere *social trip*, or a trip in which each member is pursuing his own *independent business interest*, is not a joint enterprise.

      a. **Sharing expenses:**   The fact that two parties taking a social trip, or pursuing separate business interests while travelling together, *share expenses* of the trip, is not by itself enough to establish that they have a "common pecuniary or business purpose". Rest. 2d, §491, Comment i.

   2. **Mutual right of control:**   The requirement that each joint venturer have a partial right of control over the enterprise generally means, in the case of an automobile trip, that each must have some say in how the car is to be driven. Where the occupants of the car have the "common business" purpose referred to above, it is usually found that they have at least a theoretical right of control over the car as well. This does not mean that each has the right, at any time, to grab the wheel and steer; it simply means that each is understood to have something like an equal say in how fast the car will travel, what the route will be, etc.

      a. **Social purpose:**   But where only a social trip is involved, courts often find that the passenger has no right of control over the driver.

      b. **Joint ownership:**   Many courts used to hold that the mere fact that the automobile was *jointly owned* (e.g., by a husband and wife) meant automatically that the passenger/co-owner had a right of control over the driver/owner. But this is no longer the rule. See P&K, pp. 520-21.

   3. **Passenger v. driver:**   Incredible as it may seem, a few courts have constructed, in effect, their own judicial "automobile guest statutes" by holding that where driver and passenger are joint venturers, the passenger may not sue the driver when the latter negligently causes a crash. The driver's negligence is said to be imputed to the passenger, who is then contributorily negligent and thus barred from recovery against the driver. This rule is on the wane. (But the driver's negligence may still be imputed comparative negligence by the passenger in a suit against the driver of another vehicle, as discussed *supra*, p. 288.)

V.   AUTO CONSENT STATUTES, THE "FAMILY PURPOSE" DOCTRINE AND BAILMENT

A. Bases for automobile liability: Courts and legislatures have tried particularly hard to find a solvent defendant in car accident cases. To do this, they use a number of vicarious-liability techniques, which vary from state to state.

B. Consent statutes: About one quarter of the states have enacted statutes, called "*automobile consent statutes,*" which provide that the owner of an automobile is *vicariously liable* for any negligence committed by one using the car with the owner's ***permission***.

1. **Scope of consent:**   Since the liability is based upon the "consent," if the use by the borrower (or "bailee" as he is usually called) goes clearly ***beyond*** the scope of that consent, there is no liability. For instance, if the owner expressly forbids the bailee to drive on the highway, such use would probably so exceed the scope of consent as to render the statute inapplicable.

C. **Automobile insurance omnibus clause:**   The need for automobile consent statutes is eliminated, in many states, by the fact that the standard ***automobile liability insurance policy*** covers not only the named insured (usually the head of household, who is also generally the owner or co-owner of the automobile), but also any member of the named insured's household, and any other person who uses the auto with the consent of the insured. See generally P&K pp. 592-96. The effect of this is to make the user of the car financially responsible himself, so that liability on the part of the owner is unnecessary (at least up to the policy limits).

D. **Judge-made doctrines:** Apart from consent statutes and compulsory-insurance requirements, a number of ***judge-made doctrines*** accomplish the same objective of making the car owner vicariously liable for the negligence of one she permitted to use the car.

1. **Joint enterprise:** Often the ***joint enterprise*** doctrine (*supra*, p. 322), can be used to make one member of the enterprise (e.g., the vehicle owner) vicariously liable for the negligence of another member (e.g., the driver).

2. **Family purpose doctrine:**   Another important judge-made doctrine is the *"family purpose doctrine."* The doctrine, in force in about 12 states, provides that a car owner who lets ***members of her household*** drive her car for their own personal use has done so in order to further a "family purpose" or family objective, and is therefore vicariously liable. (The doctrine is also sometimes called the *"family car"* doctrine.)

    a. **Car financed but not owned by D:**   Some cases have extended the family purpose doctrine to cover situations in which the defendant head of household does ***not own*** the car, but has made the driver's use of the car possible by giving the family-member/driver the ***funds*** with which to buy and/or ***maintain*** the vehicle.

    b. **Abandonment:**   In states adopting consent statutes, discussed above, the family purpose doctrine is usually unnecessary, since the owner is liable for the negligence of whomever she allows to use the car, whether a member of her household or not, and whether there is a family objective or not.

E. **Bailments:**   In the absence of a consent statute (and assuming the family purpose doctrine doesn't apply), the mere existence of a ***bailment*** does ***not*** make the bailor vicariously liable for the bailee's negligence.

> **Example:** D lends his shotgun to X. X, while hunting in the woods, negligently fires without noticing P nearby. Even though D is a bailor (he has lent his personal property to X), D does not thereby become vicariously liable for X's negligent use of the bailed property.

1. **Negligent entrustment by bailor:**   But the bailor may, of course, be negligent herself in entrusting a potentially dangerous instrument to the bailee where she ***should know that***

the latter may use it unsafely. In this situation, the claim is directly against the bailor for *"negligent entrustment,"* and there is no vicarious liability.

Example: In the above example, if D knew that X often hunted while drunk, D's act of entrusting the shotgun to X might itself be negligent, in which case D would be directly (not vicariously) liable to P for the injuries caused by X.

Quiz Yourself on
VICARIOUS LIABILITY (Entire Chapter)

63. Harvey Bangbang owns the Shoot 'M Up Gun Store. He strictly instructs his employees not to load guns before demonstrating them to customers. One employee, Annie Oakleaf, is having a hard time selling a gun to a customer, Long John Silver. She loads a gun and fires at a target on the wall. She accidentally shoots Silver's leg off in the process. Will Harvey be liable for Annie's negligence? _____

64. The Plen-Tee O'Food Company organizes and runs country fairs. For the Lonornament County Fair, Plen-Tee contracts with Circe du Lune, a highly respected holiday-light-show company, to run a laser-guided light show at night. Due to Circe's negligent running of the show, Patron, an audience member, is blinded. A light show of this sort is perfectly safe if proper techniques are used, which they weren't here. Circe is jugment proof. Will Plen-Tee be liable for Patron's blindness? _____

65. Allnever Tell gives his four-year-old son, Willie, a real bow and arrow set for Christmas. Willie takes it outside and fires an arrow at his neighbor, Captain Hook, hitting him in the arm. Will Allnever be liable? _____

66. Cosa Nostra Collectors, Inc. runs a debt collection service. All employees of Cosa are instructed that they should never use violence, or even threats of violence, in attempting to collect a debt. Vincent ("Big Vinny") Testarosa, one of Cosa's collectors, attempts to collect a $10,000 debt owed by Potter to a Cosa client, Carla. Potter refuses to pay even though (as Vincent knows) Potter has the money. In order to soften Potter's resistance, Vincent disregards his employer's instructions, and with an unlicensed pistol fires a slug through Potter's left kneecap, crippling him for life. Potter then pays the money. Potter (after assuming a new identity and state of residence) brings suit against Cosa for battery, under the doctrine of *respondeat superior*. Can Potter recover? _____

Answers

63. **Yes, even though Annie had strict instructions not to load the gun.** Since the tort occurred within the scope of the employment relationship, and Annie was serving Harvey's objectives (albeit in a prohibited way), Harvey will be liable. To decide otherwise would undermine vicarious liability in general, since employers would almost always escape liability by giving their employees careful instructions.

    NOTE: However, an employee's doing what he is expressly told not to do will often be <u>evidence</u> (but non-dispositive) that he was acting outside the scope of employment.

64. **Yes.** Although employers are in general not vicariously liable for the torts of their independent contractors, they *are* liable in a number of special situations. One of those situations is where the work being delegated to the independent contractor poses a "<u>peculiar risk</u>" of physical harm if not properly done. That's the case here. So even though this was not an ultra-hazardous activity (and Circe would be liable only if negligent, as it was), the mere fact that the activity posed a particular risk of harm if not conducted prop-

erly means that Plen-Tee is vicariously liable for the negligence of its independent contractor, Circe. Notice that this result occurs even though Circe was apparently well-qualified for the job when picked by Plen-Tee (so that Plen-Tee was not directly negligent in its own behavior regarding the contractor).

65. Yes. As a general rule, parents are not vicariously liable for their children's torts. However, parents can be *directly* liable for their children's torts under certain circumstances. One such circumstance exists here: when a parent allows the child to use a dangerous object which the child lacks the maturity and judgment to use safely, the parent will be liable for torts committed with the object. It's clearly unreasonable to give a four-year-old a real bow and arrow. That makes Allnever negligent, and makes him liable for Hook's injuries.

66. Yes. Even if the tort committed by servant is an intentional one, the master will be held liable for it under the doctrine of *respondeat superior*, provided that the tort was committed in some sense *in furtherance of the employer's business.* According to most courts, it does not matter that the method or action used was expressly forbidden by the employer, as long as it was done in furtherance of the employment. Since Vincent, when he fired the slug into Potter's kneecap, was attempting to collect the debt (and indeed the slug helped him succeed), a court would almost certainly find that Vincent was acting in furtherance of his employment with Cosa, so that Cosa would be liable under *respondeat superior*.

Exam Tips on
VICARIOUS LIABILITY

Vicarious liability is tested amazingly frequently, out of all proportion to the number of pages it takes to describe the rules governing it. By "vicarious liability" we mean all of the doctrines which may cause one person to become liable for the acts of another, including: (1) liability of an *employer* for acts of her employees; (2) the occasional liability for the acts of an *independent contractor* whom one has engaged; (3) liability under the theory of *"joint enterprise"*; (4) liability pursuant to an *automobile consent* statute; and (5) the now mostly-outmoded doctrine of "imputed contributory negligence." Here's how to handle each of these:

☛ Most of all, look out for places to apply *"respondeat superior" (RS).*

   ☞ You should be thinking RS whenever you have an employee doing something during the course of his job. The most-typical context: the employee is driving a car or truck for the employer. But there can be many odd-ball contexts (e.g., Employee, while on the job, incorrectly answers a question asked by a customer).

   ☞ Remember the two-part test for when RS will apply: (1) D2 must be the *"employer"* of D1, which means that D2 must have the right to *control the details* of D1's performance; and (2) D1 must be acting within the *scope of the employment* at the time he commits the act in question.

   ☞ RS applies not only to negligence by the employee, but also to *intentional torts* committed by the employee within the scope of employment. (*Example:* Employee is a truck driver, who gets into a fist-fight with P when P won't move his car so Employee can make a delivery.) Of course, the fact that the tort is intentional may make it less likely that the tort is in fact committed within the scope of employment, but if it *is* within the scope, it's covered by the RS doctrine.

☞ Most-tested issue: the distinction between an employee (where RS applies) and an *independent contractor* (where RS does not apply, though other forms of vicarious liability may, as discussed below). The main test is whether the "employer" had the right to *control the details* of how the "employee" did the job. Quick rule of thumb: *A* is an employee of *B* if, in the eyes of the community, *A* would be regarded as part of *B*'s *"regular working staff."* The real working relationship, not the contractual label, is what counts. Some examples:

  ☞ Where Finance Co. hires Repoman to repossess cars, and Repoman owns his own tow truck, sets his own hours, and does pick-ups for other companies as well as Finance Co., probably Repoman is an independent contractor.

  ☞ Where Auto Rental Co. sends cars to Repairman to be fixed, and Repairman has his own garage and tools, and buys the repair parts with his own cash (even though Auto Rental reimburses), Repairman is probably an independent contractor — Auto Rental is not controlling the details of Repairman's work.

  ☞ Where Parents hire Babysitter and pay by the hour, giving the details of what to do (e.g., "put Baby to bed at 8:00 p.m."), probably Babysitter is an employee, not an independent contractor, even if Parents don't withhold from her pay, or report it, for tax purposes.

☞ Also much tested: Was the act within the *scope* of the employee's employment? (If it's not, the employer is not liable under RS, even though the tortfeasor was clearly an employee.) Main test: Was the employee acting to *further his employer's business purposes*? If so, the act is within the scope of employment even though the means chosen were unwise or even *forbidden*. Some examples:

  ☞ Part of Employee's job is to test drapes hanging in apartments for fire-resistance. Employer's instructions say, "Never test the drapes while they are in place. Always take them down." Employee is rushing and tests while drapes are hanging, burning down a building. Employee is within the scope of her employment, because she was furthering Employer's purposes (testing of drapes) even though the way she did it was forbidden by Employer.

  ☞ Employee puts in unpaid overtime at the office on the weekend, working on an invention that Employee thinks will help Employer. Employee burns down the building. Employee is probably working within the scope of employment.

  ☞ Employee, while driving to make pick-ups of packages for Employer, makes a one-hour detour to visit her doctor to get pills for her allergies. An accident occurs while Employee is in the doctor's parking lot. This is probably not within the scope of employment, but is rather a "deviation" that doesn't trigger employer liability (i.e., a *"frolic" or "detour."*) (But if the detour is brief, and is of the sort employees frequently and foreseeably do within their working day, then a court might find it to be within the scope of employment even though it did not, strictly speaking, benefit the employer.)

☞ Keep in mind that the employ*ee* is not released from liability merely because the employer is covered by RS — both employer and employee are jointly and severally liable.

☞ Also, remember that if RS applies, the employee owes *indemnity* (full reimbursement) to the employer.

☛ If you conclude that the tortfeasor is an *"independent contractor"* rather than an "employee," the general rule is that the person who engaged him is *not* vicariously liable for the contractor's torts. But there are *exceptions,* where the person hiring the contractor is deemed to have a *non-delegable duty*:

   ☞ Most important: if the work is *unusually dangerous* (either "inherently"/"unavoidably" dangerous, or poses "peculiar risks" where not done with appropriate skill and precautions), then the person engaging the independent contractor *will* be vicariously liable.

   Example: D1, a homeowner, hires D2 to dig a hole for a swimming pool to be put in D1's back yard. D2 doesn't put up barriers, and P, a neighboring child invited to be there, falls in. Probably D1 is vicariously liable, since the nature of the work being done (excavation of a large hole in a residential neighborhood) is dangerous if not accompanied by barriers.

   ☞ Other exceptions: (1) D is a *landowner* who has a duty to *keep the premises safe* (the above example would qualify for this exception, too); (2) D is causing the contractor to do work in a *public place* (e.g., D is a city that hires a contractor to do work on a public road; D is vicariously liable for the contractor's negligent work).

☛ Be on the lookout for *"joint enterprise"* liability. When two or more people engage in an activity *"in concert"* and for shared aims, each can be held liable for the other's torts.

   ☞ Most common application: Two people go on a *car trip* together, sharing driving and/or expenses. The passenger is vicariously liable for the driver's negligence, because they were "joint venturers" or members of a "joint enterprise."

   ☞ Other contexts are possible for "joint enterprise," especially *recreational* activities. (*Example:* Golfers who engage in a "long-driving" contest; hot-rodders; a water skier and the driver of the boat.)

   ☞ A *manufacturer* of goods, and the *retailer* who sells the item to the consumer, are usually *not* found to be in a joint enterprise, or otherwise liable for each other's torts. Thus if Manufacturer is negligent in designing a product, Retailer is not vicariously liable. (Retailer may have strict product liability for selling a defective and dangerous product, but that's direct rather than vicarious liability, and is not related to anyone's negligence.)

☛ If a driver of a car gets into an accident, consider the possibility that the vehicle's *owner* may be vicariously liable even if the owner was not present. Some states have *"Automobile Consent"* statutes, whose purpose is precisely to make the owner liable for torts committed in the car by anyone who used the car with the owner's consent. But in a state without such a statute, the *mere loan* of one's car to another person does *not* make the owner liable. (Remember that the owner may have *direct* liability if the owner should have known that the driver was not competent, as where the driver was drunk or unlicensed.)

CHAPTER 13

STRICT LIABILITY

ChapterScope

The liability we have seen thus far has been based either upon intent or upon negligence. We examine in this chapter certain situations, particularly those involving *animals* and *abnormally dangerous activities*, in which liability is imposed even where neither intent nor negligence is present. Such liability is sometimes called "liability without fault" or "absolute liability." However, the more commonly-accepted term, and the more descriptive one, is "strict liability." The key concepts in this chapter are:

- **Basis for:** The basis for strict liability is that those who engage in certain kinds of activities do so *at their own peril*, and must pay for any damage that foreseeably results, even if the activity has been carried out in the most careful possible manner. Our society has made the judgment that such activities should "pay their own way." This judgment stems in part from the belief that it is generally easier for the defendant to bear the loss (probably through liability insurance) than for the injured plaintiff to do so.

- **Animals:** Court impose strict liabilities on the keepers of certain *animals*. If an animal is *"wild,"* there is strict liability for any damage that results from a "dangerous propensity" of that species. If an animal is *"domestic,"* there is only strict liability where the owner knows or has reason to know of the particular animal's dangerous characteristics.

- **Abnormally dangerous activities:** One who carries out an *abnormally dangerous* (or "ultrahazardous") activity is strictly liable — liable without regard to whether he is at fault — for any damage that proximately results from the dangerous nature of the activity.

- **Workers' compensation:** All states have enacted "Workers' Compensation" statutes. These statutes basically establish a strict liability scheme for on-the-job injuries: in essence, the employer must pay specified "damages" for any on-the-job injury suffered by the employee, even if this occurs completely without the employer's fault. Payments provided by the WC statute are generally less than would be awarded by a court in tort, and do not allow anything for pain and suffering. The WC remedy is the employee's *sole* one — in return for not having to prove fault, she must be content with a lower level of recovery, whether she wants to make this trade-off or not.

I. STRICT LIABILITY GENERALLY

A. Generally: Apart from the special situation of defective products (see *infra*, p. 358), there are three major contexts in which D can have *"strict liability"* — that is, liability regardless of D's intent and regardless of whether D was negligent. We examine those contexts in this chapter. They are:

- ❏ strict liability for keeping *wild or other dangerous animals*;
- ❏ strict liability for carrying out *abnormally dangerous* (or *"ultrahazardous"*) *activities*; and

❏ strict liability on the part of an employer for the ***employee's on-the-job injuries***, a liability that is enforced by ***"workers compensation"*** statutes enacted in all stats.

II. ANIMALS

A. Trespassing animals: The English common law rule has apparently always been that the owner of livestock or other animals is liable for property damage caused by them if they ***trespass*** upon another's land. This liability existed even though the owner exercised utmost care to prevent the animals from escaping. However, the rule applied only to animals of a sort likely to roam and do substantial damage. Thus cattle, horses, sheep and goats were included but "household" animals like dogs and cats were not. See P,W&S, p. 683.

1. **American rule:**   In most American jurisdictions, this English rule of strict liability (with its exception for dogs and cats) applies. P&K, p. 539. This is particularly likely to be the rule in the populous eastern states.

   a. **Western states:**   A number of western states, however, whose economy still depends on raising of livestock, have never adopted a broad rule of strict liability. "Fencing in" statutes in some states provide that an animal owner is not strictly liable if he attempts to fence in his animals, but that he is strictly liable if he does not. Conversely, "fencing out" statutes provide that if the plaintiff properly fences his land, he has a strict liability claim against one whose animals break in. P&K, p. 540.

   b. **Use of highway:**   Even in the eastern states, if the defendant is using a ***public road*** to transport his animals to market, he will not be strictly liable if they wander onto the land immediately adjoining the road. P&K, *ibid*.

B. Non-trespass liability: Strict liability also sometimes exists for damage other than trespass (e.g. personal injury). There is strict liability for harm done by ***"dangerous animals"*** kept by the defendant. But the definition of a "dangerous animal" depends in turn upon whether the animal is of a species that is regarded as "wild" or "domesticated".

1. **Wild animals:**   A person who keeps a ***"wild"*** animal is strictly liable for ***all damage*** done by it, provided that the damage results from a ***"dangerous propensity"*** that is typical of the species in question (or stems from a dangerous tendency of the particular animal in question of which the owner is or should be aware). Rest. 2d, §507.

   Example: D keeps a lion cub, which has never shown any violent tendencies. One day, the cub runs out on the street and attacks P. Even if D used all possible care to prevent the cub from escaping, he is liable for P's injuries, because lions are wild animals, and the damage resulted from a dangerous propensity typical of lions, that they can attack without warning.

2. **Domestic animals:**   But injuries caused by a ***"domestic"*** animal such as a cat, dog, cow, pig, etc., do ***not*** give rise to strict liability, except where the owner ***knows*** or has ***reason to know*** of the animal's dangerous characteristics. P&K, p. 542-43. This does not mean that "every dog is entitled to one free bite," an often-repeated incorrect statement. For an owner may have reason to know of his pet's dangerous tendencies because it has ***unsuccessfully*** attempted to bite someone in the past, or seems to have a generally vicious temperament, etc.

Example: D keeps a dog in the backyard. The dog escapes, and bites P, the mail carrier, in the street in front of D's house. If the dog has never attempted to bite anyone before, D is not subject to strict liability, since dogs are a domesticated rather than wild species. But if D knew or had reason to know that the dog sometimes attacks people, she would be strictly liable.

3. **Distinguishing wild from domesticated:** A domesticated species is one which "is by custom ***devoted to the service of mankind***" in the community in question. Rest. 2d, §506(2). Thus bees, bulls, and stallions are all generally held to be domesticated, even though they can be and often are very dangerous. The basis for this classification is obviously that ownership of these animals serves a social use, and should not be discouraged by excessive liability. P&K, pp. 542-43.

   a. **Fear of humans is factor:** In deciding whether a wild animal's "dangerous propensities" caused the damage in question, the fact (if true) that the ***average person fears animals of that species*** would be part of what makes the animal dangerous. So don't assume that a defanged, declawed, or generally-docile animal that is part of a wild species hasn't caused the damage, if the damage stems from the ***plaintiff's panic*** over the animal's presence.

      Example: D keeps a very tame bear in his backyard. Without negligence by D, the bear escapes, and walks into P's backyard 1/2 mile away. P, who is barbecuing, is so frightened by the bear that he suffers a fatal heart attack. The bear would not have attacked or otherwise harmed P. D is nonetheless strictly liable for P's death, because humans' fear of unrestrained bears is part of what makes bears a dangerous species.

   b. **Injury from factor that is not part of species' dangerousness:** On the other hand, if the accident or injury occurs on account of a factor that is ***unrelated*** to the "***dangerous propensities***" that are typical of the species in question, then there will ***not*** be strict liability.

      Example: D is a retired animal trainer who keeps a small tame bear that previously appeared with him as part of D's circus act. The bear is old, slow-moving, almost blind, and the size of a small dog. D keeps the bear in the fenced yard alongside his house. P is a thirteen-year-old girl who delivers newspapers to D. One day, P comes to D's home to collect for the past week's deliveries. Since she knows the bear, P opens the gate and calls the animal so that she can pet him. The bear bounds toward the place from which the sound has come, but because he is almost blind, he bumps into P. P falls to the ground, fracturing her ankle.

      P will not be able to recover against D in strict liability. Strict liability is imposed on the keeper of a wild animal, but only for harm which proximately results from a dangerous propensity that is characteristic of wild animals of that particular class. Rest. 2d, §507(2). Bears are dangerous because they bite or attack. The risk that they may clumsily knock someone over is not one which makes them more dangerous than a dog or other domestic animal, so strict liability does not apply in this scenario.

C. **Defenses:** The defenses which may be asserted in an action based on strict liability for animals are discussed *infra*, p. 337, in the general treatment of strict liability defenses.

III. ABNORMALLY DANGEROUS ACTIVITIES

A. The doctrine of *Rylands v. Fletcher:* The path to strict liability for *"abnormally dangerous"* activities was begun in the English case of *Rylands v. Fletcher*, L.R. 3 H.L. 330 (1868).

   1. Facts of *Rylands*: The defendants hired an independent contractor to construct a reservoir on their property. When the reservoir was filled up, water broke through from it into some abandoned mine shafts on the property, and then flooded into adjacent mine shafts owned by the plaintiffs. The defendants themselves were not aware of the abandoned shaft, and were therefore not negligent (although the contractor probably was).

   2. Lower holding: After the lowest court denied liability, the case came before the Exchequer Chamber, in effect an intermediate appeals court. The court reversed, holding that there was liability because " . . . the person who for his own purposes brings on his lands and collects and keeps there anything likely to do mischief if it escapes, must keep it in at his peril, and if he does not do so, is prima facie answerable for all the damage which is the natural consequence of its escape." The court analogized to the rules conferring strict liability for trespassing cattle (see *supra*, p. 330).

   3. House of Lords: The case then went to the House of Lords, the final appellate tribunal. The holding of the Exchequer Chamber was affirmed, but was significantly cut back. Liability existed because, the court said, the defendants put their land to a *"non-natural* use for the purpose of introducing [onto it] that which in its natural condition was not in or upon it", i.e., a large quantity of water. If, on the other hand, the court said, the water had entered during a "natural use" of the land, and had then flowed off onto the plaintiff's land, there would have been no liability.

B. America's slow adoption: During the first years after *Rylands*, American courts frequently misconstrued it and purported to reject it. They focused on the Exchequer Chamber version, which would have imposed liability for escaping forces even where the land is put to a natural use. P&K, p. 548. Eventually, however, the *vast majority of American courts accepted* at least the practical *result* of *Rylands*, even if not the case by name. P&K, p. 549. The rule has in fact been extended to include most activities that are extremely dangerous.

   Example: D, an exterminator, puts hydrocyanic acid gas in the basement of a commercial building one midnight, in order to kill cockroaches. The next morning, P, walking in the lobby, is almost fatally poisoned by the gas.

   Held, D's activity was "ultra-hazardous," and was not a matter of "common usage" (even though it may be common among exterminators). Therefore strict liability applies, and D must pay even though he may have exercised all due care. *Luthringer v. Moore*, 190 P.2d 1 (Cal. 1948).

C. Second Restatement's rule: The Second Restatement has, roughly speaking, codified the rule of *Rylands v. Fletcher*, to impose strict liability in cases of *"abnormally dangerous"* activities. Rest. 2d, §519.

   1. Various factors: Rest. 2d, §520, lists *six factors* to be considered in determining whether an activity is "abnormally dangerous":

    a. **High degree of risk:** "Existence of a *high degree of risk* of *some harm* to the person, land or chattels of others";

    b. **Risk of serious harm:** "Likelihood that the harm that results from it will be *great*";

    c. **Cannot be eliminated even by due care:** "*Inability to eliminate the risk* by the exercise of *reasonable care*";

    d. **Not a matter of common usage:** "Extent to which the activity is *not a matter of common usage*";

    e. **Appropriateness:** "*Inappropriateness* of the activity to the *place* where it is carried on"; and

    f. **Value:** "Extent to which its *value* to the community is *outweighed* by its *dangerous* attributes."

2. **Requirement of unavoidable danger:** A key requirement (factor (c) above) is that the activity be one which *cannot be carried out safely, even with reasonable care*.

    a. **Nuclear reactor:** One kind of activity which would almost definitely be held to fulfill the "unavoidable danger" requirement is the running of a *nuclear reactor*. Thus suits filed in the wake of Three-Mile-Island sought, *inter alia*, strict liability recovery. See *infra*, p. 336. However, Federal statues impose a maximum total liability for a single "nuclear incident" of $560,000,000. See 42 U.S.C.A. §2210(e).

3. **Value to community:** One of the factors suggested by the Restatement as working against a finding that an activity is abnormally dangerous is that it has *"value to the community"*. Thus in most parts of states such as Texas and Oklahoma, the reliance on the energy industry is sufficiently great that there is usually no strict liability for accidents arising out of oil and gas wells. (The "inappropriateness of the activity to the place where it is carried on," another Restatement factor, also leads to this result.)

    a. **Not dispositive:** But "value to the community" is not dispositive, and an extremely valuable enterprise may nonetheless have to "pay its own way" if the dangers created by it are sufficiently great.

D. **Third Restatement's rule:** The new Third Restatement *reduces the number of factors* for determining whether an activity is abnormally dangerous and thus worthy of strict liability. The Third Restatement deems an activity abnormally dangerous if it satisfies *two conditions:*

[1] the activity "creates a *foreseeable* and *highly significant risk* of *physical harm* even when *reasonable care is exercised by all actors*" and

[2] the activity " is *not one of common usage.*"

Rest. 3d (Liab. for Phys. & Emot. Harm) §20.

1. **Differences from Second Restatement:** Despite the apparently-large reduction in factors from the Second to the Third Restatement, there are only a couple of significant differences between the two:

    ❏ Most important, the last two of the six Second Restatement factors — the "*inappropriateness* of the activity to the place where it is carried on" and the "extent to which [the activity's] *value* to the community is *outweighed* by as dangerous attributes — are *eliminated* in the Third Restatement. The commentary points out that strict liability is relevant only when the defendant *does not have negligence liability*. Therefore, strict liability "rests on the assumption that the activity's advantages are apparently substantial enough as to render reasonable the defendant's choice to engage in the activity" (otherwise the defendant's mere choice to conduct the activity would itself be negligent). Rest. 3d (Liab. for Phys. & Emot. Harm) §20, Comment k. Consequently, the commentary concludes, "the point that the activity provides substantial value or utility is of little direct relevance to the question whether the activity should properly bear strict liability." *Id.*

❏ Second, the Third Restatement collapses the first two of the Second Restatement factors — existence of a "high degree of risk of some harm" and "likelihood that the harm that results ... will be great" — into a *single factor*, a *"foreseeable and highly significant risk of physical harm."* But the commentary to the new Restatement makes it clear that this is only a change in phrasing: "Both the likelihood of harm and the severity of possible harm should be taken into account in ascertaining whether an activity entails a highly significant risk of physical harm." Rest. 3d (Liab. for Phys. & Emot. Harm) §20, Comment g.

❏ Finally, the Third Restatement specifies that in deciding whether the activity is one that is risky even when reasonable care is exercised, one should assume that reasonable care is exercised *" by all actors,"* not merely by the defendant. This has the effect of *narrowing* strict liability's scope — if reasonable precautions by persons in the *victim/plaintiff's position* (or by *third persons*) could make the activity not abnormally dangerous, there will be no strict liability even though no amount of care by the defendant (the person carrying out the activity) alone could nullify the highly significant risk. Rest. 3d (Liab. for Phys. & Emot. Harm) §20, Comment h. (This means that if the situation is appropriate for *res ipsa loquitur*, it's *not* appropriate for strict liability — *res ipsa* applies only where the accident usually doesn't happen in the absence of negligence, and strict liability conversely applies only where the accident might well have happened even in the absence of negligence.)

Example: Many accidents happen involving the transmission of natural gas through underground lines. But most of these accidents occur through the negligence of parties other than the gas company who have access to the lines (e.g., other utilities doing excavation work). Therefore, the Third Restatement points out, most courts properly hold that the gas company is not strictly liable, because the use of reasonable care by *all* parties (not just the gas company) probably *would* be enough to avoid "a foreseeable and highly significant risk of physical harm." *Id.*

E. **Some contexts:** Here are some special contexts in which strict liability might be imposed:

1. **Use and storage of explosives:** A party who uses or stores *explosives* is generally held strictly liable for any damages that may result.

    Example: D stores 80,000 lbs. of explosives in a building in the suburbs of Anchorage. The building is more than half a mile from the nearest building not used for storing explosives. Thieves break into the building, and set off an explosion, causing property damage within a two-mile radius and beyond, including damage to P's property.

Held, D is strictly liable for the damage caused. Storage of explosives, like use of them in blasting operations, should be subject to a *per se* rule of strict liability, regardless of whether the place of storage was geographically appropriate, or any other factor. *Yukon Equipment, Inc. v. Fireman's Fund Ins. Co.*, 585 P.2d 1206 (Alaska 1978).

Note: The court in *Yukon* expressly rejected the Second Restatement's six-factor balancing test, discussed *supra*. Instead, as noted, the court applied a *per se* rule for explosive-storage cases.

The court also briefly addressed an interesting additional issue: was the act of the thieves, in breaking into the storage place and setting off the explosives, a **superseding intervening cause**, that would relieve D of liability? The court found that the building had been illegally broken into at least six times, usually involving the theft of explosives. Since D had knowledge of these break-ins, this particular break-in and detonation (which apparently occurred in order to cover up a prior theft) was not superseding.

2. **Crop dusting:** Strict liability is generally imposed for damage caused by ***crop dusting*** or ***spraying***.

3. **Airplane accidents:** There has been much controversy about the extent to which strict liability should be applied in cases of ***airplane accidents***.

   a. **Suit by passenger against carrier:** In suits by passengers (or their estates) against the airlines, courts have almost always held that there is ***no strict liability***. See, e.g., Rest. 3d (Liab. for Phys. & Emot. Harm) §20, Reporter's Note: "[A]viation does not fit the formal Restatement criteria for an abnormally dangerous activity." It is therefore necessary for the plaintiff to show negligence, either on the part of the pilot, the maintenance crew, the manufacturer, etc.

      i. **International flights:** By the way, liability for ***international*** flights is governed by the Warsaw Convention, which limits the carrier's liability to its own passengers to $8,300. A 1966 Montreal agreement modifies the Convention, in cases of carriers operating in the U.S., to raise the limit to $75,000, and to impose a ***modified form of strict liability***. See Epstein, 5th Ed., pp. 560-61.

   b. **Ground damage:** But most courts *do* impose strict liability for ***ground damage*** from airplane accidents. That's true for both objects that fall from aircraft, and for damage done by a crashing aircraft itself. Both the owner and the operator of the aircraft are strictly liable. Rest. 2d, §520A. (But if the owner or operator are held strictly liable, they may be entitled to indemnity from someone higher up in the distribution channel — such as the plane manufacturer — if the accident was due to a defective product; see *supra*, p. 192.) This is a variety of strict liability for ultrahazardous activities.

      Example: D operates an aircraft that crashes into P's building, causing property damage. P can recover from D (or his estate), even if D operated the aircraft without negligence.

4. **Toxic chemicals and flammable liquids:** The *storage and transport* of *toxic chemicals* and *flammable liquids* often, but not always, gives rise to strict liability. For instance, transporters of **gasoline** and **propane** have sometimes been held strictly liable for spills and explosions. See, e.g., *Siegler v. Kuhlman*, 502 P.2d 1181 (Wa. 1973) (spillage of gasoline from truck). But some courts have denied strict liability in this situation, either on the grounds that the activity is not all that *unusual*, or on the grounds that the risk could be eliminated by the exercise of reasonable care. See, e.g., *Indiana Harbor Belt Co. v. American Cyanamid Co.*, discussed *infra*, p. 337 (holding that a negligence standard would adequately handle the problem of spillage of flammable materials during transportation).

5. **Nuclear reactor:** The running of a *nuclear reactor* probably gives rise to strict liability. See *supra*, p. 333.

6. **Use of firearms:** The use of *firearms* is sometimes held to trigger strict liability. But as firearms have become more and more pervasive throughout our society, and as techniques for using them safely have become more widespread, activities involving firing of firearms are more likely to be found *not* to be abnormally dangerous.

7. **Construction activities:** Similarly, *construction activities* will generally *not* be ultrahazardous, even if they are somewhat dangerous.

> **Example:** Building an office tower in the downtown part of a densely populated city, using a crane to add each new story, is probably not ultrahazardous. That's because such activities are common in cities, the risk can be almost completely reduced by using careful precautions, and the activity is appropriate for a downtown commercial area. So if a crane operated by D falls on P, P (or his estate) will have to prove negligence by D.

8. **No strict liability for common carrier:** Although a *common carrier* has a special relationship with its passengers, placing upon the carrier the obligation to make reasonable efforts to protect them (see *supra*, p. 199), the common carrier is *not strictly liable* for harm to passengers. In other words, the common carrier merely has to act non-negligently.

F. **Incentives and economic analysis:** One of the main purposes of our tort law system is to produce *economic efficiency* (see *supra*, p. 1). That is, where an activity may injure others, we want to produce the "right" amount of it, by neither under-deterring or over-deterring it. The general regime of negligence in theory does this: if people are liable for damages stemming from their "negligence," and if we define "negligence" by balancing the costs and benefits of the defendant's conduct (see the Learned Hand formula on p. 98, *supra*), then defendants will engage in a "right" or "economically efficient" amount of dangerous activity. One corollary is that strict liability will normally "over-deter," and should therefore be imposed only where a negligence scheme will *not* be sufficient to produce the "right" amount of the activity. This is true even though there may be some irreducible danger from the activity.

> **Example:** D manufactures 20,000 gallons of liquid acrylonitrile, and puts it into a railroad car that it has leased. It then causes the X Railroad to transport this substance to a railroad yard owned by P, located in the Chicago metropolitan area. Acrylonitrile is a hazardous and flammable substance. While the car is in P's railroad yard, it leaks.

Authorities require P to decontaminate the soil at a cost of nearly $1 million. P sues D, arguing that even if D exercised reasonable care in maintaining the rail car and putting the chemical into it, D should be strictly liable because the chemical is by its nature ultra hazardous.

Held, for D. "We have been given no reason ... for believing that a negligence regime is not perfectly adequate to remedy and deter, at reasonable cost, the accidental spillage of acrylonitrile from rail cars. ..." Even though the substance is toxic and flammable, it will not leak from a properly maintained rail car. The accident here was, therefore, caused by carelessness (though it is not clear whose carelessness). Since this type of accident can be completely eliminated by the use of due care on the part of all concerned, there is no reason to make rail transport of the chemical more expensive by imposing strict liability on one party, the shipper/manufacturer. While P claims that it is unduly dangerous to ship toxic or flammable materials through a congested metropolitan area, most railroad routes involve "hubs" that are in metropolitan areas, and routing such cargo around metro areas would be prohibitively expensive and might involve other risks (e.g., the use of poorer tracks). The emphasis is and should be on "picking a liability regime (negligence or strict liability) that will control the particular class of accidents in question most effectively, rather than on finding the deepest pocket and placing liability there." For this type of activity, that liability regime is negligence. *Indiana Harbor Belt R.R. Co. v. American Cyanamid Co.*, 916 F.2d 1174 (7th Cir. 1990).

Note: The author of *Indiana Harbor Belt* was Judge Posner, who before taking the bench was a law professor well known for advocating the application of economics to law. The case illustrates an increasing judicial awareness that when a wider rule of liability is imposed than necessary, costs (in this case, shipping costs) will go up, and that the narrowest rule of liability sufficient to give actors adequate incentive to control risks is all that should be used.

IV. LIMITATIONS ON STRICT LIABILITY

A. **Limitations generally:** Despite the fact that the liability is "strict", the plaintiff does not win her case merely by showing that injury resulted from an abnormally dangerous activity or dangerous animal. One set of limitations on strict liability corresponds to the "proximate cause" limitation on negligence actions. Another set relates to the plaintiff's activities. Most of the discussion below relates to abnormally dangerous activities, though similar principles apply to dangerous animals.

B. **Scope of risk:** Generally, there will be strict liability only for damage which results from the *kind of risk* that made the activity abnormally dangerous. For instance, even though it may be an abnormally dangerous activity to transport dynamite by truck through city streets, a pedestrian run over by such a truck will not be able to claim strict liability, since the risk of hitting pedestrians is not one of the things which makes such transportation abnormally dangerous. Rest. 2d, §519, Comment e.

1. **Abnormally sensitive activity by plaintiff:** A related rule is that the defendant will not be liable for his abnormally dangerous activities if the harm would not have occurred

except for the fact that the plaintiff conducts an ***"abnormally sensitive"*** activity. Rest. 2d, §524A.

> **Example:** D conducts blasting operations, which frighten female mink owned by P, who kill their young in reaction to their fright.
>
> *Held*, D is not strictly liable. The thing that makes blasting operations unusually dangerous is "the risk that property or persons may be damaged or injured by coming into direct contact with flying debris, or by being directly affected by vibrations of the earth or concussions of the air." Here, since P's mink ranch was more than two miles away from the blasting, and there was no unreasonable interference with any other landowners at that distance, the "exceedingly nervous disposition of mink" must be held responsible for the damage, not the blast itself. Strict liability does not protect against "harms incident to the plaintiff's extraordinary and unusual use of land." *Foster v. Preston Mill Co.*, 268 P.2d 645 (Wash. 1954).

2. **Manner in which harm occurs:** In the context of negligence, we saw (*supra*, p. 155) that where the harm which occurs is the kind of danger which made the defendant's conduct negligent, but that harm occurs in an ***unforeseeable manner***, the defendant will generally not be released from liability. But in cases of strict liability, this does not seem to be the case: The defendant will usually be relieved of liability if an unforeseeable cause intervenes, even though the damage is of the same nature as that which made the activity extraordinarily dangerous.

    a. **Act of God:** Thus the intervention of an ***"Act of God"*** is often enough to relieve the defendant of strict liability. For instance, in *Rylands v. Fletcher* itself, the opinion in the Exchequer Chamber stated that the defendant could escape liability by showing that the accident occurred because of "*vis major*, or the act of God" (e.g. a storm of unprecedented severity).

    b. **Restatement view:** But the Second Restatement rejects the "Act of God" exception, as well as any exception for harm caused by the "innocent, negligent or reckless conduct of a third person" (assuming that the harm is of the sort that makes the activity abnormally dangerous). Rest. 2d, §522.

3. **Scope of liability compared with negligence cases:** In summary, most jurisdictions seem to impose liability for a narrower range of consequences in cases involving strict liability, than in cases involving negligence. See P&K, pp. 559-60. (And as previously noted, the scope of liability in negligence is generally narrower than that where an intentional tort is concerned; see *supra*, p. 8.) But the Restatement view referred to above would impose liability for at least as broad a range of consequences as in negligence cases.

C. **Plaintiff's contributory negligence no defense:** Ordinary *contributory negligence* by the plaintiff will usually not bar her from strict liability recovery. This is certainly true in those situations where the plaintiff's contributory negligence consists of being *inattentive*, and not discovering a risk which she should have discovered. In such a situation, the courts simply make a policy decision to place "the full responsibility for preventing the harm resulting from abnormally dangerous activities upon the person who has subjected others to the abnormal risk." Rest. 2d, §524, Comment a.)

1. **Unreasonable assumption of risk:** But if the plaintiff *knowingly, voluntarily* and *unreasonably* subjects herself to the danger, this will be a defense even to strict liability. Here, the plaintiff's conduct is that variety of contributory negligence which is also *assumption of risk*; see *supra*, p. 292.

   Example: Driver sees signs warning her that blasting operations will take place ahead, and that she should take a detour. She nonetheless voluntarily (and unreasonably) decides not to take the detour and is injured by the blast. Her voluntary and unreasonable assumption of the risk bars her from recovery. But if she had merely been inattentive, and had missed the sign, this ignorant contributory negligence would not have been a bar. See Rest. 2d, §524, Comment b.

2. **Assumption of risk:** As just noted, that brand of contributory negligence which is also assumption of risk (i.e., an unreasonable assumption of danger) bars the plaintiff from recovery. Beyond this, assumption of risk which is *reasonable* will nonetheless *also bar* the plaintiff.

   Example: P, an independent contractor, agrees to transport dynamite for D, in a truck owned by P. P understands that dynamite can sometimes explode spontaneously. If such an accident occurs and injures P, P cannot recover from D in strict liability, because P has assumed the risk; this is true whether P acted reasonably or unreasonably. Rest. 2d, §523, Comment d.

3. **P's comparative negligence will reduce recovery:** Furthermore, in a *comparative negligence* jurisdiction, the court will probably *reduce* P's recovery even in a strict-liability action by P's degree of negligence or other fault. For instance, the Third Restatement, in its sections on apportionment, says that comparative-fault principles apply to any person "whose *legal responsibility* has been established," and the comments make it clear that the comparative-fault allocation system should be applied even though D's liability is premised upon strict liability and P's conduct is being evaluated under a fault system. See Rest. 3d (Apport.) §8, and Comment a thereto.

   Example: D conducts blasting operations near a highway, and posts "Keep away — Blasting Danger" signs. P negligently fails to notice the signs, parks at the side of the road, and wanders into the blasting area back to bird watch. In a comparative negligence jurisdiction, P's negligence in disregarding the signs will reduce his recovery from D even if his claim against D is based on strict liability.

V. WORKERS' COMPENSATION

A. **Generally:** We consider now a type of strict liability that is completely statutory in nature: the workers' compensation statute. All states now have adopted such statutes, which basically compensate the employee for *on-the-job* injuries without regard either to the employer's fault or to the employee's. A full treatment of workers' compensation (WC) statutes is beyond the scope of this outline; indeed, most law schools offer a separate course on the subject. However, we cover here some of the most important aspects of these statutes.

1. **No fault:** Essentially, the employer is liable for on-the-job injuries even though these occur ***completely without fault*** on the part of the employer. Thus an employer who has a perfect past safety record, puts warnings on every machine, gives extensive worker training, etc., will still be liable if an employee gets his arm caught in a piece of machinery. Conversely, even considerable negligence by the employee will not reduce the statutory benefits at all — there is neither comparative nor contributory negligence, nor even assumption of risk, under the typical statute. For this reason, employers typically purchase ***insurance*** against WC liability.

2. **"Arising out of employment":** The typical statute covers all injuries "arising out of and in the course of employment." Thus activities which are purely personal are not covered.

3. **Exclusive remedy:** Both employer and employee gain something and give up something by virtue of the WC statute. The employer, as we have already seen, sacrifices the ability to assert her own non-negligence, and the ability to defend on the grounds of the employee's negligence or assumption of risk. But the employee sacrifices too: the WC statute is his ***sole remedy*** against the employer, and he generally receives payments that are substantially less than could be recovered in a common-law tort suit. Most significantly, the employee cannot recover anything for ***pain and suffering***.

   a. **No choice:** In any event, the employee gets no choice: nearly all employees are ***required*** to use the WC rather than tort-law scheme for workplace injuries, whether they want to or not.

B. **Scope of coverage:** Much litigation under WC statutes relates to whether the injury is covered at all, i.e., whether it "arises out of and in the course of employment."

   1. **Pure personal activities:** Purely personal activities, that are not in any sense "required" by the job, are not covered. For instance, if the employee is injured while at lunch, off the employer's premises, this would probably not be covered.

   2. **"To and from":** Injuries suffered by the employee while travelling ***to or from*** work — in other words, injuries while commuting — are typically ***not*** covered. This is generally true even if the employee has done work at home, and is transporting work-related materials from home to work, or vice versa. See, e.g., *Wilson v. Workers' Compensation Appeals Board*, 545 P.2d 225 (Cal. 1976) (teacher who was transporting work done at home to school at the time of a car accident, was not covered; "Because applicant performed work at home for her own convenience, transporting work-related materials to facilitate her work there was also for personal convenience, furnishing no basis for exception from the going and coming rule").

   3. **Attacks by third parties:** Increasingly, compensation statutes are interpreted to cover injuries sustained when the employee is ***attacked by third parties*** while on the job. This is now generally true even when the employee is not given the duty of dealing with the third party as part of his job, and even if the attack occurs after hours, as long as it is somehow related to the job. For instance, if a worker saw a third party carrying company property which the worker reasonably believed to be stolen, and the worker was injured while attempting to reclaim the property, there would probably be coverage even though the rescue effort took place after hours, and even though property-recovery was not an aspect of

the worker's job. See *Martinez v. Worker's Compensation Appeals Board*, 544 P.2d 1350 (Cal. 1976).

4. **Worker fault:** As noted, the worker's own *fault* is generally *not* a ground for denying him coverage of the WC statute. However, most statutes have some exceptions:

   a. **Drunkenness:** Most statutes deny compensation for an injury caused by the *intoxication* of the injured employee. See, e.g., Cal. Lab. Code, §2600.

   b. **Illegality:** Similarly, many statutes provide that if the employee is engaged in *illegality*, he will not be covered. But in recent years many courts have narrowed this exclusion in coverage. For instance, if the employer knows of and tolerates that type of illegality, then the exclusion may be found not to apply. See, e.g., *Matter of Richardson v. Fiedler*, 493 N.E.2d 228 (N.Y. 1986) (roofer who fell to his death while engaged in stealing copper from the building where he was working is covered, because the employer knew about this illegal activity and tolerated it).

   c. **Disregard of safety rules:** About 20 states reduce or bar the worker's remedy if the accident is brought about because the worker willfully disregards *safety regulations*. See Epstein, p. 1029. For instance, a worker who was repeatedly told to wear his safety goggles while welding, and who was then blinded when he refused to wear them, might well be denied recovery in one of these 20 states. (But "ordinary" negligence, as noted, will almost never bar recovery.)

C. **Benefits:** An injured worker recovers "benefits," which are tightly defined by statute. The worker is almost never allowed to recover for pain and suffering, only for direct expenses and loss of earning power. "[A]ll workers' compensation awards have a statutory base which is geared not to the severity of the claimant's injuries as such but only to its [sic] resulting "disability," that is, the degree to which it impairs the worker's earning capacity. The worker who is able to carry on without loss of income notwithstanding some physical impairment may be injured, but has not ordinarily sustained any compensable disability under the statutes." Epstein, p. 1035.

1. **Limit on maximum recovery:** Nearly all statutes place an upper limit on how much can be recovered. A typical scheme ties recovery into the *average wage* of a *typical worker* ("average weekly wage" or AWW). Then, the statute awards some portion of this AWW, for some specified length of time. In most states, a permanently and totally disabled worker receives a figure equal to about two-thirds of the AWW for the rest of the claimant's life (if she remains disabled). Epstein, p. 1036. Most states have special tables for death (typically, 400-500 times AWW). *Id.* Where the worker has lost an organ or limb, the tables also typically specify an award (e.g., 288 times AWW for loss of a leg, in New York).

D. **Exclusivity of remedy:** Probably the most important aspect of WC law, at least for our purposes, is that such compensation is the *exclusive remedy* of the employee against the employer. Thus even if the employer is clearly negligent (e.g., it permits very unsafe conditions, in violation of occupational health and safety laws), and even if the employee is completely blameless, the WC statute provides the employee's sole remedy. Since recovery under the WC statutes is typically lower than where the employee has a valid common law claim against the employer, plaintiffs' attorneys typically try to find a way around the "exclusive remedy" nature of the WC statute. Finding such "work arounds" is a burgeoning area of tort law.

1. **Intentional wrongs:**   The "exclusive remedy" rule is almost always limited to ***non-intentional*** wrongs by the employer. In other words, if the plaintiff can show that the employer intentionally injured him, the employee may pursue a common-law action.

    a. **Safety regulations:**   The most controversial question is whether an employer's knowing violation of ***safety regulations*** can, by itself, constitute an "intentional tort," thus allowing the employee to bring a common law suit against the employer.

        i. **Suit allowed:**   A few cases have allowed such suits where the employer has willfully disregarded safety regulations, even though the employer did not desire to harm the worker.

        ii. **Majority rule:**   But most courts hold that the exception is limited to "***true*** intentional torts." Epstein, p. 1042-44. The majority rule is that the employer's failure to observe safety regulations, or to repair equipment — even if that failure is "knowing" — does not transform her wrongdoing into an intentional tort, and thus does not permit the employee to escape WC as his sole remedy.

            (1) **"Substantially certain injury" not enough in some courts:**   Suppose the plaintiff worker can show that the employer not only knowingly failed to follow some safety procedure, but knew that an injury was ***"substantially certain"*** to occur because of the failure. Under traditional principles of intentional torts, being substantially certain that one's acts will cause a forbidden result is the equivalent of contending that result (see *supra*, p. 6). But courts interpreting state WC statutes have split as to whether mere knowledge of a substantially certain result — as opposed to desiring to bring about that result — qualifies for the intentional-wrong exception. The case set forth in the following statute finds that under the Kentucky statute in question, substantial certainty is not enough.

            Example: The Ds operate a uranium enrichment plant on behalf of the federal government. The Ds never disclose to the Ps (the plant's employees) that dangerous radioactive byproducts of this process are being stored at the plant. The Ps sue the Ds for the exposure, pointing out (correctly) that the Kentucky workers compensation statute does not supply the exclusive remedy where the injury occurs through the "deliberate intention of [the] employer to produce [the] injury." The Ps argue that if, as they claim, the Ds acted with knowledge that their conduct was substantially certain to produce the injury, the deliberate-intention exception applies.

            Held, for the Ds. Under the Kentucky statute, "deliberate intention to produce injury" occurs only when the employer has a *specific intent* to injure an employee — "substantial certainty" may be enough to constitute intent under general tort law, but not under the statute. *Rainer v. Union Carbide Corp.*, 402 F.3d 608 (6th Cir. 2005).

2. **Third parties:** Although the WC statute is supposed to be the "exclusive remedy" of the worker, the remedy is exclusive only as against the employer. In other words, the WC statute virtually never prevents the worker from suing a ***third party*** who, under common-law principles, would be liable for the worker's injuries.

> **Example:** P, while in the employ of X Corp., is injured by a defective drill press sold to X Corp. by D. Although all courts would hold that P is barred from suing X by virtue of the WC statute, P may nonetheless bring a strict product liability action, under common-law principles, against D. The theory behind allowing a suit between P and D is that P's give-up of his right to bring a common-law action against X is the result of a "contract" between P and X (with X purchasing insurance coverage under the WC statute), and D is not an intended beneficiary of that contract.

E. **Application to other areas:** The "no fault" approach of workers' compensation has been so successful overall that some commentators have recommended extending it to other, non-industrial, accidents, and governments have sometimes done so.

1. **Automobile no-fault:** In the area of ***automobile accidents***, about half the states have enacted some limited form of no-fault. Epstein, p. 1048. The statutes vary radically, but most seem to have these elements: (1) for less serious accidents (measured either by lack of serious/permanent injuries, or by low dollar value of property damage or medical expenses), P is entitled to receive limited compensation, generally not including pain and suffering damages, without proving that D was at fault; (2) P usually recovers from his own insurance company first, and that insurance company recovers from D's insurance company; and (3) more seriously-injured plaintiffs keep their conventional tort remedies.

2. **Childhood vaccines:** Another instance in which no-fault has been adopted is the area of vaccines. The National Childhood Vaccine Injury Act of 1986, 42 U.S.C. §§ 300aa-10 to 300aa-33, gives no-fault recovery to children injured by ***childhood vaccines***. Plaintiffs' cases are heard by a special master appointed by a federal judge. A plaintiff who can show that she took a vaccine listed in the act, suffered a malady listed as a possible side effect from that vaccine, and experienced the adverse reaction within a specified time of taking the vaccine, gets the benefit of a strong presumption of liability. In other words, P does not have to show causation directly, and does not have to show that the product was "defective".

   a. **Recovery:** P recovers actual medical expenses, cost of rehabilitation, and compensation for lost earning power. But pain and suffering is limited to $250,000, and punitive damages are not available. After going through this administrative procedure, P can reject the special master's award and sue in tort, but the Act makes a tort award somewhat difficult to obtain (e.g., an appropriate warning is a complete defense, and punitive damages are not allowable). The program design has been quite successful in inducing vaccine injury victims to accept the compensatory award and forego their right to sue in tort.

3. **Victims of 9/11:** One last instance of a federal no-fault scheme is the system set up by Congress to compensate ***victims of the 9/11 terrorist attacks.*** In the Air Transportation Safety and System Stabilization Act (ATSSSA), 49 U.S.C. §40101 et seq., Congress established an optional no-fault administrative-law system for victims who were killed or phys-

ically injured in the 9/11 attacks. About 97% of all eligible families decided to participate in the plan.

Quiz Yourself on
STRICT LIABILITY *(Entire Chapter)*

67. Bugs and Daffy are neighbors. Bugs keeps a Tasmanian Devil as a pet — a mean, vicious beast with slavering jaws. Bugs keeps the Devil in a heavy steel cage in the basement. One day, the Devil chews his way through the bars, tunnels out of the house, and goes to Daffy's house, biting him on the leg. When Daffy sues Bugs, Bugs claims he's not liable because he didn't realize the Devil's dangerous propensities, since the Devil had never escaped before. Who wins? _____

68. Guy Fawkes carefully burns a pile of leaves in his backyard; he moves all flammable objects away from the area, keeps a fire extinguisher on hand, and douses the flames occasionally to keep them under control. However, a strong gust of wind blows up, carrying sparks 50' to a neighbor's shed, setting it afire. The neighbor sues Guy, claiming he's strictly liable for the damage here. Is the neighbor correct? _____

Answers

67. Daffy. Owners of *wild* animals are strictly liable for the damage caused by their animals, regardless of the owner's knowledge of the animal's dangerous propensities. Injuries caused by *domestic* animals (dogs, cats, cows, pigs, etc.) do not give rise to strict liability unless the owner *knows or has reason to know* of the particular animal's dangerous propensities. (The concept is very loosely expressed by the not-really-correct saying "every dog is entitled to one free bite.") Here, the Devil is a "wild" animal (not domesticated, i.e., not "used in service to mankind"), so Bugs is strictly liable.

DISTINGUISHING WILD ANIMALS FROM DOMESTIC ONES: Consider customs in the community, and the utility of keeping the animal.

68. No. The use of fire is not considered an abnormally dangerous activity, and thus not a source of strict liability. Therefore, the neighbor would have to prove Guy was negligent. Since the facts here indicate he was careful, the neighbor will not recover.

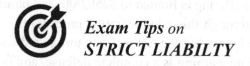

Exam Tips *on*
STRICT LIABILTY

It's easy for an issue of "strict liability" to be hidden in the fact pattern — D isn't doing anything careless, and isn't trying to hurt anyone, so you can miss the fact that D is engaging in an activity as to which strict liability might attach. In this chapter, we're only worried about two types of activity calling for strict liability: (1) the keeping of animals; and (2) "abnormally dangerous" activities.

☞ Whenever your fact pattern mentions an **animal** that does some harm, consider the possibility of strict liability.

☞ If the animal is *"wild,"* there's strict liability for any damage that results from a "dangerous propensity" of the *species*. (*Example:* If D keeps a leopard as a pet, and the leopard bites a neighbor, strict liability applies, even if this particular leopard had never attacked anyone before. This is so because the tendency to attack is characteristic of the species of leopard, and the species is wild rather than domesticated.)

　　☞ If the wild animal customarily *causes humans to be scared*, then an injury caused by P's fright *will* trigger strict liability, since fear-causing would be one of the "dangerous propensities" of the species. (*Example:* D's bear gets loose, and frightens P into having a heart attack. Even if the bear would never have hurt P, fear-causing is one of the species' "dangerous propensities," making D strictly liable.)

☞ If the animal is *"domestic,"* then there's only strict liability where the owner *knows* or has *reason to know* of the *particular animal's dangerous characteristics*. (*Example:* Suppose a dog or a horse bites a neighbor. Since both these species are domesticated, there is no strict liability unless the owner knew that this particular animal had a tendency to bite or otherwise attack, in which case the liability is not truly without regard to fault.)

　　☞ Don't say, "Every dog gets one bite free." If D knew that the dog had *tried* to bite or attack someone before and failed, D is now liable when the dog succeeds.

☛ Most questions relating to this chapter concern *"abnormally dangerous"* activities (ADA) (also known as *"ultra-hazardous"* activities).

☞ The general principle, and a good definition to quote on an exam: "One who carries out an abnormally dangerous activity is strictly liable (that is, liable without regard to fault) for any damage that proximately results from the dangerous nature of the activity."

☞ Common issue: Is the activity in fact *"abnormally dangerous"*?

　　☞ Try to remember this list of factors:

　　　　❑ Existence of a *high degree* of risk of *some* harm.

　　　　❑ Likelihood that if harm does result, that harm will be *great*.

　　　　❑ The *inability* to *eliminate* the risk by use of *reasonable care*.

　　　　❑ The *unusualness* of the activity.

　　　　❑ The *inappropriateness* of the activity to the *place* where it is carried out.

　　　　❑ The extent to which the activity's *value* to the community is *outweighed* by the activity's dangerous attributes.

　　☞ Some activities that are usually considered abnormally dangerous:

　　　　❑ Blasting or other use of *explosives*.

　　　　❑ Operation of a *nuclear power plant*.

　　　　❑ The conducting of research into contagious viruses, biochemical weapons, etc.

　　　　❑ Possibly, the *transporting* of *flammable* or very *toxic* liquids (e.g., propane).

☞ Most frequently-tested ADA issue: Did the type of harm that occurred result from the ***type of risk*** that made the activity abnormally dangerous in the first place? If not, then strict liability for ADA does ot apply. (*Example:* D uses explosive to blast through rock. The blasting frightens nearby cattle, who stampede and hurt themselves. Probably the risk of frightening animals isn't one of the special risks that makes the use of explosives abnormally dangerous. If so, D is not strictly liable for the damage to the cattle.)

☞ ***Assumption of risk*** is a defense to strict liability (whether for ADA or keeping of wild animals). (*Example:* If P sees a sign saying, "Blasting, Keep Out," and P enters anyway and gets hurt, he's probably barred by assumption of risk.)

☞ But ***contributory negligence*** is ***not*** a defense to strict liability. (*Example:* On the above example, if P negligently failed to read the sign about blasting, and didn't know blasting was going on, his carelessness would not eliminate his recovery in a contributory-negligence state.)

   ☞ On the other hand, in a ***comparative negligence*** jurisdiction, P's negligence probably *will* reduce his recovery even in a suit based on strict liability. (*Example*: On the above blasting example, P's recovery probably will reduce his recovery in a comparative-negligence state).

☛ ***Workers' compensation*** statutes are rarely tested. But if P is injured during the course of his employment by D, you should briefly mention that any recovery by P against D will probably be limited by the terms of the WC statute (and that P will not have to prove D's negligence in order to recover this limited amount).

☞ Remember that the WC statute usually provides the ***exclusive*** remedy for the employee against the owner — the employee does not have the option of suing, proving that the employer was negligent, and recovering traditional tort damages.

☞ But also remember that most WC statutes provide an ***exception*** where the employer's wrongdoing is ***intentional***. (However, most courts hold that the employer's failure to observe ***safety precautions*** does ***not*** transform the employer's wrongdoing into an intentional tort, so that WC applies even in this situation.)

CHAPTER 14

PRODUCTS LIABILITY

ChapterScope

"Products liability" refers to the liability of a seller of a chattel which, because of a defect, causes injury (usually personal) to its purchaser, user, or sometimes, a bystander. The term is used here to include both situations where P purchased the item directly from D and those where there was no contractual relationship between P and D.

- **Importance:** Products liability is the fastest-growing, and probably now the most economically significant, branch of tort law.

- **Three theories:** There are three main theories under which a seller of a chattel can be liable to one who is injured: (1) *negligence*; (2) *warranty*; and (3) *strict liability*.

- **Negligence:** The general rules of *negligence* apply to one who sells a product. Most commonly, negligence theory is used to make a manufacturer liable where he failed to use reasonable care in designing, manufacturing or labeling the product.

  - ❏ **Privity:** A negligent manufacturer is liable to a *"remote"* purchaser (one who bought from some intermediary in the distribution channel), or to a "user" or "bystander." In other words, *"privity"* is *not* required. The only requirement is that P have been in some sense a "foreseeable" victim, a requirement that is usually satisfied.

- **Warranty:** There are two main ways in which a seller of goods may be liable under a *warranty* theory when the item causes injuries:

  - ❏ **Express warranties:** A seller may *expressly* warrant that her goods have certain qualities. If the goods turn out not to have these qualities, the purchaser (or, possibly, other affected persons) may sue for this breach of warranty. Most commonly, a seller breaches an express warranty by making a false claim about the product's attributes in advertising or on the label.

  - ❏ **Implied warranty:** Alternatively, an *implied* warranty about the quality of the goods can come into existence from the mere fact that the seller has offered the good for sale.

    - ❏ **Merchantability:** Most importantly, a merchant in goods of a particular type is held to automatically warrant that they are *"merchantable"* (i.e., "fit for the ordinary purposes for which such goods are used").

    - ❏ **Fitness for particular purpose:** Also, a seller may be found to implicitly warrant that the goods are *"fit for a particular purpose"* — this warranty arises where the seller knows that the buyer wants the goods for a particular purpose, and the buyer relies on the seller's recommendation of a suitable product.

- **Strict liability:** Virtually all states apply the doctrine of *"strict product liability."* Under that doctrine, a seller of a product is liable *without fault* for personal injuries (or other physical harm) caused by the product if the product is sold: (1) in a *defective condition* that is (2) *unreasonably dangerous* to the user or consumer.

❏ **Non-manufacturer:** Strict product liability applies not only to the product's manufacturer, but also to its *retailer*, and any other person in the distributive chain (e.g., a wholesaler).

❏ **Unavoidably unsafe products:** A product will not give rise to strict liability if it is *"unavoidably unsafe."* For instance, if a prescription drug causes side effects or allergies in some patients, and there is no way to avoid these, the drug is "unavoidably unsafe" and thus not "defective."

❏ **Warnings:** A product may become "defective" because D has failed to issue a *warning* concerning its use. In general, even if a product is properly designed and properly manufactured, D must give a warning if there is a *non-obvious* risk of person injury from using the product. Similarly, D must give instructions concerning correct use, if incorrect use would create a danger.

▪ **Who may be a plaintiff:** The three theories differ as to who may be a plaintiff. The main area of controversy relates to *"bystanders,"* i.e., one who is neither a purchaser nor user of the product, but who is injured merely because he happens to be nearby. Generally, the negligence and strict liability theories protect any bystander who is "reasonably foreseeable," but courts are split as to whether the warranty theories protect such a bystander.

▪ **Who may be a defendant:** Courts differ in the details of who may be liable under the various theories. Special questions arise, for instance, with respect to sellers of used goods, lessors of goods, and suppliers of services used in conjunction with a good.

▪ **Interests that may be protected:** Special rules also apply where P's damages consist only of property damage, or solely of "intangible economic harm" (e.g., lost profits).

I. NEGLIGENCE

A. **Negligence and privity:** There is no reason why the general principles of negligence, discussed previously, could not apply in a case in which personal injury has been caused by a carelessly manufactured product. Historically, however, the use of negligence theory for such purposes was drastically limited by the requirement of *privity*, i.e., the requirement that, in order to maintain an action, the plaintiff must show that he contracted *directly* with the defendant.

   1. *Winterbottom v. Wright:* The privity requirement stems from an 1842 English case, *Winterbottom v. Wright*, 152 Eng.Rep. 402. In *Winterbottom*, the driver of a mail coach was injured when the coach broke down due to a lack of repair. He sued the defendant, who had contracted with the post office to keep the coach in good condition. The court held that since the defendant's original duty of repair arose out of a contract, that duty extended only to the other contracting party (the post office). Since the plaintiff never contracted with the defendant, his lack of privity meant that he could not recover, *either in contract or tort*.

B. **Historical development:** During the seventy years following *Winterbottom*, the courts modified that rule to permit negligence suits without privity where personal injury occurred from an "inherently dangerous" defective product. A consumer who was made sick by contaminated food, for instance, could sue the manufacturer, even though she had made her purchase from a retailer; the food was said to be "inherently" or "imminently" dangerous.

1. ***MacPherson v. Buick:*** Determining whether a product was "inherently dangerous", however, was difficult and uncertain. In 1916, Judge Cardozo rejected the "inherent danger" requirement in negligence actions, in the landmark case of ***MacPherson v. Buick Motor Co.***, 111 N.E. 1050 (N.Y. 1916), *infra*, p. 372.

   a. **Facts of *MacPherson:*** The defendant in *MacPherson*, Buick Motor Co., made a car which it sold to a retail dealer. The dealer in turn sold it to the plaintiff. Due to defective spokes in one of the wheels, the car collapsed and injured the plaintiff. Although Buick had purchased the wheel from someone else, there was evidence that Buick could have discovered the defect by reasonable inspection.

   b. **Holding:** Judge Cardozo held that the plaintiff could recover for negligence, despite the fact that he was not in privity with the defendant. His right of recovery arose out of tort law imposed by the court, not out of contract. Furthermore, it was not necessary for the plaintiff to show that cars are in general "inherently dangerous". Instead, the test should be whether the product was "reasonably certain to place life and limb in peril when negligently made. . . . " If so, a negligence action may be brought even without privity.

   c. **Significance:** *MacPherson* thus established the general principle that once the plaintiff shows that the product will be unreasonably dangerous ***if defective***, he may sue in negligence without privity. The effect of this holding was virtually to abolish the rule of *Winterbottom* in a case where a negligently made product caused personal injury.

2. **Acceptance of *MacPherson:*** ***Every state*** has now accepted *MacPherson*. It is therefore universally the rule that ***one who negligently manufactures a product*** is liable for ***any personal injuries proximately caused by his negligence.*** See Rest. 2d, §395.

   a. **Property damage:** Furthermore, most courts now allow negligence recovery where it is only ***property damage***, not personal injury, which results. See P&K, p. 683.

   b. **Economic harm:** However, if the plaintiff suffers ***only economic harm*** (e.g., lost profits suffered because a defective machine does not work), the courts are split as to whether he may recover for this harm from a remote seller. The subject is discussed more extensively *infra*, p. 405.

   c. **Bystanders:** Where the plaintiff is a ***casual bystander*** (as opposed to a purchaser or other user of the product), he can recover in negligence if he can show that he was a "***foreseeable plaintiff***". For instance, a pedestrian who is injured when a defectively made automobile crashes into him could recover if can show the manufacturer's negligence, since it is reasonably foreseeable that a defective automobile may injure a pedestrian.

C. **Classes of defendants:** Not only manufacturers, but also ***retailers, bailors,*** and other suppliers may have negligence liability.

   1. **Manufacturers:** The manufacturer is of course the person in the distribution chain most likely to have been negligent. His duty of due care includes the following aspects:

a. Design: The obligation to use due care to *design* the product in a reasonably safe way. (See *infra*, p. 372.)

b. Manufacture: The duty to set up reasonably error-free *manufacturing procedures*.

c. Inspection and testing: The duty to perform reasonable *inspections* and *tests* of the finished products.

d. Packaging and shipping: The duty to *package* and *ship* the product in a reasonably safe way. See generally, Rest. 2d, §395, Comments e and f.

e. Assembly of parts made by another: If the final "maker" of the product produces it by assembling *components* made by others, he may be negligent if he does not take reasonable care to obtain them from a reliable source. Also, he probably has an obligation to make a *reasonable inspection* of the components (or at least samples) before he incorporates them. See Rest. 2d, §395, Comment g.

f. Manufacturer of component assembled by another: Conversely, the *component-part manufacturer* will be liable if he fails to use reasonable care to design a safe product, even though that product is not sold directly to the public, but is instead incorporated into a larger unit. See the discussion of component parts manufacturers *infra*, p. 396.

2. Third person's failure to inspect: Suppose the manufacturer negligently makes the product, and someone further along in the distribution chain (e.g. the retailer) has an obligation to inspect the product, and fails to do so adequately. Does this negligence in inspection let the manufacturer off the hook? The answer is almost always "no." Thus a car maker which tried to absolve itself of liability for negligent manufacture on the grounds that its dealer had the duty to make a final inspection for obvious defects would lose; see *Vandermark v. Ford Motor Co.*, 391 P.2d 168 (Cal. 1964). See Rest. 2d, §396; see also *supra*, p. 173.

a. Effect on manufacturer's liability: Although the mere failure of the retailer to make an inspection (even one he is obliged to make) will not by itself relieve the manufacturer of liability, if the retailer *does* make such an inspection and learns of a defect, or actually learns of a danger through some other means, and fails to warn the customer, many courts hold that this conduct is so gross that it *breaks the chain of causation*, and absolves the manufacturer of liability.

3. Retailers: A retailer who merely resells the product manufactured by another is much less likely than the manufacturer to be successfully charged with negligence. The mere fact that she has sold a negligently manufactured or designed product is not by itself enough to show that she failed to use due care, since she may have had no duty to inspect, or even if she had, no chance of finding the defect. For this reason, *suits against retailers are now generally brought on warranty* (*infra*) or *strict liability* (*infra*, p. 358) theories, rather than negligence. There are, nonetheless, a few situations in which the retailer may be negligent.

a. Reason to know of danger: If the retailer knows, or should know, that the product is unreasonably dangerous, she is negligent if she does not at least *warn* her customers. Rest. 2d, §401.

   b. **Duty to inspect:** In the absence of a particular reason to believe that the product may be dangerous, the retailer ordinarily has *no duty to inspect* the goods. Rest. 2d, §402. This is true even if there is a defect which *could have been discovered* by a very simple and superficial examination.

   i. **Minority view:** But a minority of courts impose on the retailer a duty to make at least such a simple superficial examination, and if she does not do so, she is liable in negligence for any defect which she would have discovered. See Pr. L. Nut., p. 54. This is particularly likely to be the case where the retailer is a *car dealer* (either of new or used cars), where the effect of a defect is likely to be severe, and the retailer is likely to have much greater expertise in inspection than the buyer. Pr. L. Nut., *ibid.*

   c. **Sales to minor, etc.:** A seller may have negligence liability if she fails to use reasonable care to avoid selling a product to a person *incapable of using it safely.* Selling weapons to a child would be an example of such negligence. P&K, 1988 Pocket Part, p. 93.

4. **Other suppliers:** Other classes of defendants may also have negligence liability. For instance, bailors of real property (e.g., rent-a-car companies), sellers and lessors of real estate, and suppliers of services (e.g., blood transfusions) may all be negligent. The general products liability status of these persons (including their status under warranty and strict liability theories) is discussed *infra*, p. 394.

II. WARRANTY

A. **Historical importance of warranty:** Historically, a purchaser of goods has always been able to sue his immediate seller on the grounds that the goods were not as they were contracted to be. Such an action was generally brought under the name "breach of warranty". If the buyer could show that the seller made representations, or warranties, either expressly or implicitly, about the quality of the goods, and that these representations turned out to have been false, the buyer could win, *even in the absence of negligence* on the part of the seller. Thus the fact that the seller reasonably and honestly believed her representations to be true, and in fact could not possibly have discovered the defects in the product, was irrelevant; furthermore, the fact that the defects were due to someone else's negligence (or to no one's negligence at all) was also irrelevant.

1. **Hybrid between tort and contract:** Since warranties arose, at common law, only in situations where there had been an actual contract of sale, the action had many contract law aspects to it. For instance, the contract statute of limitations usually applied, as did the contract measure of damages (including damages for purely economic loss, which was not true in negligence actions).

2. **Tort aspects:** But certain aspects of tort law have also been grafted onto warranty law. Perhaps the most notable instance of this is the tendency of the last twenty years to dispense, partially or completely, with the requirement of *privity*. As is discussed below, many if not most states today allow a suit for breach of warranty to be brought against the seller by one other than the person who made the immediate purchase from that seller.

3. **Confused state of the law:** Warranty law is made even more confused by the fact that the Uniform Commercial Code (UCC), in effect in every state except Louisiana, attempts to deal statutorily with warranties. Yet the case law of warranty has gone its own way, often ignoring the UCC statutory language.

4. **Scope of discussion:** The treatment of warranty which follows addresses primarily the rules of the UCC. However, where case law has departed from the UCC, these departures are indicated.

5. **Express v. implied warranties:** There are two general sorts of warranties, "express" and "implied" ones. Because the rules governing the two classes differ in important respects, they are treated separately.

B. **Express warranties:** A seller may *expressly represent* that her goods have certain qualities. If the goods turn out not to have these qualities, the purchaser (or, possibly, other affected persons — see the discussion of privity below) may sue for this breach of warranty.

> **Example:** P buys a Model A Ford from St. John Motors, a Ford dealer. Before the sale, Ford had given its dealers brochures, one of which describes the Model A's windshield as "Triplex, shatter-proof glass . . . So made that it will not fly or shatter under the hardest impact." While P is driving the car, a pebble hits the windshield, making the glass shatter, in turn damaging P's eyes.
>
> *Held*, Ford expressly warranted that the glass was shatter-proof, and P had a right to rely on these representations, particularly since their falsity was not readily apparent. Furthermore, P may recover from Ford for breach of the warranty even though he purchased not from Ford, but from a dealer. *Baxter v. Ford Motor Co.*, 12 P.2d 409 (Wash. 1932). See *infra*, p. 441, p. 457.

1. **UCC version:** The UCC section governing express warranties is §2-313. It provides that an express warranty may be produced by an "***affirmation of fact or promise***" about the goods, by a ***description of the goods*** (e.g., "shatter-proof glass"), or by the use of a ***sample or model*** (e.g., a TV store's use of a floor model would be an express warranty to a customer that any set of the same model has the same general characteristics).

    a. **Reliance:** Under original common law warranty theory, the plaintiff had to show that he actually ***relied*** on the warranty. But the UCC, and most modern non-UCC case law, have watered down this requirement; under UCC §2-313 the only requirement is that the warranty be "part of the basis of the bargain".

    b. **Privity:** Persons not in privity with the defendant-seller, may recover for breach of express warranty. In order to do so, it is probably not necessary for the non-privity plaintiff to show that ***he himself*** was even aware of the express warranty. See Pr. L. Nut., pp. 27-28.

        i.   **Representation expected to reach plaintiff:** Some courts hold that a plaintiff not in privity with the seller must be at least a member of a class that the seller ***intended to reach*** with her express warranty. For instance, if the defendant could show that she made the warranty to a particular purchaser, in response to the purchaser's own needs, and that there was no expectation that the product would ever be re-sold, the second buyer would not be protected.

    ii. Warranties to public: But many express warranties (e.g., the warranty of shatter-proofness in *Baxter*) would probably be held to be addressed to the public at large, and a remote buyer, user, or even passer-by, might be held to be part of the general class to which the warranty was addressed.

2. **Strict liability:** Observe that a defendant's liability for breach of an express warranty is in reality a kind of *strict liability*, i.e. liability without regard to fault. As long as the plaintiff can show that the representation was not in fact true, it does not matter that the defendant reasonably believed it to be true, or even that she could not possibly have known that it was untrue.

3. **Restatement "misrepresentation" claim:** The Second Restatement establishes a tort action that is quite similar to a breach of express warranty claim. §402B imposes strict liability on a seller who "makes to the public a misrepresentation of a material fact" about the product.

C. **Implied warranty:** The existence of a warranty as to the quality of goods can also be *implied* from the fact that the seller has offered the good for sale.

1. **Warranty of merchantability:** The UCC imposes several implied warranties as a matter of law. The most important of these is the *warranty of merchantability*. §2-314 (1) provides that " . . . a warranty that goods shall be merchantable is implied in a contract for their sale if the seller is a merchant with respect to goods of that kind."

    a. **Meaning of "merchantable":** The Code offers no simple explanation of what makes goods "merchantable." But one of the factors listed by §2-314(2) is that to be merchantable, the goods must be *"fit for the ordinary purposes for which such goods are used."*

    Example: A car which, because of manufacturing defects, has a steering wheel that does not work, is not "merchantable," since it is not fit for the ordinary purpose — driving — for which cars are used. Therefore, if such a car made by Manufacturer and driven by Owner hits Pedestrian, Pedestrian may recover from Manufacturer for his injuries on a breach-of-implied-warranty theory.

        i. Packaging: To be merchantable, the goods must also be "adequately contained, packaged, and labeled. . . . " (§2-314(2)(e)). And they must conform to any "promises or affirmations of fact" that are made on the label (§2-3143(2)(f)). (If they do not, this would also be a breach of express warranty, as discussed above.)

    b. **Requirement that seller be a "merchant":** The implied warranty of merchantability arises, under the Code, only if the seller is a *"merchant with respect to goods of that kind."* This requirement imposes two important practical limitations:

        i. Requirement of businessperson: First of all, the seller must be, in effect, a businessperson.

        ii. Regular sale of that kind of goods: Second, he must regularly sell the kind of goods in question. Thus a businessperson who is selling a piece of equipment which he once used but no longer needs makes no implied warranty of its merchantability, since he does not regularly deal in that kind of machine.

c. **Used goods:** It is not clear whether there can ever be an implied warranty of merchantability for **used goods**, even if the seller deals in goods of that kind (e.g., a used car lot). Liability of such used goods dealers, including possible strict liability, is discussed *infra*, p. 395.

d. **Food and drink:** The UCC merchantability warranty applies explicitly to "the serving for value of food or drink to be consumed either on the premises or elsewhere". §2-314(1).

e. **Services:** But the Code itself does not apply to **services**, real estate transactions, or bailments. Some courts have applied portions of warranty theory to such transactions by analogy; this is discussed *infra*, p. 401.

f. **Retailers:** A retailer who did not manufacture the product is nonetheless held to have impliedly warranted its merchantability, simply because she has sold it (assuming that she deals in goods of that kind).

   i. **"Sealed container" doctrine:** However, a few jurisdictions have carved out an exception to the Code, known as the *"sealed container" doctrine*. That doctrine provides that a retailer who resells a "sealed container" does not warrant the merchantability of the contents. This is usually justified on the grounds that the retailer has no ability to inspect; but since warranty liability is not based on failure to inspect or other fault anyway, it is hard to see how this exception makes sense. Georgia, Mississippi and Tennessee are among the states applying the doctrine. Pr. L. Nut., pp. 55-56.

2. **Warranty of fitness for a particular purpose:** A seller may also implicitly warrant that the goods are *"fit for a particular purpose"*. This warranty arises, under UCC §2-315, when the seller knows that the buyer wants the goods for a particular (and not customary) purpose, and the buyer *relies on the seller's judgment* to recommend a suitable product. The warranty is that the goods are in fact suitable for that special purpose.

   Example: Consumer tells Shoe Dealer that he wants a pair of shoes for mountain climbing. Dealer recommends Brand X, on the grounds that they have good traction. If the shoes turn out not to have good traction, and Consumer falls, he can sue Dealer for breach of the implied warranty of fitness for a particular purpose.

3. **Privity:** Breach of warranty, as noted, started out as basically a contract action. Courts were therefore reluctant to permit a plaintiff to recover for breach of implied warranty against a manufacturer, or other person within the distributive chain, with whom the plaintiff had not directly contracted.

   a. **Food cases:** However, as with negligence actions, courts developed exceptions to the privity requirement. For instance, in cases of defective food, the manufacturer was held to impliedly warrant that his products were of reasonable quality, and this warranty "ran with the goods", so that anyone who consumed them could sue.

   b. ***Henningsen v. Bloomfield Motors, Inc:*** Then in 1960, the case of *Henningsen v. Bloomfield Motors, Inc.*, 161 A.2d 69 (N.J. 1960), *infra*, pp. 356, 357 drastically restricted the privity requirement in warranty cases in almost exactly the same way as

MacPherson v. Buick (*supra*, p. 349) had restricted the privity requirement for negligence actions.

i. **Facts of *Henningsen:*** The defendant, Chrysler Corporation, produced a car with a defective steering mechanism. One of its dealers, Bloomfield Motors, sold the car to Mr. Henningsen, who gave it to his wife. She was injured when the steering failed.

ii. **Holding:** The court held that Mrs. Henningsen could recover from Chrysler for breach of the implied warranty of merchantability (imposed by the then-effective Uniform Sales Act, a predecessor of the UCC). She could recover notwithstanding the fact that she never contracted with Chrysler directly.

iii. **Similarity to food cases:** The court saw no reason not to apply to this case the rationale of the food cases, referred to above, and not to require privity. "The unwholesome beverage may bring illness to one person; the defective car, with its great potentiality for harm to the driver, occupants and others, demands even less adherence to the narrow barrier of privity."

iv. **Consumer is cultivated:** Furthermore, the court said, it is clear that under modern mass merchandising techniques, the ultimate "consumer", not the initial dealer, is the person being cultivated by advertisements. It is therefore not unfair to impose on the manufacturer responsibility to this ultimate consumer.

v. **Disclaimer ineffective:** The contract that Mr. Henningsen had signed with Bloomfield Motors contained a disclaimer of all warranties (except for a limited agreement to repair defective parts). The court held that this disclaimer was an ***"adhesion contract"***, and resulted from "the gross inequality of bargaining positions" between the manufacturer and the consumer. Therefore, the disclaimer was ruled invalid. See the further discussion of disclaimers *infra*, p. 357.

vi. **Non-purchaser status of Mrs. Henningsen:** Mrs. Henningsen failed to be in privity with Chrysler in two ways: First, as noted, Chrysler had sold the car through its dealer. Second, the actual purchase was made by Mr. Henningsen, and given as a gift to his wife. The court held that this second lack of privity was no more a barrier to recovery than the first. Mrs. Henningsen was "a person who, in the reasonable contemplation of the parties to the warranty, might be expected to become a user of the automobile." Therefore, she was covered by it.

Note on vertical v. horizontal privity: Some courts have distinguished between the lack of "vertical" privity, and the lack of "horizontal privity". Mr. Henningsen failed to be in vertical privity with Chrysler, because there was an intermediate seller. Mrs. Henningsen failed to be in horizontal privity even with the dealer, because she was merely a user, and member of the same household, as the actual purchaser from the dealer. The distinction was formerly of importance, but the general abandonment of privity requirements in warranty cases (except in cases of purely economic loss — see *infra*, p. 404) renders it of only minor significance today.

c. **Reaction to *Henningsen:*** Almost all states have now accepted both aspects of the privity part of *Henningsen*. That is, they hold that a manufacturer's (or other distributor's) warranty extends to remote purchasers further down the line, and they also hold that once the final purchaser is covered by the warranty, the warranty also applies to, at least, members of the household who may reasonably be expected to use the goods.

    i. **Strict liability:** However, many of the decisions rejecting privity have been in *strict liability* suits. In general, warranty suits have been used less and less as strict liability has increased, because many of the "sales law" aspects of warranty, (e.g. the requirement that notice of the breach be given by the injured person) are really unsuited for personal injury cases.

  d. **UCC privity rules:** The original 1962 version of the UCC, in §2-318, provided that if the final purchaser was a beneficiary of a warranty, any member of his family or household, and any houseguest, was also covered, "if it is reasonable to expect that such person may use, consume or be affected by the goods", and was personally injured by the breach.

    i. **Vertical privity not mentioned:** This provision thus in effect abolished the "horizontal" privity requirement, at least for family members, houseguests, etc. But it did not say anything about vertical privity; that is, it left completely unanswered (intentionally) the question of whether a manufacturer's warranties extended to a remote purchaser. For instance, if *Henningsen* had occurred under the UCC, nothing in the Code would have indicated to the court whether Mr. Henningsen was covered by Chrysler's warranty.

    ii. **Left to case law:** Instead, resolution of this "vertical" privity question was left to case law. And, as noted, nearly every jurisdiction abolished the "vertical" privity requirement, at least in cases of personal injury.

    iii. **Rejection of Code limitations:** Most courts simply ignored the vertical privity limitations imposed by the original version of §2-318. For instance, they held that an employee of the purchaser of a defective product, or a bystander injured by the driver/purchaser of a defective car, could recover. Some courts also rejected that section's limitation to personal injury cases, and held that a person who suffered only property damage could recover in warranty against a remote seller.

  e. **1966 Amendments:** In response to this fast-moving case law, two new alternative versions of §2-318 were officially promulgated in 1966. The original §2-318, discussed above, is now called "Alternative A".

    i. **All foreseeable users:** "Alternative B" extends warranty protection to "any natural person who may reasonably be expected to use, consume or be affected by the goods and who is injured in person by breach of the warranty." Thus, the employee of the purchaser, or even a casual bystander injured by a defective car, may both sue the manufacturer for warranty, under this section.

    ii. **Property damage:** "Alternative C" goes even further. It protects all the people that Alternative B protects, and also allows them to recover even if they suffer *only property damage*. Furthermore, a *corporation* or other non-natural person may sue.

f. **Adoption by states:** Most states still have Alternative A on their books (although, as noted, courts have simply ignored its limitations in many situations). But a significant number have now adopted either Alternative B or C. New York, for instance, changed to Alternative B in 1975.

g. **Summary on privity:** In summary, virtually all states would allow one who has actually purchased goods to recover on implied warranty, even though her purchase was made from a dealer, not the defendant. Furthermore, many if not most states, either by statute or case law, would permit a non-purchaser whose use of (or presence near) the product is foreseeable, to recover against the manufacturer or other person in the distributive chain, at least if personal injury is involved.

D. Warranty defenses: Most defenses to products liability claims are discussed in a separate section *infra*, p. 406. Here, we consider three defenses that are virtually unique to warranty claims: disclaimers, limitation of remedies, and notice-of-breach requirements.

1. **Disclaimers:** A seller may, under the UCC, *disclaim* both implied and express warranties.

a. **Disclaimer of merchantability:** A seller may make a written disclaimer of the warranty of merchantability, but only if it is *"conspicuous"*. UCC §2-316(2). This is usually interpreted to mean that the disclaimer must be in capital letters or bold print, not hidden in the fine print. Furthermore, the word "merchantability" must be specifically mentioned.

i. **Implied limitations:** Apart from this express disclaimer of the warranty of merchantability, the circumstances may occasionally give rise to an *implied* disclaimer. The most common situation is when used goods are sold *"as is"*. See UCC §2-316(3).

b. **Federal warranty act:** Federal law now limits disclaimers in written warranties. The Magnuson-Moss Federal Trade Commission Improvement Act of 1974, 15 U.S.C. §2301, *et. seq.*, provides that if a written warranty is given to a consumer, there cannot be any disclaimer of any implied warranty. The manufacturer does not have to make a written warranty at all, but once he does so, the warranty must include the implied warranty of merchantability.

2. **Limitation of consequential damages:** Rather than (or in addition to) disclaiming implied warranties, a seller may often try to *limit the remedies* available for breach. Frequently, for instance, the seller will provide that any remedy is limited to *repair or replacement* of the defective product, and that there shall be no liability for consequential damages.

a. **Code restrictions:** However, the Code restricts the ways in which the seller may do this. The most important of these, at least in personal injury cases, is given by §2-719(3), which states that "limitation of consequential damages for injury to the person in the case of consumer goods is *prima facie* *unconscionable*. . . ." In other words, if the product is designed for personal (as opposed to business) use, any provision limiting remedies to repair or replacement will not be upheld by the court, if personal injury has resulted. Thus had the UCC been in effect in New Jersey at the time of *Hen-*

ningsen, the court could have knocked out the "liability limited to repair or replacement" clause without resorting to common law principles.

  i. Commercial loss: That same Code section, §2-719(3), also provides that where the loss from a breach of warranty is "commercial" (i.e., intangible economic loss in a business setting), a limitation of damages is ***not*** unconscionable.

 3. Notice of breach: Under the UCC, the buyer must "within a reasonable time after he discovers or should have discovered any breach", ***notify the seller*** of the breach. UCC §2-607(3).

  a. Plaintiff not in privity: But if the plaintiff is not in privity with the defendant, this notice-of-breach requirement is ***frequently not enforced***. This is particularly likely to be the case where the plaintiff was not a purchaser of the goods at all, but rather, a user or bystander.

E. Phasing out of warranty suits: A plaintiff not in privity with the defendant seller may therefore, in many situations, bring a warranty claim without being barred by the disclaimer, limitation-of-remedies, or notice-of-breach defenses. But once these defenses are eliminated from warranty actions, the warranty case (at least where based on an implied, rather than express, warranty) is virtually ***identical*** to a ***strict tort liability*** claim, discussed below. For this reason, the use of implied warranty claims in this situation has decreased in recent years.

 1. Useful cases: But there are still a few non-privity situations where it may be to the plaintiff's advantage to sue on implied warranty rather than strict liability.

  a. Pure economic harm: Some states may allow a plaintiff who has suffered ***only economic harm*** to recover in implied warranty against a remote seller, where this would not be allowed in strict liability. See *infra*, p. 404.

  b. Statute of limitations: Warranty actions are usually held to fall within the contract statute of limitations. In UCC cases, this is four years. Strict liability cases, on the other hand, generally fall within the tort limitations period, which is usually shorter, often two or three years. Assuming that the two statutes start to run at about the same time (not always a correct assumption), the plaintiff may therefore still have a warranty claim after his strict liability claim has been barred.

 2. Privity action: And where the plaintiff has dealt ***directly*** with the defendant, he will often be much better off suing under implied warranty. For one thing, he will have no trouble recovering a broad range of consequential damages, including lost profits and other intangible economic harm.

III. STRICT LIABILITY

A. Historical emergence: Implied warranty suits, as noted, provide for "liability without fault", in the sense that negligence by the defendant does not have to be proven. However, these actions have many contract aspects that are illogical where there is no privity between the plaintiff and the defendant. For this reason, many courts, starting with the case set forth in the following example, have abandoned the language of "implied warranty," and have allowed recovery for "***strict tort liability.***"

Example: D1 manufactures, and D2 retails, the "Shopsmith," a power tool that can be used as a saw, drill, or wood lathe. P sees one on display, and has his wife buy it for him. While he is using it as a lathe, a piece of wood clamped to the machine flies out and hits him on the head, severely injuring him. P does not give timely notice of breach of warranty to D1, as is required in warranty actions by California law.

Held, by Justice Traynor, P's failure to give notice of breach does not bar his action, since D1 is strictly liable in tort. "A manufacturer is strictly liable in tort when an article he places on the market, knowing that it is to be used without inspection for defects, proves to have a defect which causes injury to a human being." The law of sales warranties is not a good way to protect consumers like P, because of requirements (like the notice-of-breach requirement) that are suitable only for commercial transactions. (The liability of D2 was not discussed.) *Greenman v. Yuba Power Products, Inc.*, 377 P.2d 897 (Cal. 1963).

B. Restatement Second §402A: In 1965, two years after *Greenman*, a similar doctrine of strict tort liability was embodied by a Tentative Draft of the Second Restatement, in §402A. This section has become far and away the most famous and influential provision of the entire Second Restatement. Its importance is so great that we set it out here in full:

§402A. Special Liability of Seller of Product for Physical Harm to User or Consumer:

(1) One who sells any product in a defective condition unreasonably dangerous to the user or consumer or to his property is subject to liability for physical harm thereby caused to the ultimate user or consumer, or to his property, if

(a) the seller is engaged in the business of selling such a product, and

(b) it is expected to and does reach the user or consumer without substantial change in the condition in which it is sold.

(2) The rule stated in Subsection (1) applies although

(a) the seller has exercised all possible care in the preparation and sale of his product, and

(b) the user or consumer has not bought the product from or entered into any contractual relation with the seller.

1. Popular acceptance: Section 402A "literally swept the country." P,W&S, pp. 733. It is probably safe to say that a substantial majority of American jurisdictions have adopted, if not the precise rules set forth there, at least the general theory of strict tort liability for dangerously defective products.

2. Non-manufacturer: Observe that §402A applies not only to the product's manufacturer, but also to its *retailer*, and any other person in the distributive chain (e.g., a wholesaler) who is in the business of selling "such a product." Non-manufacturer liability is discussed further *infra*, p. 394.

C. Third Restatement on Products Liability: In the 30-plus years after Rest. 2d §402A was published, the law of product liability underwent massive evolution and expansion. The drafters of Restatements (the American Law Institute) decided to draft an entirely new Restatement to deal with this evolution. Therefore, a full-volume portion of the Third Restatement of Torts, a portion known as the ***Restatement Third of Torts: Products Liability***, was published in

1997. (We call it the *"Third Restatement"* here, for short.) This set of provisions represents a dramatically new approach to products liability. We reproduce the two central sections of the Third Restatement's product-liability provisions here:

§1 Liability of Commercial Seller or Distributor for Harm Caused by Defective Products

One engaged in the **business of selling or otherwise distributing products** who sells or distributes a defective product is subject to liability for **harm to persons or property caused by the defect.**

§2 Categories of Product Defect

A product is **defective** when, at the time of sale or distribution, it contains a **manufacturing defect**, is defective in **design**, or is defective because of **inadequate instructions or warnings**. A product:

(a) contains a **manufacturing defect** when the product **departs from its intended design even though all possible care was exercised** in the preparation and marketing of the product;

(b) is **defective in design** when the **foreseeable risks of harm posed** by the product **could have been reduced or avoided by the adoption of a reasonable alternative design** by the seller or other distributor, or a predecessor in the commercial chain of distribution, and the **omission of the alternative design renders the product not reasonably safe**;

(c) is **defective** because of **inadequate instructions or warnings** when the **foreseeable risks of harm** posed by the product **could have been reduced or avoided by the provision of reasonable instructions or warnings** by the seller or other distributor, or a predecessor in the commercial chain of distribution, and the **omission** of the instructions or warnings **renders the product not reasonably safe**.

1. **Our approach:** In the discussion that follows, we'll be talking about the approaches of both the Second Restatement (§402A) and the Third Restatement. Because the Third Restatement's product-liability provisions have been around for less than 20 years as of this writing, the Second Restatement's provisions have been subjected to a much wider range of judicial opinions. But the Third Restatement is becoming extremely influential, and we therefore talk about it a lot.

D. **What products meet the test:** Under the approach of the Second Restatement, the principal issue is often whether the product is *"defective"* and *"unreasonably dangerous."*

1. **Term of art:** The Comments to Rest. 2d §402A do not define the term "defective condition" apart from the term "unreasonably dangerous." Instead, the overall phrase "defective condition unreasonably dangerous" is used as a term of art. The basic idea seems to be that a product is in a "defective condition unreasonably dangerous" if it is "dangerous to an extent beyond that which would be contemplated by the ordinary consumer who purchases it, with the ordinary knowledge common to the community as to its characteristics." (§402A, Comment i).

    a. **"Viewpoint of the consumer" test:** In other words, if a reasonable consumer, knowing the true characteristics of the product, would nonetheless use it, the product is not "in a defective condition unreasonably dangerous."

2. **Third Restatement drops "unreasonably dangerous" requirement:** The Third Restatement drops the requirement that to be defective, a product must be "unreasonably dangerous," at least with respect to manufacturing (as opposed to design or warning) defects. §1 of the Restatement says that "one engaged in the business of selling or otherwise distributing products who sells or distributes a defective product is subject to liability for harm to persons or property caused by the defect." §2 then defines what constitutes a "defective product," by breaking down defects into manufacturing defects, design defects or instruction/warning defects. A "manufacturing defect" is said to exist "when the product *departs from its intended design* even though all possible care was exercised in the preparation and marketing of the product." §2(a). So a manufacturing defect exists whenever the product does not live up to the design, and there is *no need for the plaintiff to show* that the product was *"unreasonably dangerous"* (or even "dangerous" at all), as the Second Restatement required.

   a. **Design and warning defects:** But the Third Restatement does *not* abandon the concept of unreasonable dangerousness in the case of *design* defects or *warning* defects. In these latter two situations, the defect is only deemed to exist if the design or omission of warnings "renders the product not reasonably safe." Rest. 3d (Prod. Liab.) §§ 2(b) and 2(c). This is part of the Third Restatement's decision to insert negligence-based concepts, and a risk-utility approach, into the design and warning contexts. See *infra*, p. 372 (design) and p. 381 (warnings).

E. **Unavoidably unsafe products:** Some products might be thought of as being *"unavoidably unsafe."* These are products that conform to their design, and essentially do what the consumer expects them to do, yet are by their very nature *inherently dangerous*. Here are some products usually thought to be unavoidably unsafe:

   ❏ *prescription drugs* that, in order to perform their therapeutic functions, have inevitable *side effects*.

   ❏ *cigarettes*, which in order to give the smoking satisfaction that customers expect, will inevitably *cause disease* in many users.

   ❏ *handguns*, which in order to be capable of being fired in the way users expect, pose some risk of *firing unintentionally*.

   Courts and commentators have struggled for decades about the appropriate product-liability treatment for such unavoidably unsafe products.

1. **Second Restatement's exemption:** The Second Restatement, in the well-known Comment k to §402A, effectively *exempted* unavoidably-unsafe products from the general rule of strict liability. Under Comment k, so long as a product could not be made safe without *changing its fundamental characteristics*, sale of the product would not lead to product liability if the seller supplied an adequate warning of the dangers.

   a. **Rabies vaccine example:** Comment k gave the example of *rabies vaccine*: the vaccine often leads to serious side effects, yet has great value since it helps prevent an otherwise invariably-fatal disease. "Such a product, properly prepared, and accompanied by proper directions and warning, is not defective, nor is it unreasonably dangerous."

b. Criticism: However, the approach of Comment k — giving a blanket exemption to any product that could not be made safe — has been frequently criticized, on the grounds that some unavoidably unsafe products are so dangerous that society would be better off if the product was not sold at all, rather than being sold with immunity from tort liability.

2. Third Restatement takes risk-utility view: The Third Restatement takes a quite different approach to the problem of the unavoidably-unsafe product. To understand this approach, first understand that the problem posed by the unavoidably-unsafe product is essentially a *design* problem: there is no manufacturing problem (the particular cigarette or gun or drug conforms to its design), and instead the problem is that the product's design makes it inherently unsafe. But the Third Restatement does not impose strict liability at all for design defects (see *infra*, p. 373); instead, the Restatement imposes a *risk-utility* approach, under which a product is defective in design "when the *foreseeable risks of harm posed* by the product *could have been reduced or avoided by the adoption of a reasonable alternative design* by the seller ... and the omission of the alternative design renders the product not reasonably safe." Rest. 3d (Prod. Liab.) §2(b). It then follows that "no separate rule about unavoidable dangers is required under the [Third] Restatement. Instead, the question is *whether the product is reasonably safe.*" Dobbs, p. 989.

a. Whether utility outweighs risks: Under the Third Restatement's approach, it still makes *some* difference that the product is unavoidably unsafe. But the equation becomes a direct balancing of utility versus danger, with no consideration of any alternative design (because, by hypothesis, there *is* no alternative design that would reduce the risks while keeping intact the essential benefits of the product). So as one commentator summarized the effect of the new Restatement's approach to unavoidably unsafe products, "If the utility of [these] products outweighs these irreducible risks, they are *not* defective. If dangers outweigh the unavoidable risks, the logic of the risk-utility is that they *are* defective." Dobbs, p. 989 (emph. added). (But keep in mind that the product will also be deemed defective if it is not accompanied by a reasonable warning where one is feasible. See *infra*, p. 383.)

Example: Suppose that P is injured when she dives into a plastic above-the-ground swimming pool made by D. The injury occurs because the plastic bottom of the pool is slippery, and P's hands slip apart as they touch the bottom, causing her head to slam into the bottom. Assume that it is in the inherent nature of above-the-ground plastic swimming pools that their surfaces are slippery, and that there is no good way to design around this problem while still using plastic.

A court following the Third Restatement's approach would simply ask whether the utility of such a plastic pool outweighs the unavoidable danger inherent in the design. If so, P would not be permitted to recover on a defective-design theory, since the product would be deemed non-defective (assuming that all reasonable warnings were given and that there was no manufacturing defect). If, on the other hand, the court decided that the social utility of such a pool was so low that its dangers outweighed that utility, then the design would be deemed defective even though the danger was unavoidable in all above-ground plastic pools.

3. **Prescription drugs and medical devices:** *Prescription drugs and medical devices* present a special case of the unavoidably-unsafe problem. Such drugs and devices are usually of very high social utility, yet often have very serious, completely unavoidable, side effects. Courts have always tended to give an automatic or near-automatic *exemption* from liability for such drugs and devices, assuming that they have been approved by the FDA and further assuming that the warnings given with them are adequate.

   a. **Special Third Restatement rule:** The Third Restatement has a special rule for prescription drugs and medical devices. To understand why, first notice that ordinary products have essentially the same utility, and pose the same risks, to *all* consumers. Therefore, in judging such ordinary products the court can reasonably do a *single* risk-utility balance. But drugs and devices are very different: person *A* may respond very differently to a particular drug than person *B*, so the risk-reward computation would be very different for *A* than for B. Consequently, the Third Restatement says that a defective-design claim can be brought in the case of a prescription drug or medical device only "if the foreseeable risks of harm posed by the drug or medical device are sufficiently great in relation to its foreseeable therapeutic benefits that reasonable health-care providers, knowing of such foreseeable risks and therapeutic benefits, would not prescribe the drug or medical device for *any class of patients*." Rest. 3d (Prod. Liab.) §6(c). In other words, if there is even a *single group* of patients for whom the drug or device could sensibly be prescribed, then *no patient* (even a member of a different class) may bring a design-defect against the maker. The Comments to this part of the Restatement say that "given this very demanding objective standard, liability is likely to be imposed only under unusual circumstances." Comment f to §6.

   Example: D, a pharmaceutical company, sells PregLast, a prescription drug designed to prevent premature pregnancies. The company has learned from its testing that in a small number of cases, users of the drug will suffer significant heart damage for which they will require open-heart surgery. Although P is not at especially high risk for giving birth prematurely, her doctor prescribes PregLast for her. P develops heart damage caused by the drug. She sues D, alleging that the drug was defectively designed, in that its side effects outweigh its utility.

   In a court following the Third Restatement's approach, D will win as long as it can show that there is *some* group of patients for whom a reasonable doctor would conclude that the medical benefits from the drug outweigh the side effects. Cf. Rest. 3d (Prod. Liab.) §6, Illustr. 1. The fact that P may not have been a member of such a group will be irrelevant. (All of this assumes that D supplied P's doctor with adequate warnings of the side effects — if not, P will be able to prevail on a failure-to-warn theory; see *infra*, p. 381.)

   i. **Consequence:** Notice how revolutionary the Third Restatement's drug rule is. It "seems to mean that manufacturers of drugs and related products *need not exercise reasonable care under a risk-utility balance to make a safer drug*. To get this protection, the drug must provide benefits in excess of harms, but it still need not be as safe as it could be with reasonable cost or effort." Dobbs & Hayden (5th), p. 728, n. 7.

ii. Courts reject Restatement's approach: The first courts to consider the Restatement approach (promulgated in 1998) have *rejected* it. See, e.g., *Bryant v. Hoffman-La Roche, Inc.*, 585 S.E.2d 723 (Ga.App. 2003), rejecting the approach, criticizing it for "the fact that a consumer's claim could easily be defeated by expert opinion that the drug had some use for someone, despite potentially harmful effects on a large class of individuals," and stating that to date, no court had adopted it. See also Dobbs & Hayden (5th), p. 728, n. 7.

F. Unknowable dangers: Related to the *"unavoidably unsafe"* problem is the "unknowably unsafe" problem. Suppose that at the time a product is designed and manufactured, given the state of technology there is simply *no way* (at least at acceptable expense) for the manufacturer to *discover* that a particular danger lurks within the product. Suppose further that had the manufacturer somehow known of the danger, an alternate design could have been selected. When the unforeseen danger finally strikes, may the manufacturer be held liable for defective design, or for that matter failure to warn of the unknown defect?

1. Most courts answer "no": The substantial majority of courts that have considered the question have answered *"no"* — there is *no duty to either design around, or warn against, a danger that could not reasonably have been foreseen* at the time of design and manufacture. Dobbs, p. 991. As the idea is sometimes (though ambiguously) expressed, the manufacturer may assert a *"state of the art"* defense. See, e.g., *Vassallo v. Baxter Healthcare Corp.*, 696 N.E.2d 909 (Mass. 1998) ("[W]e hereby revise our law to state that a defendant will not be held liable under an implied warranty of merchantability for failure to warn or provide instructions about risks that were not reasonably foreseeable at the time of sale or could not have been discovered by way of reasonable testing prior to marketing the product.")

2. Third Restatement agrees: The Third Restatement agrees with this prevailing approach. A design defect exists only "when the *foreseeable* risks of harm posed by the product could have been reduced or avoided by the adoption of a reasonable alternative design" (§2(b)); an unknowable danger by definition does not pose a "foreseeable risk of harm," and thus cannot cause a design to be defective. Similarly, a defect due to failure-to-warn exists only "when the *foreseeable* risks of harm posed by the product could have been reduced or avoided by the provision of reasonable instructions or warnings" (§2(c)); here, too, the unknowable danger does not pose a "foreseeable risk of harm," so the failure to warn about it does not constitute a defect. (For more about warnings of unknowable dangers, see *infra*, p. 388.)

Example: D manufactures and sells fire-resistant roof construction materials, exposure to which turns out, decades later, to materially increase the risk of a particular type of Acute Lymphocytic Leukemia (ALL). Assume that this risk was not reasonably foreseeable to one in D's position at the time D sold the product to Contractor, who installed it in P's house. Years later, P gets ALL that can be traced to his exposure to the material sold by D. If P brings a suit for either product defect or failure to warn, in most courts (and under the Third Restatement), P will not prevail, because D had no duty to warn of a risk, or avoid dangers from a risk, that was not, at the time of sale, foreseeable.

G. Food products: Courts have struggled with whether there should be a separate standard for *food products*: how should the "defectiveness" of food be measured?

1. **Foreign/natural distinction:** Some courts have made a distinction between *"foreign"* material and *"natural"* material in the food. Under this approach, there is strict liability for "foreign" matter found in food (e.g., a piece of metal inside a can of tuna fish), but no strict liability for the vendor's failure to remove a naturally-occurring substance from the food (e.g., bone fragments in canned tuna, or pits in cherries). See, e.g., *Mexicali Rose v. Superior Court*, 822 P.2d 1292 (Cal. 1992) (no strict liability for chicken bone in enchilada, because the injury-producing substance "is natural to the preparation of the food served, [and therefore] was reasonably expected by its very nature [so that] the food cannot be determined unfit or defective.")

2. **The majority's "consumer expectation" standard:** Most courts, however, have applied a *"consumer expectations"* test, under which the food product is defective if and only if it contains an ingredient that *a reasonable consumer would not expect it to contain*. This is also the approach of the Third Restatement; see §7, stating that "a harm-causing ingredient of the food product constitutes a defect if a reasonable consumer would not expect the food product to contain that ingredient."

   > **Example:** Consider the chicken enchilada at issue in *Mexicali Rose, supra.* The Third Restatement's commentary says that "although a one-inch chicken bone may in some sense be 'natural' to a chicken enchilada, depending on the context in which consumption takes place, the bone may still be unexpected by the reasonable consumer, who will not be able to avoid injury, thus rendering the product not reasonably safe." Comment b to Rest. 3d (Prod. Liab.) §7.

H. Warning: A product may be held to be defective and unreasonably dangerous partially because it does not carry an *adequate warning*.

1. **Negligence aspects:** While failure to give an adequate warning is sometimes treated as giving rise to strict liability, it has strong overtones of negligence (i.e., would a reasonable person give a warning, and if so, what would she say in the warning?). The duty to warn is therefore discussed in a separate section, where both negligence and strict liability aspects are treated. See *infra*, p. 381.

I. Obvious dangers: Suppose the product's dangerousness is *obvious* to the consumer. Does this very obviousness itself prevent the product from being defective? Courts have struggled mightily with this question. The answer has usually depended on just how the court defines "defect."

1. **Second Restatement's "consumer expectation" standard may bar recovery:** Many courts follow the Second Restatement's approach to meaning of "defect," and that approach makes it hard to recover for an obvious danger. Under Rest. 2d §402A, a product is defective if, considering its reasonably foreseeable use, it is in an unreasonably dangerous condition "not contemplated by the ultimate consumer." Rest. 2d §402A, Comment g; see also Dobbs, p. 981. If that ultimate consumer can easily see that the product is dangerous in a particular way, the manufacturer has a strong argument that the product is not defective under this definition. And, indeed, many courts following the "consumer expec-

tations" test have held that a danger that is obvious to any reasonable consumer cannot constitute a defect.

> **Example:** To virtually any adult member of American society today, cigarettes are obviously dangerous, in that they cause cancer, heart disease, etc. Therefore, a court following the "consumer expectations" test might well reason that regardless of whether a safer version of the ordinary cigarette might be designed, the standard version produced today cannot be defective because its dangers are well-known. See Dobbs, p. 983.

2. **Third Restatement's approach:** The tendency of the consumer-expectations test to make obviousness a fatal bar to recovery has been much criticized, especially in design cases. In a design case, the consumer may know of the product's dangers, but not necessarily know that there are safer alternatives; in this situation, "the consumer's ignorance of safer designs hardly seems like a good reason to deny liability if a safer design is in fact cheap and useful, but the consumer expectation test has been used in just that way." Dobbs, p. 983. Therefore, the Third Restatement takes a different approach, in which obviousness is *merely one, non-dispositive, factor* on the issue of defectiveness. That Restatement's handling of the obviousness problem varies depending on whether the defect is a defect in manufacturing, design or warnings.

   a. **Manufacturing defects:** The problem of obvious defects will rarely matter in the case of a *"manufacturing"* defect, under the Third Restatement. A product contains a manufacturing defect "when the product departs from its intended design," (§2(a)) and that seems to be so even if the departure is or should be obvious. (However, in a jurisdiction applying comparative fault, plaintiff's recovery might be reduced on account of her failure to notice an obvious defect. See Rest. 3d (Prod. Liab.) §17, Comment d.)

   b. **Design defects:** It is in design-defect cases that the Third Restatement's handling of the obviousness problem is most likely to be different from the Second Restatement's consumer-expectations test. The comments to the Third Restatement's definition of design defects say that the definition "does not recognize the obviousness of a design-related risk as precluding any finding of defectiveness. The fact that a danger is open and obvious is *relevant* to the issue of defectiveness, but *does not necessarily preclude a plaintiff* from establishing that a reasonable alternative design should have been adopted that would have reduced or prevented injury to the plaintiff." Comment d to Rest. 3d (Prod. Liab.) §2.

   > **Example:** Suppose that P smokes cigarettes made by D for 20 years, then gets lung cancer as a result. Under the Third Restatement approach, even if D can show that at all times P knew that cigarettes frequently cause lung cancer, P would not necessarily lose on the issue of whether the cigarettes were defective. For instance, suppose P can show that D knew that a cigarette with satisfactory taste could be developed that would be much less likely to cause cancer and that could be manufactured for the same price. If so, under the Third Restatement P might be able to convince the court that D's standard cigarettes were defective despite the obvious risk they posed.

   c. **Failure to warn:** In *failure-to-warn* cases, by contrast, even under the Third Restatement the obviousness of the danger makes it very likely that the lack of a warning will *not* constitute a defect. The Restatement commentary says that "in general, a product seller is *not* subject to liability for failing to warn or instruct regarding risks and risk-avoidance measures that *should be obvious to, or generally known by, foreseeable product users*." Comment j to Rest. 3d (Prod. Liab.) §2. The comments explain that warnings of an obvious or generally known risk "will not provide an effective additional measure of safety," and may even have the bad consequence of "diminish[ing] the significance of warnings about non-obvious, non-generally-known risks." *Id.*

   i.   Cigarette suits: One context in which the duty to warn of arguably obvious dangers arises is that of *cigarettes*. For years, smokers have been suing the tobacco companies, arguing that cigarettes are defective. Many of these suits have been brought on a failure-to-warn theory, and the industry has defended them by asserting, among other things, that the dangers were obvious, and that product-label warnings were in any event adequate. Since the beginning of the 21st century, however, the tobacco industry has not infrequently lost or settled these failure-to-warn suits.

J.   Proving the case: The plaintiff in a strict liability case must prove a number of different *prima facie* elements. The things she must prove are not very different from those she would have to prove in a negligence case, particularly a negligence case relying on *res ipsa loquitur*. It is true that the plaintiff does not have to prove that the manufacturer (or retailer) failed to exercise due care, but she must still establish the following elements, each of which we'll consider in more detail:

❑   that the item was *made or sold by the defendant*;

❑   that the product was *defective*;

❑   that the defect *caused* the plaintiff's injuries; and

❑   that the defect *existed* when the product *left the defendant's hands.*

1.   Manufacture or sale by defendant: The plaintiff must show that the item was in fact manufactured, or otherwise placed in the stream of commerce, by the defendant. (Strict liability applies to anyone in the business of selling goods of the type in question, whether or not she is the manufacturer — see *infra*, p. 394.)

2.   Existence of defect: The plaintiff must show that the product was *defective*; the difficulties of showing this are discussed above, and also in the treatment of design defects *infra*, p. 372.

   a.   Subsequent remedial measures: To prove that the product was defective, particularly in cases of alleged design defect, the plaintiff will often try to show that the defendant subsequently *redesigned* the product to make it safer. Most courts apply a general rule that such evidence is *inadmissible* to prove the defectiveness, on the grounds that to allow it would discourage manufacturers from doing such redesigning. This rule developed in negligence cases, prior to the adoption of strict liability.

      i.   Refusal to apply to strict liability: The California Supreme Court, in a strict liability case, refused to apply a statute barring such redesign evidence, holding that the statute was intended to apply only to negligence cases. *Ault v. International Harvester Co.*, 528 P.2d 1148 (Cal. 1975).

ii. **Admissible to show cost:**   Other courts have held that despite the general rule against such evidence, the fact that the defendant made a redesign can be admitted for the limited purpose of rebutting the defendant's argument that the product is not "defective" because to remove the danger would be unduly costly, and the product is really therefore "unavoidably unsafe". Thus in *Incollingo v. Ewing*, 282 A.2d 206 (Pa. 1971), a case alleging that a drug manufacturer failed to give an adequate warning of the dangers of its drug, the plaintiff was permitted to introduce the fact that subsequent packaging contained a more detailed warning, for the limited purpose of showing that the increased warning "was not costly or burdensome to [the defendant] in relation to the risk or danger involved."

b. ***Res-ipsa*-like inference:** When P is trying to prove that there was a defect, she will often get the benefit of a *res-ipsa*-like inference, if the accident was of a type that usually doesn't occur except on account of a product defect. This inference is discussed further *infra*, p. 370.

c. **Toxic torts:**   In the increasingly-important category of cases called ***"mass toxic torts,"*** it is often especially difficult for the plaintiff to prove that the product was "defective." Here are two examples of fact patterns presenting this problem: (1) the defendant manufactures "Agent Orange," used as a defoliant in Vietnam, and Vietnam Veterans claim that they have gotten cancer years later from ingesting the substance; and (2) the defendant drug manufacturer makes a prescription drug, DES, used by pregnant women, whose children then later claim to have been injured by the drug.

i. **Epidemiological proof:**   Human beings get sick from a wide variety of causes, so it will generally be hard to say that Agent Orange, DES, or some other allegedly toxic substance in fact damages human beings. Controlled experiments on human beings will generally not be possible. Therefore, the plaintiff is left with two possible methods in most instances: (1) she can present the results of animal studies; or (2) she can introduce ***epidemiological*** evidence of defectiveness. Since substances often do not affect animals the same way they affect people, courts and juries take proof based on animal studies somewhat skeptically. Therefore, the plaintiff will often have to show defectiveness by epidemiological studies, which rely on statistical techniques. That is, the plaintiff typically offers expert testimony by an epidemiologist that, say, the daughters of women who took DES in pregnancy have five times the incidence of the cancer adenocarcinoma between the ages of 15 and 30 than do similar women whose mothers did not take the drug. A court is likely to hold that such expert testimony — based not on a showing of *how* the product harms people, but merely on the statistical proof that the condition is more prevalent when the substance is used — is enough to allow the jury to find that the product is "defective."

By the way, two terms — ***"general causation"*** and ***"specific causation"*** — have evolved to differentiate between a substance's tendency to increase the risk of a given illness, and the substance's having caused that illness in a particular individual. Thus the Third Restatement explains that " '*general* causation' exists when a substance is ***capable of causing a given disease*** [whereas] '*specific* causation' exists when exposure to an agent ***caused a particular plaintiff's disease***." Rest. 3d

(Liab. Phys. & Emot. Harm) §28, Comment c. (See *infra,* p. 371 for more about the general/specific distinction.)

3. **Causation:** The plaintiff also has to show that the product, and its defective aspects, were the *cause in fact*, and the *proximate cause*, of her injuries.

    a. **Rebutting alternative causes:** This means that she may have to rebut the defendant's suggestion that alternative events were the sole cause in fact of the accident, or that they were *superseding causes* that prevented the defect from being a proximate cause. The issue arises most frequently in the case of the defendant's allegation that the plaintiff, or some third person, was *negligent.* However, most courts are quite liberal about letting the plaintiff at least get to the jury on this issue.

    Example: P accidently tries to start his Oldsmobile by turning the ignition while the automatic transmission selection lever shows "drive"; the car starts, leaps forward, and injures P and his family. P sues the manufacturer of the automobile, GM. At trial, he produces an expert who testifies that, after the accident, he tested the car and found that it would start in the "drive" position, and that the front wheels accelerated almost immediately.

    Held, the jury could properly find that the car did indeed start in the "drive" position, and that this was a defect which existed at the time of manufacture. The trial judge's direction of the verdict for the defendant was therefore erroneous. *Friedman v. General Motors Corp.*, 331 N.E.2d 702 (Ohio 1975).

    b. **Intervening acts:** In determining whether an *intervening act* is superseding or not, the courts seem to be applying pretty much the same rules in strict liability cases as in negligence ones. Thus if the occurrence of the intervening act is reasonably foreseeable, or it is unforeseeable but causes the same type of harm as made the product dangerous, the intervention will probably not be superseding. See Prod. L. Nut., p. 250.

        i. **Slightly stricter test:** However, because strict liability does not depend on any fault by the defendant, the courts may be slightly quicker to find a superseding cause than in negligence cases, particularly where that cause is the *negligence or recklessness of the plaintiff or a third person.*

        ii. **Misuse of product:** Negligence by the plaintiff or a third person may also provide the defendant with an argument that the product was "misused", and therefore not defective at all. This defense is discussed *infra*, p. 410.

    c. **"Toxic" torts:** Causation is especially important in one category of cases, those involving a plaintiff's claim that exposure to a *toxic substance* made or sold by D caused a disease or illness in plaintiff. Such "toxic torts" frequently require the plaintiff to use epidemiological proof of causation. For more about such proof, see *infra*, p. 370.

4. **Defect existed when in hands of defendant:** As a final element of proof, the plaintiff must show that *the defect existed at the time the product left the defendant's hands*. In the case of a suit against a manufacturer, where the product has gone through several intermediate suppliers and has then been used for a time by the plaintiff before the accident, this can be a very hard thing to do.

a. Lenient courts: But here, as in the case of showing that a defect was the proximate cause of the accident, the courts are frequently lenient to the plaintiff. For instance, in *Friedman, supra*, testimony by the dealer who had sold plaintiff the car to the effect that no one had adjusted the transmission after the car left the factory, and plaintiff's own testimony that he had never tried to start the car in "drive" (thus affording no opportunity to discover the defect) were enough to allow the jury to conclude that the defect existed when the car left the factory.

b. *Res ipsa* inference: In many strict liability cases, an inference similar to that of ***res ipsa loquitur*** is permitted. That is, from the fact that the product did not behave in the usual way, plus evidence that the accident was of a kind that usually happens as the result of a product devect, plu general evidence that no one tampered with the product after it left the defendant's hands, the jury may be allowed to conclude that the product was defective, and that the defect existed when the goods left the defendant's hands.

i. Third Restatement agrees: The new Third Restatement agrees that juries should be allowed to make this *res-ipsa*-like inference. Rest. 3d (Prod. Liab.) §3, entitled " Circumstantial Evidence Supporting Inference of Product Defect," says that "It may be ***inferred*** that the harm sustained by the plaintiff was caused by a product defect existing at the time of sale or distribution ... ***without proof of a specific defect***, when the incident that harmed the plaintiff: (a) was of a kind that ***ordinarily occurs as a result of product defect***; and (b) was ***not***, in the particular case, solely the result of ***causes other than product defect*** existing at the time of sale or distribution." This section functions in a way that is almost perfectly analogous to *res ipsa*: P is relieved from proving the specific defect as long as she shows that the accident is one that would ordinarily not happen without a defect, and there is no affirmative evidence pointing to other causes.

Example: The Restatement gives this example: P buys a new car and drives it 1,000 miles without incident. When she is stopped at a red light, the seat suddenly collapses backwards, causing P to hit the accelerator, so that the car is propelled into traffic and hit by another car. The collision causes a fire that consumes the seat assembly. On these facts, the Restatement asserts that "the incident resulting in the harm is of a kind that ordinarily occurs as a result of product defect," and then concludes that consequently, P does not need to establish that the seat assembly contained either a manufacturing defect or a design defect. Rest. 3d (Prod. Liab.) §3, Illustr. 3.

K. Epidemiological proof: In ***mass toxic tort*** cases, it is likely to be especially difficult for the plaintiff to prove that the substance made by the defendant was the ***cause in fact*** of the plaintiff's injuries. As with respect to proving whether the product was "defective" at all (*supra*, p. 367), the plaintiff is likely to use ***epidemiological*** evidence in an attempt to show that the substance made by the defendant was the cause in fact of the plaintiff's own particular injuries. First, of course, P must show she used a substance made by D. Then, if P can find an expert epidemiologist to testify that a particular medical condition is, say, 10 times as likely to occur when a person uses the defendant's product than where she does not, the court may permit the jury to infer that this evidence, if believed, sufficiently establishes cause in fact.

1. **Victories by defendants:** Conversely, if the plaintiff cannot come up with epidemiological evidence in her toxic tort case, or if the defendant's evidence is more convincing, the defendant may well prevail even though the plaintiff used the defendant's product and got very sick. For example, many cases have been brought against Merrell Dow Pharmaceuticals alleging that the anti-nausea drug Bendectin, made by Merrell Dow, when taken during early pregnancy, causes birth defects. Yet, Merrell Dow has won the vast majority of these cases, because plaintiffs have been unable to come up with credible epidemiological evidence that the children of women who took the drug early in pregnancy have materially more birth defects than those who did not. More and more frequently, courts will even overturn a jury verdict for the plaintiff, on the grounds that the plaintiff's expert epidemiological testimony was not credible.

    a. **Victory by plaintiffs:** But it is now somewhat easier than before for a plaintiff to prove that the defendant's product was the cause in fact of the plaintiff's injuries, at least in federal cases. In *Daubert v. Merrell Dow Pharmaceuticals, Inc.*, 113 S.Ct. 2786 (1993), a Bendectin case, the Supreme Court *lowered the standard* for epidemiological and other scientific evidence when used in federal trials. According to *Daubert*, a scientific theory *need not be "generally accepted" to be admissible*, and even the fact that the theory or evidence has never been published or peer reviewed is not fatal — so long as the evidence is, loosely speaking, "scientific knowledge," in the sense that it has been or is capable of being "tested," it may be admitted. See the fuller discussion of *Daubert*, *supra*, p. 146.

2. **General causation used to prove specific causation:** Exactly how does epidemiological evidence work to establish "cause in fact"? Before we analyze this question in detail, recall (see p. 368) the terms *"general causation"* and *"specific causation"* — general causation is a substance's tendency to increase the general incidence of a given disease, and specific causation is the substance's having caused plaintiff's own disease. Courts normally require *proof of specific causation* as part of the plaintiff's prima facie case. However, if plaintiff's only direct proof on the causation issue is proof of general causation, courts will nonetheless permit the jury to infer specific causation if the proof of general causation is sufficiently strong, so long as there is also some evidence that the plaintiff was actually exposed to the agent.

3. **The "doubling" rule:** So how much proof of general causation ought to be required before the jury will be permitted to infer specific causation? That is, how much must the agent be shown to have raised the general incidence of the disease before the jury will be permitted to infer, if it wishes, that the agent caused the plaintiff's own disease? Many courts have imposed the so-called *"doubling rule"*: the jury will be permitted to infer specific causation if and only if P shows that the agent *more than doubles the incidence of the disease* in the population as a whole. These courts reason that without a doubling, it is not "more likely than not" (the relevant preponderance-of-the-evidence standard) that the agent caused P's particular disease.

    a. **Criticism of the doubling rule:** But the doubling rule has been heavily *criticized*. Indeed, the Third Restatement explicitly *rejects* the doubling rule, stating that depending on other factors (like whether P has been exposed to other agents that also increase the risk of the disease in question) "an increase of the incidence of disease *less than a*

doubling may be sufficient to support a finding of causation, while in another case, even an ***increased incidence greater than two may not be sufficient.***" Rest. 3d (Liab. Phys. & Emot. Harm) §28, Comment c(4).

L. **Bystanders and other non-user plaintiffs:** ***Any person who is injured*** due to a dangerously defective product may recover, even if the plaintiff never bought the product. Thus ***family members of buyers, bystanders,*** even ***rescuers,*** may all recover if their injuries are proximately caused by the defect in the product. As the idea is sometimes put, "***privity***" is ***not required*** for strict product liability.

> **Example 1:** Consumer buys a car from Dealer. The steering wheel fails due to a manufacturing defect, causing the car to swerve and hit Ped, a pedestrian walking on the sidewalk. Ped can recover from Dealer in strict product liability, because his physical injuries were proximately caused by a defective product sold by Dealer. The fact that neither Ped nor any member of his family ever purchased the product in question doesn't matter.

> **Example 2:** X buys a sport parachute from SportsStore, a sporting goods retailer. Due to a manufacturing defect, the parachute opens 2 seconds too late during a sky dive by X. X hits the ground in a remote mountainous location and breaks his leg. (He would have landed on the target, and with no injury, had the chute opened on time.) P, a paramedic, hikes with two others into the mountains to rescue X. While doing so, he falls into a crevasse and is injured.

> P can recover from SportsStore in strict product liability — the defect in the product sold by SportsStore proximately caused P's injury (it was reasonably foreseeable that a parachute's failure to operate properly due to defective manufacture would cause a rescue effort in which the rescuer might be injured), so the fact that P wasn't a user, and wasn't injured directly by the product, won't matter. Nor will it matter that SportsStore had no way to know of the existence of the defect.

IV. DESIGN DEFECTS

A. **Design defects distinguished from manufacturing ones:** There are two fundamental kinds of product defects. One might be termed a "manufacturing defect"; this is the case where the particular item that injures the plaintiff is different from the other ones manufactured by the defendant, because something went wrong with the manufacturing process. For instance, the defective spokes in *MacPherson v. Buick, supra,* p. 349 and the defective steering gear in *Henningsen, supra,* p. 354, are manufacturing defects.

1. **Design defect defined:** The other major kind of defect is usually called a ***"design defect":*** All of the similar products manufactured by the defendant are the same, and they all bear a feature whose design is itself defective, and unreasonably dangerous.

B. **Aspects of negligence:** Most design defect claims have heavy negligence aspects, even though they may be couched in strict liability terms. Normally, the manufacturer either is actually, or should be, aware of the safety attributes of his design. The manufacturer of a power mower, for instance, which does not have a guard shielding the user's foot from the blade, ought to be aware of the potential for harm. A suit against that manufacturer, therefore, whether phrased in negligence or strict tort, would involve substantially identical issues, i.e., whether the defendant chose a design that posed an unreasonable danger to the plaintiff, in view of the burdens of using some other design (e.g., a full guard).

1. **Alternative tests:** Both California and New Jersey, in fact, apply a combined negligence and strict liability test for design defects. There will be a design defect if *either* (1) the design's dangers *outweigh its utility* (negligence or risk-utility analysis) or (2) the design does not perform *as safely as a reasonable consumer would expect,* when used for an intended or reasonably foreseeable purpose (strict liability or "consumer expectations" test, see *supra* p. 360). *See Barker v. Lull Engineering Co., Inc.,* 573 P.2d 443 (Cal. 1978) (also discussed *infra*, p. 378), and *O'Brien v. Muskin,* 463 A.2d 298 (N.J 1983).

    a. **"Consumer expectations" test:** The *"consumer expectations"* test, as set out by the *Barker* court, is noteworthy for two reasons. First, it defines the "defectiveness" of a design in terms of the *consumer's expectations*; a product is defective if it fails to perform as safely as an ordinary consumer would expect. Secondly, the issue is the safety of the product when used *either* in the intended way or in a *"reasonably foreseeable"* way. Thus where the use ought to have been reasonably foreseen by the manufacturer, the manufacturer cannot defend on the ground that that use was not the "intended" one.

C. **Third Restatement's approach:** The Third Restatement adopts a *risk-utility test* as the *sole* test for defective design. Because the Third Restatement approach has already had considerable influence in the few years since its publication, we consider it in some detail here.

1. **Text of definition:** The Third Restatement defines a product as being "defective in design" "when the *foreseeable risks of harm posed* by the product *could have been reduced or avoided by the adoption of a reasonable alternative design* by the seller or other distributor, or a predecessor in the commercial chain of distribution, and the omission of the alternative design *renders the product not reasonably safe*." Rest. 3d (Prod. Liab.) §2(b).

2. **Based on negligence:** You can see that this definition is essentially a negligence-like, *risk-utility-balancing*, standard: the "foreseeable risks of harm" posed by the defendant's design are to be measured against a "reasonable alternative design" that could have been used.

    a. **Represents trend away from strict liability:** This emphasis on negligence represents a *trend* in design-defect cases. "Recent years have seen a shift, reflected in the [Third Restatement] and in some case law, *away from strict liability for design defects.*" Dobbs & Hayden (5th), p. 729.

3. **The "reasonable alternative design" (RAD):** Ordinarily, the plaintiff will have to prove that there indeed existed a *"reasonable alternative design"* (we'll abbreviate it *"RAD"*) that would have been materially safer. (There are a couple of quasi-exceptions which we'll discuss below.) This is a necessary but not sufficient condition to plaintiff's recovery: the plaintiff loses if she doesn't show the existence of an RAD, but does not necessarily win even if she does show an RAD (she still has to show that the existing design is so unsafe that failure to use the RAD "renders the product not reasonably safe").

a.   What P must prove: It's not clear just how specific the plaintiff's proof of an RAD must be. The comments to the Restatement say that it "does ***not*** . . . require the plaintiff to produce a ***prototype*** in order to make out a prima facie case." Comment f to Rest. 3d (Prod. Liab.) §2. So probably fairly ***general*** evidence about how the product could have been made safer will usually suffice.

i.   Other products' safety features: One of the best ways for plaintiff to show the existence of a reasonable alternative design, of course, is for her to show that ***similar products*** from ***other manufacturers*** already have such an alternative design.

Example: Suppose that P is badly injured in a car accident, when the car she is driving hits a barrier and rolls over; the roof crumples, crushing P's skull. P's claim against the manufacturer, D, is based on the theory that it is foreseeable for cars to roll over in collisions, and that a safer design would be one that included crash-resistant "roll bars" embedded in the roof. If P can show that many cars of the same general price, type and model year as P's have such an embedded roll bar, this showing will probably meet the requirement of a reasonable alternative design.

ii.   Cost and utility: It is clear that the ***cost*** and ***utility*** of the RAD proposed by the plaintiff are to be considered. If using the RAD would result in a doubling of the price of the whole product, for instance, that fact weighs heavily against a conclusion that the RAD is indeed a "reasonable alternative." Similarly, if the safety feature that the RAD contains causes the product to be much less useful to the category of users at whom the original product was aimed, this, too, will weigh heavily against a finding that the alternative is reasonable.

Example: D, a manufacturer of bullet-proof vests for law-enforcement, offers two models. Model A covers only the back and front of the wearer's torso, and costs $200. Model B covers not only the wearer's back and front, but also his side, and costs $400. Model A weighs three lbs, and is sufficiently flexible that the wearer can easily run and twist his torso. Model B weighs seven lbs., and makes it hard for the wearer to either run or twist. P, a police officer, is severely wounded when he is shot in the side while wearing a Model A vest. He sues D on a defective-design theory, arguing that Model B is a reasonable alternative design whose mere existence demonstrates that Model A is defective and unreasonably dangerous in its failure to provide side cover.

A court following the Third Restatement approach would almost certainly conclude that P has *not* demonstrated that Model A is defective. Model B's much greater cost and weight, and its reduction of the wearer's mobility, prevent it from being a reasonable alternative design whose mere existence renders Model A defective and unreasonably dangerous. Cf. Rest. 3d (Prod. Liab.) §2, Illustr. 10 (based on similar though not identical facts).

iii.   Consumer choice: When the reasonable-alternative-design analysis is carried out, the court will pay attention to the ***value of consumer choice*** — the fact that some other design might appeal more to *some* consumers on a cost-benefit analysis does not mean that the design under litigation is defective, because consumers don't all agree on the package of benefits and costs that they find most desirable. For instance, on the facts of the above Example, even though some police officers might prefer Model B on the theory that the greater safety is worth the extra cost and weight, other officers might still conclude that Model A is a better deal. As the Third Restatement says in its commentary on an illustration whose facts are similar to the above Example, "[t]o subject sellers to liability based on [the more expensive and cumbersome] design would unduly restrict the range of consumer choice among products." *Id.*

4. **Consumer-expectation test not dispositive:** Under the Third Restatement approach, *consumers' expectations* are a factor, but *not a dispositive one*, in determining whether a design is defective. The ultimate test is the risk-benefit analysis. The fact that the product does or does not meet "reasonable consumer expectations" is certainly a factor in the court's assessment of whether the product's risks so outweigh its benefits, compared with alternative possible designs, that the product should be regarded as defective. But the mere fact that most consumers find a particular product to meet their expectations certainly does not preventing a finding that, say, a particular safety feature (which the average consumer may never have thought about) could have provided so much benefit at so little cost that its absence makes the product defective. See Comment g to §2 (design-defect definition "rejects conformance to consumer expectations as a defense").

   a. **Significance:** So under the Third Restatement, even if a product does exactly what it was intended to do — and exactly what a reasonable consumer would expect it to do — a plaintiff who is injured when the product does what it is expected to do might still recover.

      i. **Guns as illustration:** The design of *firearms* provides a good illustration of how the Third Restatement prevents satisfaction of the consumer's expectations from giving an automatic defense to the manufacturer.

         Example: Suppose that handguns can be equipped with any of several readily-available devices that would make the gun more child-resistant, such as a heavy trigger pull and/or a child-resistant manual safety. Suppose further that D chooses to manufacture the Model A revolver, which has none of these child-safety features, and which is designed for the "home self-defense in emergencies" market, where a gun's ability to be easy-to-fire at all times is "a feature, not a bug." Assume that P, a young child of the gun's owner, shoots himself.

         Under the pure consumer-expectation test, as long as D can demonstrate that any reasonable consumer who read the Model A's packaging and bought the gun would know that it did not have any child-resistant features, D would be entitled to an automatic dismissal — the gun does what a reasonable consumer would expect it to do (fire easily), and that would be the end of the matter. But under the Third Restatement's risk-utility standard, D would probably *not* get the automatic dismissal — P would still be able to prove that the gun was defective (by showing that the utility of including child-resistant features outweighed the risks or burdens from including such features), even though the gun matched reasonable consumer expectations.

(1) Rejected by some courts: The Third Restatement's rejection of the defendant's right to argue that satisfying consumer expectations automatically makes the product non-defective has itself been *rejected* by a number of courts, including at least one court in the handgun context. See *Halliday v. Sturm, Ruger & Co.,* 792 A.2d 1145 (Md. 2002) (D markets a pistol without certain child-proofing features like a heavy trigger-pull; court continues to apply the "consumer expectations" test, under which D has no design-defect liability because an ordinary consumer who bought the gun would expect that it would lack these child-proofing features).

5. **"State-of-the-art" defense allowed:** Notice that because of the Third Restatement's focus on the availability of a reasonable alternative design, the so-called *"state-of-the-art"* defense is in effect *recognized*. That is, if the defendant can show that at the time the product was manufactured, the state of the art did not allow for production of a safer product at an acceptable price, the product will be found to be non-defective.

    a. **Safest on market at the time:** In fact, even if the defendant merely makes a lesser showing — that the product design it used was the safest *actually being sold at that time* — this lesser showing will probably, though not necessarily, be enough to demonstrate that the product was not defective. As the Restatement commentary says, "When the defendant demonstrates that its product design was the safest in use at the time of sale, it may be difficult for the plaintiff to prove that an alternative design could have been practically adopted. The defendant is thus allowed to introduce evidence with regard to industry practice that bears on whether an alternative design was practicable." Comment d to Rest. 3d (Prod. Liab.) §2.

        i. **Not dispositive:** But such evidence that no other product was safer is *not dispositive*. "If the plaintiff introduces expert testimony to establish that a reasonable alternative design could practically have been adopted, the trier of fact may conclude that the product was defective notwithstanding that such a design was not adopted by any manufacturer, or even considered for commercial use, at the time of sale." *Id.*

6. **Strict liability for reseller:** When a defective-design suit is brought against the manufacturer, the suit is not really in strict liability if the Third Restatement's approach is used — the Restatement's focus on risk-utility and foreseeability mean that negligence standards are really being used. But when the suit is against a *distributor* or *retailer*, there *is* in a sense strict liability against that reseller. That is, the reseller's liability will depend on whether the manufacturer (not the reseller) failed to achieve a good risk-utility trade-off in designing the product.

        Example: Suppose that Pete buys a hot water heater from a Sears store. The heater was manufactured by Heatco, sold by Heatco to Distribco, a distributor, and then sold by Distribco to Sears. If Pete is injured by the heater and brings a suit based on Third Restatement principles against Sears, Sears will in effect face strict liability, because whether it is liable will not depend at all on its own conduct. Instead, Sears' liability will depend on whether Heatco, in designing the heater, failed to use an alternative reasonable design that would have been materially safer. (But if Sears is held liable, it will be entitled to indemnity from Heatco. See *infra*, p. 394).

D. Types of design defect claims: Most cases claiming design defects fall within three general categories, which sometimes overlap: (1) structural defects; (2) absence of safety features; and (3) suitability for unusual purposes. We'll discuss each of these in turn immediately below.

E. Structural defects: The plaintiff may be able to show that because of the defendant's choice of materials, the product has a ***structural weakness***, which caused it to break or otherwise become dangerous. A chair built out of lightweight materials, for instance, which is likely to collapse whenever a person of more than average weight sits on it, might be held to be structurally defective.

    1. Test: The test is usually whether the product is less durable than a reasonable consumer would expect, taking into account, among other things, the price of the product. A $10 chair would not have to have the same durability as a $100 one, in order to avoid structural defectiveness.

        a. Length of product's life: A related question is ***how long the product should last*** before breaking. It is often said that the seller does not undertake to provide a product which will never wear out. But if it wears out too quickly, in relation to its cost, it may be held defectively undurable.

    2. Most durable design not required: It must be kept in mind that the defendant's obligation is not to provide the ***most*** durable design, but simply one which is not unreasonably flimsy.

F. Lack of safety features: It may be the case that a ***safety feature*** could be installed on a product with so little expense, compared with the cost of the product and the magnitude of the danger existing without the feature, that it is defective design not to install it.

    1. Defenses: The defendant to such a claim often attempts to show that competitive products similarly lack the safety feature, that the feature would be unduly expensive to install, or that it would prevent the product from being put to its intended use. At least the latter two defenses are often successful.

        a. As safe as competition's product: But more and more courts are refusing to allow the defendant's showing that his design was ***as safe as the competition's*** to be a complete defense. Such courts often point to Judge Hand's statement in *The T.J. Hooper*, *supra*, p. 105, that custom is not dispositive on the issue of negligence because an entire industry may have lagged in the installation of safety devices. This principle seems equally applicable to strict liability claims.

        b. Restatement view: The Third Restatement agrees that the fact that no safer product is on the market is not dispositive — plaintiff always has the opportunity to convince the trier of fact that a reasonable alternative design, containing the safety feature in question, was practicable. See the discussion of the "state of the art" defense *supra*, pp. 376-376.

    2. Obvious defects: The defendant may also contend that she had no obligation to install a safety device because the danger was ***"obvious."*** It is true that the obviousness of the danger may be a factor bearing on the degree of danger, and hence the need for protection (since a concealed danger is, all other things being equal, more likely to cause harm than an obvious one against which the plaintiff can protect himself).

   a. Not dispositive: But most courts now generally ***reject*** any *per se* rule automatically eliminating the need for protective devices to guard against an obvious defect.

   b. Restatement agrees The Third Restatement agrees that the "obviousness" of the design danger is not dispositive. See *supra*, p. 366.

3. Subsequently discovered precaution: What if no economically sensible safety feature exists at the time the product is manufactured, but one has been found by the time of trial? Most courts would probably allow proof of the post-manufacture solution as evidence of a feasible alternative. But the question is clearly "Was the original design reasonably safe *as of the time of manufacture and sale to plaintiff*?" Consequently, the manufacturer may show that the alternative was not in use at that time as evidence that that alternative was not yet feasible.

G. Suitability for unintended uses: Suppose a product's design poses no unreasonable dangers when the product is used for the use intended by the manufacturer, but does pose such danger when the product is put to ***some other use.*** Does the manufacturer have any duty at all to guard against the dangers from such uses?

1. Unforeseeable misuse: If the misuse of the product is ***unforeseeable***, courts generally agree that the manufacturer has no duty to design the product so as to protect against it.

   a. Third Restatement agrees: The Third Restatement agrees. To begin with, a design is defective only when "the ***foreseeable*** risks of harm imposed by the product could have been reduced or avoided by the adoption of a reasonable alternative design. . . ." Rest. 3d (Prod. Liab.) §2(b). Then, the commentary to this section says that it "impose[s] liability only when the product is put to uses that it is reasonable to ***expect a seller or distributor to foresee***. Product sellers and distributors are ***not*** required to foresee and take precautions against ***every conceivable mode of use and abuse*** to which their products might be put." Comment m to §2.

2. Foreseeable misuse: But where the "misuse," or other use not intended by the manufacturer, is ***reasonably foreseeable*** by it, most modern courts require it to take at least reasonable design precautions to guard against danger from that use. See, e.g., *Barker v. Lull Engineering Co., supra*, p. 373.

   a. Unreasonable use: However, even if the misuse is somewhat foreseeable, courts may hold that it is so ***unreasonable*** that the mere unreasonableness should result in a finding that the seller had no duty to design against it. See, e.g., Rest. 3d (Prod. Liab.) §2, Comment p ("The post-sale conduct of the user may be so unreasonable, unusual, and costly to avoid that a seller has no duty to design or warn against [it].")

   Example: D, a furniture manufacturer, makes the "BarMaster" oak chair. The back of the BarMaster consists of four horizontal wooden bars in the contour of a human back. P puts the back of a BarMaster up against a bookcase, and climbs onto the top bar to reach the highest shelf of the bookcase. The chair tips, and P falls and is injured. P sues D on a design-defect theory, alleging that the chair should have had either enough stability to support him when he stood on it or a different back that would not have permitted him to stand on it. On essentially these facts, the Third Restatement says (and virtually all courts would agree) that P's "misuse of the product is so unreasonable that the risks it entails need not be designed against." Rest. 3d (Prod. Liab.) §2, Illustr. 20.

Note: Notice that the answer to this chair hypothetical does ***not*** turn on the ***unforeseeability*** of the misuse, merely on its unreasonableness: even if D was on notice that people often stand on the backs of the BarMaster, a re-design would almost certainly not be required (though a warning might be).

b. **Warning:** Whether or not a re-design is required to avoid liability, a ***warning*** against the danger from the foreseeable misuse will often be required. See *infra*, p. 381.

3. **Second collision cases:** The most common "unintended but foreseeable use" cases involve automobile manufacturers' duty to provide a ***"crashworthy"*** vehicle. The plaintiff's theory in such cases is that, although the manufacturer is of course not liable for a car accident itself, it should be liable for not taking reasonable precautions to minimize the injuries to passengers once the accident occurs. As the idea is sometimes put, the manufacturer should take design precautions against the so-called ***"second collision"***, i.e. the collision between the passenger and the inside of his own automobile following the initial accident.

a. **Recent view:** The first courts to consider this issue held that the car manufacturer had no such obligation, since collisions were not an "intended" use, and also because there was simply no duty to make a crash-proof car. But most courts that have recently considered the issue have held that the manufacturer ***does*** have an obligation to take reasonable precautions to make the car reasonably safe in an accident.

   i. **Industry custom:** Industry custom (e.g., the fact that all other manufacturers have the same lack of special safety features) is admissible on the question of reasonableness. But the existence of the custom is not dispositive and, indeed, the custom itself may be held to be negligent.

b. **Obvious design feature:** In determining whether a vehicle is unreasonably unsafe in an accident, it may only be compared with other vehicles of ***similar general type***. Thus a Volkswagen van, with the engine in the rear and very little metal in front of the driver to absorb the force of a collision, is not defective merely because it is less safe than a typical passenger car which does have a whole engine compartment to absorb the impact of a collision. *Dreisonstok v. Volkswagenwerk, A.G.*, 489 F.2d 1066 (4th Cir. 1974).

   i. **Obvious danger:** Another way of reaching the same result is to say that a design is defective only if it is "hidden", rather than "obvious". Thus almost anyone who thought about the matter would realize that a Volkswagen van will subject its driver and front seat passenger to greater injuries from a head-on collision than would a Cadillac. (But obviousness is not usually an automatic bar to a design-defect claim, merely one factor considered by the court. See *supra*, p. 377.)

4. **Contributory negligence defense:** The defendant in a "product misuse" claim will, in addition to arguing that he had no duty to guard against misuse, also frequently argues that

the plaintiff was contributorily negligent. This defense is discussed *infra*, p. 406.

H. Unavoidably unsafe categories: Normally, when the plaintiff is alleging a design defect, she is implicitly saying to the jury, "There was a way of designing this product so that it would have been acceptably safe." But a few courts have allowed plaintiffs to say, in effect, "Even if the current design cannot be improved on, the design of the product (perhaps the design of the whole *category* of product) is such that its risks outweigh its utility. Therefore, the product should not be sold." A few courts have *allowed* plaintiffs to make this kind of argument.

> **Example:** P dives into an above-the-ground plastic swimming pool made by D. When his hands touch the bottom, they slip, and he injures his head. P claims that the vinyl liner making up the bottom of the pool was defective because of its extreme slipperiness. In P's strict liability suit against D, D shows that there was no way to make a less-slippery bottom for above-ground pools.
>
> *Held* (on appeal), a jury could reasonably find that despite the lack of alternative feasible designs, above-ground pools are simply so hazardous that their risk outweighs their utility, so that D's design is "defective." *O'Brien v. Muskin*, 463 A.2d 298 (N.J. 1983).

1. **Third Restatement's view:** The Third Restatement similarly recognizes at least the possibility that a particular product may have such a hazardous design that the design should be deemed unreasonable even if no alternative design containing the same essential features is feasible. The Restatement hypothesizes the case of a toy gun that shoots hard rubber pellets with enough velocity that children are injured. If the realism of the toy gun, and its capacity to cause injury, are viewed as essential product features, then no less-dangerous alternative, by hypothesis, would be available. In that event, the Restatement commentary says, the court could conclude that the design is unsafe and defective even though no reasonable alternative exists. Rest. 3d (Prod. Liab.) §2, Comment e.

I. Military products sold to and approved by government: If a product is *sold* to the *U.S. government* for *military use*, and the government approves the product's specifications, the manufacturer will generally be immune from product liability even if the design is grossly negligent. The Supreme Court so held in *Boyle v. United Technologies Corp.*, 487 U.S. 500 (1988), *supra*, p. 307.

1. **Facts:**   The application of this immunity is shown by the facts of *Boyle*. P, a U.S. Marine helicopter pilot, was killed when his helicopter (manufactured by D) crashed into the ocean. P survived the impact, but drowned when he was unable to escape from the cockpit; his estate argued that the escape hatch was defectively designed by D.

2. **Holding:**   By a 5-4 vote, the Supreme Court held that states cannot impose liability for design defects in military equipment if: (1) the U.S. approved *"reasonably precise specifications"*; (2) the equipment *conformed* to those specifications; and (3) the supplier warned the U.S. about any dangers in the equipment that were known to the supplier but not to the U.S.

J. Regulatory compliance defense: The "product sold to the government for military use" situation, discussed in the prior paragraph, is actually a sub-problem of a more general issue: should the fact that the manufacturer has *complied with federal or state regulations* governing the design of the product absolve it of faulty-design liability? The traditional common-law answer is *"no"* — regulatory compliance is an item of evidence that the jury may consider, but it is not dispositive.

1. **Labeling:** Most often, the issue arises in connection with federal *labeling* requirements. That is, Congress requires that some substance (cigarettes, drugs, alcohol, etc.) be labeled in a particular way. P then brings a suit for failure-to-warn (*infra*, p. 381), and argues that even though the product bore a congressionally-mandated warning, the jury should be free to find that a greater warning was required. The general rule is that unless Congress *intended* to *preempt* the states from requiring stricter or different warnings, the defendant's compliance with the federal labeling requirement does *not immunize the defendant* from failure-to-warn liability. This topic is discussed *infra*, p. 415.

2. **Design or manufacture:** Where the government regulation relates to *design* or *manufacture*, rather than to labelling, the general rule is the same: in most states, the manufacturer can show compliance as an *item of evidence*, but the jury is still free to conclude that the defendant should have used an alternative, safer design. Thus an airplane manufacturer whose design meets FAA standards, for instance, is probably not immune from a claim that a safer design was required.

3. **Restatement makes compliance non-dispositive evidence:** The Third Restatement *agrees* with the prevailing rule that *compliance with government regulation does not preclude liability for design defects*. See Rest. 3d (Prod. Liab.) §4(b): "A product's compliance with an applicable product safety statute or administrative regulation is *properly considered* in determining whether the product is defective with respect to the risks sought to be reduced by the statute or regulation, but such compliance *does not preclude as a matter of law* a finding of product defect."

4. **Statutes:** Several states have enacted statutes making regulatory compliance a defense, either generally or in specific contexts. For instance, New Jersey has such a statute for FDA-approved drugs and drug labels. See N.J. Code §2A:58C-4.

5. **Preemption:** Even under the traditional common law rule disallowing a regulatory-compliance defense, a court may still find that a federal regulation has *preempted* the alternative design that the plaintiff argues should have been used. Preemption is discussed more fully *infra*, p. 412.

V. DUTY TO WARN

A. **How the duty to warn may arise:** The presence or absence of a *warning* as to the possible dangers of a product may have a great bearing on whether the product is "defective" or "unreasonably dangerous," as may the quality of the *directions for use* given by the manufacturer.

1. **Negligence aspects predominate:** However, in determining what warnings or instructions are needed, a predominantly negligence standard is usually used, as in the case of what kind of a design is adequate (see *supra*). We discuss the negligence aspect of the duty to warn *infra*, p. 383.

B. Significance of duty to warn: The "duty to warn" is essentially an *extra* obligation placed on a manufacturer. In other words, a manufacturer who has otherwise produced a defective product cannot render the product un-defective by giving an adequate warning. On the other hand, a product that is not defectively designed and not defectively manufactured may nonetheless be treated as "defective" if warnings are required for its safe use, and those warnings are not given. To see how the "duty to warn" works in a general sense, let's consider three alternative scenarios:

1. **Manufacturing defect:** First, consider the product that is *defectively manufactured*. That is, a particular *instance* of the product has a defect not shared by the other copies made by the defendant, and this manufacturing deviation causes P's injury. In this situation, *no warning can save D from strict liability.*

    Example: D, a soup manufacturer, knows from its own quality control inspections that about one in one million cans of soup produced by it will have a small piece of glass in the soup. By spending much more money on new equipment, D could eliminate this risk of glass, but it has chosen not to do so, because it cannot afford that expense. Instead, D puts on every can of soup the following warning, in big and bold letters: "There is a .0001% chance of glass or other foreign objects in this can of soup." P happens to be the unlucky one who buys the one-in-a-million can, and cuts her gums on hidden glass.

    P will be able to recover in strict liability against D, despite D's warning — since the defect here is a manufacturing defect (i.e., D has failed to make every can of soup match the "standard" can), D's warning will be of no avail to it. (If no amount of money today could eliminate this risk, D might be able to argue that the product was "unavoidably unsafe," but this argument has rarely been accepted outside of the prescription-drug context.)

2. **Design defect:** Now, consider a product whose *design* is defective. Here, too, a warning *will almost never shield D* from product liability.

    Example: D designs a low-cost toaster. One of the ways D saves money is by not insulating the wires coming out of the toaster. The toaster retails for $7, whereas the cheapest properly-insulated toaster sells for $14. The toaster contains a large, bold warning, "To keep this toaster affordable, we have failed to insulate the wires coming out of it. Use rubber gloves when you plug in this toaster, and don't step in any water while touching the appliance." P fails to follow these directions, and is electrocuted. P shows that a conventional toaster (with insulation) would not have given P a shock. The warning will not save D from product liability.

    a. **Restatement agrees:** The Third Restatement agrees that a warning will not shield D from liability for a defective design. See Comment l to Rest. 3d (Prod. Liab.) §2 ("Warnings are not, however, a substitute for the provision of a reasonably safe design.")

3. **Properly manufactured and designed product:** Now, consider the third category, the only one in which the giving of a warning might shield the maker from liability. This is the category where the product is *properly designed*, and *properly manufactured*. If, despite the proper manufacture and design, there remains a *non-obvious* risk of personal injury,

the defendant will be liable if he does not warn. Similarly, if a reasonable consumer might *misuse* the product in a foreseeable way, *instructions concerning correct use* must be given, and D will be liable if these instructions are not given.

> **Example 1:** DES is a drug given to prevent nausea in pregnant women. D, the manufacturer, knows (or should know based on the state of science at that time) that there is a small risk that the fetus will be born with birth defects caused by DES, if DES is taken early in the pregnancy. D does not put, either on the product itself, or in material furnished to doctors, any warning of this risk. P, whose mother takes the drug in early pregnancy, is born without limbs.
>
> Even though the particular pills taken by D's mother were not manufactured defectively (i.e., they were the same as all other DES pills), and even though DES could not have been designed any differently (that is, the particular chemical compound that produces the anti-nausea effect inevitably produces some birth defects), D will be liable for its failure to warn of these risks.

> **Example 2:** D manufactures lawn mowers. D's lawn mowers are all properly manufactured, and their design is proper (in the sense that they cannot be made safer without increasing the production costs to an unreasonably high level). The mower is perfectly safe as long as one stands behind it, to the right of it, or in front of it. However, if one stands to the left of the mower, where grass cuttings are ejected, one may be injured by stones thrown free. An ordinary consumer might not realize this danger. D did not place anywhere on the mower any warning that the proper way to use it is to remain behind it. P, a 10-year-old, stands to the left of the mower while his father pushes from behind. P is struck in the eye by a stone thrown loose, and is blinded. D's failure to warn of the danger from walking to the left of the mower will render D strictly liable for P's injury.

C. Risk-utility basis for warnings liability: Some courts have implicitly treated the duty to warn as a type of strict liability. But most courts have applied *negligence-like principles* to the duty. That is, in determining whether a particular accident could have been avoided by a particular type of warning, most courts apply a *risk-utility analysis*, and balance such factors as the foreseeability of the harm, its severity, the cost of giving a warning, and the likelihood that the warning would be heeded.

1. **Third Restatement agrees:** The Third Restatement agrees that liability for failure-to-warn should be based on a risk-utility analysis. A product will be deemed defective on account of "inadequate instructions or warnings" "when the *foreseeable risks of harm* imposed by the product could have been reduced or avoided by the provision of *reasonable instructions or warnings* ... and the omission of the instructions or warnings renders the product *not reasonably safe*." Rest. 3d (Prod. Liab.) §2(c). Several aspects of the Restatement's treatment of warnings are worth noting:

   a. **Longer warning is not necessarily better:** *Longer* warnings are *not necessarily better.* As the Restatement commentary notes, "In some cases, excessive detail may detract from the ability of typical users and consumers to focus on the important aspects of the warnings. . . ." Rest. 3d (Prod. Liab.) §2, Comment i.

b. **Warnings to users who are not purchasers:** While an otherwise-required warning must normally be given to the purchaser, in some instances *persons other than purchasers* may also need warnings. For instance, where a machine is designed to be used by a business, it will often be the case that the manufacturer must see to it that *employees who will be using the machine* are warned, so that a warning to the employer-owner will not suffice; in that instance, a warning sign that is *attached to the machine itself* is likely to be necessary.

c. **Warning against inherent risks:** The fact that a particular danger is *inherent* in the use of the product (i.e., "unavoidable") does not mean that the danger need not be warned against. In inherent-danger situations, "such warnings allow the user or consumer to avoid the risk warned against by making an informed decision not to purchase or use the product *at all*. . . ." Rest. 3d (Prod. Liab.) §2, Comment i. (See also *Liriano v. Hobart Corp., infra*, p. 390, making this same point.)

D. **Drug cases:** The most common category of failure-to-warn cases involves *prescription drugs*.

1. **"Learned intermediary" defense:** Most courts, and the Third Restatement, recognize a defense that makes the manufacturer's duty to warn in prescription drug cases easier-to-satisfy: the *"learned intermediary"* defense. Where the defense is allowed, the manufacturer's duty is generally limited to warning the *prescribing physician* rather than the patient. The physician is viewed as a "learned [i.e., highly trained] intermediary" between the manufacturer and the user; the rationale is that the physician is, in most cases, in the best position to decide whether a drug should be prescribed and when and how its risks should be disclosed.

a. **Restatement adopts:** The Third Restatement basically *applies* the learned intermediary rule as the default rule (but subject to an important exception). Rest. 3d (Prod. Liab.) §6(d)(1), imposes failure-to-warn liability on a drug or medical device maker only if *"reasonable instructions or warnings* regarding foreseeable risks of harm" are *not provided* to *"prescribing and other health-care providers* who are in a position to reduce the risks of harm in accordance with the instructions or warnings."

i. **Exception:** But the Third Restatement includes an important exception to this general acceptance of the learned intermediary defense: The language quoted above indicates that if health-care providers will *not* be a position to pass on warnings, the manufacturer has a duty to give the warnings and instructions *directly to the patient*. Rest. 3d (Prod. Liab.) §6(d)(2). So, for instance, if the product is sold over-the-counter to consumers with a mass-media campaign, then warnings must be made to the consumer (e.g., via packaging inserts and/or on TV ads), not just to physicians who might recommend the item to patients.

2. **Adequacy of warning:** When a warning directly to the end-user is required, the manufacturer must provide, in language comprehensible to a lay person, a warning conveying a fair indication of the *nature, gravity and likelihood* of the known or knowable risks of the drug.

a. **Intensity:** A warning may be inadequate because it is not *intense* enough. Lack of intensity may result not only from the text of the warning itself, but also from the surrounding *advertising and publicity campaign* for the drug (which obscure the effect of the warning).

3. **Failure-to-warn as main basis for liability:** In the usual situation where a prescription drug is of net benefit to some class of patients, *defective-design* liability will not exist. (See *supra*, p. 363.) In these situations, therefore, failure-to-warn is the *only* basis for liability. Indeed, most product liability suits brought against drug companies are premised upon the failure to warn.

4. **Warnings about generic drugs:** *Generic* drugs pose a special issue concerning warnings, due to the special way that warnings on generic drugs are regulated by the federal government. This regulatory scheme creates conceptual problems with allowing any failure-to-warn-based recovery by a patient who takes the generic version, whether the patient sues the generic manufacturer or the brand-name maker.

   a. **Regulation of warnings:** First, let's look at how the regulation of warning labels by the federal Food and Drug Administration (FDA) *varies* as between labeling on the brand-name drug and that on the generic version.

      i. **Warnings on brand-name drugs:** When a company makes and proposes to market a *brand-name* prescription drug, federal law places on the manufacturer the responsibility for drafting the label for the drug; the label must contain all sorts of federally-dictated information, including such matters as usage instructions (e.g., recommended dosages), contraindications to use and a listing of the most-common and/or most-serious adverse reactions. The FDA closely scrutinizes, and must approve, the brand-name drug's label contents. Furthermore, at all times after the branded drug has gone on the market, the maker has an ongoing duty (and right) to *revise* the label in light of new safety-related information that comes to the maker's attention; importantly, the maker may do so *without prior FDA approval* (though the agency can then require that the change itself be modified).

      ii. **Warnings on generic drugs:** By contrast, the maker of a *generic* drug has far less — essentially zero — responsibility for drafting the warning label for that drug. In brief, the generic maker must place *"the same" label* on the drug as the one the FDA has currently approved for the brand-name version. So, for instance, if either the brand-name maker or the generic maker learns of some *new hazard* posed by the drug, the generic maker may not modify the label to warn of the new hazard until the FDA approves the new language (whereas, as noted, the brand-name maker may *unilaterally* change the label, subject to subsequent FDA review).

   b. **State-law tort claims, and federal preemption:** The fact that these federal rules on labeling treat brand-name and generic drugs differently has a major impact on how and when patients can bring failure-to-warn suits against the two types of drug manufacturers.

      i. **Nature of preemption:** Congress' decision to give the FDA authority to extensively regulate drug labeling has the effect of *"preempting"* (i.e., nullifying) to some extent the right of states to let patients recover against drug makers when the suit is based upon allegedly-inadequate labeling.[1]

ii. **Incomplete preemption of labeling claims vs. brand-name makers:** First, let's consider whether the existence of FDA regulation of labels on *brand-name* drugs preempts the states' right to allow state-tort-law "failure to warn" claims by patients who claim that they were injured by inadequate labeling of brand-name drugs.

    (1) **No preemption (*Wyeth v. Levine*):** The short answer is that *no preemption exists* in this situation. In *Wyeth v. Levine*, 129 S.Ct. 1187 (2009), the Supreme Court rejected claims by makers of branded drugs that as long as a drug's label was approved by the FDA, the federal regulatory scheme should be viewed as preempting the states from allowing a patient to recover based on an inadequate warning. In *Wyeth*, the Court reasoned that even after a particular label has been approved by the FDA, the regulatory system permits the maker to add a stronger warning, so that it was possible for the maker to *simultaneously comply* with both FDA and state-law-product-liability-based warning requirements.

iii. **Complete preemption of labeling claims vs. generic makers:** But the Supreme Court has reached the *exact opposite result* as to preemption in the case of the labeling of *generic* drugs. Recall (see Par. (a)(ii) above) that makers of generic drugs are required to *use exactly the same labeling* as is required for the brand-name version — even if the generic maker knows or has reason to know of a danger that is not adequately reflected in the brand-name drug's warning, the generic maker is not permitted to strengthen the warning unless the FDA first approves this change (whereas the brand-name maker can *unilaterally* change the label, subject to the FDA's power to later disapprove of the change).

    (1) **Consequence is preemption of suits:** This difference led the Supreme Court to say in a post-*Wyeth* case, *Pliva v. Mensing*, 131 S.Ct. 2567 (2011), that federal law *does preempt* the states from allowing a state-law-based failure-to-warn claim against a generic manufacturer based on a supposedly-inadequate label (assuming that the label used was the same as the one approved for the brand-name version).

c. **Possible right to sue brand-name maker if P took the generic:** Well, what about letting a plaintiff who has taken an arguably-mislabeled generic drug seek recovery not from the maker of the generic, but from the *maker of the branded version,* perhaps on a misrepresentation theory? After all, it's the branded manufacturer who has written the label (a form of representation), and who had the responsibility to update the label based on any newly-discovered hazards. The problem, of course, is that the American law of product liability has always implicitly restricted product liability suits — even suits based on inadequate warning labels — to ones brought against defendants who either *manufactured* the particular instance of the defective product that harmed the plaintiff, or who were *part of the chain that distributed* that instance. So letting the patient injured by an improperly-labeled generic drug recover from the

---

1. For a more general discussion of federal preemption of state-law product-liability suits against makers of drugs and medical-devices, see *infra*, p. 414.

creator/maker of the branded version would require abandoning a central requirement of product-liability law.

i. **Majority rule says that P is out of luck:** Indeed, the substantial majority of courts to have considered the issue have held that the plaintiff who took the generic is *simply out of luck:* in these states, there is no drug-maker from whom the plaintiff can recover. These courts have, in particular, *rejected* the theory that the plaintiff should be able to recover against the *brand-name manufacturer* based on fraud or negligent misrepresentation in creating and disseminating the incorrect labeling.

ii. **Minority approach allows recovery against branded manufacturer where P took the generic:** But a few recent cases have reached the *opposite result*, by *allowing* the plaintiff who consumed an arguably mislabeled generic drug to seek recovery on a *fraud or misrepresentation theory against the brand-name manufacturer* who drafted the text of the label used on the generic drug, even though that defendant did not manufacture or distribute the generic medication taken by the plaintiff. The case set forth in the following example is the best-known of these decisions.

Example: The Ps are minors whose mother used terbutaline (a drug to suppress premature labor). The brand-name version of this drug, Brethine, was made by D (the large pharmaceutical firm Novartis). P was never prescribed (or used) Brethine; instead, she was prescribed and used the generic version of Brethine, manufactured by a generic-drug maker the Ps have not sued. The Ps allege that the warning label for Brethine failed to warn by falsely representing that the drug was safe for use by pregnant women, and that D owed them and their mother a duty to amend the warning label on Brethine to reflect dangers of which D had become aware. (Federal law provides that because the contents of the label for Brethine were controlled by D and approved by the FDA, all makers of the generic version were required by federal law to use that label, so D owed the Ps a duty to keep the Brethine label up-to-date.)

As an additional complication, six years before the Ps were injured during their mother's pregnancy, D stopped making Brethine and sold all rights to it to a third party. But the Ps assert that despite this fact, D should be held liable for not updating the warning label while it still owned the rights to Brethine, once it learned that the drug was not safe in pregnancy.

Held (by the Supreme Court of California), for the Ps: D will be liable if the Ps can prove their core allegation that the warning label for the brand-name version of the drug (Brethine) should have been updated by D once D learned of the danger to pregnant women. Neither the fact that the Ps' mother took only the generic version made by a third party, nor the fact that when the mother took the generic version D no longer controlled the rights to make (or to modify the label for) the brand name version, is a bar to recovery.

On the basic issue of whether a brand-name drug manufacturer owes a duty of care to users of the generic version, California looks mainly to the *foreseeability of the harm*, and the *public policy justifications* for carving out an exception from the usual rule that only a party in the distribution chain can have product liability. As to the foreseeability issue, D "could reasonably have foreseen that its deficiencies in its Brethine label could mislead physicians about the safety of terbutaline, Brethine's generic bioequivalent, which was legally required to bear an identical label." As to the public policy justifications, if users of the generic version are excluded from the right to sue the only party responsible for the contents of the warning label (here, D), "consumers would insist on the brand-name drug over the cheaper bioequivalent, *inflating health costs* with no corresponding increase in safety[.]"

As to the significance of the fact that D no longer owned or manufactured the brand-name version by the time the Ps were injured, this is irrelevant, because D's sale of the rights to the drug "does not, as a matter of law, terminate its liability for injuries foreseeably and proximately caused by deficiencies present in the warning label prior to the sale." *T.H. v. Novartis Pharmaceuticals Corp.*, 407 P.3d 18 (Cal. 2017).

E. Cigarettes: A number of cases have been filed since the 1980s against *tobacco* companies, contending that *warnings on cigarette packs* were not adequate.

   1. *Cipollone* case: However, with respect to sales after 1966, this argument is *pre-empted* by federal law. That is, the Supreme Court has held that a cigarette smoker's state common-law damage claim for failure to warn is pre-empted by the federal Cigarette Labelling and Advertising Act of 1965. See *Cipollone v. Liggett Group, Inc.*, 112 S. Ct. 2608 (1992).

F. Duty to warn of unknown and unknowable dangers: If the defendant can show that it neither *knew* nor, in the exercise of reasonable care, *should have known* of a particular danger at the time of sale, the vast majority of courts hold that there was *no duty to warn* of the unknowable danger. (Liability for such *"unknowable"* risks is sometimes called *"superstrict* liability." See Dobbs & Hayden (5th), p. 736.)

   1. Restatement agrees: The Third Restatement agrees that there is no duty to warn of unknowable risks. The commentary says that "in connection with a claim of inadequate design, instruction, or warning, plaintiff should bear the burden of establishing that the risk in question was *known or should have been known* to the relevant manufacturing community. The harms that result from *unforeseeable risks* — for example in the human body's reaction to a new drug, medical device, or chemical — *are not a basis of liability*." Rest. 3d (Prod. Liab.) §2, Comment m.

   2. Testing required: Notice that it's not enough for the manufacturer to show that it was not in fact aware of the defect — it must further be the case that the manufacturer *should not* have been aware. "A seller is charged with knowledge of *what reasonable testing would reveal*. If testing is not undertaken, or is performed in an inadequate manner, and this failure results in a defect that causes harm, the seller is subject to liability for harm caused by such defect." *Id.*

   3. Compare to defective design: Just as courts generally hold that there is no duty to *warn* against an unknowable danger, they also hold that there is no duty to *design* against an unknowable danger. See the discussion of unknowable design risks and the "state of the art" defense, *supra*, p. 364.

G. Effect of government labeling standards: The scope of the defendant's duty to warn may be affected by the fact that the *government* imposes certain *labeling* requirements.

    1. Evidence: Where a defendant can show that it has complied with a federal or state labeling requirement, most courts permit this to be shown as *evidence* that the warning was adequate. This evidence is not dispositive: the jury is always free to conclude that even though the government requirement was complied with, a reasonable manufacturer would have given a more specific (or different) warning.

    2. Federal pre-emption: Where the labeling requirement is imposed by the *federal government*, the fact that the defendant has complied with that warning requirement is likely to be more significant than where the labeling is prescribed by state law. This is because of the doctrine of federal *pre-emption* of state law. When the doctrine of pre-emption is applied, the federal law takes priority over state law dealing with the same subject, because of the U.S. Constitution's Supremacy Clause.

        a. Pre-emption generally: The mere fact that federal law prescribes detailed warning labels does not by itself mean that state law has been pre-empted. The pre-emption doctrine is only applied where the court finds that Congress *intended* to pre-empt more demanding state labeling rules.

        b. Preemption found: On the other hand, if the court finds that Congress *did* intend to preempt the states from imposing additional or different warnings, then the preemption doctrine will help the defendant immensely: under the federal constitution's Supremacy Clause, if the state was not permitted to require different or additional warnings, the state is also blocked from *awarding tort damages* for the defendant's failure to warn. The net effect is that once the court finds that Congress intended that its own warning scheme preempt state law, a defendant who has complied with the federal scheme cannot be sued for failure-to-warn. For more about this, see the discussion of preemption in cases involving warning labels on prescription drugs, *infra*, p. 415.

H. Danger to small number of people: If the manufacturer knows that the product will be dangerous to a *small number* of people, may it make the decision that the need for a warning is not sufficiently great? This will usually turn on the *magnitude* of the danger; if the danger is great enough, even a small number of potential bad results will require a warning. See Rest. 3d (Prod. Liab.) §2, Comment k ("The more severe the harm, the more justified is a conclusion that the number of persons at risk need not be large to be considered 'substantial' so as to require a warning.")

        Example: Even though a person getting an inoculation against polio has only a one-in-one-million chance of contracting polio from the vaccine, that chance is still great enough that the vaccine manufacturer had a duty to warn of the danger. *Davis v. Wyeth Laboratories, Inc.*, 399 F.2d 121 (9th Cir. 1968).

I. Obvious danger: If the danger is *obvious* to most people, this will be a factor reducing the defendant's obligation to warn. But many recent decisions are reluctant to hold that the mere obviousness of the danger automatically means that there is no duty to warn, at least where there is evidence that some substantial minority of people, including the plaintiff, were not aware of the danger.

1. **Chance to use alternatives:** Why is this so? Well, even where the danger is obvious to the particular plaintiff, it does not follow that a warning is valueless. There are *two quite distinct functions* that a product warning may play: a notification of danger, but also an *explanation of the existence of a safer alternative*. Since even a warning about an obvious danger may give useful information about the existence of a safer way, courts increasingly hold that obviousness is not an automatic defense to a failure-to-warn claim.

    Example: P, a 17-year-old immigrant, works for Super, a grocery store. Super has bought a meat grinder made 30 years before by Hobart. Hobart manufactured the grinder with a safety guard, but Super has removed the guard. The grinder does not contain any warning that use of the machine without the guard might be dangerous. P uses the grinder without the guard, and loses his right hand and lower forearm when the hand gets caught inside the machine. P sues Hobart for product liability, claiming (*inter alia*) that Hobart violated its duty to warn. Hobart defends on the grounds that even if the modification by Super did not absolve Hobart of any duty to warn, the danger was so obvious that absence of a warning could not have caused the accident.

    Held, for P. "[A] warning can convey at least two types of messages. One states that a particular place, object, or activity is dangerous. Another explains that people need not risk the danger posed by such a place, object, or activity in order to achieve the purpose for which they might have taken that risk. . . . A jury could reasonably find that there exist people who are employed as meat grinders and who do not know . . . that it is feasible to reduce the risk with safety guards. . . . Moreover, a jury can also reasonably find that there are enough such people, and that warning them is sufficiently inexpensive, that a reasonable manufacturer would inform them that safety guards exist and that the grinder is meant to be used only with such guards. Thus, even if New York would consider the danger of meat grinders to be obvious as a matter of law, that obviousness does not substitute for the warning[.]" *Liriano v. Hobart Corp.*, 170 F.3d 264 (2d Cir. 1999).

J. **Warning against misuse:** Just as modern cases may require the defendant to *design* to protect against *foreseeable misuses* of the product, so he may have to *warn* against such misuses.

    Example: D manufactures a step-ladder that is not designed to hold loads greater than 350 lbs. D fails to give a warning against using the ladder for loads greater than 350 lbs. If the ladder collapses while holding P, who weighs 300 lbs. and is carrying a 75-lb. sack of cement, D's failure to warn can give rise to strict product liability

1. **Warning against removal of safety devices:** A related problem is the manufacturer's duty to warn against *removal of safety devices* that the manufacturer has installed on a piece of equipment. If a manufacturer installs a safety device on the equipment, and a third person (e.g., an employer who owns the equipment) removes the device, this third-party "tampering" is an intervening cause that probably shields the manufacturer from design-defect liability. But the manufacturer in this situation may nonetheless be liable for

failing to ***warn*** the ultimate user that using the equipment without the safety device is dangerous.

> **Example:** Same facts as *Liriano v. Hobart, supra,* p. 390. As an alternative defense, Hobart points out that Super removed the safety guard that Hobart had supplied. Hobart therefore asserts that a manufacturer has no duty to warn against substantial alterations made by third parties.
>
> *Held,* for P. It is true that a manufacturer is not liable on a design-defect theory for injuries caused by substantial alterations to the product by a third party that render the product defective or unsafe. But it does not follow that a third party's substantial alteration also removes the manufacturer's duty to *warn.* "The burden of placing a warning on a product is less costly than designing a perfectly-safe tamper-resistant product." Therefore, under New York law P should be permitted to reach the jury on the question whether Hobart violated its duty to warn. *Liriano v. Hobart Corp.,* 92 N.Y. 2d 232 (N.Y. 1998). (In this decision, the New York court was answering a question about New York law certified to it by the federal Second Circuit, where the case was pending; that Second Circuit panel issued the decision quoted *supra.*)

K. Post-sale duty to warn: To what extent does a manufacturer have a duty to make a ***post-sale*** warning about dangers of which the manufacturer was not aware at the time of manufacture? Courts' answers have varied.

   1. Duty to warn when manufacturer learns of the risk: The most common approach is to hold that at least where the manufacturer eventually ***learns about the risk,*** it has an ***obligation to give a post-sale warning*** if the risk is great and the user of the product can be identified. In this situation, a duty to warn probably exists even though the defect was ***not knowable at the time of manufacture.***

      a. Third Restatement adopts: The Third Restatement follows this approach. Rest. 3d (Prod. Liab.) §10(a) says that one who sells a product commercially has a duty to issue a post-sale warning "if a reasonable person in the seller's position would provide such a warning." §10(b) then says that a reasonable person in the seller's position would provide a post-sale warning if:

         ❑ the seller "***knows or reasonably should know*** that the product poses a ***substantial risk of harm***[;]"

         ❑ those to whom a warning might be provided "can be ***identified*** and can reasonably be assumed to be ***unaware*** of the risk of harm";

         ❑ A warning can be "***effectively communicated*** to and ***acted upon*** by those to whom a warning might be provided"; and

         ❑ the risk of harm is ***sufficiently great to justify the burden*** of providing a warning."

      Example: D makes a Model 123 power drill. Three years after putting the product on the market, D learns that under conditions of extreme use, the drill can overheat and break, badly injuring the user. The danger comes to light only because one particular drill is used on an alloy that did not even exist at the time the Model 123 was first sold. Assume that D could not reasonably have foreseen the development of the alloy, or the overheating problem, at the time the drill was manufactured. (This means that the drill was not "defective" when manufactured.)

Once D learns of the danger, it will have a duty to warn about it to users that it can identify. This is true even though the drill was not defective at the time it was sold to that user. Cf. Rest. 3d (Prod. Liab.) §10, Illustr. 1.

b. **Duty to monitor:**   Some courts have held that the manufacturer has a duty not only to warn about dangers or defects that it learns about, but also an affirmative duty to ***"keep abreast of the field"*** by ***monitoring the performance and safety*** of its products after sale. Such an affirmative duty of monitoring and testing is most likely to be found in cases involving ***prescription drugs***. Dobbs Hrnbk, §368, p. 1020. See also Rest. 3d (Prod. Liab.) §10, Comment c ("With regard to one class of products, prescription drugs and devices, courts traditionally impose a ***continuing duty of reasonable care to test and monitor after sale*** to discover product-related risks.")

   i. **Non-drug cases:**   Outside of the prescription drug area, most courts seem not to impose an affirmative duty to test and monitor post-sale, except where the manufacturer happens first to learn about a particular risk. See Rest. 3d (Prod. Liab.) §10, Reporter's Note to Comment c: "In non-drug cases there appears to be no practical post-sale duty to investigate or test a product not [originally] defective unless information comes to the attention of the product seller is that there is a problem attendant to its use."

c. **Warning about originally-defective product :**   Notice that if the product was ***defective at the time it was manufactured***, then the existence of a post-sale duty to warn doesn't matter very much. That's because the manufacturer will be liable for making the defective product in the first place, and a duty to warn — whether that duty existed at the time of manufacture or came into existence thereafter — won't add much to the plaintiff's case as a practical matter. So the existence of a post-sale duty to warn therefore really matters only in cases where the product itself was not defective at the time of manufacture (perhaps because its dangers were not only unknown but reasonably unknowable), but the manufacturer learned of significant dangers post-sale.

d. **Safety measures:**   Some cases go even further than imposing a post-sale duty to warn; they impose a duty to inform the user about a ***newly-discovered safety technology*** (e.g., a newly-available guard on a dangerous machine tool).

e. **Product recalls:**   Can a manufacturer have separate liability for ***failing to recall*** a product that it discovers, post-sale, to be defective? Where no statute or regulation requires the recall, most courts have answered ***"no."***

   i. **Third Restatement:**   The Third Restatement agrees with this general no-liability rule. Assuming that there is no statute or regulation requiring the maker to recall the product, the Restatement imposes liability for a failure to recall only if the maker "***undertakes*** to recall the product" and then ***fails to carry out the recall in a reasonable way.*** Rest. 3d (Prod. Liab.) §11.

      Example: D, to avoid a government-mandated recall, agrees to make a voluntary recall. D then fails to give notice to most of the owners whose identities it possesses. Even under the limited Restatement rule, D will be liable for the failure to follow through on the promised recall. Id., Illustr. 4.

L. **Allergies:** A manufacturer may have a duty to warn of possible *allergic reactions*. There are actually two different sorts of warnings that may, depending on the case, be needed: (1) a warning that the product *contains a particular ingredient*; and (2) a warning that the ingredient *may cause an allergic reaction*.

1. **"Commonly known" exception:** Most courts do not require a warning of allergy-related dangers that are *generally known* to consumers. This may remove the need for one or both of the above types of warnings in a particular case. As the Third Restatement puts it, for there to be a duty to warn, "The ingredient that causes the allergic reaction must be one whose danger or whose presence in the product is not generally known to consumers. When the presence of the allergenic ingredient would not be anticipated by a reasonable user or consumer, warnings concerning its presence are required. Similarly, when the presence of the ingredient is generally known to consumers, but its dangers are not, a warning of the dangers must be given." Rest. 3d (Prod. Liab.) §2, Comment k.

> **Example:** D produces an over-the-counter nonprescription medicine containing aspirin. D is aware that many consumers are allergic to aspirin. D may reasonably assume that most consumers who are allergic to aspirin are aware of their allergy. D may further reasonably assume that a consumer who is not aware of having the allergy would not be helped by a warning. Therefore, although D must warn that the product contains aspirin, it need not warn that aspirin can cause allergies. Rest. 3d §2, Illustr. 13.

2. **Balancing test:** Recent cases have adopted the same "balancing test" approach to allergy warning issues as they have in other kinds of warning cases. Thus if the plaintiff's allergic reaction, and the foreseeable reactions of others, are of only mild severity, a greater percentage of the overall population will have to be susceptible before liability is found.

3. **Hypo-allergenic claim:** If the defendant markets its product as *"hypo-allergenic"*, this may be held to be an *express warranty* that the product will not cause an allergic reaction. This would be true even if the seller neither knew or should have known of the possibility of allergy. See Prod. L. Nut., p. 215. See also the discussion of express warranties, *supra*, p. 352.

M. **Hidden causation issue:** In any failure-to-warn scenario, be sure to check that the requirement of a *causal link* between the failure to warn and the resulting injury is satisfied. If the provision of a warning *would not have prevented the accident* from occurring, then the defendant will *not* be liable for failing to warn.

1. **Plaintiff who does not read warnings or ignores them:** For example, in a case in which the injured plaintiff is the one who was the user of the product, and the claim is based upon the defendant manufacturer's failure to place a warning label on the product, evidence that the plaintiff *never read any warning labels* would prevent failure-to-warn liability. Similarly, if there is evidence that even had plaintiff read the warning, plaintiff would have *ignored the warning* and used the product in the same way so that the accident would have happened anyway, failure to warn will not be the basis for liability.

Example: D manufacturers a hand-operated power saw that is sold to P, a professional carpenter. P cuts off one of the fingers of his left hand while holding the saw with his right hand only. The saw contains a bold-faced warning label, but the warning label does not specify that the saw should only be operated with two hands. P sues D in strict product liability, alleging that the failure of the warning label to specify a need for two-handed operation rendered the product dangerously defective. D presents evidence at trial that P had over his career used many similar hand saws, that most of them had a label warning against one-handed use, and that P very frequently ignored such warnings by operating the saws with one hand only.

If the jury is convinced that P would have ignored a two-hands-only label had one been present, then P will not be permitted to recover for failure to warn.

VI. WHO MAY BE A DEFENDANT

A. **Cases involving chattels:** In the true "product" liability case (i.e., a case involving a "good" or "chattel"), both strict and warranty liability will apply to *any seller* in the business of selling goods of that kind. See Rest. 3d (Prod. Liab.) §1; UCC §2-314(1).

    1. **Retail dealers:** This means that a *retail dealer* who sells the good, but has not manufactured it, will have strict liability as well as warranty liability, even though there is nothing she could have done to discover the defect. It is in the area of retailer liability that strict liability produces a markedly different result from negligence.

       a. **Restatement agrees:** This principle that retailers (and other non-manufacturers) who sell defective goods are strictly liable is embedded in the Third Restatement's general rule of strict product liability. The Restatement does not distinguish between a manufacturer and a "downstream" wholesale or retail seller: "One engaged in the business of selling or otherwise distributing products *who sells or distributes a defective product* is subject to liability for harm to persons or property caused by the defect." Rest. 3d (Prod. Liab.) §1.

       b. **Must be in business of selling goods:** Both strict and warranty liability are triggered only if the seller is "in the business" of selling goods. Thus a private individual who sells his car has neither liability, since he does not make a business of such sales. Similarly, a businessperson who makes a sale outside of the usual course of his business (e.g. he sells all his furniture because he is relocating his office) will not have liability.

          i. **Sales need not be major part:** But as long as the sale is part of the business, it will give rise to liability even if it is not the predominant or even an important part; thus strict liability applies to "a motion-picture theater's routine sales of popcorn or ice cream, either for consumption on the premises or in packages to be taken home." Rest. 3d (Prod. Liab.) §1, Comment c.

       c. **Indemnity:** If the retailer is held liable in this way, she will be entitled to *indemnity* from the manufacturer or wholesaler, as long as the retailer was not herself negligent.

Example: Manuf makes an electric heater, and sells it to Wholesaler. Wholesaler sells the heater to Retailer. Retailer sells to Consumer. Due to a manufacturing defect, the heater catches fire, and burns Consumer badly. Consumer sues Retailer. As noted,

Consumer will be able to recover against Retailer for selling a defective product, even without showing that Retailer was negligent.

Then, however, Retailer will be able to obtain indemnity from either Manuf or Wholesaler, as long as these are unable to show that Retailer was negligent in failing to spot or warn of the danger. See Rest. 3d (Apport.) §22(a)(2)(ii), giving a person indemnity where "the indemnitee . . . was not liable except as a seller of a product supplied to the indemnitee by the indemnitor and the indemnitee was not independently culpable."

Note: Also, if in the above example Consumer recovers from *Wholesaler*, Wholesaler will be entitled to indemnity from Manuf. In other words, a faultless seller who has to pay a products-liability claim can always obtain indemnity from an upstream supplier.

2. **Used goods:** There is much controversy about whether there can be strict or warranty liability upon the seller of *used goods*, particularly used cars. A number of courts, probably a majority of those that have considered the question, have held that there is *no such liability.*

> **Example:** P1 and P2, young children, are walking home from school when they are hit by a used car. A suit claiming that the car's brakes were defective is brought against the driver and the used car dealer.
>
> *Held*, strict liability will not be imposed upon the used car dealer, absent a showing that the defects were created by him. Otherwise, "the used car dealer would in effect become an insurer against defects which had come into existence after the chain of distribution was completed, and while the product was under the control of one or more consumers." *Peterson v. Lou Bachrodt Chevrolet Co.*, 329 N.E.2d 785 (Ill. 1975).

     a. **Restatement generally has no strict liability:** The Third Restatement agrees, in most instances, that there is *no strict liability for used goods.* In the typical situation where a reasonable consumer in the buyer's position would expect the used product to present a *somewhat greater risk of defect* than if the product were new, there will be no liability in the absence of negligence. See Rest. 3d (Prod. Liab.) §8 and Comment b thereto (stating that the section "subject[s] commercial sellers of used products to liability without fault only under special circumstances.")

         i. **Consumer expectation:** So if the used product sells for a significantly lower price than a comparable new product, or is marked "as is," or is obviously quite old, under the Restatement these factors will be deemed to put the buyer on notice that the risk of defect is greater than in the case of the new product, and will prevent strict liability from occurring.

> **Example:** D1, a commercial seller of snow blowing equipment, sells a used snow blower to P. The blower was manufactured by D2. The blower is five years old and has obviously been extensively used. The price charged by D1 is 1/3 less than the price for a new blower with comparable specs. The blower is marked "sold as is." Because of a manufacturing defect (which may have existed at the time the blower was originally manufactured), P is injured by using it. Assuming that P cannot

show negligence on the part of D1 (e.g., in failing to spot the particular defect) or D2, he cannot recover against either. Cf. Rest. 3d (Prod. Liab.) §8, Illustr. 15, on approximately these facts.

ii. **Sold as "nearly new":** On the other hand, if the goods are sold as being *remanufactured* or *"nearly new,"* so that a reasonable consumer in the buyer's position would be justified in believing that the risk of the dangers defect would be *no greater* than if the product were new, then the seller *will* be strictly liable. See Rest. 3d (Prod. Liab.) §8(b).

Example: D is a car rental company. It advertises that the average car in its fleet is only six months old. D makes a three-day rental of a car to P. The odometer reading on the car at the time of lease is 8,000 miles. P is injured when a defect in the car causes him to crash. D will be strictly liable, because the situation would have led a reasonable consumer in P's position to believe that the risk of a defect would be no greater than in the case of a new car. Cf. Rest. 3d (Prod. Liab.) §8, Illustr. 19. (Lessors of personal property are generally held to strict liability on the same terms as sellers; see *infra*, p. 400.)

3. **Component manufacturers:** The manufacturer of a part which is defective, and which is then *incorporated* as a *component* in a larger product, will be strictly liable if the defect causes injury. See Rest. 3d (Prod. Liab.) §5(a) ("One . . . who sells or distributes a component is subject to liability for harm . . . caused by a product into which the component is integrated if: (a) the component is defective in itself . . . and the defect causes the harm[.]")

    a. **Warranty:** The same result should follow where the suit is brought for breach of implied warranty. See Prod. L. Nut., pp. 47-48.

4. **Fulfillment services:** The rise of *Internet retailing* has led to an important issue about who is a seller. The emergent case law about whether and when *providers of Internet services are sellers* has focused on *Amazon*, the overwhelmingly-dominant Internet merchant; therefore, we'll refer to "Amazon," but what we say will apply not just to Amazon but to other Internet-based companies that offer services that facilitate the sale of goods.

    a. **Amazon wears two hats:** When the Amazon.com website offers goods for sale on its Internet website, it may be wearing one of two quite different "hats."

        [1] **"For sale by Amazon" hat:** Amazon wears one of these hats when it conducts the sale under the label of *"For Sale by Amazon."* In this scenario, Amazon.com is acting as a true classic retailer: it buys the product from a supplier (and thus *takes title* to it), advertises the product as being sold by Amazon and fulfills the order. When the sale occurs under this "For Sale by Amazon" label, it's clear that Amazon is the actual seller of the product, and will be strictly liable if the product causes personal injury or property damage — Amazon is a seller just the way a brick-and-mortor store is a seller of the same product.

        [2] **"Amazon Marketplace," and "Fulfilment by Amazon":** But the substantial majority of product sales that occur on Amazon.com occur while Amazon is wearing its *other* hat, that of *"aggregator"* or *"facilitator"* of a sale in which a third

party (not Amazon) is the one who **holds title** to the product at the time of sale. On Amazon.com, these product offerings are typically labeled as being from *"Amazon Marketplace."* There are actually two different flavors of Amazon Marketplace sales, depending on whether the goods are (1) stored and shipped by Amazon or, instead, (2) stored and shipped by the merchant who holds title. The more interesting legal issue concerning Amazon's possible liability as a seller stems from flavor (1), where the Marketplace sale is made under the program called *"Fulfillment by Amazon,"* or *"FBA."*[2]

In the FBA program, the merchant who holds title to the goods (1) initially ships them in bulk to Amazon for storage in an Amazon warehouse, and (2) relies on Amazon to (a) **receive the order** on the Amazon.com website, (b) "pick" the goods for the order from the warehouse and (c) **ship** the goods to the customer. For the merchant seller, a key benefit of using the FBA program is that the order becomes automatically eligible for *"Amazon Prime,"* so that the goods will arrive within two days at no extra cost to the Prime customer.

b. **The legal issue under FBA:** As you might imagine, when a customer buys a dangerously defective product from a merchant who uses Amazon to fulfill the order via FBA, the key issue is **whether Amazon is a "seller"** of the product for purposes of strict product liability. Cases dealing with this issue are quite **split**, with some saying Amazon is a seller and others saying it is not. (See *infra*, p. 400, for our summary of this split of authority as of early 2022.) In Par. (c) below, we'll look at the leading case holding that Amazon was *not* a seller when the shipment was fulfilled by Amazon under the FBA program, and in (d), we'll discuss the leading case reaching the opposite conclusion.

c. **Amazon wins (*Erie Ins. v. Amazon.com*):** In *Erie Ins. v. Amazon.com*, 925 F.3d 135 (4th Cir. 2019), Amazon prevailed — the court concluded that Amazon was *not* a "seller" of the defective product even though it fulfilled the shipment under the FBA program.

   i. **Facts:** In *Erie Ins.*, a consumer residing in Maryland (Trung Cao) bought a headlamp that was manufactured by Dream Light and offered for sale on Amazon.com via the FBA program. Cao gave the headlamp to friends as a gift. The batteries malfunctioned, igniting the friends' house and causing $300,000 in damage. P (Erie Insurance, the friends' homeowners insurance company) paid for the damage and, acting as "subrogee,"[3] brought a strict product liability suit against Amazon.

   ii. **Details of FBA:** Under the FBA arrangement, Amazon received the order from the customer, retrieved the headlamp from the Amazon warehouse (where it had been "consigned" in bulk by Dream Light), packaged and shipped it to Cao via

---

2. The substantial majority of Marketplace sales occur through the FBA program, not via fulfillment by the merchant who holds title.

3. Under the doctrine of "subrogation," an insurer who pays a property or personal injury claim automatically takes over the claimant's right to sue the party whose tortious behavior caused the damage. The insurer is known as a "subrogee."

UPS, collected payment from Cao and, after withdrawing its service fee, remitted the balance to Dream Light.

iii. The parties' contentions: The suit was a diversity action, so the issue was whether the tort law of Maryland (where both Cao and the friends lived) would treat Amazon as having been a "seller."

iv. Amazon wins: The Fourth Circuit found *in favor of Amazon:* the company was not a "seller" of the headlight. The court relied completely on the fact that *Amazon never held title to the headlight.* Construing Maryland's products liability law, the court concluded that the state imposes strict product liability only on *"owners of personal property who transfer title* to purchasers of that property for a price."

    (1) Firms that "render services to facilitate" sales: Thus under Maryland law, firms are not sellers if they "do not take title to property during the course of a distribution but rather render services to facilitate that distribution or sale[.]" The court listed various types of *"service facilitators"* who, because they do not take title at any point in the distribution chain, are not sellers: *"shippers, warehousemen, brokers, marketers, auctioneers,* and *other bailees* or *consignees*[.]"

d. Amazon loses (*Oberdorf v. Amazon.com*): But in another Federal Court of Appeals case decided the same year as *Erie Insurance, supra,* the court reached exactly the *opposite* conclusion, that under the law of the relevant state (Pennsylvania), Amazon *was* a seller even though it *never took title* to the defective product. The case was *Oberdorf v. Amazon.com Inc.*, 930 F.3d 136 (3d Cir. 2019).[4]

i. Facts more favorable to Amazon: The facts of *Oberdorf* were roughly similar to those of *Erie Insurance.* But the details of the order and shipment were, if anything, *more* favorable to Amazon's position in *Oberdorf* than in *Erie.* That's because in *Oberdorf*, the third-party supplier/seller did not use the Fulfillment by Amazon (*supra*, p. 396) process; instead, it used the *non-FBA version* of Amazon Marketplace, under which the customer's order on Amazon.com was *processed directly by the supplier*, and it was the *supplier*, not Amazon, who shipped the product to the customer.

    (1) Details: P (Oberdorf) bought a dog collar on Amazon.com. When she put the collar on her dog, the dog lunged, causing the collar to break and the leash to hit her eye, blinding her. The collar was sold by a third-party vendor, The Furry Gang, which listed it on Amazon Marketplace and shipped it to P. P sued Amazon (in part because she was not able to locate The Furry Gang for service).

    (2) Issue: As with *Erie Insurance, supra,* the only issue was whether Amazon was a "seller" under the relevant state product liability law (that of Pennsylvania).

---

4. It's unclear whether the opinion in *Oberdorf* represents official case law in the Third Circuit. The opinion was by a standard three-judge panel, and because of that opinion's unusual procedural posture, it's not clear whether the entire corps of Third Circuit judges would view the result as being the law of that Circuit.

ii. Court holds Amazon to be a seller: But in contrast to *Erie*, the court (the federal Third Circuit) held that under Pennsylvania law, Amazon was a seller, even though it never took title.[5]

iii. Four factors in test: As the *Oberdorf* court noted, the Pennsylvania Supreme Court had previously announced the following test: whether an actor (i.e., the defendant) is a "seller" is to be determined by considering *four factors* (none of which was whether the defendant took title):

[1] Whether the defendant was the *"only member of the marketing chain available to the injured plaintiff for redress"*;

[2] Whether "imposition of strict liability upon the [defendant] serves as an *incentive to safety"*;

[3] Whether the defendant is "in a better position than the consumer to *prevent the circulation of defective products"*; and

[4] Whether the defendant *"can distribute the cost of compensating for injuries* resulting from defects by *charging for it in his business*, i.e., by adjustment of the [sale] terms."

iv. All factors against Amazon: The *Oberdorfer* court concluded that if the Pennsylvania Supreme Court were considering the facts of the case, that court would find that *all four factors cut in favor* of holding Amazon to be a seller:

[1] As to factor [1] (whether Amazon was "only member of the marketing chain *available to the injured plaintiff for redress"*), neither P nor Amazon had been able to "locate" The Furry Gang for purposes of instituting suit. Therefore, Amazon was indeed the only member of the marketing chain from whom P could obtain redress.

[2] As to factor [2] (whether the imposition of strict liability on Amazon would "serve as an *incentive to safety"*), Amazon argued that because it did not have a *"relationship with the designers or manufacturers* of products offered by third-party vendors" (like The Furry Gang), imposing strict liability on it would not be an incentive for safer products. But the court noted that Amazon *"exerts substantial control"* over third-party vendors, because its agreement with that type of vendor gave Amazon complete *power to remove any product listing* and/or *terminate any service* offered to such a vendor. Amazon was "fully capable, in its sole discretion, of *removing unsafe products"* from its website. Therefore, imposing strict liability on Amazon would indeed incentivize it to pursue safety.

[3] As to factor [3] (whether Amazon was "in a *better position than the consumer* to *prevent the circulation* of defective products"), the court pointed out that

---

5. Because *Oberdorf* (like *Erie Ins.*) was a federal diversity suit, under classic *Erie v. Tompkins* doctrine, the federal court had to decide whether under the tort law of the state where the injury occurred, Pennsylvania, Amazon was a seller. More precisely, the federal court had to predict how the Pennsylvania Supreme Court would resolve the issue.

Amazon was "uniquely positioned to ***receive reports of defective products,***" because it "retains the ability to ***collect customer feedback***." In fact, Amazon's contracts with third-party vendors specified that if a vendor wanted to communicate with Amazon users who buy the vendor's products via the site, the vendor could do so *only* by using "tools and methods that [Amazon] ***designate[s]***." Thus Amazon's ability to receive consumer reports about product defects put it in a better position than individual consumers to prevent circulation of defective products.

[4] The last factor, [4], was whether Amazon "can ***distribute the cost*** of compensating for injuries resulting from defects by ***charging for it in [its] business***[.]" The court noted that neither P nor Amazon had been able to ***locate*** the third-party vendor in the case, The Furry Gang. Amazon's customers (like P) are ***"particularly vulnerable"*** in situations where it's hard or impossible to locate the vendor. But if there had been an incentive for Amazon to keep track of its third-party vendors (and to charge higher fees to vendors of dangerous products), the company might have done this. Thus this final factor, too, cut in favor of treating Amazon as a seller.

e. **Summary of split of opinion:**   Here is a summary (as of early 2022) of the case law on whether Amazon should be treated as a seller for product liability purposes when (a) only a ***third-party vendor, not Amazon, ever holds title*** to the item; and (b) Amazon merely ***facilitates*** the sale by making available the Fulfillment by Amazon or some other Amazon Marketplace service:

> "By and large, U.S. courts have held that Amazon is ***not strictly liable*** for the goods sold by third parties on Amazon's website. ... With that said, the tides may be ***turning***, with several recent decisions ***holding Amazon liable*** for defective products sold by third-party sellers on its website."
>
> Monestier, *"Amazon as a Seller of Marketplace Goods Under Article 2,"* 107 Cornell L. Rev. 705, 717-718 (March 2022).

B. **Lessors of goods:**   Courts usually impose strict liability upon a ***lessor*** of defective goods. Thus a number of ***car rental*** companies have been held strictly liable when defective cars they rented have injured the lessee, a passenger in the car, or a pedestrian. See P,W&S, p. 787, n. 3. However, the lessor must be in the "business" of leasing.

1. **Third Restatement:** The Second Restatement's strict item liability provisions apply only to "sellers," and are silent about lessors. But the Third Restatement expressly ***applies*** to people who do not sell but who "otherwise distribute" a product, including lessors. See Rest. 3d (Prod. Liab.) §20(b).

2. **Negligence liability:**   The lessor may, of course, also be liable for negligence in failing to discover the defect. See *supra*, p. 351.

3. **Warranty:**   A court might also allow recovery on an implied warranty theory by analogy to the UCC.

C. **Sellers of real estate:**   Sellers of ***real estate*** have also, again by analogy, sometimes been subjected to strict and warranty liability when the property turns out to have been defective.

1. **Third Restatement:** Thus the Third Restatement allows the possibility of strict liability on the part of sellers of real estate, saying in its section defining "Product" that "Other items, such as real property ... are products when the context of their distribution and use is *sufficiently analogous* to the distribution and use of tangible personal property that is *appropriate* to apply" the strict-product-liability rules. Rest. 3d (Prod. Liab.) §19. The Comments to this section explain that courts have traditionally resisted holding real estate sellers strictly liable, but that this has begun to change, so that at least, a building contractor who *sells a building* that contains *appliances* or other *manufactured equipment* will likely be held to be a seller of these products and thus strictly liable if they are defective. *Id.*, Comment e to §19.

   a. **Building itself:** In fact, the Third Restatement indicates that the seller of a building may be strictly liable for defects *in the building itself* in two situations: (1) where the building is *"prefabricated"* (e.g., manufactured housing, such as a trailer); or (2) if the buildings are dwellings that are built, even on-site, "on a *major scale*, as in a *large housing project*." *Id.*

2. ***Schipper* case:** The best-known case imposing strict liability on a seller of real estate is *Schipper v. Levitt & Sons, Inc.*, 207 A.2d 314 (N.J. 1965). There, the defendant, a mass-producer of homes, was held strictly liable for breach of an implied warranty of "habitability" when the infant plaintiff was injured by the house's defective hot-water system.

3. **Privity requirement:** In *Schipper*, the plaintiff was not the purchaser of the house, but the purchaser's child. Many courts, however, although willing to recognize an "implied warranty of habitability", or strict liability, have applied it only where the plaintiff is the actual contracting party.

   a. **Remote purchaser:** This has been particularly true where the injured person was not even a family member of the original purchaser, but instead, a *subsequent purchaser*, or a member of that person's family.

4. **Seller who did not build house:** Another limitation frequently imposed is that the defendant must be the *actual builder*, not merely a prior occupant. Such a result can be justified because defendant-homeowner is not in the "business" of selling homes, and should not bear "enterprise liability" for defects as a mass-producer should.

   a. **Concealment of known dangers:** But even such an "amateur" seller may be liable if there were defects of which he was aware, and which he actively concealed. See *supra*, p. 255.

D. **Lessors of real property:** *Lessors of real estate* have also, in a few cases, been held to impliedly warrant the habitability of the premises. But in many states, the lessor does not even have full negligence liability, let alone strict or warranty liability. See the discussion of negligence *supra*, p. 251.

E. **Services:** One who sells *services*, rather than goods, does not fall within the Second or Third Restatement's strict liability provisions, nor within the UCC implied warranties (except that sales of food and drink in a restaurant are within the Code). See, e.g., Rest. 3d (Prod. Liab.) §19(b): "Services, even when provided commercially, are not products."

1. **Electric utilities:** Electric utilities, and others who *supply electricity* as some aspect of the service they sell, are good examples of this "no strict liability for services" principle. At least where the electricity has not yet been delivered to the customer (e.g., at the time of the accident it's passing through a telephone pole or power station maintained by the utility), a plaintiff bystander who gets *electrocuted* will have to show that the utility or service provider behaved negligently.

   > **Example:** Utility puts up a wooden pole next to the street, containing high-voltage power lines. Due to a defect in the insulation on a bolt that Utility fastens at shoulder height onto the pole, the bolt carries a high-voltage charge. When P, a passerby, touches the bolt, he is electrocuted.
   >
   > P will not be able to recover in strict product liability against Utility, because Utility sold a service (electricity), not a defective product (the pole or the bolt). (Operation of high-voltage lines might conceivably be held to be an ultrahazardous activity leading to strict liability on that count, but that wouldn't be strict "product" liability. Also, if the electricity had already passed into the house of a customer before the accident, a court might hold that the electricity had become a "product" that could give rise to strict product liability.)

2. **Construction workers:** Another good illustration of the principle that service providers won't have strict product liability is *construction work.* Suppose a construction company (call it Contractor) does work using a construction product that is not being "sold" by Contractor to the customer, and some bystander is injured. Contractor won't have strict product liability, because it didn't sell the defective product.

   > **Example:** Contractor does tiling in Customer's apartment. In doing so, Contractor uses a high-temperature torch made by Manco. The torch, due to a design defect, sprays its flame too widely, and ignites a piece of pre-existing wall. The resulting fire releases toxic fumes that leak into the neighboring apartment, injuring Neighbor. Neighbor won't be able to recover against Contractor in strict product liability, because Contractor didn't "sell" the torch, making the fact that the torch was defective irrelevant. (But Neighbor could recover in strict product liability against *Manco*, because the torch was defective, was at some point in the distribution chain sold by Manco, and proximately caused the injury to Neighbor.)

3. **Product incorporated in service:** However, if a product is furnished *in combination with a service*, then most courts (and the Restatements) will apply strict liability if the product turns out to be defective. See, e.g., Rest. 3d (Prod. Liab) §20(c), making the standard product-liability provisions of the Restatement applicable to one who "provides a combination of products and services."

   > **Example:** P goes to D's beauty parlor to get a permanent. D uses a solution made by a cosmetics company, X, which is defective and causes acute dermatitis on P's scalp. Most courts would allow P to recover against D for either breach of implied warranty or strict liability for supplying a defective product, even though D also supplied a service together with the product.

   a. **Services by professionals:** But where the services are rendered by a *health professional,* she will almost never be liable in either strict tort or warranty, even if she uses a product which is defective. See, e.g., *Magrine v. Krasnica*, 227 A.2d 539 (N.J. 1967), aff'd 241 A.2d 637 (1968) (D, a dentist, not strictly liable for using a defective needle on P's jaw).

   i. Hospitals: Similarly, courts have generally declined to make *hospitals* strictly liable for medical devices that they (or doctors operating inside the hospital) supply to patients. See, e.g., *Hector v. Cedars-Sinai Medical Ctr.*, 225 Cal. Rptr. 595 (Ct. App. Cal. 1986) (hospital not strictly liable for injuries from implantation of a defective pacemaker performed in the hospital, because such liability would raise medical costs, and because the hospital does not select the pacemaker so is in a poor position to protect itself by testing, using a different brand, etc.).

VII. INTERESTS THAT MAY BE PROTECTED

A. Property damage: Products liability is generally involved with *personal injury*, and the rules discussed previously in this chapter were generally formulated in such cases. But the plaintiff's damages in some cases may consist of *property damage.* If so, may he recover on the same basis as if there were personal injuries?

1. Recovery allowed: The answer is generally "yes", assuming that the court finds that the damage in question really was *"property damage"*, as opposed to what might be called *"intangible economic harm"* (e.g., *lost profits*), discussed below.

   a. Restatement view: Thus the Third Restatement makes its standard rules of product liability applicable to "harm to persons *or property* caused by the defect." Rest. 3d (Prod. Liab.) §1. For instance, if a defect in a wood-burning stove causes it to catch fire and burn down the plaintiff's house, the plaintiff can recover for the loss of the house.

   b. Negligence: The same result would follow under negligence theory, assuming that the defendant's failure of due care could be demonstrated.

   c. Warranty: But a plaintiff not in privity with the defendant might have trouble suing on an implied warranty; such a suit against a remote seller does not fall within the versions of UCC §2-318 in force in most states, i.e., Alternatives A and B. Those sections both apply only where the non-privity plaintiff is injured "in person" by breach of the warranty.

   i. Exceptions: But Alternative C does not contain this limitation. Furthermore, case law in a particular state may give protection for such property damage, even though this is not within the language of Alternative A or B.

2. Property damage defined: Courts have not always agreed on what kind of harm falls within this "property damage" class, as opposed to intangible economic harm.

   a. P's property apart from the product itself: Clearly, sudden destruction of *plaintiff's property apart from the defective product itself* qualifies. Thus in our earlier hypothetical of a defective stove that burns down P's house, the house is obviously "property apart from the defective product," so P can recover for its value in strict liability.

b. Damage to the product itself: What if the defect causes the *defective product itself* to be *destroyed*? Here, courts are split — some treat this as "property damage" and allow strict-liability recovery, but most view it as intangible economic loss (see *infra*, pp. 404-405), for which contractual and warranty recovery, not strict product liability, are the appropriate forms of relief.

    i. Restatement does not allow recovery: The Third Restatement follows the latter view, disallowing strict-product-liability for damage to the product itself. The commentary to the Restatement says that in the case of damage to the product itself, "a majority of courts have concluded that the [contract] remedies provided under the Uniform Commercial Code — repair and replacement costs and, in appropriate circumstances, consequential economic loss — are sufficient." Rest. 3d (Prod. Liab.) §21, Comment d.

    Example: D Rubber Co. sells a conveyor belt to P, an automobile manufacturer. P installs the belt on an assembly line, on which it is making its hot new car model. The belt breaks due to a manufacturing defect, and this belt causes the entire line to be inoperable for several days, until a substitute belt can be installed. P loses many days of production at a time when the new model has just started appearing in showrooms. In P's strict liability suit against D, expert witnesses testify for P that the breakdown cost P $1 million in profits that P will never recoup.

    Most courts, and the Third Restatement, would agree that P should not be permitted to recover its lost profits on a strict-liability theory, because P has suffered no physical injury, and the only property damage has suffered is damage to the defective product itself. Therefore, P will have to recover on a warranty theory or not at all. Cf. Rest. 3d (Prod. Liab.) §21, Illustr. 3, posing essentially these facts, and concluding that because P's losses do not derive from injury to persons or to property other than the defective item itself, P cannot recover under the Restatement's product-liability rules.

c. Loss of bargain: Now, suppose the plaintiff's damages stem from the fact that his product simply *doesn't work* because of the defect, or is *worth less* with the defect than it would be without it. Here, too, courts are in dispute. Most would treat this as intangible economic harm, for which strict liability will generally *not* be allowed. See P,W&S (9th), p. 774, n. 1.

    i. Warranty: Where the plaintiff claiming a loss of bargain is not allowed to recover in strict liability, her recourse will generally be to use a *warranty* theory. But disclaimers and problems with privity usually make warranty law less attractive. See *supra*, p. 351.

B. Intangible economic harm: Where the plaintiff's damages are found to be solely *intangible economic* ones, as opposed to personal injury or property damage, the plaintiff will have a much harder time recovering, particularly if he is not suing his immediate seller. The profits lost by a businessman when a piece of equipment failed to work because it was defective would, for instance, be such an intangible economic loss.

1. Direct purchaser: If the plaintiff is suing the person who sold the goods to him, his best bet is suing for breach of *implied or express warranty.*

a. **Measure of damages:** Whether the warranty breached is express or implied, the direct purchaser can recover the difference between what the product would have been worth had it been as warranted, and what it is in fact worth with its defect. (UCC §2-714(2)). He can also recover consequential damages, (e.g. *lost profits*) if these result from "general or particular requirements and needs of which the seller at the time of contracting had reason to know. . . . " (§2-715(2)).

b. **Strict liability and negligence:** Since the measure of damages in warranty is quite generous to the plaintiff in this position, it is rare that he would want to assert a strict liability or negligence claim. This might, however, happen if the seller had some UCC warranty defense (e.g., a *disclaimer of liability*). In that event, a court would almost certainly hold that the plaintiff is not entitled to recover on a strict liability or negligence theory for the intangible economic harm.

Example: Recall the example on p. 404, where a defective belt brings P's assembly line to a halt. Since P has suffered only intangible economic harm, P may not recover in strict liability (or negligence), and must recover on a warranty theory if at all.

2. **Remote purchasers and non-purchasers:** Where the plaintiff is suing not his own seller, but a remote person (e.g., the manufacturer) he will find it difficult to recover anything if his only harm is an intangible economic one.

a. **Warranty:** A few courts might allow him to recover on implied warranty, particularly states in which Alternative C to §2-318 is in force (although that section may be limited to economic harm resulting from "property damage," not intangible harm). Most courts, however, would probably deny the implied warranty claim, on the grounds that the plaintiff must sue his own immediate seller for such breaches. See, e.g., W&S, p. 395-398 ("We agree with the courts that have refused to allow recovery of consequential economic loss to remote buyers.")

i. **Express warranty:** Of course, if the plaintiff could show that the remote seller or manufacturer had made an *express warranty* and breached it, and that he, the plaintiff, was within the class of persons expected to be reached by the warranty, he would have a good chance of recovering under the UCC, even if his harm was only economic. Thus in *Seely v. White Motor Co.*, 403 P.2d 145 (Cal. 1965), the plaintiff purchaser of a farm truck was permitted to recover from the defendant manufacturer for lost profits, as well as part of the purchase price, when the truck did not live up to the business uses that the defendant had expressly warranted it for. (However, the court indicated that had the plaintiff been suing merely on a strict liability theory, he would not have been permitted to recover for lost profits; since the law generally prevents disclaimers of strict tort liability, it would be unfair to force every manufacturer to be responsible for its ultimate customers' loss of business profits.)

b. **Strict liability:** The remote buyer will not recover for his economic harm in *strict liability*, in almost all courts that have considered the question. See, e.g., Rest. 3d (Prod. Liab.) §21, Comment a: "Some categories of loss, including those often referred to as 'pure economic loss,' are more appropriately assigned to contract law and the [warranty] remedies set forth in . . . the Uniform Commercial Code."

    i. **Non-buyers:** This rule applies not only to remote purchasers who are suing people further up the distribution channel with whom they have no direct contractual relationship, but also to ***non-purchasers*** who have suffered economic harm as a result of injury to the person or property of ***someone other than themselves.***

        Example: P owns a restaurant, located next door to an office building that is owned by X Corp. and occupied exclusively by X Corp's employees. D manufactures a faulty boiler, which it sells to X Corp. The boiler explodes, damaging X Corp's building extensively. The building damage causes X Corp. to suspend operations for one month while repairs are made. During that month, P's restaurant loses 50% of its revenues, and all its profits, due to the absence of X Corp. employees as customers.

        Even though the defective boiler has caused property damage to X Corp. (for which X will be able to recover on a strict liability theory), *P* will not be permitted to recover in strict liability (or, for that matter, in negligence) because she has suffered only intangible economic harm. Cf. Rest. 3d (Prod. Liab.) §21, Comment d ("[A] defective product may destroy a commercial business establishment, whose employees patronize a particular restaurant, resulting in economic loss to the restaurant. The loss suffered by the restaurant generally is not recoverable in tort and in any event is not cognizable under product liability law.")

  c. **Combined with other harm:** On the other hand, if the plaintiff *can* show that he has received either physical injury or "property damage," he may then be able to "tack on" his intangible economic harm as an ***additional*** element of damages. This would certainly be the case in a negligence action (e.g., profits lost by the plaintiff-businessman when he can't work due to physical injury). It might also be true in a strict liability or warranty action, although this is less likely.

VIII. DEFENSES BASED ON THE PLAINTIFF'S CONDUCT

  A. **Introduction:** Since courts began recognizing strict product liability in the 1960s, they have struggled with the significance that should be given to "bad" conduct by the plaintiff. What happens if the plaintiff negligently fails to notice that the product is defective? What happens if the plaintiff knowingly continues to use the product after consciously realizing that it is unsafe? What if the plaintiff misuses the product, putting it to a use which she knows or should know is not intended by the manufacturer? Courts have always varied tremendously in how they answer these questions, and the "majority" rule on a particular issue, if one ever existed at all, has tended to change over time. The student will not find much certainty in this area.

  B. **The Second Restatement and early decisions:** When the Second Restatement formulated the concept of strict product liability in 1965, that concept focused on manufacturing defects, as opposed to design defects and failure-to-warn. At that time, contributory negligence was an absolute bar to a plaintiff's recovery in virtually every state. Given this absolute bar, if the Second Restatement had allowed contributory negligence to be a defense to a strict product liability action, the advance of strict liability — and the shifting of the risk of non-negligent manufacturing defects from consumer to manufacturer — would have been nearly stopped in its tracks.

1. **Contributory negligence no defense:** Therefore, the Second Restatement adopted the view that ***contributory negligence*** — at least in the sense of the plaintiff's ***failure to discover a product's defects*** — was ***not*** a defense to a strict liability action. See Comment n to Rest. 2d §402A ("The user's negligent failure to discover a defect, or to take precautions against the possibility of its existence, is not a defense to a strict liability action.")

2. **Assumption of risk:** On the other hand the Second Restatement *did* recognize the defense of ***assumption of risk***, even in a strict-liability action. If the plaintiff knowingly, voluntarily and unreasonably subjected himself to a particular product risk, this would be a complete bar to strict-liability recovery. Rest. 2d §402A, Comment n. (We'll talk more about assumption of risk *infra*, p. 408.) (The Second Restatement seems to have implicitly assumed that all plaintiff misconduct can be classified as either failure-to-discover-the-defect or knowing-assumption-of-risk; as we'll see below, there are in-between situations that are important.)

3. **Courts agreed:** In the first decades of the rise of strict liability, most courts agreed with the Second Restatement's approach of disallowing the plaintiff's negligence to be a defense, except in the case of knowing assumption of risk.

4. **Problems with the Second Restatement approach:** But in the late twentieth century, comparative negligence replaced contributory negligence nearly everywhere. (See *supra*, p. 282.) Furthermore, courts began to see that even in many actions denominated "strict" liability, there were large negligence components; this was true, for instance, in virtually every design-defect and failure-to-warn claim. Since plaintiff's negligence would merely reduce rather than eliminate recovery, and since the defendant was usually being evaluated based on quasi-negligence rather than strict-liability criteria, the Second Restatement's practice of completely eliminating plaintiff's negligence as a defense seemed increasingly ***inappropriate***.

C. **The Third Restatement / modern approach recognizes comparative fault:** Consequently, most modern decisions ***allow the plaintiff's negligence to be asserted as a defense in product liability actions.*** Epstein Tbk, §16.15, p. 430. The Third Restatement agrees with this approach: *whatever* the jurisdiction's standard method of dealing with plaintiff's negligence is (typically comparative negligence of one sort or another), ***that method applies to product-liability actions***. See Rest. 3d (Prod. Liab.) §17(a): "A plaintiff's recovery of damages for harm caused by a product defect may be reduced if the conduct of the plaintiff combines with the product defect to cause the harm and the plaintiff's conduct fails to conform to generally applicable rules establishing appropriate standards of care." The commentary notes that "[a] strong majority of jurisdictions apply the comparative responsibility doctrine to products liability actions." Comment a to Rest. 3d §17.

There are a number of different ways in which a plaintiff might behave negligently with respect to a product. Therefore, to see how the modern approach works, we need to consider each of these ways separately.

1. **Failure to discover the risk:** First, the plaintiff might ***"negligently" fail to discover that there is a defect at all.*** Here, the modern approach essentially agrees with that of the ear-

lier Second Restatement: if the plaintiff's only fault is to fail to discover the defect, this is probably not really "negligence" at all, since a person is normally entitled to assume that a product is not defective. Therefore, in the ordinary case plaintiff's failure to discover the defect will not cause any reduction in her recovery.

> **Example:** P opens a can of tuna fish manufactured by D. Absent-mindedly, P takes a large forkful of the tuna without looking at it. Had P looked, he would have seen a large, sharp, metal sliver, which he would not have put in his mouth. P's mouth is slashed, and he brings a strict-liability action against D.

> Even though a consumer of ordinary attentiveness might well have looked at his food before eating it, and would have discovered the risk, most courts will not apply comparative negligence to reduce P's recovery, on the theory that a consumer is entitled to expect that a product will not contain a manufacturing defect. See Rest. 3d (Prod. Liab.) §17, Comment d ("In general, a plaintiff has no reason to expect that a new product contains a defect and would have little reason to be on guard to discover it.")

2. **Knowing assumption of risk:** Second, the plaintiff might be fully aware of a product's defectiveness (whether of a manufacturing or design nature), yet voluntarily and unreasonably decide to "assume the risk" of that defect. In this situation, the modern trend is to ***treat assumption-of-risk as a form of comparative negligence***: to the extent that the plaintiff's decision to use the product in the face of the known risk was unreasonable, it will cause plaintiff's recovery to be reduced proportionately (and will ***not*** serve as an ***absolute bar*** to recovery).

> **Example:** P is driving a new car manufactured by D. A warning light suddenly flashes, saying "Overheated engine. Stop immediately." As it happens, P has just carefully read the car's instruction manual, and knows that an overheated engine can often lead to an explosion, with consequent physical danger. P then looks under the hood, and sees that a water hose has ruptured, causing the engine to receive too little water. (Assume that this rupture constitutes a manufacturing defect for which D will be liable under standard strict-liability doctrine.) Nonetheless, P continues to drive for 100 more miles in 90 degree temperatures, even though he is merely taking a pleasure drive. The engine explodes, injuring P.

> Under the traditional Second Restatement approach, P's conduct would be viewed as assumption of risk, and he would probably be completely barred from recovery. But under the Third Restatement and modern approach, P's conduct — though it consists of a voluntary encountering of a known risk — will be treated the same as any other type of plaintiff's negligence. In a pure comparative negligence jurisdiction, therefore, P's recovery will be reduced by an amount representing P's portion of the combined "responsibility" of P and D, but P will still be allowed to make some recovery.

a. **Complete bar in some courts:** But a minority of courts still treat a plaintiff's voluntary encountering of a known product defect to be assumption of risk, and to be a complete bar to recovery. Thus on the facts of the above example, some courts would find that P was not entitled to recover anything, because his continuing to drive after knowing of the danger of an explosion constituted an assumption of risk.

3. **Conduct that is high-risk apart from defect:** There are some types of culpable plaintiff behavior that fall in between the "negligent failure to discover the defect" and "intentional assumption of the risk from the defect" situations that we've discussed so far. One of these occurs where the plaintiff *knowingly pursues* an activity that would be *high-risk even in the absence of a defect*, and the activity *combines with a defect* to create an accident, or to make an accident worse. In this situation, as in the prior two situations, the modern approach is to simply treat plaintiff's behavior as being one sort of negligence that is to be thrown into the comparative-fault hopper, and weighed against the manufacturer's culpability.

> **Example:** P buys a new car made by D. P drives the car while intoxicated, and hits a guardrail while traveling at 40 mph. Had P not been intoxicated, the collision would probably not have occurred. Immediately following the collision, P is thrown against the drivers-side door. Due to a defective latch on that door, the door opens, and P is thrown into the roadway, where he is hit by another car and seriously injured. Had the latch not been defective, the door would probably not have opened, P would not have been thrown out, and his injuries would have been much less severe.
>
> A court following the modern / Third Restatement approach will treat P's driving-while-intoxicated on a comparative-fault basis. Assuming that the jurisdiction applies pure comparative negligence (or that it applies modified comparative negligence, but that P's responsibility is found to be less than D's responsibility) P's recovery will be reduced by his percentage of the total responsibility, but will not be eliminated. Implicit in this result will be the conclusion that P's driving while intoxicated and D's manufacture of the defective latch were both proximate causes, and causes in fact, of P's injury. (To the extent that D can demonstrate that some of P's injuries would have occurred even had the latch not failed, P will recover nothing for those injuries, since the defective latch did not in any way cause those injuries.)

4. **Ignoring of safety precaution:** Another "in between" situation arises where P *consciously fails to use an available safety device*, and is then injured by a product defect that would not have led to injury had the safety device been used. In some situations, the safety device is one provided by the manufacturer of the defective product; in other cases, it is provided by a third party. The analysis is pretty much the same in both types of situations — in most courts the plaintiff's failure to use an available safety device is generally fault that *reduces* (but does *not eliminate*) plaintiff's recovery.

> **Example:** P, a consumer, purchases a Slicer-Dicer made by D. The Slicer-Dicer is designed to slice, dice, chop, and puree a variety of household products. The Slicer Dicer comes with a hand guard, which when installed prevents the user's hand from getting near the cutting blades. The hand guard is purposely designed to be removable for easy cleaning; the device and its instruction manual both contain a bold-faced warning that the device should not be operated without the hand guard. P removes the hand guard because he finds it easier to use the machine without it; he realizes that there is a greater danger of cutting his hand, but decides to risk it. P's hand slips, and is severely cut by the blades. P sues D on the theory that D's permitting the guard to be removed for separate cleaning constituted a design defect.

In a modern comparative-negligence jurisdiction the court would probably hold that P's use of the product without the guard should reduce, but not eliminate, his recovery.

> **Note:** However, P's "misuse" of the product by permanently removing the guard might cause the court to invoke one of several doctrines that might prevent P's recovery *entirely*. For instance, the removal might be found to be such a misuse of the product that it constituted a ***superseding cause***. Alternatively, the court might conclude that such a removal was so ***unforeseeable*** that the temporarily-removable design was ***not defective at all***. See *infra*, immediately below, for a discussion of the various ways that product misuse might affect the outcome in a litigation.

D. **"Misuse" of the product:** Courts sometimes speak of ***"product misuse"*** as if it were a single defense or doctrine that could defeat a plaintiff's claim. But the reality is that plaintiff's misuse of a product is merely a description of facts, not an independent doctrine or defense. Dobbs, p. 1026. The plaintiff's misuse of the product can lead to at least three different legal consequences, depending on the precise facts:

[1] it may lead to a ***reduction in plaintiff's recovery***, under comparative-fault principles;

[2] it may indicate that the product was ***not defective at all***; and

[3] it may prevent the defect from being deemed to be the ***proximate cause*** of plaintiff's injuries.

We consider each of these possible effects in turn.

1. **Reduction in recovery:** The misuse will often, of course, constitute ***"fault"*** on the part of the plaintiff, which will then under comparative-fault principles result in a reduction in the amount of the plaintiff's recovery. This is the type of consequence which we have discussed extensively *supra* (e.g., the overheated-engine, drunken-driver and Slicer-Dicer examples on pp. 408, 409 and 409-410 respectively.)

2. **Indication that product was not defective at all:** In some circumstances, the fact that the accident came about only after the plaintiff's misuse may indicate that the product was ***never defective in the first place***. This is especially likely to be so in the case of a ***design-defect*** claim. Recall that a design is defective only if it fails to reduce the risks of ***foreseeable*** harms, and that there is no duty to design a product that will remain safe when used in unforeseeable manner. (See *supra*, p. 378.) It follows that if plaintiff's misuse was so unusual as to be considered unforeseeable, the fact that the accident occurred will say very little about whether the product was defective.

> **Example:** Recall the example from p. 378, in which P climbs up the back of a chair made by D in order to reach the top of a bookshelf. On these facts, the Third Restatement concludes that the chair is not defectively designed, because P's "misuse of the product is so unreasonable that the risks it entails need not be designed against." Rest. 3d (Prod. Liab.) §2, Ilustr. 20.

a. **Foreseeable misuse:** But remember that if the misuse is ***reasonably foreseeable***, and could be designed against without undue cost or sacrifice of product features, a design that does not prevent the misuse may well be defective. The classic example is a car:

speeding may in some sense be a "misuse" of the product, but if the car's maker does not make at least reasonable efforts to design a car that will be crashworthy in the event of a high-speed collision, the lack of crashworthiness is likely to be found to be a design defect.

b. **Unavoidably unsafe:** However, you cannot assume that merely because a particular type of misuse is foreseeable, a product whose design does not protect against that misuse is necessarily defective. Remember that a design defect exists only where an ***alternative reasonable design exists***, such that the dangers of the design actually chosen by the defendant outweigh the benefits of that design. (See *supra*, p. 373-374). A design that fails to guard against a particular type of misuse may nonetheless be non-defective under this risk-utility analysis — this typically happens in the case of "unavoidably unsafe" products.

Example: Suppose that D, a liquor manufacturer, makes a particular brand of 100-proof rum in 40-ounce bottles. (Assume that rum is commonly sold in such a 100-proof version, though less potent variations are also often sold.) P chug-a-lugs an entire 40-ounce bottle, and dies of acute alcohol poisoning. P's estate sues D on the theory that D should have designed the rum differently by reducing its alcohol content.

P is unlikely to prevail, because the court is likely to conclude that uncontaminated 100-proof rum is simply not defective — its alcoholic content is characteristic of this type of rum, and a reduction in the alcohol content would have turned it into a different product materially less attractive to consumers. In other words, it cannot be said that the 100-proof version had dangers that outweighed its benefits, viewed in the context of alternative types of rum.

3. **Misuse as superseding cause:** Finally, the plaintiff's (or someone else's) misuse of the product may be a ***superseding cause***, i.e., a cause that prevents the defect from being deemed to be a ***proximate cause*** of the harm. (See our discussion of superseding causes in general negligence cases *supra*, p. 162.) When this occurs, the plaintiff will be ***completely barred*** from recovery, since the usual tort rules on proximate cause apply: D cannot be required to pay anything on account of an injury for which its conduct was not a proximate cause.

a. **Foreseeability of misuse:** Generally, the proximate cause issue revolves around *foreseeability*: if the misuse was foreseeable, it is not a superseding cause, but if it was unforeseeable, it *is* superseding. Dobbs, p. 1029.

i. **Extreme misuse required:** This foreseeability standard means that it takes a ***very extreme misuse*** to be superseding in a strict product liability case. So, for instance, the mere fact that the defendant ***warned against*** a particular use won't be enough to establish misuse when the plaintiff engages in that use. And in any event, courts will narrowly construe warnings.

Example: D manufactures an all-electric sports car that can go from 0 to 90 mph in 4.7 seconds. The user's manual states in bold letters on the cover, "Using the full acceleration capability of this car is dangerous. Do not accelerate faster than 0-80 in 5.0 seconds, because any faster rate will impose G-forces in excess of 2, which may cause neck and spine injuries." P reads the manual, doesn't focus on this cover language, and figures, "Let's see how fast this can accelerate." P floors it, and his head snaps back when he accelerates at 3 G-forces. Due to a lack of a head rest that would accommodate the accelerations of which the car is capable, P's neck is fractured. He sues D in strict product liability, claiming that the lack of a proper head rest was a design defect.

A court would be *unlikely* to hold that P's conduct, including the ignoring of the warnings, constituted misuse of the sort that would be superseding. Since the car was manufactured in a way capable of acceleration more rapid than the head rest could support, P's use of that rapid-acceleration capability would be "foreseeable," and thus not superseding. Therefore, any misconduct by P would be classified as comparative negligence that will reduce his recovery, not as a superseding cause that would negate recovery entirely.

b. **Removal of safety device by employer:** If the misuse is unforeseeable, it may be superseding even if done by a *third person* rather than by the plaintiff. The most common illustration is an *employer's removal of a safety device* from a machine: where the removal is deemed to be unforeseeable, it will be superseding, and will block even a completely innocent user from recovering against the manufacturer.

Example: D makes a commercial meat grinder with an integrated hand guard that cannot easily be removed. The machine is sold to X, a supermarket. In an attempt to increase productivity, X hires a machine shop to remove the hand guard by use of a blowtorch and other specialized tools. P, an employee of X, loses three fingers when his hand slips while using the guard-less grinder. Had the guard been present, the accident would not have occurred. P sues D on a design-defect theory, alleging that the grinder should have been designed so that if the guard was removed, the machine would become inoperable.

The court will first determine whether removal of the hand guard was reasonably foreseeable. On these facts, is likely that the court will conclude that the removal was not reasonably foreseeable. In that event, X's conduct in removing the guard will probably be deemed to be a superseding cause, relieving D of all liability to P. If, however, the court decided that the removal *was* reasonably foreseeable (e.g., because there was evidence that, prior to the manufacture of this particular unit, D had heard that other users were removing the guard for productivity reasons), the removal by X would not be superseding, and P *would* be permitted to recover if he proved that D's design was defective. (Even here, however, it would be hard for P to show that D's failure to make the machine inoperable without the handguard present constituted a design defect.)

IX. DEFENSES BASED ON FEDERAL REGULATION, MAINLY THE DEFENSE OF PREEMPTION

A. **Preemption:** The federal government regulates many aspects of products. For instance, the design, marketing and labeling of medical devices are heavily regulated, as are the advertising and labeling of tobacco products. This federal regulation can have an important impact on consumers' state product-liability rights. In particular, under the doctrine of *"preemption,"* federal regulatory action may *limit the states' freedom to apply their usual rules of tort liability* to cases involving the regulated product.

1. **The Supremacy Clause:** The concept of preemption is based on the *Supremacy Clause* of the U.S. Constitution. That clause says, in essence, that federal law *takes priority over conflicting state law*.

2. **Preemption, generally:** The rules of preemption, then, are simply rules about how to apply the Supremacy Clause to state action that's alleged to be inconsistent with federal action. Here is a brief summary of how preemption works in the context of product-liability law.

    a. **Express preemption:** First — and usually easiest to apply — is *"express"* preemption. This occurs when Congress explicitly says that it intends to take away the states' ability to regulate in a particular way. When it is clear that Congress has meant to do this, the Supremacy Clause nullifies any attempt by a state to do what Congress has said the state may not do.

        i. **Express preemption in medical-device cases:** Express preemption is likely to be found, for instance, where the Food and Drug Administration *pre-approves* a newly-developed *medical device* such as a pacemaker or heart valve. Once this happens, a user of the device will generally not be permitted to recover under state tort law for the device's defectiveness. That's because the court will likely conclude that the federal approval expressly preempts a state from awarding tort damages premised on the device's defectiveness. See, e.g., *Riegel v. Medtronic Inc.*, 128 S.Ct. 999 (2008) (where FDA gives pre-market approval to a particular medical device, this fact preempts states from hearing common-law claims alleging that the product is unsafe or ineffective).

    b. **Implied preemption:** Most real-life controversies involving preemption in tort law, however, involve *"implied"* rather than express preemption. That is, Congress (or a federal agency acting under direction from Congress) does not explicitly tell the states that they may not take a particular tort-related action. Instead, Congress or the federal agency enacts a statute or regulation, and a litigant (usually the manufacturer of the product) argues that the federal enactment should be interpreted as displacing a particular state tort-law rule. There are two different ways in which implied preemption can occur in a tort-law context — a *direct conflict* and a federal decision to *occupy* an *entire field*.

        i. **Direct conflict:** Sometimes analysis of the federal law and the state law shows that the two are in *direct conflict*. When this happens, as you'd expect, the state law must yield. The direct conflict can be of two sorts:

            (1) it is *impossible* for the maker of a product to *comply simultaneously* with the federal regulation and the state regulation; or

            (2) the *objectives* behind the federal regulation and the state regulation are *inconsistent*.

                Example of (1) (compliance with both is impossible): Suppose that Congress says that every package of cigarettes must contain a label stating, "the

Surgeon General has determined that smoking may be hazardous to your health." Suppose then that North Carolina, a tobacco-growing state, passes a statute saying "No health warnings are required in this state on any package of cigarettes." Obviously there is a direct contradiction between the federal and state regulatory schemes — a given cigarette package cannot comply with both. Therefore, the state regulation is invalid.

Example of (2) (conflicting objectives): Suppose that Congress says, "it is the desire of Congress that auto manufacturers be encouraged to install airbags in every automobile produced after the date of this act." To further that objective, Congress gives auto manufacturers a $200 tax credit for every car that is made with an airbag. Texas then passes a statute saying, "in any tort litigation in which the occupant of a vehicle alleges that he or she has been injured by the inappropriate inflation of an airbag, the burden of proving the non-defectiveness of the airbag shall be placed upon the manufacturer." A court might well hold that in view of the strong federal interest in encouraging airbag installation, the Texas statute has a sharply conflicting objective — making airbag installation more burdensome to manufacturers — and that the Texas statute should therefore be deemed impliedly preempted by the federal legislation.

ii.   **Occupation of entire field:** The second form of implied preemption occurs where the federal government is found to have *intended to occupy an entire field of regulation*. If such an intent is found, then even a state law that does *not directly conflict* with the federal law will be preempted.

   Example: Congress has given the Food and Drug Administration (FDA) full power to license most types of medical devices, and to prescribe how such devices may be marketed. Assume that as to a particular device, the FDA has not actively examined or approved the device (making the situation different from *Riegel, supra,* p. 413, where the FDA explicitly pre-approved the device). A state then imposes additional licensing requirements on that device. A court would likely hold that because Congress intended to occupy the *entire field* of licensing that type of device, the additional state requirements are preempted even though the state requirements don't conflict with any actual federal requirement.

   (1) Need for uniformity: When a court is deciding whether Congress intended to occupy the entire field, the court will give special weight to indications that Congress perceived a need for a *uniform national rule*, rather than varying state rules. So, for instance, in the medical-device-labelling field, the need for manufacturers to have a *single nationwide system of labels* (not state-by-state variations) would be an important factor pointing a court towards the conclusion that Congress intended to occupy the entire field.

c. **Implied preemption of state common-law tort remedies:**   The most interesting and controversial question involving preemption occurs when a manufacturer argues that federal regulation preempts the states from allowing a plaintiff to recover for a *common-law tort*. In this scenario, there is no explicit state "regulation" — the state is not passing a statute or enacting an administrative regulation that is alleged to be inconsistent with the federal approach. Instead, the defendant manufacturer is typically making the argument that merely ***allowing a plaintiff to recover in tort*** would itself constitute an ***implicit*** sort of "regulation" that is inconsistent with the federal regulatory scheme. So these are cases of "implied" (rather than express) preemption of state law by federal law.

i.   **Needs direct conflict or impeding of federal enforcement:** It is not easy for a manufacturer to defeat a common-law tort claim by use of an implied preemption defense. As a good rule of thumb, the manufacturer (D) will win with such a defense *only* if it can show that *either:*

[1] the conduct that P argues D was required to take under state common-law rules ***conflicts*** with the federal regulation; or

[2] allowing the tort recovery sought by P ***would impede enforcement*** of the federal regulatory scheme.

Dobbs, § 373, p. 1037. Manufacturers will often have a tough time making either of these showings.

ii.   **Implied preemption in prescription-drug cases:** Cases involving ***prescription drugs*** will often be found to involve only "***implied***" preemption. Although Congress has given the FDA authority to regulate prescription drugs just as it allowed the agency to regulate medical devices like the one in *Riegel* (*supra*, p. 413), Congress has ***not expressly dealt with preemption*** in the prescription-drug context. Therefore, prescription-drug cases are harder for the defendant manufacturer to win on a preemption theory than are medical-device cases, because an implied-preemption defense tends to be harder to establish than an express-preemption one.

Example: P receives an anti-nausea drug, Phenergan, made by D. The warnings on the label for Phenergan had been approved by the FDA. There are several ways to administer Phenergan, one of which is by putting it directly into the patient's vein (the "IV-push" method). The IV-push method is the most dangerous, because if the drug is mistakenly put into an artery instead of a vein, it is likely to cause gangrene. That's what happens to P, who ends up having her arm amputated. P claims that the drug was improperly labeled by D, in that D should have instructed practitioners to avoid the IV-push method.

D makes two sorts of preemption claims in defense: (1) that since the FDA had already given pre-market approval of D's labelling, it would have been *impossible* for D to *simultaneously comply* with the federally-imposed requirements and with any state-law duty to warn against the dangers of the IV-push method (dangers that apparently didn't become known until after the pre-market approval by the FDA); and (2) the *purposes* of the FDA regulatory scheme would be impeded by allowing state common-law recovery based on the label.

Held (by the Supreme Court 6-3), no implied preemption occurred here. As to the impossibility defense, "impossibility preemption is a demanding defense," and D hasn't shown that the FDA wouldn't have retroactively approved D's revision of its label to include strengthened warnings (a process that the FDA regulations generally allow).

As to the inconsistent-purposes defense, Congress knew how to expressly forbid state-law suits where it thought such suits posed a danger to congressional objectives, as Congress had long done in the case of medical devices (as in *Riegel, supra*). So in the context of prescription drugs, the fact that Congress remained silent rather than enacting such a ban indicates that Congress did not view such suits as being inconsistent with its objectives. Consequently, Congress has not impliedly preempted state-law suits. *Wyeth v. Levine*, 129 S.Ct. 1187 (2009).

B. **Compliance with government standards:** Don't confuse the defense of federal preemption of state law with a separate defense, the so-called *"regulatory compliance"* defense. The latter defense asserts that because a product complies with a particular government regulation scheme, that compliance automatically means that the product is not defective. Most jurisdictions do *not* accept this defense — the plaintiff is free to show that even though the product meets the relevant federal regulatory requirements, the product is nonetheless defective. (However, nearly all states at least allow the fact that the product meets federal regulatory requirements to be admitted as non-dispositive *evidence* of non-defectiveness.) The regulatory compliance defense is discussed *supra*, p. 380.

Quiz Yourself on

PRODUCTS LIABILITY *(Entire Chapter)*

69. Slip 'N' Slide Floor Polish, which is poisonous, looks like Flopsy Cola, a popular soft drink, and comes in a soda-like bottle with an easily removable lid. The bottle has a warning, reading: "This product is poisonous. Keep out of reach of children." Little Bobo, three years old, finds a bottle of polish under the kitchen sink, pops the lid off, and drinks the contents of the bottle, making himself seriously ill in the process. Could Slip 'N' Slide be strictly liable for Bobo's injuries? _____

70. Count Dracula enters the hospital for an operation to correct internal hemorrhaging. During the operation he receives a transfusion of blood infected with the HIV virus, and as a result he contracts AIDS. Can he successfully sue the hospital in strict product liability? _____

71. Americus Gothic is justly famous in his neighborhood for his delectable acorn jelly. He's not in the retail business, but occasionally he sells a jar to a lucky neighbor. Although Gothic is careful, one batch of his jelly is contaminated and, when his neighbor, Uneeda Purifyre, buys a jar and eats some, she becomes violently ill. Can Uneeda hold Gothic liable in strict liability? _____

72. Scrubby Dubdub Inc. manufactures equipment for automatic car washes. Spit 'N' Polish reconditions old car wash equipment, rebuilds it, and resells it. The Hot Wax Car Wash buys reconditioned equipment from Spit 'N' Polish. The equipment fails as Lydia Puttputt is getting her car washed. The brushes go crazy and smash her car. She is seriously injured as a result. She sues Scrubby Dubdub in strict liability. Could Scrubby Dubdub be liable? _____

73. Campfire Soup Company is in the business of making canned soups. It uses only the latest, state-of-the-art machinery to blend, cook, and can the soups; it maintains high safety standards; and it conducts rigor-

ous inspections constantly. A particular can of the company's Cream of Snail soup is sold to Wholesaler, who is a distributor for Campfire's products. Wholesaler resells the can to Retailer. In Retailer's store, it is bought by Charles, a consumer. Charles prepares the soup, and serves it to Gaia, a houseguest and friend of his. As Gaia is eating the soup, she bites down, and suffers a terrible gash in her gum. The gash turns out to have been caused by a small fragment of glass in the soup. All available evidence suggests that the glass was in the soup at the time the can was opened by Charles. The glass is a type used in Campfire's canning equipment, and the most likely (though still somewhat speculative) explanation is that there was a once-in-a-million breakage of the machinery during the making of the batch that included this can. Gaia has sued all people concerned (Campfire, Wholesaler, Retailer, and Charles). Against which of them can she recover, assuming that she produces no evidence other than that already described in this question? 74

74. Frieda is driving her 2022 Newmobile when she is struck from the side by a speeding driver who drives away and is never found. The impact on Frieda's car is great enough that it causes the car to go through a barrier at the side of the road, where it tumbles over and falls into a seven-foot-deep ravine. The car finally lands on its roof, and Frieda is seriously injured. Medical evidence shows that the only serious injuries to Frieda occurred when the car landed on its roof, the pieces of steel supporting the roof buckled, and the roof therefore collapsed onto Frieda's head and neck. The evidence also shows that had a "roll bar" been installed in the car to maintain the structural integrity of the passenger compartment in a roll-over accident, Frieda would not have sustained her injuries. There is evidence that other manufacturers of similar cars have installed roll bars for this reason.

Frieda sues Newmobile in strict product liability. Newmobile defends on the grounds that a manufacturer of a defective product only has liability when the product is put to its intended use, and that collisions and roll-overs are not the intended use for cars. Will Newmobile prevail with this defense? _____

75. United Automobile Corp. manufactures a 2019 Weep four-wheel-drive vehicle, and sells it to Dealer, who resells it to Tim. The car comes with no express warranties by United, and with whatever implied warranties are implied by law in such sales. Tim, after using the car for a year, sells it to Peggy. One day, due to a defect in the design of the Weep's radiator, the radiator becomes clogged, the engine temperature heats up to an unbearable extent, and the engine catches fire. (There is no evidence that United was negligent in the way it designed the radiator — the flaw in design only became apparent long after Peggy's Weep was made, after a couple of fires like the one in Peggy's car.) Peggy escapes the car without injuries, but the car is completely destroyed by the fire. Can Peggy recover for the value of the car against United? If so, on what theory? _____

Answers

69. **Yes.** Strict liability applies to products in a defective condition unreasonably dangerous to consumers. Here, it is foreseeable that children will find the bottle, and Slip 'N' Slide designed theirs to look like soda pop. As such, Slip 'N' Slide will likely be strictly liable. The warning won't exculpate Slip 'N' Slide -- a reasonable warning is an <u>additional</u> requirement, added to the requirement that a product not be sold in a defective/unreasonably dangerous condition.

RELATED ISSUE: Slip 'N' Slide would probably also be liable in negligence, since it is unreasonable to put a poisonous product in a container like Slip 'N' Slide's. (Furthermore, it is easy for Slip 'N' Slide to redesign the bottle with a childproof top and different shape.)

70. **No.** Strict liability can only be imposed for the sale of defective products, not services. Blood transfusions are generally considered a service, not a product, and as a result strict liability cannot be imposed for infusion with infected blood.

71. No. Strict liability can only be imposed against one who is in the *business* of selling goods of the type in question. A casual transaction between neighbors, like this, cannot be the basis of strict liability. Instead, the seller must be a manufacturer, wholesaler (or other middleman), or person in the business of retailing.

72. No. The equipment was substantially altered after it left Scrubby Dubdub — Spit 'N' Polish rebuilt it. Strict liability requires that there be no substantial change in the product after it leaves defendant. Thus, Scrubby Dubdub will not be liable.

73. Campfire, Wholesaler, and Retailer, but not Charles. Campfire, Wholesaler, and Retailer will all have *strict product liability* — each sold a product that was both defective and unreasonably dangerous. Since they did so, it does not matter that they may all have behaved with more than reasonable care. It does not even matter that Wholesaler and Retailer had absolutely no chance to discover the defect no matter how diligent they were — since they were in the business of selling products of this type, they became liable for dangerous defects in the product without reference to their level of care. But the same is not true of Charles — since he was not in the business of selling soups, he can be liable only for his negligence, and the facts do not suggest that he was negligent here. (But if he should have noticed the glass and through inattention did not, then he would be liable to Gaia for negligence). See Rest. 2d, §402A, and Illustr. 1 thereto.

74. No. Strict product liability will be found whenever the product is dangerously defective if used in a *"foreseeable"* way, not merely when used in an "intended" way. Since it is quite foreseeable that a car may be involved in an accident, including a roll-over accident, Newmobile is unlikely to prevail with this defense. (Newmobile might prevail by showing that installation of a roll bar would be prohibitively expensive in light of the infrequency with which it would prove beneficial, but this is another matter.)

75. Yes, probably, but only on a warranty theory. Most courts (and the Third Restatement) would say that since the damage here consists solely of damage to the defective product itself, strict products liability does not apply. That is, most courts would treat this as a form of intangible economic loss, not "property damage," and strict products liability generally doesn't apply to intangible economic loss. In such a court, Peggy will have to proceed on a warranty theory (since by hypothesis there was no negligence.) The problem is that United didn't sell directly to Peggy but rather to Tim, who re-sold to Peggy. States vary in whether they find that the implied warranty of merchantability (which would probably cover this fact pattern) applies to a subsequent purchaser — Peggy will probably win in a state following Alternative C to UCC §2-318 but not in a state that follows Alternatives A or B (since the only non-privity plaintiffs who are covered by those Alternatives are ones who are injured "in person" by breach of the warranty).

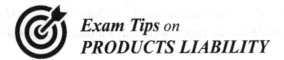

Exam Tips on
PRODUCTS LIABILITY

You'll almost always know when you've got a products liability issue — in the typical situation, some "product" will be sold, and someone will be injured when the product does not perform the way a consumer would expect it to. The hard things to do are: (1) to articulate the various theories on which P can recover; (2) to structure your answer into a sensible order; and (3) to spot and analyze the various sub-issues (e.g., Can a bystander recover? Was the product unavoidably unsafe? Was there a design defect? Was there a failure to warn?).

☛ As to structure, you may want to organize your answer into the following order:

(1) At the top level, arrange it by plaintiff-defendant pair (all claims by P1 against D1, then those by P1 against D2, P2 against D1, etc.);

(2) Then talk about the theories that could be used in each P-D pair. (*Example:* "P1's suit against D1 could be based either on strict product liability, negligence or breach of express and implied warranty. Probably P1's best results will come from the strict liability theory, because…");

(3) Then, talk about each special issue presented by the fact pattern, discussing all theories of recovery in the context of that special issue. Thus do a complete discussion of the failure to warn (as to negligence, strict liability and warranty), followed by a complete discussion of, say, design, and so on. (*Example:* "Was the product properly designed? For the negligence claim, the issue is whether the design was done with 'reasonable care.' For the strict product liability theory, the issue is whether the product was designed 'defectively,' which most courts interpret to mean 'designed in such a way as to satisfy the expectations of a reasonable consumer about how the product would perform.…'")

☛ Whenever you have injuries caused by a "product" (as distinguished from a service or an activity), remember that there are ***three main theories*** on which liability might be founded:

(1) ***Negligence*** (the manufacturer's or retailer's failure to use reasonable care in the design, manufacture, labelling or marketing of the product).

(2) ***Breach of warranty*** (which can come in three types: express warranty, implied warranty of merchantability, and implied warranty of fitness for a particular purpose).

❑ "Misrepresentation" is an offshoot of warranty, applicable mainly to cases of inadequate labelling or false advertising.

(3) ***Strict product liability*** (imposed without regard to fault, for a "defective" and "unreasonably dangerous" product).

Note: You should be sure to list and discuss *each of these theories in each instance*, if there's any chance that it might be applied. (Even if the theory won't be successful, it's probably worthwhile to say why it won't be.) (*Example:* "Because the facts tell us that Manufacturer could not have found the manufacturing defect even through the exercise of due care, probably a recovery against it based on negligence will not be possible.")

☛ In considering recovery for ***"negligence,"*** here are the main things to look for:

☞ Remember that the ordinary rules of negligence apply — there's nothing very special about negligence in the product context.

☞ ***"Privity"*** doesn't matter — as long as P was a "reasonably foreseeable" plaintiff, the fact that she was a remote purchaser, or even a bystander, doesn't prevent her from a negligence recovery against a negligent manufacturer. This is true even if the product went through several different sellers (wholesaler, retailer, original purchaser, etc.).

☞ Your analysis will differ depending on the particular defendant's place in the ***distribution channel***.

   ☞ Where D is the ***manufacturer***, the question is always, "Did D use reasonable care in making the product?" This includes component-selection, design, manufacture, post-manufacture inspection, and labelling. Generally, negligence theories are most useful against the manufacturer (as opposed to people further down in the distribution chain).

   ☞ Where D is the ***retailer***, a negligence claim is much less likely to succeed. In the typical case of a manufactured product shipped in a sealed package, the only ways the retailer is likely to be negligent are: (1) he saw or should have seen from the outside of the package that something was wrong; or (2) he knew or should have known that this particular manufacturer was likely to be producing bad goods (e.g., a safety recall is in place, which the retailer ignores or negligently fails to know about).

      ☞ Most important: the retailer has ***no duty*** to ***inspect*** the goods he sells, so the fact that an inspection would have disclosed a problem is irrelevant.

      ☞ Also, the manufacturer's negligence is ***not imputed*** to the retailer.

   ☞ Where D is a lessor, bailor, or user (i.e., a "non-seller"), negligence may be your best theory of recovery (because warranty and strict product liability are not always imposed on non-sellers).

☞ ***Contributory (or comparative) negligence*** can be a defense to a negligence product liability claim, as in other types of negligence cases. (*Example:* If P should have noticed that a food product made or sold by D was rotten from its smell, it's probably contributory/comparative negligence for P to eat it.)

☛ Be sure to mention ***breach of warranty*** whenever you analyze a product situation. This is the theory of recovery that students most frequently omit.

   ☞ One type of breach of warranty is breach of ***express*** warranty. This occurs where the product fails to live up to explicit statements that D has made about it. In the product context, this comes in two main forms: (1) D ***advertises*** the goods as having a certain characteristic (e.g., "doesn't cause drowsiness"); or (2) the ***labelling*** contains statements about the product.

      ☞ Also, the manufacturer's use of a ***picture*** or ***model*** can be an express warranty. (*Example:* If the box containing a helmet shows a person riding a motorcycle with the helmet on, that's probably an express warranty that the helmet is suitable for use as a motorcycle helmet.)

      ☞ A ***retailer*** is deemed to have "made" any express warranty that is contained on the product (and probably to have made any warranty contained in the manufacturer's advertising).

      ☞ The warranty is ***"strict"*** — it doesn't matter that D used all reasonable care to make the product conform to the warranty, or reasonably thought the product did conform.

☞ Whenever a label or advertising is incorrect, also mention that P can sue for common-law *misrepresentation*. Cite to Rest. §402B, establishing liability for one who "makes to the public a misrepresentation about a material fact" concerning the product. This theory is useful if the state's warranty law (controlled by the UCC) is narrower than usual (e.g., it allows a disclaimer that would not block misrepresentation liability, or it applies a narrow version of privity cutting off bystanders).

☞ When a product is sold by a *"merchant"* (one in the business of selling goods of that kind), the merchant is deemed to make an *implied warranty* that the goods are *"merchantable."*

☞ In your discussion of merchantability, you should define the term: "Goods are 'merchantable' if they are 'fit for the *ordinary purposes* for which such goods are used.'" There will often be an issue about whether the goods breached this warranty. (*Example:* P has a rare allergic reaction to a drug. Probably this does not make the drug "unmerchantable," because the "ordinary person" doesn't have this rare allergy.)

☞ Normally, the merchantability suit is against the retailer. But the suit can also be against the manufacturer, as long as the manufacturer was in the business of selling goods of that kind.

   ☞ Sometimes tested: Can a merchantability suit be brought against one who *"leases"* rather than sells the goods? Answer: most courts allow warranty liability here.

☞ Occasionally, you should mention the implied warranty of *fitness for a particular purpose*. Look for this fact pattern: D (almost always the retailer, not the manufacturer) knows that P has *special requirements*, and makes a *recommendation* of a particular make and model, which P follows. (The existence of a warranty of fitness for a particular purpose does not displace the warranty of merchantability — both apply.)

☞ For all three types of warranty (express, merchantability, and fitness for a particular purpose), you generally don't have to worry much about *privity*.

   ☞ All of these warranties are now generally held to extend to a *remote purchaser* ("vertical" privity).

   ☞ In virtually every state, every member of the purchaser's *household* is also covered. In most states, users who didn't buy, and even *bystanders*, are covered — but since a few states don't extend the warranties this far, you should mention this as an issue if the injured person is a bystander or other non-purchaser.

☞ Warranties can be *disclaimed*. Most-often tested: a product is marked *"AS IS."* This marking generally serves to disclaim the two implied warranties (merchantability and fitness); it's not clear whether the marking wipes out an express warranty contained elsewhere on the product's labelling, though a handwritten notation probably does disclaim any implied warranties on the pre-printed label.

☞ If P's sole damages are *intangible economic harm* (e.g., lost profits), warranty theory may be P's best bet. P's claim for economic harm is strongest where P bought the item directly from D under an express warranty; it's weakest where P sues on implied warranty and was not a purchaser (e.g., P is a "bystander" whose business is interrupted when the product explodes and cuts off electrical service in the neighborhood).

☛ The bulk of your analysis will typically concern *strict* product liability, since most of the time this furnishes P with the best overall chance of recovery.

☞ Start your analysis of strict product liability with a definition. A good one is from the Rest. 3d: "One engaged in the *business of selling or otherwise distributing products* who sells or distributes a defective product is subject to liability for *harm to persons or property caused by the defect.*"

☞ Here is a *checklist* of requirements for the strict liability doctrine:

❑ D must be a *"seller"*;

❑ D must have been in the *business* of selling or distributing products *of this type*;

❑ The product must be *"defective"*;

❑ The product must have been expected to, and did, reach the consumer *without substantial change* in its condition;

❑ P must have suffered *personal injury or property damage* (not just economic loss); and

❑ The product (and in fact its defectiveness) must have been the *cause in fact*, and the *proximate cause* of the damage to P.

☞ Two major things to keep in mind:

☞ In the usual case of a manufacturing defect, it doesn't matter that D *used all possible care* in designing and manufacturing the product;

☞ The doctrine applies to non-manufacturers who sell, most notably *retailers* (even though they couldn't possibly have known of the defect or danger).

☞ Commonly-tested: Was the product in fact *"defective"*?

☞ For manufacturing defects, quote the Rest. 3d's test: "A product contains a *manufacturing defect* when the product *departs from its intended design even though all possible care was exercised* in the preparation and marketing of the product."

☞ If the product is *food*, anything *"foreign"* is probably a dangerous defect if it could cause physical injury. (*Example:* Slivers of metal in canned tuna fish.) Anything *"natural"* to the food before processing (e.g., in bones in canned salmon) may or may not be a defect — some courts say that natural items in food can never be a defect, but most now say that anything a consumer *wouldn't expect to find* in that type of food is a defect, even if it's "natural."

☞ If the product *breaks* or *wears out* before a reasonable consumer thinks it would/ should, this can be a defect.

☞ *"Design defects"* are the most commonly-tested type of defect. Here are the general principles:

❏ Quote the Rest. 3d's definition: "A product is ***defective in design*** when the ***foreseeable risks of harm posed*** by the product ***could have been reduced or avoided by the adoption of a reasonable alternative design*** by the seller or other distributor ... and the ***omission of the alternative design renders the product not reasonably safe.*** " Notice that this is essentially a ***negligence-based***, risk-utility standard.

❏ Availability of a ***safer*** design is important evidence that the design actually used was "defective."

❏ The fact that "everyone else in the industry designs it this way" is probative, but not binding, on whether the design was defective.

❏ D's failure to include a cost-effective technologically-available ***safety feature*** will often be a design defect. (*Example:* If the technology exists to make a car not start when the seat belt is not attached, it may well be a design defect not to include this feature.)

❏ The ***"state of the art"*** defense will be accepted in design cases — if at the time of manufacture technology did not yet exist (or wasn't cost-effective) to design the device a certain way, the fact that this design became feasible later (before trial) is irrelevant.

☞ In any design-defect or failure-to-warn case, be on the lookout for a possible ***preemption*** defense: if the particular design or warning-label that P says was faulty was imposed by ***Congress***, and the court finds that Congress intended to ***preempt*** the states from requiring stricter or different designs or warning labels, then D has a defense. Remember that this is always a question of ***congressional intent:*** did Congress intend, by imposing the requirement, to block the states from allowing strict product liability against a D who followed the federal rules?

☞ ***"Unavoidably unsafe"*** products often turn up on exams. There are two different problems:

☞ *Case 1:* The defect slips in during the manufacturing process, and no better production process, and no amount of inspection, would prevent this particular unit from being "broken" (different and more dangerous than the "standard" one off the assembly line), or allow D to separate that item from the non-broken ones. Courts are split as to whether the product here is "unavoidably unsafe," but the Rest. 3d's view is that the unavoidability of the defect is ***no defense***.

☞ *Case 2:* Here, ***each*** copy is unsafe, in the sense that the items are all the same, and each poses the same dangers. Here, "unavoidably unsafe" is usually a defense, at least if the product's overall benefits outweigh its overall dangers.

☞ In this category, the most common example is ***prescription*** drugs. Even if the drug has rare side effects, or causes allergic reactions in a few people, as long as D gives adequate warnings and the drug produces a net benefit to *some* group of patients, then at least according to the Third Restatement the drug is not defective, and the particular P who is injured cannot recover. (But note that most courts *disagree* — even in prescription drug cases, these courts let P win on a strict liability theory if D did not at least make reasonable efforts to make the drug as free from side-effects or allergic reactions as it could.)

☞ Be sure that the product was defective *when it left D's hands.* Often-tested: the product is OK when it leaves Manufacturer's plant, but because of bad shipping, bad handling by retailer or bad care by purchaser, its condition changes to a dangerous condition. (*Example:* A bottle leaves Manufacturer's plant OK, gets broken in transit, and P gets glass in her mouth. Manufacturer is not strictly liable.)

☞ Many questions involve *"failure to warn."* The duty to warn is basically an *extra* obligation.

☞ Thus if the product is basically dangerous either because of a manufacturing defect or a design defect, D can't cure this defect by warning of the dangers.

☞ Even if the product is designed in a "non-defective" way, D still has a duty to warn of any *non-obvious* dangers. Failure to carry out this duty is evaluated in a way that has aspects of both negligence and strict liability.

❏ Commonly-tested: D must warn that certain *uses are not appropriate*. (*Example:* If a ladder can't take more than a certain amount of weight, and a reasonable consumer would think that it could take more stress than it really can, it's a violation for the manufacturer not to warn of the real limit.)

❏ Usually, failure-to-warn arises in connection with the *label*. So if the fact pattern tells you something about what the label says, that's a tip-off to look for a failure-to-warn problem.

❏ Be especially on the lookout for failure-to-warn in *prescription drug* cases — there's almost always some side effect or allergy potential, and courts today say that virtually any risk (however small) must be warned of.

❏ Common scenario: The warning booklet (or box containing the warning) is part of the package when the product leaves the manufacturer, but it's *lost* in shipping or lost by the retailer. The manufacturer is protected here by the "when it left defendant's hands" rule, except for situations where the danger is so great that a reasonable exercise of the duty-to-warn required putting the label right on the product itself instead of on packaging. (*Example:* A power mower probably needs a warning on a metal plate attached to the mower, not just on the box.)

❏ If the danger wasn't *knowable* at the time of manufacture, most courts say there's no duty to warn of it. This is the *"state of the art"* defense. (*Example:* If after all reasonable testing, a prescription drug manufacturer doesn't know that a particular side effect can happen, it's not a violation to fail to list this effect.)

❏ But if the manufacturer *later learns* of the danger, most courts will impose on it a *post-sale duty to notify* the prior buyer or user of the danger, if that person's identity is known.

☞ There is no duty to warn of a danger that would be *obvious* to an ordinary person. (*Example:* It is obvious that a kitchen knife can cut someone, or that the user of a ladder might fall off. Manufacturers therefore do not have to warn of these dangers.)

☞ The most important category of failure-to-warn cases involves *prescription drugs.*

    ☞ Keep in mind the *"learned intermediary"* defense for drug makers. Where the defense is allowed (as it is in most states), the manufacturer's duty is generally limited to warning the *prescribing physician* rather than the patient. So if the manufacturer warned the physician, but the physician didn't adequately warn the patient, the manufacturer is off the hook in a state that allows the intermediary defense.

    ☞ Where P took a *generic drug*, consider the possibility that P may be able to bring a failure-to-warn suit not against the maker of the generic, but instead against the maker of the *brand-name version.* Courts sometimes allow suit against the brand-name maker (even though it didn't sell the generic that P took) because it's the brand-name maker, not the generic maker, that has the *responsibility* for making sure the *warning label* adequately discloses the risks of the drug. (The generic maker's duty is simply to use the same warning label as the brand name.)

☞ Don't forget *causation*, especially *proximate* cause. Even in strict liability (and warranty), these elements must still be proved. So the "defect" (not just the product) must be the proximate cause of D's injuries.

    ☞ Most common scenario: Purchaser *misuses* the product in a way that is virtually *unforeseeable*. This constitutes a *superseding cause*. (*Example:* P tries to cut his hair with a lawnmower.) But *foreseeable* misuse is *not* superseding, and most misuse these days is found to be "foreseeable."

        ☞ If the manufacturer warns against a particular misuse, and P (or whoever is using the product) *consciously disregards* the warning, that's probably superseding. (But P's negligent failure to notice the warning is not superseding.)

☞ Causation is especially important in *failure-to-warn* cases. Most important context:

    ☞ If D can show that P *wouldn't have read* a warning even if one had been given (or would have *ignored* the warning if it had been given and P had seen it), then the failure to warn wasn't the proximate or "but for" cause of the accident, and D won't be liable.

☞ A *reaction* to an initial danger is often foreseeable, and thus not superseding. (*Example:* P1 is injured, and P2 tries to help, or just panics. Either way, if P2 gets injured, that's probably a foreseeable response, and thus not superseding.)

☞ If Manufacturer discovers a problem and tries to *recall* the product to fix it (at Manufacturer's cost), Owner's refusal to allow this is probably superseding. (*Example:* Manufacturer recalls cars at its own cost; O1 refuses to cooperate; O1 sells to O2; O2 crashes into P when the car breaks. P loses, because Manufacturer got off the hook once O1 refused to cooperate with the recall.) But if Manufacturer *charges* for the attempt to fix, it's not clear whether O's refusal is superseding. (Certainly that refusal is not superseding if Manufacturer's charge to fix was unreasonably high.)

☞ Consider some possible defenses to strict product liability:

    ☞ Courts vary on whether **contributory and comparative negligence** are defenses to strict product liability. The modern/Rest. 3d view is that these defenses **apply the same way** as they would in a negligence action.

    ☞ **Assumption of risk** is a defense, if P acted **unreasonably** in encountering the danger. (*Example:* If Manufacturer warns against using a ladder to hold more than 200 lbs., and P knowingly puts 250 lbs. on, P has assumed the risk.) But if P is reasonable in ignoring the warning, and the warning unfairly limits the product compared with what a reasonable consumer would expect, P probably is not bound by AOR. (*Example:* If the reasonable consumer expects a step-ladder to hold at least the weight of an average 175-lb.-man, a warning not to put more than 100 lbs. on probably won't be effective to trigger AOR if P disregards the warning.)

    ☞ **Compliance** with **governmental safety regulations** is usually **not** a defense.

        ☞ Watch out for the possibility that the federal government has **pre-empted** the area. For instance, if the federal government has prescribed warning labels, this may mean that the feds have occupied the entire field of labelling. In that case, states can't impose failure-to-warn liability if the federal labelling rules have been followed. (This is clearly true for cigarettes — makers who conform to federal cigarette labelling guidelines can't be sued for failure to warn.)

☞ Regardless of the theory of recovery, examine carefully whether P falls within the class of **persons who may sue**.

    ☞ Where P is a **"remote"** purchaser (he bought, but not directly from D), P can probably recover. At least where physical injury occurs, this lack of "vertical" privity is never a defense today, whether the suit is based on warranty (express or implied), negligence or strict product liability.

    ☞ Where P is a "user" who is **not** a purchaser, P is again clearly covered under strict product liability and negligence. Whether she's covered under warranty depends on the precise version of the UCC in force in the state (with some states limiting warranty recovery to purchasers and to members of the purchaser's family).

    ☞ If P is a **"bystander"** (neither a purchaser nor a user), the question is closer. Bystander liability is the most commonly tested aspect of who may sue.

        ☞ Under negligence, the bystander may recover if he was **"reasonably foreseeable,"** which he will usually be found to be. (*Example:* If a plane crashes into P's house due to a manufacturing defect, P will be allowed to recover, because it is foreseeable that someone on the ground might be hurt by a defective plane.)

        ☞ Under warranty, P's right to recover depends on state law (as it does for "users" who didn't purchase, discussed above).

        ☞ Under strict liability, most courts protect virtually any bystander. (*Example:* People injured when a defective car or plane crashes, or when defective scaffolding falls down on them as they walk by, are all permitted to recover.)

    ☞ If the way a bystander gets hurt is really strange, consider the possibility that proximate cause is not present because the manner of harm was too unforeseeable. (*Example:* D makes a prescription drug, and doesn't warn users of possible drowsiness. X uses the product, gets drowsy, drives his car and crashes the car into a pole, knocking it down; when the pole falls it hits a propane truck, starting a fire, that injures P, a nearby pedestrian. Probably this was not a foreseeable risk from the mislabelling, in which case there would be no strict liability for D.)

☛ Be careful to examine whether *D* is the sort of person *who can be liable.*

    ☞ If D is a *retailer,* strict liability and warranty, not negligence, are the best theories.

    ☞ If D has sold *used* goods (e.g., used cars), courts are split. Most courts say that D is not liable in strict liability or implied warranty. But there can still be negligence liability (e.g., D fails to warn of what he knows to be a defect in the item).

    ☞ If D is a *lessor* of goods, courts differ about whether to apply strict liability and warranty. The trend is probably to cover this situation. Certainly D can be liable in negligence under ordinary principles.

    ☞ If D is a supplier of *services*, with the product used by D only as a *tool* during provision of the service, strict liability and warranty do not normally apply. (*Example:* D, a tattoo artist, uses special needles in doing the tattooing. D would not be strictly liable or liable under warranty, because he was not selling needles. But the manufacturer of the needle could be liable.)

    ☞ Where *title* to the item is *transferred* to P as part of the service, courts are split. In cases involving *health-care professionals*, most courts *don't* recognize strict liability or warranty liability. (*Example:* D, a surgeon, puts a pacemaker into P. If the pacemaker breaks, D is probably not strictly liable or liable under warranty, since the dominant aspect of his performance was as supplier of services, not as reseller of goods.)

    ☞ If D is a company that *supplies fulfillment services* but *doesn't take title* to the goods, remember that some courts now *allow* P to sue D even though D wasn't truly a "seller."

    Example: Suppose X lists a product on the Amazon.com website and uses Amazon's "Fulfillment by Amazon" service (where Amazon stores, picks, ships and bills the goods, but never takes title) to fulfill the order. Mention that some courts now allow an injured buyer to sue Amazon, especially where the actual seller is a foreign company that can't be found for service.

    ☞ If D is a *"user"* of goods, rather than a seller, D has no strict liability to a bystander. This is an often-tested aspect.

    Example 1: D is a carpenter using power tools. As P passes by, a part of the tool flies off and hits him. D is not strictly liable, because D wasn't making any sale. But the manufacturer of the tool could, of course, be strictly liable.

Example 2: D is a store owner who causes an escalator to be installed. P, a customer, is injured on the device. D is not strictly liable because he didn't sell the item to P.

☞ If D is a **gift-giver**, he is not strictly liable. (*Example:* D buys a teddy bear, and gives it to P as a gift. P chokes on a button from the teddy bear. D is not strictly liable, because D did not make a sale.)

☞ If D sells the item, but sells as an **"amateur"** (i.e., not one in the business of selling goods of that kind), D is not strictly liable. (*Example:* D owns a candy store. D sells a slightly-used lawn mower that she has used a few times to cut the grass in front of the store. Since D is not in the business of selling goods of this type, D is not strictly liable to the buyer if the mower is dangerously defective.)

☛ Don't overlook **damages**.

☞ For negligence and strict liability, there must normally be some **physical impact or injury**.

☞ If there's only **emotional** damage, then probably the same **"zone of danger"** rule applies to strict liability as to negligence, whatever that rule is. (*Example:* In a state maintaining the zone-of-danger rule for negligence cases, Wife sees Husband mangled by a power mower 30 yards away. Even in strict liability, Wife probably can't recover against the manufacturer of the mower, because she was not physically at risk.)

☞ P can probably recover for **property damage** under all three theories (though a few states don't allow recovery for property damage under a warranty claim if no physical injury).

☞ If the only damage suffered by P is **"intangible economic harm"** (e.g., lost profits) then the choice of theory makes a difference.

☞ For **negligence**, not all courts allow recovery for intangible economic harm, and those that do require P to be a member of an "identifiable class."

☞ For **implied warranty**, P can recover if he was a direct purchaser. (In this situation, implied warranty is clearly superior to negligence or strict liability as a theory.) If P was a remote purchaser, courts are split. If P was a bystander, most courts do not allow recovery for pure economic harm.

☞ For **strict liability**, most courts **don't** allow recovery for pure economic harm. (*Example:* Dentist buys a new drill made by Maker. The drill breaks as it's being used on a patient. If Dentist suffers a loss of reputation leading to lost profits, he can't recover in strict liability against Maker.)

☛ If P can recover against a retailer under warranty or strict liability, the retailer may obtain complete **indemnity** from the manufacturer.

☛ Look for the possibility that federal law has **preempted** state common-law tort recovery.

☞ This is especially likely in **labeling** cases, where, say, if the maker follows FDA drug or device labeling rules, it can't at the same time follow state common-law failure-to-warn rules requiring extra or different warnings. State common-law recovery is pre-empted in this situation.

CHAPTER 15

NUISANCE

ChapterScope

The term "nuisance" refers not to a type of tort, but to a ***type of injury*** which P has sustained. There are actually two types of nuisance: "public nuisance" and "private nuisance."

■ **Public nuisance:** A "*public* nuisance" is an ***interference with a right common to the general public***. If D releases noxious odors or harmful chemicals into the air, cuts off the use of a public road, or maintains an unlicensed business, all of these may be public nuisances.

■ **Private nuisance:** A "*private* nuisance" is an ***unreasonable and substantial interference*** with P's ***use and enjoyment of his land***.

I. NUISANCE GENERALLY

A. Confusion surrounding the term: Although courts often use the term "nuisance" as if they were talking about a particular tort, the term really refers to a ***kind of injury*** which the plaintiff has sustained. In the case of "public nuisance," this injury is the loss of any right that the plaintiff has by virtue of being a "member of the public." In cases of private nuisance, the plaintiff's injury consists of interference with his ***use or enjoyment of his land***. See generally P&K, pp. 616-19.

1. Significance of nuisance: Therefore, instead of viewing the rules set forth in this chapter as circumstances under which the "tort" of nuisance may be maintained, you should instead think of them as definitions of what constitutes sufficiently great damage to the plaintiff that he is entitled to sue. The suit itself may have as a basis any of the types of culpable defendant behavior we have examined so far: (1) intentional interference with the plaintiff's rights; (2) negligence; or (3) abnormally dangerous activities or other conduct giving rise to strict liability.

> **Example:** A gas well being drilled by D explodes, throwing noxious chemicals on P's property. In order to show the kind of damage required for "private nuisance," P must show that his use and enjoyment of his property have been substantially impaired (which he will almost certainly be able to do). But he must also show that D's conduct was either intentional (e.g., D knew that the well was substantially certain to interfere with P's property), negligent (e.g., D carelessly neglected to take adequate safety precautions) or abnormally dangerous.

II. PUBLIC NUISANCE

A. Definition of public nuisance: A "public nuisance" is an interference with *"a right common to the general public."* (Rest. 2d, §821B(1)).

1. Lack of more definite rule: We talk more below about what is a right "common to the general public." See *infra*, p. 430. Generally, activities that interfere with *public waterways, air purity,* or *public roads and facilities* are the most likely to be found to satisfy this standard.

2. **Factors:** The factors which will be looked at in determining whether something is a public nuisance include "the *type of neighborhood*, the nature of the thing or wrong complained of, its proximity to those alleging injury or damage, its frequency, continuity or duration, and the damage or annoyance resulting. . . . " *Culwell v. Abbott Constr. Co., Inc.*, 506 P.2d 1191 (Kan. 1973).

   a. **Substantial harm required:** A public nuisance will not be found to exist unless the harm to the public is *substantial*.

3. **Statutes and ordinances:** In addition to types of conduct that are commonly recognized by courts as giving rise to "common law" public nuisance (the examples in (1) above are instances of this), particular *statutes and ordinances* in each jurisdiction may make certain things public nuisances (e.g., "black currant plants" — see P,W&S, p. 802).

4. **Need not be crime:** Traditionally, it was generally held that for conduct to be actionable as a public nuisance, it must also be a *crime*. But the Second Restatement (in §821B) and most modern decisions no longer impose such a requirement (although the fact that conduct *is* a crime will make it more likely to be held a public nuisance).

B. **"Right common to general public":** As we noted above, the key element of a claim of public nuisance is that the right that is being unreasonably interfered with must be a "right that is *common to the general public.*" (Rest. 2d, §821B(1)).

1. **Has impact:** This requirement of a right common to the general public has considerable *impact*, in that it prevents many widespread harms from being eligible to be considered public nuisances. As the Second Restatement puts it, to be a right common to all members of the general public the right must be "*collective in nature* and *not* like the *individual* right that everyone has not to be assaulted or defamed or defrauded or negligently injured.*" Id.* at Comment g.

   a. **What qualifies:** As one court has put it, the term "public right" is limited to those *"indivisible resources shared by the public at large*, such as *air, water, or public rights of way*." *State of Rhode Island v. Lead Industries Association, Inc.*, 951 A.2d 428 (R.I. 2008).

      i. **Interference with just some people:** Even if the interference *is* with a shared resource like air or water, the interference won't qualify if by its nature it affects *only a few isolated landowners, not the public at large.* Thus the Restatement says, "the pollution of a stream that merely deprives 50 or 100 lower riparian owners of the use of the water for purposes connected with their land does not for that reason alone become a public nuisance. If, however, the pollution prevents the use of a public bathing beach or kills the fish in a navigable stream and so deprives *all members of the community* of the right to fish, it becomes a public nuisance." Rest. 2d, §821B(1), §Comment g.

      ii. **Interference that takes place within individual properties:** The "common right" requirement means that typically, a claim that a product has had a particular effect on a piece of *privately-owned real estate not accessible to the public* at large will *fail* the common-right test. Thus claims that manufacturers have infiltrated *guns* into neighborhoods, or that manufacturers of *paints* have failed to remove lead from buildings painted with those paints, thus injuring children living there, have tended to fail the "common right" standard.

C. Requirement of particular damage in private suits: Courts sometime say that a *private citizen* may *recover for his own purely economic damages* stemming from a public nuisance, but only if he has sustained financial damage that is different in *kind*, not just degree, from that suffered by the public generally. However, it's not clear how much impact this so-called requirement has anymore; many newer decisions seem to ignore it.

> **Example:** P is a tenant of a small novelty store on the boardwalk of a famous beach which contains hundreds of merchants. D, an oil exploration company, negligently causes an offshore oil spill that fouls the beach for the entire summer, causing P's profits to drop 50% or $20,000, and doing approximately the same to hundreds of the other merchants. It's likely that P can recover from D in public nuisance for his lost profits, notwithstanding that hundreds of other merchants have suffered the same sort of harm to their collective right to an unfouled beach.

1. **Injunction:** Even in courts still requiring a a "different kind" of harm, the requirement will *not* necessarily be imposed in suits for an *injunction*, as opposed to one for damages. Rest. 2d, § 821C, indicates that an injunction may be obtained not only by a plaintiff who could obtain damages, but also by a public official, and by a private citizen who has "standing to sue as a representative of the general public, or as a citizen in a citizen's action or as a member of a class action." (These standing requirements are determined by the local court's civil procedure standing rules.)

D. Within "control" of defendant at time of harm: For public nuisance, courts require that the defendant have had *control over the instrumentality* at the *time of damage* — it's *not* enough that defendant had control at some *earlier* point (e.g., at the time of a sale of a product).

> **Example:** A state, acting on behalf of children injured by ingesting lead-based paint used in apartments, sues the Ds, who manufactured the paint. *Held*, for the Ds, in part because the state has not shown that when the children were ingesting the lead, the Ds still had the right to abate the nuisance by removing the paint. The fact that the Ds had control of the contents of the paint at the time of the much *earlier* sales to the building owners is irrelevant — the "control at the time of the harm" requirement is not satisfied. *State of Rhode Island v. Lead Industries Assoc., Inc.*, 951 A.2d 428 (R.I. 2008).

III. PRIVATE NUISANCE

A. Nature of private nuisance: A *private nuisance* is an unreasonable interference with the plaintiff's *use and enjoyment* of his land. See Rest. 2d, §822.

1. **Distinguished from trespass:** Whereas trespass is an interference with the plaintiff's right to *exclusive possession* of his property, nuisance is an interference with his right to use and enjoy it. For instance, a condition near the plaintiff's property that interferes with her peace of mind (e.g., explosives stored in a dangerous way) would be a nuisance, since it interferes with her use and enjoyment, but not a trespass, since nothing physically enters her property.

a. **Overlap:** However, it frequently happens that conduct by the defendant is both a nuisance and a trespass. For instance, if the defendant conducts blasting operations near the plaintiff's land, the noise, threat of harm, and vibrations, will all be aspects of nuisance, while the throwing of rocks onto the plaintiff's land (and, in a few courts, even the shock waves themselves — see *supra*, p. 43) will be trespasses.

2. **Must have interest in land:** The critical thing to remember is that plaintiff can sue based on a private nuisance only if he has an *interest in land* that has been affected. For instance, the fishermen in *Burgess, supra,* could not have sued for private nuisance, because although their livelihood was affected, no interest in land they held was affected.

a. **Tenants and family members:** But the interest in land does not have to be a "fee simple." *A tenant* may have such an interest; also, *members of the family* of the owner or tenant may sue, on the grounds that they have a *de facto* interest in using and enjoying the land. See Rest. 2d, § 821E.

3. **Elements of the case:** The plaintiff must demonstrate two principal elements in order to recover for private nuisance: (1) that his use and enjoyment of his land was interfered with, in a *substantial way*; and (2) that the defendant's conduct was either negligent, abnormally dangerous, or intentional.

B. **Interference with use:** The interference with the plaintiff's use and enjoyment must be *substantial*. Recovery for nuisance is therefore very different from that for trespass (at least where the term "trespass" is used in its modern-day sense to include only intentional invasions) — the trespass plaintiff may recover nominal damages, even where she has suffered no substantial harm (see *supra*, p. 41).

1. **Inconvenience:** If the plaintiff is personally injured, or her property receives physical damage, the interference will always be "substantial." But if the plaintiff's damage consists in her being *inconvenienced* or subjected to unpleasant smells, noises, etc., this will be substantial damage only if a person in the community of *normal sensitivity* would be seriously bothered.

a. **Abnormally sensitive plaintiff:** So a *"hypersensitive plaintiff"* will *not* be able to recover for nuisance no matter how great the harm to the plaintiff's use and enjoyment, if an ordinarily sensitive person would not be unduly bothered. Rest. 2d, §821F, Comm. d.

Example: P is an invalid who is thrown into convulsions by the ringing of a nearby church bell, the sound of which would not be disturbing to an ordinary member of the community whose house was located the same distance from the church as P's. P cannot recover for nuisance, because he is hypersensitive. Rest. 2d, §821F, Illustr. 1.

b. **Nature of locality:** What constitutes a "substantial interference" will generally depend in part on the *neighborhood*. For instance, a plaintiff living in a residential neighborhood will be required to submit to less noise, industrial smells, etc., before these are substantial, than one who lives over a store-front in a busy commercial neighborhood. This is really the same kind of balancing that goes on in determining whether the defendant's conduct is unreasonable (see *infra*).

C. Defendant's conduct: There is *no general rule of "strict liability" in nuisance*. In other words, the plaintiff must show that the defendant's conduct fell within one of the three principal classes we've examined thus far, i.e., *negligence, intent,* or *abnormal dangerousness*.

> **Example:** D, a public electric utility, is charged with spewing pollutants into the air, which damage cars being processed and stored by P. No claim is made that D's conduct is abnormally dangerous.
>
> *Held,* unless D's conduct is shown to have been intentional (in the sense that D intentionally injured P's enjoyment of his property, or knew that the injury was substantially certain to result), or was negligent in causing the injury, D is not liable. *Copart Industries, Inc. v. Consolidated Edison Co. of New York, Inc.,* 363 N.E.2d 968 (N.Y. 1977).

1. **Negligence:** If the plaintiff wants to base her nuisance claim upon the defendant's negligence, she must meet the same requirements of proof as in any other negligence action. Thus she must show that the utility of the defendant's conduct was outweighed by the harm to the plaintiff (i.e., that the defendant's conduct was *"unreasonable"*).

2. **Abnormally dangerous:** The plaintiff may be able to show that the defendant's conduct was an "abnormally dangerous activity", giving rise to, in effect, "strict nuisance liability". For instance, if she can show that the defendant had stored explosives near the plaintiff's property in a residential area, this may be sufficient.

D. Intentional: Most nuisance claims arise out of conduct by the defendant that can be called *"intentional."* This does not mean that the defendant has *desired* to interfere with the plaintiff's use and enjoyment of her land, but simply that he *knows with substantial certainty* that such interference will occur.

> **Example:** D operates a coal-burning electric generating plant. The plant spews 90 tons of sulphur-dioxide gas into the atmosphere each day; this gas settles on the fields of local farmers (including the Ps), causing damage to crops and other harms. D claims that it has used due care in the construction and operation of its plant, and that it is therefore not negligent. Consequently, it argues, it cannot be held liable for nuisance.
>
> *Held,* the emissions from D's plant constitute a nuisance for which D must compensate the Ps. The nuisance here was intentional: "[A] continued invasion of a plaintiff's interest by non-negligent conduct, when the actor knows of the nature of the injury inflicted, is an intentional tort, and the fact that the hurt is administered non-negligently is not a defense to liability." (Also, the fact that the economic and social utility of the operation of the plant may have been greater than the utility of the Ps' farming operations is irrelevant — D must still compensate the Ps for the damage to their property.) *Jost v. Dairyland Power Cooperative,* 172 N.W.2d 647 (Wis. 1970) *infra,* p. 434.

1. **Unreasonableness requirement:** In nuisance cases based on negligence or abnormal danger, a requirement that the degree of interference with the plaintiff's interests be "unreasonable" is built-in, because of the very definition of negligence and of abnormal dangerousness (see *supra,* p. 332). But where the defendant's conduct is intentional, the

courts have ***also imposed a requirement that the interference with plaintiff's interests be unreasonable***. P&K, p. 623.

    a. Significance: This means that even if the defendant intentionally interferes with the plaintiff's rights, he will have a kind of "privilege" to do so, as long as the interference is not unreasonable. "Life in organized society, and especially in populous communities, involves an unavoidable clash of individual interests. Practically all human activity, unless carried on in a wilderness, interferes to some extent with others. . . . It is an obvious truth that each individual in a community must put up with a certain amount of annoyance, inconvenience, and interference, and must take a certain amount of risk in order that all may get on together. . . . " Rest. 2d, §822, Comment g.

    b. Balancing test: To determine whether the interference is "unreasonable," courts have traditionally done a simple ***balancing test***, weighing the utility of the defendant's conduct against the harm to the plaintiff. In some cases, this has meant that the plaintiff cannot get damages, ***no matter how substantial the harm to her***, as long as the utility of the defendant's conduct was greater.

    c. Rejected by Restatement: The Second Restatement has rejected the "balancing test" as the sole test for "reasonableness." Instead, the interference will be deemed unreasonable if ***either***: (1) the harm to the plaintiff outweighs the utility of the defendant's conduct; ***or*** (2) "the harm caused by the conduct is substantial, and the financial burden of compensating for this and other harms does not render infeasible the continuation of the conduct." Rest, 2d, §826. This idea is rephrased in Rest. 2d, §829A, which states that the interference is unreasonable if it is substantial and ***"greater than the [plaintiff] should be required to bear without compensation."***

        i. Significance: To put it another way, once the plaintiff shows that the harm is substantial, then no matter how meritorious and socially useful the defendant's activity, the defendant will have to pay for the harm to the plaintiff if it is "unfair" that such payment not be made. The only exception to this is that if there are so many people situated in the same position as the plaintiff that to pay damages to all these people would make it impossible for the defendant to continue his activity, and the utility of that activity outweighs the harm it causes, the defendant will not have to pay.

        ii. Pollutants: The Restatement approach ("pay for the damage even if your activity is socially useful") is illustrated by *Jost v. Dairyland Power Cooperative, supra*, p. 433. Even though the operation of the electric utility was socially beneficial, and even though that plant's social utility probably outweighed the harm to the farmers, the utility was nonetheless required to pay for the damage it caused.

2. Nature of neighborhood: One important factor in determining whether the defendant's interference is "unreasonable" is the ***kind of area or neighborhood*** in which the defendant and plaintiff are located. The ***zoning*** of the area is likely to be important in this respect.

    a. Supermarket operation: For instance, in *Winget v. Winn-Dixie Stores, Inc.*, 130 S.E.2d 363 (S.C. 1963), the court held that the defendant's operation of a ***supermarket*** was not a nuisance as to plaintiff's residence. The court relied on the fact that the store was located in an area of the city zoned for such use. (The plaintiff's house was just on the other side of the zoning border, in a residential neighborhood, but this was treated as practically irrelevant by the court.) However, the court held that the *manner* in which the defendant conducted its business (e.g., air conditioning fans directed towards the plaintiff's shrubbery, and use of floodlights after closing hours) was unreasonable.

3. **Action taken for spite:** An action taken by the defendant for *spite* — that is, an action of *little or no benefit to the defendant*, and taken for the *purpose* of *annoying or injuring* the plaintiff — is especially likely to be found to be unreasonable and thus a nuisance.

   Example: P and D, who are neighbors, quarrel. Out of anger at P, D then puts up bright lights and a large "spite fence," both of which are of little benefit to D and a major detriment to P's enjoyment. The cost/benefit analysis, coupled with D's harmful intent, will likely lead the court to conclude that D's conduct was "unreasonable." If so, D will be found to have created a nuisance.

E. **Interference with water:** Where a landowner has a stream, lake, pond, or other *water* on or adjacent to her property, she has a right to be free of interference with her continued use and enjoyment of that water. Interferences are evaluated by reasonableness rules similar to those applicable to nuisance.

   1. **Restatement test:** Thus the Restatement evaluates one landowner's interference with another's use and enjoyment of water use by considering such nuisance-like factors as:

      ❏ the *purpose* of the competing uses;

      ❏ the *suitability* of the uses to the stream, lake, etc.;

      ❏ the *economic value* of the uses;

      ❏ the *social value* of the uses;

      ❏ the practicality of *avoiding the harm* by *adjusting the use or quantity* being made by one owner or the other;

      ❏ the need to *protect the existing value* of land;

      and the like. Rest. 2d, §850A.

      Example: A stream runs from D's property to P's property next door, and has done so for years. Both are vacation homes. P has never physically entered the stream, but enjoys looking at it. Recently, D built a dam that created an ornamental pond on D's land, but that completely stopped the flow of water to P's property.

      A court will likely enjoin the dam (i.e., require D to remove it), on a nuisance-like theory that D has unreasonably interfered with P's use and enjoyment of her property.

F. **Remedies:** P may have one or more of three possible *remedies* for private nuisance.

   1. **Damages:** If the harm has already occurred, she can recover *compensatory damages*. If it is not clear whether the harm will continue in the future, she can usually recover only for the damages sustained up till the time of suit, and she must bring successive actions for subsequent harm. But if it appears that the nuisance will probably be a permanent one (e.g., a polluting factory that is likely to stay in business), she can and must recover all damages, past and *prospective*, in one action.

2. **Injunction:** If the plaintiff can show that damages would not be a sufficient remedy, she may be entitled to an ***injunction*** against continuation of the nuisance. (Since courts typically regard every parcel of land as having a unique use, the plaintiff will frequently be able to make this showing that compensatory damages are not an adequate remedy).

   a. **Balancing test:** But there is one crucial difference between the showing that the plaintiff must make to get an injunction and that required for damages. Under the new Restatement approach summarized above, the plaintiff can get damages as long as she can show that it is "unfair" for her to bear the harm without payment, even if the utility of the defendant's conduct outweighs the harm to the plaintiff. But to get an injunction, the plaintiff must show that the harm to her (probably added to the harm to others similarly situated — see Rest. 2d, §827, Comment b) actually ***outweighs*** the utility of the defendant's conduct.

      Example: D operates a large cement plant, which employs 300 people, and which cost more than $45 million. Ps, neighboring landowners, sue for nuisance, because of dirt, smoke and vibrations from the plant. A lower court finds that the damage to the Ps totals $185,000.

      Held, an absolute injunction against D should not issue, in view of the great disparity between the economic consequences to D and its employees (as well as the local economy) in closing down the plant, and the consequences to the plaintiffs in allowing it to continue. However, it is fair to require D to pay for the harm it causes, regardless of the utility of the plant. Therefore, a temporary injunction will be issued, to be suspended if D makes payment of permanent damages to the Ps. *Boomer v. Atlantic Cement Co., Inc.,* 257 NE.2d. 870 (N.Y. 1970).

      A dissent contended that the court's holding amounted to "saying to the cement company, you may continue to do harm to your neighbors so long as you pay us a fee for it." Also, the dissent noted, once the damage was repaired, the incentive to find a cure for the pollution would disappear.

3. **Self-help abatement:** In some situations the plaintiff may have the right to use the ***"self-help"*** remedy of ***"abatement"***. That is, she may have the right to enter the defendant's land to remove the nuisance. But she may use only reasonable force to do this, and must ordinarily first complain to the defendant and wait for the latter to refuse to remedy the condition himself. See P&K, p. 642.

G. **Defenses:** The defendant may raise a number of affirmative defenses to a private nuisance claim. In particular, we examine here situations in which the ***plaintiff's conduct*** may give rise to the defenses of contributory negligence or assumption of risk.

   1. **Contributory negligence:** Where the claim is based on the defendant's ***negligent*** maintenance of a public or private nuisance, contributory negligence will normally be a defense.

   2. **Assumption of risk:** The defense of ***assumption of risk*** is similarly applicable where the defendant behaved negligently, and possibly where his maintenance of the nuisance was a combination of intent and negligence, as described above. The defense may also apply where the defendant conducted an abnormally dangerous activity (e.g., the plaintiff refuses to heed the defendant's sign that it is conducting blasting activities and that

bystanders should stay out).

a. **"Coming to the nuisance":** One controversial aspect of the assumption of risk defense is whether a plaintiff will be barred if he has ***"come to the nuisance"***, i.e., purchased his property with advance knowledge that the nuisance exists.

   i. **Restatement view:** Older decisions sometimes treat "coming to the nuisance" as an absolute defense. But the modern view, exemplified by §840D of the Second Restatement, is that the fact that the plaintiff has come to the nuisance is merely "a factor to be considered" in determining whether the plaintiff wins.

   ii. **Locality:** The court is much more likely to hold that "coming to the nuisance" is a defense if the defendant's activity is suitable for the area where it occurs, and the plaintiff's own use is out of step with that area.

Example: D has operated a cattle feedlot (producing "over a million pounds of wet manure per day") for many years, in a completely rural area outside Phoenix. P, a developer, builds a development called "Sun City", one portion of which adjoins the feedlot. The flies and odor make this portion of the development unhealthy and almost unusable for residential purposes.

Held, P has "come to the nuisance", and if its interests were the only ones at stake, it would not be entitled either to damages or to an injunction. But since the rights of innocent third parties (the inhabitants of Sun City) are also involved, D will be enjoined from operating the feedlot, and forced to move. However, again because it has come to the nuisance, P will have to ***indemnify*** D for its costs in moving. *Spur Industries, Inc. v. Del E. Webb Development Co.*, 494 P.2d 700 (Ariz. 1972).

Quiz Yourself on
NUISANCE *(Entire Chapter)*

76. Gore 'N Guts Byproducts opens a factory in which it processes entrails into pet food. Next door is the home of Charles Nifferoo, a fragrance analyst with a necessarily ultra-sensitive nose. Gore does what it can to control the smell associated with its product, but mildly foul odors occasionally emanate from the plant. While most of the neighbors find it a little unpleasant, it drives Charles' sophisticated nostrils crazy. Can Charles recover for private nuisance? _____

77. Ghosts have become a serious problem to society, including Phantasm Town. The town is happy when the Ghostbusters open up their ghost collection facility there, primarily because it creates jobs for 500 people, and the town is a victim of high unemployment. One of the unfortunate (and unavoidable) by products of ghost collection is that neighboring property occasionally gets "slimed." When Amelia Nebbish's nearby property is slimed, it causes $100,000 in permanent damage. She sues Ghostbusters for private nuisance, seeking damages and an injunction. What likely result? _____

78. Eyyon, a large oil refiner, owns a large tanker, the SS Eyyon. As the SS Eyyon, filled with oil, is approaching the port of Zedlav, its captain fails to notice a large iceberg in the ship's path. The SS Eyyon slams into the iceberg, and discharges tens of thousands of gallons of oil into the bay surrounding Zedlav. Evidence later shows that the captain was seriously intoxicated at the time of the accident. The oil kills nearly all fish in the bay. The economy of Zedlav is a diversified one, but commercial fishers make up a significant (though minority) chunk of its local industry. The fishers bring a class action against Eyyon

Corp. for their losses.

    (a) On what tort theory should the fishers sue?   _____

    (b) Will they recover? _____

Answers

76. No. A private nuisance requires creation of a condition which poses an unreasonable, substantial interference with plaintiff's use or enjoyment of his property. This is an objective test: the interference would have to be offensive, annoying, or inconvenient to an average member of the community; and it would have to be substantial. Since most people are only mildly bothered by the smell, and Charles is driven crazy only because he's ultrasensitive, Gore will win.

COMPARE: Torts like battery, where defendant takes plaintiff "as he finds him," sensitivities and all.

77. Yes to the damages, no to the injunction.

A private nuisance is an unreasonable interference with the use and enjoyment of land, caused by deliberate, negligent, or hazardous conduct. If damages would not be an adequate remedy, plaintiff may be entitled to an injunction, if the harm to plaintiff outweighs the utility of defendant's conduct. The wrinkle in these facts is the *social value* of Ghostbusters' conduct — you're told in the facts how valuable it is, due to the number of jobs it creates. Because shutting the plant down would do serious harm, a court would probably not enjoin its operation. However, since the harm created is serious and there's no indication that paying the damages will shut it down, the damages are likely to be awarded. Rest. 2d §826(b).

78. (a) They should sue on a "public nuisance" theory. That is, they should sue Eyyon for having "unreasonably interfered with a right common to the general public" (see Rest. 2d, §821B(1)). In this case, the right common to the general public would be the right to an unpolluted waterway.

(b) Yes, probably. The fishers must show, in addition to the fact that Eyyon unreasonably interfered with a right common to the general public, that Eyyon's conduct fell within one of the three usual classes of tortious behavior (intention, negligent or abnormally dangerous activity). Here, the fishers' best hope is to show that Eyyon was negligent — the captain was clearly negligent in failing to see the iceberg, and his negligence will be imputed to Eyyon by the doctrine of *respondeat superior*. The most significant issue is whether the fishers suffered a "harm of a kind different from that suffered by other members of the public...." as is required for public nuisance suits by the Restatement (see Rest. 2d, §821C(1)) and some courts. Probably the fishers will meet this test if it applies, since the subject matter of their livelihood — the fish — was directly killed by Eyyon's creation of the nuisance.

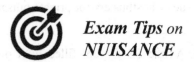

Exam Tips on NUISANCE

It's easy to miss a "nuisance" issue, because it can seem like a number of other torts (e.g., trespass, abnormally dangerous activity, negligence, etc.). In fact, any fact pattern that can be nuisance might also be one or more of these other torts (though usually, the other torts will involve a direct physical impact and nuisance will usually not.)

☛ The name of the tort is a good clue to what type of fact pattern you should be looking for: if in colloquial usage what D is doing would be called a "nuisance" by a lay-person, then the tort of nuisance is worth at least thinking about. Look mostly for fact patterns where D has *not* caused a *physical impact* with P's person or property.

☛ You have to distinguish between public and private nuisance, of course (more about the distinction below). But the *same types* of activity by D tend to characterize the two types of nuisance. Here is a representative sampling of D's conduct that might be either a public or private nuisance:

❑ D makes persistent *loud noises.*

❑ D releases *noxious odors.*

❑ D releases *harmful chemicals* into the air.

❑ D cuts off the use of a *public road.*

❑ D cultivates *disease-ridden animals.*

❑ D maintains an *unlawful business* that lowers the local quality of life (e.g., an unlawful bar, gambling parlor or brothel).

❑ D interferes with *water* that flows onto P's property (e.g., D dams a stream, preventing it from flowing onto P's property).

☛ You need to distinguish between public and private nuisance. It's the nature of *P's interest* that distinguishes the two. Public nuisance is an interference with a right "common to the general public." Private nuisance is an interference with P's use and enjoyment of his land. The same act by D can be both a public and private nuisance. Normally you should analyze whether the act is a private nuisance first (since that's the better claim for P), and then go on to public nuisance if you conclude that it's not a private one.

☛ For *private* nuisance, check for three main things: (1) does P have an *interest in land* that has been interfered with?; (2) is that interference *"unreasonable"* and *"substantial"*?; and (3) was D's conduct *negligent, abnormally dangerous* or *intentional*?

  ☞ The most commonly-tested aspect is the requirement that P have an *"interest in land"* that has been affected. (*Example:* P is a fisherman whose livelihood is ruined because D discharges pollution into the coastal waters. P can't recover in private nuisance because his interest in land hasn't been affected. This is true even if P owns land near the coast, because his *use* of the land he owns hasn't been affected by D's wrongdoing.)

    ☞ The interest of a *tenant* suffices.

    ☞ If P does own an interest in land that has been interfered with, there's no requirement of "particular harm," i.e., no requirement that P's interest be different from that of others (as there is for public nuisance). (*Example:* If D discharges odors into the air, each local landowner who gets substantial smells on his property has met the "interest in land" requirement, and can sue.)

  ☞ The requirement that the interference with P's use be *"substantial"* is also often tested.

    ☞ If the interference causes *personal injury* to P, or *direct injury* to his property, the injury is by definition "substantial." (*Example:* Pollutants that cause house paints to become discolored, or that cause plants to die, are a "substantial" interference.)

☞ If the interference doesn't cause physical injury or property damage, it's only "substantial" if a person of *normal sensitivity* in the community would be seriously bothered. For instance, *noises* or *smells* will be measured by this "normally sensitive person" standard. This *"ultra-sensitive plaintiff"* issue is often tested.

☞ D's conduct must be *"unreasonable."* Courts consider the magnitude of the interference with P's interests. Some also consider the *social utility* of D's conduct. (*Example:* D runs a large factory that employs many people, and that cannot stop releasing unpleasant smells and noises without prohibitively costly measures. Some courts are more likely to find a private nuisance here than where D's interests are less "weighty." Other courts *only* consider the magnitude of the interference with P's interests, not the size of D's countervailing interests.)

☞ D's conduct must be shown to be either *negligent*, *abnormally dangerous* or *"intentional."* In other words, there is no general strict liability for nuisance.

☞ Most nuisance conduct is "intentional," meaning that the interference was *known* to D to be *substantially certain* to occur (not that D "desired" that interference). (*Example:* D runs his factory carefully. Unbeknownst to him, the factory one day sends out non-dangerous but annoying pollutants that interfere with P's property. This is not private nuisance, because D has not acted negligently or abnormally dangerously, and did not know with substantial certainty that the interference would occur. But if P complained repeatedly, and D didn't change his practice, then D's knowledge that the interference was occurring would turn the interference into an "intentional" one.)

☞ Lastly, the defense of *"coming to the nuisance"* is sometimes raised. Look for this whenever the fact pattern tells you that D was engaging in his activity *before P moved in*. Usually, the fact that P "came to the nuisance" is *not an absolute defense*, merely one non-dispositive factor in deciding whether D's conduct was unreasonable.

☛ For *"public nuisance,"* there's no real definition, only the vague "interference with a right common to the general public" standard. Anything that an entire community would find dangerous or annoying, but that doesn't result in a direct physical impact, is a candidate.

☞ Requirements: (1) there must be an interference with rights common to the *public at large* (not just P's interests); (2) the interference with the public's interest must be *"substantial"*; and (3) in some courts, P's own harm must be *different in kind* from that suffered by the public at large (the requirement of *"particular harm"*).

☞ Overwhelmingly, the most commonly-tested aspect is the *"right common to the public"* requirement. Every time you have a possible public nuisance issue, you should discuss whether the harm involved a right common to the general public.

Example: Where Ds (manufacturers of lead-based paint) didn't remove the paint from buildings in which young children later ate the paint, freedom from lead poisoning wasn't a "right common to the public at large," so an individual child who ate lead couldn't recover.

Chapter 16

MISREPRESENTATION

ChapterScope

The independent tort of "misrepresentation" usually describes a situation where a misstatement causes intangible pecuniary loss. There are two types of misrepresentation, "intentional misrepresentation" and "negligent misrepresentation."

■ **Intentional misrepresentation (deceit):** To recover for *"intentional misrepresentation"* (also called *"deceit"* or *"fraud"*), P must establish the following elements:

❏ **Misrepresentation:** A *misrepresentation* by D;

❏ **Scienter:** *Scienter* (i.e., a culpable state of mind — either knowledge of the statement's falsity or reckless indifference to the truth);

❏ **Intent:** An *intent to induce P's reliance* on the misrepresentation;

❏ **Third-party recovery:** Even if D did not intend to influence P, however, P can recover if she can show that she is a member of a *class* which D had reason to expect would be induced to rely, and the transaction is of the same sort that D had reason to expect would occur in reliance.

❏ **Reliance:** *Justifiable reliance* by P; and

❏ **Damage:** *Damage* to P, stemming from the reliance.

■ **Negligent misrepresentation:** Today, most courts also allow recovery for *"negligent* misrepresentation," even where P suffers only intangible economic harm.

❏ **Same requirements:** Most requirements for a negligent misrepresentation action are the same as for intentional misrepresentation.

❏ **Business relationship:** However, most courts add the requirement that D's statements be made in the course of his *business or profession*, and that D have had a *pecuniary interest* in the transaction.

❏ **Liability to third persons:** The maker of a negligent misrepresentation is liable to a much *narrower class* of third persons than is the maker of a fraudulent statement. In most courts, D is liable for negligent misrepresentations only to a *"limited group of persons"* whom D either: (1) *intends to reach* with the information; or (2) knows the *recipient intends to reach*.

■ **Strict liability:** Generally, a person has no liability for an "innocent" misrepresentation — that is, there is no strict liability. But there are some exceptions (e.g., where two parties are involved in a sale transaction, and one makes a representation to another).

I. INTRODUCTION

A. Misrepresentation generally: Misrepresentation has been discussed in the context of several of the torts we have already examined. For instance, where a negligent representation leads to physical harm (e.g., a truck driver carelessly signalling a motorist to pass him when it is unsafe), an ordinary negligence action may be brought; see *supra*, p. 96. Similarly, if a seller of products makes an express warranty about them, and this warranty turns out to be false (e.g., car with "Shatter-proof" windshield — see *Baxter v. Ford Motor Co., supra*, p. 352), a products liability action may be brought. In these situations, the misrepresentation is simply one aspect, one method of accomplishing, the more general tort of negligence, strict liability, etc.

1. **About this chapter:** In this chapter, we are concerned with misrepresentations that cause only ***intangible pecuniary loss***. Because courts have always been more reluctant to impose liability for this kind of loss than for direct physical injury or property damage, special rules have grown up governing those misrepresentations that have this effect. Most of this chapter will be devoted to intentional misrepresentation, which corresponds to the common law action of "deceit". The growing willingness of courts also to impose liability for negligent misrepresentation, and, in some cases, for innocent misrepresentation (i.e., strict liability) is also discussed.

II. INTENTIONAL MISREPRESENTATION ("DECEIT")

A. **Common law action:** The common law action of ***"deceit"***, or ***"fraud"***, corresponds to what we would call today "intentional" misrepresentation.

1. **Elements of cause of action:** To recover for intentional misrepresentation, the plaintiff must establish the following elements:

   a. A ***misrepresentation*** by the defendant;

   b. ***Scienter*** (i.e., a culpable state of mind, either knowledge of the statement's falsity or reckless indifference to the truth);

   c. An ***intent to induce the plaintiff's reliance*** on the misrepresentation;

   d. ***Justifiable reliance*** by the plaintiff; and

   e. ***Damage*** to the plaintiff, stemming from the reliance.

   See P&K, p. 728.

B. **Misrepresentation:** The defendant must make a misrepresentation to the plaintiff. Normally, this will be in ***words***, (e.g., "The lot that I am selling consists of 26 acres").

1. **Actions:** But the defendant's ***actions*** may also constitute a misrepresentation. For instance, if a used car dealer turns back the odometer on a car from 60,000 to 18,000 miles, he is making a misrepresentation as to the mileage. Rest. 2d, §525, Illustr. 1.

2. **Concealment:** Furthermore, if the defendant intentionally ***conceals*** a fact from the plaintiff, he will be treated the same way as if he had affirmatively misstated that fact. Rest. 2d, §550.

   > **Example:** D, the owner of a Cadillac, trades it in to P, a car dealer, as part payment on a new car. Previously the engine block cracked, and prior to the trade-in D has a service station paint over the cracks to conceal them.

This is a positive act of fraudulent concealment. Therefore, D will be liable for fraud.

3. **Nondisclosure:** Suppose the defendant simply *fails to disclose* a material fact (as opposed to taking positive steps to conceal it).

   a. **Common law:** At common law the defendant was almost *never liable* for fraud in the "mere nondisclosure" scenario. This was particularly true in cases involving business transactions, where the rule was pretty much "every man for himself" and "caveat emptor."

   b. **Modern rule:** Today, the *general rule* remains that *failure to disclose by itself does not constitute misrepresentation.* (But as we'll see below, there are important exceptions.)

   Example: D proposes to buy a parcel of rural land from its absentee owner, P. D, who is a petroleum engineer, knows that oil has recently been discovered beneath adjacent lands. P does not know this. D offers a price about equal to the market value the land would have as farmland, which is far below what an oil company would now pay given the local oil discoveries. D says nothing about the discoveries, nor makes any other statement about the value of the land. P agrees to sell, closes on the sale, and then discovers that D knew about the oil discovery. P sues D for intentional misrepresentation.

   P will lose. This scenario falls within the general rule that one party to a proposed transaction ordinarily has no duty to make disclosure to the other about a material fact which the former knows and the other does not. There are exceptions (see *infra*) but none applies here. (But if D said, "I'm an oil engineer, and I can tell you that no oil has been or is likely to be discovered around here," that's an affirmative misrepresentation that *would* be the basis for liability.)

   c. **Exceptions:** But there are some important *exceptions* to the general rule that nondisclosure will not trigger liability for deceit. The Second Restatement, in §551(2), lists several situations in which one party to a business transaction has an obligation to make disclosure to the other. Among these are the following:

      i. **Fiduciary relation:** Matters which must be disclosed because of a *fiduciary relationship* between the two (e.g., a bank and its depositor);

      ii. **Half-truth:** Matters which must be disclosed in order to prevent a *partial* statement of the facts from being misleading (discussed below);

      iii. **Subsequent information:** *Newly-acquired* information which, if not disclosed, would make a *previous statement* misleading; and

      iv. **Facts basic to transaction:** Most importantly, *facts basic to the transaction*, if the party with knowledge "knows that the other [party] is about to enter into [the transaction] under a mistake as to them, and that the other, because of the relationship between them, the customs of the trade, or other objective circumstances, would *reasonably expect a disclosure* of those facts." (§551(2)(e)).

(1) Termite cases: The duty to disclose is frequently invoked in *"termite"* cases. A homeowner selling his home today is often held liable to the purchaser for his failure to tell the latter that the house has had termites. This modern rule represents a change in doctrine.

d. Rescission: Although the plaintiff's ability to get *damages* for non-disclosure is even today, as noted, somewhat limited, he has always been able to obtain *rescission* (i.e., a cancelling of a contract) for nondisclosure of a material fact. Thus if the plaintiff in *Swinton* had brought an equitable action to rescind the contract, he probably would have won.

e. Extension to other defects: Courts have become more lenient in what they consider a *"basic fact"* required to be disclosed. Thus a real estate developer who sold lots without indicating that the land had such a heavy salt content that shrubbery or trees could not be grown on it, was held to have failed to disclose a basic fact, and was therefore liable. *Griffith v. Byers Constr. Co. of Kansas, Inc.*, 510 P.2d 198 (Kan. 1973).

f. Non-disclosure by buyer: Courts are less likely to hold that a *buyer* has a duty to disclose (even if he knows that the item is much more valuable than the seller thinks it is) than to hold that a seller has such a duty. See P&K, p. 739. The oil-in-the-ground example on p. 443 is an illustration.

C. Scienter: To maintain the common law action of deceit, the plaintiff must show that the defendant had that culpable state of mind called *"scienter."*

1. What constitutes scienter: The defendant acted with scienter if he either:

a. *knew* or *believed* that he was not telling the truth; or

b. did not have the *confidence* in the accuracy of his statement that he *stated or implied* that he did; or

c. knew that he did not have the *grounds* for his statement that he stated or implied that he did. See Rest. 2d, §526.

2. Negligence not enough: The main function of the *scienter* requirement is to prevent merely *negligent* misrepresentations from being actionable. This rule was derived from the well-known case of *Derry v. Peek*, set forth in the following example.

Example: Ds, who are directors of the Plymouth, Devonport & District Tramways Co., issue a prospectus in order to obtain capital for the company. The document states that the company has obtained, by special Act of Parliament, the right to use steam power to run a tramway, and that this will make the line more efficient than ones operated by horses. P buys shares in reliance on this prospectus. It turns out that the consent of the Board of Trade is necessary for use of steam power, and the Board refuses to allow steam over most of the line. The company goes bankrupt, and P sues the Ds in deceit.

Held, "In order to sustain an action of deceit there must be proof of fraud, and nothing short of that will suffice. . . . Making a false statement for want of care falls far short of, and is a very different thing from, fraud, and the same may be said of a false representation honestly believed though on insufficient grounds." Since there was evidence that the Ds expected to receive the approval of the Board of Trade as a matter of course, their representation was not fraudulent. (But, it was noted, if the Ds had "shut [their] eyes to the facts", they would have lacked an actual belief in the truth of their statements, and would be liable for deceit.) *Derry v. Peek*, 14 App. Cas. 337 (Eng. 1889), *infra*, pp. 445, 454.

   a. Why negligence action not used: Since the plaintiff in *Derry* could have shown that the directors made their representations negligently, one might wonder why he did not bring an ordinary negligence action. The answer is that until recently, recovery was not allowed in ordinary negligence actions for pure intangible economic loss, without any personal injury or other direct physical damage. (This rule also has implications in products liability, which are discussed *supra*, p. 404.)

      i. Rescission: If the plaintiff, instead of bringing a deceit action, merely wants to *rescind* a contract which she has been induced to make by means of misrepresentations, she has a much easier task. In this situation, the courts have always been willing to allow rescission merely on a showing of *negligent* misrepresentation. Thus even the *Derry* court itself noted that "Where rescission is claimed it is only necessary to prove that there was misrepresentation; then, however honestly it may have been made, however free from blame the person who made it, the contract, having been obtained by misrepresentation, cannot stand."

3. Stating belief as knowledge: If the defendant says that he knows something to be the case when in fact he *doesn't know whether it is the case or not*, this will furnish the necessary scienter.

4. Negligent and innocent misrepresentation: Many courts have now either relaxed or abandoned the strict scienter requirement, and allow recovery for negligent misrepresentation, and even in some instances for innocent misrepresentation (i.e., strict liability). These theories of recovery are discussed *infra*, pp. 454 and 457, respectively.

D. Right of third persons to recover: Can a plaintiff ever recover if the fraudulent misrepresentation was made not to her, but to some other person?

1. Common law rule: The traditional common law rule has been that the defendant is only liable to those persons whom he has *intended* to influence by his misrepresentation, and not to others, even though their reliance may have been foreseeable.

2. Relaxation of rule: However, this rule requiring intent to induce reliance has been *relaxed* substantially in recent years. The Second Restatement recognizes a number of circumstances in which a person will be liable for misrepresentations to one other than the recipient, even though not made for the purpose of inducing the plaintiff to rely. The most important of these are the following two:

   a. Use in commercial document: One who incorporates a misstatement in a *commercial document* (e.g., a product label) is liable to anyone who suffers loss through his justifiable reliance on the truth of the statement. For instance, a company which markets clover seed in bags intentionally labelled "alfalfa seed" would be liable to anyone who planted the seeds in reliance on the label, and suffered loss, whether the company "intended" to reach that person or not. Rest. 2d, §532, Illustr. 2.

b. **"Reason to expect":** The defendant is liable to any member of a "class of persons" whom he has *"reason to expect"* will **learn of and rely on** the misrepresentation, if the reliance occurs in the *"type of transaction"* in which he has reason to expect them to engage because of such reliance. Rest. 2d, §§531, 533. In other words, the plaintiff to whom no misrepresentation has been directly made must, in order to recover under this section, show two things:

   i. that she is a member of a class which the defendant had *reason to expect* would be induced to rely; and

   ii. that the transaction is of the *same sort* that the defendant had reason to expect would occur in reliance.

c. **Change from former law:** The Restatement's position is thus more liberal than that of most earlier cases, such as *Peek v. Gurney*.

   i. **Not same as foreseeability:** But even the Restatement's test is not the same as one based on "foreseeability." The reliance by the third person must be more than foreseeable; it (or other reliance by other similarly situated plaintiffs) must be "expectable." (The Restatement leaves a Caveat to §531 as to whether there may be circumstances in which mere "foreseeability" will be enough.)

d. **Negligent misrepresentation:** In jurisdictions recognizing the possibility of an action for *negligent* misrepresentation, most courts have understandably been even more reluctant to find liability to persons with whom the defendant has not dealt directly. But a few decisions have held the speaker (e.g. an auditor) liable to anyone who foreseeably relied on the representation. See the discussion of this question, including the treatment of *Ultramares v. Touche Niven & Co., infra*, p. 455.

E. **Justifiable reliance:** The plaintiff must also show, to establish deceit, that he in fact *relied* on the misrepresentation, and that his reliance was *justifiable*.

1. **Causal question:** With respect to the "reliance in fact" aspect of this requirement, the principal issue is whether the plaintiff has relied when he has made an additional *investigation* on his own, and his action is the product of reliance both on the misrepresentation and on his own investigation.

   a. **Misrepresentation need not be sole factor:** In this situation, it is generally held that the plaintiff has met the reliance requirement, as long as the defendant's misrepresentation was a *substantial factor* in inducing his reliance, despite the fact that his own investigation also was a substantial factor. See Rest. 2d, §546, Comment b and Illustr. 2.

      i. **Reliance solely on investigation:** But if, after receiving the defendant's misrepresentation, the plaintiff makes his own investigation, and *relies totally* or almost totally upon this investigation, he will be held not to have met the reliance requirement. Rest. 2d, §547(1).

2. **Justifiability of reliance:** The plaintiff must also show that his reliance was *justifiable*. Many of the cases involving the justifiability of reliance involve opinions, statements of "law," and predictions and statements of intention; these subject areas are discussed at various places later in this chapter.

   a. **Duty to inspect:** Apart from these issues, the principal question is whether it is ever unreasonable for the plaintiff to rely on the defendant's representation without making an *independent investigation* of his own.

      i. **No general duty to investigate:** In general, the plaintiff has *no duty to investigate* on his own, even where an investigation could be easily done, and would disclose the falsity of the defendant's statements.

         (1) **Disbelief by court:** However, in some cases the court may simply disbelieve the plaintiff's claim that the representation in question was made, or his claim that he relied on it. In such situations, for procedural reasons courts may hold that the plaintiff could so easily have investigated that his failure to do so made his reliance unreasonable.

      ii. **Obvious falsity:** Although the plaintiff seldom has a duty to investigate, he does have a duty not to overlook the *"obvious."* Thus Rest. 2d, §541, Comment a, makes the plaintiff's reliance unjustified if the representation's falsity "would be patent to him if he had utilized his opportunity to make a cursory examination or investigation."

         (1) **Contributory negligence:** But the plaintiff's *contributory negligence* is not by itself a defense to a deceit action. The fact that a person of reasonable prudence would not have believed the defendant's misrepresentation is irrelevant, as long as its falsity is not obvious.

3. **Materiality:** The plaintiff must also show that the fact he relied on was *material* to the underlying transaction. For instance, if the defendant, acting as agent, sells the plaintiff a tract of land, and in so doing falsely states that his principal is left-handed, the plaintiff will not be able to recover in deceit, since the representation was not material. (See P,W&S, p. 1048, note 6.)

   a. **What is material:** Generally, a representation is material if a "reasonable man would attach importance to [its truth] in determining his choice of action in the transaction in question." Rest. 2d, §538(2)(a).

      i. **Special knowledge by defendant:** In addition to this, if the defendant has some reason to know that the plaintiff attaches a particular importance to the fact in question, even though a reasonable person would not do so, the representation will be treated by the court as material. Rest. 2d, §538(2)(b). For instance, if the defendant knew that the plaintiff believed in astrology, and induced him to buy stock in a particular company by falsely stating that the horoscopes of all the company's officers predicted success, the representation would be held to be material. Rest. 2d, §538, Illustr. 1. (Observe the Restatement's implicit position on the reasonableness of believing in astrology!)

F. Opinion: Courts have always been reluctant to allow a plaintiff to recover based on any statement that could be called an ***"opinion."***

Example: D sells P some farm land by saying that it contains "about" 150 acres of timber, that the timber can be sold for $4 per cord, and that the land can be cultivated so as to produce 100 bushels of potatoes per acre. P sues D for fraud. *Held*, for D: these statement were merely "speculative expressions of opinion", and "mere trade talk"; they are therefore not actionable. This is so even though D may have known perfectly well that there were less than 150 acres of timber, that the wood would not bring $4 per cord, or that an acre would never produce 100 bushels of potatoes. *Saxby v. Southern Land Co.*, 63 S.E. 423 (Va. 1909).

1. **More liberal rule:** Today, courts are somewhat more willing to allow suit based on a false expression of opinion than they were in the time of *Saxby*. It is still generally true that even if the defendant says that something is his opinion, when it is really not his opinion, the plaintiff cannot recover in deceit. However, in a few situations, discussed below, modern courts are sometimes willing to recognize the possibility that reliance may be justified.

2. **Opinion of adverse party:** Where the defendant was an ***"adverse party"*** to the plaintiff at the time of the misstatements (e.g., buyer and seller, or any other pair of negotiating parties), Rest. 2d, §542, lists the following situations in which the plaintiff may be justified in relying on the defendant's expression of opinion:

   a. **Special knowledge:** The defendant "purports to have ***special knowledge*** of the matter" that the plaintiff does not have.

   Example: The Ps, experienced restaurant operators, negotiate with D (Prudential Insurance), a company that owns a vacant building that the Ps propose to lease for use as a restaurant. During the negotiations, D's representative, Powell, tells the Ps, "The building is in perfect condition. ... This [is] a very new building; [I was] present at the very beginning of this building and watched it all the way through. ... There [has] been nothing wrong with the place at all." After the Ps sign the lease and begin remodeling the property, they learn from multiple sources that there was previously a hamburger restaurant there, Hudson's Grill, and that Hudson's operations were harmed by the building's "very very bad odor." Evidence shows that while Hudson's was still operating, Powell personally experienced the odor and described it as "almost unbearable." The Ps sue D to recover damages for fraud (and to rescind the lease). D defends on several grounds, one of which is that Powell's statements were statements of opinion.

   Held (by the Texas Supreme Court), Powell's statements about the building's suitability for the Ps' planned restaurant give rise to a fraud claim. Even if, as D argues, Powell's statements are properly considered "pure expressions of opinion,"[1] Powell's and D's ***"one-sided knowledge of past facts*** makes these ... representations actionable[.]" Where a lessor has ***"superior personal knowledge,"*** a prospective tenant is "entitled to rely on the fact that [the lessor] ***will not actively conceal material infor-***

---

1. The court disagreed with this characterization, saying that the statements concealing the odor problem were "more properly statements of fact, not pure expressions of opinion." But the court was willing to assume for the sake of argument that these were statements of opinion.

*mation." **Italian Cowboy Partners, Ltd. v. Prudential Ins. Co. of Am.**,* 341 S.W.3d 323 (Tex. Sup. Ct. 2011).

b. **Fiduciary relationship:** The defendant "stands in a ***fiduciary*** or other similar relation of trust and confidence" to the plaintiff.

c. **Confidence:** The defendant "has successfully endeavored to secure the ***confidence***" of the plaintiff.

d. **Other:** There is some other "special reason" to expect that the plaintiff will rely on the defendant's opinion.

   i. **Defendant knows of plaintiff's gullibility:** For instance, if the defendant knows that the plaintiff is particularly ***gullible*** or unintelligent, and therefore has reason to believe that the plaintiff will be misled by a false statement of opinion, this will be actionable. This would be a "special reason" to expect the plaintiff to rely; see Rest. 2d, §542, Comment i.

3. **"Puffing" still not actionable:** *"Puffing",* or *"trade talk,"* is still not actionable under the Restatement test. Thus if a car dealer says, "This is the best little two-door car you're gonna find for the money anywhere on the market," the plaintiff can't sue even if he can prove that the dealer doesn't really believe that the car is a particularly good one. Rest. 2d, §542, Comment e.

4. **Opinion of apparently disinterested person:** Where the opinion is expressed not by one of the parties to a business deal, but by someone whom the plaintiff reasonably perceives as being *"disinterested,"* courts are much more willing to find the plaintiff's reliance on it reasonable.

   a. **Rationale:** Whereas in the "adverse party" situation discussed above, the plaintiff is presumed to understand that her adversary is likely to stretch the truth to make the deal, this factor is not present where the defendant seems to be disinterested. See Rest. 2d, §543.

   Example: P buys a pair of shoes manufactured by D1. When she wears the shoes on her vinyl kitchen floor, she slips, and hurts herself. She sues not only D1, but also D2, a publisher who publishes Good Housekeeping Magazine, which has given the "Good Housekeeping Seal of Approval" to the shoes. D2 is on record as stating that it has satisfied itself that products receiving the Seal of Approval are "good ones".

   Held, for P against D2. Since D2's purpose in granting Seal of Approval to products was to induce people to buy them, it will not be heard to say that its representation that the product was a "good one" was merely opinion. D2 "held itself out as a disinterested third party which had examined the shoes, found them satisfactory, and gave its endorsement. By the very procedure and method it used, [D2] represented to the public it possessed superior knowledge and special information concerning the product it endorsed." Therefore, D2 can be liable for negligence. *Hanberry v. Hearst Corp.,* 81 Cal. Rptr. 519 (Cal. Ct. App. 1969).

5. **Opinion implying fact:** The above discussion applies only to those opinions which are "pure opinion", and which do not state or imply concrete facts. There are, however, many opinions which do either ***express or imply facts***. When such an opinion is given, the plain-

tiff may be able to establish that his reliance on such expressed or implied facts is reasonable.

a. Lack of knowledge of inconsistent facts: Thus an opinion will often contain an implied statement that its maker knows of no facts *incompatible with* that opinion. If the plaintiff can show that the defendant was in reality aware of facts incompatible with his opinion, he may be able to recover. See Rest. 2d, §539(1)(a).

b. Line between opinion and fact: Also, it does not take much to cross over the line from opinion to statement of fact. Thus while a simple *statement of value* (e.g. "This land is worth $5,000 per acre") is an opinion, "Land just like this is selling for $5,000 across town", "I paid $4800 for this land last year", and "I've already been offered $4950 for this acre" are all statements of fact, and the plaintiff can sue and win on a deceit theory if he can show that the defendant knew they were false. See P&K, p. 758. See also P, W&S, p. 1050.

Example: D, the manufacturer of a vacuum cleaner line, sells P equipment for making the vacuum cleaners, and the patents to them. D claims that the machines are "absolutely perfect in even the smallest detail", that they will last a lifetime, that their use of water power is the most efficient form of cleaning, etc. D also represents that these vacuum cleaners have never before been sold on the market. After the deal is done, P comes to disagree with this evaluation, and sues for deceit.

Held, the claims of quality are mere "puffing" or "dealers' talk", and are not actionable. This is so because P, as purchaser of the business, had ample opportunity to check out the claims. (A similar result, the court indicated, might not be reached if P were merely a consumer buying one machine.) However, the statement that no cleaners had been sold previously went beyond the realm of opinion, and P is entitled to recover if he can prove that sales were made. *Vulcan Metals Co. v. Simmons Mfg. Co.*, 248 F. 853 (2d Cir. 1918).

G. Statements as to law: Statements as to *questions of law* were almost always held to be opinions, and therefore not to be relied upon, at common law.

1. Modern view: But today, statements involving legal principles are generally treated the same as any other kind of statement. For instance, if the statement is fairly read as being solely an opinion, it may be relied on only in those limited circumstances discussed *supra*, p. 447. Rest. 2d, §545(2).

a. Implied factual statement: The most important consequence of this more liberal rule is that if the defendant's representation of law includes an *implied statement* as to *factual matters*, the plaintiff may rely upon this implied statement as he could upon any other factual representation. Rest. 2d, §545(1).

Example: T is about to become a tenant in a New York City building owned by L, a landlord. As L knows, T proposes to operate in the building a business that converts restaurant garbage into fertilizer. The lease contains a representation by L that for zoning purposes, the premises are in an "unrestricted zone," so that the proposed use will not be in violation of the zoning ordinance. Before T signs the lease, L also tells T orally that L "guarantees" that the proposed use will be valid. P signs the lease, moves in, and starts to convert garbage. However, it turns out that three years before the lease was signed, New York City modified its zoning ordinance so as to reclassify the building from an M-3 district (with odor standards that T's use would have complied with without T's needing to modify its equipment) to an M-1 district (with much stricter odor standards that would require T to bear a significant added expense to meet those standards). The city now declares that T's use violates the M-1 standard, and closes down the business. T sues L for fraud. L defends on the grounds that "only a misrepresentation of law rather than of fact is involved," and that misrepresentations about whether the law allows a particular use are always statements of pure opinion, for which state law does not allow recovery in fraud.

Held (by the highest court in New York), for T. The false statement about the building's zoning status was not a pure expression of opinion about the law, but rather a mixed statement of fact and law: when L said that it knew the premises were in an unrestricted district, T properly understood this to mean that L "knew, as a fact, that the zoning [code] did not restrict the use of the particular premises." Therefore, the false statement was a statement of fact (what the zoning resolution contained by way of legal requirements for that particular building); it was "hardly [an] opinion[] as to the law, albeit matters to be found in a law." *National Conversion Corp. v. Cedar Bldg. Corp.*, 246 N.E.2d 351 (N.Y. Ct. App., 1969).

H. Prediction and intention: Courts distinguish between statements of *"prediction"* and statements of *"intention."*

1. **Prediction:** If the defendant *predicts* that a certain thing will happen, this will almost always be held to be merely an opinion, and is at best something that can relied upon only in those situations where other opinions could be relied on (e.g., a fiduciary relationship between defendant and plaintiff). Thus if the defendant, trying to sell the plaintiff a piece of land, says "The value of this parcel is bound to increase 20% a year for the next ten years", the plaintiff will almost certainly be unable to establish that his reliance was justifiable.

   a. **Defendant's lack of knowledge of contrary facts:** But as with other opinions, such a prediction generally contains an implicit statement that the maker knows of no facts inconsistent with it. Thus if the defendant landseller mentioned above knew that the property was likely to be condemned, or to sink in a marsh, her statement about value would probably be held to be actionable. (In any event, plaintiff could also probably show "fraudulent concealment"; see *supra*, p. 442.)

2. **Intention:** But where the defendant, instead of making predictions about things beyond her control, makes a statement as to her own *intentions*, plaintiff's reliance will often be justifiable. As one well-known statement put it, "The state of a man's mind is as much a fact as the state of his digestion." *Edgington v. Fitzmaurice*, L.R. 29 Chi. Div. 359 (Eng. 1882).

   a. **Means of avoiding contract defenses:** One party to a contract will often try to avoid various *contract defenses* by suing on a theory that the other party never intended to keep the contract, and therefore fraudulently misstated his intent to do so. Where the necessary intent can be shown, most courts hold that neither the Statute of Frauds, the parol evidence rule, the illegality of the transaction, lack of consideration, or any other contract defense will bar liability. See P,W&S, p. 1060.

Example: As part of a transaction, D promises P that he will pay a $500 mortgage so that P will not have to pay it. He fails to do so, and P sues on the theory that D never intended to keep the promise, even at the time he made it. (P couldn't sue for breach of contract, because of the Statute of Frauds.)

Held, if D never intended to keep the promise, this was a fraudulent misrepresentation which is actionable. Furthermore, the Statute of Frauds does not bar the suit. *Burgdorfer v. Thielemann*, 55 P.2d 1122 (Or. 1936).

  b. Statement as to intent of others: Essentially the same rules apply to statements as to the present intentions of *others*; if the plaintiff can show that the defendant has knowingly misstated these intentions, he will have an action for fraud.

I. Damages:

  1. Proximate cause: Once the plaintiff has met the requirements for deceit, he may recover any damages which are found to have been ***proximately caused*** by the defendant's misrepresentations. He must show that he sustained actual damages, and may not recover nominal ones (as he could for other intentional torts; see *supra*, p. 8).

    a. Decline in value: The issue of proximate cause arises most frequently in situations where the plaintiff has purchased stocks or bonds in reliance on a misrepresentation about them, and their market value declines due to causes entirely *unrelated* to the misrepresented matters. Despite the fact that the misrepresentation is the "but for" cause of plaintiff's loss in this situation (i.e., if there had been no misrepresentation, the plaintiff would not have purchased, and would not have been in a position to suffer losses), such recovery is generally ***not allowed***, on the grounds that the loss was not a "reasonably foreseeable" result of the misrepresentation. See Rest. 2d, §548A, Illustr. 1.

  2. Measure of damages: Courts have applied essentially two different ***measures*** of damages: (1) one which attempts to put the plaintiff in the position he was in before the misrepresentation (which in contract law would be called the ***"reliance"*** measure — see the Emanuel Law Outline on *Contracts*); and (2) one which, where the plaintiff and defendant have made a contract, puts the plaintiff in the position he would have been in had the misrepresented facts been true (in contracts, the ***"benefit of the bargain"*** or "expectation" measure).

    a. Reliance measure: About 12 courts consistently apply the reliance measure in all deceit actions. (P&K, pp. 767-68.) Thus if the defendant fraudulently induces the plaintiff to buy an object for $10,000, and it is really worth only $7,000, the reliance or "out of pocket" recovery is $3,000. This is so regardless of whether the entire $3,000 discrepancy is due to the fact that the object was not as warranted, or is rather due in part to this but also in part to the fact that the plaintiff would have made a bad bargain anyway, even without the misrepresentations (e.g., by paying $10,000 for something worth only $9,000).

b. Benefit of the bargain: A *majority* of American courts, however, give the plaintiff his "*benefit of the bargain*" or "*expectation*" damages, at least in those situations where the defendant is someone with whom he has made a contract. These courts reason that even though the deceit action is not on the contract, it is fair to give the plaintiff the contract measure of damages, and to punish the defendant. Thus if the plaintiff paid $10,000 for something worth $7,000, and the thing would have been worth $15,000 if the misrepresentations about it had been true, the plaintiff will receive damages of $8,000 from these courts (i.e., the difference between what the item was worth in reality, and what it would have been worth if it had been as represented).

    i. Repair bill as estimate of expectation damages: The plaintiff seeking the benefit of his bargain will often have a hard time showing what the actual value of the product was (as opposed to what it would have been worth if it had matched the representations made about it). In this situation, he will sometimes be able to recover the costs of *repairing* it to bring it up to the condition it was represented to be in.

c. Restatement view: The Second Restatement, in §549(2), allows the "benefit of the bargain" measure where expectation damages are "proved with reasonable certainty."

d. Where reliance damages greater: In some situations the reliance measure will be *greater* than the expectation measure (as where the plaintiff has made such a bad bargain that even if the item had been as represented, it would still not have been worth what he paid for it). In this situation, all courts agree that the plaintiff has the option of choosing to recover reliance damages. That is, he will receive the difference between what he paid and what the product was really worth.

e. Consequential damages: The plaintiff may also recover *consequential* damages. For instance, where the plaintiff was sold a horse which was represented to be gentle, and which kicked him, he was allowed to recover for his injuries. *Vezina v. Souliere*, 152 A. 798 (Vt. 1931). See P,W&S, p. 1063, n. 7.

f. Financial loss required: Most courts say that plaintiff can recover *only* for *pecuniary* (i.e., *financial*) loss for the deceit.

    i. No recovery for emotional distress: Thus plaintiff *cannot* recover for *emotional distress* that resulted from the deceit.

    Example: D, offering to sell P D's rural land for $100,000, tells P that oil has been discovered on nearby parcels. P knows that this would be a cheap price if oil had really been discovered nearby. P gets very excited about his wonderful prospective purchase. Before signing a contract, P performs due diligence, and discovers that no oil has been discovered nearby, and that D knowingly misrepresented that oil had been discovered. P suffers great emotional distress at the loss of the opportunity he thought he had. P never signs a contract for the land, but sues D for deceit.

    P cannot recover, because he has suffered no pecuniary loss, and damages for emotional distress (as distinguished from pecuniary loss) may not be recovered in a deceit action.

III. NEGLIGENT MISREPRESENTATION

A. Historical view: *Derry v. Peek, supra*, p. 444, established that the action of deceit could not be used for a misrepresentation that was merely negligent, rather than intentional.

  1. Direct physical damage required: Nor, until recently, could the victim of a negligent misrepresentation bring an ordinary negligence action when only his intangible economic interests had been harmed. That is, to bring a conventional negligence action, the plaintiff had to suffer either personal injury or direct property damage, not mere intangible economic harm (e.g., lost profits, or a bad contract).

  2. Changing view: But in the last 20 or so years, most American courts have begun to allow some kind of recovery for *negligent misrepresentation*, even where only intangible economic harm is suffered. Some courts have done this by allowing a special action for "negligent misrepresentation" analogous to deceit; others have simply assimilated the intangible-harm case into the conventional negligence action.

   a. Same requirements: In either case, most requirements for the action are generally the same as for a deceit action. For instance, the plaintiff must show that his reliance was justifiable, and the standards for justifiability are at least as strict as in deceit.

B. Business relationship: The courts have been most willing to allow recovery for negligent misrepresentation where the defendant's statements are made in the course of his *business or profession*, and he had a *pecuniary interest* in the transaction.

> **Example:** P, an importer, is expecting goods to come in by ship to be stored by D. P wants to insure the goods, so he calls D, and asks whether and where they are stored; he is told that they have been docked and are stored at "Dock F, Weehauken". He gives this information to the insurance company to get insurance. It turns out that the goods have not yet arrived; when they do, they are stored at Dock D, not F, and are then destroyed by a fire. P can't collect on the insurance because of the misdescription, so he sues D.
>
> *Held*, P may recover for this negligent misrepresentation. P and D were not strangers; instead, they had a bailor/bailee business relationship. This relationship was enough to give D the burden of exercising due care in his statements. *International Products Co. v. Erie R.R. Co.*, 155 N.E. 662 (N.Y. 1927).

  1. Direct compensation not required: Most courts, and the Second Restatement, hold that it is not necessary for the plaintiff to show that the defendant *directly* received compensation in the transaction giving rise to the misstatements. See Rest. 2d, §552, Comment d. For instance, if a prospective client comes to a lawyer's office, and as part of a "free first consultation", is negligently given incorrect advice, she may sue, despite the fact that she has not paid for the services.

   a. Curbstone opinion: But where a statement is made totally outside of the defendant's usual business or professional work, there is no liability. Thus in the case of a *"curbstone opinion"*, "as when an attorney gives a casual and offhand opinion on a point of law to a friend whom he meets on the street", there is no liability. Rest. 2d, *ibid.*

C. Liability to third persons: The maker of a *fraudulent* misstatement will be liable not only to the recipient of the statement, but to any person who the maker has "reason to expect" may rely on it. (*Supra*, p. 446.) But the maker of a negligent misrepresentation is liable only to a *much narrower class of third persons.*

1. Persons intended to be reached: The Second Restatement, in §552(2), makes the defendant liable to a *"limited group of persons"* whom the defendant *intends to reach* with the information, or whom he knows the *recipient intends to reach.* That is, whereas the fraudulent misrepresenter is liable to anyone whom he should have "reason to expect" will learn about the statement and rely on it, the negligent misstater is liable only to a limited group, and that group must be composed of persons whom the defendant either intends to reach or knows that the recipient intends to reach.

> **Example:** D, a firm of accountants, negligently prepares a certified audit of the books of X Corp. D is aware that the results of this audit will be shown to banks, factors, and other persons from whom X wants to borrow money (but is apparently unaware of the precise identity of any of these potential creditors.) In reliance on the audit, P, a factor, lends money to X, which goes bankrupt. P sues D for negligent misrepresentation.
>
> *Held*, D had no duty of care to P, and therefore cannot be liable. Otherwise, "a thoughtless slip or blunder, the failure to detect a theft or forgery beneath the cover of deceptive entries, may expose accountants to a liability in an indeterminate amount for an indeterminate time to an indeterminate class." Also, this would make the scope of liability for negligence as great as it is for actual fraud, which would be illogical. (But, the court noted, if the members of D lacked even a genuine *belief* that the audit was correct, they could be found to have made a fraudulent misrepresentation, and their liability would extend to creditors, like P, who relied.) *Ultramares Corp. v. Touche, Niven & Co.*, 174 N.E. 441 (N.Y. 1931).

    a. Restatement view of *Ultramares*: The Second Restatement accepts the result of *Ultramares*; Rest. 2d, §552, Illustr. 10. But under the Restatement, if the defendant was aware that the representation would be passed on to a *limited number* of people, he may be liable to one or more of those people, even if he didn't know their precise identities. For instance, if an accounting firm's client says that he will use a certified statement to negotiate "a bank loan," and does not mention a particular bank, the accountants will be liable to whatever bank is finally approached by the client and suffers loss. Rest. 2d, §552, Illustr. 7. Other instances in which the defendant may be liable to a limited class whose precise members are unknown include:

        i. Information supplied to bidders: Information supplied by engineers to the owner of a construction project, who passes it on to *bidders* on that project; if a bidder then suffers loss as a result of the information's incorrectness (e.g., by submitting too low a bid for excavation work based on an unduly favorable soil engineer's report), the engineer will be liable.

        ii. Abstractors: Abstractors of title who furnish a *title report* on a piece of property to the owner, knowing that it will be given to prospective purchasers;

        iii. Surveyors: Land surveyors who should know that their *surveys* will be given to prospective purchasers;

iv. Lawyers: A *lawyer* who drafts a will which negligently cuts out certain *intended heirs*.

v. Public duty: Persons having a *public duty* to give correct information; (e.g., a government food inspector who negligently stamps a seller's beef as "Grade A" when it is inferior, and which is then bought by the plaintiff; see Rest. 2d, §552, Illustr. 18.)

D. Contributory negligence: The plaintiff's *contributory negligence* will be a defense to an action for negligent misrepresentation to the same extent that it would be a defense to any other kind of negligence action. See Rest. 2d, §552A.

E. Damages limited to pecuniary harm: Damages for negligent misrepresentation are limited to *pecuniary harm.* This principle has several important consequences:

[1] Emotional harm: Plaintiff *cannot* recover for *emotional harm* suffered as the result of the misrepresentation.

Example: D offers P a contract to purchase stock in D's new startup company, telling P that D is about to sign a large and profitable contract with the U.S. government. P signs the contract, and anticipates making millions of dollars on his investment. Before P has closed on the contract or paid money to D, the U.S. government rejects the proposed deal. D honestly (but negligently) believed that the deal would go through when he made the statement to P. D allows P to rescind the agreement. P suffers severe emotional distress from having his hopes of profit dashed. If the contract had gone through, P would indeed have made an enormous return on his investment.

P cannot recover for negligent misrepresentation, because he has suffered only emotional, not pecuniary, loss.

[2] Benefit of bargain: Plaintiff *cannot* recover for the *"benefit of her bargain."* That is, if the misrepresentation relates to a contract, P may not recover the difference between the actual value received by P and the value that P would have received that the facts been accurately stated.

Example: On the facts of the above example, P cannot recover the difference between the price of the stock he contracted to buy and the value the stock would have had if D's representation about the government contract had been true.

[3] Reliance damages: But plaintiff *can* recover the difference between the *value* of what P has *received* and what P *paid* in purchase price or other value. So P gets, in effect, *"reliance damages."*

Example: On the facts of the above Example, if P had paid $100,000 for the stock, and without the government contract the stock was worthless, P would be entitled to a return of the $100,000 as damages for negligent misrepresentation.

See generally Rest. 2d, §552B.

IV. STRICT LIABILITY

A. **Increasing willingness to allow:** Just as courts were reluctant to recognize a cause of action for negligent misrepresentation until fairly recently, so they have been even less willing to impose *strict liability* for "innocent" misrepresentations. But there are now at least two kinds of situations in which a substantial number (perhaps even a majority) of courts allow recovery for losses due to a misrepresentation that is neither intentional nor negligent.

B. **Sale, rental or exchange:** If two parties are involved in a *sale, rental* or *exchange* transaction, and one makes a material misrepresentation to the other in order to close the deal, he will be liable even if the misrepresentation was not negligent or fraudulent. Rest. 2d, §552C(1).

> **Example:** D, a developer, induces the Ps to buy a particular house by giving them a survey which shows that the house is 20 feet from a particular boundary of the lot, as is required by local zoning laws. After Ps move in, they discover that in fact the house is less than 2 feet from that boundary, and that not only is this a violation of local zoning laws, but a trespass on their neighbor's property occurs every time anybody goes in or out of the house.
>
> *Held*, even if D's misrepresentation was completely innocent (as opposed to negligent), D is liable. *Richard v. A. Waldman & Sons, Inc.*, 232 A.2d 307 (Conn. 1967).

1. **Comparison with warranty:** In the vast majority of cases in which such a recovery based on misrepresentation made in a sale, rental or exchange is available, plaintiff could also sue on an implied or express *warranty* theory. But one big difference between warranty recovery and strict tort liability is that in warranty suits, a number of contract defenses, including most importantly the *parol evidence rule*, may be asserted. In strict tort, they may not be.

   a. **Illustration:** Thus in the above example, the plaintiffs had taken title by a deed, which under the parol evidence rule dissolved any warranties which had been given in the contract of sale or orally. The court held that this did not bar the plaintiffs from suing for innocent misrepresentation.

2. **Service transactions:** A few courts have been willing to apply strict liability where the transaction between plaintiff and defendant involves a *service* rather than a sale, rental or exchange. For instance, if an insurance company agent told the plaintiff that the policy he was buying would cover him against a certain kind of liability, and it didn't, the plaintiff might be able to recover in strict liability, without showing negligence on the part of the agent.

3. **Must be privity:** The sale, rental or exchange must have been directly between plaintiff and defendant. For instance, if a manufacturer makes a representation to a retailer, who passes it on to the plaintiff to induce her to buy, there will be no strict liability under Rest. 2d, §552C. See Comment d to that section.

C. **Misrepresentation by seller of chattels to consumer:** A seller of goods who makes any misrepresentation on the label, or in public advertising, will be strictly liable for any *physical injury* which results, even if the injured person did not buy the product from the defendant. Rest. 2d, §402B. This provision is essentially part of products liability law, and is similar to the "express warranty" provisions of the UCC. See, e.g., *Baxter v. Ford Motor Co., supra*, p. 352, which was decided on substantially the theory of §402B.

Quiz Yourself on

MISREPRESENTATION *(Entire Chapter)*

79. Noah and Judas are neighbors, who frequently do each other favors. One night, Judas is visiting Noah, and, as he leaves, Noah says: "I'll come out with you as far as the barn. It looks like rain, and I want to make sure the unicorns are securely shut in the barn." Judas says, "Forget it. I'll check on my way home." Judas has no intention of checking, figuring Noah's just being a worrywart. In fact, the unicorns are not securely penned, and they run away and drown in the subsequent flood. Had they been penned, they would have survived. Noah sues Judas for misrepresentation. Judas claims he didn't misrepresent a past or present fact, so the claim will not lie. Who's correct? _____

80. Betty Omen is considering buying passage on the first voyage of the Titanic. She is at a cocktail party and sees Captain Smith, who is going to command the voyage. Betty walks over and asks the Captain, "Is the Titanic safe?" He responds, "Madame, the Titanic is capable of surviving any impact whatsoever — missiles, nuclear weapons, icebergs, you name it." In fact, Smith doesn't know if this is true; he hasn't seen the ship itself or any technical specifications. Her worries calmed, Betty buys a ticket. The Titanic sinks, but Betty survives. She sues Smith, who has also survived, for intentional misrepresentation. Will she win? _____

81. Nysen Shiny, travelling cookware salesman, knocks on the door of the Gingerbread House, where Wicked Witch lives. She invites him in. When he tells her he sells cookware, she says, "Oh, good. Do you have a pot large enough to hold two small children?" He responds, "Oh, yes. Our HG pot is the one for you." He excuses himself to make a phone call, and Witch rifles through his briefcase, finding a spec sheet which shows that the HG pot is clearly not large enough to hold two children, and in fact there aren't any that can. However, when Nysen returns, Witch sweetly orders the HG pot, figuring a pot big enough for one kid at a time will have to suffice. The pot arrives, and Witch sues Nysen for misrepresentation. Assume that Witch suffered financial loss from the fact that she could boil only one kid at a time (lower productivity, translating to loss of revenue from sale of magic potions made from the boiled children). Can Witch recover? _____

82. E. F. Mutton, the hottest stock broker in New Zealand, is at a cocktail party in the U.S. Yves Dropper, another guest at the party, overhears Mutton telling a third guest, Little Lamb, that, based on his confidential sources, the Embraceable Ewe Sweater Company is about to announce a huge quarterly profit, and it's a great time to invest. In fact, Mutton knows that Embraceable Ewe lost big bucks, and Mutton is just trying to buy time in which to unload his own shares. Relying on his statement, Yves invests, and takes a "bleating" when the market drops. Is Mutton liable to Yves for deceit? _____

83. Darlene owns a five-story apartment building in Pound City. Darlene offers the building for sale to Percy. She gives Percy a sheet she has prepared, which states, "The current rent roll is $5,000 per month, consisting of ten apartments at $500 each." She does not disclose to Percy a fact well known to her, namely, that under the Rent Stabilization ordinance in force in Pound, the highest rent properly chargeable for any of the apartments is $400, and that any tenant who becomes aware of his rights can sue to have the rent reduced to that amount. Percy is aware that the Rent Stabilization ordinance exist, and is also aware that there are records at the Pound City Hall showing, for each apartment building, the highest rent that can be charged per apartment. Percy decides that Darlene looks honest, so he neglects to check the town records, even though he could easily do this. He buys the building at a price that appears economically sensible to him based on a $5,000 per month rent roll, but that he would not have paid had he known the legal rent roll was only $4,000.

Shortly after the closing, the tenants discover their rights, bandd together, and successfully sue to have each person's rental reduced to $400. Percy sues Darlene for fraudulent misrepresentation and/or non-disclosure. Darlene defends on the grounds that: (1) she has no liability for what was essentially non-disclosure; and (2) in any event, Percy was not justified in relying, because he could have easily performed his own investigation which would have disclosed the true facts. Which, if either, of these defenses has merit? _____

84. Pia is contemplating the purchase of a painting which the seller represents to be by the great master Rubens. Pia brings the painting to her friend Dimitrius, who Pia knows to be one of the world's great experts in Old Masters paintings. Pia asks Dimitrius to give his opinion on whether the painting is really by Rubens. Dimitrius looks at the painting, and said, "Yes my dear, I'm nearly certain that it really was painted by Rubens himself." In fact, Dimitrius is very unsure whether the painting is by Rubens or rather by one of his students, but he is too embarrassed to tell Pia (whom he longs after romantically) of his uncertainty. Pia buys the painting, and suffers financial loss when it is later conclusively shown to have been by one of Rubens' students. Pia sues Dimitrius for fraudulent misrepresentation. Dimitrius defends on the grounds that he was only stating, as Pia knew, his own opinion. May Pia recover?

Answers

79. **Noah.** Statements of intention are treated just like statements of fact for misrepresentation purposes. Thus, they can be the source of justified reliance. Here, Noah is justified in modifying his conduct based on Judas' statement of intent. *Note that Noah would have to prove that Judas didn't intend to follow through with his stated intent <u>when he made the statement</u>*.

RELATED ISSUE: It's *predictions* which typically cannot be misrepresentations, as long as the speaker knows nothing to prevent the prediction from coming true.

NOTE: For intentional torts, an intervening cause (like a flood) is much less likely to break the chain of causation, relieving defendant of liability, than in a negligence claim. If Noah's claim were based on negligence (e.g., Judas negligently forgot to check the unicorns), the flood would probably be considered a superseding cause as an unforeseeable "Act of God" breaking the chain of causation from Judas to the loss of the unicorns, such that it would relieve Judas of liability.

80. **Probably.** Misrepresentation requires a misrepresentation, knowledge of falsity or reckless disregard for the truth (scienter), intent to induce reliance, actual, justified reliance and damages. Here, Smith didn't know whether the Titanic was sinkable or not (and knew he didn't know), but he assured Betty it wasn't. Thus he satisfies the "scienter" requirement with a reckless disregard for the truth, and, as Captain of the ship, his assurance induces justified reliance.

NOTE: Were the Captain merely negligent — offering an opinion based on unreliable information — he could be liable for negligent misrepresentation.

81. **No.** Misrepresentation requires proof of the misrepresentation itself, knowledge of falsity or reckless disregard for the truth (scienter), intent to induce reliance, actual, justified reliance and damages. Here, Witch <u>investigated</u> and found the fraud and hence <u>didn't rely</u> on the misrepresentation. That means that the actual reliance (causation) element of intentional misrepresentation is missing. Although she was under no duty to investigate, once she did so she was not justified in relying on Nysen's statement.

82. No. Deceit (a/k/a intentional misrepresentation) requires proof of the misrepresentation itself, knowledge of falsity or reckless disregard for the truth (scienter), intent to induce reliance, causation, justified reliance and damages. Here, Mutton did not intend to induce reliance in Yves, so the "intent" requirement of misrepresentation is not satisfied.

RELATED ISSUE: Say that Mutton *did* intend that Yves rely on his statement. Then he *would* be liable, even though his statement is not a statement of fact and therefore not a source of justified reliance. However, here Mutton would be liable, since he has superior knowledge which Yves does not share; furthermore, he knows facts that indicate his opinion is wrong. These elements mean Yves *could* pursue a misrepresentation claim against him.

83. Neither. First, Darlene has not merely failed to disclose; she has made a material (and fraudulent) misrepresentation in the form of a "half truth." That is, she has told Percy that the current rent roll is $5,000, but has not given him the additional facts (that the current rents being charged are illegal) necessary to make the statement that she did make not misleading. See Rest. 2d, §529, Illustr. 2. Second, it is not a defense to a fraudulent misrepresentation action that the other party failed to perform an investigation which he could reasonably have performed — a party to a transaction has no duty to investigate, even if his failure to do so is unreasonable and thus amounts to contributory negligence. See Rest. 2d, §540. So Percy will recover for fraud.

84. Yes. A statement of opinion will not usually give rise to liability for intentional misrepresentation. However, courts are quicker to find liability for an opinion when the opinion is expressed by one who is not an "adverse party" to the listener, i.e., where the two parties are not on opposite sides of a business transaction. Here, Dimitrius and Pia were not on opposite sides, as they would have been had Dimitrius been trying to sell the painting to Pia; therefore, a court will be quicker to find Dimitrius liable than if he were the seller. Also, the courts are quicker to find liability even for an opinion, where the other party believes that the speaker has reason to know special facts which the listener does not. Here, Pia reasonably understood Dimitrius to be implying that he knew facts sufficient to lead him to his opinion of the genuineness of the painting. Therefore, Dimitrius will be liable since he knew that he did not have such facts. See Rest. 2d, §539, Illustr. 3.

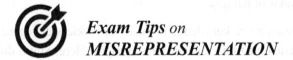

Exam Tips on
MISREPRESENTATION

Whenever one party in your fact pattern **makes a statement** to another, and the statement turns out to be **untrue**, be on the lookout for a "misrepresentation" claim. A misrepresentation issue is usually not one of the major torts contained in a complex multi-issue fact pattern; it's usually hidden away as one of the more minor issues.

☛ When you talk about "misrepresentation" as an independent tort, you're generally looking for misrepresentations that cause only **intangible pecuniary loss**. For misrepresentations that cause personal injury or property damage, usually the general tort of negligence (if the falsehood was unintentional) is the better tort to concentrate on.

☛ Remember, of course, that the tort of misrepresentation can be committed intentionally (the action called "fraud" or "deceit," as well as "intentional misrepresentation" — we'll use "fraud" here for shorthand) or, in some states, negligently. For each misstatement, first analyze and discuss whether fraud has been committed, and go on to discuss negligent misrepresentation only if you conclude that fraud hasn't (or may not have been) committed.

☞ For the most part, the requirements for fraud and negligent misrep. are the same. We'll talk about most exam issues here under "fraud," and under negligent misrep., we'll just focus on the elements that are different.

☛ Here's what to look for on **fraud**:

☞ Memorize this list of requirements (it's easy to forget one):

❑ A **misrepresentation** by D;

❑ **Scienter** (culpable state of mind by D, essentially either **knowledge** of falsity or **reckless indifference** to the truth);

❑ An intent to **induce P's reliance** (or at least a reason to expect that the class of which P is a member would be likely to rely);

❑ **Justifiable reliance** by P; and

❑ **Damage** (usually pecuniary) to P stemming from the reliance.

☞ Don't forget to check that the representation was **false**. This won't always be obvious. (*Example:* Insurer says to Claimant, "You have no legal case against us." Claimant settles. It's not clear that this representation was false, so you should discuss the falsity issue.)

☞ Remember that an affirmative act to **conceal** a fact from P is the same as asserting the non-existence of the fact. (*Example:* Seller repaints a cracked engine block in his car. He then sells to Buyer. That's misrepresentation to Buyer concerning the status of the engine block.)

☞ Also, **silence** can occasionally (though not usually) be the equivalent of an assertion of fact. The most important situations where silence will be an assertion: (1) D has a **fiduciary relationship** to P (*Example:* Lawyer to Client); or (2) D knows that P is mistaken about some **fact basic to the transaction** (*Example:* Buyer says to Dealer, "I'm paying you $100,000 because I know that's a Picasso"; Dealer stays silent knowing that the picture is a fake or by a lesser artist. Dealer's silence equals misrepresentation because P's mistake is about a fact basic to the transaction.)

☞ The fact that D has **more knowledge** about the situation than P is not by itself enough to turn D's silence into misrepresentation, especially where D is the buyer. (*Example:* Buyer is a jeweler; Seller is an amateur owner; Seller thinks the going rate for used diamonds is $2 per carat when Buyer knows it's $3 per carat — Buyer's silence is not a misrepresentation.)

☞ Look out for statements of **intention** where D **promises** to do something; the fact that D doesn't keep the promise, doesn't alone make it a misrepresentation. But if D **never intended** to keep the promise, this is misrepresentation.

☞ Also, look out for statements of *opinion*. A statement of opinion isn't normally a "representation."

    ☞ But in some situations, it is a misrepresentation for D to say that something is her opinion when it's not. In an "adverse party" situation (P and D are on opposite sides of a proposed transaction), the main example of misrepresentation of present opinion occurs where D has *special knowledge* that P doesn't. (*Example:* "As an art dealer, it's my opinion that this is a Picasso" — if Dealer doesn't really believe this, it's a misrepresentation because of Dealer's supposed special knowledge.)

    ☞ Statements of *law* are often held to be non-actionable statements of opinion. But if a statement includes an implied statement concerning the underlying facts, that implied statement can be a misrepresentation. (*Example:* "This house conforms to the zoning code's set-back requirements" — that's an actionable statement of fact, not opinion, about how the house is positioned on the lot.)

☞ Check that D had *scienter*. In essence, D must either *know* the statement was false, lie about *how much knowledge* as to the statement's truth, or *recklessly disregard* the fact that he doesn't know the truth.

☞ Check that D meant to *induce P to rely*. If the statement is made directly to P, usually this isn't a problem.

    ☞ D is also liable to *third persons* if they are members of a *class* which D had *"reason to expect"* would rely, and the transaction is of the *sort* that D should foresee would or might occur in reliance. (*Example:* If D knowingly mislabels goods, D is liable to anyone, even a non-purchaser, who reads the label and relies.)

    ☞ Common test issue: D makes a statement to X, who *repeats* it to P. Here, D is not liable, if he had no reason to expect the statement to be repeated to P or relied on by a class of which P is a part.

    ☞ Often, exams test the *"overheard"* remark (addressed to X, but overheard by P) — normally, the speaker turns out not to be liable, because she had no reason to expect the overhearing. (*Example:* Art Expert falsely says to Friend at Dealer's store, "That's a Picasso." Customer overhears, and offers to buy from Dealer without disclosing that she overheard Expert's statement. Expert isn't liable, because he had no intent to induce Customer to rely, and Customer wasn't a member of a class Expert should have expected to rely.)

    ☞ An *endorser* can have fraud liability to a member of the buying public. (*Example:* Olympic Champion says, "I made money with my BurgerQueen franchise." Any member of the buying public who relies by buying a franchise can probably sue Champion if Champion knew his statement was false.)

☞ Check two aspect's of P's *reliance*: (1) that there was "actual" reliance; and (2) that the reliance was justifiable.

☞ P must have ***actually*** relied. Often-tested: P ***spots the untruth*** but does the transaction anyway. Here, P couldn't have relied. (*Example:* D sells P a car, saying that it was never in an accident. In fact, the engine block was cracked in an accident, and had been painted over. P inspects closely and spots the broken engine block, but says nothing, and buys. P has not "actually relied" on the misrepresentation.)

☞ P's reliance must be ***"justifiable."*** So if the falsity would be ***"obvious"*** to an ordinary person in P's position, P can't recover. But P has ***no duty to investigate***, and P's ***contributory negligence*** is ***not*** a defense so long as the falsity is not obvious.

☞ If you conclude that P can recover for fraud, discuss the ***measure of damages.*** In the usual case where P has bought something based on the misrepresentation, courts differ about the measure: (1) some courts give P ***"expectation damages,"*** a/k/a the ***"benefit of the bargain"*** (the difference between what the item was really worth and what it would have been worth if it had been as represented); (2) other courts limit P to ***"reliance"*** damages (difference between the amount paid and the real value, without reference to what it would have been worth if it had been as represented). (*Example:* D says, "That's a Picasso worth $200,000, but you can buy it for $150,000." It's really a fake worth only $1,000. Some courts give P $199,000, in expectation damages, whereas others give $149,000, in reliance damages.)

☞ Whichever measure of damages is to be used, don't forget to subtract the ***actual value*** of what P got. (P doesn't get to tender the item back to D in return for not having this subtraction.)

☞ Also, look for ***consequential damages***. (*Example:* If a car said to be in working order breaks down while P is going to an important meeting, and P has to rent a replacement car, P can recover the cost of the rental as an additional item of damages on top of expectation or reliance.)

☛ If you conclude that P can't recover for fraud, consider a recovery for ***"negligent misrepresentation"*** (NM).

☞ Not all courts allow NM where there's only intangible economic harm, and not personal injury or property damage. Point this out in your answer.

☞ The differences between an action for fraud and one for NM: (1) D's mental state must be merely negligent, not "intentional" or "reckless"; (2) D must have made the statement ***during the course of his business*** and with a ***pecuniary interest*** in the transaction; and (3) P must be a person or member of a ***"limited group"*** that D ***intended to reach, or who D knows a recipient*** of the information intended to reach.

☞ A ***"re-publisher"*** can be liable for NM. (*Example:* X tells Newspaper, "There's no danger of salmonella from chicken as long as it is cooked for at least five minutes at 300 degrees." If Newspaper prints this as a quotation without checking its accuracy, Newspaper may be liable for NM, at least if we ignore the "who may sue" issue discussed below.)

☞ Most commonly-tested issue in NM: D must make the statement in the course of his ***business or profession***, and have a ***pecuniary interest*** in the transaction.

☞ The "pecuniary interest" requirement knocks out *"curbstone opinions,"* i.e., statements by professionals that take place outside the office and outside of a paid professional relationship. (*Example:* Attorney gives unpaid advice to a friend at a cocktail party.)

☞ The "pecuniary interest" requirement also knocks out situations where D is speaking to a customer, but on a subject that is outside of the business relationship with the customer. (*Example:* Storekeeper, owner of a hardware store, gives Customer advice about how to make a will. Since the advice has nothing to do with the sale of any product by Storekeeper, probably Storekeeper will be held to have had no pecuniary interest in the transaction.)

☞ A person making an NM is liable to a *narrower group* than the defrauder: he is not liable to those whom he has "reason to expect" will rely, but merely to a *"limited group"* that he either *intended* to reach, or that he knew the *recipient* intended to reach. (*Example:* D, a newspaper, negligently reports greater earnings by X Corp. than really occurred. Reader buys the stock, and loses money. Because the readership of a general newspaper is not a "limited class," probably Reader may not recover for NM.)

☞ *Contributory negligence* is a *defense* to NM. So if a reasonable person would investigate, P loses if he didn't. (Contrast this with the "no duty to investigate" rule for fraud.)

☞ For both fraud and NM actions, pay attention to the *measure of damages:*

☞ P can only recover *pecuniary* damages, not damages for *emotional distress* (e.g., disappointment that the representation turned out not to be true).

☞ P can't usually recover the *"benefit of her bargain,"* i.e., the amount by which P would have profited had the representation been true.

☞ Very occasionally, *strict liability* for misrep. is tested. Most common situations: P and D are parties to a sales or service transaction. Since these situations must involve privity (P and D dealt face-to-face), strict liability here is based as much in contract as in tort.

☞ Also, a seller who *mislabels* a product has, in effect, strict liability for misrepresentation for any *physical injury* that results. Cite to Restatement §402B on this labelling issue.

CHAPTER 17

DEFAMATION

ChapterScope

A person's interest in his *reputation* is protected by the tort actions for *"libel"* and *"slander,"* collectively called *"defamation."*

- **Libel vs. slander:** *Libel* is caused by a *written* statement, and *slander* is caused by an *oral statement*. Most of the rules governing the two tort actions are identical.

- **Defamation generally:** To establish a case for either libel or slander, P must prove:

  - ❑ **Defamatory statement:** A *false* and *"defamatory"* (i.e., reputation-damaging) statement concerning P;

  - ❑ **Publication:** A *communicating* of that statement to a person other than P (a "publication");

  - ❑ **Fault:** *Fault* on the part of D, amounting to at least negligence if D is a media defendant, and either knowledge of falsity or reckless disregard of the truth if P is a "public official" or "public figure";

  - ❑ **Special harm:** In the case of certain types of slander, *"special harm,"* i.e., harm of a pecuniary nature.

- **Constitution:** Some of the above rules are imposed by the U.S. Constitution. Most importantly, Supreme Court decisions interpreting the First Amendment are the source of the rule that where P is a public figure or public official, he must show that D acted with either knowledge of the statement's falsity or reckless disregard of whether it was true or false.

I. GENERAL PRINCIPLES

A. Prima facie case: To establish a prima facie case for either libel or slander, the plaintiff must prove the following elements:

1. **Defamatory statement:** *A false* and *defamatory* statement concerning him;

2. **Publication:** A *communicating* of that statement to a person other than the plaintiff (a *"publication"*);

3. **Fault:** Fault, amounting at least to *negligence*, on the part of the defendant (except perhaps if the defendant is not part of the media), and in some instances, a greater degree of fault;

4. **Special harm:** Either *"special harm"* of a pecuniary nature, or actionability of the statement regardless of the existence of such special harm. See generally, Rest. 2d, §558.

II. DEFAMATORY COMMUNICATION

A. Injury to reputation: To be defamatory, a statement must have a ***tendency to harm the reputation*** of the plaintiff. Rest. 2d, §559.

   1. Special activity of plaintiff: The particular business carried on by the plaintiff may be significant in determining whether a statement about him is defamatory. For instance, it would be defamatory to say that a kosher meat dealer sells bacon; see P&K, p. 776.

   2. Reputation not actually injured: For the statement to be defamatory, it is not necessary that it have ***actually*** injured the plaintiff's reputation; it must simply be the case that, if it had been believed, it would have had this effect. Thus even if the defendant can show that everyone who heard the statement believed that it was false, this will not prevent the statement from being defamatory.

   a. Special damage: However, in most cases of slander, and in cases of libel where the defamatory meaning is not apparent from the face of the statement, the plaintiff will generally have to prove "special damage", i.e., that his reputation was ***in fact*** damaged, and that he suffered a pecuniary harm from this; see *infra*, p. 472. But this special damage requirement does not have anything to do with whether the statement itself is defamatory; it is simply an additional requirement in certain kinds of cases.

B. Effect limited to one segment of public: Certain allegations will, if believed, diminish a person's reputation only in the eyes of ***certain segments*** of the community. It is usually held that a statement is defamatory as long as a significant and "respectable" minority of persons would draw an adverse opinion of the plaintiff from it, even if most people would not. Rest. 2d, §559, Comment e.

   Example: D, a magazine, prints a piece in which P, a lawyer, is referred to as having been a "legislative representative for the Massachusetts Communist Party."

   Held (in an opinion by Judge Learned Hand), the allegation is defamatory, regardless of whether "right-thinking" people would hold it against P if he were a Communist Party member or sympathizer. "It is enough if there be some, as there certainly are, who would feel so, even though they would be 'wrong-thinking' people if they did." *Grant v. Reader's Digest Ass'n*, 151 F.2d 733 (2d Cir. 1945).

   1. Element of disgrace: But there must nonetheless be an element of ***"disgrace"*** connected with the allegation. If a Democrat were called a Republican, "it is quite probable that unpleasant feelings would be aroused against him in the minds of some other Democrats; but [this statement] can scarcely be regarded as defamatory." P,W&S, p. 840, n. 4.

   2. "Respectable" group: Also, the minority who might draw an adverse opinion must be ***"respectable."*** For instance, if the plaintiff is accused of having ***informed*** to the authorities as to the activities of his former partners in crime, this would probably be held not to be defamatory, on the grounds that only criminals would draw an adverse inference.

C. Meaning to be attached to statement: Many statements can be interpreted in more than one way. Where this is the case, the statement is defamatory if ***any one*** of the interpretations is one which a reasonable person might make, and the plaintiff shows that at least one of the recipients did ***in fact*** make that interpretation.

1. **Judge-jury allocation:** It is up to the court to determine whether the statement has *at least one possible, reasonable, meaning that is defamatory*. If the court decides that it *does*, it is then up to the jury to decide whether *at least one recipient took this interpretation.* Rest. 2d, §614.

   a. **Recipient's belief in statement's truth not required:** However, as noted, it is not required that the recipient have *believed* the statement to be true, either in its defamatory sense or otherwise. For example, suppose that in a libel case against a magazine publisher, P, produces a witness who said "I read the article, and I thought the author was accusing P of dishonesty, but I didn't believe a word she said against him"; the jury can find that the statement was libelous.

D. Reference to plaintiff: The plaintiff must show that the statement was reasonably interpreted by at least one recipient as *referring to the plaintiff.* At common law, there had to be a formal allegation in the complaint that the statement was so interpreted; this allegation was called the *"colloquium."*

1. **Defendant's intent irrelevant:** But the plaintiff does not necessarily have to show that the defendant *intended* to refer to him, rather than to someone else. Until recent constitutional decisions, in fact, there was essentially strict liability, and it was completely irrelevant whether the plaintiff was the person to whom the defendant intended to refer; see *infra*, p. 476.

2. **Groups:** The defendant's statement may concern a *group*, rather than an individual. If the plaintiff is a member of this group, the statement will generally be defamatory as to him only if the group is a *relatively small one*. Rest. 2d, §564A. It is unlikely that the plaintiff could recover if the group were larger than, say, about 25 persons. Thus a statement such as "All lawyers are shysters" would not be defamatory as to any particular lawyer (in the absence of other evidence indicating that the statement was intended to refer to the plaintiff in particular).

   a. **Reference to part of class:** If the statement by its terms applies to only a *part* of a class, the plaintiff's chances of recovering are even smaller. In addition to showing that the group is sufficiently small, the plaintiff probably has to show that a substantial portion of the group has been included. For instance, a statement that one person out of a group of 25 has stolen an automobile would not defame any particular member of that group; see Rest. 2d, §564A, Comment c.

3. **Reference need not be by name:** If a non-explicit reference to the plaintiff is reasonably understood as in fact referring to him, it is not important that the plaintiff is referred to by a *different name* or characterization. Nor will recovery be denied merely because the publication is labelled as a *"novel"* or *"fiction"* (again, assuming that a reader will reasonably understand the reference to be to the plaintiff).

   a. **Some changing of the facts:** In fact, as long as some reasonable readers or viewers would think that is the plaintiff who is being referred to, the fact that the publisher has *changed some of the facts to deviate* from the plaintiff's actual life won't furnish a defense. So, for instance, if D portrays a supposedly fictitious character who has a strong resemblance to P, but D attributes to the character some disreputable traits, the fact that P doesn't really have those traits not only won't furnish a defense, but may itself constitute a libel.

E. Truth: A statement is not defamatory if it is *true*. At common law, it was generally held that the *defendant* had the burden of proving truth.

    1. Effect of constitutional decisions: However, Supreme Court decisions limit a state's ability to put the burden of proving truth on the defendant:

        a. Matter of public interest: If the statement involves a matter of *"public interest,"* the First Amendment requires that the *plaintiff bear the burden* of proving that the statement was false, at least where the defendant is a *media* organization. *Philadelphia Newspapers v. Hepps*, 475 U.S. 767 (1986). This is true even though the plaintiff is a *private figure*. (If the plaintiff is a *public* figure, she too must clearly bear the burden of proving falsity, since the statement will probably by virtue of the plaintiff's public figure status alone be of "public interest.")

        b. Private figure, no public interest: If the statement is *not* of public interest, and the plaintiff is a private figure, it is not clear whether the state may require the defendant to bear the burden of proving truth. Thus on facts such as those in *Dun & Bradstreet, Inc. v. Greenmoss Builders, Inc.* (discussed more fully *infra*, p. 473), a state may be allowed to make the defendant credit reporting company bear the burden of showing that its credit report of P's bankruptcy was true.

        c. Non-media defendant: Also, it is possible that a *non-media* defendant may be required to bear the burden of proving the truth of his statement, even if the statement relates to a matter of public interest. The Court in *Hepps* explicitly declined to decide this question.

        d. Where defendant's statement not specific: There may be times when the defendant's allegedly defamatory statement is so *vague* that it would be unfair to require the plaintiff to come forward with evidence proving its falsity. For instance, if the defendant has stated that the plaintiff is a storekeeper who short changes his customers whenever he gets the chance, how can the plaintiff prove the falsity of this statement unless the defendant first comes forward with specific instances when this is supposed to have occurred? See Rest. 2d, §613, Comment j.

    2. Substantial truth: For truth to constitute a barrier to recovery, it is not necessary that the statement be *literally* true in all respects. Instead, it must merely be *"substantially"* true. See Rest. 2d, §581A, Comment f.

        Example: Suppose that D writes that P "was convicted of larceny in connection with the theft of $10,000 from his previous employer." Assume that in reality, D was convicted of embezzlement in connection with the theft of $11,000 from that employer. Almost certainly, a court would find that P may not recover against D, because what D wrote was "substantially" true even though it was not true in all respects.

        a. Proof of different offense: On the other hand, if the defendant has made one charge of wrongdoing against the plaintiff, he may not establish truth by proving a *materially different* charge. If the defendant has stated that the plaintiff stole a watch from A, "It is not enough to show a different offense, even though it be a more serious one, such as stealing a clock from A, or six watches from B." P&K, p. 841. See, e.g., *Kilian v. Doubleday & Co.*, 79 A.2d 657 (Pa. 1951) (where D accused P of having knowingly encouraged the mistreatment of American soldiers, the fact that D was convicted of mere neglectful "permitting" of such mistreatment was not enough to establish the defense of "substantial truth").

F. Opinion: Can a person's expression of *"opinion"* constitute defamation? The brief answer today is that a statement of *"pure opinion"* cannot be defamatory, but a statement of opinion that implies an assertion of an *underlying fact* can trigger defamation liability for that assertion of fact. Let's look at these principles in more detail:

1. **Pure opinion:** A *"pure"* expression of opinion cannot be defamatory. That is, where the statement of opinion does not also make an express or implied statement about some *fact* that supports the opinion, there can be no liability. The reason is that a defamation action can only exist for a "false" statement, and a pure expression of opinion is neither "true" nor "false." As the Supreme Court has expressed the idea, the statement must be "*provable* as false." *Milkovich v. Lorain Journal Co.*, discussed *infra*.

   Example: If D were to write in the local newspaper, "In my opinion, Mayor Jones shows his abysmal ignorance by accepting the teachings of Marx and Lenin," this could not be a defamatory statement (at least assuming that Mayor Jones really does accept the teachings of Marx and Lenin, and the only dispute is over whether the Mayor is "abysmally ignorant" in doing so). (This hypothetical, and this analysis of it, are from the Supreme Court's decision in *Milkovich, infra*.) The reason is that the teachings of Marx and Lenin are neither "probably true" nor "provably false," and therefore the assertion that acceptance of these teachings is "abysmally ignorant" is also neither provably true nor provably false.

2. **Implied assertions of fact:** But where a statement of opinion implies the assertion of *underlying facts*, and those underlying facts are provably false, then the statement of opinion *can* give rise to liability for defamation. The Supreme Court so decided in *Milkovich v. Lorain Journal Co.*, 497 U.S. 1 (1990).

   a. **Holding:** The Court in *Milkovich* conceded that to be defamatory, a statement must be "provable as false." But, the Court said, this does not mean that there should be a "wholesale defamation exemption for anything that might be labeled 'opinion.'" If a statement *implies an assertion of objective fact*, then there can be defamation liability for that implied assertion of fact if it is false.

      i. **Illustration:** The Court gave the following illustration: the statement, "In my opinion Mayor Jones is a liar" contains within it a statement of fact that could be proved false (i.e., that Jones is in fact a liar). Therefore, that statement, though couched in the form of an opinion, can be defamatory.

3. **Hyperbole:** How, then, is the Court to determine whether the defendant's statement is a "pure" expression of opinion, or, rather, implies assertions of provable fact? Clearly one factor is whether the statement appears to be dry and literal or, on the other hand, filled with *hyperbole*, figurative speech or other *non-literal language*. The more it tends toward the latter, the less likely that the court will find it to contain assertions of provably false fact.

Example: In a review of a play, the reviewer's use of the words "rip-off," "fraud" and "a snake-oil job" are not actionable, because a reasonable reader would inevitably view them as pure expressions of opinion. *Phantom Touring, Inc. v. Affiliated Publications*, 953 F.2d 724 (1st Cir. 1992).

4. **Context:** Similarly, the ***context*** of the statement will be considered in determining whether it implies an assertion of provably false fact. Thus if the statement is part of a column called "My View" or "Opinions," it is less likely to be found to contain factual assertions (though it may still be found to do so) than if it is contained, say, in a front page pure news story. Similarly, a letter printed on a "Letters to the Editor" page is more likely to be found to be pure opinion than, say, a story by the newspaper's own staff.

5. **Reviews:** One especially controversial area is whether ***reviews*** of products, restaurants, movies, etc. are entitled to greater constitutional protection from defamation actions than are other types of stories. The Supreme Court has never spoken on this issue.

   a. **Subjective:** Most reviews are understood to contain large subjective elements that should probably be read as pure opinion. Thus a statement like, "Service was slow," or "This is the worst action drama of the year," would almost certainly not be found to contain a provably false assertion of fact, and would thus be free of liability for defamation.

      i. **Assertion of fact:** But even a review may be found to contain an express or implied assertion of fact, in which case there can be defamation liability. See, e.g., *Mr. Chow of New York v. Ste. Jour Azur S.A.*, 759 F.2d 219 (2d Cir. 1985), holding that a restaurant reviewer's statement that the Peking Duck dish "was made up of only one dish (instead of the three traditional ones)," was sufficiently "laden with factual content" as to be potentially defamatory.

      ii. **Context matters:** However, keep in mind that a statement which, if it were to appear in a news column, might be found to contain an "assertion of provably false fact," is more likely to be found to be pure opinion when contained in a review — this is so because the reader understands that a review is essentially the reviewer's opinions. Thus in *Mr. Chow, supra,* somewhat factual-sounding statements (e.g., "The sweet and sour pork contained more dough . . . than meat" and "The green peppers . . . remained still frozen on the plate") were found not to contain assertions of fact, and thus not to be even potentially defamatory.

   b. **Public figure:** Also, in the case of reviews, keep in mind that the corporate or individual plaintiff is likely to be found to be a ***"public figure."*** If so, under *New York Times v. Sullivan* there can only be liability for defamation if the plaintiff proves "actual malice." Thus in *Mr. Chow, supra,* even the "factually laden" statement about a Peking Duck dish was found not to have been made with "actual malice," and thus not to be defamatory.

G. **Who may be defamed:** Any living person may be defamed.

1. **Deceased persons:** There can be no defamation of a ***dead person***, and therefore neither his estate nor his survivors may sue.

2. **Corporation:** *A corporation* may be defamed, but only if the statement "tends to prejudice it in the course of its business or to deter others from dealing with it." Rest. 2d, §561. Thus a statement that one of the officers of a corporation was an adulterer would not be held to be defamatory of the corporation, unless this were shown to hurt its business directly. This same rule applies to *partnerships* and *associations*. Rest. 2d, §562.

III. LIBEL VS. SLANDER

A. **Significance of distinction:** The common law developed the distinct torts of libel and slander. While the problem of determining which category a particular statement fits into is a complicated one, discussed below, the significance of the distinction is fairly clear: To establish slander, the plaintiff must show that he suffered an actual "special harm" of a pecuniary nature (unless the statement falls into one of four special categories, discussed below). To prove libel, on the other hand, the plaintiff does not have to show such special harm (although some courts require him to do so if the defamatory nature of the statement is not evident on its face). Thus for a plaintiff who cannot point to any specific financial harm, and whose only complaint is that his friends have turned against him, the distinction between libel and slander remains of major importance.

B. **Libel:** Libel consists, first of all, of all *written or printed matter*.

1. **Embodied in physical form:** Additionally, many modern courts, and the Second Restatement, §568, hold that it includes any communication embodied in *"physical form"*. Thus a phonograph record or a computer tape would be libelous rather than slanderous. The Restatement in fact extends its definition of libel to include "any other form of communication that has the potentially harmful qualities characteristic of written or printed words." *Ibid*.

   a. **Illustrations:** For instance, the Restatement takes the position that if the defendant hires men to "shadow" the plaintiff, and they do so until the shadowing becomes well-known throughout the community, this is libel. Rest. 2d, §568, Illustr. 1. Similarly, if the defendant places a wax figure of the plaintiff among a collection featuring various murderers, this is libel. *Ibid*, Illustr. 3.

2. **Dictation to stenographer:** A spoken statement that is intended to be written down, and is so, is libellous. Thus if a person dictates to a *stenographer*, and the stenographer writes the statement down in shorthand, this is libel even if no one ever sees the writing. (This also probably constitutes a "publication" of the libel; see *infra*, p. 475. However, the dictation may be qualifiedly privileged; see *infra*, p. 480.)

3. **Radio and television:** If a program is broadcast on *radio or television*, all courts agree that it is a libel if the program originated with a *written script*.

   a. **No script:** But if the program is "ad-libbed", courts are in dispute. Thus in *Shor v. Billingsley*, 158 N.Y.S.2d 476 (Sup. Ct. N.Y.Co. 1956), this was held to be libel, on the grounds that "the broadcast of scandalous utterances is in general as potentially harmful to the defamed person's reputation as a publication by writing."

b. Restatement view: The Restatement, in §568A, provides that all such broadcasting is libel, whether or not it is read from a manuscript. But statutes in most states now provide exactly the contrary, that all broadcasts are slander. See P,W&S, p. 857, n. 2.

C. Slander: All other statements are *slander*. An ordinary oral statement is the most common form of slander.

D. Special harm: As noted, plaintiff may generally establish slander only if he can show that he has sustained some *"special harm."* This harm is usually required to be of a *"pecuniary nature."* Thus where the plaintiff proved merely that the defendant's statements about him upset him so much that he became ill, this was held insufficient to constitute "special harm," since there was no evidence that other people's opinion of plaintiff was lowered. (Mere apprehension by plaintiff that this would occur was insufficient.) *Terwilliger v. Wands*, 17 N.Y. 54 (N.Y. 1858). Similarly, it is not enough that the plaintiff shows that his friends have rejected him, since friendship is not ordinarily something having economic or pecuniary value. See Rest. 2d, §575, Illustr. 4.

1. **Tacking on of damages:** But if the plaintiff can show the requisite pecuniary loss, he may then "tack on" his damages for emotional distress, loss of friendship, etc. This rule is similar to that which does not allow recovery for pure emotional distress in negligence actions, but permits recovery for such distress once physical injury is proved; see *supra*, p. 218.

2. **Harm caused by repetition:** In proving his special harm, the plaintiff may, in addition to showing the harm caused directly by the defendant's own statement, point to harm caused by certain *repetitions* of the statement by third persons. However, this will generally only be true if the defendant authorized the repetition, or it was either reasonably to be expected or "privileged". See Rest. 2d, §576. Thus if the defendant makes a defamatory statement to one person, and makes her agree that the material will not be repeated to anyone else, harm caused when this person breaches his agreement and goes around spreading the tale probably would not count as special harm (or be recoverable as damages).

3. **Cases where no special harm necessary ("slander per se"):** There are *four kinds of utterances* which, even though they are slander rather than libel, *require no showing of special harm*. These categories derive from a variety of historical factors, but their common element is that they are by their very nature especially likely to cause pecuniary harm. Such slander is generally called *"slander per se."* See P&K, p. 788-93. The categories are as follows:

   a. **Crime:** Statements imputing *criminal behavior* to the plaintiff. However, an accusation of a minor crime (e.g., a parking ticket) is not generally enough. The Restatement requires that the conduct imputed to the plaintiff either be "punishable by imprisonment" or "regarded by public opinion as involving *moral turpitude*." Rest. 2d, §571.

   b. **Loathsome disease:** An allegation that the plaintiff currently suffers from a *venereal* or other loathsome and communicable disease. The theory behind this exception is that others will be afraid of catching the disease from the plaintiff; therefore, an allegation that the plaintiff once had the disease, and is cured, will not be sufficient. Rest. 2d, §572.

c. **Business, profession, trade or office:** An allegation that adversely reflects on the plaintiff's *fitness* to conduct her *business*, trade, profession or office.

> **Example:** P is a storekeeper. D tells a friend F, "P cheats his customers." Since this statement reflects on P's fitness to conduct her business, P can recover without showing any pecuniary loss from the statement. So as long as P can show emotional distress (e.g., from when F repeats the remark to P), P can recover even though there's no evidence that F believed the statement, or that anyone stopped patronizing P's store.

> i. **Must be relevant to office:** But the allegation must relate directly to the plaintiff's fitness to conduct these activities. Thus an allegation that a stenographer does not pay her bills, is not sufficient, since her creditworthiness has nothing to do with whether she is a good stenographer. See Rest. 2d, §573, Illustr. 7.

> ii. **Disparagement of goods not included:** Also, if the plaintiff is a manufacturer or seller of goods, it is not sufficient that the quality of the goods themselves (as distinguished from the plaintiff's own personal reputation) is criticized. Rest. 2d, §574, Comment g.

d. **Sexual misconduct:** Statements imputing serious *sexual misconduct* to the plaintiff. In general, this has been applied only to women, and has included not only adultery but also fornication. The Fourteenth Amendment may, however, be interpreted so as to require that a state give equal tort protection to men. It also may be that allegations of *homosexual activity* will be included within this category; see P,W&S, p. 860, n. 4.

4. **Libel:** In the case of *libel*, by contrast, the traditional common-law rule was that if the defamatory nature of the communication was apparent from the statement itself, *actual harm did not need to be proved — "presumed"* damages could be awarded. Thus the plaintiff could recover a sizeable sum in approximation of the damage that would "normally" flow from a defamatory statement like the one at issue, even though he produced no evidence of pecuniary harm, and in fact no evidence of *any* actual harm (e.g., humiliation or loss of friendship). However, Supreme Court decisions have substantially cut back on the right of courts to award such presumed damages.

a. **Matters of public concern:** If recovery is allowed without proof of "actual malice" (i.e., proof that the defendant knew the falsity of his statements or recklessly disregarded the truth), presumed damages *may not constitutionally be awarded*, according to *Gertz v. Robert Welch, Inc.*, discussed *infra*, p. 477. (Recovery without a showing of "actual malice" may not in any event be allowed to a plaintiff who is a "public figure," under *New York Times v. Sullivan*, *infra*, p. 477.)

b. **Matter of purely private concern:** A Supreme Court plurality opinion, *Dun & Bradstreet, Inc. v. Greenmoss Builders, Inc.*, 472 U.S. 749 (1985), *supra*, p. 468, further complicates the presumed damages issue. Under *Dun & Bradstreet*, if the defamatory statement does not involve a matter of *"public concern,"* presumed damages *may* be allowed, even without a showing of "actual malice." Apparently this result will rarely if ever benefit a traditional "media" defendant (i.e., a newspaper or broadcaster), since matters covered by the media will almost always be found *ipso facto* to involve the "public interest."

Example: The facts of *Dun & Bradstreet* indicate the type of situation in which an award of presumed damages may occur even without a showing of "actual malice." In that case, D was a credit reporting agency, which sent to several subscribers a written report falsely stating that P, a corporation, was insolvent. Since the statement was not of "public interest," it was not unconstitutional for P to be awarded $50,000 in presumed damages (plus $300,000 in punitive damages), even though P did not show that D either knew of the falsity of its statements or recklessly disregarded the truth (and although P did not show that its reputation was in fact harmed or its economic interests adversely affected).

   c. **Actual malice:** When the plaintiff does show "actual malice" (i.e., either the defendant's knowledge of falsity or his reckless disregard for the truth), presumed damages may apparently constitutionally be awarded, even if the plaintiff is a public figure, and even if the matter is one of public interest. (But Rest. 2d, §621, in a Caveat, declines to take a position on whether presumed damages may be awarded in this situation.)

   d. **Libel per quod:** There are some statements which are not defamatory on their face, but which become defamatory if the recipient is aware of certain **extrinsic facts**. In cases involving such "libel **per quod**," the common law has required proof of "special harm" (i.e., pecuniary loss). However, this requirement seems to have fallen into disfavor, and Rest. 2d, §569, Comment b abandons it. Under the Restatement approach, even in cases of libel per quod, the plaintiff may recover for actual harm of a non-pecuniary nature (e.g., distress, loss of friendship, etc.)

IV. PUBLICATION

   A. **Requirement of publication generally:** The plaintiff must show that the defamation was *"published"*. "Publication" is a term of art, not meaning "disseminated by writing", but rather, *"seen or heard by someone other than the plaintiff"*.

   1. **Must be intentional or negligent:** The defendant's publication must have been either *intentional or negligent.* That is, there is *not* (and never has been) any *"strict liability"* as to the publication requirement. For instance, if the defendant makes a defamatory statement to the plaintiff himself, and purely by some hard-to-foresee accident someone else overhears it, no publication as to that third person has occurred.

      Example: While D and P are dining together alone in a restaurant, D calls P a thief for stealing a sum that D invested with P. A waiter overhears and understands the remark. Unless D knew or should have known that the waiter (or at least someone other than P) would likely hear the remark, D can't be liable to P for defamation even if the statement was false.

   2. **Must be understood:** The plaintiff must show that the third person not only heard or saw, but also *understood*, the communication, and perceived its defamatory aspects.

      Example: One of D's clerks says, in English, to P, a Greek, that P has stolen a handkerchief. Another clerk states the same accusation in Greek.

Held, the first clerk's statement was not a publication, because it was addressed to (and heard by) only P. The second was not a publication because there was no evidence that any of those who heard it, other than P, understood Greek. *Economopoulos v. A.G. Pollard Co.*, 105 N.E. 896 (Mass. 1914).

3. **Dictation to stenographer:**   If the defendant dictates defamatory matter to a *stenographer* who takes down shorthand notes of it, this is generally held to be publication, and of a libel rather than slander (even if the words are never transcribed). This is the view of Rest. 2d, §577, Comment h. See *supra*, p. 471.

4. **Defamation by will:**   If a decedent has inserted defamatory matter into his *will*, some courts have held that the reading of the will by the executor constitutes a publication by him, and have therefore held the estate liable. See P&K, p. 801.

B. **Publication by plaintiff:**   As noted, the making of a communication *to the plaintiff* is not publication. If the plaintiff then passes the statement on to someone else, this will also generally not constitute publication. But there are a few situations in which it will.

1. **Blindness:**   For instance, if the plaintiff is blind, and receives a defamatory letter, there will be publication if he gives this to a friend or relative to be read to him.

2. **Job application:**   Similarly, if the plaintiff is fired by the defendant, who in the course of doing so defames him, the plaintiff's repetition of this material to a new prospective employer will be a publication, at least where the employer asks "Why did you leave your last job?"

C. **Repeater's liability:**   One who *repeats* a defamatory statement made by another is held to have published it, and is liable as if she were the first person to make the statement. And this is true even if she indicates that she herself *does not believe* the statement. See Rest. 2d, §578, Comment e.

> **Example:** Citizen is arrested by the police. Sometime later, he calls a press conference, and says to the reporters assembled there, "When I was arrested, Officer Jones beat me." D, a newspaper, publishes an article stating, "Citizen said he was beaten by Officer Jones." If Citizen's statement was not true, then D has committed libel in repeating it. This is true even if the reporting by D states, "This newspaper has been unable to determine the truth of Citizen's charges," or even, "This newspaper's investigation has turned up evidence that Citizen's charges may well have been false." (A court might recognize a privilege for "neutral reportage" in this situation; see *infra*, p. 482.)

1. **Newsdealers, libraries, etc.:**   However, one who merely *distributes* or sells defamatory matter will not be liable if he can show he had no reason to believe the materials were defamatory; see *infra*, p. 479.

2. **Reading of written defamation:**   A person who reads out loud a previously written defamation has published a *libel*, rather than a slander. P&K, p. 786.

D. **Single or multiple publication:**   If many copies of a book are sold, is each one a separate defamation, or are they all to be treated as one defamation? The question is important for purposes of such issues as venue and statute of limitations.

1. **Single publication rule:** Most American courts now hold that an entire edition of a book or periodical is to be treated as one publication. This is called the *"single publication rule."* See, e.g., Rest. 2d, §577A, which says that "[a]ny one edition of a book or newspaper, or any one radio or television broadcast, exhibition of a motion picture or similar aggregation communication is a single publication," for which only one suit may be brought.

   a. **Internet postings:** In cases involving statements *posted on the Internet*, most courts have applied the single-publication rule. That is, the posting of a web page containing an unchanging defamatory statement is deemed to be a *single publication,* no matter how long the web page stays up or how many people independently view it over time.

      Example: P is an employee of D (New York State). The state inspector general releases a report that is highly critical of P's job performance, and the state Education Department puts the report (which P alleges to be defamatory) on the Department's website. The statute of limitations for bringing a defamation action is one year. More than one year after the Department first posted the report, P sues the state. P claims that each "hit" by a person viewing the report about him is a new publication, giving him another year to sue. P also claims that the Department's one-time modification of its website by adding another report not related to P constituted a new publication.

      Held, for D: P's claim is time-barred. Under the single-publication rule which New York applies, all viewings of a website that contains an unchanging statement constitute a single publication, just as all sales of a particular print edition constitute a single publication. And the fact that D added some new report having nothing to do with P to its site did not cause a republication of the original statement about P, "for it is not reasonably inferable that the addition was made either with the intent or the result of communicating the earlier and separate defamatory information to a new audience." *Firth v. State of New York*, 775 N.E.2d 463 (N.Y. 2002).

V. INTENT

A. **Common law strict liability:** Libel and slander were, at common law, essentially *strict liability* torts. While the plaintiff had to show that the *publication* occurred due to the defendant's intent or negligence, neither intent nor negligence was required as to any of the other aspects of the tort.

   1. **Falsity:** Thus it was irrelevant that the defendant had every reason to believe that the statement was *true*. Similarly, it was irrelevant that the statement was intended to refer to A, and through no negligence on the defendant's part, was interpreted to refer to B. As the idea was expressed by one court, "The question is not so much who was aimed at as who was hit." *Corrigan v. Bobbs-Merrill Co.*, 126 N.E. 260 (N.Y. 1920).

B. **Constitutional decisions:** However, over the last few decades, the U.S. Supreme Court has virtually eliminated the freedom of state and federal courts to impose strict liability for defamation. The Court's decisions have held that the plaintiff's right to recover for defamation gives way, to a certain extent, to the defendant's First Amendment free speech and free press rights.

1. *New York Times v. Sullivan:* The Court's first major decision in this area was *New York Times Co. v. Sullivan*, 376 U.S. 254 (1964), *supra*, pp. 473, 499. In that case, the plaintiff was a public official part of whose duties was the supervision of the Montgomery, Alabama police department. He alleged that the Times had libelled him by printing an advertisement that stated that the Montgomery police had attempted to terrorize Martin Luther King and his followers.

   a. **Holding:** The Court held, *inter alia*, that the plaintiff was a *"public official"*. As such, the First Amendment required that he recover only if he showed that the Times printed the advertisement either with *knowledge that it was false* or in *"reckless disregard"* of whether it was true or not. The Times had not been shown to have either of these states of mind, the court said.

      i. **"Actual malice":** The Court unfortunately tried to encapsulate these two states of mind, knowledge of falsity and recklessness as to the truth, in the phrase *"actual malice"*. But it is clear from this case and its successors that the plaintiff is not required to show malice in the sense of "ill-will" on the part of the defendant.

   b. **Reference to plaintiff:** The Court in *New York Times* also noted that the advertisement in question never mentioned the plaintiff by name or by position, and that his case was based solely on the theory that the advertisement contained an "implicit" criticism of him as the person who was in control of the police. The Court implied that it might be constitutionally impermissible to allow recovery for such oblique references, even apart from the question of the defendant's state of mind.

2. **Meaning of "reckless disregard":** The Court interpreted the phrase "reckless disregard of the truth" in *St. Amant v. Thompson*, 390 U.S. 727 (1968). The Court stated that in order to make such a showing (which, under *New York Times*, any plaintiff who is a public official would have to do), it is not enough to show that a "reasonably prudent man" would not have published, or would not have published without further investigation. Rather, there must be evidence to permit the conclusion that "The defendant *in fact entertained serious doubts* as to the truth of his publication."

3. **Public figures:** The *New York Times* "actual knowledge or reckless disregard of the truth" test was extended to include *"public figures"* in *Curtis Pub. Co. v. Butts*, 388 U.S. 130 (1967). In this and a related case, both the University of Georgia football coach and a prominent retired Army General were held to be public figures.

4. **Private figures:** But if the plaintiff is neither a public official nor a public figure, there is *no constitutional requirement* that he prove knowledge of truth or reckless disregard of the truth. See *Gertz v. Robert Welch, Inc.*, 418 U.S. 323 (1974).

   a. **Facts:** In *Gertz*, the plaintiff was a locally well-known lawyer who represented the family of a youth who was killed by a police officer. Plaintiff was falsely attacked as a criminal and Communist by defendant, publisher of a John Birch Society magazine.

   b. **Main holdings:** The Court, after concluding that plaintiff was a private figure, made two holdings concerning the defendant's state of mind required in actions brought by private figures: (1) The First Amendment requires that *strict liability* not be sufficient; in other words, the plaintiff must prove either that the defendant knew his statement was false, or that he was at least negligent in not ascertaining its falsity. (2) The states are *free to decide* whether they wish to establish *negligence, recklessness,* or *intent* as the standard.

c. **Who is a private figure:**   *Gertz* also indicates that a person does *not* become a "public figure" merely because he has *become involved in a controversy of public interest.* The plaintiff in *Gertz* was a lawyer who brought a civil suit against a police officer accused of homicide; the Court held that he did not become a public figure merely because newspapers took a great interest in the lawsuit and surrounding events.

d. **Rejection of "public interest" rule:**   Prior Supreme Court decisions had given the media the same freedom to comment upon any matter of "general public interest" as *New York Times* gave for comment about public officials. But *Gertz* **repudiated** these decisions.

   i. **Rationale:**   The *Gertz* Court distinguished between public officials and public figures on the one hand, and private individuals on the other. The Court reasoned that public officials "usually enjoy *significantly greater access* to the channels of effective communication and hence have a more realistic opportunity to counteract false statements than private individuals normally enjoy." Therefore, private figures should not be subject to the same constitutional limitations on defamation recovery, whether they are involved in a matter of general public interest or not.

   ii. **States can require at least reckless disregard:** But the states are still free to impose, as a matter of *state* (non-constitutional) law, the requirement that such private individuals prove at least reckless disregard by the defendant.

e. **Presumed and punitive damages not allowed:**   The court in *Gertz* also held that at least where the state elects to allow private figures to recover based on less than a showing of reckless disregard for truth, *presumed and punitive damages may not be awarded*. (However, where no matter of "public concern" is involved, this aspect of *Gertz* is apparently no longer valid, in light of the later case of *Dun & Bradstreet v. Greenmoss*, discussed *infra*, p. 486.) Presumed and punitive damages are discussed further *infra*, p. 486.

5. **Application to non-media:**   Both *New York Times* and *Gertz* involved *media* defendants, and the Court relied heavily on freedom of the press considerations. It is not clear whether the same constitutional rules apply where the defendant is a private person or other *non-media defendant.* Thus it is possible that such non-media defendants might as a constitutional matter: (i) be held liable without a showing of reckless disregard or knowledge of falsity when they defame a public official or public figure, and (ii) even be held *strictly liable* where they defame a *private figure.* The Supreme Court has simply never spoken on either of these constitutional questions.

   a. **State common-law rules**   However, virtually all states — as a matter of *common law*, not federal constitutional law — refuse to allow private-figure plaintiffs to recover against even non-media defendants unless the plaintiff *shows at least negligence.* In other words, as a common-law matter, all defamation suits require *at least a showing that the defendant negligently failed to make reasonable efforts to ascertain the statement's truth or falsity.* Rest. 2d, §580B(c).

Example: D fires P. P seeks a new job from X. X asks D for a reference. D writes back, "We fired P because P sexually harassed a co-worker." If D's belief that P harassed a co-worker was reasonable, under state common-law principles P cannot recover from D for libel, even if P can prove that the accusation was completely false.

6. **Private aspects of public figures:** Even if the plaintiff is a public official or public figure, it is quite likely that some aspects of her life are so peculiarly *private* that the defendant's statement as to these aspects will not be protected by the *New York Times* "reckless disregard" requirement. See Rest. 2d, §580B. This would probably be true, for instance, of a politician's sex life, as long as it did not amount to "misconduct" reflecting on his fitness for office.

VI. PRIVILEGES

A. **Privileges generally:** Even if the plaintiff succeeds in surmounting all of the hurdles discussed thus far, she may still lose because the defendant establishes that he had a *privilege* to make the defamatory statement. Privileges are divided into "absolute" ones and "conditional" ones.

1. **Distinction:** The distinction between these two classes is that an "absolute" privilege applies regardless of whether the defendant was activated solely by malice or other bad motives, whereas a "conditional" privilege applies only where the defendant acts for certain well-defined purposes.

B. **Absolute privileges:** The following classes of absolute privileges are usually recognized:

1. **Judicial proceedings:** Judges, lawyers, parties, and witnesses are all absolutely privileged in what they say during the course of *judicial proceedings*, regardless of the motives for their statements. For instance, even if a judge tells the jury, for purely personal and malicious reasons, that the defendant should be convicted because he is a born crook and liar, the defendant cannot win a slander suit.

   a. **Must be relevant to proceeding:** The one limitation on this privilege, however, is that the defendant's statement must have *"some relation"* to the matter at issue. See Rest. 2d, §§585-589.

   b. **Quasi-judicial proceedings:** Absolute privilege may extend to quasi-judicial proceedings, such as private arbitration or grievance hearings. P&K 1988 Pocket Part, p. 115.

2. **Legislative proceedings:** A similar privilege exists for *legislators* acting in furtherance of their legislative functions (e.g., making a speech on the floor), and witnesses before legislative proceedings. Rest. 2d, §§590-590A.

   a. **Hearings:** The privilege extends to *legislative hearings*. But it does not extend to a "newsletter" published by a legislator, and probably not to press conferences held by him, although these may be protected by the "Speech or Debate" clause of the Constitution. See Rest. 2d, §590, Comments a and b.

3. Government officials: Certain government officials may also have an absolute immunity from defamation, as to statements issued in the course their jobs.

   a. Federal officials: The Supreme Court has held ***all federal officials***, no matter how low their rank, have this absolute privilege. *Barr v. Matteo*, 360 U.S. 564 (1959).

   b. State officials: All states agree that the governor, and other high state officials, have a similar immunity. But states disagree about whether this absolute immunity extends down to the lower ranks (e.g., police officers).

   c. Must be within course of duty: Even where the absolute immunity exists, it applies only if the defamatory statement occurs in the course of, and in furtherance of, the defendant's job.

4. Husband and wife: Any communication between a ***husband and wife*** is absolutely privileged. Rest. 2d, §592.

   a. May count as publication: But if a defamation originates with a third person, and is relayed by a husband to his wife, this repetition will still be a publication, and the third person will be liable for the harm caused by it. This is so under the rule that one who publishes a defamation is liable for any damage caused by the privileged repetition of it; see Rest. 2d, §576(a).

5. Consent: Any publication that occurs with the ***consent*** of the plaintiff is absolutely privileged. This is true even if the plaintiff has attempted, for the purposes of establishing a defamation suit, to maneuver the defendant into repeating a previously privileged statement. For instance, if the defendant has defamed the plaintiff during the course of a trial, and the plaintiff says to him, "Step outside the courtroom and repeat that, so I can sue you," the repetition will be privileged. See P&K, p. 823.

   a. Attempt to find out what is said: But if the plaintiff has merely attempted to find out what the defendant is saying about her, and asks him to repeat it for this purpose, this is not held to be consent to the previous defamation. P&K, *ibid.*

C. Qualified privilege: In addition to these absolute privileges, there are a number of *"conditional"*, or *"qualified"* privileges. The distinction between them and the absolute privileges is that the conditional ones will be lost if the defendant is acting primarily from *malice*, or for some other purpose not protected by the privilege.

1. Protection of publisher's interest: The defendant is conditionally privileged to ***protect his own interests***, if these interests are determined to be sufficiently important, and the defamation is directly enough related to those interests. Rest. 2d, §594. Some of the interests which are generally held to be of sufficient importance include the following:

   a. Protection of property: Protection of the defendant's ***property***. Thus if the defendant's property has been stolen (or he reasonably believes that it has been) he may tell his suspicions of the plaintiff to the police. (But he may be held to have ***abused*** this privilege, by acting recklessly, or by spreading the defamation more widely than necessary; see *infra*, p. 484.)

b. **Protection against defamation of defendant:** The defendant may be conditionally privileged to protect *himself* against defamation by the plaintiff. For instance, he may have a qualified privilege to call the plaintiff a liar, even if she isn't.

c. **Competition not sufficient interest:** But a businessperson's attempt to obtain a *competitive advantage* is not a sufficient interest to qualify for the conditional privilege. Thus a businessperson has no right to say that one of his competitors does shoddy work, merely in order to gain a customer for himself (although, of course, he will not be liable if he can show the truth of this statement).

2. **Interest of others:** Similarly, the defendant may be qualifiedly privileged to act for the protection of the *recipient* of his statement, or some other third person. But the Restatement limits this privilege to situations where the recipient is "a person to whom [the statement's] publication is . . . within the generally accepted standards of *decent conduct*." Rest. 2d, §595(1)(b).

a. **Definition of "decent conduct":** In determining what is within these standards of "decent conduct," the Restatement attaches considerable importance to the fact that the statement is made "in response to a *request* rather than volunteered by" the defendant. *Ibid*, §595(2)(a).

b. **Family or other relationship:** Another factor tending to make the statement "decent conduct" is that there is a family or other *relationship* between the defendant and the person to whom he makes the statement.

i. **Old boss to new boss:** Thus an ex-employer generally has the right to give information about his *ex-employee* P to a new, prospective, employer if asked by the latter. That's true even if the ex-employer repeats his own or another's suspicion of wrongdoing by P that the ex-employer is negligent in believing. (But there is no privilege if the ex-employer passes on suspicions that he does not in fact believe or whose truth he recklessly disregards.) See Rest. 2d, §595, Comment i.

c. **Credit-reporting agencies:** A number of states have held that *credit-reporting agencies* have a conditional privilege to give their subscribers credit-worthiness reports on potential customers. See Rest. 2d, §595, Comment h. But again, this privilege may be abused, as it almost certainly would be by recklessness, and perhaps even by negligence. See *Dun & Bradstreet, infra*, p. 486, where punitive damages were awarded upon a showing that was apparently no more than negligence.

3. **Common interest:** The defendant may have a conditional privilege because of the fact that he and the recipient have a *common interest*. Rest. 2d, §596. For instance, one member of a club might be conditionally privileged to tell his co-members that a proposed applicant should not be admitted because he is a thief.

4. **Where recipient can act in public interest:** There may be a conditional privilege where a communication is made to one who has the power to *act in the public interest* (usually a public official). Rest. 2d, §598. For instance, a private citizen's accusation about *crime* made to a police officer or district attorney would have this privilege.

5. **Report of public proceedings:** At common law, there was a qualified privilege to report on *public proceedings*, such as *court cases*, *legislative hearings*, etc.

a. **Public figures:** To the extent that such reports concern *"public officials"* or *"public figures,"* the privilege is *less frequently needed* than it was before *New York Times v. Sullivan*.

i. **No "actual malice":** If the defendant making the report (typically a publisher or broadcaster) did not have "actual malice" as that term is used in *New York Times* (i.e., it did not know the statement in the public proceeding to be false and did not recklessly disregard whether it was true or false), the privilege is no longer needed in this "public official or public figure" situation. This result follows directly from *New York Times*.

ii. **Actual malice:** But if the defendant does have "actual malice," then the privilege can still be useful even where the plaintiff is a public figure. In particular, the privilege allows the newspaper or publisher to print statements made in a public proceeding even though the publisher has ***serious doubts*** about the truth of the statement.

Example: X, on trial for the crime of resisting arrest, testifies, "I did not resist arrest, and the arresting officer, Officer Jones, beat me savagely." A reporter for D newspaper, having heard all the evidence at the trial, subjectively believes that X is lying and that the beating never occurred. D publishes a story stating that "At X's trial, X testified that Officer Jones had beaten him."

In a libel suit by Officer Jones against D, the privilege to report on public proceedings will turn out to be both applicable and useful. Because D (or its reporter) had actual serious doubts about the truth of X's statement, D has "actual malice" (as that phrase is used in *New York Times v. Sullivan*), and under ordinary libel principles could be held liable. But because the statement being reported upon was made at a "public proceeding," i.e., the court case, D is protected by the privilege.

b. **Private figures:** If the public proceeding being reported concerns a ***private figure***, the "actual malice" requirement of *New York Times* will ***not*** be applicable. The Supreme Court rejected an argument that the "actual malice" requirement should be extended to all reports of judicial proceedings, in ***Time, Inc. v. Firestone***, 424 U.S. 448 (1976). In this situation, the *Gertz* standard (requiring only that strict liability not be permitted, and that punitive damages not be allowed on a mere showing of negligence) is the sole applicable constitutional principle. Consequently, the qualified common-law privilege for reports of judicial proceedings may be of value not only where the defendant publisher has actual doubts about the truth of the statements being republished, but also where the defendant has been ***negligent*** (as opposed to "reckless") in publishing the statement. (See the discussion of abuse of qualified privileges *infra*, p. 484.)

c. **Report of pleadings:** The traditional privilege for reporting proceedings has generally been held not to apply to reports of ***pleadings*** filed in court which have not yet been acted upon. See P,W&S, p. 891, n. 9.

6. **The "neutral reportage" privilege:** Suppose a publisher or broadcaster repeats a statement made by someone ***outside*** of a "public proceeding." Obviously, the privilege for "reports of public proceedings," discussed just above, does not apply. Remember that one who repeats another's defamatory statement is himself liable for defamation, even if the repeater states that he does not believe the truth of the re-published assertion. (See *supra*, p. 475). Even with the protection given by *New York Times v. Sullivan*, a media defendant can be placed in a situation where it becomes liable for reporting statements concerning controversies of interest to the public; paradoxically, the defendant's greatest danger of liability comes when it investigates the charges and develops substantial doubts about their truth. To deal with this gap in the coverage of *New York Times v. Sullivan*, some lower courts have recognized a relatively new *"neutral reportage"* privilege.

a. Situation: There are two main situations where a defendant who republishes another person's statement made outside of formal proceedings may find itself liable for defamation unless a "neutral reportage" provision is recognized:

i. Charge against public official: First, consider the situation where a person makes charges about a *public official or public figure*, and the charges are newsworthy.

Example: Suppose that Antrim and Bellows are colleagues on the City Zoning Board. Antrim tells a reporter that he thinks Bellows accepted an illegal kickback from a property owner. The reporter investigates, concludes that the charges are probably false, but also believes that the mere fact that a public official (Antrim) is accusing another public official of wrongdoing is itself a matter that the public should know about. Therefore, the reporter writes a story stating that Antrim has accused Bellows of an illegal kickback, and indicating that the newspaper has been unable to substantiate the charge. Without a "neutral reportage" privilege, Bellows can sue the reporter and the newspaper for libel — the reporter and the newspaper have repeated Antrim's defamatory statement, and their indication that they don't believe it is not a defense, as discussed *supra*, p. 475. Also, even though Bellows is a "public figure," the Ds had "actual malice" (since they had serious doubts about the statement's truth but published it anyway), so they are not protected by *N.Y. Times v. Sullivan*. See 86 Nw. U.L. Rev. 417.

ii. Charge against private figure: Second, the problem may arise where a person makes charges about the conduct of a *private figure*, but the charges are nonetheless of public concern. Again, the publisher or broadcaster may be blocked from reporting a matter of public interest, for fear of defamation liability.

Example: Recall the example on p. 475: Citizen tells a press conference, "Officer Jones beat me when he arrested me." At least if there had been widespread reports of police brutality, Citizen's statement is relevant to a matter of public controversy. Yet because Officer Jones is presumably a "private figure," Newspaper will be liable for defamation when it accurately reports Citizen's accusation, if Newspaper is shown to have been even negligent (let alone reckless) in not having determined that Citizen's charges are false. (Even more dramatically, Newspaper gets no protection for investigating, concluding that Citizen's charges are probably false, and saying so.) Again, a "neutral reportage" privilege could protect Newspaper.

b. Privilege recognized by a few courts: The Supreme Court has never squarely determined whether there should be a "neutral reportage" exception as a matter of constitutional law. However, a few lower-court cases have ***recognized*** such a privilege on constitutional grounds.

    c. Requirements: Those courts that have recognized the "neutral reportage" privilege — whether on constitutional or non-constitutional grounds — have not always agreed on what the requirements for that privilege should be. Here are some of the requirements that have been imposed:

       i. Correct reporting: All courts recognizing the privilege seem to agree that it applies only where the media defendant ***correctly reports*** the charges, so that the only truth/falsity issue is whether the charges themselves are true.

      ii. Neutrality: All courts also seem to agree that the privilege should apply only where the defendant behaved ***"neutrally"*** with respect to the underlying controversy. Thus if the reporter states that he ***agrees*** with the charges, or ***distorts*** those charges to make the plaintiff look even worse, the privilege will be lost.

     iii. Relates to public controversy: Most courts have required that the report relate to a ***public controversy***. Thus if Newspaper reports, "X has written us a letter stating that his neighbor P is an adulterer," probably the privilege would not apply to this news item, since it does not relate to an area of significant public concern.

    d. Rejected: Some courts have ***rejected*** the "neutral reportage" privilege, in least in those situations where the defendant had serious doubts about the truth of the charges that it was repeating.

D. Abuse: Even where a qualified privilege exists, it may be ***abused*** (and therefore forfeited) in a number of different ways.

    1. Knowledge of falsity or reckless disregard: The privilege will be lost if the defendant ***knew that his statement was false***, or acted in ***reckless disregard*** of whether it was true or not.

      a. Rejection of negligence standard: Prior to *Gertz v. Robert Welch, supra,* p. 477, many courts held that a privilege was abused if the defendant was merely ***negligent*** in not ascertaining the falsity of his statement. But since, under *Gertz,* negligence is required in most cases, as part of the plaintiff's prima facie case, it would not be sensible to hold that a qualified privilege is lost through negligence; this would mean, in any case in which less than reckless disregard was shown, that the privilege was abused as soon as the necessity for it (i.e., the establishment by the plaintiff of his prima facie case) was shown. See Rest. 2d, Ch. 25, "Special Note on Conditional Privileges and the Constitutional Requirement of Fault." Probably, therefore, most courts will allow the privilege even where the defendant was ***negligent*** (but not reckless) in not ascertaining that the statement was false.

      b. Publication of rumor: Even if the defendant knows or believes that the defamatory matter is not true, he will not abuse a qualified privilege if he states that the matter is ***rumor or suspicion***, and publication of the statement is otherwise reasonable. For instance, if D tells his friend X that he has heard a rumor that P, X's employee, is dishonest, this would not constitute an abuse of the qualified privilege to protect X's interest. See Rest. 2d, §602, Illustr. 1.

2. **Purpose of the privilege:** A qualified privilege will also be lost if the ***primary purpose*** behind the defendant's statement is something other than protecting the interest for which the privilege is given. For instance, where a person connected with the plaintiff's ex-employer made allegations to the plaintiff's new boss concerning his honesty, it was held that a jury could find that this communication was simply an attempt to coerce the plaintiff into returning certain materials to the defendant, or to find out whether the plaintiff had started work for the new boss before quitting the old job; in either event, this would be an abuse of the privilege of protecting the new boss's interests. *Sindorf v. Jacron Sales Co., Inc.*, 341 A.2d 856 (Md. App. 1975).

3. **Excessive publication:** The privilege is abused if the statement is made to persons to whom publication is ***not reasonably necessary*** to protect the interest in question. Rest. 2d, §604. Similarly, if more damaging information is stated than is reasonably necessary for the purpose, the privilege is abused. For instance, if the defendant reported to a police officer his suspicions that the plaintiff had committed a theft, and added his belief that the plaintiff was a homosexual, this would probably constitute an abuse. See Rest. 2d, §§605 and 605A.

E. **Statutory privileges:** Many states, and the federal government, have enacted a number of ***statutory privileges.***

1. **Internet Service Providers:** One of the most important of these is the federal immunity given to ***Internet Service Providers*** (ISPs) under the Communications Decency Act of 1996 (CDA). Part of the CDA, 47 U.S.C. § 230(c)(1), says that "***no provider or user*** of an interactive ***computer service*** shall be treated as the ***publisher or speaker of any information*** provided by ***another information content provider.***" This provision amounts to a grant of ***immunity*** from state defamation liability for "publishing false or defamatory material so long as the ***information was provided by another party.***" *Carafano v. Metrosplash.com, Inc.*, 339 F.3d 1119 (9th Cir. 2003).

> **Example:** D is the corporate owner of the matchmaker.com Internet dating service. Some unknown person, using a computer in Berlin, Germany, posts a dating profile of P (the actress whose stage name is Chase Masterson) on the matchmaker.com site, without P's consent. The posting is done in the form of answers to a questionnaire that D requires posters to fill out; many of the questions are in multiple-choice format. The posting includes P's picture, her home address, her e-mail address and various sexually-oriented statements (e.g., that she is "looking for a one-night stand" and that she likes to be "controlled by a man, in and out of bed.") People who send e-mail to the e-mail address are then given P's home phone number. As a result, P receives numerous phone calls, voice mail messages and e-mails, some of which are sexually explicit or threatening. She sues D in state court, alleging defamation and various privacy-related torts (e.g., misappropriation of identity, as to which see *infra*, p. 496). D defends on the grounds that the CDA gives it immunity against all such claims by P. P responds that the CDA immunity does not apply where D supplies part of the defamatory content, and that that is what happened here, since most of the content was formulated in response to matchmaker.com's detailed questionnaire.
>
> *Held*, for D. The immunity given by the CDA was intended by Congress to be ***"quite robust."*** It is true that the immunity does not apply where the defendant func-

tioned as an "information content ***provider***" for the portion of the statement or publication at issue. But here, the fact that some of the content was formulated in response to D's questionnaire does not mean that D was the provider of the content in question. In this case, ***"the selection of the content was left exclusively to the user."*** And the fact that D's site structured and standardized the poster's answers (e.g., by supplying multiple-choice answers for dozens of questions) did not turn D into a supplier of the content in the profile, especially since the objectionable information, such as P's phone number, was "transmitted unaltered to profile viewers." *Carafano v. Metrosplash.com, Inc., supra.*

VII. REMEDIES

A. **Damages:** A successful defamation plaintiff may, of course, recover ***compensatory*** damages. These can include not only items of ***pecuniary*** loss (e.g., lost business), but also compensation for humiliation, lost friendship, illness, etc., even though these items would not count as ***"special harm"*** for purposes of slander (see *supra*, p. 472).

1. **Punitive damages:** In *Gertz v. Robert Welch, supra*, p. 477, the Supreme Court that ***punitive damages*** may not be awarded upon less than a showing that the defendant knew his statements were false or recklessly disregarded the truth. Thus in those states that allow recovery by a private figure upon a mere showing of negligence, *Gertz* appeared to mean that punitive damages are not allowable. However, the post-*Gertz* case of ***Dun & Bradstreet, Inc. v. Greenmoss Builders, Inc.***, 472 U.S. 749 (1985), cuts back this aspect of *Gertz* to cover only those suits by private figures that involve a matter of "public interest"; as to these, it remains the case that punitive damages may only be awarded upon a showing that the defendant knew his statements were false or recklessly disregarded the truth. As to matters that are of merely ***private concern, mere negligence will suffice***, as a constitutional matter.

   a. **Facts of *Dun & Bradstreet*:** Thus in *Dun & Bradstreet* itself, D, a credit reporting agency, falsely reported to a few subscribers that P, a corporation, was insolvent. Because the credit report did not involve any matter of public concern, a punitive damage award in favor of P was affirmed by the Supreme Court, despite the absence of any showing that D was more than ordinarily negligent.

   b. **No majority opinion:** The precise significance of *Dun & Bradstreet* is especially hard to ascertain, since there was no majority opinion in that case. A three-justice plurality opinion argued that *Gertz* simply never addressed the issue of punitive damages in cases where the false statement did not concern a matter of public interest. Two additional members of the Court (Burger and White) joined the result reached by the plurality, but on the broader ground that *Gertz* should be overruled in its entirety. One aspect of *Dun & Bradstreet* that is especially unclear is what constitutes a matter of "public interest" — all we know from *Dun & Bradstreet* is that a credit reporting service's report about a relatively small corporation, distributed to four or five subscribers, does not involve a matter of public interest.

2. **Presumed damages:** The common law allowed, in cases of libel (except libel per quod) and slander per se, the award of "***presumed***" damages. That is, even if the plaintiff could

not show that she suffered any actual harm (whether of a pecuniary or non-pecuniary nature), she could recover a sometimes substantial sum representing the harm that would "ordinarily" stem from a defamatory statement like the one at issue. Presumed damages could be awarded even where the only witnesses put on by the plaintiff testified that they never believed the defamatory statement (so that there was no proof that the plaintiff's reputation was in fact damaged). However, *Gertz, supra,* p. 477, held that the plaintiff may only recover "actual damages (i.e., compensatory ones) if she does not establish at least reckless disregard of the truth. Thus in states that allow a private figure to recover upon a showing of mere negligence, *Gertz* bars such a plaintiff from recovering presumed damages.

 a. **Cases of private interest:** However, on this issue, too, the *Dun & Bradstreet* case cuts back the scope of what had appeared to be the holding in *Gertz*. Under *Dun & Bradstreet,* presumed damages may be awarded even on a showing of mere negligence, if the matter is not one of "public interest." (Where the matter *is* one of public interest, *Gertz* still bars the award of presumed damages unless the plaintiff establishes at least reckless disregard of the truth.)

3. **Nominal damages:** Even a plaintiff who has suffered no direct loss will, in order to "clear her name," often have a powerful incentive to try to establish defamation, and to recover *nominal* damages. *Gertz,* insofar as it allows a plaintiff to recover only "actual" damages if she does not establish reckless disregard of the truth, may mean that nominal damages are no longer awardable upon a showing of mere negligence. Such a result would be undesirable, since it would prevent a plaintiff who has not suffered actual damage from "clearing her name." (In any event, if the statement does not involve a matter of public interest, *Dun & Bradstreet* clearly allows nominal damages to be recovered.)

B. **Retraction:** Almost two-thirds of the states, in order to discourage defamation suits, have enacted so-called *"retraction"* statutes. Some of these statutes hold that if the defendant publishes a retraction of a defamatory statement within a certain period of time, this bars recovery. Others merely require a news medium to grant a right of response to the plaintiff, without providing that this eliminates the defamation action. See P,W&S, pp. 935-36.

Quiz Yourself on

DEFAMATION *(Entire Chapter)*

85. Ratso is a small-time criminal who likes to hang around with shady types. John Dillinger circulates the lie that Ratso is a "stoolie" who's ratted on various local criminals to the police. Ratso sues John for defamation. Was John's statement "defamatory?" _____

86. Clara Bow is an up-and-coming Hollywood starlet. Brunhilda, jealous of Clara's success, spreads the lie that Clara has been intimate with an entire college football squad. When Clara sues Brunhilda for defamation, must she prove that she suffered pecuniary harm? _____

87. Socrates is up for parole. Defamitus testifies to the parole board that the parole should be denied because Socrates is a menace to society — he has been known to solicit sexual favors from young boys. This is not true, although Defamitus has good reason to believe it's true. Can Socrates successfully sue Defamitus for defamation? _____

88. Pierre Exposee, a reporter for the Paris *Clarion du Jour,* publishes a story that the Emperor Napoleon falsified his war record. Pierre has heard the story from a friend, and actually believes it. Nonetheless, the story is wrong — Napoleon's record is bona fide (as Pierre could have determined with only a little further investigation). However, Pierre has despised Napoleon ever since he stole Pierre's girlfriend, Josephine, and Pierre is glad the story hurt Napoleon's reputation. Napoleon sues Pierre for defamation. Can he recover? _____

89. Gil Ibble, reporter for the Washington Rag during the Lincoln administration, hears a guy in a bar say: "The only way Abe Lincoln got elected was by stuffing ballot boxes!" Ibble figures this would make a great story, and he writes it, fully believing it's true, and not unearthing any evidence to the contrary. In fact, "Honest Abe" didn't stuff any ballot boxes, and he sues Ibble for defamation. Can Abe recover? _____

90. Dumbo, a home-loving elephant who teaches piano for a living, likes to keep to himself. While reading the local paper one day, he's horrified to see an item in the gossip column, saying that he had just been in the hospital for ear implants. In fact, had the gossip columnist checked her sources, she would have found that Dumbo was in the hospital for an operation on his deviated septum; he's never had an ear implant, his ears are just *naturally* that large. Dumbo sues the paper for defamation. Can Dumbo recover? (Assume that defamation suits by animals follow the same rules as for humans.) _____

91. Mrs. Tolstoy is jealous of the beautiful and popular Anna Karenina. In an effort to destroy her reputation, Mrs. Tolstoy circulates the story that Anna is an adulteress — she's having an affair with Vronsky. Will the fact that this is true absolve Mrs. Tolstoy from liability, even though she was trying to wreck Anna's reputation? _____

92. In Smalltown USA, Martha Washington tells her neighbor, Betsy Ross, "Dolly Madison told me Benedict Arnold is a Communist." Arnold is not a Communist, and he sues Washington for defamation. She asserts truth as a defense, proving that Madison, in fact, told her Arnold is a Communist. Will the defense prevail? _____

93. Newspaper, in a story on the general subject of how organized crime figures have infiltrated legitimate business, states, "And Joe's Casino, the big Atlantic City casino, is probably mob-controlled, because Joe Picolo, owner of record, has been linked by law enforcement authorities to the mob." Joe brings a libel suit against Newspaper. At the trial, Newspaper does not come up with any evidence to show that Joe has links to the mob, but Joe does not come up with evidence to show that he does not. Assuming that the truth of Newspaper's allegations is the only issue in the case, who will win the suit? _____

94. Newspaper, a local paper in the town of Chippewa, publishes an article called "Police Blotter" in every day's paper. The Blotter purports to be a reprinting of crimes handled by the local police (and listed on the police department's blotter) the prior day. In one edition, the Blotter article says, "John Smith was charged by the police with a burglary at 123 Main Street, at the home of John Brown." In fact, this item has not been taken from the blotter, but is the result of a conversation between the cub reporter on the police beat and Officer Flatfoot of the Chippewa Police Dept. Because the reporter was inexperienced and tired, the article as printed reversed the names — it was really John Brown who was charged with a burglary at the home of John Smith at 123 Main. A reporter of average professional standards would have read his notes back to Flatfoot before leaving the police department, but the cub reporter did not know to do this. Neither the reporter nor Newspaper or any of its other employees knew that the item printed was false. John Smith, a local resident of no special prominence, brings a libel action against Newspaper. May he recover? _____

Answers

85. No. A defamatory statement is one tending to harm one's reputation so as to lower him in the eyes of a respectable segment of the community. The statement here is not defamatory because it didn't tend to harm Ratso's reputation in a respectable segment of the community. The fact that small-time cons give him the cold shoulder doesn't satisfy the "respectable segment" requirement.

86. No. While in the normal case of slander pecuniary damages (known as "special" damages) must be proven, imputing serious sexual misconduct is one of the four exceptions to the rule, known as "slander per se." Thus, Clara will not have to prove special damages in order for her claim to succeed.

Traditionally, only women plaintiffs could get the benefit of having allegations that they committed serious sexual misconduct treated as slander per se. But the 14th Amendment's Equal Protection clause probably means that a state today must protect plaintiffs of either gender the same way, so an allegation that a man has committed, say, fornication or adultery would probably also constitute slander per se.

87. No. The statement is subject to a "qualified privilege" because Defamitus is speaking in the public interest. A qualified privilege means the speaker will not be liable for otherwise defamatory statements unless he (1) exceeds the scope of the privilege, or (2) either lacks reasonable grounds for believing the statement, or acts recklessly in determining its truth or falsity (states are split on the reasonable/reckless issue). Neither applies here.

RELATED ISSUE: Were Defamitus speaking without a qualified privilege, the statement would be slander per se, since it imputes both serious sexual misconduct and a crime of moral turpitude — molesting little boys. Thus, Socrates would not have to prove special (pecuniary) damages in a defamation suit against Defamitus.

RELATED ISSUE: Say Defamitus made the statement not because he cares at all about society, but because he wanted to seduce Mrs. Socrates, and figured his chances would be better with Socrates in the slammer. He'd be liable for defamation, because he wouldn't have a qualified privilege — the privilege only applies when the defamer speaks *in furtherance* of the interest protected, not in an attempt to *injure* the plaintiff.

88. No. For plaintiffs who are "public figures," the fault level required for defamation is "actual malice." Actual malice is knowledge of the defamatory statement's falsity, or a reckless disregard for whether it's true — not spite or ill will, which is what's present in these facts. Since Pierre believed (even if unreasonably) that the story was true, there is no malice and the defamation claim will not lie.

NOTE: Here, Pierre was *negligent* (but not reckless) in not investigating the story. As a public figure whose public stature has been attacked, Napoleon cannot recover. If he were a *private figure* he could, since mere negligence is enough to support a defamation claim against a media defendant.

COMMON LAW RULE: Defamation was a strict liability offense, so no fault had to be proven.

RELATED ISSUE: Had the story libeled Napoleon's private life, on an issue not bearing on his fitness for public life, he could probably have recovered on the same basis as a private individual (i.e., a mere showing of negligence).

89. No. In order to recover damages from a media defendant for defamation involving an issue of public interest or concern, a plaintiff who is a public figure or public official must prove "actual malice." Actual malice is knowledge of a defamatory statement's falsity, or reckless disregard for its truth. Recklessness is measured subjectively here, and requires proof that defendant *actually had serious doubts* about the truth of his story. Here, Ibble believes the story is true, so there's no "malice."

NOTE: At common law, defamation was a strict liability offense, so no fault had to be proven.

RELATED ISSUE: Had Ibble asked Lincoln himself, and Lincoln had denied the charge, Ibble might have been reckless in printing the story anyway. (However, not checking sources in and of itself is generally only negligence, not recklessness.)

90. No. The "*New York Times* privilege" protects the media when it publishes matters of public interest or concern about a *public figure* or public official, as long as the publisher doesn't act with *"actual malice"* (knowledge of falsity or a reckless disregard for the truth). Since Dumbo is a private figure, the paper doesn't get the benefit of the *Times* privilege. However, that doesn't mean that Dumbo won't have to prove *any* fault; he'll still have to prove at least *negligence*.

NOTE: Negligence can be shown by, for instance, a failure to check sources. Recklessness, however, requires a subjective evaluation: whether the reporter entertained serious doubts about the truth of what he was printing.

91. Yes. In defamation, truth is always an absolute defense. (Of course, Mrs. Tolstoy could be guilty of other torts, like invasion of privacy through publication of private facts about Anna.)

NOTE: If the defendant is a media defendant and the defamation involves a matter of public concern, the *plaintiff* has to prove the statement is false; otherwise, plaintiff only has to *allege* that it's false — defendant has the burden of proving truth as an affirmative defense.

92. No. While the entire statement need not be literally true in a truth defense, the defamatory "sting" must be proven true. Here, it doesn't matter who said it, it matters that Arnold was called a Communist. For a truth defense to fly, Washington would have to prove Arnold is a Communist.

NOTE: For media defendants and public matters, the *plaintiff* has to prove the statement is false; otherwise, the plaintiff only has to *allege* falsity, and the defendant has to prove truth as an affirmative defense.

93. Newspaper. If the statement involves a matter of public interest and the defendant is a media organization, the First Amendment requires that the plaintiff bear the burden of proving that the statement was false. This is true even if the plaintiff is a private figure. See *Philadelphia Newspapers v. Hepps*. Therefore, even though it may seem unfair to Joe to make him prove a negative fact (very difficult to do), this is what Joe must do, and he loses since he did not do it.

94. Yes. John Smith is clearly a "private figure." As such, the *New York Times* "actual malice" requirement does not apply to his libel suit. Therefore, to recover he only has to prove that Newspaper and its reporter were negligent, not intentionally false or reckless. Also, because the item originated with the unofficial words of Officer Flatfoot, the conditional privilege to report on public proceedings does not apply.

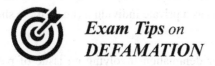

Exam Tips on
DEFAMATION

Defamation issues are pretty easy to spot — you're looking, of course, for situations where someone is saying something that damages somebody else's **reputation**. But spotting and analyzing the sub-issues can be difficult, especially because of the Supreme Court's constitutional rulings.

☛ Don't get too hung up on the *libel/slander* distinction. It only matters when you're worrying about whether P has to prove "special harm," i.e., pecuniary loss. Use the term "defamation" if you're not sure whether the suit is for libel or slander.

☛ Memorize this list of requirements for defamation (both libel and slander):

   ❏ A *false* and *defamatory* statement by D about P;

   ❏ A *"publication,"* i.e., a communicating of that statement by D to one other than P;

   ❏ The appropriate level of *fault,* which is always at least negligence (except possibly in the case of a private figure suing a non-media defendant), and is "actual malice" if P is a public official or public figure;

   ❏ If the action is for slander that is not "slander per se," *"special harm,"* i.e., damages of a pecuniary nature.

☛ Check that the statement was *"defamatory."* The term means "having a tendency to harm the *reputation*" of P.

   ☞ Commonly-tested: the fact that the listener/reader *doesn't believe* the statement is *irrelevant* on the issue of whether the statement is defamatory. (But this may be relevant to whether "special harm" has been shown, where the suit is for slander.)

   ☞ Some statements would, if believed, hold P up to disgrace or ridicule in the minds of *some* but *not other* listeners. Here, so long as a *"significant and respectable minority"* would have this negative opinion of P, the statement is defamatory even though other people would not have a negative opinion. (*Example:* "P is gay" is probably defamatory, because a sizeable minority of law-abiding — though perhaps not politically correct — Americans thinks poorly of gay people.)

   ☞ Check the meaning of the statement. Where the statement is *ambiguous*, it's defamatory if a *"reasonable person"* might interpret the statement in a defamatory way, and at least one person in fact took this interpretation.

☛ Check that the statement referred (and was understood to refer) to *P, not someone else*.

   ☞ If the statement *doesn't name* P, but refers to P in a way that some listeners *understand* to be a reference to P, that's enough. Often, the *context* will make it clear that P is the one referred to. (*Example:* "A leading member of this college faculty stole a computer" qualifies, if there are people who previously knew that P was the one under suspicion.)

   ☞ If the statement refers to an *entire group*, it's defamatory as to the whole group if the group is a small one (probably less than 20 members). If the statement pertains to only one or a few unnamed members of a larger group, the statement is probably not defamatory if there's no way for listeners to know which members are meant.

☛ Check that the statement was *false*. If it's true, the Constitution *forbids recovery*.

   ☞ "Falsity" can occasionally be tricky to determine. Watch out especially for statements that are a charge of *criminality*, whose truth or falsity depends on technical details about the crime. (*Example:* D says, "P stole my tools when he quit working for me." If P took the tools by mistake but then failed to return them, this isn't common-law theft, so the statement would probably be ruled to be "false.")

☞ But remember that *"substantial"* truth will bar recovery, not just literal truth. (However, if D accuses P of one crime, D can't defend by showing that P really committed a different crime, even a closely-related crime.)

☞ Statements of *"pure opinion"* can't be defamatory. (*Example:* "Our City Manager can't govern his way out of a paper bag" is an opinion, and thus can't be defamatory even if spoken with hatred and a desire to harm.)

☞ But a statement of opinion that contains an *implicit* assertion of related *facts* can be defamatory as to those facts. (*Example:* "In my opinion, P is an alcoholic" contains the implicit statement that D knows facts that would support this opinion; if P never drinks, D loses.)

☞ If the statement relates to a subject of controversy and public interest, D gets some leeway for *hyperbole* and non-literalness. (*Example:* "P's position on this issue shows that he must have been high on something" probably isn't intended to be taken literally, so it's an opinion, not a statement of fact.)

☛ Check that D had the requisite degree of *fault*. Most-often tested: D's degree of fault relative to the *truth or falsity* of the statement.

☞ If P is a *"public figure"* or *"public official,"* P must prove that D acted with *"actual malice."* Remember that this is a term of art, meaning not malice but either: (1) D had *knowledge* of the statement's falsity; or (2) D *recklessly disregarded* the truth. (Cite to *New York Times v. Sullivan* on this issue.)

☞ Also, remember that D is "reckless" only where D *"in fact entertained serious doubts"* about the statement's truth. If D was extremely careless in not checking the story, but had no doubts, that's not "reckless disregard" of the truth for *New York Times v. Sullivan* purposes.

☞ If P is a *private* figure, and D is a *media* defendant, P must prove *at least negligence* by D in failing to discover the statement's falsity. In other words, states can't impose strict liability here. (Cite to *Gertz v. Robert Welch* on this point.)

☞ If P is a *private* figure and D is *not* a media defendant, the Supreme Court has never imposed a constitutional requirement of negligence or greater. (The Supreme Court simply hasn't spoken on this issue.) So the states are theoretically free to find D *strictly liable*. However, as a matter of common law, virtually no states impose strict liability as to fault — they all require at least negligence.

☞ This issue is frequently tested despite the fact (or perhaps because of the fact) that it's relatively obscure.

Example: D, P's former boss, says to X, "P is the most dishonest employee I've ever had." D has a reasonable, non-negligent belief that P stole from D. In fact, however, P never committed any crime. Although there's no constitutional rule preventing a state from imposing strict liblity on D, no state would do so — P would always be required as a matter of state common law to prove at least that D was negligent in not ascertaining the statement's truth or falsity.

☛ At some point in your answer, you should try to determine whether the defamatory statement was *libel* or *slander*.

☞ Essentially, libel is *written*, and slander is *spoken*. Broadcast statements are clearly libel if they're done from written scripts; if the broadcast is ad-libbed, courts are split as to whether it's libel or slander.

☞ There is only one reason you have to worry about the distinction. For libel, P doesn't have to prove "special harm," i.e., that P's financial interests were harmed. For slander, P *does* have to prove *"special harm,"* i.e., that his financial interests were harmed — unless the slanderous statement falls into one of four special cases (collectively, "slander per se").

☞ The four classes making up *slander per se:* (1) most important (and most often-tested), a statement accusing P of *criminal behavior*; (2) a statement that P has a *loathsome disease*; (3) a statement adversely reflecting on P's fitness for *conducting her business* or profession; or (4) an allegation of *sexual misconduct* by P. [

Example 1. P works for D. D orally tells his friend X that P has stolen D's property. P in his slander suit need not show that he has suffered "special harm," i.e., financial harm from D's statement — D accused P of criminality, and the case is thus for slander per se.

Example 2: Same basic facts, but now D tells X that P was a completely incompetent employee. Unless P can show that he suffered some financial loss from this statement, P can't recover even nominal damages.

☞ Where the hearer/reader *doesn't believe* the statement, the requirement of special harm (assuming it applies) will virtually never be met.

☛ Check that *"publication"* occurred.

☞ Most often tested: "Publication" is communication to *one other than P*. (*Example:* D says to P, "You're a crook." If no one else overhears this, there's been no publication. This is true even if P then repeats the defamatory statement to another.)

☞ [Courts do *not* impose *strict liability* on the publication issue. Thus if D neither knows nor has reason to know that anyone other than P will hear/read the statement, D is not liable. (*Example:* D writes a letter to P, saying, "You're a crook." X, P's wife, opens the letter and reads it. If D didn't know and didn't have reason to believe that anyone other than P would read the letter, D is not liable.)

☞ A *repeater* is a "publisher," and thus is liable for defamation, on the same rules as the person who originally made the statement.

☞ Most-often tested: It doesn't matter that the repeater says, "I'm just repeating what so-and-so says," or even, "I'm quoting so-and-so." It doesn't even matter that the repeater says, "But I *don't believe* the statement that I've just repeated." If the underlying statement is false, the repeater faces liability (subject to the rules on fault, e.g., the repeater must have "actual malice" if P is a public figure).

☛ Look for *privileges* that might apply as defenses. Here are the most commonly-tested:

☞ The privilege of "protection of the *publisher's interest*." Most common illustration: D tries to protect/regain his *property*. (*Example:* D thinks P has stolen his property, and he yells, "Stop thief," or accuses P to the police. Even if D's belief is wrong, he is protected by the privilege, so long as he doesn't spread the defamation wider than needed or otherwise abuse the privilege.)

☞ The privilege of "protection of *another's interest*." Most common illustration: X asks D for a *job reference* concerning D's former employee, P. Even if D's statement about P is wrong, D is protected by the privilege.

☞ The privilege of "protection of *common interest*," i.e., an interest shared by D and the person to whom D speaks. (*Example:* D, an officer of one bank, says to X, an officer of another, "I hear that P's been passing bad checks. Have you heard the same?" Since D and X are both interested in stopping bad-check passing, D is protected even if wrong.)

☞ The privilege of *"neutral reportage."* This is used especially by media reporting on allegations that the reporter has serious doubts about but thinks need public airing. (*Example:* D, a reporter, writes, "Well-informed sources inside the D.A.'s Office say P [a public official] is believed to have taken bribes." Even if the reporter thinks that P probably didn't take the bribes, the reporter is protected if she reasonably thinks the accusation is important for the public to know about.) (Only a few courts have recognized this privilege so far.)

☞ But remember that all of the above privileges are just *"qualified"* ones, so they're *lost* if *abused*. Generally, a privilege is abused if used out of malice, if used for a different purpose than that furthered by the interest (e.g., idle gossip), or if the statement is spread more widely than needed. The privilege is also lost if D's belief as to the statement's truth is *reckless*. Courts are *split* about whether the privilege is lost if D is merely *negligent* in his belief that the statement is true.

☛ Remember that courts are limited in when they can award *"presumed"* damages. Presumed damages are compensatory (as opposed to nominal) damages awarded without actual proof of loss, on the theory that such an amount "would normally" be inflicted by the statement in question. At least where D is a *media defendant* and the issue relates to a matter of *public concern*, even a private-figure plaintiff can't be awarded presumed damages unless he shows that D acted with "actual malice" (not just negligence).

CHAPTER 18

MISCELLANEOUS TORTS

ChapterScope

This chapter covers several torts that have little to do with each other:

- **Invasion of privacy:** The tort of "invasion of privacy" is actually a cluster of four different, but related, torts.

  - ❏ **Misappropriation of identity:** *"Misappropriation of identity"* occurs where P's *name* or *likeness* has been used by D for D's financial benefit, without P's consent.

  - ❏ **Intrusion on solitude:** *"Intrusion on solitude"* occurs where D *invades* P's *private space* in a manner which would be highly offensive to a reasonable person in P's position.

  - ❏ **Publicity of private life:** *"Publicity of private life"* or "public disclosure" occurs where D publicly discloses a non-public detail of P's private life, where the effect would be highly offensive to a reasonable person in P's position.

  - ❏ **False light:** *"False light"* occurs where D publishes *false statements* about P which, although not defamatory, would be highly offensive to a reasonable person in P's position.

- **Misuse of legal procedure:** Three related tort actions protect P's interest in not being subjected to unwarranted judicial proceedings:

  - ❏ **Malicious prosecution:** The tort of "malicious prosecution" protects P's interest in not having wrongfully instigated a criminal proceeding against him.

  - ❏ **Wrongful institution of civil proceedings:** The tort of "wrongful institution of civil proceedings" is similar to "malicious prosecution," except that the original proceedings are civil rather than criminal.

  - ❏ **Abuse of process:** "Abuse of process" occurs where a person involved in criminal or civil proceedings uses various litigation devices (e.g., subpoenas) for improper purposes.

- **"Business torts":** There are three related torts that protect *business interests*:

  - ❏ **Injurious falsehood:** The action for *"injurious falsehood"* protects P against certain false statements made against his business, product or property (e.g., D makes false statements disparaging P's goods or business).

  - ❏ **Interference with contract:** The tort of *"interference with contract"* protects P's interest in having others perform *existing contracts* which they have with her. The claim is against one who *induces* another to breach a contract with P.

  - ❏ **Interference with prospective advantage:** If due to D's interference, P loses the benefits of *prospective, potential* contracts (as opposed to existing contracts), P can sue for *"interference with prospective advantage."*

I.   INVASION OF PRIVACY

A. Right generally: The so-called "invasion of privacy" cause of action is essentially four distinct mini-torts. They have in common not much more than the fact that they involve various aspects of the plaintiff's "right to be let alone." The four are:

[1] *misappropriation* of P's name or picture;

[2] *intrusion* on P's solitude;

[3] undue *publicity* given to P's *private life*; and

[4] the placing of P in a *false light*.

We consider each one in turn below.

B. Misappropriation of identity: The plaintiff can sue if her *name or picture* has been *appropriated* by the defendant for his own financial benefit. The action is said to be for *"misappropriation of identity"* or *"right of publicity."*

> **Example:** D1, a baker, runs an advertisement for his bread in D2's newspaper. The ad states, "Keep that Sylph-Like Figure by eating more of Melts' rye and whole wheat bread, says Mlle. Sally Payne, exotic red-haired Venus." By mistake, the ad contains a picture of P in a bathing suit rather than a picture of Sally Payne.
>
> *Held*, "The unauthorized use of one's photograph in connection with an advertisement or other commercial enterprise gives rise to a cause of action. . . . " Furthermore, P is entitled to nominal damages if she cannot prove actual damages. *Flake v. Greensboro News Co.*, 195 S.E. 55 (N.C. 1938).

1. Statutory regulation: A number of states have enacted statutes preventing such appropriation. See, e.g., New York Civil Rights Law §§50-51, which prohibits the use of any person's name or likeness without his consent for "advertising purposes" or for "purposes of trade."

2. Evoking a celebrity: There is dispute about whether the defendant should be liable for common-law misappropriation of identity if all he has done is to *"evoke"* the identity of a *celebrity*. Several courts have answered "yes" — even though the celebrity's name or "likeness" is not used, if advertising causes the reader to think that the celebrity is being *referred to* for the advertiser's financial benefit, that's enough to constitute common-law appropriation.

> **Example:** D, a manufacturer of VCRs, runs an ad depicting a robot, dressed in a wig, gown and jewelry which D has consciously selected to resemble the hair and clothing of P (TV personality Vanna White). The robot is posed next to a game board which is recognizable as the *Wheel of Fortune* game show set. D refers to this ad internally as the "Vanna White ad." P does not consent to the ad, nor is she paid. She sues for, among other things, violation of her common law right of publicity.
>
> *Held*, for P. D has violated P's common law right of publicity, by appropriating P's "identity." It does not matter that D has not appropriated P's name or "likeness." The right of publicity will be deemed to have been violated whenever a person's *"celebrity value"* is *exploited* by the defendant, regardless of the means by which this is done.

(But a dissent argues that the majority's opinion is a "classic case of overprotection," and that courts should not make it tortious to simply "remind the public of a celebrity" or to simply "evoke the celebrity's image in the public's mind.") *White v. Samsung Electronics America, Inc.*, 971 F.2d 1395 (9th Cir. 1992).

C. Intrusion: The plaintiff may sue if his *solitude* is *intruded upon*, and this intrusion would be "highly offensive to a reasonable person." Rest. 2d, §652B.

1. **Must be private place:** This "intrusion upon seclusion" branch of invasion of privacy is triggered only where a *private place* is invaded. Thus if the defendant takes the plaintiff's picture in a public place, this will normally not be enough.

   a. **Wiretaps and electronic surveillance:** The use of *wiretaps* and other kinds of secret electronic surveillance equipment will generally constitute an intrusion into a "private place."

   Example 1: P, consumer advocate Ralph Nader, plans to publish a book attacking the safety of automobiles manufactured by D (General Motors). In order to stop P from doing so, D harasses P by making threatening phone calls, conducting surveillance of P in public places, interviewing P's acquaintances, having women accost P with illicit proposals, tapping P's phone, and eavesdropping on P with electronic equipment. P sues D for invasion of privacy.

   Held, P has a cause of action for invasion of privacy, but only for the wiretapping and electronic eavesdropping. "[T]he mere gathering of information about a particular individual does not give rise to a cause of action for [invasion of privacy]. Privacy is invaded only if the information sought is of a confidential nature and the defendant's conduct is unreasonably intrusive." *Nader v. General Motors Corp.*, 255 N.E.2d 765 (N.Y. 1970).

   Example 2: Suppose that P and D are roommates at college; they share a suite, but each has his own small bedroom. D hides a web-cam in P's room, and uses it to stream video on the Internet of P having sex with X. P (as well as X) will have a claim against D for the intrusion-on-solitude branch of invasion of privacy: the use of hidden electronic equipment to monitor P's private space is an intrusion that would be "highly offensive to a reasonable person."

D. Publicity of private life: The publicizing of details of the plaintiff's *private life* may be an invasion of his privacy. As in the case of "invasion of seclusion," the effect must be "highly offensive to a reasonable person." Rest. 2d, §652D.

   Example: D, a frustrated creditor of P, puts up a notice in the window of his store stating that P owes him money and has not paid him. This is an invasion of P's privacy. Rest. 2d, §652D, Illustr. 2.

1. **Must be truly "private":** The details divulged must be truly "private" ones, which are *not* contained anywhere on the *public record*. This requirement was spelled out, as a constitutional principle, in *Cox Broadcasting Corp. v. Cohn*, 420 U.S. 469 (1975). In that case, the defendant broadcasting company broadcast the name of a deceased rape victim, in violation of a state law. The Supreme Court held that the girl's parents could not constitutionally be given recovery for invasion of privacy. The Court relied on the fact that the

name of the victim was given in indictments made available for public inspection at the rapists' trial, and held that the First Amendment required that dissemination of such *publicly-available information* not be prohibited.

2. **Truthful matter not on any public record:** *Cox* leaves open the question of whether it is constitutional to allow a tort recovery for the publicizing of truthful matter that is *not* contained on any public record. In a post-*Cox* case, the Supreme Court has held that only if the state is protecting *"a state interest of the highest order"* may the state punish (or allow a private plaintiff to sue for) publication of "truthful information about a matter of public significance," even where that information is not on the public record. *Florida Star v. B.J.F.*, 491 U.S. 524 (1989).

   a. **Hard burden to meet:** The facts of *Florida Star* show that this will be a hard burden for the state, or the private plaintiff, to meet. In *Florida Star*, P, like the plaintiff in *Cox Broadcasting*, was a rape victim. Florida law made it a crime to publish the name of a rape victim. Unlike the *Cox* situation, in *Florida Star* the information was not truly public — the newspaper obtained it from the local sheriff's department, which had put it in the press room. The Supreme Court overturned the jury award for P, because the "state interest of the highest order" requirement was not satisfied here — the state here was adopting no-fault (strict) liability, plus it was punishing only media, not private individuals who might disseminate the same information.

      i. **Consequence:** So it remains possible, but by no means clear, that a tightly-written state statute preventing the intentional publication of the name of a rape victim by anyone (not just by a media defendant) may give rise to an invasion-of-privacy action if the information was not part of the public record.

3. **Must not be of legitimate public concern:** In addition to the requirement that the details be "private" ones, it is probably also required for an "invasion of private life" action that the material *not be of legitimate public concern*. See Rest. 2d §652D(b).

   Example: P is tried for murder and is then acquitted. After the trial is over, D, a newspaper, publishes extensive reports on P's pre-trial history and his daily life. A court would almost certainly conclude that these details are of legitimate public concern, given P's status as a public figure on account of the murder trial. If so, P cannot recover under the publicity-given-to-private-life branch of invasion of privacy, no matter how offensive or embarrassing the details may be. Cf. Rest. 2d, §652D, Illustr. 13.

4. **Must be publicized:** The private details must be widely *publicized*, as opposed to being released to a few people. For instance, if a creditor notifies his debtor's employer about the debt and the debtor's refusal to pay it, this is not an invasion of privacy. Rest. 2d, §652D, Illustr. 1.

5. **Already-public information:** Conversely, the requirement that the details be widely publicized by the defendant means that recovery is not allowed where the information is *already known or available to the public*, and defendant merely gives extra publicity to this publicly-available information. Rest. 2d, §652D, Comm. b.

Example: At a public meeting of the Muni Zoning Board, Fred complains that his next-door neighbor Nan has been sunbathing nude, and getting drunk, in her outdoor hot tub, which Fred (and only Fred) can see from a particular window in his house. Newspaper, whose reporter is present, accurately reports Fred's remarks, identifying Nan. Nan cannot recover for publicity-of-private-life against Newspaper, because the information had already been made public at the zoning meeting.

E. **False light:** The plaintiff can sue if he is placed before the public eye in a *false light*, and this false light would be highly offensive to a reasonable person. Rest. 2d, §652E.

> **Example:** P is a war hero. D makes a movie about P's life, which contains much material concerning a fictitious private life of P, including a non-existent romance with a girl. D is liable for invasion of privacy. Rest. 2d, §652E, Illustr. 5.

1. **Constitutional limits:** At least where the plaintiff is a public figure, he may bring such a "false light" action may only if he can show that the defendant either *knew* it was portraying its subject in a false light, or acted in *reckless disregard* of the risk of a false-light portrayal. *Time, Inc. v. Hill*, 385 U.S. 374 (1967). (In *Time, Inc.*, the Court consciously applied the defamation standard defined in *New York Times v. Sullivan, supra*, p. 477.)

2. **Distinguished from defamation:** In many "false light" cases, the material will also be defamatory of the plaintiff. But this is *not necessarily* the case. For instance, in the example of the war hero given above, P can sue for invasion of privacy even though the movie does not hold him up to ridicule (and even portrays his private life in a manner which some people would find dashing and romantic). However, the presentation must be "highly offensive to a reasonable person," and trivial deviations from the literal truth will not be enough. Rest. 2d, §652E, Comment c.

F. **Privileges:** Most courts, and the Second Restatement, hold that the absolute and conditional *privileges* allowable in defamation actions are also available in invasion of privacy actions. Rest. 2d §§652F and 652G.

1. **Consent:** For instance, if the plaintiff consents to an appropriation of her name, publication of private information about her, etc., this consent will be a defense (assuming that its scope is not exceeded). Rest. 2d, §652F, Comment b.

II. MISUSE OF LEGAL PROCEDURE

A. **Three torts:** Three related tort actions protect the plaintiff's interest in not being subjected to unwarranted judicial proceedings. These are:

1. *malicious prosecution;*

2. *wrongful institution of civil proceedings;* and

3. *abuse of process.*

B. **Malicious prosecution:** To make out a prima facie case of malicious prosecution, the plaintiff must prove the following elements: (1) that the defendant instituted *criminal proceedings* against him; (2) that these proceedings terminated *in favor of the plaintiff* (the accused); (3) that the defendant had *no probable cause* to institute the proceedings; and (4) that the defendant was motivated primarily by some purpose other than bringing an offender to justice. See Rest. 2d, §653; P&K, p. 871.

1. **Initiating proceeding:** The plaintiff must show that the defendant took an *active part* in instigating and encouraging the prosecution. For instance, if the defendant merely states what she believes to be the facts to the prosecutor, and leaves to the latter the decision whether to prosecute, this will probably not be "institution" of proceedings. But if the defendant has attempted to influence a district attorney to prosecute, or has lied so as to make prosecution more probable, this will be sufficient. See P&K, p. 872-73.

   a. **Prosecutorial immunity:** The prosecutor himself is almost always immune from malicious prosecution suits. P&K, p. 873. (For exceptions to this rule, see generally P&K, pp. 1059-1062.) This immunity is also generally given to police officers, as long as they act within the general scope of their duties. P&K, p. 873.

2. **Favorable outcome:** The criminal proceedings must *terminate in favor of the accused* (the plaintiff). This requirement is met not only where there is an acquittal, but also where the prosecutor ultimately decides not to prosecute because he does not think he has a good case, or a grand jury refuses to indict, or any other disposition that indicates the weakness of the case.

   a. **Plea bargain:** But a *plea bargain*, in which the plaintiff pleads guilty to some other offense, will not meet the "favorable disposition" requirement. Rest. 2d, §660(a).

3. **Absence of probable cause:** The plaintiff's biggest hurdle is likely to be the requirement that he show that the defendant *lacked probable cause* to institute the proceedings. In general, the defendant will be held to have had probable cause if she correctly or reasonably believed that the plaintiff had committed certain acts, and that these acts constitute the crime charged. Rest. 2d, §662.

   a. **Mistake:** The defendant may have been mistaken either as to the facts (i.e., whether the plaintiff committed the acts in question) or as to the law (i.e., whether those acts constitute the crime charged). But as long as her mistake is *reasonable*, she does not lack probable cause.

      i. **Mistake of law:** But a lay person's erroneous belief that certain conduct constitutes a crime is quite likely to be held to be unreasonable, if it is not arrived at after consultation with a lawyer or prosecutor. Once the defendant *does* receive assurances of her lawyer or the prosecutor that these facts constitute a crime, however, she has probable cause (assuming that she has made full disclosure of the facts known to her). See Rest. 2d, §662, Comment i and §666.

   b. **Effect of outcome:** The outcome of the criminal proceeding may, but does not necessarily, affect the existence of probable cause. If the plaintiff was convicted, this will always mean that the defendant had probable cause. If the complaint is dismissed by a magistrate, or a grand jury refuses to indict, most courts hold that this is *prima facie* evidence that no probable cause existed. P&K, p. 880.

      i. **Acquittal:** But an *acquittal* of the plaintiff does not establish lack of probable cause, and is not even admissible as evidence to that effect. The obvious reason for this is that the plaintiff can obtain an acquittal merely by showing a reasonable doubt, yet the existence of such a doubt is not incompatible with the existence of probable cause. See Rest. 2d, §667(2).

   ii. Retrial in tort action: The consequence of this is that even if the plaintiff has been acquitted, the defendant has a right to *retry the plaintiff's guilt* in the course of the tort action. If she can show, by a *preponderance of the evidence*, that the plaintiff was guilty of the crime charged, she has established probable cause.

4. **Improper purpose:** Lastly, the plaintiff must show that the defendant acted out of *malice*, or for some other purpose than bringing an offender to justice. For instance, if the crime charged is the obtaining of money by false pretenses, the plaintiff might meet the "improper purpose" requirement by showing that the defendant was his creditor, and was trying to coerce him into paying the debt. See Rest. 2d, §668, Comment g.

5. **Damages:** It is usually held that the plaintiff does not have to prove actual pecuniary loss. But the common law principle of allowing "presumed damages" for harm to reputation, in the absence of an actual showing of such harm, is probably unconstitutional in light of *Gertz v. Robert Welch, supra,* p. 477 (except where no matter of "public interest" is involved — see *Dun & Bradstreet, supra,* p. 486). To the extent that plaintiff can prove such actual harm to his reputation, emotional distress, lost income, etc., stemming from the proceedings, he may recover for these losses.

C. **Wrongful civil proceedings:** The tort of "malicious prosecution," as noted, formally relates only to unwarranted *criminal* proceedings. Most states, however, have granted a similar tort action for wrongful institution of *civil* proceedings. While this tort is also often called "malicious prosecution," the better term is "wrongful use of civil proceedings" (the Restatement's term) or something like it.

1. **Elements:** In general, the plaintiff must prove the same elements as for the criminal proceedings case.

2. **Institution of proceedings:** The "civil proceedings" which the defendant has initiated can include not only the ordinary civil lawsuit, but also insanity or bankruptcy proceedings, administrative proceedings, ancillary attachment proceedings, etc.

3. **Probable cause:** The defendant must be shown to have acted without probable cause.

   a. **Easier standard:** However, one has probable cause to institute civil proceedings on a significantly less certain knowledge of the facts than would suffice for a criminal proceeding (because of the difference in the burden of proof ultimately imposed, as well as the usually less severe hardship imposed on the person defending the action).

   b. **Mistake of law:** Similarly, the institutor of civil proceedings is less harshly penalized for a mistake of law than one who starts criminal proceedings; it is enough if she reasonably (though mistakenly) believes that there is a *respectable chance* (even if less than 50%) that she will be able to convince a court or jury of the legal merits of her claim. Rest. 2d, §675, Comment e.

4. **Improper purpose:** The civil proceedings must have been instituted for an *improper purpose*. The only proper purpose for such proceedings is "securing the proper adjudication of the claim on which they are based". Rest. 2d, §676. Thus if the suit is a "nuisance" suit or "strike suit", which the plaintiff knows has no real chance of succeeding, and which

is brought solely for the purpose of extorting a settlement, this is an improper purpose. The same would be true of a ***counterclaim*** asserted solely for the purpose of delaying proceedings. Rest. 2d, §676, Comment c.

5. **Favorable termination:** The civil proceedings must have terminated in favor of the person against whom they were brought.

   a. **No re-litigation:** This first adjudication cannot be relitigated on the merits, as it could in the case of a criminal acquittal. That is, it is not open to the person defending the "wrongful civil proceedings" claim to show that she should have won on the merits at the first trial, and is therefore not liable. (But she may, of course, show that she had probable cause to start the suit.)

D. **Abuse of process:** Even if a criminal or civil proceeding is brought with probable cause, and for allowable motives, a person involved in it may use various litigation devices available to him during the course of it for improper purposes. If so, he will be liable for ***"abuse of process."***

1. **Writ of arrest:** Thus in one case a judgment creditor, in order to avoid the trouble of having the sheriff seize the debtor's property and sell it off to satisfy the judgment, improperly obtained an arrest warrant. (At the time, a debtor could be imprisoned until he paid the debt.) As the creditor hoped, this arrest coerced the debtor into paying the judgment directly. The court allowed a cause of action for abuse of process, even though the underlying suit (which gave rise to the judgment) had not been terminated in the debtor's favor. *Ash v. Cohn*, 194 A. 174 (N.J. 1937).

2. **Subpoena:** Similarly, the use of a ***subpoena*** against a person to harass him or make him settle a suit, rather than for the proper purpose of obtaining his testimony, would be an abuse of process. See Rest. 2d, §682, Illustr. 3.

III. INTERFERENCE WITH ADVANTAGEOUS RELATIONS

A. **Three business torts:** A cluster of three tort actions protects certain business interests that are not protected by any of the actions previously discussed. These three are commonly referred to as:

1. *injurious falsehood;*

2. *interference with contract;* and

3. *interference with prospective advantage.*

B. **Injurious falsehood:** The tort action for ***"injurious falsehood"*** protects the plaintiff against certain false statements made against his business, product, or property. The action is most often helpful to a businessperson whose competitor has made false statements disparaging the plaintiff's ***goods or business***. In such a case, the tort is often called ***"trade libel"***. The plaintiff must generally prove the following elements:

1. **False disparagement:** First, he must show that the defendant made a false statement disparaging the plaintiff's goods, business, etc.

   a. **Falsity:** The plaintiff bears the burden of proving the statement's falsity.

b. **Clear reference to plaintiff:** The statement must *clearly refer* to the plaintiff or his product. P&K 1988 Pocket Part, p. 138.

c. **Not co-extensive with defamation:** A statement can disparage the plaintiff's business or product even though it is not defamatory as against the plaintiff. For instance, if the defendant tries to get people to buy from her rather than from the plaintiff by saying that the plaintiff is dead or out of business, this is disparagement, even though it's not defamatory of the plaintiff (since it does not hold the plaintiff up to ridicule or disgrace).

2. **Publication:** Plaintiff must show that the statement was "published", as that word is used in defamation cases.

3. **Intent:** The plaintiff must also show *scienter* on the part of the defendant. Unlike common law defamation, for which the defendant could be liable if she either innocently or negligently failed to ascertain the falsity of her statement, the trade libel defendant must have either: (1) known her statement was false; (2) acted in reckless disregard of whether it was false; or (3) (according to some courts) acted out of ill-will or spite for the plaintiff, or to interfere with the plaintiff's business in some impermissible way. See Rest. 2d, §623A and Caveat thereto.

4. **Special damages:** The plaintiff must prove *"special damages"*. This "special harm" is defined the same way as in defamation; i.e., the harm must be "pecuniary."

a. **General lost business:** Courts used to hold that it was not enough for the plaintiff to show that his business suffered generally, and required him to point out specific lost sales. However, the modern view seems to be that this requirement will not be imposed where it is unreasonable to do so. For instance, if the disparagement is widely circulated, the plaintiff may be permitted to recover for the general reduction in the volume of his business if he can show that there is no other reasonable explanation for this drop apart from the defendant's statement; see P&K, pp. 972-73.

5. **Defenses:** The defendant can raise a number of defenses, some of which are as follows:

a. **Truth:** The defendant can, of course, attempt to show that the statement was true. As noted, it is generally up to the plaintiff to show that the statement is false.

b. **Privileges:** Any of the absolute and qualified privileges that could be raised in a defamation case (*supra*, p. 479) may be raised by a trade libel defendant.

c. **Competition:** Furthermore, courts recognize a privilege that does not exist in the defamation context, that of *pursuing competition by fair means.*

   i. **General comparisons:** In particular, the defendant is privileged to make *general comparisons* between her product and the plaintiff's, stating or implying that her product is the better one. But this privilege only extends to statements that are in the language of misrepresentation, "puffing"; see *supra*, p. 449. If the defendant makes *specific* false allegations against the plaintiff's product, she will not be protected.

Example: P and D both make devices for testing industrial material. D sends to P's present and prospective customers a false report that the U.S. government has found P's product to be only about 40% as effective as D's.

Held, this statement goes beyond the bounds of privileged "unfavorable comparison". A statement that another's product is only "40% as effective" as one's own is already too specific to qualify for this privilege; the matter is even worse when a false allegation is made that this conclusion has been reached by the U.S. Government. *Testing Systems, Inc. v. Magnaflux Corp.*, 251 F. Supp. 286 (E.D. Pa. 1966).

6. **Slander of title:** A similar tort action is given where the defendant falsely disparages *property rights* in land, goods, or intangibles. This action is commonly known as one for *"slander of title"*. See Rest. 2d, §624.

   a. **Liens, mortgages and executions:** One common way of slandering title is to file a false mortgage, attachment, lis pendens, levy of execution, etc., which interferes with the plaintiff's right to hold or dispose of his property.

   b. **Patents, trademarks and copyrights:** Another way of committing the tort is for the defendant to state that the plaintiff's goods infringe the defendant's patent, trademark, or copyright.

   c. **Intent:** The plaintiff is required to meet the same scienter requirement as for trade libel. That is, he must prove knowing falsehood, reckless disregard of the truth, or malice.

   d. **Privileges:** The defendant has defenses and privileges similar to those of trade libel.

      i. **Rival claimant's privilege:** In particular, she has a conditional privilege to assert an *inconsistent legal interest* of her own. For instance, if she reasonably believes that she may have a right to land which is ostensibly owned by the plaintiff, she may file a lis pendens to prevent the plaintiff from selling the land until its ownership can be adjudicated. Similarly, if she believes that she may have a valid trademark or patent infringement claim against the plaintiff, she may assert this. See Rest. 2d, §647.

      ii. **Abuse:** But since the privilege is conditional, it is lost where it is *abused.* It is abused if it is asserted in bad faith, or out of malice toward the plaintiff.

C. **Interference with existing contract:** The tort of *"interference with contract"* protects the plaintiff's interest in having others perform existing contracts which they have with him. The tort claim exists against one who *induces* another to breach a contract with the plaintiff.

   Example: P runs a theater, and has a contract with an opera singer under which she will perform for P, and will not perform for anyone else during a certain period. D induces the singer not to perform her contract with P. *Held*, P has a cause of action against D for inducing this breach. *Lumley v. Gye*, 118 Eng. Rep. 749 (Q.B. 1853).

1. **Contracts as to which inapplicable:** Certain kinds of contracts *cannot serve* as the basis for this "inducing of breach" cause of action.

a. Illegal contracts: For instance, if a contract is *illegal* or "contrary to public policy", the defendant may induce a breach of it with impunity. Rest. 2d, §774. This would be true, for instance, if the contract violates the antitrust laws.

b. Contract terminable at will: If a contract is *terminable at will*, most courts hold that the defendant is not liable for inducing one party to terminate it.

    i. Restatement view: But the Second Restatement, and a growing minority of modern courts, hold that inducing the breach of a terminable-at-will contract *does* constitute interference with contract. See Rest. 2d, §766, Comment g. The theory behind this view is that until the contract has been in fact terminated, it is a valid and existing one, and the plaintiff has a right to expect that it will not be tampered with.

    ii. Damages: However, even under this emerging minority view, the fact that the contract could be terminated at any time will be a factor tending to *reduce the damages* that the plaintiff has suffered; for instance, if the defendant can show that the other contracting party was unhappy with the service or price he was getting, and would have terminated the contract anyway, this will reduce or eliminate the plaintiff's damages.

    iii. Privilege: Also, if the defendant acts for *reasonable competitive purposes* (i.e., getting the business for herself), her conduct is very likely to be held to be *privileged* if the contract is terminable at will, as it would be if only the "prospective advantage" of the plaintiff had been interfered with. See Rest. 2d, §768, Comment i. But if the defendant acts for other, improper, motives (e.g., desire to drive plaintiff out of business for pure spite) her conduct will not be privileged.

2. "Interference" by defendant: The defendant is liable only if she has *actively interfered* with the contract.

a. Mere offer of better price: Thus the defendant does not become liable merely by *offering a better price* to the third person, or routinely soliciting his business, even if she knows that an acceptance would cause the third person to breach his contract with the plaintiff. Rest. 2d, §766, Comment m. But if the defendant says, "I'm offering you a better price than you have with P; if you take me up on it, you'll save enough that you can settle your contract with P and still come out ahead," the defendant has stepped over the line and actively induced the breach. Rest. 2d, §766, Illustr. 3.

3. Intent: The defendant's interference must be *intentional*. If she has merely negligently prevented another from performing his contract with the plaintiff, the tort of interference with contract has not occurred.

a. Knowledge of contract required: For the defendant to have the required intent, it must be shown that she *knew about the contract*. Rest. 2d, §766, Comment i.

4. Damages: The plaintiff may recover the pecuniary loss he has sustained as a result of the interference (including the profits he would have made from the contract). Many courts also allow him to recover for *emotional harm* suffered.

5. Privileges: The defendant's interference may have been *privileged*.

a. Business competition: The defendant's desire to *obtain business* for herself, however, is *not* by itself enough to make her privileged to induce a breach of contract. Rest. 2d, §768(2).

   i. Contract terminable at will: One exception to this general rule, however, is that if the contract is merely *terminable at will*, the defendant is privileged to induce a termination of it solely for the purpose of obtaining the business for herself (assuming that the court is one which even recognizes the possibility that such an at-will contract can give rise to the tort.) Rest. 2d, §768(1).

   ii. Improper means: Even this limited privilege will be lost, if the defendant uses *improper means* (e.g., threats, violence, illegal boycotts, etc.) to induce the termination of the at-will contract. Rest. 2d, §768(1)(b), and Comment e thereto.

b. Defendant protecting her own contract rights: If the defendant is not trying to gain business for herself, but trying to protect her *existing contract rights*, she will generally be privileged to induce a breach. For instance, if D has a contract to buy widgets from X, and she knows that X can't deliver unless he breaks his contract to sell the same widgets to P, D can request that X favor her (and probably even threaten to sue if he doesn't). See P&K, p. 986.

c. Social interests: The defendant may be privileged if she is acting not primarily in furtherance of her own interests, but for *valuable social* interests. Thus in the classic case of *Brimelow v. Casson*, 1 Ch. 302 (Eng. 1923), the defendant labor leader was held privileged to induce various theater owners to cancel their contracts with the plaintiff troupe manager, where the wages paid by the latter to his female troupe members were so low as to force them into prostitution (including cohabitation with an "abnormal and deformed dwarf").

6. Interference with plaintiff's own performance: A closely related tort action exists where the defendant has interfered with the *plaintiff's own performance* of a contract. This can occur not only by forcing the plaintiff to breach, but also by making performance more burdensome or more expensive. Rest. 2d, §766A.

a. Illustration: For instance, if the defendant intentionally prevented the plaintiff's truck from delivering merchandise to a customer, or forced the truck to take an extensive detour, this would be actionable.

b. Same rules: In general, the same rules as to intent, damages, and privileges, apply as where a third person is induced to breach the contract with the plaintiff.

D. Interference with prospective advantage: Suppose that through the defendant's interference, the plaintiff loses not the benefits of an existing contract, but simply the benefits of *prospective, potential*, contracts or other relationships. In this situation, the plaintiff may be able to recover for the tort that is usually called *"interference with prospective advantage."*

1. Same rules except for privilege: Essentially the same rules apply to this tort as to "interference with contract," discussed *supra*, p. 504. But there is one major difference: since the plaintiff's interests have not ripened into a present, existing contract, they are somewhat less worthy of protection, and the defendant has a correspondingly greater scope of *privilege* to interfere.

a. **Competition:** The most important practical consequence is that the defendant's desire to ***obtain business for herself*** will be enough to give her a privilege, where she would not be privileged to interfere with an existing contract for this purpose.

b. **Interference must be wrongful:** Most courts hold that the defendant's interference must be *"wrongful,"* and that plaintiff bears the burden of showing wrongfulness. Since the defendant's attempt to protect its own legitimate business interests will not be "wrongful," this is usually a hard showing for plaintiffs to make.

Example: D (Toyota motors) wishes to prevent Lexus cars made by it that have been imported into the U.S. from being re-exported to Japan, since these re-exported cars compete with D's own Japanese sales efforts. P is an American in the business of buying Lexuses from U.S.-based Lexus dealers and exporting them to Japan at a profit. To stop these re-exports, D warns its U.S. Lexus dealers that anyone who does business with people like P may be punished. As a result, the dealers refuse to sell to P, and P's business dries up. P sues D for interfering with the purchases that P could have made from other dealers. The trial judge requires P to prove that D's conduct was "wrongful," and the jury then finds for D. P appeals on the grounds that the burden of proof on wrongfulness should have been placed on D.

Held, for D. It is important to distinguish sharply between claims for the tortious disruption of an *existing* contract and claims that a *prospective* contractual relationship has been interfered with. Courts should give less protection to the latter, and should recognize that "relationships short of [a contract] subsist in a zone where the rewards and risks of competition are dominant." Therefore, the trial judge was correct to require P to prove that D's interference was wrongful. *Della Penna v. Toyota Motor Sales, U.S.A., Inc.,* 902 F.2d 740 (Cal. Sup. Ct. 1995).

   i. **Intent to bankrupt plaintiff:** In fact, as long as the means used are not unlawful or wrongful in themselves (e.g., price fixing, attempted monopolization, etc.), the defendant may even use methods that are intended to ***drive the plaintiff out of business***.

c. **Pure malice:** IHowever, if the plaintiff is lucky enough to be able to prove that the defendant acted not primarily to obtain economic advantage for herself, but rather, solely or primarily out of ***sheer malice***, the defendant's conduct will not be privileged.

   i. **Mixed motives:** But as long as furtherance of business interests is a significant motive on the defendant's part, the fact that she also bears the plaintiff ill-will will not cause her to lose the privilege.

2. **Honest advice:** One who gives ***honest advice*** to another against doing business with the plaintiff will not be liable for interference with prospective advantage. This is likely to be true, for instance, of advice given by a lawyer, friend, or relative. See Rest. 2d, §772.

3. **Unconstitutional zoning ordinance:** A city may be liable for interference with prospective advantage if it enacts an ***improper zoning ordinance*** (e.g., one that prevents the owner from signing a lease with a particular tenant). P&K 1988 Pocket Part, p. 140.

4. Interference with non-business expectation: It may also be tortious to interfere with the plaintiff's *non-business* expectations of financial gain. For instance, the defendant might be liable if he induced the plaintiff's grandfather to leave the plaintiff out of his will.

    a. Interference with prospective legal claim: Similarly, several courts have held that it can be tortious to interfere with a plaintiff's potential *legal claim*. Examples of such interference include: (1) D tampers with medical records or tape recordings; (2) D disposes of potentially revealing evidence she had agreed to preserve; and (3) D conceals facts that, if P knew them, would reveal to P that he has a cause of action. Even mere *negligence* by D may make him liable in this way (especially if a special relationship exists between D and P, such as where P is injured when the bus he is riding is hit by a car, and the bus company negligently fails to get the car's license plate number). P&K 1988 Pocket Part, pp. 140-41.

E. Common-law trademark, copyright and unfair competition claims: Related to these general business torts are common-law claims based upon *trademark, copyright* and *unfair competition*. Although major portions of these areas are governed by explicit federal statutes (e.g. the federal Copyright Act), certain cases involving these subjects are decided on general common-law tort principles.

    1. Preemption: However, the plaintiff's common-law rights may in some cases be *preempted by federal laws* governing the subject area.

        Example: P holds a patent on a "pole lamp," an almost exact copy of which is being sold by D. The patent itself has been held to be invalid under federal law for "lack of invention" (a technical patent term). However, P now seeks a state-law ruling that D has nonetheless unfairly competed with P by selling an item which the public will confuse with P's own product.

        Held (by the U.S. Supreme Court), federal patent law has preempted the domain in question. Since the patent is invalid, a state may not award P damages for unfair competition arising out of D's copying of P's non-patentable item. (But the state *may* require that two otherwise indistinguishable items each be labeled, so that there will be no confusion as to source.) *Sears Roebuck & Co. v. Stiffel Co.*, 376 U.S. 225 (1964).

IV. INTERFERENCE WITH FAMILY AND POLITICAL RELATIONS

A. Interference with family relations: A family member's interest in having the continued affections of the other members of his family is sometimes protected against outside interference by tort claims for "alienation of affections" and the like.

    1. Husband and wife: A jilted *spouse* may, in a number of states, bring either of two tort claims against an outsider who has interfered with the marital relation:

        a. Alienation of affections: Recovery for *"alienation of affections"* is available in some states against anyone who has caused the plaintiff's spouse to lose his or her affection for the plaintiff.

i. **Not necessarily romantic rival:** The defendant can, but does not necessarily have to, be a romantic rival who has lured the spouse away. The tort can also lie against a friend or relative who has convinced the spouse to leave the plaintiff. See Rest. 2d, §683.

ii. **Privilege:** But the defendant, particularly if he or she is a friend or relative (rather than romantic rival) may be ***privileged*** to interfere; this is the case, for instance, if the defendant acts "primarily to advance what is reasonably believed to be the welfare of the alienated spouse." Rest. 2d, §686.

b. **Criminal conversation:** A person who has ***sexual intercourse*** with one spouse may be liable to the other for ***"criminal conversation."*** Rest. 2d, §685.

   i. **Initiator irrelevant:** At least in the Restatement's view, it is not a defense that the spouse, rather than the defendant, made the overtures that led to the act. It is also irrelevant that the spouse falsely represented that he or she was unmarried. See Rest. 2d, §685, Comment f. (But this would be a defense to the tort of "alienation of affections," since knowledge or belief that the person is married is necessary for that tort. Rest. 2d, §683, Comment i.)

c. **Statutory abolition:** Many states have eliminated both of these causes of action by statutes, commonly known as "Anti-Heart Balm" statutes. See, e.g., §80-c, N.Y. Civil Rights Law.

2. **Parent's claim:** A ***parent*** will not usually have a tort claim against one who alienates his ***child's affections***. Rest. 2d, §699. But there are at least a couple of special situations in which a parent may sue for interference with filial relations:

a. **Causing minor to leave home:** He will have a claim against a person who causes his minor child to ***leave home***, or not to return home. Rest. 2d, §700.

   i. **Moonies:** This has been the basis for a number of tort suits against Rev. Sun Yung Moon and his followers; such suits are aided by the fact that it is no defense that the defendant may have acted out of motives of kindness or affection to the child, or believed that his not returning home was in the child's best interests. Rest. 2d, §700, Comment b.

   ii. **One parent against other:** If a child's parents are divorced, and one has been awarded sole custody, that parent may maintain an action against the other for abducting the child or otherwise inducing him to leave the former's home. Rest. 2d, §700, Comment c. But if there has been no judicial determination on custody, or an adjudication of joint custody, there can be no such suit. (*Ibid.*)

   iii. **Marriage:** One who induces a minor child to leave home in order to ***marry*** him or her is privileged, and therefore not liable. Rest. 2d, §700, Comment f.

b. **Sexual intercourse with minor female:** The parent has a tort claim against anyone who has ***sexual intercourse*** with the parent's minor ***daughter*** (but not son). Rest. 2d, §701. (But if the defendant is the daughter's husband, there will be no liability). (*Ibid.*)

    c. **Adoptive parent's claim:** If D induces the P's to *adopt* a child by misrepresenting the facts (e.g., by concealing the child's violent tendencies), D may be liable. P&K 1988 Pocket Part, p. 129.

  3. **Alienation of parent's affection:** A child will not usually be allowed to sue for the alienation of a *parent's* affections. Thus in *Nash v. Baker*, 522 P.2d 1335 (Okla. 1974), five children were denied recovery against a wealthy widow who had lured away their father from their mother "with a finer home, sexual charms, and other inducements." See also, Rest. 2d, §702A.

  4. **Indirect interferences:** The right of family members to recover for indirect losses through physical injury to a spouse, child, or parent, is discussed *supra*, p. 270. See also the discussion of wrongful death recovery *supra*, p. 272.

B. **Interference with political and civil rights:** There may be liability for interfering with the plaintiff's *political rights* (e.g., his right to vote), his *civil rights* (e.g., his right to make a public protest) or his *public duties* (e.g., his duty to serve on a jury). Such areas are frequently governed by statutes, which often contain explicit civil damage provisions.

  1. **§1983 suits for state violation of federal rights:** The most important statute allowing recovery for civil rights violations is the famous federal *"section 1983,"* 42 U.S.C. §1983. Section 1983 allows a person to bring a tort action against any person who, *"under color of" state law*, deprives the plaintiff of "any rights, privileges, or immunities" secured by the *federal Constitution or a federal statute*. So the basic effect of §1983 is to permit a tort suit by anyone who is injured when a *state or local official* violates the plaintiff's federal rights, typically her *constitutionally-guaranteed civil rights*. Dobbs, §44, p. 82.

    a. **Constitutional provisions:** Most §1983 actions allege that state or local officials have violated one of these three federal constitutional provisions:

      [1] the 14th Amendment's guarantee of *substantive and procedural due process* of law, and its guarantee of *equal protection* of the laws;

      [2] the 4th Amendment's prohibition of *unreasonable searches and seizures*; and

      [3] the 8th Amendment's ban on *cruel and unusual punishment. Id.*

      Example (Fourth Amendment): Suppose that Officer, an officer in the City police force, arrests P without probable cause, and then brutally beats P in an unsuccessful attempt to extract a confession. P can recover tort damages from both Officer and City under §1983. Officer has acted "under color of" state law — that is, he has used his official position as justification for his acts. And Officer's conduct amounts to an "unreasonable seizure" under the 4th Amendment. City is vicariously liable under the doctrine of *respondeat superior* (*supra*, p. 315).

    b. **Inaction:** Probably the most controversial issue in connection with §1983 suits is the extent to which government officials and government itself can be liable for a *failure* to act, when that failure is a failure to protect the plaintiff from harm by non-governmental persons. § 1983 case law has essentially followed the common-law approach to this problem: government has *no affirmative duty to protect citizens*, except where government has somehow "undertaken" to act.

Example: City learns that P, a young boy who lives there, is being repeatedly beaten by his father. City fails to intervene. The father eventually beats P so badly that he becomes permanently brain-injured.

P cannot recover against City under §1983. That's because a person has no constitutional due process right to affirmative governmental aid, even if such aid is needed to protect a liberty or property interest of which the government could not itself deprive the person. Cf. *DeShaney v. Winnebago County Dept. of Soc. Serv.*, 489 U.S. 189 (1989).

   i.   Undertaking: But where the state ***affirmatively steps in*** to render protection, then this ***"undertaking"*** may impose a duty to act non-negligently, just as under the common law (see *supra*, p. 202). For example, suppose the state takes ***physical custody*** of P, as where P is a prisoner or has been involuntarily committed to a mental institution. Here, it's clear that the government must take reasonable measures to protect P against physical harm by third persons.

c.   Limitations: Supreme Court decisions over the last few decades have placed two important *limits* on the extent to which suits brought under §1983 can supplement state tort law recoveries.

   i.   Must show actual damage: First, compensatory damages may not be awarded based on the abstract *value* or *importance* of the constitutional rights that were violated.

   Example: P, a teacher, is dismissed from his public school teaching post in violation of his First Amendment right to academic freedom. *Held*, P may not recover "presumed" damages under §1983, only "actual" damages such as emotional distress, loss of wages, etc. *Memphis Community School Dist. v. Stachura*, 477 U.S. 299 (1986).

   ii.   Negligence: Second, where the deprivation of a constitutionally-guaranteed right results from a public official's *negligence* rather than intent, §1983 *may not be used at all*.

   Example: P, a prisoner, is attacked by X, a fellow prisoner. Prior to the attack, a prison guard working for D (the state) negligently fails to heed P's warning that X plans to attack him. *Held*, for D: §1983 protects only against intentional, rather than negligent, deprivations of Due Process. So P has only his state-law tort remedies (which, apparently, don't exist here because of sovereign immunity). *Davidson v. Cannon*, 474 U.S. 344 (1986).

d.   Implied right of action from constitutional provision: Section 1983 allows only actions against state and local government officials, not federal ones. However, when a federal official violates a citizen's constitutional rights, the citizen is often permitted to bring a federal tort-like suit against the official. This occurs because the court finds an ***"implied private right of action"*** for violation of the constitutional provision.

   i.   4th Amendment violation: For example, suppose that a federal law-enforcement official violates P's 4th Amendment right to be free from unreasonable searches and seizures. The Supreme Court has held that P has an implied right to bring a federal civil-damages suit against the official for this violation. See *Bivens v. Six Unknown Named Agents of FBI*, 403 U.S. 388 (1971) (civil suit for money damages allowed against FBI agents for search and arrest made without probable cause).

Quiz Yourself on

MISCELLANEOUS TORTS *(Entire Chapter)*

95. To cash in on the allure of the famous spy Mata Hari, the Madame X Lingerie Company introduces a line of Mata Hari jewelled bras without Mata Hari's permission. Has the Company committed an invasion of privacy? If so, of what sort? _____

96. Mr. Magoo is driving his car when he hits a pedestrian, Elastic Man. Elastic files a personal injury claim against Magoo, claiming he's wheelchair bound. Magoo's insurance investigator doesn't believe Elastic's as injured as he says he is. The investigator gets a tip that Elastic's going to be at the park for a picnic, and sure enough, at the appointed time, Elastic shows up at the park. The investigator sits 50 yards away, taking photographs of Elastic as he runs around and contorts himself into a pretzel. Someone mentions to Elastic that he's being photographed. He sues the investigator for invasion of privacy. Will Elastic recover? If so, for what variety of invasion? _____

97. Vivien Lee is at a Chinese restaurant, and she gets a fortune cookie for dessert. The fortune inside reads: "A phone call tomorrow will make you a millionaire." Thrilled, Vivien stays home all day for the phone call. In the process, she misses her audition for a Civil War movie. The phone call never comes. Furious, she visits her lawyer, Sid Sharky, and he tells her: "You have a valid criminal fraud case against the fortune cookie company." She presses criminal charges against the Phu Yuc Fortune Cookie Company, which produced the fortune. The case is dismissed, and Phu Yuc sues Vivien for malicious prosecution. Will Yuc prevail? _____

98. Hansel and Gretel are law students at the Gingerbread Law School. There is a bar review expo at school, where all the competing bar review courses display their wares on tables in an auditorium, in an attempt to sign up students. Hansel and Gretel are standing at the Barcrusher Bar Review table, avidly listening to a sales pitch. They're just about to sign up, pen in hand, when Wicked Witch walks over to them and says, "Don't sign up for this before you talk to me about <u>my</u> course. My materials are better than these; they work like magic. Anyway, I have free chocolate chip cookies and beer at my table." (Assume that these statement are arguably true — they're not clear misstatements of the facts.) Witch leads them away by the elbow, and they wind up signing up for Witch's course instead of Barcrusher's. What's Barcrusher's best claim against Witch, and will it succeed? _____

99. Dogged, a notorious papparazzo, makes his living photographing celebrities (usually against their will) and selling the photographs to magazines. Peggy Pulchritudinous, a famous movie star, hates publicity, and especially hates to be photographed. Rumors have spread that Peggy, while still married, has been carrying on an affair with one of her co-stars, Siegfried Sensitive. Each night for a week, Peggy and Siegfried go for an evening stroll, sit on their favorite park bench, and have a cup of coffee at a sidewalk cafe. Each of those nights, Dogged snaps at least one picture of the couple doing this, although they ask him to stop. Dogged then causes two of the pictures showing the couple holding hands (one while they are walking down the street, the other while they are sitting at the cafe) to be published in a national magazine. Peggy wishes to bring a tort action against Dogged. Is there any claim she can make successfully, and if so, what? _____

Answers

95. Yes, of the "misappropriation of identity" variety. Appropriation is the defendant's unauthorized use (appropriation) of plaintiff's name or likeness for defendant's own commercial or business purposes. That's what Madame X did, so it's liable. Note that with a celebrity like Mata Hari, the damages will focus on the *reasonable value* of Madame X's use, such that Madame X won't profit from the appropriation.

NOTE: Consent is a valid defense to invasion of privacy; so, if Mata Hari had consented to the use of her identity, her claim would be defeated.

96. No — Elastic will lose. The only plausible invasion-of-privacy claim is for "intrusion on solitude." Intrusion requires intrusion on plaintiff's affairs in a way that would be objectionable to a reasonable person. The intrusion must be into something private; that is, where plaintiff has a reasonable expectation of privacy. That's not the case here; there's no reasonable expectation of privacy in a public park, so there can't be an intrusion.

RELATED ISSUE: Say that the investigator set up a high-powered camera at the top of a ladder at the edge of Elastic's yard, so he could photograph him in his bedroom at night through Elastic's upstairs window. This *would* be an intrusion, since there's a reasonable expectation of privacy in a room not visible from the street.

97. No, probably. Malicious prosecution requires wrongful institution of criminal proceedings against the plaintiff, lack of probable cause, favorable termination for plaintiff, and damages. Here, the "lack of probable cause" element is missing. Probable cause requires a reasonable ground for belief of the accused's guilt. Vivien initiated the proceedings based on Sharky's legal advice that plaintiff was guilty. This was probably enough to give Vivien probable cause to believe in Phu's guilt. Thus, the prima facie case is defeated.

98. Barcrusher's best claim is for interference with prospective advantage, but it'll probably lose. Interference with prospective advantage requires proof of defendant's act, with knowledge and purpose of interference, adversely affecting plaintiff's prospective advantage (a contract is not required). However, anyone can use fair, commercially-acceptable <u>competitive tactics</u> to lure customers away from competitors *before* they sign a contract. That's all Witch did here. As a result, she's not liable.

99. Probably not. Obviously, Peggy would like to allege invasion of privacy. "Invasion of privacy" is not a single tort, but is rather four different torts, three of which might conceivably (but probably would not) apply here. Peggy might claim that her solitude was intruded upon. However, this tort is generally committed only when the defendant has intruded into a private place — here, everything Dogged captured in his photographs was visible to a member of the public, so Peggy will probably not win on this claim. Alternatively, Peggy could claim that her likeness and name had been appropriated. But the problem with this theory is that the tort is usually found to exist only when the defendant makes use of the plaintiff's name or likeness to publicize a product. A newspaper's publication of a photograph of a public figure, even where the item's news value is weak, is unlikely to be held to be the sort of "appropriation" that is protected against.

Finally, Peggy could claim that the details of her private life have been unreasonably publicized. However, the tort does not exist when the material that is publicized is of "legitimate concern to the public." Here, since Peggy is a "voluntary public figure" (she has sought her stardom), probably even the somewhat personal details of her romantic life would be held to be of legitimate public concern. Also, the First Amendment might prevent

514   Ch. 18 — MISCELLANEOUS TORTS

states from making Dogged liable on these facts. So in summary, Peggy probably loses on all three of her invasion of privacy claims. See Rest. 2d, §§652B, 652C & 652D.

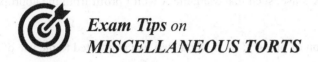

Exam Tips on MISCELLANEOUS TORTS

Most of the torts in this chapter will appear on exams only as "minor" torts thrown into fact patterns that also involve the "major" torts from other chapters. For instance, the various "invasion of privacy" torts are most likely to be encountered in the same fact pattern as defamation and intentional infliction of emotional distress.

☛ The various *"invasion of privacy"* torts are overwhelmingly the torts from this chapter that you're most likely to be tested on.

☞ You'll get very little credit for just noting that P may be able to sue for "invasion of privacy." The four types are so different that to get credit for spotting the issue, you've got to identify the right one.

☞ Memorize this simplified list of definitions:

❑ *"Appropriation of identity"* occurs where P's name or likeness has been appropriated by D for D's financial benefit, without P's consent.

❑ *"Intrusion on solitude"* occurs where D invades P's private space in a manner which would be highly offensive to a reasonable person in P's position.

❑ *"Publicity of private life"* or *"public disclosure"* occurs where D publicly discloses a non-public detail of P's private life, if the effect would be highly offensive to a reasonable person in P's position.

❑ *"False light"* occurs where D publishes false statements about P which, although not defamatory, would be highly offensive to a reasonable person in P's position.

☞ For *"appropriation of identity,"* you're typically looking for an *advertisement* that claims that P uses or endorses the product.

☞ P doesn't have to be a public figure or celebrity to win.

☞ It's no defense that the statement is true. (*Example:* P, a famous comedian, says on TV, "I always smoke X-Brand cigars." X Co. takes out ads saying, "P smokes only our brand." X is liable.)

☞ If the disclosure is *"newsworthy,"* that's a defense. However, this defense is usually available only to "news stories," not "advertisements," so anything that looks like an endorsement probably won't qualify for this exception. (*Example:* If the *National Enquirer* runs a photo of a famous comedian on the cover as part of a news story about the comedian's problems, the fact that the newspaper is "using" the comedian's likeness to sell newspapers is irrelevant — the "newsworthy" defense applies.)

☞ The "newsworthy" exception applies even if the item is of interest only to a small portion of the viewers/readers.

☞ P doesn't have to show that D had "malice" of any sort, even if P is a public figure or public official.

☞ For *"intrusion on solitude,"* look for a *physical entry* into P's *private place* (typically a *home*, *office* or *vehicle*). (*Example:* D breaks into P's office, rifles through P's desk or safe, and copies down information found there.)

☞ Make sure the intrusion would be *"highly offensive* to a reasonable person." (*Example:* If D is a reporter who interviews P at her home, then without permission goes into P's bathroom to snoop, this probably doesn't meet the "highly offensive" test.)

☞ So long as there has been the requisite physical entry, the information does *not* have to be *publicized* in order for the tort to occur — the intrusion itself constitutes the tort.

☞ Surveillance of P done from and in a *public place* doesn't qualify. (*Example:* "Paparazzi" who dog P and shoot her photo constantly while she is in public aren't committing the tort.) If binoculars or telescopes are used from a public place to peer into P's house through a window, this probably qualifies (since it's certainly "highly offensive to a reasonable person").

☞ For *"publicity of private life,"* look for the disclosure of *details* that are highly private (and that a reasonable person would find highly offensive to have disclosed). (*Example:* The precise details of a minor celebrity's sexual preferences and sexual habits would probably qualify.)

☞ The fact that the details are true (and thus the publication is not defamatory) is irrelevant, and in fact this tort is almost always committed by accurate disclosures.

☞ Most commonly-tested aspect: The detail must not be anywhere in the *public record*. If it's in the public record (even buried away where no one except a reporter has ever noticed it), this is a defense. (*Example:* If the county real estate records disclose how much P paid for his house and how much he pays in property taxes, this information can be disclosed, even though a reasonable person would find it very offensive and even though no member of the public has ever known the information before.)

☞ Also, if the item is of *"legitimate public concern,"* that's a defense. (*Example:* If P is now on trial for theft, or is now running for public office, the fact that many years ago P was accused of theft by a former boss is probably of "legitimate public concern.")

☞ For *"false light,"* look for a fact pattern in which P is not defamed, but some *untrue statement* about P is published. Often, this statement will make P "look *better*" than the truth would have. (*Example:* P is falsely said to have been a hero, or to have won a prize.)

☞ The statement need not be defamatory.

☞ The main issue is whether the reasonable person would be *"highly offended."* "Embarrassed" isn't enough. (*Example:* A false statement that P has won a door prize or raffle probably isn't sufficient.)

☞ If P is a *public figure*, P must show *"actual malice"* (that D either knew the statement was false or recklessly disregarded its truth). (Cite to *Time v. Hill* on this point.)

    ☞ Undecided issue: The Supreme Court has never said whether P has to show "actual malice" where P is a *private figure*. Point out this uncertainty if your fact pattern involves a private figure.

☛ The *"misuse of legal procedure"* torts (malicious prosecution, wrongful use of civil proceedings and abuse of process) are rarely tested. Just try to memorize the basic definitions and scenarios for these torts.

☛ The three "business torts" are also not often tested.

☞ If D makes false statements disparaging P's goods or services, that's *"injurious falsehood."*

☞ If D *induces X to breach an existing contract* which X has with P, that's *"interference with contract."*

    ☞ If the contract is *"at will"* (terminable at any time on little or no notice), courts are split about whether and when D can be liable for interfering with it. If D is acting out of spite, or to drive P out of business, D is probably liable; but if D is just offering a better price or better deal to get the business for himself, he is probably not liable.

☞ If D interferes with P's chance to make a contract (or otherwise do business) with X in the *future*, that's *"interference with prospective advantage."* Basically the same rules apply as for interference with existing contract, except that D has a broader set of privileges to use as defenses. (*Example:* If D is *competing*, that's clearly protected by the privilege, whereas D's desire to compete is not protected by the privilege where an existing non-at-will contract is involved.)

ESSAY EXAM
QUESTIONS AND ANSWERS

The following questions were asked on various Harvard Law School First-Year Torts examinations. The questions are reproduced as they actually appeared, with only slight modifications. The sample answers are not "official" and represent merely one approach to handling the questions. The page references in parentheses are to the main text of the outline.

QUESTION 1: At points where a trail entered his property in a sparsely settled area, Farmer posted signs warning, "No trespassing. Snowmobilers and other unauthorized persons keep off. Violators assume all risks." Boisterous intruders continued to run snowmobiles through his property at night. Farmer then erected a barbed wire barrier across the trail at each edge of his property and again about 100 yards in from each edge. He piled brush over the two barbed wire barriers at the edges of the property, but left the barbed wire uncovered at the barriers farther in. Joyce, operating a snowmobile owned by Jimmy, her passenger, maneuvered around a barrier at the edge of Farmer's property, returned to the trail, and while proceeding at high speed, crashed into one of the inner barriers. Joyce, not having her seat belt fastened, was thrown off the snowmobile into a snowbank, unhurt. The snowmobile, uncontrolled, crashed into Farmer's barn, a quarter of a mile off the trail, and started a fire. Jimmy unfastened his seat belt and dragged himself away from the fire, severely injured. Farmer rushed out to the barn and tried to control the fire. Joyce appeared, discovered Jimmy's condition, and asked Farmer to take them to the nearest hospital, 40 miles away. When Farmer refused and continued his efforts to control the fire, Joyce, threatening Farmer with a knife, took Farmer's car keys and forced Farmer to help carry Jimmy to Farmer's car. Joyce then drove Jimmy to the hospital, where Jimmy was found to be suffering from exposure as well as the injuries from the crash. Farmer returned to the barn to fight the fire, but without success.

What torts? Explain.

QUESTION 2: During his 63rd year, defendant D's wife died and he retired on his social security and a small pension. He moved out of the house he had lived in with his family for 35 years, into a smaller wood frame one in a residential neighborhood. About a year later, he became aware that an ailanthus tree was growing into the brick foundation. He consulted a friend who was a small time building contractor, and was told that unless he did something about the tree he would eventually have to replace that part of the foundation, at a cost of at least $50,000. He then called a local company that was in the business of pruning and removing trees. They told him that it would cost him about $10,000 to have the tree cut down and taken away.

$10,000 was his income for a month, so he decided to do the job himself. He was in good health. He owned a chain saw and some ropes, and he had often spent his lunch hour watching tree surgeons at work. The tree was about 30 feet high, but he knew that ailanthus wood is light and weak, being mainly water.

From his attic window, he tied a rope around an upper branch and then went outside and cut through about six of the 12 inches of the trunk. He pulled on the rope, in order to cause the tree to fall away from the street, along the side of his house, and into his back yard. What he didn't realize was that he had made the cut on the wrong side of the tree (only an expert would have known this) so that, given its angle and the distribution of its foliage, the natural direction of its fall was toward the street. The tree wouldn't budge, no matter how hard he pulled on the rope, and he found himself quickly out of breath and a little dizzy. He picked up the chain saw and cut further into the trunk, until he realized that the tree had begun to fall — toward the street! He tried to push it back and over into the right direction. He would probably have succeeded had he been a vigorous young man of 20. But he was too weak, and the tree fell into the street, severing an electric power line.

The power line had been put up twenty years before the accident by the Power Company, acting under technical specifications that had been approved by the state power regulatory commission. Two years before the accident, the regulatory commission had approved the Power Company's proposal to replace all old power lines with new ones. The new model is strong enough to withstand the impact and the weight of a tree like that which D cut down. But at the time of the accident the company had fallen six months behind in the implementation of the replacement program. Had it not been for the delay, a new wire would already have been installed on D's block.

It was a Sunday afternoon, and normally there would have been little if any traffic in D's street. But it happened that P, an out of town motorist who had gotten lost, came down the street just as the tree was falling. If he had been obeying the 20 m.p.h. speed limit, instead of going 25, it wouldn't have hit him, but it did. He was very frightened but unhurt by the impact. The roof of his car was dented. He slammed on the brakes and jumped out, stepping on the live power line and electrocuting himself.

His widow sues both D and the Power Company for the damage to her husband and to the car. Assume that she has the same rights her husband would have had if he had been injured instead of killed (i.e., there is no problem about interpreting a wrongful death statute in this case). Discuss the pros and cons of the issues that will arise in the case.

QUESTION 3: In the early 2010s the Dow Drug Company developed a compound called XYZ, which its researchers hoped would prove effective in treating certain unusual blood diseases. By 2016, after experimentation with almost a thousand human subjects, the drug was approved by government authorities for distribution to only a few specially qualified physicians, who would themselves inject it into patients. Dr. Mary Jones, a specialist in blood diseases who practices in Ames City, is qualified to administer the drug. She became fully apprised of the drug's potentialities and side effects through the instructions sent to physicians by Dow with the drug. The instructions noted that short-term adverse side-effects were judged to be relatively slight — nausea, light-headedness, and blurring of vision, all normally expected to pass within five to ten hours after the drug was injected. The blurring of sight was related by experimenters to very slight hemorrhaging of the retina, and there was thought to be a theoretical possibility (not realized with any experimental subject) of more serious hemorrhaging and eye damage, particularly after repeated injections. Also, a handful of the experimental subjects reported continued nausea lasting on and off over a period of months, even from a single injection.

Early in 2018 Fred Smith, a 32-year-old construction worker, was referred to Dr. Jones by his family physician. Smith was afflicted with Price's syndrome, a rare condition of the blood for which no recognized treatment was available. Smith complained of characteristic symptoms of the Syndrome: a constant dull aching throughout his body and phases of debilitating listlessness which interfered with his work so much that he feared he might be fired.

After a thorough examination, Dr. Jones explained that there was no recognized treatment for his illness but added that a new drug just on the market might conceivably prove to be the answer, though no one could tell for sure. Smith, stating that he didn't want to spend the rest of his life feeling poorly and uncertain about employment, concluded that if the doctor thought this drug might work, he would try it. Dr. Jones replied that "on balance" she thought it worthwhile to go ahead. She injected Smith with the recommended dose of XYZ. Dr. Jones then said that, though the side-effects of the drug were apparently limited to "some mild discomfort that passes in a matter of hours," the drug still was "experimental", and therefore they should monitor its effects closely. Smith agreed to come back for a check-up the following week.

That night Smith was troubled by nausea, but he felt fine the next morning as he set out in his car to drive to the construction site where he worked. While on a little-travelled three-lane highway, Smith rounded a curve and saw that his lane was blocked by a stopped car about 50 yards ahead.

The car belonged to Elmer Brown, a senior official of the Ames City Health Department. Brown was to deliver the main address in one hour at a special state-wide meeting of health officers called to discuss the grave public health problems caused by recent heavy rains and flooding. His car's right rear tire had blown out. Brown's travelling companion had advised Brown to pull off the road before trying to change the tire, but Brown had rejoined that the side of the road was so muddy that they would probably get stuck there. As Smith approached, Brown was working furiously to change the tire, knowing that his chances of arriving on time for his lecture were decreasing.

When Smith saw the Brown car he maintained his speed but started to pull out into the middle lane to pass. There was no on-coming traffic. But at that moment Smith suddenly suffered serious retinal hemorrhaging and near total loss of vision. He hit the brakes but couldn't control direction or avoid a glancing collision with Brown's car.

Both cars were damaged in the collision, and both Smith and Brown were hospitalized with fractures. Tests showed that Smith's impairment of vision was irreversible.

Discuss the tort actions that Smith and Brown might bring. The State of Ames, where the relevant events occurred, is a common-law jurisdiction with respect to auto accidents; the Ames courts follow the rule of "pure" (not "partial") comparative negligence.

QUESTION 4: Prime Textiles Corporation purchased a 30-year-old building in an industrial section of Amesville in late 2019 and converted its interior to a plant for the manufacture of brightly colored fabrics to be sold to dress manufacturers. Prime has been a successful innovator in designs and even in a year of recession shows a handsome profit. Its sales are at an annual rate of about $120 million, and it employs 400 workers and technicians at this, its only plant.

In early 2020, Dead-em Insecticides, Inc., constructed for $80 million a plant in the same industrial section of Amesville, five blocks (1/4 mile) distant from Prime. It employs 200 workers and technicians. Dead-em is a leading producer of insecticides for use against household pests — bees, roaches, etc. In 2021 it developed a new and commercially successful product, Strike, that has proved to be remarkably effective while meeting all safety requirements. The new process of manufacture necessarily involves the emission of gases and other by-products different in chemical composition from the by-products of the manufacture of the earlier type of insecticides.

By mid-2022, Prime began to receive complaints from its vendees that the colors on about 1/2 of its fabrics were not proving "true" or "fast." They faded after several months, and some took on a different tint. After investigation, Prime determined that the recent gaseous emissions from Dead-em had permeated its building and adversely affected certain of the dyes that it used for coloring fabrics.

Prime has retained your firm to advise it of what recourse it has against Dead-em. Your preliminary inquiry reveals the following additional information. (1) No other industrial producer in this section of Amesville has been adversely affected by these emissions. (2) The alternatives open to Prime, if it has no recourse against Dead-em, are to abandon a profitable and important part of its production involving certain standard, adversely affected dyes; to remove at great and perhaps prohibitive expense to another location; or to renovate its building (doors, windows, year-round air conditioning) to exclude the interfering gases. This last alternative would cost about $20 million, a serious expenditure that, in a competitive industry, would sharply reduce profits. (3) Prime's 2003 loss of profits (on many warranty claims from its vendees and then reduced sales) is estimated at $5 million.

The senior partner in your firm requests a memorandum outlining (a) the possible legal recourse against Dead-em, (b) your analysis of the difficulties in litigation and assessment of the chances of success, and (c) your recommendation of how Prime should proceed. No recent decision of the Supreme Court of Ames addresses this type of problem.

ANSWERS

SAMPLE ANSWER 1: I will discuss the possible torts in the chronological order in which they occurred.

Trespass by Joyce and Jimmy: It seems clear that both Joyce and Jimmy have committed a trespass on Farmer's land. As trespassers, they are liable for virtually all consequences (p. 41), probably including the burning of the barn (even if this was not foreseeable, and even if it was not the result of any negligence). Even though Jimmy was not the driver, he will almost certainly be held to have actively participated in the trespass, and he will be ***jointly and severally liable*** with Joyce for the barn-burning.

However, if Farmer is found to have committed a battery, this might constitute a superseding cause relieving Joyce and Jimmy of liability.

Nuisance by Joyce and Jimmy: Farmer could sue Joyce and Jimmy on a private nuisance theory, since they (in combination with other snowmobilers) substantially interfered with his use and enjoyment of his property. However, in view of his trespass claim, it is unlikely that Farmer would bother to assert nuisance.

Battery by Farmer: The use of the barriers by Farmer might be a ***battery*** against Jimmy and Joyce, if they can show that Farmer either intended to cause the contact with their bodies or snowmobile, or knew that such a contact was substantially certain to follow (p. 6). In trying to prove this, Joyce and Jimmy will want to point to the fact that the outer barriers were covered up, which indicates that Farmer was trying to hurt snowmobilers, not merely keep them out. On the other hand, Farmer could show that the barrier that was crashed into was uncovered, and could claim that he was just trying to keep people off the trail once they got onto the property.

In any event, Farmer is certainly likely to assert that he was ***privileged*** to erect the barriers, to prevent trespass. To sustain this privilege, he will have to show that he used no greater degree of forced than seemed reasonably necessary, and that this force was ***not deadly*** (i.e., not likely to cause death or serious bodily injury). Since Farmer knew that most of the snowmobiling took place at night, on what are presumably unlit trails, the use of such barriers does seem likely to cause serious harm. If so, the case would be similar to *Katko v. Briney* (p. 75), and there would be no privilege, since Farmer's own safety, and the sanctity of his dwelling, were not in danger.

Even if Farmer succeeds in showing that the barrier should not be considered deadly force, he may lose his privilege by virtue of his failure to ***warn*** of the device's existence (p. 76).

Negligence by Farmer in erecting barrier: Even if the erection of the barrier is not a battery by Farmer, it might be ***negligence*** on his part, if it constituted a failure to use ordinary care. However, the duty of care owed by a landowner to trespassers is limited.

Jimmy and Joyce might be found to have been "constant trespassers on a limited area" (the trail), in which case Farmer would have at least a duty to warn them of dangers they were unlikely to discover for themselves (p. 240), of which the barrier is probably an instance. Alternatively, if Jimmy and Joyce are children (the question does not indicate whether they are), Farmer might have a duty of care towards them, if he knew that many of the snowmobilers typically were children (p. 242).

Even if Farmer were found to have been negligent, Jimmy might be held to have assumed the risk, or to have been contributorily negligent. These defenses are discussed in the treatment of his suit against Joyce, below.

Negligence by Joyce towards Jimmy: Joyce's conduct in driving at high speeds was probably negligent as to Jimmy. However, she will be able to assert several defenses based on his own conduct. First, he may be held to have ***assumed the risk***. Normally one assumes the risk only as to ***particular*** risks that one is aware of; however, in this instance, Jimmy might be held to have assumed the risk of unknown dangers (p. 295), especially ones that are incident to a dangerous activity like snowmobiling in the dark. However, even if Jimmy assumed the risk of a barrier, he did not necessarily assume the risk that Joyce would drive at high speeds; this would be a question of fact, turning on whether she had driven fast on other occasions with him, giving him reason to know that she was likely to do so again.

Alternatively, Jimmy may have been ***contributorily negligent*** in riding with Joyce. Again, this is likely to turn on whether he knew that she would drive too fast, or had an opportunity to get off when he saw that this was the case.

Lastly, there may be an ***automobile guest statute*** broad enough to include snowmobiles (e.g., a statute including "all motorized recreational vehicles), which would allow Jimmy to recover only if Joyce was "grossly" or "wantonly" negligent.

Assuming that Joyce is liable for negligence, she would certainly be liable for Jimmy's injuries from the collision. She may also be liable for his ***exposure*** injuries. She will argue that the exposure injuries are the direct result of Farmer's refusal to help, which should be treated as a superseding intervening cause. However, it seems probable that the exposure would be held to be reasonably foreseeable, even if Farmer's intransigence was not; the case would then fall under the rule that where the harm was foreseeable, and the manner of its occurrence not, there is liability (p. 160).

Negligence by Farmer in his refusal to help Jimmy: Farmer's refusal to aid Jimmy might be negligence. The general rule is that one has no duty to rescue a stranger, even when this could be done at little danger to oneself. (p. 198). However, since Jimmy's injuries were the result of an instrument under Farmer's control, this would probably be enough to give rise to a duty on the part of Farmer to render reasonable assistance (p. 201).

But even if Farmer had such a duty to give reasonable assistance, he may have been privileged not to so do because of his right to preserve his property (by fighting the fire). This question would depend on what a reasonable person would have done in the circumstances; normally human life is considered more important than property, but since Joyce was available to take Jimmy to the hospital, Farmer may have behaved reasonably. A court might also hold that Farmer's duty of care was lessened because of the fact that Jimmy was a trespasser (although this would contradict the rule that once a landowner discovers a particular trespasser on his property, he must behave with ordinary reasonable care towards him; p. 241).

Assault by Joyce: Joyce's use of the knife to threaten Farmer is probably a prima facie case of ***assault***. Joyce's threat was a ***conditional*** one, but the general rule is that this is still an assault unless she had the legal right to make Farmer comply with the threat (by taking Jimmy to the hospital) (p. 16). She had such a right only if this fell within Farmer's duty of reasonable care, an open question as discussed above. In any case, even if she did have a legal right to compel him to take Jimmy, her use of a knife may have constituted an unreasonably violent way of accomplishing this result. (See paragraph J(1)(a), p. 16).

Conversion or trespass to chattels by Joyce: Joyce's use of Farmer's car to take Jimmy to the hospital may have been either conversion or trespass to chattels. It will be the latter rather than the former unless the inconvenience and harm to Farmer was substantial, which the question does not indicate it to have been.

Assuming that there was at most merely trespass to chattels, even this may fall within Joyce's privilege of ***private necessity***. This will be so if there was no better way of getting Jimmy to the hospital. (p. 80).

SAMPLE ANSWER 2:

(1) P vs. D: P can pursue two general lines of attack against D: negligence and strict liability. After discussing these two, I will discuss the proximate cause issues that are common to both. (I will treat the plaintiff as being P, rather than his widow, for simplicity).

Negligence suit against D: In order to establish a negligence cause of action against D, P must first show that D bore him a duty of care. This should not be hard to do, since a landowner's duty to persons outside the premises is generally one of reasonable care, at least where an activity, rather than a natural hazard, is concerned.

Assuming that D had the duty to behave as a reasonable person would, the principle issue is whether D should be held to the standard of care of persons habitually engaged in tree surgery (i.e., *experts*), or the standard of care of a non-expert. (Disposition of this issue is obviously critical, since by cutting on the wrong side of the tree, D violated the former standard but not the latter)

In arguing for imposition of a "reasonable expert" standard, P can point out that the whole reason most tree surgery is done by experts is that it is a dangerous activity if not done correctly, and society has a strong interest in not being forced to run the risk of bungling amateurs. A person who performed medical surgery would certainly be held to the standard of a reasonable doctor, whether she had a license to practice medicine or not; similarly, a child who engages in dangerous activities usually pursued by adults will be held to an adult standard of care (p. 104). P can make a strong argument that these principles should be extended to impose on D the standard of care which would be shown by a reasonable tree surgeon.

In response to this, D can argue that imposing a higher standard on him than that of a reasonable non-expert landowner would be grossly unfair. There was no way he himself could have met such a standard, since by definition it is one met only by experts. Nor did he behave unreasonably in not going to an expert, since to do so would have cost him a month's income, and the risk of accident did not seem to justify such a painful expenditure. Furthermore, D can contend, this situation is different from that of the unlicensed person holding herself out as a doctor; D has not represented to any one that he is an expert, and no one has relied on any indication of expertise.

Assuming that D is held to an ordinary reasonable person standard, and was therefore not negligent in the way he cut the tree, it could still be argued that he was negligent in not pushing the tree back in the right direction once it started to fall. Normally a person's physical attributes (in this case, his weakness and age) are taken into account, and not held against him, in determining what constitutes reasonable conduct. (p. 100.) But the fact that D was weak, and not equipped to deal with an emergency, may be a factor indicating that it was not reasonable care on his part to start the cutting process in the first place; certain activities require an ability to react well in an emergency, and the actor will be negligent if he performs them without this capacity (e.g., a bus driver with slow reflexes; see p. 107).

Strict liability for abnormally dangerous activity: As a second line of attack, P can argue that tree surgery in this situation was an ***abnormally dangerous activity***, and that D should be strictly liable for the resulting accident. However, it is usually held that this kind of liability will apply only where the activity is such that substantial risk cannot be eliminated even by due care. Since a professional tree surgeon could probably have brought down the tree with almost no risk of this kind of accident, this condition seems not to be met.

Proximate cause: For each of these theories, P will have to establish that D's conduct was the proximate cause of his harm. To do this, he will have to overcome a number of hurdles.

First, D will contend that damage to the power lines was not a foreseeable result of his activity. But from the sound of things, given that P was negligent (or that the activity was abnormally dangerous), the risk of damaging power lines seems to be within the "cluster" of risks that made the conduct negligent or ultrahazardous.

But even if damage to the power lines was foreseeable, and thus a proximate result of D's conduct, it doesn't follow that the damage to P's car was also foreseeable. This was a sparsely travelled street, and there was very little danger that a motorist would happen to be passing by when the tree fell. D could plausibly argue that P was really in a *Palsgraf*-like position, an essentially "unforeseeable plaintiff." But P could convincingly argue that the Third Restatement's test should be applied: D will escape liability on proximate-cause grounds only if the harm was "different from the harms whose risk made [D's] conduct tortious." Here, the risks that make it negligent to cut a tree so that it falls onto the public road almost certainly include the risk that the tree will fall on a passing car, so D's negligence ought to be viewed as the proximate cause of the collision with P's car.

However, even assuming that D's act was the proximate cause of the damage to the car, it does not by any means follow that D is also the proximate cause of P's death. D will start by contending that he never imposed an unreasonable risk of bodily harm on P at all, and that P is in a *Palsgraf*-like position with respect to his personal injuries, even if he was not in such a position with respect to the damage to his car. However, D will probably lose with this *Palsgraf* argument; the court is likely to hold that once P was placed in danger for his personal property from a falling tree, he thus established himself as a foreseeable plaintiff, and any other harm arising to him in the same general episode would be D's responsibility. This result could be supported by analogy to those cases allowing recovery for negligent infliction of emotional distress to a parent who sees a child harmed, and who is himself within the "zone of danger" (i.e, put in risk of bodily harm); see p. 213.

Next, D has a string of several "superseding intervening cause" arguments. First, he can try to blame the whole accident on Power Co., for having delayed in putting in a power line that would have withstood the tree. But this contention is very unlikely to succeed; Power Co.'s negligence was almost certainly not "gross," and its ordinary negligence is unlikely to be considered a superseding cause. (The most this argument will get D is joint-and-several liability with Power Co.)

Then, D can claim that P's travelling above the speed limit was a superseding cause (or, alternatively, contributory negligence per se). But this argument is not likely to work either. P's fast driving did not increase the danger of the accident, at least as far as anyone observing from P's position before the accident would have been able to tell. (See the discussion of *Marshall v. Nugent*, p. 163).

Lastly, D can contend that P's leaving the car and stepping on a live power line was an irrational and bizarre act which should be superseding (or, alternatively, that it was contributory negligence). He could point to Illustration 2, §445 of the Second Restatement, which indicates that where a passenger, after being frightened by a near collision, panics, opens the door, and throws out her child, this is a superseding act for which the person who has caused the near-miss is not responsible. (See p. 165.) But P ought to be able to distinguish this example fairly easily, by stating that he merely got out of the car as a reasonable person would have, and didn't notice the power line. In any event, this was an emergency of sorts, and P should only have to live up to the standards of a reasonable person in such an emergency (p. 106), which he probably did.

All in all, unless D succeeds in showing that he should be held to the standard of care of a reasonable non-expert, not a reasonable tree-surgeon, he is likely to be held liable for both the damage to the car and P's death.

(2) P vs. Power Co.: P may proceed against Power Co. under either a negligence or a strict products liability theory. And there is a remote possibility that he might succeed on a "strict liability for abnormally dangerous activities" theory.

Negligence: In order to establish that Power Co. was negligent, and that this negligence was a proximate cause of his damages, P will have many hurdles to overcome.

First, Power Co. will argue that the regulatory commission's approval of the technical specifications conclusively established that its conduct met the standard of reasonable care. While such compliance will probably not be conclusive on this issue, in the same way that a statutory violation would conclusively establish "negligence per se," the court might consider this compliance as *evidence* that Power Co. met reasonable standards of care. (p. 120.) But it would do even this only on a showing that these technical specifications were drafted after consideration of safety needs imposed by possible storms, rotten trees, etc.

Even if Power Co.'s conduct was reasonably careful twenty years ago, however, this does not mean that it did not later become negligent by not replacing the power line. As stronger materials became available, the durability of the minimum reasonable installation surely increased; the question then becomes whether there is an obligation to go to the expense of substituting the newly-available materials. This question has generally been answered affirmatively in highway design cases, in which states have been held to be under an obligation to use newly-developed safe-design knowledge to remodel old roads now known to be unduly dangerous. (See p. 105.)

Even if Power Co.'s delayed installation of the new lines would not otherwise be negligence, it may have become "negligence per se" once the plan was approved by the regulatory commission, and then not followed. (This assumes that the commission approved not only the overall plan, but also the timetable, which was not met). Power Co. could counter this negligence per se argument by contending that its new program went far beyond the requirements of reasonable care, and that it should not be penalized for adopting an ambitious plan. Also, the court might hold that an administrative body's determination should not be accorded the same deference as the legislature's safety statutes.

Proximate cause: To show that Power Co.'s negligence (if established) was the proximate cause of the damage to the car, it will not be necessary for P to show that this particular accident (i.e., bad tree surgery) was reasonably foreseeable. The risk that trees might fall for other reasons (e.g., storms), was itself substantial, and this accident would probably be held to be an illustration of the principle that where a foreseeable kind of harm occurs in an unforeseeable manner, there will be liability. See, for instance, *Gibson v. Garcia*, p. 168, in which the defendant was held liable for a negligently maintained wooden pole next to the street, where it was knocked over by an unforeseeable car accident.

Power Co.'s next line of defense would be that even if it was negligent with respect to damage to the car, it was not negligent with respect to danger of electrocution. But again, danger of some sort of electrocution was probably one of the risks that made the conduct negligent in the first place, so the fact that this may have occurred in an unforeseeable manner (i.e., panic as the result of being hit by a tree) would not be enough to be a superseding cause.

Power Co. could try to blame the whole thing on D's negligence, arguing that his negligence contributed so much more directly to the accident that he should be the only one to be liable. But since Power Co.'s negligence was clearly a "but for" cause of the accident, and otherwise appears to have been a proximate cause of it, D's own negligence (surely not "gross" negligence) is unlikely to get it off the hook. The best that Power Co. can hope for from this argument is the right to ***contribution*** from D, according to an estimate of their relative degrees of fault.

Lastly, Power Co. can, like D, argue that P's speeding was the superseding cause, since he wouldn't have been electrocuted if he had been within the speed limit (since he wouldn't have been hit by the tree, and therefore not have gotten out of the car). But this argument is no more likely to succeed for Power Co. than for D; P's speeding did not increase the perceivable risk of the electrocution, so it will not even be contributory negligence, let alone a superseding cause.

Strict products liability: P might try to argue that the Power Co. line was a "defective" product, and that Power Co. should have strict tort liability for it.

Normally, some kind of sale, rental or other transfer has been necessary for strict products liability. Here, since Power Co. has simply put up the power line for its own purposes, such a transaction seems to be missing. But D can argue that Power Co. was supplying a service (electricity) and should have strict liability for any physical product used in supplying that service. (He could analogize to *Newmark v. Gimbel's*, the beauty shop case, p. 402). Then, the argument would continue, Power Co. would be liable to P as a "bystander", just as a car maker would be liable to a pedestrian injured by a defective car.

But even if a court were willing to extend strict products liability to this considerable extent, this probably wouldn't get P too far. He would still have to show that the product was "defective," and to do so, he would probably have to make the same kind of showing that the benefits of the new, stronger, lines outweighed their costs, that he would have to make in a negligence action. He might draw some support from the many cases holding that a design is defective if it doesn't meet a reasonable consumer's expectations as to safety (p. 373); he might be able to show that the average driver or homeowner reasonably believed that a power line would withstand having a fairly light tree fall on it, or that it would go dead once severed.

Abnormally dangerous activity: Lastly, there is a very small chance that D might be able to establish that weak power lines constituted an abnormally dangerous activity, giving rise to strict liability. P could point, for instance, to *Lubin v. Iowa City*, 131 N.W.2d 765 (Iowa 1965), holding that a town which buries water mains and intentionally leaves them there till they start leaking has such strict liability. However, this case seems to be distinguishable on the grounds that it involved a danger which was almost certain to materialize, whereas the power lines were not at all certain to be hit by a falling tree.

SAMPLE ANSWER 3:

Smith v. Dow Drug: Smith can bring a ***products liability*** claim against Dow Drug. Unless he can prove negligence in the testing procedures, he will have to proceed on either a strict liability or implied warranty cause of action. Because of possible privity problems with a warranty claim, this strict tort liability claim looks like his best bet, and this is what I will consider.

Smith will have to demonstrate that the product was ***"defective"***. Dow will undoubtedly argue that even if the product was dangerous, it was ***"unavoidably dangerous,"*** since extensive experimentation failed to disclose the danger. The question is really whether the product's safety should be judged as of the state of medical knowledge at the time it was given to Dr. Jones, or as of the time of trial. (p. 360.) Most courts would probably hold that the former is the time for evaluating the danger, and that the product was therefore unavoidably unsafe.

Dow can also point out that it was not engaged in mass distribution of the drug, but merely a new level of carefully supervised experimental testing. Particularly since this testing stage was approved by the government, Dow can make a powerful claim that it should not be held liable; otherwise, it would be impossible to test a drug sufficiently to market it. On the effect of government approval of the drug, Dow could assert a "regulatory compliance" defense, recognized by some courts, which would shield it from liability since XYZ was approved by an appropriate government agency (p. 380).

Warning: Smith can also contend that even if the product was otherwise unavoidably unsafe, Dow at least bore the duty of giving an adequate warning of possible bad side effects. It is usually held that a drug manufacturer has no duty to warn of bad side effects of which it is unaware at the time of sale (p. 384). But since Dow was aware of at least the theoretical possibility of retinal hemorrhaging, it might well be held that it had a duty to warn of this possibility. (I am assuming that severe retinal hemorrhaging was not mentioned to Dr. Jones as a possibility, although the question is unclear on this issue.)

Smith may also contend that it was not enough that the warning was transmitted to Dr. Jones, and that Dow had an obligation to see that the patient himself received the warning. However, this argument is unlikely to prevail; it is usually held that a warning to the dispensing doctor is sufficient (the "learned intermediary" doctrine).

If Smith does make out his prima facie case that the product was defective, he will probably also be able to establish that the defect was a proximate cause of both his impairment of vision and the accident. As to the latter, even if the danger of severe hemorrhaging was only theoretical, there was a well-established danger of blurring vision; the accident would then fall within the principle that where the harm is foreseeable, but occurs in an unforeseeable manner, it is a proximate result. (See p. 160.) It is possible, however, that the court will apply a narrower standard of proximate cause in a case based upon strict liability than in the usual negligence case.

Smith v. Dr. Jones: Smith has two theoretical causes of action against Dr. Jones, one for products liability and the other for malpractice.

He is unlikely to be successful on his products liability claim. Such liability has almost never been imposed on **professionals** who supply a product in the course of rendering a service. See, e.g., the *Magrine* case, p. 402.

Smith has a much stronger case against Dr. Jones for **malpractice** (i.e., professional negligence). Jones does not seem to have acted negligently in recommending the drug's use, since Smith appears to be the sort of candidate for whom its use was indicated. However, Smith has an excellent chance of showing that his **informed consent** was not obtained. (See p. 112.)

Prior to the injection, Smith was not informed of any of the possible side effects. Assuming that Dr. Jones was aware only of the minor side effects, and not of the possibility of severe hemorrhaging, she might be able to persuade the court that these side effects were so minor that a reasonable person in Smith's position would have taken the drug even had he known of them, and that they were therefore not material considerations required for informed consent. On the other hand, Jones' statement that "on balance" she thought the drug would be worth while seems to indicate that she did not regard these side effects as all that trivial, and should therefore have told Smith about them.

Assuming that Jones did not know about the risk of severe hemorrhaging, it seems very unlikely that communication of that risk to Smith was necessary for his informed consent. Informed consent is generally a matter of professional standards, and a professional could hardly be expected to warn of risks that he was not aware of. (Informed consent is not yet a matter of strict liability.) If my assumption that Jones did not know of the theoretical danger of severe hemorrhaging is incorrect, then it seems highly likely that she failed to gain Smith's informed consent. This would seem to be so even though the danger was only "theoretical", since a person in Smith's position, suffering a non-fatal disorder, might well decline to take the drug on account of this danger.

It may also have been negligent of Dr. Jones not to warn of the danger of on-and-off nausea for several months. Again, this is a factor that might well have been material to one in Smith's position. It seems probable that even though this particular risk never materialized in his case, its omission from Jones' description of the drug should be held against her for purposes of determining whether she was negligent. The question ought to be whether, taking all the undisclosed risks together, Smith was given enough information to make a reasonable choice.

If Dr. Jones is found to have been negligent in not obtaining Smith's informed consent, the court will then have to decide whether this negligence was the proximate cause of either the hemorrhaging or the auto accident. It seems likely that it will be a proximate cause of at least the hemorrhaging, since this was one of the risks (although theoretical) the non-disclosure of which was negligent. If this is so, then the car accident also ought to be a proximate result, since it is highly foreseeable that one who suffers a hemorrhage will do so while driving and get into an accident. Furthermore, since there was a danger of blurred vision anyway, the accident would, as noted, fall within the "foreseeable harm but unforeseeable manner" principle, as it would in Smith's case against Dow.

Brown v. Smith: Brown can try to maintain an ordinary negligence action against Smith. His biggest problem will be in showing that Smith was negligent, since there is no indication that Smith had any knowledge of the danger to his vision. Nor is there any indication that Smith was negligent in maintaining his speed when he moved to pass.

If Brown does somehow establish Smith's negligence, he would still be faced with a potent comparative negligence defense by Smith. Brown might be able to combat this by showing that it would have been unreasonable for him to have tried to change the tire at the side of the road, and risk getting stuck, particularly in view of the extreme social importance of his being on time for his speech. (In general, the value of the interest being pursued by the plaintiff will be taken into account in determining whether he was comparatively negligent.)

If there is found to have been comparative negligence, Brown's recovery will be reduced by the proportion which his negligence bears to the combined negligence of Smith and himself. If the jurisdiction is one in which *last clear chance* is still allowed as a defense despite comparative negligence (p. 284), Brown might have a chance at having this doctrine applied. However, it doesn't seem that Smith, suffering as he was from a hemorrhage, really had a last clear chance to avoid the accident.

Brown v. Dow Drug: Brown might bring a strict tort liability claim against Dow. He would have to make the same showing as to defectiveness and lack of warning as Smith would. Beyond that, he would have to convince the court to extend the strict tort doctrine to cover him as a bystander. Most jurisdictions have been willing to make such an extension, particularly where the bystander is a pedestrian or motorist injured in a car accident. (However, most such cases have involved defective automobiles, where the risk of bystander injuries is probably greater than it is from a defective drug.) The proximate cause issue is likely to be resolved the same way as in Smith's suit against Dow for his fracture and the damage to his car.

Brown v. Dr. Jones: If Brown brought a negligence action against Dr. Jones, he would have to establish negligence on the same informed consent basis as would Smith. His biggest obstacle, however, would be in establishing that Dr. Jones bore him a *duty of care*. A court might well hold that even assuming that there was a significant enough danger of hemorrhaging that Jones should have warned Smith of this, the danger to a passing motorist is slimmer, and the motorist might be in a *Palsgraf* position. On the other hand, Brown can point out the fact there was also a danger of an accident occurring through temporarily blurred vision, and that he was a foreseeable victim of such an accident.

Even apart from this, there remains the broader question of whether a doctor should ever be liable for injuries to third persons arising from side effects of a drug (whether or not there was informed consent). Suppose that Dr. Jones had made all required disclosure, and Smith elected to go ahead with the use of the drug; it would certainly seem unfair to hold Jones liable for Brown's injuries in this event. The old *Palsgraf* question arises again: why should Brown be able to take advantage of Jones' negligence (lack of informed consent) vis-à-vis Smith? All in all, it seems unlikely that a court would hold Dr. Jones liable.

SAMPLE ANSWER 4:

Prime can proceed on either a trespass or a nuisance theory. On either of these theories, it can attempt to get compensatory damages for past and/or future harm, as well as an injunction against future wrongdoing by Dead-em.

Trespass: Prime should first try to show that the permeation of its plants by the Dead-em gases constituted a trespass. Until fairly recently, courts refused to recognize that gases and fine particles could constitute a trespassory invasion, and required a suit based on nuisance. But a number of courts now permit a trespass suit in this situation. For instance, in *Martin v. Reynolds Metals*, (p. 43), a suit in trespass was allowed where gases and particles from an aluminum reducing plant ruined the plaintiff's farmland.

To maintain a trespass action, Prime will have to show that the gaseous invasion was "intentional". It will not have to show that Dead-em intended or knew that damage to the dyes would result, but it does have to show that Dead-em knew that the gases would enter the plant (i.e., that the trespassory contact was intentional). This may be difficult (at least prior to Prime's giving notice to Dead-em of the problem), since the two plants are some distance apart.

If the court accepts the argument that there has been a trespass, we should have no problem getting compensatory damages for the lost profits in 2023. Prime may also be able to get an injunction against future trespasses of this nature. It would have to show that permanent compensatory damages (i.e., an estimate of the harm caused in the future) would not be an adequate remedy. If the court is disinclined to give an injunction, there is a good chance that we could get it to award the $20 million required to gas-proof the plant.

Nuisance: If we fail to sustain the trespass theory (e.g., because the court won't recognizes gases as trespassory), we will have to resort to a private nuisance theory. We can certainly satisfy the basic requirement, a showing that Prime's use and enjoyment of its property has been substantially impaired. (See p. 431-432.)

We will also have to show that Dead-em's interference with Prime was either intentional, negligent, or abnormally dangerous. At at some point after Prime discovered the damage, I assume that it made a complaint to Dead-em. As to any damage occurring after this time, we would almost certainly be able to show that the nuisance should be treated as "intentional", since Dead-em knew that the gaseous invasion was occurring. But prior to our giving notice, I think we will have trouble showing that there was either negligence, intent or abnormal danger. We may simply have to write off the $500,000 loss during 1993.

We face several additional hurdles in trying to get prospective damages or an injunction on a nuisance theory. First, Dead-em is almost certain to argue that Prime's manufacturing process constitutes an ***"abnormally sensitive activity,"*** and that it should not be liable for this. Dead-em could cite *Rogers v. Elliott* (p. 432), where a plaintiff who was sent into convulsions by the defendant's church bell was not allowed to recover for nuisance due to his abnormal sensitivity. On the other hand, what constitutes "abnormal" is determined in part by the plaintiff's location; since Prime is located in an industrial area, surely a suitable place in which to run a manufacturing and dying plant, its use might not be held to be abnormally sensitive.

An additional requirement that Prime will have to meet is a showing that Dead-em's interference was "unreasonable." Dead-em will be able to show not only that its plant employs a lot of people, and represents a large investment, but also that there is a substantial social good resulting from its product (i.e., freedom from bugs with safety).

Until the late 20th century, many courts would have simply determined whether the harm to Prime was greater or less than the social utility of Dead-em's product, and if the former was less than the latter, would have refused damages. Now, however, there is an increasing tendency to hold that even if the defendant's conduct has benefits outweighing the detriments to the plaintiff, the defendant must still pay for the harm he causes. This is the view of the Second Restatement (p. 434-434). We would still have to show that requiring Dead-em to pay permanent compensatory damages (probably the $2 million required for gas-proofing) would not put it out of business, but I think we can make this showing.

I don't think we have much of a chance of getting an injunction on a nuisance theory. Here, the court will definitely balance the benefits of Dead-em's product against the harm to us, and I don't think we'll come out ahead. Even though we employ more people than Dead-em, the fact remains that we could keep the same employment merely by investing $20 million, whereas Dead-em would probably be put out of business, or at least have to slash a good portion of its working force (as well as giving up a socially useful product) if the injunction were granted. The court is likely to point to *Boomer v. Atlantic Cement* (p. 436) as authority for denying a permanent injunction.

Final recommendations: In summary, we might as well try both trespass and nuisance theories. We should try to develop facts which will push back as far as possible the date on which Dead-em knew or should have known of the invasion of the plant by its emissions, so that we will be able to get recovery for the 2023 lost profits. We should probably not devote much of our resources to trying to get an injunction, since this seems futile; instead, we should try to recover the $20 million it would take to gas-proof Prime.

MULTISTATE-STYLE QUESTIONS

Here are 30 multiple-choice questions, in a Multistate Bar Exam style. These questions are taken from *"The Finz Multistate Method,"* a compendium of 1100 questions in the Multistate subjects written by the late Professor Steven Finz and published by Aspen Publishing. To learn more about this book and other study aids, go to www.AspenPublishing.com.

1. Prescott, who owned an appliance repair shop, was at a cocktail party when he saw Dresden, one of his competitors. Approaching Dresden, Prescott said, "I'm glad to run into you. I was hoping that we could discuss the possibility of going into partnership instead of competing with each other." Dresden responded, "I wouldn't go into business with you because you're the most incompetent person I've ever known." Audit, a customer of Prescott's, overheard the conversation. As a result, the following day, Audit cancelled a contract which she had with Prescott.

   If Prescott asserts a claim against Dresden for defamation, Prescott will be successful if

   (A) Dresden knew or should have known that the statement was defamatory when he made it.

   (B) Dresden knew or should have known that the statement was false when he made it.

   (C) Dresden knew or should have known that the statement would be overheard when he made it.

   (D) Dresden knew or should have known that harm would result from the statement.

2. Preston purchased a box labeled "Generic Breakfast Cereal" from Riteway Supermarket. While he was eating it, he broke a tooth on a stone which the product contained. The product sold by Riteway and labeled "Generic Breakfast Cereal" is furnished by three different companies: Acme, Birdco, and Cullen. Each sells an approximately equal quantity to Riteway. In addition, all package their product in identical wrappers, so that it is impossible to tell which of them furnished any given box of breakfast cereal. Although the companies compete with each other, at Riteway's request they worked together to design the product wrapper.

   If Preston is successful in an action for damages against Riteway, it will probably be because

   (A) Riteway, Acme, Birdco, and Cullen were involved in a concerted action in the manufacture and marketing of the product.

   (B) Riteway, Acme, Birdco, and Cullen established standards on an industry-wide basis, which standards made identification of the product's manufacturer impossible.

   (C) the negligence of either Acme, Birdco, or Cullen resulted in harm to Preston under circumstances such that it was impossible to tell which of them caused the harm; and Riteway is vicariously liable for that negligence.

   (D) either Acme, Birdco, or Cullen manufactured a defective product, and Riteway sold that product while it was in a defective condition.

Questions 3-4 are based on the following fact situation.

Dan, a thirteen-year-old boy, was a member of Survival Scouts, a national young people's organization. As part of a Survival Scout project, he planned to spend an entire weekend camping alone in the woods. Napper, who knew about the project, phoned Dan's mother Mabe the day after Dan left home. Napper said, "We have your son. We've already beaten him up once, just to hear him scream. Next time, we might kill him." Napper instructed Mabe to deliver a cash ransom to a specified location within one hour. Since there was no way to locate Dan's campsite in the woods, Mabe could not find out whether Napper was telling the truth. Horrified that her son might be beaten and injured or killed, she delivered the ransom as instructed. She remained in a hysterical state until Dan returned from his camping trip, and Mabe realized that the ransom demand had been a hoax. Mabe, who already suffered from a heart ailment, had a heart attack the day after Dan's return.

3. If Mabe asserts a claim against Napper for assault, the court should find for

   (A) Mabe, because Napper was aware that his conduct would frighten her.

   (B) Mabe, because the court will transfer Napper's intent.

   (C) Napper, because Mabe did not perceive injury being inflicted upon Dan.

   (D) Napper, because Mabe had no reason to expect to be touched by Napper.

4. If Mabe asserts a claim against Napper for damages resulting from her heart attack on a theory of intentional infliction of mental distress, the court should find for

   (A) Napper, because the heart attack occurred the day after Dan's return.

   (B) Napper, if Mabe's pre-existing condition made her especially susceptible to heart attack.

   (C) Mabe, if the heart attack was caused by Napper's outrageous conduct.

   (D) Mabe, because Napper should have foreseen that his conduct would result in harm.

5. Dusty was a "crop duster," an occupation which required her to spray insecticides onto growing crops from an airplane which she flew within fifteen feet of the ground. In locating the fields of her customers, she used a map which the county published for that purpose, and on which every parcel of real estate in the area was identified by a parcel number. Arrow, a farmer, hired Dusty to spray his fields with insecticide. Arrow knew that his farm was identified on the county map as parcel 612, but by mistake told Dusty that it was parcel 621. As a result, Dusty sprayed the farm which the county map identified as parcel 621. That farm belonged to Plower, who had contracted to grow his crop without chemical insecticides and to sell it to an organic produce distributor. As a result of Dusty's spraying, Plower was unable to fulfill his contract and sustained serious economic losses.

If Plower asserts a claim for damages resulting from trespass to land, the court should find for

   (A) Plower, because crop dusting is an abnormally dangerous activity.

   (B) Plower, because Dusty intentionally flew through the air space above his land.

   (C) Dusty, because she reasonably believed that the farm which she was spraying belonged to Arrow.

   (D) Dusty, because there was no damage to Plower's land.

6. Nichol, who was 11 years of age, was playing with Paul, who was ten years of age. While they were playing together, Nichol offered to show Paul his new air rifle. The air rifle was manufactured by the Loly Company. Nichol purchased it from Storr, with money which he earned by mowing the lawns of several of his neighbors. While demonstrating the air rifle to Paul, Nichol accidentally shot him with it, severely injuring Paul's eye. Paul subsequently asserted a negligence claim against Storr.

If Paul is successful in his claim against Storr, it will be because a jury finds that

   (A) any negligence by Loly Company in the

design of the air rifle should be imputed to Storr.

(B) the air rifle was defectively designed.

(C) the air rifle was defectively manufactured.

(D) it was unreasonable for Storr to sell the air rifle to Nichol.

Questions 7-8 are based on the following fact situation.

Pellum was employed by Denner as chief field mechanic. When he received his salary, Pellum noticed that he had not been paid for the overtime which he had worked the previous month. When he complained to Denner about it, Denner said that all company employees were expected to put in extra time when necessary, and that he had no intention of compensating Pellum for the excess hours. Pellum resigned immediately and advised Denner that he would hold the tools which Denner had issued to him until he received payment.

7. Assume for the purpose of this question only that after Pellum's resignation, Denner wrote him a letter in which he said, "You were never any good as a mechanic, and in addition you were the most dishonest employee this company ever had," and that these statements were false. Pellum's mother, who lived with Pellum and frequently opened his mail, read the letter as soon as it arrived. In an action by Pellum against Denner for defamation, a court should find for

(A) Pellum, because Denner's statements were published to Pellum's mother.

(B) Pellum, only if Denner had reason to know that someone other than Denner would open and read the letter.

(C) Denner, because the statements contained in the letter were communicated only to Pellum.

(D) Denner, because of the employer's privilege.

8. Assume for the purpose of this question only that Pellum applied for a job with Nuco, and that Nuco wrote to Denner asking for an evaluation of Pellum's honesty and ability. Denner wrote a letter to Nuco which stated, "When Pellum left my company a valuable set of tools left with him. This disappearance has never been properly explained or straightened out." As a result, Nuco did not hire Pellum. If Pellum asserts a claim against Denner for defamation, Pellum should

(A) lose, if Pellum did not return the tools which he took when he left Denner's employ.

(B) lose, because Denner's statement was made in response to a specific request by Pellum's prospective employer.

(C) win, because Denner's statement could not have benefitted Denner's own business interests.

(D) win, if Denner's statement accused Pellum of stealing the tools.

9. Arnold was driving north on Canal Street. As he approached the intersection of First Avenue, he noticed that the traffic light was red against him. Preparing to stop, he stepped on his brake pedal. Because the brakes were not working properly, he could not stop, and continued into the intersection. Burger, who was driving east on First Avenue, saw Arnold go through the red light. Because the light was green in his favor, however, Burger did not stop, but continued into the intersection, believing that he could avoid striking Arnold by steering around him. The two vehicles collided in the intersection. Although damage to Arnold's car was minimal, Burger's car was totally destroyed. The jurisdiction has a statute which prohibits entering an intersection against a red traffic signal light and another statute which adopts the all or nothing rule of contributory negligence.

In an action by Burger against Arnold, the court should find for

(A) Arnold, since Burger had the last clear chance to avoid the accident.

(B) Arnold, if it was unreasonable for Burger to enter the intersection when he did.

(C) Burger, if Arnold's violation of statute was a substantial factor in producing the damage.

(D) Burger, since Arnold's conduct was negligence per se.

10. Fridge was the operator of an appliance store. Once, while testing a refrigerator prior to selling it, she discovered a defect in its wiring. Realizing that the defect would make it dangerous for a person to touch the refrigerator while it was plugged in, she resolved not to sell it. Instead, she placed it on the sidewalk in front of her store to attract the attention of passersby. After two years, the refrigerator became so dirty that she decided to get rid of it. In crayon, Fridge wrote "AS IS - $25" on its door. Pally, who was building a food smoker, needed the body of a refrigerator. When he saw the one in front of Fridge's store, he bought it. As she was loading it onto Pally's pickup truck, Fridge said, "I hope you know that this refrigerator doesn't work." Pally said that he did. When Pally got the refrigerator home he plugged it in, and received a severe electrical shock while attempting to open its door.

In an action by Pally against Fridge for damages resulting from his injury, the court will probably find for

(A) Pally, if it was unreasonable for Fridge to sell the refrigerator without warning him about the wiring defect.

(B) Pally, since the refrigerator was unfit for ordinary use.

(C) Fridge, since Pally purchased the refrigerator "AS IS."

(D) Fridge, if it is found that Pally had the "last clear chance" to avoid being injured.

11. The Chemco insecticide factory was located on the edge of the city of Pinetree. When the wind blew from the east, foul-smelling waste gases from Chemco factory chimneys were blown over Pinetree, causing most of the residents to experience a burning of the eyes and throat. Packer was a resident of Pinetree. On several occasions, she attempted to persuade the City Attorney to seek an injunction against Chemco. The City Attorney refused, however, because the City Council was afraid that doing so would drive Chemco from

the area. If Packer seeks an injunction by asserting a claim against Chemco on a theory of public nuisance, which of the following would be Chemco's most effective argument in defense?

(A) The City Attorney's decision is binding.

(B) Packer has not sustained harm different from that of the general public.

(C) A private citizen may not seek an injunction against environmental polluters.

(D) A private citizen may not sue on a theory of public nuisance.

12. When Darren entered a restaurant for lunch, she hung her coat on the coat rack. When she was leaving, she removed from the rack a coat which looked like hers, but which actually belonged to Perdu. At the time she took it, Darran believed it to be her coat, but when she had driven two miles from the restaurant, she realized that it was not hers. She turned around and was driving back to the restaurant when she was involved in an automobile accident. Perdu's coat was completely destroyed in the accident.

If Perdu asserts a claim against Darran for trespass to chattel, the court should find for

(A) Perdu, because the coat was completely destroyed after Darran took it.

(B) Perdu, unless the automobile accident in which the coat was destroyed occurred without fault by Darran.

(C) Darran, because she believed the coat to be her own when she took it.

(D) Darran, if she was making a reasonable effort to return the coat when it was destroyed.

13. Michael, who was eleven years old, received a sled manufactured by Rosebud from his uncle as a Christmas present. Since he already had a better sled, Michael sold the Rosebud to his neighbor Petey. Petey was riding the Rosebud sled down a snow-covered hill when one of the bolts which held it together broke, causing the sled to over-

turn and injure Petey severely. The bolt broke because of a crack which existed when the sled left the Rosebud factory, but which was too minute to be discovered by reasonable inspection. If Petey brings an action against Rosebud, the court should find for

(A) Petey, if the cracked bolt was a defect.

(B) Petey, but only if Michael did not use the sled before selling it to Petey.

(C) Rosebud, since the sale by Michael was outside the regular course of business.

(D) Rosebud, because the crack was too minute to be discovered upon reasonable inspection.

14. Stabel owned and bred horses, and was an excellent rider. He purchased a horse known as Thunder even though he had heard that Thunder was wild and dangerous, because he hoped that he would be able to "break" or train him. Each time Stabel attempted to approach the horse, however, Thunder reared and kicked at him. Finally, Stabel hired a professional horse trainer named Parte to break Thunder. After explaining that Thunder had repeatedly attacked him, Stabel showed Parte to Thunder's corral. While Stabel stood outside watching, Parte entered the corral holding out his hand and making soft murmuring noises to attract Thunder's attention. When Thunder saw Parte, the horse kicked him, fracturing Parte's leg.

If Parte asserts a claim for damages against Stabel, the court should find for

(A) Parte, since Stabel knew that Thunder had a propensity to attack human beings.

(B) Parte, since Thunder was a wild animal.

(C) Parte, since Stabel acted unreasonably in permitting Parte to enter the corral under the circumstances.

(D) Stabel, since Parte knew that Thunder was dangerous when he entered the corral.

15. Penny was attending a nightclub at which Dr. Hypno was performing. Before the show began, a request was made for a volunteer to assist Dr. Hypno with her act, and Penny volunteered. She was taken backstage to Dr. Hypno's dressing room where she and Dr. Hypno had a conversation. Following their conversation, Penny agreed to participate in Dr. Hypno's show. During the course of the performance, Dr. Hypno attempted to hypnotize Penny on stage. She then touched Penny's skin with an electric cattle-prod (a device which produces an electric shock and is used for handling stubborn cattle) causing her great pain and discomfort.

Penny subsequently instituted an action against Dr. Hypno. In it, she alleged that Dr. Hypno committed various intentional torts against her by touching her with the cattle prod. If one of the following facts were established at the trial, which would be most helpful to Penny in responding to Dr. Hypno's defense of consent?

(A) During the conversation in Dr. Hypno's dressing room, Dr. Hypno stated that she was going to attempt to hypnotize Penny on stage, stated that she was usually successful in hypnotizing volunteers, and stated further that if she was successful, the cattle prod would cause Penny no discomfort.

(B) During the conversation in Dr. Hypno's dressing room, Dr. Hypno promised to pay Penny $100 for participating in the show; she never did pay her; and, in fact, when she promised that she would pay Penny, she did not intend to do so.

(C) During the conversation in Dr. Hypno's dressing room, Dr. Hypno stated that the electric cattle-prod produced a mild electric shock which would cause no real discomfort, when she knew that this was not true.

(D) When Penny consented to participating in Dr. Hypno's act, she did not know that contact with the electric cattle-prod would result in great pain and discomfort.

16. The state governor was attending a major league baseball game when a member of the home team

hit a home run. The governor jumped to his feet and cheered loudly, along with the rest of the crowd. Frank, a freelance photographer, snapped the governor's photograph while he was cheering. When the photograph was developed, Frank had it imprinted on targets. Packaging them with toy plastic darts, Frank marketed them under the name of "The Cheering Governor Dart Board Game," selling several thousand. The governor sued Frank for invasion of privacy.

On which of the following theories is the governor most likely to be successful in his action against Frank?

(A) Appropriation of identity.

(B) Public disclosure.

(C) Intrusion.

(D) False light.

17. Alice was driving her automobile on Country Road in the rain when she rounded a bend and saw a cow standing directly in her path. She immediately jammed on her brakes and pulled the steering wheel to the right in an attempt to avoid striking the cow. As a result, she lost control of her car which skidded off the road and into Basil's yard. Basil, who was in the process of installing an automatic watering system, had dug a trench across the yard for pipes. When the wheels of Alice's car hit the trench, the car stopped abruptly, throwing Alice forward into the windshield, and causing her to be injured. In an action by Alice against Basil for negligence, will a court decide that Basil owed Alice a duty of reasonable care?

(A) Yes, if it was foreseeable that persons driving on Country Road might lose control of their vehicles and skid into Basil's yard.

(B) Yes, if, but only if, the cow was in the road because of some conduct by Basil.

(C) No, because it was not unreasonable for Basil to dig a trench on his own land.

(D) No, because Alice was a trespasser.

Questions 18-19 are based on the following fact situation.

Carp, who was building a house on his own property, had posted a sign which said, "No Trespassing." He was working on the framework of his roof when he found that he had brought the wrong hammer onto the roof with him. Without looking to see if anyone was around, he tossed the hammer to the ground, shouting "Heads up!"

Truck was a truck driver assigned to deliver lumber on the street where Carp was building a house. Carp had not ordered lumber, but when Truck saw Carp working on the roof of an unfinished house, he incorrectly assumed that Carp was the person to whom he was supposed to deliver the lumber. He parked his truck at the curb and was walking across Carp's property toward the unfinished house to talk to Carp about the delivery, when he was struck in the head by the hammer thrown by Carp. Truck cried out in pain, and then fell to the ground, unconscious and bleeding. Carp saw it happen, but merely shrugged and continued working.

A moment later a passerby who had seen what happened called an ambulance. When it arrived, Truck was still unconscious. The driver, Ann, loaded Truck into the ambulance and began driving to the hospital. Because of Ann's negligent driving, the ambulance struck a pole. Truck was killed in the crash.

18. Assume for the purpose of this question only that the representative of Truck's estate instituted an appropriate action against Carp, alleging that Carp's failure to call for medical assistance after he saw the hammer strike Truck was negligence. Which of the following comments is most accurate regarding that allegation?

(A) Carp owed Truck no duty to call for help if Truck was a trespasser.

(B) Truck's estate is entitled to punitive (exemplary) damages if Carp was substantially certain that there was a possibility of harm resulting from his failure to act.

(C) Carp's failure to call for medical aid was not a factual cause of harm to Truck, since someone did call a moment later.

(D) Truck was an invitee since he was a user of the public street who had entered upon adjacent private land.

19. If the representative of Truck's estate instituted an appropriate action against Ann under the state's "wrongful death" statute, the court would be most likely to find for

(A) Ann, if Carp's conduct was foreseeable

(B) Ann, since a rescuer is not under an obligation to use reasonable care in the face of an emergency

(C) Truck's estate, since Ann's negligence was a proximate cause of Truck's death

(D) Truck's estate, unless Carp is found to be liable for Truck's death

20. Darby was towing a small travel-trailer with his automobile when the hitch which attached the trailer to the car broke, causing the trailer to collide with the vehicle of Venden which was parked at the curb. A statute in the jurisdiction provides that "No person shall operate a motor vehicle or trailer on the roads of this state unless said motor vehicle or trailer is covered by a valid policy of liability insurance." Darby was in violation of that statute in that he knew that his trailer was not covered by a valid policy of liability insurance at the time of the accident. Is his violation of statute relevant to the issue of negligence in an action brought against him by Venden?

(A) Yes, because the statute was designed to protect the victims of automobile and trailer accidents.

(B) Yes, because the reasonable person does not knowingly violate a statute.

(C) No, because the law encourages the purchase of automobile insurance, and therefore absolutely prohibits disclosure to the jury about whether or not a defendant was insured.

(D) No, because compliance with the statute does not prevent automobile or trailer accidents.

21. One night police officers Axel and Barber received a message that a burglary was in progress at the Super Grocery Store. Rushing to the location, they discovered that the back door of the store was open. Entering cautiously, they saw two burglars hiding in the storage room. In the ensuing attempt to effect an arrest in the dark, Axel and Barber knocked over several stacks of merchandise, including cases of bottled soda-pop manufactured by Popco. When the stacked groceries fell over during the chase a bottle broke, and a fragment of flying glass struck Officer Axel, injuring him. If Axel institutes an action against Super, Axel will

(A) win, since the fact that he was attempting to apprehend a criminal who was burglarizing Super's store made him an invitee.

(B) win, if but only if Super's conduct was a physical cause of the harm.

(C) lose, since he was a bare licensee at the time the injury occurred.

(D) lose, if it was unforeseeable that persons would be chasing around the storeroom in the dark.

Questions 22-23 are based on the following fact situation.

Collins was a well-known collector of art. Dillon was an art dealer who operated a gallery in which she sold paintings and other works of art. One day, while Collins was visiting Dillon's gallery, Dillon showed him a new painting called "The Petticoats" which she had received that day.

"The artist didn't sign it," Dillon said. "But I'm sure it was painted by Degas. That would make it worth at least $250,000."

Collins answered, "It's by Degas, all right. It's worth every cent you're asking. But I already have several paintings by Degas in my collection, and I don't need another."

Barton, who was browsing in Dillon's gallery, overheard the conversation between Collins and Dillon. Barton knew very little about art, but had just inherited a large sum of money. Because he knew that Collins and Dillon were art experts, he believed what he heard them saying. After Collins left the gallery, Barton asked Dillon if she would accept $200,000 for "The Petticoats." Dillon said that she would not take anything less than $250,000. After negotiation, Barton purchased it for $225,000.

Barton subsequently learned that "The Petticoats" had not been painted by Degas, and was worth only $600.

22. If Barton asserts a tort claim for misrepresentation against Dillon, which of the following would be Dillon's most effective argument in defense?

(A) A statement of opinion cannot be construed as a misrepresentation, since there is no such thing as a false idea.

(B) Barton did not sustain damage as a result of his reliance on a statement by Dillon.

(C) Dillon did not know that Barton would rely on the statements which she made to Collins.

(D) The value of any work of art is a matter of opinion.

23. If Barton is successful in a tort action for misrepresentation, the court is likely to award him a judgment for

(A) $250,000 (the value which Dillon stated).

(B) $250,000 (the value which Dillon stated), on condition that Barton return "The Petticoats" to Dillon.

(C) $225,000 (the price which Barton paid to Dillon).

(D) $224,400 (the price which Barton paid to Dillon less the value of "The Petticoats").

24. Dalton was an elderly man who lived in a house with a swimming pool in the back yard. Although Dalton enjoyed swimming in the pool, his age and physical infirmity made him unable to clean or maintain the pool himself. Instead, he agreed to allow his fourteen-year-old neighbor Nellie to swim in the pool anytime she wanted to without notifying Dalton or asking his permission, in exchange for Nellie's services in cleaning and maintaining the pool.

On Friday morning, Nellie thoroughly cleaned Dalton's pool. Later that day, Dalton drained all the water from the pool and did not refill it. Saturday morning, Nellie woke up early and decided to go swimming in Dalton's pool. She put on her bathing suit and went into Dalton's yard, running onto the diving board of his swimming pool and diving in without looking first. Nellie was severely injured when she fell to the concrete bottom of the empty swimming pool.

If Nellie asserts a negligence claim for her injuries against Dalton in a jurisdiction which has a pure comparative negligence statute, the court should find for

(A) Nellie, because the pool constituted an attractive nuisance.

(B) Dalton, because Nellie was a trespasser.

(C) Nellie, if it was unreasonable for Dalton to drain the pool without warning her.

(D) Dalton, if the reasonable person in Nellie's position would have known the risk of diving into an empty swimming pool.

25. Carolyn was driving to visit her fiance who was staying in Smallville, about fifty miles away. Before she left, her friend Frieda asked her to deliver a small package to someone in Smallville. The package contained a bottle of caustic chemical. Because she was afraid that Carolyn would refuse to carry it if she knew its contents, Frieda wrapped the package in brown paper and did not tell Carolyn what was in it. Carolyn placed the package in the glove compartment of her car and began driving to Smallville. Along the way, Carolyn saw Harold hitchhiking by the side of the

road. Since they had gone to high school together, Carolyn offered Harold a ride. While Harold was sitting in the front seat beside Carolyn, the package in the glove compartment began to leak, dripping liquid onto Harold's trousers. Without saying anything to Carolyn, Harold opened the glove compartment and removed the wet package. As soon as the caustic liquid touched Harold's hand, it burned his skin severely.

If Harold commences a negligence action against Carolyn in a jurisdiction which has no automobile guest statute and which applies the all-or-nothing rule of contributory negligence, which of the following would be Carolyn's most effective argument in defense?

(A) Harold was a mere licensee, and was only entitled to a warning of those conditions which Carolyn knew were dangerous.

(B) Carolyn could not have known or anticipated that the contents of the package would cause harm to a passenger in her car.

(C) Harold was contributorily negligent in touching the wet package.

(D) Harold assumed the risk of injury resulting from contact with the wet package.

26. Six months after Dr. Danh performed surgery on her, Peck was x-rayed by another doctor. The x-ray disclosed a surgical instrument inside Peck's chest. Danh was the only person who had ever performed surgery on Peck. Peck subsequently asserted a medical malpractice claim against Danh, alleging that Danh had negligently left the surgical instrument inside her while operating on her.

If an expert testifies that surgeons do not usually leave instruments inside a patient's body unless they are acting unreasonably, may Peck rely on *res ipsa loquitur* in her claim against Danh?

(A) No because the doctrine of *res ipsa loquitur* is not applicable to a claim for professional malpractice.

(B) No because a jury of laypersons is not competent to infer that a physician was negligent.

(C) Yes because a surgeon is under an absolute duty not to leave instruments inside a patient's body.

(D) Yes because Danh was the only person who had ever performed surgery on Peck.

27. When Perl, a law student, told her cousin Joe that she needed a place to study, Joe gave her the key to his mountain cabin and said that she could use it. Because Perl had never been there before, Joe drew a map and wrote instructions on how to find it. Perl followed the map and instructions, but when she arrived she found five identical cabins in a row and did not know which one was Joe's. She tried the key which Joe had given her. When it opened the door of one of the cabins, she went inside, believing the cabin to be Joe's.

Actually, the cabin which Perl entered did not belong to Joe, but to his neighbor Darrin. Joe knew that his key fit the doors of all five of the cabins, but had forgotten to mention it to Perl. While Perl was inside the cabin, she attempted to turn on the gas stove. Because of a defect in the stove, it exploded, injuring Perl.

If Perl asserts a claim against Darrin for her injuries, the court should find for

(A) Perl because the stove was defective.

(B) Perl if Darrin should have anticipated that a person would enter his cabin by mistake.

(C) Darrin only if Perl was a trespasser at the time of the explosion.

(D) Darrin unless Darrin knew or should have known that someone would be injured by the stove.

Questions 28-29 are based on the following fact situation.

One evening in Alfred's tavern, Yeong, who was

17 years old, drank alcoholic beverages which Alfred sold her. Yeong then left and went to Barney's tavern where she drank alcoholic beverages which Barney sold her. When Yeong left Barney's tavern, she attempted to ride home on her motorcycle. Because Yeong was intoxicated, she struck and injured Palco, a pedestrian. Palco subsequently asserted claims against Alfred and Barney under a state law which provides as follows: "If a minor under the age of 20 years injures another while intoxicated, any person who sold said minor the alcohol which resulted in said minor's intoxication shall be liable to the injured person."

28. Assume for the purpose of this question only that Alfred did not sell Yeong enough alcohol to make Yeong intoxicated, and that the alcohol which Barney sold Yeong would have made Yeong intoxicated even if Alfred had sold Yeong no alcohol at all. In determining Palco's claim against Barney, the court should find that

   (A) Barney's conduct was not the cause of Yeong's intoxication because Alfred's conduct was a substantial factor in making Yeong intoxicated.

   (B) Barney is liable under the statute even if Barney's conduct did not cause Yeong to become intoxicated.

   (C) Barney's conduct was a cause of Palco's injury because Yeong would not have become intoxicated if Barney did not sell Yeong alcoholic beverages.

   (D) Barney's conduct was a cause of Yeong's intoxication, but was not a cause of Palco's injury because Yeong's driving superseded it.

29. Assume for the purpose of this question only that the amount of alcohol which Alfred sold Yeong would have made Yeong intoxicated even if Barney sold Yeong no alcohol at all, and that the amount of alcohol which Barney sold Yeong would have made Yeong intoxicated even if Alfred sold Yeong no alcohol at all. Which of the following statements is/are most correct?

   I. Alfred did not cause Palco's injury because

Barney subsequently sold Yeong enough alcohol to make her intoxicated.

   II. Barney did not cause Palco's injury because Alfred had previously sold Yeong enough alcohol to make her intoxicated.

   (A) I only.

   (B) II only.

   (C) I and II.

   (D) Neither I nor II.

30. Drinker was obviously intoxicated when he entered Barr's tavern one night and ordered a drink of Old Wheatstraw alcoholic liquor. A statute in the jurisdiction prohibits serving alcoholic liquor to any intoxicated person. Barr knew that Drinker was intoxicated, but because Drinker was a good customer, Barr opened a new bottle of Old Wheatstraw and poured him some of it. After drinking the liquor, Drinker left the tavern and began driving home.

The liquor which Barr served Drinker had been manufactured by Wheatstraw. Before the liquor left Wheatstraw's factory, Fuller, an angry employee, added a poison to it which could not have been discovered by reasonable inspection. While Drinker was driving in a reasonable manner, the poison caused him to die. As a result, Drinker's car struck Prill, injuring her. If Prill asserts a claim against Barr based on Barr's violation of the above statute, which of the following would be Barr's most effective argument in defense against that claim?

   (A) Barr did not serve Drinker enough liquor to make him intoxicated.

   (B) The statute was not meant to prevent people from drinking liquor which had been poisoned.

   (C) Serving liquor to Drinker was not a cause of Prill's injuries.

   (D) Fuller's conduct was a superseding cause of Prill's injuries.

ANSWERS TO
MULTISTATE-STYLE QUESTIONS

1. C   Although liability ordinarily results from the publication of false defamatory statements about the plaintiff, the courts have always required that publication be either intentional or the result of negligence. Dresden's statement to Prescott was not a publication, since Prescott is the plaintiff. The fact that it was overheard by Audit does not satisfy the requirement of publication unless either Dresden intended that Audit hear it or Audit heard it as a result of Dresden's unreasonable conduct in the face of the foreseeable risk that Audit would hear it. If Dresden knew that Audit would hear it, he intended the publication. If he should have known that Audit would hear it, he acted unreasonably in saying it.

    The courts have never required proof that the defendant knew the statement to be defamatory, so **A** is incorrect. The United States Supreme Court has held that in some defamation cases the plaintiff must prove that the defendant knew or should have known that the statement was false when he made it. **B** is incorrect, however, because the requirement has not been applied to a defamation action brought by a private person against a non-media defendant. **D** is incorrect because knowledge that harm will result is not an essential element of any defamation case.

2. D   Strict liability is imposed on the seller of a product which is in a defective condition when sold. Thus, if Riteway sold the product while it was defective, Riteway would be strictly liable no matter who manufactured it.

    Parties who work together to accomplish a particular result are involved in a concert of action which may make any one of them vicariously liable for torts committed by the others. **A** is incorrect, however, because the facts indicate that the manufacturers and retailer did not work together on manufacturing or marketing the product. It has been held that where there are a small number of manufacturers in a particular industry, where all belong to an industry-wide association which establishes industry standards, where those standards result in their products' being defective, and where all members of the industry and the association are named as defendants, liability may be imposed on an industry-wide basis. **B** is incorrect, however, because there is no indications that the number of cereal manufacturers is small or that they belong to an industry-wide association which sets standards or that their standards made the product defective or that all members of the industry and their association have been named as defendants. Under the alternative liability theory, where two or more defendants commit identical acts of negligence under circumstances which make it impossible to tell which one injured the plaintiff, it will be presumed that all of them factually caused the plaintiff's injury. **C** is incorrect, however, because there is no indication that all of the parties named committed identical acts of negligence or that any of them was negligent at all.

3. D   Assault occurs when, with the intent to induce such apprehension, the defendant induces in the plaintiff a reasonable apprehension that a harmful or offensive contact with the plaintiff will occur. Since Mabe did not fear contact with herself, she was not assaulted.

    A and **B** are incorrect because Napper's conduct did not induce Mabe to apprehend contact with herself. If Napper's conduct did give Mabe reason to apprehend contact with herself, it would not matter whether she had perceived contact with Dan. **C** is, therefore, incorrect.

4. C   A defendant is liable for intentional infliction of mental distress if, with the intent to cause mental distress, he engages in outrageous conduct which causes serious mental suffering. The defendant intends the plaintiff's mental distress if he desires or knows that it will result from his conduct. Because of the affection normally associated with the parent-child relationship, Napper probably knew (i.e., intended) that his threats to injure or kill Dan would cause his mother to experience mental distress. If his conduct was outrageous and caused her to experience mental distress, Napper is liable to her for the mental distress and any physical manifestations of it.

        A is incorrect because the passage of time is not sufficient to prevent liability for an injury which was caused by the defendant's tortious conduct. If the reasonable person would not have experienced any suffering as a result of Napper's conduct, then a plaintiff who did experience suffering might not be permitted to recover for it because the law does not seek to benefit a supersensitive plaintiff. If the reasonable person would have experienced some suffering, however, the plaintiff will be permitted to recover for her suffering even if a pre-existing condition makes it unusually severs. (This rule sometimes leads courts to exclaim, "The defendant takes the plaintiff as he finds her.") **B** is, therefore, incorrect. **D** is incorrect because liability for intentional infliction of mental distress requires intent, not merely a foreseeable risk.

5. B   Trespass to land is an intentional entry on realty possessed by the plaintiff. For this purpose the air immediately above the ground is regarded as part of the realty.

        Without intent, there is no trespass liability. **A** is incorrect because participation in an abnormally dangerous activity does not satisfy the requirement of intent. **C** is incorrect because intent means a desire to enter the land or air space above it (without regard to knowledge of the plaintiff's right). **D** is incorrect because damage to the realty is not an essential element of trespass to land.

6. D   The facts specify that Paul's claim is for negligence. Negligence is unreasonable conduct. It may be unreasonable to sell a device as dangerous as an air rifle to an eleven-year-old, because the risk that he will use it to shoot another child is foreseeable. In any event, D is the only finding listed which could result in a judgment for Paul.

        A is incorrect because negligence of a manufacturer is not imputed to a retailer. **B** and **C** are incorrect because there is no indication that the harm resulted from any defect in the air rifle or that such a defect resulted from negligence.

7. B   There can be no liability for defamation unless the defendant intentionally or negligently communicated the defamatory statement to a person other than the plaintiff. Communication of the accusation to Pellum's mother would satisfy this requirement only if Denner knew or should have known that she would see the contents of the letter which contained them.

        A is, therefore, incorrect. **C** is incorrect because the statements actually were communicated to Pellum's mother, who read the letter. Courts have sometimes held that an employer who defames a former employee in a communication with a prospective employer of that former employee is privileged if he believes reasonably and in good faith that his statements are true. This reasoning does not apply to the facts given, however, because Denner's statements were not being made to a prospective employer of Pellum. **D** is, therefore, incorrect.

8. **D**   A statement is defamatory if it would tend to hold the plaintiff up to shame, disgrace, or ridicule in the minds of a substantial group of respectable people. Since most respectable people believe that theft is disgraceful, an accusation that the plaintiff is a thief is probably defamatory. In a defamation action, a statement means what the reasonable person reading it would think it means. The reasonable person reading Denner's statement might believe that it accuses Pellum of stealing tools. Whether this is so is a question for the jury, but it is clear that *if* Denner's statement accused Pellum of stealing tools it was defamatory and might lead to liability.

If Pellum did not return the tools, Denner's statement is literally true. Since a statement means what the reasonable person hearing it would think it means, and since the reasonable person might think that Denner's statement accused Pellum of theft, the literal truth of the statement would not prevent Denner from being liable. **A** is, therefore, incorrect. A defendant may be privileged to make defamatory statements in a reasonable and good faith attempt to protect a legitimate interest. In deciding whether a former employer was acting in good faith when making a defamatory statement to a plaintiff's prospective employer, courts frequently look to whether the former employer made the statement gratuitously (making it less likely that he was acting in good faith) or in response to a request for information (making it more likely that he was acting in good faith). **B** is incorrect, however, because this fact alone is not sufficient to privilege a defendant's publication. **C** is incorrect because if the defendant was acting reasonably and in good faith, the interest which a former employer has in common with a prospective employer might be sufficiently legitimate to make the privilege apply.

9. **B**   Under the all-or-nothing rule of contributory negligence, a plaintiff is completely barred from recovering damages if his own unreasonable conduct contributed to their occurrence. Since Burger saw Arnold in the intersection, he was probably guilty of contributory negligence.

The doctrine of last clear chance does no more than negate the effect of a plaintiff's contributory negligence. If a defendant had "the last clear chance" to avoid injuring the plaintiff, the defendant might be liable in spite of the plaintiff's negligence. The plaintiff never loses a case, however, simply because that plaintiff had "the last clear chance" to avoid being injured. **A** is, therefore, incorrect. **C** and **D** are incorrect for two reasons: first, the presumption which results from a defendant's violation of a statute (sometimes called negligence per se) may ordinarily be rebutted by proof that the violation resulted from circumstances beyond the defendant's control; and, second, even if Arnold could not rebut the presumption that he was negligent, Burger's contributory negligence is still available to him as a defense.

10. **A**   Although the phrase AS IS disclaims implied warranties of merchantability or fitness for a particular purpose, it does not free a seller from the duty of acting reasonably. Since it probably was foreseeable that the purchaser of a refrigerator would plug it in even after being advised that it did not work, Fridge had a duty to take reasonable precautions against the harm which might result therefrom. If her failure to warn Pally was unreasonable, it was negligence which was a proximate cause of harm and would result in liability.

B is incorrect because the phrase AS IS is an effective disclaimer of the implied warranty of merchantability (i.e., fitness for ordinary use). **C** is incorrect because Fridge is still liable under a negligence theory. **D** is based on a misinterpretation of the doctrine of "last clear chance" which accomplishes nothing more than undoing the effect of a plaintiff's contributory negligence. (If a defendant had "the last clear chance" to avoid injuring the plaintiff, the defendant might be liable in spite of the plaintiff's negligence. The plaintiff never loses a case, however, simply because that plaintiff had "the last clear chance" to avoid being injured.)

11.　B　A private individual can successfully assert a claim for public nuisance only if the harm which she sustained was different from that sustained by the general public (i.e., "particular" harm). Since no fact indicates this to be so of Packer, she may not assert the public nuisance claim.

　　　　A is incorrect because if Packer had sustained "particular" harm, the decision of the City Attorney would not prevent her from suing for damages. Although it is generally held that a private individual may not seek an injunction on a public nuisance theory, **C** is incorrect because there are other theories on which a private individual may receive an injunction against environmental polluters. **D** is incorrect because a private individual who sustains particular harm as a result of a public nuisance may sue for damages.

12.　A　Trespass to chattel is intentional interference with the plaintiff's chattel resulting in damage. For this purpose, intent consists of a desire or knowledge that the chattel will be involved, without regard to whether the defendant knows that the chattel is the plaintiff's or that the plaintiff's rights are being violated. Interference can consist of any act regarding the chattel which only its rightful possessor is entitled to perform. Since Darren desired to take that particular coat, she had the necessary intent, regardless of her belief that the coat was her own. Since only Perdu was entitled to take the coat, Darren interfered with it. Since the coat was destroyed while Darren possessed it, her interference resulted in damage to Perdu. Darren is, therefore, liable to Perdu for trespass to chattel.

　　　　B is incorrect because the tort was committed when Darren took the coat and the tort led to the coat's destruction. In trespass to chattel, intent does not require knowledge that the chattel belongs to another or that the defendant's act will affect the rights of another. **C** is, therefore, incorrect. Trespass to chattel was committed when Darren took the coat. If she had succeeded in returning the coat, damages might have been mitigated (i.e., reduced), but the tort would not have been undone. **D** is incorrect because her unsuccessful attempt to return the coat could not even mitigate damages.

13.　A　Strict liability is imposed on the seller of a product which is in a defective condition when sold. Since the bolt was cracked when the sled left the Rosebud factory, Rosebud would be liable if the crack constituted a defect.

　　　　B and C are incorrect because the use and/or sale by Michael would not prevent the imposition of strict liability if the sled was defective when it left Rosebud's factory so long as such use or sale did not substantially change its condition. **D** is incorrect because strict liability in tort does not depend on unreasonable conduct by the defendant.

14.　D　One who voluntarily encounters a known risk assumes that risk, and is not entitled to damages resulting from it.

A, B, and **C** are all incorrect since assumption of risk is available as a defense in claims based on negligence or strict liability. In addition, **B** is incorrect because horses are not regarded as wild animals, and **C** is incorrect because the fact that Parte, a professional horse trainer, had been warned of the animal's propensity indicates that Stabel's conduct was reasonable.

15.   C   Consent means willingness, and the affirmative defense of consent is effective because of the rule that a plaintiff who is willing for a particular thing to happen to her has no right to complain when it does. For this reason, a defendant does not commit a tort when she does something to which the plaintiff has consented. If the defendant induces plaintiff's consent by fraud, however, the consent does not have this effect, and does not privilege the defendant's conduct. A defendant induces consent by fraud when she knowingly misrepresents the nature of the act to which the plaintiff is consenting. Thus, if Dr. Hypno told Penny that the cattle prod would produce no real discomfort when she knew that this was false, she fraudulently induced Penny's consent to contact with it, and was not privileged by her consent.

In **A**, Penny consented to the contact even though she was aware that Dr. Hypno was not always successful in hypnotizing volunteers and that if she was not successful in hypnotizing her, the cattle prod might cause discomfort. Since she knew the nature of the act to which she was consenting, her consent would furnish Dr. Hypno with a privilege. **A** is, therefore, incorrect. In **B**, although Dr. Hypno defrauded Penny by promising money which she did not intend to pay, the fraud did not relate to the nature of the act to which Penny was consenting. Dr. Hypno would, therefore, be privileged by her consent, and **B** is, therefore, incorrect. A mistake leading to a consent does not destroy the effect of that consent unless the defendant is aware of the mistake. Since there is no indication in **D** that Dr. Hypno was aware of Penny's mistake regarding the effect of a cattle prod, her consent privileged Dr. Hypno, and **D** is, therefore, incorrect.

16.   A   Appropriation of identity is committed when the defendant, without the plaintiff's permission, uses the plaintiff's identity for a commercial purpose. Since Frank sold games which were imprinted with the governor's likeness, a court could conclude that he is liable for appropriation.

Public disclosure is committed when the defendant publicly discloses a private fact about the plaintiff the disclosure of which would offend the reasonable person in the plaintiff's position. Since a photo of the governor's face as it appeared in a public place is obviously not a private fact, **B** is incorrect. Intrusion is committed by intentionally invading the plaintiff's private space in a manner which would offend the reasonable person in the plaintiff's position. Since Frank snapped the photo in a public place, he did not invade the governor's private space, and **C** is incorrect. False light is committed by publishing false statements about the plaintiff which, although not defamatory, are in some way embarrassing or damaging. Since Frank did not publish any statements about the governor, **D** is incorrect.

17.   A   Holders of land owe a duty of reasonable care to travelers who foreseeably deviate onto the land for reasons related to their use of the adjacent public way.

B is, therefore, incorrect. **C** is incorrect because although the reason given explains why Basil's conduct was not negligent, it fails to explain why he had no duty. Although a landholder generally owes no duty of reasonable care to a trespasser, **D** is incorrect because a strayed traveler as described above is entitled to reasonable care as an exception to the general rule.

18. **C**   Conduct is a factual cause of harm if the harm would not have occurred without it. Since medical assistance was summoned just a moment later, and since the facts do not indicate that Truck was worse off for the momentary delay, Carp's failure to summon aid was not a cause of harm.

Most jurisdictions agree that a landholder owes no duty of reasonable care to a trespasser. When the landholder knows of the trespasser's presence, however, and knows that the trespasser has been imperiled by some affirmative act of the landholder, the landholder does have a duty to act reasonably to protect the trespasser from that act. Since Carp knew that his act of throwing the hammer created the need for aid, he probably did owe Truck a duty to act reasonably in summoning it. **A** is, therefore, incorrect. Punitive damages may be available against a defendant who intended harm by his act. Intent requires a substantial certainty that the harm will probably occur, however. Knowledge that harm is *possible* is not intent, and is not sufficient to result in liability for punitive damages. **B** is, therefore, incorrect. A user of the public way who enters upon private land foreseeably and in connection with his use of the public way is entitled to some measure of reasonable care. **D** is incorrect, however, because he does not thereby become an invitee, and, further, because Truck's entry onto Carp's realty was not connected with Truck's use of the public way.

19. **C**   Since the death would not have occurred without Ann's negligence, her negligence factually caused it. Since it is obviously foreseeable that an automobile accident will result in the death of a passenger, Ann's negligence was also a legal cause of the harm.

A is incorrect because Carp's conduct preceded Ann's, and is, therefore, not an intervening cause of Truck's death. Although "reasonable care" may require less in an emergency than it does under ordinary circumstances, one faced with an emergency is still required to act as a reasonable person would under similar circumstances. **B** is, therefore, incorrect. Even if Carp is liable for Truck's death, Ann would be liable also if her negligence proximately caused it. **D** is, therefore, incorrect.

20. **D**   Violation of statute is relevant to the question of negligence only if the statute violated was designed to protect a class of persons to which the plaintiff belongs against risks like the one which resulted in harm to the plaintiff. Since insurance would not have prevented the trailer hitch from failing, the statute was not designed to protect against the risk that it would. Its violation is, therefore, not relevant.

A is, therefore, incorrect. **B** is incorrect because the violation is not relevant unless the statute was designed to protect against the risk involved. Public policy generally prohibits disclosing to a jury that a defendant was or was not insured. Such disclosure is not *absolutely* prohibited, however, since there are circumstances under which such disclosure could be made to a jury (e.g., to establish ownership of a vehicle). **C** is thus based on an overinclusive statement of the law, and is therefore incorrect.

21. **D**   Negligence is the breach of a duty of reasonable care. A defendant owes a plaintiff a duty of reasonable care when the defendant's conduct creates a foreseeable risk to the plaintiff. If it was unforeseeable that persons would be running about the storeroom in

the dark, the stacked groceries did not pose a foreseeable risk to the plaintiff. There would, therefore, be no duty to protect him against them and no negligence.

A is incorrect because an invitee is only entitled to reasonable care, and unless Super's conduct was unreasonable, the duty to Axel was not breached. **B** is incorrect for the same reason, since unless the conduct was negligent there is no liability. The fact, alone, that Axel was a licensee would not be sufficient to defeat his case, since even a licensee is entitled to reasonable warnings about known hidden dangers on the premises. **C** is therefore incorrect.

22. C   An essential element of tort liability for misrepresentation is the defendant's intent to induce the plaintiff's reliance on the defendant's statement. If Dillon did not know that Barton would rely on the statements which she made to Collins, she could not have intended to induce Barton's reliance on those statements. Since there is no indication that Dillon was aware that Barton had overhead her conversation with Collins, C is correct.

A is overinclusive, and, therefore, incorrect: statements of opinion, especially when made by experts, may be regarded as assertions of fact (i.e., the fact that the speaker actually held that particular opinion). Since Barton paid $250,000 for something worth only $600, based on his belief in what he had overheard Dillon saying, he did sustain damage as a result of his reliance on Dillon's statement. **B** is, therefore, incorrect. **D** is incorrect for two reasons. First, as indicated above, an expert may incur misrepresentation liability by stating that she holds an opinion which she doesn't actually hold. Second, Dillon's statement was not only an evaluation of the painting's value, but included a statement about who had painted it.

23. D   Since Barton received something for his money, the measure of his damage must consider the value which he has received. In some jurisdictions, damage for misrepresentations is measured by the difference between what the plaintiff received and what the defendant told him he would be receiving (benefit of the bargain theory). In this case, that would be $250,000 less $600, or $249,400. In other jurisdictions, the damage is measured by the difference between what the plaintiff paid and what he actually received (out of pocket theory). In this case, that would be $225,000 less $600 or $224,400. D is, therefore, correct. **A** and **C** are incorrect because they ignore the value of what Barton actually received. **B** is incorrect because it describes a rescission remedy, which may be available in a claim for breach of contract, but is not available in this tort claim for damages.

24. C   Under pure comparative negligence statutes, a plaintiff's recovery in a negligence action is diminished in proportion to the plaintiff's fault, but is not barred by the plaintiff's own negligence. Thus, Nellie would be entitled to recover part of any damages which she sustained as a result of Dalton's conduct if Dalton's conduct was unreasonable.

In most jurisdictions, a landholder owes a duty of reasonable care to an invitee, but owes no duty of reasonable care to a trespasser. For this purpose, an invitee is one whose presence confers an economic benefit on the landholder, and a trespasser is one who enters without permission. Since Nellie's use of Dalton's pool was consideration for valuable services which she rendered, she was an invitee. Under the "attractive nuisance" doctrine, a trespassing child may be entitled to reasonable care, but it is inapplicable here because Nellie was an invitee rather than a trespasser. **A** and **B** are, therefore, incorrect. If Nellie's conduct was unreasonable, the amount of her damages would be diminished accordingly. **D** is incorrect, however, because in a pure comparative negligence system, the plaintiff's negligence does not completely bar her recovery.

25.   B   Negligence is a failure to act reasonably in the face of a foreseeable risk. If it was not foreseeable that the contents of the package would cause harm to a passenger in her car, Carolyn's conduct with respect to the package could not have been negligent. Although it is not certain that a court would come to this conclusion, the argument in B is the only one listed which is supported by the facts.

A is incorrect because the rule limiting the duty owed to a licensee applies only to conditions of realty occupied by a defendant. Contributory negligence is unreasonable conduct by plaintiff which contributes to the happening of the accident. Since Harold could not have known that the contents of the package were caustic, there is no reason to conclude that his conduct was unreasonable. **C** is, therefore, incorrect. A plaintiff is said to have assumed the risk when he voluntarily encounters a known risk. **D** is incorrect because Harold did not know that the contents of the package were caustic, and touching it did not, therefore, constitute an encounter with a known risk.

26.   D   Under the doctrine of *res ipsa loquitur*, an inference that the defendant acted unreasonably can be drawn from the facts that the injury involved was one which does not usually occur without unreasonable conduct and that the defendant was the only person whose conduct could have caused the injury (i.e., the defendant was in exclusive control of the circumstances). If an expert witness testifies that surgeons do not usually leave instruments inside a patient unless they are acting unreasonably, Peck can rely on the inference established by *res ipsa loquitur* if she can show that Dr. Danh was the only person who could have left the instrument inside her. Since Danh was the only person who had ever performed surgery on Peck, Danh is the only person who could have left the instrument inside her.

A is incorrect because it is based on an inaccurate statement of law; there are many medical malpractice cases in which the plaintiff is permitted to rely on *res ipsa loquitur*. (Indeed, these cases frequently involve foreign objects which were left in the plaintiff's body during surgery). Ordinarily, in drawing an inference of negligence under the doctrine of *res ipsa loquitur*, a jury relies on what it knows about human experience to determine whether a particular accident is of a kind which does not usually occur without negligence. Because of its lack of specialized knowledge, a jury is not competent to decide whether the particular result of a professional's conduct is one which would not usually occur without negligence. Once a jury has heard testimony to that effect from an expert witness, however, it may base an inference of negligence on its decision about whether or not it believes that witness. This is a decision which a jury is uniquely competent to make. For this reason, **B** is incorrect. **C** is incorrect because *res ipsa loquitur* is not dependent on the existence of any "absolute duty," but rather on circumstantial evidence which justifies the inference that a particular defendant acted unreasonably.

27.   D   In general, there are only three potential bases for tort liability: intent, negligence, and liability without fault. Liability without fault is ordinarily imposed upon a person who knowingly engages in abnormally dangerous activities or who is a professional supplier of products. Since Darrin was neither, liability without fault cannot be imposed. Inten-

tional tort liability is imposed upon a defendant who knew to a substantial degree of certainty that his act would harm the plaintiff. Unless Darrin *knew* that the stove would hurt someone, he cannot be liable for committing an intentional tort. Negligence is unreasonable conduct in the face of a risk about which the defendant should have known (i.e., a foreseeable risk). Unless Darrin *should have known* that his stove would injure someone, he cannot be liable for negligence.

Although liability without fault (i.e., strict liability) may be imposed upon a professional supplier who sells a defective product, **A** is incorrect because Darrin was neither a professional supplier of stoves nor did he sell the defective stove. If Darrin should have anticipated that a person would enter his cabin by mistake, he might have owed Perl a duty to act reasonably. **B** is incorrect, however, because there is no fact indicating that he breached that duty by acting unreasonably. It is often held that a landholder owes a trespasser no duty of reasonable care. Thus, if Perl was a trespasser at the time of the explosion, Darrin would probably not be liable to her for negligence. Even if she was not a trespasser, however, Darrin would not be liable unless he knew or should have known that the stove would injure someone. Perl's trespass is, therefore, not the *only* thing that would result in a judgment for Darrin. **C** is, therefore, incorrect.

28.   C   Under the "but for" rule of causation, defendant's conduct is a cause in fact of plaintiff's injury if the plaintiff's injury would not have occurred without it. Since Palco would not have been injured without Yeong's intoxication, and since Yeong would not have become intoxicated without Barney's conduct, Barney's conduct was a cause in fact of Palco's injury.

A is incorrect for two reasons: first, under the given facts it is uncertain whether Alfred's conduct was a substantial factor in making Yeong intoxicated; and, second, even if Alfred's conduct was a cause of the harm (i.e., a substantial factor in producing it), Barney's conduct was also a cause of that harm. **B** is incorrect because the language of the statute (" ... any person who sold said minor the alcohol which resulted in said minor's intoxication ... ") indicates that liability depends on a causal relationship between the defendant's conduct and the minor's intoxication. Since Palco's injury would not have occurred without Yeong's intoxication, any cause of Yeong's intoxication must also have been a cause of Palco's injury (see above explanation of "but for" rule). **D** is, therefore, incorrect.

29.   D   Under the "substantial factor" rule of causation, defendant's conduct is a cause of a particular consequence if it was a substantial factor in bringing that consequence about. Conduct which would have produced a particular consequence all by itself was a substantial factor in producing that consequence even if other factors happened to combine with that conduct to bring the consequence about. Since either Alfred's conduct alone or Barney's conduct alone would have made Yeong intoxicated, each was a substantial factor in making Yeong intoxicated. Each was, therefore, a cause of Yeong's intoxication. Under the "but for" rule of causation, a condition is a cause of harm if the harm would not have occurred without that condition. Since Palco's injury would not have occurred had Yeong not been intoxicated, Yeong's intoxication was a cause of Palco's injury. Since the conduct of Alfred and Barney were causes of Yeong's intoxication, and since Yeong's intoxication was a cause of Palco's injury, the conduct of Alfred and Barney were causes of Palco's injury. For this reason, neither I nor II is correct.

30.   B   Violation of a statute may establish the violator's negligence (or liability) in a particular
            case if the statute was designed to protect against the risk which led to the plaintiff's
            harm. Prill was hurt not because Drinker was drunk, but because Drinker had been poi-
            soned. (Note that the facts indicate that Drinker was driving reasonably.) If the statute
            was not meant to protect against the risk of drinking poison, then its violation would not
            be relevant in the case of an injury which resulted from drinking poison. Since poison
            could as easily be drunk in non-alcoholic drinks, it is unlikely that the statute in this case
            was designed to protect against drinking poison.

            A is incorrect because the language of the statute appears to prohibit the sale of alcohol
            to a person who is already intoxicated, without regard to how he got intoxicated. **C** is
            based on an inaccurate statement. Conduct is a cause of harm if that harm would not
            have resulted without the conduct. Since Drinker's death and the resulting accident
            would not have occurred if Drinker had not drunk the poisoned liquor, service of the
            liquor was a cause of Prill's injuries. **C** is, therefore, incorrect. If an intervening cause of
            harm was unforeseeable, it may be called a superseding cause and relieve a defendant of
            liability by resulting in the conclusion that his conduct was not a "legal" or "proximate"
            cause of the injury. Causes which existed or occurred prior to the defendant's conduct
            are not intervening causes, however, and, therefore, cannot be superseding causes of
            harm. **D** is incorrect because Fuller's conduct preceded Barr's service of liquor to
            Drinker.

TABLE OF CASES

TABLE OF *RESTATEMENT SECOND* REFERENCES

TABLE OF *RESTATEMENT THIRD* REFERENCES

Note: References to "Rest. 3d (Liab. for Phys. Harm)" are to the Rest. 3d's volumes whose full title is "Restatement 3d, Liability for Physical and Emotional Harm."

SUBJECT MATTER INDEX